SERVICES MARKETING

SERVICES MARKETING

S.M. JHA *Ph.D.,D.Lit.*
Professor,
Department of Commerce and Business Administration,
L.N. Mithila University,
Darbhanga - 846008.
India.

First Edition : 1991
Second Edition : 1997
Third Edition : 1998
Fourth Edition : 2000
Fifth Edition : 2002
Sixth Edition : 2003
Reprint : 2004, 2005, 2006, 2007, 2008
Seventh Revised and Enlarged Edition : 2011
Edition : 2013, 2014, 2015, 2017, 2018
Edition : 2022, 2024
Edition : 2026

Published by : Mrs. Meena Pandey
for **HIMALAYA PUBLISHING HOUSE PVT. LTD.,**
Vishal Industrial Estate, 1st Floor, Office No. 63/64,
Bhandup Village Road, Subhash Nagar (Opp. CEAT Tyres),
Nahur (W), Mumbai - 400 078. **Phone:** 022-35131464/65/66/67
E-mail: himpub@bharatmail.co.in; **Website:** www.himpub.com

Branch Offices :

New Delhi : "Pooja Apartments", 4-B, Murari Lal Street, Ansari Road, Darya Ganj, New Delhi - 110 002. Phone: 011-23270392, 23278631; Fax: 011-23256286

Nagpur : Kundanlal Chandak Industrial Estate, Ghat Road, Nagpur - 440 018. Mobile: 09325409992, 09325908881

Bengaluru : Plot No. 91-33, 2nd Main Road, Seshadripuram, Behind Nataraja Theatre, Bengaluru - 560 020. Phone: 080-41138821; Mobile: 09379847017, 09379847005

Hyderabad : No. 3-4-184, Lingampally, Besides Raghavendra Swamy Matham, Kachiguda, Hyderabad - 500 027. Phone: 040-27560041, 27550139

Chennai : No. 34/44, Motilal Street, T. Nagar, Chennai - 600 017. Mobile: 09380460419

Pune : "Laksha" Apartment, First Floor, No. 527, Mehunpura, Shaniwarpeth (Near Prabhat Theatre), Pune - 411 030. Phone: 020-24496323, 24496333; Mobile: 09370579333

Cuttack : Plot No 5F-755/4, Sector-9, CDA Market Nagar, Cuttack - 753 014, Odisha. Mobile: 09338746007

Kolkata : 3, S.M. Bose Road, Near Gate No. 5, Agarpara Railway Station, North 24 Parganas, West Bengal - 700 109. Mobile: 09674536325

Printed at : Geetanjali Press Pvt. Ltd., Nagpur. On behalf of HPH.

FOREWORD

Service sector is a new frontier for marketing strategy. Not unexpectedly service contains to be an ever more important part of the gross national product of developing and developed nations. Health care, tourism, recreation, engineering services, telecommunication, education, financial services and similar activities are vital to the health and prosperity of every nation. Yet, relatively little has been written about the marketing of services compared to the marketing of tangible products. The approaches necessary to create customer satisfaction in the delivery of goods versus services are dramatically different. This book helps practitioners and academicians understand the critical difference and how to develop marketing strategy in meeting customer needs and the firms desire for a strong bottomline.

Quality becomes the critical competitive factor in the services marketing mix. It is the primary factor which separates the delivery of one service from another one. Consistent service quality is difficult to achieve because precise specifications for development and delivery are harder to establish and maintain than in manufacturing. Customers, because of the intangible nature of services, also find it more difficult to articulate the attributes they are seeking in services than in products. The quality of service can vary from customer to customer, from day to day, and producers. Thus, not only the service outcome but also the process of service delivery is important.

An additional difference is that most services are fundamentally perishable. Doctors and dentists, for example, cannot recover revenue lost because of an unfilled schedule. Tickets to a football game or an airline flight are only good for the day sold. Additional services cannot be transported. Medical care, for example, is available only at a doctor's office. The result is that services are very labour-intensive, which limits economies of scale. Also, many services must be personally produced and customised to meet the needs of each consumer.

Strategically, the core services are the primary benefits that consumers seek from the services provider. The core service often becomes a commodity as a service industry matures. Consumers expect the firm to be competent in providing the core service. The result is that the peripheral services often become the way in which the customers heart is won. For example, customers expect a high quality of healthcare in a hospital. However, the differentiating factor between one hospital and another may be the presence of valet parking, the quality of the food, the availability of a private room, an in-room phone, or an in-room television.

Professors Leonard Berry and Parasuraman at Taxas A&M University have determined that several key factors — word-of-mouth communications, personal needs, past experience and external communications — influence customer's expectations. They define service quality in marketing terms as a discrepancy between customer's expectations and perceptions. The key dimensions to service quality thus become reliability (the ability to perform as promised), responsiveness (willingness to help customers and to provide prompt service), competence (the skills and knowledge necessary to perform the service), courtesy (politeness of contact personnel), credibility (honesty in the eyes of the customers), security (freedom from risks), communication (communicating with customers in ways they can understand and respond to), and understanding the customers (making the effort to know customers and their needs). These variables are the keys to success in developing marketing strategy for services in meeting customer expectations.

In summary, this book helps the readers understand the key ingredients for competitive succession in the various sectors of the services economy, how to meet and exceed customer expectations, and how to meet and exceed customer expectations, and how to make the delivery of services more efficient and productive. This book will make a difference. It has something for everyone.

J. BARRY MASON

Dean and Russell,
Professor of Business Administration,
The University of Alabama,
USA

PREFACE

Change is a natural phenomenon. Time cycle necessitates a change in concept and percept because all of us do not venture to go against the wind. Yesterday, the perception of service was confined to work and advice only with service motto. Today, the services have been commercialised and professionalised. Of course, it is due to corporate culture followed by material culture in which financial health of an organisation or an individual proves to be an important base for evaluating soundness, perfection and excellence. It is against this background that individuals as well as the organisations have been found making professionalised efforts to earn and multiply as much as they can. The unfair, unethical, unlawful practices are found common. The laws and regulations have proved to be insensitive and ineffective. A stage of fierce competition is now existent. Profiteering appears to be legalised. Unfair practices are suitably rewarded. Intelligents are found misusing their intelligence for manipulation. These negative developments complicate the task of professionals. We go through the marketing problem in an age of techniculture where new generation of sophisticated technology has been found establishing an edge over the expertise and excellence of human resources. The boardrooms prefer to use sophisticated technology in place of employing more people since they find it cost-effective. The professionals evince their keen interests in promoting the use of sophisticated technology because they find it convenient to manage them. Thus, the goods manufacturing or service generating organisations are found arranging a transcendental priority to the techno-driven and user-friendly marketing.

Management thoughts have changed substantially over the last one century. It started with a rationalistic approach, passed through different phases by shifting emphasis on the organisation of the group activity, the motivation of an individual and the stimulation of satisfaction of users' needs and requirements and finally have arrived at a holistic view which has considerably enlarged the functional boundaries of a corporate decision-maker. The holistic approach makes it essential that the boardrooms, senior executives and executives develop a positive feeling towards serving and subserving the social interests. Of course, it is one step ahead of the customer satisfaction. In the business world of today, an organisation is supposed to assign an overriding priority to social interests. Further, it is also pertinent that the process of value orientation is accelerated. Of late, even in the less developed countries like ours, we find boardrooms advocating much in favour of social-oriented and value-based decisions. An attitudinal change in the armoury of management has sizeably increased the functional responsibilities of almost all who are involved in the process. We now need to ensure that organisations are working not just for profits.

Till now, we have concentrated on marketing tangible and therefore the services sector could not be developed in a right fashion. With corporatisation followed by globalisation, we find services sector gaining popularity. The public sector banks and insurance corporations, the transport organisations, the hotel and tourism, the educational institutions and hospitals, the political and social and even religious organisations have started practising marketing which on the one hand has made the organisations financially solvent while on the other hand has also increased the number of satisfied group of users. We cannot negate that private sector services generating organisations where we find world-class professional excellence have been establishing an edge over the public sector. Though the process of practising marketing has been switched on but the public sector still lags behind specially in terms of professionalised efforts. It is in this context that we make a strong advocacy in favour of conceptualising aggressive marketing in the public sector organisations.

The developed countries have been practising innovative marketing and the MNCs working in India have also been found assigning due weightage to marketing. We do not find any exaggeration in saying that they treat their customers more than a guest and therefore we find their success graph very high. They keep on moving the practices of innovating their strategic group of customers. Contrary to it, the public sector organisations are yet to adopt it as a part of their decision-making process.

Sky is the limit for quality. Whatever the perception we nurture today regarding the quality cannot remain productive even for tomorrow. The increasing sophistication in info-tech has been found playing an incremental role in defining and redefining quality. The MNCs keep themselves aware of the changing levels of expectations of users and manage them in such a fashion that task of developing a product profile commensurate with the changing taste preferences of users is found much more easier.

The innovative marketing considerably helps in bringing the derailed systems back on the rail. With the support of techno-driven information system, we come to know the latest developments in the levels of expectations of users. We innovate services and activate the elimination and inclusion processes to take competitive advantages both in the domestic and global markets. Product attractiveness is made possible and with the help of creative promotional measures, the marketing professionals find it convenient to inform, sense, sensitise, persuade and transform the potential users into actual users and the actual users into habitual users. We start getting the repeat orders and develop brand loyalty. The cycle of qualitative transformation thus never takes a rest and if we continue to work on this line, our efforts for becoming a quality leader is found proactive.

Of late, we find a majority of the service generating organisations promoting the use of new generation of technology for improving the quality of their services. The process has continued during the yesteryears and will continue even in the years to come. This makes it essential that almost all categories of organisations practise marketing and make professionalised efforts to satisfy the customers because it is the only thing that would engineer a sound foundation for striking a balance between organisational and social considerations.

The marketing professionals need to strengthen their realisation that nothing is to be possible unless we have a team of dedicated, committed and value-based people. The vanishing work culture in almost all the public sector organisations makes it essential that they devise a new system of human resource management. The increasing domination of trade unions in the public sector organisations is found to be an important reason for a sharp fall in the level of efficiency. Unless we improve the quality of people, all our techno-driven efforts are to be turned into a fiasco.

The present book in its new form has studied a number of problems which could not be studied in the previous editions. A number of services have been studied, viz., Bank, Insurance, Mutual Funds, Portfolio Management, Factoring, Transport, Tourism, Hotel, Consultancy, Retail, Personal Care, Education, Hospital, Political, Day-care, Courier, Entertainment, Mass Communication, IT, Electricity and Automobile. The application of modern marketing principles in the services sector would open new vistas for qualitative-cum-quantitative improvements. The quality of services would be improved, the level of operational efficiency would be increased, the rate of profitability would be maximised, the leadership would be established and the most neglected dimensions in the today's context e.g., social considerations and value-orientation would also get due place. We find the unemployment problem at its peak and the services sector would be very much instrumental in creating new job opportunities.

Actually, we do not find a boundary for perfection. I have made sincere and honest efforts to make the book useful to the academics, practitioners, policy makers, students and many others who keep their interests alive in qualitative improvements but when we find the sky limit for quality, whatever the lapses and shortcomings the readers identify would be welcome.

I acknowledge with sincere gratitude, the co-operation of my friends and colleagues in preparing the new edition of Services Marketing.

Department of Commerce and
Business Administration,
L.N. Mithila University,
Darbhanga.

S.M. JHA

CONTENTS

BRIEF CONTENTS

CHAPTER

THE FOUNDATION OF SERVICES MARKETING

"Services are going to move in this decade to being the front edge of the industry."

– *Zeithmal & Bitner*

Chapter Objectives

Introduction – Services: The Concept – Goods and Services: A Comparative Analysis – Salient Features of Marketing Services – Services Marketing: The Concept – Why Marketing of Services? – Significance of Services Marketing – The Behavioural Profile of Users of Services – The Role of Culture in Services – Marketing Information System – Market Segmentation – Emerging Key Services – Building Service Aspirations – Technology in the Services Sector – Consumer Protection in Services – Summary – Key Terms – Review Questions – Application Exercises – Endnotes.

Learning Objectives

The motive of this chapter is to develop awareness of the readers regarding some of the basics of services marketing which will prepare a sound foundation for the development of knowledge in the related areas. It is essential for the service marketers to know the outstanding features while marketing services so that they find their decisions having an edge over their rivals. The behavioural profile of users, the marketing information system and market segmentation would help them in studying and understanding the customers in a right fashion. The role of culture in services will simplify their task of decision-making in an emerging multi-cultural society. The instrumentality of technology will make the ways for promoting techno-driven services. The professionals will also find it easier to build service aspirations and to formulate a sound marketing mix.

INTRODUCTION

Corporatisation considerably influenced by globalisation has opened new vistas for the development of techniculture. The increasing domination of technology on the services sector of the economy has been successful in accelerating the pace of economic transformation. This has made possible a significant increase in the levels of disposable and discretionary income. What to talk of the developed countries of the globe when we find even in developing countries like ours an apparent change in the lifestyle. Materialism is the result of materialistic gains which has engineered a sound foundation for the development/material culture. It is against this backdrop that we need to keep on moving the process of economic transformation specially with the help of tertiary sector.

We cannot negate that during yester years, the services sector has made significant contribution to the process of economic transformation but we have yet to capitalise on tremendous opportunities to prove ourselves the world leader. It is right to mention that world-class professional excellence would help us in this endeavour. The corporate leaders of today need to be professionally sound. They have to devise innovative practices for getting the desired level of success. The corporate policy makers need an attitudinal change so that the formulation of a sound policy in tune with the incoming global requirements is made possible. Excelling competition necessitates formulation of a sound strategy. The service marketers in the changing environment are required to accept the responsibility of formulating a sound strategy which helps them in touching the target. The processes at different stages must be cost-effective so that we not only get success in becoming a quality leader but also succeed in becoming a price leader which provides us an opportunity to adopt and strengthen pricing as a motivational tool.

Our focus here is on the conceptualisation of innovative marketing principles with a professional touch. We need a new vision to accelerate the pace.We need personal touch to increase the number of star performer. We need value orientation for the projection of a fair image. We need human orientation for cohesion. It is not only significant that we have tremendous opportunities. It is equally important that we have an appropriate strategy to capitalise on. The government policy makers need to ensure due protection to the investors — domestic or foreign.

Expectations and satisfaction move together. The process of technological sophistication has been found very much instrumental in increasing the levels of expectation. The service-providers are also afraid of the gap due to new generation of technology. The quality gap due to wrong operation, handling and maintenance of new generation of technology would make ways for disappointment and frustration. It is only professional excellence of our people which would play a catalytic role. Concept and percept never remain static. Of late, we find a change in our perception of quality. We define quality and keep on moving the process.

Gone are the days when the perception of services remained confined to work with only service motto, without charging any fee or without accepting any obligation. The time cycle coiling more dynamism in its nature necessitates a change as willingly or unwillingly, we don't venture to go against the wind. The mechanised system of development has now paved ways for socio-economic transformation which has made possible an increase in the level of disposable income. When we earn more, we like to spend more. We evince interest in utilising our leisure time and availing the modern amenities and facilities. We can't deny the fact that the imbalance in the demographic structure has complicated the task of policy makers, specially in terms of creating and expanding the job opportunities. There is no doubt in it that the goods manufacturing organisations have been contributing a lot to the process but the service generating organisations find it difficult to cope with the mounting problem aggravated by the developed countries of the world. In the Indian perspective, the services sector has not been contributing substantially to the process of socio-economic transformation.

In the 21st century, the business environmental conditions are likely to be more volatile. The multi-dimensional developments in the information technologies, activated and energised by the developed countries, have made ways for sophistication in almost all the areas. It is against this background that leading service generating organisations of the world have been found believing in making things happen. The invention and innovations have been paving avenues for a qualitative transformation in almost all the areas. This has been successful in increasing the level of expectations of customers. The globalisation and liberalisation has opened new vistas for the development of service generating organisations. The intensity of competition is found moving upward. The organisations active in enriching their strength have been found establishing an edge and compelling the weak organisations to make a final good-bye. This makes it essential that even in the Indian condition, the service generating organisations make sincere efforts to make themselves stronger and stronger, if they have to survive and thrive. They have to explore profitable avenues and practise innovating marketing since quality or world-class services with innovative marketing would help them in proving their excellence nationally and internationally competitive.

It is against this background that we talk about the marketing of services. In the present world, it is not possible that we keep ourselves isolated. To be more specific when we have advanced information technologies and quality professionals, we don't find any sense in continuing with the traditional technologies and negative attitudes.

We need positive attitude, creative approach and innovative strategies which would make our efforts productive. This requires a fair blending of performance orientation and employee orientation. Our services as product are to be of world-class and our employees are to be professionally sound. This requires an in-depth knowledge of quality and its changing perception. This is due mainly to the fact that sky is the limit for quality.

Both the sectors, public as well as the private need to understand the new corporate culture in which employees need to have personal commitment. The business environment is more competitive and this makes a strong advocacy in favour of quality generation. We can't negate that by and large in almost all the public sector service generating organisations, the fast deteriorating quality has been a matter of serious concern. The policy of liberalisation has made ways for leading multinationals to enter the market and to excel competition which is found throwing a big challenge to the existence of public sector undertakings. If they are found surviving, it is just due to the attitudinal support of the masses. Sooner or later, we expect a shift in their attitudes and this would compel the public sector service generating organisations to leave the ground free for the private sector. To be more specific in the Indian condition, we don't find it a positive development since the prospects/customers in a majority of the conditions would face the implications of a high price structure. The foreign companies would start exploiting the masses and the national economy would be thrown back in the reverse gear. Thus, it is high time that the public sector organisations start and activate the innovation process and prove themselves to be strong enough to face the challenges and threats in the market.

Of late, the technologies have been found dominating the services sector and the organisations depending on traditional technologies or manual services have been facing a rough time. This makes it essential that we promote the use of technologies but at the same time also keep in our minds the implications of the use of sophisticated technologies on the generation of employment opportunities. Since we are facing the problem of unemployment, the policy makers can't negate this dimension of development. In a true sense, we need a policy that makes the ways for quality generation but at the same time is also not to create the problem of retrenchment. A fair synchronisation of technology and human resources is considered significant to make the process of development proactive.

In some of the service generating organisations, we face the problem of strong trade unionism dominating decision-making with a negative attitude. We can't negate that such a development has been making an invasion on the efficiency of employees *vis-a-vis* gearing back the profitability index of an organisation. The trade unions need to change their attitudes. If they continue to remain as fighters, the ultimate sufferers would be the workers/employees. If they make the organisations financially sick, the problems of retrenchment would reach at an alarming stage. This makes it pertinent that trade unions work as an efficiency generator. They keep in their records, the efficiency index of employees and based on that continue to champion their claims and subserve their interests.

In view of the above, it is right to mention that application of modern marketing principles would help almost all the organisations in enriching their efficacy. If the potentials are enriched, we become strong. And if we are strong, the resistance power is increased. This simplifies the task of facing the rough weather. The worldwide economic depression is not to be slowed down. The customers in almost all the cases and areas are likely to be more sensitive to price. Thus, the cost-effectiveness would play a decisive role in developing and thriving an organisation. The organisations offering quality services at a reasonable price structure would prove to be a leader. The innovative marketing strategies would help them fantastically. It is in this context that we make an advocacy in favour of the application of marketing principles in almost all the areas.

Thus, we need professional excellence to get the best result. The professionalism makes the ways for innovation. This makes it essential that our employees working in different sectors and areas are only not efficient but in addition they are also committed, dedicated and value-based. Almost all the organisations need to have an ongoing training programme for the development of sound professionals. Performance orientation is thus the first task which would help an organisation in offering the world-class services to the customers. At the same time, we also need employee orientation which would redress the interests of employees by offering to them suitable incentives. In this context, it is important to mention that efficiency would be the focal point around which our strategies would cluster. By promoting inventions and innovations, we would develop a new perception of quality which would require involvement of efficient personnel. If we continue to offer to the efficient personnel, the incentives based on their efficiency, the inefficient personnel would have no option but to improve their efficiency. This would start a circle in which total quality management would be required to be practised in a right fashion.

This book studies the marketing problems in a number of organisations where the problem of inefficiency is found at an alarming stage. The Public Sector Banks have been found facing a rough weather. The State Transport Corporations have been declared financially insolvent, the Life Insurance Corporation lacks work culture, the Government-managed hospitals are in a depleted condition, the educational institutions, specially managed by the government have been found offering substandard services to the masses, the tourism industry has miserably failed in contributing to the process of generating foreign exchange, the hotel industry is facing a rough weather, the supply of electricity to the different sectors is found presenting a gloomy picture. This makes it clear that by and large almost all the service generating organisations have become insensitive and unproductive. On the other hand, we are promoting liberalisation which has been found inducing the leading multinationals to enter the business and get a success. The result is obvious that they succeed in establishing an edge over the domestic companies and sooner or later the control of national economy would go to the hands of multinationals. This makes it essential that the service generating organisations in general innovate their policies and the policy makers make possible an attitudinal change.

The conceptualisation of modern marketing principles in the services sector would make the business environment much more competitive and only those organisations would continue to succeed in the volatile business environment who keep on moving the process of enriching their professional excellence. In addition to the organisations found traditionally sound, the new categories of organisations would also be required to practise innovative marketing with a new vision and a holistic touch. The techniculture will show its domination and the material culture will gain prominence. The process of corporatisation will gain a rapid momentum and the retail services are to be much more sophisticated. The professional excellence of retail marketers will help in emerging the new faces of retail marketing. The mall culture will gain popularity and the shopping will be considered a device for getting pleasure. Since a number of new sectors will start becoming financially sound, we cannot negate the possibility of stock markets and financial institutions becoming stronger and stronger. This will make the ways for the development of portfolio management services. Almost all categories of players will evince their keen interests in channelising investments and they will essentially require portfolio management services considerably helping and guiding for them for making profitable and the risk-free investments. The stock markets, banks and insurance companies will be the avenues for making investments and the guidelines from the financial experts showing a professional touch will be productive specially to the small and marginal investors found fully unaware of the changing scenario. To keep on moving the process of development, the corporate sector will require adequate financial support which will pave avenues for mutual fund services. The domestic players will get an opportunity to capitalise on. Acting as a close link between the investors and the capital market, the mutual fund services will find new vistas of development and tremendous opportunities to tap. The world-class professional excellence and the innovative marketing practises would make the task much more result-oriented.

The most important role in the changing perspective is to be played by the IT sector. The development sectors in general and the IT sector in particular cannot initiate the process of quantitative or qualitative improvements without professional excellence and personal touch. The multi-faceted uses of IT in all the three sectors of development such as primary, secondary and tertiary will open new doors for the development of this sector and in this context, we cannot undermine the role of marketers. The managerial proficiency rests on professional excellence. The service marketers having world-class professional excellence would be efficacious of excelling the ever increasing competition.

This focuses our attention on the innovative marketing for the services sector which should be techno-driven. While practising marketing, they need to keep into consideration the multi-dimensional improvements in the global business environment. Identifying the changing level of expectations and fulfilling them to the desired level would significantly increase the number of satisfied group of customers.

SERVICES: THE CONCEPT

In common parlance, the term can't be only personal services like auto repairing, haircutting, services of dentists, legal consultants and so on. The marketing experts view the problem in a bit different way. They feel that the contents of services are much more wider. There is no doubt in it that a number of experts have attempted to define the services but no single definition has been accepted universally. It is quite natural that as and when we attempt to clarify the perception, a number of comments crop up.

According to US Government's Standard Industrial Classification, "Establishments primarily providing a wide variety of services for individuals, business and government establishments and other organisations, hotels and other lodging places, establishments providing personal services, repair and amusement services, educational institutions, membership organisations and other miscellaneous services are included."[1]

On the basis of the classification made by the Standard Industrial Classification, it is clear that different types of services are an important base for the services establishments offering services to both categories of customers, the individuals as well as the organisations.

Another expert says,

"Services refer to social efforts which include even government to fight five giant evils, e.g., want, disease, ignorance, squalor and illness in the society."[2]

This opinion focuses on the organisations offering social services where hospitals or medicare or health centres, communication organisations, educational institutions are found important. Thus, the social efforts and the organisations taking part in the process are supposed to be studied in the very context.

Another opinion throws light on human efforts. An expert says,

"Services can also be defined as a human effort which provides succour to the needy. It may be food to a hungry person, water to a thirsty person, medical services to an ailing person and education to a student, loan to a farmer, transport to a consumer, communication aid to two persons who want to share a thought, pleasure or pain."[3]

The definition given above clarifies that services are human efforts. The focus is on the point that services are not meant services for the sake of services or say, services without charging any fee.

One expert says,

"Services can also be defined an action(s) of organisation(s) that maintains and improves the well-being and functioning of people."[4]

It can't be refuted that the definition presented by Yakeshel Hasen Field and other through small covers everything which the services need. The well-being functioning of people are important and we can't ignore it while clarifying the perception of services.

The American Marketing Association defines services in the following way, "Services are activities, benefits or satisfaction which are offered for sale are provided in connection with the sale of goods." This definition makes it clear that services are activities, benefits or satisfaction and we find their uses for selling products which may be tangible or even intangible.

GOODS AND SERVICES: A COMPARATIVE ANALYSIS

Services and goods are not tantamount. There are a number of salient features that establish a clear-cut difference between the two. Something which can be physically touched, verified, attracted or exchanged with or even without making profits are known as goods. On this basis, goods are food, clothes, books, other domestic and industrial items that can be carried home, can be stored at a place and are tangible. On the other hand, the services are hotel business, personal care, legal or medical services, banking services, insurance services, transportation services and many other services which can't be stored at a place and one has to hire someone else to perform the services. The effects are pleasure, joy, entertainment, a relief from ailment or so. The following points clarify the difference between the two:

1. **Tangibility:** By tangibility, we mean anything which can be viewed. On the basis of tangibility, goods are found tangible since we can view the goods bought by us. Contrary to it, the services are found intangible because it is not possible to view the services. We can just realise the services used by us.

2. **Transferability:** On the basis of transferability, the goods can be transferred from one place to another. We can carry goods bought by us. We find transfer of goods from the point of sale to the point of use. Just reverse to it, it is not possible to transfer the services from the point of sale to the point of use.

3. **Existence:** The goods bought by us remain existent. The durables continue for a long time and even the non-durables have limited existence. We don't find the same thing with the services since we find services non-existent in nature.

4. **Heterogeneity:** On the basic of heterogeneity, the services can hardly be standardised. Contrary to it, the goods can be standardised. It is very difficult to measure the quality of services but it is easier to measure the quality of goods.

5. **Reselling:** The goods bought by us can be resold. After a limited use, the owners are in a position and they do also possess a legal right to resale the same. We don't find the same thing with the services. If we buy a seat in the aircraft, if we book a room in a hotel, if we buy a seat in a cinema hall; we have no option but to use or surrender. We don't bear the right of reselling the same.

The aforesaid differences between the goods and services are obvious. It is right to mention that being a marketer we treat both of them as a product. Of course, the services product have distinct features or properties which generate numerous problems, specially in the marketing process but we call them product because the combination of different types of inputs result into the generation of a service output. In addition to the financial resources, we find investment in human resources for generating the services. It is against this background that we go through the problems in the marketing of services based on their salient features. The service generating organisations need professionally sound employees who prove to be high performers. This necessitates an in-depth study of its salient features.

SALIENT FEATURES OF MARKETING SERVICES

Services have some salient features which necessitate a new vision, a distinct approach and a world-class professional excellence to market effectively and profitably. The professionals not well aware of the properties find it difficult to make creative decisions. It is against this background that we go through the salient features with the viewpoint of their instrumentality in making the marketing decisions.

1. Intangibility: Intangibility is an important consideration that complicates the functional responsibility of a marketing manager, specially while influencing and motivating the prospects/customers. The goods of tangible nature can be displayed, the prospects or buyers can have a view, they can even test and make a trial before making the buying decisions. The selling processes are thus found easier. We are aware of the fact that services are of intangible nature and it is intangibility that complicates the task of decision-makers. While motivating, they find it difficult to perform and display and the positive or negative opinions regarding the services come up only after the completion of the using process. The customer can't touch the services, they albeit can't smell them. In a true sense, it is not a physical object. It has mental connotations. According to Carman and Uhl, a buyer of products (goods) have an opportunity to see, touch, hear, smell or taste them before they buy.[5] Of course, we don't find the same thing with the services product. It is the professional excellence of decision-makers that counts here, that influences the entire process and that helps them substantially. While selling or promoting services, we need to concentrate on benefits and satisfaction which a buyer can derive after buying. We can hardly emphasise the service itself. As for example, the banking organisations promote the sale of credit cards by visualising the conveniences and comforts the holders of the credit cards are likely to get from the same. Services carry with them a combination of intangible perceptions. As for instance, an airline sells the seat from one destination to another. Here, it is a matter of consumers' perception of the services and their expectations not smelling or tasting the services. They expect safe, fast, decent services. A service by nature is an abstract phenomenon. Thus, it is right to mention that due to intangibility, the selling and marketing of services become much more complicated.

2. Perishability: Another point complicating the task of a professional is the nature of perishability that we find in the services. The goods if not sold today can be stored, preserved for further selling. Thus, the risk element is here in a different form. But in the context of services, if we fail to sell the services, it is lost only not for today but even for the future. If a labour stops to work, if a seat in the aircraft remains unsold, if a bedroom in a hotel remains unbooked, a chair in a cinema hall remains vacant; we find the business non-existent and the opportunities are lost and lost forever. The services can't be stored or preserved. Unutilised or underutilised services are found to be a waste. A building unoccupied, a person unemployed, credit unutilised, vacant beds in a hospital are economic waste. Of course, this is due mainly to its perishability. This makes it essential that decision-makers or the executives by using their professionalism minimise the possibilities of economic waste. The opportunities come and you need to capitalise on the same by using your excellence.

3. Inseparability: This is also a feature that complicates the task of professionals while marketing the services. The inseparability focuses on the fact that the services are not of separable nature. Generally, the services are created and supplied simultaneously. Like the dancers, musicians, dentists and other professionals create and offer services at the same time. In other words, the services and their providers are the same. Donald Cowell says, "Goods are produced, sold and then consumed whereas the services are sold and then produced and consumed."[6] It is inseparability that makes the task of marketing services a bit difficult. The goods are produced at one point and then distributed by others at other points. In the services, we find the selling processes making ways for the generation of services. The professionals while marketing the services thus bear the responsibility of removing or minimising the gap between the services-promised and services-offered. Goods are produced, sold and then consumed but the services are sold, produced and then used. The inseparability thus makes it essential that the service-providers are acting and behaving professionally so that the marketing processes are not to pave the avenues for a degeneration in the quality.

4. Heterogeneity: Another feature is heterogeneity which makes it difficult to establish standard. The quality of services can't be standardised. The prices charged may be too high or too low. In the case of entertainment and sports, we find the same thing. The same type of services can't be sold to all the customers even if they pay the same price. The consumers rate the services in a different way. Of course, it is due to the difference in the perception of individuals at the levels of providers and users. The heterogeneity factor makes it difficult to market efficiently. The professionals by using their excellence bear the responsibility of minimising the problem.

5. Ownership: It is also ownership that makes it significant to market the services in a bit different way. The goods sold are transferred from one place to another, the ownership is also transferred and this provides to the buyers an opportunity to resell. In the case of services, we don't find the same thing. The users have just an access to the service. As for example, a consumer can use personal care services or medicare services or can use a hotel room or swimming pool, however the ownership rests with the providers. An expert opines, "A service is any activity or benefit that one party can offer to another that it is essentially intangible and does not result in the ownership of anything."[7] Here, it is clear that ownership is not affected in the process of selling the services. The issue of ownership has also been clarified by another expert. He says, "Services are those separately identifiable, essentially intangible activities which provide want satisfaction and that are not necessarily tied to use sales of a product or another services. To produce a service may or may not require the use of tangible goods. However, when such use is required, there is no transfer of permanent ownership to these tangible goods."[8] The same theme of not transferring the ownership has also been supported by Batesan.[9] Here, the focus is on the point that transfer of ownership simplifies the task of a marketer since he/she can use it as a motivational tool. In case of services, the professionals experience difficulties because we don't find any scope for the transfer of ownership. The professionals thus need to be more careful while selling or marketing the services.

6. Simultaneity: Services can't be delivered to customers or users. Services don't move through the channel of distribution. For availing the services, it is essential that the users are brought to the providers or the providers go to the users. It is right to say that the services have limited geographical areas. Carman and Uhl say, "Producers of services generally have small-sized operations than do producers of goods, largely because the producers must travel to get the services or *vice versa.* When the producers travel to the buyer, time is taken away from the production of services and the cost of those services is increased. It also costs time and money from buyers to travel to producers of services and these economies of time and travel provide incentive to locate more services centres closer to prospective customers which results in smaller service centre."[10] This can be clarified by a suitable example. Hotel rooms can't be brought to the users, aeroplane can't be brought to the customers, etc.

7. Quality Measurement: The quality of service requires another tool for measurement. We can't measure it in terms of service level. It is very difficult to rate or quantify the total purchase. As for example, we can quantify the food served in a hotel but the way a waiter or a carrier serves it or overall environment or behaviour of other staff can't be ignored while rating the total process. Hence, we can determine the level of satisfaction at which the users are found satisfied. A firm sells atmosphere, conveniences, consistent quality, status, anxiety, moral, etc.

8. Nature of Demand: While going through the features of services, we can't underestimate the factor related to the nature of demand. Generally, the services are found of fluctuating nature. Particularly during the peak season, we find an abnormal increase in the demand. As for example, the mobility of passenger is found increased, specially during the marriage season or during an important festival. The tourists prefer to go the tourist spots or resorts specially during summer when we find the weather condition suitable. The cricket stadiums are used in winter. The golf courses remain unused during the winter. The public transport facilities are used considerably during the beginning and end of office hours. There are a number of examples to prove the peak hour when we find an abnormal increase in the demand position.

The aforesaid features of services make it clear that the professionals working in the services sector need excellence to make available to the customers the promised services without a gap. If the executives working in the different service generating organisations bear the potentials to understand the specialities in the services to be sold, they can do the best possible to understand the expectations of customers. This simplifies the process of satisfying the customers. It is not meant that the professionals working in the goods manufacturing organisations don't need excellence. The focus is on the point that since the services as a product are found of sensitive nature and the expectations of customers are found high, it is essential that the professionals understand the services *vis-a-vis* the customers. This makes an assault on the multi-dimensional problems likely to crop up in the process of selling services.

SERVICES MARKETING — THE CONCEPT

We term marketing a function by which a marketer plans, promotes and delivers goods and services to the customers or clients. In the marketing of services, the providers are supposed to influence and satisfy the customers or users. An institution or an individual may act as a provider who requires professional excellence to influence the impulse of prospects and to transform them into actual customers. When we buy services-offered by a service generating organisation in a true sense we buy the time, knowledge, skill or resources. The application of marketing principles in the services sector is the main thing in the services marketing.

We can't deny the fact that the concept "services marketing" has gained prominence very recently. The emergence of a number of service generating organisations in almost all the areas engineered a strong foundation for the development of services marketing, specially in the developed countries of the West which could get a place in the developing countries like ours in the due course. The end of the decade 1950s paved avenues for services marketing since a number of financial institutions and to be more specific, the insurance companies realised the instrumentality of the quality of services in making the environmental conditions conducive. The service generating organisations like banking organisations, insurance companies and others felt that application of marketing principles in the service management would initiate qualitative transformation which would simplify their task of increasing the market share and establishing leadership.

The perception of service marketing focuses on selling the services in the best interest of users/customers. It is concerned with a scientific and planned management of services which makes possible a fair synchronisation of the interests of providers as well as the users. With a change in the perception of management, we witnessed multi-faceted changes which necessitated an analogous change in the concept of services marketing. The service generating organisations realised the interests of customers and thereafter they were compelled to assign due weightage to the interests of society in the face of the holistic concept of management.

Marketing a service is meant marketing something intangible. It is marketing a promise. It is more selling yourself. We can't deny the fact that selling of promises complicate the task of marketers since they find it difficult to identify the stage or time where the services start degenerating or where the promises fall. Of late, we consider marketing a customer satisfaction engineering. There is no doubt in it that the organisational goals like making profits, establishing a leadership, innovating the marketing resources are found significant but the focal point is the user's satisfaction. In the marketing of services, we go through a number of problems directly or indirectly influencing the business index. The problems like market segmentation, marketing information system, behavioural management are studied minutely which simplify the task of formulating a sound mix for marketing, such as Product mix, Promotion mix, Price mix and Place mix. It is important to mention that we find "People" an important mix of marketing services.

Marketing is also defined as a managerial process by which the products are matched with market and through which the consumer is enabled to use or enjoy the product.[11] In the present definition, the product is an all inclusive term which includes services as well as physical goods. It is also said about marketing that it is the managerial process by which products are innovated. Modern management regards marketing and production an interdependent subsystem. It is against this background that in the marketing management, a number of problems are discussed, such as personal selling, advertisement, publicity, sales promotion, pricing, placement and management of marketing people. The combination of marketing controllables used to market a product or a service is often described as the marketing mix. In addition, the marketing management is also responsible for the continual adjustment of marketing controllables used to market tangibles or intangibles. A Life Insurance Company which basically sells the service of protection expects its marketing staff to provide information about the potential buyers or the prospects and the kinds or types of insurance services they need and want. They are also supposed to provide channels through which the services are made available to the prospects, make potential buyers aware of the types and nature of services-offered and participate in the determination of prices that would be acceptable to the potential buyers and yield profits to the company. Whether the service is dancing instruction, travel advice or hairstyle, marketing is found responsible for the inward flow of income to the organisation.[12]

The aforesaid facts make it clear that marketing is a vital function in both profit and no-profit making organisations. Traditionally, we study marketing only from the viewpoint of profit-seeking institution but recently we have the marketing type problem of even the no-profit making organisations like educational institutions, hospitals, political and social organisations or so.[13] Of late, we evince our interests in studying the marketing problems of service generating organisations. The banks making available to the customers the savings and investment facilities, the insurance companies sharing the risks of insured persons, the transport organisations offering to their customers quality, safe and economic services, the tourist organisations, the hotels, the communication organisations and many others are found studying the problems of marketing with the motto of satisfying the customers, subserving the social interests and enriching their potentials to face the challenges and threats in the market. By and large, almost all the service generating organisations are found practising marketing for accomplishing the organisational goals.

In view of the above, we observe the following key points regarding the concept or perception of services marketing:

- It is a managerial process of managing the services.
- It is an organised effort for providing a sound foundation for the development of an organisation.
- It is a social process helping an organisation to understand the emerging social problems and to take part in the social transformation process to justify its existence in the society.

WHY MARKETING OF SERVICES?

Of late, we find a phenomenal growth in the services marketing. The developed as well as the developing countries have been found making multi-dimensional efforts to market services in a right fashion. The public as well as the private sector organisations have been making innovative efforts to market services. The services sector has been found contributing substantially to the development process. The multi-faceted developments in the services sector and the mounting intensity of competition generated by the well-established multinational corporations have been engineering a strong foundation for the application of modern marketing principles in the service generating organisations so that they not only survive and thrive but in addition to these things also make a significant contribution to the process of socio-economic emancipation. It is in this context that we find it pertinent to think in favour of practising marketing principles in the services sector. The following facts make it clear that application of modern marketing principles by the service generating organisations would pave avenues for qualitative-cum-quantitative transformation.

1. Upward Trend in the Disposable Income: We can't negate that of late the disposable income of masses has been found moving upward. This trend is found even in the developing countries like ours where the development-oriented sector has opened new job opportunities and the liberalisation of economy is opening new vistas for development. The development of corporate sector makes ways for the transformation of industrial economy. If we find more job opportunities, the masses get an opportunity to earn more and when they earn more, it is quite natural that they want to spend more. The positive developments in the development sector thus open doors for an increase in the disposable income. The moment we find an increase in the disposable income, the process of demand generation gains a rapid momentum provided the pressure of inflation and the economic depression are not to slow down the tempo. These facts are a mute testimony to the proposition that even in the Indian economy we find positive developments which have been creating new opportunities for the development of services sector. The intensity of competition is found at its peak and this necessitates application of marketing principles.

2. Increasing Specialisation: We are living in an age of specialisation in which only perfection is to be rewarded suitably. More and more sophistication in the process of economic transformation is mainly due to the increasing specialisation. In the industrial economy, the magnitude of technological sophistication is found increasing. Of course, this is due to the growing importance of specialisation. The organisations have now no option but to promote specialisation since this helps them in making possible cost-effectiveness. The firms prefer to engage specialists for almost all the purposes. Experts and professionals like the management consultants, legal advisers financial experts, technocrats play a decisive role in managing an organisation. We can't negate that even in the years to come the importance of specialisation would be increased further which would require excellent professionals in almost all the areas. This makes it clear that increasing importance of specialisation would activate the demand cycle which would make ways for the development of banking services, insurance services, transportation services, communication services and many other services would be motivated. The promotional services would induce advertising agencies, the marketing information system would be influenced by the inventions and innovations in the field of information technology and legal services would flourish to protect the interests of all. Thus, it is right to mention that due to growing specialisation, the service generating organisations would need a new culture influenced by the corporate culture and the marketing practices would help the same.

3. Growing Fashion: With the development of corporate culture and the emergence of a well-established services sector, there would be a basic change in the lifestyles. Since the information technologies would show their influence in almost all the areas, it is natural that fashion would take shape of an industry. The hair dressing, beauty parlours, jogging and gym centres would flourish since the masses would be found more conscious to their physical health. The westernisation of culture, craze for western living conditions, the tidal wave of pop culture, the dresses and hairstyles would throw a big impact on the society. This makes it clear that there would be a conducive environment for the development of beauty parlours, modelling centres, dry-cleaning centres, studios, hair dressing, tailoring or almost all the centres directly or indirectly helping us in looking smart, handsome and attractive. This makes it essential that we think in favour of practising modern marketing principles in all the selected areas.

4. Professionalism in Education: The development of human resources would be given a transcendental priority by almost all the organisations either producing goods or generating services. Of course, the corporate culture makes an advocacy in favour of performance orientation but it is not possible unless we assign due weightage to employee orientation. The professional excellence thus would get a new priority and the masses would be tempted to the professional education. We can't deny that the business environmental conditions for all the sectors would be conducive and the organisations developing professionals and the institutions preparing professionally sound human resources would get a profitable opportunity. Excellence, perfection, professionalism would be the attractions which would require development of world-class educational institutions for almost all the disciplines. The tourism services, hotel services, banking services, insurance services, communication services, entertainment services, educational services, medicare services, consultancy services, personal care services thus would be professionalised in which only the world-class human resources would get place. The application of marketing principles would make the task easier.

5. Information Explosion: Of late, the developed countries have been found making sincere efforts to build a superhighway for communications. The inventions and innovations in the field of communications have been found fuelling information explosion. It is in this context that we now find globe like a village. To be more specific after the development of satellite communication facilities, we find beginning of a new chapter in almost all the areas. The tremendous opportunities generated by communications would influence almost all the sectors.

The entertainment industry, the advertising industry, the fashion industry and many others would be influenced by the latest developments that we find in the world of communications. It is in this context that we find it essential to practise the modern marketing principles so that the marketing information system plays a positive role in improving the quality of decisions. The decision-making, decision supporting systems would have a new look, the micro-computers would assist decision-makers in many ways. The intensity of competition would be at its peak and an organisation assigning due weightage to the quality of decision would be successful in establishing an edge over the organisations managing things traditionally.

6. Sophistication in Market: With the development of communication services, it is natural that we find sophistication in the market where customers' expectations would be found high. The westernised lifestyles would change the hierarchy of needs and requirements and fashion-oriented, comforts-generating household items would have a profitable market. The living conditions would be changed, the food habits would be changed, the dresses and hairstyles would be changed, the drinks would be changed, the vehicles would be changed and the style of homes and apartments would be changed and so on and so forth. This makes it clear that multi-dimensional changes in almost all the areas would change the nature of market *vis-a-vis* the products/services required for that market. The supermarket culture, the departmental store culture, the fast food culture, the telemarketing culture, the tele-education culture would influence masses.

7. Increasing Governmental Activities: The expanding governmental activities mainly due to the participation of state in almost all sectors of the economy would also make ways for the development of services sector. The trade and cultural exchange policies, the global partnership, the convention industry, the hospitality industry, etc. would have a profitable market.

The aforesaid facts make it clear that the services sector has a bright future. A number of service generating industries would get place in the Indian market. The domestic as well as the foreign companies would act as business partners in which efficiency would suitably be rewarded. Willingly or unwillingly, the government would be compelled to make the market free. This would make the market competitive in which only efficient, value-based organisations would survive. This makes it essential that the service generating organisations view the problem with a new vision and make their strategic decisions innovative. They show world-class performance, offer world-class services, behave decently, show empathy and perform excellently. They create a quality gap by promoting making things happen. They maximise the frequency in innovation and establish an edge over their competitors. If they work with this motto, the opportunities would be capitalised on profitably. The modern innovative marketing principles would help them in many ways. This would help them in improving the quality of their services. The promotional decisions would be creative and sensitive, the price charged would be reasonable and moderate and the offering processes would be decent. The human resources or the marketing personnel would be professionally sound and thus qualitative improvements in almost all the areas would help them fantastically in increasing the market share and establishing the leadership.

SIGNIFICANCE OF SERVICES MARKETING

The services sector if marketed in a right fashion contributes substantially to the process of development. The speed of socio-economic transformation can be increased sizeably if the innovative marketing principles are practised. We can't deny the fact that in the years to come the services sector would get a conducive environment with profitable opportunities. If we market the services in a right direction, the available opportunities can be capitalised on optimally. It is against this background that we make an advocacy in favour of services marketing. The following facts are a staunch testimony to this proposition that an optimal development of the services sector would pave copious avenues for the development of national economy.

1. Creation and Expansion of Job Opportunities: The mounting problem of unemployment specially in the Indian perspective makes it essential that whatever the development plans we formulate are instrumental in creating and expanding the job opportunities. We can't deny that the development of services sector would open doors, search new vistas for the development of even those sectors which have either remained untapped or have partially been tapped. If we turn our eyes on the different components of the services sector, such as personal care services, education services, medicare services, communication services, tourism services, hospitality services, banking services, insurance services, transportation services, consultancy services and even other services; the existing conditions compel us to think that an organised and a systematic development would create tremendous job opportunities. It is also right to mention that marketing practices would play an incremental role in making the organisations commercially viable which would signal positive developments in the national economy. It is important to mention that in the Indian context, we have not been successful in tapping the potentials of the services sector since in the USA more than 85 per cent of job opportunities come from the services sector.[14] This confirms the significance of services sector to the creation of job opportunities. Our prime attention on raising the contribution of the services sector to the GNP or the national economy would establish a new circle of development which would invite multi-faceted positive developments.

2. An Optimal Utilisation of Resources: The most important thing in the development process is to make possible an optimal development of the different types of resources available in a country. Since we have been facing the problem of a non-optimal demographic structure, it is pertinent that we make an assault on the misuse of resources. It is in this context that we find the services marketing important since this sector of the economy if marketed properly regulates the unproductive use of resources. By marketing services, we prefer to use resources which remain unutilised or underutilised generally found to be a burden on the exchequer. The personal care services, the entertainment services, tourism services, hotel services help developing the economy without consuming the natural resources. It is high time that the policy planners realise gravity of the situation and regulate the non-optimal use of natural resources so that we don't complicate the magnitude of problem for the coming generations. To be more specific in an over-populated country, it is much more impact generating that the development policies assign due weightage to the conservation of natural resources. Of course, the services marketing simplify our task of conserving the valuable natural resources for the coming generations.

3. Paving Avenues for the Formation of Capital: To energise the process of development, it is essential that we speed up the process of capital formation so that the problem of inadequacy of financial resources is minimised. It is against this background that we need to assign due weightage to the development of services sector. The formation of capital is substantially influenced by the contributions of production processes to the national economy. If our investments are found to be productive, we contribute substantially to the development process. The increasing GNP paves avenues for the development of income which opens doors for investment. For accelerating the rate of capital formation, it is essential that we explore opportunities and identify important or the profitable services. It is also significant that we keep in mind the potentials available and plan accordingly. It is important to mention that in the economy of US, an individual spends about 49 per cent of a dollar on service.[15] This makes the development conditions favourable and investment opportunities are capitalised on profitably. An important task before the development planners is to raise the contribution of GNP to the national economy which is even below 40 per cent in the Indian context.[16] It is a crying need of the hour that the development planners make sincere efforts to accelerate the rate of capital formation and the services sector would not disappoint them.

4. Increasing the Standard of Living: The philosophy of development is coiled in the essence of improving the living conditions of masses which in turn help increasing the standard of living. If we offer quality living conditions for the masses, the faculty of development would be proved to be productive. The qualitative developments in the society are substantially influenced by the pattern or system of development adopted by the policy makers. If we turn our eyes on the standard of living of the Indian society, of course, we find ourselves far behind the developed countries. At the same time, it is right to mention that we find good auguries and are optimistic. For increasing the standard of living, it is only not essential that we make available to the masses opportunities to earn more but it is also essential that we make sincere efforts to increase public awareness so that they know how to spend, where to spend, what to eat, how much to eat, how to develop our personality, how to keep the health sound and so on. These things contribute considerably to the standard of living. It is right to mention that with an increase in the standard of living, we succeed in enriching the potentials of human resources. The development of service generating organisations inform and sense the customers in a right fashion.

5. Environment-friendly Technology: Of late, we find use of technologies even in the services sector since almost all the services are now found technology-driven. To be more specific, the developed countries have been found practising the same. There is no doubt in it that we find a beginning even in the Indian condition but it is at the nascent stage. The basic difference that we find in the nature and types of technologies used for managing and offering the services is its negligible or even dismal negative effective on the environment. The banking services, insurance services, tourism services, hostel services, communication services, education services and by and large almost all the services are now technology-driven but environment-friendly. If we talk about the technologies used for manufacturing organisations, the harmful effects on environment can't be negated. This makes it clear that technology-driven service generating organisations offer world-class services even without polluting the environment.

The aforesaid facts make it clear that marketing of services is found significant to the service generating organisations, users and even to the employees serving the organisations in many ways. The service generating organisations succeed in improving the quality of services and increasing the market share. This further simplifies the process of establishing leadership. The users are found benefited since they get the world-class services because the service generating organisations are supposed to improve the quality of their services as an ongoing process. The users thus get quality services and the decent behaviour. We find all possibilities of fulfilling their expectations since the marketing processes assign due weightage to the behavioural management. In addition, the employees are also benefited because they get suitable incentives and other benefits. It is against this background that we find services marketing important. It is also important to mention that the generation of employment opportunities is the number one positive impact of marketing the businesses of the services sector. To be more specific in the Indian condition where we find problem of unemployment at its peak, the development of services sector needs an intensive care.

In this context, it is also pertinent to mention that the instrumentality of this sector is substantially influenced by the excellence of professionals who manage the services. The employee-orientation occupies a place of outstanding significance because in absence of the same, we can't think about performance orientation. Since both of them are interrelated, it is important that the policy makers and decision-makers specially for sharpening the instrumentality of this sector make possible a fair blending of the two. Of course, we find use of technology in the services sector and by and large, almost all the organisations have been found promoting sophisticated technologies for improving the quality but keeping in view the Indian condition, the policy makers and the senior executives are supposed to make the use of technology rational so that the cases of retrenchment of employees are checked. Though automation has been instrumental in raising the level of expectations of customers and they are found tempted to the technology-driven system, it is also right to opine that just to fulfil their expectations we should not aggravate the problem of retrenchment and unemployment. The main thing in the process is to improve the quality and to influence the customers. A rational use of technology in the face of national conditions would, on the one hand, improve the quality of services while on the other hand would also counter the negative effects.

THE BEHAVIOURAL PROFILE OF USERS

We agree with this view that the first commandment of marketing is to know they market which draws our attention on understanding the behavioural profile of buyers. Buyer's behaviour is viewed as an orderly process whereby an individual interacts with his/her environment for the purpose of making marketplace decisions on products and services.[17] The decision process used by the users of services moves through different stages, e.g., recognition of problem, search for information, evaluation of information, purchase decisions and post-purchase

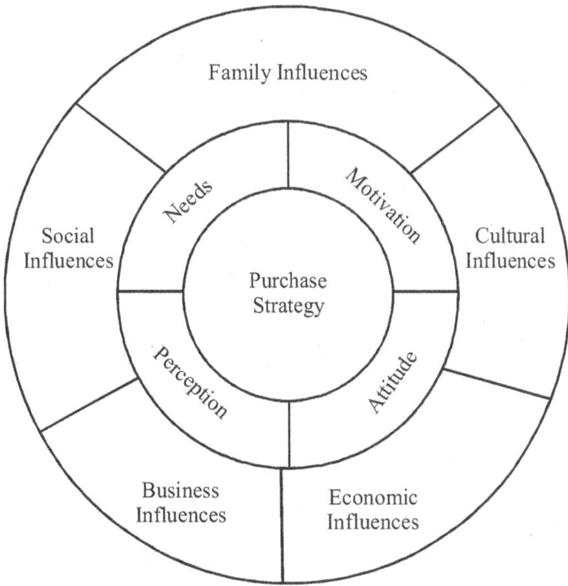

Fig. 1.1: Environmental and Cultural Influences

evaluation. At the marketplace, an individual's specific behaviour is governed by internal factors like need, motives, perception and attitudes as well as by external factors or environmental influences, such as the family, social groups, cultural, economic and business influences.[18] C. Glenn Walters in his important contribution on Consumer

Behaviour has shown the environmental and individual influences in a circle.[19] The environmental and culture influences as shown in Figure 1.1 make it clear that the purchase strategy is influenced by a number of factors and an in-depth study of these influences are essential to understand the behavioural profile of users.

The formal explanation of buyer behaviour has been initiated by the economists since their studies of income and personal consumption and the concept of discretionary income are found helpful in comprehending the behaviour of users. The economic theory describes man as a rational buyer who has complete information about the market and uses it to obtain optimum value for his buying efforts and money. In this context, we find price as an effective motivational force. The economists feel that markets are homogeneous. They advocate that heterogeneity not homogeneity characterises markets. Another way to explain buying behaviour is in terms of what the buyers are trying to do.

The Sorting Theory explains different stages starting from conglomerations, going through the various types of sorting and concluding with assortments.

This also conveys that the consumer enters the market as a problem solver.[20] The economic theories explain competition among sellers by emphasising innovative competition, product differentiation and differential advantage. It is advocated that each item is differentiated from all others by the characteristics of its products, its services, its geographic location or its particular combination of all these features. It is against this background that the survival of a firm depends upon its efforts for offering differential advantages over other firms. The goods manufacturing or the service generating organisations found successful in establishing distinction are found successful in getting a positive response.

There are a number of economic factors influencing consumers or users while spending their incomes for personal consumption, e.g., disposable personal income, size of family and family income, expectations of consumers, liquid assets of consumers and consumer credit. We can't ignore the fact that goods as well as the services are produced for consumption. The transformation of production into consumption is substantially governed by the purchasing power and the disposable income which represents for the potential purchasing power in the hands of consumers. It is clear that the income after discharging the tax liability is called the disposable income.

The social scientists view marketing as involving the activities of groups of people motivated by group pressures as well as by individual desires. The significance of reference groups, individual's concept of social role, the diffusion process and social classes are found instrumental in influencing the human behaviour. The studies made by them have demonstrated the importance of social factors in anatomising and influencing the consumer behaviour.

The cultural-anthropological influences are also found significant while studying the consumer behaviour. Every culture evolves unique patterns of social conduct. As for instance, the Japanese culture provides for certain pattern of eating, dress and hairstyles and social interactions. The American culture provides for different patterns. And both are found different from those prevalent in the Indian culture. In the USA, again we find different patterns. It is said that many aspects of American culture and subcultures within the US are unique, including the role of ethnic groups, religion, influence of women in society, leisure hour and fashion as well as the composition of population itself.[21] There are a number of factors included in the cultural influences like religion, ethnic groups, role of women, leisure time and fashion and a study of behavioural profile which necessitates an in-depth study of all.

The psychologists have discussed the psychological influences. They study attitudes and learning for understanding the consumer behaviour. Concepts borrowed from the learning theory help in answering a number of questions as mentioned below:

- How do consumers learn about products offered for sale?
- How do they learn to recognise and recall these products?
- By what processes they do develop buying or consuming habits?

The aforesaid facts make it clear that economic, social, psychological factors help us in understanding the behaviour of buyers. It is important to mention that an in-depth study of the behavioural profile requires a sound management of information and for which we need support of sophisticated information technologies. This makes it significant that the service generating organisations assign due weightage to the marketing information system. Understanding human behaviour is, of course, a difficult task. We find lifestyle a distinct mode of living in a dynamic society. The lifestyle research measures help us in understanding the interests of buyers, their opinions and certain basic demographic characteristics.[22] The lifestyle research answers to a number of questions like:

- What do women think of the job of housekeeping?
- Do they participate in the community activities?
- Are they interested in the future?

It is right to mention that lifestyle segmentation is related to people rather than products. It classifies them into different lifestyle groups naturally each with a unique style of living. The justification for the lifestyle approach is that consumer is not interested in the product *per se* or by himself but in its effect upon himself.[23] We accept the fact that recently the lifestyle segmentation has provided a more global look at the behaviour of buyers.

Of course, the aforesaid factors help us in understanding the behaviour of buyers. However, the study of human behaviour is found a tough task. The task is much more difficult when we are required to study the behaviour of buyers. It is right to say that a picture cut into different pieces can't be set right unless the missing piece is available. This makes it clear that a number of factors influence the behaviour of buyers and in the process of study, it is natural that we often commit a mistake. Thus, dealing with a diverse, obscure and complex personality requires more professionalism. To be more specific in the marketing of services where we find the users enigmatic; it is essential that we make possible an in-depth study of the different factors directly or indirectly influencing the behavioural profile of buyers.

SEARCH vs. EXPERIENCE vs. CREDENCE PROPERTIES OF GOODS AND SERVICES

The classification of properties in the goods and services is found in a different way. The economists distinguish between the two properties of consumer products, viz., the search properties and experience properties. The search qualities make it clear that a consumer can determine before purchasing the product whereas the experience qualities or properties make it clear that consumers can be discerned only after the purchase or during consumption. In the search qualities, we include colour, style, price, fit, feel, hardness and smell. In the experience qualities, we include taste and wearability. If we talk about automobiles, clothing, furniture and jewellery; they are found high in search qualities because the consumers can determine their attributes and evaluate them before purchase. Goods and services such as vacations and meals of restaurants are found high in experience qualities. This is due to the fact that we come to know about their properties only after we experience.

The credence qualities focus our attention on the characteristics which cannot be evaluated even after purchase and consumption. A majority of the consumers find it difficult to evaluate the medical and mechanical skills. They do not know the justifications for services or they find it difficult to know about the quality of services-offered.

The three properties thus presented in Figure 1.2 make it clear that the service marketers need to know the differences for studying and understanding their behavioural profile.

Fig. 1.2: Search, Experience and Credence Qualities

The three categories we find in Fig. 1.2. A number of services are found high in experience qualities and credence qualities. Just reverse to it, we find a number of goods high in search qualities. The evaluation process is found easier where we find goods of search qualities but it is found difficult where we find experience and credence properties. Thus, the evaluation process is found much more complicated when we talk about services. This forces consumers to rely on the different cues and processes while evaluating services.

The services are found dominated by the experience and credence qualities.

In Fig. 1.2, we find major goods in the left continuum whereas the major services in the right continuum. In the left end of the continuum, we find clothing, jewellery, furniture and houses which can easily be evaluated. In the centre of the continuum, we find automobiles, restaurant meals, vacation, haircuts. We find them high in experience qualities and therefore difficult to evaluate. The goods and services in the right end of the continuum such as television repair, root canal, auto repair, medical diagnosis and legal services are much more difficult to evaluate.

The above-mentioned properties make the evaluation process much more difficult in services. It is against this background that the consumers are found employing different processes for evaluation, specially when they make use of services. The orders in the decision-making process in a very natural way will be found different in respect of services.

In the context of services, when we talk about need recognition, we find social, ego and self-actualisation needs important. This is the first stage for decision-making. In the second stage, we find information search and for services, the consumers rely on the personal sources. This is due to a number of reasons, first mass and selective media communicate little about experience qualities and second the non-personal sources of information cannot be available. In the next stage, we find evaluation service alternatives and here we find less alternatives. When the services are of non-professional nature, they have alternative of hiring. In the fourth stage, we find purchase and consumption of services where we find moods and emotions playing an important role. The moods and emotions of both providers and users are found here significant. So far as the fifth stage is concerned, we find services considerably influenced by information.

THE ROLE OF CULTURE IN SERVICES

Transmission is an essential feature of culture. Being multi-dimensional in nature, we find culture learned and shared to be transmitted from one generation to another. In the context of services marketing, we find culture playing an outstanding role. The interaction of people serving the organisation considerably rests on culture. We find its role assuming a place of outstanding significance specially in the field of international services marketing. This does not meant that we need not consider this factor in the domestic marketing because even in this context we find culture governing the market conditions. With the changing faces of corporatisation and increasing domination of Multinational Corporations (MNCs), we find emergence of a multi cultural or cross-cultural society. Taking services from one country and offering the same in another necessitates an in-depth study of culture. The professionals need to understand culture because they are supposed to go through the same in each and every stage of decision-making process without which the quality of decisions would considerably be affected. It is against this background that we find it essential to study the role of culture in services marketing in general and the marketing of international services in particular.

Here we quote, "Everybody looks at the world from behind the windows of a cultural home, and everybody prefers to act as if people from other countries have something special about them (a national character) but home is normal. Unfortunately, there is no normal position in cultural matters."[24] Of course, it is not in good taste that we find a majority of us viewing other cultures through cluttered lens of our own. In the United States of America, we find a majority of Americans viewing foreigners as underdeveloped Americans. The focus here is on the fact that particularly when we talk about the marketing of services in the global perspective, the marketing professionals having an in-depth idea of cultural patterns are to be efficacious of making quality marketing decisions. This makes it essential that professionals are sensitive to culture.

We find cultural universals as manifestations of the lifestyle or the way of life of any group of people and the marketers need to understand them in a right fashion. We find role of culture or even domination of culture in the decision-making practices for services. The culture remains to be a guiding force as we find it clear in Figure 1.3.

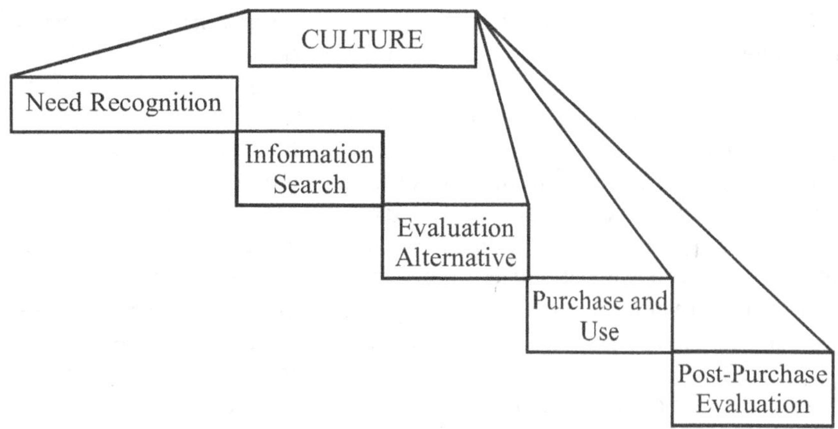

Fig. 1.3: Culture — A Guiding Force

The service marketers bear the responsibility of developing their awareness of the cultural universals which we find manifesting our lifestyles or the way of life. The values and attitudes differ across cultures and therefore our sensitivity to the emergence of a cross-cultural society in the wake of globalisation needs due attention. The manners and customs help us in identifying the behavioural profile. If we talk about the service encounter, this is directly influenced by manners and customs. So far as the habits are concerned, we find them considerably influenced by culture. This is in this context that we find Japanese preferring to use long holidays in place of holidays of one or two days. And if they take the holidays of suppose ten days, the direct benefit that we find goes to the tourism industry as during this period they make use of package benefits. The material culture is another important dimension which we find as the tangible products of culture. It is against this background that we find Americans Mexicans, Indians, having distinct character of shopping and travelling. The aesthetics refer to cultural ideas about your taste and apparance. The ideas about aesthetics differ across culture. The educational and social institutions happen to be the transmission agent of culture. The healthcare delivery systems and the interaction between doctors and patients also reflect our culture.

The five categories of consumer behaviour as shown in Figure 1.3 reflect the difference between goods and services, such as need recognition, information search, evaluation of service alternatives, service purchase and consumption and post-purchase evaluation. In this context, we go through the following problems helping marketers in understanding the instrumentality of culture in the services sector. The important issues are: Values and Attitudes, Manners and Customs, Material Cultur, Aesthetics and Educational and Social Institutions.

Values and Attitudes: The service marketers bear the responsibility of understanding the behaviour of their customers and for this, they need to develop their awareness of values and attitudes. We cannot negate that values and cultures help marketing professionals in identifying the thinkings and studying the minds of customers. If we find masses having temptation of fascination to national excellence, this is to affect the culture and behaviour. An attitudinal change in the customers of services cannot be negated in the very context. It was due to this that when Mexicans developed their fascination to national excellence, this affected their attitudes and they stopped making use of American products. Particularly when we go through the problem in the global context, the marketing professionals need to consider the changes they feel due to the behavioural changes. No doubt in it that the task of marketing professionals is considerably simplified when they have right perception of the values and attitudes of customers of those countries where they have to market.

Manners and Customs: The marketing professional having an in-depth idea of manners and customs find it convenient to identify the appropriate ways of behaving. Since we find them affecting the service encounter, it is pertinent that professionals develop their awareness of the existent differences between the two.

We find habits similar to customs influencing the marketing decisions. The marketing professionals need to know about the manners and customs helping them in making their decisions much more effective. The travel industry, hotel industry, transportation in general and civil aviation in particular are considerably influenced by the manners and habits. Since we find them directly affecting the service encounter, the service marketers cannot overlook their influences. The customers in a very natural way evaluate services considerably governed by manners and customs.

Material Culture: The systems and patterns of economic transformation substantially affect the formation of material culture. When materialistic gains start dominating the behaviour, we find its impact on culture. It is also right to mention that domination of services or tertiary sector on the economy governs our culture in a different way. This is due to the fact that we find its two-tier impact. The services sector considerably affect the process of economic transformation in which we find development of high aesthetic sense. Thus, qualitative and quantitative impact on economy and behaviour stimulate the formation of material culture. The way of displaying our material possession cannot be identical in different parts of the globe. The Japanese behave in a different way, the Americans have a different behavioural profile and the Indians have also a different style of behaviour. With the development of corporate sector in the developing countries like ours, we find a significant increase in the level of income of masses which have been resulting into the materialistic, display in different forms. In a true sense when we start earning more; our behavioural profile is changed and the materialism starts dominating the behaviour. Taking pleasure in displaying the materialistic gains is normally found at the initial stage of development. Gradually when we find development becoming a part of or way of life, it becomes non-existent.

Aesthetics: In aesthetics, we find focus on our taste and beauty. We find general masses developing attractions to beauty because it is natural. We find reflection of aesthetics in art, music, colour, dresses, service environment or environment at the place where services are rendered. Aesthetic preferences may vary from culture to culture and country to country. The marketing professionals need to assign due weightage to aesthetic management. In the hospitals and healthcare services, we find aesthetic management playing a significant role in improving the quality of treatment and minimising the period of recovery. In the tourism and hotel industry, we find aesthetic sense of people working or serving there and aesthetics displayed at the workplace playing an important role.

Educational and Social Institutions: We find both the social institutions working as an agent of culture. The impact of culture on both the sources of formation of social assets cannot be negated. The pattern of classroom lectures vary from country to country. In India, Japan and America, we find a different scenario during the classroom lectures. The pattern of treatment, doctor-patients relations also vary from country to country. The marketing professionals need to be aware of the impact of culture on the quality and types of services.

Service Experiences Differ Across Cultures

Based on the study results, we go through, the differences in the service experiences that we find between United States of America and Japan. Of course, we find there cultural variation and this has a telling impact on the service experiences.

In the United States of America, we find personal authenticity and promptness dominating whereas in Japan, we find caring and concern as the focal point. In the United States, we find emphasis on individualism whereas in the Japan, we find focus on empathy. Of course, we find civility emerging as a common feature in both the countries but with a different meaning. In the United States, we find focus on attention and quality service whereas in Japan we find it to be patient and fair. In the United States, we find authenticity an important dimension but this is not so in Japan. Thus, the service providers need to develop their awareness of the culture which plays an effective role while providing the services.

The service differences across the national boundary require to be received in a right fashion. Now, we need to go through the problem in a systematic way because with the emergence of a cross-cultural society, the cultural influences draw a priority attention of the service marketers. It is in this context that they have to understand the following:

Authenticity: In the United States, the clerks work independently but in the Japan, we find artificial style because every clerk has the same type of smile. In this context, we find variation in treatment.

Caring: In Japan, this is considered to be the most important dimension because they consider customer as God but we do not find the same thing in the United States.

Control: In the United States, we find control an important dimension but this is not so in the Japan.

Courtesy: In Japan, we find courtesy occupying a place of outstanding significance but in the United States, it is not so important.

Formality: In the United States, we find informal treatment whereas in Japan, it is formal.

Friendliness: In the United States, the friendliness is expected whereas in Japan friendliness can be disrespectful.

Personalisation: In the United States, we find service very much personalised and therefore we find use of names frequently but this we do not find in Japan where they treat like the same person.

Promptness: In Japan, we find people preferring quick services whereas in the United States, we find people expecting chat.

The service marketers need to go through the variations that we find in the behaviour due to cultural variations. It is in this context that we find Europeans presenting a very different picture. Of late, we find emergence of a cross-cultural society and therefore the marketing professional cannot undermine the variations due to cultural influences.

MARKETING INFORMATION SYSTEM

We are living in an age of information technologies in which a sound management of information plays an important role in improving the quality of managerial decisions. The mounting intensity of competition makes it essential that we make possible frequency in the process of innovating the decisions so that our task of making things happen is simplified considerably. It is in this context that we talk about the instrumentality of information-based decisions in making the marketing processes proactive. Almost all the organisations either producing goods or generating services need to manage information in a right fashion. Of late, we have sophisticated information technologies and the professionals bear the responsibility of managing the marketing information system.

We can't remain unilluminated specially about a river in which we venture to float our crafts. It is pertinent that we understand the river, collect information regarding the movement of winds, shallow and deep points, possibilities of a tidal wave and only then start the process of sailing. This help us in minimising the magnitude of risk. Like this, it is essential that the service generating organisations are well aware of the recent developments in and around the business and formulate policies and decisions which cater to the changing needs. If the banking organisations are not familiar with the latest developments in the socio-economic environmental conditions, the requirements of business and industries, the expectations of different categories of customers; the task of making sensitive policy decisions would be difficult. If the hotels and tourism organisations are not aware of the emerging trends in the tourism industry *vis-a-vis* the expectations of potential tourists and guests, the policy decisions would show a lukewarm response. Like this, the personal care service generating organisations are supposed to enrich their knowledge bank, specially regarding the requirements of the potential customers failing which we find their task difficult. These facts are a mute testimony to this proposition that by and large, almost all the organisations need to manage the marketing information and it is against this background that we make an advocacy in favour of developing a technology-driven marketing information system.

The main purpose of marketing information system is to make possible co-ordinated, systematic and continuous collection of information. It is an organised set of procedures, information-handling routines and reporting techniques designed to provide the information required for making marketing decisions.[25] It reduces the domination of intution-based decisions as relevant and useful information from both the internal and external sources are collected. Further, it also provides a mechanism for reducing the often overwhelming flood of available marketing information to pertinent usable amounts.[26] The responsibility for an effective MIS rests with the system analysts who are found highly skilled in information-gathering and information-handling techniques. An advisory group of representative from marketing, finance and accounting, operations research, data processing and other organisational units not only assist a system analyst but also maintains continual surveillance over the MIS, suggests modifications to meet the company's evolving marketing information needs and the initial design.

It is important to mention that the identification of desired information outputs is the most critical aspect of MIS design. Essentially, system designer is required to focus on the nature of decisions required for combating the marketing problems. The job of MIS is to process large quantities of marketing data and to present it to management in the most usable form effective for decision-making. A sophisticated processor computer is required for the handling of data. The processor is controlled by a data bank, a statistical bank and a model bank. The real challenge in designing an MIS is to determine what kind of and how much information is how often needed by each executive in the marketing organisation.

The MIS information inputs come from diverse sources, both within and outside the organisation. The internal sources provide the major information flows, found routine or of continuous nature, e.g., the controller, research and development department. These sources provide for operating and sales analysis data. The external sources provide three forms of marketing information, e.g., marketing intelligence, marketing forecasts and marketing research.

In making the marketing decisions, the operating data has been found significant. The marketing executives use such data almost daily which help them in identifying problems, developing alternatives, appraising them and deciding courses of action. The sources of operating data are company's own financial, accounting, sales and production records. The sales analysis data is also an important operating data. Analysis of a company's sales records makes it possible to detect various marketing strengths and weaknesses. In the context of external sources, we find marketing intelligence important which is considered to be an organised procedure to collect regularly from diverse sources the information of potential usefulness for the making of marketing decisions. It includes raw data, summary statistics, qualitative inferences, expert and lay opinions, impressions and albeit rumours. In this context, a majority of the items are collected from the public sources. Another important source is sales forecasting. It is an estimate of sale tied to a particular marketing programme and assuming a particular set of economic and other forces outside the forecasting unit. The forecast may be both, sophisticated and unsophisticated. Naturally, the sophisticated forecasts have greater accuracy in their performance. Regression analysis and econometric model building are the two most widely used methods, however, the third one is also used which is the survey of consumers' buying power. The unsophisticated methods are jury of executive opinion, poll of salesforce opinion and projection of post-sales.

It is important to mention that an MIS is made of different subsystems. If a system has to aid in decision-making, it is essential that the system analysts are well aware of the nature of information needed. Hence, the decision-makers are required to speak of the nature of information required by them. This helps decision-makers in thinking through the decision process in great detail which simplifies the task of system analysts.

Like the goods manufacturing organisations even the service generating organisations are found using MIS to improve the quality of their decisions. In Fig. 1.4, we find the process of managing the information in the MIS.

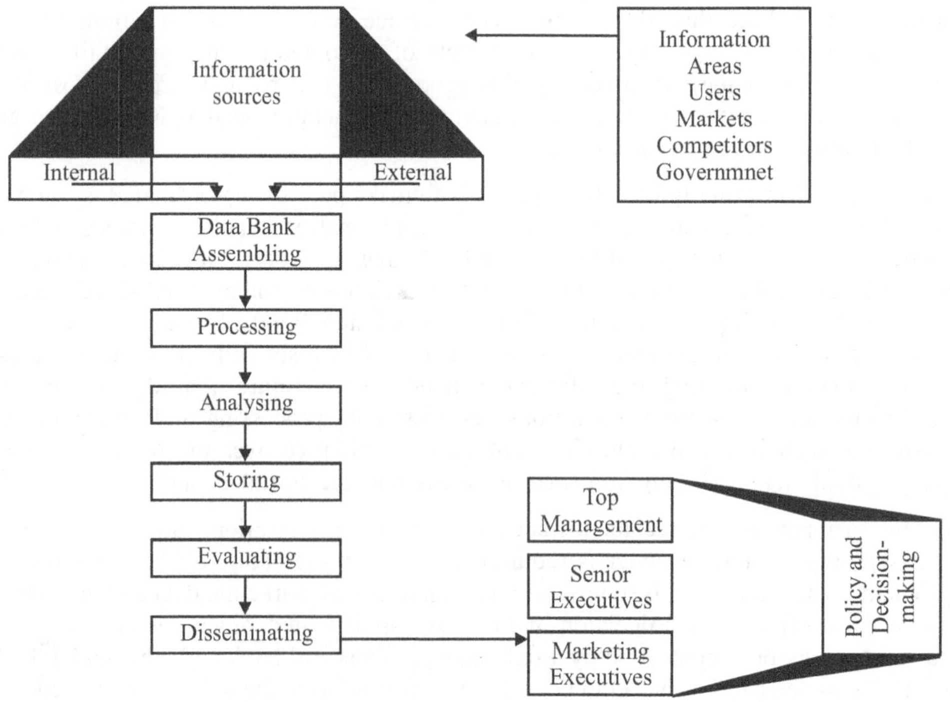

Fig. 1.4: Marketing Information System

Assembling of data, processing of data, analysis of data, storage of data, evaluation of data and the dissemination of data are the different functions of the MIS as shown in the Figure 1.4. The richness of data bank is an important consideration which requires due attention on the collection of information. The availability of sophisticated information technologies is also significant to influence the accuracy and time in managing the information. The quality of computer professionals also influences the process considerably. The senior executives working in an organisation are required to assign due weightage to the development and management of the system. If the organisations have been found managing the information with the help of new generation of information technologies, we find its immediate effect on the quality of decision. It is important to mention that of late we also find micro computers assisting executives in making the decisions. Thus, in the years to come, we expect new developments in the discipline which would make it essential that the service generating organisations assign an overriding priority to the development of an MIS.

MARKET SEGMENTATION

Markets rather than being homogeneous are really heterogeneous. No two buyers or potential buyers of a product are ever identical in all respects. They represent every income group, every age group, every section of the country. We find both sexes and even a single mother in the process of making the decisions. Despite all, we find existence of a group of individuals with common characteristic as buyers. Knowing the market is found important to a marketer's success. An optimal marketing strategy becomes a must and the task of formulating the same is found difficult if we don't have an in-depth study of market segmentation. It is against this background that almost all the service generating organisations are required to study the problem of market segmentation.

Market segmentation is a division or subdivision of market. It is the recognition that market is composed of different buyers who have different responses to market offerings. Robert E. Pitts says, "Market segmentation is the recognition that market is composed of different buyers who have different responses to market offerings. No one approach to the market will satisfy all buyers. Each segment represents a somewhat different opportunity for the organisation. In its most fundamental form, market segmentation recognises that a company or its product/ service offering cannot be all things to everyone."[27] Harper and Massy opine, "Process by which a firm partitions its prospective customers into subgroups or sub-markets is known as market segmentation."[28] There is no doubt in it that we find market segmentation a play of divide and rule. By segmenting the market, we divide the market into different groups and subgroups which help us in understanding the complexities and similarities found in a particular segment.

In view of the above, the following key points are observed:

- Market segmentation is the division and subdivision of markets.
- It gives formal recognition to the fact that wants and desires of consumers are diverse.
- It is grouping of two or more consumers for a product/service.
- It is based on the modern concept of marketing which focuses on the demand side.
- It is a strategy of 'divide and rule'.

Of course, we agree with the view that in all the services we don't find market segmentation essential. To be more specific in the services where we need to maintain uniformity, the market segmentation becomes ineffective. The instrumentality of market segmentation is involved in the essence of making available to the customers the right goods and the quality services. The latest studies in the field of behavioural science make it clear that the behaviour of consumer can't be uni-dimensional, rather than they find it multi-dimensional. This in a natural way increases the instrumentality of segmentation.

The segmentation reflects reality in the market situations, ensures higher customer satisfaction and brings qualitative improvements in the effectiveness of the marketing programmes. It is a customer-oriented marketing philosophy that sensitises the marketing policies, strategies and programmes.

For market segmentation, we use a number of bases like geographic, demographic and psychographic. The geographic consideration becomes significant since the needs and requirements of customers are also influenced by the geographical incidence. The market is divided into different territories and regions and the needs and requirements of customers can't be uniform in different segments. Within different parts of a nation, we find sufficient variation in the consumption patterns, such as food habits, dresses, household requirements and so on. These variations may result from the differing cultural heritage or topography. Thus, a change in the hierarchy of needs and requirements due to geographical variation makes it essential that marketers while formulating marketing strategies assign due weightage to the same. The urban segment and rural segment present a different look, specially when we study their needs and requirements *vis-a-vis* the behavioural patterns. The size and population of a town or city also influence the taste and temperament.

Demographics are the most frequently used base for market segmentation. This is mainly due to the fact that the process of measurement is easy and the market differentiation is simple. Income, age, education, social class, sex, occupation, religion also influence the needs and requirements and therefore while segmenting a market we should also consider different related components. The persons with low income are found hard pressed and therefore they find it difficult to manage even the basic necessities, such as food, clothing and shelter. The education is also a base for segmentation since we find a change in the needs and requirements and level of expectations of educated and illiterate persons. Cultural type of entertainment, such as opera, legitimate theatre and ballet appeal primarily to the educated segment of the society. Wrestling matches, roller derbies and carnivals appeal most strongly to the less educated segment. Market segmentation by stage in the life cycle is found another dimension considered as a base for market segmentation. Expenditure on some of the selected items vary with the stage in the life cycle. The gender or sex is also to influence the hierarchy of needs *vis-a-vis* the behavioural patterns. In addition, the status, occupation, religion are also found influencing our needs and requirements. It is important that the professionals are well aware of the different demographic considerations and segment market accordingly.

Psychographic bases are also required to be taken into consideration while segmenting the market. Personality influences the use of a number of services, the status, profession, position influence the taste and temperament. An aggressive personality may be reflected in the choice of ostentatious clothing, furniture and automobiles. Life-style is another important segmentation basis.[29]

Swingers home-family types, social or political activists, all of them have different lifestyles. These lifestyles influence the allocation of income across consumption categories as well as among types and brands. The swingers bear different clothing, buys different recreation equipment, even eat differently.[30]

The aforesaid bases for market segmentation makes it clear that the service generating organisations also need to segment market since even in the services we don't find uniformity in the choice. While segmenting, there are a number of factors to be taken into active consideration, such as the emerging trends in competition, the homogeneity of product, life cycle of the product, the homogeneity of customers, availability of the financial resources and regulatory support extended by the government. We can't deny the fact that the emerging changes in the social, political and economic conditions also govern our decisions.

Important to the professionals' success is the availability of information related to the different segments. If the marketers/professionals are found successful in enriching their knowledge bank, the task of understanding the market is simplified considerably. The marketers are not expected to forget that all the customers don't buy the same services with the same motive. Unless they know about the customers, it is a bit difficult to identify the motive. This makes it essential that the marketers know the market, understand the features in a right perspective and formulate the marketing strategies accordingly. Since the market is small, the task is not so difficult. It is also important to mention that needs and requirements are also found changing. With the passage of time, a change in the lifestyles can't be negated. This necessitates a continuous study of the changing market conditions so that the strategic decisions are not to undermine the same. It is against this background that by and large almost all the service generating organisations have been found assigning due weightage to market segmentation.

We can't deny the fact that even for right segmentation, we need a well-developed information system. Since we expect a number of changes influenced by the changing social and economic conditions, the marketing information system would simplify the task of marketers. It is in this context that the information technologies have been found playing an important role in segmenting the market in a right fashion. Of late, we find nucleus marketing gaining popularity the world over. Not only the goods manufacturing organisations but even the service generating organisations have been found talking about the same. This focuses our attention on understanding the changing needs and requirements of all the members in a family and assigning due weightage to the same while formulating the strategic decisions. The market segmentation thus occupies a place of outstanding significance and the marketers need to realise its importance in making the marketing decisions.

EMERGING KEY SERVICES

Sky is the limit for marketing services. Almost all the countries of the world, of late, have been seen assigning a transcendental priority to the development of services sector. Sky is the limit for quality. This complicates the task of marketers since they need to make the innovative efforts more and more competitive which requires world-class professionalism. Sky is the limit for perfection. This needs to fuel the process of development. It is against this background that the service generating organisations have been found intensifying innovative efforts to excel competition which simplifies the task of establishing leadership. We have failed in making possible an optimal utilisation of the services sector though we have world-class potentials. We have failed in assigning due weightage to an optimal development of marketing resources though we have world-class professional excellence. We can't negate the fact that it is the fastest growing sector in the economy of the developed countries which has been attempting to reserve an elbow room even in the developed countries like ours. Of late, in the advanced countries of the world, we find the services sector contributing about 70 per cent in the job markets. It is in this context that we make an advocacy in favour of the services sector since the mounting problem of unemployment can be countered effectively. The public as well as the private sector, the domestic as well as the foreign companies, the national as well as the multinationals need to focus on the services sector.

Today, we market a number of services. This has engineered a sound foundation for the development of service generating organisations. The emerging key services in which we find enough potentials to serve the society and economy need innovative marketing strategies. Like the goods manufacturing organisations even the service generating organisations need to realise the importance of quality in managing the development processes. Scientific inventions and innovations have energised information explosion and we find information technologies playing an incremental role in improving the quality of services. The professional excellence makes ways for qualitative-cum-quantitative improvements. There is no doubt in it that we have been making efforts to tap the potentials in the services sector but our efforts have been found getting a lukewarm response. This makes it essential that almost all the service generating organisations working in the Indian perspective make sincere efforts to make the services internationally competitive. This requires a fair synchronisation of performance orientation and employee orientation. A new corporate culture is waiting for innovation. The policy planners and the senior executives need an attitudinal change. The boardrooms need a new vision.

There are a number of services likely to be productive if the policies and strategies are innovated. The banking services, the insurance services, the transportation services, tourism services, hotel services, consultancy services, communication services, education services and hospital services are to mention a few waiting for a major change. The personal care services, entertainment services, electricity services have tremendous potentials. We need a sound policy to make possible an optimal utilisation of the potentials and to make the development process proactive *vis-a-vis* productive.

Exhibit 1.1 BANKING SERVICES

In the group of service generating industries, we find banking services occupying a place of outstanding significance. We can't deny the fact that with the development of economic activities, the banking sector could emerge as an industry. The public as well as the private sector has been found owning, managing and controlling the banking services. It is right to mention that scientific inventions and innovations made ways for the use of technologies in almost all the sectors and the developed countries activated the process of promoting the technology-driven, user-friendly services. A number of information technologies got important place in the management of banking services. In the past, the banking sector did not get any attraction in the Indian economy because of the low level of economic activities and the meager business prospects. Of late, the business prospects are bright, the trade and commerce has been found getting a conducive environment, the development-oriented activities are motivated, the welfare-oriented programmes are given due weightage, the international trade has been found gaining popularity and these positive developments in the economic world have engineered a sound foundation for the development of banking industry. It is against this background that we find different types of banks serving the different segments of the Indian economy.

In the Indian banking industry, the contours of development underwent radical changes specially after the first phase of nationalisation of commercial banks way back in 1969. The nationalisation was with the motto of raising the contributions of public sector commercial banks to the development and welfare heads but they failed in doing such. The job security to bank employees and domination of trade unions paved the avenues for a degeneration in the quality of customer services. The process of degeneration reached to its peak which developed a bias and the customers in general are found dissatisfied with the services of the public sector commercial banks. Meanwhile, the foreign banks and a few of the private banks got an opportunity to display their excellence and with the support of high-performing bank employees and technology-driven services; they got success in establishing an edge over the services of public sector banks. Of course, the regulation of the Reserve Bank of India demotivated the private sector banks and especially the foreign banks while expanding their network which has minimised the intensity of competition, however they have been successful in building and projecting a positive image. It is in this context that we talk about the application of modern marketing principles in the banking services.

Of late, the policy makers have realised gravity of the problem since they appear interested in discussing and deliberating upon the problems of customer services even in the boardrooms. With the increasing level of customer expectations, it is essential that to be more specific, the public sector commercial banks innovate strategies and promote technology-driven, user-friendly services to increase the market share vis-a-vis to project a positive image. This makes a strong advocacy in favour of bank marketing since its application in a right fashion would answer to a number of unsolved questions.

Exhibit 1.2 INSURANCE SERVICES

Wherever there is uncertainty, there is risk. Wherever there is business, there is risk. The risk can't be averted. We do not have any command on uncertainties since there are a number of uncontrollable factors. The insurance is a co-operative device to accumulate funds to meet uncertain losses. The industry, the business and the individuals appear interested in using the insurance services. The involvement of public sector in the insurance business has made possible a number of changes in its functional areas and responsibilities. The behaviour of insuring institutions, the work culture and the quality of services are presenting a gloomy picture. Of course, a number of steps have been taken to improve the insurance business much more widely and in particular to the rural areas and to socially and economically backward classes with a view to reaching almost all segments of the society but a degeneration in the quality of service has been a matter of serious concern. It is against this background that we talk about the insurance services, specially under the public sector.

Of late, we find different types of services offered by the insurance corporation to the individual and industrial customers. The General Insurance is also managed and controlled by the public sector. Thus, in the Indian perspective, we find the Life Insurance Corporation of India and the General Insurance Corporation engaged in the insurance business. The insurance business was nationalised with the motto of improving the quality of services. In addition, it was also expected that the insurance business would benefit the rural sector of the economy and the weaker sections of the society would get an opportunity to develop. It is right to mention that they have failed in doing such which has engineered a foundation for the entry of private sector in the insurance business. The regulatory barrier is delaying their entry. The task of insurance corporation is found difficult as well as challenging. This necessitates a change in the service profile of the public sector insurance business.

A change in the product mix would naturally require involvement of rural agents having adequate training facilities. The behavioural profile of insurance employees working in the public sector is to be given due weightage. The performance orientation is to be made possible. The domination of trade unions is to be minimised. The promotional efforts are to be made innovative. The gap between the services-promised and services-offered is to be bridged. And all these reforms need conceptualisation of modern marketing principles. The policy makers vis-a-vis the insurance employees need an attitudinal change. The boardrooms need to review the policy decisions in the face of recent developments.

Since we find a number of private insurance companies very much operational in the business, the service marketers would be required to formulate a sound marketing mix where in addition to the traditional four Ps, the extended three mixes would also be practised. The recent changes in the provisions mainly due to IRDA 1999 make the business environment much more volatile. Not only the Insurance Companies but we find even banks entering in the insurance business. This focuses our attention on the professional excellence specially in the public sector where due to managerial deficiency, the foreign insurance companies have been found snatching the business.

With the development of information technology, we now find a changed scenario both in bank and insurance sectors. The internet services have virtually revolutionised the operational mechanism. The database is to make possible a significant change in the decision-making process. We find computerisation making ways for a number of qualitative and quantitative improvements in the insurance sector.

Of course, the leading foreign insurance companies have been found tapping the urban markets and they are also making efforts even to tap the rural markets. They have a team of dedicated and committed marketing professionals and therefore we find their marketing efforts much more result-oriented. Undoubtedly enough, we also find public sector making efforts to initiate the process of innovative marketing but still they need miles and miles to go.

The public as well as the private insurance companies need to tap the non-life business which in the Indian condition is found very low. With the influx of foreign big players, we find good auguries and expect that in the years to come, the non-life business will also show an upward trend.

Capitalising on the opportunities requires world-class professional excellence. The professionals, specially in the Indian perspective also need rural orientation.

Exhibit 1.3 **MUTUAL FUND SERVICES**

Acceleration in the pace of economic transformation makes it essential that flow of capital gains a rapid momentum both at domestic and global levels. We find a close relation between savings and investment. And both, the processes are found interlinked with the emerging trends in the economy. In the annals of transformation of Indian economy, we find the decade 1980s known for a number of positive developments which remained instrumental in engineering a sound base for corporatisaton. It is in this context that we find even the public sector financial institutions evincing keen interests in the mutual funds specially during the late 1980s. The State Bank of India, Canara Bank, Life Insurance Corporation of India, Unit Trust of India, Bank of India, General Insurance Corporation etc. are found showing special interest in the operation of Indian financial market. Of late, we find a number of schemes for the investors and the credibility for the same goes to emergence of a strong savings market. We cannot negate that during 1980s, the Indian economy witnessed a good number of positive developments. This in a very natural way made ways for the development of Indian financial sector. The mutual funds actually worked as a close link between savings and the capital market.

The increasing domination of corporate sector instrumentalised the process of corporatisation and this was mainly due to liberalisation and globalisation. Since 1990, we find a turning point in the Indian economy. The liberal business and economic regulations started motivating the foreign investors. The Indian Stock Market started becoming stronger and stronger. The pace of economic transformation was found accelerated. The flow of capital in the stock market started marching forward and this, of course, was a challenge before the institutions engaged in the mutual funds services. The globalisation of Indian economy in a very natural fashion made ways for the globalisation of Indian financial sector and in the process the institutions promoting mutual funds services experienced a number of threats and challenges. The globalised efforts based on world-class professional excellence made it difficult for the domestic players to excel competition.

It is against this background that mutual funds services need a new vision, a new strategy and a new device so that not only the big players but even the small players get an opportunity to make their savings and investments much more productive. The household savings has been found increasing and therefore the potential investors can be transformed into the actual investors if the mutual funds players take the support of professional excellence. Sensitising the domestic investors makes it essential that our marketing efforts are of innovative nature. We cannot deny the confidence of small domestic savers on the domestic mutual funds players and therefore the only thing the financial institutions need to activate is world-class professional excellence. The conceptualisation of modern marketing principles would make their task much more easier. The quality managerial decisions bear the efficacy of turning the negative into positive.

Exhibit 1.4 **PORTFOLIO MANAGEMENT SERVICES**

It is not only sufficient that we keep on moving the process of economic transformation. It is equally important that we create a condition in which investors have additional attractions. Since we find a number of positive developments in the process of national economic transformation, it is natural that there would be wider avenues for the channelisation of investments by almost all categories of the investors. In the Indian perspective, the investors in a majority of the cases lack sensitivity. They find themselves unaware of the emerging trends in the volatile business environment. Where to invest, how much to invest and when to invest are some of the essential considerations making our investments either productive or unproductive. A number of Indian investors have poor risk bearing capacity. This makes a strong advocacy in favour of portfolio management services helping, guiding, sensing and sensitising potential investors for transforming them into actual and habitual investors by ensuring a profitable return of their investments.

We cannot negate that the financial services in India have been witnessing a boom and the trend is to continue even in years and decades to come. The professionals have tremendous opportunities for channelising the productive investments and therefore we find conceptualisation of marketing practices much more significant. The portfolio managers need world-class professional excellence for communicating and motivating the investors. In the process-we find people, technology and equipment playing a very positive role. The strategic decisions play a very effective role in the entire process. The portfolio managers with the help of a sound marketing mix may be successful in formulating a strategy that would be helpful in satisfying the investors. The relationship considerably influenced by professionalism bears the efficacy of activating the transformation process in which even the intangible services would be tangible in the minds of investors.

With the changing faces of economic transformation, we find copious avenues for the development of stock markets. This makes it essential that portfolio managers bearing the potentials of managing financial and marketing activities develop professional excellence so that the tremendous opportunities available in the stock markets are successfully capitalised on. Service blueprinting, servicescapes, service encounters would help marketing and financial professionals in many ways. Development of a sound marketing information system will help professionals in many ways. The marketing reports, their minute scanning, emerging trends in the stock markets at both the domestic and global levels, attitudinal change in investors, changing behavioural profile of investors and potential investors are some of the important areas to be instrumental in increasing the potentials of professionals.

A gigantic leap that we find in the portfolio management services will continue even in future. The most important thing is to conceptualise innovative marketing and to make use of world-class professional excellence. The market is becoming much more competitive in which the excellation process needs priority attention on professionalism.

Exhibit 1.5 FACTORING SERVICES

Corporatisation makes the ways for economic transformation in which we find development of a number of economic activities to be instrumental in activating the process of development. The financial activities, if gaining a rapid momentum, open new vistas of development in which we find place for the growth of new types of business. It is in this context that we find the emergence of factoring services in the Indian business environment.

Factoring service includes in its purview the services related to financing and collection of receivables in both the domestic and global sectors. The small and medium enterprises are found involved in the factoring services which are found gaining popularity in the Indian business environment. We find factor responsible for providing finance against bills receivables and trade debts, undertaking the books and accounting process, providing the insurance services, offering consultancy services to the concerned organisations. We find factoring an arrangement in which the receivables on account of sale of goods or services are sold to the factor at a discount who gets the title to the goods and services on account of the factor contract. This makes him responsible for controlling the credit, debt collection, sales accounting, etc.

The above-mentioned facts make it clear that factoring is to offer a package of services to the clients for which the factor works. Particularly in the Indian context, we find strong justifications for the development of factoring services as the development of small and medium organisations for which the factoring services are found significant have been getting priority attention of the government. It is also found that in absence of factoring services, the concerned organisations find it difficult to realise dues from the large-scale enterprises and the government companies and departments. This obstructs the process of development of small and medium organisations. With factoring arrangement, an organisation will be in a position to increase its business activities which would improve its financial performance. The cash flow position of the concerned organisation can be increased with the help of prepayment facilities upto a certain percentage which may normally vary from 80 to 90 per cent of the value of assigned invoices if the circumstances necessitate so. It was against this background that specially for the development of small-scale sector, the Vaghul Committee on money market had strongly recommended development of such a system that facilitates factoring. The Committee opined that banking and the non-banking financial institutions particularly in the private sector should be encouraged to set up institutions for factoring services. Further, the Kalyansundram Committee also made a strong advocacy in favour of factoring services which were accepted by the Reserve Bank of India in principle but in practice the services could not be popular. Lack of awareness is an important reason for the same which makes it essential that the factoring organisations take part in the sensitisation process.

Exhibit 1.6 TRANSPORT SERVICES

For speeding up the process of socio-economic transformation, we find transportation services occupying a place of outstanding significance. Of late, this sector is considered to be a facto barometer of national economy. It has also been successful in transforming the globe into a village. Besides, it has even contributed to the evolution of civilisation by transmitting ideas and inventions to the people of different countries. It removes barriers to physical separation, momentises the inflow and outflow of different types of resources and instru-mentalises the process of delivering goods to the national economy. In the modern age, we can't imagine the development of society if there is a bottleneck in the transport network. In a country like India, the development of transport network in which different modes take part is felt essential. There are a number of services generating organisations engaged in the process of making available to us the transportation facilities. The public sector as well as the private sector organisations take part in the process but all of us feel that the quality of service, risk element, time schedule, fare and freight decisions are required to be innovated. This is essential to improve the quality of service vis-a-vis to maintain the commercial viability of the transport organisations.

The road transportation, rail transportation and air transportation are the important modes where we need professionalism. It is right to mention that by and large almost all the State Transport Corporations have been facing the problem of financial bankruptcy. The cases of accidents are frequent, the fare and freight structure are not judicious, the overcrowding is a general problem, the time schedule is not maintained and so on. The rail transportation services used by the millions and millions of the rail users have been found deteriorating. Since they don't have any competition, the users' services fail in getting due weightage. The Indian Railways have been found depending on the central assistance. The Air transportation services have been facing the problem of fierce competition. In the Indian context, both the Indian Airlines and Air India have failed in delivering quality services. Besides, they are also facing the problem of financial imbalance. The international market is found more competitive and Air India finds it difficult to compete. The quality of service is poor, the fare structure is found exorbitant, the time schedule is not maintained, the safety provisions are hardly practised. Thus, all the three modes of transportation have been facing a critical situation which is found questioning the commercial viability of the service generating organisations. It is against this background that we need to take up the problem with a new vision.

In the Indian perspective, it is pertinent that we make possible qualitative-cum-quantitative improvements which necessitate a new policy, an innovative strategy and a team of dedicated and committed personnel. Our policy decisions are required to be reviewed while practising marketing principles in all the transport organisations since this would only not make ways for profit generation but would also make possible qualitative improvements in their service mix.

Exhibit 1.7 TOURISM SERVICES

Of late, we find tourism not associated with aristocracy, since even ordinary persons can afford. With the passage of time, the tourism has become almost a part our normal life. It is virtually a mass phenomenon. It has grown to such an extent that we consider it an important industry contributing substantially to the national economy vis-a-vis the foreign exchange reserve. The promotion of tourism as an industry serves multi-pronged interests, such as promoting our art and culture, preserving our cultural heritage, interaction between different religions, exchange of views, enrichment of knowledge, generation of foreign exchange and so on. It is against this background that tourism organisations like Global Tourist Organisation, Pacific Area Travel Association, International Union of Official Travel Organisation, etc. have been found promoting the tourism industry. We find this industry an economic bonanza. It is also considered to be a potential force for making possible world peace through mutual appreciation and international understanding. The success of tourism industry is considerably influenced by consumer orientation which necessitates integrated development of all the related components like transportation facilities, hotel, communication, availability of travel agents, tourist guides, etc. The tourism product can only be experienced. It is a service product found of perishable nature. The providers are a heterogeneous group of people. The success of this industry depends upon the integrated efforts of providers. Since it is an amalgam of different industries, the task of developing professional excellence requires due cooperation of all the constituents.

In the Indian context, we find this industry in a critical condition because the amalgamating components lack world-class excellence and the policy makers appear least interested in making them competitive. Of course, we have world class potentials but our contributions to the world tourism is 0.40 per cent. This speaks of the fact that tourism services need a new strategy for development so that we make the tourist spots a point of attraction and promote with the support of innovative devices which help us in projecting our positive image. It is right to mention that image problem has been playing a negative role in the development of tourism industry in India. There is no doubt in it that the most important thing for the development of tourism industry is ensuring safety to the tourists and we find our efforts dismal at least in relation to the law and order situations in the country. The world tourists are found to be the worst sufferers as treatment with them in Kashmir, Bodh-Gaya or even while travelling compel us to form a negative attitude. We have attractive tourists centres, world-class hotels, most sophisticated communication facilities, rich cultural heritage, modern transporation facilities but nothing can attract tourist if we find a threat to their safety and security. It is in this context that we find it an important dimension, specially in the Indian perspective.

It is high time that the policy makers assign an overriding priority to the image problem and activate concerted efforts to develop this industry in a right fashion. The tourist organisations and other amalgamating forces need to change their functional style. We make a strong advocacy in favour of tourism marketing.

Exhibit 1.8 HOTEL SERVICES

The recent developments in the transportation and communications services, the liberal cultural exchange policy of government, the development of tourism as an industry, the development of corporate culture, a change in the lifestyles of masses are some of the important factors opening new vistas for the development of hotel industry in India. The growing instrumentality of managerial proficiency in the hotel industry has made it essential that we develop this industry in the changed socio-economic scenario and create new job opportunities in this neglected sector. Today, the customer services are planned, automated, audited for quality control and regularly reviewed with the motto of initiating qualitative improvements which make the industry internationally competitive. We find a new vision for the development of hotel industry the world over and it is essential that hotel planners assign due weightage to the same even in the Indian perspective. The moment we find a change in the taste and preferences of customers, it is pertinent that we make possible an analogous change in our service mix.

We are well aware of the fact that like the tourism industry, the hotel industry is also influenced by the multi-dimensional developments in the allied areas. The development of tourism industry paves avenues for the development of hotel industry and like this, the development of corporate culture paves avenues for the development of both the tourism industry as well as the hotel industry. This makes it essential that we plan development of hotel industry in tune with the changing preferences of customers. Of late, the high spending tourists prefer to stay in a cottage having all the facilities like a five star hotel. They like peace. It is against this background that we make an advocacy in favour of a new vision. The policy makers, the hotel planners, the tourist organisations need an innovative strategy for the development of hotel industry. In the Indian perspective, we find a beginning in the development of corporate culture which signals positive signs for the development of hospitality industry in a new fashion which makes it a point of attraction.

The hotel services are found based on customer services and therefore we need to identify the changing behavioural profile of guests so that our marketing resources are found to be productive. The development of hotel buildings, the location of hotels, the infrastructural facilities, the safety and security provisions, the development of hotel personnel, the innovative promotional devices, the hotel tariff are some of the important factors to be given due weightage. We find the future bright provided our efforts are positive, strategies are innovative and the marketing resources are internationally competitive. It is against this background that we need to develop the hotel industry both in national and international background. On the one hand, we need luxurious expensive hotels for high spending tourists while on the other hand we also realise the urgency of developing economic hotels for masses or the low spending tourists who can't afford luxurious hotels. Thus, we need to identify the changing preferences, likes and dislikes of different segments of market and to market the services accordingly. This is possible when we practise modern marketing principles in the hotel industry which right now is facing a problem of poor occupancy ratio.

Exhibit 1.9 CONSULTANCY SERVICES

Providing consultancy or advice is not a recent phenomenon. We have witnessed the practise even during the ancient days when a king used to keep ministers for consultation and advice for which they were suitably paid. At the same time, we also find cases when the religious saints, gurus and hermits offered free of cost services which was the result of their deep meditation. With the passage of time, the concept of commercialisation gained the momentum. A firm, an organisation or an individual required specialised knowledge, expertise for the smooth functioning of the business. An individual needed legal, financial, medical advices. An organisation used consultants for generating profits and an individual used consultation for his/her personal gains. This engineered a foundation for the development of consultancy organisations in different areas. Of late, a number of public and private organisations have been found selling their expertise. The mounting intensity of competition in the business world and the increasing requirements and expectations of the individuals are some of the points injecting strength to the consultancy business. It is in this context that we find profitable avenues for the development of consultancy business.

Excellence, innovative efforts, new ideas, research, dedications, considerably determine the quality of our results. It is not possible that all the organisations have a special wing for different consultants for different purposes. It is not possible that an individual develops expertise in all the required areas. Hence, the use of consultancy services remains the lone solution. It is in this context that we feel a profitable future of the consultancy business even in the Indian context. This is due mainly to the fact that we find multi-faceted developments in almost all the areas. The intensity of competition is increasing fast. The small-scale and large-scale businesses have been found developing. The growing significance of specialised knowledge and skill, instrumentality of specialised services by the firms and confirmation of their views by the experts are some of leading factors responsible for the development of consultancy services. The present is bright, the future is prosperous. The medicare services, the legal services the financial services, the technical services, the managerial services are likely to be much more profit generating in the years to come. This makes it essential that the consultancy organisations market their services in a right way.

The application of marketing principles in the consultancy business would help the consultancy organisations in many ways. The very success of the consultancy business is influenced by the excellence and behaviour of the consultants, the personal attention paid by the consultants to the interests and well-being of their clients/ customers, the consultancy fee charged for the services rendered and their image in the business world. The formulation of a sound marketing mix is to help the consultancy organisations/individuals in different ways. The management of information is considered to be an essential part of the consultancy services. This in a natural way draws our attention on innovative marketing which helps an organisation, an individual or the users at large by making available to them the world-class services.

Exhibit 1.10 RETAIL SERVICES

With the increasing domination of corporatisation, we find a significant increase in the level of discretionary income. The burgeoning middle class has been found expanding avenues for the development of retail sector. The development of mall culture is the gift of corporate culture. The retail services in the changing business environment need a new look and a new approach. It is in this context that we realise the instrumentality of professionalisum for the world-class development of retail sector. In the Indian context particularly during the decade 1990s, we find different new faces of retail services. What to talk of the cosmopolitan towns and cities when we find development of mall culture even in the small towns and cities. The changing new faces of retail sector make it clear that the Indian retail trading has been moving in the new directions. Of late, the retail sector has been witnessing an upsurge and the foreign investors appear to capitalise on the opportunities. The regulations need due care of government.

The Chain of Stores, Convenient Store, Franchise, Departmental Store, Supermarket, Hypermarket, Shopping Mall, Shopping Plaza, Discount Stores, Factory/Secondary Stores and Kiosks are the different faces of retail sector gaining popularity even in the Indian society. The days are coming when we will find the retail services prospering like Thailand, Brazil, Malaysia, Poland and China. This is due to the changing lifestyle for which credibility is to the developing corporate culture. According to the Survey of NCAER, we find middle class touching 65 per cent of the Indian household. Against this background, we find positive trends in. the development of retail sector in the Indian perspective.

This in a very natural way draws our attention on the professional excellence of retail marketers. The conceptualisation of innovative marketing in the retail services would simplify our task in many ways. We need to bridge the knowledge gap, quality gap, delivery gap and communication gap for which the professionals need world-class excellence. The primary sector is also found opening new avenues for the development of retail services. The agri-business is found emerging as a new area where new faces of retail services are to be much more popular.

Of course, we find a number of woes in the development of new faces of retail sector which would considerably be regulated with the help of professionalised services. The increasing cases of theft, shoplifting, administrative errors, frauds and inventory shrinkages are found increasing fast. In a country like India where we find budding or upcoming youths not developing a temptation to the value engineering process, the marketing people serving shopping malls have been found creating numerous problems. We need to regulate the multi-faceted woes because we cannot regulate the development of retail sector. The professionals need to develop a techno-driven marketing information system identifying the retail opportunities and capitalising on the same in a right way. The retail traffic cannot work suitably if we find lack of world-class professional excellence.

Exhibit 1.11 PERSONAL CARE SERVICES

With the development of corporate culture, we find a change in our lifestyles which makes ways for the personal care services. The development of industrial economy, growing significance of globalisation, sophistication in the process of communications, multi-culturism management, transformation of globe into a village are some of the important factors contributing substantially to the development of personal care services even in the Indian setting. To be more specific, the emerging positive trends in the level of income has paved avenues for an organised development of personal care services so that the users get the quality services and the organisations succeed in generating profits. A change in taste and fashion, increasing awareness for maintaining sound physique, growing temptation for corporate services engineer a sound foundation for the development of personal care services. It is against this background that we find development of beauty parlours, hair dressing centres, gym and jogging, steam bath or so. There is no doubt in it that our words impress and throw an imprint on the psychology of an individual but the make-up narrates our feelings and ideas, taste and temperament even without a face-to-face communication. In a country like India where we find the problem of unemployment at its peak, the development of personal care services may create job opportunities and may sizeably counter the problem of unemployment. Of course, a number of organisations have been found engaged in offering the personal care services but we find much scope for developing the same so that the organisations are found internationally competitive.

The application of marketing principles in the personal care services thus requires a priority attention. The framing or designing of marketing mix requires professionalism and if we develop the services in an organised way and activate systematic efforts to make the services internationally competitive, the users would get world class services vis-a-vis the organisations would get profitable opportunities to capitalise on. The product mix is required to be designed in the face of changing preferences of prospects of different segments. The beauty parlours bear the responsibility of making your face impressive and attractive but it is not meant that they always focus on western lifestyles. We find enough scope for the development of our own lifestyles to promote our culture. The jogging and gymnastic centres bear the responsibility of making your body sound and smart and the Indianised efforts with a fair mix of Yoga would create profitable opportunities not only in the Indian markets but even abroad. The use of herbal products need due attention so that we succeed in promoting our own products. The beauty parlours are meant not only for the women but in the changing lifestyles which are substantially influenced by the corporate culture even men would need the services of beauty parlours. We can't say that personal care services are meant only for a particular segment since almost all the segments, such as men and women, child and youths, kids and teens, rural and urban need the services related to personal care. This makes it essential that pricing strategies are formulated in the face of the level of incomes. Thus, the need of the hour is to organise and innovate the personal care services so that the customers get quality services. This makes a strong advocacy in favour of personal care marketing.

Exhibit 1.12 EDUCATION SERVICES

Today we pay for excellence. Education is an important device to enrich the credentials which help in generating excellence. It is not only fair but even judicious that all the segments of the society get an opportunity to enrich their potentials. If we succeed in developing knowledge, our success in developing professional excellence can't be negated. If we succeed in developing professional excellence, the managerial proficiency would help both the profit and not-for-profit making organisations in subserving the organisational interests vis-a-vis the social interests. Contrary to it, if we fail in developing excellence even the world-class inputs and sophisticated technologies would fail in delivering good. It is in this context that we talk about the education services which have been found in a critical condition. The educational institutions, of course, bear the responsibility of enriching the credentials but the task becomes much more difficult when we find them in a depleted condition. Except a few, almost all the educational institutions have been found facing numerous problems which have been making an attack on their potentials to deliver the world-class services. The primary education, secondary education, college education and university education need a structural change. With the passage of time, we find multi-dimensional changes in the socio-economic conditions and this makes it pertinent that the educational institutions assign an overriding priority to the total quality management. It is against this background that we go through the problem of general and professional education.

The process of socio-economic transformation is sizeably influenced by the instrumentality of human resources. The human capital formation thus occupies a place of outstanding significance. The educational institutions energise the process of human capital formation by producing quality human resources supposed to be productive. The rationale behind applying the principles of marketing in the education services is securing to the users the world class services and at the same time making the educational institutions financially sound at enrich the inputs used in the process. We can't negate the fact that educational services are based on the quality of inputs and in most of the cases we find the educational institutions not in a position to manage the quality inputs. The principles of social marketing make it essential that the educational institutions are given freedom to generate their own funds for improving the quality of educational aid. This necessitates a fundamental change in the policy decisions. The formulation of a sound marketing mix is found essential since this would help educational institutions in increasing their strength and making the services nationally and internationally competitive. To be more specific, the educational institutions owned, managed and controlled by the government have been facing a rough weather condition. This has been questioning the quality of their outputs. It is high time that the educational institutions realise gravity of the situation and apply the principles of marketing. It is need of the hour that the policy makers and intellects realise gravity of the situation and formulate such a policy that makes available quality education to the masses. It is pertinent that the corporate sector takes part in the process of promoting the educational services. This is possible when we think in favour of education marketing.

Exhibit 1.13 HOSPITAL SERVICES

Human resources are the precious endowment in a country. The success of a plan or development of the national economy or an increase in the physical quality life index is substantially influenced by the effective measures taken for education, health, skill and well-being of the masses. This in a natural way draws our attention on the medicare services made available to the human resources. The development of healthcare facilities is not only influenced by the opening of healthcare centres and hospitals but more so by their effective administration and value-orientation. If the hospitals or the healthcare centres are well managed, we can't deny quantitative-cum-qualitative improvements in the healthcare services. Of course, the healthcare services have not received due attention of the policy planners which have been found deteriorating the quality of services made available by the hospitals. To be more specific, the government hospitals are found in a depleted condition. The doctors, para-medical personnel and even the low echelon staff lack a sense of commitment. In a country like India where the poor sections of the society are not in a position to afford the expensive medicare services offered by the private hospitals, it is not a good sign. Hence, it is high time that the policy makers, medical and para-medical personnel, managerial personnel realise gravity of the situation and make possible the necessary changes in the administration of hospitals so that the masses are made available the world-class medicare services.

There are a number of private hospitals offering to the society the world-class medicare services but it is not possible that urban and rural poor use the expensive services of these hospitals. Of course, we find the management of medicare services a costly affair since a big budget is needed to promote the research facilities, to procure sophisticated plants and equipments, to operate and maintain the hospitals. We can't deny the fact that the world-class excellence can't be promoted unless we intensify world-class education and research facilities. Except a few almost all the government medical college hospitals fail in doing such partially on account of the budgetary constraints and partially on account of poor management. The private hospitals have been found assigning an overriding priority to the work culture which is the result of a well managed education and training programme. It is against this background that we make a strong advocacy in favour of hospital management in which the marketing of hospital services occupies a place of outstanding significance. The defined principles of social marketing make it essential that both the public and private hospitals consider hospital a social institution.

The quality of service, the behaviour of medical and paramedical personnel, the structure of fee, the inculcation of mass awareness are some of the aspects to be given due weightage while marketing the healthcare services. In the Indian perspective, the hospitals irrespective of the fact that they are public or private bear the responsibility of expanding their services to the rural areas where the masses suffer a lot. This in a natural way requires a new approach, a new strategy, a new vision. It is against this background that we talk about hospital marketing which would make the ways for multi-dimensional developments.

Exhibit 1.14 POLITICAL SERVICES

Political organisations bear the responsibility of serving and subserving social interests and protecting and promoting national interests. They are considered to be socially, morally and constitutionally bound to think and act for society. The party members, workers, volunteers need to make the working conditions much more conducive. This makes it essential that the political parties are well aware of the services they need to deliver to the society. With the help of a techno-driven political information system, they can study and understand the society in a right fashion. The multi-faceted changes in the society, the emerging social, economic and cultural problems draw priority attention of society. The increasing levels of expectations of people need due attention of political leaders.

Making possible a fair blending of core and peripheral services is considered an important functional responsibility of political organisations. Making an invasion on the rivals and getting a success in the race requires high degree of professional excellence. They need to build a fair image and for that it is essential that the political parties offer innovative core and peripheral services. The core services focus our attention on the contributions of political organisations to the process of socio-economic transformation. This makes it essential that they have an indepth knowledge of the emerging trends. The socio-economic conditions of different segments of society need due attention. The primary education facilities essential supporting infrastructural facilities, basic health and medicare, availability of potable water and sanitation services need due weightage on the development agenda of political parties. The core services cover all those services found essential for protecting the interests of humanity in the society. The women and child care deserve an intensive care. While offering the core services, they need to make it sure that the services included in their election manifesto are fulfilled.

In addition to the core services, they have also to manage the peripheral services. In the context of peripheral services, we find focus on supportive services to be instrumental in improving the quality of services. Sensitising the masses and developing mass awareness, regulating social evils, promoting informal education, national, social and communal harmony, activating community welfare coming forward to counter natural calamities, etc. need due weightage. In a true sense, we do not find any boundary for the peripheral services. This is due to the fact that peripheral services if innovative in nature and distinct in character help political organisations in the building and projection of a fair image. Besides, they will also find it easier to counter the rival parties. Establishing an edge over the rivals is the motto and this task will be found easier it they keep, on moving the process of innovating the peripheral services.

Managing things with the help of professional having world-class excellence is the crying need of the hour. Value engineering process, of late, is found on the bottom of almost all the political parties. This requires an intensive care because political parties witnessing ethical imbalance cannot serve the society.

Exhibit 1.15 DAY-CARE SERVICES

The day-care services or day-nursery services, of late, have been found gaining popularity and the credibility for the same goes to the development of culture. We find it an institution meant for the working mothers who due to lack of time find it difficult to look after their children. The centres are either run independently or as a part of the kindergarten school. It is found located in the urban areas and offers to the children not only the essential services related to their proper nursing but also some of the peripheral services to develop them for the primary pre-primary schools. The composite day-care and the exclusive day-care are the two important dimensions of day-care services. In the exclusive day-care, we find only care whereas in the composite day-care we also find the kindergarten. The day-care centres are supposed to offer a friendly environment and ensure proper care for an overall development of children enrolled therein. We also call them creches. The children get there a number of services such as love and affection, parental guidance, educational services, child care, recreation and sports, development of character and civic and aesthetic sense. The parental affection and parental guidance are the two different aspects of day-care services and the day-care centres fail in providing the parental affection.

We cannot negate that pre-education age is the most sensitive and receptive stage in our life cycle because this portrays a picture which cannot be removed for the long time. Since we find our temptation for corporate culture and material culture increasing very fast, we cannot check the development of day-care centres. The only thing that we can do is to regulate the services harming the interests of children. In a true sense, we find materialism opening new vistas for the development of day-care culture. If we find a prosperous future for the corporate culture, the material culture will gain popularity and this will open doors for the development of day-care culture. The day-care centres in the changing perspective need to profeesionalise their services in the larger interests of children vis-à-vis the parents. The increasing urbanisation, burgeoning middle class, increasing domination of corporate sector, mounting temptation for corporate and material culture are a few of the key factors making the business environment much more conducive. The opportunities are there and the professionals need to capitalise on.

The strategic decisions for the day-care centres need an innovative approach. Since the day-care centres bear the responsibility of serving the children of working mothers, well educated mothers, fully aware and conscious mothers and specially those mothers developing temptation for material culture; the professionals managing the affairs need innovative services to be effective in satisfying them. We also find cases where the day-care centres have been found engaged in unfair and unethical practises and therefore our focus must be on the quality services in tune with the changing levels of expectations of working parents. Working couples nurture a dream of developing their kids and the day-care centres are supposed to fulfil. This in a very natural way requires a professional touch and a new vision. Despite all, we do not find any substitute for parental affection.

Exhibit 1.16 COURIER SERVICES

With the increasing pressure of work and decreasing level of efficiency, the Department of Posts failed in managing the mailing services which made ways for the development of an alternative system catering to the changing needs of trade as well as the household sectors. The courier services came into existence and a number of formal and informal organisations started offering the services at regional, national and international levels. Of course, from the time immemorial, we find organised and unorganised services for this purpose but the services of Department of Posts assumed a place of outstanding significance due to its global network and cost economy. Since 1907 till present, we find Department of Posts using the Railway Mail Services for qualitative and quantitative transformation in the postal system. A number of services are included in the courier such as despatching letters and packets both at national and international levels, despatching valuables, despatching boxes and offering to the individuals and organisation the services included in their purview. Of late, we find a number of small courier organisations not efficacious of offering the quality services as they lack the supporting infrastructural facilities. They, of course, are defaming the privately managed courier services and consequently making an invasion the image of courier sector. We do not welcome such a negative trend in the courier services and feel that high degree of professional excellence and availability of adequate supporting infrastructural facilities will be helpful in rebuilding the lost glory.

The most important thing in this context is networking which majority of the courier organisations lack and therefore the formation of a consortium or syndicate mainly with the support of leading national and international courier organisations is found essential. The leading courier organisations find it difficult to expand their services to the rural areas and if we find an integrated approach with the help of small courier organisations, there will be a significant improvement in their services even at the micro level. The leading courier organisation need to feel that they have a profitable market even in the villages because with the expansion of job markets in the urban areas, we find migration of rural population to the big towns and cities and for diverse motives they make use of the courier services. Rural-urban networking and national-global networking are the two important aspects of courier services drawing priority attention of leading courier organisations.

The courier organisations need a sound service profile which will help them in building and projecting a fair image. They also need to assign due weightage to the behavioural profile of their workforce who lack personal touch and commitment. A majority of the users of services specially in the small towns and cities appear dissatisfied with the services of courier organisations. Managing courier services with a professional touch is considered essential for improving the quality of services. Despite significant developments in the field of IT services, the courier services will remain in existence. The opportunities are there and they have to devise ways of capitalising on the same which would be made easier by the professionals.

Exhibit 1.17 ENTERTAINMENT SERVICES

Temptation for recreation is a natural phenomenon. If we undermine the law of nature, the environment for concentration, meditation, efficiency generation can't be conducive. This may result into monotony and the process of degeneration may gain momentum. Particularly in the modern age, the human beings in general have been found experiencing multi-faceted problems. They are supposed to follow the busy schedule to earn more and at the same time are also required to be a high performer. In addition, the management of family is also an important responsibility. This necessitates entertainment. The incoming changes in the taste and temperament of masses, the increasing disposable income, the changing lifestyles due to the development of corporate sector have paved avenues for the development of healthy entertainment facilities. Opening of new air-conditioned cinema halls, open air theatres, drama centres, music centres, pub, club, art and handicraft and painting centres have been found gaining popularity. A number of new budding, upcoming entrepreneurs have been seen evincing their interests in promoting the entertainment services. They by doing such only not entertain masses but also perform the responsibility of inculcating awareness, promoting education and developing knowledge. It is against this background that we focus on the development of entertainment services in a right fashion.

The development of entertainment services requires professionalism. The movies, dramas, songs bear the efficacy of educating the masses. The application of marketing principles in the entertainment services would make ways for the development of healthy entertainment services and in addition would also be successful in making the services commercially viable. The use of sophisticated technologies for promoting the entertainment services has virtually revolutionised the nature and character of entertainment services. The blind use of sophisticated devices has been found making an invasion on our culture. The healthy entertainment services like circus shows, dramas are found disappearing. The tidal wave of pop culture has been found gaining popularity. The domination of western culture has very much been instrumental in derailing the new generation. The TV culture has been found making the new generation more crazy. The use of sex and violence in the TV serials, and cinemas have been misguiding the youths. This makes it essential that we think over the problem with a new vision. The entertainment marketing would only not be effective in making the organisations commercially viable but would also be helpful in promoting the healthy entertainment services. To be more specific in the Indian perspective where we find a majority of the population illiterate, the organisations engaged in promoting the entertainment services bear an outstanding responsibility of inculcating awareness, sensing the masses and channelising the entertainment services even in the rural areas of the country. Since a majority of the population are found below the poverty line, it is also essential that the pricing strategy adopted for the entertainment services assigns due weightage to the poor paying capacity of the weaker sections. The entertainment facilities are required to be channelised even in the rural areas and this requires an overriding priority to the taste and temperament of rural masses. We find marketing principles effective in simplifying our task in many ways. It is in this context that we need to implement the principles of marketing in the entertainment services. The entertainment marketing thus appears to be a productive approach to initiate qualitative-cum-quantitative improvements.

Exhibit 1.18 MASS COMMUNICATION SERVICES

With the development of satellite, we find significant strides in the field of mass communication services. Sophistication paves avenues for complications. Scientific inventions and innovations, no doubt, have made possible a number of positive developments in the field of mass communications but at the same time have also opened doors for numerous negative developments. We cannot negate that globalisation of economy gained a rapid momentum mainly due to the sophisticated communication and information technologies and resulting from which the general masses could get an opportunity to taste the fragrance of world-class goods and services. The multi-faceted developments in the socio-economic fabrics are the outstanding contributions of mass communication. But other side of the coin presents a very disappointing result. The mounting social tension and dissension, upward moving graph of violence contracting respect for elderly people amongst the upcoming youths, disintegrating Indian families, increasing selfishness, aggravating craze for an open sexual behaviour and developing temptation for material culture are a mute testimony to this proposition that we are moving in the wrong directions. If scientific inventions and innovations start paving ways for negative developments in the socio-cultural areas, the development processes need a microscopic audit. The mass communication services need due attention of policy decision-makers.

The mass communication services include both the information media and the entertainment media such as telecasting, broadcasting and print media. The beginning of the decade 1980s initiated a new era and the credibility for the same goes to the satellite. The significant developments in the field of IT services have virtually revolutionised the mass communication services. The mass communication considered to be a process of communicating to a very large number of people or masses need professional excellence. The instrumentality of communication organisations engaged in the process is considerably influenced by the quality of messages to be transmitted which rests on new generation of sophisticated technologies and the quality professionals.

We are well aware of the multi-faceted developments in the field of communication technologies reverberating the process of qualitative and quantitative transformation in the field mass communication. In an age of information explosion, the spread in the dissemination of information has proved to be an index of national prosperity. In a democratic set-up, we assign due weightage to public participation which in a true sense rests on the transmission of right information on right time. This necessitates high degree of accessibility to mass communication. World-class professionals and new generation of communication technologies simplify our task.

The mass communication services have also been benefiting the corporate sector in different ways. We find new generation of print technology making available to them a number of benefits while promoting. Besides, the broadcast and telecast services also play a positive role in the development process. Offering quality services is considered to be a crying need of the hour. Either we talk about social transformation or our focus is on cultural and economic dimensions, the contributions of mass communication are significant.

Exhibit 1.19 IT SERVICES

With the increasing domination of corporatisation, the decision-making practices started diverting the attention of corporate big players. In this context, we find focus on the computer-driven or technology-driven decisions. Due to some regulatory barriers, it was not possible to develop the IT industry earlier and this trend continued till the late of 1980s. But with the beginning of 1990s, the contours of development have undergone radical changes. The liberalisation, globalisation and increased pace of corporatisation opened new vistas for the development of IT industry. Almost all categories of organisations realised the instrumentality of IT in the development process and this considerably affected the demand side. The liberal governmental regulations removed the barriers and a good number of organisations started making use of IT. The process of economic transformation was accelerated which made ways for the development of IT industry.

The modern product is found marketed with the help of traditional marketing. This necessitates innovative marketing prcatises for the IT product. In a true sense, we find three-tier developments in the field of information technology, first the development of a chip, second the development of satellite communication technology and a sharp fall in the cast. It is in this context that we find almost a boom in the IT industry and whatsoever the developments that we find in the management and marketing activities in the IT industry are due to its demand side. The application of software, professional services, system integration, maintenance services, education and training, techno-driven application and software packages are found important in the very context.

Since we find multi-faceted uses of IT in all the three sectors of development, viz., primary, secondary and tertiary; it is natural that the boom that we find in this industry will continue even in the years to came. The sophistication in the information and communication technologies will keep on moving. There will be a significant increase in the demand side and this makes it essential that supply side is also given a new shape. All the components related to the development of IT need professional excellence, managerial efficacy and marketing potentials. The innovative products of 21st century need innovative marketing. The liberal business regulations and the positive mindset of government make it essential that we make ways for professional excellence.

The IT services have been found gaining popularity in almost all the areas right from the manufacturing of goods to the generation of services. This trend will continue even in future. A large number of organisations are to be the potential customers. How to transform the potential customers into actual and habitual customers is found significant in the very context. The managerial proficiency rests on professional excellence. The intensity of competition will be at its peak. The organisations marketing IT services in the face of professional excellence will be successful in excelling competition. It is against this background that we need to go through the problem of marketing IT services in the changing global business environment where both the demand and supply sides need professional excellence.

Exhibit 1.20 ELECTRICITY SERVICES

A very important feature of the energy scenario in rural India is the predominance of non-commercial energy as against commercial energy like coal, petroleum products and electric power. Energy is the basic element of human activity and an indispensable input to energise the process of socio-economic transformation. The present energy scenario has diverted the attention of scientists, the planners and the publics alike realising that the process of overall development can hardly be geared up in the right direction unless adequate energy supply is made possible. The US has approximately 6 per cent of the world population but they use near about 40 per cent of *the total energy in the world. When India became independent in 1947, the power generation capacity in the country was merely 1300 MW. Now after more than 50 years of the planned development of course we find an increase in the capacity to the level of 60000 MW but keeping in view the demand position, we find the supply position non-optimal. This has been found generating numerous problems on almost all the fronts. The development-*oriented *welfare plans are hardly implemented in time, the masses fail in using the electric, power-based domestic appliances, the agricultural sector is adversely affected and we can't negate the fact that due to the inadequate supply position, the speed of development slowed down. This makes it essential that the organisations engaged in generating and distributing the electric power think over the problem with a new vision. We find almost all the government managed electricity boards and corporations in a depleted condition. On the other hand, the demand position is found increasing substantially. The private sector has been seen making sincere efforts but the regulatory barrier has been found standing as an obstacle. This makes it essential that both the public and private sector organisations engaged in generating and distributing electricity practise marketing to deliver goods. It is against this background that we go through the problem of electricity marketing.*

We find energy an essential input of economic development and an important source for improving the quality of life and the standard of living. But due to non-optimal supply position, the users fail in getting the required units. The industrial, agricultural, services and the domestic sectors find it difficult to initiate qualitative transformation. The application of marketing principles would pave avenues for the generation of electricity. The process of generation would be cost effective which would minimise the cost of generation and would make the services economic. Of late, we find frequent use of electric power-based appliances, equipments, plants and machines. The productivity of all the assets used in the process would substantially be accelerated if the supply position is improved. By and large almost all the organisations generating and distributing energy have been found generating losses which has been forming a vicious circle. The increased cost of generation and distribution has been instrumental in increasing the overall cost and masses find it difficult to use the services in the required units. The marketing principles would help in adopting a sound pricing strategy which subserves the interests of all. The organisations would be commercially viable and the masses vis-a-vis the primary, secondary, tertiary sectors would be benefited considerably.

Exhibit 1.21 AUTOMOBILE SERVICES

With the increasing pace of economic transformation, we find wider avenues for the development of automobile services. This is due to the fact that increasing level of income makes the ways for the development of public or private road transportation services. The automobile services focus our attention on the development of inputs by the servicing centres so that their services are commensurate with the changing technology and increasing levels of expectations. Emerging trends in the lifestyles, increasing sophistication in the motor vehicle technology and mounting domination of corporate sector in the process of national economic transformation are some of important factors reverberating the movement of people from one place to another for diverse motives and reasons. With the development of a new culture in which comforts and luxuries get top priority, we expect a sizeable increase in the number of different categories of motor vehicles. The emergence of corporate culture and growing prominence of material culture have fuelled the process resulting from which we find a number of new generation of vehicles on roads. It is in this context we find justifications for the development of automobile services.

The emerging trends indicate that a number of automobile servicing centres would be required to be developed and for that the supporting infrastructural facilities would be essential. To cater to the changing technology, the automobile centres would need a large number of skilled people. Managing technology and managing people and in addition, managing the supporting infrastructural facilities would be found essential in the changing perspective. Since we find change both in quantitative and qualitative terms, the automobile services would require high degree of managerial proficiency. The organised and systematic development of automobile servicing centres equipped with new generation of technology in tune with the latest development in technology would be found essential. Not only the big towns and cities but even the small towns and cities would have opportunities for the development of automobile servicing centres. How and in what way we capitalise on the existent opportunities would depend on our managerial excellence.

With the development of corporatisation as a major impact of globalisation, we find a number of leading auto manufacturing companies establishing their production units. It is natural that for providing after-sale services they also develop the automobile servicing centres. The dealers and private parties have a profitable market for the some. The location point for the development of automobile services, the environmental conditions for the centres, service designing and service blueprinting, service encounters and the service quality gap are some of the key issues for the development of automobile servicing centres. In addition to other dimensions, the automobile centres also need to study the behavioural profile of users because we find a basic change in their attitudes related to the frequency of change of vehicles.

BUILDING SERVICE ASPIRATIONS

Aspirations make the ways for the generation of demand. Aspirations pave the avenues for the offering of quality services to the users. If we talk about the service aspirations of organisations engaged in generating the services, our emphasis is on the offering of quality services. And when we make an advocacy in favour of the service aspirations of users, our focus is on the creation of demand, expansion of market and tapping of the market potentials. The service generating organisations while formulating strategies need to build service aspirations so that the process of demand generation gains momentum. It is not only sufficient that they formulate a sound marketing plan. It is much more impact generating that they build up service aspirations so that the employees engaged in offering the services make available the users the promised services. As and when we find a gap between the services-promised and services-offered, it is due mainly to the lukewarm efforts of the service generating organisations while building the service aspirations. The stagnation in demand is also influenced by the same because the prospects stop thinking about the services regarding which the organisations evince least interest in translating the aspirations into demand. It is against this background that we find it significant to focus on the service aspirations. The professionals working in an organisation bear the responsibility of building the service aspirations. We can't negate the fact that with the development of corporate sector and a strong emphasis on the services sector, it is high time that the service generating organisations make sincere efforts to build up services aspirations.

At the outset, we talk about the service aspirations of an organisation where the employees engaged in offering the services are supposed to work with the motto of offering quality services to the users. In a majority of the cases, we find that the policy makers promise the services and make a provision for the world-class services but due mainly to the lack of employee orientation *vis-a-vis* the work culture, a gap between the services-promised and services-offered remains existent. The employees serving an organisation lack training; the policy makers fail in initiating employee orientation and resulting from which the promised services never reach to the users. If the employees are not interested in serving the users, this is due to the fact that the policy makers *vis-a-vis* the professionals have not assigned due weightage to the development and motivation of human resources. The training facilities are inadequate, the policy decisions are not proactive and the professionals are found disinterested. In Figure 1.3, it is clarified that building of service aspirations requires employee orientation. If the employees are imparted proper training facilities; if they are motivated reasonably; we find employee orientation which engineers a sound foundation for serving the users. Performance orientation necessitates employee orientation and the employee orientation requires proper training and adequate incentives. If the front line staff are not working properly; if they are deliberate in creating a gap; this is because of deficient management and faulty policy decisions. Thus, it is pertinent that the policy makers as well as the senior executive realise the instrumentality of building the services aspirations and plan to train and motivate the employees in a right fashion. The executives bear the responsibility of translating the plan into action which make a strong advocacy in favour of professional excellence.

The building of service aspiration also draws our attention on the potential users or the prospects. Here, our emphasis is on creating aspirations among the prospects so that they appear interested in using the services-offered by an organisation. This makes ways for creating awareness and sensing the prospects so that they realise the importance of services to be demanded. The innovative promotional measures simplify the process of building service aspirations among the prospects or customers. Unless you aspire, the process of demand generation can't be activated. Thus, an important problem before the professionals is to switch on aspiration by activating the aggressive promotional devices. There is no doubt in it that with the development of corporate culture, we find a change in our lifestyles which have been found constructing a base for using the services of different types of organisations. The professionals if evince interests in switching on the process, the task is not much more difficult. The banks and other agencies have been issuing credit cards. The service aspirations at the end of an organisation are well managed because the employees are found promoting the same. Here, it is important that the professionals sensitise prospects in a right fashion so that they aspire for using the credit cards. The market for cellular phone is not capitalised on optimally due to the fact that the service generating organisations fail in sensitising the prospects for aspiring the use of cellphone. This speaks of the fact that building of service aspirations at the users' end is also significant. In Figure 1.5, we find the service aspirations a result of the sensitising process.

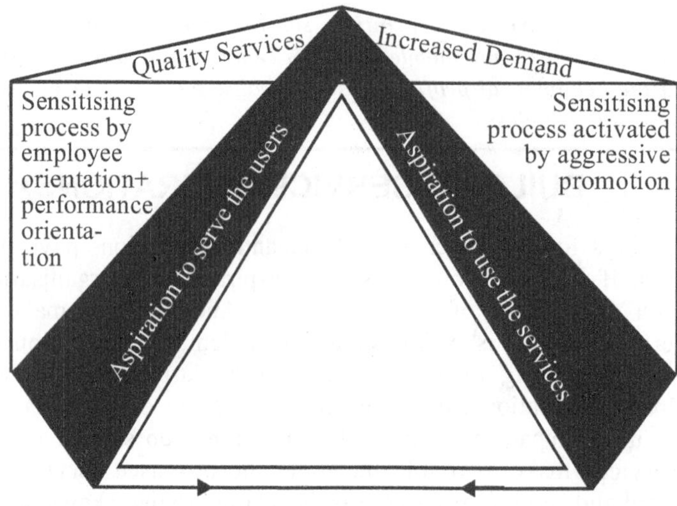

Fig. 1.5: Service Aspiration.

In view of the above, it is right to mention that building of service aspiration is essential. Of late, we find development of service generating organisations and a number of quality services are found available in the market. The prospects in a majority of the cases are not aware of the new developments. Of course, they have desire, capacity but aspirations at the very nascent stage. They fail in making demand and the opportunities are lost. We can't negate the fact that prospects of today are the customers of tomorrow. If we make sincere efforts to understand their aspirations, if we make initiative efforts to transfigurate their aspirations into demand; the process of demand creation is only not activated but keeps on moving for the years and years to come.

TECHNOLOGY IN THE SERVICES SECTOR

We cannot negate that the process of technological sophistication has influenced almost all sectors of the economy. We agree with this view that technology is dramatically changing the nature of services making ways for tremendous potentials for the offerings of new services which no doubt was difficult to imagine just a few years back. The new generation of technology is significantly changing the perception of service quality. During the yester decades, the services were confined to home locations but now we find them crossing the geographical and national boundaries. In the process, we find a number of technology but we consider Internet — the king of technology — acting as a vehicle for the travelling of services. The service-providers and service-users, of course, get a number of benefits but we also find paradoxes and the dark side. There are cases when both the employees and customers become critical to the use of technology. The customers feel that this may invade on their privacy whereas the employees resist to the new changes in the work process. Besides, we find lack of personal and human touch when we find new generation of technology used in the process of service offerings. Absence of interaction between the providers and users makes the evaluation process much more difficult. In addition, we also find involvement of costs and the additional responsibility before the professionals to educate and train the employees so that they are aware of the new generation of technology. However, we find a craze for promoting the use of technology in almost all the countries be it developed or be it developing like ours.

We appreciate the outstanding contributions of technology to the development of services sector but at the same time also find adverse remarks to be instrumental in generating the quality gap. This is due to the high level of expectations of customers which if not fulfilled mainly on account of misuse of technology or also due to fault in technology create a gap between the offerings and the expectations. The developing countries like ours face this problem in almost all the sectors. A majority of the banks making use of core banking services and located in suburbs or small towns and cities face such type of problem. Such a quality gap due to technology needs priority attention of policy makers. If we make use of new generation of technology, our efforts must be to make available to the users the benefits they expect.

The new generation of technology, no doubt, has proved to be the basic force behind service innovations such as automated voice mail, interactive voice response systems, fax machines, ATMs and other common services are the gift of new generation of technology. The satellite communication services virtually have revolutionised the information system. We are now considerably depending on new generation of technology and even cannot imagine a day having a communication gap. The Internet services have dramatically changed the scenario as a host of services more through internet. Whatsoever the qualitative or even the quantitative improvements that we find in the services are due to the emergence of new generation of sophisticated technology which has made ways for the emergence of techniculture.

We do not find any exaggeration in accepting internet as a king of technology because a majority or the services considerably depend on their functioning. A large number of services are on the horizon which in the days to come would benefit the customers in many ways. Actually, internet provides a way to offer the new services. Internet-based bill paying service for customers, map and routing, software for cars to enable drivers to know the services available on roads, directing drivers to specific locations, weather forecasts, and warnings, are some of the features redefining the internet services *vis-à-vis* fostering the outstanding contributions of new generation of technology. The mobile internet, accessing the web via cell phones, charging vending machine and gasoline purchases through cell phones and delivering advertising messages via cell phones are now rewriting the contributions of new generation of technology.

Of late, we also find technology for the offerings of services. The basic customer service functions such as bill paying, questions, checking account records, tracking orders, retail and business-to-business transactions has virtually changed the concept and percept of service offer. Actually, we have shifted from face-to-face service to the telephonic service and now even to wireless service. Not only this today, we also find technology helping in making purchases. In the banking business, we find a number of services online. Without human intervention, we can make use of the benefits of new generation of technology. Thus, we cannot negate that technology has been successful in the service innovation process and more so the internet has redefined the quality of services. Service can now be provided on the internet via e-mail, website robots, FAQ and online chat.

The above-mentioned facts make it clear that with the emergence of new generation of technology we find scope for innovations and innovative services offered to the customers play a vital role in redefining the quality. We also find expectations of customers changing because they demand choice on phone, automated voice systems via fax or e-mail or through internet services. Expectations if not fulfilled in the desired way pave avenues for frustrations. The new generation of sophisticated technology, of course, has been successful in increasing the levels of expectations but where we find lack of work culture or not suitable or unfriendly environment for techniculture; the customers/users find it difficult to avail the benefits.

In the Indian perspective, we find possibilities for the same as a number of obstacles are found in offering the benefits of technology to the masses. The supporting infrastructural facilities considerably influence the defined role of technology. The new generation of technology requires minute observation and active operation and for that we need professional excellence.

We cannot deny that even in the years to come a number of new services are to be included in the list of techno-driven services and in the changing environment, we need to develop our awareness of the new techniculture making ways for material culture.

CONSUMER PROTECTION IN SERVICES

With the increasing domination of buyers' market, we find new dimensions in the marketing of services. With the mounting intensity of competition, we find service generating organisations redefining their functional responsibilities. With the increasing rate of mass sensitivity, we find professionals becoming much more conscious while formulating and implementing the strategic decisions. Gone are the days when organisations exploiting and misleading consumers were found thriving. In the today's business world, we find a number of regulations to protect them. Particularly in the Indian context where we find rate of literacy presenting a gloomy picture and common masses looking insensitive to their problems and further the ethical dimensions not getting due place on the development agenda of corporate sector; it is pertinent that we not only make provisions for the protection of the right of consumers but a step forward makes it sure that regulatory provisions are not violated.

After 1990 when the globalisation became instrumental in diverting the attention of corporate policy makers, the tertiary sector started gaining popularity. The corporatisation considerably benefited the services sector and it was against this background that the services sector was found contributing significantly to the process of national economic transformation. The globalisation and liberalisation fuelled the process of development and the race and pace of economic transformation witnessed satisfactory trends in acceleration. The multi-faceted developments in the society also made ways for exploitation of consumers. This necessitated priority attention of government policy makers on the consumer protection regulations. It was against this background that a number of changes were made in the Consumer Protection Act of 1986.

Right to safety, Right to be informed, Right to choose and Right to be heard are some of the dimensions of consumer rights which at the early stage of development were found neglected. In the Indian perspective, of course, a number of steps were taken during the yesterdecades but the exploitation of consumers continued and even till date partially due to insensitivity and partially due to attitudinal transformation we find violation of the provision of Act. The protagonisits of Consumer Protection Act, 1986 need due attention on the increasing violations of the provisions of this Act.

Our focus here is on the administration of provisions of this Act in the services sector. The term "service" has a variety of meanings. It may mean any benefit or any act resulting in promoting interests of happiness. It may be contractual, professional, public, domestic, legal, statutory and so on. The concept of "service" is found to be very wide which is mentioned in the Act under Section 2(0). The concept of "Consumer" is found in the Act under Section 2(d). At the outset, it is essential to perceive the concept of Consumer and Service.

As per Section 2(d), Consumer means any person who buys any goods for a consideration which has been paid or promised or partly paid or partly promised or under any system of deferred payment and includes any users of such goods other than the person who buys such goods for consideration paid or promised or partly paid or partly promised or any system of deferred payment when such use is made with the approval of such person but does not include a person who obtains such goods for resale or for any commercial purpose or hires or avails of services for a consideration which has been paid or promised or partly paid or partly promised or under any system of deferred payment and includes any beneficiary of such services other than the person, who hires or avails of the services for consideration paid or promised or partly paid or partly promised or under any system of deferred payment when such services are availed of with the approval of the first mentioned person (but does not include a person who avails of such services for any commercial purpose).

According to the Section 2(d) of the Consumer Protection Act, it is not merely the buyer of goods or hirer of services who is called a consumer but any other person who uses such goods or avails of such services with the approval, of the original buyer/hirer is also a consumer.

Further the above definition makes it clear that the Consumer Protection Act primarily brings under its purview all goods and services but Section 1(4) says as otherwise expressly provided by the Central Government by notification, this Act shall apply to all goods and services. Though the law makers provided an option to the Central Government to exempt certain categories of goods and services from the ambit of the Act, no such exemption has been contemplated so far. In this context, it is also essential that we go through the explanation in the Case of Lucknow Development Authority vs. M.K. Gupta, Supreme Court.

The definition of the service as given in Consumer Protection Act under Section 2(0) reads as under:

"Service means service of any description which is made available to potential users and includes (but not limited to) the provision of facilities in connection with banking, financing, transport, processing, supply of electrical or other energy, boarding or lodging or both (housing construction) entertainment, amusement or the purveying news or other information but does not include the rendering of any service free of charge or under a contract of personal service.

Since we go through the services sector, it is essential that we go through the provisions of the Act 80 that service providing organisations are aware of the regulatory provisions and at the same time, the service-users and potential users also come to know that how and in what way they can be successful in protecting their rights.

Contract of personal service and contract for personal services are the two different things because the former is the service relationship of a master and servant whereas the latter is the professional or technical services.

A service must be made available to potential users who are willing to pay for the service. It must be rendered for remuneration. Service free of charge not come under the definition and hence are outside the scope of the Consumer Protection Act.

It is in this context that medical services rendered free of charge in a government hospital are not found within the purview of the Act. The free services rendered by the municipalities or corporations like sanitation, roads, street lights, parks and so on are also outside the purview of this Act. Actually, we find these services managed out of the tax amount paid by the citizens. The Supreme Court observed in the case of *Commissioner, Hindu Religious Endowment, Madras vs. Shri Lakshmindra Thirtha Swaminar* that these taxes do not constitute consideration for the service ostensibly rendered gratis by the state to its citizens. Like this, a case related to a claim pension by employee from his employer is not covered under the Act. Regarding the relationship between the doctor and patient, the Supreme Court observed that the relationship between a medical practitioner and patient carries within it a certain degree of mutual confidence and trust and therefore the services rendered by the medical practitioner can be regarded as service of personal nature but since there is no relationship of master and servant between the doctor and patient, the contract between medical practitioner and his patient cannot be treated as a contract of personal service and as contract for services and hence not covered by the exclusionary part of the definition of service.

Professional Services

We consider profession as an occupation requiring intellectual or manual skills controlled by the intellectual skill. Thus, the occupations which are regarded as profession have the following features:

- The work found skilled and specialised and a substantial part of the same is mental rather than manual.
- Commitment to moral principles and duty to a particular client or patient.
- The Associations of professionals regulating admission and seeking to uphold the standards of profession through professional codes on matters of conduct and ethics.
- High status in the community.

Educational Services

We consider imparting of education a mission or a noble vocation. Imparting education cannot be treated as a trade or business specially in India. We consider it a religious duty or a charitable activity. We go through the problem with the viewpoint of Consumer Protection Act. Because we consider students as consumer, the different commissions such as the Maharashtra State Commission, the Harayana State Commission and the Tamil Nadu State Commission have observed that the education falls within the purview of Consumer Protection Act.

Education is one of the most valuable services in the human society and this service is not rendered free and therefore the students are the consumers. Actually, we find relationship between the students and educational institutions of provider and users. If we find educational institutions making tall claims and creating big business by collecting from the students high fees, such a relationship of provider and user we cannot deny. A student is virtually a consumer of services in an educational institution; therefore when there is no service there is no right with the college to appropriate fees. If it insists on collecting fees without imparting education, it will amount to deficiency.

As per Section 2(i)(g) of the Consumer Protection Act, deficiency means any fault, imperfection, shortcoming or inadequacy in the quality, nature and manner of performance which is required to be maintained by or under any law for the time being in force or has been undertaken to be performed by a person in pursuance of a contract or otherwise in relation to any service. It is a breach of obligation — statutory, contractual or otherwise to maintain a particular quality, nature and manner of performance of service. The expression of deficiency is synonymous with negligence.

In the context of professional services, we find medical and healthcare services occupying a place of outstanding significance. This is due to the fact that we find these services essential in nature and required by each one of us in the society. This makes it essential that a medical practitioner attends on the patient and exercises reasonable care while treating. A medical practitioner found negligent in his/her professional career is found liable under the

Consumer Protection Act is also to be remembered that wrong diagnosis is not considered to be negligence unless it is negligence *per se*. The paramedical services such as scanning centres, diagnostic centres and medical laboratories also come under the purview of Consumer Protection Act.

Illegal Strike and Disruption of Services

Disruption of services due to illegal strike also come under the purview of Consumer Protection Act. On account of illegal strike by the Flight Engineers' Association, passengers were in trouble. A Voluntary Consumer Organisation filed a case on a common cause with the National Commission. The National Commission observed that the persons employed on salary in an organisation, which is rendering service for consideration are equally covered by the provisions of the Consumer Protection Act, along with their management, if they resort to illegal strike. If a strike appears to be imminent and the concerned organisation (bank) has received a strike notice served by their union of employees, it is essential that the notice related to the strike is published in the newspaper so that small amount holders, pensioners get an opportunity to withdraw money.

The service-providers bear the responsibility of developing their awareness of the provisions of Consumer Protection Act so that they do not throw their organisations in the reverse gear and create image problem.

SUMMARY

You have gone through the foundation of services marketing. Before starting another chapter, be sure that the following facts are well versed:

Services – the Concept: Services can be defined as an action(s) of an organisation(s) that provides a number of services to the individuals and organisations. Services are activities, benefits or satisfaction.

Goods and Services: Services and goods are not tantamount. Services are intangible, perishable, inseparable but the goods are tangible, separable and transferrable.

Salient Features of Services: Service have a number of features related to intangibility, perishability, inseparability, heterogeneity or so.

Services Marketing: Marketing a services is meant marketing something intangible. It is marketing a promise. It is more selling yourself.

Why Marketing of Services: Upward trend in the disposable income, increasing specialisation, growing fashion, professionalism in education, information explosion, sophistication in market, increasing governmental activities are some of the reasons entailed behind marketing services.

Significance of Services Marketing: Creation and expansion of job opportunities, an optimal utilisation of resources, paving avenues for the formation of capital, increasing the standard of living, use of environment-friendly technology are the important points in favour of services marketing.

The Behavioural Profile of Users: It is a study related to the behavioural profile of users of the services where we find emphasis on the needs, requirements, preferences, attitudes and expectations, The social, economic, family and business influences are found here significant.

Marketing Information System: It is a combination of different subsystems to transform the data into information either manually or with the support of information technologies to simplify the task of executives in making creative and effective marketing decisions.

Market Segmentation: Market segmentation is a division or subdivision of market to make it small to study and understand the customers. It is based on the principle of divide and rule. While segmenting a market, we divide it into different small segments which helps us in understanding the behavioural profile of users/prospects.

Emerging Key Services: The key services on which we find focus are banking services, insurance services, transportation services, tourism services, hotel services, consultancy services, education services, hospital services, personal care services, entertainment services, electricity services and telecom services. We can't negate the fact that all these services need application of marketing principles to offer quality services to the users and to maintain commercial viability for the development of organisations engaged in generating the services.

Building Services Aspirations: In the context of building services aspirations, our emphasis is on acting on two fronts, such as generating aspirations to serve the users and generating aspirations to use the services,

This activates the process of demand generation since the employees work with the motto of serving the users who are sensitised to buy the services.

Role of Culture in Services: Everybody looks at the world from behind the windows of a cultural home. We consider culture a software of mind and cultural universals as the manifestations of life of any group of people. With the emergence of a cross-cultural society, the service marketers need to have an in-depth knowledge of values and attitudes, manners and customs, material culture aesthetics and educational and social institutions affecting cultural and behavioural patterns, specially in the global perspective. Actually, service experiences differ across cultures.

Technology in Services: In an age of sophisticated technology, we find the emergence of techniculture where new generation of sophisticated technology has been found dominating even the services sector. In a true sense, the technology has proved to be a basic force for activating the process of service innovations such as automated voice mail, interactive voice response system, fax machines, ATMs, etc. The basic customer functions such as bill paying, questions, checking account records, tracking orders, retail and business to business transactions are now done with the help of new generation of technology. Shifting from face-to-face services to the telephonic and wireless services are the contributions of technology.

Customer Protection in Services: Protection of the rights of customers is an important consideration in the services sector. With the Consumer Protection Act 1986, we find application of this Act even in the services sector. Right to safety, Right to be informed, Right to choose and Right to be heard are considered key dimensions of this Act. Since in the Indian society we find customers in general almost insensitive even to their own interests, we expect a lot from this Act. A number of qualitative improvements are possible in the education and health care services if we find application of this Act in the right perspective.

KEY TERMS

Corporate Culture
Multinationals
Professional Excellence
Common Parlance
American Marketing Association
Disposable Income
Discretionary Income
Information Explosion
Sophistication
Behavioural Profile
Sorting Theory
Culture in Services
Material Culture
Aesthetics
Marketing Information System
Market Segmentation
Technology-driven Banking Services
Service Profile of Insurance
Mutual Fund Services
Portfolio Management Services
Factoring Services
Transport Network
Superstructure
Occupancy Ratio
Retail Services
Mall Culture
Paramedical Personnel
Human Capital Formation
Upcoming Entrepreneurs
TV Culture
Electricity Marketing
Mass Communication
Satellite Services
Day-care Services
Peripheral Services
Value Engineering
Automobile Services
Courier Organisations
IT Services
Service Aspirations
Techniculture
Consumer Protection Act
Professional Services
Illegal Strike
Technology Gap
Quality Gap

Review Questions

1. What do you mean by Services? Distinguish between goods and services.
2. Focus on the salient features of services which complicate the task of marketing services effectively.
3. "Marketing is a vital function in both profit and not-for-profit making organisations." Discuss this statement.
4. Explain fully what the Services Marketing Concept is all about. What reasons are there for believing that services marketing would be more significant in future?
5. Point out and explain the important reasons for a substantial growth in the service markets.
6. Focus on the significance of services marketing in the Indian perspective.
7. 'The first commandment of marketing is to know the markets which draws our attention on understanding the behavioural profile of users.' Comment on this statement and focus on the environmental influences governing the behaviour of users.
8. Explain the instrumentality of marketing information system in making the creative decisions for marketing services.
9. 'Market segmentation recognises that a company or its main product/service can't be all things to everyone.' Do you agree? Defend your opinion.
10. Write a brief note on the emerging key services in the Indian perspective.
11. Focus on building service aspirations found instrumental in improving the quality of services and at the same time activating the process of demand generation.
12. Explain the role of technology in the services sector.
13. "Culture considerably influences the services." In the light of this statement discuss the role of culture in improving the quality of services.

Application Exercises

1. Give examples of how during the last ten years, the services sector have made significant contributions to the national economy of India.
2. Prepare a list of at least ten services that you have used during the yestermonths and mention the impact of new generation of technologies there.
3. Select a service generating organisation of your choice and show that how each of the seven Ps of marketing have been conceptualised there.
4. As a marketing professional, clarify the role of culture in the decision-making process.
5. The service marketers feel that service experiences differ across cultures. What are your reactions?
6. As a marketing professional, comment on the news of a majority of Indians that imparting education cannot be treated as a trade or business.
7. Focus on the services where the Consumer Protection Act are effective.

Endnotes

1. Sasser W.E., Oison R.P. and Wyckoff D.D., *Management of Service Operations,* Allyon & Bacon Inc., 1978, p. 2.
2. Sir William Beveridge, *Report on Social Insurance and Allied Services,* London, HMSO, 1942.
3. Rao A.V.S., *Service Sector Management in India,* Allied Publishers, Hyderabad, 1986, p. 24.
4. Hasen Field Y. and Richard A.E., *Human Services Organisations;* The University of Michigan Press, 1974, p. 1.
5. Carman James M. and Kenneth P. Uhl, *Marketing Principles and Methods,* Homewood III, Richard D. Irwin, 1973, p. 362.
6. Donald Cowell W., *The Marketing of Services,* CAM Foundation and Institute of Marketing, London, 1984, p. 25.
7. Kotler P., *Principles of Marketing,* Prentice-Hall, 1982, p. 264.
8. Stanton W.J., *Fundamentals of Marketing,* McGraw-Hill, New York, 1981, p. 441.
9. Bateson J., *Do We Need Service Marketing — Marketing Consumer Services,* Marketing Science Institute, Boston, 1977, New Institute Reports, pp. 75-115.
10. Carman J.M., and Kenneth, *op. cit.,* p. 364.
11. The American Marketing Association, *American Marketing Association Definitions,* Chicago, 1960, p. 15.
12. John M. Rathwell, *Marketing in the Services Sector,* Cambridge, 1974.
13. Webster F.E., *Social Aspect of Marketing,* Prentice-Hall, 1974, pp. 73-92.

14. Sanjiv Bhatt, Marketing Services, *The Economic Times,* 28th April, 1988.
15. *Ibid.*
16. Times Magazine, *The Times of India,* December 1988-Jan. 1989, p. 5.
17. Cundiff Still and Govoni, *Fundamentals of Modern Marketing,* Prentice-Hall of India, 1982, p. 128.
18. Walter C. Glenn, *Consumer Behaviour,* Homewood, 1978, pp. 7-17.
19. *Ibid.,* p. 1.
20. Alderson W., *The Analysis Framework for Marketing,* Proceedings of the Conference of Marketing Teachers from the Far Western States, p. 18.
21. Walter A. Henry, Cultural Values do Correlate with Consumer Behaviour, *Journal of Marketing Research,* May, 1976, pp. 121-127.
22. Joseph T. Plummer, The Concept and Application of Lifestyle Segmentation, *Journal of Marketing,* January 1974. pp. 33-37.
23. Frederick F., Webster Jr. and Yoram Wind, *Organisational Buying Behaviour,* Prentice-Hall, 1972.
24. G. Hofstede *Culture and Organisations*, Software of Mind, McGraw-Hill 1991, New York, p. 235.
25. Cundiff, Still and Govoni, *op. cit.,* p. 65.
26. *Ibid.,* p. 66.
27. Reidenbach E.R. and Pitters R.E., *Bank Marketing,* p. 57.
28. Harper B. Jr. and William Massey, *Marketing Management,* 1972, p. 87.
29. Joseph T. Plummer, *op. cit.,* pp. 33-37.
30. Elizabeth A. Richard and Stephen Sturman, Lifestyle Segmentation in Appeal Marketing, *Journal of Marketing,* October, 1977, pp. 87-91.

KEY ELEMENTS IN SERVICES MARKETING

"Services Marketing once a tiny academic field championed by a handful of pioneering Professors has now become a thriving area of activity with exciting future."

– *Lovelock*

Chapter Objectives

Introduction – Service Environment – Service Blueprinting – Demand-Supply Management – Management of Service Capacity – Management of Service Relationships – Relationship Marketing – Service Recovery – Customer – Service Expectations – Service Encounters – Service Quality – Service Quality Gap – Service Quality Audit – SERVQUAL – Development of New Service Product – Branding Service Product – Service Leadership – Service Strategy – Service Mission – Service Triangle – Summary – Key Terms – Review Questions – Application Exercises – Endnotes.

Learning Objectives

The motive of this chapter is to sensitise the readers to some of the key elements helping a marketing professional in making quality decisions. The environmental conditions and blueprinting for services are found important in the very context. The Demand-Supply management or Sycromarketing helps them in maintaining a balance and relationship marketing simplifies their task of creating and capitalising on the opportunities. Service recovery, service encounters, service expectations play an outstanding role in making our efforts professionally sound. Service quality issues and the multi-faceted gap need due attention of professionals. SERVQUAL helps in measuring service quality. The development of new services, formulation of a service strategy, service mission, service triangle are some of the important issues in services marketing.

INTRODUCTION

Professional excellence makes the ways for qualitative-cum-quantitative transformation. Managerial proficiency paves copious avenues for making the process cost-effective. Conversely, the managerial deficiency contracts avenues for the same. This makes a strong advocacy in favour of professional touch in the process of making the managerial decisions. A number of factors for making the marketing decisions sound necessitate priority attention of marketing professionals because the process of excelling competition cannot be successful unless we have excellence of world class. In the Indian perspective, we have tremendous opportunities. How and in what way we capitalise on the existent opportunities depend on our sincere efforts for making the policy decision-making processes much more result-oriented.

The problems like service environment and service blueprinting help them in making their decisions proactive. The demand-supply management studies simplify their task of balancing the position. The multi-faceted studies of relationship considerably influence the marketing processes. Building relationship and capitalising on the same in the best interests of service providing organisation makes the marketing efforts much more result-oriented. The scope for service recovery help service marketers in winning their confidence and tapping their potentials. The problems like service encounters, service expectations help marketing professionals in many ways. In a true sense, they cannot undermine these sensitive issues considerably influencing their success.

In an age of globalisation, we are suitably rewarded for quality. The organisations not assigning due weightage to service quality fail in excelling competition. On the other hand, the organisations defining and innovating quality prove to be a quality leader because they establish themselves as a service leader. The studies related to quality assume a place of outstanding significance. We cannot refute that development processes in the modern business world are sizeably influenced by the quality of technology used by an organisation. The organisations making use of new generation of sophisticated technology succeed in establishing an edge over those who continue to make use of traditional technology. But in this context, they also need to make it sure that quality is not to create a gap. A study of gap model will help service marketers in improving the benefits of technology to the users. The marketing professionals also need to go through the problem of service quality audit as this is to keep on moving the process of technological sophistication. In this context, we also find SERVQUAL an important scale for measuring the service quality.

The formulation of a sound service strategy is found significant to the service marketers. They need to work with a holistic touch. They need new vision, new approach and innovative strategic decisions. Identifying the sorespots and based on their sense of judgements and techno-driven information modifying them in tune with the changing situational requirements appear to be the need of modern business world.

SERVICE ENVIRONMENT

Mary Jo Bitner in her paper "Servicescapes[1]: The Impact of Physical Surroundings, Customers and Employees", published in Journal of Marketing, 56, 1992 used this terminology for Service Environments. This focuses our attention on the style and appearance of the physical surroundings and other experiential elements encountered by customers at service delivery sites. We consider service environment an art consuming much more time and efforts. It is designed and built by experts and are not always easy to change. We cannot deny that the studies related to service environment are the field of environmental psychology. The service marketing academics have conceptualised the theories for developing their understanding and managing customer responses to service environment.

What are our feelings regarding a particular service or our perception of a firm's image and positioning are shaped in the face of service environment. For users, it becomes much more difficult to, assess service quality and therefore we find customers preferring service environment as an important quality signal. It is very natural that a well designed service environment makes customers feel good and increase the level of satisfaction *vis-a-vis* the productivity of service operation. The environmental psychologists make a strong advocacy in favour of environmental impact on our mindset. The Stimulus-Response Model of Mehrabian-Russell[2] holds that environmental conditions influence our feelings, and we cannot deny the impact of feelings on our behaviour.

The key dimensions of service environment[3] are ambient conditions which may include music, colours and scents and environmental fragrance throwing a major impact on our behaviour. Besides, the layout, signs, symbols and artifacts also become a part and parcel of service environment. In the lobby of hotels, presence or absence of background music, type of music, tempo and volume bring an important difference in the perception of satisfaction. Actually, the perception of quality combines or coils in its essence a number of items and the professionals need to take care. It is in this context that we find aesthetic management becoming an integral part of corporate culture because we cannot negate its major impact on adding additional attractions to environmental fragrance. What about others when we find its positive impact in hospitals particularly on increasing the recovery rate or minimising the duration of recovery. In almost all the service generating organisations, the service environment has been found throwing a major impact on the feelings and behaviour of customers. Of course, the professionals need to plan everything in the face of nature and types of services and the quality of users/customers.

The different dimensions of service environment as displayed in Fig. 2.1 draw our priority attention so that professionals succeed in injecting additional attractions. The ambient conditions, (music, scent, colour), spatial layout, signs, symbols and artifacts and more so people as a part of service environment chance our perception of quality.

SERVICESCAPES

Physical surroundings affect our behaviour. It is essential that the service marketers are aware of the environmental conditions where the services are offered. Of course, it is a subject related to environmental psychology and against this background we find M.J. Bitner developing a comprehensive model that she named the Servicescapes (Journal of Marketing, 56, April 1992, pp. 57-71, Servicescapes: The Impact of Physical Surroundings on Customers and Employees).

According to Bitner, the ambient conditions, space/functionality and signs, symbols and artifacts are the part and parcel of service environment. Likes and dislikes cannot be identical. Beauty lies in the eyes of beholder and is subjective. Rap music may be pleasent to some customer segments but at the same time sheer torture to others. Enhancing the productivity of front line staff and the quality of service they deliver are considerably influenced by service environment. An in-depth study of the various dimensions of physical environment is thus found essential.

DIMENSIONS OF PHYSICAL ENVIRONMENT

The ambient conditions include temperature, quality of air, noise, music, and colour. The space includes layout, equipment, furnishing. The sign and artifacts include signage, personal artifacts, style of decor. In Figure 2.2, we find a framework for understanding the relationships of users of services to the environment.

Ambient Conditions: In the ambient conditions, we find focus on the five senses. We perceive ambient conditions both separately and holistically. This includes the background characteristics of the environment.

Temperature: If we find customers/users or employees spending considerable time in the servicescape, the temperature influences the behaviour. People visiting a hall where the air-conditioning has failed and the air is hot and stuffy will be uncomfortable and its reflection will be found on their feelings. If we find the temperature and air quality within a comfort tolerance zone, the ambient factors will remain unnoticed.

Music: We find music throwing a powerful impact on perceptions and behaviour. The structural quality of music such as tempo, volume and harmony are found important in this context. The fast-tempo music and high volume music increase arousal levels. In the hospitality industry or even in other areas, the adjustment of tempo and volume of music play an important role in influencing the customers and working employees. We find relaxing music found effective in minimising the stress levels in a waiting room of hospital's surgery. The effectiveness of music is found in a number of areas but the main thing is the volume and type of music.

Scent: An ambient smell pervades the service environment. The service fragrance is found very much related to the ambient smell. We cannot confine it to a particular product. The customers/users feel the power of smell in almost all the conditions and therefore we find it a part of servicescape.

The smell awares us of our hunger and also suggests a solution. The scent throws a strong impact on mood, responses and purchase intentions and behaviours. These things make it clear that marketing professionals need to assign due weightage to the fragrance in the service environment.

Colour: We find colour calming, stimulating, expressive, symbolic, impressional and even disturbing. Colour pervades every aspect of our lives and it has a strong impact on our feelings. The psychologists have defined colours as hue, value and chroma. Hue clarifies the pigment of the colour such as orange, red, yellow, green, blue, violet. Value is considered to be the degree of darkness or lightness of the colour indicating its degree. Chroma refers to hue intensity, saturation or brilliance. The researches reveals that a majority of the people prefer service environment having warm colour such as red, orange, yellow. In the context of service environment, the marketing professionals need to make it sure that colours have a match with the servicescape for a particular service.

Spatial Layout and Functionality: We find a correlation between service environment and our purposes or needs. In this context, the spatial layout and functionality of the service environment are found significant. The spatial layout refers to the size and shape of furnishing, counters and potential machines and equipment and also focuses on the way of arrangement and positioning. The functionality throws light on the potentials of those items to facilitate the performance service transactions. The marketing professionals need to perceive that spatial layout and functionality affects the behaviour of customers and the levels of satisfaction.

Signs, Symbols and Artifacts: In the service environment, we find a number of things acting as explicit or implicit signals communicating the image of an organisation. As and when the customers witness servicescape, they need a signal which helps them in proceeding for obtaining the desired services. If they do not find any signal there, they may be confused and resulting from which we may also find anger and frustration. The service designers are required to use signs, symbols and artifacts to guide customers through the process of service delivery. The directional cues are found important particularly for the new customers and the marketing professionals cannot be sure that there will be any day when the new customers will not enter the service environment. It is right to mention that new customers entering the service environment are generally found shy of asking anyone and the signposts, symbols and artifacts considerably help them in the process of searching the service points they want to reach.

PEOPLE IN THE SERVICE ENVIRONMENT

Service environment creates impression and the appearance and behaviour of both service providers and customers can detract or reinforce from the impression already created. This makes it clear that people in the service environment play a very effective role in influencing the behavioural profile of customers.

Service environment, no doubt, is considered important for the formation of service expectations but in the entire process we find people playing a decisive role. The service providers and the customers are responsible for both the conditions — attraction or detraction. The dimensions talked earlier, no doubt, play a very positive role in the creation of impression but if we find service providers not playing the desired role by projecting their facial expression and guiding the customers suitably, our efforts show a lukewarm response. The marketing professionals are supposed to play here an outstanding role by attracting customers who not only appreciate the ambience but also add attractions in the ambience by their appearance and behaviour.

DESIGNING OF ENVIRONMENT WITH A HOLISTIC VIEW

If we talk about the holistic view of service environment, our focus is on artistic designing emphasizing on specific types of servicescapes. In the hospitality industry, we find experts concentrating on restaurants, bars, clubs, cafes and bistros, retail outlets and even the health care services. Actually, the interior designers create hotel lobbies around the world. The experts need to view the servicescapes with holistic approach which makes it essential that no dimension of the design is given a shape in its isolation. If they see servicescapes holistically, they would not forget that everything depends on everything. They need to elicit the desired consumer responses and therefore the elements like background music, colour mixing, scent, environmental fragrance are required to be considered. Distinctive or unique servicescapes viewed holistically add additional attractions and create a distinct service expectations. The small things like colour of floors, materials of the furniture, lighting arrangements and promotional materials and positioning of the firm make servicescapes much more productive. Thus, holistically designed servicescapes and professionally displayed service environment bear the potentials of adding additional attractions.

DO NOT FORGET CUSTOMERS WHILE DESIGNING

Of course, the professionals need to think about the aesthetic values and the artistic touch but they are not supposed to forget the customers who are going to use them. The high profile service environments must be foolproof and best efforts are to be made to identify and remove the flaws. Ron Kaufman opines,[4] "It's easy to get caught up in designing new things that are 'cool' or 'elegant' or 'hot'. But if you don't keep your customers in mind throughout, you could end up with an investment that's not." We find a number of cases where the designers have not taken into consideration the customers who are going to use them. In Jordan, a new Sheraton Hotel was opened without clear signage from the ballrooms to the restrooms. The signs etched in muted gold on dark marble pillars failed in attracting the attention of customers. Of course, the designs must be user-friendly.

Another case that we find related to the airport. At the Dragon Air lounge in the new airport of Hong Kong, a partition of colourful glass hanging from the ceiling created a number of problems to the customers. We need not forget that a lounge in the airport is a heavy-traffic area where we find people moving in and out round the clock. The designers need to make the signposts and further to position or display them at the place where the customers/users do not face any problem.

While designing a number of factors need due care. The customers/users would not allow or digest even minor things because they have a high level of service expectations. If they divert their attention on ambient conditions and witness that store is dirty, shopping centre is too hot, music is too loud, bad smell is in the store, they would definitely react. Like this, when they go through using the services, they find no mirror in the dressing room, inadequate or vague directions; this will again create problem.

The aforesaid facts make it clear that the designers need to consider even the small things particularly in the high profile services where we find customers having a high level of expectation. If they undermine, this is to make the service environment user-unfriendly.

FACTORS TO CONSIDER FOR DESIGNING SERVICESCAPES

While designing servicescapes, the professionals need to understand the customers in a right way. The following tools are to be helpful:

- Observation of the behavioural profile of customers and responses of management, supervisors and managerial and front-line staff regarding the service environment.
- Feedback from the front-line staff and customers and for that purpose different research tools may be used.
- Field experiments for bringing or incorporating necessary changes. The professionals may use computer-stimulated virtual tours for that very purpose. This helps in knowing the impact of changes. The alternatives layouts, styles, furnishing and colour may be tested.
- Service mapping is also found essential. This helps in including the physical evidence in the environment.

In view of the aforesaid facts, it is right to say that service environment plays a major role in shaping the perception of customers regarding the image of an organisation. Building of a fair image becomes easier if we find professionals assigning due weightage to the designing of service environment coiling much more fragrance.

The above-mentioned studies related to servicescapes make it clear that in a majority of the service providing organisations, the different dimensions of service environment draw priority attention of designers supposed to have world-class excellence. The exteriors and interiors cannot be undermined. They need a holistic view and to consider even the minor things attracting the customers and visitors. Besides, the conveniences and inconveniences of working people also need due care. Ultimately, we do everything for customers for which the services are created. Everything depends on everything else and therefore the professionals need a holistic view. We cannot design anything in isolation.

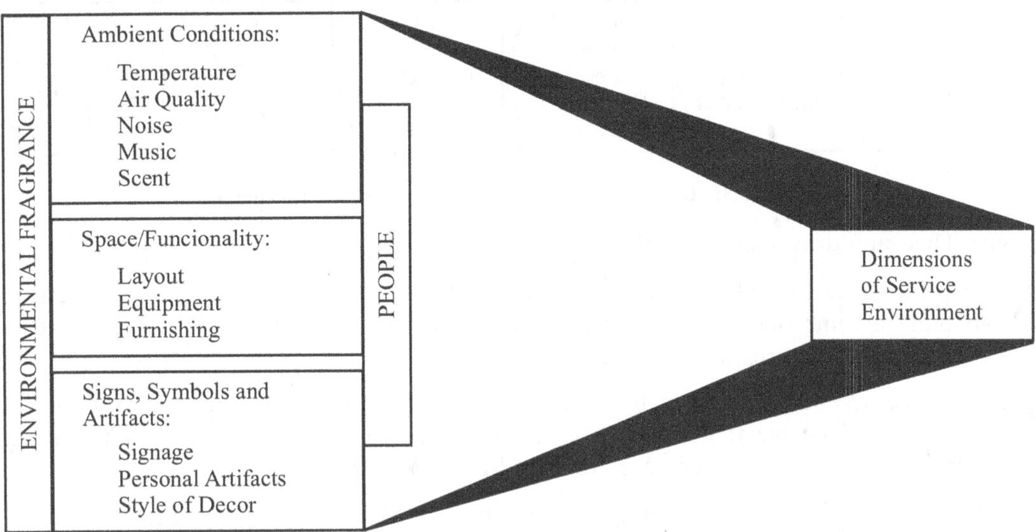

Fig. 2.1: Dimensions of Service Environment

Environmental psychologists also opine that ambient conditions generate fragrance in services. Our services considerably rest on servicescapes. It is but natural that likes and dislikes cannot be identical. We need to add additional attractions to our services and servicescapes generated and designed with the help of professional designers having world-class excellence may be much more proactive. The very success of corporate culture rests on attractions and fragrance. How to add much more attractions and how to increase the fragrance in tune with the taste and temperament of customers as well as the service providers need excellence. Servicescapes designing, of course, is an art but at the same time, we also consider it a profession. It requires a microscopic study of the likes and dislikes of users and providers and the designers are required to dance in tune with their preferences.

SERVICE BLUEPRINTING

Blueprinting becomes essential particularly in the manufacturing and construction industries because we cannot expect a car, a computer or even a toy being built without concrete and detailed plans, engineering drawings and specifications. But services even of complex nature can be introduced without any formal depiction of the process.

We find blueprinting a picture or a map virtually portraying the service system so that the providers understand them in a right fashion. At the designing and redesigning stages of development of new services, we find blueprinting useful. It magnifies the process of service delivery, the points of customers' contact, the roles of the customers and employees are supposed to play and the visible elements of the service. The Figure 2.2 clarifies it.

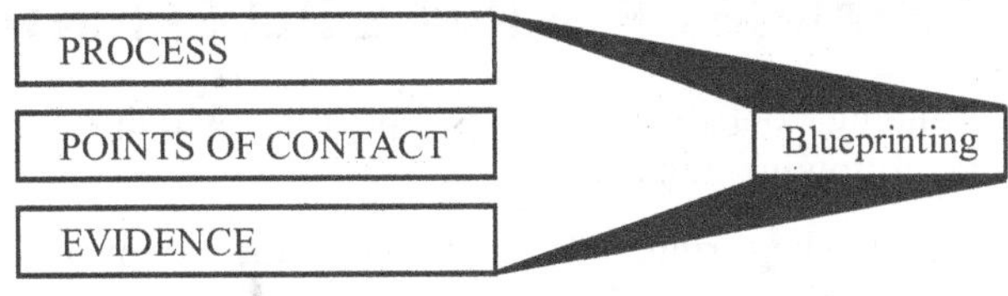

Fig. 2.2: Service Blueprinting

BUILDING A BLUEPRINT

Building a service blueprint moves through different stages. The process of developing blueprint helps in achieving the intermediate goals. The multi-faceted intermediate goals are clarification of the concept, development of a shared service vision, recognition of complexities and intricacies of the service found initially not to be apparent and delineation of the roles and responsibilities. The basic steps in building the blueprint have been shown in the following:

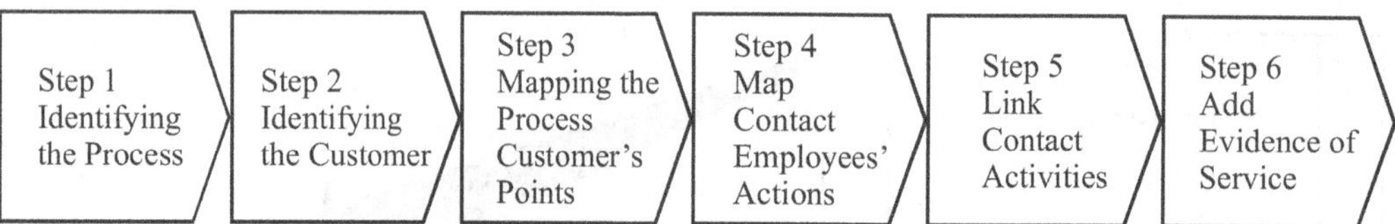

Fig. 2.3: Basic Steps in Building a Service Blueprint

First Step: This step draws our attention on identifying the process to be blueprinted.

We find blueprinting developed at a variety of levels. In some of the services, we find just basic service concept level whereas in some others we find variation in the face of segmentation. When the blueprinting is found specific, the specific features are clarified.

Second Step: The second step in the blueprinting process identifies the customers or customer segment experiencing the service. Since we find a variation in the needs and requirements of different segments, there must be difference in the features of services for the different segments.

Third Step: The third step of blueprinting concentrates on blueprinting from the viewpoints of customers. This step involves charting of the choice and actions performed and experienced by customers in the process of purchasing, using, and evaluating the services. In this context, we find processes and steps not influenced by customers becoming insignificant.

Fourth Step: This step draws our attention on the actions of map contact employees which may be both onstage and backstage. In the process, we find firstly the lines of interaction and visibility and then mapping of the points of view of the contact persons. In the context of technology-driven services, the required actions of technology interface are mapped. If we do not find help of employees in the process, then the area can be relabeled, such as 'onstage technology action. If we find interactions of both technology and people, a horizontal line would separate 'onstage contact employee actions' and 'onstage technology actions.'

Fifth Step: In the fifth step, we find link contact activities to the required supported functions. In this respect, we find direct and indirect impact of internal actions on the customers becoming apparent. The line of internal action can be drawn and linkages from contact activities to internal support functions can be identified in this step.

Sixth Step: This is the last step of blueprinting which can be added to blueprint to illustrate the experiences of customers. We agree that at this stage, the photographic blueprinting including photos, slides or video of the process can be very useful.

Of course, some of us do not realise the significance of blueprinting in the services sector but the organisations making use of the same have been found getting considerable benefits. Actually, service blueprinting becomes productive particularly in the today's techno-driven services sector. The service generating organisations may substantially be benefited and even the users of services are also found benefited. But the blueprinting must be scientific.

IMPORTANCE OF SERVICE BLUEPRINTING

We cannot negate the outstanding contributions of blueprinting which helps developing the service sector organisations in many ways. The following facts testify it:

- **An Overview to Employees:** The service blueprinting provides an overview to the working people which provides a customer/user-oriented focus. They find themselves in a position to make an anatomy of the services-offered and making the customer-friendly.
- **Helps identifying the weaknesses:** The chain of service activities may develop some of the weaknesses and blueprinting helps you in removing the same for improving the quality. If the points of failures are identified, remedial measures are adopted; our quality improvement programmes get a success.
- **Illuminating the customer's role:** The service blueprinting makes ways for an interaction between the external customers and employees and thus illuminates the customers' role and demonstrates where we find customers experiencing quality. This is considered to be an important contribution to the informed service design.

- **Facilitating the rational service design:** In the process of service blueprinting, we find line of visibility that promotes a conscious decision on what customers/users should view and which employees would be in contact with customers/users. The process thus facilitates rational service design.
- **Clarifying interfaces across the departmental lines:** The service blueprinting strengthens quality improvement programme. In the blueprinting process, we find line of internal interaction clarifying interfaces across the departmental lines with their inherent interdependencies which strengthens our quality improvement programmes on a regular basis.
- **Stimulating strategic decision:** The service blueprinting also stimulates strategic decisions by illuminating the elements and connections bearing the potentials of constituting the service. The persons participating in the strategic sessions are found exaggerating the significance of their own special functions and perspective unless a common ground for the integrated view of the service is provided.
- **Providing a basis for identifying and assessing cost:** We find service blueprinting making available a sound basis for the identification and assessment of cost, revenue and capital invested.
- **Constituting a rational basis for internal and external marketing:** The service blueprinting makes available a rational basis for both — the internal and external marketing. Overviewing a service and making a choice make the promotional and other measures effective.
- **Facilitating approaches to quality improvement:** The blueprinting also facilitates top-down and bottom-up approaches for improvement in the quality of services. Further, it enables professionals to identify channel and activate quality improvement efforts specially of grass root employees working as front-line or as support team.

DEMAND-SUPPLY MANAGEMENT

Balancing supply and demand sides of a service industry is not easy. The professionals managing or striking a balance between the two make difference. In a number of service generating organisations, we find much more fluctuations between demand and supply sides, such as restaurants, courier services, consultancy services and vacation resorts. The impact of seasonal fluctuation is found of high magnitude which complicates the task of a professional. This makes it essential that professionals assign top priority to this problem. Assessing demand and improving the supply position are the two problems necessitating excellence of marketing professionals. In any case, the mismatch between the two is to be reduced to the extent it is possible. It is in this context Kotler talked about Sycro-marketing[5] which focuses on synchronising demand and supply.

MANAGING DEMAND SIDE

There are a number of approaches for managing the demand side and the professionals need to study the situations and then to adopt a particular measure. The professionals may not take any action in the first condition where the supply side is low but the demand side is high as it may irritate customers. Another condition may be reverse when we find supply side high but the demand side low because here we find waste of capacity.

In the second condition, the professionals may reduce demand by increasing price particularly in less profitable and desirable segments we may not find this prescription so much effective. The third condition prescribes an increase in demand. In this case, the profitable segments are given priority. The two additional conditions we find pertaining to inventory demand by reservation system and by formalised queuing.

The role of a marketer while managing the demand is found of significant nature. This focuses our attention on the different mixes of marketing helping in managing demand. Of course, we find price to be instrumental in managing demand but other mixes of marketing also influence the process.[6]

MARKETING MIX vs. DEMAND SIDE

Managing Product: Variations in product help us in managing the demand. The goods and services, of course, have a different nature. The services having seasonal fluctuations draw a close attention of marketing professionals. In a particular season, we find a sharp increase in demand. The variation may be found even during the different hours in a day. The hospitals and hotels both have a different nature. In some of the resort hotels, we find a different package of services for different hours. During peak season, we find an increase in demand but during off season, we find an adverse condition. The professionals need to know about the nature of product *vis-a-vis* the seasonal impact. In some of the centres, we find high influx of tourists and the officials are forced to develop a marketing campaign for regulating the influx. The service product offerings are changed and the pressure of people is discouraged because the supply side is not optimal to meet the demand side.

Managing Promotion: The marketing professionals while managing the demand side also need to manage the promotion mix. The promotional measures have a two-fold impact. We find professionals advertising to motivate and even to demotivate. The relevant informations are transmitted to the customers and potential customers so that they take a decision in tune with their conveniences. The changes in price, product and distribution are communicated to the customers to make use of their options. Creativity in advertisement compaigns helps customers in different ways. The publicity measures are also found effective in the very context. Peak times and off-peak times are the two different conditions particularly when we talk about the tourism industry. Since the influx of tourists is to be checked, it is essential that professionals make use of messages and campaigns motivating tourists in visiting the place during the off-peak seasons. Since a number of incentives are offered to them, the advertisement messages and slogans may be used for this purpose. During New Years' Day, Xmas, Holi, Dipawali, Id, we find more pressure on the Department of Post. They make use of promotional measures so that users avail the opportunities before the start of peak hour. We also find business where demand regularly exceeds the supply side and in this context, the professionals make a strong advocacy in favour of queuing or reserving. In the Indian Railways where we find demand regularly exceeding the supply side, the provision of reservation on a first-come first-serve basis is found.

Managing Distribution: For managing the demand side, we also find professionals making use of this mix of the marketing mix. The modifications in the place and timing are found in this context. In the first condition, there will be no change in the location point. Because we may find the supply side increasing fast, this strategy is not considered to be suitable. The second strategy focuses our attention on changing the time. This facility is in the face of convenience of customers. In the theaters and cinema complexes, we find different time for shows keeping in view the leisure hours of users and potential users. During festive season, we may also find an increase in the frequency. In addition, we may also find third strategy in which the services are offered to the customers or users at a new location point. All the three strategies are used in the face of changing demand position.

Managing Price/Fee: The fourth marketing mix is related to pricing and of all the submixes, we find pricing the most effective mix for optimising the demand position. We cannot negate that particularly in balancing the demand position, the marketing professionals make use of this submix very carefully. A change in price/fee structure is used for controlling the supply. A number of service generating organisations are found conceptualising pricing for controlling and regulating the demand position. In this context, it is also significant to mention that on the one hand the lure of cheap prices would act as a motivational force to increase demand during off-peak season while on the other hand, the high price during peak season would act as a demotivational force. We find such a case in the tourism industry where to regulate the influx of tourists during peak season, the pricing is used as a demotivational tool. When to use it as a motivational tool and when to use it as a demotivational tool depends on certain conditions such as demand position, duration of peak season and a temptation or craze for visiting the place. The professionals find pricing a tool to regulate supply because it becomes difficult for them to increase supply or to regulate demand. In this context, they may take the support of Demand Curve which will help them in identifying a situation and taking a decision regarding pricing. The movement of demand curve would provide to them a guideline.

In Fig. 2.4, a sample demand curve is presented. The shape and slope of a demand curve will help professionals in taking a decision regarding pricing. The objective is to maximise revenue from each segment. Of course, it is very difficult for the marketing professionals to determine the nature of various demand curves. In the graphic representation, we find different conditions for room price and room demand during high season and low season. YO shows the price per room. and OX shows the demand for room. B_1 shows the the business travellers in high season. B_2 shows the business travellers in low season. T_1 shows the tourism in high season and T_2 shows the touristsm in low season.

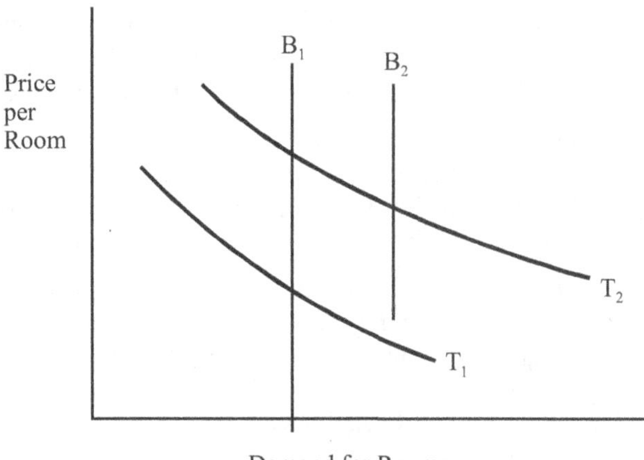

Fig. 2.4 : Demand for Rooms

In view of the above, it is right to say that for managing demand, the marketers make use of all the different submixes of marketing where multi-faceted measures create a condition where the customers/users regulate their demand.

MANAGEMENT OF SERVICE CAPACITY

We find conditions where marketing professionals need to manage the capacity. Expansion and contraction in the demand side make it essential that we also focus our attention on the supply side. It is also right to mention that we also find conditions where the expansion in capacity reaches to the point of saturation and the professionals have no option but to regulate the demand side. The types of services and the market mechanism are the different conditions responsible for the development of two different situations. Here, we go through the problem that how and in what way the service capacity can be managed. The following factors influence the service capacity of an organisation.

1. People: We cannot negate that expansion and contraction in the service capacity of an organisation are influenced by the people managing the affairs. Of course, the use of new generation of technology has been found minimising the importance of people in the service generation process, however the people occupy a place of outstanding significance. Increasing the number of people for improving the service capacity and conversely decreasing the number of people for regulating the capacity are the normal conditions which remain instrumental in an age of traditional or old generation of technology. Currently, we find use of sophisticated technology in almost all the service generating organisations which has reduced the importance of people in the service generation process. With a fall in demand, the professionals need to manage the people in such a way that alternative work schedule is undertaken. The professionals may also allow holidays during the off-season when the demand is low. In case of increase in demand, the professionals may also employ part-time staff. During peak season, the professionals also hire extra workers. Thus, we find management of service capacity to manage the demand side.

2. Supporting Facilities: For meeting demand, we find use of a number of supporting facilities. Since the demand side cannot remain static or we find a big fluctuation in it, the professionals need to rent the facilities in lieu of procuring the same. The extra space may not be useful in the off-season. Thus, depending on the conditions we find arrangements for increasing the supporting facilities.

3. Machine and Equipment: Of late, we find a large-scale use of technology in almost all the service generating organisations. The modern sophisticated technology, no doubt, has helped service generating organisations in defining the service quality but we find them much more expensive and therefore not affordable. Because in some of the organisations, we find much more fluctuation in the demand side, the procuring of machine and equipment cannot be a productive proposition. This makes it essential that just to meet seasonal demand, the organisations share extra facilities. A formal sharing agreement may be signed for this purpose. The process will also bring economy in the service cost.

4. Adjusting the Time: For balancing the service capacity, the professionals may also think in favour of balancing the time. If we allow to work for longer hours, the capacity can be increased. Of course, there are obstacles in the process of increasing the time because this may be inconvenient to the users.

5. Cross-training the Employees: For improving the supply position, the professionals may also think in favour of providing an opportunity of cross-training to the employees so that they are in a position to perform a variety of tasks. An arrangement of shifting to bottleneck points may be an option to make use of the unutilised capacity. The total system capacity thus is found increased and the problem of unutilised capacity is also resolved.

The aforesaid measures help professionals in balancing the supply position. The key problem in this context is to adjust capacity to match demand. We also find experts suggesting tailoring of the overall capacity to match variations in demand. This is known as chasing demand which was suggested by Fitzsimmons in Service Management: Operations Strategy and Information Technology. Further W. Earl Sasser Jr. also advocated in favour of chasing demand in Service Industries in Harvard Business Review (Nov-Dec 1976). We also find cases where the capacity remains unutilised not in the overall capacity but in a particular segment. Such type of problem is found in hotels, railways and aircrafts. This focuses our attention on upgrading to adjust the seats. Or, it draws our attention on designing of physical facilities in such a way that easy adjustments are possible.

We also find some capacity of elastic nature and bearing the potentials of absorbing the extra demand. It is against this provision that we find provisions for standees in the buses. In the civil aviation services, the professionals may also think in favour of replacing the aircrafts having higher capacity particularly during the peak hours. Another alternative may be in favour of using the facilities for the longer periods. The offering of evening classes by the universities and institutes and provisions in the restaurants for early dinner and late suppers are considered suitable examples. Stretching capacity or shrinking capacity thus help in balancing the supply.

The aforesaid facts make it clear that there are a number of options or solutions for balancing the supply for balancing the demand but the suitability of a particular prescription depends on a particular type of service and the specific demand hour. All solutions cannot be effective for all the conditions. It is upon the marketing professionals to take into account the timing and the market conditions where the demand and supply can be adjusted.

MANAGEMENT OF RELATIONSHIPS

We live in an age of loyalty-based business and therefore our prime task is to identify the customers having the potentials to be loyal. We need to target, acquire and retain the right customers. Not only building loyalty but we also need to maintain it which rests on our well-conceived relationship marketing strategies. It is not advisable that professionals waste their time, expertise and energy on all segments and all people who cannot be transformed because they are potentially deficient. They need to make it sure that which type of customers they can serve well. The moment we find professionals getting a success in selecting the right customers; the efforts for building relationship and transforming them to loyal customers may be activated. We cannot deny that both the tasks related to identification and transformation are found to be much more complicated.

Understanding customers in a right way depends upon the professional excellence of a marketing manager. If we have a right perception of the potentials of customers, our efforts for developing relationships and building loyalty are found positive. In a true sense, we find both the terms interrelated.

UNDERSTANDING THE CUSTOMER RELATIONSHIP

By relationship marketing, our focus is on the extended relationship with the customers. Nicole Coviello, Roderick Brodie and Hugh Munro writes that there are four distinct types of marketing, such as transactional marketing, database marketing, interaction marketing and networking marketing. In the group of relationship marketing, we find database, interaction and networking. The possibilities for building relationship are found wider where we find enough scope for exchange of information. Currently, the marketing activities are considerably governed by the management of information where the information technology has been playing a dominating role.

Transactional Marketing: In the context of transactional marketing, we find relationship marketing almost non-existent. The exceptions are, of course, in a very small number when we find consumers buying manufactured goods for household purposes and rarely thinking about a formal relationship. They never have a relationship with the dealer or other intermediaries. We find the same case in the context of cinema and food service. Thus, we find marketing in this context without any mutual recognition between the customers and employees.

Database Marketing: In the database marketing, we find exchange of information and therefore we find scope for developing relationship with the targeted customers. It becomes easier for the marketers to retain the patronage of their customers but at the same time it is also right to say that the relationship in the database marketing is not found to be close. Instrumentality of technology plays an important role in the entire process. With the help of technology, the actual and potential customers are identified and efforts are made to personalise the relationship. The services like electricity, gas and cable TV are considered suitable examples for the database marketing.

Interaction Marketing: We cannot negate that if we talk about relationship, our focus must be on the relationship based on one-to-one or face-to-face interaction. Of course, we find quality of services offered playing an important role in the building of relationship. However, value addition through interaction and societal approaches cannot be undermined. In the emerging banking and insurance services, the interaction marketing has been found much more effective in building relationship because there we find a relationship based on interaction and trust. Both the parties are found aware of the profile of each other and therefore the interaction is found effective. The relationship marketing is found based on confidence and trust and the prevailing local environments, regional affiliation, image of the marketers make the interaction process result-oriented.

Network Marketing: We find network marketing based on mutual interest. The network of relationship with customers, distributors, suppliers and the media and further with trade associations, governmental agencies and rivals help development of relationships in the network marketing. We find network marketing relevant even in the field of consumer marketing where we find customers encouraging to refer friends.

Thus, the above mentioned types of marketing are found successful in developing relationships. The effectiveness of a particular method depends on the prevailing conditions. The most important thing in relationship marketing is one-to-one or face-to-face relationships where interaction determines the magnitude of success.

TYPES OF RELATIONSHIP WITH CUSTOMERS

While going through the types of relationship, Evert Gummesson in *Total Relationship Marketing* (1999) identified 30 types of relationships within the broader context of total relationship marketing.[8] Formalised and Informalised relationships are the two different conditions between the service-providers and the service-users.

FORMAL RELATIONSHIP OR MEMBERSHIP RELATIONSHIP

We find membership relationship a formal relationship found between the firm and an identifiable customer where both the parties are found availing benefits of special offer. In this context, we find an opportunity to create an ongoing relationship. The process of transformation is found in two way — first by selling the service in bulk and second by offering extra benefits to customers who prefer to register with the firm. We find marketing professionals in this context getting an opportunity of knowing the details such as identities and addresses.

RELATIONSHIP MARKETING

Influencing the impulse of potential users is found essential for activating the transformation process and building the personal relationship. Of late, we find professionals assigning due weightage to the process of relationship building. Developing rapport with the actual and potential beneficiaries is considered essential for relationship building. In the process, the professionals select a sensitive segment, identify the loyal users and make use of their experiences for influencing the impulse of other users. If we succeed in building relationship, our tasks of making customers loyal are considerably simplified. It is in this context that we talk about relationship marketing for the services sector.

In the services sector, we find development of personal attachment turning into personal relationship. In the banking and insurance sectors, the agents or advisors find it easier to get the business if they have been successful in developing emotional attachment with the potential customers. The governing force for influencing the impulse of customers/users considerably rests on emotional attachment. The professionals with the help of information system come to know the details regarding the potential customers and develop personal attachment with them by interaction. The marketers need not to be influenced by this perception that in all the condition, the selected group of customers are high spenders. It is also to be accepted that they may interact with customers who are indecisive in nature and indecent in behaviour. The good customers are to be targeted for relationship marketing and the professionals for this purpose would be required to develop their awareness of the portfolio for appropriate customers having much more sensitivity for smooth transformation.

AN APPROPRIATE CUSTOMER PORTFOLIO

The success rate of marketing professionals while developing personal relationship with the customers and potential customers would, of course, be high when they have an in-depth knowledge of the portfolio of an appropriate customer. It is in this context that we go through the portfolio which focuses our attention on customers having a sound base. When we find banks thinking about the portfolio management, the motive is to identify the most profitable segment and for that purpose formulating a sound mix of different investments in the face of changing needs and requirements and the risk preference. Like this, in the context of marketing when we make use of the term portfolio, our focus is on developing a mix in which we find inclusion of profitable customers. We cannot negate that different segments offer a different value for a service generating organisation. An anatomy of different segments keeping in view the short- and long-term effects is to be done by the marketing professionals. They need to consider that some of the customers may not be profitable in the short-run but in the long-run they may be profitable and therefore the personal relationship is required to be established even with that category of segment.

Developing a portfolio combining good quality of customers cannot be undermined by a marketing professional. An expert David Maister[9] says that marketing is about getting better business not simply more business. We agree with this view that business clients magnifies the image of an organisation. Only volume cannot be a measure of excellence. It is knowledge bank of a professional particularly regarding the different categories of customers that would help him in identifying quality customers found to be potentially sound. The experts talk about the Customer Pyramid as shown in the following Fig. 2.5.

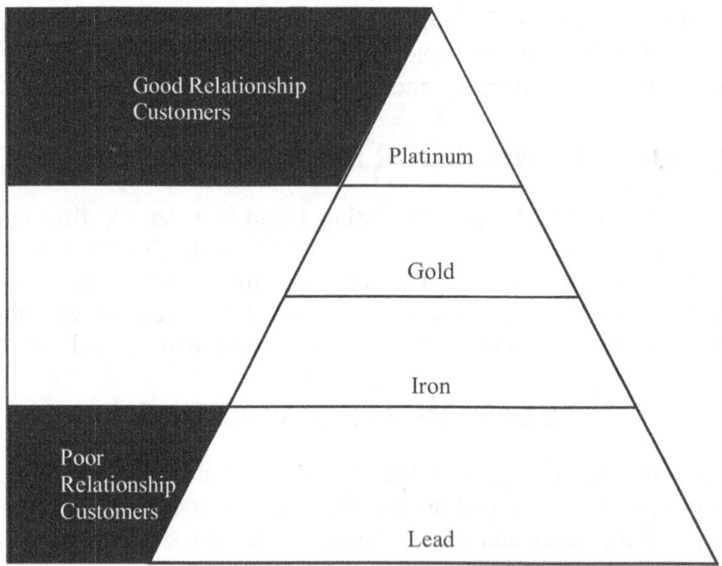

Fig. 2.5: The Customer Pyramid

Zeithmal, Rust and Leman[10] talked about such a pyramid in California Management Review, 43/3, 2001. Only making efforts for transforming different segments of people in the portfolio whose potentials have not been tested should not be the motive of marketing professionals. We find customers potentially sound for good relationship and at the same time we also find customers who lack the traits for good relationship. A strategic approach is required to be essential to develop a sound portfolio. The marketing professionals while developing a portfolio may require to retain, upgrade or even terminate the segments not found to be potentially sound.

A four-level pyramid has been given due weightage in the process of developing a portfolio of customers. The good relationship customers and the poor relationship customers are the two different categories combining Platinum, Gold, Iron and Lead tiers. Studying and understanding the customers coming from different segments depend on the professional excellence of marketers.

Platinum: It is very natural that platinum category of customers constitute a very small percentage of the customer base but contributes a very large percentage of profit. Of course, the platinum segment is less sensitive to price but much more sensitive to the quality. The professionals need to identify the platinum segment and to develop personal relationship with them.

Gold: The gold segment or tier constitutes a larger percentage of customers. They are found contributing less profit to the organisation than the platinum category. We find them a bit sensitive to price and not having so much commitment to the firm as found in the Platinum category.

Iron: This tier provides a strong base for business to an organisation. We talk about cost-effectiveness and economies of scale and the iron tier provides to us a sound base for this purpose. The professionals need to consider that this segment though not so much profitable but would simplify their task of developing a sound infrastructural base for serving the gold and platinum categories.

Lead: We find this category of customers generating low revenues but costing more and therefore from a firm's perspective, they are found to be a loss-making segment.

Developing a portfolio protecting and promoting organisational as well as social interests requires world-class professional excellence. They need to retain, upgrade and terminate customers and such a tailoring process would provide to an organisation a portfolio which is considered to be appropriate.

RETAINING, UPGRADING AND TERMINATING CUSTOMERS

Developing an appropriate customer portfolio considerably depends on the professional excellence of marketers. The profit making service generating organisations would take into consideration profitability as an important criteria whereas the non-profit organisations would have to assign due weightage to the social welfare criteria.

The professionals would be required to divert attention to the platinum category of customers because they contribute siganificantly to the process of profit generation. The professionals may think in favour of offering some additional services to the platinum segment. It is in the larger interests of the organisation to retain platinum category.

Another category we find is gold category. The benefits level of gold category would have an edge over the iron and lead levels. The professionals would like to retain even the gold category.

We find iron category in a very good number because an organisation gets major chunk of business from that segment. The professionals may think in favour of upgrading them if the business conditions and the existent situations permit.

The lead category needs due attention of professionals so that they are upgraded and clubbed in the iron group.

We find some of the relationships not considered to be profitable and therefore strategically the professionals need to bring a change in the strategy. The tailoring process requires a clear understanding of customers and the market forces so that relationships are found to be productive.

ESSENTIALS OF RELATIONSHIP MARKETING

The service generating organisations need to assign due weightage to relationship marketing. The professionals serving there are required to be aware of the different essentials for relationship marketing as mentioned below:

- Identifying the need for relationships in the organisations where they serve. Understanding the nature and types of services offered by the concerned organisation.
- Knowing the prospects or potential customers of the related services. Collecting data regarding potential customers, actual customers and habitual customers.

- Carefully screening the list of prospects or potential customers/users and actual and habitual customers.
- Designing programme for building relationships with them and in this contex, the professionals need to be aware of their details.
- Formulating plans for contact. Frequently approaching and reapproaching based on the contact programme.
- Developing packages for enhancing relationships with them. Developing contact with the potential customers and actual customers with the motto of enhancing relationship.
- Developing packaging for maintaining relationships specially with the habitual customers who are considered to be loyal.
- Preparing a team of marketing people for developing relationship with the different categories of customers. Developing team of dedicated and committed marketing people well aware of the behavioural dimensions.
- Designing the system, infrastructure and supportive services which would be efficacious of the developing relationships.
- Executing the relationship development programme.
- Designing a feedback system and making marketing people aware of the system.
- Collecting feedback from the different groups of customers and storing them in the marketing information system.
- Based on feedback making an appraisal of the efforts made and steps taken for developing relationships. Incorporating the aspects considered to be essential.
- Relationships must be based on personal touch.
- Multi-dimensional personalised services are to be added.

The aforesaid facts draw priority attention of marketing professionals bearing the responsibility of developing and maintaining relationships. Business relationships if transformed into personal relationships make ways for transformation of actual customers into the habitual customers. Even in the age of technology, we do not find options for personalised relationship. Face-to-face communication is a must for personal relationships.

RELATIONSHIP MARKETING vs. TRADITIONAL MARKETING

A number of differences are found in between relationship and traditional marketing. Traditional marketing is also known transaction marketing.

Exhibit 2.1 RELATIONSHIP VS. TRADITIONAL MARKETING

Relationship Marketing	Traditional Marketing
Relationship Marketing focuses on transforming a customer to be loyal.	In the Traditional Marketing, we find focus on making sale.
In this marketing, we focus on the benefits of products.	We focus on features of products.
In relationship marketing, we find long-term focus.	In this marketing, we find short-term focus.
In the relationship marketing, we find maximum emphasis on customer services.	In the traditional marketing, we find relatively minimum emphasis on customer services.
In this marketing, we find high commitment to customers.	Here, we find low commitment to customers.
The level of customer contact in the relationship marketing is found high.	We find moderate customer contact in the traditional marketing.
In the relationship marketing, we find quality a concern of all	In the traditional marketing, we find quality a concern of production.
In the relationship marketing, we find customer retention.	In the traditional marketing, we find customer satisfaction.

Exhibit 2.2 CUSTOMER RELATIONSHIP MANAGEMENT IN DIFFERENT FORMS

ECRM	Enterprise Customer Relationship Management
e-CRM	Electronic Customer Relationship Management This is web-based CRM
PRM	Partner Relationship Management
mCRM	Mobile Customer Relationship Management
SRM	Supplier Relationship Management
OCRM	Operational Customer Relationship Management
ACRM	Analytical Customer Relationship Management

SERVICE RECOVERY

We do not find anything wrong in the saying "To err is human; to recover, divine." It is but natural that we commit mistakes; it is immoral that we do not confess. Theodore Levitt opines,[11] "One of the surest signs of bad or declining relationship is the absence of complaints from the customer. Nobody is ever that satisfied, especially not over an extended period of time." In a true sense, we find service recovery an umbrella terms for systematic efforts by a firm to resolve or correct a problem. We agree with this view that service recovery makes ways for service satisfaction. If your customers are not complaining, it is meant that almighty God is not favouring you. Oren Harari[12] wrote one article with this theme which was entitled, "Thank Heavens for Complainers", which was published in Management Review; March, 1997. Getting a dissatisfied customer simplifies your task of making almost all of them satisfied. Actually, dissatisfaction paves avenues for satisfaction. If we find something going wrong with our customers/users; our prime responsibility is to receive them in a right perspective and to recover them at the earliest possible. Customers/users not complaining make our task much more difficult.

The professionals bear the responsibility of increasing the number of satisfied group of customers and this task will remain unfulfilled if customers are hesitant of making complaints. The rate of retention witnesses a galloping increase if we welcome complaints and try to resolve them without making a delay. It is against this background that complaint handling counter is considered a profit center not a cost center. The research shows that on an average only 5 in 10 per cent of dissatisfied group of customers complain. The percentage may even be lower. TARP — a customer satisfaction and measurement firm — has identified reasons for customers not making complaints. They observe that time constraints and unawareness of dissatisfied group of customers are the important factors restricting them of making complaints. A majority of us feel that complaining would not be pleasent and some of us also feel that inviting confrontation would disturb them. In this context, it is also felt that low power or say inability to influence or control the transaction also obstructs the process.

The professionals are required to resolve the problems by minimising the barriers to the extent it is possible. For this, they may also use impersonal channels such as internet which would be easy for them to use. But in no case, the professionals should be influenced by this perception that there is nothing wrong with their services because they are not getting any complaints from the users of services.

The researches reveal that people in the higher socio-economic levels are more likely to complain than the users living in the lower levels. The standard of education, level of income and greater social involvement provide to them confidence and they complain as and when they encounter problems. Actually, we need to make the process of receiving complaints much more easier.

SERVICE RECOVERY PARADOX

We find two different cases, the first when the customers complained about the failure of services and the providers resolved them to their best satisfaction. And the second case when the customers did not have any problem in the first place. It is found that future responses of first type of customers have been much more positive. Since they were confident that as and when they would have problem, the resolutions are must. But in any case we should not welcome the repeated service failures because this makes an invasion on the goodwill of providers. Thus, we find service recovery paradox referring to the sometimes observed effect. We consider it a paradox due to the fact that responses of customers experiencing excellent resolutions have an edge over the customers who have not faced any problem.

We also find studies questioning the existence of service recovery paradox. A major study conducted by Andreassen[14] with the help of 8,600 telephonic interviews observed that after a service recovery, customers' attention to repurchase and their perceptions of an attitude towards the company, never surpassed the ratings of satisfied group of customers who did not experience a service problem in the first place. It happened even when the service recovery was very well and the complaining customers were satisfied with the steps taken for recovery.

The service recovery is found very difficult in some of the cases. It is quite difficult for us to recover the holidays already ruined. But we also find adverse conditions when the customers are found delighted. A lost reservation in hotel, or railways where we find recovery in the form of upgradation which allows the delivery of a superior product no doubt delights the customers as we find customers very much hopeful that even in future this will happen.

The aforesaid facts make it clear that we find different conditions in which the customers act and react in a different way. The best strategy is to do it right the first time and never provide a second opportunity of making complaints to your customers. In any case, you cannot assure customer dismal possibility of making complaints because we find frequent cases where human faults or technological faults keep you in an uncertain situation and you find possibilities of making complaints. It is not so much important that you find possibilities of making complaints by your customers. It is much more important that you are very honest and sincere to the problem of resolution and make best of your efforts to check the possibilities of repetition.

A number of factors are found responsible for providing quality services to the service-users. In the process, if we find anything to emerge as a paradox, 'it is silence of your customers regarding complaints'. We find much more strength in this assumption, "Thank Heavens for Complainers".

RESPONSES OF CUSTOMERS/USERS TO SERVICE RECOVERY

Identifying a dissatisfied customer is the prime responsibility of a professional. We should not think that customers making complaints do not provide any chance to correct or resolve. We find a majority of the users proving an opportunity and therefore the professionals should restore relationships with the complainer which would provide to them an opportunity to get the business. We cannot negate the service recovery is like an umbrella which safeguards you and provide to you an opportunity to correct. We agree with this view that service recovery plays an important role in restoring the satisfaction of customers or in minimising the dissatisfied group of customers. Your excellence, of course, is coiled in the essence of fulfilling your commitments to quality and any obstacle making your task difficult needs to be removed.

Service recovery if found effective benefits an organisation in many ways. This makes it essential that professionals formulate an effective service recovery strategy which is considered to be a difficult task. The recovery process is not only to be made easier but also to provide an assurance to the complainers that their complaints would be removed. The moment they feel that providers are dishonest and perceive that they are not to redress their grievances or their recovery efforts are to be weak, the task of professionals would be much more difficult. Conversely, if they feel that you are honest and their complaints would get a positive response we find enough opportunities for rebuilding and retaining the relationships.

SERVICE RECOVERY vs. CUSTOMER LOYALTY

Effective service recovery makes ways for customer loyalty. If customers find that their complaints are satisfactorily resolved, they are found loyal. The researches of TARP reveal[15] that intentions to repurchase for different types of products vary from 9 to 37 per cent, when customers were dissatisfied but did not complain. The retention rate increased from 9 per cent to 19 per cent when customers complained, a sympathetic hearing was also found but the company was not able to resolve. The same retention rate jumped to 54 per cent when the complaints were resolved to the satisfaction of customers.

This makes it clear that just getting complaints would not harm you if you are serious and sincere to their resolutions. Hence, the professionals need to form this perception that avenues should be made wider for making complaints, the processes should be made easier and sincere efforts should be made for their honest resolutions. If you do not get complaints, you need to be much more serious. It is against this backdrop that we also call service recovery a paradox. Making customers loyal is your target and your honest resolutions of customers' recovery would help you in achieving it.

COMPONENTS OF EFFECTIVE SERVICE RECOVERY

Service recovery must be effective. Making the system of service recovery is influenced by a number of factors and the professionals need to develop their awareness of the guiding principles. We find three important dimensions in this context, such as make it easy for your customers to give feedback, make service recovery much more effective and establish appropriate levels of compensation.

EASY FOR CUSTOMERS/USERS TO GIVE FEEDBACK

Professionals need to make special efforts so that customers feel free of making complaints. The complaint-collection procedures need innovative efforts. We find some of the suitable measures for this such as adding special toll-free phone, links on websites, display of customer comment cards, video terminals for recording complaints.

EFFECTIVE SERVICE RECOVERY

The professionals need to make the process of service recovery much more effective. The procedures should be proactive, planned, trained and empowered.

If we make a strong advocacy in favour of proactive recovery, our focus is on initiating the service recovery on the spot, even before customers have a chance to complain.

Our efforts must be planned which focus our attention on the contingency plans especially for problems cropping up frequently. We also need to educate and train the customers and in this context our focus is on making customers aware of the recovery skills.

By empowered employees, our emphasis is on service recovery efforts which should be flexible and the employees should be empowered to use their judgement and communication skills.

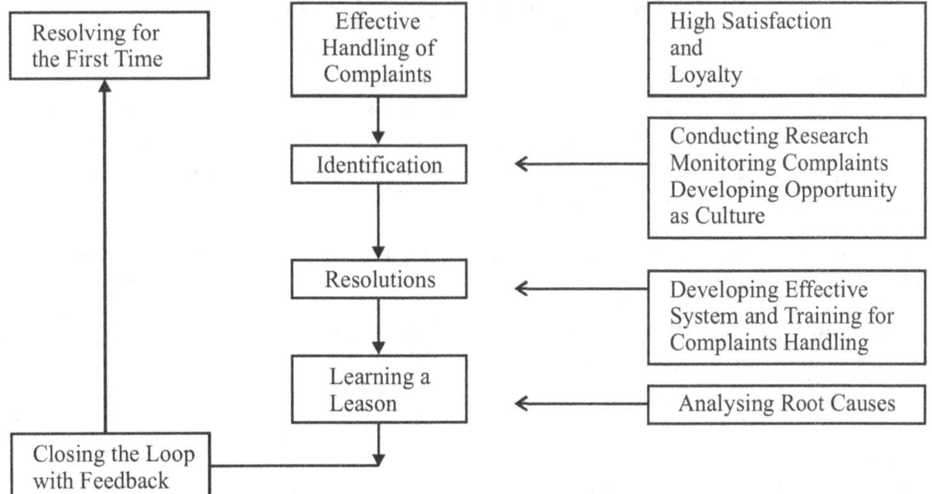

Fig. 2.6: Service Recovery

SERVICE EXPECTATIONS

Concept of Service Expectations

At the outset, it is essential that we go through the conceptual aspect of service expectations. Beliefs of customers about service delivery functioning as standards or reference-points against which we rate performance are known as customer expectations. We find customer expectations critical to service marketers due to the fact that customers compare their perception of performance with the service standards or reference points when they start making an evaluation of service quality with the help of knowledge they have acquired. When we think about delivering the quality services, the first thing that we find critical but essential to know is developing our awareness about customers. The expectations of customers about the services are found to be the results of their aspirations about the standards, specifications and quality. Expectations thus may be the effects of developments in quality shaping our perception. Increasing flow of information and developing modes of transportation are the two important factors sizeably instrumental in the formation of expectations. Our beliefs about the quality that we expect are known as expectations. It is right to mention that customer expectations embrace several elements such as desired level, adequate service, predicted service and zone of tolerance that falls between the desired and adequate service levels.

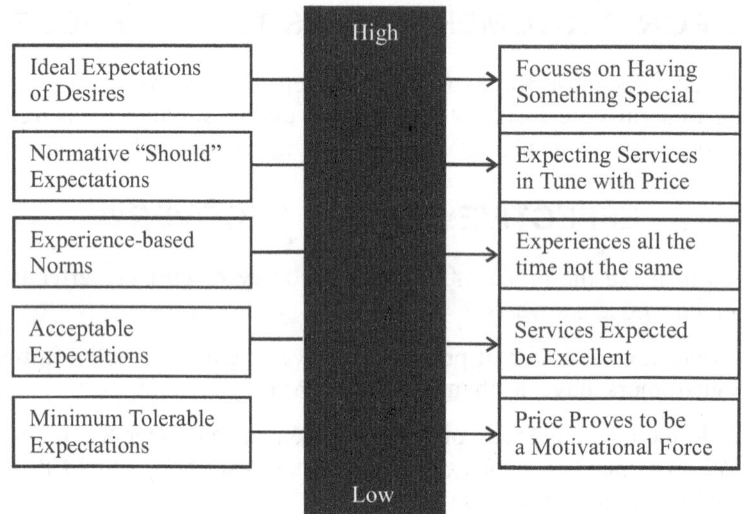

Fig. 2.7: Levels of Expectations

LEVELS OF EXPECTATIONS

The Figure 2.7 shows a continuum in which we find different types of service expectations moving from low to high. The expectations at each and every stage have been named. The perception regarding the performance rests on the expectations. In some of the cases, we find high level of services quality even much more than our expectations and conversely we also find cases where we get much less than our expectations. Thus, a study of the levels of expectations are fond important.

The different levels that we find in the context of expectations are the desired level, adequate level, predicted level and a zone of tolerance level.

Desired and Adequate Levels: We also call it a "Wished for" level. The level of services is desired by the customers. We find a majority of the customers of realistic nature and based on their realism, they are of the view that in all the cases, the organisations cannot deliver the desired level of services. It is due to the fact that they also nurture a threshold level which focuses our attention on the adequate level of expectations. This is actually the minimum level of services expected by the customers. We find both categories of expectations reflecting explicit and implicit promises by the providers. The setting of this level of expectations depends on situational factors affecting the performance and level of service which may be anticipated form the alternative suppliers.

Predicted Level: The level of a service anticipated by a customer is known as the predicted level of expectations. This is considered to be adequate level on that very occasion. This makes it clear that the level is set by the prediction of an individual. If we find prediction of good service, the adequate level of expectations will be higher specially in the condition when we predict poor service. Here, we find predictions of customers considered to be important which would be different in a specific situation. The predictions depend on certain conditions. If we find something abnormal in the situations where we find users availing the services, the predictions will vary.

Zone of Tolerance: The customers have resistance power and the extent to which we find customers resistive to accept the variation, we call it zone of tolerance. If we find level of performance going down the adequate level, the customers would be found frustrated and they would be found dissatisfied. We are aware of the fact that services are of heterogeneous nature resulting into variation in the levels of services across providers, across employees form the same providers and even with the same set of people. If the service performance is found higher, than the zone of tolerance at the top and where performance exceeds desired service, the customers would be found very pleased. We may also consider zone of tolerance as the range or window in which customers do not notice the performance of service. But when we find it falling outside the range which may be either very low or very high the service draws attention of customers in either a positive or negative way. If you are standing in the queue, you have in your minds the acceptable range for waiting. Till the expected range, we do not find a customer reacting but when he/she is out of the range, he/she may notice. Conversely when we find more frontline people coming to different windows and servicing them much earlier than the expected range, the customer may find the service excellent.

The above-mentioned facts make it clear that zone of tolerance varies from customer to customer as we find different customers possessing different zones for tolerance. A few of the customers have narrow zone whereas a few have also a greater range.

When we find the customers busy, they would not like to spend more time for availing the services and therefore the zone of tolerance in that case would have less wait times. There are a number of factors influencing the zone of tolerance. In this context, we find price an important factor which is considered to be a controllable factor to be regulated by the organisation. When the customers have to pay high prices for the service to be availed, the customers become much more sensitive to quality and they do not accept the poor quality of services. In this case, we find the zone of tolerance moving downward because the adequate service level shifts upward.

The zone of tolerance also varies from service to service. The different service attributes or dimensions determine the zone of tolerance. When the services are found not to be reliable, the zone of tolerance is found low. In a true sense, the fluctuations in the zone of tolerance of an individual customer are the result of incoming changes in the adequate service level, considerably influenced by the situational forces. Accumulated experiences play here an important role. We find desired service relatively idiosyncratic and stable compared with the adequate service.

The above-mentioned facts make it clear that the boundaries of customer's expectation of services can be expressed with two different levels of expectations, such as desired service and adequate service. In the desired level, we find less scope for change when in the adequate service level we find much more scope for a change. It is zone of tolerance that separates the desired and adequate levels.

FACTORS INFLUENCING SERVICE EXPECTATIONS

The service marketing need an in-depth study of those factors which considerably influence the levels of service expectations. We find expectations playing an outstanding role in the marketing decision-making processes and this makes it essential that the professionals study and understand the factors instrumental in shaping them. A number of controllable and uncontrollable factors are found involved in the shaping process.

1. Influences of Desired Service: We find personal needs or conditions essential to the physical or psychological well-being of the customers. What do we expect from services considerably depend on our personal needs. There are a number of categories of personal needs such as physical, social, psychological and functional. If you feel yourself thirsty, hungry or you urgently need money, the levels of your expectations would be different to the persons who do not have such a condition. The physical conditions thus shape the levels of expectations. If we do not have staff to do a great deal of our work for insurance broking, own expectations from broker would be high. Conversely, if we have staff to do our business, the use of broking services would be minimum. We also find some of the customers more demanding than others and in that case, the levels of expectations would be high. Personal service philosophies and derived service expectations elevate the level of desired service. In a few cases, we find customers having much more awareness of the services based on their customer's personal experience such as the waitresses or waiters have a deep idea regarding the standard of services of restaurants and therefore their levels of expectations would be high. It is right to mention that we find these factors related to the desired service expectations.

2. Influences of Adequate Service Expectations: In this context, we find influences having much more fluctuations than the desired level. The important factors influencing the adequate service are transitory service intensifiers, perceived service alternatives, customer self-perceived service role, situational factors and predicted service. The transitory service intensifiers develop our awareness of the service. The personal emergency situations influence the level of expectations of adequate service. Thus, the nature of our problem influences the level of expectations. The perceived service alternatives are other providers from whom the customers obtain the services. If the customers have multiple service providers, the level of expectations would be higher than those of customers who have a perception that it is not possible to get better service elsewhere. In this context, it is essential that the service marketers are aware of the complete set of options viewed by the customers as perceived alternatives. The customer's self-perceived service role focuses our attention on customer perception of the degree to which customers are found exerting an influence on the level of service they receive. Here, the expectations of customers are partly shaped by how well they believe that they are performing their own role in service delivery.

The levels of adequate service are also influenced by the situational factors. We also call them service performance conditions viewed by the customers. As and when we find abnormal conditions, the situations are not found to be normal. A situation forcing personal emergencies creates a different condition in which the level of expectation is found high.

Predicted service is an estimate or calculation of the service a customer will receive. The predicted service also influences the adequate service. This type of service expectation can be viewed as predictions made by customers about what is likely to happen. If customers predict good service, the levels of adequate service are likely to be higher.

SOURCES OF DESIRED AND PREDICTED SERVICE EXPECTATIONS

When customers are interested in purchasing the services on the basis of information received from different sources, we find both the desired and predicted service expectations active. In addition to the external search, the customers may also conduct an internal search by reviewing the information. Explicit service promises, implicit service promises, word-of-mouth communications, and past experiences of customers influence the desired and predicted service expectations. Explicit service promises are based on personal and non-personal statements about the service generated by an organisation. The statements communicated by the salespeople are known as personal whereas they are considered non-personal when we find them coming from advertising, brochures, and other written publications for promotion. The explicit services throw a direct bearing on the desired service expectations. We also find cases when explicit service promises influence both the desired and predicted service expectations. The implicit service promises are considered to be service related cues dominated by price, and tangibles associated with the service. The importance of word-of-mouth communications are found for both the predicted and desired services. Particularly when the customers find it difficult to evaluate the services, we find word-of-mouth communications much more effective. Whatsoever the past experiences, the customers have gained are found significant to the shaping of predictions and desires.

The above-mentioned facts make it clear that expectations of customers are influenced by a number of factors where some of them are controllable and some of them are also uncontrollable. We find customers holding different types of expectations such as desired service reflecting what customers want; adequate service what customers are willing to accept; predicted service what customers believe they are likely to get. The service marketers are supposed to command the explicit service promises and implicit service promises found of controllable nature. The less controllable factors are enduring service intensifiers, personal needs, transitory service intensifiers, perceived service intensifiers, word-of-mouth communications, past experience, situational factors and predicted service. The marketing professionals having world-class excellence can command all variables; of course the degree of command may vary.

In an age of information technology where we find high frequency of flow of information and due to sophisticated mode of transportation changing perception of speed and distance, it is very natural that we find much more frequency in the changing levels of expectations of customers/users. When we find our counterparts leading a sophisticated modern lifestyles, and witness our relations and friends availing new amenities and facilities for a luxurious life condition; our expectations for the same level of services cannot be unnatural. We cannot deny that the shaping of the levels of expectations is a natural process. It is against this background that we find our hierarchy of needs considerably influenced by information and transportation. Since we find process of inventions and innovations moving forward with much more frequency, the expectations follow the same and the professionals delaying the inclusion and adoption suffer a lot. According to Daniel Bethamy of American Express, consumers want memorable experiences, not gadgets. The incoming changes in the behavioural profile customers/users provide an opportunity to the service generating organisations to understand and perceive them in a right fashion and to make ways for an analogous change in their product profile so that they are potentially sound for capitalising on the opportunities.

We cannot negate that expectations change over time which are considerably influenced by advertising, pricing, new technologies and service innovation as well as social trends, promotional efforts by consumer organisations and increased access of information through the media and internet. Of course, all the factors are found instrumental in the formation of the levels of expectations but in this context we cannot devalue the role of discretionary income which during the yesterdecades have witnessed a galloping increase. The globalisation of economy is found to be the root-and-branch cause for the same.

If we recollect the development scenario in the Indian perspective, it is right to mention that during post 1990s, we find a visible increase in the level of income of common masses in general and the middle class in particular. The credibility of course goes to the globalisation of economy. An increase in the level of income made ways for a different lifestyle which was influenced by western culture and therefore the socio-cultural conditions started dancing in tune with their behavioural patterns. Accessibility to information started injecting life, strength and continuity to the processes of change and formation of expectations and high speed transportation facilities started translating them into realities. The innovations in the field of marketing communication fuelled the process of demand creation and the market forces were found much more effective. Thus, a number of incoming changes in globalised economy has played a constructive role in the formation of expectations.

SERVICE ENCOUNTERS

At the outset, we need to understand the conceptual aspect of Service Encounter which is also known as moment of truth. For organisations, we consider it a device to testify the quality and for customers/users, we call it a moment for interacting and viewing the quality of services provided by an organisation. It is right to mention that service encounter is a period of time during which customers/users directly interact with a service.[16] We also consider it a point or an opportunity where promises are either kept or broken. It is due to this that we also call it real-time marketing. Because we find users of services getting an opportunity to view, we also call it a process for building of the perception of users regarding quality. The customers/users also find service encounter as a way of having a snap of the quality of services of the concerned organisation. The delivery steps in some of the services are found very limited whereas in few services we find multiple steps. The expectations and evaluations of services depend on the interaction process. While interacting with the service generating organisations, the customers/users come to know the information related to the employees, impersonal delivery system such as websites, physical facilities and other customers/ users of services which influence their expectations and evaluation. This makes it essential that at each and every step of service delivery, the providers try their best to perform excellently.

Thus, while going through the service encounter, the following points are observed:

- Service encounter is a period of time during which we find a direct interaction with the service.
- It is also known as Moment of Truth because we find customers/users getting an opportunity to view.
- It is considered a device to testify quality.
- It is a moment for interacting and viewing.
- It is a point where promises related to services are either kept or broken.
- It is also considered a real time marketing.
- It is a process for building of the perception of customers/users regarding quality.

TYPES OF SERVICE ENCOUNTER

The service encounters are found of different types. We can expect longer service encounters in some of the services. The encounters may be with the people providing the services and it may also be with the equipment. If may be high and it may also be low. It may be remote, and it may also be on phone or face-to-face. We find some of the services having contact whereas in some of the services we find non-contact. The different types of service encounters[17] have been shown in Fig. 2.8.

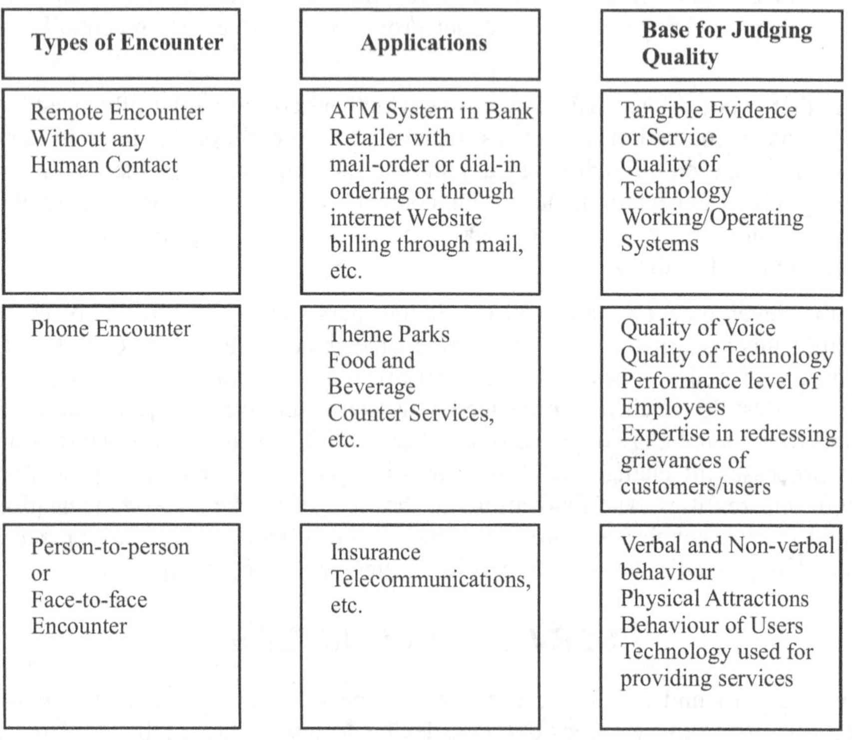

Types of Encounter	Applications	Base for Judging Quality
Remote Encounter Without any Human Contact	ATM System in Bank Retailer with mail-order or dial-in ordering or through internet Website billing through mail, etc.	Tangible Evidence or Service Quality of Technology Working/Operating Systems
Phone Encounter	Theme Parks Food and Beverage Counter Services, etc.	Quality of Voice Quality of Technology Performance level of Employees Expertise in redressing grievances of customers/users
Person-to-person or Face-to-face Encounter	Insurance Telecommunications, etc.	Verbal and Non-verbal behaviour Physical Attractions Behaviour of Users Technology used for providing services

Fig. 2.8: Service Encounter

1. Remote Encounter: Since we find remote encounter without any human contact, we call it remote encounter. In this system, we find technology playing a significant role in providing the service to the ultimate users. The ATM services in Banks or in the mail-order system, we find absence of human contact. With the advent of internet services, we find remote encounter in a number of services. The users here get an opportunity to view the services and therefore the quality of services made available to them is an important consideration for the formation of perception of quality. The techno-driven services considerably rest on the quality of technology and the experts operating or handling the same. Of late, we find use of new generation of technology in the banking and insurance services and therefore the shaping of high level of expectations is but natural. Hence, the providing organisations need to care that technology and the operating people are aware of the high level of expectations of users. The errors in technology in some of the cases are found dissatisfying and frustrating the users. There is no doubt in it that internet services have virtually revolutionised the banking services and the CBS have formed a high level of expectations of the users of services but due to failure of linkage in the communication technology, we find the services badly affected and virtually making an invasion on the perception of users. Hence, we also find cases where the promised quality of services depends on the functioning of the total system and in this case, a fault at one stage affects the quality for which neither the providing organisations nor the working people are at fault. Particularly in the remote areas where we find services network badly affected, the users fail in getting the promised quality. Of course, diffusing tension of users is an important task before the working people but this excuse will not serve their purpose for the long time. Hence, an improvement in the network of services needs priority attention of professionals.

2 Phone Encounter: With the new generation of information and communication technology, we find formation of a high level of expectations. In the insurance, telecommunications and even the banking services we find cases of phone encounter. We find agents, advisors, telemarketers working in different capacities making efforts to provide the promised quality of services. The users realise the quality of services in the process of telephonic conversation and therefore the quality of voice, quality of technology and expertise in the field of redressal of customers/users grievances are found important for judging the quality. The performance level of employees providing the services is also found an important dimension affecting the quality of services. The encounters may be at different stages of conversation and therefore the professional excellence of employees attending the phone calls plays here a decisive role. If you start with high tone, you are not sincere to the volume and flow, you undermine a balance in pause, you try to make your users insignificant; the users are found disappointed and in a very natural way we find an invasion on their perception. How do you conclude determine the magnitude of your success. The quality of phone that you use and your professional excellence in marketing communication also help in fulfilling your promises.

3 Person-to Person Encounter: The third type of encounter is found one-to-one where we find a direct in interaction playing an important role. The frontline staff or the staffs facing the users or the salespeople influencing the customers play here a dominating role. The behavioural profile of providers contains a number of factors. The communication excellence of the frontline staff, the body language and the personal care services determine the quality of services. It is in this context that we find physical attractions getting a significant place in the marketing mix. The dresses and uniform of employees offering or providing the services and their facial expression are important for maintaining the quality of promised services. The employees may also use technology for this purpose and therefore the contribution of technology is also found to be important factor for influencing the quality.

TECHNO-DRIVEN SERVICE ENCOUNTERS

Satisfaction and dissatisfaction are the two terms governed by a number of factors. The marketing professionals need to develop their awareness of the governing variables so that they succeed in serving and satisfying them to the desired level of their expectations. It is significant to mention that a number of factors shape the level of expectations and the most sensitive variable is the process of technological sophistication. Of late if we find providers of techno-based services defining and innovating services and satisfying the customers in a distinct way, the credibility for the same goes to the techniculture. The researches now reveal that the factors underlying satisfaction is techno-based service encounters. The outstanding contributions of internet services, automated phone service, services delivered through CD or video technology, kiosk services offer to the customers an opportunity to witness the world-class services and the process of encountering thus makes ways for high level of expectations and the desired levels of satisfaction. The experiences of customers/users with self-service technologies (SSTs) has defined new perception of satisfaction and dissatisfaction and the marketing professionals assigning due weightage to them succeed in offering to their encountered levels. We find personal encounters between customers/users and the people of service generating organisations which we name interpersonal services help in satisfying the customers. At the same time, we also find cases, where due to failures of technology, the customers fail in getting the desired level of services and resulting from which they were found dissatisfied.

Self-service Technologies thus work in both ways. The SSTs satisfy them when we find customers thrilled that the technology would bail them of a difficult situation. They find their intensified needs fulfilled or when they get better than the alternative or when the technologies worked and served as it should. In all the three cases, the customers enjoy the benefits of new generation of techno-based services. The technologies must be convenient for them, they find them better than the alternative and in addition, easy to use, helpful in saving time and as per the requirements. The technologies must work in the desired order and they do not witness the cases of failures of technology.

We cannot deny the cases of dissatisfaction when we find customers/users not encountering the desired level of expectations. The cases of failures of technology encounter a condition where we find much more scope for dissatisfaction. The failure of process also results into dissatisfaction. The failure of back-office or follow-up process also results into dissatisfaction because we do not find the process as per their assumptions. The dissatisfaction may also cause when we find design of technology poor which has been causing to them confusions or even menu options are not clear. We cannot deny the situations where due to knowledge or due to poor know-how or due to unawareness of using the technology in proper way, the customers experience dissatisfaction.

Thus, we find both the cases of satisfaction and dissatisfaction, but in a majority of the cases we find new generation of technology successful in defining the perception of satisfaction.

SERVICE ENCOUNTER OR MOMENTS OF TRUTH

In a true sense, we find service encounters as moments of truth. How do we make use of moments with professionalised efforts determines the magnitude of our success. Richard Norman coined this Spanish terminology from the show of bullfighting. Normann says,[18] "We could say that the perceived quality is realised at the moment of truth, when the service provider and the service customer confront one another in the arena. At moment, they are very much on their own.......It is the skill, the motivation and the tools employed by the firm's representative and the expectations and behaviour of the client which together will create the service delivery process."

If we get an opportunity to witness or view bullfighting, we watch there the moments of truth. In the bullfighting, we find life of bull or matador at stake. We find matador a person whose task is to kill the bull in the show of bullfighting. Thus, in the show bullfighting, we find skill of a bullfighter playing a very important role. A minor mistake, delay or lapse may cause a major injury resulting into the death of a bullfighter. The moment of truth is the instant at which the matador deftly slays the bull with his sword. Normann feels that it is the life of relationship that is on stake. Since we find bullfighting a show, a large number of audience watches the moment where even a minor mistake may result a major injury found of irreparable nature.

Another expert Jan Carlzon, the former CEO of Scandinavian Airlines Systems (SAS) used the moments of truth for transforming SAS from an operation-driven business into a customer-driven airline. He comments,[19] "Last year, each of our 10 million customers came into contact with approximately five SAS employees and this contact lasted an average of 15 seconds each time. Thus, SAS is created 50 million times a year, 15 at a time. These 50 million moments of truth are the moments that ultimately determine whether SAS will succeed or fail as a company. They are the moments when we must prove to our customers that SAS is their best alternative."

The above-mentioned two cases are the different situations where we find use of moments of truth. The first condition where we find moments of truth clarifies that in the show either bull or the matador would have to go. Hence, it is the skill or expertise or making use of an opportune moment by the matador that determines the success of show.

We find another case where the communication excellence of working employees determines the magnitude of success. While conversing with the users of services, we find a moment of a few seconds where the feedback that you get from the customers and the efforts that you make to convince that you are number one depend on the use of moments by serving or communicating people.

IMPORTANCE OF SERVICE ENCOUNTER

The service marketers need to determine customer satisfaction and loyalty and for which we find service encounter playing an important role. For getting the effective result, the marketing professionals should make sincere efforts to initiate the process at the very early stage. If we find customers encountering the services for the first time, the initial encounter is found instrumental in creating a first impression of the organisation. Because the customers do not have any basis for judging the service quality whatsoever the service quality they encounter play an important role in creating and projecting the organisational image. The positive and negative interactions with a firm result in projecting a positive or negative image. Many positive interactions result in a compositive image of high quality whereas many negative interactions cause opposite effect. If we find a mix of positive and negative interactions, the customers are found indecisive.

The service encounter also helps in building and continuing relationship. Of course, we do not find all the encounters bearing the potentials of building relationships. However, there are certain conditions when certain encounters prove to be the key to customer satisfaction. In a majority of the conditions, we find early encounters to be much more effective. In the hospitality industry, we find early encounters helping customers in forming an opinion about the service quality. In the hospital services, we find encounters with nursing staff to be effective.

The service encounters may be common and at the same time also momentous. The marketing professionals need to develop their awareness of the momentous encounters which if found negative may bind a customer to an organisation for life long. The service marketers need to remember this proverb "One bade apple," simply ruins the rest and drives the customer away, no matter how many or what type of encounters have occurred in past.

The above-mentioned facts make it clear that service encounters, no doubt, have a positive impact on the perception of customers regarding service quality but the encounters must be impressive. The professionals also need to make it sure that customer visiting the centres do not get even a single opportunity when they are not witnessing even the basics or the minimum level of services quality. We cannot negate the outstanding role of services encounters in building perception of quality and providing an opportunity for satisfying the customers. Perceptions may be favourable and at the same time also unfavorable. How do we make the perceptions favourable occupy an important place.

The professionals managing the servicescapes, of course, play here an important role. The tangibles provide to customers an opportunity to witness the moments of truth for developing the perception of service quality. If they evidence everything right, the formation of a positive opinion is a must. Conversely, if they witness anything wrong, the formation of a negative image cannot be denied.

Service Encounters: A Strong Foundation for Satisfaction and Service Quality

We consider services encounters or moment of truth as a strong foundation for customer satisfaction *vis-à-vis* the service quality. We also consider encounters as building blocks for satisfaction and quality. We find it a place where promises are either kept or broken. The customers here get an opportunity for the formation of perception. We also find services encounters as real-time marketing. From customers' perspective, we find service encounters making available to them vivid impression. Providing to the customers a snapshot is significant for shaping of perception and the service encounters make it possible. When we find customers entering a hotel and viewing the arrangements in the rooms, experiencing while eating in the restaurants, requesting for a wake-up call and checking out; the customers get an opportunity to encounter the quality which becomes instrumental in satisfying them. In the Figure 2.9, we find a services encounter cascade.

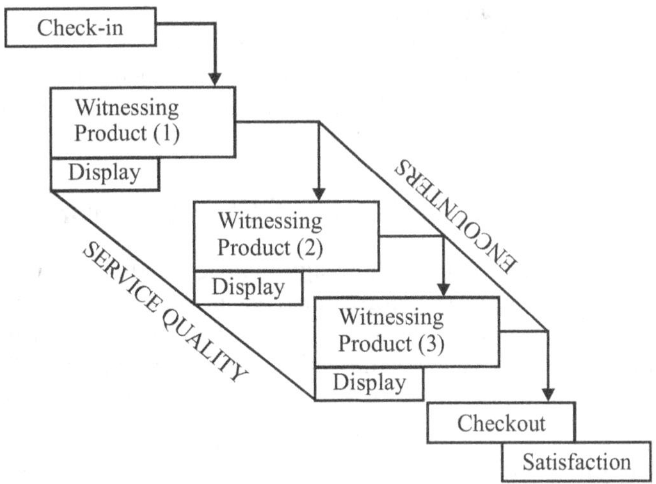

Fig. 2.9: Service Encounter Cascade

In Figure 2.9 where we find services encounter cascade, the moments of truth have been linked. In encounters, we find customers witnessing everything personally which may help shaping of perception regarding service quality. At each and every encounter, the professionals get an opportunity to satisfy the customers. From the viewpoint of an organisation, each and every encounter provides to the professionals an opportunity to prove the existent potentials.

Thus, we can say that service encounters provide an opportunity to display the positives you have. The customers get an opportunity to witness the quality and the providers get an opportunity to display their potentials. The customers form a perception of quality and because they get the services in tune with the perception they have in their minds, we find them satisfied. A snapshot is essential and the services marketers need make it possible.

SERVICE QUALITY

A majority of us believe that service quality is more a function of attitude rather than of technology but now it appears just a myth. An individual or an institution succeeds in thriving, if they do not fix any boundary for service quality. Professional excellence rests on perfection which makes a strong advocacy in favour of innovations. Optimism plays an incremental role in the entire process. If we keep on and continue with the process of innovations, the new vistas are opened for devising new perception of quality. Of course, we find process of technological sophistication activating the process of value additional in the service creation but at the same time we cannot undermine the role of quality marketing people. Service quality satisfaction becomes essential to capitalise on the opportunities and to establish a brand name. Quality can be split into technical quality and functional quality and if we synchronise both of them optimally, the desired results are achieved. It is in this context that service quality assumes a place of outstanding significance amongst the key elements in the services marketing.

Concept: According to Crosby[20] (1984), we define quality as, 'conforming to requirements'. This focuses our attention on the fact that the service generating organisations first need to establish requirements and specifications and then to comply so that the promised quality of services are made available with the users. Juran[21] (1982) opines that quality is all about fitness for use. This definition is found based on satisfying the needs of customers. In both the opinions, we find focus on customers playing an important role in defining quality. Swan and Combs[22] 22 (1976) identified two important dimensions of service quality, viz., instrumental and expressive. The instrumental dimension describes the physical aspects whereas the expressive dimension is found related to psychological and intangibility aspects. An expert, Gronroos[23] (1984) identified technical and functional quality as the two important dimensions of quality. The technical quality refers to the relatively quantifiable aspects of service which are made available to the customers in the interaction process. We consider it an important base for measuring service quality. The functional quality cannot be measured as objectively as the technical quality.

The conceptual aspect of service quality thus makes it clear that we cannot draw a line between the two as the expectations of customers/users of services and the offering by the providers are influenced by a number of developments taking place in the society each and every day. It is also to be made clear that we find service quality influenced by knowledge of the customers/users of services the quality of technology used for adding value to the services and the professionalism of marketing people engaged in the process. In addition, attitudes of people, their appearance and facial expression and service environment also influence the service quality. The conceptualisation of service quality begins by addressing the abstract expectations perceived by customers/users in respect of quality.

IMPORTANCE OF SERVICE QUALITY

Services quality assumes a place of outstanding significance in almost all categories of service generating organisations. The pace and race of economic transformation considerably depend on the contributions and domination of services sectors to the national economy. The task of image building and image projection rest on quality be it an individual; be it an institution; be it a goods manufacturing organisation; be it a service generating organisation, be it a profit making organisation or a non-profit making organisation. The following facts justify the importance of quality in the services sector:

1. Quality for image projection: The organisations making sincere efforts to innovate and define quality get an opportunity for image projection. Both the facets — image building and image projection are found correlated. Our sincere and concerted efforts for inventions and innovations, research and development activities make ways for the new perceptions of services having an edge over the rivals. The common masses start realising the positive contributions of an organisation to the process of socio-economic transformation. If we do something positive for society, if we contribute something concrete to the economy and if we keep on moving the process of protecting and promoting nature, our promotional measures throw a positive impact and we find ourselves in a position to establish our identity. The general masses and beneficiaries start realising their contributions to the transformation of society and development of national economy.

2. Quality makes ways for cost-effectiveness: Of late, we find an age of techno-driven services and therefore the service generating organisations making use of new generation of technology are found successful in creating and expanding the markets. Since we find a significant increase in the number of customers/users, it is natural that cost economy is maintained. Making possible cost-effectiveness becomes essential for developing countries like ours where we find common masses not having a high rate of affordability. The educational institutions and healthcare sectors in particular need to make their services affordable. Increasing the number of customers/users and making possible cost economy depend on the qualities of services that we offer.

3. Quality benefits the employees: Quality services generated by an organisation create a sense of confidence among people serving the organisations. They are duly motivated and therefore work with a sense of confidence. We also find high morale on account of lucrative incentives. The organisations realise their contributions and reward them suitably. The cycle of qualitative transformation keeps on moving and benefits organisations, customers and employees in many ways. They find themselves successful in establishing a distinct identity in the society.

4. Minimising the risk factor: The service quality also minimises the risk factors and the users of services develop a sense of confidence. The word-of-mouth promotion helps transmission of information regarding the quality element and this makes ways for reliability and dependability which contracts avenues for risk.

Creation of doubts in the minds of customers and potential customers cannot be considered to be positive for the creation of demand and expansion of markets. Once you prove your leadership in the market, the customers start depending on your services. Contrary to it, when you develop an image problem due to poor quality of services; your task of creating the confidence is found much more difficult. The patients using the services of quality hospitals, the students using the services of quality educational institutions. The bank and insurance companies attracting customers on the basis of their quality services maximise possibilities for dependability and minimise possibilities for doubts and suspicion. The customers and providers both the sides are found confident which simplifies the process of market penetration. Business without risk or with a minimum risk keeps both the sides intact and the marketing activities gain a rapid momentum.

5. Quality helps creation of value system: The service generating organisation defining quality in the face of multi-faceted developments in the socio-economic system find it easier to switch on the process of value engineering. The marketing activities are found expanding, scope for profit generation is found increasing and unethical practices are found in the reverse gear. Since we find business with a holistic touch, the providers have no options but to respect the value system as the moment customers/users start realising that they are cheated, a negative attitude will start working which will make an invasion on their confidence and trust.

The above-mentioned facts make it clear that quality constitutes to be an essential element for the existence or prosperity of an organisation. If we keep on moving the process of maintaining and defining quality, our task of getting success in the business world is considerably simplified. Conversely, if we fail in maintaining quality, this ultimately tarnishes our image. And once we find our image tarnished, the possibilities of recovering are the least possible. The government managed hospitals and educational institutions have been found facing image problems and we find the same thing in other government sectors.

Quality thus benefits the service generating organisations in many ways. In almost all the service generating organisations, we find use of technology which has been found redefining the service quality. Service quality satisfaction becomes essential for capitalising on the opportunities. It is also important to mention that world-class professional excellence and the world-class services creating technologies have changed the perception of customers regarding service quality. There is no doubt in it that the side-effects of qualitative improvements have paved avenues for quality gap because we find the expectations of customers almost at peak. Even a minor mistake on the part of providers and minor faults in the technology used create big quality gap.

SERVICE QUALITY GAP

Quality paves avenues for expectations. Expectations if not fulfilled make the ways for gap. The multi-faceted attempts for improving service quality have made possible a significant increase in the levels of expectations of customers/users. World-class professional excellence, new generation of supplicated technology and number one physical amenities and facilities have shaped high level of expectations of service users and of the providers. Service quality gap draws priority attention of professionals so that they make it sure that promised quality of services are made available to the customers.

Zeithmal, Berry and Parsuraman[24] (1988) identified four potential gaps which may lead to the serious gap between the expectations of users and offerings of providers. It is also significant to mention that Lovelock[25] (1994) has enlarged the gap to seven. All the seven gaps can be grouped into two major parts such as internal and external. The standard gap, delivery gap, and internal communication gap[26] are known as internal gap whereas the knowledge gap, perception gap, interpretation gap and services gap are of external nature. The internal gap occurs between different functioned and departments within the organisation and therefore we call them internal gap. Contrary to it, the external gap is influenced by the four external conditions and therefore we call them external gap. This is shown in Figure 2.10.

Internal	Quality Gap	External
Standard gap Delivery gap Internal Communication gap		Knowledge gap Perception gap Interpretation gap Service gap
Influence of Internal Forces		Influence of External Factors

Fig. 2.10: Internal and External Service Quality

1. The Knowledge gap: It focuses our attention on the difference between the service-provider's beliefs and the expectations of customers/users. If the services providers and services users do not believe and expect in the same in the way, we find the knowledge gap.

2. The Standard gap: In this gap, we find the difference between management perception of customers/ users expectations and the quality standards for delivery. May be that customers have high levels of expectations and they do not find the services to that desired level and then we find the standrd gap. The professional failing in forming a right perception of expectations invite this type of gap.

3. The Delivery gap: This type of gap due to the difference between the specified delivery standards and the actual performance of the services providers related to these standards.

The providers promise and we find multi-faceted arrangements for delivery. If we find delay or indecency in the offering process, the delivery gap is created.

4. The Internal Communication gap: This is the gap that is found between what the organisations think about advertising and salespeople such as levels of service quality, features of product and performance. Of late, we find the communication processes much more effective as technology governs the operation. The gap may be created due to faulty operation and ineffective communication.

5. The Perception gap: We find this gap as the difference between what is in fact delivered and what the customers/users perceive. Since we find technology governing the quality of services, the customers develop perception of delivery and in case if we find the delivery not in tune with the perception, there will be gap.

6. The Interpretation gap: It is the difference between the service-providers and service-users particularly in terms of interpretation. We find such type of gap in advance of service offerings. The providers may interpretate in a different way and the users may not receives in the desired way. Or just reveres, the users or customers may interpretate in a different way and the providers may not receive in the desired way.

7. The Service gap: We find such type of gap between what the customers expect to receive and their perception of the services actually offered to them. We find cases where the customers are influenced by this perception they would be offered high level of services but they do not get to the desired level and we find a gap.

Whatsoever the standard of technology we have, we cannot devise a system that is found to be foolproof. Whatsoever the quality of people we have, we cannot be sure that there would not be any gap. Actually, it is not due to one side; indeed we find both sides such as providers and users responsible for the same.

BRIDGING THE SERVICE QUALITY GAP

Development is a natural phenomen on and like this, we also find gap a natural phenomena. Professional excellence coils in its essence that we diagnose the gap at the earliest possible and make sincere and honest efforts to bridge the gap. It is in this context that we find marketing experts prescribing the following prescriptions:

Prescription-1: We need to understand the expectations of customers/users in a right way. This makes it essential that the marketing professionals make sincere efforts to interact with the service users. This in a very natural way will enable them to know the changing levels of expectations influenced by a number of factors. The organisation using new generation of technology, much more sincere to the availability of physical amenities and facilities and fortunately working or serving with a team of super or star performers interact with the customers in a right way.

Prescription-2: This prescription focuses on establishing the right service quality standards and in this context your efforts must have customer orientation. Proper training facilities are required to ensure that your working people are well aware of the goals. You need to take the best possible efforts to sensitise them.

Prescription-3: This prescription focuses on ensuring that the service performance meets the service standards. It is also to be made sure that the marketing people are well aware of the role they have to play for satisfying the customers/users. The technology supports may be taken for improving the quality of services.

Prescription-4: In this prescription, it is to be ensured that the communication promises are realistic in nature. The services providers have to preview the advertisements before they are exposed to the customers/ users. Innovtive advertisement campaigns are to be developed.

The above mentioned prescriptions are for bridging the quality gap. The marketing professionals need to make of the suitable prescription that helps them in resolving the problems.

MEASURING SERVICE QUALITY

For managing things in a right and effective way, it is essential that we are in a position to measure them. This is due to the fact that without measuring the service quality, the marketing professionals would not be in a position to know the intensity of problem and the emerging gap in quality. It is in this context that we find two-tier measures for measuring the service quality often practised by the marketing professionals. We call them soft and hard measures.

Soft Measures: The measures cannot easily be observed. It is found based on an interaction with customers/ users, employees and others. We find soft standards providing direction, guidance and feedback to employees. It can be quantified by measuring the perception and beliefs of customers/users. In this context, the organisation are required to establish ongoing listening system by using multiple methods among the different group of customers. We find ongoing research to be effective in the process.

Hard Measures: The hard measures of measuring service quality refer to operational processes or outcome with the data such as uptime, service response times, failure rate and delivery costs. By contrast hard standards times, our focus is on these characteristics and activities that can be counted, timed and measured through audit.

The organisations interested in offering quality services make use of both the measures. We find those organisations good who listen to both customers and employees. Identifying right conditions and applying appropriate measures help an organisation in getting the desired success. Professional excellence contracts avenues for service-quality gap as at both the stages the concerned parties such as service-providers and service-users receive the difficulties of each other in a right way. Particularly in the Indian setting, we find quality gap a matter of serious concern and this is, of course, due to managerial deficiency which is to be replaced by managerial proficiency.

REASONS FOR SERVICE QUALITY GAP

We cannot negate that each gap is the result of inconsistencies and deficiencies in the process of quality management. The professional managing the affairs need to develop their awareness of the emerging gap.

The Perception gap: This gap is the result of poor understanding of expectations of customers which may trigger a chain of wrong decisions resulting into poor quality perception. The reasons entailed behind the perception gap are insufficient marketing research, wrong information from the system, wrong interpretation of information, lack of demand analysis, the research activities not concentrating on the quality of services, absence of interaction between management and customers, inadequate upward and downward internal communication, too many organisational layers or levels, lack of market segmentation and lack of focus on relationships.

The Quality Specification gap: This gap occurs due to mistakes in the planning process, lack of customer-friendly standards, absence of formal process for determining the service goals, lack of management commitment, vague service design, haphazard new service development process and lack of cooperation and support from the management.

The Service Delivery gap: The service delivery gap occurs due to complex process specifications, faulty polices of human resource such as recruitment, compensation, lack of empowerment, improper evaluation, poor management of services operations, mismatch between demand and supply, ineffective internal marketing, poor quality of customers, etc.

The Market Communication gap: The market communication gap may occur due to failures of company while integrating market communications with service operations, high level of promises while initiating external communication gap campaign, inability of managing the expectations of customers and not maintaining the specified norms for performing.

The Service Quality gap: The service quality gap occurs due to bad reputation or negative image, increasing in the number of lost customers, bad reputation, negatively confirmed quality and negative corporate or local image. The professionals may experience difficulties in identifying the reasons.

The Knowledge gap: The knowledge gap occurs due to unawareness of provider regarding customers and *vice versa.* The professionals and other marketing people acting as providers lack of information The variations in believes and expectations of both the providers and users help developing knowledge gap.

The Interpretation gap: We find occurring of interpretation gap due to misunderstanding between the providers and customers. We can also call it ineffective expression by both the parties, viz., providers, and users.

SERVICE QUALITY AUDIT

The service generating organisations, of late, have been facing a number of challenges and one of the greatest challenges is to ensure that customers/users are getting quality services on a continuous basis. The achievements of a particular method cannot be ensured simply by the design of effective quality management process. The professionals are required to be able to gear the system towards efficient functioning. Since we find service system functioning in a dynamic environment, it becomes essential that the system is capable of adopting itself to the emerging changes. This focuses our attention on an audit system which helps us in identifying the deficiencies, discrepancies and limitations at various processes. The GAP Model of Service Quality if implemented properly may serve our purpose. We also call it Conceptual Model of Service Quality.

GAP MODEL OF SERVICE QUALITY

Thus, the conceptual model shown in Figure 2.11 transmits a clear message to manage evincing keen interest in improving the quality. These models being with the process of improving the service quality. We need to perceive here the nature and extent of the customer's gap. This necessitates a strong focus on the customers and in this context the marketing professionals have to enrich their knowledge bank about the customers. If we understand customers in a right fashion, the formulation of a sound service strategy is sound easier.

The different types of gap in quality related to delivery and marketing of services focus our attention on the existent gap between expectations and perceptions. The marketing professionals bear the responsibility of bridging the gap. As long as the process of technological sophistication continues, the creation of gap will also remain in practice. This is due to the fact that adoption of new generation of technology in the services sector has been making ways for defining and redefining and quality. The innovative service help in changing the perception of quality. The customers starts expecting much more from the service providing organisations. If we find everything working smoothly and properly, the customers get the desired level of services, but when we find technologies not working properly and the working people not operating the technology as per specified norms, the possibilities for a quality gap cannot be negated. The service providing organisations also play an important role in increasing the levels of expectations by making use of creative promotional measures. The increasing flow of information becomes very much instrumental in aggravating the flow and intensity of expectations. Thus, the side-by-side movement of innovations and multi-pronged gap. The marketing professionals are supposed to make use of the prescriptions to be instrumental in resolving their problems.

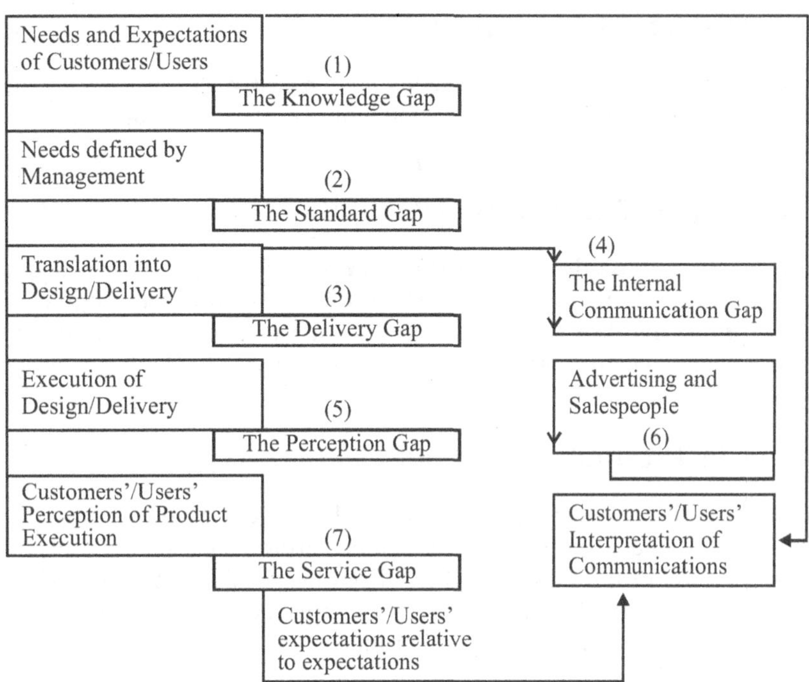

Fig. 2.11: Service Gap (Adapted from Christopher Lovelock Product plus McGraw-Hill, New 1994, p.112).

ACCELERATING SERVICE PRODUCTIVITY

Productivity focuses our attention on a proportionate relationship between input and output. Accelerating the rate of productivity is considered essential even in the service providing organisations. Of course, the marketing professionals will find it difficult to increase the productivity of the services found of tangible nature. Particularly when the measurement of productivity is found related to the information-based services, the task is much more difficult. Because the task of defining output is found difficult in the service sectors, the measurement of productivity also proves to be complicated. In the people processing services, such as hospitals and educational institutions, we can look at the number of patients treated and in case of educational institutions, the number of patients treated and in case of educational institutions, the number of students passed out from the institution. However, the processes are found to be much more complicated. Since we find variation in the nature and types of patents, to be admitted at different times and the recovery ratio also to be different due to the complicated patients, a judicious approach for measuring productivity appears to be difficult.

Organisational Strategy to Accelerate Productivity

The operation manager serving an organisation bears the responsibility of accelerating the rate of productivity. Even in the service producing organisations the following measures are to be effective:

1. There must be a careful control of cost at each and every step in the process. The cost-effectiveness needs professionalised conceptualisation.
2. Do not keep people and equipment partially tapped or untapped. The productivity capacity is to be matched to the average level of demand not the peak level.
3. New generation of technology is to be promoted.
4. Make available to the people equipment with databases which would enable them to work faster.
5. Inculcate and cultivate to the people the habits of performing in a right way, minimising possibilities for mistakes and errors.
6. Broaden the array of tasks which the people can perform.
7. Practise expert systems which would allow paraprofessionals to accept the work responsibility earlier performed by more experienced people.

Customer-based Strategies to Accelerate Productivity

In the service sector, we find even involvement of customers in the process on generating the services. The marketing professionals are required to adopt the following strategies so that the customers behave in more productive ways.

A Change in the Timing of Customers' Demand

We often find cases of pressure on the demand side. The service are found crowded and congested, seasonal or cyclic peaks in demand. Thus, we also find cases where during the off-peak periods, the managers find very few customers. Making a productive use of assets requires shift in demand by changing the time of services. Of course, we also find demand which cannot be shifted so easily but a number of services make ways for a shift.

Involving Customers in Production Process

In a number of cases, we find scope for self-service and therefore involvement of customers in the service production process. Of late, we find many companies making efforts to encourage customers who have access to internet so that the transmission of information directly from the firm's corporate. Even we find five-star hotels with traditionally high levels of personal services asking their guests to do more of their work. We find these steps very much effective in accelerating the rate of productivity.

In view of the above, it is right to say that the service providing organisations can make ways for cost economy which would help them in the productivity acceleration process. Making the services cost-effective is need of the hour which would make the services not only affordable but also to be successful in excelling competition.

SERVQUAL

Expectations and satisfaction never remain static. The service marketers bear the responsibility of developing their awareness of the changing levels of satisfaction in relation to the different aspects of service quality. Noted marketing experts, Parasurman, Zeithmal and Berry in 1988 developed an instrument to measure the levels of customer satisfaction and we call this instrument as SERVQUAL.[27] The basic thene that we find in the SERVQUAL model is comparison of perceptions with expectations. It is found applicable to all the service industries. In this model, we find five dimensions such as tangibility, reliability, responsiveness, assurance and empathy. Strongly agree and strongly disagree are the two different sides. We find SERVQUAL a scale involving a survey containing 21 services attributes grouped into five dimensions as mentioned above. The data collected from the SERVQUAL Scale can be used for a number of purposes as mentioned below:

1. For each service attribute determining the average gap between perceptions and expectations of customers.
2. Assessing the service quality with the help of five dimensions of SERVQUAL.
3. Tracking expectations and perceptions of customers over time.
4. Comparing scores of SERVQUAL with the scores of rivals.
5. Identifying and examining the segments of customers significantly found different.
6. Assessing internal service quality rendered.

We find application of SERVQUAL for the measurement of the quality of service in the multiple contexts, cultures and countries. Even in the public sector organisations, we find use of this scale. This scale is found applicable all over the world in the service sector. The contexts where we find use of SERVQUAL are real estate brokers, doctors in private practice, the programmes related to public recreation, clinic of a dental college, placement centre of a Business School, a tire store, an accounting firm, discount and department stores, gas and electric company, hospitals, banking dry cleaning, higher education and fast food.

The two different areas where we find SERVQUAL are Consumer Service Context and Industrial Product Context. The five dimensions of SERVQUAL are the criteria for evaluation. The two similar banks of USA were selected by the Australian Bank for testing the SERVQUAL. The important points observed by them are the following.

Tangibility

The banks with the outstanding performance would have:

1. The banks will have new generation of sophisticated equipment.
2. They will have physical facilities with a visual appeal.
3. Employees have awareness of personal care services. They have aesthetic sense. They are neat and clean and well-dressed.
4. The materials having a high appeal such as brochure or statements.

Reliability

The excellence banks will have the following:

1. They promise and fulfill.
2. Evincing keen interests in resolving the problems.
3. They perform well.
4. They maintain error-free records.

Responsiveness

1. The customers are told when the services are performed.
2. The customers are offered prompt services.
3. The employees show interest in serving the customers.
4. The employees know the answers to the questions of customers.

Assurance

The employee's servicing there:

1. have confidence in customers.
2. are courteous to customers.
3. answer to the questions of customers.
4. ensure safety in transactions with customers.

Empathy

The banks will:

1. provide personal attention to customers.
2. keep operating hours convenient to customers.
3. receive the specific needs of customers.

Of course, the observations are related to banks but we find them relevant to a number of services providing organisations. The organisations setting up a measuring system to track service quality at regular intervals succeed in improving the quality of services.

Not only in the context of consumer services but we find SERQUAL significant even to the industrial product. We cannot negate the instrumentality of SERVQUAL for identifying the required level of performance improvement and further for assessing how much improvement is needed. It helps in evaluating the impact of efforts made for improvement.

The SERVQUAL scale was first published in 1988 and since then it has witnessed a number of improvements and modifications. On the basis of two different formats, one for perceptions and another for expectations, we measurement of service quality. The dimensions related to perceptions are tangibility, reliability, responsiveness, assurance and empathy whereas in the expectations we find measurement of minimum level with the desired level.

A majority of the service generating organanisations make use of SERVQUAL but we find doubts expressed by a majority of regarding conceptual foundation and methodological limitations. Gerhard Mels, Christo Boshoff, and Denon Nel[28] made an analysis of the data from banks, insurance brokers, vehicle repair firms, electrical repair companies and life insurance firms. They feel that SERVQUAL scores measure only two factors such as intrinsic service quality and external service quality. In the intrinsic service quality, we find emphasis on functional quality whereas in extrinsic quality, the focus is on tangible aspects of service delivery or technical quality. We also find critics arguing that we do not find anything wrong in the SERVQUAL scale, indeed the researchers have committed mistakes and have altered the list of statements for measuring the service quality. Anne M. Smith[29] in his paper entitled "Measuring Service Quality: Is SERVQUAL Now Redundant?" published in the Journal of Marketing Management, 11/1995 was not of the view that SERVQUAL has lost its relevance. Thus, it is right to mention that the scale for measuring service quality may be used even in today's perspective. A survey research instrument developed by marketing experts is used by a majority of the service generating organisations. We are aware of the facts that the scale is based on the premise that customers can evaluate a firn's service quality by making a comparison of their perceptions with the expectations. A generic measurement tool can be applied across a broad spectrum of service industries.

The success of SERVQUAL is considerably influenced by the role of researchers. The list of statements should not be modified or altered. In addition, the researchers also need to be aware of the conceptual foundation and methodological limitations. The mistakes committed in the process will adversely affect the findings and will tell upon the effectiveness of SERVQUAL.

DEVELOPMENT OF NEW SERVICE PRODUCT

At the outset, let's go through the conceptual aspect of new service product. The service product found totally innovative, generated and offered by the company to the globe for the first time and a new experience to both the providing organisations and using customers is called a new service product. Improved versions and adaptive replacements cannot be known as new product. Booz, Allen and Hamilton talked about six categories of new products as mentioned below:

Really Innovative: The products are innovative and we find the customers/users witnessing the product for the first time. Since the globe has not witnessed the product earlier and it is a new experience for both the providers and users, we call them really innovative product.

New Product Lines: We find the products not new to the market but new to the organisation. A company may add a new product to the existing one and may enter the market for the first time.

Additions: Here, we find organisation adding new product in their existing product lines with the motto of strengthening the same.

Improvements: A company may also modernise its products by adding new features or values or replacing the existing services with the improved services.

Repositioning: This is targeting of existing products in the new markets.

Cost reductions: We also find companies developing new services with the same performance but at the lower cost.

Of course, we find different categories but as and when we talk about new service product, our focus is on the fact that services are totally innovative and both the parties such as providing companies and using the customer's experience for the first time. Inventions and innovations make the ways for the development of new product. The organisations intensifying research and development activities prove to be an innovator and get an opportunity to offer the new product in the market. The customers/users are found tempted or fascinated to the new product as they find the new product as the status symbol. This provides to the service generating organisations a new opportunity to capitalise on with almost dismal competition.

STAGES IN THE DEVELOPMENT OF NEW SERVICES

The development of new product moves through different stages and at each and every step, the professionals need to divert due attention. The outstanding feature that we find with the services that their production and consumption processes move together. The production process is found where we find providers encountering with the service-users. It is also significant here to mention that we consider service users as co-produce. In addition to other aspects, we find involvement of customers whose attitudes, potentials and involvement play a decisive role. Of course, the supporting infrastructural facilities, service environment and potentials of providers are also found significant in the very context.

The researches reveal that products developed through different stages and introduced in a structured planning framework have more possibilities of getting a success in the market than those products which has not been developed within a framework. The intangibility features of services is found relevant even to the development of new services. The four basic characteristic are found significant even for the development of new services such as, the product must be objective not subjective; it must be precise, not vague; it must be fact-driven and it must be methodological, not philosophical.

In the development of new services, we find subjective options of professionals and employees very much instrumentals. The objective designs of services such as incorporation of new data about the perceptions of users, market needs and feasibility are found less significant in the entire process. We find services produced and consumed simultaneously normally based on the interaction of employees and customers. A number of experts have been found critical to the fact that development of new services should be in the face of an interaction between the employees and the customers. Because we find employees interacting with the customers; they have the real perception of their changing likes and dislikes. This makes it essential that employees are involved in the process of developing new services. We find contact employees psychologically and physically close to customers and therefore the identification process related to the changing likes and dislikes of customers would be much more proactive. Thus, we find strong advocacy in favour the involving employees in the design and development process of new services. We also find arguments that because customers often participate in service delivery, they should also be involved in the processes of development of new services. There is no doubt in it that this argument is found much more logical particularly in cases where the customers personally carry out part of the service process. We find a number of organisations involving guests particularly in the designing of the hotel rooms is found much more effective. Of course, the features and placement of furnishings in the rooms should be for the guests and not just for the staff or architects bearing the responsibility of designing the room.

The different stages in the development of new services have been presented in Figure 2.12. Right from generation of new ideas to the stages of commercialisation of services, the professional need much more care and excellence. The steps can be practised in any type of new services or services design. No doubt that we find almost the same stages for the development of manufactured goods but in the context of services, the adaption process assumes a place of outstanding significance. Besides, we also find variation in the process of implementation. A new idea can be dropped at any stage of the process if they do not satisfy the criteria for success at the particular stage and therefore at each and every stages, we find the checkpoints which mention these requirements found to be essential for that new service.

The Figure 2.12 presented below has two sections, viz., first front-end planning and second back-end planning implementation. The front-end planning focuses on the development of service concept whereas the back-end throws light on the implemention. We cannot consider the development of new service a linear process as we find scope even for skipping.

Front-end Planning and Back-end Planning: In this context, we find development of business strategy. The vision and mission of a service generating organisation is reviewed in the first step. The first stage that we find here is idea generation. The ideas must be screened in the face of new service strategy. The second stage that we find in this step is development of concept and evaluation. In this context, the professionals need to test the concept with customers and employees. The third stage is business analysis where we find test for profitability and feasibility. All the three stages we find related to front-end planning. The second step in the back-end planning where the first stage focuses on services development and testing. This necessitates conducting service prototype test. The second stages in the back-end planning is market testing where we find emphasis on test service and other market mix elements. The third stage is commercialisation. Further post-introduction evaluation is also to be made.

The figure 2.12 makes it clear that business strategy development, new service strategy development and post-introduction evaluation are the three important steps covering different stages from idea generation to commercialisation.

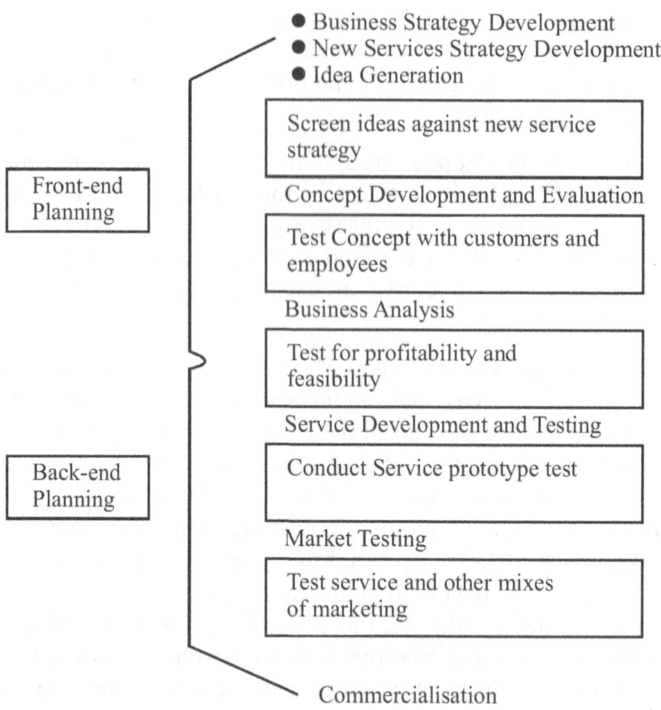

Fig. 2.12: Service Development Stages

Business Strategy Development: In an organisation, we find an overall vision and mission and the first step focuses our attention on reviewing the vision and mission. In almost all the organisations, we find strategic picture and it is essential that the new service strategy and new service ideas must fit within the large strategic picture of an organisation.

New Service Strategy Development: The researches reveal that a new service strategy is significant because without a clear picture of strategy, the task of desiring a well-planned portfolio of new products and services would be difficult.

We cannot negate that a product portfolio strategy and a well-defined organisational structure for the development of new services are considered to be the foundations for success. The organisational goals, vision, potentials and growth plans will determine the suitability of a particular service product in a particular condition.

The moment find task of defining in a new service strategy is over, an organisation will be in a better position to switch on the process for the generation of specific ideas.

For the formulation of a new service strategy, the professionals may take the support of a New Service Strategy Matrix as shown in Figure 2.13.

OFFERINGS	MARKETS	
	Current Customers	New Customers
Existing Services	Share Building	Market Development
New Services	Service Development	Diversification

Fig. 2.13: New Service Strategy Matrix

The matrix as shown above will be helpful to the professionals in formulating a new service strategy for identifying the growth opportunities. We may find this matrix as a catalyst for creative ideas, which later may also be used as an initial idea screen. The matrix suggests that the service generating organisations can develop a growth strategy around current and can focus on current offerings or new services offerings.

Idea Generation: The next stage in the process is idea generation. There are a number of methods and avenues for the generation of new service ideas. The common approaches like formal brainstorming, solicitation of new ideas from employees and customers, lead user research and learning about offerings of the competitors may be used by professionals for searching out new service ideas. The new service ideas can be screened in the face of new services strategy. The professionals need to observe customers that how they do make use of their services to be helpful in the generation of creative ideas.

Service Concept Development and Evaluation: Once the process of generation of new idea is over, we find the stage set for initial development. This stage of the process is found complicated particularly for the services mainly due to intangibility. It is significant that at this stage, the agreement is reached by involving the multiple parties in sharpening the concept. After clear definition of the concept, a description of the service can be produced which would represent its specific features and characteristics and then would determine initial customers' and employees' responses to the concept.

Business Analysis: Determining feasibility and potential profit implications after development of concept. At this stage, we find demand analysis, projection of revenue, analysis of costs and assessment of operational feasibility. We find this stage involving preliminary assumptions about the costs of hiring and training people, enhancement of the delivery system and other projected operation costs. We find this test mainly for profitability and feasibility.

Implementation

We find beginning of the implementation stage after crossing the front-end planning hurdles.

Service Development and Testing: This stage involves construction of prototypes of the products and testing for consumer's acceptance. This stage of service development and testing is found difficult and therefore should involve all who have a stake in the new service such as customers and contact employees as well as the functional representatives from marketing, operations and human resources. At this stage, we find refining of the concept. Conducting service prototype test is the main thing that we find in this stage.

Market Testing: Due to its inherent characteristics, the professionals at this stage need to adopt alternative ways for testing such as offerings to the employees of the organisation and their families to assess their responses to variations in the marketing mix. Or it may also prefer to test variations in price and promotion mixes. The professionals need to believe that there is simply no substitute for a proper rehearsal when introducing a new service.

Commercialisation: At this stage, we find the service live and their introduction to the marketplace. This stage has two primary objectives such as building and maintaining acceptance of the new service among large numbers of service delivery people found responsible for service quality and monitoring all aspects of the service during introduction and through the complete service cycle. Careful monitoring needs due attention.

Post-introduction Evaluation: At this stage, we find reviewing of the information collected during the stage, of commercialisation. If essential, the required changes are incorporated in the face of actual market response to the offering. Since we find change — a natural phenomena, no service will ever stay the same. The changes will take place which may be deliberate or unplanned. This makes it essential that we formalise the review process with the motto of improving the service quality.

The different stages of new services development need due attention of professionals. Any service generating organisation cannot be sure about the timing and process of developing new services. Since we find intensity of competition at its peak, the professionals may expect more frequency in the development of new services.

BRANDING SERVICE PRODUCTS

A term 'Product' previously used in the manufactured goods is now also used by the service-driven organisations. In true sense, we find much more similarities in the business environment of both types of organisations. We find product implying a defined and consistent 'bundle of output'. If we conceptualise the term product in the goods manufacturing organisations, the problem of reception of perception is not found there. But we do not find the same thing with the service. In a number of services generating organisations offering of a line of product rather than a single product we also find some of the product found distinctly different to each other. We find a number of hotel brands and many of the hotel chains offering a family of brands such as hotels reports, courtyard, fairfield inn, residence inn, spring hill suites and vacation club. We find each brand promising a mix of benefits distinct to each other. We cannot negate that the task of targeting customers is found much more easier with such a provision of umbrella brand. The strategy of brand extension aims at encouraging customer to continue patronising units within the brand family. Not only in the context of hotel services but we find this concept even in the context of civil aviation services as a number of air travel service products are offered by the British Airways. In the group of intercontinental offerings, we find four such as Deluxe Subsonic Service, Club World (Business Class), World Traveller Plus (Premium Economy Class) and World Traveller (Economy Class). In the intracontinental group, we find two such as Club Europe (Business Class) and Euro-traveller (Economy Class).

Brand has meaning for customers. It can be both at corporate and product levels by almost any service business. In a well-managed firm, the corporate brand is not only easily recognised but we find its special meaning for the customers. The sub-brands under the umbrella of a corporate brands reflects the values of the latter. The sub-brands also communicate the experiences and benefits associated with a given service process. Like the manufactured product, we find service product also availing the benefits of brand. An important functional responsibility for marketing professionals is to become brand champions. The nation of branded services experience any be related to the Flower of Service metaphor by emphasising the need for consistency in the colour and texture of each petal.

Branding is found a way of doing business. Like the goods manufacturing organisations, the service generating organisations are also found making efforts to establish brand loyalty and in this context, the professionals play a very significant role. Since brand carries a special, meaning for the customers, the professionalism makes it essential that sincere efforts are made to image which is totality of the impressions about the brand.

SERVICE LEADERSHIP

Articulating a vision and helping to bring it about is considered to be the most important dimension helping an individual or an institution to thrive, prosper and establish leadership. This task, of course, remains unfulfilled if we find in an organisation lack of human leaders who bear the potentials of setting the standard for service quality, initiating important innovations, promoting new generation of technologies for getting the competitive advantage, defining and refining quality which may help excelling competition and establishing leadership. May be that due to the domination of situational forces, an organisation succeeds in attaining the position of a leader in the respective markets and industries but this is not to secure the leadership position unless they have a team of potentially-sound human leaders who bear the efficacy of taking them ahead in the right direction, setting the right strategic priorities and ensuring that the concerned strategies will be implemented throughout the organisation. The aforesaid facts are a staunch testimony to this proposition that the most important dimension for attaining and retaining leadership is the quality of human leaders.

We consider John Kotter, the best-known authority on leadership. He opines[30] that most successful change management processes, people need to move through eight complicated and often time-consuming stages.

1. Creating a sense of urgency to develop the impetus for change.
2. Putting together a strong enough team to direct the process.
3. Creating an appropriate vision of where the organisation needs to go.
4. Communicating the new vision broadly.
5. Empowering employees to act on that vision.
6. Producing sufficient short-term results to create credibility and counter cynicism.
7. Building momentum and using that to tackle the tougher change.
8. Anchoring the new behaviours in the organisational culture.

Development of vision and strategies is considered significant in the process for which empowerment of people overcome to obstacles and make the vision happen cannot be undermined.

Kotter says, "Leadership works through people and culture. It's soft and hot. Management works through hierarchy and systems. It's harder and cooler. The fundamental purpose of management is to keep the current system functioning. The fundamental purpose of leadership is to produce useful change, especially non-incremental change. It's possible to have too much or too little of either. Strong leadership with no management risk chaos; the organisation might walk right off a cliff. Strong management with no leadership tends to entrench an organisation in deadly bureaucracy."[31]

LEADERSHIP vs. MANAGEMENT

The two terminologies "Leadership" and "Management" are found different to each other.

We find leadership considered to be the primary forces behind successful change which is found related to vision and strategies. It is also related to the empowerment of people to remove the obstacles and making the vision happen. Conversely, we find management operating through planning, budgeting, organising, staffing, controlling and problem solving. An authority Warren Bennis and another Burt Nanus opine[32] that leaders emphasise the emotional and even spiritual resources of an organisation whereas managers concentrate on physical resources such as raw materials, technology and capital. Another expert Kotter says, "Leadership works through people and culture. It's soft and hard but management works through hierarchy and systems. It's harder and cooler. The management aims at keeping the current system functioning whereas the fundamental purpose of leadership is to produce useful change, especially non-incremental change.

LEADERSHIP QUALITIES

Leonard Berry feels that service leadership requires a special perspective. He says. "Regardless of the target markets, the specific services, or the pricing strategy, service leaders visualise quality of service as, the foundation for competing".[32] The service leaders have no option but to believe in the people who work for them and interact with the employees on a priority basis. Love for the business is considered an important dimension for service leadership. The enthusiasm must be natural to motivate individuals to teach the business to others, Another expert Berry says, "A critical role of value-driven leaders is cultivating the leadership quality of others in the organisation and he further notes that value-driven leaders rely on their values to navigate their companies through difficult periods."[33]

In addition, we find a number of experts writing on leadership and we find it a service in its own right. Vision, charisma, persistence, high expectations, expertise, empathy, persuasiveness and integrity are found to be the essential qualities for leadership. Sam Walton highlighted the role of managers as servant leaders and Jim Collins observed that a leader does not require a larger than life personality. Currently, we find transformational leadership drawing our attention which is considered as the preferred style in achieving work outcomes. In this context, we find personal values getting priority attention. The transformational leaders make use of charisma, inspirational, motivation, intellectual stimulation and individual consideration. Charisma provides a sense of vision and mission, the inspirational motivation communicates high level of expectations, the intellectual stimulation promotes rationality, logic and careful problem solving and the individual consideration pays close attention to individual differences among employees and advising staff through personal attention.

Market leadership draws due attention of professionals. It is right to say that for any organisation achieving and maintaining leadership without human leaders is quite difficult. This is due to the fact that leaders bear the potentials of articulating and communicating vision and in the process, of course, they get support of individuals having expertise. Service leadership requires high level of performance. We find a number of levels in the process of attaining service leadership and the human resource managers will classify whether it is a service loser, or a service non-entity; a service professional or a service leader.

We cannot say that leadership is confined only to the selected echelons of management such as Chief Executives or other top managers. Actually, the leadership trait may be useful even for low echelons of employees holding supervisor or managerial position including those heading teams.

Of late, the business environment is becoming much more competitive and for excelling competition we will require leadership which would help an organisation in thriving. While concluding, it is right to mention that by service leadership, our focus will be multi-dimensional. We can view things also in terms of market leadership in which we find emphasis on companies considered as a leader in a particular service industry. Or alternatively, we can also think in terms of associating leadership with individuals thinking of the role of chief executive in leading an organisation or of leadership position at different levels in a service business. We can be unrealistic in perceiving the perception in a right fashion. If we lack human leaders, it is difficult to think about leadership.

It is natural that all the service generating organisations make sincere and honest efforts to attain and retain service leadership but only those organisations succeed in their efforts whose approaches are well supported by a value-driven leader, a service leader who trusts on the people working for him. A number of qualities and traits are needed for a successful market leader and in the process, we inculcate the faculties required fro establishing market leadership. Unless we find articulation of a vision, our efforts for achieving leadership will get a lukewarm or even negative results.

Across the globe, we find multi-faceted changes in the business environment. The intensity of competition is found mounting everyday. The corporate world makes a strong advocacy in favour of innovations, new generation of technologies and world-class professional excellence. Only leaders having essential traits may be effficacious of initiating and activating the process of innovative developments.

SERVICE STRATEGY

We consider strategy an integrated and coordinated set of commitments and actions designed to exploit our potentials and gain competitive advantage. We also find strategy combination of our competitive efforts and business approaches practised by mangers by showing their professional excellence to please customers, excel competition and accomplish the organisational objectives. Actually, it is a game plan that determines the magnitude of our success. It helps us in touching the target by making use of our potentials in a right way. For the development of an organisation, it is not only sufficient that they are potentially sound but it is also essential that they are strategically profound. In a true sense, we find our resources becoming unproductive, if we lack managerial or professional excellence.

Of late, we find the business environment becoming much more volatile. The magnitude of competition is found moving upward. The organisations getting a success in the formulation and implementation of a sound marketing strategy succeed in excelling competition and becoming a leader. Our strategic moves and approaches and further their effective implementation determine the magnitude of our success. We need professional excellence to formulate a sound strategy and to make possible its time-honoured and cost-effective implementation, it become significant that we have world-class professional excellence.

With due focuses on globalisation, we find service sector considerably contributing to the development process and it is against this backdrop that even in the developing countries like ours we find intensive efforts for the development of this sector. The increasing domination of tertiary sector to development of global economy makes it essential that our strategic decisions related to marketing have an edge over the rivals. It is in this context that we make a strong advocacy in favour of service strategy.

STRATEGIC PLANNING PROCESS

Formulation of a sound strategy requires world-class professional excellence. The marketing professional bearing the responsibility of formulating a sound service strategy need to go through a number of problems as mentioned below:

- Which of the services are to be much more productive?
- What is our business area at present?
- How should we develop our business?
- How should we satisfy our customers/users?
- How should we excel competition?

- What should be our efforts to respond to the changing markets?
- How should we achieve the strategy and financial results?
- How should we manage the financial units?
- How should we manage the functional units?
- How should we build relationships with customers/users?
- How should we build relationship with suppliers?
- How should we satisfy the stakeholders?
- How should we protect and promote social interest?
- How should we strengthen the value-engineering process?
- How should we establish and prove our leadership?

The Steps in Strategic Planning Process

Normally, we find the following steps in the strategic planning process as mentioned in the following Figure.

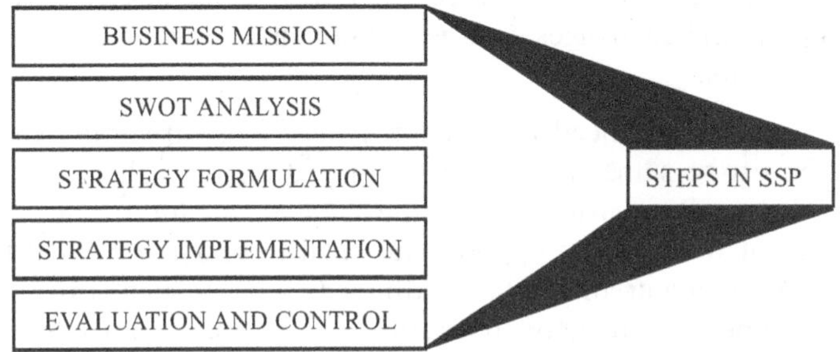

Fig. 2.14: Steps in the Strategic Planning Process

SERVICE MISSION

We find mission a value treatment around which the entire corporate strategy clusters. Of course, it is much more difficult to define the purpose and mission of a business but unless we define it our task remains much more complicated. Our responsibilities related to the setting of objectives, formulation of strategies are found much more complex if we fail in defining our mission. Though we cannot deny that almost all categories of organisations need to justify their existence in the society but it is also essential that professionals serving the organisation keep into consideration the fact that they practice management by performance. A mission statement defines the scope of the business and the long-term vision of an organisation.

A mission statement needs the following:

- Defining aspirations of the concerned organisation.
- Allowing creative growth and disallowing negative ventures.
- Making the organisation distinct to others.
- Evaluating or auditing organisational efforts.
- Ensuring that organisation has been optimally contributing to the social welfare programmes.
- Developing an action plan commensurate with the changing requirements.
- Justifying its existence in the society.

We find two categories of service generating organisations, for example, profit making and non-profit making. And the mission of both of them may be to justify their existence in the society, of course in line with defined motives.

The profit making organisation would make it sure that they create tremendous job opportunities and contribute to the process of social transformation whereas the non-profit making organisations would justify their social existence by protecting and promoting social interests in different forms.

SWOT ANALYSIS

It is essential that an organisation is strong enough to face the multi-faceted challenges in the volatile business environment. The S denotes strength of an organisation focuses our attention on its financial, technological as well as the managerial proficiency. It is very natural that the evaluation of strength of an organisation would be in face of its rivals. The strategic decisions would focus on making an evaluation and enriching the strength. The W denotes for weaknesses and in this context, our focus will be on identifying the deficiencies in relation to finance, technology and management. A number of new generation of technologies are used in the services sector and the organisation depending on traditional technology and manual operations fail in delivering goods. The strategic decisions make it essential that due weightage is given to the measures to be effective in removing the deficiencies. The O represents for opportunities. Of course, we find tremendous opportunities in the service sectors specially after globalisation and an organisation found technologically, financially, managerially proficient has been found capitalising on the opportunities. The strategic decisions need priority attention on identifying the opportunities and capitalising on the same in a right way. A mechanism requires to be developed for that very purpose. The T focuses our attention on threats. Since we find the business environment much more volatile, it is natural that a number of threats and challenges emerge. An organisation found to be stronger would be efficacious of facing the challenges and threats.

The service generating organisations need to prepare a list of its strengths, weaknesses, opportunities and threats. A periodical evaluation of the same would help policy decision-makers in formulating a sound strategy that helps organisation in achieving its mission. It is significant to mention that strengths and weaknesses are related to the internal environment whereas the opportunities and threats are related to the external environment. An organisation may also think in favour of strategic alliances with respect to product or service, promotion, logistics and pricing, creative thinking and innovative efforts. An action plan needs to be designed in the face of emerging trends in the business environment.

FORMULATION OF STRATEGY

Strategy is considered to be a game plan. In the process of formulating a strategy, it is essential that professionals are well aware of the strategic competitiveness. They may get necessary inputs from SWOT analysis. The competitive strategy is found a bit different because in its context we find low-cost provider, differentiation, cost provider and focussed strategies. The professionals bear the responsibility of formulating a strategy.

Low-cost Provider Strategy: Since we find a number of customers much more sensitive to price, the low-cost provider strategy may help service generating organisations in establishing an edge over their rivals. On the basis of cost-effectiveness, the professionals succeed in minimising the cost which makes the price/fee structure affordable to the common masses.

Differentiation Strategy: In the context of service generating organisations, we find differentiation strategy occupying a place of outstanding significance. The strategy focuses on variation in price, keeping in view the customers and their paying capacity. How to make the services distinct so that we find additional attractions is found to be an important functional responsibility before the professionals. Of course, the innovative services considerably help them in the process. The organisations assigning top priority to the research and development activities succeed in activating the process of innovation. Peter F. Drucker suggests that for innovating the business ideas, the seven sources of innovation need due attention of professionals. They are unexpected occurrences, incongruities, process needs, industry and market changes, demographic changes, changes in perception and new knowledge. In this context, Theodre Levitt opines that a powerful new idea becomes ineffective if we find organisations not making efforts for putting ideas to work and a number of organisations fail in transforming the ideas into action. Making the services distinct to the rivals is the main theme that we find in this strategy which provides an organisation smooth ways for becoming an innovator.

Best Cost Provider Strategy: This strategy focuses our attention on making available to the customers the best value of their money. The customers form a perception that they are getting more than they pay. An organisation for successful implementation of this strategy needs to make the services cost-effective and for that they would be required to promote the use of new generation of technology. The operational efficiency, rate of productivity of assets and people are some of the important factors helpful in practising cost economy. We find services a result of different types of costs which may be good or bad. John Carlson talked about good and bad costs. Good costs are found directly productive and very much instrumental in improving the potentials of service generating organisations, e.g., costs on front-line operations, support operations, training, physical goods required for the generation of services and their offerings. We call them good costs because we find them helpful in improving the quality of services. Whatsoever the perception that we find in the minds of customers/users regarding quality can be translated with the help of good costs. On the other hand, we find bad costs responsible for increasing the total costs of services such as costs on operational and administrative routines, too many and too heavy management levels, unnecessary bureaucracy and supervision costs. We also call them evil costs and therefore the professionals need to minimise them to the extent they find it possible.

SERVICE TRIANGLE

Christian Gronross has the creditability of developing one of the most popular strategic models for services marketing which is known as Service Triangle. He identifies three important groups playing a significant role in the accomplishment of organisational goals, e.g., company (top management), employees and customers. Thus, according to the model of Gronross, the formulation of overall marketing strategy for an organisation requires three-dimensional approach. The model makes a strong advocacy in favour of Internal Marketing, External Marketing and Interactive Marketing. This is shown in the following Figure 2.15.

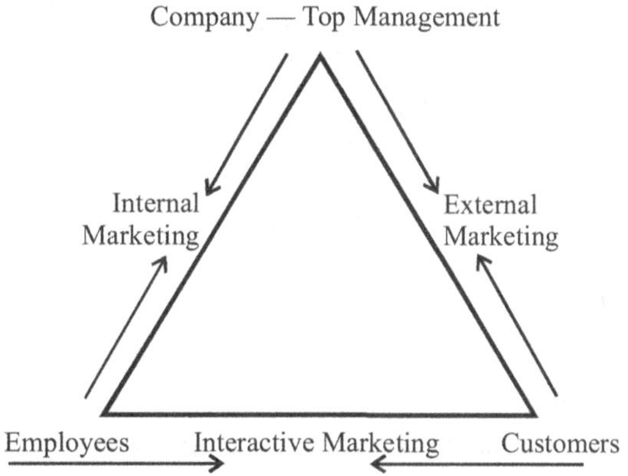

Fig. 2.15: Service Marketing Model

The model suggests development of a special marketing programme for company and its employees which is known as internal marketing. The external marketing programme which is found between the company and its customers. The third marketing programme is between employees and customers.

Internal Marketing: All of us are well aware of the outstanding role of people in an organisation. If we have a team of quality people, our task of accomplishing the organisational goals is considerably simplified even if we find design, system and supportive services not upto the mark. The underlying philosophy in the internal marketing emphasises on the facts an organisation needs to satisfy the people on a priority basis because the working people should be viewed as the first market for the service generating organisation to serve. The top management and the marketing professionals need to make it sure that strategic decisions are very much proactive to the working people. They are to be motivated suitably and for that pay, promotion and packages of other benefits are required to be made much more lucrative. All possible efforts are to be made to promote their morale. If we expect from them high level of efficiency, personal-touch-in-service and a sense of commitment, our focus must be on the motivational factors. A group of satisfied group of people may be successful in protecting and promoting the interests of customers and organisation *pari passu.*

External Marketing: The success of an organisation rests on its customers. The external marketing focuses our attention on reading and understanding the customers in a right fashion. The professionals serving the organisation bear the prime responsibility of developing their awareness of customers. This necessitates an in-depth study of their behavioural profile. The levels of expectations cannot remain static. The increasing flow of information and sophisticated mode of transportation shape the level of expectations provided we find the discretionary income moving upward. If we find marketing professionals well aware of their changing levels of expectations, the portfolio mix of service can be designed in tune with their taste and temperament which would have a proactive response. We cannot negate the fact that customers play a decisive role in the designing of service mix. The service generating organisations cannot undermine their customers. The strategic decisions need to assign top priority to the levels of expectations. If we find customers participating in the process of generation of services, they can evince interests in using them.

Interactive Marketing: Interactive marketing is found based on an interaction between the people and customers. We also call it service encounters. The employees serving an organisation are found well aware of their customers. When we talk about the generation of services, there are a number of forces found instrumental in the process such supporting services, systems, techniques and tangibles. The services process not having an interactive base cannot be proactive. This makes it essential that working people assign due weightage to the customers.

The above-mentioned service triangle helps in the formulation of a sound marketing strategy. The strategic decisions related to the development of an organisation make it essential that tremendous opportunities are created and tapped for the development of an organisation. The strategic decisions related to working employees/people necessitate a dedicated and committed team which cannot be possible unless we find them duly motivated. And finally the strategic decisions related to customers/users focus our attention on quality and cost-effective services commensurate with their changing needs and requirements. Thus, we find model developed by Gronross to be suitable and effective for the service generating organisations.

Formulation of an overall marketing strategy is found significant to the development of an organisation. The model developed by Gronross would help professionals in different ways. Organisational prosperity makes the ways for the protection and promotion of the interests of people and their customers. We consider it a special marketing programme serving the multi-pronged interests.

SUMMARY

In this chapter, you have gone through the key elements of services marketing. Before starting another chapter, be sure that the following facts are well versed:

Service Environment: Servicescapes or Service Environment focus our attention on the style and appearance of the physical surroundings and other experimental elements encountered by customers at the sites where services are delivered.

Service Blueprinting: We find blueprinting a picture or a map portraying the service system so that the providers understand them in a right fashion. It magnifies the process of service delivery, the points of customers/ contact, the role to played by customers and employees and the visible elements of the service.

Demand-Supply Management: It is a managerial process of balancing the demand and supply position, keeping in view the capacity of providers and demand generated by the users. Assessing demand and improving the supply position are the important dimensions. Particularly in the industries having seasonal fluctuation, we find a study of demand and supply position important. The management proficiency helps in removing or minimising the mismatch between the two.

Relationship Management: Studying and understanding customers in a right way is an important consideration in the relationship management. In an age of loyalty-based business, the professionals are supposed to identify the loyal customers for developing relationship for marketing the services.

Relationship Marketing: By relationship marketing, our focus is on the extended relationship with the customers. Database, interaction and networking are the important aspects of relationship marketing. So far as the transactional marketing is concerned, we find the relationship marketing almost non-existent in the very context. Particularly areas where we find exchange of information assuming a place of outstanding significance, the relationship marketing is found relevant. Developing personal relationship is the main theme of relationship marketing. Customer retention is the result found.

Service Recovery: The concept of service recovery is influenced by the theme that "to err is human and to recover divine". We find services recovery an umbrella for systematic efforts by a firm to resolve or correct a problem. Getting complaints and recovering them without making any delay are the steps involved in the process. In the process, the service marketers bear the responsibility of getting the feedback and making service recovery and further to establish appropriate levels of compensation.

Service Expectations: We find customer expectations embracing the desired level and adequate level of service. It is also the predicted level of service. Expectations are considerably influenced by information, transportation and the level of income. The levels of expectations are found fluctuating.

Service Encounter: We also consider service encounter as moment of truth. It is a period of time during we find a direct interaction with the service. This process is adopted for interacting and viewing. We find it a point where promised services are either kept or broken. We also consider it a process for building the perception of customers regarding quality. The customers or users here get an opportunity to have a snap of the quality of services.

Service Quality: A majority of us feel that service quality is more a function of attitude rather than of technology. No doubt that it is now a myth. Quality can be split into technological quality and functional quality and if we synchronies both of them optimally, the desired levels of quality are achieved. Quality is all about fitness for use. In developing the perception of quality, we find customers occupying a central position. Quality constitutes to be an essential element for the existence or prosperity of an organisation.

Service Quality Gap: There are seven types of quality gap such as knowledge gap, standard gap, delivery gap, internal communication gap, perception gap, interpretation gap and service gap. In the gap model of service quality, we find internal and external gap combining all the seven types of gap in the service. The internal gap occurs between different functions and departments within the organisation whereas the external gap is influenced by the external conditions.

SERVQUAL: We find SERVQUAL a scale for measuring the quality of services. The basic theme that we find in the SERVQUAL model is comparison of perception with expectations. It is found applicable to all the service generating organisations. Even in the public sector organisations, we find conceptualisation of SERVQUAL. The real estate brokers, doctors in private practice, the programmes related to public recreation, a tire store, an accounting firm, discount and department stores, gas and electric company, hospitals, banking, dry cleaners, higher education and fast food are the key areas where the SERVQUAL has successfully been implemented.

Development of Service Product: The service product found totally innovative, generated and offered by the company to the globe for the first time and a new experience to both the providing organisations and using customers is called a new service product. The new product moves through different stages such as development of strategy, generation of ideas, screening of ideas, product testing, profitability and feasibility test, service prototype test and test service.

Service Product Branding: Brand has meaning for customers which can be used both at corporate and product levesl. The corporate brand is not only easily recognised but we find its special meaning for the customers. The sub-brands under the umbrella of a corporate brand reflects the values of latter. Branding is found a way doing business. Image is considered to be the totality of the impressions about the brand.

Service Leadership: Leadership works through people and culture. It is to produce useful change. Service leadership requires a special perspective.

Service Strategy: We consider strategy an integrated and coordinated set of commandments and actions designed to exploit our potentials and gain competitive advantage. It is also considered combination of our competitive efforts.

KEY TERMS

Service Environment
Ambient Conditions
Artifacts
High Profile Service Environment
Layouts
Portraying
Front-line or as Support Team
Influx of Tourists
Management of Relationship
Database Marketing
Network Marketing
Customer Portfolio
Personalised Services
Service Recovery Paradox
Service Expectations
Moment of Truth
ATM Services
Kiosk Services
Matador
Gap Model
SERVQUAL
Innovative Product
Service Product Branding
Service Strategy
Service Triangle
Servicescapes
Aesthetic Management
Holistic View
User-friendly Design
Blueprinting
Onstage Technology
Sycro-marketing
Service Capacity
Transactional Marketing
Interactive Marketing
Relationship Marketing
Customer Pyramid
Service Recovery
Empowered Employees
Services Encounter
Remote Encounter
Self-Service Technologies
Bullfighting
Service Quality
Service Quality Audit
Empathy
Front-end and Back-end Planning
Service Leadership
Service Mission

Review Questions

1. What do you mean by Service Environment? Focus on the different dimensions of Service Environment.
2. Explain the designing of service environment with a holistic view and discuss the role of customers in the process of service designing.
3. Explain the concept of Service Blueprinting. Discuss the different steps in building a service blueprint.
4. Do you find service blueprinting important to the services sector? Present arguments in your favour.
5. What do you mean by Sycro-marketing? Explain your role in synchronising demand and explain.
6. How would you manage the marketing mix for managing the demand side. Explain.
7. Write a descriptive note on the management of service capacity.
8. Define Relationship Marketing. Discuss the different types of relationship marketing.
9. Explain the different types of relationships with the viewpoint of customers.
10. Focus on the Customer Pyramid.
11. State and explain the essentials of relationship marketing.
12. Distinguish between Relationship Marketing and Traditional Marketing. What are the different forms of Customer Relationship Management.
13. What do you mean by Service Recovery? Is it a paradox? Comment.
14. Explain the responses of customers to service recovery?
15. What do you mean by effective service recovery? Explain its components.
16. Define Service Expectations. Explain the change playing a constructive role in the formation of expectations.

17. What do you mean by Service Encounters? Discuss the different types of service encounters.
18. Write a note on techno-driven service encounters.
19. Do you find service encounters as moments of truth?
20. Define Service Quality. Explain the importance of quality to the service sector of the economy.
21. Explain the Service Quality Gap Model.
22. Suggest measures to bridge the quality gap. Explain Service Quality Audit.
23. Why do you mean by SERVQUAL? Focus on its various dimensions for measuring service quality.
24. Explain the different stages for the development of new service product.
25. Define Service Leadership. Focus on leadership qualities.
26. Define Service Strategy and explain strategic planning process.
27. Explain the following:
    (a) Service Triangle
    (b) Service Mission
    (c) Internal Marketing
    (d) External Marketing
    (e) Interactive Marketing

Application Exercises

1. As a market professional, focus on the ambient conditions throwing a major impact on the behaviour of customers.
2. Design servicescapes for a Five Star Hotel in Indian Perspective.
3. As a service marketer, throw light on the role of aesthetic management in a hospital.
4. Build a Blueprint for a service sector of your choice.
5. As a marketing professional, you have to manage the demand side. Explain the practises to be followed by you in a service generating organisation of your choice.
6. Explain the relevance of database marketing for the electricity services.
7. Throw light on the essentials for relationship marketing.
8. As a marketing professional, you are not getting any complaint from your customers. Show your reactions.
9. You act as a service marketer in an organisation. Focus on the factors you need to consider in the formation of expectations.
10. In the Insurance business, explain the role of phone encounter.
11. Explain the application of remote encounter in the context of a public sector bank in India.
12. In the capacity of a marketing professional, prescribe measures for bridging the quality gap.
13. You are acting as marketing professionals, in a bank. Practise SERVQUAL for measuring the quality of services.
14. As service marketer, you have to develop a new product for your organisation. Explain the stages you need to cross.
15. Focus on the steps that you need to go through in the Strategic Planning Process.

Endnotes

1. Mary Jo Bitner, "Servicescapes: The Impact of Physical Surroundings on Customers and Employees", *Journal of Marketing*, 56, 1992, pp. 57-71.
2. James A. Russell: A Circumplex Model of Effect, *Journal of Personality and Psychology*, 36/6, 1980, pp. 1161-68.
3. Lovelock Christopher, Jochen Wirtz, *Services Marketing*, 5th Edition, pp. 292-99.
4. Ron Kaufman, *Service Power: Who were They Designing* Its for Newsletter, 2001.
5. Kotler P., Sydney J. Levy, *Demarketing, Yes Demarketing*, HBR, 1971, Nov-Dec, pp. 74-80.
6. Lovelock, *op. cit.*, pp. 267-71.
7. Coviello N.E., Roderick J. Boride and Hugh J. Munro, Understanding Contemporary Marketing Development of a Classification Scheme, *Journal of Marketing Management*, 13/6, 1995, pp. 501-22.

8. Evert Gummesson, *Total Relationship Marketing,* Oxford England Butterworth Heinemann,. 1999, p. 24.
9. David H. Maister, *True Professionalism*, Free Press, NY., 1997.
10. Zeithmal, Rust and Lemon, The Customer Pyramid — Creating and Serving Profitable Customers; *California Management Review,* 43/4, 2001.
11. Theodore Levitt.
12. Oren Harari, Thank Heavens for Complainers, *Management Review,* March, 1997, pp. 25-29.
13. TARP (Technical Assistance Research Programme) Institute, Consumer Complaints Handling.
14. Tor Andreassen: From Disgust to Delight — Do Customers Hold a Grudge?, *Journal of Service Research*, 2001, pp. 39-49.
15. TARP, *op. cit.,*
16. Lovelock, *op. cit.,* p. 32.
17. Zeithmal, *op.cit.,* pp. 102-04.
18. Richard Normann, Services Management; *Strategy and Leadership in Service Businesses*, 2nd Edition, pp.16-17.
19. Jan Carlzon, Moments of Truth; Cambridge, Ballinger, 1987, p. 3.
20. Croby P.B, Quality Without Tears, New America Library, NY., 1984.
21. Juran J.M., Upper Management and Quality; Juran Institute, NY., 1982.
22. Swan and Combs, Product Performance and Customer Satisfaction: A New Concept, *Journal of Marketing,* April, 1976.
23. Gronroos C., A Service Quality Model and its Marketing Implication, *European Journal of Marketing,* Vol. 18/4, pp. 36-4.
24. Zeithmal, *op. cit.,* pp. 532-37.
25. Lovelock, *op. cit.,* pp. 411-13.
26. Gronross C., *op. cit.*
27. Parsuraman, Zeithmal and Berry, Understanding and Improving Service Quality: A Literature Review and Research Agenda.
28. Gerhard Mels, Christo Boshoff and Denon Nel, The Dimensions of Service Quality: The Original European Perspective Revisited, *The Service Industries Journal*, 17/1997 pp. 173-189.
29. Anne M. Smith, Measuring Service Quality: Is SERVQUAL Now Redundant?, *Journal of Marketing Management,* 117/1995.
30. John P. Kotter, *What Leaders Really Do?*, Boston: Harvard Business School Press, 1999, pp. 10-11.
31. *Ibid.*
32. Warren Bennis and Burt Nanus, On Great Service, 9.
33. Leonard L. Berry, *Discovering the Soul of Service*, The Free Press, NewYork, 1999, p. 44.

★★★

MANAGEMENT OF SERVICES MARKETING

"The marketing mix philosophy implies that there is an optimal mix of the four factors for a given market segment at a given point of time. Because services are usually produced and consumed simultaneously; the customers often look for tangible. The expanded submixes of marketing thus draw our attention."

Chapter Objectives

Introduction – Marketing Mix: The Concept – The Product Mix – Levels of Product – Product Line – Product Development – Proactive Process – Reactive Process – Developing a Package – Product Attractiveness – Promotion Mix – Components of Promotion Mix – Advertising – Publicity – Sales Promotion – Personal Selling – Word-of-mouth Promotion – Telemarketing – Cause-related and Sponsorship Marketing – Price Mix – Place Mix – Expanded Mix for Services Marketing – Process – Physical Evidence and Attractiveness – People – Capacity Planning – Capacity Scheduling – Internal Marketing – External Marketing – Interactive Marketing – Summary – Key Terms – Review Questions – Application Exercises – Endnotes.

Learning Objectives

This chapter aims at clarifying the managerial process for marketing services. The formulation of a sound marketing mix is considered essential and the service marketers need to develop their awareness of all the submixes of marketing such as the Product Mix, Promotion Mix, Price Mix, Place Mix, Process, Physical Evidence and Attractions and People. The problems like capacity planning, internal marketing, external marketing and interactive marketing have also been discussed here to enrich the knowledge bank of marketing professionals. The motive of this chapter is to clarify the basics in the formulation of a sound marketing mix.

INTRODUCTION

Emerging national economic scenario is the gift of services sector which has significantly contributed to the process of national economic transformation. We have tremendous opportunities for the development of services sector and therefore our professional excellence must be of global standard. On the one hand, we have to pave avenues for the development of traditional services sector while on the other hand we also need to develop the partially tapped or untapped areas like tourism, consultancy, courier, mass communication, retail, IT, Automobile, portfolio management, mutual funds and hotel. In an age of material culture considered dominated by technicul-ture, we find high level of temptation for materialistic gains. We earn more and need new avenues to spend more. The burgeoning middle class has been found considerably contributing to the development of consumerism. The race will have high level of pace which would engineer a sound foundation for the development of service-based national economy.

It is against this background that the service marketers require world-class professional excellence so that the existent opportunities are capitalised on and the benefits of economic development are ploughed back for reverberating the development process. Managerial proficiency in the world of marketing makes it essential that a sound marketing mix is formulated in which extended submixes need due weightage. The four Ps of marketing and the additional three extended Ps if well synchronised with professional touch and holistic approach would be much more result-oriented. The marketing professionals need to develop their excellence in right processing, time-honoured processing, decent processing so that the promised services are made available to them. The physical soundness of a place where the services are created and delivered. Innovative and creative atmosphere making the service environment much more productive. The quality marketing professionals commensurate with the changing global requirements or say Process Mix, Physical Evidence and Attractions and People need priority attention in this volatile business environment. A fair synchronisation of all the seven marketing mixes requires the services of world-class professionals.

Managerial proficiency bears the efficacy of changing the negatives into positives. Against this background, we find management of marketing activities occupying a place of outstanding significance. New mixes are to be incorporated, innovative strategies for marketing are to formulated and the world-class marketing professionals are to be given an opportunity to prove their excellence. In the changing global economic order, we have a large number of potential customers. The service marketers need to test their innovation efforts. Service leadership is the motive. Social interest is the mission. Organisational prosperity is the target.

The management of marketing activities assumes a place of outstanding significance since the development of marketing resources is substantially influenced by the quality of management. If we use world-class expertise to develop the marketing resources, the results are, of course, to be proactive. We are well aware of the fact that there are a number of service generating organisations engaged in offering the services but only a few of them have been found successful in offering the world-class services. The rate of profitability is also found disappointing in a majority of the cases mainly due to the development of poor quality of marketing mixes. This speaks of the fact that we need professional excellence while developing the marketing resources since the market is competitive and expectations of users can't remain static. It is against this background that we need to assign due weightage to the formulation of marketing mix.

In almost all the organisations either producing goods or generating services, the formulation of product mix occupies an important place. The product mix for the services sector draws our attention on the services to be offered to the users. Generally, we find two types of services such as the core services and the peripheral services. The core services are directly related to our promises for which the users are charged. But the peripheral services add attractions to our service mix and provide to us an opportunity to establish an edge over the competitors. It is in this context that the service generating organisations need a strong emphasis on the blending of the core and peripheral services in such a way that their service mix is found very much instrumental in excelling competitions. This draws our attention on the formulation of a sound product mix. It is natural that in the very context the marketers are well aware of the emerging changes in the level of expectations of prospects/users so that the inclusion, elimination processes are carried on in a right fashion. It is professional excellence that would help in designing a sound product portfolio in which different types of services/schemes would be given due place in the face of present and future conditions. While formulating a sound service mix, there are a number of factors to be given weightage but of all the factors, we find quality of services deserving top ranking position.

It is only not sufficient that we offer quality services. It is much more impact generating that our prospects/users come to know that they are using the world-class services. This is found significant to build service aspirations. This focuses our attention on the second important mix of the marketing mix known as the promotion mix. There are a number of components to be managed properly in the very context, such as the advertisement, publicity, sales promotion, personal selling, word-of-mouth promotion and the latest one, the telemarketing. The professionals bearing the responsibility of formulating a sound promotion mix are supposed to use the different components in such a way that projection of a positive image is made possible.

The pricing decisions are found a challenging task since the customers in general are found sensitive to price. Like the goods manufacturing organisations, the service generating organisations are also supposed to make the process cost-effective so that they are in a position to use pricing as a motivational tool. The formulation of a sound pricing strategy thus is found significant in the very context which requires professional excellence.

The placement decisions become significant with the viewpoint of making available the promised services to the users in a decent way. We can't negate that a gap between the services-promised and services-offered is to jeopardise our all efforts to offer the quality services. Of course, we don't find delivery of services like the delivery of goods but the people bearing the responsibility of making available the services to the ultimate users play here an incremental role. The policy makers and senior executives make provisions for generating the world-class services but the indecent behaviour of employees responsible to offer the services may turn all their efforts into a fiasco. This draws our attention on managing people in a right way so that the services are offered in a decent way. The location of service generating organisations also becomes significant and therefore, the policy makers and the senior executives need to assign an overriding priority to the problem of location.

The aforesaid facts make it clear that formulation of a sound marketing mix is an important problem and the organisations assigning due weightage to employee orientation succeed in getting efficient professionals who make the ways for performance orientation. It is important to mention that the formulation of a sound marketing mix is an ongoing process because we don't find any limit to perfection. The changing market conditions and the increasing expectations of customers make it essential that we perform the responsibility of innovating the mixes much earlier than our competitors. This necessitates more frequency in the innovation process and only the efficient personnel can make it possible.

The senior executives are required to be vigilant to have a correct picture of their potentials. It is natural that in a competitive market, the organisations either producing goods or generating services need to analyse their strength in the face of changing prospects and increasing threats. This draws our attention on capacity planning. Unless we know about the quality and volume of strength required to counter the challenges and threats, our efforts can't be proactive. If we study and understand the market in a right fashion, it becomes easier to assess our own strength. Not only this, it also helps us in assessing the strength of our competitors. This simplifies the process of increasing the potentials and excelling the competition. It is against this background that capacity planning plays a decisive role in the formulation of marketing mixes. This chapter of the book studies two problems, such as the formulation of a sound marketing mix and the capacity planning. The formulation of marketing mix would be in the face of changing market conditions. The study of capacity planning would focus on "Strength". The formulation of an ideal plan for increasing the strength would be the focal point of discussion. As and when we talk about planning, the formulation process requires the support of a well developed information system. This makes a strong advocacy in favour of technology-driven marketing information system.

MARKETING MIX — THE CONCEPT

Under the product, we include both — goods as well as the services with the prime motto of satisfying the customers/users. The marketers are supposed to make sincere efforts for merchandising customer benefit and services with the help of customer-oriented marketing decisions. This draws our attention on the formulation of a sound marketing mix. Like the goods manufacturing organisations even the service generating organisations are required to formulate market-oriented programmes and policies. The more innovative the service mix, the more proactive are the results. The formulation of a sound marketing mix requires professional excellence. At the outset, it is essential that we go through the concept of marketing mix.

The term 'Marketing Mix' was first introduced by Prof. Neil H. Borden of the Harvard Business School.[1] Both the term and concept have since been adopted throughout the world. In the initial stage of industrialisation, a company fixed its production facilities at first and then adjusted all other functional activities around it. A number of authorities realised that marketing is something that takes place after the manufacture of product. With the passage of time, we find rapid industrialisation which paved avenues for the inclusion of a number of products in the latest product. Thus, the stress could no longer be confined to manufacturing and gradually we find development of service generating organisations. The conceptual framework of marketing mix has been designed by different experts in different ways but the perception by and large is the same. Kotler, Keeley and Lazar, Davar and many others have gone through the term, but all of them agree that it is a fair combination of product mix, promotion mix, price mix and the place mix. The ultimate goal of different mixes is to deliver standard goods or services to the customer/users. The product mix includes product line and quality, brand, packaging and services. The promotion mix includes, advertising, public relations, sales promotion, word-of-mouth promotion, personal selling and telemarketing. The price mix includes strategic decisions related to the use of pricing as an operational as well as a motivational tool. The place mix includes the distribution processes or say, a study of the distribution channel. All these mixes help management in making and innovating the marketing decisions. These four elements make up what is commonly known as the marketing mix or the four Ps. The elements of the marketing mix can be combined in different ways just as the ingredients of a cake can be varied in different recipes as shown in Figure 3.1.

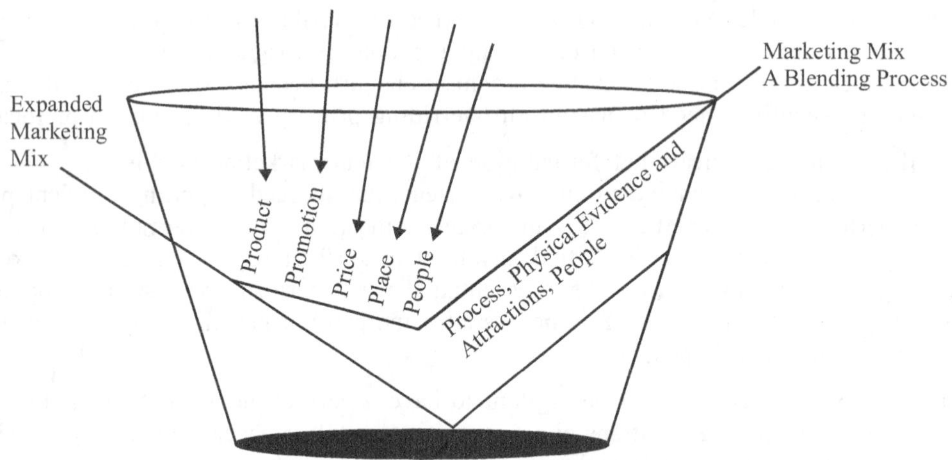

Fig. 3.1: Formulation of Marketing Mix

In recent years, some authors have suggested that the four Ps should be extended to include other aspects of marketing such as packaging. Whilst the case for factors such as packaging is less clear-cut, there is a growing body of support for the inclusion of People as fifth P. The standard of customer service provided is increasingly recognised as a key factor in determining a company's success or failure. Authors like Peters and Waterman pinpointed the way in which a company's employees behave as the main factor distinguishing their successful American companies — a finding that has since been confirmed in almost all parts of the world.

In the formulation of different ingredients, the professional excellence of marketers plays a significant role. It is essential that different decision-making areas are studied carefully and the required changes are incorporated optimally so that the marketing decisions are found of quality.

While formulating the product mix, the marketers bear the responsibility of introducing a new product, deleting old product line, modifying the product design, changing the packaging and improving the product specification. Since we go through the marketing of services, it is pertinent that our efforts keep into consideration the blending of core and peripheral services in the mix. Your professional excellence is coiled in the essence of making the peripheral services distinct so that you succeed in using the same as a motivational tool. It is not meant that you underestimate the core services. You are supposed to be careful that your core services are of world-class.

In the context of promoting your services, it is pertinent that the promotional measures are found efficacious in informing and sensing the customers. The more innovative the promotional measures, the more productive would be your efforts to persuade the customers/users. The different components of promotion, such as advertising, publicity, sales promotion, word-of-mouth promotion, personal selling and telemarketing need due attention. By offering the quality services, you make efforts to build a positive image and by enriching the promotional measures you make sincere efforts to project a positive image.

The pricing decisions become significant because the users in general are found sensitive to price. The strategic decisions related to pricing help you in using pricing as an operational as well as a motivational tool. This necessitates that your efforts are cost-effective and economy is maintained at different stages of offering the services. You are required to avoid a stage like price war.

The placement decision focuses on the distribution processes you follow to make available the services to the ultimate users. The decisions related to the point of location also become significant in the very context.

The decisions regarding people become important since quality services can't be offered if the employees serving your organisation lack dedication, commitment and personal-touch-in-service.

THE PRODUCT MIX

We are well aware of the fact that services product are found of intangible nature. In addition, we also find the services product perishable which make it essential that the marketers show their world-class excellence while formulating the product mix. The standard of living is substantially influenced by the level of income. If we find positive trends in the level of disposable and discretionary incomes, the demand for the use of different types of services is found increasing. This is due to the fact that when we earn more, we like to spend more. This makes it essential that almost all the service generating organisations are familiar with the emerging trends in the level of incomes. The sophistication in the process of communications also appears to be a dominating factor since the telecast media in particular make effective efforts to change the lifestyles *vis-a-vis* the needs and requirements. The quality of services in a hotel is considerably influenced by the quality of users. The line of services offered for the personal care are found influenced by professionalism in education and multiculturism in which we find transverse section of the society and their culture dominating our needs and requirements. The product mix of the financial services or to be more specific the banking services depends substantially upon the emerging trends in the business environment and the governmental regulations. The consultancy services are governed by the consciousness of the business markets to use the innovative technologies and expertise for getting the productive results. The entertainment services and their line of product depend upon the location of services and qualitative developments in the related area. The transportation services are influenced by emerging trends in the industrialisation, urbanisation and lifestyles. In this way, the different categories of services require due weightage on some of the selected components while formulating the product mix.

We can't negate the fact that strategies for designing or framing the product mix determine the magnitude of success, intensity of profit and level of satisfaction to the customers. In the case of personal care services, the taste, temperament and lifestyles play a dominating role. The beauty parlours in the Indian context are found influenced by the western culture and therefore we find western hairstyles and use of cosmetics gaining popularity. The beauty parlours interested in innovating their product mix may prefer to promote the Indian culture by promoting Indian hairstyle, long hair culture, use of herbals, minimising the use of cosmetics with more side-effects and so on. In respect of hotel services, we find the product mix substantially influenced by international trade relations, cultural exchange, development of corporate culture, emphasis on convention industry or so. The marketers thus bear the responsibility of formulating a sound product mix and at the same time, they also need to make innovation an ongoing process by making possible frequency and consistency. The leading service generating organisations prefer to innovate their services much earlier than the dominating competitors. This makes their marketing efforts productive. We can't deny the fact that successful new products substantially command the higher profit margins than the products found at the stage of maturity or stagnation. Generally, the new services are found profitable at least for a while since it takes sufficient time for the competitors to come up with their own products, enter the market and compete.

This makes it pertinent that the service generating organisations minify, magnify, combine and modify the existing services and formulate a package to suit and meet the needs and requirements of customers. In a competitive market, the task of selling profitably is found difficult because by and large almost all the service generating organisations offer the core services of identical nature. Here, it is important to mention that the formulation of an innovative package, or launching of a new product provide profitable opportunities to capitalise on. It is not to be forgotten that the customers buy the solution to their problems, not the goods or services such as the customers buy nutrition;

not bread; beauty; not cosmetic; warmth; not fuel oil, bill-paying conveniences; not cheques or credit cards, risk; not insurance, pleasure and adventure; not tour or so. The service generating organisations while formulating the product mix need to think over these problems on a priority basis.

The important dimensions to be given due consideration while making the product decisions are the development and introduction of new product, deleting or eliminating the old product, modifying the old product, improving the product specification and making continuous efforts to develop world-class product. Here, it is significant that the marketers study the product life cycle and identify the emerging trends. The new product requires invention and innovations *vis-a-vis* the intensive research. The service generating organisations bear the responsibility of studying and understanding the emerging trends in the product life cycle which is the result of the changing trends in demand. We can't negate the fact that the professional excellence of marketers is coiled in the essence of identifying the emerging trends and declaring their product obsolete much earlier than their competitors. Innovative services are found expensive but the prospects are found tempted to the use of new services which help in creating demand and earning profits. Since the innovation processes are found expensive, the service generating organisations in general prefer to modify or formulate a package. It is important to mention that the professionals are supposed to take a decision regarding innovation or modification in the face of the emerging trends in the market *vis-a-vis* the product life cycle. We don't find any limit to quality upgradation. Sky is the limit for qualitative transformation. This makes it essential that the service generating organisations interested in increasing their market share and planning for establishing leadership make continuous efforts to set a new standard by initiating the process of quality upgradation. The organisations believing in making things happen by intensifying research and offering new product get a success. This makes it impact generating that the service generating organisations are well aware of the changing needs and requirements, likes and dislikes, lifestyles and make the marketing decisions accordingly.

We accept the fact that the designing of a sound product portfolio is the prime responsibility of a professional. Our emphasis is here on the fact that the marketers are also supposed to be responsible for including different types of services in the mix found at different stages of the product life cycle so that a crisis-like situation is averted. It is not your wisdom that you earn more profits today but present a very disappointing result tomorrow. This necessitates that in the product portfolio, you have shown your excellence by blending the product with existing and future potentials.

A sound product portfolio makes the ways for a positive response *vis-a-vis* ensures the future.

What to diffuse and what to include; How much to diffuse and how much to include; When to diffuse and When to include are some of the important decision-making areas testifying the professional excellence of marketers. It is not only sufficient that we innovate; it is not only significant that we declare our product obsolete; indeed it is much more impact generating that we have selected an opportune moment for performing our defined responsibilities. A sound product portfolio is essential but its process of constitution is difficult. An organisation with a sound product portfolio gets a conducive business environment and succeeds in increasing the sensitivity of the marketing decisions. The service generating organisations also need to design a sound product portfolio which helps them in getting a positive response in the market not only at present but also in future. This draws our attention on portfolio analysis which can help an organisation in identifying those services or schemes which need additional efforts to improve the quality of results. In addition, it is also significant that the organisations are well aware of the schemes or services performing badly. This helps them in eliminating the services or in innovating the promotional efforts.

LEVELS OF PRODUCT

An important decision-making area in the formulation of a sound product mix is related to the level of product. The levels of product help marketers in knowing the details about the product to incorporate necessary changes in the product as a whole. Kotler[2] has divided the level into five parts as shown in Figure 3.2. The levels are core product, generic product, expected product, augmented product and potential product.

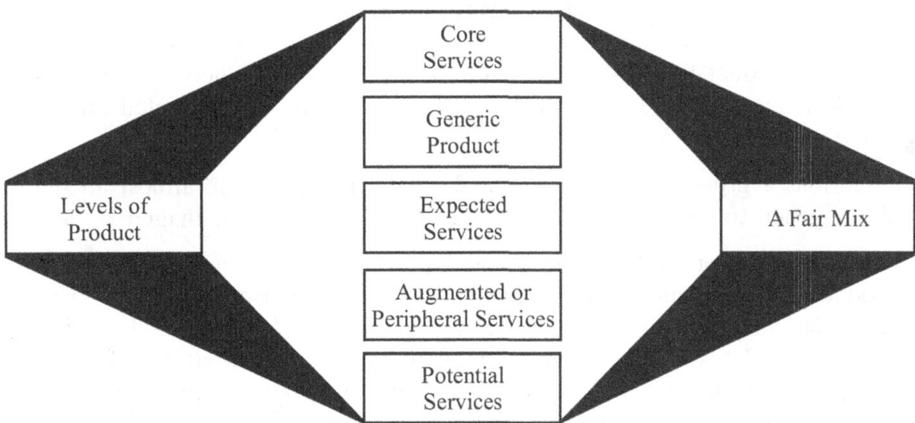

Fig. 3.2: Levels of Product

Core Product: About the core product or services, it is said that core product is what the buyer is really buying. If we talk about the banking services, the core product is the service that you are really buying. In the hotel services, the core product is a room where you stay. In the aviation services, the core product is the seat made available to you in the aircraft.

Generic Product: The marketers are supposed to turn the core benefit into generic product also known as the basic version of the product. The supermarkets and most of the departmental stores are found selling generic product. We also call it the basic product.

Expected Product: This is the product with features which have developed over a period of time shaping the standard specification. In the expected product, we find the minimum requirements which the customers expect from you. In the banking services; the customers expect quick transaction, in the aviation services the users like safe and fast service, in the consultancy services, the clients like world-class expertise, in the insurance services, the users expect safety and security.

Augmented Product: The augmented product is additional attraction which is with the motto of establishing an edge over the competitive firms. Of late in almost all the services, we find the concept of augmented product helping marketers in making the marketing efforts proactive. We also call it the peripheral services. The peripheral services helps substantially in motivating the users/prospects since by and large almost all the service generating organisations offer identical core services.

This makes it clear that more innovative or creative the peripheral services, more responsive would be the marketing efforts. A fair blending of core and peripheral services is possible when the marketers are found professionally sound.

Potential Product: Almost all the organisations are found instrumental in unlocking the full potentials by discovering new ways of attracting and holding customers/users. If the banking organisations start operation on Sunday or in night shift, if they start paying interest on the current account deposits, the available potentials are tapped.

In view of the above, it is right to mention that the marketers are supposed to know the different levels of product since this helps them in developing, modifying, altering, preparing a package or so. Almost all the organisations need to blend the core and peripheral services optimally and this requires an in-depth study of the levels of product. The service generating organisations also need to know the competitors' strategies and to formulate an attractive package. A study of the levels of product thus helps marketers in many ways. The motive is to formulate a fair mix which simplifies the task of getting a positive response. It is in this context that we find the levels of product occupying a place of outstanding significance. Your professionalism right from the core services to the augmented and potential services determines the magnitude of success. Of late, we find the intensity of competition at its peak and this makes it essential that the service generating organisations make sincere efforts to understand the instrumentality of the changing level of product. The five levels of product as shown in Figure 3.2 make it clear that the product levels ultimately help in formulating a fair product mix. In addition to other aspects, the marketers need to know and understand the levels of product so that they succeed in tapping the available potentials optimally. The untapped or partially tapped potentials make your marketing resources unproductive.

PRODUCT LINE

Kotler says about the product line, 'A product line is a group of products that are closely related because they perform a similar function, are sold to the same customer groups, are marketed through the same channels or make up a particular price range.'[3]

In the product line thus a group of product is found impact generating in almost all the organisations either manufacturing goods or generating services. Each product line is usually managed by a different executive.

The managers managing the product line need two types of information — first, they must know the sales and profits of each product in the line and second, they must know how their product line compares with competitors' product line. He/she is also supposed to know the percentage of total business and profits contributed by each item in the line. In addition, he/she is also required to review that how and in what way the product line is positioned against the product line of competitors. The decision regarding the length is also found essential which focuses on an optimal product line length. It is natural that the product lines tend to lengthen over time. Thus, a number of decisions draw our attention when we talk about the product line.

Like the goods manufacturing organisations, the service generating organisations also need to manage their product line. As and when we find organisations incorporating a number of services or schemes in the product line, the customers get additional attractions and are found motivated. It is against this background that we find the service generating organisations exploring avenues for the inclusion of a number of schemes or services benefiting the customers of the same group. It is the professional excellence of managers that determines the quality of services or schemes to be included in the product line. The strategic planners are supposed to know the properties to be instrumental in establishing an edge over the services or schemes of their competitors. They are also required to know the results of items included in the line earlier. The policy planners need to forecast the latest developments in the area with the help of senior executives and are required to incorporate necessary changes in the items or schemes to be included in the product line. The executives bear the responsibility of implementing the scheme or selling the services to the users. The positioning of product line is found significant which requires an in-depth knowledge of competitors' product line. The positioning strategy helps executives in many ways. He/she is supposed to know about the results and to communicate the same to the senior executives. In addition, a time-to-time analysis of the results of new schemes or services also looks pertinent to get the desired results.

The aforesaid facts make it clear that the product line is an important decision-making area to be more specific when we talk about the formulation of product mix. The marketing information system simplifies the task of executives while making an analysis of the results of items included in the product line. Since we are supposed to know about the strategy of dominating competitors, the task of formulating a sound product strategy is simplified considerably. This makes it essential that the organisations attempt to have a sound product line which make their marketing resources productive.

PRODUCT DEVELOPMENT

Development of product is an ongoing process. Today, we declare one product obsolete and right from today itself, we start the process of launching a new product. Almost all the organisations interested in thriving prefer to declare their product obsolete much earlier than their competitors. The service generating organisations also need to make efforts to develop new services with the prime motto of adding attractions. We also find organisations developing a package by combining different services and schemes. By minifying, magnifying, combining and modifying; the service generating organisations design a package which caters to the changing needs and requirements of customers. We agree with the view that the frequency in the development of a new product is considerably influenced by the changing needs and requirements of customers *vis-a-vis* the increasing intensity of competition. This makes it essential that the executives serving the organisation are well aware of the recent developments in market conditions. Generally, we find two processes followed for the development of product as shown in Figure 3.3. The first process is known as proactive because in the said process, the needs of the target market are anticipated and highlighted. The second process is reactive and in this context, the service generating organisations respond to the expressed needs of the target.

Proactive Process

In the proactive process, we find development of product to the changing market needs. This makes it essential that executives are familiar with the changing needs of the target market. There are six stages for the development of product in the proactive process as explained below.

1. Idea Generation: A constant supply of idea is needed to keep on moving the process of product development. For a product that fails at a particular stage, the process may require to revert back to an earlier stage, i.e., beginning with a new idea. The idea for new products come almost from anywhere. The customers and employees help an organisation substantially in the generation of a new idea. In a true sense, we find the front-line staff as the 'eyes and ears' of an organisation. Being a direct contact with the customers, they of course are found in a sound position to recommend improvements to the product. Most importantly, they can identify the potential gap in the market where the needs of customers are yet to be satisfied. The well established organisations are found conducting research for that very purpose since they have an independent wing for intensifying research.

2. Product Concept Screening: This is the second stage in which we find screening of product concept. The aim of the screening process is to narrow down the list of the idea generated to a small number of concepts which are further worth investigating. Some of the product ideas are found shifted out since they are considered inappropriate to the existing potentials and weaknesses of an organisation. Once a product concept is considered serious, the service generating organisations may carry out value engineering study to weed out products which might be impractical or uneconomic.

3. Assessing the Market Potentials: The next stage in the process is to assess the market potentials. The marketing department is found responsible for this at the apex level. The executives can estimate the market potentials. Assessing the market potentials is found significant to minimise the intensity of risk *vis-a-vis* to formulate a sound product mix.

4. Product Cost Analysis: The next stage in the process is to analyse the cost which helps an organisation in knowing the results of cost-benefit analysis. This includes different types of financial involvement in the services/ schemes to be developed and the benefits the organisations would get from the same.

5. Test Marketing: This is a stage just before the final launching of the product which is found essential to minimise the risk element. If we launch a new scheme in the market, without knowing the test result, the intensity of risk is likely to be high. Such a test is to be conducted in a segment in which we find potential customers/ prospects in a good number. The main thing in the process is to select a responsive market and to seek the co-operation of dedicated and value-based researchers.

6. Final Launch: This is the final stage where we find launching or introduction of a new product. Once a product is found successful in the test market, the necessary preparations are made for its final launching.

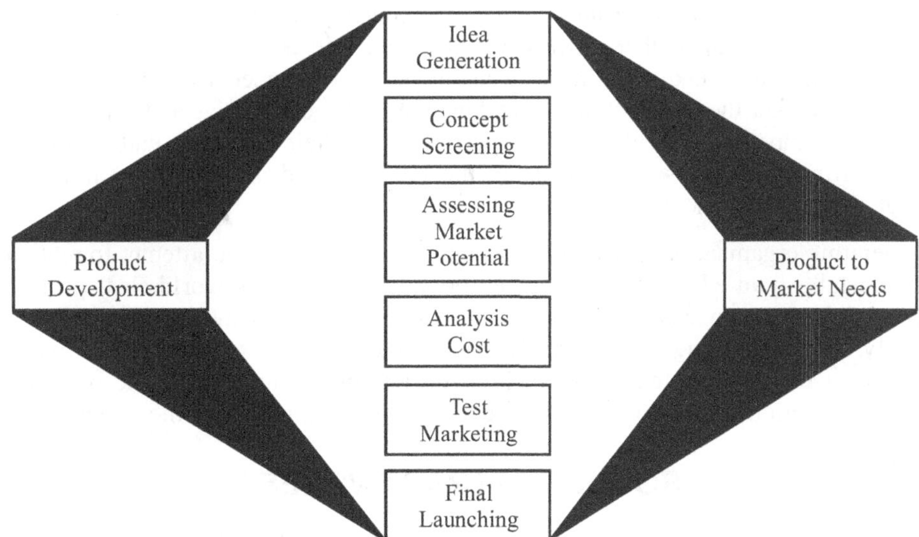

Fig. 3.3: Product Development

Reactive Process

In the reactive process, the service generating organisations are supposed to respond to the expressed needs of the target and therefore, we also call it market needs to product. The different development processes are explained below:

1. Need Identification: This is the first stage in which we find identification of needs. The process draws our attention on the identification of market needs. It is natural that needs can't remain static and therefore for introducing a new scheme or service, we find it essential to identify the emerging trends in the market.

2. Size of the Market: Before we develop, it is essential that we have an idea of the size of the market for which the product is to be developed. This would let the executives know the details regarding the development programme with the motto of rating the capacity.

3. Cost-benefit Analysis: This stage is related to the cost-benefit analysis. The service generating organisations here are supposed to know the involvement of finance in the introduction of new services or schemes and in addition also to assess the demand in the market.

4. Introduction: This is the final stage where we find introduction of the product which is already developed. We also call the process launching or final commercial launching.

The aforesaid processes are found essential to develop, modify, change the services or schemes to be developed by the service generating organisations. The development of a product is an ongoing process and the professionals bear the responsibility of identifying a suitable time for the same.

DEVELOPING A PACKAGE

In the formulation of a sound product mix, it is important that the organisations also think about developing a sound package because it is not possible to develop the new product frequently and more so, we don't find it a commercially viable proposition. The term 'packaging' focuses here on the formulation of an effective mix of different services and schemes which is efficacious in attracting the customers/users. We can't negate that the development of an effective or attractive package requires professional excellence and therefore, the executives serving an organisation bear the prime responsibility of understanding the preferences of customers/users and to design a package in tune with their changing taste and temperament. What the package should basically be or do for the particular target is found significant. We are aware of the fact that a number of schemes and services are included in the service mix and it is quite natural that all the services are not preferred by all the customers. This makes it essential that the executives have an in-depth knowledge of the changing needs and requirements of customers/users of different segments. The motive is to influence them. The tourist organisations, the banking organisations, the transport organisations and albeit others are found developing a package to tap the market potentials. The importance of packaging thus can't be undermined considering the functions it performs in attracting and satisfying the customers. In addition to other aspects, we also find it instrumental in creating the market potentials since a number of users/customers take a positive decision being influenced by the outstanding properties of a package. The executives here bear the responsibility of making the package attractive and competitive. This necessitates a study of the emerging competitors, identifying the properties of their package, understanding the preferences of customers, incorporating the necessary changes in the package and offering the same to the customers in a decent way and at the right moment.

The service generating organisations thus with the help of a sound package attempt to motivate the customers. They are supposed to establish an edge over the competitors and this requires world-class professional excellence. The combinational of different services, schemes in one package act as a motivation tool, if the professionals perform it intelligently. The main thing is to make the package attractive *vis-a-vis* competitive. It is an important component of the product mix and the executives while formulating or innovating the mix need to know about the same. It is right to mention that an ideal package succeeds in minimising the promotion budget.

PRODUCT ATTRACTIVENESS

We accept the fact that the task of selling is found more difficult to be more specific when the market is found competitive. The professional excellence of executives plays here an incremental role. At the same time, it is also impact generating that services generated and offered are of world-class which succeed in establishing an edge over the services of competitors. This makes it essential that the professionals show their excellence in adding attractiveness to their service mix. In a true sense, the customers don't buy the goods or services or the core product but the package or the benefits of the package made available to them. The service generating organisations work with the twin objectives in mind — conveying the benefits of the core services and projecting a product difference with the services offered by their competitors.[4] Thus, the main task is to make the services attractive. It is against this background that the service generating organisation need to devise ways that how and in what way the services included or to be included in the mix can be made attractive. We agree with this view that strategically, the core services are the prime benefit that the customers seek from the provider. The core service often becomes a commodity as a service industry matures. The customers expect that the service generating organisations are sound enough to provide the world-class core services for which they are charged. The result is that the peripheral services often become the way through which we inject attractiveness to our services and scheme and thus succeed in winning the heart of customers. The more attractive the services we offer, the more easy the process of sensitising the prospects/customers. We should not forget that the key dimension to service quality is reliability which is the ability to perform as promised. It is also responsiveness which is meant the willingness to help customers and to provide prompt service. It is security which is meant freedom from risk. It is a combination of a number of benefits which is meant product attractiveness. It is a combination of a number of benefits which is meant as attractive package.[5] Thus, the task is to make the services attractive and this is possible when we make our services different to others by incorporating the outstanding properties. It is in this context that we focus on some of the properties or features helping the organisations substantially in making the services attractive *vis-a-vis* competitive.

1. Enrich the peripheral services: We find a number of service generating organisations concentrating on the core services resulting from which we find the peripheral services neglected. The organisations enriching their peripheral services thus succeed in attracting the customers. This makes it essential that the service generating organisations make innovative efforts to enrich their peripheral services and simplify the task of winning the heart of customers.

2. Understanding the service quality expectations: In almost all the service generating organisations, we consider it to be an important force to sensitise the impulse of customers/prospects. The expectations of customers can't remain static. The innovative services of the leading organisations help in shaping and reshaping the expectations which change the perception of standard specification or quality. It is impact generating that the professionals bear the capacity of understanding the expectations and to make efforts to improve the quality.

Like the goods manufacturing organisations, they are also required to promote the principle of making things happen, which makes an advocacy in favour of creating a quality gap by momentising the process of innovation. Innovation makes the ways for attraction.

3. An overriding priority to the behavioural profile: Making the services attractive is an art that in addition to the quality that you develop also requires decent way of offering the services. This makes it essential that we assign due weightage to the behavioural profile of customers and intensify efforts to make available to the providers an in-depth knowledge of behavioural management. Of course, a majority of the service generating organisations hardly incorporate this dimension of the mix while offering the services. There is no doubt in it that you bear the responsibility of offering the world-class services but at the same time you are also supposed to offer the same in a decent way. Your behaviour, dialogues, approaches, attitudes and more so your empathy play an incremental role in transforming the negative into positive. Maybe that your customers are aggressive, short-tempered; may be that regulations and laws are making your task a bit difficult but you should not forget that your behaviour while dealing with the customers occupies a place of outstanding significance.

4. Take the support of information technologies: Being a professional, you bear the responsibility of making your service mix attractive and this makes it essential that you promote the use of technologies helping you in serving the customers/users fantastically. The well established service generating organisations have been found using technologies for different purposes, such as billing machines, computers for filing and documentation, tele-marketing to make the services convenient, credit-debit machines used by a few of the banking organisations, ATMs by the banks for fast services or so. By using technologies, they serve the customers in many ways and at the same time also keep their records crystal clear. The use of fax machines, e-mail, internet services help them substantially in dealing with the large-sized customers. We can't deny the fact that the use of technologies simplifies your task of building and projecting a fair image.

5. Product for all: Of late, we find nucleus marketing gaining popularity in the business world. We talk about the attractiveness in the services-offered. Your service mix should assign due weightage to the customers of different age groups and both sexes representing a family. If some of the services are for youths, we also find some of the services for kids and teens. If some of the services are for women, we also find some of the services are for men. If some of the services are for affluents; we also find some of the services for poor sections. Thus, you promote the concept of nucleus marketing and get an opportunity to tap the available total market potentials. It is essential that you are well aware of the changing needs and requirements of the different sections/ segments and formulate a service mix that subserves the interests of all.

The aforesaid properties if incorporated in your service mix optimally, would provide to you ample profitable opportunities to tap on. Your services would be distinct to your competitors and the customers would conveniently be motivated. Attraction simplifies promotion.

PROMOTION MIX

The second important submix of the marketing mix is found instrumental in informing, sensing and persuading the prospects/customers. The marketers bear the responsibility of using the different components of promotion in such a way that the measures adopted for promoting the goods or services are found productive. The promotion communicates to customers information on the other elements of marketing mix, such as product, pricing and place. The advantage of product itself, details on the place through which it is sold and details on the pricing are transmitted through promotion. We can't negate the fact that more creative the promotional measures, more proactive we find our sensitising efforts. Creativity is found to be an integral part of communication. It is against this background that we find even the service generating organisations very much instrumental in using the different components of promotion. We go through the different components of the promotion mix as shown in Figure 3.4.

Fig. 3.4: Components of the Promotion Mix

Advertising

Advertising is a paid form of persuasive promotion since we find it playing an effective role in informing and sensing the customers. The creativity is found to be an essential aspect of advertising which increases the importance of professional excellence in making the advertising processes productive. The professionals are supposed to take into consideration the following facts while advertising. This would help them in making possible creativity besides optimising the advertisement budget. The service generating organisations also need to advertise carefully.

1. Finalising the advertisement budget: The involvement of finance is an important consideration and any organisation either producing goods or generating services can't undermine it. We need to formulate a pragmatic budget so that the financial constraint is not to aggravate the problem. It is very natural that the scale of business of an organisation would be a dominating factor while designing the advertisement budget. The professionals are supposed to know about the budgets of the leading competitors and to incorporate necessary changes felt essential to make the advertisement attractive and informative. They are also required to know the stages through which their services or schemes move. This would help them in rationalising the financial requirements.

2. Selecting a suitable vehicle: Another consideration that requires due attention of the professionals is the suitability of vehicles through which the advertisements regarding the services product move. There are a number of devices to advertise such as print media, broadcast media and the telecast media. The nature of product, intensity of competition, the quality of target market are some of the considerations to be given due weightage while selecting a medium. The involvement of cost and the rate of sensitivity in different media can't be uniform. We can't negate that telecast media is found very much effective but at the same time very expensive. All the organisations can't make a provision for TV advertising. The broadcast media has a big network and some of the organisations also prefer to advertise through Radio. It is right to mention that the broadcast media is found economic but not very much effective. To be more specific for the service generating organisations, we find print media suitable since it is economic as well as effective in throwing a positive impact. The organisations requiring more space for placing the message find the print media suitable. The professionals need to select a suitable vehicle depending upon their potentials and requirements.

3. Making possible creativity: It is important to mention that promotion without creativity carries no meaning. By creativity, our emphasis is on the attractive and innovative measures which have not been adopted by the competitors. The messages, appeals, slogans are instrumental in sensitising the customers. Of late, there are a number of adversting agencies where world-class professionals are engaged for making possible creativity. The creativity in advertisement would substantially simplify the task of professionals since the persuasion process would be found proactive.

4. Testing the effectiveness: It is only not sufficient that we advertise. It is much more impact generating that our advertisements are effective. This is meant we are getting a profitable return for our investments in advertisement. The messages, slogans, appeals continue for a long time and the persuasion processes are found instrumental in transfigurating the prospects into customers. Our focus is here on the life expectancy of advertisements. We can't deny that creativity and sensitivity make the ways for effective advertising.

5. Instrumentality of executives: The executives bear the responsibility of advertising locally at micro level. They are supposed to have an in-depth knowledge of local market and target population. Of course, we find a budget at apex level or at macro level but provisions at micro level are found very much productive. If we talk about the cause-related marketing, the professionals working locally know about the local events, customers, prospects problems or so. How to influence the local population for getting a positive response. The professionally sound executives can make it possible.

6. Characters and themes: The sensitivity of advertisement is considerably influenced by the characters, themes, events selected for advertising. It is essential that while advertising, the professionals know about the characters and themes.

Public Relations/Publicity

Almost all the organisations need to develop and strengthen the public relations activities to promote their business. This component of promotion is found effective though the organisations don't make any payment for publicity because we find it a non-paid form of communication. This focuses on the instrumentality of professionals in developing rapport with media people or others who can be helpful in getting the business. The service generating organisations need to develop this element of the promotion mix because the professionals meant to perform as PROs or contact persons require some of the attributes which are not found in common people. Since they bear the responsibility of developing and strengthening public relations, it is much more impact generating that they have ability to communicate effectively besides having a handsome physique. The appeal of public relations is based on high credibility, offguard and dramatisation. When we talk about credibility, our emphasis is on promoting new features and stories since we find them more effective in projecting a positive image. By the off guard, we propose to touch those prospects who could not be influenced by advertisement or other promotional efforts. In this context, the messages go to the customers as news rather than as advertisement. In respect of dramatisation, our emphasis is on dramatising the product of the organisations. Thus, the three elements of public relations are found instrumental in sensitising the customers provided the professionals responsible to perform evince interests in developing rapport with the media people. We can't deny the fact that in the service generating organisations, the effectiveness of public relations is of high magnitude. It is in this context that we find strong emphasis on the designing of promotion mix in the service generating organisations.

In the goods manufacturing organisations, of course we find advertisement playing a commanding role but so far as the service generating organisations are concerned we find instrumentality of personal selling and public relations establishing an edge over advertisement. It is not meant that the service generating organisations are not supposed to advertise but here we mean that they need to assign due weightage to both the submixes, such as public relations and personal selling. The most important thing in the context of public relations is the instrumentality of executives in projecting a positive image of the services-offered. They should have the potentials to throw a positive imprint on the prospects. In addition, it is also significant that they know the art of developing rapport with the media people. They frequently organise a meeting with them and try to influence them. The coverage in newspapers would, of course, be helpful to the creation of market.

The aforesaid facts make it clear that the service generating organisations are required to develop and strengthen the public relation activities. How to publicise is an art and the professionals bearing the responsibility to perform as PROs should have the efficacy to promote your business by projecting a fair image regarding the services offered and promised. We find here strong emphasis on the communicative ability of the professionals. Smiling face and a handsome personality help them fantastically in impressing the media *vis-a-vis* the prospects.

Personal Selling

An important submix of the promotion mix, the personal selling is found instrumental in promoting the business of service generating organisations. We consider personal selling a process of informing the customers besides persuading them to purchase products being influenced by personal communication. It is just a process of communication in which an individual exercises his/her personal potentials, tact, skill and ability to influence the impulse of prospects and to transform them into customers. Since we get an immediate feedback, the personal selling activates process of communication very effectively. The sensitising process is so quick that customers are influenced in a positive way. Personal sale thus provides the right volume and complexity of information for each potential customers.[6]

Nothing happens unless somebody sells something and nothing is sold unless someone communicates something. The task of motivating the customers is found difficult if the people managing the selling activities lack professional excellence. The oral presentation in conversation bears the efficacy of turning motivation into persuasion, provided the management of salesforce is sound. Personal selling is just another name for persuasion. We find persuasion playing an effective role in the service generating organisations. The personal selling is an art of persuasion. It is highly distinctive form of promoting sale. In the personal selling, we find interpersonal or two-way communication that makes the ways for feedback. There is no doubt in it that the goods or services are half sold when their outstanding properties are well told. This art of telling and selling is known as personal selling in which an individual based on his/her expertise or professionalism attempts to transform the prospects into customers.

Personal selling is basically a method of communication. It involves not only individual but the social behaviour too; each of the person in face-to-face contact, salesmen and prospect influence the other.[7] Thus, we find personal selling a personal communication, seller-buyer interaction, interpersonal communication and more so direct selling. The following facts are observed regarding the personal selling:

- It is a direct personal relation between the buyer and seller.
- It is an oral presentation in conversation.
- It is two-way communication.
- It is personal and social behaviour.
- It is an exercise for selling the goods or services.
- It is found more effective in the service generating organisations.

- It is based on the professional excellence of an individual.
- It is an important element of the promotion mix.

The aforesaid facts thus make it clear that to be more specific the service generating organisations need to use this component of the promotion mix preferably in a creative way. An individual is supposed to be high performer to get the desired result. This makes it essential that the service generating organisations make sincere efforts to develop such a professional who shows his/her expertise in touching and influencing the impulse of prospects/customers. Thus, this element of the promotion mix needs adequate training facilities to develop professional excellence.

Sales Promotion

Creation and generation lack any meaning unless we do something positive for expansion. We create impulse buying though personal communication, generate a gap with the help of advertisements but nothing is to be stable unless we do something extraordinary to stimulate the impulse buying. To monitor efficiently the plan of expansion, it is pertinent that we supplement and coordinate the personal selling and advertising, get a missing link which backs up the pre-selling done by advertising and stimulate the impulse of buyers. Sales do not occur automatically. To be more specific in the business environment where we find the intensity of competition moving upward, it is not possible to go and remain at the top for a long time to come, unless we prepare the ground or set the stage for future expansion and evolve new ideas for creating favourable selling conditions. It is sales promotion which backs up pre-selling and stimulates the impulse buying. It attracts the prospects and keeps moving the actual customers behind the product. Thus, it succeeds in winning and keeping the customers. It is against this background that we make an advocacy in favour of sales promotion. American Marketing Association says:

'Those marketing activities other than personal selling, advertising and publicity that stimulate customers and dealers effectively, such as display shows, exhibitions, demonstrations and various non-recurrent selling efforts not in the ordinary routine are the sales promotion measures.'[8]

R.S. Davar opines, "Sales promotional activities are devices aimed at reaching the consumer at home or in his business establishment. The tools are generally in the form of samples, contests, demonstrations and coupons. Sales promotion directed at consumers may be done with a view to increase the product's rate of use among existing customers or to attract new customers to the company's product. It may also be undertaken to retaliate against a competitor's sales promotion or other activities."[9]

In view of the above, it is right to mention that it is an important element of promotion mix in which a number of tools are used as shown in Figure 3.4. The incentives in the sales promotion are offered for a particular period and therefore we find the measures of temporary nature.

The innovation in sales promotion is found essential to establish an edge over the competitors' efforts to promote sale. To be more specific for the service generating organisations, it is found significant to motivate both the concerned parties, such as the providers and the customers. A senior executive at the apex level or a manager at the macro level is supposed to see that the tools of sales promotion are instrumental in promoting sale. The organisations have been found using the tools of sales promotion at the different stages of the product life cycle. The sales promotional measures while launching the product are offered with the motto of creating a conducive market condition. The organisations also use this element of the promotion mix when we find the product at the declining stage. In this context, the motive is to clear the old product which would be declared obsolete in the near future. We also find use of this component of the promotion mix when the products are found at the maturity stage. Here, the tools of sales promotion are found effective in increasing and maintaining the market share.

TOOLS OF SALES PROMOTION

As shown in Figure 3.5, we find different tools of sales promotion effective in promoting sale.

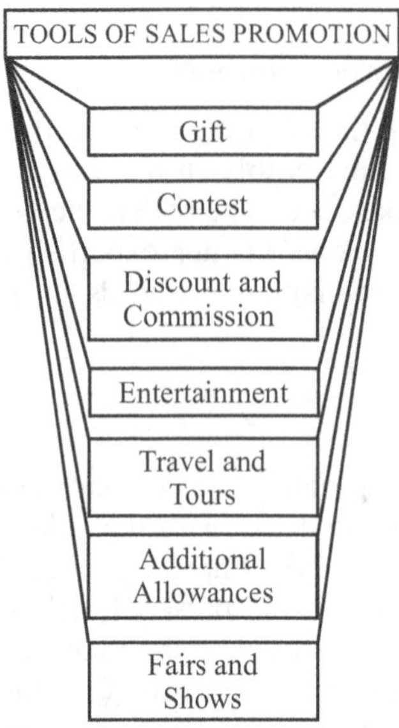

Fig. 3.5: Tools of Sales Promotion

Gift, contests, discount and commission, entertainment, travel and tours, additional allowances, fairs and shows are some of the important tools of sales promotion offered to both, the providers as well as the users. The motives are increasing the selling activities, touching the target, excelling the competition, increasing the market share, clearing the old products to be declared absolute in the near future or so. This makes it clear that the instrumentality of sales promotion is substantially influenced by the sensitivity of tools selected for the said purpose. More innovative the tools of sales promotion, more positive would be the results. It is not wisdom that you just copy the measures adopted by the competitors. Your wisdom and professional excellence would make the ways for innovative measures. We can't deny the fact that the tools of sales promotion should be for both the parties involved in the process such as the providers or traders who offer the goods or services and the customers who ultimately consume or use. A hotel company distributed a small gift pack to its customers. The customers were advised to open the pack at their homes and after opening they found in the pack seeds of an attractive plant with suitable instructions for plantation and transplantation. The trees started blooming and the attractive flowers of the said tree was found point of attraction. The friends, relatives, bypassers asked about the plant and the narration of facts promoted the business of that hotel for years and years to come. This makes it clear that the tools of sales promotion, if innovative, become very much instrumental in promoting sales. The professionals serving the organisations bear the responsibility of innovating the tools so that the process of making the buying decisions being influenced by the sales promotion is found effective.

Word-of-mouth Promotion

Much communication about the performance of the service generating organisations actually take place by word-of-mouth information which is also as word-of-mouth promotion. In the service generating organisations, we find use of different components of the promotion and in this context, we find this element of the promotion mix very effective. The word-of-mouth recommendations by the hidden salesforce make the process of communication effective. This is testified by the fact that whatever we receive from our friends, relatives or the persons having domination in the society have a far reaching effect on our buying decisions. The process is to cost nothing but to throw a positive effect on the impulse of the prospects/users. The local leaders, social reformists, popular leaders are found dominating the social behaviour and therefore whatever we receive from them influence our impulse sizeably *vis-a-vis* govern the buying decisions considerably. It is against this background that we find it significant to talk about this component of the promotion mix. We can't negate the fact that the high magnitude of effectiveness of this tool is due to the high level of trust. The growing sensitivity of the words and experiences of hidden salesforce simplify the task of promoting the business. The advertisements, sales promotion measures, the personal selling may of course be effective but the word-of-mouth recommendations are found acceptable in all the conditions by almost all the prospects. If we keep on moving the process of satisfying the users, our task of increasing the numbers of hidden salesforce is simplified considerably.

The executives and the front-line staff serving the organisations need to assign an overriding priority to this element of the promotion mix. We call the process two-step flow of communication in which messages are directed to the opinion leaders in society rather than to the masses. About the opinion leaders, it is right to mention that persons having domination on the social behaviour are known as opinion leaders. The representatives of mass media, social workers, leaders of an organisation or even others having a say in the society can act as opinion leaders. We can't negate that even the satisfied group of users also act as opinion leaders. This makes it pertinent that the service generating organisations assign a transcendental priority to the quality of services offered. The task of word-of-mouth promoters or the hidden salesforce is found much more difficult when the quality of service product is found poor.

An important question regarding the word-of-mouth promotion is related to its intensity of sensitivity and acceptability. Why do we find this element of the promotion mix so much effective? Of course, a plain answer to this question is the positive and right opinions. If the word-of-mouth promoters start advocating the wrongs, the acceptability would be minimised considerably. If our friends communicate to us the specialities of their positive feelings about the services of a particular organisation; we trust on them blindly albeit without a detailed narration. If our relatives convey to us their feelings about the outstanding services offered by a bank or hotel in which they stayed, we try to use the services as and when we get an opportunity. It is in this context that this element of the promotion mix is found significant to the service generating organisations. We find a strong emphasis on the quality of services-offered failing which the promotion processes would hardly be effective.

Telemarketing

Telemarketing is found instrumental in promoting the business and even the service generating organisations have been found using this element of the promotion mix. The telemarketing helps in activating the process of advertisement in addition to its instrumentality in increasing the sale. The service generating organisations in general and the banking, insurance, transport, hotel, tourism organisations in particular have been found using telemarketing with the two-fold objectives of selling and advertising. The instrumentality of telephones and televisions are found effective in the process of promoting the business. The transmission of information regarding services or schemes help the customers/prospects in developing their awareness, specially regarding the new product. They if informed and sensed in a right fashion and persuaded in a right way go to the telephone numbers, make necessary queries or enquiries, if they need so or, even send their representatives to collect detailed information and/or, call the numbers and let them know their decisions. This makes it clear that we find advertising even in the process of selling since the users/prospects before the television screen come to know about the new developments or arrivals. It is right to mention that advertisements persuade the users and the telemarketing also instrumentalises the same process, of course, in a bit different way. The instrumentality of telemarketing in persuading the users is substantially influenced by the quality of personnel supposed to discharge the responsibility. The creativity is found to be an important aspect and this makes it essential that advertising professionals are well aware of the expectations and attitudes of users/prospects. It is against this background that we find increased temptation for this element of the promotion mix not only in the developed countries but even in the less developed countries like ours.

In the present world when we find it much more difficult to manage the people, the telemarketing occupies and would continue to occupy a place of outstanding significance. The telemarketing, no doubt, minimises the dependence of service generating organisations on the salespeople since just a counter or a centre listed in the call numbers serves multi-dimensional purposes. The interested person(s), organisation(s) come to the centre and get further information or they can do everything even on their phones or they can also send their representatives. Since we have a perception of everything automated, it is possible with the frequent use of developed or sophisticated communication technologies, we find telemarketing gaining popularity and the process would continue even in future. In the Indian perspective, we find only the beginning but in the coming days, it is to gain momentum. A number of foreign banks, hotels and tour operators have been seen promoting telemarketing. We have a big network of the telecom and telecast services and therefore, the future looks prosperous.

The aforesaid facts make it clear that an important submix of the promotion mix, i.e., telemarketing is a process of promoting the business. Both the goods manufacturing as well as the service generating organisations can rationalise their selling expenses fantastically if they assign due weightage to telemarketing. Not only the selling processes but albeit advertisement processes find telemarketing instrumental in their desired goals of offering more but taxing less.

THE PRICE MIX

This element of the marketing mix is related to the decisions influencing the fee structure, rate of interest, commission charged and paid by the service generating organisations. It is considered to be the most critical component of the marketing mix. Both from economic and social standpoint, the management of pricing is important but at the same time more critical and challenging. This makes it essential that the service generating organisations formulate a sound strategy for pricing so that the commercial viability is maintained. We are well aware of the fact that there are some of the organisations, such as the not-for-profit making organisations who don't have a legitimate right of making profits but albeit in such category, we find pricing decisions important because the pricing decisions are to influence the maintenance, development and expansion plans of an organisation. Of course, the educational institutions, hospitals, voluntary social organisations, political organisations, charitable trusts don't have a legitimate right of making profits but they, of course, need adequate finance to offer the world-class services. Thus, the no-profit organisations need to use this element of the marketing mix in a different way so that whatever they charge as fee is found sufficient to implement the development and expansion plans. It is in this context that we need to go through the problem of pricing carefully and intelligently. We use pricing both as an operational and a motivational tool. The professionals bear the responsibility of identifying the conditions when pricing is to be used as a motivational tool.

The professionals need to go through a number of considerations while setting or fixing the fee and interest. Modern marketers except in rare cases enjoy considerable freedom in making the pricing decisions. The freedom comes from their success in manipulating other controllables like products, distribution and promotion.[10] If they are successful in optimising the costs on inputs; successful in minimising the promotional expenses; if they are successful in minimising the promotional expenses; if they are successful in rationalising the distribution costs, the avenues for optimising the cost and rationalising the price structure are broadened considerably. While selling or promoting the business, to be more specific in the service generating organisations, we find quality factor more sensitive. The users/customers in general are found sensitive to quality. It is important to mention that the emerging trends in economic depression influence the process of sensitising the users substantially. Of late, the customer/users have been found sensitive to price even while using the services. The pricing decisions are influenced by a number of internal and external conditions. This makes it essential that the executives while blending or compounding the marketing mix regard price as a variable to be traded off against product quality and promotion rather than as an absolute where the lowest price is most desirable.[11] Pricing policies are used as general guide-lines in making the pricing decisions over long periods. The pricing policies are general and long-run while the pricing strategies are specific and short-run. Pricing setting procedures vary with the emerging trends in competition. The regulatory control on the management of pricing is a built-in-feature all over the world. In almost all the countries, we find such control specially to regulate profiteering. To be more specific in the Indian perspective where we find users sensitive to price, it is pertinent that the service generating organisations make ways for cost-effectiveness since this would pave copious avenues for optimising the cost structure.

THE PLACE MIX

Another important element of the marketing mix is place mix which focuses our attention on the offering of services by the providers to the ultimate users and the place of location for the service generating organisations. In some of the cases, we find that providers have no option but to locate the units/branches as per the instructions of the apex body. The locational advantages simplify the task of implementing the marketing principles. But in a majority of the cases, we find freedom to the executives to locate units or the branches as per his/her choice. In both the cases, the location is preferred at the points where we find some of the essential features, such as easy and convenient accessibility, safety or protection availability of the infrastructural facilities, attractive and healthy surroundings or so. We can't negate that these features make available to the units/branches the locational advantages which simplify the task of marketing effectively. If we undermine these features, the task of professionals in a command area is found much more difficult. The hotels, tourist organisations, offices of the tour or transport operators, bank branches, insurance branches get the locational advantages when we find their location close to the populated area or in the cities precincts. Thus, the place occupies a place of outstanding significance and the service generating organisations are supposed to select a place having the essential features mentioned earlier.

In addition, we need to gravitate our attention on the providers of the services. To be more specific in the service generating organisations where we don't find direct distribution of services due mainly to intangibility, it is pertinent that the front-line staff who bear the responsibility of offering the services to the ultimate users, don't create a gap between the services-promised and services-offered. The policy makers and the senior executives make provision for services with certain specifications and standard which take the shape of promises. The front-line staff are supposed to make available the services-promised to the ultimate users. If they commit a mistake in offering the services, we find a gap which makes the ways for dissatisfaction since a degeneration in the quality is found existent. This makes it essential that the service generating organisations make it sure that the services-promised reach to the ultimate users in a decent way. Here, we find the instrumentality of people. If they have dedicated, committed and efficient people to manage the services, the possibilities of degeneration in quality are minimised considerably. It is against this background that some of the experts make an advocacy in favour of fifth P, i.e., People.

The development of employees in tune with the changing expectations of users is found significant in the very context. The service generating organisations bear the responsibility of imparting proper training facilities to the employees so that they make possible performance orientation. Besides the policy makers are also supposed to pave avenues for employee orientation which make it essential that the employees serving the organisations get adequate incentives. If they make possible employee orientation, the doors are cleared for performance orientation. It is not only sufficient that we improve the quality of service. It is much more impact generating that the services-promised reach to the ultimate users without any distortion. This is possible when the service generating organisations blend the two important dimensions optimally.

EXPANDED MIX FOR SERVICES MARKETING

The service marketers mainly due to the distinct features of services find it difficult to market them. The features like intangibility and perishability complicate their task. This makes it essential that the marketing professionals expand the areas of marketing mix and against this background we talk about the additional three mixes such as Process, Physical Evidence and Attractions and People.

Process focuses our attention on the actual procedure adopted for generating the services. This also includes in the purview the mechanism and flow of activities for delivering the services. The service delivery and operating systems are also related to process mix.

Physical Evidence and Attractions are concerned with a number of factors such as the environment, the tangible components in the delivery process and the attractions of serving people and the service environment. The tangible components like brochures, letter-adding head, business cards, report formats, signage and equipment. The factors additional attractions in the service environment or servicescapes and making the physical amenities and physical appearance to be effective in throwing a positive impact on the mindset of customers and visitors, the ambience, the colours, the aesthetic management also need due attention.

People draw our attention on the working marketing people who bear the responsibility of offering or delivering the services.

With the development of techniculture, we find a basic change in the attitudes of customers. They expect quick services and at times cost-effective services. They prefer services to be offered in a decent way. They are found tempted to the attractive service environment. These developments make it essential that the expanded mixes of marketing get due attention of service marketers. In the process of formulating a sound marketing mix, the marketing professionals also need to blend all the seven Ps.

Process

Additional mix of marketing focuses our attention on the processing of services. With the use of new generation of sophisticated technology, we find a basic change in processing. We find some of the services of complex nature and they go through a number of processes before delivery. The processes are offered with the support of employees and technologies used in the process.[12] The operational flow of service is considerably influenced by generation of machines used for this purpose. Particularly in the highly bureaucratised services, we find extensive series for the processing of services. The promised quality of services cross the different stages and at each and every stage we find instrumentality employees and machines used for processing. The professionals need to make it sure that the services reach to their destination on time and without any distortion. The most important role in the process is played by the front-line staff who deliver the services to the ultimate customers.

The processes provide evidence to the customers of the quality of services made available to them. The processing influences the quality of services and therefore the professionals need to make it sure that employees working there or equipments or machines used in the process perform in a right way.

Physical Evidence and Attractions

The service environment, of course, occupies a place of outstanding significance. This mix of marketing includes a number areas such as tangible representations of the service such as brochures, letterhead, business cards, report formats, signage and equipment.[13] Besides, we also find in this context the physical facilities at the point where the services are offered. We often talk about the servicescapes in which we concentrate on the arrangements at the service place for improvement the quality. We cannot negate that physical evidence can provide tremendous opportunities to an organisation for transmitting messages regarding the organisational objectives, intended market segments and the nature of service. We also find areas where physical facilities become irrelevant such as telecommunication services but in that case we find tangibles like billing statements playing an important role in judging the quality. In an age of technology, we find much more scope for displaying of the technology helping an organisation in different ways.

Another important dimension of this marketing mix is related to the physical attractions. We agree with this view that corporate culture considerably rests on attractions. The customers and visitors coming to an organisation prove to be an evaluator. The physical appearance of employees, the dresses used by them, their physical fitness, their facial expression, their hairstyle, the displays related to aesthetic sense are some of the dimensions adding additional attractions to the providers. The service environment carrying everything but not assigning due weightage to physical attractions would fail in projecting an image that is distinct to others. It is in this context that we find personal care services becoming an important aspect of physical fitness. We agree with this view that service generating organisations are required to assign due weightage to this submix of marketing. In the MNCs, we find this getting due place. In the government organisations, we do not find it diverting due attention. But we find none of them rejecting this submix as all of us have temptation for attractions. In the Indian perspective, we find a clear-cut difference between that public and private sectors as the employees serving the public sector banks do not develop a temptation for personal care whereas the same group of people serving the private sector banks have no option but to develop that sense.

People

The people serving an organisation play a dominating role in its development. The quality of technology, no doubt, determines the magnitude of success but ultimately we find people working there governing the process. The corporate sector needs quality people who prove to be a star performer. They need to be personally- and professionally-committed.

In addition, they also need to be value-based. Because we find character to emerge as a power, the organisations compromising with values would have to bid a good-bye.

People mix in an organisation constitute all the human actors who are concerned with the process such as employees serving the organisation, customers/users who are directly concerned with services of the organisation and other customers in the service environment who sooner or later may affect the process.[14] The marketing people taking part in the delivery process make available to the customers cues regarding the services. They play a very significant role in the entire process of service delivery. The three important properties need due attention of professionals while developing people in the marketing department.

The people need to be thematically sound. This focuses our attention on the subjective knowledge of world-class which the marketing people are to be made available on a continuous basis. Brushing up the knowledge by incorporating significant changes with the help of education and training programme appears important. The marketing professionals need priority attention on the working marketing people. Particularly in an age of globalisation where we find emergence of multi-cultural society, the marketing people need to develop their excellence in a different way so that they do not commit mistake while identifying and understanding the customers. The emergence of a society influenced by material cultural makes it essential that the marketing professionals develop people who have an in-depth knowledge of emerging culture and changing behaviour.

Personal and professional orientation needs an intensive care. The marketing people need personal-touch-in-service and in addition, they also require professional commitment. In an age of marketing, the service marketers cannot undermine the significance of personalised services influenced by holistic touch. We need a new vision and a distinct approach commanding the volatile business environment.

Gone are the days when service marketers succeeded even by practising profiteering. The rivals are in search of an opportunity helping them in distorting or tarnishing your image. It is in this context that we make a strong advocacy in favour of value orientation in the process of marketing decisions. We cannot negate that character is to emerge as a dominating power. This makes it essential that marketing professionals activate the process of value engineering.

Developing quality people is their prime responsibility and this is not possible unless we find people having all the three properties. While selecting and recruiting people, while motivating people and while educating and training people; they can make ways for cultivating and inculcating the additional properties they lack.

The three expanded submixes of marketing need due attention of marketing professionals for making and innovating the marketing decisions.

CAPACITY PLANNING

It is not sufficient that we are interested only in managing our present. It is much more significant that we keep our eyes open, minds active to know about the future and continue to enrich our potentials to manage the future. Of late, we find a good number of organisations who concentrate their energy on current development plans but undermine the developments to take place in future. This makes ways for the emergence of numerous complications. The organisations not managing the future fail in managing the demand and supply position, make it difficult to optimise the development of marketing resources to cope with the changing requirements, make possible a contraction in their resistance power and both on quantitative and qualitative fronts, we find them moving backward. It is against this background that we need to assign due weightage to capacity planning. By capacity planning, our emphasis is on the management of strength. It is, of course, due to deficient management that we improve the supply position but the process of demand generation is energised non-optimally. We invest on resources but fail in getting the return and thus a vicious circle is formed which questions the soundness of our strength. If we assign due weightage to the management of strength and continue to activate the process of enriching the potentials, we find ourselves in a sound position to make an attack on the multi-dimensional threats and challenges in the business environment. The capacity planning focuses on the management of strength in the face of changing scenario.

The service generating organisations have been found practising frequent innovation and the organisations not aware of the future find it difficult to increase their strength. This makes it essential that they have an in-depth knowledge of future. They make possible a microscopic evaluation of their strength in tune with the world-class developments; they know about the strength of their competitors they perceive an idea of the emerging trends in demand and they are sound enough to improve the supply position which caters to the changing needs and requirements of prospects/users. Thus, we find emphasis on strength both in quantitative and qualitative terms. To be more specific in the Indian perspective, we find a majority of the service generating organisations not efficacious in managing the future which often creates an imbalance in the demand and supply position. This makes it essential that we assign a transcendental priority to capacity planning.

Capacity planning is known as planning the capacity in the face of future. This throws light on both the aspects — first, the organisations are supposed to know the demand position so that the potentials are enriched to increase the quantity or capacity of generating the services and second, the organisations are also required to know about the likes and dislikes, preferences, expectations, attitudes which make an advocacy in favour of quality generation. In simple words, you know about the tastes and expectations of prospects/users and improve your capacity to offer the same. Thus, the professionals need excellence to study the market conditions and further to rate their potentials so that lapses are identified and the corrective measures are taken. If the users expect sophistication in services, the organisations need to use sophisticated technologies to fulfil their expectations and this is not possible unless we think in favour of capacity planning.

The capacity planning thus focuses our attention on the strategic planning, which makes an advocacy in favour of the formulation of an action plan to enrich strength. It is natural that in the years to come, the intensity of competition would go up which would make it essential that the service generating organisations keep on moving the process of qualitative transformation. On the one hand, they need to improve the quality of services and on the other hand also to inject additional attractions to their service mix by innovating the peripheral services. On the whole, they need to offer world-class services found competitive both at national and international levels. It is high time that they think in favour of making things happen and intensify research activities to innovate the marketing resources.

The strategic plan would make the ways for the mobilisation of financial resources to cater to their increasing requirements. We can't deny the fact that if an organisation succeeds in maintaining the process of profit generation, the financial health of that organisation becomes so sound that the task of satisfying the employees and investors is simplified considerably. This makes it pertinent that like the goods manufacturing organisations even the service generating organisations also carry forward the task of making health sound. If you are physically sound, the task of countering the diseases is found much more easier. If an organisation is strong, the task of facing the challenges and threats in the markets is simplified considerably. It is against this background that strategic planning assumes a place of outstanding significance. When we talk about capacity planning, our prime focus is on strategic planning since the process of enriching strength can't be made possible within a couple of days. The foreign leading commercial banks, the airways, the consultants, the tourist organisations, the hotels, the educational institutions, the hospitals and many other service generating organisations assign an overriding priority to the capacity planning which make them efficacious enough in facing the multi-dimensional threats and challenges in the markets.

The aforesaid facts make it clear that the formulation of an action plan is essential to march ahead in the right direction. Of late, the leading service generating organisations have been found making concerted efforts to manage information with the help of sophisticated information technologies which make possible more sensitivity in their decisions. They forecast the problems, the needs and requirements, the intensity of competition and formulate such a service mix which is of world-class, of course, strong enough in excelling competition, increasing the market share, establishing the leadership and dominating the business world. In the Indian perspective, it is much more impact generating that the service generating organisations promote the use of sophisticated information technologies for improving the quality of their decisions. A decision related to the supply side is found based on the demand side. There are a number of factors to influence the process of demand generation and the service generating organisation have to switch on the process by innovating the promotional measures since the other factors found of uncontrollable nature are not within their control. The quality of marketing mixes influences the sensitivity of marketing decisions and the formulation of a sound marketing mix is not possible unless you identify the errors and intensify corrective measures much earlier than the side-effects start troubling you.

The professionals bear the responsibility of matching the offerings to the market demand. The matching of demand and supply optimally is a difficult task that requires excellence. There are a number of factors to be taken into consideration.

- The task of predicting the behaviour of users is found critical since a number of factors influence the same. The emerging trends in the environmental conditions influence our behavioural profile and a majority of them are found of uncontrollable nature. The fluctuating trends in the money and stock markets govern the behaviour of investors and the deteriorating law and order conditions influence the travelling plan of tourists.
- Inavailability of sufficient lead time is also an important factor making the task difficult to the professionals and the decision is so quick that the professionals find themselves helpless.
- In the process of the utilisation of available capacity, the smaller production/assembly/packaging cause wastage. The nursing services make it clear.
- Higher annoyance is expected due to the lack of alternatives. If the users fail in getting the services on time, the level of dissatisfaction is found at its peak. The users/customers using the services of airways are found annoyed if the flights are delayed or the time schedule is not maintained.
- The cost on account of round-the-clock services affects the benefit relationship for extraordinary setting of performance standards.

The aforesaid complexities, of course, make the task of optimising the demand and supply difficult.

CAPACITY SCHEDULING

How much of what (service) will be needed to achieve its predetermined goals is an important consideration that makes an advocacy in favour of capacity planning and scheduling. However, approximate we find the analysis of demand, the service generating organisations bear the responsibility of planning for the capacity. There are a number of critical variables requiring due consideration in the process such as, goals of the service firm, availability of capital and the quality of human resources, market segments served and the level of service quality aimed at. A detailed scheduling of man, materials, money and machines (Four Ms) is essential for each element of the service mix on a time map.

INTERNAL MARKETING

We agree with this view that services are predominantly people-based. In the service generating organisations, we find personnel of the marketing department as well as others very much instrumental in performing the marketing function. This makes it essential that we clearly understand the common purpose and spirit of the tasks to be performed and its backward and forward linkages with the other tasks. Internalising the marketing function is an important task found of critical nature. This makes an advocacy in favour of internal marketing with the motto of employing quality people.

Bringing home the concept of internal customer focuses on marketing internally to the internal market of employees. This makes an advocacy in favour of employing a higher number of skilled personnel in the service generating organisations. The service firms valuing investments in people as much as investments in machines, using technology to support men or people on the front line, making recruitment and training as crucial for sales clerks and housekeepers as for managers and senior executives and linking compensation to performance for employees at every level not just at the top need a new model for managing services.

The task of internal marketing is simplified considerably with the help of internal interactive communication, internal mass communication, market and image research, external mass communication and advertising. The task of raising the customer consciousness is difficult and the following issues are found having a far reaching effect:

- Sponsoring employees for training programmes in the areas of marketing. The behavioural management needs an intensive care.
- Increasing the involvement of staff in activities like deposit mobilisation, customer service campaigns, undertaking market surveys, formulation of branch budget or so.
- Organising the marketing conference and workshops, activating capsule course relating to the marketing of services.
- Sharing of the findings of customer surveys, image and other studies.
- Motivating the staff by offering awards and rewards both on an individual and a group basis.
- Provision for guiding on the customer service with the help of a house journal, special newsletters and other printed leaflets.
- Setting up of marketing/customer cells.
- Maintaining visibility through strengthening public relations activities.

Increasing Business Mindedness

An important task is to increase the business mindedness of employees. The following activities may be helpful in the process:

- Sharing of performance results vs. budgets and problems facing the organisations.
- Allocation of specific goals to staff and close monitoring of the day-to-day developments.
- Training for the development of detailed customer call programmes.
- Exposure of staff to the criteria of cost-benefit.
- Development of teamwork among staff.

- Promotion of education programmes.
- Encouraging the use of suggested services.

The personal commitment is an important dimension for increasing the business mindedness and the service generating organisations need to develop employees so that performance orientation is made possible. We can't negate that employee orientation would make the ways for performance orientation which focuses on enriching the credentials and making the compensation plans attractive.

EXTERNAL MARKETING

Stimulating market is found essential to get a positive response. In the purview of external marketing, we include all our communication campaigns to inform, sense, sensitise, persuade and transform the potential customers into actual and habitual customers. The providers make creative efforts to get positive result. We find information occupying an outstanding position in the communication campaigns. The organisational objectives are to be accomplished and this makes it essential that the service providing organisations are sincere to the multi-dimensional themes of promotional campaigns and in the process, the service marketers having world-class professional excellence are supposed to play a dominating role. The themes related to communication campaigns are in Figure 3.6.

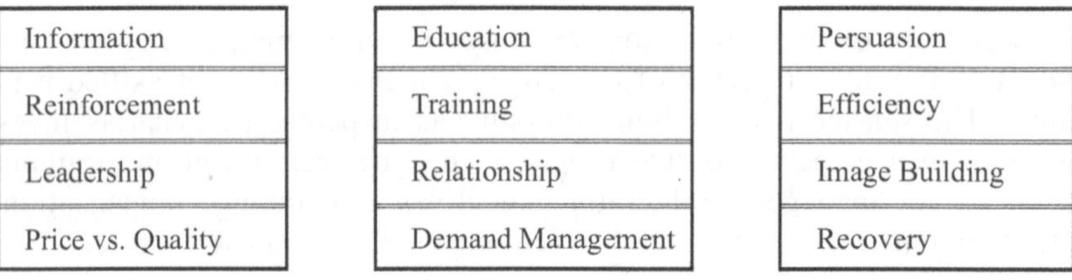

Fig. 3.6: Campaign Themes in External Marketing

Information: The communication themes for sensitising the campaigns are found very much related to the quality and timing of information. In the marketing process, there are a number of stages when the service marketers for making decision depend on information. The information related to the package of services, offering of a new or modified services, offering of services in a new market, changes in marketing mix are some of the important information related to the marketing communication campaigns.

Education: Studying and understanding the customers in a right way and on right time are the important considerations in the campaign themes. The expectations of customers cannot remain static. A number of factors related to socio-cultural and economic dimensions influence them. The service marketers bear the responsibility of managing service promises and expectations. Thus, Customer Expectations Management and Provider Promises Management are the two important areas necessitating due attention of service marketers. In the management of promises, the service providing organisations need to make it sure that unrealistic promise, are not made. While injecting life and strength to service the promises, it is also essential that the service providing organisations assure compensation in case of service deficiency or service failure. In the formation of the levels of expectations, the promises made by the service providing organisations also play an outstanding role and therefore, they need to be careful while making promises. We find scope for realism and unrealism in both the specified areas of promises and expectations. The services marketers with high professional excellence can strike a balance between the two.

Persuasion: The communication process if persuasive help the making of quality marketing decisions, influencing the customers to make the buying decisions. The professionals bear the responsibility of transforming the potential customers into actual and habitual customers and for that they need to activate the persuasion process. The target market is to be identified and persuaded by the professionals and in the process, they need to present the special benefits and outstanding features of the product. The approaches may be offensive or even defensive but the persuasive communication has to play a positive role.

Reinforcement: The customers must be loyal and development of loyalty makes it essential that the customers are well aware of the factors like credibility, reliability and continuity of the quality factors. The customers get an assurance that they would have similar or even better experiences after using the services. This factors helps in reducing cognitive dissonance and supports and strengthens the earlier decisions of using the services. The customers are encouraged to continue and gradually they prove to be a habitual customer.

Training: We consider consumer the co-producers. This is due to the fact that whatsoever they are found using are of their choice. The service providers identify some of the users who may help them in the process of developing the product profile. They must have ability and expertise to participate in the service production process. The marketing professionals bear the responsibility of training the customers. It is significant to mention that in the product process, we find three phases such as joining phase, production process phase and detachment phase. The customer support system requires to be developed and suitable training facilities are made available to the customers. It is also not to be forgotten that production processes developed with the help of quality customer are found proactive.

Efficiency: The professionals need to identify their achievements and to project them in such a fashion that customers are impressed. The growth rate during a particular period, the expansion of market and networking, loyal consumer network, the percentage of success in service, networking of relationship with other services and the size and strength of the corporate group in the economy are some of the bases for projecting efficiency. The messages must be communicated in an authentic way so that the customers are found convinced.

Leadership: Leadership constitutes a place of outstanding significance. The quality leaders bear the efficacy of influencing and attracting the prospects or potential customers. Such a leadership positioning may be either in terms of market share or innovative efforts. The leaders would be in a position to attract the prospects by communicating to them their increasing market share or a continuous innovations. Both at corporate or local levels, the leaders may be effective.

Relationship: Building relationship and further maintaining them in a right perspective is found important. The service marketers need to activate special campaigns for this purpose. Not only retention but making customers loyal to brand are the motives of relationship. When the customers are found loyal to a particular brand, they start acting as an ambassador. Transforming potential customers into an actual customer and then turning them as a habitual customer and loyal customer make ways for using as an ambassador who promotes the services in a very effective way.

Image Building: We find image a consideration of our contributions. An individual or an institution significantly contributing to the process of development paves avenues for the building of a fair image. Just reverse to it, if they do not contribute something concrete or make negative contributions; the image problem makes their task difficult. All the supporting infrastructural facilities in an organisation can be bought; even the quality people can be hired but the image is only built not bought. World-class excellence in the services paves avenues for the building of a fair image. Firstly, the service generating organisations need to make significant contributions to the process of quality innovations and thereafter, the image building campaigns are to be made.

Price vs. Quality: We cannot deny that the customers around the world are becoming much more sensitive to price and quality. This makes it essential that the service generating organisations strike a balance between the two. On the one hand, they keep on moving the process of quality innovations while on the other hand also make sincere efforts to make the process cost-effective. This will help them in offering quality services at an affordable price/fee. For excelling competition, this is considered to be the most effective prescription.

Demand Management: Optimising the demand and supply position is considered essential. This focuses our attention on the fact that the service generating organisations consider both the issues. They can balance demand in different ways such as by changing the fee/price structure and also by changing the time. From peak periods to the slack periods and from high rate of tariff to the subsidised or concessional rate of tariff help in striking a balance.

Recovery: We cannot claim that in all the cases, our efforts are foolproof. We find possibilities for failures and deficiencies because human errors or even faults in machines are but natural. However, the service generating organisations need to think about recovery due to the mistakes committed by them. It is the responsibility of service marketers that they develop their awareness of the failures and deficiencies *vis-a vis* the financial losses to the customers/users and make sincere, honest and time-honoured efforts to recover. This will help them in many ways. The customers will be found satisfied and the projection of a fair image will be easier.

INTERACTIVE MARKETING

Marketing processes based on an interaction between the contact employees, service providing companies and the consumers are known as interactive marketing. We consider it a managerial process to initiate interactions between the several generating organisations and the consumers with the motto of facilitating efficient participation in service production and consumption to be instrumental in satisfying the needs of the consumers and further successful in creating or innovating quality perception in tune with the customer's taste and temperament. It is very natural that serving employees and the customers both of them have a different perception of quality. Interactive marketing is considered a process to perceive quality in tune with the perception of customers. Thus, customer's perceived quality if adopted and made available to customer's makes ways for high level of satisfaction.

The key areas in the interactive marketing are involvement of customers in the process, identification of contact employees supposed to interact, operational processes and the system and the physical resources and equipment available at the place where services are generated. When we talk about service production system, the most important thing we find is the active participation of customers. Therefore, we call them a resource generating quality. The contact persons are those employees who bear the responsibility of interacting with the customers. A number of processes are followed for interaction. The service marketers need to make it sure that the employees who directly contact and interact with customers have a communication excellence. The contact persons may belong to any echelon of management. The interactions may be direct or even indirect on the phone, fax, mail or internet. In addition to contact persons, we find the system and technology adopted by an organisation influencing the interaction process. This makes it essential that whatsoever the systems and technologies we have are not complex or complicated. In the context of physical resources and equipments, we find other tools used in the process of generating the services. Both the technical and functional qualities rest on the quality of technology used by an organisation in the service generating process.

The contact persons interacting with the customers need to be aware of the facts, they have to consider while communicating. Location and exterior of the service outlets, tools, furnitures, equipments as we find them of tangible nature. The system and process followed for offering or delivering the services and signage and other communications material such as signboards, directions, display of rules and regulations, caution, etc. The peripheral services made available to the customers such as drinking water, sanitation and ventilation.

In the interactive session, the customers encounter everything and the contact employees are supposed to study and understand them in a right way so that they have a right perception of customers' perceived quality. The interactions include negotiations and sharing of insights in both directions.[15] We find some of the organisations effectively combining database and interaction marketing.

SUMMARY

You have gone through the dimensions of managing the service marketing. Before starting another chapter, be sure that the following facts are well versed.

Marketing Mix: It is a combination of different submixes of the marketing mix, such as product mix, promotion mix, price mix and the place mix. Some of the experts also talk about submixes like People, Physical evidence and Process. The term marketing mix was first coined by Prof. Neil H. Borden.

Product Mix: While managing the services product, it is essential that the marketers assign due weightage to the levels of product, product line, product process, packaging and product attractiveness. The management of different elements of the core and peripheral services become significant in the very context.

Promotion Mix: This submix of the marketing mix focuses on different elements of promotion, such as advertising, publicity, sales promotion, word-of-mouth promotion, personal selling and telemarketing. The management of promotional measures is the main theme in the very context.

Price Mix: The management of pricing in the service generating organisations is related to the management of fee, interest, commission or so. The service generating organisations need to manage this mix, specially with the motto of getting a profitable return from the marketing inputs used in the process.

Place Mix: The management of place draws our attention on the problem of location and the process of offering the services. It is essential that the service generating organisations make it sure that the promised services reach to ultimate users without any distortion. In addition, the point of location also becomes significant in the very context.

Internal Marketing: By internal marketing, we mean internalising the marketing function, Bringing home the concept of internal customer is the main thing in the internal marketing which is to market to the internal market of the employees.

Processing: This submix of the marketing mix focuses our attention on the actual procedures adopted for generating the services. This also includes in its purview the mechanism and flow of activities for delivering the services.

Physical Evidence and Attractions: The service environment is found to be the focal point in this submix. The tangible components like brochures, business cards, report formats, signage and equipments are included in this mix. The ambience, the colours, the aesthetic management and the attractions generated by the working employees are also included in this mix. The additional attractions in the service environment or servicescapes, physical amenities and physical appearance are the problems related to this mix.

People: This submix draws our attention on the working marketing people. The thematical competence of people, the personal commitment and personal-touch-in-service and value orientation are the important items of this mix. In almost all the organisations, we find people playing a decisive role. This draws our attention on developing professionally sound and value based human resources who contribute substantially to the development process. The organisations need performance orientation which is not possible unless we make possible employee orientation.

Capacity Planning: The capacity planning is related to the planning of strength which draws our attention on strategic planning. The motive is to enrich the potentials of an organisation in respect of four Ms so that the capacity to counter the challenges is sizeably maximised.

Capacity Scheduling: The scheduling of capacity is a detailed scheduling of men, materials, money and machines (Four Ms). This helps in knowing the changing requirements of users.

Internal Marketing: By internal marketing, we mean internalising the marketing functions. Bringing home the concept of internal customer is the main theme in the internal marketing.

External Marketing: In external marketing, we include all our communication campaigns to inform, sense, sensitise, persuade and transform potential customers into actual and habitual customers. In this context, the service providing organisations are required to be aware of the multi-dimensional promotional campaigns.

Interactive Marketing: In this context, we find interactive sessions between the contact employees and the customers. It is considered a process to perceive quality in tune with the perception of customers, regarding quality. The customers are involved in the process.

KEY TERMS

Sycro -marketing	ATMs
Global Economic Order	Peripheral Services
Product Portfolio	Core Services
Capacity Planning	Capacity Scheduling
Techno-driven Marketing	Marketing Mix
Packaging	Perishable Product
Product Life Cycle	Beauty Parlours
Generic Product	Expected Product
Augmented Product	Potential Product
Product Line	Target Market
Proactive Process	Concept Screening
Test Marketing	Reactive Process
Cost-Benefit Analysis	Service Quality Expectations
Behavioural Profile Credit-Debit Machine	ATMs
Cause-related and Sponsorship Marketing	Public Relations
Personal Selling	Word-of-Mouth Promotion
Telemarketing	No-Profit Organisations
Profiteering	Physical Evidence and Attractions
Thematically Sound	Strategic Plan

Review Questions

1. What do you mean by Marketing Mix? Focus on the different traditional submixes of the marketing mix.
2. Throw light on the different key decision-making areas in the management of product of a service generating organisation.
3. Explain the different components of Promotion Mix.
4. Discuss the instrumentality of Personal Selling in the marketing of services.
5. Focus on the pricing decisions in a service generating organisation.
6. "The management of place draws priority attention of service marketers." Comment on this statement.
7. Explain the expanded submixes of the Marketing Mix for the service generating organisations.
8. What do you mean Capacity Planning? Explain strategic planning with the viewpoint of capacity planning.
9. What do you mean by Internal Marketing? Justify its relevance in the marketing of services.
10. Explain External Marketing. Focus on the campaign themes in external marketing.
11. What do you mean by Interactive Marketing? Explain in brief its role in services marketing.

Application Exercises

1. As a marketing professional, focus on the relevance of formulating a sound marketing mix. Explain your reactions about the expanded marketing mix.
2. You act as a service marketer in a service generating organisation. Throw light on the key decision-making areas when you develop a product mix.
3. You have been assigned the responsibility of formulating a promotion mix for your organisation. Explain the components to be blended.
4. Focus on the role the personal sellers are required to play in a service generating organisation.
5. You have been asked to make the process of generating services much more cost-effective. Suggest the measures in Indian perspective.

Endnotes

1. Borden Neil H., The Concept of Marketing, *The Journal of Advertising Research,* Vol. IV/2, 1964, p. 27.
2. Kotler P., *Marketing Management,* Prentice-Hall of India, p. 430.
3. *Ibid.,* p. 436.
4. Saxena K.K., Bank's Unique Selling Proposition, The Financial Express, October, 2, 1984.
5. Mason J. Bary, (Foreword to the Book) *Services Marketing,* By S.M. Jha, Himalaya Publishing House, Mumbai, 1994.
6. Reidenback E. R. and Pitts R.E., *Bank Marketing*, p. 152.
7. Cundiff, Still and Govoni, *Fundamentals of Modern Marketing,* Prentice-Hall of India, pp. 381-82.
8. American Marketing Association, *Journal of Marketing,* October, 1984, p. 24.
9. Davar, R.S., *Modern Marketing Management,* p. 456.
10. Rosemarie Stefanou, *Marketing,* pp. 136-37.
11. Mclver and Naylor, *op. cit.,* p. 65.
12. Zeithaml & Bitner, *Services Marketing*, Tata McGraw-Hill, New Delhi, 3rd Edition p. 25.
13. *Ibid.,* p. 25.
14. *Ibid.,* p. 24.
15. Lovelock & Wirtz, *Services Marketing*, Pearson Education, Fifth Edition, p. 357.

★★★

TOTAL QUALITY MANAGEMENT

"Total Quality Management is the management approach of an organisation centered on quality, based on the participation of all its members and aiming at long-term success through customer satisfaction and benefits to all members of the organisation and to society."

– *ISO*

Chapter Objectives

Introduction – Service Quality? – Measurement of Service Quality – Total Quality Management (TQM) – Seven Management Gurus on Total Quality Management – Dimensions of Total Quality Management – Implementing TQM in the Services Sector – Roadmap for TQM – Controlling Quality – Effects of Total Quality Management – Quality Circle – Summary – Key Terms – Review Questions – Application Exercises – Endnotes.

Learning Objectives

This chapter aims at clarifying the different dimensions of Total Quality Management. The opinions of seven management gurus on TQM would help readers in knowing the concept of TQM. The readers also come to know the different dimensions of TQM in which we find focus on management of people, management of technology and management of infrastructure. The implementation of TQM in the services sector will help readers in practising the same. Besides, the problems like roadmap for TQM, controlling quality and effects of TQM will simplify the task of readers in perceiving the right ways for application and evaluation.

INTRODUCTION

We agree with this view that no management concept has contributed as much to the development of industrial economy as the TQM. The 20th century, no doubt, has the credibility of producing a number of illustrious management thinkers whose impact on secondary and tertiary sectors particularly for the purpose of social transformation has widely been appreciated. Of course, we are lucky to have a team of quality experts representing both East and West. The Quality Gurus like W. Edward Deming, Joseph M. Juran, Philip Crosby, Tom Peters, Kaoru Ishikawa, Shigeo Shingo and Genichi Taguchi virtually have revolutionised the concept of Total Quality Management.

Journey towards excellence remains incomplete if we delay conceptualisation of Total Quality Management. And today we cannot think of achieving excellence, if we are not committed to quality. In an age of globalisation, we cannot think of excelling competition if our products, systems and services do not have an edge over the rivals. If Japanese have been found moving fast towards excellence, it is due to their consistent efforts for defining quality. Not only the technical issues but they have seriously taken up soft issues such as leadership, culture of organisation, attitude towards customers, motivation of employees and finally the contributions of quality to the organisational excellence. This focuses our attention on the overall function of an organisation which simplifies the task of achieving world-class excellence.

The conceptualisation of the philosophy of TQM to the services sector of the economy is found significant as the domination of this sector has been found galloping even in the developing countries like ours. ISO 9000:2005 defines service quality as degree to which a set of inherent characteristics fulfil requirements. Of course, in the services sector, we cannot measure quality in the quantitative terms indeed in the subjective terms. Here, it is also important to mention that in banking, insurance, travel, security, and sanitation sectors we find offering of only services whereas in hospitability and healthcare, we also find some physical elements such as food and machines. It is against this background that in the services sector, we find quality a result of performance and expectation.

Increasing the contributions of services sector to the process of socio-economic transformation is our motto. The intensity of competition is found at its peak. At this juncture, it is only TMQ that would make our task much more easier. The process of corporatisation is found increasing fast, the domination of techniculture in the development of corporate culture has been found moving forward and the temptation of masses to the material culture is also found moving upward. A prescription which is to be much more effective in the changing perspective is application of Total Quality Management.

Sooner or later today or tomorrow, we are suitably rewarded for our excellence. Our dedication, commitment, optimism play an incremental role in generating excellence which is the result of perfection. An individual or an institution succeeds in thriving if there is no boundary for quality. Sky is the limit for perfection. Innovation makes new ways for achieving perfection. This makes it essential that we assign a transcendental priority to the total quality management. It is in this context that almost all the organisations have been found making innovative efforts to develop a new perception of quality which helps them in achieving the desired results.

Service quality is more a function of attitude than that of technology. Most of us believe in this proposition which is yet to be testified. We don't find strong justifications in this assumption to be more specific when we find sophisticated technologies engineering a base for techniculture, found very much instrumental in improving the quality of services that we offer. Of late, the information technologies have been found helping banks, insurance companies, transport companies, tour operators, educational institutions, hospitals, consultation companies, and many others in offering fast and right services to the customers. The service generating organisations operating manually find it difficult to compete with the organisations operating with the help of sophisticated technologies. The technology-driven services, of course, have been successful in establishing an edge over the manually-operated services. Thus, we find arguments to authenticate the instrumentality of technologies improving the quality of services.

We agree with this view that the quality of service is substantially influenced by the quality of personnel or human resources. The inefficient personnel find their task of satisfying the customers much more difficult even if they have the support of a well developed technology-driven system. Contrary to it, we find high-performer employees serving an organisation and satisfying the customers more effectively though the system is manually-driven. This focuses on the behavioural profile of providers who are found responsible to offer the services. Efficient, decent, submissive, personally-committed employees may establish an edge albeit over the technology-driven system. When we talk about the total quality management, our strong emphasis is on the quality of employees serving an organisation. In the modern world, the infrastructural facilities no doubt contribute significantly to the process of quality generation which focuses on the availability of infrastructural facilities to the service generating organisations. The customers of today assign due weightage to the amenities and facilities they are made available while using the services. Thus, we find it an important element of total quality management. In the bank, insurance, airways offices, you feel comfortable if air-conditioning, furnishing, light, water and sanitation facilities are of quality.

The use of billing machines has improved the functioning of the hotels and other organisations. The credit-debit machine has improved the functioning of banking organisations. The fax and e-mailing facilities have improved the services of a number of organisations. The use of computers has revolutionised the functional properties of hotels, airways, railways, tourist organisations and many others. These illustrations are a staunch testimony to this proposition that the use of information technologies has improved the quality of services. Thus, while managing quality, the service generating organisations also need to take the support of technologies which help them in making available to the users quality services.

The management of technologies *vis-a-vis* the management of people need world-class professional excellence. The availability of services or offering of services has been found significant in almost all the organisations. We agree with this view that a shoddy service quality does not necessarily cost less than the superior service quality. The banking organisations offer quality services but the bankers misbehave with the customers. In this context, the quality becomes inferior but the cost of services is not minimised. We can't negate the fact that to be more specific in the service generating organisations, we need to manage the service-providers very carefully and intelligently. All positive and sincere efforts of the policy decision-makers are transformed into a fiasco if the people engaged thereon lack a sound behavioural profile. The total quality management, thus, makes it essential that the policy decision-makers intensify multi-cornered efforts. They are serious to the innovation of service mix and side-by-side make possible efforts to intensify the use of technologies. The technology-driven system can fulfil the expectations of customer/users. They need to assign an overriding priority to the comforts, conveniences and users' interests and make the services technology-driven *vis-a-vis* user-friendly. They need to intensify research to understand the changing needs and requirements of customers. They are supposed to educate and train people so that they are well aware of the behavioural management. The total quality management thus necessitates to activate multi-dimensional measures.

In view of the above, it is right to mention that the service generating organisations bear the responsibility of energising the process of qualitative transformation. In the Indian perspective where we find users unorganised and unconscious, the policy makers need to bring a positive change in their attitudes. An attitudinal change in the boardrooms is thus a crying need of the hour. The banking organisations, transport organisations, insurance corporations, hospitals, educational institutions have to realise that the users in general lack a time-tested perception regarding the quality of services-promised to them but not offered. If they continue to go ahead with the attitude of exploitation, the masses would face a number of problems. It is against this background that the service generating organisations in general and the public utility undertakings in particular bear an outstanding task of inculcating awareness. Let the users know about the quality promised and only then attempt to rate your performance.

The Total Quality Management (TQM) thus draws our attention on people, technology, quality control, quality generation which help in shaping a new and internationally competitive perception of service quality instrumental in adding attractions. Quality excellence for organisational excellence is the main theme of TQM.

SERVICE QUALITY?

It is a combination of two words, Service and Quality where we find emphasis on the availability of quality services to the ultimate users. The term quality focuses on standard or specification that a service generating organisation promises. We can't have a clear-cut boundary for quality. Sky is the limit for quality generation. Scientific inventions and innovations make the ways for the generation of quality. More frequency in innovations, less gap in the process of quality upgradation. Like the goods manufacturing organisations even the service generating organisations are found instrumental in promoting research and devising something new that makes the services, schemes distinct to the competitors and creates profitable market opportunities to capitalise on. It is against this background that in the developed countries, the process of innovation is found more frequent. The created quality shapes the boundary of expectations since the users tasting the sweetness, of world-class services expect the same from other organisations. The expectations pave the avenues for satisfaction or dissatisfaction. If we succeed in fulfilling the expectations of users, they are found satisfied and the satisfaction makes the ways for increasing the market share.

It is right to mention that the service quality satisfaction is the outcome of the resources and activities expanded to offer service against the expectations of users from the same. It is also opined that the service quality can be broken into technical quality and functional quality.[1] For the purpose of improving the levels of the quality of services that we offer. The service generating organisations are required to identify the reasons entailed behind mounting dissatisfaction amongst the users and to activate appropriate measures (technical or functional) to minimise it. The technical measures draw our attention on the inventions and innovations in the field of technologies that help to improve the quality of services. It focuses on the use of technology or prefer to have a technology-driven service. The functional measures gravitate our attention on improving the quality of services offered by the employees, which pave ways for style of functioning, work culture, formulation of a profitable package, behavioural profile of employees or so. The frequency in the process of technological innovations *vis-a-vis* the growing influence of high-performer employees develop technology-driven and user-friendly service with a new quality. The functional quality of employees can be improved by strong emphasis on behavioural areas such as attitudes, service-mindedness, accessibility, interpersonal relations, appearance, commitment. It is right to say that poor quality of services or service failures are not designed into the system by the choice of the senior management.[2]

The aforesaid facts make it clear that the perception of service quality keeps on changing and the governing factors are use of new generation of technologies, development of quality people and an attitudinal change in the boardrooms. The top management and the senior executives bear the responsibility of shaping the perception of service quality by promoting the use of sophisticated technologies and increasing the number of personally-committed employees. This makes it essential that the service generating organisations prefer to practise the principle of making things happen which focuses on quality generation.

MEASUREMENT OF SERVICE QUALITY

An organisation producing goods or generating services requires to measure the quality of product/services-offered to the ultimate customers/users. This enables them to identify the errors and to follow up the corrective measures. We believe in this principle that sky is the limit for quality upgradation. There are a number of questions to be answered suitably if we have a desire to thrive in this competitive business world.

- Do we find any gap between the services-promised and services-offered?
- Do we assess the quality of services-offered?
- Do we find our employees maintaining the time schedule?
- Do we find our employees showing decent behaviour?
- Do we find our front-line staff showing empathy?
- Do we find accessibility?
- Do we find our services of world-class?
- Do we make a time-to-time rating of our services?
- Do we assign due weightage to the customer's complaints?
- Do we find the redressal measures sufficient?

The service generating organisations aware of the aforesaid problems and making sincere efforts to find out the right solutions succeed in making things happen. They frequently innovate their services and energise efforts to improve the quality of marketing resources. An organisation interested in establishing leadership intensifies the research activities and comes to know the changing needs and requirements of users. They identify the level of their expectations and innovate marketing efforts to fulfil them. Thus, they succeed in satisfying the users and increasing the market share. We can't negate that generation of profit is an important consideration without which the goods manufacturing or the service generating organisation can't exist but at the same time we also agree with this view that our professional excellence is coiled in the essence of generating profits by satisfying the users. If we succeed in satisfying the users, we also get a success in increasing the market share which makes the ways for establishing leadership. It is against this background that we make an advocacy in favour of innovating the marketing efforts which simplify our task of satisfying the users. Of course, we have a legitimate right of making profits but in no case, we are supposed to promote profiteering.

The aforesaid facts make it clear that the service generating organisations need to promote the concept of Total Quality Management (TQM). A number of goods and service generating organisations of world repute have been found making sincere efforts to practise the concept of total quality management. This makes it essential that the policy decision-makers make multi-cornered efforts to have a new perception of quality. By doing such, they can be successful in excelling competition. A number of foreign banks, insurance companies, airways, hotels, tourist organisations, educational institutions, hospitals have been found practising total quality management which have been helping them substantially in making their marketing resources innovative *vis-a-vis* productive. It is high time that even in the Indian perspective we make possible TQM.

TOTAL QUALITY MANAGEMENT (TQM)

World-class excellence makes the ways for world-class services. There is no limit for quality generation. Optimism paves avenues for having world-class goods or services. The innovators define and shape the perception of quality which determines the level of satisfaction. It is against this background that the world over we find a race for having a new quality that is to be internationally-competitive. This necessitates total quality management (TQM). The concept of total quality management focuses our attention on managing everything directly or indirectly instrumental in improving the quality of services that we propose to offer. Thus, we find TQM an innovative effort to help an organisation in getting a number one position. The TQM thus focuses our attention on the following:

- Quality is an aim ranking top position.
- Sky is the limit for quality generation.
- Best in the world applies to the effective management of human resources/employees.
- The employees serving an organisation are supposed to be problem solvers.
- The employee orientation is an essential consideration for quality upgradation.
- The performance orientation draws our attention on developing personally-committed employees.
- The use of sophisticated technologies injects new properties to the perception of quality.
- The professional excellence is coiled in the essence of making the entire process cost-effective.
- The innovative efforts are needed to enrich the core and peripheral services.
- The policy makers need a positive attitude. The holistic concept of management needs to be promoted even by the service generating organisations.
- The gap between the services-offered and services-promised is required to be bridged over.
- Offer more than the promises.

The aforesaid issues need a priority attention when we think over the concept of total quality management. The elements of TQM are People, Technology and Quality Control. The people or the management of human resources occupies a place of outstanding significance. A fair synchronisation of subjective and supportive knowledge is essential to develop quality people. By educating, training and motivating, you keep on moving the process of developing the personally-committed employees who simplify your task in many ways. A fair blending of performance orientation and employee orientation is thus found possible. By using the sophisticated technologies, you get success in offering quick, right services. This helps you in keeping your records crystal clear. The task of maintaining and controlling the quality is simplified considerably if you make possible an optimal use of information technologies. Thus, your task of remaining at the top is found easier. The techniculture simplifies your task.

TQM: CONCEPTUAL EXPOSITION

According to the Total Quality Forum of the USA, the TQM is a people-focused management system that aims at continual increase in customer satisfaction at continually lower cost. TQM is a total system approach (not a separate area or program) and an integral part of high-level strategy. It works horizontally across functions and departments, involving all employees, top to bottom and extends backward and forward to include the supply chain and the customer chain.

The ISO (International Standard Organisation) defines TQM as follows:

"Total Quality Management is the management approach of an organisation, centered on quality, based on the participation of all its members and aiming at long-term success through customer satisfaction and with benefits to all members of the organisation and society."

The globe is marching forward to excellence. This necessitates a broader concept of quality of products and services. Not only the quality concept but one step ahead the organisational excellence also becomes essential to cross the journey toward excellence. We name this concept as the Total Quality Management. It is also considered to be a philosophy for an optimal utilisation of resources with the motto of benefiting all the stakeholders of the organisation including the society at large.

SEVEN MANAGEMENT GURUS ON TOTAL QUALITY MANAGEMENT

Combined wisdom of seven quality gurus on Total Quality Management coming from both East and West has virtually made possible a qualitative improvement in the concept and percept of TQM. The following seven management gurus such as W. Edward Deming, Joseph M. Juran, Philip Crosby, Tom Peters, Kaoru Ishikawa. Shigeo Shingo and Genichi Taguchi have considerably influenced the TQM movement.[3] The service marketers need to develop their awareness of the Total Quality Management.

W. Edward Deming

Born in 1990, W. Edward Deming is famous for his work in Japan as an advisor of General MacArthur. He played a very constructive role in shaping the post Second World War Japanese economy. The industrial economy of Japan was virtually found derailed from the track and the concept of Deming not only helped bringing back the economy of Japan on the rail but helped a lot in dominating the changing global economic order. It was against this background that Japanese started increasing their share in the American markets. For his excellence in quality, Japanese remember. Deming and in his honour has also instituted the Deming Award. Deming made a strong advocacy in favour of 14-point approach as mentioned below:

1. Innovations should be both continuous and endless. A better way to make money is to stay in business and provide jobs through innovation, research, constant improvement and maintenance.
2. A new belief system in which mistakes and negativism are unacceptable. Management needs to take leadership for change.
3. Eliminate the need for mass inspection by building quality into the product.
4. End awarding business on price and aim at minimising the total cost.
5. Improve constantly the product.
6. Institute training.
7. Institute leadership.
8. Drive out fear. People must feel secured.
9. Break down barriers between the departments. Control goal conflict.
10. Eliminate slogans, exhortations and numerical targets for the workforce.
11. Remove barriers to taking pride in workmanship.

12. Eliminate numerical quotas or work standards.
13. Institute a programme for educating people.
14. Special Management Team for Quality Mission.

Joseph M. Juran

Born in 1904, Juran was a contemporary of Deming. His first book published in 1951 on Quality Control made him internationally famous. We find Quality Trilogy as his famous contribution such as Quality Planning, Quality Improvement and Quality Control. Juran has suggested a 10-step approach for improving the quality.

- Developing awareness of opportunities
- Setting goals for improvement
- Organising to achieve goals
- Providing training
- Carrying out projects to solve problems
- Reporting for progress
- Providing recognition
- Communicating the results
- Keeping score
- Maintaining momentum

It is also important to mention that Juran was of the opinion that in addition to the end-users we also need to develop our awareness of internal customers. At the intermediate stages of production or delivery of services to the internal customers, it is to be ensured that services are fit for use. The customer chain within the organisation must be strong. For ensuring quality, we cannot undermine the internal customers.

Philip Crosby

Born in 1926, Philip Crosby has the credibility of propounding the "Zero-Defect" movement. Crosby promoted the concept of "Do it Right First Time" and made a strong advocacy in favour of four absolutes of Quality Management as mentioned below:

1. Perceive Quality not as "goodness" or "elegance" rather than in tune with our requirements.
2. Prevention causes quality not the appraisal.
3. Performance standard must be zero-defects not "that is close enough."
4. Measurement of quality is the price of non-conformance not indices.

In the 14-step Programme of Crosby, we find him about Management Commitment, Quality Improvement Team, Quality Measurement, Cost of Quality Evaluation, Quality Awareness, Corrective Action, Zero-Defects Planning, Supervisory Training, Zero-Defects Day, Goal Setting, Errors Cause Removal, Recognition, Quality Councils, Do it all over Again.

In his noted contribution 'Quality without Tears' Crosby says "The main problem of quality as a management concern is that it is not taught in management schools. It is not considered to be a management function, but rather a technical one. However, either the pressure on quality erupting worldwide and the difficulty in getting senior management to do something about it, it becomes apparent that a new management is needed for quality."

Tom Peters

We find Tom Peters linking quality with leadership. Peters talks about twelve elements as mentioned below:

Management Obsession with Quality, Passion, Measurement of Quality, Reward for Quality, Training for Quality, Constitution of Multi-function Teams, Perceiving Small is Beautiful, Creating Endless Hawthorne Effect,

Parallel Organisational Structure for Quality, Involvement of All, Quality Minimises Cost, Considering it a Never-ending Journey.

Kaoru Ishikawa

Born in 1935 Ishikawa, a Professor at Tokio University is well-known for his writings on Quality Control. He has the credibility of simplifying the statistical techniques for quality control. The famous cause and effect diagram of Ishikawa provides a powerful tool for problem solving and quality improvement. The Quality Circle Movement was pioneered in Japan by Ishikawa. He has also the credibility of developing Company-wide Quality Control movement whose proper application results in reduction of effects and improvement in the quality of product. It also helps in reducing the wasteful work and rework. The cost of product can be minimised with the help of CWQC which may help in accelerating the rate of productivity. The maintenance of equipment is found rational and human relationships are found cordial. It is right to mention that CWQC engineered a sound foundation for the development of TQM.

Shigeo Shingo

Born in 1909 with industrial engineering background, Shigeo Shingo is known for his idea that once the defect has occurred during any process, the process should not be allowed to continue further. Shingo is known for his non-statistical innovations for reducing defects. The concept of 'Poka-Yoke' or mistake-proofing was developed by Shingo. Besides, he also succeeded in reducing delays and minimising bottlenecks. He developed Single Minute Exchange of Dies (SMED) and the Just-in-Time System while working in Toyota, Japan. The system made possible immediate supply of inputs without any delay. Shingo has also propounded new concepts in production management in his famous book 'Toyota Production System.'

Genichi Taguchi

Born in 1924, Taguchi is best known for his innovative application of statistical theory to manufacturing problems. Loss function is considered to be his famous contribution. Besides we also find "offline" and "on-line" as his important contributions. He made possible wider application of quality assurance. The following facts clarify the feelings and observations of Taguchi:

- Quality is the loss imparted to the society from the time product is shipped.
- Quality improvement and cost economy are necessary for staying in business.
- Six Sigma is the practical application of continuous quality improvement.
- Quality loss function magnifies the customer's loss due to a product's performance.
- Engineering design of the product plays an outstanding role in fixing cost and determining quality.
- By exploiting the non-linear effects of the product and process the performance variation can be reduced.
- Statistical planned experiments can be used to determine the settings of product and process parameters.

DIMENSIONS OF TOTAL QUALITY MANAGEMENT

In the face of mounting competition and increasing level of expectations of customers, the service generating organisations bear the responsibility of managing the different dimensions of total quality management in an effective way. It is right to mention that for total quality management we need concerted efforts at different stages and levels influencing the quality directly or indirectly, marginally or substantially. The three important elements sensitise the process of improving and maintaining the quality of services offered by the service generating organisations. It is quite natural that the management of people/employees serving the organisations needs a transcendental priority because the quality human resources keep on moving the development processes (Figure 4.1).

MANAGEMENT OF PEOPLE

The human resources/employees serving an organisation influence the level of success. Almost all the organisations either producing goods or generating services need to assign due weightage to the management of people failing which even the sophisticated technologies would hardly be successful in improving the quality of services. It is against this background that the marketing experts, of late, consider 'people' as a dominating submix of the marketing mix. We talk about corporate culture, we also talk about the work culture but fail to manage the people who make the ways for the same. We use sophisticated technologies, we expect quality results from the same but fail to manage the people who operate, handle and maintain the technologies. This makes it clear that all our development-oriented efforts are to be turned into a fiasco if we don't have quality people.

Quality people draws our attention on the people instrumental in generating efficiency and at the same time also making it easier to the technologies to deliver quality services to the ultimate users in a decent way. They are supposed to be personally-committed. It is only not sufficient that they are available and work during the defined working hours but it is also essential that their presence at any point, at any time promote the interests of organisations in which they work. They are relaxing but thinking about the organisations. They are walking, talking but thinking about the image of organisations in which they work. They are in the supermarkets and departmental stores for shopping but their actions directly or indirectly are not to make an invasion on the image of the organisations in which they work. Thus, in addition to efficiency, there are a number of factors to be given due weightage while developing quality people.

In the Indian perspective or in almost in all the less developed countries of the world, we find the perception of quality limited to the efficiency. The multi-dimensional serious implications and complications crop up due mainly to our wrong perception of quality. We have efficient professionals but they are found promoting profiteering. We have efficient faculty but not assigning due weightage to ethical values. We have efficient bureaucrats but making ways for corruption. We have efficient technocrats but we find them very much instrumental in using their excellence for a degeneration in quality just to promote personal interests. We have world-class entrepreneurs but we find them using their entrepreneurial excellence in exploiting the employees and users/customers. These illustrations are a mute testimony to the proposition that we have been successful in developing efficient employees but have miserably failed in using their excellence for promoting values. It is in this context that we don't find work culture in any of the organisations either manufacturing goods or generating services. If in a few of the private sector organisations, we find work culture, this is due mainly to job insecurity not on account of their human values.

The management experts feel that by developing quality people our emphasis is on developing such employees who are not only efficient but at the same time also efficacious in promoting the ethical values. Unless we make it possible, the work culture is not possible and unless we find work culture existent, the corporate culture would hardly gain the momentum. The service generating organisations, specially working in the Indian setting need to promote work culture which makes a strong advocacy in favour of a fair blending of performance orientation and employee orientation.

We can't negate the fact that the task is difficult but not so difficult as we feel. A well-knit education and training programme to develop human resources in the face of the defined principles of the holistic concept of management may make it possible. It is right to mention that the efficiency-based incentive plan would simplify the task of professionals while developing quality people. The educational institutions, the parents, the telecast media, the voluntary social organisations bear the responsibility of engineering a sound foundation for the development of value-based human resources. At the later stage, the organisations bear the responsibility of brushing up their faculties and sensing them suitably.

In the Indian perspective, the trade unions, workers', employees' associations have been found playing a negative role and unless we find them working with a positive attitude, the task is to remain much more difficult. This draws our attention on the attitudes of trade unions which by and large in almost all the cases have been seen making ways for inefficiency, value degeneration or so. We don't expect an attitudinal change in the trade unions. This draws our attention on promoting contractual job system where efficient personnel would suitably be rewarded whereas the inefficient would have to make a good-bye.

We talk in favour of using sophisticated technologies in the service generating organisations and in this context, it is pertinent that they are made available training facilities to operate, maintain, repair the technologies used or to be used. A number of service generating organisations like the Indian Railways, the Life Insurance Corporation of India, the Public Sector Commercial Banks have been found promoting the use of technologies but in a majority of the cases, we find even the sophisticated technologies not delivering quality services since the computer professionals lack excellence. This makes it essential that whatever the technologies we use or propose to use, our employees are well aware of the same. This would only not improve the quality of services but would also make the process of operation cost-effective.

MANAGEMENT OF TECHNOLOGY

Of late, we find even the service generating organisations making use of sophisticated information technologies for improving the quality of services. We can't deny that the use of technologies has helped them in many ways. If we find foreign banks and insurance companies establishing an edge over the public sector commercial banks and the LIC of India, an important reason entailed behind the process is the use of technologies. Not only the banks and insurance companies but we find even other service generating organisations using technologies with the prime motto of improving the quality. It is against this background that we focus on the management of technology.

Inventions and innovations make the ways for technological sophistication. Since we find development an ongoing process, it is natural that almost all the organisations either producing goods or generating services activate sincere efforts to energise the process of qualitative transformation. This makes it essential that they are well aware of the emerging trends in competition and speed up the process of innovation accordingly. The frequency in innovation is substantially influenced by the intensity of competition. We can't negate that the potentials to deliver the world-class services is fantastically influenced by the technological competence. Since we talk about total quality management, it is pertinent that the service generating organisations also create a quality gap with the support of sophisticated information technologies.

The banking companies, insurance companies, transport organisations, the hotels, the tour operators are some of the leading organisations making use of information technologies for improving the quality of their services. The advent of Electronic Fund Transfer System, Direct Pay Roll, Point of Sale System, Credit and Debit Cards, Pre-authorised transfer, Automated Clearing Houses, Billing Machines, ATMs, Credit Deposit Machines, Super computers and Micro Computers, Fax Machines, Internet and Intranet, E-mailing are to mention a few which have revolutionised the functional properties of the service generating organisations. We can't deny the fact that use of these technologies have made available to the users quality services.

The aforesaid facts testify that a number of service generating organisations now make use of sophisticated technologies which has, of course, changed the perception of customer services. The perception of expectations is also taking a new shape and therefore the users availing manually-operated services are found dissatisfied. The management of information technologies has simplified the process of making the creative decisions since the decision supporting system is found helping the professionals. The speed, accuracy, perfection are the new terms to be included in the expectations of customers. The use of technology is found common in the private sector but so far as the public sector organisations are concerned they have not been successful in making the use of information technologies in an effective way. This in a natural way draws our attention on the management of technology so that the use of technology is not only instrumental in offering the user-friendly services but also efficacious in making the process cost-effective.

The maintenance and operation of sophisticated technologies require proper care and skill. The atmospheric conditions, the ventilation and temperature, the use of materials for delivering goods require an intensive care. Sophisticated technologies, of course, bring frequency in operation but here it is essential that the professionals bearing the responsibility of maintenance and operation are well aware of the technicalities. The Public Sector Commercial Banks, the Indian Railways, the Life Insurance Corporation of India, the Air India and many others have been making use of sophisticated technologies to improve the quality of their services but in a majority of the cases we find the life expectancy of technologies very poor mainly due to faulty operation and maintenance. The dust particles, the temperature conditioning are not managed properly which ultimately affect the operational quality.

We can't deny that globalisation has engineered a strong foundation for the emergence of techniculture since the market conditions are now more competitive and organisations delaying the application have no option but to make a good-bye. The significant developments in the information technologies have virtually changed the entire scenario where the perception of users' satisfaction is found changing. There are a number of arguments to justify the use of technologies in the service generating organisations.

Fast disposal: The front line personnel who bear the responsibility of making available to the users the services-promised find it convenient to work fast, specially with the help of sophisticated technologies. The reservation counters, the reception counters, the complaints and grievances redressal counters, the operation counters would not face the problem of overcrowding if we find use of technologies. Today, the users prefer to have quick disposal which is not possible with a manually-driven system. Thus, it is right to say that the service generating organisations find it convenient to increase the speed of offering the services which would be very much instrumental in saving the time.

Maintaining Accuracy: In almost all the organisations, we find the problem of documentation filing, maintaining records, preparing list, listing the complaints, or preparing the reports. The users using the banking services, the tourists availing the services of tour operators and airways, the business executives using the services of hotels expect accuracy in the offering of services. The technologies make the task easier. The records can be made crystal clear, the information transmitted can be made authentic and reliable, the data made available would be found authentic or so. The information technologies help in maintaining accuracy.

Understanding the Behavioural Profile: The use of technologies make it easier to manage the information related to the behavioural profile of users. The professionals find it convenient to have information related to the changing needs and requirements, attitudes, expectations or so. The scanning of behavioural profile in a right fashion makes it easier to manage the marketing inputs optimally. The professionals find it convenient to sensitise the impulse of users. The innovation processes rest on the emerging trends in the behavioural profile. The survey results, the competitors' strategies are studied and analysed properly with the help of technology-driven marketing information system.

Effective Communication: The communication processes can be made more effective specially with the help of technology-driven services. Of late, almost all the organisations have been making use of communication technologies to sensitise the communication processes. The fax machines, e-mailing, e-commerce, sophisticated telephone instruments, Internet and Intranet services have paved avenues for transmission of information. The cases of miscommunication, confusion and misunderstanding are found minimised considerably. The organisations thus are found efficacious in making the communication process more effective.

Performance Evaluation: Making an appraisal of the services of different employees is essential to make the incentive plans rational. By evaluating performance, an organisation succeeds in identifying the high performers and rewarding them suitably that makes the ways for performance orientation *vis-a-vis* employee orientation. The imparting of training facilities, the organisation of refresher courses, capsule courses are found in tune with our requirements and therefore we succeed in evaluating the performance. The computers simplify the task substantially.

Cost-effectiveness is possible: Almost all the organisations need to make the processes cost-effective, specially to minimise the operational cost. The use of technology minimises the administrative expenses since an organisation requires the less number of personnel. To be more specific, the number of front-line personnel can be minimised sizeably with the use of sophisticated technologies. This makes possible only not qualitative improvement in the services-offered but also minimises the cost.

The aforesaid facts make it clear that the use of technology would gain popularity even in the years to come. We can't deny that the technology-driven system makes the ways for user-friendly services but at the same time, we also find technologies showing a number of harmful effects in the Indian perspective. The possibilities of retrenchment of employees in almost all the service generating organisations where we find use of sophsiticated technologies can't be negated. In a country like India where the problem of unemployment is found at its peak, the use of sophisticated technologies, no doubt, would fuel and aggravate the intensity of the problem. This makes it essential that the service generating organisations while using technologies also think over the problem seriously and intensify efforts to make a rational use of technology. We are not opposed to a technology-driven system but can't make an advocacy in favour of a system that aggravates the problem of unemployment. Besides, the mounting problem of unemployment would make youths jobless. The human resources getting employment would get more incentives but the human resources found unemployed would face the problem of survival.

One segment of society earning more and another segment earning nothing would make the ways for dissatisfaction and social tension. The unfair, unethical and illegal practices would get a sound nexus. The masses would naturally be more crazy as we find in the USA where the new generation is found dissatisfied. The use of technologies would help a contraction in the development faculties since the decision-making and supporting systems would increase our dependence on technologies. The human minds taking rest become insensitive and unproductive.

IMPLEMENTING TQM IN THE SERVICES SECTOR

In the process of economic transformation, we find services sector in a dominating position. However, the incredible opportunities existent in the Indian economy are yet to be capitalised on. The corporatisation of services sector has gained a rapid momentum and even in the years to come, the trend will continue. We need to establish an edge over the rivals and this is to be easier if the TQM is practised. The plan for implementation needs due care. The most difficult thing in the conceptualisation process is to show measurable results through the implementation of tools and techniques with the proper behaviour and attitude of people involved in the process. In a majority of the cases, we find even excellent plans floundering. Strategical and tactical issues need due care of professionals in the implementation process. The issues like organisational structure, policies, building of competence and cultural transformation may be helpful in the implementation process.

A holistic organisational view is found essential in the present changing scenario. This focuses our attention on pleasing both the external as well as the internal customers. A narrow departmental focus is not to serve our purpose. Conceptualisation of the 9th rule of Deming "Break down barriers between staff areas" in which we find, the goals of all functions aligned to the organisational objectives and mission; needs due care. Interdependence of various departments simplifies the task of professionals.

We find TQM an organisation-wide initiative. This makes it essential that the management board is found sincerely involved in the process of overall guidance and control. The success of TQM rests on the interdepartmental and intradepartmental co-operation. In this context, the steering committee is required to play an important role. Approval of the TQM plan, provision of resources, periodical reviews for monitoring of progress, resolving interdepartmental problems while implementing TQM and advising on the corrective actions to keep the plan on track are areas where we find the Steering Committee playing an important role.

Based on the mandate of the TQM steering committee, development of a project document is found essential which should essentially have well-defined objectives, constitution of a project team including a leader, list of resources allocated and a schedule of project activities. The initial step in the implementation of TQM is concerned with the development of departmental mission based on organisational vision and mission and critical success factors. We cannot negate that the most critical success factor in the TQM is customer satisfaction. The professionals here bear the responsibility of satisfying the internal customers who will make ways for the satisfaction of external customers. The development of specifications is found essential which will define the requirements of internal customers. Since dissatisfaction of internal customers results into the dissatisfaction of external customers, it is essential that internal customers should be fully satisfied.

In each and every organisation, we find critical success factors. The professionals bear the responsibility of identifying the critical factors and then to identify the areas of improvement in various departments. Assessment of progress becomes essential for planning development.

ROADMAP FOR TQM

Careful planning and effective implementation of TQM necessitate a roadmap.[4]

1. **An Assessment of organisation:** The first thing in the roadmap is to carry out an assessment of the organisation on the scale of excellence. The weaknesses and their causes are to be identified. It is also to be deliberated that TOM is likely to be the appropriate initiative.
2. **Sensitising and developing awareness:** The unions and staff are to be taken into confidence that the conceptualisation of TQM would not have any adverse impact an the job security and working conditions. An awareness programme will let working people know the need, concept, benefits and justifications for TQM.
3. **Establishing vision, mission and objectives:** The organisational objectives should be based on the mission of customer focus besides broader applicability and pragmatism. The objectives are to be communicated throughout the organisation.

4. **Translating goals into practice:** At functional level, the goals are to be developed and the efforts to be made for functional improvement are to be linked with the organisational objectives.
5. **Involving customers:** An interactive session with customers will help in knowing their needs and perceptions of the organisation.
6. **Studying the current process:** The existing processes are to be studied and documented. The standards of current processes are to be measured against the processes to be followed.
7. **Taking up improvement projects:** The required teams are to be constituted and projects are to be allocated to them. The work of these project teams are to be monitored.
8. **Learning needs are to be identified:** The achievements of the goals of TQM are to be evaluated. The adequacy of current knowledge and its shortfalls are to be assessed.
9. **Training and enriching the potentials:** The materials required for training are to be procured and the resource persons to; train them are to be identified. The satisfaction and motivation factors need due attention. The effectiveness of training to be evaluated by studying the performance of trained persons.
10. **Assessing the progress:** The progress is to be assessed and for that questionnaire to be designed. The weak areas of weaknesses and the reasons far the same are to be identified.
11. **Continuing improvement:** The objectives are to be revised, if necessary. The experiences of past need due attention in the very context.

CONTROLLING QUALITY

It is only not sufficient that you promise. It is also pertinent that you make available the services-promised to the ultimate users. This makes it essential that the service generating organisations make sincere efforts to control quality. Control is an important element of total quality management. The banking organisations promise but the users fail to get the same. The Insurance Corporations promise but the policyholders find a big gap between the services-promised and services-offered. The Airways promise but they fail in maintaining the time schedule. Thus, a big task before the service generating organisations is to minimise the gap and this necessitates quality control.

Quality control focuses our attention on monitoring and controlling the variables directly or indirectly related to the offering of promised services. It is a progressive science with tremendous opportunities. It explores avenues for quality generation and makes it sure that the machines, people, infrastructure used in the process are not to generate problems. It is a device to increase efficiency by making things happen. The scientists and their inventions and innovations play a decisive role in maintaining and controlling the quality. The quality control covers in its compass stage-to-stage evaluation, identification of errors and devising ways to correct them. The men, machines, infrastructure are used in a defined way which simplify the task of defining the standards, specifications and the results of inputs used in the process.

In the Indian perspective, we realise the need for controlling the quality since we often face the problem of quality degeneration. The service generating organisations promise the world-class services but the services-promised hardly reach to the ultimate users. It is against this background that a majority of the service generating organisations have been facing image problem. We find cases of quality degeneration in almost all the public utility undertakings. The Public Sector Commercial Banks, the Insurance Corporations, the Indian Railways, the Indian Airlines and Air India have been facing the problem of quality degeneration. This has been found welcoming leading foreign companies to throw a challenge to the domestic companies which makes it essential that the service generating organisations assign due weightage to the problem of quality control.

Standards, specifications define our target. We employ people, take support of sophisticated technologies and make available a number of infrastructural facilities to maintain and offer the service of promised standard and specifications but generally fail in doing such since the quality control measures are not taken in a right way. In some of the cases, the human resources become ineffective and in some other cases, the technologies become unproductive. The policy decision-makers find it difficult to control the men since the trade unions often stand as a barrier. The technologies fail in delivering goods since the human resources are not made available the required training facilities. Thus, we find mismanagement in both the areas which complicate the task of maintaining the quality. The professionals bear the responsibility of setting standards, engaging men and machines and making available to the ultimate users the services-promised. The quality inspectors bear the responsibility of monitoring the ways for maintaining and controlling the quality.

Quality control is a deliberate and planned activity having for its object the determination of the quality of a product with a view to accepting it as such in case it satisfies the stipulated requirements, or in case it does not satisfy these requirements to take necessary measures to correct the quality appropriately.[5] Control of quality is best exercised during the course of production actually starting with the inputs going through the various processing stages and ending up with the final product paying due attention to packing, storage and transport. When we talk about the control of quality in the service sector, our emphasis is on controlling the process of offering the promised services to the users.

Standards or specifications of quality are prerequisites of quality control because unless quality characteristics are assessed, specified and measured, quality control cannot be implemented. Sometimes the specifications are given by the buyers himself. For several products, we find Indian standards specified by the Bureau of Indian Standards. The international standards are specified by the bodies like International Standards Organisation (ISO) and International Electrochemical Commission (IEC).[6]

The service generating organisations are also supposed to control quality and for that we find standards or specifications. The services found internationally-competitive need standards to be specified at international level. The professionals bear the responsibility of maintaining and controlling the quality which make it essential that they are particular to the quality of people, machines, infrastructural facilities used for offering the services.

Quality improvement is a prerequisite for competing successfully in the highly competitive market. We don't find a limit to quality upgradation since the inventions and innovations and use of sophisticated technologies in the process of offering the services shape and reshape the perception of quality. The service generating organisations believing in making things happen prefer to innovate their services frequently. Thus, by momentising the innovation process, they create a quality gap. The competitive organisations find their services of inferior quality and therefore find it difficult to compete. The gap is also created by the providers in the process of offering the services. The service generating organisations make a promise for certain specific quality or standard but the people engaged in the process create a gap by degenerating the quality of services-offered. Thus, we find creation of a big gap at both the stages. A gap in quality generated by the innovation process makes possible a qualitative improvement in the quality of services whereas a gap in quality created by the providers makes possible degeneration in quality. When the users get quality of services which they did not expect, we also find satisfaction at its peak and contrary to it, when the users don't get the quality promised, we also find dissatisfaction at its peak. The first gap is found of positive nature whereas the second gap is of negative nature. In a majority of the cases to be more specific in the Indian perspective, we find a gap in quality created by the providers himself. While controlling quality, it is to be made sure that the providers are not to create such a gap that makes the ways for dissatisfaction. It is against this background that we find quality control assuming a place of outstanding significance since a degeneration in the process is to aggravate the image problem.

The elements of Total Quality Management (TQM) thus need an intensive care even in the service generating organisation (Figure 4.1).

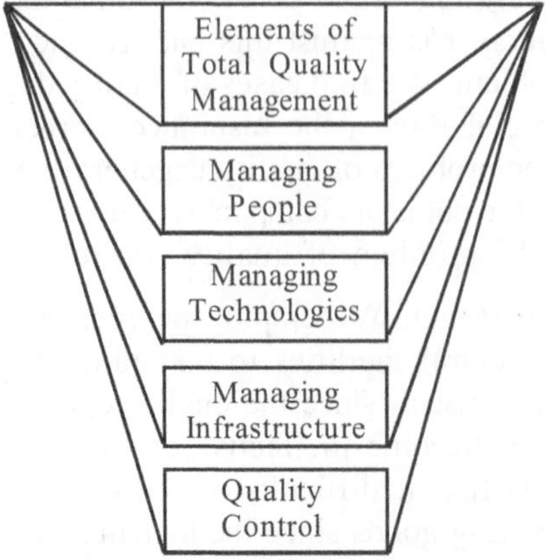

Fig. 4.1: Total Quality Management (Elements)

In the present business world where we find the intensity of competition moving upward, it is pertinent that the policy decision-makers assign due weightage to the different elements of total quality management. At the outset, they need to manage people. In the total quality management, we find management of people playing a decisive role since the performance orientation is considered to be the most vital aspect of quality generation. We need efficient, dedicated, personally-committed employees who are supposed to know how to work efficiently even if the working conditions are not conducive. The high performers simplify our task. The professionals bear the responsibility of managing people.

The second task is to manage technology. It is well-known that of late even the service generating organisations make use of a number of sophisticated technologies to improve the quality of their services. The management of technology draws our attention on using appropriate technology, maintaining and operating the technologies as per the required norms, making available to the technologies the required working conditions, such as power, temperature, ventilation or so. Gentle handling, proper switching are found significant in the very context,

In addition, the service generating organisations also need to manage the infrastructure playing an incremental role in improving the quality of services, such as light, furnishing, water and sanitation facilities, safety provisions or so. The quality control focuses our attention on setting the standards, monitoring the operations, making it sure that the promised services are made available to the ultimate users without any distortion.

EFFECTS OF TOTAL QUALITY MANAGEMENT

For the projection of a positive image, it is essential that the service generating organisations keep on moving the process of quality upgradation. We find enough scope for a qualitative transformation and it is upon the professionals to identify the opportune moment and to initiate the process. There are some of the positive aspects of quality generation and an organisation assigning due weightage to them succeeds in excelling competition. The following effects of total quality management make it clear that the service generating organisations assigning an overriding priority to TQM succeed in creating and capitalising on the profitable opportunities.

1. Total Quality Management helps in energising the innovation process: Innovation occupies a place of outstanding significance in almost all the organisations either producing goods or generating services. The organisations believing in making things happen intensify research and make their marketing decisions innovative. The inventions and innovations focus on the services very much instrumental in sensitising the prospects. It is natural that prospects have a craze for using the innovative services which have not been used by their counterparts. The TQM is based on an intensive research. The core or peripheral services of innovative nature makes the marketing decisions proactive. The innovative services, promotional measures, way of offering the services, instrumentality of pricing as an operational tool simplify the task of marketers. The professionals find it convenient to market the services profitably. Since the organisations promote innovation, the followers keep themselves engaged in copying the services. The task for the competitors is found much more difficult when they find in the markets new services much earlier they adopt the old one.

2. TQM makes the ways for cost-effectiveness: Maintaining cost economy is essential for surviving or thriving the organisation. This makes it essential that whatever we invest is found optimal to our requirements. We do minimise our requirements and further are careful while investing or spending. It is well-known that the service generating organisations make use of a number of resources for making available quality services to the users. We find a number of employees of different echelons. The infrastructural facilities also need huge investment. Of late, the use of sophisticated technologies is also common. The research and development activities can't be of world-class unless we take support of value-based efficient researchers and a well developed marketing information system which is technology-driven. Thus, the multi-dimensional requirements to make possible total quality management need huge financial investment. The organisations promoting TQM are supposed to make their resources productive. They need to explore ways for optimising their requirements. While developing new services or while developing a package, they need to assign due weightage to cost-benefit analysis. While engaging employees, imparting training facilities, introducing an incentive plan; we find them considering the benefits they expect from their investments. The use of sophisticated technologies is found based on service plus economy. The professionals bear the responsibility of making a step-to-step evaluation of cost. This helps them in controlling the expenses at different stages. If they succeed in maintaining cost economy, the quality service are offered at a reasonable fee structure. The total quality management thus makes the ways for maintaining cost-effectiveness. Of late, the cost-effectiveness is found occupying due attention since the users/customers are now found more sensitive to price. The increasing sensitivity of price/fee in making the buying decisions makes it essential that cost-effectiveness continues to get due attention. The productive use of inputs is thus found possible if we promote total quality management.

3. The Productivity is accelerated: We are aware of the fact that economy or cost-effectiveness makes the ways for high productivity. If we find organisations successful in optimising the investments/expenses; if we find the marketing resources proactive; the rate of productivity is maximised. The service generating organisations assigning a transcendental priority to TQM devise ways for optimising the cost. The efficient, dedicated, personally-committed employees; the fast, reliable services made available by the sophisticated technologies; the high quality of infrastructural facilities used for offering the services; sincere and honest efforts while maintaining and controlling the quality are some of the positive developments which pave avenues for high productivity. The productivity of human resources, technologies and infrastructure if keep on moving upward; we find an increase in the rate of overall productivity. This makes it clear that the total quality management carries forward the task of accelerating productivity.

4. The Profitability is found high: Of course, we find a correlation between cost-effectiveness and productivity. Since the TQM makes possible cost economy, it is found easier to accelerate the rate of productivity. We find a direct impact of high productivity on the rate of profitability. If the productivity is high, the profitability is also to show the same trend. Thus, the service generating organisations having a legitimate right of making profits find it convenient to increase the rate of profitability. We can't deny the fact that high profitability makes the ways for the maximisation of assets which enrich the potentials of an organisation to deliver goods even in the future. The service generating organisations successful in maintaining the process of profit generation are found efficacious in subserving the interests of all. A circle of positive developments keeps on moving the process of qualitative-cum-quantitative developments.

5. Projection of a fair image: The TQM, thus, paves avenues for the projection of a fair image since the organisations maintaining consistency in profit generation process motivate all the concerned parties. The masses form a positive opinion about the organisations, the users get quality services, the employees get handsome incentives, the investors get a profitable return and these positive developments simplify the task of professionals. Building and projection of a positive image rest on the quality of services an organisations offers.

The aforesaid facts are a staunch testimony to this proposition that the total quality management has a far reaching effect on the strength of an organisation. The TQM paves copious avenues for a sound health.

QUALITY CIRCLE

We consider Quality Circle, a key to quality products. Quality circle can fulfil the promises of maintaining quality by optimising the performance of both individuals and organisations. It is a unique tool for making available to the customers or users, goods or services of high quality. It is right to mention that quality is never an accident but a result of consistent, intelligent efforts.[7] Japanese after the World War II skilfully integrated the American Behavioural Sciences and statistical theories and techniques in the development of quality circles (QCs). Right from 1945 till present, they have successfully made possible quality circles which has helped them substantially in maintaining and improving the quality of goods or services. Ishikawa (1963) recommended that foremen should establish book reading circles within their work groups to promote quality concept. His suggestion gradually was taken up the world over. The work-based groups moved from theoretical study to problem-solving which emerged into QCs. This move focused on group decentralisation and participative decision-making. Education and training in quality control concepts and techniques were extended to include every level in the organisation from the top management to the shop floor. A Quality Control Audit (QCA) was introduced and computers were used for quality control activities. Thus, we find emergence of the concept of quality circle which is considered to be a voluntary group of 5-15 people who do the same work and meet regularly under the leadership of foremen. Japanese thinking about QCs is that the real cause of problem is often unknown and that only by providing employees with adequate tools and techniques the process would be instrumental in solving the problems. The QCs are thus aimed at:

- Making possible self and mutual development.
- Increasing quality and cost awareness.

- Utilising the creativity of the workforce.
- Improving the morale of workers.
- Developing managerial ability and leadership.
- Building team spirit through participative decision-making.
- Implementing and managing the accepted ideas.
- Improving task-resulting in a better product and process at work.
- Improving productivity.

The success of QCs depends upon the establishment of effective communication among their members. The mutual trust between the management and workers is a must. The workers must be convinced that management is really interested in their suggestions and these suggestions finally lead to the betterment of the individual as well as the organisation. The Japanese see their people as the most valuable resources. This is evident in saying "Making Every Man Manager." The training requirements are found very critical to the success of QCs. Dr. Ishikawa feels that training should be a part of an overall company programme. QC training involves training of communication, human relations and skills to complement technical requirements. The participative management techniques are taught along with statistical tools like Pareto Charts, Ishikawa diagram, histogram, scatter diagram, checksheet and control charts. An adequate time is given for training to ensure widespread acceptance and systematic exposure.

QCs are found process-oriented and the processes deal with the system of production indirectly due to their predominantly preoccupation with production analysis and the collective development of production improvement plans. To implement QCs, an organisation is required to make necessary preparations.

The following steps are found important:

- A dialogue between the management and the people closest to the means of production is found useful. The neutrally knowledgeable third party consultant may perform this responsibility.
- The current organisational climate requires an intensive audit.
- The QC leaders and members need proper education and training and for this, the allocation of resources is essential.
- Establishment of objectives involving supervisors and middle managers.
- In all phases of implementation, the involvement of unions is found impact generating. The unions need to feel that the QCs do not infringe upon the collective bargaining process.
- After the formation of QCs, the education and training programmes should be intensified at all levels of the organisation. All the employees should be given an opportunity to assume leadership.
- After processing, the impact should be measured and the objectives should be evaluated and revised, if necessary.
- The QCs are found effective when we allow to implement their own suggestions.
- The problems regarding incentives should be resolved by measuring the value of contributions.
- High degree of trust and co-operation, open communication between workers and managers is found essential.

We can't deny that the formation of QCs would be effective even in the service generating organisations. Of course, the approaches would be a bit different. The service generating organisations need the cooperation of employees. This makes it essential that the organisations assign due weightage to the properties to be inculcated during the education and training programmes. The sensitivity rate of people is found of high order and therefore the service generating organisations need to modify their education and training programmes in the face of recent developments. Of late, the use of sophisticated information technologies is found increasing and this makes it essential that the employees are well aware of the technologies to be used in the process. Effective communication is an essential part of QCs and the instrumentality of the technologies of new generation is found successful in sensitising the communication processes. The technological awareness would simplify the task considerably.

The QCs make an advocacy in favour of a sound relation between the management and employees. The services generating organisations, specially in the public sector are found unionised. The domination of unions is so high that the implementation of policies is often delayed. This makes it essential that the service generating organisations seek the cooperation of trade unions failing which the task would remain difficult and the problems would hardly be unlocked.

The Quality circles would help the service generating organisations in many ways. The figure 4.2 focuses on the formation of quality circles.

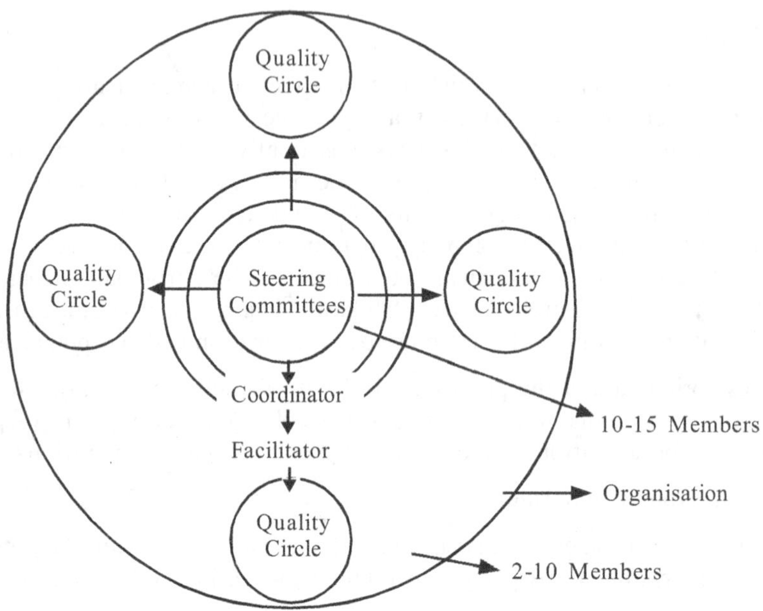

Fig. 4.2: Formation of Quality Circles

The steering committee would help the organisations in formulating sound policy decisions which would simplify their task of quality innovation. The innovative services or schemes if well coordinated and facilitated would be instrumental in making the services internationally-competitive. The service mix would be in the face of emerging trends in the level of expectations of users/prospects. The excellence of quality circles would depend upon the instrumentality of coordinators and facilitators. If they have effective communication, a well developed technology-driven marketing information system; the innovation in the peripheral services would make the ways for product attractiveness. This would pave copious avenues for demand generation. If the users are found influenced by the services of foreign banks, insurance companies, airways, hospitals, educational institutions; this is due mainly to the fact that they innovate their peripheral services frequently. The Quality Circles would devise new ways of innovating the peripheral services. The facilitators are supposed to be aware of the changing preferences of users; they are also supposed to know the innovative efforts of competitors and to transmit the facts to the coordinators. The coordinators bear the responsibility of informing the messages to the steering committee who in consultation with both of them would make possible a change in the policy decisions.

In view of the above, it is right to mention that the formation of quality circles would make possible total quality management. The organisations would find the present profitable and the future prosperous. The potentials would be enriched, the resistance power would be maximised, the threats and challenges in the markets would effectively be countered and a sound foundation would be engineered for the qualitative and quantitative improvements. Since the market is competitive, the organisations would be required to make it an ongoing process. The growing influence of techniculture makes it pertinent that the service generating organisations prefer to have a technology-driven system.

SUMMARY

You have studied in this chapter different components of TQM. After going through the chapter, be sure that following facts are well-versed:

Service Quality?: The term 'Service Quality' draws our attention on the quality of services made available to the organisation. The perception of service quality keeps on changing and the governing factors are the use of sophisticated technology, development of professionally-sound and personally-committed people and availability of supporting infrastructural facilities.

Measurement of Service Quality: In the measurement of service quality, we focus on total quality management which is related to maintaining and controlling the quality of people, technology and infrastructure. The aggregation of all the four essentials helps in managing the quality of services. We also call them various elements of service quality.

Total Quality Management: The word 'Total' focuses our attention on involvement of all the departments at all levels. The word 'Quality' draws our attention on organisational excellence not only the quality of product. The term 'Management' is not only confined to a technical discipline, indeed it is a management function. Thus, the TQM is a people-focused management system.

Seven Management Gurus on TQM: The experts or management gurus are W. Edward Deming, Joseph M. Juran, Philip Crosby, Tom Peters, Kaoru Ishikawa, Shigeo Shingo, Genichi Taguchi. They have contributed significantly to the management concept.

Dimensions of TQM: The different dimensions of TQM draw our attention on Management of People, Management of Technology, Management of Infrastructure and Quality Control.

TQM in the Services Sector: The conceptualisation of TQM in the services sector necessitates a holistic organisational view. The external as well as the internal customers need due attention. The professionals need interdepartmental and intradepartmental cooperation while practising TQM. Development of departmental mission based on organisation vision and mission need due care.

Roadmap for TQM: Effective implementation of TQM requires a roadmap.

Quality Control: Quality control focuses our attention on monitoring and controlling the variables directly or indirectly related to the offering of promised services. It is a progressive science with tremendous opportunities.

Effects of TQM: The multi-dimensional effects of TQM are energising the innovation process, making the ways for cost-effectiveness, acceleration of productivity rate of profitability and projection of a fair image.

Quality Circle: It is a unique tool for making available to the customers goods or services of high quality. It is a key to quality products.

KEY TERMS

Quality Gurus	Quality Triology
Techno-driven Services	Quality Mission
Billing Machines	Zero-defects Day
Credit-debit Machines	Six Sigma
Boardrooms	Non-linear Effects
Shoddy Service Quality	Roadmap
Service Quality	Toyota Production System
Front-line Staff	Quality Circle
Empathy	Quality Control Audit
Holistic Concept of Management	Electronic Fund Transfer System
Seven Management Gurus on TQM	Direct Payroll
Deming Award	Automated Clearing Houses

Review Questions

1. Focus on the term Total Quality Management. Explain the relevance of quality to the service generating organisations.
2. What do you mean by the Total Quality Management? State and explain the different dimensions of TQM.
3. "Measurement of the services-offered to the ultimate users is essential to identify the errors and make the services upto the expectations of users." Comment.
4. Throw light on the observations of seven management gurus on Total Quality Management.
5. Focus on the effects of Total Quality Management in the context of service generating organisations.
6. Prepare a Roadmap for Total Quality Management in Indian perspective.
7. Discuss the effects of Total Quality Management on the service generating organisations working in India.
8. What do you mean by Quality Circle? Do you feel that a formation of quality circles is essential for total quality management? Justify your answer.
9. What do you mean by Quality Control? Explain the importance of Quality Control to the service generating organisations.
10. "There is no doubt in it that different elements of total quality management are important for quality generation but of all the elements, we find management of people playing a commanding role in managing quality." Comment on this statement with suitable examples.
11. "In an age of techniculture where sophisticated information technologies play an incremental role in improving the quality of services, the total quality management is difficult unless we make use of information technologies." In the face of this statement, focus on the role of technologies in improving the quality of services.

Application Exercises

1. As a marketing professional, focus on the role of technologies in improving the quality of services in the public sector banks in India.
2. You have been serving an insurance company as a marketing manager. Explain your role in attaining organisational excellence.
3. "Measurement of the services-offered to the ultimate users is essential to identify the errors and to make the services upto the expectations of users." Comment on this statement as a marketing professional.
4. As a service marketer, justify the formation of quality circles for conceptualising Total Quality Management.
5. You have not been getting the expected level of support of your team of marketing people. Do you feel that it is to affect the application of Total Quality Management in your organisation?
6. Prepare a roadmap for implementing TQM.
7. Do you feel that 14-point approach of Deming will be sufficient for the application of TQM in an organisation?
8. Explain the viewpoints of Ishikawa in the formation of quality circle.
9. Do you feel the TQM is a people-focused management system?

Endnotes

1. Singh, J.D., Bank Marketing in India, *International Journal of Bank Marketing,* 3/2, 1985, pp. 48-63.
2. *Ibid.*
3. H. Lai., *Organisational Excellence through Total Quality Management,* New Age International Publisher, 2008, pp. 111, 122.
4. *Ibid.,* p. 250.
5. Benentt R.C., The Service Sector in India, Some Heretical Thoughts, *Indian Management*, pp. 12-16.
6. Collier D.A., *Services Management*; Prentice-Hall Inc., Englewood, N.J., 1987.
7. Pemse M.L., *Quality Circles: A Key for Quality Product Management;* Vol, II/1, 1985, pp. 8-14.

★★★

Bank Marketing

A corollary to the major challenge of delivering quality services to the customers may be to practise modern marketing principles. The conceptualisation of innovative marketing in the public sector commercial banks is a crying need of the hour.

Chapter Objectives

Learning Objectives

The motive of this chapter is to practise marketing principles in the banking organisations facing a number of challenges and threats. The bank professionals will be successful in developing their awareness of the various submixes of marketing and their conceptualisation in the banking services. With the electronics banking, we find a number of new developments in the banking services. The public sector commercial banks need to practise the modern marketing principles which helps them in maintaining and retaining their market share. This chapter aims at sensitising the readers to the modern marketing practices adopted by foreign banks. With a holistic approach and a professional touch, the public sector commercial banks are required to innovate the marketing strategies.

INTRODUCTION

We agree with this view that India's journey of globalisation has not been marked by crisis or bloodshed. The national economy has moved from managing the external sector to implementing an optimal integration of domestic and external sector and the global economy. Banking business in India is getting redefined; of course, it is likely to face myriad challenges and opportunities specially during the second decade of 21st century because by that time they would be fully exposed to competition. Indian banks are bracing themselves to be ready through the adoption of new generation of sophisticated technology, to be efficacious of strengthening their capital base. We cannot deny that the structure of Indian banking system is expected to undergo a transformation, led by consolidation, convergence and technology. The process is already switched on and we expect the complete transformation by the second decade of this century. From large number of small banks to small number of large banks; the scenario that we expect tomorrow. Indian banking system is increasingly becoming competitive and is getting integrated with global banking. Customer acquisition is found at war footing. Service delivery standards are being benchmarked to global standards and the competitive advantage is coming from technology and marketing. The new generation of sophisticated technology has accelerated the value addition process and the additional attractions of peripheral services have tempted customers to such an extent that the process of snatching business from public to private banks are found with an accelerated pace. Internet banking has virtually made ways for a number of qualitative improvements in the banking services. Frequent use of debit and credit cards, electronically transfer of funds, online accounting system, electronically payment and settlement system, tax information network of Income Tax Department, doorstep banking cellphone banking, internet banking, web-based banking and virtual banking have lured customers of almost all the segments.

When technology starts governing the functional behaviour, the perception of quality of services is found considerably influenced. The service blueprinting and servicescapes are now found changing. The service environment and service ambience are also found in a new shape. But what we need to do more is inculcation of service culture in which we are still lagging far behind. Technological sophistication cannot serve our purpose, if we lack service fragrance. We need professionals having world-class excellence. We need a new vision and a holistic approach. Since it is an age of compete or perish, the only prescription that can help us in excelling competition is a team of dedicated and committed, value-based and professionally-sound bankers. The private sector banks have been successful in increasing the number of star or super performers and the public sector banks have to create a condition for that.

Greater presence of international players in Indian financial system has been found creating a condition in which some of the Indian banks would become global players. The roadmap drawn by the Reserve Bank of India makes it clear that just by the beginning of the second decade of 21st century, the foreign bank in India would be at par and will have a level playing field with Indian banks.

The satisfaction index is substantially influenced by the quality of services made available to the customers/ users. If we feel that the Indian economy is moving on the right path of progress; if we realise that the Indian consumers are now more conscious, a radical change in the marketing practices of the banking organisations is required essential. In the past, the banks did not find any attraction in the Indian economy because of the low level of economic activities and meager business prospects. Today, we find a positive change in the business regulations and development strategies and therefore it is natural that strategies designed earlier show a lukewarm response. More than a century back in 1858, the then Finance Minister of the Governor General's Council realised the need of a national bank. With this, the Government was found evincing interest in the development of the organised banking system in the Indian economy. Accordingly, the State Bank of India was set up for extending credit facilities to hitherto neglected areas of the country. However, the needs and requirements, hopes and aspirations of the masses remained neglected till the dawn of independence in 1947.

With the attainment of independence, the contours of development underwent radical changes. The Constitution of India assigned an overriding priority to social welfare and regional imbalance. The policy makers realised that the establishment of small affluent islands around the vast sea of backwardness was not the real purpose of promoting the financial institutions. The beginning of the planned concept of development way back in 1951 opened new vistas for the development of banking sector. The policy makers felt that the banking sector is not contributing substantially to the development and welfare of Indian society due mainly to the fact that they are working under the private sector with the sole motto of making profits. This engineered a strong foundation for the nationalisation of commercial banks. The process of nationalisation took a final shape and in 1969 we find nationalisation of fourteen commercial banks. The main purpose of nationalisation was to make possible a basic change in the working style and functional properties of the commercial banks so that they contribute sizeably to the development of the poorer sections and the backward regions. The nationalised commercial banks made possible qualitative improvements in the implementation of development-oriented welfare plans which could not be implemented in past mainly due to the financial constraint. The second phase of nationalisation was found in 1980. In due course, the list was enlarged but the contributions to the generation of quality services were found disappointing.

The mounting participation of public sector commercial banks in the organisation of the processes of socio-economic transformation made it essential that the policy makers audit their strategic decisions. The degeneration in the quality of services-offered by the public sector commercial banks was found at its peak. The expectations of customers increased substantially but the service profile of banks failed in fulfilling the same.

In a development-sensitive welfare economy, the formulation of marketing mix is, of course, a difficult task. The growing magnitude of social costs again makes it more complicated. The regulations of the Reserve Bank of India stand as a major obstacle while making and innovating the policy decisions. Of late, the foreign banks and a few of the private sector domestic banks have been found establishing an edge over the public sector commercial banks. The customers are found satisfied with the quality of services made available by them. This makes it essential that the public sector commercial banks also practise the principles of modern marketing which may initiate the process of qualitative transformation. A shift in the psychology of investors and general customers has made it urgent that the policy decision-makers assign due weightage to the marketing decisions. A corollary to the major challenge of offering quality services to the customers may be to initiate an overall improvement in the banker's behavioural management. This would help bankers fantastically while transforming the prospects into users. It should not be forgotten that even unfounded rumours relating to the behavioural profile of bankers can jeopardise all efforts to get the business. It is against this background that the banking organisations, of late, have been found assigning due weightage to the marketing dimension of the bank management.

The beginning of the decade 1980s brought a significant change in the concept of bank marketing. There is no doubt in it that the concept emerged even in the late 1950s but the process could be activated only after the use of sophisticated information technologies in the banking sector. The advent of electronic fund transfer system in late 1970s made the ways for the induction of ATMs, Direct Deposit of Payroll, Pay by Phone, Point of Sale, Credit and Debit Cards, Automated Clearing House, Credit Deposit Machines, Auto-banking or so. Thus, the process of development started gaining the momentum. Futurologists forecast some more changes and reforms in the banking operation since the foreign banks have made the services more competitive by promoting work culture and welcoming techniculture.

The downward moving share of the public sector commercial banks to the process of socio-economic transformation make it essential that they audit their policies and strategies. On the one hand, they are expected to subserve social interests while on the other hand, they also bear the responsibility of generating profits and maintaining commercial viability. This is not possible unless we find a big increase in the banking business. It is right to mention that the public sector commercial banks find it difficult to work since the interference of government makes it difficult to make the services competitive.

We find liberalisation of economy opening up new vistas in the Indian banking system resulting from which a number of foreign and domestic banks have been found initiating the required changes in their strategic decisions. Global Trust Bank, Indus Ind Bank, Times Bank have been seen rescheduling their functional areas. The term lending institutions like IDBI and ICICI have also set up their own commercial banks. The market situation continues to be competitive and we don't expect a change even in the functional style and properties of the public sector commercial banks. This draws our attention on the marketing of banking services.

The use of sophisticated technologies particularly by the foreign banks has sizeably increased the expectations of customers. In the years to come, we expect more sophistication in the information technologies. This is likely to bring about a radical change in the marketing of banking services. In an age of electronic banking, the manually operated public sector commercial banks would find it difficult to survive. This makes it essential that even the public sector commercial banks promote the use of technologies. It is high time that they innovate their marketing efforts and continue to keep their market share high. Of course, we find the RBI obstructing the development processes by regulating the business conditions but at the same time, we also find policy makers working with negative attitudes. An attitudinal change in the boardrooms is thus a crying need of the hour. The policy makers have no option but to make the working conditions conducive *vis-a-vis* the services internationally competitive. The perception of customer satisfaction is to be reviewed in the face of changing level of expectations of customers. In addition, the social orientation needs an intensive care since the principles of social marketing are also required to be conceptualised. The banking and other service generating organisations have to think that their services are not engineering a foundation for value degeneration. They, in addition to the generation of profits, have also to search ways for users' satisfaction and social orientation.

The conceptualisation of marketing in the required fashion is thus found an urgent need and the public sector commercial banks where a big quality gap is existent till now are required to bridge over the gap on a priority basis. Of course, we find a number of factors responsible in the process but the innovative marketing practices bear high sensitivity. It is against this background that the private sector commercial banks and the foreign banks have been found assigning due weightage to the perception of customer satisfaction. In the present condition, it is not only sufficient that the banking organisations confine themselves to the core services but it is much more impact generating that they make possible frequency in the innovation of peripheral services. The inclusion of a good number of peripheral services would make the ways for product attractiveness which would simplify the task of bank professionals.

The aforesaid facts make it clear that the banking business is now becoming competitive and the intensity of competition is likely to move upward. This makes it essential that the policy makers change their attitudes and the professionals prove themselves personally committed. In the present condition, only the high performers can make the marketing resources proactive. It is in this context that we make an advocacy in favour of innovative marketing practices for the banking sector. Innovation makes the ways for demand generation. Innovation paves the avenues for profit maximisation. Innovation opens new vistas for increasing the market share. Like other organisations even the banking organisations also need to promote innovation.

This makes it essential that they have technology-driven marketing information system. New services, schemes, profitable services, lucrative packages, and new peripheral services with decent behaviour bear the efficacy of making the marketing resources productive. If the public sector commercial banks make possible frequency in innovating the marketing decisions, the future marketing would prove to be proactive.

BANK MARKETING — THE CONCEPT

Earlier, the attitude about the marketing of banking services was that it was not professional to sell one's services and was unnecessary in the sense that traditional relationships and quality of products were sufficient to carry forward our task. The evolution of marketing concept in the banking profession is traced in the West. Deryk Weyer of Barclays Bank came out by far with the most comprehensive definition of bank marketing. He considered it as consisting of identifying the most profitable markets now and in future, assessing the present and future needs of customers, setting business development goals, making plans to meet them, managing the various services and promoting them to achieve the plans — all in the context of changing environment in the market.[1] It is right to mention that the conceptual exposition of bank marketing presented by Weyer expanded the marketing areas in the banking industry.

With the passage of time, we find significant developments which has further widened the definition and scope of bank marketing. It is said that marketing should gear itself more to the well-being of the society and therefore the term 'Social Marketing' has been coined.[2] Hartley prefers to call it responsive marketing[3] which suggests an attuning or responding to the changing needs of customers, society and environment. In the responsive marketing, an organisation naturally looks to long-term profit goals. However, Gist[4] looks to the social dimensions with a different angle. He says because marketing activities lead to the creation of new products and services, because marketing activities promote new ideas to the society which is being served and because marketing activities play an important persuasive role in the formation of public opinion, marketing is unavoidably a social concern.

Thus, the new concept of bank marketing assigned due weightage to customer satisfaction. In a true sense, the hallmark of the changed concept aimed at having a full view of customer's needs, fulfilling the identified needs in the best possible way by required services, identification of potential customers and conducting the activities at the branches on the basis of market segmentation. Marketing was thus accepted to be as an organisational imperative. Earlier, the marketing came into banks not in the form of marketing concept but in the form of advertising and promotion concept. Gradually, it was realised that marketing transcends advertising and friendliness.[5] Thus, regarding the bank marketing concept, it is right to mention that it is a managerial process by which services are matched with markets. The matching of services with marketing is meant formulation of overall marketing strategies which suit the taste, temperament, needs and requirements of customers.

In view of the above, it is said that marketing of banking services is concerned with product, promotion, pricing and place. In addition, a number of experts also advocate in favour of People, Process and Physical appearance. The different mixes of marketing are found influenced by the changing business conditions. The marketing experts feel that to be more specific in the service generating organisations, we find People playing a decisive role. This draws our attention on the quality of bankers recruited and developed by the banking organisations which focuses on the development of human resources for the banking services. We can't negate that in almost all the organisations the quality of human resources plays a decisive role.

The aforesaid facts are a mute testimony to this proposition that bank marketing is a managerial-cum-social approach. The professional excellence becomes instrumental in drawing a balance between the two opposite considerations. The qualitative transformation in the process is quite natural since the market is competitive and the customers of today are more receptive. It is against this background that we find it a profession which sets the right direction. In the present-day world, we also find marketing a social process since the strategic decisions necessitate due weightage to the social considerations. The core and peripheral services are required to be designed in the face of social transformation programmes and policies. The promotional measures are to be formulated and innovated in the face of the sensitivity of a particular segment. The interest and fee are also to be charged with the motto of subserving the social interests. The professionals thus are found searching ways for social orientation which makes it a social process.

Thus, we find bank marketing an approach to give right direction to banks *vis-a-vis* multi-dimensional benefits to the different segments using the services of banks. The modern marketing principles if conceptualised in a right fashion make the ways for establishing a balance between the organisational and social interests. In an age of electronic banking, the perception of bank marketing requires a new vision. This is due to the fact that use of sophisticated technologies by the banking organisations has made possible a major change in the quality of services. The customers using the services of foreign banks have a different perception regarding the quality of banking services. The word-of-mouth communication makes possible smooth transmission and the customers using the services of manually operated public sector commercial banks come to know about the quality of services their counterparts already avail. Thus, the shaping of expectations is found switched on which necessitates a change in the perception of service quality. The marketing of banking services paves the ways for the shaping of expectations.

The bank marketing is thus an approach to market the services profitably. It is a device to maintain commercial viability. It is an art to project a positive image. It is a method to energise performance orientation. It is a tool to activate employee orientation and more so, it is a managerial approach to excel competition. The changing perception of bank marketing has made it a social process. The significant properties of the holistic concept of management has made bank marketing a device to establish a balance between the commercial and social considerations, often considered to be the two opposite wings. A compendium of two words 'Bank' and 'Marketing' thus focuses our attention on the following:

- Bank marketing is a managerial approach to market the services.
- It is a social process to subserve social interests.
- It is a fair way of making profits.
- It is an art to make possible performance orientation.
- It is a professionally-tested skill to excel competition.

JUSTIFICATIONS FOR PRACTISING MARKETING PRINCIPLES

Marketing principles, if practised in a right fashion, bear the efficacy of enriching the business potentials, satisfying the customers and subserving the social interests. The innovation in the perception becomes essential to cater to the changing needs and requirements of the users belonging to different segments. It is against this background that we focus on the points justifying the application of marketing principles in the banking organisations.

The professionals bearing the responsibility of conceptualising marketing need world-class excellence to make the marketing resources productive.

1. Understanding the customers: The concept of bank marketing is, of late, well supported by sophisticated information technologies. In an age of information explosion, the banking services depend substantially on the marketing information system. With the help of different subsystems and to be more specific with the instrumentality of marketing research, the bankers get an opportunity to study and understand the changing levels of expectations of customers. Since while marketing we segment the market and intensify research, it is easy to identify the magnitude or the emerging new trends. The lifestyles, likes and dislikes, preferences, attitudes or the behavioural profile can't remain static. The multi-dimensional developments in the business environment influence the process of change. If the professionals perceive the emerging changes in a right fashion, the marketing decisions can be made proactive. The marketing practices simplify the task of formulating creative policies and strategies which contain more sensitivity. It is against this background that the banking organisations of today need to practise marketing. A good number of foreign banks and even some of the domestic private sector banks have been found conceptualising marketing and getting the desired results.

2. Satisfying the customers: In almost all the organisations, the first and foremost task is to satisfy the customers. If we understand the customers in a right perspective, the success rate reaches at its peak. If the marketing processes help us in understanding the customers, the task of satisfying them is found easier. The formulation and innovation processes of the marketing mixes move in a right and desired order. The customers get the services in tune with their changing requirements which help banks in expanding the market, increasing the market share and activating the process of mobilising the savings and deposits. The process of excelling competition is geared up and the profitability is maximised. Thus, we create market potentials and capitalise on them optimally.

3. Excelling competition: The modern marketing principles are conceptualised in the banking organisations also with the motto of excelling competition. Of late, the intensity of competition is found moving upward. Even the banking organisations have been facing numerous problems on that account. The leading foreign banks have made the business environment so competitive that the task of excelling competition is found difficult to the public sector commercial banks. The public sector banks would find it easier to excel competition if they practise marketing and keep on moving the process of innovation since the foreign banks till now emerging as the leading competitors have been found promoting innovation frequently. This makes it essential that the marketing principles are practised. The need of the hour is to enrich the peripheral services so that the mobilisation process gains momentum. It is important to mention that the leading foreign banks have been found promoting the use of new technologies to improve the quality of their services but the public sector commercial banks have been facing strong opposition of trade unions on that account. The application of marketing principles would also help banks in optimising the requirements for the use of technologies.

4. Formulating and innovating the mixes: We can't negate that the quality factor assumes a place of outstanding significance, specially in getting the new business *vis-a-vis* retaining the old one. If we turn our eyes on the product mix of the private sector banks, we find peripheral services of world-class which add additional attractions to their service mix. The private sector banks have been found promoting consumer financing in tune with the emerging trends in consumerism but the public sector commercial banks have not assigned due weightage to this dimension in their service mix. This makes it essential that while formulating or innovating the product mix they assign an overriding priority to the peripheral services since the core services in almost all the banks are by and large the same. While promoting, we need to use sophisticated technologies and the cooperation of advertising professionals to make the process creative. While setting fees, rate of interest or commission, the public sector commercial banks need to go through the strategies followed by the leading competitors. We also need due weightage to the development of people since the personally-committed human resources are found efficacious in solving the numerous problems. The recruitment and training facilities, the organisation of refresher and capsule courses, the incentive plans the performance appraisal are some of the important dimensions influencing the quality of human resources.

5. Social orientation: It is not only sufficient that we offer to the consumers the world-class services and the profitable schemes. It is not only significant that we promote in a right fashion. It is not only sufficient that our pricing policies are motivational. It is not only sufficient that the working employees are well aware of the behavioural management. In addition, it is more impact generating that the policy makers have a positive attitude towards the social costs and the boardrooms assign due weightage to social interests while formulating the policy.

To be more specific in the Indian setting, we find this aspect assuming a place of special significance since the masses have high expectations from the banking organisations in general. How to increase our contributions to the process of social transformation is an important task that, in addition to the application of marketing principles, also requires due attention of the policy decision-makers.

The aforesaid facts justify the application of marketing principles in the banking services. We can't deny that the public sector commercial banks have not assigned due weightage to the conceptualisation of marketing principles which has been found generating numerous problems. We expect that marketing practices would simplify the task of bank professionals responsible for managing the marketing mix. Application and frequent innovation would make the ways for qualitative transformation. The policy decision-makers as well as the RBI need to think over the problems on a priority basis. The bankers serving the public sector commercial banks need to realise the gravity of the situation.

THE USERS OF BANKING SERVICES

The users/customers constitute a place of outstanding significance. The line of services, the planning and development of services, the offering of services, the pricing strategies or the interests charged for the services made available and the promotional strategies depend substantially upon the nature and type of users using the services of an organisation. It is against this background that a study of different categories of users is found significant. The emerging trends in the level of expectations affect the formulation of marketing mix. Innovative efforts become essential the moment we find a change in the level of expectations. Yesterday, the users did not expect fast, decent services but today they expect. Yesterday, the consumer financing was not so much important but today, the banks appear to think about the same on a priority basis. Yesterday, the industrial users did not expect credit facilities on liberal terms and conditions but today, they expect. These changes make it clear that the level of expectations contain dynamism *vis-a-vis* influence the marketing decisions.

We find two types of customers using the services of banks, such as general customers and the industrial customers as shown in Figure 5.1.

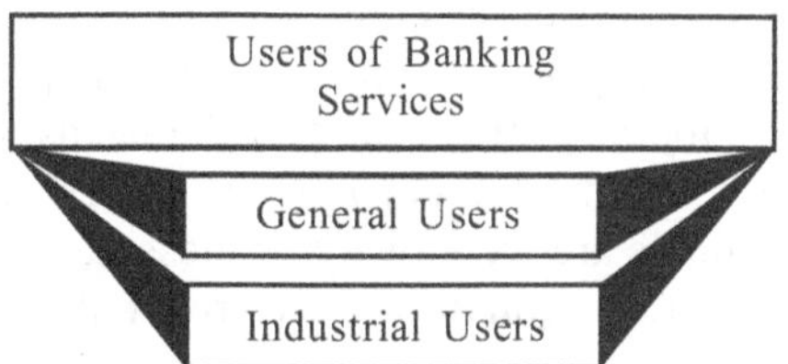

Fig. 5.1: Users of Banking Services

General Users: Persons having an account in the bank and using the banking facilities at the terms and conditions fixed by a bank are known as general users of the banking services. Generally, they are found small-sized customers.

Industrial Users: The industrialists, entrepreneurs having an account in the bank and using the credit facilities and other services for the establishment and expansion of their business are known as industrial users. Generally, they are found large-sized.

Prospects: It is also essential to clarify the term, 'Prospects'. The general or industrial prospects do not use the banking services at present but they have the potentials to become a customer if induced or motivated in a right fashion.

The aforesaid facts make it clear that the banking organisations transact with different types of customers. The behavioural profile of the two types of customers can't be identical. Both the customers are found important to the marketers and their professional excellence is coiled in the essence of studying and understanding the customers in a right perspective. The marketing resources instrumentalise the process of transforming the prospects into customers/users.

THE BEHAVIOURAL PROFILE OF USERS

The psychologists opine that it is very difficult to study the behavioural profile of customers. Of course, they are right since a study of diverse, obscure, complex personalities is not an easy task. This makes it essential that the marketers are well aware of the behavioural science. Of late, the role and range of the behavioural scientists can't be confined to the personality and moral rather can be expanded to the study of the behavioural profile of prospects/customers using or likely to use the services. It is in this context that we focus on the behavioural profile of customers. The buyers' decision-making process may be simple or elaborate, static or dynamic, gregarious or distinct or a combined endeavour of all. The behavioural psychology developed by Prof. J.B. Waston brought a significant change in the management of marketing resources. He was of the view that stimulation has the necessary response. A well-known experiment made by Pavlov on the dogs proved that when dogs were conditioned to associate the ringing of the bell with the offering of food, the saliva dropped from their jaws as and when the bell was rung, albeit the food was not served. This speaks of the fact that our actions, decisions have a close relation with our habits and behaviour. Later on, the psychoanalysis developed by Freud in 1930 focused on the domination of behavioural scientists.

The formulation of marketing mix is directly or indirectly related to the changing behavioural profile of customers. A gradual change in the behavioural profile is quite natural if we find a change in the environmental conditions. The increasing rate of literacy, the changing level of income, the significant developments in the field of transportation and communications, the domination of corporate sector in activating the process of development influence our behaviour *vis-a-vis* the needs and requirements and the lifestyles. It is pertinent that the bank professionals are well aware of these developments so that they don't commit a mistake in studying and understanding the expectations.

The management's experts feel that a change in the behavioural profile of customers is to influence the business plan *vis-a-vis* the strategic planning and strategic marketing. They argue that an apparent change in the behavioural profile affects the lifestyles which govern everything. The psychologists feel that a study of behavioural profile is a challenging task since even two customers can't be identical. However, we club a number of persons into a segment and the behavioural profile of all customers related to that segment is found by and large the same. They dissect the behaviour of customers into different compartments which simplify the process of study. An in-depth study of the behavioural profile of different categories of customers would help bank professionals in understanding their expectations and the strategic marketing would help them in fulfilling the same. There are a number of factors influencing the behavioural profile, such as the needs and requirements, level of discretionary income, emerging trends in the national economy, the emergence of corporate culture, the intensity of competition or so. It is pertinent that the bank professionals are well aware of these developments. The creativity in the marketing decisions would be possible if the bank professionals are aware of the behavioural profile.

In the 21st century, the service generating organisations in general and the banking organisations in particular would have to make a final good-bye if they fail in assigning due weightage to the changing behavioural profile of users. The main thing in the process is to identify the level of their expectations so that the strategic marketing decisions fulfil and satisfy the same. In the Indian context, the public sector commercial banks have been found neglecting the behavioural dimension which is likely to be very damaging, specially with the viewpoint of future marketing. An in-depth study of behavioural profile of users is thus a crying need of the hour.

FACTORS INFLUENCING THE BEHAVIOURAL PROFILE OF USERS

There are a number of factors found instrumental in influencing the behavioural profile of both the categories of customers — general and organisational. It is natural that they make decisions on the basis of their changing needs and requirements which are influenced by the emerging trends in business environment. The important factors governing the behavioural profile, such as social, economic, psychological and political need due attention of bank professionals. Unless they understand their behavioural profile, the marketing decisions can't be creative and unless the marketing decisions are creative, the market share can't be increased.

The public sector commercial banks in particular need to overhaul their marketing strategies. The organisational customers would require more support from the banking organisations since they are also supposed to activate the process of innovation. The general customers of almost all the segments would also have high expectations since they are also supposed to have a different lifestyle. The organisational customers or the large-sized customers would require more financial support from the banks on liberal terms and conditions. The general customers would have a craze for sophisticated domestic/household items which would make an advocacy in favour of consumer financing. These changes make it essential that the bank professionals are familiar with the changing behavioural profile of customers. In Figure 5.2, the factors influencing the behavioural profile of customers make it clear that the bank professionals have no option but to keep their eyes moving so that the changing hierarchy of needs have a correlation with the service mix. It is in this context that we focus on the influencing factors.

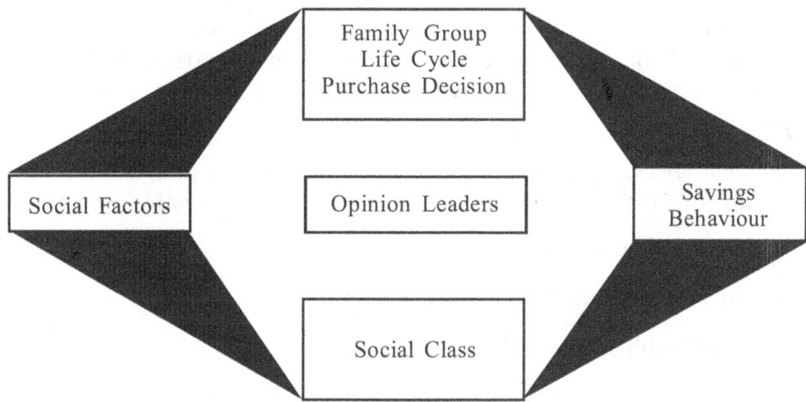

Fig. 5.2: Social Factors Influencing Savings

Social Factors: At the outset, we go through the social factors influencing the behavioural profile of users. Among the social factors, the lifestyles constitutes a place of outstanding significance. Right from the unmarried stage to the stage of marriage, the lifestyle passes through different stages. In this respect, the marital status, age of family members, size of a family and status of the head of a family influence the savings behaviour. It is natural that the family budget of a married couple is different to the budget of an unmarried individual. In a family where there are a number of children, the rate of saving is found woefully low. Like this, we find investment behaviour of middle-aged persons different to the youths. The middle-aged group is considerably influenced by the rate of interest and other financial incentives.

To be more specific in the Indian setting where the virus of dowry is found spreading like a wildfire, the family budget of an individual in which we find daughters in a good number is found different to others. It is also confirmed that lifestyle has a direct bearing on the saving potentials. If we invest with the motto of earning interest, the study of life cycle assumes an outstanding significance. The propensity to save is found almost dismal, specially in the age-group 20-35.

In a family, the purchase decision also influences the saving potentials. We classify a family into four parts, such as a family where a husband dominates, a family where wife dominates, a family where both of them take a joint decision and a family where children dominates. If we find domination of husband, the saving potentials is found high provided the husband is free from the ill habits. If we find domination of wife, the saving potentials may be high but not liberal to banks but to purchase ornaments, gold, and fixed property.

The bank professionals are also to be aware of the opinion leaders and intermediaries, specially while sanctioning loans. This is based on the logic that opinion leaders make decisions without any considerations whereas the intermediaries are guided by a number of factors.

An increase in the social status of an individual or a family also influences the saving potentials. Of course, we find high class of the society earning more and therefore having the potentials to save. But the impact of consumerism can't be underestimated. The lower class of the society is found interested in saving but mainly due to low income we find potentials showing a negative trend.

The aforesaid facts make it clear that our saving habits are influenced by social variables and here, in addition to the problems explained earlier, we find lifestyle an important factor. Both the aspects — propensity to save and propensity to spend — are considerably influenced by the lifestyle that we follow.

Economic Factors: The economic factors play a decisive role since the emerging trends in the economy influence the level of income. We can't negate that ultimately it is income that influences the behavioural profile *vis-a-vis* the lifestyles. If we earn more, we spend more, we save more. If we earn less, we spend a major portion of our income and so save less. The Wharton study[7] revealed that in urban families with lower incomes, average personal consumption spending exceeded income. It also showed that the average propensity to consume declined rather than rapidly since income rose above the poverty line. Like this, the income expected and avenues for getting additional also influence the behavioural profile. The national economy showing positive trends of developments make the business environment conducive and the banking organisations get a favourable milieu for development. Contrary to it, the economic depression contracts avenues for development and the negative trends in the economy activate the vicious circle. The pressure of inflation is found here significant since the mounting pressure brings down the discretionary income and the banking businesses are adversely affected. It is in this context that we find different dimensions of national and international economies influencing the behavioural profile.

Psychological Factors: It is right to say that no single theory of consumer motivation is complete enough to explain the behaviour of customers. The attitudes and learning, motivation, conditioning are the key factors in the very context. The study of attitudes and learning answer to the questions mentioned below:

- How do the users learn about the product?
- How do they learn to recognise and recall these services?
- By what process they develop using habits?

In a true sense, learning is a process in which total functions are altered and rearranged to make them more useful. In the banking industry, a study of attitudes is found important provided the sources used for the study are reliable. The information regarding the innovative peripheral services if transmitted through a reliable source would simplify the motivation process.

Motivation is found instrumental in governing his/her condition or activities. Human motivation is considered to be a subject with considerable interest. For the banking organisations, the task of motivation is not so difficult provided the services-promised are made available to the users without any distortion. The banking organisations need to innovate their services since this simplifies the process of motivation.

Conditioning is considered to be a way of learning. The conditioned response establishes a behavioural pattern but of a temporary nature. It may disappear if the reinforcement is not up-to-mark. The banking organisations need to condition their customers that the services-offered to them are internationally competitive and of world-class.

The aforesaid social, economic and psychological factors can't remain static. This makes it essential that the bank professionals keep their eyes open and make possible an intensive study of the changing emerging trends.

MARKETING INFORMATION SYSTEM

We can't remain unilluminated, specially about a river on which we plan to float a craft. It is believed that information is the ever moving mighty river on which the marketing craft is floated. In the management parlance, the management of information becomes important since this helps in making and innovating the decisions in a right perspective. The creativity is made possible and the task of marketers is simplified considerably. We can't negate that considerable judgement and keen insight are needed in discriminating the major and minor problems. The time and cost considerations force bank professionals to make some of the decisions based on their intuition. But a majority of the marketing decisions are required to be information-based. In making intuitive decisions, the professionals depend upon their past experiences. But the major marketing problems require information-based decisions, specially to inject creativity. The formulation of marketing mix is an important functional responsibility and it is essential that the policy decision-makers attempt to make the decision-making processes information-based.

The main purpose of the Marketing Information System is to make possible coordinated, systematic and continuous collection of information. MIS is an organised set of procedures, information-handling routines and reporting techniques designed to provide the information required for marketing decisions.[8] It reduces the volume of intuition-based decisions as relevant and usable information both from the internal and external sources to make the decisions proactive. Further, it also provides a mechanism for reducing the often overwhelming flood of available market information to pertinent, usable amounts.[9] The responsibility for an effective MIS rests with the senior executives, assisted by their juniors. The design and operation of an MIS is delegated to specialists or the system analysts, supposed to be highly skilled in information gathering and handling techniques. An advisory group made up of representatives from marketing, finance and accounting, operations research, data processing and other organisational units not only assist a system analysts but also maintains continual surveillance over the MIS.

In the banking organisations, the MIS is found instrumental in helping the policy decision-makers in different ways. The emerging trends in competition, the developments in the stock and money markets, the emerging trends in the level of incomes, the changes in the lifestyles, the increasing impact of communications, the domination of consumerism are some of the key factors playing a decisive role in the banking services. The task of making creative decisions is made easier if the banking organisations have a well developed and technology-driven information system. Though an MIS is found instrumental at all the three levels, such as branch level, regional level and corporate level but we find it more instrumental at micro level or branch level. The effective execution of market development plans rests on the MIS, specially at branch level. The objectives of MIS at regional level are regional planning, implementation and reviewing of the situation. At the corporate or apex level, the objectives are corporate planning, setting of business objectives and goals, identification of profitable opportunities, knowing about the leading competitors or so.

There are a number of sources for collecting information at the apex level but at the micro/branch level, the branch managers face numerous problems while collecting the information. If the branch managers get right and up-to-date information on time, the strategic decisions at micro level of the bank can be made more proactive. The potential customers would be identified, the areas for distributing the services would be finalised and the task of formulating marketing planning and budgeting would also be made easier. A review of the performance of different areas would be possible. These facts testify that MIS simplifies the task and responsibility of branch managers. The nature of information required at the branch level has been shown in Figure 5.3.

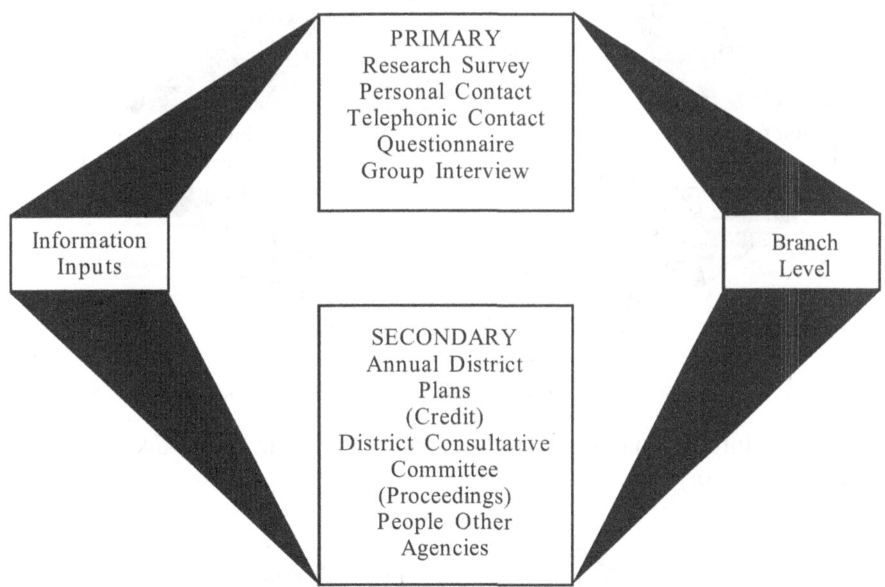

Fig. 5.3: Information Inputs for Branch

In the primary source, the informations are collected from the researchers who make a survey, personal contact, telephonic contact, mail questionnaire, group interview or so. In the secondary source, the small district plan is found helpful as the credit plans include profile of the districts, blocks, population, agriculture, industries, infrastructural facilities of the concerned district. So far as the cost factor is concerned, the data collected from the primary source is found more expensive than the data collected from the secondary source. Here, it is right to prefer the secondary source. It is felt essential that there should be a provision for cross-checking of data, specially when we collect the same from the secondary source.

Segment-wise Collection of Information

Detailed analysis of fact is possible from the segment-wise collected data. This consists of individual and corporate segments. In Figure 5.4 and 5.5, we find individual segment, information inputs and corporate segment information inputs.

Practically, it is very difficult to collect information from the segment in which we find a heterogeneous combination. These informations are found useful, specially with the viewpoint of placing the incremental income of the concerned party into deposit schemes or for contributing to the Provident Fund, Gratuity, etc.

To energise the banking transactions, it is essential that banks collect information regarding corporate segment. The National Dailies like, The Economic Times, The Financial Express, Financial Weeklies, The Business Weeklies, etc. may feed information or the back-up materials.

We can't negate that a detailed analysis of fact is possible from the segment-wise collected data. The individual and corporate segments as shown in Figure 5.4 and Figure 5.5 clarify it. Of course, it is difficult to collect data since we find the segments a heterogeneous combination but we find it important and meaningful, specially with the viewpoint of placing the incremental income of the concerned party into deposit schemes or for continuing to their Provident Fund and Gratuity.

The Dailies, Beneficiaries, Life Insurance Corporation of India, Census and Electoral Rolls are the key sources to feed data for the individual segment.

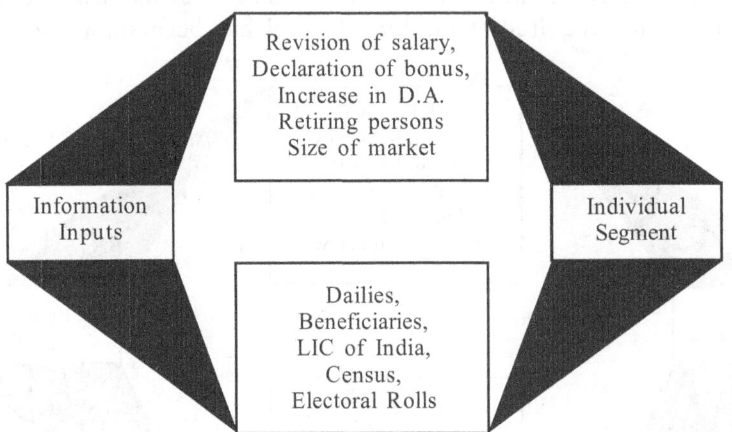

Fig. 5.4: Information Inputs from Individual Segment

In Figure 5.5, we find the information inputs for the corporate segment. The banking organisations are supposed to assign due weightage to the corporate segment since the large-sized customers are found profitable.

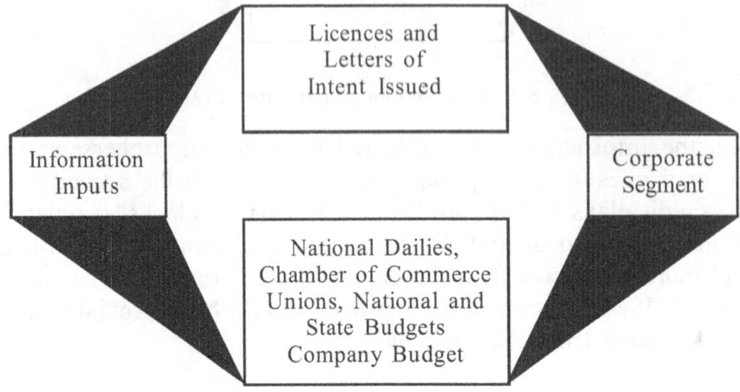

Fig. 5.5: Information Inputs from Corporate Segment

The licences and letters of intents issued become the information for the corporate segment for which the inputs are the national dailies, trade associations, Chambers of Commerce, the budgets of Union Government, State Governments and Corporate Budget. The bank professionals are supposed to collect information and the information system would let them know the emerging trends and the future opportunities. The Marketing Information System, thus, would simplify the task of policy decision-makers in many ways.

SIGNIFICANCE OF MIS TO THE BANKING ORGANISATIONS

We agree with this view that marketing information system is found significant to almost all the organisations but here it is right to say that the banking organisations find the system very much instrumental in making the creative decisions and getting a right direction. In the modern world, it is important that we are well aware of the day-to-day developments. The leading business organisations always look forward. It is not only sufficient that they maintain their existence. It is much more impact generating that they thrive and succeed in excelling competition. This makes it essential that they move with the time and use sophisticated information technologies in the system to get the right information. Knowledge is power. Information improves the quality of knowledge. The banking organisations find the system useful. The following facts testify it.

1. MIS develops knowledge: World-class management of business organisations require world-class management of information. If we agree with this view that knowledge is power which simplifies the task of making creative decisions, an overriding priority to the technology-driven marketing information system is need of the hour. Unless we feed to the system quality inputs (date), we can't expect quality outputs (information). We are well aware of the fact that the MIS is a process of transforming the data into information. The collection of right information, in right time from all the possible sources and their processing in a right fashion help bank professionals in formulating a time-tested strategy. If we have more information, it is very natural that we have enough potentials to study and understand the market.

2. Helpful in identifying the profitable opportunities: In the banking services, it is pertinent that we search profitable opportunities and make innovative efforts to capitalise on the same much earlier than our competitors. If we have right information, the task of identifying profitable opportunities would not remain difficult. The multi-dimensional changes in the different categories of customers *vis-a-vis* the business environment have a far reaching impact on strategic decisions. The system makes available to the bank professionals information related to the different areas. This helps them in identifying a profitable market or a profitable segment. We can't negate the fact that mainly due to the inavailability of time-honoured information, the branch managers often fail in identifying the profitable opportunities.

3. Diagnosing the emerging trends in competition: Your potentials, excellence carry no meaning, if you fail in excelling competition. The task of excelling competition is not difficult, if you know and understand your competitors. The MIS helps bank professionals in identifying the intensity of competition. We can't deny that, of late, the foreign banks in particular have been throwing a big challenge to the public sector commercial banks. The emerging trends in the market share of the leading competitors and their strategic decisions help the competing organisations substantially. This makes it clear that the MIS helps banking organisations in diagnosing the intensity of competition which is found essential for innovating the marketing inputs. Here, it is pertinent that the system is technology-driven.

4. Helpful in business expansion: The expansion or contraction in the product line, the inclusion of new services or schemes in the product mix, the elimination of old services and schemes not getting a positive response, the diversification and standardisation in the product mix are sizeably influenced by the information that we get from the system. With the help of marketing information system, the banking organisations find it convenient to formulate and innovate decisions regarding their future expansion plans. By collecting data from the primary and secondary sources and further by transforming the same into information with the help of a technology-driven marketing information system, the banks find it convenient to plan for the future.

The system helps in answering to a number of questions helping bank professionals in many ways.

- Who are the prospects?
- Who are likely to be your prospects in future?
- What changes in the position of users would create new opportunities?

- What changes in the socio-economic and political conditions would create new problems and opportunities?
- What changes in the legal environment would necessitate a change in the functional areas?

The aforesaid questions if suitably answered would help bank professionals in identifying the profitable business opportunities. The task, of course, is difficult but the MIS would help them in the very context.

5. Helpful in image projection: It is not sufficient that we are fair. It contains an outstanding significance that we look fair. It is against this background that the projection of a positive or a fair image constitutes a significant place in the world of business. The marketing information system helps bank professionals in projecting a fair image. When we take stock of our performance, or when we insist on self-evaluation, or when we frame or formulate marketing strategies, the task of image projection becomes easier. We are well aware of the fact that for the development of banking organisations, the development of strong public relations system becomes important. The public relations activities make ways, for the projection of a fair image. In view of the above, it is right to mention that a technology-driven marketing information system helps the banking organisations in many ways.

The banking organisations find it convenient to formulate and innovate the marketing strategies which make their marketing efforts proactive. The task of excelling competition is found easier. It is in this context that the leading foreign banks and even some of the private sector domestic banks have been found assigning a transcendental priority to the management of information. Of late, we find the public sector commercial banks in trouble.

This is due to the fact that they have failed in assigning due weightage to the management of information. The marketing decisions of the public sector commercial banks are not of world-class. Of course, the regulations of the RBI obstruct their development plans but it is also right to mention that in a majority of the cases they are not serious to their efforts. It is high time that they realise gravity of the situation and seek cooperation of a well-developed, technology-driven marketing information system.

INSTRUMENTALITY OF MARKETING RESEARCH IN THE BANKING ORGANISATIONS

Out of the different subsystems that we use for managing the information, the marketing research occupies a special place. The marketing research considered to be a systematic gathering, recording and analysis of data makes the ways for making and innovating the marketing decisions. The information collected from the external sources by conducting surveys helps bank professionals in different ways.

In the banking services, the formulation of overall marketing strategies is considered significant with the viewpoint of tapping the potentials, expanding the business and increasing the market share. An integral part of the MIS, the marketing research provides information inputs and simplifies the task of making creative marketing decisions. In the banking services, the intensity of competition is found moving upward. The increasing domination and gaining popularity of foreign banks, the profitable schemes of the non-banking organisations, the mounting craze among the customers for private banks have made the task of influencing the impulse of customers a bit difficult. A microscopic study of the emerging trends in competition, market share, craze appears essential to initiate the process of qualitative transformation which is found very disappointing, specially in the public sector commercial banks.

The marketing research simplifies the task of studying the magnitude of competition by opinion surveys and the feedback from customers. The multi-dimensional changes in the service mix can be made productive if it is based on marketing research. The formulation of a sound marketing mix is possible if we use this system in a right fashion.

The banking organisations need to make a time-to-time appraisal of their performance. The results of sales analysis, if indicate a sharp fall in the deposits, would be successful in identifying the reasons responsible for the same. If the competitive banks propose to offer a new service or a new scheme and the market test is to be conducted, the marketing research would make available the preferences and reactions of the prospects. If the old services or schemes are not getting a positive response, the marketing research would suggest ways to innovate the marketing resources. If the promotional measures in general and the sales promotion measures in particular are not getting the desired response, the marketing research would identify the reasons entailed behind the process.

In view of the above, it is right to say that marketing research helps bank professionals in many ways. The marketing decisions would hardly remain proactive, if we stop the process of conducting surveys or undertaking research. There is no doubt in it that in the banking services we also find the marketing intelligence system effective. Here, it is important to mention that the intelligence system is practised to know about the day-to-day performance. The difference between the two is like the difference between a flash bulb and candle. The light of a flash bulb is not found static but the light received from a candle is found static. The intelligence system is like a candle whereas the marketing research is like a flash bulb. It is against this background that while managing the information, the banking organisations also need to use the marketing intelligence system. It can't be denied that the success rate of marketing research is sizeably influenced by the instrumentality of researchers. If they are honest, value-based and sincere; the research results would undoubtedly be helpful to the bank professionals.

MARKETING INTELLIGENCE SYSTEM FOR THE BANKING ORGANISATIONS

The marketing intelligence system is defined as a set of procedures and sources used by executives to obtain their everyday information about important developments. It is essential that the bank managers make a day-to-day scanning of the environment. The scanning may be in different ways.[10] It may be undirected viewing which is without any specific purpose in view, it may be conditioned viewing which is without looking to a clear area, it may be informal research which is limited effort to gather specific information and it may also be formal research which is with a well-defined objective and purpose into any specific area. Generally, in social get-together or in a club, we witness undirected viewing. A bank manager may come across a lot of information just by his/her presence. The main thing here is the alertness of a manager in picking up the bits and making use thereof. The conditioned viewing is looking to a clear area. A bank manager witnesses conditioned viewing in get-togethers specially meant for bankers and customers. Here, it is pertinent that a bank manager gets an opportunity to look to a clear area. Like this, the informal research is carried on to collect specific information whereas the formal research is undertaken with a well-defined approach.

In the formulation of marketing strategies, the instrumentality of marketing intelligence system assumes an important place. This is mainly due to the fact that in the banking services we find involvement of a number of financial agents and therefore we can't deny frequent changes in the strategic decisions. This makes an advocacy in favour of undirected and conditioned viewing of the emerging problems. The decision-making in the banking services is substantially influenced by the happenings data which is supplied by the marketing intelligence system. A bank manager carries on marketing intelligence mostly by reading newspapers, weeklies, trade publications and even by talking to the customers. To get an optimal result from the marketing intelligence system, it is essential that bank professionals have been imparted the necessary training facilities and are motivated to spot and report new developments. Further, it is also essential that the banking organisations evince interest in motivating the bankers and agents to pass on important intelligence information. It is also possible that some of the banks have established an internal marketing information centre to collect and circulate marketing intelligence. Here, the employees scan major publications, abstracts, relevant news and disseminates a new bulletin to the managers. The staff assist managers in evaluating new information. There is no doubt in it that these services improve the quality of information.

In view of the above, it is right to say that the marketing intelligence system, an important subsystem of the marketing information system, is found helpful to a bank manager. He/she can use intelligence for improving the functions of branch or even regions. The intelligence system would help bankers even in making a spot study of the problems experienced by customers in getting the services promised. The emerging trends in business also become significant and the intelligence system would help bank managers in identifying the trends. The attitudinal changes in customers can be identified in a right fashion. These facts are a mute testimony to this proposition that the banking organisations should make intensive efforts to develop a sound intelligence system which simplifies the task of bank professionals.

MARKET SEGMENTATION

An organisation is supposed to cater to the changing needs of customers. It is natural that all customers have their own likes and dislikes. They have some uniqueness which throw a big imprint on their lifestyles. This makes the task of understanding the customers a bit difficult. It is in this context that we go through the problem of market segmentation in the banking services.

A study of the needs of customers invites a plethora of problems since in addition to other aspects, the regional considerations also influence the hierarchy of needs. To be more specific in the banking services, the banking organisations are supposed to satisfy different types of customers living in different segments. The segmentation of market makes the task of bank professionals easier. If the market segmentation is done in a right fashion, the task of satisfying the customers is simplified considerably. The modern marketing theories advocate the formulation of marketing policies and strategies for each segment which an organisation plans to solicit.

The market segmentation is based on the principle of divide and rule. If we divide the market into different segments, the size of a market is made small and the process of study is found convenient. We find market segmentation division and subdivison of a market based on certain considerations. It is against this background that E.R. Reidenback and R.E. Pits opine that market segmentation is the recognition that market is composed of different buyers who have different responses to market offerings. No one approach to the market will satisfy all buyers. Each segment represents a somewhat different opportunities for the organisation. In its most fundamental form, market segmentation recognises that a company or its product/service offering can't be all things to everyone.[11] The definitions presented by the marketing experts clarify that market segmentation is the grouping of customers or strategy of dividing market in order to conquer them. It helps in making and innovating the marketing decisions. It is against this background that the market segmentation assumes a place of outstanding significance particularly in the banking organisations.

The bank professionals have to segment the market in such a way that the expectations of all the potential customers are studied in a right perspective and the marketing resources are developed to fulfil the same. The marketing efforts can be made more proactive if the process and bases of segmentation are right. It is essential that the bank professionals assign due weightage to the difference that we find in market behaviour due to geographical, age, sex, nationality, educational background, income classes, occupations, social and other considerations. If they overlook or underestimate key bases while segmenting, the study results can't be proactive to the formulation of creative marketing decisions. This makes it essential that the bank professionals are well aware of the criteria for market segmentation. This would make the segmentation process right *vis-a-vis* the results proactive. The agricultural sector, industrial sector, services sector, household sector are found important in the very context. The gender segment is found important no doubt but we can't underestimate institutional and professional segments. Since the banking organisations serve different sectors and segments, the segmentation should be done carefully.

IMPORTANCE OF SEGMENTATION TO THE BANKING ORGANISATIONS

Like other goods manufacturing and service generating organisations, we find segmentation important even to the banking organisations. The following facts testify it.

1. Instrumental in exploring opportunities: We find segmentation very much effective in exploring the profitable opportunities. It is well-known to us that while segmenting, the market is divided into different groups and subgroups and this simplifies the process of studying and understanding the customers in a right perspective. If we know about the rural segment, the opportunities are explored in the rural areas. If we know about the women segment, the opportunities are identified in that area. If we know about the low income group, the opportunities are explored in that group. Thus, the segmentation helps bank professionals in exploring the profitable opportunities.

2. Instrumental in designing a sound marketing strategy: We can't deny that market segmentation makes it easier to formulate a sound strategy. Since the bank professionals are aware of the changing needs and requirements of a segment, the marketing resources can be developed in tune with the needs and requirements of a segment. The formulation of a package is found significant and the bank professionals can do it successfully on the basis of market segmentation. The promotional measures can be sensitised in the face of the receiving capacity of a particular segment. The pricing strategy can be made operational and the sales promotion measures can be made productive.

3. Helpful to the policy planners: In addition, the policy makers also find segmentation important since they are well aware of the emerging trends in the business environment. They get detailed information about the changing needs and requirements of a segment. The planning is an ongoing process. The bank professionals transmit necessary information to the policy planners which simplify the process of making a sound policy.

4. A sound management of budget is possible: Formulation of a pragmatic plan and an optimal budget has a far reaching effect on the rate of success. As and when we talk about planning, the budgetary provisions, allocation in the face of changing requirements, optimal distribution of funds to different heads, monitoring of expenses become important. If we know about a segment, we also know about the requirement of that segment.

At branch level, the segmentation provides necessary information to a branch manager that helps him in studying the requirements of the command area in which the study is undertaken.

5. Enriching the marketing resources: In addition to other aspects, we find segmentation instrumental in enriching the market potentials. If we know about the preferences, needs, requirements, attitudes, lifestyles; it is found easier for us to develop the marketing resources accordingly. This in a natural way makes it convenient to develop the marketing resources. The process of innovation can be activated. The services, the promotional measures, the pricing tool and the process of offering can be made more competitive. The development of world-class marketing resources thus makes it convenient to influence the impulse of prospects. The bank professionals find it easier to get the positive results for their productive marketing efforts.

CRITERIA FOR SEGMENTATION

Segmentation in a right fashion makes the ways for profitable marketing. This helps policy planners in formulating and innovating the policies and at the same time also simplifies the task of bank professionals while formulating and innovating the strategic decisions. The following criteria make possible right segmentation.

1. Economic System: An important criterion for market segmentation is the economic system in which we find agricultural sector, industrial sector, services sector, household sector, institutional sector and rural sector requiring due weightage while segmenting. The Figure 5.6, Figure 5.7, Figure 5.8, Figure 5.9, Figure 5.10, Figure 5.11 and Figure 5.12 present different segments in the different sectors.

A. Agricultural Sector: In the agricultural sector, there are four categories since the needs of all the categories can't be identical.

Agricultural Segment				Sub-segment
	10 acres and above	①	Sub-segment	
	5 to 10 acres	②	Sub-segment	
	2 to 5 acres	③	Sub-segment	
	Marginal	④	Sub-segment	

Fig. 5.6: Agricultural Segment

The mechanisation of agriculture, the improved or scientific system of cultivation, the help of nature, the magnitude of risk, the availability of infrastructural facilities influence the level of expectations *vis-a-vis* the needs and requirements. The banking organisations are supposed to know and understand the changing requirements of different categories of farmers.

B. Industrial Sector: The banking organisations subserve the interests of the industrial sector. The large-sized, small-sized co-operative and tiny industries use the services of banks. The expectations of all the categories can't be uniform. In Figure 5.7, we find the industrial sector.

Industrial Segment				Sub-segment
	Large-sized	①	Sub-segment	
	Small-sized	②	Sub-segment	
	Co-operative	③	Sub-segment	
	Tiny	④	Sub-segment	

Fig. 5.7: Industrial Segment

The banking organisations are supposed to have an in-depth knowledge of the changing needs and requirements of the industrial segment. The emerging trends in competition, the pressure of inflation, the use of sophisticated technologies, the business regulations, the foreign exchange regulations are some of the important aspects influencing the hierarchy of needs.

C. Services Sector: It is an important sector of the economy where the banking organisations get profitable business. The two categories of organisations, such as profit-making and not-for-profit making are found important in the very context. In Figure 5.8, we find different segments which can be regrouped into different sub-segments.

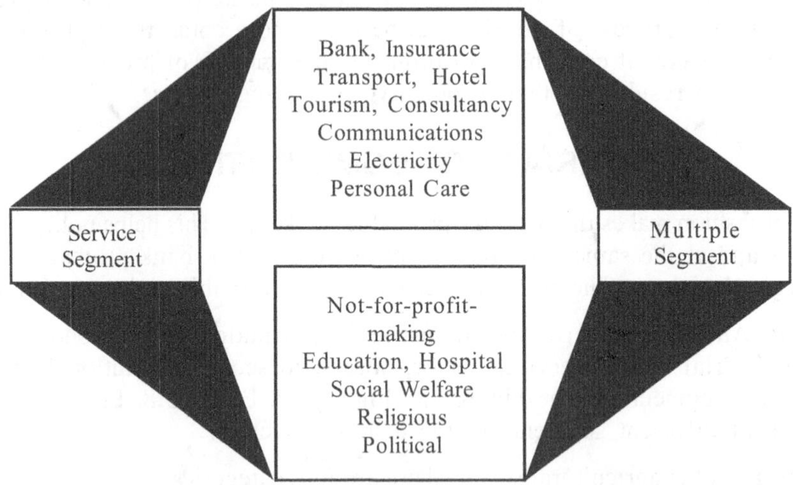

Fig. 5.8: Segmenting the Services Sector

The banking organisations need to identify the changing needs and requirements of the services sector. With the frequent use of information technologies and with the mounting pressure of inflation and competition, we find a change in the hierarchy of needs.

2. Household Sector: This also constitutes an important sector where different income groups have different needs and requirements. In Figure 5.9, we find the different segments of the household sector.

Household Segment

High Income	①	Sub-segment
Middle Income	②	Sub-segment
Low Income	③	Sub-segment
Subsistence	④	Sub-segment
Marginal	⑤	Sub-segment

Sub-segment

Fig. 5.9: Household Sector

A. Household Segment: The high income group, middle income group, low income group, subsistence level group and marginal income group have different hierarchy of needs which influence the level of their expectations.

B. Gender Segment: In the gender segment, we find male and female having different needs and requirements. The banking organisations are supposed to identify the level of expectations of both sexes, as shown in Figure 5.10.

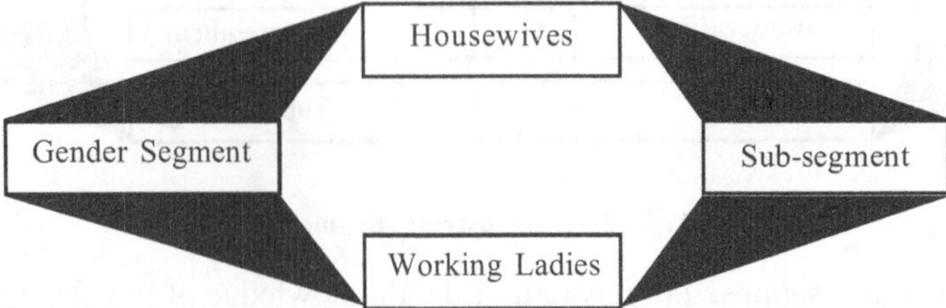

Fig. 5.10: Gender Segment

Some of the women are housewives and therefore they have different needs and requirements whereas some of them are working ladies having different needs and requirements.

C. Profession Segment: In the profession segment, we find different categories of professions and therefore we find a change in their needs and requirements. As shown in Figure 5.11, the change in profession influence the hierarchy of needs.

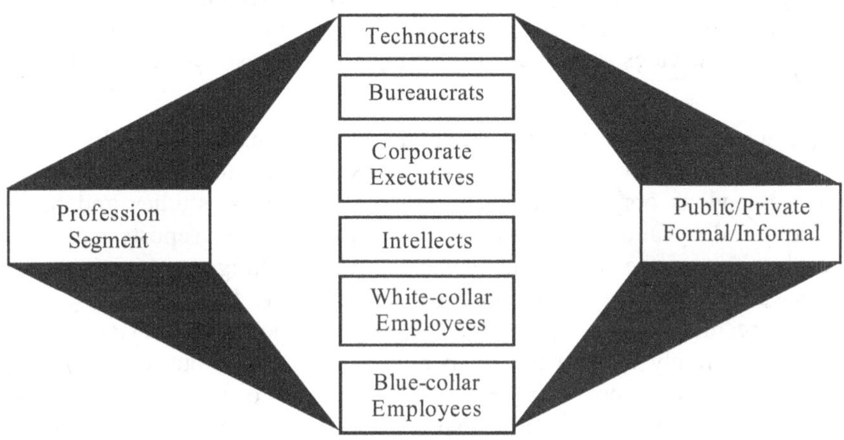

Fig. 5.11: Profession Segment

The technocrats, bureaucrats, corporate executives, intellects, white- and blue-collar employees have different needs and requirements and therefore the banking organisations should know their expectations.

3. Institutional Sector: In this sector, as shown in Figure 5.12, we find different categories of organisations. Some of the organisations are known as cultural organisations, some of them are charitable, some of them are industrial, some of them are not-for-profit making, some of them are philanthropic and some of them are related to trade and commerce. It is natural that the needs and requirements *vis-a-vis* the level of expectations can't be identical in all the cases. To satisfy and to increase the market share, it is pertinent that the banking organisations are familiar with their changing needs and requirements. The emerging trends in the social transformation process determine the hierarchy of needs.

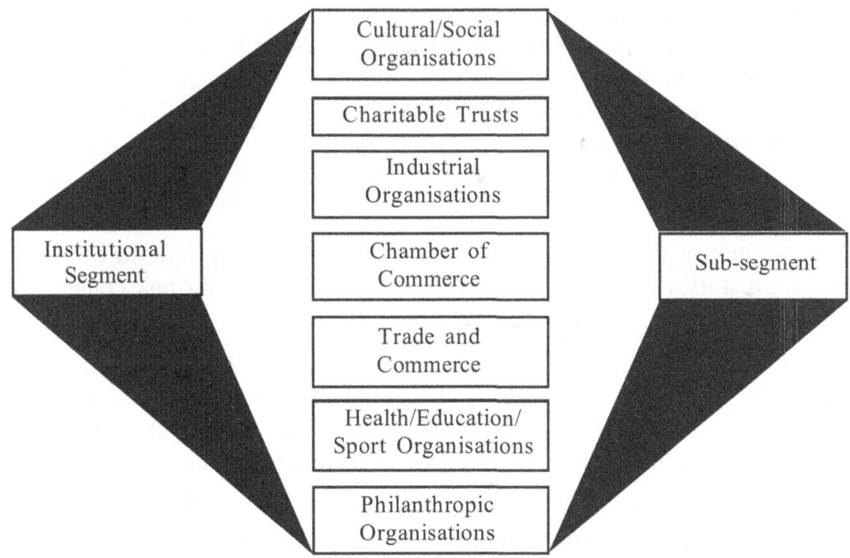

Fig. 5.12: Institutional Segment

The bank professionals bear the responsibility of understanding the changing level of their expectations further to fulfil the same.

Market segmentation thus simplifies the task of understanding the customers/prospects. The bank professionals find it convenient to formulate and innovate the marketing mix of world-class which simplify the process of excelling competition. The policy planners find it easier to make their policies and programmes development-sensitive *vis-a-vis* internationally acceptable. The strategic decisions are made condition-oriented. These facts are a mute testimony to this proposition that with the help of market segmentation, the banking organisations may be successful in increasing their market share. The services, schemes subserving the interests of different segments would get a positive response.

In the Indian perspective where we find agrarian economy contributing substantially to the transformation of national economy, it is pertinent that the banking organisations assign due weightage to the rural sector of the economy where we find tremendous opportunities. There are a number of studies and researches related to the emergence of rural segment and by and large, almost all the findings and reports make a strong advocacy in favour of rural-based development of the marketing resources. The banking organisations need to make their savings and investment plans sensitive to the rural sector of the economy. It is in this context that we realise the instrumentality of banking organisations in tapping the profitable opportunities existing or to be existent in the rural India. The urbanisation is likely to gain the momentum and villages, outskirts of big towns and cities are to be developed on a priority basis. Almost all the organisations are to get tremendous opportunities there. The marketing resources if of innovative nature would make the ways for capitalising on the same profitably.

MARKETING MIX FOR THE BANKING SERVICES

The formulation of marketing mix for the banking services is the prime responsibility of the bank professionals who based on their expertise and excellence attempt to market the services and schemes profitably. The innovative efforts of the professionals become essential to make the services internationally competitive. It is in this context that we talk about the formulation of marketing mix.

The needs and requirements, the likes and dislikes, the preferences, the attitudes, the expectations and the lifestyles can't remain static. There are a number of factors influencing the process of change. Today, we sell credibility and therefore a basic change in the perception of marketing is quite natural. This is essential for fulfilling the increasing level of expectations and even for increasing the market share. Innovation makes the ways for perfection which helps you substantially in maximising profitability and establishing leadership. The bank professionals having world-class excellence make possible frequency in the innovation process which simplify their task of selling more but spending less. It is against this background that we go through the formulation process. The marketing mix, a combination of different submixes has been deliberated by a number of marketing experts. The four traditional submixes — Product, Promotion, Price and Place — are found significant even to the banking organisations but in addition to the traditional combination of recipes, the service marketers also talk of about three additional submixes of marketing such as Process, Physical Evidence and Attractions and People. While formulating a sound marketing mix, the service marketers need to blend them in the face of changing socio-economic conditions.

Process draws our attention on the processing of services so that the promised services reach to the users on time without making any distortion. The concept and percept of processing has considerably been influenced by the use of new generation of technology in the banking services.

Physical Evidence and Attractions focus on two dimensions. The servicescapes are found very much related to the physical evidence where we find exteriors and interiors and other tangibles important. In addition, we also go through physical attractions which draws our attention on the personal appearance of employees serving banks. The dresses they wear, the physique they have and the body language they use are found important in physical attractions.

People also draw our attention. It is right to mention that the quality of people serving the banks play an important role in the entire process of creating and delivering the services. The banking organisations need due care on the quality of people they have. This requires a strong emphasis on thematically-sound people who have an in-depth knowledge of banking activities around the globe and in addition, they are aware of the emerging trends in the banking services. The people serving banks need to be personally committed. Personal touch in service helps bankers in satisfying the customers. Besides, they are also required to be value-based. The marketing experts also talk about empathy in the very context.

THE PRODUCT MIX

We find banks primarily engaged in offering services and therefore the formulation of a sound product mix is found significant. With the use of new generation of technology, we find a basic change in the service mix of banking organisations. Of late, we find banks offering a number of innovative services, e.g., Debit and Credit Cards, electronic payment, and settlement system, electronically transfer of funds, online accounting system, tax information network of Income Tax Department, funds and non-funds information flows, public key information structure and other services absolutely different to the traditional services.

The changing attitudes, increasing levels of expectations, rising levels of income, changing lifestyles, increasing domination of foreign banks and the changing needs and requirements of customers at large make it essential that the banking organisations innovate their services and make them of world-class.[12] The development of new generic product, specially when the business environment is volatile appears to be difficult. However, it is pertinent that banks formulate a package in tune with the changing business conditions. Against this background, we find it significant that the banking organisations minify, magnify, combine and modify their service mix.

In the formulation of service mix, the banks can follow two guidelines, first is related to the processing of product to market needs and the second is concerned with the processing of market needs to product. In the first process, the needs of the target market are anticipated and visualised and therefore, we expect the process likely to be productive. In the second process, the banks react to the expressed needs and therefore we consider it reactive. It is essential that every product is measured up to the accepted technical standards. This is due to the fact that no consumer would buy a product which contains technical faults. Technical perfection in service is meant prompt delivery, quick disposal, presentation of right facts and figures, right filing, proper documentation or so. If computers start disobeying the command and the customers get wrong facts, the use of technology would be a minus point, and you don't have any excuse for your faults.

Marketing aims not only offering but also at creating/innovating the services/schemes found new to the competitors *vis-a-vis* to the customers. The enhanced customer patronage would be a reward to the bank. The additional attractions, the product attractiveness would be a plus point of your mix which would help you in many ways. This makes it essential that the banking organisations are sincere to the innovation process and try to enrich their peripheral services much earlier than the competitors. In Figure 5.13, we find the products portfolio of banks. While formulating the services mix, it is also pertinent that the bank professionals make possible a fair synchronisation of core and peripheral services. To be more specific, the peripheral services need an intensive care since the core services are found by and large the same. Innovating the peripheral services thus appears to be an important functional responsibility of marketing professionals. We can't deny the fact that if the foreign banks have been getting a positive response, the credibility goes to their innovative peripheral services. Thus, the formulation of product mix is found to be a difficult task that requires world-class professionalism.

PRODUCT PORTFOLIO

The bank professionals while formulating the product mix need to assign due weightage to the product portfolio. By the concept product portfolio, our emphasis is on including the different types of services/schemes found at the different stages of the product life cycle. The portfolio denotes a combination or an assortment of different types of products generating more or less in proportion to their demand. The quality of product portfolio determines the magnitude of success. It is excellence of bank professionals that help them in having a sound product portfolio. It is quite natural that all the services/scheme included in the portfolio can't be equally profitable. We find some of the services at the maturity stage generating more profits to banks whereas we also find some of the services/schemes just launched and likely to get a profitable market in the future. In almost all the organisations such a balanced product portfolio is essential because we cannot expect uniform return from all the product. If we concentrate on the profitable product and ignore or undermine the new product likely to be profitable, the returns in future will be found insecured. The professionalism makes an advocacy in favour of blending both types of product. It will be difficult for an organisation to thrive unless profitable opportunities are left for the future.

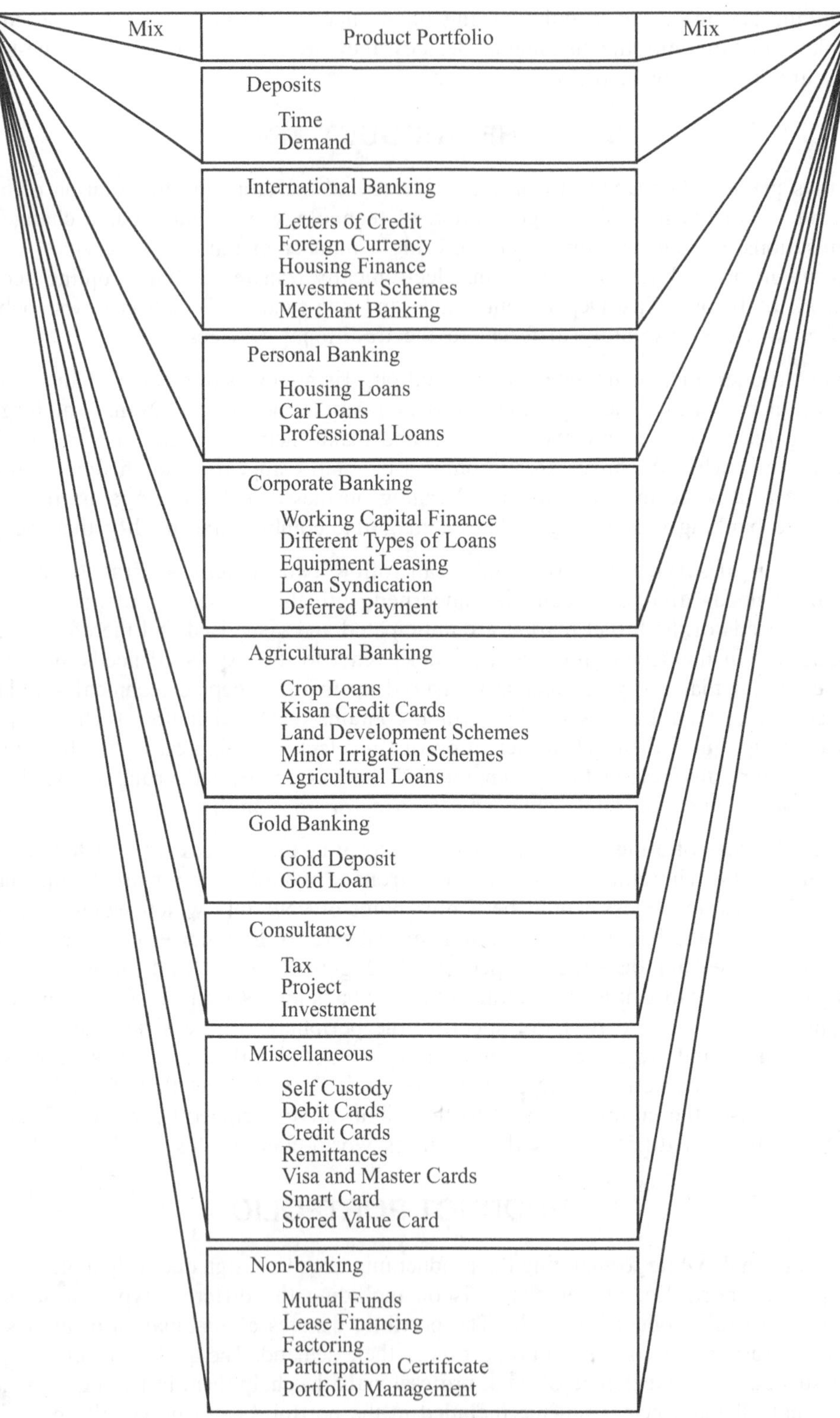

Fig. 5.13: Product Portfolio of Bank

We find the composition of a family sound, if members of all the age-groups are given due place. Like this, the composition or blending of a service mix is considered to be sound, if well established and likely to be profitable schemes are included in the mix. It is against this background that a study and analysis of product portfolio is found significant. The bank professionals are supposed to perform the responsibility of composing the same.

What to diffuse and what to include; How much to diffuse and how much to include; When to diffuse and When to include are some of the important questions to be answered suitably and the professional excellence of bankers occupies a place of outstanding significance in the very context. It is not only sufficient that you innovate; it is not only sufficient that you declare your product obsolete. Of course, it has far reaching effects that you have selected an opportune moment for discharging your functional responsibilities. A sound product portfolio is essential but its process of constitution is difficult. An organisation with a sound product portfolio gets a conducive environment and succeeds in increasing the sensitivity of marketing decisions. The banking organisations need a sound product portfolio and the bank professionals bear the responsibility of getting it done suitably and effectively.

If the banks rely solely on their established services and schemes, the multi-dimensional problems would crop up in the long-run because when the well established services/schemes would start saturating or generating losses, the commercial viability of banks would, of course, be questioned. Conversely, an overreliance on young services prove equally dangerous because of the heavy financial burdens created by the cash injections which the growing schemes need. The survival rate of newly launched schemes is generally found notoriously low and most of them don't last long albeit to repay the investment made. This makes it essential that banking organisations formulate a mix of profitable nature. An analysis of portfolio would let professionals know about the services/ schemes not responding well or performing badly or very badly which are required to be dropped. The Boston Matrix devised by the Boston Consulting Group in the USA during the 1960s enabled organisations in assessing whether they have a balanced range of products by making their classification on the basis of relative market share and relative market growth. The RMS is considered to be a more useful concept than the market share. It is evaluated by dividing the market share of an organisation by the market share of its largest competitor.

Designing of a sound product portfolio is found important to an organisation. This helps professionals in knowing that they have eliminated a scheme because it is not getting a profitable return. For the commercial launching of a product or even for identifying that a scheme is getting a profitable return, the product portfolio is found significant. In addition, the product portfolio also helps in knowing that a particular scheme is to get a profitable return in future. The bank professionals bear the responsibility of blending the different categories of schemes in such a way that the commercial viability of the organisation is found secured. Any organisation can't rely on any service or scheme for the long time to come. Sooner or later, it is to be eliminated. The banking organisations relying substantially on a profitable scheme and doing nothing for a new scheme likely to get a profitable market in the future is to face a crisis-like situation. It is in this context that we find designing of a sound product portfolio essential to an organisation. We can't deny that the product portfolio of the foreign banks is found sound since they keep their eyes moving. The innovation, diffusion, adoption and elimination processes are taken due care. The public sector commercial banks need to innovate their services and this makes a strong advocacy in favour of analysing the product portfolio.

DESIGNING AN ATTRACTIVE PACKAGE

In the formulation of product mix for the banking organisations, the designing of package is found important. In this context, we find packaging decisions related to the formulation of a mix of different schemes and services. Developing an attractive package requires professional excellence and therefore, the bank professionals are required to be aware of the different key issues influencing the formulation process. What the package should basically be or do for the particular target. We are aware of the fact that a number of schemes and services are included in the service mix of bank product and all the services or schemes can't be preferred by all. It is quite natural that different groups or segments like different packages. This makes it essential that a bank manager has an in-depth knowledge of the needs and requirements of customers living in different segments of his/her command area. The motive is to make the package motivational and competitive. We can't deny that such an effort mainly taken by the foreign banks and some of the private sector commercial banks have substantially been effective in influencing the customers. Of course, we find some of the public sector commercial banks now evincing interests in developing a package but till now, they have been found at the very nascent stage. This makes it essential that a bank manager thinks in favour of developing a package. The importance of packaging can't be underestimated considering the functions it performs and the effects which we witness in the process of attracting and satisfying the customers. In addition to other aspects, it is also pertinent that a bank manager is familiar with the package developed by the leading competitive banks since this would help them in innovating the package.

In the banking services, we talk about packaging in a bit different way. This is mainly due to the fact that like goods, we can't think regarding the development of an attractive and durable packaging for the services. In the banking services, our emphasis is on combining different services or schemes in such a way which offer to the customers benefits and conveniences. This makes it essential that the services/schemes included in the package act as a motivational tool. For example, in a bank, we find provision of some incentives when we talk about the term. deposit schemes. It is in this context that we go through the packaging problem in the banking or other service generating organisations. It is an important component of the product mix and a bank manager while formulating or designing a package needs to assign due weightage to the formulation process. While developing a package, it is essential that the packages offered are efficacious in establishing an edge over the packages of competitors. Thus, the needs and requirements and preferences of the target market in addition to the packages offered by the competitors need due weightage while designing a package.

In the designing process, the bank professionals can make a package, an ideal combination of both, the core and peripheral services. The main thing in the process is to make it profitable, convenient and productive to the customers so that they prefer to transact with the bank. For the bank professionals, it is an important persuasive effort that helps in increasing the business even without developing or innovating the services or schemes.

PRODUCT DEVELOPMENT

In almost all the organisations and in almost all the services, the development of a product is an ongoing process. Today, we declare one product obsolete and right from today itself start the process of including a new product in the mix. The banking organisations also need to develop new services and schemes. We can't deny that the development of product specially in the banking services is found difficult since they don't have any discretion, however they can do it, of course in a limited way. By minifying, combining, modifying and magnifying, the banking organisations can give to the services or schemes a new look. The regulations of the Reserve Bank of India, no doubt stand as a barrier but professionally-sound marketers make it possible even without violating the rules and regulations. The banking organisations in general have been found developing product by including some new properties or features. This makes it essential that the bank professionals at both the levels, micro and macro are familiar with the recent developments. Generally, we find two processes for the development of product as shown in Figure 5.14. The first process is found proactive since the needs of the target market are anticipated and highlighted. The second process is reactive and in this context the banks respond to the expressed needs of the target.

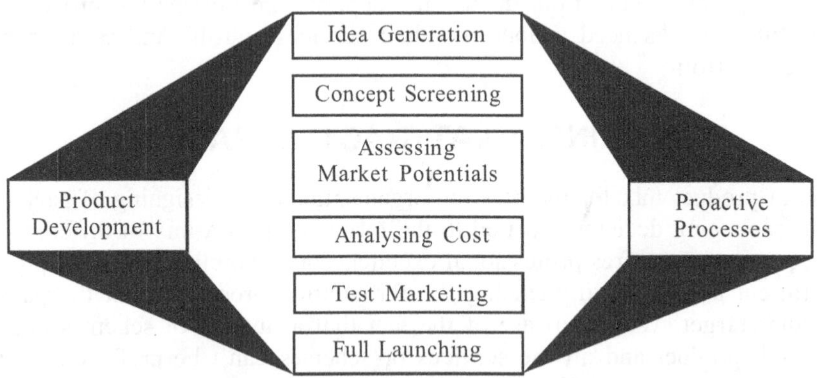

Fig. 5.14: Product to Market Needs

Proactive Process: In the proactive process, we find product to market needs. This makes it essential that the branch managers are aware of the changing needs of the target market. There are six stages for the development of the product, such as idea generation, screening of the concept, assessing of market potential, analysing the cost, test marketing and final commercial launching. The bank professionals have to be careful at all the stages so that whatever the services or schemes are developed are found instrumental in getting a positive response. Idea generation is the first stage in which we need a constant supply of idea which may come almost from anywhere. The customers and competitors help bank professionals substantially in generating a new idea. The screening of the product concept focuses on the process of narrowing down the list of the ideas generated to a small number of concepts. The banks may adopt value engineering process for that purpose, specially to weed out products which might be too impractical or uneconomic.

The assessment of market potential is the third stage in which we find scanning of the market potentials at the apex level. The branch managers can assess the potentials in their command areas.

The fourth stage draws our attention on analysing the cost on the basis of a cost-benefit analysis and the fifth stage before launching is test marketing which is found instrumental in minimising the risk element. And finally, we find commercial launching.

Reactive Process: In the reactive process, the banks are supposed to respond to the expressed needs of the target and therefore, we also call it market needs to product. The development processes are identification of needs, knowing about the size of the market, cost-benefit analysis and introduction. The identification of needs gravitates our attention on the scanning of market needs. It is natural that market needs can't remain static and therefore for introducing a new scheme or service, we find it essential to identify the emerging trends in the market.

The next stage is an analysis of the size of market. Before we develop, it is pertinent that we have an idea of the size of market for which the product is to be developed. This would let the bankers know the details about the development programmes and the banks would assess their potentials to cover the market.

The third stage is cost-benefit analysis and at this stage, the banks are supposed to know the involvement of cost and the benefits to be received after launching the product. The fourth stage is introduction in which we find final commercial launching.

The aforesaid facts make it clear that the development of product requires professional excellence and the bankers taking the problem seriously succeed in developing a profitable service or scheme. Both at apex and branch levels, the bank executives are supposed to think in favour of product development so that they offer something new much earlier than their competitors. Of late, we find even the public sector commercial banks very much instrumental in formulating a new package. We can't deny that new attractive packages of the foreign banks have compelled them to think in favour of formulating a package. But in this context, it is also essential that they think in favour of developing a new product which is found a bit different to the package. The new services or schemes are new to both — the customers as well as the competitors. This requires more excellence, more studies, intensive researches and open eyes. The bank professionals bear the responsibility of developing new services or schemes. In the Indian perspective, we find the business environment regulated and this makes it essential that the provisions, regulations, restrictions are given due care while processing the development of new services or schemes. The Reserve Bank of India is also required to make the regulations liberal so that the public sector commercial banks get an opportunity to make their services or schemes internationally competitive. The unfair practices, illegitimate steps should be checked but fair practices should essentially be promoted to make the business environment conducive.

PROMOTION MIX

In the formulation of marketing mix, the bank professionals are also supposed to blend the promotion mix in which different components of promotion, such as advertising, publicity, sales promotion, word-of-mouth promotion, personal selling and telemarketing are given due weightage. The different components of promotion help bank professionals in promoting the banking business.

Advertising

We are well aware of the fact that advertising is a paid form of communication. Like other organisations, the banking organisations also use this component of the promotion mix with the motto of informing, sensing and persuading the customers. While advertising, it is essential that we know about the key decision-making areas so that its instrumentality helps bank organisations both at micro and macro levels.

- **Finalising the budget:** This is related to the formulation of a budget for advertisement. The bank professionals, senior executives and even the policy planners are found involved in the process. The formulation of a sound budget is essential to remove the financial constraint in the process. The business of a bank determines the scale of advertisement budget. In addition, the intensity of competition also plays a decisive role since in a majority of the cases, we find an increase in the budget due to a change in the competitors' strategies.

- **Selecting a suitable vehicle:** Another task at apex level of the bank is to select a suitable vehicle for travelling the messages. There are a number of devices to advertise, such as broadcast media, telecast media and the print media. In the face of budgetary provisions, we need to select a suitable vehicle. Of course, we find the telecast media very much effective but it is found very expensive. For promoting the banking business, the print media is found economic as well as effective. The latest developments in the print technology have made print media effective. The messages, appeals can be presented in a very effective way.

- **Making possible creativity:** In advertising, we find creativity playing a decisive role in making the process effective. The advertising professionals bear the responsibility of making the appeals, slogans, messages more creative. The banking organisations should seek the co-operation of leading advertising professionals for that very purpose. By creativity, we mean making the advertisement programmes distinct to the competitive organisations which are active in influencing the impulse of customers and successful in informing and sensing the customers. This requires an in-depth knowledge of the receiving capacity of the target market for which the advertisements are designed.

- **Testing the effectiveness:** It is not only sufficient that we advertise. It bears an analogous significance that our advertisements are effective in influencing the impulse of customers by energising persuasion. For making the process effective, it is essential that we test the effectiveness before launching of the commercial advertisements. The life expectancy if increased makes advertisements cost-effective since the returns for our investments are found productive.

- **Instrumentality of branch managers:** At micro level, a branch manager bears the responsibility of advertising locally in his/her command area so that the messages, appeals reach to the target customers of the command area. Of course, we find a budget for advertisement at the apex level but the business of a particular branch is considerably influenced by the local advertisements. If we talk about the cause-related marketing, it is the instrumentality of a branch manager that makes possible the identification of local events, moments and make advertisements condition-oriented.

- **Characters and themes:** At the apex level, it is also important that while advertising, the senior executives watch the process minutely and select events, characters having a regional orientation. The popular characters and sensational moments are likely to be impact generating. The theme for appeals and messages also need due attention. Of course, they have a legitimate right of advertising but it is not meant that like the goods manufacturing organisations, the service generating organisations also start making an invasion on our culture. We need to regulate a bias to gender, profession, region or so.

The aforesaid facts make it clear that while advertising, the banks need to assign due weightage to the limitations failing which the advertisements would outlive their utility. We consider advertisement the most sensitive component of the promotion mix but in a majority of the cases, we find misuse of this tool. In addition to other negative effects, the unproductive advertisements would also increase the financial burden therefore utmost precautions are needed to make the entire process productive. The professionals bear the responsibility of determining the share of this component to the promotion mix since we can't be disproportionate.

Public Relations

Almost all the organisations need to develop and strengthen the public relations activities to promote their business. We find this component of the promotion mix effective even in the banking organisations.

The appeal of public relations is based on high quality, off guard and dramatisation. When we talk about high credibility, our emphasis is on the promotion of new stories and features since we find them more effective. By the offguard, our emphasis is on touching the prospects who could not be influenced by advertisements. In this context, the messages go to the customers as news rather than as advertisements. In respect of dramatisation, we focus on dramatising the product of the banking organisations. Thus, the three elements of public relations are found instrumental in sensitising the customers provided the executives responsible for strengthening public relations activities evince interests in developing rapport with the media people. We can't deny that in the banking services, the effectiveness of public relations is found of high magnitude. It is in this context that we find a bit difference in the designing of the mix for promoting the banking services. Of course, in the consumer goods manufacturing industries, we find advertisements occupying a place of outstanding significance but when we talk about the service generating organisations in general and the banking organisations in particular, we find public relations and personal selling bearing high degree of importance. It is not meant that the banking organisations are not required to advertise but it is meant that the bank executives unlike the executives of other consumer goods manufacturing organisations focus on public relations and personal.

Personal Selling

The personal selling is found instrumental in promoting the banking business. We consider personal selling a process of informing the customers.

The persuasion is based on transmission through personal communication. It is just a process of communication in which an individual exercises his/her personal potentials, tact, skill and ability to influence the impulse of the customers. Since we get an immediate feedback, the personal selling activities energise the process of communication very effectively. The sensitising process is so quick that customers are influenced in a positive way. Personal sale, thus, provides a one-to-one communication vehicle which can be customised to provide the right volume and complexity of information for each potential customer.[13]

Nothing happens unless somebody sells something and nothing is sold unless the buyers are motivated. The task of motivating the customers is found difficult, if the forces managing the selling activities lack professional excellence. The oral presentation in conversation bear the efficacy of turning motivation into persuasion, provided the management of salesforce is sound. Personal selling is just another name for persuasion. We find persuasion playing an affective role in the banking business. The personal selling is an art of persuasion. It is a highly distinctive form of promoting sale. In personal selling, we find interpersonal or two-way communication that makes the ways for a feedback. There is no doubt in it that the goods or services are found half sold when the outstanding properties are well told. This art of telling and selling is known as personal selling in which an individual based on his/her expertise attempts to transform the prospects into customers.

Thus, we find personal selling a personal communication, seller-buyer interaction, interpersonal communication, a direct selling or so. The following facts are observed regarding the personal selling:

- It is a direct personal relation between the buyer and seller.
- It is oral presentation in conversation.
- It is two-way communication.
- It is personal and social behaviour.
- It is selling of goods and services.
- It is found more effective in the service generating organisations.
- It is based on the professional excellence or expertise of an individual.
- It is an important element of the promotion mix.

In the Indian perspective, we find this submix of the promotion mix not getting due weightage. A number of potential customers remain unilluminated of the new services or schemes launched in the market. To be more specific, the rural prospects fail in getting the information since the agents, dealers, motivators prefer to concentrate in the urban areas. For increasing the sensitivity of the marketing decisions, it is important that we draw our attention on transactions supposed to be complementary, crossed and hidden. The transaction is the basic unit of communication instrumentalising the process of stimulation and thus making possible positive results. In the transaction of different types, we find a bit variation in the nature of conversation. The complementary transaction makes possible smooth conversation.

We consider transactional analysis as a lever spring of personal selling. The transactional analysis is likely to be convenient, if the branch managers have an in-depth knowledge of the behavioural profile of the customers. Here, the branch managers are supposed to study the ego states found of dynamic nature. The identification of ego states can be through tone, words, postures, gestures, manners and language. From the standpoint of study, we classify ego state into different parts, such as parent ego state, child ego state, and adult ego state. The parent ego state is made up of attitude and behaviour. The imprints of attitude and behaviour, specially during the childhood are found significant in the formation of parent ego state.

Noted psychologist Clements says, "Our childhood perceptions and experiences were stored in our heads like video tape recordings. And like video recordings, we replay them today, often using the same words, gestures and expressions those grown up many years ago."[14] The behavioural aspect characterises parents as controlling and nurturing. The Child ego state covers the degree of freedom enjoyed as a child. A distinction between free child and adapted child is to be studied. The words used by free child are, I want. Contrary to it, the words used by adapted child are, I wish. The free child relaxed, seductive, animated and exaggerated whereas the adapted child are sad, dejected and controlled. The Adult ego state is found different to the child or parent ego state. In the adult ego state, the decisions are made after considering the pros and cons and therefore it is natural that the decisions are rational. Clements describes adult ego state as the computer of the personality. He says like a computer, the adult logically and generally is not influenced by emotion. It operates with reality of the here and now situation.[15]

For raising the sensitivity of personal selling, it is essential that the managers go beyond the various influences on customers and come to know that how and in what circumstances, the customers make their buying decisions, the type of buying decisions and the steps in the buying process.[16] Noted expert John Dewey listed the steps in problem-solving to explain the process an individual goes through in arriving at a decision and he viewed consumer behaviour as a process rather than as a discrete act on the part of consumer.[17] The processes as detailed by him are the recognition of problem, search, alternative evaluation, choice and outcome. In the personal selling, the knowledge of buyers' behaviour is found essential.

DYNAMICS OF PERSONAL SELLING

The dynamics of personal selling are found instrumental in activating the selling activities. Sales preparations are considered most crucial for the actual sales. Pre-sale activities and post-sale services can't be left neglected to improve the marketing activities. McIver and Naylore[18] have compared the sale of financial services with the sandwich. They opine, "We prefer to think that in the financial services, the actual selling interview, important as it is, the filling in the sandwich of which pre-sale activities and post-sale services are the bread and butter. It is important to mention that the preparations for the actual sales interview are vital for getting a positive response. An efficient salesmen is required to prepare himself in the face of questions to be asked. It is natural that before switching on the buying activities, the customers may prepare themselves. Some of the general informations are the main features of the services-offered, their uses and benefits, relationship of the services with the customers and the justifications for the services-offered. The customers may be interested in knowing the main features of the services, how a particular service would help them, rationale behind the technical services and proof in regard to its uses. The pre-sale activities would bring the positive results, if preparations are adequate.

It is important to mention that all the customers have varying degree of awareness about the financial markets as shown in Figure 5.15.

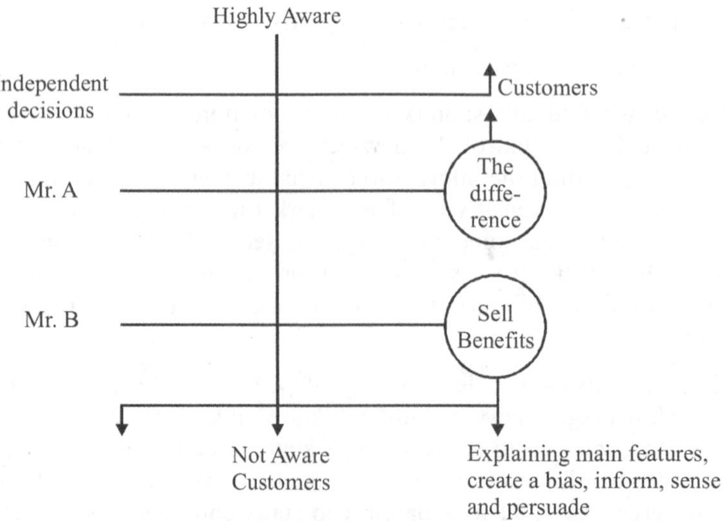

Fig. 5.15 : Degree of Awareness

Some of the customers are found highly aware of the developments, they are found well-informed. On the other hand, we also find other category of customers who are in dark. Here, the branch managers are expected to match the level of awareness of customers. As for instance, Mr. A goes up the matrix but Mr. B has not enough time for the branch managers. The branch managers are supposed to prepare a synopsis of their sales talk. Not surprisingly, the highly aware customers are found in apposition to make independent decisions and know all about. While selling to the less aware customers, the managers should stress on the main features of the services and the expected benefits of these services. To this class, we are supposed to sell the benefits, not the service....the benefit which is of no interest to the man in front of you is no benefit for that sale.[19]

The aforesaid facts make it clear that personal selling is an important dimension of the promotion mix. The banking organisations need to make use of this dimension with the help and cooperation of efficient and personally-committed salespeople. If we find salespeople having an in-depth knowledge of the sales dialogue, sales technique, behavioural profile of the customers, the task of transforming the dialogue into a business is found easier. This requires an intensive training programme. The personal selling is based on the personal skill of salespeople. If they know in detail about the prospects to be interviewed, the questions to be asked by the prospects/representatives of business houses, it is possible for them to convince.

Sales Promotion

More innovative the tools of sales promotion, more positive are the results. It is not wisdom that you just copy the promotional measures adopted by the competitors. Your execllence is coiled in the essence of offering the innovative measures. It is natural that like other organisations, the banking organisations also think in favour of promotional incentives both to the bankers as well as the customers. The banking organisations make provisions for incentives to the bankers and we call this bankers' promotion. Like this, the incentives offered to the customers are known as customers' promotion. There are a number of tools generally used in the different categories of organisations in the face of the nature of goods and services sold by them. The gift, contests, fairs and shows, discount and commission, entertainment and travelling plans for bankers, additional allowances, low interest financing and retailitary are to mention a few found instrumental in promoting the banking business.

As and when the banking organisations offer new services and schemes, the tools of sales promotion are required to be innovated. This is with the motto of stimulating the new and old customers. An important thing in the very context is the changing needs and requirements of customers/prospects. The tools like gifts, fairs and shows, discount and commission, additional allowances to bankers are of traditional nature. In this context, the bank professionals need to innovate the measures, such as offering a travelling plan to the bankers, provision for gifts having long lasting life and memories, low rate interest for house construction and conveyance or so. But the sales promotion should be linked to the business results and based on their performance, the decisions regarding promotional tool should be made final.

In addition, the customers/prospects are also offered incentives and we call it consumer promotion. We can't negate that incentives to customers would be linked to the offering of a package if a particular scheme is taken by an individual. It is natural that being influenced by the incentives, they evince special interests in the services and make sincere efforts to transact and share substantially to the bank business. We agree with this view that the tools of sales promotion would change in the face of market conditions. The bank professionals bear an outstanding task of studying the competitors' strategies which would help them in initiating the process of innovation. Here, it is important to mention that promotional incentives to the customers would focus on decisions related to the selection of a tool. There are a number of considerations to streamline the process. The bank professionals are supposed to study the market conditions and to make necessary suggestions, specially regarding the incentives.

It is a blending process and the bank professionals have to be sure that whatever the provisions, they are fulfilled on a priority basis. In the sales promotion, not only the consumers but even the bankers are to be involved and therefore we find an ideal sales promotion synchronising the interests of both the parties. More incentives, more efficiency or a *vice versa* condition, more efficiency, more incentives motivate bankers substantially.

Word-of-mouth Promotion

Much communication about the banking services actually take place by word-of-mouth information which is also known as word-of-mouth promotion.[20] In the banking industry, we find use of different components of promotion and in this context, it is essential that we also talk about word-of-mouth communication which makes the process of influencing the prospects effective by sensitising the word-of-mouth recommendations. If your friends, relatives, or other well-wishers recommend you about the excellent services of a particular bank or the outstanding properties of a particular scheme, the process of influencing the impulse becomes effective and you try to avail the services of that bank as and when the opportunities come. We call the persons engaged in communication, the hidden salesforce who play an incremental role in increasing the demand. The process is to cost nothing but to contribute more to the stimulation process since we believe or trust the deliberations made by our friends or relatives. It is against this background that we talk about the role of word-of-mouth promotion in the banking services. We can't negate that the high magnitude of effectiveness of this tool is due to the high level of trust. If we keep on moving the process of satisfying the customers, the circle of word-of-mouth promotion would keep on moving for the long time to come.

An important question regarding the word-of-mouth communication is related to its intensity of sensitising the persuasion process. Why do we find this tool of promotion so much effective? Of course, a plain answer to this question is the positive opinion of the promoters. If our friends communicate to us the specialities of their positive feelings about the services of a particular bank, we trust on them blindly. It is in this context that this component of promotion is found significant to the banking organisations and the bank professionals are required to seek the cooperation of opinion leaders for that very purpose. The problem before the bank professionals is to identify the persons to be included in the list of word-of-mouth promoters. It is supposed that a bank manager is well aware of the social composition of his/her command area. They at the very outset are required to prepare the list and to invite them on dinner or get-together and to explain to them the new schemes to be launched in the market. It is natural that being influenced by the services of that bank they don't need any clarification regarding the quality of services. You need to explain to them the salient features of new schemes or services for his/ her personal cooperation in getting the business. You also need to think in favour of offering to them small gifts. They would start the process of influencing the customers and prospects. This is an organised effort to make the process effective.

In this context, it is also significant to mention that the oral publicity plays an important role in eliminating the negative comments and improving the services. This helps you know the feedback which may simplify the task of improving the quality of services. An organisation distributed a packet to the invited guests which in a true sense included the habitual customers. Along with this packet, they also supplied instructions. After going home, the habitual customers opened the packet and found seeds of a plant. The transplantation process was mentioned inside the packet. The long lasting plant worked as a point of memory. The promotion process was switched on. People ask them about the plant and they narrate the story which in a natural way includes the services of the organisation who distributed the packet. This draws our attention on the fact that while distributing gifts to the opinion leaders or vocal persons or habitual customers we should try to be innovative.

The social reformists, popular cine artists, TV artists, opinion leaders, vocal persons may act as word-of-mouth promoters. It is important that a branch manager has an in-depth knowledge of his/her command area and a list of word-of-mouth promoters is prepared. Organising dinner, offering to them a gift and seeking their cooperation are the processes to use this tool of promotion. Here, it is also right to mention that if the banks have been offering the world-class services, the task of word-of-mouth promoters is simplified considerably. A satisfied group of customers is considered to be the most successful hidden promoters. A branch manager showing his/her excellence in improving the quality of services in his/her command area, establishing an edge over the services of the competing banks, promoting LGD marketing (lunch, golf, dinner marketing) succeeds in instrumentalising the word-of-mouth promotion. It is against this background that this component of the promotion mix is found getting due place.

In view of the above, it is right to mention that this component of the promotion mix is not to influence your budget adversely or to generate additional financial burden. By improving the quality of services and by offering small gifts to the word-of-mouth promoters, you can get more business in your command area. We can't deny that the foreign banks have been seen using this component of the promotion mix and their efforts have also been found productive. The public sector commercial banks, of course, need to use this tool but we can't negate the fact that the instrumentality of this tool is minimised considerably if we find the quality of services poor. The word-of-mouth promoters can't be successful in influencing the customers if the quality of service is poor. Thus, it is not to be forgotten that ultimately you are paid for your quality.

The aforesaid facts make it clear that word-of-mouth promotion is an important component of the promotion mix but its instrumentality is influenced by a number of factors. The most dominating factor is the quality of services-offered. The bank professionals, the front-line staff and the senior executives should realise that a degeneration in quality would make this tool ineffective. We spend a lot on advertisement, we also have a big budget for sales promotion, we offer a number of incentives to the salespeople, we also spend on media people and therefore we find a strong case for offering something to the word-of-mouth promoters. Of course, the senior executives can do something concrete in the very context.

In this component of the promotion mix, we find two important considerations, first the bank professionals are required to make it sure that the promised services reach to the ultimate users and second, the word-of-mouth promoters are offered small but new incentives which have not been offered by their competitors. The list of word-of-mouth promoters is to be based on a survey result or on the personal experiences of a branch manager. A revision in the list is made possible as and when the circumstances necessitate so. The innovative peripheral services-offered by the banks are well publicised and the word-of-mouth promoters focus on the same intelligently.

Telemarketing

An important component of the promotion mix, telemarketing has gained popularity particularly in the developed countries. In the Indian perspective, we find just a beginning and the process has, of course, been initiated by the foreign banks. The telemarketing is a process of promoting the business with the help of sophisticated communication network. The television services fuel the process of telemarketing significantly. Thus, the telephonic services and the telecast services determine the instrumentality of telemarketing.

Of late, telemarketing is likely to be a major marketing tool. The telemarketing blossomed in the late 1960s with the introduction of inbound and outbound Wide Area Telephone Service (WATS). With IN WATS, the marketers can offer customers and prospects toll-free numbers to place orders for goods or services stimulated by print or broadcast advertisements, direct mail or catalogues or to make complaints and suggestions. With OUT WATS, they can use the phone calls to sell directly to consumers and businesses, generate or quality sales leads reach more distant buyers or service current customers or accounts. The automatic dialing and recorded message players (ADRMPs) can dial numbers, play a voice-activated advertising message and take orders from interested customers on an answering machine device or by forwarding the call to an operator. Telemarketing is increasingly used in business marketing.

Television is found to be a growing medium for direct marketing both through network and cable channels. Television is used in two ways to market products directly to consumers. The first is through direct response advertising. Another television marketing approach is becoming shopping channels where an entire television programme or the whole channel is dedicated to selling goods and services. Thus, we find telemarketing either working independently or working with the support of television. Thus, it is natural that the significant developments in the field of satellite communication influence the development process in the field of telemarketing.

In the Indian perspective, the telemarketing diverted attention of marketers in the beginning of the decade 1990s but nothing concrete was visible specially in the banking services unless the foreign banks used this tool of promotion. Here, it is right to mention that even in the Indian context, the telemarketing can be used effectively if the public sector commercial banks evince interest in marketing through the telephones. Today, we have sound communication network and the main thing that we need is to make available to the branches sophisticated telephonic services.

The telemarketing also helps in activating the process of advertisement. The banking organisations telecasting their messages on the TV screen are benefited in two ways. The first that the customers come to know the information regarding the services or schemes, their salient features and relative merits and second they are also persuaded in a right way. The transmission of information regarding the services or schemes help the customers/prospects in developing their awareness, specially regarding the new services or schemes. They if informed, sensed and persuaded in a right way may approach to the telephone numbers, make necessary queries or enquiries if they need so.

They can send their representatives to collect information at the information centres or may call the numbers. This makes it clear that we find advertising even in the process of selling since the customers/prospects before the television screen come to know about the advertisements and the messages transmitted or appeals made regarding a particular service or scheme. The banking organisations can use this component of promotion even for advertising. This is supported by the fact that while watching TV, the messages on screen attempt to persuade the customers/ prospects. It is well-known that advertisements persuade the customers/prospects and the telemarketing also activate the same process. Of course, the instrumentality of telemarketing is involved in the essence of people working as telemarketers and the quality of messages, appeals, slogans transmitted on the screen. If the advertisement professionals make possible creativity in the messages to be transmitted, the telemarketing succeeds in advertising the goods or services effectively. This makes it essential that the advertisement professionals are well aware of the attitudes and expectations of customers/prospects and while designing the messages, they assign due weightage to the target audience. It is in this context that we find television playing a contributory role in the entire process. We can't negate that the intensity of success of telemarketing is substantially influenced by the sophistication in the telephonic and television services.

The aforesaid facts make it clear that telemarketing is found instrumental in advertising the banking services and the banking organisations can use this tool of the promotion mix both for advertising and selling. This, of course, minimises the dependence of banking organisations on the salespeople and just a counter or centre as listed in the call numbers may serve multi-dimensional purposes. The interested person/persons, organisation/ organisations can seek the cooperation of telemarketers even for lodging complaints and the telemarketers can make efforts for their redressal and ring back the feedback to the concerned person(s). Since of late, we have a perception of everything automated, it is possible. It is not to be forgotten that in a majority of the branches of the public sector commercial banks we don't find telephonic services in a right order. This makes it essential that the branches are made available sophisticated telephonic services and professionally-sound telemarketers are engaged for that very purpose.

In view of the above, it is right to mention that telemarketing is likely to play an incremental role in marketing the banking services and in the years to come even the public sector commercial banks would have to realise its instrumentality in promoting the banking business. The leading foreign banks and even some of the private sector commercial banks have been found promoting telemarketing and they have also been getting a positive result for their efforts. In the Indian perspective, we find tremendous opportunities for telemarketing and it is high time that the senior executives and the bank professionals realise the gravity of the situation and promote the use of telemarketing both for selling and advertising as well. In addition, they can also use telemarketing for the redressal of the grievances of customers. The telemarketing would be successful where the public relations officers have failed. The telemarketers are supposed to be professionally sound and therefore his/her professional excellence can activate the process of selling and advertising.

Cause-related and Sponsorship Marketing

Of late, we find almost all the organisations identifying opportunities for effective promotion. Since we find social responsibility getting priority attention of corporate sector, the banking organisations also appear interested in promoting through cause-related and sponsorship marketing. Particularly, the public sector commercial banks have been found significantly contributing to the process of social welfare. As and when we find cases of natural calamities or abnormal conditions, the banks are supposed to come forward and to help the sufferers or victims. This provides to them an opportunity to display their posters, banners and other materials such as brochures, leaflets, information regarding innovative products and contribution of banks to the process of social transformation. Projection of fair image with the help attractive publicity materials is found much more easier. We call it cause-related marketing because it is found serving the social cause. The sponsorship marketing focuses our attention on sponsoring a particular event with the motto of fulfilling social responsibility. The fund collected through a programme is used for social welfare. Like cause-related marketing, the professionals also get there a suitable place for business promotion. Since we expect assembling of customers and potential customers there; the advertisement materials are expected to be much more effective. Both the measures for promotion need due care of not only the public sector banks but even the private sector banks.

Projection of a fair image considerably rests on our efforts made for building the image. The banking organisations if contributing to cause-related and sponsorship marketing would find it easier to build a fair image. Identifying the opportunities and capitalising on the same with a professional touch is essential. Organising events and mobilising funds, displaying publicity materials and sensitising the masses simplify the process of relationship building. Thus, we find both the aspects very much instrumental here, viz., social transformation and promotion.

With the development of corporatisation, we find a good number of foreign banks coming to India. Of course, they have been contributing to the process of economic transformation but if we talk about their contributions to the process of social transformation, we find a very disappointing result. The foreign banks in particular need priority attention on their contributions to the social welfare activities. They should not forget that their minor contributions to the process of social transformation would provide to them a platform for business promotion.

The different submixes of promotion mix are to be blended in such a way that the processes are not only effective but also cost-effective. While promoting, the professionals need to be much more creative so that they succeed in informing, sensing, sensitising, persuading and transforming the potential customers into actual and habitual customers.

THE PRICE MIX

In the formulation of product mix, the pricing decisions occupy a place of outstanding significance. The pricing decisions or the decisions related to interest and fee or commission charged by banks are found instrumental in motivating or influencing the target market. The Reserve Bank of India and the Indian Banking Association are concerned with the regulations. The rate of interest is regulated by the RBI and other charges are controlled by the Indian Banking Association. To be more specific in the Indian setting, we find this component of the marketing mix significant because the banking organisations are also supposed to subserve the interests of weaker sections and the backward regions. The public sector commercial banks in particular are supposed to play developmental role with societal approach.[21] It is natural that this specific role of the public sector commercial banks complicate the problem of pricing. In making the pricing decisions, the Government of India instrumentalises or commands everything as a shadow policy maker. This complicates the task of bank professionals found responsible for managing the banking transactions.

Pricing policy of a bank is considered important for raising the number of customers *vis-a-vis* the accretion of deposits. Of course, there are a number of factors to influence the process but it is also right to mention that the key role in the entire process is played by the Reserve Bank of India. A National Consumer Survey conducted by the L.H. Associates reveals that the quality of customer service was one of the three top issues and the consumers ranked the quality of their bank relationships as even more important than the fees charged for the services.[22] This makes it clear that specially in the banking services, we find customer services ranking top position. However, it is not practical that we underestimate the decisions related to interest and fee. To be more specific when we find a number of domestic and foreign banks working in the Indian economy, the Reserve Bank of India bears the responsibility of making the business environment conducive. The non-banking organisations and foreign banks have been found attracting customers by offering to them a number of incentives. The potential customers or investors frame their investment plans in the face of pricing decisions made by the banking organisations. It is right that the policy makers consider price an important variable to be traded off against product quality and promotion rather than as an absolute where the lowest price is most desirable.[23] While formulating the pricing strategies, the banks have also to take the value satisfaction variable into consideration. The value and satisfaction can't be quantified in terms of money since it differs from person to person. Keeping in view the level of satisfaction of a particular segment, the banks have to frame their pricing strategies. In a competitive market, the buyers and sellers must have the feeling of winning the transactions. If this in not made possible, the transactions would hardly take place. As for instance, the sellers are satisfied with cost-plus-profit whereas the buyers look for satisfaction in return for the prices paid by them. The policy makers are required to be sure that the services offered by them are providing satisfaction to the customers concerned. The pricing decisions may be to a bit liberal, if the potential customers are found shifting to the non-banking investments. In this context, it is pertinent that pricing is used as a motivational tool.

The formulation of pricing strategies can't be purposeful if the RBI fails in assigning due weightage to some of the key factors like the strategies followed by companies, socio-economic developments, intensity of competition in the market, rising level of income or so. We can't negate that these components have an important bearing on the formulation of strategies related to pricing. The banking organisations are required to frame two-fold strategies. First, the strategy is concerned with interest and fee charged and second, the strategy is related to the interest paid. Since both the strategies throw a *vice versa* impact, it is pertinent that banks attempt to establish a correlation between the two. It is essential that both the buyers as well as the sellers have a feeling of winning as shown in Figure 5.16.

The transactions would not take place if either of the two have a feeling of loss. The banks have to take the value satisfaction variable into consideration while designing the pricing strategies. McIver and Naylor opine that a marketing manager has to regard price as a variable to be traded off against product quality and promotion rather than as an absolute where the lowest price is not desirable.

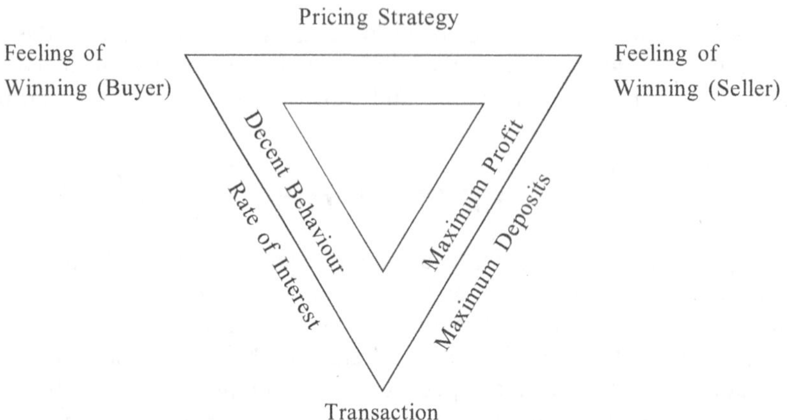

Fig. 5.16: Game of Buying-Selling

In view of the above, it is right to mention that in a highly controlled banking industry, the task of formulating the price mix is critical as well as challenging. The RBI has to be more liberal so that the public sector commercial banks make decisions in the face of changing business conditions. The mounting intensity of social costs has made it essential that a stage of financial disaster is prevented and for that the public sector commercial banks in particular need autonomy. There is no doubt that the commercial banks bear the responsibility of energising the socio-economic development programmes. In tune with the principles of social marketing, they are also supposed to bear the social costs. It is also right that the foreign banks have been found making the business environment more competitive. These emerging trends necessitate a close look on the pricing problem. The policy makers find it difficult to bring a change since the regulations of the RBI make things more critical. The public sector commercial banks thus find it difficult to work. They are forced to make the social costs disproportionate to their potentials and this creates a vicious circle. The expenses are not regulated by the RBI and the banking organisations are forced to increase the budgetary provisions. The sources of revenue are regulated which complicates the task of bank professionals. This makes it essential that the Reserve Bank of India, the Government of India and the banking organisations think over this complicated issue with a new vision.

THE PLACE MIX

This component of the marketing mix is related to the offering of services. Whatever the provisions we find in the service mix of banks move through different windows, such as the bank executives and the front-line staff. The services are sold through the branches. The two important decision-making areas are making available the promised services to the ultimate users and selecting a suitable place for bank branches.

The selection of a suitable place for the establishment of a branch is significant with the viewpoint of making the place accessible and in addition, the safety and security provisions are also found important. The banking organisations are not free to open a branch since the Reserve Bank of India regulates the subject of branch expansion but so far as the management of branch is concerned, the branch managers have option to select a place which is convenient to both the parties, such as the users and the bankers. The task of selecting a suitable place for branch is significant that requires to be considered carefully. A place easily accessible is the first consideration and therefore the availability of all-weatherproof roads needs an overriding priority. The availability of infrastructural facilities can't be underestimated since in today's perspective we find frequent use of sophisticated information technologies to improve the quality of services. In the Indian perspective, the protection to the bank's assets and safety to the users and bankers need due weightage. The vulnerable areas or regions need adequate provisions to make the branch safe. The management of office is also found significant with the viewpoint of making the services attractive. The furnishing, civic amenities and parking facilities can't be overlooked. Of late, we find aesthetic management getting due place in the foreign branches. This draws our attention on beautifying the office and premises and making the place environment-friendly. Thus, these considerations need due weightage while managing the branches of a bank.

Another important decision-making area is related to the offering of services. This draws our attention on the behavioural profile of bankers. The bankers in general and the front-line staff in particular bear the responsibility of making available the services-promised to the ultimate users without any distortion. Often, a gap is found generated by the front line staff that makes an invasion on the image of a bank. The bank professionals or a branch manager is required to be sure that whatever the promises have been made regarding the quality of services are not distorted. A gap in the distribution process is to be bridged over and this is not possible unless we find a team spirit. A branch manager and his/her team has the responsibility of making it sure that whatever the expectations their competitors have shaped regarding the quality of services in the minds of the ultimate users are fulfilled. If we find cases of indecent behaviour by the bankers, the promises would hardly reach to the ultimate users. This would complicate the task of a branch manager since the inconveniences to the customers would act as a demotivational tool and the dissatisfied group of customers would start word-of-mouth to propagate reverse remarks regarding the bank that would affect the future business of a bank. It is in this context that we find the instrumentality of a branch manager of high magnitude in the very context.

If we find the Reserve Bank of India interested in setting things in the right direction, a number of problems would automatically be solved. The number of branches, the location of a branch office, the placement of bankers, the behavioural profile of bankers are some of the sensitive issues affecting the image *vis-a-vis* the quality of services. The RBI and the different public sector commercial banks are required to manage the distribution process intelligently and professionally. Thus, the place mix is found to be an important decision-making area which requires due attention, both at macro and micro levels. If the banking organisations sell the promises, it is essential that the end-users get the same without any distortion.

EXPANDED MARKETING MIX FOR BANKING SERVICES

With the multi-dimensional development in the banking services, the business environment is found becoming much more competitive. Particularly the leading foreign banks with the help of their innovative services have been found complicating the task of public sector commercial banks. This makes a strong advocacy in favour of the three additional marketing mixes for them which would help them in satisfying the customers.

Process

The processing of banking services is found significant with the viewpoint of making the services much more friendly to the customers. With the use of new generation of technology used in banks, we find processing occupying a place of outstanding significance. The standardised and customised flow of activities in the banking organisations of today make a strong advocacy in favour of processing. We find processing the actual procedures, mechanism and flow of activities by which the service is delivered.[24] In the processing of banking services, a number of technologies and professionals are found involved. The motive is to deliver the promised quality of services on time, without any distortion and discrimination. We find process characteristics of the banking services a form of evidence used by the customers/users to judge the quality. Since they get an opportunity to encounter, a change in perception is but natural. We cannot negate that the process of encounter increases the levels of expectations of customers. The customers visiting the banks get an opportunity to witness and expect standardised services.

The techno-driven services in a very natural fashion increase the flow of banking activities. The processing of banking services thus now is becoming easier because the computer-based services minimise a scope for stepping. The most important thing while processing is right handling and functioning of machines and equipments used for this purpose. The availability of supporting infrastructural facilities is also an important consideration. We find a number of cases when the public or private sector banks working in Indian environment find it difficult to process due to power breakdown. The benefits of new generation of technologies cannot be made available to the customers if we do not find uninterrupted power and communication services. The delivery of core banking services are becoming a challenging task, specially in the areas where the power and communication services are found disturbed. The service environment included in its purview the availability of all the supporting infrastructural facilities essential for delivering the promised quality of services. Technology facilitates order and at the same time technology also leads to disorder. Technology leads to feelings of intelligence and efficacy and at the same time also the feelings of ignorance or ineptitude. Technology can facilitate involvement, flow or activity and technology can also lead to disconnection, disruption and passivity. These facts make it essential that techno-driven processing requires intensive care of banking professionals.

Right processing, time-honoured processing and fault-free processing are the key areas in the modern banking.

Physical Evidence and Attractions

The service environment is considered to be an important dimension of bank marketing. The environment in which the banking organisations deliver and where the bankers and customers interact and any tangible components that facilitate performance or communication of the banking services are studied in the context of physical evidence. We can say that the physical evidence of banking services includes all of the tangible representations of the service such as brochures, letterhead, business cards, signages and equipments used for delivering the services. We also call it servicescape as, for example, the retail banking services. Physical evidence cues provide excellent opportunities for the banking organisations where they get an opportunity for fair projection and transmission of a positive message. Thus, we find two things in the Physical Evidence servicescape and tangibles. In the group of servicescape, we find facility exterior such as exterior design, signage, parking, landscape, surrounding environment and in addition we also find facility interior such as interior design, equipment, signage, layout, air quality and temperature. Besides we also include tangibles such as business cards, stationery, billing statements, reports, web pages, brochures and virtual servicescape.

In the modern banking services, we find all the aspects of physical evidence important helping not only an improvement in the quality of banking services but in addition also simplifying their task of projecting a fair image. Exterior and interior components draw priority attention of banking professionals. The private sector foreign banks, of course, have been found more sincere to the physical evidence but so far as the public sector banks are concerned we find the situations by and large not so impressive. The banking professionals while making provisions for exterior designing need to make it sure that all the dimensions are getting due attention. In a majority of the public sector banks, we find facility exterior not even at the bottom of their development agenda. Particularly parking and landscape and ambience are found insignificant to them. The exterior designing also presents a gloomy picture. The policy decision-makers need priority attention failing which they would find it difficult to project a fair image. Of course, a few of the dimensions of other tangibles have been found getting attention such as brochure, billing statements, stationery, business cards but even in these respects we find foreign banks establishing an edge over them. The banking professionals need priority attention because the servicescape cannot be undermined. They also need priority on the web pages.

Thus, in the changing scenario, the banking organisations need due attention on physical evidence and in this context, they have to make the exterior, interior and other tangible of global standard. This is an essential ingredient of service environment which helps banks in projecting their image. Incorporating additional attractions to our services has been found drawing priority attention of foreign private banks. Let the Public Sector Commercial Banks activate the process.

The Physical Attractions

Of late, we also find emphasis on the employees looking smart, handsome, and impressive. With the development of corporate sector and with the emergence of corporate culture, we find this dimension of the management of people getting a new place in the marketing mix. This draws our attention on the management of body which helps you in projecting your personality and adding physical attractions. The personal care services would help employees in developing their physique and looking impressive and attractive. To be more specific in the banking organisations, we need to assign due priority to this component since this would help bankers in adding additional attractions to their personality. You are professionally-sound, personally-committed, value-based and at the same time also looking smart and attractive. This makes you sound enough to attract the customers. You are not supposed to look like a philosopher. Since you bear the responsibility of promoting the banking business, it is your prime responsibility that you by your behaviour, with your actions and by your physique impress upon the prospects and succeed in transforming them into the habitual customers. This in addition to other properties make an advocacy in favour of personal care.

The front-line staff, a branch manager need to manage their physique in tune with the changing expectations of customers. If you go to the foreign banks and turn your eyes on the physical make-up of the employees of different echelons working there, a sea change is apparent in the public sector commercial banks. Your dresses, your physique, your hairstyle, your aesthetic sense, your taste make a strong sense in the today's corporate world.[26] It is against this background that we find the foreign banks assigning due weightage to the physique and make-up of employees working there. We should also not forget that physical attractions help us in getting the business. We should also not forget that attraction is a result of aggregation of different properties. Attraction in product is, of course, essential but at the same time attraction in salespeople is also found impact generating. The public sector commercial banks need to think over the issue on a priority basis.

A decade back when we talked about the personal care services for men, it was not accepted by masses. Today, all of us feel that this dimension assumes a place of outstanding significance. It is against this background that we find it emerging as a submix of the marketing mix. In the years to come, we expect significant changes in the expectations of customers and this makes it essential that we make sincere efforts to identify them and activate necessary steps to correct them. The employees serving the banking organisations need to remember that they bear the responsibility of promoting the business. The employees serving the foreign banks have no option but to manage their physique and personality. The public sector commercial banks where we don't find this dimension of the marketing mix getting due place need to think over the issue with a new vision.

Uniqueness is found getting the desired results. By uniqueness, we mean our services, our schemes, our bankers, our banks projecting a world-class image. You offer the world-class services, you should have decent behaviour, you need to show empathy, you are value-based, looking smart and attractive; your task of promoting the business is found easier.

The People

Sophisticated technologies, no doubt, inject life and strength to our efficiency but the instrumentality of sophisticated technologies start turning sour if the human resources are not managed in a right fashion. We can't deny the fact that if foreign banks are performing fantastically, it is not only due to the sophisticated information technologies they use but the result of a fair synchronisation of new information technologies and a team of personally-committed employees. The moment they witness lack of productive human resources even the new generation of information technologies would hardly produce the desired results. In addition to the professional excellence, the employees working in the foreign banks are generally value-based. Thus, we accept the fact that generation of efficiency is substantially influenced by the quality of human resources. It is against this background that a majority of the management experts make a strong advocacy in favour of developing quality people and of late, the people management has been included in the marketing mix of organisations in general and the service generating organisations in particular.

What do we mean by the term "Quality People"? Quality is related to a number of properties or attributes. It is an aggregation of all the properties which are found essential for generating the efficiency and projecting a fair image. A professionally sound banker may be efficient but only efficiency is not to solve the problem. A professional found efficient, showing diligence but making a good-bye to the ethical values can't be termed to be quality people. This is supported by the fact that short-term generation makes the ways for a long-run degeneration. If they satisfy you in the short-run by practising unfair practices, they certainly harm you in the long-run by damaging your interests because the unfair, unethical, illegal practices grow and spread like a wildfire and the vicious circle throws an organisation in the reverse gear. This makes it clear that efficiency should essentially be supported by ethical dimension, humanity, humanism or so.

Not only the public sector commercial banks but almost all the public sector organisations and albeit other government departments, of late, have been facing the problem of quality people resulting into inefficiency, deceleration in the rate of overall productivity and profitability or so. The public sector commercial banks are found infected. The front line staff are rough and indecent, the branch managers are helpless and even the bankers have been found involved in the unfair practices. It is in this context that we find justifications for treating people as an independent submix of the marketing mix of the banking organisations.

The aforesaid facts make it clear that the public sector commercial banks need to assign an overiding priority to the development of quality people. We appreciate the fact that a majority of the management experts have realised the significance of quality people in the development of an organisation and the boardrooms are also found changing their attitudes. The first task before the banking organisations at the apex level is to overhaul the recruitment processes. While fixing criteria for selection, they need to assign due weightage to the ethical values. The identification process would not be difficult if we start testing their family background. The psychologists can successfully scan their negative traits, if they cross and interview the candidates minutely. The education and training facilities are required to be innovated. The process of identification and inculcation need to be managed carefully.

The bankers serving the private sector banks are found committed to their profession but the same lot of persons if recruited in the public sector banks disappoint us by their actions and behavioural profile. The main reason for the beginning of the degeneration process is job security and the domination of trade unions both at the macro and micro levels. The foreign banks and the private sector commercial banks reward for efficiency and at the same time, also demotivate the inefficient bankers. This helps them in improving the efficiency of even the inefficient people. It is in this context that we find work culture in the private sector banks.

Of course, it is high time that the public sector commercial banks think over the issue on a priority basis and the policy makers at the apex level make possible a basic change in the service conditions of bankers. The beginning of a contractual job system appears to be the most suitable solution to generate efficiency and make possible value orientation. The problem of inefficiency if not arrested at the beginning stage is likely to infect the entire process.

The development of human resources makes the ways for the formation of human capital. We can't negate that all our efforts for innovating the technology and improving the quality of services would turn fiasco if we don't manage people properly. It is against this background that the management experts the world over have been found assigning due weightage to the development of HUMAN, HUMANE, HUMANISM. The three terms if found in the human resources would simplify our task of developing productive people. The subjective knowledge is, of course, essential but in addition, we also realise the sensitivity of supportive knowledge which focuses on the people having the feelings and realisation of right and wrong, fair and unfair, ethical and unethical.

Incentives, of course, inject efficiency and the organisations offering more incentives succeed in motivating the people. In the Indian perspective, we fail in having a right perception of incentives because we also find cases where an organisation like IOC offering more incentives to its employees fail in motivating the employees who prefer to serve an organisation where they get an opportunity to earn more by adopting the unfair practice.

BANK MARKETING IN INDIAN PERSPECTIVE

Cellphone Banking, Internet Banking, Web-based Banking, Virtual Banking are now becoming common terminologies albeit in the Indian Banking System which till late of 1990s was dominated by the traditional banking system. Credibility, of course, goes to globalisation which has opened doors for new generation of technology resulting into the emergence of techniculture. A number of innovative services and a big list of product offered by the leading foreign banks made it essential that even the traditionally-managed public sector commercial banks open new vistas of development. What to talk of the banking services when banks started performing a number of non-banking services such as mutual funds, lease financing, factoring services to customers, dematerialisation of physical certificates, portfolio management, consultancy and personal investment. Agricultural cards, Visa cards, Master cards, Smart cards, Stored Value cards started changing our lifestyles. Services at our doorstep transformed the functional character of banking services. A non-stop innovation in the process of development made the business environment much more volatile.

The formulation of policies is substantially influenced by the emerging trends in the national and global business environment. The level of income, expectations, rate of literacy, geographic and demographic considerations, rural and urban orientation, domination of technology in the process of economic transformation are some of the key factors governing the development plan of an organisation. To be more specific in developing countries like ours, the public sector commercial banks are supposed to play a decisive role in fuelling the process of socio-economic emancipation. This makes it clear that the banking organisations need a new vision, a holistic approach and a professional touch. Willingly or unwillingly, they have also to bear the social costs.

In a development-sensitive welfare economy, the banking organisations are required to play a constructive role in shaping the economic destiny. It is right to mention that particularly in the Indian setting, the contours of development have undergone radical changes, specially after mid-1980s. Of course, the development process started moving in the positive direction after the adoption of planned concept of development in 1951 but the race and pace were not commensurate with the national socio-economic requirements. The nationalisation of Reserve

Bank of India, no doubt, is a landmark in the development of Indian Banking System but a number of ups and downs in the socio-political and economic environmental conditions failed in engineering a sound foundation for reverberating the process of economic transformation. We cannot even imagine about socio-economic transformation if the banking organisations are not involved in the process. Despite all, the attainment of independence and the nationalisation of Reserve Bank of India are the two important developments which in a true sense paved avenues for qualitative-cum-quantitative improvements. Acquisition of extensive powers of supervision and control by the Reserve Bank of India under the Banking Regulations 1949 opened new vistas for the expansion of banking facilities. The structure of public sector bank was further strengthened in 1959. To curb concentration of economic power and promote a judicious use of the financial resources for the economic development activities, the banking system was regulated and supervised by the RBI. Subsequently, in 1969, the Government acquired a direct control over a substantial segment of the banking system signifying its commitment to reshape the banking system so as to meet progressively and serve better the needs of the development of economy in conformity with the changing national policy and objective. The fruitful results of nationalisation of 14 commercial banks in 1969 encouraged government to nationalise more commercial banks in 1980. These developments necessitated a fundamental change in the functional responsibilities of the public sector commercial banks. Here, it is pertinent to mention that nationalisation was with the motto of improving the quality of services but the public sector commercial banks started disappointing the masses. Of late, the quality of services is so poor that customers in general are found dissatisfied. This makes it essential that the Reserve Bank of India and the policy makers of the public sector commercial banks think in favour of conceptualising modern marketing principles which would bring a radical change in the process of quality upgradation.

The first task before the public sector commercial banks is to formulate the marketing mix which suits the national socio-economic requirements. They need to synchronise the core and peripheral services in such a way that product attractiveness is increased substantially. To be more specific, the peripheral services need frequent innovation, since this would be helpful in excelling competition. The designing of a sound product portfolio is found significant to maintain the commercial viability of the public sector banks. The promotional measures need an intensive care so that masses come to know about the positive contributions of banks towards the development of socio-economic activities. The different components of promotion, if become instrumental, the inculcation of awareness is found possible. To be more specific, the personal selling and public relations activities need an intensive care. It is pertinent to mention that the leading foreign banks have been found promoting telemarketing and the public sector commercial banks need to make it possible. Since we have world-class communication technologies, the task is easier. The word-of-mouth promotion also needs due care and for that we need to improve the quality of services *vis-a-vis* the cooperation of opinion leaders. The pricing strategy needs due weightage since the instrumentality of pricing as a motivational tool would help banks in increasing the market share. The Reserve Bank of India and the Indian Banking Association need an attitudinal change. The boardrooms also need to change their attitudes. The gap between the services-promised and services-offered is required to be bridged over. This requires professional excellence. The professionals need to make possible a fair synchronisation of performance orientation and employee orientation. This is not possible unless the banking regulations are made liberal. The quality of people/employees serving the banking organisations needs an overriding priority. The bankers need to know about the behavioural management. The front-line staff need empathy in their behaviour. This requires intensive training facilities. The domination of trade unions is required to be minimised. The contractual job system needs due attention. The bank professionals need to assign due weightage to their physical properties. They are supposed to look smart, active and attractive. Thus, we need multi-dimensional transformation which make a strong advocacy in favour of implementing the innovative marketing principles.

In view of the above, it is right to mention that in the face of new perception of quality developed by the foreign and private sector commercial banks, the public sector commercial banks have no option but to improve the quality of services. The marketing principles bear the efficacy of initiating qualitative improvements. It is against this background that we go through the problem of bank marketing. Of late, the foreign banks have been found promoting the use of sophisticated information technologies. This makes it essential that we realise gravity of the situation and make possible a rational use of technologies which is not to aggravate the problem of retrenchment. The marketing principles would be helpful in making an assault on the multi-dimensional problems. Of course, we find good auguries because the policy makers have been found exploring ways for implementing the marketing principles but till now, the efforts are at the very nascent stage. It is high time that the public sector commercial banks conceptualise innovative marketing for bringing the banking system on the rail.

The Citi Bank, Standard Chartered, SBI, ICICI Bank, American Express, HSBC, HDFC, Centurian, ABN Ambro, Bank of India, IDBI Bank need to continue the process of technological sophistication and the banks playing as innovators would prove to be a leader. The Standard Chartered Bank, a leader in the foreign bank segment and the State Bank of India, a leader in the public sector segment bear the responsibility of activating the innovations so that the all categories of customers get the world-class services. In the Indian perspective, we find particularly the public sector banks not very much sincere to the servicescapes. They should perceive that attractions make ways for business promotion. The cycle of corporatisation cannot be reverberated if we find service ambience missing service fragrance. The exteriors, interiors, aesthetic management are some of the dimensions not getting due weightage specially in the public sector banks particularly working in small cities and towns. Like the foreign banks, they have to adopt a uniform policy irrespective of the fact that the branches are in the cosmopolitan towns or in the small towns. Of course, the innovations have been delayed in the Indian banking system. It is high time to activate.

If we turn eyes on the global scenario, we find banking and financial services undergoing a dramatic transformation over the yesterdecades. Effective use of technology has greatly helped the banking sector to transform the multi-faceted challenges into opportunities. Actually, we find three phases of technological development to reduce their operating costs by improving their operational efficiency. In the process, they streamlined their back-office and eliminated error-prone manual inputs of data. In the second phase, the customers witnessed qualitative improvements in services as the innovative services were offered and in the third phase, the banks could be efficacious of developing and implementing sophisticated risk and information management systems and techniques with the help of powerful data analysis and storage and analysis technologies.

Unlike the global banks, the banks in India could hook on computerisation drive by the 1980s and 1990s. The beginning was with the PC-based systems and from that they moved to Total Branch Automation (TBA) and later to networking and implementation of Centralised/Core Banking Solutions (CBS). A number of large banks have confined the CBS facility to 30 per cent of the branches which has deprived of the mass customers of getting the fruits of modern technology. The latest innovations in wireless technology, low-cost ATMs, Point of Sales (PoS) terminals, smart cards, etc. have of course been successful in serving the remote villages.[27]

Despite the implementation of CBS, the ATM channel, the flip side is that we find a big variation in the quality of services of different branches of the same bank. Since the process of technological transformation has been without enriching the supporting infrastructural facilities, the service is not found free from occasional disruptions like communication link failure, non-replenishment of cash on time, etc. All strategies for technological sophistication need a realisation that their business has to drive technology and plans should be based on the principle that any investment in IT should be helpful in adding business value to the bank and its customers. The operational risks emanating from the large-scale dependence of technology in banking operations have to be mitigated to the acceptable level through appropriate business continuity plans.

We cannot negate that in the years to come the banks and financial institutions will continue to experiment new generation of technology and electronic and information-based services to the customers. We need proper alignment of technology strategies with business goals that would ensure commensurate value addition to banks.

SUMMARY

In this chapter, you have gone through the different dimensions of bank marketing. Before starting another chapter, be sure that the following facts are well versed:

Bank Marketing: The Concept: It is application of modern marketing principles in the banking organisations. We consider bank marketing a managerial process to market the banking services. It is also a social process to serve social interests.

Justifications for Practising Marketing: Understanding the customers, satisfying the customers, excelling competition, formulating and innovating the mixes and social orientation justify application.

Behavioural Profile of Users: The bank professionals need to be aware of the behavioural profile of users which focus on needs and requirements, level of expectations, attitudes and lifestyles. The multi-dimensional changes in the business environment influence behaviours.

Factors influencing Behavioural Profile: Social, economic and psychological factors influence behavioural profile.

Marketing Information System: The MIS focuses on managing the information related to the market conditions which help in making and innovating marketing decisions.

Importance of MIS: Development knowledge, identifying the profitable opportunities, diagnosing the emerging trends in competition, helping business expansion, image projection are some of the important contributions of MIS to the banking organisations.

Market Segmentation: It is to divide and group the markets into small segments so that the identification process is simplified.

Marketing Mix: The bank professionals bear the responsibility of formulating a sound marketing mix such as product mix, promotion, place, price, process, physical evidence and attractions and people.

The Product Mix: The professionals formulate a sound product mix combining both the core and peripheral services.

The Promotion Mix: The different components of promotion such as advertising, publicity, sales promotion, personal selling, telemarketing, cause-related and sponsorship marketing and word-of-mouth promotion are conceptualised in the banking organisations.

The Price Mix: The professionals here go through the problem of interest, discount and commission affecting the banking services.

The Place Mix: In this mix, the problems related to the location of a branch and channels for delivering the services are discussed.

Process: This mix draws our attention on processing of services from the first point to the point of delivery. We find technology playing here an important role.

Physical Evidence and Attractions: The problems related to servicescape and physical appearance of employees are discussed here.

The People: The submix goes through the problem of different categories of people serving the banking organisations.

Bank Marketing in Indian Perspective: Here, the problems in the Indian setting are discussed.

KEY TERMS

Internet Banking	Debit and Credit Cards
Online Accounting System	Public Key Infrastructure
Plastic Money	ATMs
Direct Deposit of Payroll	Automated Clearing House
Auto Banking	Core and Peripheral Services
Social Marketing	Prospects
Industrial Users	Behavioural Profile
Organisational Customers	Wharton Study
Marketing Information System	Creativity
Intuiting-based Decisions	Marketing Intelligence System
Happening Data	Market Segmentation
Philanthropic Organisations	White-collar Employees
Physical Evidence	Product Portfolio
Synchronisation	Factoring
Lease Financing	Boston Matrix
Attractive Package	Cost-Benefit Analysis
Personal Selling	Ego States

Word-of-mouth Promotion	Hidden Promoters
Telemarketing	Wide Area Telephone Service (WATS)
Automatic Dialing and Recorded Message	Players (ADRMPs)
Cause-related Marketing	Sponsorship Marketing
Buying-Selling Game	Servicescape
Exterior and Interior	Physical Attractions
Quality People	Humane

Review Questions

1. What do you mean by Bank Marketing? Explain its origin and growth in Indian perspective.
2. State and explain the various types of users of the banking services. Write a note on the behavioural profile of users of the banking services.
3. Focus on the factors influencing the behavioural profile of users of banking services.
4. What is Market Segmentation? Discuss the different bases for market segmentation with a reference to the banking services.
5. Explain the importance of segmentation in the banking organisations.
6. Focus on the instrumentality of Marketing Information System in making the marketing decisions in the banking organisations.
7. Write a short note on the formulation of marketing mix for the banking organisations.
8. Discus the three additional marketing mixes in the banking services.
9. What do you mean by Product Portfolio? Explain it in the context of banking organisations.
10. Discuss the different processes for the development of product in the banking organisations.
11. What do you mean by service package? Explain it in the context of banking services.
12. Focus on the different components of promotion mix for promoting the banking services in Indian perspective.
13. Define Personal Selling. Explain its role in the banking services.
14. "Word-of-mouth promotion is an important component of the promotion mix." Comment on this statement with a reference to the banking services.
15. Focus on the future of telemarketing in the banking services in Indian perspective.
16. Should banks promote through cause-related and sponsorship marketing? Justify your arguments.
17. In the formulation of marketing mix, the pricing decisions are found critical. In the light of this statement, comment on the barriers obstructing the process.
18. "Offering of services and location point for a bank need due attention of bank professionals." Discuss.
19. Focus on the role of people in improving the quality of banking services.
20. "Servicescape needs due attention of bank professionals." Comment.

Application Exercises

1. As a marketing professional of a public sector bank, you have been assigned the responsibility of studying the behavioural profile of users. Focus on the factors you need to go through.
2. The business of your branch is not showing an impressive result. Suggest the measures you expect to be effective for motivating the different categories of depositors.
3. You are serving a private sector bank in a cosmopolitan town. A new branch has been opened in the same town where you have been deputed to establish the branch. Throw light on the servicescape you will take care while establishing.
4. Focus on the role of Marketing Information System helping you in studying and understanding the users coming from different segments.
5. As a marketing professional, comment on the expanded submixes of marketing helping you in different ways.
6. The business of your branch is going down. Explain the innovative peripheral services helping you in regaining the business.
7. The front-line staff of your bank are not working satisfactorily. You have frequently been getting the complaints of customers. As a branch manager, how you will resolve the problem?
8. You have been facing a number of challenges from a leading foreign bank who has recently established its branch. Throw light on the promotional measures you find to be effective.

9. You have been working as a manager of a public sector commercial bank. You find people serving your branch not assigning due weightage to physical attractions. The high profile customers do not like to visit your branch. Focus on the measures helping you in resolving the problem.
10. As a marketing professional, you are supposed to take a decision regarding the location point of your branch. How would you discharge your responsibility?
11. Being a bank professional, you need to design your service package in such a way that proves to be motivational *vis-à-vis* competitive. How and in what way you will design a profitable package? Explain.
12. You realise the need for strengthening the publicity measures. Explain your role as a bank professional.

Endnotes

1. Sanjiv Bhatt, Bank Marketing, *The Economic Times,* Sept. 1, 1988.
2. Fieldman, L.P., Societal Adoption, A New Challenge for Marketing, *Journal of Marketing,* p. 54.
3. McIver and Nylor, *Marketing Financial Services by Banks,* p. 5.
4. Ronald Gist, *Marketing and Society,* pp. 14-15.
5. Sullivan M.P., *Bankers,* Vol. 164, July-August, 1981, p. 27.
6. Watson J.B., Do *We Need Service Marketing?* Marketing Science Institute, Boston, 1977.
7. Steuart R. Brit, *Applying Learning Principle of Marketing Business Topics Spring,* 1975.
8. Cundiff, Still and Govoni, *Fundamentals of Modern Marketing*, Prentice-Hall of India, 1982, p. 102.
9. Smith Samuel V., Brien Richard H. and Stafford James E. (Ed.), *Marketing Information System – An Introductory Overview* in Readings in MIS, Boston, 1968, p. 7.
10. Francis J. Aguliar, *Scanning the Business Environment,* Macmillan, New York, 1967.
11. Reiden Back, E.R. and Pitts, R.E., *Bank Marketing,* 1986, p. 57.
12. Jha S.M., The Framing of Marketing Mix for the Banking Services, *'The Banker',* Vol. 16/12, February, 1990.
13. Lorraine W., When Banks looked like Banks – A Pictorial Review, *"The Business Magazine",* September-October 1983, p. 43.
14. Clements Ron, *A Guide to Transactional Analysis*, p. 4.
15. *Ibid.,* p. 6.
16. Kotler P., *Marketing Management,* Prentice-Hall, p. 142.
17. Eagle Blackwell, Kollat, *Consumer Behaviour,* pp. 21-22.
18. McIver and Nylor, *Marketing Financial Services by Banks,* p. 110.
19. Edlund, Sidney, *There is a Better Way to Sell,* 1981, p. 91.
20. Jha S.M., The Innovative Marketing for the Banking Services, "*The Pigmy Economic Review*" , 33/12, 1989.
21. Varde V. and Singh S., Profitability of Commercial Banks, *Journal of NIHM*, 1983, pp. 43-45.
22. Bankers, *Differentiating Customer Services in Branches*, March-April 1984, p. 70.
23. McIver and Nylor, *op. cit.,* p. 65.
24. Zeithmal V.A. and Bitner M.J., *Services Marketing*, Tata McGraw-Hill, New Delhi, 2003 p. 25.
25. *Ibid.*, pp. 24-25.
26. Jha S.M., *Bank Marketing*, Himalaya Publishing House, Mumbai, 2003, pp. 366-67.
27. The Analyst: *Indian Banking 2005-06*, October.

★★★

Insurance Marketing

The wave of liberalisation is in full swing in India and so in the insurance sector. Let the insurance marketers realise it.

Chapter Objectives

Introduction – Insurance Marketing: The Concept – Users of Insurance Services – The Behavioural Profile of Users – Market Segmentation in the Insurance Organisations – Significance of Segmentation in the Insurance Business – Impact of Technology on the Insurance Sector – E-Insurance – Marketing Information System for Insurance Organisations – Insurance Product – Product Planning and Development – The Formulation of Marketing Mix for Insurance Organisations – The Product Mix – The Promotion Mix – Advertising – Publicity – Sales Promotion – Personal Selling – Word-of-mouth Promotion – Telemarketing – Cause-Related and Sponsorship Marketing – Price Mix – Place Mix – Extended Marketing Mix in Insurance – Recommendations of Malhotra Committee – Insurance Marketing in the Indian Environment – Summary – Key Terms – Review Questions – Application Exercises – Endnotes.

Learning Objectives

This chapter aims at sensitising the readers to the various dimensions of insurance marketing. The market is becoming much more competitive and the big foreign players have been making it more volatile. The public sector insurance organisations in particular need world-class professional excellence to maintain and retain their well established leadership. The insurance marketers need to conceptualise innovative marketing with a professional touch. The readers come to know about the application of seven mixes for marketing the insurance services. The marketing professionals also need to promote techniculture in the insurance sector so that the insurance organisations succeed in defining and redefining the service quality.

INTRODUCTION

The race and pace of economic transformation make ways for the development of financial institutions. With the conceptualisation of globalisation, the Indian economy witnessed myriad of challenges and resulting from which new vistas were opened for the development of almost all the financial institutions in which the policy makers assigned due weightage to professional excellence. It was in this context that we find development of insurance sector in which the foreign-based insurance companies played a significant role. Earlier, the government sector dominated the business which was almost working in a monopolistic condition. The traditional product of public sector insurance business witnessed a threat when the leading private sector insurance companies based on world-class professional excellence and managerial proficiency started establishing an edge over them. They had innovative product and the marketing processes of world-class making the business environment much more challenging for the public sector insurance business. Of course, the governmental regulations provided to them a strong protection but the process of liberalisation gained a rapid momentum and the government had no option but to make the business environment for insurance business much more productive and against this background, the IRDA made liberal provisions for the private sector insurance business.

The IRDA Act 1999, provided for three categories of insurance business in India, such as a public company with two categories of operation — public limited and public unlimited companies set up mostly in the USA were not allowed to do insurance business in India and similarly the private limited companies were also not allowed to do insurance business. The second category that we find of a society incorporated under the Cooperative Societies Act 1912 in India or under any other law relating to cooperative societies. And the third category that we find of a body corporate incorporated abroad under the law of that country not being in the nature of a private company. Further, the provision for disinvestment is to allow the fourth category that is Public Unlimited Companies in future which would have a major impact on the insurance business.

The multi-faceted developments in insurance sector have made the business environment much more volatile and the intensity of competition is found almost at its peak. The big players with a professionalised approach have been making the task of government managed insurance business much more challenging. This makes a strong advocacy in favour of innovative marketing practices. The innovative services with high level of managerial proficiency will be an effective prescription to resolve the problems before the insurance sector. Of course, we have covered a long journey and have witnessed a number of developments during the yesterdecades but this age appears to be an acid test of our organisational and managerial excellence. Let's have a brief knowledge of development scenario.

Wherever there is uncertainty, there is risk. The risk can't be averted. It involves multi-faceted losses. Risk is uncertainty of a financial loss. We don't have any command on uncertainties. This makes it essential that we think in favour of a device that becomes instrumental in spreading the loss. It is in this context that we think about insurance which is considered to be a social device to accumulate funds to meet uncertain losses. The main functions of insurance is to provide protection against the possible chances of generating losses. It eliminates worries and miseries of losses at destruction of property and death. Further, it provides capital to the national economy since the accumulated funds are invested in the productive heads. The industries, businesses, individuals are considerably benefited by the services of insurance organisations.

The earliest traces of insurance are in the form of marine trade losses or carriers' contracts. In 'Rigveda', the references are made to the concept of "Yogakshema" which is more or less akin to the well-being and security of people. This makes it clear that the traces for sharing the future losses were available even in the ancient India. However, there is no evidence of a particular form or shape, specially before the 12th century. The oldest form of insurance is the 'Marine Insurance'. The travellers by sea or by land very much exposed to the risk of losing their assets, vessels and merchandise required measures to cover risk. The piracy on the open seas, highway robbery or fear of sinking of the vessels in the deep water necessitated a device which spreads the financial losses. The Marine Insurance was found suitable for the purpose.

After the marine insurance, we find development in the field of 'Fire Insurance'. It started from Germany in the beginning of the 16th century. The great fire in England in 1666 which resulted in the burning of 85 per cent of the houses to ashes injected life, strength and continuity to the concept of fire insurance. With the colonial development of England, the fire insurance spread all over the world. In India, the General Insurance started working in 1850. The credibility for the same goes to the Triton Insurance, Kolkata.

The Life Insurance was found existent in England in the 17th century. The policy of life of William Gybbons on June 18, 1633 is the first recorded evidence. Even before this, the annuities were found common in England. The first registered life office was the "Hand-in-Hand Society" which was established in 1696. In USA, the Life Insurance could not flourish mainly due to an abnormal fluctuation in the death rate.

In India, the first Life Insurance Company was established in the Bengal Presidency in 1818 which was known as the Oriental Life Insurance Company. In the annals of Indian Insurance, the year 1870 is a landmark. Experiencing so many ups and downs, the insurance business was found in a changed shape, particularly after the attainment of independence and to be more specific after nationalisation in 1956. Further, the General Insurance was nationalised in 1971. Thus, the insurance business in India is found under the public sector which is managed by a corporation. There is no doubt in it that a number of small companies are working under the private sector but their insignificant contributions to the society right now keep them out of the purview.

The public sector insurance business, of course, made possible numerous changes in the functional areas of the insurance corporations but at the same time it also made ways for a degeneration in the quality of services. We can't deny the fact that after nationalisation, a number of steps have been taken to spread the insurance business much more widely to the rural areas and specially to the socially and economically backward regions with a view to reaching all the potential users of the services. The insurance network has gained the momentum and now even the rural masses are well aware of their contributions.

In India, the Life Insurance Corporation of India and the General Insurance Corporation of India are managed and controlled by the Union Government and therefore, the responsibility of qualitative improvements or even a degeneration in quality is found on their shoulders. For the expansion of insurance business, it is essential that the potential policyholders are identified and marketing resources are used optimally to transform them into the actual users. This naturally requires professional excellence and a strong sense of determination. The over ambitious objectives of the Corporation necessitate a change in its management. This makes a strong advocacy in favour of practising the marketing principles. The formulation of marketing mixes is required to be given due weightage. The quantitative and qualitative improvements are to be made possible.

At the outset, it is essential that the insurance corporations think about their service profile. Of course, we find inclusion of a number of policies and programmes for the welfare of the policyholders but when we make a comparative analysis of their contributions with the foreign well established insurance companies, a sea change in the profiles of both can't be negated. The policyholders in a majority of the cases feel that the agents, front-line staff have hardly been offering to them the services-promised. The behavioural profile of insurance personnel is found presenting a disappointing result. We also find cases of misbehaviour by the staff. Of course, we find the service mix in the face of changing socio-economic requirements but a gap in the services-promised and services-offered is found expanding. This has been inviting numerous problems to the insurance organisations. We accept the fact that the work culture which was at a satisfactory level only a decade back is now moving in the reverse gear. The agents, staff hardly evince their interests in promoting the insurance business. The boardrooms have not been found sincere to the emerging problems. An attitudinal change appears to be an urgent need of the hour that requires a basic change in the policy decisions.

By conceptualising modern marketing principles, the insurance business can be improved, the profitability can be increased and the quality of services can be matched to the changing expectations of users. In addition to the world-class core services, they would also be in a position to innovate the peripheral services adding attractions to their service mix and making it distinct to the competitors. This is the first and foremost task before the public sector insurance organisations where a degeneration in the quality of services has been found engineering smooth ways for the leading foreign insurance companies. While marketing the services, it is also pertinent that they think about the innovative promotional measures. It is not only sufficient that you perform well. It is also important that you let others know about the quality of your positive contributions. It is in this context that they need to use the different components of promotion. The creativity in the promotional measures is need of the hour which would help insurance organisations in informing and sensing the users in a right fashion. The advertisement, public relations, sales promotion, word-of-mouth communication and telemarketing need due care and the personal selling requires an intensive care. It is right to mention that the business of insurance is based on the skill and excellence of agents and this makes a strong advocacy in favour of personal selling. We can't negate that while promoting business, the foreign insurance companies have been found creative *vis-a-vis* innovative in their approaches. The public sector insurance organisations have to learn a lesson. The pricing decisions become impact generating with the motto of persuading the prospects/users. The public sector insurance organisations need to make their services/ schemes lucrative so that they succeed in using it as a motivational tool. The decisions related to premium, bonus and other incentives to the policyholders need due care. In addition, the public sector insurance organisations also need to think about the way of offering the services so that the promised services reach to the ultimate users without any distortion. The agents and the front-line staff need to show their excellence in the process of offering. Further, it is also significant that the location point for an insurance branch is given due weightage. It should easily be accessible and the infrastructural facilities should also be available to make the services comfortable. Since the use of information technologies is found getting a due place in the insurance business, it is important that uninterrupted power facilities are made available to the insurance branches.

The marketing professionals also make a strong advocacy in favour of three additional submixes such as process, physical evidence and attractions and people. Since we find technology playing an important role even in the insurance sector, the processing occupies a place of outstanding significance. The new generation of technology operated by professionals having expertise in the related area would bridge the gap between the services-promised and services-delivered. The front-line staff find themselves helpless when they find the technology used in the process not helping them properly.

In the fast changing and developing insurance sector, we need due emphasis on physical evidence and attractions. We are aware of the fact that exteriors and interiors and use of new generation of technology considerably add to the service environment. The customers, visitors coming there get an opportunity to witness the physical surroundings. They find themselves convinced because everything they watch in an operational condition. Further, the physical attractions containing the physical appearance of employees working there in different capacities help shaping of a positive opinion in the minds of customers coming for availing the services. They watch everything such as business and non-business. The ambience containing additional attractions resulting into service fragrance make the task of professionals much more easier. Though the business policy is sold earlier but the process keeps on moving.

In addition, we also find significant role of insurance people. They need an in-depth and up-to-date knowledge of emerging new trends in the business environment. It is this context we need insurance professionals to have world-class professional excellence. They need to be thematically sound, of course, in a position to establish an edge over their rivals. Excelling competition requires topmost priority and to make it possible they need personal-touch-in-service. Professional commitment is considered essential to offer the promised quality of services. To touch the target, they are not supposed to adopt unfair or unlawful practices.

In the changing business environment, the public or private sectors need world-class professional excellence. Innovative services are to be included in the product mix and further the creative promotional measures are to be intensified. If we find leading foreign insurance companies getting a success in snatching the business from the public sector, it is mainly due to their world-class professional excellence. We cannot deny that even till date, the general masses have been found preferring the service of public sector but this is not going to be a permanent feature. Hence, the most important thing in the changing scenario is to conceptualise modern marketing principles. Among the selected leading insurance companies, we find the LIC, ICICI Prudential, Bajaj Alliance, HDFC Standard, Birla Sun Life, Tata AIG, SBI Life, Max New York, Aviva, Kotak Mahindra promoting life insurance whereas the New India, Oriental, National, United India, ICICI Lombard, Bajaj Alliance, IFFCO-Tokio, Tata AIG, ECGC, Royal Sundaram have been found promoting general insurance. LIC of India and New India are the market leaders. To maintain and retain leadership, they have to practise innovative marketing failing which it will be difficult for them to hold leadership.

INSURANCE MARKETING — THE CONCEPT

The marketing concept in the banking and insurance services emerged with the publication of an article entitled, "Banks and Savings Institutions in the Television Age." The article focused that in the recent past, the banking and saving institutions have assigned due weightage to their austere dignity rather than the friendliness. The marketing experts advocated that marketing transcends advertising and friendliness.[1] Later, it was realised that marketing is not more than smiling, friendliness. This necessitated customer convenience and injected new life and strength to the marketing concept in the banking and insurance and even in other financial institutions. Marketing was accepted as an organisational imperative. It was felt that conceptualisation of marketing in the insurance business would identify the most profitable markets now and in future; would be helpful in assessing the present and future needs of the users; would be instrumental in setting business development goals; would be successful in formulating time-honoured plans and would manage various customer services, in addition to their promotion in the socio-economic parlance. These outstanding properties of marketing make it clear that insurance business like the banking business finds it easier to expand and flourish if the marketing decisions are taken in a right fashion.

The term 'insurance marketing' refers to the marketing of insurance services with the motto of customer orientation and profit generation. A fair blending of profit generation and customer satisfaction makes the ways for development and expansion. The insurance marketing focuses on the formulation of an ideal mix for the insurance business so that the insurance organisations survive and thrive in a right perspective. The quality of services can be improved by formulating a fair mix of the core and peripheral services. The persuasion process can be speeded up with the support of creative promotional measures. The premium and bonus decisions can be made motivational, the gap between the services-promised and services-offered can be bridged over, the quality and value-based personnel can make possible performance orientation and these developments can make the insurance organisations stronger enough to face the challenges and threats in the markets. It is meant managerial proficiency which makes an assault on unethical and unfair practices by regulating profiteering. The organisations thus are found successful in increasing the market share, maximising the profitability and keeping on the process of development.

In the Indian perspective where rural orientation needs a prime attention, the insurance marketing may prove to be a device for combating regional imbalance by maintaining the sectoral balance. As an investment institution, the rural development-oriented projects make ways for the transformation of rural society. Like the banking services, we find automation playing a decisive role in fuelling the process of devlopment. In a true sense, we find use of sophisticated information technologies in both the services that pave avenues for quality upgradation. It is right to mention that the marketing concept in both the banking and insurance businesses is a matter of recent origin. Marketing is to excite the interest of insurance and stock brokerage companies although they have a long way to go in applying marketing effectively.[2] The marketing concept in the insurance business is concerned with the expansion of insurance business in the best interest of society *vis-a-vis* the insurance organisations. There is no doubt in it that a few of the insurance companies have effective marketing operations, however, there are a number of typical insurance companies where the marketing function is diffused throughout the organisation with no one executive responsible for the overall marketing performance. The lack of coordination results in overemphasising the marketing activities, such as advertising at the expense of others, providing adequate customer service at teller's windows.[3] On the other hand, it is also found that some of the insurance companies have recognised the significance of marketing concept where executives are made responsible for overall marketing performance. However, it is right to mention that the insurance companies lag behind most manufacturers in recognising the marketing concept in their organisations. Insurance companies tend toward a strong sales orientation, since the services they sell, although certainly necessary ones, rarely sell themselves. Potential policyholders are reluctant to think about the disaster and death. So they postpone planning for these possibilties unless they are contacted and influenced by insurance agents. Thus, the insurance company's mutual orientation is toward sales, not marketing.[4] But in the modern business world, the marketing concept insists on fixing of accountability for overall marketing performance.

The selection of risks (product planning), policy writing (customer service) rating or actuarial (pricing) and agency management (distribution) — all marketing activities[5] make up an integrated marketing strategy. We can't negate that during the yester decades, there have been considerable developments in the perception of customer servicing firms like banking and insurance companies. Particularly in the developing countries like ours, the organisational objectives adovcate spreading of insurance services much more widely and in particular to the rural areas and specially to the economically backward classes with a view to reaching all insurable persons. This naturally necessitates an integral marketing strategy. In other words, market orientation in place of sales orientation is need of the hour. Hence, the marketing concept in the insurance business focuses on the formulation of marketing mix or a control over the whole group of marketing activities that make up an integrated marketing strategy.

In view of the above, we observe the following facts regarding the concept of insurance marketing:

- It is a managerial process.
- It is conceptualisation of marketing principles.
- It is a process of formulating the marketing mix.
- It is a device to make possible customer orientation.
- It is an attempt to help profit maximisation.
- It is another name for marketing professionally.
- It is even a social process that paves avenues for social transformation.
- It is to make possible product attractiveness.
- It is to energise the process of quality upgradation.

USERS OF INSURANCE SERVICES

The formulation of creative marketing decisions is not possible unless we are well aware of the different categories of users using the services of insurance organisations. It is natural that different categories of users are guided by different considerations. The general users assign due weightage to their own interests whereas the industrial users assign an overriding priority to the interests of their organisations. The emerging changes in the socio-economic conditions and governmental regulations influence the interests of both categories of users. It is against this background that an in-depth study of users is found significant to the insurance organisation. Of course, they are working in a regulated environment but even till now, we find enough scope for incorporating necessary changes in the marketing decisions. An individual or an institution, a person or a group of persons availing the services are termed to be the actual users of the insurance organisations. On the other hand, both the categories of prospects having potentials, bearing the willingness but not using the services right now are termed to be the potential users. We also call them prospects. It is well-known that the services made available by the Life Insurance Corporation of India and the General Insurance Corporation of India and other private insurance companies are used by both categories of users. In the insurance business, we find prime focus on the policyholders and therefore an individual or an institution taking the policies is known as the actual policyholder(s) whereas the persons or organisations willing to do so but waiting for the creative persuasive efforts of the agents are known as the potential policyholders. We are well aware of the fact that insurance marketing is an effort to transform the prospects into actual users. As shown in Figure 6.1, the different categories of users of the insurance services need due attention of the marketers.

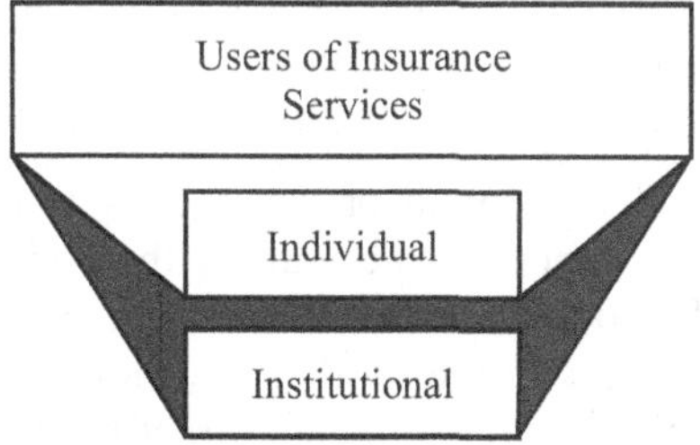

Fig. 6.1: Users of Insurance Services

The needs and requirements can't remain static. The business environmental conditions influence the process of change. The expectations mainly influenced by the competitive efforts of the leading insurance organisations of the world are found of dynamic nature. The professionals engaged in servicing the insurance organisations bear the responsibility of understanding the changing level of expectations of the different categories of users at first than activating sincere efforts to develop marketing inputs which energise the transformation process. Some of the users are educated, some of the users are illiterate. Some of the users are of small size whereas some of the users are large-sized. Some of the users live in the rural areas whereas we also find some of them living in the urban areas. It is natural that the behavioural profile *vis-a-vis* expectations of all categories of the users can't be identical.

THE BEHAVIOURAL PROFILE OF USERS

The behaviour of users is viewed as an orderly process whereby an individual acts with his/her environment for the purpose of making marketplace decisions.[6] Needs, motives, perception and attitudes known as the internal factors and the external influences[7] like family, social groups, culture, economic and business conditions are found instrumental in guiding the behavioural profile of an individual. When we turn our eyes on the service profile of insurance organisations, the policyholders appear to play an incremental role in shaping the product portfolio. Of course, the business of an insurance organisation is considerably influenced by the changing behavioural profile of both categories of users. The insurance organisations are supposed to study their behavioural profile so that they succeed in fulfilling their expectations. The large-sized organisational users also use the services of insurance organisations with diverse motives. They expect borrowing facilities at liberal terms and conditions in addition to the safety of their assests. The shaping of expectations is substantially influenced by the performance and quality of services offered by the leading competitors. We can't negate that the leading foreign insurance companies have made their service profile lucrative, attractive and productive. They innovate their marketing mix frequently and assign due weightage to the changing needs and requirements of prospects. The marketing information system is well managed by the new generation of sophisticated information technologies which helps them in identifying the level of expectations. This makes their insurance decisions proactive. It is also right to mention that the public sector insurance organisations find it difficult to improve their rank profile since the expectations of users are not given the due weightage.

The needs and requirements of rural and urban segments, men and women segments, teens and youths segments, affluent and weaker segments, individual and institutional segments can't be identical. There are a number of factors to influence the hierarchy of human needs. The emerging trends in economy, the social transformation processes, the changing inflationary pressure, the amendments and reforms in governmental regulations, the instrumentality of sophisticated technologies in offering the services are some of the key factors governing the hierarchy of needs *vis-a-vis* the expectations. In addition, the innovative efforts made by the leading insurance companies also play an important role. The insurance professionals in general and agents in particular bear the responsibility of identifying the emerging new trends and to develop marketing resources accordingly.

The Life Insurance Corporation of India and the General Insurance Corporation of India, the well-established public sector insurance organisations in the Indian perspective need to study the behavioural profile of users so that the formulation of marketing mix is made optimal to the changing expectations. The core and peripheral services are required to be made of world-class. The profitable opportunities in the rural sector are required to be capitalised on effectively. The behavioural profile of insurance personnel needs an intensive care. The premium structure and bonus decisions are to be made rational. The creativity in the promotional measures is to be made possible. And all these dimensions are directly or indirectly related to the behavioural profile of users of the insurance organisations.

The Life Insurance Corporation of India is found preserving its faith in the virtue of thrift and saving for a future objective. What the rural prospects expect is the loan of the sum assured so that they can dig or deepen their well or reclaim wasteland or start a poultry farm. This makes it clear that if the public sector insurance organisations want to tap the available potentials in the rural areas, they have no option but to study the behavioural profile of that segment. The services sector has now been found attracting the upcoming entrepreneurs, the investment is likely to be commercially viable and therefore, the insurance organisations need to innovate their service mix. Thus, it is clear that the insurance companies can't be successful in making their marketing decisions proactive unless they are aware of the changing requirements of different segments. They need to enrich the information system which would help them substantially in studying the changing trends.

We are well aware of the fact that the insurance business rests on the professional excellence of agents. The agents and the rural career agents promote the business and they based on the face-to-face communication get a feedback that plays a decisive role in innovating the marketing decisions of the insurance organisations. The insurance professionals need to accept the responsibility of making it sure that the suggestions given by the sales personnel are given due treatment while formulating or innovating the marketing decisions.

In addition to the general users, the insurance organisations are also concerned with the industrial organisations. It is important to mention that the corporate securities are an important medium for the investment of insurance funds. In the Indian perspective, we find insurance organisations preferring investment in the government securities. Unlike other countries, the public sector insurance organisations in India are found liberal to the government. In almost all the countries of the world, we find insurance companies investing substantially in the corporate securities. An attitudinal change is felt essential to make the insurance business commercially viable. Justice Chagla while submitting the report on the business transactions of the Life Insurance Corporation of India relating to the purchase of share in Mundhra Concerns recommended that the government should not interfere with the working of autonomus statutory corporation. The funds of LIC of India should be used for the benefits of the policyholders only not for any extraneous purpose. If they are to be used for any extraneous purposes, the purpose must be in the larger interest of the country. Thus, it is high time that the public sector insurance organisations realise the significance of corporate investment for making their investments productive. The business prospects of insurance organisations can't be bright unless they keep on protecting the multi-dimensional interests of customers/users by offering to them profitable services and schemes. They bear the prime responsibility of safeguarding the interests of policyholders.

The General Insurance Corporation of India needs more care, specially while transacting with the industrial users. The Corporation is found engaged in fire insurance, marine insurance and miscellaneous insurance businesses of course with the support of its subsidiaries. The users of the General Insurance services are subsidiary companies, e.g., National Insurance Company, New India Insurance Company Ltd., Oriental Fire and General Insurance Company Limited.

All the subsidiary companies are found promoting fire and marine insurance to the concerned users. Here, the insurance organisations are supposed to study the changing level of different categories of users so that the formulation of marketing decisions is processed in a right fashion.

We can't deny the fact that the leading foreign insurance companies have been assigning due weightage to the behavioural profile of users and it is against this background that we find them very much successful in fulfilling their expectations. They believe in making things happen and keep themselves engaged in intensifying research to promote innovation. If we turn our eyes on their service profile, it is apparent that the users/policyholders *vis-a-vis* their interests are given top priority. They attempt to add attractions to their product mix by making their peripheral services innovative which help them in snatching business and increasing the market share. Of course, they work in a regulated environment, however their professionals are found devising new services and schemes. We also find them using sophisticated information technologies which help them considerably in knowing and understanding the behavioural profile of prospects.

In view of the above, it is right to mention that an in-depth study of the behavioural profile of the users of insurance services is important to the insurance professionals. They by doing so can make their product mix motivational. The public sector insurance organisations are also supposed to study the same so that the temptation of users to the foreign insurance companies is minimised. It is in this context that we find it essential to the time-honoured fulfilment of users' interests and their expectations. We can't check the process of change. We can't stop the process of development. We can't make the business conditions liberal. The only thing that we can do is improving the quality of services. In the Indian perspective, the insurance organisations would get a profitable rural market in future and therefore to promote future marketing, they have no option but to study the changing level of expectations of the users in the 21st century. They can't devalue the instrumentality of behavioural profile of users, if they have to survive and thrive.

In addition, it is also impact generating that the insurance organisation in general and the public sector insurance organisations in particular assign an overriding priorty to the behavioural profile of insurance professionals and agents. A very few of the insurance organisations find it esential to use time and money for identifying the nature and behaviour of insurance personnel. If the personnel dealing with the customers lack even the fundamentals of behavioural management, the task would remain difficult and unfulfilled. We are not supposed to make the marketing resources unproductive and the resources developed without knowing the behavioural profile would hardly carry any meaning. Hence, a study of the behavioural profile of both — the end-users and the insurance professionals — would benefit the insurance organisations in many ways.

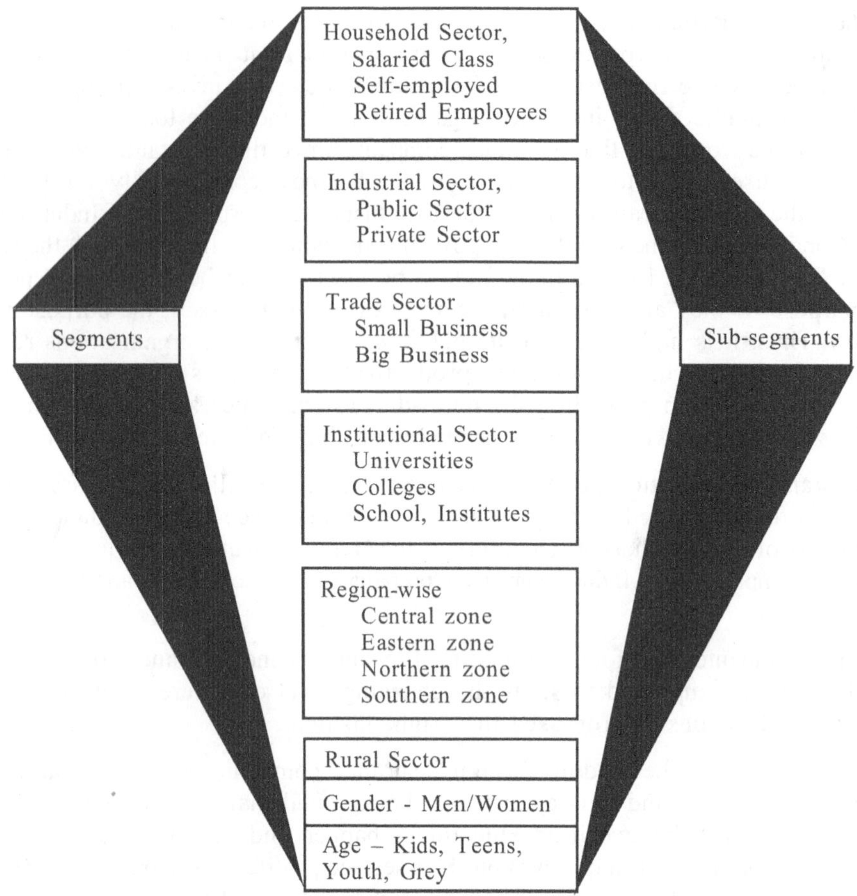

Fig. 6.2: Market Segmentation for Insurance

MARKET SEGMENTATION IN THE INSURANCE ORGANISATIONS

Before the adoption of mass production, the markets were automatically segmented because each product or service was tailored to the needs of buyers or users who had ordered for supply. With an increase in the scale of operation, the segmentation occupied a place of significance. This was due to the fact that the scale of production large in size was found unmanagable. 'Know thy market' was made a difficult process and the consumption processes were found complicated. To get a success, it was essential that we know the different segments consuming/using our goods/services. In the insurance organisations, the task of formulating the overall marketing strategies can't be performed efficiently unless we segment the market. It was against this background that marketing studies engineered a sound foundation for segmenting the markets of insurance business. The market for the insurance business is found vast, the potential policyholders are in a very good number and their needs and requirements are not identical. The segmentation helps the insurance organisations in dividing and subdividing the market into small segments in which the needs and requirements are found by and large identical. In Figure 6.2, we find different segments for the insurance.

SIGNIFICANCE OF SEGMENTATION TO THE INSURANCE BUSINESS

Like the banking services, we find market segmentation important even to the insurance business. If the market segmentation is done in a right fashion, the marketers find it convenient to identify the level of expectations of users. The main purpose of market segmentation is to know the market. Unless we know the needs and requirements and identify the level of expectations of the policyholders, it is difficult to formulate a sound marketing strategy. Spotting of opportunities in right time is found essential to influence the target market. It is quite natural that the needs and requirements of different users living in different segments, regions are not identical. The marketers bear the responsibility of identifying the difference in preferences so that the strategic decisions are formulated in line with the same. This helps in sensitising the marketing resources. The marketing inputs are found instrumental in developing the required marketing outputs.

In the Indian perspective where we find a large number of users living in the rural areas, the emergence of a strong rural sector can't be negated. The region-wise segmentation simplifies the task of having a microscopic study of culture, language, likes and dislikes. This helps in making the marketing decisions creative. It is essential that the insurance organisations capitalise on the available opportunities in the market. They need to increase their market share. This makes it essential that they succeed in informing, sensing and persuading the different segments where the potential users are available. It is not productive to concentrate on only one segment. The insurance professionals need to do business in all the segments, such as rural and urban, men and women, agricultural and industrial or so. The need of the hour is to spread the insurance business even to the agricultural sector of the economy. We appreciate the and cattle insurance facilities for furthering the interests of the agricultural sector, we feel that the insurance organisations come to know the changing needs and requirements of the rural sector and innovate their services/schemes accordingly. In addition to the mobilisation of savings, we also need to promote investments. This requires an overriding priority to the industrial sector or the corporate sector. The insurance organisations also need to identify profitable opportunities in the services sector.

Knowing and understanding the market is considered significant to the insurance professionals since the process helps them in scanning the changing needs and requirements. The formulation of an optimal marketing strategy is not possible unless we know a segment. The needs and requirements of industrial sector would be different to the needs and requirements of the agricultural sector. Like this, the needs and requirements of rural sector would be different to the needs and requirements of urban sector. A study of segmentation would help insurance professionals in formulating a sound marketing strategy. The product mix would be competitive and all the prospects would have additional attractions in using the services. The product portfolio would be sound which would make the marketing processes productive not only for the present but even for the future. The formulation of a sound package would act as a motivational tool. It is in this context that we find segmentation important to the formulation of product mix of the insurance organisations.

The segmentation would help insurance professionals in making the promotional measures creative which would be very much instrumental in sensitising the prospects. The advertisement professionals would make advertisement appeals, messages, campaigns proactive to the receiving capacity of the target audience. The sales promotion measures can also be innovated to get a positive response. The personal selling may be effective since the sales personnel/agents are supposed to be aware of the needs and requirements of customers/users. Thus, the segmentation would help marketers in many ways. The pricing/fee decisions can also be rationalised and the weaker sections of the society would get substantial benefits. The main thing in segmentation is perceiving the expectations of users/prospects in a right fashion. If we succeed in understanding the users, we also succeed in making the marketing decisions proactive. These facts are a mute testimony to this proposition that market segmentation would prove its instrumentality in knowing and understanding the changing level of expectations which would simplify the task of insurance professionals. They can also have an idea of identifying the emerging profitable segment of the future. In the Indian perspective, we find rural market to be a profitable market for both the bank and insurance organisations in the 21st century. If the insurance professionals assign due weightage to the rural segment, they can make their services/schemes rural-oriented and such orientation would make the ways for positive developments. It is against this background that we find market segmentation an essential component of managing the marketing activities and the insurance organisations are supposed to intensify research for exploring new markets found more productive but generating less complications. We can't negate that the foreign insurance companies assign due weightage to market segmentation and it is due to the fact that they have an in-depth idea of the emerging profitable markets.

The purpose of insurance business is to cover the maximum possible potential policyholders. In addition, it is also pertinent that liquidity, safety and profitability are given due weightage. Mobilisation of savings and channelisation of investments, if done in a right way would make the insurance business productive. A market is composed of different users and the corporate objectives focus on covering all the segments so that a sound product portfolio is designed in which the services/schemes of present and future are blended optimally. The market segmentation would make possible formulation of a sound market planning which would make the strategic decisions sensitive.

A closer view of smaller market aggregate would permit the planner to spot opportunities. The development of most profitable or attractive package of insurance services/schemes would also be possible with the help of segmentation. To maximise the rate of profitability, the marketers need to identify the profitable segments. Since we also expect privatisation of insurance services or deregulating the business conditions, it is high time that the public sector insurance organisations in particular know about the emerging profitable segments.

In view of the above, it is right to say that segmentation needs a priority attention of insurance professionals. How to reach and influence the target market is found meaningful to accomplish the corporate objectives. The segmentation would help marketers in transforming the prospects into users.

IMPACT OF TECHNOLOGY ON THE INSURANCE SECTOR

We agree with this view that inventions and innovations in the field of information and communication technology have posed serious challenges and threats for the insurance sector in India. The insurance companies have been found promoting the use of new generation of technology showing a direct impact on the productivity of resources and a sweepening impact on making the entire process cost-effective. For the speedy and correct issuance of documents, expeditious disposal of insurance claims and proper accounting, the use of innovative information technology has been seen sizeably benefiting the financial management. This speaks of the fact that the insurance business, of late, has been revolutionised by technology at a high pace. The importers, exporters, shipping companies and financial institutions have been frequently making use of information technology. In a true sense, the software solutions have made ways for crossborder trade to become even paperless. The Database Management System, Data Warehouse, Decision Support System, Group Linking Software, Imaging and Workflow Technologies, Mapping, Call Centre Technology, Video Linking, Cat Models[9] have considerably improved the functional quality of insurance companies. The insurance marketers have been seen promoting the use of technology for developing awareness, settlement of claims, payment of premiums, handling of customer grievances and intermediary analysis.

Database Management Systems: New Personal Computer and Reduced Instruction Set Computing have made it possible to keep millions of policies on a device with thousands of bites of data per policy/client/agent. Reviewing of data simplifies the process of identifying the lapsed and surrendered policies.

Data Warehouse: Based on the integration of a number of information systems, this technology helps in developing one-stop shopping to have a national network. The data warehousing also provides a regional focus. This helps minimising the cost. The Transactions Processing Systems help in developing the MIS. Besides, the DSS can also be easier with the help of Data Warehouse.

Group Linking Software: It helps sharing of information. In the large-scale insurance business, it is found effective.

Mapping: The mapping technology is found helpful in identifying the loss-prone areas and analysing its network.

Call Centre Technology: The Interactive Voice Response Services (IVRS) is considered to be helpful in making possible customer-friendly services which is found based on the concept of call centre technology. This helps in receiving the grievances of customers and also helps in removing their confusions.

Video Linking: It helps in linking the two remote units of an insurance company. The broking services can be activated with the help of video linking.

Cat Models: We also call it catastrophic model helping in predicting the property of insurance in case of natural disasters.

Intranet, Extranet and Internet: Intranet is a method of integrating different offices of the same business. Extranet is a network for communicating with the business partners. Internet is a global network of many computer networks.

IT for Insurance Marketing: Of course, we find IT playing a very significant role in almost all the functional areas but we find its role assuming a place of outstanding significance in marketing the insurance services. The formulation of a sound marketing mix considerably rests on IT. The services marketers in general and the insurance marketers in particular use IT for the following purposes:

- **Developing awareness:** In the marketing process, the most significant aspect is making customers and potential customers fully aware of the features of product. We cannot negate that IT has made the task much more easier. The internet services help in informing and sensing the customers. The different insurance companies use the different pages of Web and from there the customers come to know about the salient features of product. As and when we find new products launched by the insurance companies, the customers get an opportunity to view not about the products but they also come to know incentives time-to-time offered by the insurance companies. In a true sense, the task of insurance marketers is considerably simplified with the help of IT.
- **Service orientation:** We find insurance business based on customer services. The leading big foreign players have virtually sensitised the customers. It is natural that before taking a decision, the customers need different types of information and IT helps dissemination of information. The marketing research activities can be much more effective. The targeting of customers and their segmentation help serving the customers. The payment of premiums, settlement of claims, tracking of brokers and agents are found easier with the help of IT. The redressal of customers' grievances is possible on time. Thus, the services can be made friendly to customers. The insurance marketers *vis-à-vis* the insurance customers are found immensely benefited.

E-INSURANCE

Today, we find all the systems and subsystems considerably influenced by techniculture. Like other sectors, the technology has also been found searching ways for dominating the insurance sector. It is right to mention that the process of corporatisation cannot gain a rapid momentum, if we find new generation of information and communication technologies not getting due weightage. A new area we find taking a shape even in the Indian context known as E-Insurance.

With the entry of foreign insurance companies, we find a big change in the insurance sector. The intensity of competition is found mounting everyday. The big players have been found promoting the use of new generation of technology in the insurance sector. We cannot deny that unlike banking and broking services, the insurance services have not been so much techno-driven. But now we find a big shift. It is in this context that we find E-Insurance drawing due attention of insurance policy makers albeit in the Indian business environment. Though we find a majority of us not accepting the success of E-Insurance in the Indian perspective where we find general masses even till date not developing temptation to the IT. However, we cannot outright reject the concept of E-Insurance.[10]

Selling of insurance product "online" is the main theme that we find in the E-Insurance. It is also argued that both the public and private insurance companies should explore the possibilities of practising E-Insurance markets. The expanding software industry is found signaling green light for E-Insurance in the Indian setting but we should also accept that even in the global scenario, this concept has not been widely accepted. Despite all we need to think over E-Insurance which is to benefit the insurance business in many ways. The customers would be in a position to get the information which would be both authentic and cost-effective. The issue of policies and settlement of claims would be possible at a high speed. The services would be customised and flexible. The global accessibility is an additional benefit the customers can get from the E-Insurance. The collection of premium would be on time and the costs on sales force would considerably be minimised. The customers would have round-the-clock services.

We cannot deny good auguries in the field of E-Insurance in India because we find a galloping increase in the number of net users. In the years to come, the number of net users in India will be more than 250 million. Since the intensity of competition is found mounting, the E-Insurance will benefit both the providers and users in many ways. At the initial stage, the E-Insurance may be cost-ineffective but in the long-run, it may prove to be a profit driver.

Despite all, we need to debate its conceptualisation because it may aggravate the problem of unemployment and in a country like India, may not be a welcome step.

MARKETING INFORMATION SYSTEM FOR INSURANCE ORGANISATIONS

The emerging multi-dimensional changes in the socio-economic and business conditions make it essential that like other organisations, the insurance organisations also manage information with the help of sophisticated information technologies. The technology-driven marketing information system has already been promoted by the foreign insurance companies and this has helped them in making the marketing decisions creative. We need to promote information-based decisions and the senior executives and the policy planners have to think about a well developed technology-driven information system. A continual surveillance over the MIS would be effective in preparing an initial design. Here, it is pertinent to mention that designing of blueprints is a difficult task and if it is done satisfactorily, the system analysts would find it convenient to finalise the growing and changing information requirements of insurance organisations. It is high time that the system designer is vigilant so that the nature of information required is studied in a right perspective.

Like banking, the insurance business is also done with the support of different branches. This makes it clear that an MIS is to be useful at all the three levels, e.g., Corporate level, Regional level and Branch level. At the apex level, there are a number of measures for collecting information but to be more specific at the branch level, from where the business comes, the management of information is found very poor. This makes it essential that the branch managers realise gravity of the situation and enrich their information bank related to his/her command area. The marketing planning and budgeting can't be productive unless the branch managers are well informed. In Figure 6.3, we find the information inputs for branch.

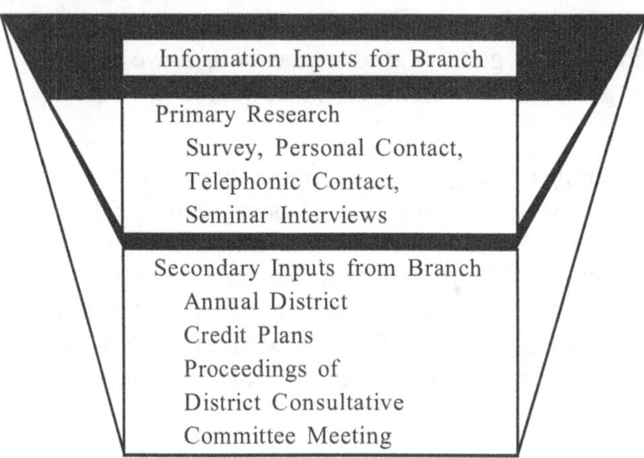

Fig. 6.3: Information Inputs for Branch

SEGMENT-WISE DATA

It is natural that segment-wise collected data simplifies the task of branch managers, specially while identifying a profitable segment. In this context, the important sources are the commercial banks where the branch managers can get detailed information regarding the current income of existing employees, retired persons, pensionholders, small and big business houses or so. A direct link with the concerned organisation would also serve the purpose. To be more specific in the insurance business, it is found more impact generating that the branch managers prepare a list of salaried persons, employees working in the formal and informal sectors and different categories of agriculturists with the support of related organisation and village level committees. The agents and the rural career agents, the electoral roll, district census would also help the process of enriching the information bank.

The segment-wise information sources is presented in Figure 6.4. The nature of information and the possible sources are shown in different boxes. The management of information particularly with the viewpoint of making creative marketing decisions simplifies the task of branch managers. With the support of agents, rural career agents and front-line staff, the branch managers can be efficacious in collecting information related to his/her command area. At the branch level, the management of information becomes significant since the multi-dimensional developments in the command area can be studied and the necessary informations can be transmitted to the senior executives and the policy makers. Even at the regional and corporate levels, the management of marketing information is found significant since the changes required in the policy decisions can't be made possible unless the branches and regions make available the necessary information.

The aforesaid facts make it clear that the marketing information system is found significant to the smooth working and future prosperity of the insurance organisations. To be more specific when we find the intensity of threats and challenges moving upward, it is pertinent that the insurance organisations in general and the public sector insurance organisations in particular enrich the information bank and keep themselves engaged in innovating their marketing decisions. This would have a far reaching effect on the service mix of the insurance organisations since they can offer innovative services or schemes and can add attractions to their services by innovating the peripheral services. The formulation of an attractive package would also be possible which would act as a motivational tool. In addition, the decisions related to other mixes of the marketing, such as promotion, premium and bonus, offering of services, instrumentality of insurance professionals, development of dedicated and personally-committed personnel would also be made creative to sensitise the prospects. It is against this background that the management of marketing information with the help of a technology-driven system needs due attention of the insurance organisations.

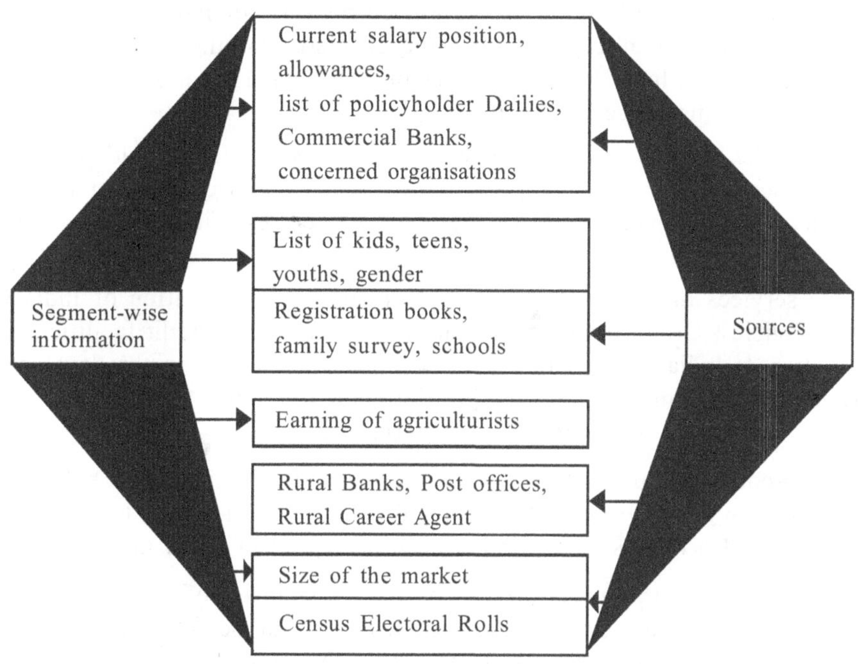

Fig. 6.4: Segment-wise Information Sources

INSURANCE PRODUCT

The insurance business is concerned with the guaranteeing compensation in the event of loss, damage to property or death. The present-day insurance, or the protection as provided by the Life Insurance Corporation of India and the General Insurance Corporation or other companies and agencies in the private sector pertaining to life, fire and marine has its basic concept that the individuals or groups of companies seeking protection must earn a surplus over the cost of maintaining and then pay a premium out of the income. For this purpose, the insurance business is based on a mutual and basic desire to protect the loss of one's property and loss due to death of an individual.

What do we produce are known as our product. If we produce goods, our emphasis is on tangible product and when we produce or generate services, our emphasis is on intangible service product. The insurance organisations produce or generate services in different forms. A product is both what a seller has to sell and what a buyer has to buy. Thus, any enterprise that has something to sell, tangible goods or not is selling products.[11] In the insurance business, the insurance organisations are found selling services and therefore, we find services as their product. Thus, a product is also called a bundle of utilities consisting of various product features and accompanying services.[12] When an individual or a company buys a policy from the insurance organisations, not only the policies are bought but the agents's assistance and advice, the prestige of the insurance organisations, the facilities of claims and compensations are also bought.

In the Indian perspective, the Life Insurance Corporation of India and the General Insurance Corporation of India are the two leading organisations engaged in offering insurance services to the concerned users. We call them public sector insurance organisations. The General Insurance Corporation through its four main subsidiaries offers fire and marine insurance services. The important products are shown in Figure 6.5 and Figure 6.6. The key services or shemes of the Life Insurance Corporation are policies, annuities, credit facilities to the individuals and companies and in addition, they also offer the consultancy services. The General Insurance Corporation offers policies, agents to subsidiaries, consultancy services to the subsidiaries, reinsurance, etc. as the key services. It is pertinent to mention that the General Insurance Corporation is found mainly engaged in supervising and controlling the activities of its subsidiaries but the moment it feels that they are not carrying on their business satisfactorily, the business can be conducted by the General Insurance Corporation of India. Of late, the General Insurance Corporation is found formulating suitable policies for the efficient working of its four main subsidiaries, e.g., National Insurance Company, New India Insurance Company, Oriental Fire and General Insurance Company and United India Fire and General Insurance Company.

In Figure 6.5 and 6.6, the key services of both the insurance organisations would give an idea that the services or schemes of the public sector insurance organisations need to be reviewed in order that the services are made internationally-competitive. This problem would be discussed while presenting the formulation of product mix by the insurance organisations.

In Figure 6.5, the services and schemes of the Life Insurance Corporation of India have been classified into six subheads, viz., Policies, Group Insurance, Annuities, Consultancy, Credit facilities and Underwriting. The Life Insurance Corporation of India as a public sector organisation focuses on the development of public sector organisations by promoting government securities. The policies are found of different types which have been designed to cater to the needs and requirements of different segments.

In Figure 6.5, the product of Life Insurance has been classified[13] into eight subheads, viz., Endowment, Money Back, Pension, Women/Child/Girl/Couple, Disabled, Whole Life Polices, Investment Plus Risk and Term Insurance. Both the public and private sectors need to make the product much more innovative and competitive.

In Figure 6.6, the services and schemes offered by the subsidiaries of the GIC have been presented. We can't negate that like the Life Insurance Corporation, the General Insurance Corporation also requires to innovate their services, specially to make them productive and internationally-competitive. With the development of corporate sector, we find opening of new vistas for the development of the business of General Insurance Corporation of India. The four subsidiaries offer policies, consultancy services, credit facilities and some special and miscellaneous services.

In Figure 6.7, we find Typology of Non-life Insurance. The different heads are Fire Insurance, Automobile Insurance, Marine Insurance, Health Insurance, Rural Insurance, Social Insurance and Miscellaneous.

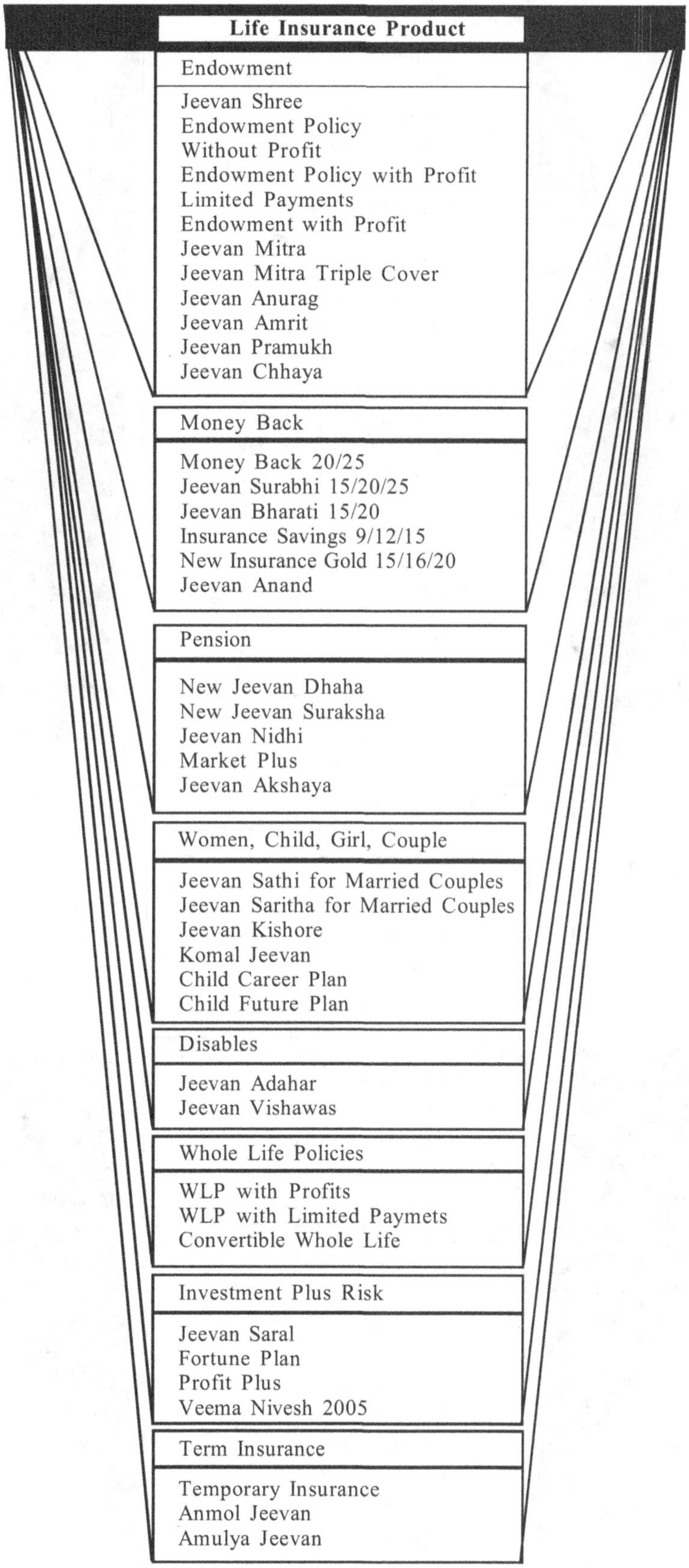

Life Insurance Product

Endowment
- Jeevan Shree
- Endowment Policy Without Profit
- Endowment Policy with Profit Limited Payments
- Endowment with Profit
- Jeevan Mitra
- Jeevan Mitra Triple Cover
- Jeevan Anurag
- Jeevan Amrit
- Jeevan Pramukh
- Jeevan Chhaya

Money Back
- Money Back 20/25
- Jeevan Surabhi 15/20/25
- Jeevan Bharati 15/20
- Insurance Savings 9/12/15
- New Insurance Gold 15/16/20
- Jeevan Anand

Pension
- New Jeevan Dhaha
- New Jeevan Suraksha
- Jeevan Nidhi
- Market Plus
- Jeevan Akshaya

Women, Child, Girl, Couple
- Jeevan Sathi for Married Couples
- Jeevan Saritha for Married Couples
- Jeevan Kishore
- Komal Jeevan
- Child Career Plan
- Child Future Plan

Disables
- Jeevan Adahar
- Jeevan Vishawas

Whole Life Policies
- WLP with Profits
- WLP with Limited Paymets
- Convertible Whole Life

Investment Plus Risk
- Jeevan Saral
- Fortune Plan
- Profit Plus
- Veema Nivesh 2005

Term Insurance
- Temporary Insurance
- Anmol Jeevan
- Amulya Jeevan

Fig. 6.5: Insurance Product (Life Insurance Corporation of India)

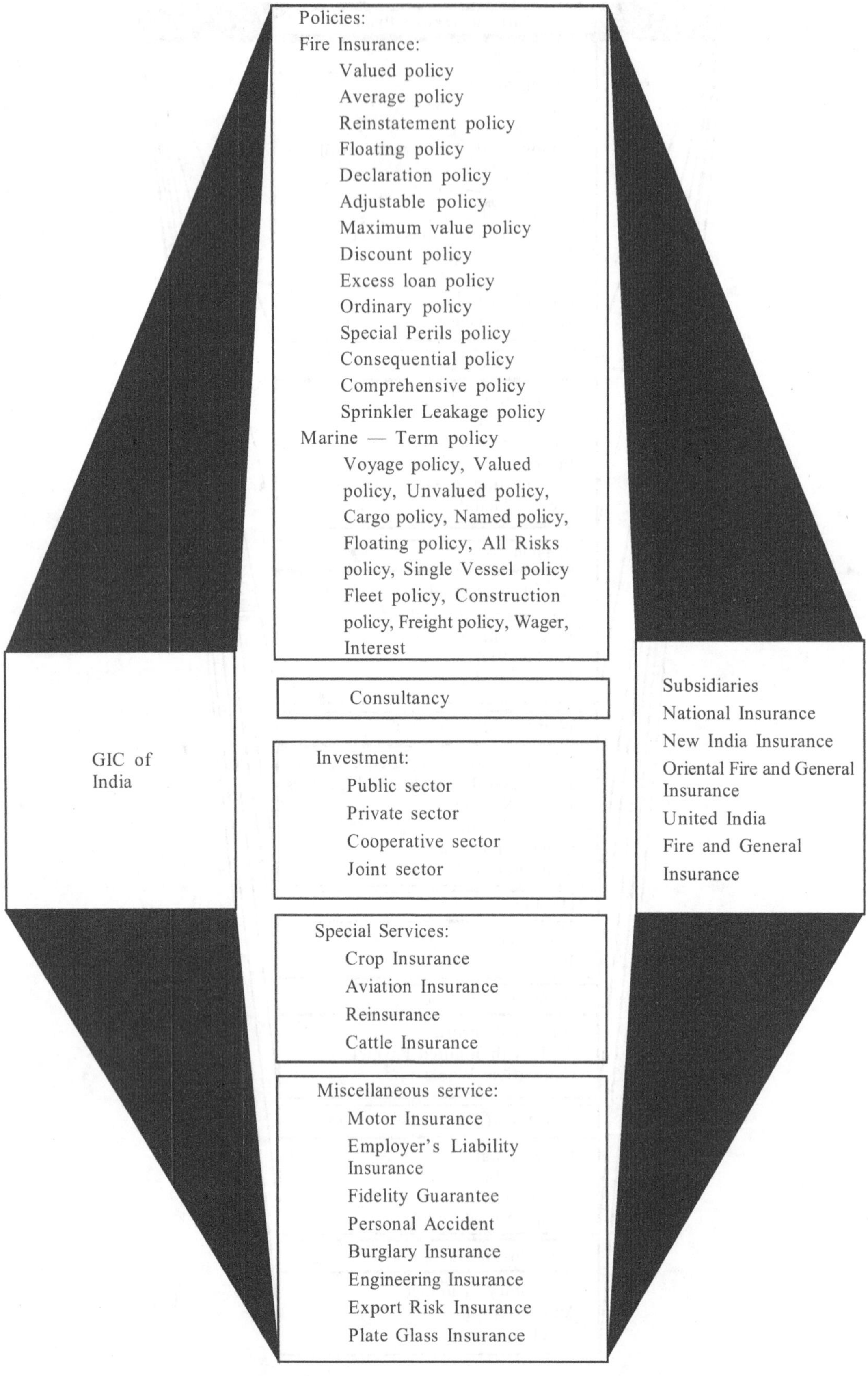

Fig. 6.6: Insurance Product (General Insurance Corporation)

TYPOLOGY OF NON-LIFE INSURANCE
FIRE INSURANCE
Standard Fire Policies Floater Policies Decleration Policies Reinstatement Value Polices Consequential Loss Policies

AUTOMOBILE INSURANCE
Act Policy Comprehensive Policy

MARINE INSURANCE
Hull Insurance Cargo Insurance Freight Insurance Protection & Indemnity Insurance

HEALTH INSURANCE
Central Government Health Scheme Employee State Insurance Scheme Mediclaim, GIC Bhavishya Arogya Insurance Policy Jeevan Asha — LIC Asha Deep — LIC Hospital Cash Daily Allowance Policy Bajaj Allianz Health Guard Bajaj Allianz Critical Illness Bajaj Allianz Health Shield Royal Sundaram Employee Managed System NGO System

RURAL INSURANCE
Aqua Culture Insurance Cattle Insurance Failed Well Insurance Framers' Package Insurance Fish Insurance Floriculture Insurance Sprinkler/Lift Irrigation Scheme Horticulture/Plantation Scheme Poultry Insurance

SOCIAL INSURANCE
Krishi Bima Yojana — GIC Krishi Shramik Samajik Suraksha Yojana – LIC Janashree Bima Yojana — LIC

MISCELLANEOUS
Project Insurance Engineering Insurance Burglary Insurance Fidelty Guarantee Scheme Business Insurance Personal Accident Insurance Horse, Cycle Rickshaw, Plate Glass, Pedal Cycles, Household Appliances, LPG Dealers Insurances

Fig. 6.7: Typology of Non-Life Insurance

PRODUCT PLANNING AND DEVELOPMENT

The success of an organisation is substantially influenced by the time-honoured development of product that requires the formulation of an intelligent as well as a realistic plan. The purpose of insurance business is to generate profits besides subserving the social interests. The present business environment is volatile and even the insurance business is likely to be more competitive. The foreign insurance companies have been found planning and developing their services and schemes in the face of emerging trends in the socio-economic conditions. The public sector insurance organisations need to realise the gravity of the situation and to activate efforts for planning and developing their services and schemes not only with the motto of generating profits but also to energise the process of social transformation. Planning is a process directed towards making today's decision with tomorrow in mind and means of preparing for future decisions so that they be made rapidly, economically and with as little disruption to the business as possible.[14] Further, it involves process of developing and maintaining a viable fit between the organisation's objectives and resources and its environmental opportunities.[15] We find numerous changes in the needs and requirements of different categories of users. If the insurance organisations have to thrive, they have no option but to assign due weightage to the product planning and development. It is against this background that we go through different dimensions of product planning and development.

Product is like a stage on which the entire drama of successful marketing is acted. It is the gateway from which roads to success of an organisation start and lead to a blissful state of organisational prosperity. It is like the engine that pulls the rest of the marketing programmes. It is in this context that product management of an organisation needs an intensive care. We can't negate that during the yesterdecades, we have witnessed a number of developments in the business environment. This in a natural way gravitates our attention on the planning and development of product. The strategy for the same rests on the emerging new trends in the social, economic, political, technological, legal environmental conditions. In addition, the incoming changes in the natural environment also influence the strategic decisions.

Yesterday, the policyholders had limited hopes and aspirations but today, they expect more and they would like even something more tomorrow. This focuses on the fact that strategic decisions are influenced by the environmental conditions. The public sector insurance organisations need to realise the fact that failing the planning and development of services, they would not be successful in increasing their market share. The recent developments in the business environment make it essential that both the public sector insurance organisations (LIC of India and the GIC of India) think over the problem on a priority basis.

The product development needs a new vision, a new approach and a new strategy. Till now, the public sector insurance organisations have not made possible an optimal utilisation of their marketing resources specially in the rural areas where tremendous opportunities are found available. This makes it essential that they assign due weightage to the development of services and schemes which cater to the changing needs and requirements of the rural segment.

It would be more prudent that the LIC of India is allowed to pursue a policy of Direct Investment for Rural Development instead of indirect financing. It may grant direct loan to Community Development Block authorities for implementing development-oriented schemes in their command areas. Besides, a provision for direct loan to the co-operative societies for financing their main activities and direct and indirect financing for house construction activities in the rural areas need an overriding priority. The numerous schemes for financing house construction activities introduced by the LIC of India so far show an avert leaning towards urban population. This is required to be changed.

In the development of product, the co-operative investments need due priority. At present, the Corporation is found concentrating on the governmental securities and private investments are found of secondary importance. In almost all the countries, we find insurance companies channelising corporate investments. This influences the rate of profitability of the insurance companies and in addition also contribute considerably to the socio-economic transformation process. It is important to mention that in USA and Canada, we find more than 50 per cent of the life funds invested in the corporate securities. Of course, we find the underwriting activities gaining the momentum in the Indian context but till now it is at the nascent stage.

Of late, a number of new policies have been included in the product mix of both the public sector insurance organisations but keeping in view the strategic decisions of the foreign insurance companies, they need to speed up the process of product innovation. While innovating the services or schemes, they need to keep in their minds that policies covering the maximum possible lives are given due weightage. New annuities and policies activating the process of savings generation and energising the process of welfare orientation would serve our purpose. The insurance business is to be looked at as a concept of Perpetual Corpus. It can best be studied in the face of past social concepts, changing conditions and expectations of the prospects.

In the years to come, we expect a substantial increase in the number of potential policyholders. This naturally necessitates product planning and development in tune with the changing socio-economic conditions. The objectives of the LIC of India are to spread life insurance much more widely and in particular to the rural areas and to socially and economically backward classes with a view to reaching all insurable persons in the country and providing them adequate financial cover against death at a reasonable cost to maximise the mobilisation of people's savings by making insurance-linked savings adequately attractive; bear in mind the investment of funds, the primary obligation to its policyholders whose money it holds in trust, without losing sight of the interest of the community as a whole, the funds to be developed to the best advantage of the investors as well as the community as a whole, keeping in view the national priorities and obligations of attractive return; conduct business with utmost economy and with full realisation that the money belongs to the policyholders; act as trustees of the insured public in their individual and collective capacities; meet the various life insurance needs of the community that would arise in the changing social and economic environment; improve all people working in the interest of the insured public by providing efficient service with courtesy and promote amongst all agents and employees of the corporation a sense of participation, price and job satisfaction through discharge of their duties with dedication towards achievement of corporate objectives.[16]

In view of the above, the following key points emerge:

- Inclusion of new product or policies having a rural bias.
- Due weightage to the socially and ecomomically backward classes.
- Maximising the mobilisation of savings by offering lucrative schemes.
- Assigning due weightage to the interests of investors.
- Maintaining economy in the business by promoting cost-effectiveness.
- Acting as a trustee of the policyholders.
- Keeping in mind the emerging trends in the business environment.
- Improving the quality of customer/user services.
- Promoting a sense of participation.

The General Insurance Corporation of India bears the responsibility of fulfilling the following objectives:

- Making provision for grants to its subsidiaries.
- Advising the subsidiaries in respect of management, cost, commission.
- Advising the subsidiaries in the investment of funds.
- Advising the subsidiaries in conducting the insurance business with a view to excel competition.
- Starting the business of general insurance as and when it is felt essential.

In view of the aforesaid objectives of the GIC of India, it is pertinent that the development of product is assigned due weightage. This requires a change in the nature and form of services, schemes, policies which cater to the changing needs and requirements of the users. It is also significant that rural orientation is required to be assigned a transcendental priority. In addition, it is also significant that the process of mobilisation of savings of small classes is promoted. The quality of customer services draws due attention of the management.

Of course, the LIC of India has been found fuelling the process of fulfilling the corporate objectives but even today, we find tremendous opportunities to be capitalised on profitability. We can't negate the fact that the corporation, has not been serious to the tapping of profitable opportunities in the different segments. This makes it essential that the insurance organisations conceptualise marketing. It is right to mention that in the Indian perspective both the public sector organisations have devalued the customer services which in due course is to complicate the task of business expansion. The customers at large feel that the foreign insurance companies have been instrumental in protecting the interests of the policyholders whereas the public sector insurance organisations take it very lightly. This is an unpleasent development which needs an attitudinal change and for that the insurance organisations have no option but to implement innovative marketing so that the interests of policyholders are protected and at the same time, copious avenues are paved for channelisation of investments *vis-a-vis* the generation of profits. It is in this context that we make a strong advocacy in favour of formulating the marketing mix in the face of recent developments. This draws our attention on innovative marketing for promoting the public sector insurance business.

THE FORMULATION OF MARKETING MIX FOR INSURANCE ORGANISATIONS

The insurance organisations in general and the public sector insurance organisations in particular need to assign due weightage to the formulation of marketing mix for the insurance business. The moment we find the market competitive, the organisations either producing goods or generating services are required to innovate the marketing decision. We can't negate the fact that to be more specific the public sector insurance organisations have not been formulating and innovating the marketing mix to cater to the changing needs and requirements and the increasing level of satisfaction of the users. This has been found increasing the image problem since in a majority of the cases, we find users dissatisfied with the service profile. They often complain regarding the deteriorating quality of services and this has been engineering a sound foundation for snatching of business by the foreign insurance companies. The emerging trends indicate that if the insurance organisations delay the process of formulating a sound marketing mix for their business, there would be a sharp fall in their market share in the future, which would bring down the rate of profitability. It is against this background that we go through the problem of marketing mix for the insurance services. This makes it essential that we turn our eyes on the different submixes and make sincere efforts to innovate the same in the desired fashion. We discuss all the submixes of marketing, such as the product mix, the promotion mix, the price mix, the place mix, the people, the process and the physical evidence attractions. It is important to mention that the marketing experts of today make a strong advocacy in favour of managing people since they find human resources contributing substantially to the development processes.

THE PRODUCT MIX

The formulation of product mix for the insurance business makes it significant that we turn our eyes on the services and schemes of insurance organisations. We know about their product portfolio and assess the process of formulating a package. It is natural that the users expect a reasonable return for their investments. It is quite natural that the insurance organisations want to maximise profitability. Both the dimensions are found interrelated. It is profitability that makes the ways for a reasonable or profitable return to the users. And it is the contribution of policyholders that influence the business of insurance organisations *vis-a-vis* their profitability.

Of course, to be more specific after the nationalisation of private insurance companies, we find inclusion of a good number of services and schemes by both the Life Insurance and the General Insurance but we can't appreciate their efforts to make the services or schemes motivational. The Group Insurance is required to be promoted, the Crop Insurance is required to be expanded and new policies, schemes having a rural bias are required to be included in the product portfolio. We are aware of the fact that a majority of our population live in villages. The landless labourers, unemployed youths, non-traditional farming, rural artisans, fishermen, potters, etc. deserve due care. It is well-known that the key objectives of the insurance business are mobilisation of savings and channelisation of investments. This makes it essential that the insurance business is made lucrative so that the users/potential users get incentives to buy a policy or to invest in the insurance organisations.

In the yesterdecades, the Life Insurance Corporation has intensified efforts to promote urban savings but so far as the rural savings are concerned, we don't find it impressive. The introduction of Rural Career Agent's Scheme has been found instrumental in inducing the rural prospects but the process at the very nascent stage requires more professional excellence. The policy makers are required to activate the efforts. It would be prudent that the LIC is allowed to pursue a policy of Direct Investment for Rural Development.[17] This makes a strong advocacy in favour of innovating the services and schemes. It is high time that the policy makers and the senior executives think in favour of profitable policies and schemes for rural masses. This would be instrumental in mobilising the rural savings. The investment policy of the organisation needs due care of the policy makers. It is pertinent to mention here that the practices of promoting pro-government securities are required to be stopped and the interference of government in the business policy of the insurance organisations is to be checked. The channelisation of investment in the private sector would make the ways for the maximisation of profitability. The insurance organisations also need to promote the underwriting activities which would activate the process of arresting the regional imbalance. We can't deny the fact that the insurance organisations have, of course, been liberal to the development of urban areas but the backward provinces and the neglected areas have failed in getting even the due. Paradoxically, the developed states like the Gujarat, Maharashtra, Punjab, Haryana have received considerable benefits from the policies and schemes of the insurance organisations but the backward states like Bihar, Orissa and Assam have been discriminated. This necessitates an overhauling of the investment policy with a positive attitude and a new vision and a good-bye to the policy of step motherly treatment.

In the context of formulating the product mix, it is essential that the insurance organisations promote innovation and in the product portfolio include even those services and schemes which are likely to get a positive response in the future. In an agrarian economy, the insurance organisations are supposed to play a positive role by promoting Cattle Insurance, Crop Insurance so that the farmers develop their potentials to resist the natural calamities. We can't negate that the product innovation process would require a change in the regulatory provisions. The Life Insurance Corporation Act 1956, the Marine Insurance Act 1963 and the General Insurance Act 1972 need amendments in the face of the recommendations of Malhotra Committee. The corporate objectives indicate that the insurance organisations are required to be careful, specially while launching a new policy. It is not only sufficient that the policies generate enough premium but it is also important that our policies cover even the persons working in the informal sector, serving as porters, working as manual labourers, or engaged in the farm sector.

In view of the above, it is right to mention that new policies and schemes are required to be included in the product portfolio of the insurance organisations. In addition, they need to formulate a sound package that proves to be more motivational. While formulating a package, the insurance professionals need to assign due weightage to the interests of rural India. The package if profitable proves its instrumentality as a motivational force and simplifies the task of insurance professionals. In this context, it is also important that the insurance organisations think in favour of eliminating those services which are not getting a profitable return. This would pave avenues for the mobilisation of savings.

The formulation of a sound product portfolio is thus found important to the public sector insurance organisations which, of late, have been facing a rough weather. The regulations, no doubt, stand as a barrier but they have no option. It is the need of the hour that the insurance organisations make their service mix internationally competitive. In the insurance business, the mounting intensity of risks and uncertainties make it significant that the insurance organisations assign due weightage to the innovation of product strategy. The inclusion of new policies in the product portfolio keeping in mind the changing business conditions and the future scenario would help insurance organisations in many ways. The private sector insurance organisations have been found making their service mix internationally-competitive. This makes a strong advocacy in favour of innovative product strategy for the public sector insurance organisations.

In view of the above, the following aspects need due attention of policy makers, senior executives and branch managers:

- The formulation of product mix should be in the face of innovative product strategy. The strategies adopted by the foreign and private insurance companies should be taken into consideration while initiating the innovation process.
- The Data Processing Department is supposed to collect necessary information related to the changing level of expectations of prospects so that the senior executives make the product portfolio productive to the users and profitable to the insurance organisations.
- It is also significant that the insurance organisations initiate the process of elimination of the services, schemes not profitable to them. This necessitates a study of the product life cycle.
- The formulation of product strategy should assign due weightage to the rural segment emerging as a big profitable segment specially in the 21st century. It is right to mention that the policies, schemes should

also have rural orientation so that the backward and neglected regions of the country get priority attention and the problem of regional imbalance is minimised.

- In this context, it is also pertinent that the insurance organisations make possible welfare orientation and include in the product portfolio even those policies and schemes which become instrumental in safeguarding the interests of the weaker sections of the society.
- The formulation of a package is also found important. We find the foreign insurance companies designing a package on the basis of the needs and requirements of the concerned segment. This would make the product mix competitive.
- There are some of the profitable areas which till now are found either partially tapped or even totally untapped. The agents, rural career agents, the branch managers bear the responsibility of identifying the profitable segments of future and helping the senior executives in tapping the potentials optimally.
- A sound product portfolio is the need of the hour and therefore the regulatory barriers or constraints in activating the innovation process should be minimised.

THE PROMOTION MIX

In the formulation of marketing mix, the promotion mix occupies a place of outstanding significance. Like other organisations, the insurance organisations are also supposed to realise the instrumentality of this submix of the marketing mix which would help them substantially. It is in this context that we go through the various dimensions of the promotion mix. In the promotion mix, we include a number of submixes, such as the advertising, public relations, sales promotion, word-of-mouth promotion, personal selling and telemarketing. We can't deny the fact that all the components of promotion need due attention of the insurance professsionals. This is based on the logic that the public sector insurance organisations right now facing the image problem have to adopt a big push theory in which all the components need to contribute optimally. It is not only sufficient that we are contributing substantially to the processes of socio-economic transformation. It bears an analogous significance that the users at large feel that you are really making a significant contribution. While making promotion decisions, the insurance professionals have to assign due weightage to creativity. This would help them in sharpening the instrumentality of promotional tools. It is against this background that we go through different components of promotion.

Advertising

Advertising, a paid form of persuasive communications, is found important to promote the insurance business. Of late, we have sophisticated devices to advertise. In addition, we have executives having world-class professional excellence. The advertising professionals bear the responsibility of making the advertisement slogans, appeals, campaigns creative so that the process of sensitising the prospects is found proactive. We talk about a group of target audience found unconscious, unorganised, illiterate, insensitive or so. This increases the functional responsibilities of advertisement professionals. It is in this context that we make a strong advocacy in favour of creativity.

We advertise through telecast media, broadcast media and the print media. We can't negate that the insurance organisations need to make possible an optimal use of all the three media. So far as the vulnerable sections of the society are concerned, we find the telecast media more effective in the sensitising process. With the help of audio/visual exposure, the rate of acceptability of the messages can be increased sizeably. If the advertising professionals are well aware of the receiving capacity of the prospects, they can make the advertisement slogans, and messages creative. Being a big organisation, the Life Insurance Corporation of India is found efficacious in having its own advertisement wing for that purpose. However, they can seek the co-operation of other agencies if they find it essential. The motive is to make the slogans creative. We can't deny that the telecast media is expensive but to promote the insurance business we have no option but to assign due weightage to the same.

The broadcast media can also be used for that very purpose. Since we have a big transmission network and a well-developed system, the insurance organisations are supposed to use even the broadcast media. If we find the messages sensitive, the rate of acceptability would also be high. Another benefit of this media is to reach the messages even to the remotest parts of the country. It is the responsibility of insurance professionals that they with the support of advertisement professionals make possible creativity in the messages and slogans and increase the effectiveness of broadcast media. The media being economic in nature offers additional benefit that would collect more support on the financial ground.

The print media can also be used for promoting the insurance business. Being economic in nature and impressive in expression, the print media, of late, has been found gaining popularity. The sophistication in the print technologies has made the media more attractive. It is against this background that now almost all the organisations assign due weightage to this. The insurance organisations need to promote the print media since this would simplify their task of making the appeals effective by using regional languages. The detailed explanation is another property that requires due place while making decisions related to the selection of a suitable vehicle for travelling the messages.

An important consideration while making the decision is the budgetary constraint. Since we find insurance organisations working on a large scale, we don't find this constraint standing as an obstacle. They can afford even the expensive telecast media and therefore they should assign top priority to the acceptability factor. Of course, we find the public sector insurance organisations advertising properly, but there must be a close relation between the services-offered and the services-advertised. If we find a gap or an exaggeration, the sensitivity rate of our messages would go down. This focuses our attention on building up of a positive image by offering the promised services to the users. Advertisement helps us in projecting a positive image but if we find nothing positive in our accounts to advertise, the sensitivity in messages is not possible.

The LIC of India and the GIC of India, the two leading public sector organisations bear the responsibility of offering the promised services to the users. We can't deny the fact that private insurance companies are found instrumental in building up of a positive image since, the quality of their services is found of world-class. It is unpleasent to comment that the public sector organisations have not been assigning due weightage to the quality upgradation and therefore whatever they advertise are not positive in effects. Of course, they need to advertise but their advertisement messages should have a close link with the quality of services they offer. It is against this background that the insurance professionals while advertising services need to make the advertisement message realistic. The main thing is creativity and this necessitates seeking the co-operation of world-class advertising professionals who show their excellence.

In view of the above, it is right to mention that advertisement, an important dimension of the promotion mix requires due attention of senior executives so that whatever the lapses we find in the advertisment programming are sorted out. We need to use this tool in a right fashion. We need to avoid the misuse of this tool. Of late, there are a number of devices to make possible sophistication in promotion and the insurance professionals are supposed to remember it. There must be a proportionate use of the different components of promotion.

Publicity

In addition to advertisement, the insurance professionals also need to think in favour of publicity since this component of promotion if used in a right fashion makes our promotional efforts proactive. The advertisements may be insensitive, but we find publicity effective since the messages, views, opinions, facts, figures are publicised by media or the vocal leaders. It is a device to promote business without making any payment and therefore we also call it an unpaid form of persuasive communication bearing high rate of sensitivity. It is against this background that we make a strong advocacy in favour of strengthening and innovating the public relation activities so that our positive contributions reach to the prospects in time. Developing rapport with media is an important aspect of publicity. This makes it essential that the public relations officers working in the insurance organisations or the branch managers or even the senior executives develop rapport with the media people, organise a press conference, distribute to them small gifts, offer to them lunch/dinner and persuade them to write something in their favour by making a story or in the form of news cover. All of us are aware of LGD marketing gaining popularity the world over. L (Lunch), G (Golf), D (Dinner) focus on the fact that in the business world, the executives bear the responsibility of managing business favourably, this way or that way. If we find coverage in the newspapers, magazines, the prospects are to be influenced.

Strengthening the public relations activities is another dimension requiring due attention of the senior executives and the branch managers. At the apex and regional levels, the public relations officers bear the responsibility of projecting a positive image of the organisation and at the branch level, we find this responsibility upon the shoulders of branch managers. The PRO is considered to be a professional having the world-class excellence in influencing the prospects, users, others. He/she bears an important responsibility of informing, sensing and persuading. He/

she is found responsible for managing the sales dialogues. This makes it essential that we find selection of suitable persons for the said purpose and in addition also intensify training programmes, refresher courses, capsule courses to educate and train them in tune with the changing business conditions. The receptionists, secretaries, front-line staff publicise your business with their gesture and posture. The *modus operandi* and *modus vivendi* become important in the very context. They are supposed to know-how to talk, how to initiate, how to impress and how to conclude. They should look smart and attractive and should also have quality communicative ability. It is an art which is found based on certain properties. We need to educate and train them properly so that they with the help of their dialogues and body communications succeed in impressing upon the prospects/users. If they are well aware of the changing level of expectations of customers, the task is made easier.

In view of the above, it is right to mention that this dimension of promotion needs due care of senior executives of the insurance organisations. The foreign insurance companies have quality public relations officers but in the public sector insurance organisations, we don't find public relations activities of world-class which makes our task of publicising insensitive. It is in this context that we need an overriding priority to this dimension of promotion.

Sales Promotion

We find sales promotion a device to promote sale to meet a certain target. It is a temporary device which is withdrawn after a particular period. It is meant for both — the end-users of the services and the channels found instrumental in promoting the services. In the insurance business, the incentives to the policyholders/users or to the agents, rural career agents or even to the insurance personnel for promoting the business are the sales promotion tools. Almost all the organisations are found using the tools of sales promotion in a different way. Since the business environment is likely to be more competitive, it is pertinent that the insurance organisations offer innovative tools of sales promotion and increase or decrease the duration depending upon the business conditions *vis-a-vis* the emerging trends in business. It is against this background that we make a strong advocacy in favour of sales promotion for promoting the insurance business. It is upon the senior executives and the policy makers to think in favour of innovative tools.

Incentives to the end-users for taking a policy play an incremental role in promoting the insurance business. It is in this context that we need to think about the tools of sales promotion for the policyholders. Since the insurance business is also related to the achievement of a particular target, it is pertinent that the policy makers assign due weightage to the same and the senior executives as well as the branch managers promote the same on a priority basis. In addition, the branch managers as well as the agents and the rural career agents should also accept the responsibility of making this component of the promotion mix popular *vis-a-vis* proactive. The offering of small gifts during a particular period, the rebate, discount, bonus can be instrumental in increasing the business of insurance organisations. It is right to mention that such incentive to the policyholders/prospects would be successful in increasing the busines. It is the responsibility of the insurance professionals that they keep on activating the process of innovation so that the foreign insurance companies find it difficult to compete with the public sector insurance organisations. We can't deny the fact that the governmental support to the public sector insurance organisations, specially in the shape of income tax exemption makes the business conditions a bit different. The moment such an exemption is withdrawn, the task of public sector insurance organisations would be much more difficult.

The agents and the rural career agents play an incremental role in promoting the insurance business. It is against this background that we need to promote them for getting more business. The promotional tools for the agents and the rural career agents and even for the branch managers and the front-line staff need due attention of the senior executives of the insurance organisations. Since they bear the responsibility of promoting the insurance business, it is judicious as well as logical that the promotional tools for them are frequently innovated. Such an incentive would help the insurance organisations in many ways. If we feel that rural segment needs an intensive care, they should be given more incentives for promoting the business in the rural areas. This makes it clear that incentives to the users/policyholders as well as to the agents and the rural career agents would be instrumental in promoting the insurance business, provided the insurance professionals innovate the same, much earlier than their competitors.

Personal Selling

We can't deny the fact that out of all the components of promotion mix, the personal selling occupies a place of outstanding significance. This is due to the fact that the insurance business is substantially influenced by the instrumentality of agents and the rural career agents. If they are aware of the art of informing, sensing and persuading the potential policyholders, the task of insurance organisations is simplified considerably. It is in this context that we talk about this component of the promotion mix.

We are well aware of the fact that personal selling is based on the excellence of an individual. This focuses our attention on the ability of an individual to influence the impulse by activating the persuasion process. This makes it significant that the agents as well as the rural career agents have certain outstanding properties or attributes, such as patience, communicative ability, attractive personality and commitment to the profession. The insurance business can't exist if the agents stop working. Hence, the insurance organisations are supposed to assign due weightage to the excellence in an individual who is assigned this responsibility. They need to provide due incentives to the agents so that they work satisfactorily and keep on moving the process of informing and persuading the policyholders/prospects. While recruiting agents, the insurance professionals need to be careful so that persons with high communicative ability, an attractive physique and everlasting patience are assigned the responsibility of acting as an agent. The branch managers bear the responsibility of managing and developing the agents by monitoring their contributions to the process of increasing the insurance business. They are supposed to organise refresher courses to develop the agents so that the emerging trends in the investment potentials of a command area *vis-a-vis* the changing level of expectations of the policyholders/prospects are transmitted to them in a right fashion and on time.

Since we find the rural segment likely to emerge as a profitable segment in the near future, it is the prime responsibility of the rural career agents that they perform the responsibility of informing, sensing and persuading the rural prospects. It is quite natural that the business conditions in the rural segment is to be a bit different. The rural prospects in a majority of the cases are found illiterate, unorganised and ill informed. They don't know about the insurance business. The public sector insurance organisations bear the responsibility of promoting the rural segment and therefore, it is pertinent that they develop and promote the rural career agents. The rural career agents should have high communicative ability and a hero of regional languages. This simplifies their task of influencing the impulse. We can't negate that in the Indian perspective, the rural career agents lack patience. They avoid to go to villages. They don't know the art of influencing the rural prospects. They lack rural orientation. They are not personally committed and these negative traits stand as a barrier, specially while persuading the rural prospects. It makes a strong advocacy in favour of developing the rural career agents in a bit different way. They need special training programmes, refresher courses and special incentives to stay and work in villages like a professional. Almost all the segments in the rural areas have tremendous potentials, and the rural career agents are supposed to capitalise on the opportunities optimally. The personal selling thus requires an intensive care. It is high time that THE CAREER AGENTS' SCHEMES and the RURAL CAREER AGENTS' SCHEMES are promoted.

Word-of-mouth Promotion

If you serve well; if you behave well; if you perform well the customers/users have no option but to assign due weightage to your contributions may be not today, may be not even tomorrow but must a day after tomorrow. If the organisations serve well, the users have no option but to appreciate their contributions and to adopt them. It is against this background that we talk about this component of the promotion mix in the context of insurance services.

The word-of-mouth communications result into wider publicity which substantially sensitise the process of influencing the impulse of users/prospects of the insurance services. The satisfied group of customers, the opinion leaders, the social reformists, the popular personalities act as word-of-mouth communicators. The insurance organisations like the banking organisations need to assign due weightage to the quality of services made available to the users so that the satisfied group of customers accepts the responsibility of promoting the services. The insurance professionals are also supposed to seek the co-operation of opinion leaders, vocal persons for promoting the business and for that the offering of small gifts to them is required essential. The branch managers bear the responsibility of identifying the popular personalities in their command areas and to motivate them to promote their business. The word-of-mouth communicators are also known as the hidden salesforce who promote the insurance business sizeably. It is in this context that we talk in favour of this component of the promotion mix.

Another dimension of this component of the promotion mix is to seek the co-operation of users who are satisfied with the services. They are habitual users and therefore it is natural that they talk to their friends and relatives about your positive contributions. The advertisement slogans may be insensitive, the publicity measures may also be insensitive, even the sales promotion measures may be ineffective but the positive feelings of your friends and relations communicated to you can't be ineffective. This makes it clear that the most important thing in the promotion of any business is the quality of services that you offer to your users/customers.

Thus, the word-of-mouth promotion makes it significant that the senior executives, the branch managers keep on moving the process of improving the quality of services and at the same time also identify the opinion leaders and vocal persons in a command area. In almost all the segments and in almost all the command areas, we find such persons having a domination on the behavioural profile of the select segment, command area. The hidden salesforce become very much instrumental in publicising your services for which you need to develop a rapport with them. It is essential that you organise a meeting of opinion leaders and offer to them small gifts that may activate the process of promoting your business. Thus, with a nominal investment, you succeed in getting the big business.

In view of the above, it is right to opine that this component of the promotion mix needs due care of the insurance professionals. We can't deny the fact that the private insurance companies have been found promoting their business with the support of hidden salesforce. The public sector insurance organisations need to assign due weightage to this component of the promotion mix which till now is found neglected.

Telemarketing

Of late, we find telemarketing emerging as an important component of the promotion mix. We are aware of the fact that this dimension of the promotion mix promotes business with the support of two communication devices, viz., telephones and televisions. The foreign banking and insurance companies have been seen assigning due weightage to this component of the promotion mix and they have also received a positive response. This makes it essential that the public sector insurance organisations also think in favour of this component.

The telemarketing is a device to promote business in which a person with a high communicative ability acts as a telemarketer and keeps on moving the process of informing, sensing and persuading the customers/users/prospects. The queries, questions asked by the prospects/users are suitably answered and the telemarketers attempt to convince them. With the development of satellite communication facilities and to be more specific with the expansion of television network, we find telemarketing gaining popularity the world over. The insurance organisations in general and the public sector insurance organisations in particular need to promote telemarketing. This would help them in many ways. Of late, we find a sharp fall in the quality of services of the public sector insurance organisations. The customers' complaints/grievances are not given due weightage and the redressal measures remain unnoticed due to the deficient management. This makes it essential that the public sector insurance organisations promote telemarketing to intensify the complaints/grievances redressal measures. We can't deny the fact that telemarketing may help the insurance professionals substantially.

In this context, it is pertinent that they recruit a person or a group of persons bearing the potentials of communicating efficiently. He/she is supposed to be well aware of the telephonic language/code so that the task of satisfying the customers/users or answering to the queries/questions of the users/prospects or even others is not to consume much more time. This is found helpful in informing and sensing the users and therefore, the telemarketers are required to talk intelligently, professionally so that the projection of a positive image is also possible. Of late, we have advanced communications network and therefore it is presumed that almost all the branches of insurance organisations have the sophisticated telephonic devices to promote telemarketing. We can't deny the positive contributions of sophisticated system in getting the desired results.

In view of the above, it is right to mention that telemarketing as an important component of the promotion mix is required to be promoted and for that purpose the public sector insurance organisations are required to recruit efficient personnel who can discharge their functional responsibility in a right fashion. We can't deny the fact that in a majority of the small branches of the public sector insurance organisations, we don't find even the telephonic services in perfect order. Since, for getting the best output, it is pertinent that efficient personnel and sophisticated technologies are available, it is essential that the insurance organisations think in favour of developing the same on a priority basis. The foreign insurance companies have been seen developing telemarketers since they have realised the outstanding contributions of this component of the promotion mix.

Cause-related and Sponsorship Marketing

In addition to other components of promotion, the insurance marketers need due focus on cause-related and sponsorship marketing. Building and protection of a positive image rest on the contributions of an organisation.

It is not only significant that we protect and promote the interests of our policyholders and employees. It is equally important that we also discharge our defined responsibilities to the society. It is in this context that we throw light on this component of promotion which has not received due weightage by the insurance companies. Whatsoever we do for our policyholders, this is in tune with the defined organisational responsibility. The corporate social responsibility makes it essential that even our products should have a holistic approach and this is not to be possible if we confine ourselves to the customers.

The public or private insurance companies need due focus on cause-related marketing. This is marketing to promote the social cause of an organisation. In the context of insurance business, it is possible in two ways such as including welfare-oriented policies and schemes in the product mix and identifying opportunities to take part in the social activities specially for the welfare of the poorest of the poor. They can also organise social welfare activities in case of natural calamities. If they take part in the process, the opportunities are there to project a fair image. They can display there the posters and banners which would have a positive impact on their social image. Particularly, the leading foreign insurance companies where we do not find sincere and honest efforts commensurate with the social requirements, the policy makers need to make it sure that it gets due priority on their development agenda. Besides, the public sector insurance organisations have also to increase their contributions to the process of social transformation.

The sponsorship marketing as a component of promotion draws our attention on sponsoring events and donating the money received as revenue to the social organisations or institutions for which the same has been generated and mobilised. As and when we find cases of natural calamities or problem due to war refugees or some of the urgent problems not getting due attention of government policy makers or to help and strengthen an individual or a group of people; the insurance companies may organise special events and sponsor them. The expenses on organising of the events would be sponsored by that organisation but the revenues would be donated. Actually, it proves to be a place for promotion where masses come to know the positive contributions of that organisation.

The public and private both the sectors are now in the insurance business. Of course, we find them accepting it as a component of promotion but not so much sincere and honest in conceptualising or practising them in tune with their potentials. "Protect the Society" and promote the Business, they need priority attention on this slogan.

PRICE MIX

The pricing decision in the insurance business is found a bit different to other organisations. We consider it a delicate actuarial exercise. The insurance premium, which is the sales price, is collected before stipulated services which is claim. While making the pricing decisions, the adequacy of rate is an important consideration to enable insurance companies to pay claims and meet other expenses. The rate must be moderate or reasonable. There must be justifications for the rate we charge. It should not be so much excessive that makes your task of getting business much more difficult because the market is competitive. The rate must not be the same for hetro groups and must not be different for home groups. It should not be unfairly discriminatory. We should also think over simplicity because failing it our decisions may create doubts and confusions.

The pricing decisions in life insurance and non-life insurance cannot be identical. The life insurance adopts simple class rating systems whereas in the non-life business we find complicated several rating systems. In the pricing of life business, we find stability but we find more fluctuations in the non-life business. In the life insurance business, we do not find scope for "ifs and buts" because the claim is known in advance. In the non-life business, we find a stage of uncertainty.

We are well aware of the fact that legal environment considerably influences the pricing decisions. In the insurance sector in India, we have witnessed the process of privatisation which has also affected the pricing decisions. The conditions are now changed and therefore the organisations not fair in pricing will have to suffer a lot. This focuses our attention on a policy that is transparent and not creating any doubts in the minds of customers. At the same time, it is also essential that the pricing decisions are efficacious of meeting the organisational needs.

In the process of formulating the price mix for the insurance business, the decisions related to premium are found much more significant. The principle of equivalence followed by actuaries for setting fair premium helps insurance companies in meeting all costs such as claims costs, administrative costs, cost of obtaining the capital. In this context, we find the following equation:

$$P = E(S) + k + R$$

In the equation, E(S) represents for the mathematical expectation of claims, k denotes ongoing running costs and R is a risk premium for the coverage of unforeseen deviations in the claims amount to be paid. It is considered to be a standard pricing mechanism helping insurance companies in getting the normal profits.

In the General Insurance, we find Tariff Advisory Committee playing an important role which also revises the rates of premiums based on experiences of claims from different categories of risk insured. In the deregulated regime of insurance, we need a transparent pricing regime found equitable to both insurance and the insuring public. The establishment and servicing costs have to be kept to the minimum. A realistic rationalisation is felt essential to control the current high cost ratio of insurers. The fixed management expenses and cost of processing business need an optimal relation. A detariffed price regime will answer to the problem of imbalance pricing.

In the insurance business, the pricing decisions are concerned with the premium charged against the policies interest charged for defaulting the payment of premium and credit facilities, commission charged for underwriting and consultancy services. The formulation of pricing strategies becomes significant with the viewpoint of influencing the target market or prospects. To be more specific in the Indian context where the disposable income in the hands of prospects is found low, the increasing inflationary pressure has been instrumental in contracting the discretionary income, the increasing consumerism has been making an assault on the saving potentials of masses, it is pertinent that the insurance organisations in general and public sector insurance organisations in particular adopt such a strategy for pricing that makes it a motivational tool and paves the ways for increasing the insurance business. Of course, a motivational pricing stratgey is required to be given due weightage. This necessitates a new vision for setting premium structure and paying the bonus and charging the interest.

It is against this background that we find pricing decisions occupying a place of outstanding importance in the marketing of the insurance services. The strategy may have a new vision in the sense that the insurance organisations prefer to make a mix of high and low pricing strategy. To be more specific when we find the public sector insurance organisations instrumental in offering policies, schemes for the weaker sections, it is pertinent that the pricing strategy is rationalised to cater to the low paying capacity of the concerned segment. However, the insurance organisations would be required to think in favour of a high pricing strategy for the affluent section of the society. The motive is to make the premium structure commercially-viable so that the insurance organisations succeed in having a sound product portfolio besides fuelling development orientation.

In the tangible product, we find fixation or setting of prices on the basis of cost of production. Even in the insurance business, it is found to be an important consideration and a dominating base. This makes the cost of insurance a decisive factor for charging premium. The important bases for determining the cost are rate of death, rate of interest and the expenses incurred on the insurance business. The mortality table helps the determination of death rate. It is such data which records the past mortality and is put in such a form that can be used in estimating the course of future data. It is to predict future mortality. A majority of the persons are selected and observed for death and survival rates. The best method of construction of mortality table is to select a large number of persons at attained age which is meant age close to the birth rate. The second important element is the rate of interest. On the basis of mortality rate, it is estimated that when and how much amount is to be received as premium and would be paid as claims but on the basis of interest rate, it is estimated that how much interest can be earned by investing the insurance funds. The interest table is prepared for computing the rate of interest. The last element is cost which focuses on different types of expenses. There are certain expenses which are incurred at the time of inception of the policy. This necessitates determination of the nature of expenses.

In addition, we also find recurring expenses which are incurred every year and certain expenses incur only at the time of end of the policy. The determination of expenses according to occurrence and equal distribution of the expenses every year for equitable distribution of loading are found significant to make possible a sound management of expenses.

In view of the above, it is right to say that in the making of pricing decisions, the calculation of premium rate is influenced by a number of factors. The growing management and administration expenses or the increasing unproductive expenses/investments are proved to be a burden. Contrary to it, if the insurance funds are invested in the private companies the rate of profitability would multiply. The expenses to be incurred on policy also aggravate the cost of insurance. These facts make it esssential that the cost-effectiveness in the process of managing the expenses is made possible. We can't deny the fact that cost economy would make the ways for a rational price structure.

The pricing decisions make it essential that the insurers keep in their minds the nature of policy *vis-a-vis* the segment to which the prospects belong. An important task before the policy makers is to optimise the cost structure failing which the pricing decisions can't be rational. The insurance executives bear the responsibility of managing the pricing decisions in such a way that a rational premium structure is possible. There are a number of factors influencing the rate of premium, such as the positive developments in the socio-economic environment, growing healthcare facilities, rising standard of living of the masses, increasing discretionary income, increasing rate of literacy, attitudinal change in investors or so. The investment decisions of insurance organisations are also found instrumental in influencing the costs. The insurance organisations need to feel that to counter the rate of unproductive expenses, an important step is to promote the private investments which pave avenues for profitability. Just reverse, we find public sector insurance organisations concentrating on public sector investment which is not helping the cost optimisation process. This makes a two-tier arrangements, first the unproductive expenses should be rationalised and second, the avenues for private sector investments should be broadened.

An important dimension aggravating the cost of insurance is social costs. It is right to mention that being a public sector undertaking, the LIC of India and the GIC of India are expected to bear the social costs. Of course, it is essential to subserve the interests of backward regions and the weaker sections but we also need to maintain a balance. They are supposed to channelise their investments in the social development heads but it is not to be forgotten that mounting social costs is not to imbalance the entire process of price management. In tune with the principle of holistic concept of management and to be more specific in the face of the defined principles of social or societal marketing, the insurance organisations are supposed to rationalise the social costs. This necessitates a control on the government interference. Of course, we favour that public sector as well as the private sector organisations bear the responsibility of social costs but there must be a limit.

It is in this context that we talk about rationalising the social costs. Almost all the financial as well as the management experts feel that in the Indian perspective, the mounting social costs is found jeopardising the financial management of public sector organisations. This trend needs a departure. The LIC of India has been found promoting welfare in a big way by promoting the development-sensitive, welfare-oriented projects for the development of backward areas and the weaker sections. We are not opposed to it but can't favour channelisation of investments to the public sector.

The process of rate fixation in the insurance organisations is not so scientific that we can identify the cases of moral hazard. Of course, it is easier to identify the physical hazard but the task of identifying the moral hazard is found difficult. The premium charged is to be made rational to cater to the payment of claims on a priority basis including the catastrophic losses, management expenses and margin of profit. It is essential that various factors related to both the hazards are estimated in a scientific way. In addition, the tariff offices follow the collective system of tariff rating which is found in practice specially after the nationalisation of insurance companies. The actual process of rating consists of three steps, e.g., classification, discrimination and scheduling. We divide the properties into three main parts, such as common or ordinary, hazardous and doubly hazardous. The rate structure in the fire insurance is determined in three ways — personal judgement, tabulated experience and schedule. The fire insurance business is governed by the tariff formulated by the Tariff Advisory Committee which is a statutory body established under the provision of the Insurance (Amendment) Act 1968, specially to control and regulate the rates, advantages, terms and conditions that may be offered by the insurers in respect of General Insurance.

In past, there has been a phenomenal growth in the standard of living of the masses. The medicare facilities have also been found increasing to a considerable extent. The level of income shows a positive trend. These positive developments have made possible a sharp fall in the death rate. Particularly in the life insurance business, the rate of premium is directly linked to the death rate. Higher the death rate, higher the premium and lower the death rate, lower the premium are the principles to keep on moving the defined principle of fixing the premium. It is right to mention that these provisions are not taken into consideration while fixing the premium. We can't deny that death rate is coming down but the rate of premium is not showing a proportionate downward trend. This makes it essential that the policyholders are induced or motivated by rationalising the rate of premium. In this context, the important decision-making areas are:

- Making possible cost-effectiveness.
- Restructuring of premium.
- Due priority to profit generating investments.
- Rationalising or optimising the social costs.
- Paving avenues for channelising the productive investments.
- Assigning due weightage to the policies meant for the socially and economically backward classes.
- Making the ways for maximising profitability.

Place Mix

Another component of the marketing mix is related to the place decisions in which our focus would be on the two important facets—managing the insurance personnel and locating a branch. The management of agents and insurance personnel is found significant with the viewpoint of maintaining the norms for offering the services. This is also to process the services to the end-users in such a way that a gap between the services-promised and services-offered is bridged over. In a majority of the service generating organisations, such a gap is found existent which has been instrumental in generating and aggravating the image problem. The policy makers make provisions, the senior executives specify the standards and quality and the branch managers with the co-operation of front-line staff and others bear the responsibility of making available the promised services to the end users. The public sector insurance organisations have failed in both the areas. The agents, rural career agents, the front-line staff and even a majority of the branch managers become a party to the gap. Of late, the end-users feel that the Life Insurance Corporation of India and the various subsidiaries of the General Insurance Corporation of India have not been processing the services as promised and distortion is due to the fact that the employees serving the insurance organisations lack professional excellence. It is in this context that we go through both the problems.

The transformation of potential policyholders into the actual policyholders is a difficult task which depends upon the professional excellence of insurance personnel. The regulations governing the LIC and GIC of India require due weightage to the management of insurance personnel of different echelon. The agents and the rural career agents acting as a link lack professionalism. The front-line staff and the branch managers are found not assigning due weightage to the degeneration process. The trade unions dominate the scene and come ahead to protect their interests. If in a majority of the branches of the LIC and GIC, we don't find work culture, this is mainly due to the fact that the senior executives fail in managing the people. This draws our attention on the recruitment, training and development processes which with the passage of time need a change. We can't negate that the private insurance companies assign an overriding priority to this dimension which helps them substantially in managing the quality. The insurance personnel if not managed properly would make all of our efforts insensitive. Even if the policy makers make provisions for quality upgradation, the promised services hardly reach to the end-users. This makes it significant that the insurance organisations in general and the public sector insurance organisations in particular keep in their minds the changing expectations of customers/users and the prospects. The behavioural profile of insurance personnel is studied in a right fashion and the changes required due to the changing perception of expectation are incorporated.

In the Indian perspective, we find a critical situation. The rural segment is found neglected and while developing insurance agents or other personnel, the insurance professionals fail in making them professionally sound so that they could have an in-depth idea of the prospects living in the villages. The rural career agents need an intensive care since they are supposed to go to villages and inform, sense and persuade the prospects in an effective way.

It is essential that they have rural orientation and are well aware of the lifestyles of the prospects/users. We consider agents and the rural career agents as the leverspring or kingpin of the insurance business. They are required to be given adequate incentives to show their excellence. While recruiting agents, the branch managers need to prefer local persons and by conducting refresher courses to brush up their faculties so that they know the art of influencing the users/prospects. This would simplify the task of capitalising on the rural opportunities optimally. Of course, we find Career Agents Scheme, but it is also essential that they attain a satisfactory level of excellence. In addition to the agents, the front-line staff also need an intensive training programme. In a majority of the insurance branches, we find the front-line personnel not aware of the behavioural management that plays an effective role in bridging over the gap between the services-promised and services-offered. This makes it essential that an ongoing training programme is organised by the branch managers which focuses on the behavioural management.

Another important dimension of the place mix is related to the location of insurance branches. While locating branches, the branch managers need to consider a number of factors, such as smooth accessibility, availability of infrastructural facilities and the management of branch offices and premises. We can't deny the fact that smooth accessibility would help the insurance personnel and the users in reaching to the branches conveniently. The availability of infrastructural facilities draw our attention on all-weatherproof roads, power facilities, communication services or so. Since we make an advocacy in favour of using sophisticated information technologies by the insurance branch offices, it is impact generating that uninterrupted power facilities and communication services are available to the branches. In addition, it is also significant that the branch managers assign due weightage to the safety provisions. The places found of vulnerable nature should not be selected for the location of branch offices and the users' safety *vis-a-vis* the safety of insurance personnel and cash need due attention. The management of offices makes it significant that the branch managers are particular to the office furnishing, civic amenities and facilities, parking facilities and interior office decoration. The foreign insurance companies are found serious to this component of place management which helps them in attracting the users. We can't negate that almost all the branches of public sector insurance organisations are found mismanaged where these aspects don't get any significance. Besides, the management of premises is also an important component since of late the management experts make a strong advocacy in favour of aesthetic management for generating the work culture and motivating the users. The plantation, gardening, dustbin, drains, signposts are some of the important facets which make your premises attractive and healthy.

In view of the above, it is right to opine that the place management of insurance branch offices needs a new vision, a distinct approach and an innovative strategy. This is essential to make the workplace conducive, attractive, proactive to the generation of efficiency or so. The motives are to offer the promised services to the end-users without any distortion and making the branch offices a point of attraction. The branch managers need professional excellence to make place decisions productive.

EXTENDED MARKETING MIX IN INSURANCE

The insurance marketers bearing the responsibility of formulating a sound marketing mix for the insurance business need due attention on the additional three submixes as mentioned below:

Process

The insurance services are ultimately delivered to the policyholders but before offering, a number of formalities are to be completed by different persons responsible for that, of course, with the help of information and communication technologies now frequently used in the process. In the modern insurance business, we find a number of changes initiated and activated by the leading foreign insurance companies. The computer-based operations have virtually changed the functional character of insurance companies. The insurance services, no doubt, have actually revolutionised the process of offering. Speedy and correct issuance of document, expeditious disposal of insurance claims and proper accounting are with the help of new generation of technology. The processing must be on time and for that it is essential that both the technology and people are working properly. We agree with this view that with the use of new generation of technology, we find an increase in the operational flow of services. The insurance marketers need to make it sure that the promised quality of services reach to the users on time and even without any distortion. The front-line staff plays an important role in the delivery process because we find them directly related to the customers. Any gap in the process is to be bridged and for that the professionals have to make it sure that all the supporting infrastructural facilities are uninterruptly made available to the machines and equipments used in the process. The service delivery and the operating systems are the two important aspects influencing the desired and expected processing of services. The recent developments in the insurance sector have been simplifying the process of delivery as we also find doorstep delivery of services. In the techno-driven processing, we find much more scope for gap and therefore the marketing professionals need to be careful.

Physical Evidence and Attraction

Like the banking services, we find service environment instrumental even in the insurance sector. The tangible representation also need due care. The physical surroundings can provide tremendous opportunities to the insurance organisations for transmitting messages regarding the organisational objectives. The service environment where we find focus on exteriors and interiors provide to the professionals an opportunity to display where the customers and visitors come, witness and perceive the positives while encountering. The most important thing in this context is an opportunity to encounter. Because we find modern insurance offices equipped with a number techno-driven amenities and facilities, the professionals need to display and position them in such a way that the customers get an opportunity to view. The insurance marketers need to make it sure that machines and equipment are well maintained and operational. The faulty machines are to be removed from the sight.

The special layout and functionality are the two important dimensions drawing priority attention of insurance marketers. In the special layout, we find focus on furnishing, counters and potential machines and equipments, their arrangements and positioning found instrumental in creation of a positive image. In a true sense, the physical surroundings have an important bearing on the service fragrance.

Physical Attractions throw light on the different dimensions of personal care services. The physique, dresses, facial expression of marketing people are found helpful in the value addition process specially when we talk about the service ambience. The insurance people working in offices or interacting with the customers in the field need to look neat and clean, smart and attractive. The facial expression body language, dresses they wear assume a place of outstanding significance. The displays related to aesthetic sense add attractions and inject fragrance to the ambience. The insurance marketers cannot undermine these things while managing the ambience. Creation of a positive impression is essential and the service ambience simplifies the process of injecting service fragrance.

The People

Of late, the management scientists make a strong advocacy in favour of managing the insurance people because they recognise them as an important submix of the marketing mix. This focuses our attention on the development of world-class insurance professionals. Sophistication in the process of technological innovations makes the ways for the development of people in such a way that an organisation succeeds in making possible a productive utilisation of technologies already in use or likely to be used. The thematical requirements for insurance professionals change with a passage of time because technology develops and evolves. Almost all the echelons of management serving insurance organisation and specially the marketing people need to enrich their knowledge bank. Convincing people and thereafter persuading them, of course, appear to be a difficult task. We accept that during the yesterdecades, there have been multi-dimensional developments in the nature and character of information and communication technology. The professionals need to make it sure that people serving the organisation are well aware of the technology to be used.

The insurance business considerably rests on the performance of insurance advisors and agents. They bear the responsibility of transforming the potential customers into actual and habitual customers. The process of persuasion is found much more complicated particularly in the insurance business. This is due to the fact that potential customers in a majority of the cases perceive and nurture negative feelings about the insurance investment. This necessitates that advisors and agents have a high degree of communication excellence. Let them perceive that excellence is not an art but a habit. The insurance marketers in general need nurture this perception of excellence. Personal-touch-in-service necessitates transcendental priority for the insurance people. The insurance people in general need a sense of commitment and conviction.

With the development of satellite communication facilities, we find more sophistication in the process. It is against this background that the insurance organisations have been found making use of sophisticated information technologies to improve the quality of their services. The use of computers, microcomputers, fax machines, sophisticated telephonic services, e-mailing, internet and intranet services have been found throwing a big impact on the perception of quality of services. The foreign insurance companies and even the public sector insurance organisations have been found promoting the uses of technologies. This makes it essential that the insurance organisations also think in favour of developing personnel in line with the development and use of information technologies.

This gravitates our attention on the education and training facilities to the insurance personnel. The front-line staff as well as the branch managers are required to be given the training facilities so that they are in a position to make possible an effective use of the technologies. In a majority of the public sector undertakings, we find use of information technologies gaining momentum but the professionals managing the technologies lack excellence. They are not aware of the skill for managing the same which make the processes of productive use and quality upgradation almost futile. The Indian Railways, the Department of Posts, the Public Sector Banks and many others no doubt use technologies but professionals managing the same lack world-class excellence. This makes it essential that the insurance organisations make it sure that efficient professionals are available and they are offered training facilities before the installation of new generation of technologies. Almost all the echelons of management require training and development facilities. We can't deny the fact that the foreign insurance companies take it seriously and develop credentials of employees in the face of use of technology. This helps them in making possible a productive use of technology.

In view of the above, it is right to say that the insurance organisations bear the responsibility of developing the credentials of their employees. In this context, it is also significant that they think about the behavioural profile of insurance personnel. It is pertinent that the employees are well aware of the behavioural management. They know and understand the changing level of expectations of users and make sincere efforts to fulfil the same. In this context, it is also significant that the senior executives while recruiting, training and developing the insurance personnel make it sure that employees serving the organisation have a high behavioural profile in which empathy has been given due place. The psychological attributes become significant with the viewpoint of influencing the prospects or retaining the users. It is in this context that we need a rational plan for the development of insurance personnel.

RECOMMENDATIONS OF MALHOTRA COMMITTEE

The insurance sector required multi-dimensional reforms in the face of global developments and in this context, a Committee under the chairmanship of R.N. Malhotra (1994) recommended the following measures. The Bill was passed in 1999 and now the Insurance sector is privatised with entry of foreigners upto 26% holding. Accordingly, we find IRDA set up in 1999 and amended in 2002. The IRDA laid guidelines for ownership, management, commission, etc. for both the life and non-life companies. The major recommendations are the following:

1. Setting up of a strong and effective Insurance Regulatory Authority on the lines of SEBI for the capital market.
2. Registration of LIC as a company under the Companies Act and its paid-up capital be raised from ₹5 crore to ₹200 crore with government holding upto 50% only and the rest by public at large.
3. The zonal offices of LIC should have more powers. The decentralisation of decisions and authority be made possible.
4. The GIC should be allowed to function independently and all the four subsidiaries of GIC should work as independent companies.
5. The paid-up capital of GIC should be raised to ₹ 200 crore of which 50% should be held by the Government and the rest by private.
6. The mandatory investment of insurance funds in the government sector should be reduced in phases from 75% to 35%.
7. Entry of private and foreign companies be allowed into insurance business subject to certain guidelines.
8. Co-operative sector and Postal Departments may be permitted to undertake life insurance business.
9. All the insurance companies would have to transact a minimum business from the rural areas.
10. Tariff Advisory Committee should be linked from GIC and should function independently and should advice on tariff matters.
11. Computerisation of LIC and GIC and development of an MIS in both the officers be made possible.
12. The insurance companies should have freedom to assign right job to right purveyors who have training for the jobs.
13. Pension schemes should be linked to savings with some tax relief to pensioners.
14. The institution of Ombudsman should be set up to settle disputes on personal claims upto ₹ 5 lakh.

On the recommendations of Malhotra Committee, we find a number of reforms in the insurance sector but still a number of steps are to be taken to remove centralisation of decision and bureaucratisation of the administration. The market leaders LIC and GIC have virtually created a monopolistic condition. The government and policy makers need liberal attitudes to make the insurance business much more competitive.

INSURANCE MARKETING IN THE INDIAN ENVIRONMENT

Liberalisation has opened new vistas for the development of insurance business in the Indian perspective. The liberal provisions of IRDA 1999 opened doors for the entry of foreign insurance companies which made the business environment much more competitive and volatile. Bajaj Allianz, ICICI Lombard, IFFCO-Tokio, TATA AIG, ECGC, Royal Sundaram, New India, Oriental, National in the field of General Insurance and LIC, ICICI Prudential, Bajaj Allianz, HDFC Standard, Kotak Mahindra, Birla Sun Life in the field of life Insurance are the big players dominating the insurance sector. The life and non-life insurance business included in their product profile a number of innovative products. The 21st century thus exposed the insurance sector to numerous challenges. The era of liberalisation, privatisation, globalisation, and deregulation became instrumental in increasing the intensity of competition. This necessitated world-class professional excellence.

We cannot deny that ultimately corporatisation determines the race and pace of industralisation. The process of economic transformation cannot be accelerated if we find the corporate sector not evincing keen interests in the development of corporate culture. And the very success of corporate sector rests on the development of techniculture. The inventions and innovations in the field of technological advances resulted into the development of sophisticated technology of new generation and the techniculture started dominating the corporate sector. Since the process of economic transformation gained a rapid momentum, it was natural that the financial institutions get profitable opportunities for development. It was against this backdrop that we find new developments in the field of insurance sector.

On the one hand, we find big players in the insurance business while on the other hand we also find the traditionally managed insurance sector. The conceptualisation of marketing in the insurance sector was found new for the insurance organisations managed by the public sector. This helped the big foreign players to snatch the business from the LICI and GICI. Gradually, they realised the significance of innovative marketing and now we find even the public sector insurance organisations practising marketing, of course, not so much professionally-sound in comparison to their counterparts.

Though we cannot deny a positive change in the attitudes of potential customers in the Indian environment. Of late, we find people showing interests in insurance investments and therefore the public sector insurance organisations need to capitalise on the tremendous opportunities found due to high rate of economic transformation. They can do it very successfully if we find their efforts much more friendly to customers. This makes a strong advocacy in favour of innovative marketing.

It is right to mention that both the developed and developing countries do not face the identical problems. The magnitude of problem is found of high order specially in the developing countries. In the development-oriented, welfare-sensitive developing countries, the financial institutions are supposed to shoulder the financial burden on account of social costs, the making of marketing decisions of an organisation occupies a place of outstanding significance. If an organisation is financially sound, its capacity to subserve social interests multiplies like anything. In the Indian setting, the public sector banks and insurance organisations are supposed to play an important role in the emancipation of socio-economic development processes. The masses have high expectations from these public sector organisations. The backward regions and the weaker sections expect a lot from them. The development-sensitive industries depend upon them. If these institutions are financially solvent, the expectations of different segments of the society can be fulfilled optimally.

The changing corporate culture, the mounting domination of corporate sector and the upward moving consumerism have changed the hierarchy of needs *vis-a-vis* the lifestyles. The increasing use of sophisticated information technologies by the service generating organisations in general and the banking and insurance organisations in particular have changed the perception of customer services. Of late, we find more frequency in the product innovation processes. The race for quality upgradation is now found at its peak. The leading foreign insurance companies have been developing new perception of customer services. This has made the task much more difficult to the public sector insurance organisations.

The two aforesaid conditions make it essential that the public sector organisations in general and the banking and insurance organisations in particular, conceptualise innovative marketing to fulfil the expectations of different categories of users. It is against this background that we find it essential to focus on the marketing decisions since by innovative marketing decisions, an organisation succeeds in improving its financial health. We can't deny the fact that the public sector insurance organisations have not been successful in fulfilling the increasing expectations of their customers. The image problem is found increasing day by day. The users find it difficult to continue their business relations with the public sector insurance organisations since they feel that their counterparts using the services of foreign insurance companies, have been getting much more satisfaction from the quality of services offered to them. In a true sense, we don't find any exaggeration in the fact that the foreign insurance companies assign a transcendental priority to the customer services whereas the public sector insurance organisations don't consider it essential even to include the same in their agenda. This is found creating a quality gap between the services of the two. It is in this context that the public sector insurance organisations need to think in favour of managing the marketing activities, with the help and cooperation of world-class professionals. It is right to opine that professional excellence makes the ways for quality generation which plays a decisive role in building and projecting a positive image. This makes it essential that the insurance organisations think about conceptualising the holistic concept of management which assigns an overriding priority to societal marketing.

The nationalisation of Life Insurance in 1956 and of General Insurance in 1971 opened new vistas for the development of insurance business in the Indian perspective. The vulnerable areas, the weaker sections got substantial benefits after nationalisation. The policy makers realised the significance of promoting the insurance business in the rural areas and making their investment plans liberal to rural orientation. A sense of participation was promoted against all agents and insurance employees through discharge of their duties with dedication towards accomplishment of corporate objectives. The over ambitious objectives of the LIC of India necessitated a change in the management practices. The increasing domination of sophisticated information technologies in the foreign insurance companies necessitated multi-dimensional qualitative improvements in their business profile. This made it essential that even the public sector insurance organisations think in favour of technology-driven, user-friendly perception of insurance business.

The marketing management of an organisation plays a contributory role in fuelling the processes of qualitative-cum-quantitative improvements. This makes a strong advocacy in favour of managing the marketing activities of public sector insurance organisations. The different mixes are required to be innovated to cater to the changing needs and requirements of the different categories of users. The product mix necessitates a fair synchronisation of core and peripheral services, the product portfolio is required to be made optimal, the packages need due attention in the formulation process, the new services are required to be incorporated, the unprofitable services or schemes are required to be eliminated and the effective fulfillment of development needs require world-class insurance professionals who by making their decisions innovative are found successful in having a sound product mix. In addition, the promotion decisions also need a new vision, a distinct approach and a new strategy. The sophistication in the process of advertising, the creativity in advertisement messages and slogans, the well managed public relation activities, the innovative tools of sales promotion, the word-of-mouth communications, the personal selling, and the telemarketing need due attention of marketing executives. The premium, bonus, commission policies need to be made rational and the place decisions require due weightage. The management of insurance personnel requires an overriding priority and the physical attractions of insurance professionals are to be given due weightage. These developments can't be possible if we devalue the instrumentality of marketing in improving the quality and generating the profitability.

In view of the above, it is right to opine that the marketing practices need a new look, an innovative approach and the conceptualisation of the holistic concept of management can make it possible. The defined principles of social or societal marketing if practised in a right fashion would pave avenues for the blending of three important considerations, such as profit generation, customer satisfaction and social orientation. It is in this context that the public sector insurance organisations need to realise gravity of the situation and to assign an overriding priority to the management of marketing activities. The foreign insurance companies have been found making it possible and the public sector insurance organisations have been seen making efforts to conceptualise marketing. We cannot deny that the application of innovative marketing principles in the insurance organisations would make the ways for multi-dimensional positive developments.

The recommendations of Malhotra Committee focused on the contributions of insurance sector on the development of rural economy. In this context, the private sector insurance companies need to be much more positive. They need to ensure that their products not only remain confined to the urban areas but also pave avenues for rural orientation. Like the rural career agents in the public sector insurance, they have also to make provisions for the rural advisors who evince keen interests in rural welfare schemes. The IRDA Regulations 2000 make it compulsory for the insurer's existing and new to promote the social insurance.[18] Similar to the requirement for the rural sector, the regulations also prescribe for undertaking benchmark percentages for insurances in the social insurance sector for the players. The social sector is defined as including the unorganised sector, the informal sector, the economically vulnerable or backward classes and other categories of persons both in rural and urban areas.

The IRDA regulations 2000 make it compulsory for the insurers existing and new to promote the rural insurance.[19] The rural sector has been defined as a place which as per the latest Census, the population is not more than 5000, the density of population is not more than 400 per sq.km. and at least 75% of the male working population is engaged in agriculture.

In the years to come, the insurance business will grow at a faster rate. This in a natural way will increase the intensity of competition. The most important task before the LIC and GIC is to maintain and retain their leadership in the market. This makes it essential that they practise innovative marketing. Of course, the process of computerisation has been initiated in the public sector insurance organisations but we find a number of branches where techno-driven operation is still to be initiated. The management of information is also an important dimension and in this context, they need to practise Marketing Information System. It is not only significant that we initiate the process of computerisation. It is much more important that we find them working in a right order. The interrupted supply of power and frequent failures of communication network considerably harm the techno-driven operation. If we advocate for the use of new generation of technology, it is pertinent that we also make provisions for their smooth and speedy operation which sizeably rests on infrastructural penetration. Let's hope that in an age of techniculture, the insurance organisations in general strike a balance between organisational and social considerations.

SUMMARY

In this chapter, you have gone through different components of insurance marketing. Before starting another chapter, be sure that the following facts are well versed.

Insurance Marketing – The Concept: It is the application of marketing principles by the insurance organisations and to professionalise the process of marketing in such a way that the organisations start believing in the principle of making things happen.

Users of Insurance Services: We find different categories of users using the services of insurance organisations, such as the individuals and the institutions, the rural areas and the urban areas, the weaker sections and the affluents.

Behavioural Profile of Users: A study of the behavioural profile of insurance users focuses on the needs and requirements, lifestyles, attitudes and expectations.

Market Segmentation: It is a process of dividing and subdividing the market into different segments and sub-segments so that the insurance professionals find it convenient to study the changing level of expectations and formulate the marketing mix accordingly.

Marketing Information System: Innovation in the process of making the marketing decisions is found significant. A technology-driven information system makes the ways for an in-depth study of the behavioural profile of users and their hierarchy of needs and requirements.

Insurance Product Mix: An important task before the insurance professionals is to formulate such a service mix in which we find a fair blending of core and peripheral services. The packaging decisions and the product portfolio decisions are also found significant in the very context. The motive is to make the product mix of world-class which is found internationally-competitive.

The Promotion Mix: The different components of promotion mix, such as the advertising, public relations, sales promotion word-of-mouth communication, personal selling and telemarketing have been studied in the context of insurance business. Of course, we find all the components of promotion having a far reaching impact on the projection of a positive image *vis-a-vis* business expansion but personal selling, telemarketing, word-of-mouth communications need due attention of the insurance professionals.

The Price Mix: The decisions related to premium, bonus, fee are found important in the insurance business. The insurance professionals need to make pricing a motivational tool which requires a change in the governmental regulations.

The Place Mix: This draws our attention on two important issues, first regarding the channelisation of services and the second related to the location of insurance branches. The services must reach to the end-users on time. The places for the location of insurance offices are to be accessible, safe and equipped with all the supporting infrastructural facilities.

The Process: With the increasing importance of technology in the insurance organisations, the processing focuses our attention on right and time-honoured processing so that services are delivered to the end-users without any distortion. Proper handling and maintenance of machines and equipments are important in this context.

Physical Evidence and Attractions: The physical surroundings if attractive make the service environment much more productive. The exteriors and interiors also play here an important role. The positioning and placement of machines help in the creation of a positive impression. The service ambience adds additional attractions to the service environment.

In addition, the insurance people working either in offices or in field need to be well dressed, neat and clean and to look smart. The different dimensions of personal care services become significant in the very context.

The People: The insurance people working in different capacities are considered to be a bit different to others. This is due to the fact that they need to exercise much more creative efforts persuading and transforming the potential users of services. They should have an in-depth knowledge of the emerging trends in the insurance business. Besides, they also need personal-touch-in-services and value-based efforts.

KEY TERMS

IRDA	Autonomous Statutory Corporation
Group Linking Software	Rural Career Agents
Monopolistic Condition	Peripheral Services
Mapping	Perpetual Corpse
Disinvestment	Household Sector
Call Centre Technology	LGD Marketing
Yogakshema	Institutional Sector
Video Linking	Special Costs
Boardrooms	Crop Insurance
Cat Models	Physical Hazards
Automation	Cattle Insurance
Intranet, Extranet, Internet	Special Layout
Integrated Marketing Strategy	Attractive Package
E-Insurance	Physical Surroundings
Product Attractiveness	Database Management System
Marketing Information System	Service Ambience
Behavioural Profile	Data Warehouse
Information Inputs	Service Fragrance

Review Questions

1. What do you mean by Insurance Marketing? Throw light on the instrumentality of insurance marketing in promoting the insurance business.
2. State and explain the different categories of users of insurance services. Focus on their motives.
3. Explain the behavioural profile of insurance users. Discuss the different factors influencing their expectations.
4. Comment on the role of Marketing Information System in improving the quality of managerial decisions in the insurance business.

5. Defined Market Segmentation. Explain the significance of segmentation to the promotion of insurance business.
6. What do you mean by the Marketing Mix? Explain the different components of marketing mix for marketing the insurance services.
7. Define Insurance Product. Focus on the formulation of a sound product mix for the insurance business.
8. Throw light on the different components of promotion mix. Do you find telemarketing emerging as an effective tool of promotion? Define your arguments.
9. Write a note on the Insurance Pricing.
10. Explain the place mix for the insurance business.
11. Throw light on the different extended marketing mixes for the insurance services.
12. Write a note on the marketing of insurance services in the Indian perspective.
13. Explain the impact of technology on the insurance business.
14. Focus on the major recommendations of Malhotra Committee for multi-dimensional reforms in the insurance sector.

Application Exercises

1. Formulate a sound marketing mix for insurance services in the Indian perspective.
2. As a marketing professional, segment insurance marketers for having an in-depth knowledge of the behaviour of insurance services.
3. Design a Product Mix for the insurance business in an age of technology.
4. As a service marketer, justify the role of Marketing Information System for the insurance business.
5. Keeping in view the Indian conditions, design a promotion mix to be effective and cost-effective in the Rural India.
6. Practise the additional three Ps in the Insurance business in India.
7. Do you feel that insurance business in India requires adoption of new generation of technology? Comment as a marketing professional.
8. As a marketing professional, suggest the measures the LICI requires to improve the quality of services.
9. As an insurance marketer, comment on the role of designing interiors and exteriors of insurance offices for adding additional attractions to your services.

Endnotes

1. Sullivan M.P., *Bankers' Magazine*, Vol., 164, 1981, p. 27.
2. Kotler, P. *Marketing Management*, p. 29.
3. Cundiff, Still and Govoni, *Fundamentals of Modern Marketing*, p. 39.
4. *Ibid.*, p. 40.
5. *Ibid.*
6. *Ibid.*, p. 128.
7. Walters C. Glenn, *Consumer Behaviour*, 1978, pp. 7-17.
8. Report on the Hon'ble Mr. M.C. Chagla, Chairman of the Commission of Enquiry into the Affairs of the LIC of India, 1958, pp. 21-31.
9. *Information Technology*; IC 21, Insurance Institute of India, Mumbai, 2000.
10. *Ibid.*
11. Cundiff, Still and Govoni, *op. cit.*, p. 156.
12. Wrone Alderson; *Marketing Behaviour and Executive Action*, 1957, p. 274.
13. Insurance Ready Reckoner, 2008.
14. Warren K.E., Long-range Planning, *The Executive Viewpoint*, 1966, p. 5.
15. Kotler P., *op. cit.*, p. 76.
16. Thirty-third Report of the LIC of India for the year ended 31st March, 1990.
17. Raj Kumar, Life Insurance in Rural Areas: Problems and Solutions, *The Economic Studies,* Kolkata, 23/2, 1982, pp. 173-75.
18. IRDA Annexure *22-A*.
19. *Ibid.*

★★★

Mutual Funds Marketing

In a volatile business environment, we consider mutual funds the best option before the small investors.

Chapter Objectives

Introduction – Mutual Funds: The Conceptual Exposition – Mutual Funds Services: An Overview – Types of Mutual Funds – Mutual Funds Marketing: The Concept – Users of Mutual Funds Services and their Behavioural Profile – Market Segments for Mutual Funds – Managing Information for Mutual Funds Services – Marketing Mix for Mutual Funds Services – The Product Mix – The Promotion Mix – The Price Mix – The Place Mix – Process – Physical Evidence and Attractions – People – Mutual Funds Marketing in Indian Perspective – Summary – Key Terms – Review Questions – Application Exercises – Endnotes.

Learning Objectives

The motive of this chapter is to sensitise the readers to the various dimensions of mutual funds marketing. The readers need to develop their awareness of the users of services who generally come from the segment of small investors. Studying and understanding the expectations of customers and making efforts to fulfil them by practising the innovative marketing principles are the key areas the marketers come to know. The marketing professionals also need to practise marketing to get the desired results. An in-depth knowledge about the portfolio helps marketers in inducing the investors. The application of marketing not only instrumentalises the mobilisation of savings but also activates the channelisation of investments.

INTRODUCTION

Mobilisation of financial resources plays a catalytic role in accelerating the pace of economic transformation. It is much more significant that investors have profitable avenues for channelising their investments. Inculcating investment habit to the rural and semi-urban segments becomes essential to ensure participation of a majority of the people in the development process who lack awareness, expertise and are found risk-prone. Corporatisation with the help of mass participation in which albeit the small savers get an opportunity to make corporate investment is the main theme that we find in the Mutual Funds.

Associations or trusts of public members who wish to make investments in the financial instruments or assets of the business or corporate sector for the mutual benefits of its members are known as mutual funds. The funds collected from the members are invested in a diversified portfolio of financial assets with the motto of reducing risks and maximising income. Thus, we find Mutual Fund a concept of mutual help of subscribers for portfolio investment and management of these investments by the experts. We find it an important link between savings and capital market.

The accelerated pace of economic transformation paves avenues for the mobilisation of savings. The small savers in particular are found unaware of the avenues where they can channelise their savings. They have almost dismal risk bearing capacity. This necessitates expertise which they do not have. Thus, to cater to the increasing needs of the savings market, we find emergence of mutual funds services. Of course, it is not a new proposition in the Indian context because it was way back in 1964 that Unit Trust of India engineered a foundation for mutual funds services which since late 1980s have been found gaining popularity when the public sector banks following an amendment in Banking Regulation Act in 1983 empowered the RBI to permit the banks to carry on non-banking business and the process started in 1987. The beginning of 1990s opened new avenues for mutual funds when in 1993, it was found open even for private and foreign sectors.

New avenues, new institutions, big foreign players and the increasing financial requirements have made the business environment much more competitive. When we have new challenges and new opportunities, we find an acid test of our professional excellence. Since the results of economic transformation appear to be positive, the marketers by exercising their excellence can capitalise on the profitable opportunities. Informing, sensing, sensitising, persuading and transforming the potential small and rural investors into actual investors appears to be a challenging task particularly in the Indian perspective where insensitivity is found of high order. The marketing professionals with world-class excellence can turn the negatives into positives.

The emerging positive trends in the Mutual Funds, particularly generated and mobilised by the private and foreign players, are a testimony to this proposition that in the markets of today, the organisations facing the image problem suffer and contrary to it, the organisations protecting and promoting the interests of their customers thrive. Since the beginning of the 21st century, a number of new developments took place in the business environment of mutual funds. The three different categories of institutions engaged in the business of mutual funds such as UTI, Public sector and Private sector during the first seven years of 21st century show a very surprising result. If we make an analysis of the results, we find private sector contributing 82.5% Gross, 84.1% Net, Public sector contributing 11% Gross and 11.4% Net and UTI contributing 6.4% Gross and 4.2% Net to the process of resource mobilisation. What happened to UTI; what happened to public sector, of course their results create so many doubts in our minds. If we make an anatomy of their functional behaviour, it is almost clear that due to managerial deficiency and also due to their involvement in scams; they experienced an image problem and investors had a ready-made better option which turned things in their favour.

The above-mentioned facts make it clear that both the UTI and public sector need to conceptualise innovative marketing practices. Since we find positive trends in the Indian economy, they have a profitable market. Opportunities are already in the MFs market and opportunities will remain there even in future. Capitalising on the opportunities in a right fashion requires priority attention of UTI and public sector. They, of course, need professionalised approach, dedicated and committed efforts of fund managers and sincere and honest team of agents and advisors. The image problem is to be removed on a priority basis. The people of almost all the echelons of UTI and Public Sector Banks and insurance need an attitudinal change. If we do something concrete and if we contribute something positive; our efforts for sensitisation and persuasion are found result-oriented.

The innovative marketing practices thus may be an effective prescription. Let's hope that mutual funds marketers realise the problems in a right perspective and make sincere and honest efforts to conceptualise marketing with the help of professionals having world-class excellence. The mounting uncertainties in the national economy have been tempting savers for future investments. The mutual funds houses need to capitalise on the same.

MUTUAL FUNDS — THE CONCEPTUAL EXPOSITION

Mutual funds are trusts or associations of public members interested in making investments in the financial instruments or assets of the business sector or corporate sector for the mutual benefits of its members. We find it a concept for the mutual help of subscribers for portfolio investment and management of these investments by experts. The mutual funds are also considered a device to reduce risks and maximise their income and capital appreciation for distribution to its members on a *pro rata* basis. The mutual funds are set up under the Indian Trusts Act. The members collectively enjoy the benefits of expertise in investment by specialists. We find mutual funds an alternative savings avenue with a better rate of return linked to stock market movement. Enriching the knowledge bank of rural and small investors and making available to them the expertise services for minimising risks and maximising benefits are the prime objectives for which we find the mutual funds services. We also consider mutual funds a device to increase the mobilisation of investible funds of the community by pooling the resources of a large number of small savers for corporate investment. Mutual funds are also supposed to be a method including and promoting the savings and investment habits.

In view of the above, the following facts are observed regarding the conceptual framework of mutual funds:[1]

- Mutual funds are trusts or associations of public members.
- We find mutual funds a concept for the mutual benefits of its members.
- We consider it a device to reduce the risk in the process of channelising investments.
- Mutual funds are an alternative savings avenue.
- Mutual funds are a device to increase the mobilisation of investible funds of the community.
- We consider mutual funds a device to inculcate savings habits specially amongst the small and rural savers of the community.
- Mutual funds are regulated by the Indian Trusts Act but the Mutual Funds of UTI are partially managed by their own provisions.
- We find mutual funds a result of the amendment to the Banking Regulation Act 1983 which empowered the RBI to permit the banks to carry on non-banking business such as leasing, mutual etc., under Section 6 of this Act.
- Mutual funds are for both the national and offshore investors.

Thus, we find Mutual Fund an investment company pooling money from the shareholders and investing in diverse securities, viz., stocks, bonds and short-term money market instruments or other securities. We find "Fund Manager" playing an important role in the process and discharging the responsibility of trading the funds, realising capital gains or loss and collecting the dividend or interest income. The conceptual exposition would be much more clear with Figure 7.1.

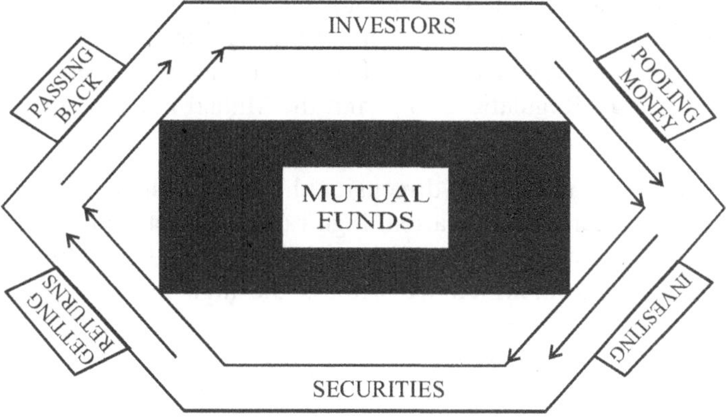

Fig. 7.1: Concept of Mutual Fund

The investors generally coming from small groups and also from rural areas with the help and co-operation of Agents, Advisors and Fund Manager channelise their investments in securities for getting the returns and then pass back the same to the investors. A majority of the investors are found unaware of the avenues where they can get a profitable return. This requires expertise knowledge and a Fund Manager makes available the same.

MUTUAL FUNDS SERVICES: AN OVERVIEW

As and when we find positive trends in the savings market, the new doors are opened for channelising the investments. The small savers also evince interests in making corporate investments both from the urban and rural areas. It is in this context that we talk about the mutual fund services. We consider it a process of investment for those savers who lack expertise of managing savings. Initially when the UTI entered in the business, this was confined to a particular segment. With the motto of tapping small savings, the UTI came with a few of the schemes such as Unit Scheme 1964, Unit Scheme 1971 (Unit-Linked Insurance Plan), Unit Scheme for Religious Trusts and Registered Societies (1981), Capital Gains Scheme (1983), Children's Gift Growth Fund Unit Scheme (1986) and Parents' Gift and Growth Fund Unit Scheme (1987); covering multi-segments of society. The monopolistic conditions of UTI continued till 1986. In 1987, a few Public Sector Banks and the Life Insurance and GIC of India entered the mutual funds business. In 1993, the private sector banks also entered in the business of mutual funds.

This in a very natural way made the market much more competitive. Of course, the economic liberalisation programme initiated and activated during late 1980s and 1990s made the business environment volatile. And against this backdrop, it was imperative to regulate the activities and SEBI came into existence. The three-tier objectives of the policy reform measures such as mobilising the resources, creating healthy competition and making ways for innovations helped development and consequently the mutual funds activities gained a rapid momentum. Creditibility to the positive developments goes to the policy reform measures. We cannot negate that the last two decades have proved to be a golden age for the development of national economy *vis-a-vis* the mutual funds.

With the entry of foreign players, the market was found dominated by the professionals having world-class excellence. It became inevitable that public sector banks and particularly the UTI also initiate innovative marketing practices. The foreign players were found successful in speeding up the resource mobilisation process and they virtually dominated the mutual funds business. However, the market witnessed a negative trend since 1996 and it was due to two important developments, first poor performance of UTI and second a number of scams in which banks and UTI were found involved. Thus, side-by-side, we find a downward trend in the business of banks and UTI and at the same time, an upward trend in the business of foreign players. It is right to mention that the domestic players were witnessing an image problem which created a favourable condition for the private and foreign players. In early 2002, a scheme was introduced for protecting the interests of investors and the UTI was also brought under the surveillance of SEBI like other mutual funds. In October 2002, the UTI was split into two parts such as UTI-I comprising US-64 and all assured return schemes which were taken over by the government under its own administration and UTI-II later renamed as UTI Mutual Fund taken over for private and professionalised management. This resulted into a number of qualitative improvements, e.g., organisational beef up, improved level of transparency, mergers of schemes, better risk management, delegation of powers and introduction of innovative product.

In April 2003, the SEBI allowed the Mutual Funds to invest in equity of listed overseas company provided they have a shareholding of at least 10% of the net assets of the fund in these securities. In 2005-06, the Mutual Funds were permitted to share the Unique Client Code of their schemes with their unitholders. Further in January 2006, SEBI amended the Mutual Funds Regulations to permit the Mutual Funds to introduce Gold Exchange Traded Fund Scheme.[2]

The multi-faceted steps resulted into multi-dimensional reforms, such as healthy regulations, structural transformation, increased level of resource mobilisation, high rate of investment and strict supervision and control of SEBI. The inclusion of foreign and domestic big players in the Mutual funds business increased the intensity of healthy competition and resulting from which we witness the high level of operational efficiency.

TYPES OF MUTUAL FUNDS

In the mutual funds houses, we find different types of mutual funds. The organisations issue them with diverse objectives. Some of the mutual funds are found close-ended. This focuses our attention on the mutual funds in which contributions from members are collected during a definite time-frame which may be for a few days or even for a few months. The "Cangrowth" was for a few days whereas the "Dhanraksha" of "LIC" was for a few months.

Another type of mutual funds is open-ended under which units are purchased and sold throughout the year and a member can enter the scheme any time or walk out of it also any time. We find those schemes of perpetual nature without an end in which each individual member enjoys the benefits of expert investment in the form of income growth, such as the UTI scheme of 1964.

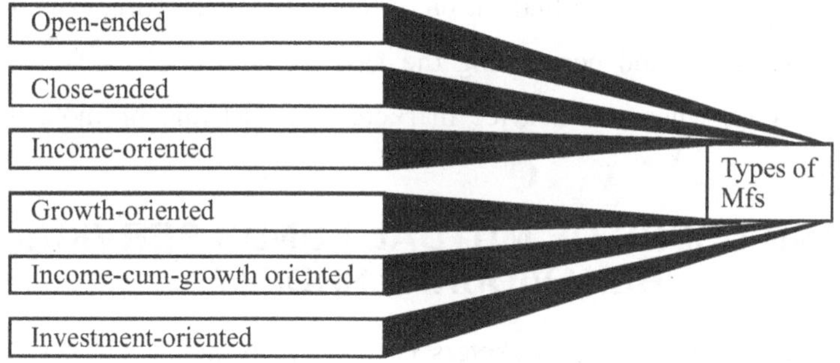

Fig. 7.2: Types of Mutual Funds

The mutual funds can also be classified into three more parts such as income-oriented, growth-oriented and income-cum-growth oriented. In the income-oriented mutual funds schemes, the motives of the members are confined to the maximisation of income whereas in the growth-oriented mutual funds schemes, we find focus on capital appreciation. In the third type of mutual funds scheme, we find a fair blending of both the motives because the members not only get the benefit of capital appreciation but in addition, they also get the income.

Even these funds can also be classified into various types, specially based on the pattern of investment, such as some of the mutual funds are invested in debentures alone or fixed interest securities like the government bonds and treasury bills whereas others may be invested in variable dividend securities like equities or shares of companies. A few may confine their investments in government and semi-government bonds; whereas a few may also confine to the real estate. In addition, we also find scope for investment in Art fund. The different types of mutual funds help marketers in identifying the defined objectives of members.

MUTUAL FUNDS MARKETING: THE CONCEPT

The conceptual exposition of Mutual funds marketing focuses our attention on the two different terminologies. When we talk about the mutual funds our focus is on trusts or associations of public members acting as an intermediary, regulated by the Indian Trusts Act with the motto of saving-mobilisation, investment penetration and income generation meant for both the national and offshore investors.

With the use of word Marketing, we find a change in the conceptual framework. Thus, the Mutual Funds Marketing draws our attention on the conceptualisation of marketing principles in the mutual funds operation. The professionals implementing the principles will be known as Mutual Funds Marketer and their operations will be called mutual funds marketing. Because we find Mutual Funds working as an industry, it is imperative that marketing of the services of Mutual Funds is given due weightage. The marketers bear the responsibility of sensitising the users and potential users of services. In addition, they are also supposed to protect and promote the interests of customers. In the Indian context where we find lack of awareness, the sensitisation process occupies a place of outstanding significance. The users of services and the potential users are to be educated, particularly those living in rural and semi-urban areas need an intensive care. In addition, it is also essential that organisational interests are well protected. Almost all categories of investors expect protection of money and further they also want profitable returns. The investors as well as the intermediaries have a legitimate right of promoting fair practices for multiplying their saving and investments. This task can be successfully done by the professionals having world-class excellence helps in accomplishing the organisational goals. Serving the customers and subserving organisations are the two opposite considerations which require a professional touch which can be made possible by the marketers. In the marketing process, we find interests of customers at the top and even in the mutual funds marketing, the interests of customers (members) are to be at the top. Satisfying the customers and creating and widening the market help mutual funds marketers in making the profits. The customers expect innovative services (product), they prefer cost-effective services and both are to be possible with the application of marketing.

In the Mutual Funds Marketing, we find correlation matrix significant where we find organisation, product and customer affecting the process. Sensitising and persuading the savers, channelising their investments into productive heads, generating the targeted returns and passing back the same to the savers to cycle and recycle the process are the areas to be successfully conceptualised by the service marketers.

- Mutual Funds Marketing is thus conceptualisation of innovative marketing principles in the MFs operations.
- It is a process of sensitising and persuading the savers.
- It is a managerial process where the service marketers protect and promote the interests of savers and intermediaries.

PROVIDERS AND USERS OF MUTUAL FUNDS SERVICES AND THEIR BEHAVIOURAL PROFILE

The first responsibility before the service marketers is to develop their awareness of the different categories of users of mutual funds services. It is but natural that the marketers will be successful in diagnosing the attitudinal differences which would make their decisions proactive.

Users of UTI: At the very outset, we talk about UTI, the pioneer in the field of mutual funds in India. It is right to mention that UTI has a larger range of customers coming from almost all the segments. They have products for rural savers and at the same time even for the urban and foreign savers. An institution working with development-cum-welfare orientation has schemes even for the retired and aged investors. The diversified ranges, the multi-segment customers and the mix of domestic as well as the foreign or offshore customers actually form a large group. Influencing, persuading and transforming them for making investments or say, pooling money from their pockets need professional excellence. The marketing professionals working there would be required to segment them and to make an anatomy of their behavioural profile. Sensitising the stimulants becomes too much difficult if we find an organisation experiencing the image problem. We cannot deny the long duration of services offered by UTI to the Indian community and even we cannot negate the contributions of UTI to the process of savings mobilisation and national economic transformation. But at the same time, they have been facing the problem of managerial deficiency. In addition, the image has also been aggravating the intensity of their problem. Because the intensity of problem is at its peak, the UTI needs a microscopic analysis of the behavioural profile of customers as only the right diagnosis makes our prescription right.

A study of savings behaviour makes it clear that there has been a significant increase in the levels of income of almost all the segments. It is also right that increasing or say mounting inflationary pressure has made an invasion on their disposable income. However, the savers and potential savers have willingness to save depending on the instrumentality of marketing professionals that how and in what way they persuade and transform. In this context, it is also pertinent to mention that savers specially coming from rural and semi-urban segments have a special temptation for UTI. Even minor efforts of professionals are to be effective in the transformation process. Innovative services and creative promotional efforts of UTI will be successful in accomplishing the organisational goals. The regulatory barriers need due care of the professionals in the entire process. If the savers feel themselves protected and expertise of fund managers help them in getting the profitable returns, the process of resource mobilisation would satisfactorily be recycled and geared. A registered portfolio manager under the SEBI Regulations 1993, considered as manager and marketer of offshore funds, needs to activate its portfolio management services.

Users of Public Sector Banks: In the public sector banks, the State Bank of India, Canara Bank, Punjab National Bank, Central Bank of India, Bank of Baroda, Bank of India and in the Insurance Sector, the LICI and GICI are found promoting their own mutual funds. They have investors from almost all the segments. With a change in regulations in 1992, we find beginning of a new era in the mutual funds business when the public sector banks were allowed to have their own MFs. Because the Indian customers in general have a high level of confidence on the public sector banks, the different schemes launched by different banks and institutions got a positive response. We are aware of the fact that mutual funds based on the pattern of their investments are classified into various types. Some of the funds are invested in debentures alone or in fixed assets securities like the Government Bonds and the Treasury Bills. The investments may also be in equities or share of companies. We also find a temptation for making investments in the real estate. We find investors even preferring to invest in government securities and bonds.

Thus, we find different categories of investors and different categories of MFs and therefore multi-pronged variations in their attitudes. An in-depth study of attitudes of investors and potential investors is found significant in the very context. But savers from any segment cannot make a compromise with the safety and moderate returns. It is also found that some of the government banks are in joint venture with some of the leading fund management companies. It is natural that banks working in the Indian conditions have an in-depth knowledge of the changing attitudes and therefore they know well about the levels of expectations of savers and potential savers. SBI Mutual Fund is a joint venture between the SBI and Society General Assets Management of France, one of the world's leading fund management companies and therefore the SBI would not have any problem while using the expertise services.

Users of Private Sector Banks: With Regulatory Reforms activated by SEBI in 1992, we find beginning of the entry of private sector and joint sector mutual funds since 1993. This broadened the mutual funds business in India. The important examples in this sector are Birla Sun Life Mutual Fund, Kotak Mahindra Mutual Fund, Reliance Mutual Fund, Tata Mutual Fund, HDFC Mutual Fund, JM Finance Mutual Fund.[3] It was natural that with the entry of private sector in the mutual funds business, we find a major change in the trends. On the one hand, the regulatory reforms initiated and activated by SEBI and on the other hand, the success of economic liberalisation programme of the government brought a positive change in the market behaviour. The private sector succeeded in getting a positive response and could win the heart and confidence of investors of almost all the segments.

Mutual Funds players coming from almost all the segments need to perceive that in the Indian business environment, they have tremendous opportunities. In a true sense, we find an attitudinal change which has been motivating savers for channelising investments in the shares and securities. The corporate sector has been found gaining popularity and the corporate culture has been taking a new shape.

The providers of services need to study the behavioural profile of users so that they are in a position to motivate them. We find users influenced by diverse motives. A few of the investors prefer high rate of return even the current income and the safety levels are low. There are also investors who prefer moderate current income and safety but high rate of return. We also find some of the investors interested in high level of safety of their funds even if they get not high but a moderate return. When we find investors investing in mixture of bonds, preference and common stocks, they want the current income and long-term growth in addition to the high rate of safety. On the other hand, when they invest in permissible stocks/debentures, they want tax reliefs and growth, the safety is high but the current income is moderate. Thus, we find a number of investors in the markets and the motives of investments are not identical.

The mutual fund marketers bear the responsibility of studying and understanding the changing behavioural profile of different categories of users. The two important dimensions are protecting the interests of investors and ensuring a profitable return. Since we find the business environment for mutual fund industry showing a positive trend, the marketing professionals on the basis of intensive survey would be in a position to identify their motives of channelising the investments. The investors, of course, are found adversely influenced by the scams but they believe that the various provisions of SEBI would protect their interests.

The mutual fund marketers have sufficient reasons to believe that today investors have enough funds and albeit positive attitudes for investing in different schemes. Choosing a portfolio is, of course, a difficult task and a portfolio manager having expertise in the related areas can help investors by suggesting to them the avenues for a productive investment. At the outset, they need to study their motives and thereafter to make efforts to convince them. The attitudes of government policy makers, emerging trends in the mutual funds market and the motives of investors are some of the factors drawing priority attention of portfolio managers, specially for pooling the money from the hands of investors.

Satisfying the users is the prime responsibility of service-providers. The marketing professionals serving UTI, public sector banks and insurance organisations need an intensive care because they lack professional excellence. Undoubtedly enough, the private sector has been found doing well in the mutual funds business. Studying the emerging trends in the business environment, identifying the attitudes of different categories of users, offering the innovative schemes commensurate with the changing needs and requirements of investors are some of the sensitive problems for which the fund and portfolio managers need adequate information.

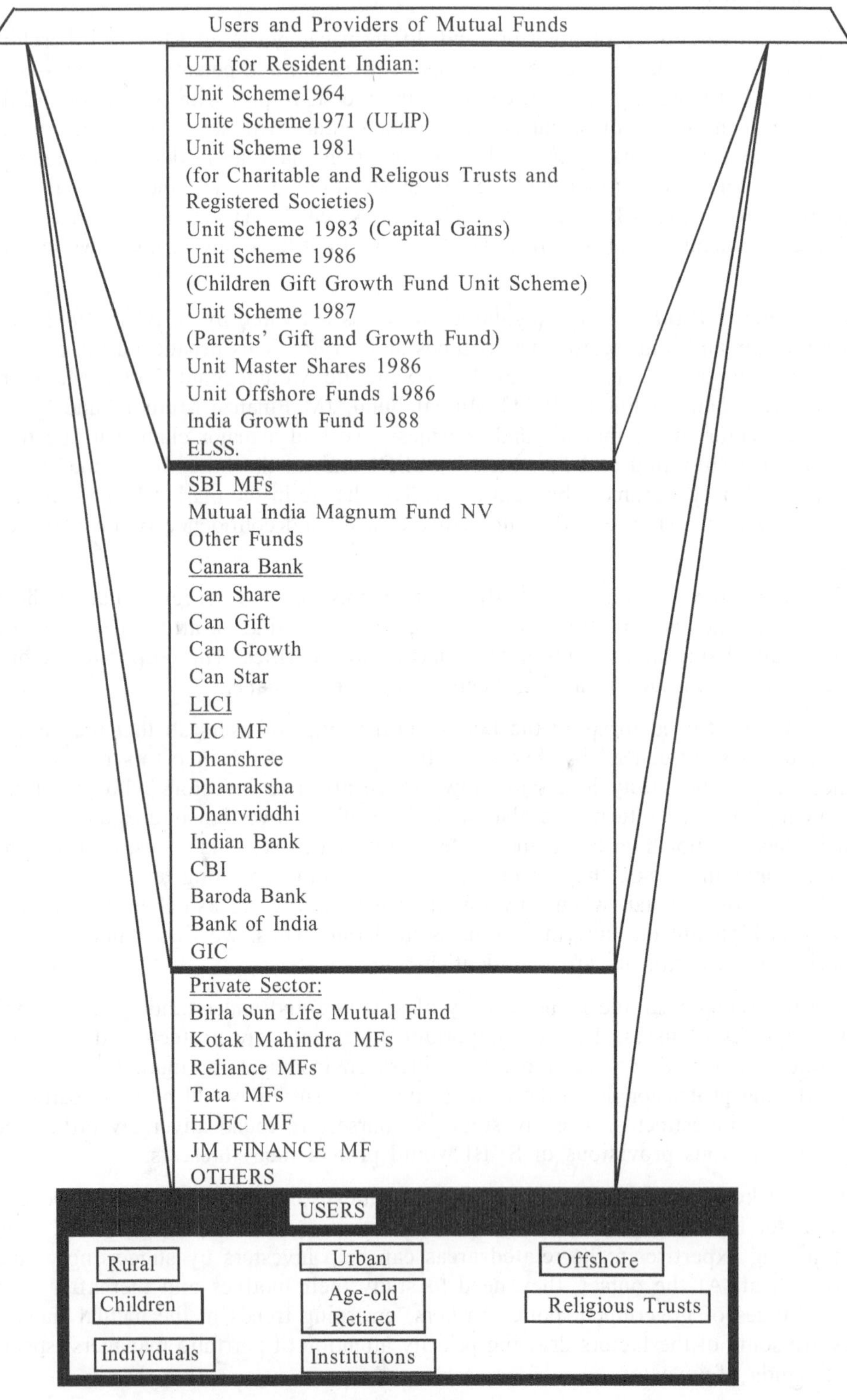

Fig. 7.3: Users and Providers of Mutual Funds

MARKET SEGMENTS FOR MUTUAL FUNDS

Studying and understanding the investors occupy a place of outstanding significance for speeding up the resource mobilisation process. The marketers have a different task of undertaking a survey so that they develop their awareness of the changing behavioural profile of investors. The markets for mutual funds cover almost all the segments investing their savings with diverse motives. If we find marketing professionals having an in-depth knowledge of their levels of expectations, they can make their marketing decisions much more proactive. It is in this context that we make a study of different segments.

Rural and Urban Investors: In the mutual funds, we find both the rural as well as the urban segments channelising their savings. In a majority of the cases, we find rural savers expecting much more safety of their investments. They do not prefer to invest in schemes where the safety provisions are low or the risk is high. They expect moderate return for their investments but the schemes having low profile of risks.

On the contrary, a majority of the urban investors prefer high rate of return for which they invest even in the schemes where the risk is high.

It is against this background that we find UTI MFs becoming much more popular particularly amongst the rural and semi-urban savers. So far as the urban savers are concerned, they prefer to invest in the ELSS of UTI and the Mutual Funds of private sector. The banks are found to be their second option.

Men and Women Investors: With corporatisation of Indian economy, we find some of the positive developments in the Indian savings market. There has been a significant increase in the number of working ladies specially in the corporate sector. This has resulted into an increase in the levels of income of married couples and unmarried women. The savings patterns in the income segment are found a bit different to the men segment. Women in general prefer to save but the risk bearing capacity of this segment is found relatively low. Since we find a significant increase in the number of middle class, the couples belonging to the middle class prefer to invest in funds making possible a high rate of return. For better future, they prefer even to bear high risk.

Investors of Different Age-groups: We find working couples making a saving plan for their children. On the other hand, the youths found unmarried and leading a single life show their temptation to the high rate of returns even if the risk factor is high. Normally, they prefer UTI or Banks long duration investments or private sector mutual funds. The senior citizens generally coming from the retired people segment have less risk bearing capacity and therefore they prefer to channelise their investments in the mutual having the lowest or dismal risk. They appear interested in return of short duration. The retired people belonging to pensionholder segment have a different temperament. Normally, they have less to save but for getting the tax benefits, they invest. The scheme offering tax reliefs get a positive response of this segment.

Return-based Investors: In the mutual funds, we find some of the schemes offering long-term return whereas some of the schemes have provisions for a short-term return. The mutual funds also include schemes having provisions for time-to-time regular return. The marketers are here required to divert their attention on the levels of income and in addition, the professions in which the investors are engaged. The burgeoning middle classs serving the corporate sector have temptation for long-term returns. They prefer high rate of returns; even the degree of risk is found high. The employees serving the public sector are found tempted to the schemes offered by the UTI and Public Sector Banks and LIC. But even in this segments we find investors preferring schemes offering tax reliefs.

Risk-prone Segment: We also find investors having the high risk bearing capacity. They are sensitive to high rate of returns and for that they have to bear the risk. The executive rank of corporate people prefer those schemes which can provide to them high rate of returns. They are found very tempted to those schemes which within the short duration can provide to them high rate of returns. They generally prefer the schemes of private sector mutual funds houses. Contrary to it the pensionholders or people serving the public sector and belonging to low income groups do not prefer those schemes which cover high risks.

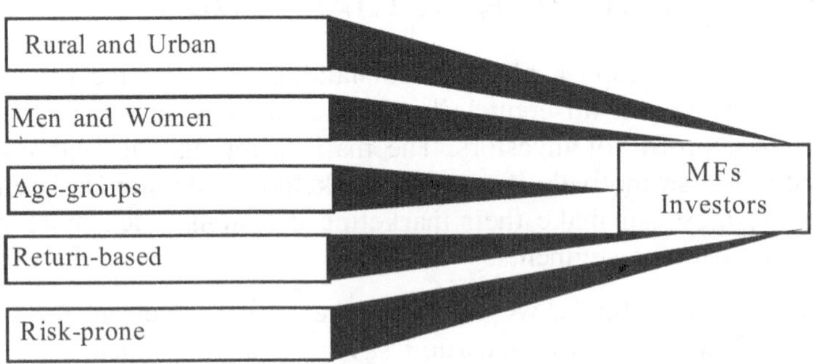

Fig. 7.4: Investors of Different Segments

Thus, the marketing professionals before formulating the marketing mix need to go through the changing attitudes of different segments. This helps them in making the marketing decisions result-oriented. The taste and temperament, likes and dislikes, the changing levels of income, the emerging trends in the economy are some of the factors influencing the behavioural profile. The marketers need an in-depth study of savings patterns on which the marketing of mutual funds rests.

MANAGING INFORMATION FOR MUTUAL FUND SERVICES

If you know about the customers, you know about the markets. And if you know about the markets, your decisions are proactive. The marketing managers bear the responsibility of developing their awareness of the customers. In the context of Mutual Funds Services, the fund managers and the portfolio managers are supposed to play a dominating role. They find tremendous opportunities in the Indian business environment but unless they have an in-depth knowledge of the emerging trends in the financial markets, whatsoever the decisions they make are found to be ineffective. The task of mobilising savings depends on our ability of identifying the attitudes of savers. The risk bearing capacity of all of the savers cannot be uniform. The expectations of all the savers cannot be identical. Of course, a majority of the savers expect a profitable return but we also find a segment that invests primarily with the motto of getting tax reliefs. The people engaged in processing the marketing activities need information related to all the segments of users.

The product must be innovative. A number of schemes are launched in the markets. Our schemes/services are to be competitive. We need to know about our rivals. The marketing professionals need right information not only about the savers but also about the emerging profitable avenues so that choice of a particular portfolio to be productive in result helps them in investment cycling and recycling. The information coming from stock markets, the information coming from savings market, the information coming from the financial institutions and the information coming from government policy makers cannot be overlooked to get the desired results and accomplish the organisational objectives. The process of resource mobilisation sizeably rests on information transmission. It is in this context that MF marketers need priority attention on the management of information related to the marketing decisions.

We live in an age of information technology and therefore it is easier to have time-honoured accessibility to the information. The UTI, LICI, GICI and Public Sector Banks need priority attention on the management of marketing information. Professional excellence of a portfolio manager or fund manager considerably depends on the quality of information made available to them. Of course, they have a big service network and therefore we find justifications even for the Marketing Information System. The leading private sector companies have a sophisticated information network. Besides, they also have a team of professionally-sound marketers.

The numbers of mutual fund houses are increasing as we find many of the foreign mutual funds setting up funds in India. We also find cases of mergers and acquisitions. Of course, the mutual funds have been taking shape of an industry and this makes a strong advocacy in favour of techno-driven information management. The quality of our decision rests on the quality of information made available in the process. The information system will also simplify the process of making an effective evaluation of the returns from the schemes. The redressal of grievances of investors will be much more easier with the networking of information.

MARKETING MIX FOR THE MUTUAL FUNDS SERVICES

In the mutual funds houses, the marketers play a decisive role. They bear the responsibility of formulating a sound marketing mix so that the processes of offering innovative services, application of creative promotional measures, smooth and convenient channelisation of services and further the pricing decisions help them in getting the desired results. It is against this backdrop that we go through the formulation of a marketing mix for the mutual funds services. In the mutual funds operations, we find involvement of a number of people at different stages and therefore, the people mix cannot be overlooked.

THE PRODUCT MIX

In any organisation, we find product assuming a place of outstanding significance. The mutual funds houses offer financial services found of tangible nature. This in a very natural way complicates the functional responsibility of marketing professionals. The business environment for mutual funds is found to be much more volatile. This is primarily due to the fact that in the stock market operations we find the intensity of competition almost at its peak. The rivals also make the market operations a place for unhealthy competition. The three big providers through which we find mutual funds operations are UTI, Public Sector Commercial Banks and LICI and GICI. In addition, we also find entry of private domestic and foreign players. While offering different types of schemes considered as the product of mutual funds industry, the intermediaries need to consider the interests of investors on a priority basis. On the one hand, the protection of invested funds and on the other hand, profitable returns on the invested funds make it essential that portfolio managers have made use of their expertise and professional excellence. Unlike banks and insurance companies, the mutual funds houses are supposed to shoulder a number of functional responsibilities. They do not have operational freedom as we find in banks and insurance companies.

The suitability of a product depends on the emerging market conditions. The schemes of mutual funds are to be investment-oriented. This necessitates a careful designing of the mutual funds schemes. The emerging trends in the stock markets need priority attention of marketers because a minor mistake in studying and understanding the market conditions may result in major losses. What are the existent trends in the stock markets and what trends are expected to emerge; the marketers need a right diagnosis. Besides, the emerging trends in the savings markets also draw attention of marketers. The segment to be targeted and the savings potentials of that segment need due weightage. The professionals need to establish a correlation between the market segments and investment instruments. The new product of mutual funds not considering savings and investment behaviour would be found much more risky. The different segments have different levels of expectations, such as some of them expect high rate of return whereas some of the segments expect regular income. We also find segments interested in getting the tax reliefs.

In some of the segments, we find investors expecting much more safety to their funds. The marketers need to identify avenues that how and in what way, they can fulfil the expectations of investors. Since we find SEBI regulating the operations of mutual funds, it is also to be made sure that provisions of regulations are given due weightage while formulating the product mix.

In the process of designing a sound product, it is pertinent that mutual funds marketers intensify market research to develop their awareness of the changing levels of expectations of investors. The future trends are to be forecasted specially related to the stock markets. The emerging trends in national economy, the political activities, global relationships, stability or instability of government, pace of corporatisation are some of the factors guiding the behaviour of stock market. The marketers on the basis of intensive research of different segments would be in a position to forecast the future trend.

The different processes for the development of product are to be followed before final launching of the product. Right from the screening of ideas to the testing product, the marketers need an intensive care. Since we find SEBI imposing controls on the mutual funds, the professionals have to make it sure that schemes and their provisions are not making an invasion on regulations. The emerging trends in demand and the changing attitudes of investors would help marketers in different ways.

Professionals also need to show their excellence while selecting a brand name. The related segments, inherent benefits of the schemes, objectives of investment and loyalty of customers are found important in the very context. In a true sense, the name of a product will convey the segment for which the product is meant. If the products are related to the child segment, the brand name explains it, viz., Children's Gift Growth Fund Unit Scheme for the segment of children, Unit Offshore Funds, India Growth Fund for Non-resident Indians, Can Gift of Canara Bank, Unit Scheme 1981 for Charitable Trusts and Registered Societies are some of them. The marketers need to realise that name conveys the features, the properties, the benefits so that the task of promotion becomes easier.

The marketing professionals cannot undermine the interests of tax payers who invest with the motto of getting the tax reliefs. They have to follow the provisions of SEBI and to offer product under the different sections covering tax benefits. The timing of launching of the product is found significant in this context.

In the process of formulating a sound product mix, the marketers are required to divert their attention also on the rural segment so that mass participation in the resource mobilisation and investment channelisation help accelerating the process of national economic transformation.

The product mix must be innovative and competitive. The elimination and inclusion process need due care. The regulatory barriers cannot be undermined. The multi-faceted interests of different segments are required to be protected and promoted.

THE PROMOTION MIX

The mutual funds marketers need to develop their awareness of the promotional measures so that they are efficacious of informing, sensing, sensitising, persuading and transforming the potential investors into actual and habitual investors. It is not only sufficient that the innovative and competitive schemes equipped with so many features are launched and available. It is much more impact generating that we activate the promotional measures and for that purpose develop a sound promotion mix. Effectiveness and cost-effectiveness are the two important considerations in the development of a sound promotion mix. It is natural that the investors of different segments are not equally sensitive and receptive. Highly educated segment and rural segment cannot be equally receptive. The child segment would expect in a different way and the senior citizens would expect in a different way. Keeping in view their levels of sensitivity, the creative promotional measures are to be adopted.

While advertising, it is to be made sure that messages, posters, campaigns have a correlation with the segment. If we find the scheme for the women segment, the selection of magazines, newspapers in tune with the taste and temperament of women is found essential. If we find our schemes for the child and senior citizens; we should advertise in the concerned magazines preferred by them. The print media, of course, have an edge over others specially when we talk about promoting the mutual funds services. The sensitisation process would be found much more effective if we make use of electronics media specially for the rural segment. The marketers need to make it sure that advertisement materials make available to the investors all the required information they need. The timing and selection of media need due care of professionals.

In the mutual funds promotion, the marketers also need to practise publicity because this will help them in many ways. The outstanding features of a particular scheme need to be narrated. The academics and media people are to be impressed. The characters having a positive image are to be approached. The public relations activities have a special bearing on the transformation process. Because we find it a non-paid form of persuasive communication, the marketers need to make use of this component even for the mutual funds industry.

The schemes for sales promotion need much more precautions. The incentives to investors and agents or advisors must be in tune with the regulatory provisions. The marketing people promoting the business need to furnish right information to the investors and potential investors.

The personal selling measures need due attention of marketing professionals because the agents or advisors play a very effective role in influencing the investors and promoting the business. They need high communicative ability to narrate facts and influence investors. The confusions regarding the schemes must be removed. Because the intensity of competition is high, it is pertinent that this component of promotion draws priority attention of UTI, Banks, LICI and GICI so that their agents and advisors initiate and activate the promotional measures in an effective way.

Promoting through telemarketing cannot be undermined because the telemarketers with the sophisticated audio-visual facilities would only not furnish the required information but would also be helpful in removing the confusions of potential investors.

The word-of-mouth promotion moves in its own way. If the mutual funds product/schemes or services are found offering to the investor's profitable returns, the concerned investors become your promoters. They virtually start acting as a hidden salesforce. In addition, the behavioural profile of your agents and advisors directly related to the investors also influence the word-of-mouth promotion. This speaks of the fact that fund managers and portfolio managers play a decisive role in the mutual funds operations. The decisions they have taken and the responses they get prove to be an indicator for activating the word-of-mouth communication.

The SEBI has some guidelines for promotion in general and advertisement in particular. The concerned providers while advertising need not to forget the following:

- Advertisement should be truthful, fair and clear.
- Advertisement should not be exaggerated or misleading. It should be factually correct.
- While advertising, they should not make any promise or guarantee of income of appreciation or other gains.
- Product advertisement should not refer to corporate performance.
- Advertisement should not contain glorifications or non-factual titles.
- No models, celebrities or financial characters should be displayed in the proposals.
- No incentives should be given with the motto of special favour.

The promotional measures must be effective and cost-effective. Creativity needs an intensive care specially when we find the potential investors very conscious. Sensitising the target investors is found significant in the very context. The marketers need to keep into consideration the motives or hidden motives of investors and potential investors. The emerging trends indicate that a majority of the investors have been found interested in getting the tax reliefs. It is also found that some of the investors have developed their temptation for long-term investments fetching profitable returns. The risk bearing capacity of investors is also found moving upward.

The marketing professionals need to develop a sound promotion mix. The weightage of a particular component of promotion depends on the situational requirements. But it is almost clear that in an age of advanced print technology, the print media can be useful to professionals in many ways. Either for transmitting information or for persuasion, the print media have an edge over others specially for the mutual funds industry.

THE PRICE MIX

In the marketing process, the pricing decisions assume an important position. We find mutual funds houses, of course, taking the shape of an industry but the results coming from the investments are influenced by a myriad of factors found instrumental in the business environment. The SEBI governs the operations of mutual funds and therefore we do not find much more options before the marketers to influence the process. The purchasing and selling prices of units/shares are the important dimensions of pricing policy of mutual funds. The RBI guidelines clarify that the maximum spread between the purchase and selling prices of units or shares should not be more than 5%. Further, it is also mentioned that the total cost of managing any scheme under a fund, including management fees and other administrative costs should be kept within 5% of the total income of the scheme. The SEBI regulations clarify that the Asset Management Company may charge the mutual fund with investment management and advisory fees which should have been disclosed fully in the prospectus subject to the following ceilings:[4]

(a) 1.25% of the weekly average net assets outstanding in the current year for the scheme concerned as long as the net assets do not exceed ₹ 100 crore, and

(b) 1% of the excess amount over ₹ 100 crore where net assets so calculated exceed ₹ 100 crore.

In addition, the Asset Management Company may charge the MFs with the following expenses:

(a) mutual issue costs of sponsoring the fund and its schemes,

(b) recurring expenses including:

(i) marketing and selling expenses, agent's commission, if any,

(ii) brokerage and transaction cost, and

(iii) registrar services for transfer of shares sold or redeemed.

The fees payable to the trustees shall be charged to the mutual funds and the fees payable to the custodian for safe keeping of fund assets and related matter shall be charg to the mutual fund. The initial issue expenses should not exceed 6% of the funds raised under each scheme. In any case, the total of all the expenses charged to the fund except the initial issue expenses should not exceed 3% of the weekly average net assets outstanding during the current year and the same shall be disclosed through advertisement, accounts, etc. All expenses should be clearly identified and appropriately attributed to the individual schemes. All mutual funds must distribute a minimum of 90% of their profits in any given year.

It is right to mention that the prices of mutual funds are inextricably linked with returns. In this context, it is also important to know about the face value of the units of mutual funds. In the pricing, we include incentives, brokerages, agency commission and other expenses such as registrar services, marketing and selling expenses. The value of a share of the mutual fund known as the NAV (Net Asset Value) is calculated on the daily basis on the total value of the fund divided by the number of shares purchased by investors.[5] Calculating NAV of mutual fund is found easy. At the outset, we take the current market value of the fund's net assets which are securities held by the fund minus any liabilities and divide by the number of shares outstanding. SEBI has approved a standard format for prospectus and specified the procedures of calculating the NAV.

NAV = (Market Value of Securities held under scheme – liabilities of the scheme)/Number of units outstanding under the scheme.

The SEBI has made it mandatory to the mutual funds houses to publish NAV weekly.

The above-mentioned facts make it clear that the pricing decisions in the mutual funds industry are governed by a number of factors. As and when we find an increase in the different costs as mentioned above, its direct impact would be on the pricing decisions. Since the market is competitive, it is pertinent that fund managers regulate the expenses. Making the process cost-effective appears to be an effective prescription for minimising the cost *vis-à-vis* the price.

There are a number of measures which may bring down the costs on the management of mutual funds. So far as the costs on agent's commission and brokerage are concerned, we cannot make an advocacy in favour of a drastic cut because they actually play a decisive role in pooling the money from the pockets of investors. But we find avenues for minimising the establishment costs. The fees to be paid to the trustees are also to be rationalised. In addition, the fees payable to the custodians for safe keeping of fund assets and related matters also draw our attention. The main thing is to bring down the costs to the extent it is not going to influence the processes of savings mobilisation *vis-à-vis* the investments channelisation.

THE PLACE MIX

The mutual funds services pass through different channels. The fund managers play an important role particularly while pooling the money from the pockets of investors/customers. They need to play a role of professional so that the investors are found satisfied and impressed upon. The impulse investment acts as a stimulant for persuasion. The investors in a very natural way are interested in getting high rate of returns from their investments. An in-depth study of portfolio is found significant in the very context. The portfolio managers with the help of Sharpe Index Model would be in a position to assess that which of the investments would provide high rate of returns. The fund managers are supposed to know about the potentials existent in a portfolio. Actually, we find Sharpe Index Model[6] also helping an investor in knowing the fate of their investments.

We are well aware of the fact that success rate of mutual funds is considerably influenced by the channel of distribution selected for channelising the investments. The providers of services are the UTI, LICI, GICI and the Public Sector Commercial Banks and the private sector companies. They with the help of fund managers, portfolio managers make available the services to the investors. On the other hand, they are also supposed to have a correct idea of the changing market behaviour specially to diagnose that which of the portfolio is to get the profitable returns. We also find one more stage when the profitable returns are passed back to the investors.

Thus, we find both upward and downward behaviour of channels for offering the mutual funds services. We cannot negate that the study of changing market behaviour helps fund managers and portfolio managers in coming to a right conclusion. With the help of Figure 7.5, we can perceive the channels for the distribution of mutual funds services.

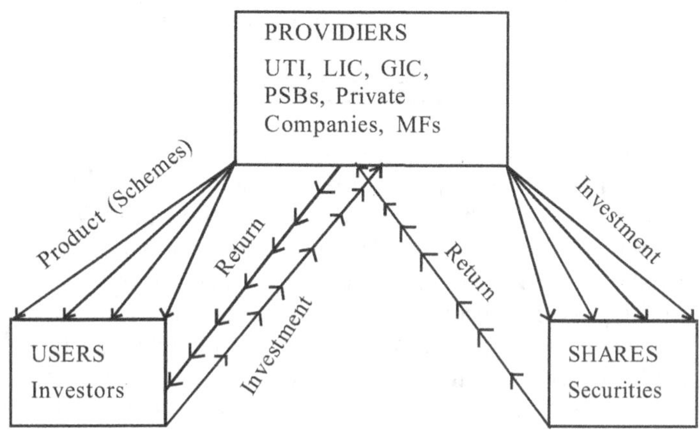

Fig. 7.5: Channels for Mutual Funds Services

Thus, the most important role in the collection process is played by the agents and advisors of the concerned organisation. They bear the responsibility of motivating the investors and potential investors. After the selection of mutual funds schemes by the investors, the fund managers and portfolio managers play an outstanding role. With the help of a sound market information system, they can help investors in the decision-making process.

PROCESS

The mutual funds services are processed with the help of a team of people at different levels and stages. The services start from the providers who are UTI, LIC, GIC public sector banks and private companies and reach to the ultimate users considered as members who buy the product normally through agents and advisors. This is one way of processing. Another way is related to the payment of returns to the users of services. The money invested by the users in the mutual funds schemes are channelised into shares, securities, debentures and bonds. Here, we also find processing determining the future of mutual funds. The fund managers with the help of expertise services of portfolio managers invest in portfolio expected to be profitable. Now, the last process is found related with the payment of returns to the members. The concerned users get the returns from the providers where the funds have been invested.

This makes it clear that the mutual funds services considerably depends on the performance of intermediaries involved in the process. The marketing professionals bear the responsibility of managing the intermediaries in such a way that the users feel themselves satisfied. Of course, we also find use of technologies for the processing of services, especially when the investors' funds reach to the providers. But the most important thing in the processing is related to the instrumentality of agents or advisors working for the providers. The role of funds manager and the involvement of agents or advisors and in addition their behavioural profile plays a significant role in determining the services quality. But different to other industries, we find processing of mutual funds services sizeably governed by the efficiency of people working in different capacities.

Right processing, time-honoured processing, techno-supported processing, information-based processing of mutual funds services draw priority attention of professionals.

PHYSICAL EVIDENCE AND ATTRACTIONS

Because the services are delivered by the agents and advisors at the doorsteps of the users, we find this submix of marketing mix not so much significant to the mutual funds services. However, we can make them partially effective specially when we talk about the role of exteriors and interiors or the physical surroundings of the offices where services take a shape. The users occasionally may visit the offices where the surroundings may create a positive impression. The agents and advisors and the marketing people having face-to-face communication with the users need to look impressive. The dresses used by them, their body language and physique throw a positive impact on the users of services. They should assign due weightage to the different dimensions of personal care instrumental in adding additional attractions to the services. The impression of your organisation depends on the impression that you create with the help of personal care services.

THE PEOPLE

Like other services, the mutual funds services also rest on the levels of efficiency of people serving the mutual funds operations in different capacities at the different stages. Particularly when the users of services are found unaware of the product (schemes), the marketers are supposed to play a meaningful role. In a majority of the cases, we find users of mutual funds services lacking right information about the profitable avenues for investments and the degree of risk involved in the investment. Inadequate information regarding the portfolio makes it essential that the people working as intermediaries and agents and advisors make available to them the right information on time. This is possible when they have an in-depth knowledge of portfolio. Thus, the first thing that we find essential for people focuses our attention on the knowledge bank of intermediaries. The emerging trends in the share markets, the fair and unfair practices in the markets, the portfolio bearing high potentials and the portfolio bearing high magnitude of risks are some of the key factors for communicating and motivating the investors. The thematically competence of marketers simplifies the process of persuasion.

The agents and advisors working for mutual funds services play the role of an informer. This is the first stage from where we find investors and potential investors knowing about the product of mutual funds houses. If the performance level of past investments is satisfactory and the investors are found satisfied with the returns they have received in past, the task of agents and advisors is found easier. Contrary to it, they find it difficult to persuade the investors when the organisation has been facing the image problem due to unfair practices or scams. The agents and advisors virtually act as a personal seller. This makes it essential that marketing professionals organise short-term training programmes or refresher courses to brush up their knowledge. The agents or advisors find it difficult to persuade the investors coming from rural background or semi-urban town and cities. If they have done their home task of building relationships with the investors, the persuasion process is found effective. The agents and advisors need to verse themselves preferably in the regional languages which would help them in showing personal-touch-in-service. The sincerity and honesty, personal commitment, personal-touch-in-service high communicative ability and high degree of resistance power help them in persuading the investors.

The fund managers responsible for managing funds coming from different schemes also play an important role. They need coordination with the agents and advisors as well as with the portfolio managers. The time-lag between the funds coming from the investors and getting them channelised in the shares and securities need to be minimised. With the help of information system, they can document information received from different sources. The fund managers act as an important intermediary.

Portfolio managers are the professionals rendering services for the management of portfolio of anybody, namely, clients or customers with the help of experts in Investment Advisory Services. An individual or an organisation can make use of the services of portfolio managers. The organisations offering mutual funds services also use the services of portfolio managers. In this context, we need not to forget the guidelines of SEBI which has given permission to Merchant Bankers of category I to do portfolio management. Only those who are registered and pay the required license fee are eligible to operate as portfolio managers. SEBI has prohibited the portfolio managers to assume any risk on behalf of the client. They are also not permitted to assure any fixed return to the client. The SEBI has imposed a number of obligations and a code of conduct on them.

In the management of people for the mutual funds services, we cannot negate the outstanding role of portfolio managers. The providers of the services lack expertise in the concerned areas. In this context, it is pertinent that they make use of the services of portfolio managers who would help them in many ways. In the mutual funds operations, the portfolio managers evaluate the performance of portfolio and identify the sources of strengths and weaknesses. The evaluation of portfolio provides a feedback about the performance to evolve a better management strategy. Of course, the evaluation of the performance of portfolio is found to be the last stage in the process but it makes ways for future investments. A number of managed portfolios are found in the capital market.

The above-mentioned facts make it clear that mutual funds houses need to have quality people because only a team of dedicated and committed people can help them in the process of persuading investors, getting funds from them, channelising their investments and making available to them the profitable returns. The users appear interested in getting the profitable returns. Making use of professionalised services in such a manner that they are further induced and the processes of savings mobilisation and investments channelisation keep on moving.

The government policy makers are also interested in promoting mutual funds operations. It is against this background that we find provisions for tax reliefs. The recently announced Equity Linked Savings Scheme (ELSS) is a staunch testimony to this proposition. The LIC and GIC have additional benefits of insurance cover. Now, the UTI has also received equal status for tax purposes. Thus, we find tremendous opportunities in the markets.

Despite fluctuating trends in the stock markets, we find good auguries in the national economy of India. In the face of mounting uncertainties in the economy, the masses are found tempted to savings. The people working in different capacities determine the speed of savings mobilisation. The professionals are required to show their excellence which would be an acid test of their managerial proficiency. If they keep on moving the process of maximising their returns, the channelisation of investments cannot be denied.

MUTUAL FUNDS MARKETING IN INDIAN PERSPECTIVE

In the Indian economy, the contours of development have undergone radical changes, particularly after the economic liberalisation programme initiated and activated during and after 1990s. The economic reforms have affected almost all segments of national economy and resulting from which the savings markets, money markets and stock markets have witnessed multi-dimensional qualitative-cum-quantitative improvements. The general masses are found tempted to the stock markets because there has been a significant increase in their levels of income. The policy reforms influenced the savings patterns and to meet the increasing financial requirements of national economy, the banks and other financial institutions brought a basic change in their investment patterns. It was against this backdrop that the emerging positive trends in the stock markets just within the span of two years (from January 2006 to January 2008) made possible a galloping increase in the sensex from 10,000 to 21,000. As and when we find a sharp increase in the markets, we also apprehend a sharp fall. The results of worldwide economic depression considerably affected the Indian stock markets and the development journey witnessed a negative trend. The sensex started moving downward and the investors started witnessing a number of uncertainties and threats. However, we expect reversal in the trend.

The mutual funds taking the shape of an industry sizeably rest on the savings behaviour. The increasing levels of income make the ways for mobilisation of savings. We cannot negate that the emerging corporate sector and developing corporate culture made possible a significant increase in the levels of income of general masses. The government policy makers with the motto of mobilising small savings in particular made provisions for tax reliefs and a number of mutual funds schemes were preferred by the savers specially for getting the tax reliefs. The significant changes in the provisions of SEBI engineered a sound foundation for the development of mutual funds houses and thus not only the UTI but in addition, the public sector banks, LIC and GIC also started offering the mutual funds services. Further with the beginning of the decade 1990s, the SEBI opened doors even for the private sector companies for taking part in the mutual funds operations. This in a very natural way accelerated the pace of savings mobilisation *vis-à-vis* national economic transformation because the process of investment channelisation gained a rapid momentum.

The UTI considered pioneer in the mutual funds business offered a number of schemes. In addition, the Public Sector Banks, LIC and GIC also offered schemes with diverse motives. The leading private companies started attracting the investors by offering schemes with the motto of providing tax reliefs to the savers under Section 80-C. This benefited the economy in two ways, first savings habits were inculcated and second flow of finance for the development purposes was found sizeably increased.

The entry of private sector companies revolutionised the mutual funds operations and they started sharing even more than 85 per cent of the contributions of resource mobilisation.[7] In the private sector, the HDFC and in the public sector, the SBI succeeded in establishing leadership in the market. In addition, Birla Sun Life, Tata, JM Finance, Kotak Mahindra, Reliance were in the dominating position in the private sector mutual operations whereas the SBI, UTI, LIC and Bank of Baroda dominated in the public sector. The market environment was found much more competitive and volatile. The SEBI a regulatory body succeeded in controlling the unfair practices. Despite a number of odds, we find future of mutual funds industry prosperous.

In the changing scenario, we need to practise innovative marketing principles so that the providers as well as the users are found benefited. If we find both of them benefited, the process of resource mobilisation and economic transformation would also gain a rapid momentum. The organisations engaged in mutual funds operations need to be professionally-sound. Capitalising on the opportunities existent in the savings market requires world-class professional excellence which all the mutual funds houses have to do on a priority basis. Excelling competition requires conceptualisation of innovative marketing.

All categories of mutual funds houses, public or private, need innovative schemes. The Equity Linked Savings Scheme of UTI has been found getting a positive response. Since we find the levels of income of women sector increasing very fast mainly due to corporatisation, the mutual funds houses need to think about innovative schemes exclusively for this segment of the society. Not only the schemes with the motto of providing tax reliefs but also with the purpose of making available to them a profitable return seems to be essential. The modern society has been found offering gifts to their children on different occasions. The mutual funds houses need to capitalise on the opportunities. We find senior citizens of the society also emerging as an important segment. Either for tax reliefs or for profitable returns for their investments, the mutual funds need to think about the incorporation of innovative schemes.

The emergence of a new trend in the society has been found paving new avenues for the mutual funds innovative schemes. The Real Estate Mutual Fund is also an option which can be used by them because we find a large scale investment in new sectors like Shopping Complex, Apartment Complex, Office Complex, Hotel Complex. In expanding economies like ours, we find scope for the development of real estate where huge amount is invested. This makes it essential that mutual funds houses design an innovative scheme in which we find investors evincing a special interest.

The mutual funds houses should not overlook the Art Fund. We find a number of examples where old paintings have been sold at a very high price. But such type of investment is not for small investors because they do not have high resistance capacity. The market for Art Fund appears to be prosperous because the individuals and organisations — both the customers pay high price for the Art Product. However, the SEBI has not given permission for Art Fund but the organisations may obtain the permission in near future.

The marketing professionals need to offer innovative schemes so that the investors get additional attractions. We cannot negate that upcoming youths, considered as backbone of the modern corporate sector, have high risk bearing capacity. They show their temptation to long-term investments for getting the high rate of returns. The women segment, a new emerging segment, need priority attention of mutual funds houses. Increasing craze for corporate investments amongst the new wave society appears to be a positive sign for the development of mutual funds industry.

The professionals also need innovative efforts for creative promotional measures. The guidelines of SEBI are to be followed while advertising for the mutual funds schemes. The masses are to be made aware of the recent trends and their profitable options. Informing, sensing, sensitising, persuading and transforming the actual and potential investors in such a fashion that they develop the potentials of distinguishing between high return and low return; high risk and low risk; short-term gain and long-term gain appear to be an important task before the mutual funds marketers. Creative and cost-effective promotional measures need due attention.

The agents, advisors, fund managers and portfolio managers bear an outstanding responsibility of capitalising on the opportunities and therefore they need professional excellence so that the investors continue to get profitable returns for their investment and the process of mobilisation of savings and channelisation of investments keep on moving. The SEBI has to think over the issue and strengthen policy reforms so that the negative trends in the stock markets start moving in the reverse gear. The ups and downs in the share markets can be brought to an optimal point if we find the service providing organisations not involving themselves in the unhealthy and unlawful practices. In a true sense, they need multi-cornered attempts; such as offering innovative schemes and for that understanding the changing levels of expectations of investors; developing a team of dedicated and committed marketing people and for that they need to educate, train, develop and motivate agents and advisors considered to be the leverspring of mutual funds operations; getting profitable returns for their investments and for that making use of expertise services of portfolio managers.

Like other business houses, the mutual funds houses have also to perceive that innovations are to be their culture so that innovative schemes help investors in getting the profitable returns for their investments. Schemes covering multi-segments, benefiting all would engineer a sound foundation for the development of mutual funds industry. The marketers have to develop a mix in tune with the changing behaviour of investors and the emerging trends in stock markets. New gizmos of benefits commensurate with the new wave society would get a positive response. Let the professionals strengthen their perception that obsolescence is the outcome of innovation.

SUMMARY

In this chapter, you have gone through different dimensions of mutual funds marketing. Before starting another chapter, be sure that the following facts are well versed:

Mutual Funds: The Concept: We find mutual funds an alternative saving avenue with a better rate of return linked to stock market investment with the help of intermediaries. It is a community by pooling the resources of a large number of small savers for corporate investments.

Mutual Fund Services in India: The UTI has been a pioneer in the field of mutual funds in India. Gradually, we find involvement of public sector banks and LIC and GIC in the mutual funds operations in 1987. Further, the SEBI made provisions even for the private sector companies to take part in the mutual funds operations in 1993.

Mutual Funds Marketing: By mutual funds marketing, our focus is on the conceptualisation of modern marketing principles in the mutual funds services so that the users and providers both are benefited.

Users of Mutual Funds Services: The users of mutual funds services belong to different segments but the small savers/investors for which this business is meant occupy an important position.

Behavioural Profile of Different Segment: The different segments of investors invest in mutual funds with diverse motives. Some of them invest for getting the tax reliefs whereas others invest for getting the short-term or the long-term gains on the invested funds. The levels of expectations of all the segments are not identical.

Market Segments for Mutual Funds: Men and women, rural and poor, youths and old/senior citizens/pensionholders, high risk bearing and the low risk bearing; high profit making and the low profit making are the different segments making investment in mutual funds.

Marketing Information for Mutual Funds: The marketing professional need information to understand the changing behavioural profile of investors and further for studying and understanding the changing trends in the stock markets. The information helps in making sound marketing decisions.

Marketing Mix for Mutual Funds Services: The professionals bear the responsibility of formulating a sound marketing mix covering the following submixes:

Product Mix: The different schemes of mutual funds are the product and the concerned organisations have to design an innovating scheme which makes available to the investors high rate of return.

Promotion Mix: The professionals have to devise creative, effective and cost-effective promotional measures for promoting the mutual funds business. They are supposed to formulate a sound promotion mix so that they succeed in informing, sensing, sensitising, persuading and transforming the potential investors into actual and habitual investors.

Price Mix: In the formulation of price mix, the marketers need to minimise the costs. A number of costs such as agent's commission, brokerage, establishment expenses, marketing and selling expenses, registrar services, payment to portfolio managers are included in the cost.

Place Mix: The services pass through different channels. The schemes offered by the mutual funds houses reach to the users through the agents and advisors. They make available the proposals to the providers who with the help of experts channelise them to the shares and securities. The returns available to the providers are paid to the users.

Process: The processing of services are done at different stages and at different points. The schemes launched by the providers reach to the users through agents and advisors. This is the first stage of processing. The agents or advisors deposit the same at the offices of the providers. This is the second stage. The providers with the help of funds managers and portfolio managers invest them in the shares and securities. This is the third stage. The returns through the providers finally reach to the users. This is the fourth stage. The professionals are supposed to process them in the right way.

Physical Evidence and Attractions: Though in the mutual funds services, we do not find this submix so much significant but the exteriors and interiors of concerned offices and the personal care dimensions for the agents, advisors and other marketing people play a positive role.

People: A number of people are found involved in the process of offering the mutual funds services. The agents, advisors, fund managers and portfolio managers need to have an in-depth knowledge of changing market conditions. They need professional excellence, personal commitment, personal-touch-in-service and value orientation.

Mutual Funds services in Indian Perspective: In the Indian context, we find UTI as a pioneer for offering mutual fund schemes. With the amendments in Banking Regulations, the Public Sector Banks, LIC and GIC and with the SEBI regulations, the private sector companies entered in the mutual funds business.

KEY TERMS

Mutual Funds Services	Non-banking Business
Market Segments	Persuasive Communication
UTI	Offshore Investment
Burgeoning Middle Class	Personal Selling
Public Sector	Mutual Funds Marketing
Return-based Investors	Asset Management Company
Stock Markets	Resource Mobilisation
Information Technology	Net Asset Value
Public Members	Government Bonds
Product Mix	Sharpe Index Model
Pro rata Basis	Treasury Bills
Volatile	Scams
Indian Trusts Act	Joint Venture
Brand Name	Innovation Culture

Review Questions

1. What do you mean by Mutual Funds Service? Focus on the development of mutual funds services in India.
2. Throw light on the concept of Mutual Funds Marketing. Explain the providers of Mutual Funds Services.
3. Discuss the behavioural profile of mutual funds users in the Indian perspective.
4. Examine the role of different segments of users in improving the functioning of mutual funds houses.
5. Do you feel that an in-depth study of different segments of users is essential to know their behaviour? Justify your arguments.
6. Focus on the different submixes of marketing for the mutual funds services.
7. Explain the key mutual fund schemes of UIT and LIC.
8. Explain the role of innovative mutual fund schemes and creative promotional measures in the development of mutual funds business.
9. Enumerate the Process and People as important submixes of mutual funds marketing.
10. The submixes like Price and Place need due attention of marketing professionals. Comment.
11. Write an essay on the marketing of mutual funds services in the Indian perspective.

Application Exercises

1. As a marketing professional, how would you improve the operational efficiency of intermediaries for the mutual funds schemes of your organisation.
2. You are working as a marketing managers of a Public Sector Bank and you have been assigned the responsibility of persuading the investors for a new mutual fund scheme which has been launched very recently. Focus on the steps you would take in this direction.
3. Formulate a marketing mix for the mutual funds services in the Indian perspective.
4. You have fixed a target for the agents and advisors. They need necessary guidelines from you. How would you organise a training programme for them? Explain.
5. You have been assigned the responsibility of managing mutual funds in your company. Explain the steps you would take for investing in portfolio for getting the profitable returns for your investors.
6. You are working as a marketing manager of LIC. Explain the steps you would take for motivating the investors of different segments.
7. Throw light on the strengths and weaknesses of Indian economy with the viewpoint of a mutual fund market.

Endnotes

1. RBI Guidelines to Mutual Funds.
2. Report on Currency and Finance, 2007-08, RBI, New Delhi.
3. *Indian Journal of Finance,* II/5 September 2008, New Delhi.
4. SEBI Regulations on Mutual Funds.
5. *Indian Journal of Finance, op. cit.*
6. *Ibid.*
7. *Indian Journal of Commerce,* 60/4, 2007.
8. *Ibid.*

Portfolio Services Marketing

Volatile market and risk-averse customers necessitate conceptualisation of marketing in the portfolio services with the help of portfolio managers having world-class professional excellence.

Chapter Objectives

Introduction – Portfolio Management: The Conceptual Exposition – Portfolio Management Services: An – Overview or Users of Portfolio Services and their Behavioural Profile – The Portfolio Managers – Market Segmentation for Portfolio Services – Information for Portfolio – Decisions – Markeing Mix for Portfolio Services – The Product Mix – Promotion Mix – Pricing/ Fee – Place Mix – Process – Physical Evidence and Attractions – People – Portfolio Services Marketing in Indian Perspective – Summary – Key Terms – Review Questions – Application Exercises – Endnotes.

Learning Objectives

This chapter aims at studying the different dimensions of portfolio management. The Conceptualisation of Marketing in the marketing of portfolio management services is the focal point of this chapter. The behavioural studies, market segmentation and information management are the basis to formulate a sound marketing mix for portfolio management. The portfolio managers need to develop the awareness of innovating marketing so that they succeed in practising marketing for satisfying the clients by maximising the returns and minimising the risks. In a highly volatile stock market, it is imperative.

INTRODUCTION

With the corporatisation of Indian economy, the stock and money markets could get a conducive nexus for development and prosperity. A majority of the investors evinced interests in channelising their investments in the shares and securities. The flow of money started gaining a rapid momentum and the portfolio management services of world-class professionals started injecting new life to the investment process. The community of investors albeit not aware of the art and tact of stock markets operations were not successful in getting high returns for their investments. The credibility for the same goes to the portfolio management services.

We cannot negate that the current massive carnage in the stock markets have been swift, sharp and gainful. However, we hope an early departure of this carnage and normal economic activities back on the rail. It is amazing that just within a short duration of two years, i.e., from January 2006 to January 2008, an increase in the sensex from 10,000 to 21,000 and just within eight months, a big fall in the sensex from 21,000 to below 10,000 till October 2008 and again a sharp increase from 10,000 to 17,600 till June 2010 has made some of us financially solvent whereas some others bankrupt. Volatility with high intensity complicates the task of investors. If we find money floating in the stock markets, the national economy will come back on the rail. Optimism is considered to be the most effective prescription for activating the process of national economy transformation. An individual or an organisation has no option but to remain optimistic for life long, if they want to nurture dreams and to harness the benefits of development.

Portfolio management helps investors in knowing what to sell and what to buy. It helps proper management of money in terms of investment in tune with the asset preference of investors and further minimises the risks and ever risk phobia and paves avenues for high rate of returns. The portfolio managers considered to be expert in the designing of a sound portfolio manage and channelise investment patterns in such a fashion that both the parties—users and providers are found satisfied. The concerned agency plays a decisive role in the entire process. It takes the responsibility of using the funds effectively for getting the desired results. The agency converts the funds into compatible portfolios on the basis of objectives and constraints of the investors. It makes a time-to-time evaluation and adjustments for better results.

Portfolio management services, of course, are an important dimension of financial management but the portfolio managers need to develop their professional excellence even in the field of marketing. We cannot deny that marketing in a volatile environment is a difficult task. Intangible services need professionally-sound tangibilisation for adding additional attractions to the services.

Particularly when the services are found intangible, the marketers need to expose tangibility and this complicates the task of a portfolio manager. The responsibility of portfolio managers while conceptualising marketing is not only confined to designing a mix that helps investors in getting the handsome returns but in addition also related to the communication excellence for motivating and satisfying the investors. Thus, they are supposed to play a dual role as a financial manager and also as a marketing manager. The responsibility aggravates further when we find the stock markets much more volatile. The level of expectations of investors are found increasing as the emerging positive trends in the markets make ways for an attitudinal change. What to sell and what not to sell; what to buy and what not to buy; specially in a globalised economy may confuse the portfolio managers. The changes in the US economy; the changes in the Asian economy or changes in other parts of the globe throw a telling impact on the functional behaviour of stock markets. The portfolio managers are also supposed to have an in-depth knowledge of the emerging trends in the stock markets *vis-a-vis* the changing behavioural profile of investors.

A mix of portfolio and a mix of marketing both are found to be different dimensions of management. The interests of clients or customers are linked with both the dimensions. On the basis of a sound mix of portfolio, the investors expect their investment to be much more productive and on the basis of a sound mix of marketing; the customers expect desired level of services delivery and recovery. While conceptualising innovative marketing, a portfolio manager requires to formulate a sound marketing mix. All the seven mixes of marketing draw their attention, such as the product mix, promotion mix, place mix, price mix, process, physical evidence and attraction and people.

An in-depth study of behaviour of different segments of investors requires a techno-driven information management. Making available to the clients multi-faceted facilities such as formulating a sound portfolio, enabling them to get the tax reliefs and minimising risks are some of the important services provided by a portfolio manager on a discretionary or non-discretionary basis. Clients may be an individual or an institution. The services offered by a portfolio manager are considered a part of the product. The service are required to be promoted in an effective way so that the users come to know about the quality of services. The portfolio managers also charge fee for their services and this is a part of the pricing decision. The services ultimately reach to the clients which we consider a subject of place mix. Besides, the processing of services would focus on the networking and physical evidence would focus on the ambience at the premises, professional looking décor of the premises and people mix concentrate on the quality of portfolio manager and the quality of people working with him.

The motive is to deliver quality services and even to make the ways for service recovery.

PORTFOLIO MANAGEMENT: THE CONCEPTUAL EXPOSITION

At the outset, it is essential to develop a conceptual framework regarding the portfolio management. The term portfolio refers to the list of investment held by investors or combination of Securities.[1]

As per the SEBI norms, the portfolio management refers to professional service made available for management of portfolio of anybody known as clients or customers with the help of experts in Investment Advisory Services. The management of services include advice to the clients regarding the worthwhileness of any particularly investment or advice what to buy and what not to buy and what to sell and what not to sell. The advice also may be regarding timing for transactions such as when to buy and when to sell. The portfolio management also includes in its purview managing investment with or without discretion for the client as per the requirements.

Regarding the conceptual aspect, it is also said that portfolio management focuses our attention on the services to be made available to the clients, for making possible the best possible effective utilisation of funds. In the process, the funds are converted into compatible portfolio in the face of objectives and constraints of the investors. Further, it evaluates the funds and makes the necessary adjustments for getting the best possible results. According to SEBI, only registered merchant bankers are to be allowed to render portfolio management services. Allocation of investments for this purpose the required strategical decisions; timing of investments and disinvestments are the important dimensions of portfolio management. A periodical valuation and review in the face of the changing market condions cannot be disintegrated with the management of portfolio. Optimising the results and minimising the risks are the important functional responsibilities of a portfolio manager.

The portfolio management services are regulated by SEBI who has given permission to Merchant Bankers of Category I to do Portfolio management of anybody. As per the guidelines of September, 1991, a separate category of Portfolio Managers is licensed by SEBI for which guidelines were given in January 1993. Merchant Bankers of categories I to IV were abolished by SEBI in 1996-97.

The following facts are observed regarding the portfolio management:

- It is a professionalised service meant for the management of portfolio.
- It is a managerial process meant for advising the investors known as clients.
- It is a process of managing investment with or without discretion for the clients.
- It is a process of converting the funds into compatible portfolios.
- It is a process for allocation, investments and disinvestment.
- It is regulated by the SEBI.
- It is an organised and systematic effort to select securities.
- It is a method of distribution of total amount of investment by the investors in different securities with the motto of minimising risks and maxmising returned.

PORTFOLIO MANAGEMENT SERVICES : AN OVERVIEW

The SEBI norms clarify portfolio management services as professional service made available for management of portfolio to anybody called as clients or customers with the help of experts in the Investment Advisory Services. The multi-faceted services are provided by a portfolio manager as mentioned below:

The services are of discretionary and non-discretionary nature made available by the portfolio managers to their clients.

Non-Discretionary Services: In the context of non-discretionary services, we find investors making their own decisions. The responsibility of a portfolio manager is found confined to the execution process. The investors of large category are found making use of non-discretionary services. The firm makes available to the clients suitable advice. Regarding the day-to-day services, the orders are also received on telephones. For safe accessibility and safety of funds, a password is made available the clients. The firms also make available a monthly report to their clients regarding transactions, portfolio valuation and the balance in the accounts of clients.

Discretionary Services: The discretionary services are made available to those clients who leave the management of their portfolios in the hands of a portfolio manager. We cannot deny that the discretionary services are found much more convenient to the portfolio managing firms because they get freedom of managing things where they exercise their minds and make use of their professional excellence. Of course, the interests of clients are found confined to better reurns. The delegation of the rights to buy and sell the securities is performed within a framework designed by the client with the help of a portfolio manager. While designing a framework, the interests of the parties such as providers and users are taken into consideration.

Optional Services: In the category of optional services, the providers offer in the beginning non-discretionary services and after the firm is well established, the discretionary services are also offered, provided the clients are interested in getting the same. In addition to the core services, the providers also offer some of the peripheral services to their clients such as organisation of counselling sessions, borrowing against securities, circulation of odd lots within the client's portfolio, facility of temporary overdraft and organising quarterly meetings of investors.

The above-mentioned services are made available to the clients (investors) by the providers (Portfolio Managing Firms). Keeping in view the increasing volatility in the stock markets, we find the role of portfolio managing firms and portfolio managers becoming much more challenging. They need world-class professional excellence to satisfy and benefit their clients. Expertise of portfolio managers plays a decisive role in determining the magnitude of success.

USERS OF PORTFOLIO SERVICES AND THEIR BEHAVIOURAL PROFILE

Investors in general are found risk-averse. And for getting maximum returns, we have no option but to bear risk. Minimising the intensity of risk and maximising the possibilities for high rate of returns are the two underlying objectives in the portfolio management services. The investors of different categories are the users of services and we find their behavioural profile influenced by a number of factors. However, all the investors expect high rate of returns from their investments. Particularly when the intensity of volatility in the stock markets is found galloping, the designing or developing a portfolio proves to be a challenging task for the portfolio managers. The price of a particular share or security which is high today may be low tomorrow and *vice versa.* Developing the art of designing an optimal mix having high risk bearing capacity, no doubt, proves to be an acid test of portfolio managers, specially when we find global economy witnessing a phase of depression. Globalisation of economy has virtually created a condition in which developments at one end of the globe affect the economies of almost all the countries.

In the Indian perspective, the race and pace of globalisation gained a rapid momentum during and after 1990s and resulting from which intensity of the expectations of general investors were found at its peak. We cannot negate that changing business environment has an important bearing on the levels of our expectations. Since there was a major change in the performance of stock markets, it was natural to have an analogous change in the behaviour of investors. It is natural that we find a variation in degree from one segment to another. The people serving the corporate sector and holding a high position have a high risk bearing capacity. The upcoming youths have a high degree of risk bearing capacity. By and large, we find the same condition with the institutional investors. But the risk bearing capacity of people investing their savings with the motto of getting short-term gains cannot be identical.

The portfolio managers bear the responsibility of studying and understanding the changing behavioural profile of users of different segments. Influencing the clients or customers is possible when we fulfil their expectations. The tax benefits and rate of return are the two important considerations necessitating due attention of professionals to increase the levels of satisfaction. We also find investors who in addition to tax reliefs and investment incentives expect innovative peripheral services from the providers. The professional need to motivate their clients because in a majority of the cases we find them expecting a package of benefits.

Developing portfolio commensurate with the changing levels of expectations of users, specially when the intensity of volatility is at its peak, appears difficult. The portfolio managers would require an in-depth knowledge of changing global scenario without which the forecasting would be a challenging task. Uncertainties prevail in the stock markets and nobody is in a position to formulate a strategy that simplifies the marketing processes.

The Portfolio Managers: The success of a portfolio management firm rests on the performance of portfolio managers. There are some guidelines and provisions for the portfolio managers because layman cannot hold the position of a portfolio manager. An applicant interested in acting as a portfolio manager in addition to expertise requires the supporting infrastructural facilities. At least two persons with required experience and qualifications in the field of portfolio management with a minimum networth of ₹ 50 lakh are eligible to apply. The certificate once granted is found valid for three years. At present, the fee required for registration is ₹ 2.5 lakh annual for two years and ₹ one lakh for the third year. From the fourth year onwards, the registration fee is ₹ 75,000 subject to a time-to-time revision by the SEBI.

The portfolio managers should have world-class professional excellence. The SEBI has imposed a number of obligations and a code of conduct for portfolio managers. According to the code of conduct, they should have a high degree of integrity, honesty, sincerity and should not have been convicted of any economic offence or moral turpitude. He/she should not resort to rigging up of the prices, insider trading or creating false markets. Their books of accounts are subject to inspection and audit by SEBI. They are also required to submit the periodical reports and documents as may be required by the SEBI from time to time.

The SEBI has prohibited the Portfolio Manager to assume any risk on behalf of their clients.[2] Besides, they cannot assure any fixed return to the client. The investment made or even advised by the portfolio managers are subject to risk which the clients have to bear. The portfolio manager is also prohibited to do lending, badla financing and bills discounting as per the SEBI norms. They are not supposed to put the funds of their clients in any investment not permitted by the contract entered into with the clients. They can make investments both in capital and money market instruments. The money of client would be deposited in the public sector banks and would not be mixed up with their own funds or investments. The portfolio managers act only on a contractual basis or on a fiduciary basis. The contract with the portfolio manager would not be for less than one year. The final settlement and termination of contact will be as per the contract or after the time period agreed upon.

The portfolio managers need professional excellence. They bear the responsibility of managing the portfolio of anybody, well call them clients or customers. Serving the clients or customers as per the SEBI norms and showing their excellence in managing the portfolio so that the clients are motivated and the image of the firms, managing the portfolio, is not tarnished need due attention of portfolio managers. We are well aware of the fact that the SEBI has given permission to Merchant Bankers of Category I to manage portfolio with the help of professionals having expertise in the related area.[3]

MARKET SEGMENTATION FOR PORTFOLIO SERVICES

Segmentation is a process of dividing and subdividing a market into different groups and sub-groups. If you divide; your task of ruling the market is considerably simplified. Particularly when we find the stocks and money witnessing much more frequency in fluctuation, the decision-making process becomes much more complicated. We are well aware of the fact that by nature and character, the stock and money markets are found volatile in which high intensity of stability is not considered to be a good sign.

The portfolio managers need an in-depth study of market and if they segment, it will be easier for them to understand. The customer sclients come from different segments and the attitudinal differences in their behavioural patterns are but natural. The clients of different segments complicate your task because the motives of all the segments are not found to be identical. The individuals, associations, public sector, private sector, trade sector, youths, old citizens, level of income are the different segments from where we find the portfolio management firms getting the clients or customers. It is significant that they are well aware of their attitudinal and motivational variations which will not only improve the quality of their marketing decisions but would also make the process of decision-making much more easier. The task of undertaking market research would successfully and effectively be done by the researchers in a segmented market.

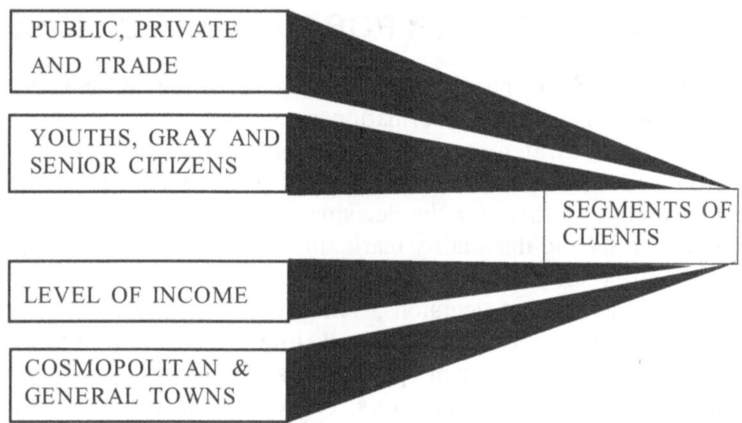

Fig. 8.1: Segments for Portfolio Services

The customers coming from different segments make use of the services of portfolio managers with diverse motives. Some of them are found interested in getting the tax reliefs and some others are found tempted to high rate of return. Some of them have high risk bearing capacity and some of them have low resistance power. Some of them prefer returns in short-run whereas some other are found interested in getting the long-term gains. The portfolio in all the conditions cannot be uniform. If the portfolio managers make possible a microscopic study of market on the basis of segmentation, the portfolio developed by them will be found result-oriented.

Public, Private and Trade Sectors: The clients coming from the public sector segment are found less resistive. They prefer short- or long-term gains with the dismal or nominal risks. Since we find much more stability in their job, they in a majority of the cases are found very calm and cool in their behaviour and temperament. The portfolio managers need to study and understand them in a right way because in the Indian perspective, they are in a very good number.

The people serving the private sector find their job profile insecured. Due to job insecurity and high level of income, particularly after globalisation, we find an apparent change in their attitudes. They prefer high returns even the intensity of risk is high. We find a significant increase in their number during the post-globalisation period.

The clients coming from trade sector or business sector, no doubt, are found interested in multiplying their investments but at the same time, they also prefer a portfolio minimising the intensity of risk.

Youths, Gray and Senior Citizens: We need to strengthen our realisation that age is an important factor influencing our attitudes and behaviour. Of course, we also find their correlation with the profession.

The youths particularly serving the private sector and holding top position are found friendly to stock investments. They prefer high rate of return. Since they are found very resistive in nature, the professionals will develop a different portfolio for them.

The gray and old citizens both of them are found almost in the same boat. The age is found to be a barrier when we talk about our capacity to resist.

The customers coming from the segment of pensionholders prefer their investments to be much more safe.

Level of Income: The portfolio managers need to understand that we find a correlation between attitudes and the levels of income. If we make a microscopic study of the different segments of customers, it is found that level of income and nature of profession have a close relation. With the same level of income, we find attitudinal variations in the clients serving the public and private sectors. Normally, the people having high level of income are found much more resistive to risk. They prefer high returns from their investments.

Cosmopolitan Towns and General Towns: The professionals cannot negate the attitudinal variations on account of township considerations. The people living in or working in the cosmopolitan towns and cities are found much more resistive to high risk and tempted to the corporate investments. Normally, we do not find the same thing with the people living in general towns and cities. They are found low resistive to risk.

The portfolio managers need to study and understand them.

INFORMATION FOR PORTFOLIO DECISIONS

The marketing professionals bear the responsibility of making marketing decisions. Keeping in view the changing scenario of stock markets, the management of information occupies a place of outstanding significance for the portfolio marketers. Developing their awareness of the behavioural profile of clients or customers and enriching their knowledge bank regarding the emerging trends in the market behaviour considerably rest on the quality and timing of information made available to them for the decision-making purposes. It is in this context that we focus on management of information for making the quality marketing decisions. A well-equipped information technology may help them in knowing about the information needs of the client. Like the providers, the users also need right and fast information for making investment decisions. The providers need to develop their awareness and for this purpose, they have to conceptualise techno-driven marketing information. We agree with this view that the availability of information on the existing investment opportunities as well as the techniques used to make an anatomy of the scrips helps in building the confidence of investors. Particularly in the volatile stock markets, this deserves an intensive care.

The emerging trends in the stock and money markets and the changing behavioural profile of investors and potential investors are the two important facets determining the success rate of portfolio management. In a true sense, the professional excellence of a portfolio manager depends on the quality of information. The information related to the performance of shares and securities is found essential for the designing of a portfolio. Like this, the information concerned with risk bearing capacity and attitudes of clients become significant for identifying the changing levels of their expectations. And for both purposes, the portfolio managers need quality information.

Global networking of information becomes significant in the present world of globalisation because the developments at one place trap others and start influencing their operational mechanism. The portfolio managers need to develop their rapport with the brokers who will provide to them the latest developments taking place around the globe. Ultimately, the customers depend on the information made available to them by the portfolio managers and therefore they are supposed to keep themselves well-equipped. Information networking with the help of new generation of information technology will simplify the process of managing information.

The updating of portfolio management services is essential and for this, the services of marketing research wing can be obtained. An interaction with brokers helps portfolio managers in knowing about the recent emerging trends and on that basis, they can invest the money of their clients. The status report can be given to the clients on time if they have IT networking. The corporate announcements become important to both the providers as well as the users.

The above-mentioned facts testify the role of information in the portfolio marketing decisions.

A majority of the investments are with the objective of getting the long-term benefits. This makes it essential that the portfolio managers pick only the strong scrips which can be done with the help of a fundamental analysis of the scrips. The preparation of reports and thereafter company-wise preparation and analysis of reports help portfolio managers in many ways. The portfolio managers can make use of annual reports which would let them know about the company. In a number of organisations, we find research departments for this purpose who bear the responsibility of maintaining and updating the data. Of late, we find development of so many software packages for this purpose. Some of the firms have been found using 'Capital Line' and 'Scriptech' packages for this purpose. But at the same time, we also find brokers believing in their gut and working confidently in the markets and even getting a positive result.

The companies maintaining portfolio management services in house are found to be financially sound. They are in a position to develop a sound information system with the help of new generation of technology. The development of marketing intelligence system will help them in getting the happening data regarding the stock markets activities. Thus, the Marketing Intelligence System and the Internal Reporting System can be used by those portfolio management firms who have been doing business on a very large scale. The development of Marketing Information System becomes essential because the portfolio management services sizeably rest on the intelligent allocation and time-honoured development of portfolio. With the help of marketing research, the system will get the required input for forecasting the trend in the stock and money markets. With the help of techno-driven information system, the task of portfolio managers would considerably be simplified. Quick decision, intelligent decision and time-honoured decision help professionals in developing a portfolio commensurate with the changing requirements. However, they need to make use of intuition which will help them in exercising the sense of judgement.

In view of the above-mentioned facts, it is right to mention that professionals accepting the responsibility of managing the portfolio of their clients or customers need to update themselves and only a techno-driven system can make it possible. Particularly in an age of globalisation, it needs our priority attention. Increasing sensitivity to the accessibility of information necessitates development of a sound information system.

MARKETING MIX FOR PORTFOLIO SERVICES

Developing portfolio in tune with the needs and requirements of customers or clients so that they remain satisfied and keep on moving the process of channelising investments is the main thing in the marketing of portfolio management services. Despite so many odds in the stock markets, the increasing temptation or fascination to the corporate investments cannot be reversed. The opportunities are and will remain even in future. The marketers with the help of a sound marketing mix will be in a position to inform, sense, sensitise, persuade and transform the potential customers into actual and habitual customers. Here, we go through the different submixes in the marketing of the portfolio management services.

THE PRODUCT MIX

In the context of portfolio management services, when we talk about the product, our focus is on the development of portfolio as a core product of the firm and offering of a number of other services in the name of peripheral. The designing of a portfolio throws light on the mix of shares and securities in a portfolio. It is also a combination of the product of share and money markets. The marketing professionals here need to formulate a sound product mix in which a package of services made available to the customers satisfies them. In the portfolio management, the services are both of discretionary and non-discretionary types and therefore the professionals need much more care while offering or delivering the services. In the case of services of discretionary nature, we find the judgement on the part of providers significant whereas in case of non-discretionary services, the providers are supposed to be much more customised. It is significant here to mention that the optional services like tax counselling, borrowing against securities, circulation of odd-lots within the portfolio of clients, facility of temporary overdraft, across the counter facility and quarterly meetings of customer add additional attractions to the product mix.

In the formulation of product mix, the portfolio managers at the very outset make use of all the tools of research such as fundamental and technical analysis. Besides, we also find a study of risk-return for making decisions on buying and selling. After the formulation of portfolio strategy, the portfolio managers do the construction and allocation of funds which result into the development of a portfolio. After the building of portfolio, the portfolio managers have to review them so that professionalised monitoring helps in identifying the weaknesses.

While designing the product mix, the marketing professionals need to know about the inclusion and elimination processes in tune with the emerging trends in markets and changing levels of expectations of customers. This necessitates time-to-time review of the results of portfolio developed by the professionals. A mix of share markets and money markets will make the product mix much more sound.[4] The professionals need to consider a number of factors while developing portfolio for their clients.

The portfolio managers need to divert their attention on two important aspects — first, whether it is worthy to invest money in individual security or individual project and second whether the investment would be diversified. Expected return and expected risk become significant in this context. The rate of return is influenced by the market price of shares at different points of time which results into variation in the rate of return and we call this variation as risk. The expected rate of return is the weighted average of returns under different possible conditions of economy. This makes it clear that expected returns and risks are found associated with the investment decisions.

In this respect, the intuitive art and mood of the market are also found significant. The valuation of share actually depends on the emerging trends in the market. The sense of judgement exercised by the professionals is found related to the mood of investors. What to do in the prevailing market conditions also depends on the sense of judgement of intuition.

In the process of formulating a sound product mix, the portfolio managers also depend on the feedback received from the brokers. The brokers have an in-depth knowledge of changing market conditions. They are found in a position to forecast and their forecast results guide the portfolio managers.

The product mix or portfolio developed by a portfolio manager thus requires to include in the mix both the instruments, such as high risk bearing and low risk bearing. The bank deposits or deposits of Post Office are known as risk-free returns. The diversification of investment into a number of scrips is essential because scrip has its own risk profile. An optimal mix is not based on a theory indeed the market conditions.

A portfolio manager needs to take into consideration that Modern Portfolio Theory is found based on free and perfect information flow and the notion of dominance. If we find in the market high rate of absorption of information, the investors can choose the scrips with the lowest possible risk. By diversifying investments in a number of companies, this is possible. No investor should invest in one company alone, if we find two or more companies carrying the same intensity of risk.

Offering the best to clients who are your customers is considered to be the main thing in the formulation process. You need to make it sure that your customers are satisfied with the product made available to them. The core product in the form of a portfolio carries the lowest possible risk and ensures to them the handsome incentives for their investments. In addition, you also need to offer to them a number of optional services such as tax counselling, borrowing against securities, facility of temporary overdraft etc. A mix of the two — core and peripheral — would help you in satisfying your clients.

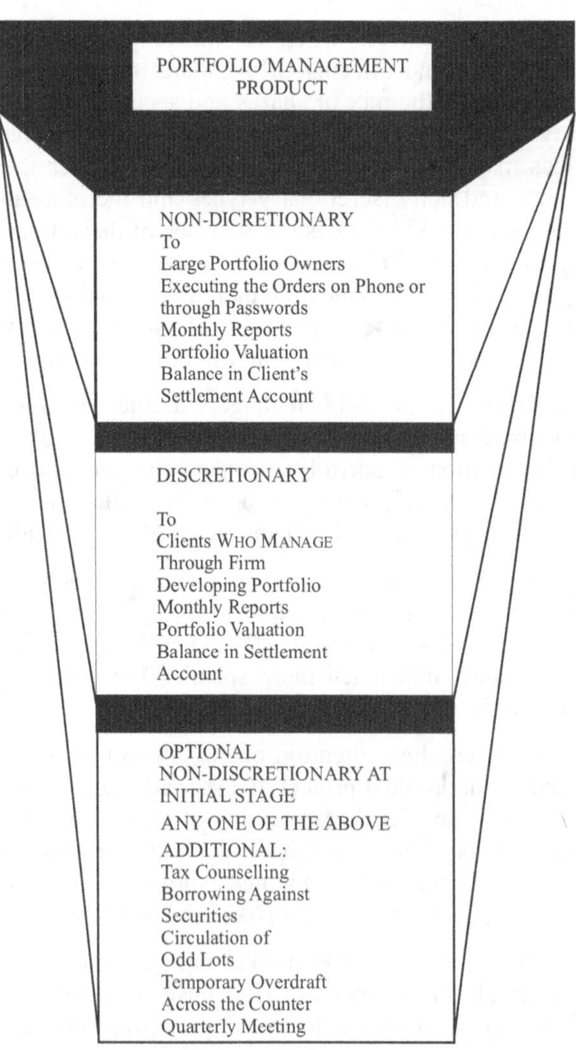

Fig. 8.2: Portfolio Management Product

The most important thing in the process of developing a portfolio is fair blending of the investments in the share and money markets. While designing a portfolio, the brokers make available to the portfolio managers the emerging trends and their valuable experiences. While developing a portfolio, the professionals also consider the intensity of risk in a particular portfolio *vis-a-vis* the risk bearing capacity of their clients.

In the marketing mix, we find product assuming a place of outstanding significance. This makes it essential that the portfolio managers watch the results very carefully and bring a change in the larger interests of their clients. The portfolio making available to the clients the high rate of returns may be considered the best portfolio. Expertise of professionals and timing of decisions determine the magnitude of success.

PROMOTION MIX

The portfolio management firms not only need to offer quality services to their clients but in addition, they also bear the responsibility of promoting their business in an effective way. The clients or customers are to be made aware of the outstanding features of their services. They make use of different components of promotion with the motto of sensitising the customers and persuading them in a right way so that the transformation process is simplified. The promotion budget in a very natural way will depend upon the scale of operation of the firm. Creative, effective and cost-effective promotional measures need due attention of professionals. If we find a firm undertaking in-house arrangements for the management of portfolio, the task of promotion is found easier.

While advertising, the portfolio management firm should not overlook a common code for advertising which focuses our attention on submission of the marketing literature and advertisements issued to the SEBI.[5] When they issue publicity brochures, nothing would be concealed and further nothing would be misleading. In the posters and leaflets, they would clarify the objectives of investments. The print media may be suitable for portfolio management firms not only with the viewpoint of cost-effectiveness but also with the objective of making the messages much more effective. The professionals need to assign due weightage to the needs and requirements *vis-a-vis* the capacity of reception of the segments for which they are advertising. The leading newspapers having wider circulation and preferred by a particular segment for which they are advertising or the magazines preferred by the concerned segment should be given weightage while advertising. But in any case, the portfolio managers should not cross the limits and should follow the guidelines of SEBI. For wider publicity of their services, the portfolio managers should develop rapport with the financial experts and academics having recognition in the financial stream.

In the process of selecting a component for promotion, the professional also need to think about telemarketers. Because they have a network of technology; the task can be made much more easier by the telemarketers having a high communicative ability. The queries of clients can be removed and their problems can be redressed with the help of telemarketers. The professionals in the very context are required to make it sure that communication and information technology used for this purpose are in right order. In the process of service recovery, the telemarketers can play an effective role.

The professionals need to make a sound promotion mix so that the clients or the potential clients are found impressed and persuaded. But at each and every stage, they need to be sincere to the guidelines and limitations so that the cases of violation of provisions are not detected. Your messages, slogans, campaign need professional touch.

PRICING/FEE

This submix of the marketing mix is found related to the payment of fee to the portfolio managers for the services they render to their clients. We find a number of arrangements for charging fee between the portfolio managers and the clients. We also find cases where no fee is charged from the clients but a minimum certain rate of return is fixed to a limit of return and with an increase in the return, we find an increase in fee. We also find provision for 'Times Guaranty'.

While charging fee, the portfolio management firm computes a number of expenses. In a majority of the cases, we find portfolio management firm making use of the services of brokers. In that condition, the firm will also include the commission paid to brokers for that purpose, i.e., Brokerage. The brokerage may vary from 0.5% to 2.5% which will be included in the price/fee charged by the portfolio management firm. The brokers also charge service charge of 5% which may vary from time to time. In addition to the brokerage, the establishment expenses are also included in the cost.

Since the portfolio management firms make available three-tier services, the fee charged in all the three conditions cannot be uniform. The large portfolio owners make use of the non-discretionary services of the firm where they simply use the guidelines or advice of the portfolio managers. The fee is charged only for the expertise advice given to them. But the small portfolio owners considerably or totally depend upon the portfolio management firms and therefore we find a different fee structure for them. We also find a mix of both and the optional services and even in that case the fee structure will be different.

While charging fee, the portfolio management firms also need to develop their awareness of the guidelines of SEBI. The SEBI has been found restricting a minimum return or capital appreciation and other incentives to regulate the unfair practices in the stock markets. The provisions for even discount are now regulated by the SEBI.

The fee for the services varies from company-to-company or from firm-to-firm. We find different portfolio management firms or managers charging different percentage of fee. We also find some of the portfolio management firms charging transaction fee at a fixed rate on the value of portfolio. Actually, it becomes difficult for the SEBI to regulate the unfair and unlawful practices adopted by the portfolio management firms for motivating the clients.

PLACE MIX

The portfolio management services pass through different stages. The users of services are the individuals and the providers of the services are the portfolio managers who with the help of brokers make available the services to the ultimate users known as clients or customers.

In the channelisation of services, the brokers play an important role. We find brokers the persons having an in-depth knowledge of the activities of the stock markets. They charge fees for their services. We also find firms having in-house brokers. But those firms who do not have in-house brokers make use of the services of a panel of brokers found to be approved by the SEBI. It is better to use the services of a panel because they frequently check the prices. Orders to brokers may be sent on a hot-line or when they visit the firms.

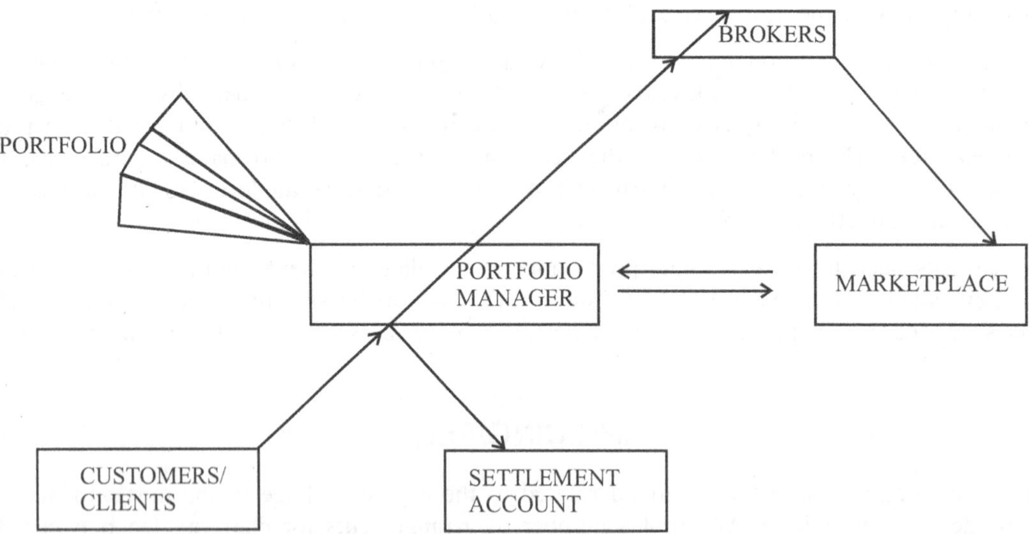

Fig. 8.3: Channelisation of Portfolio Services

The portfolio managers on the advice of brokers make investments on the basis of portfolio developed by them for this purpose. They are supposed to have an expertise in the concerned area. Normally, they should prefer a mix of stock and money markets. An interaction with the clients and brokers helps them in formulating a strategy for portfolio management. For the services rendered, the portfolio managers charge fees. The SEBI has prohibited the portfolio manager to assume any risk on behalf of the client. The portfolio managers work on the basis of a contract with the clients and final settlement and termination of contract is as per the contract and for the time period agreed upon. Notice of termination of contract is also as per the contract.

The clients are the customers using the services from the portfolio managers for which they pay fee as per the contract. They invest with diverse motives such as getting returns for investment, getting tax reliefs, using the optional services of portfolio management firm, etc.

PROCESS

This additional mix of marketing is found related to the processing of services. The professionals need not to forget that a process based on tangibilisation gives better mileage. In an age of technology, the portfolio management firms need to process and deliver the services with the help of new generation of technology. The portfolio management services are considerably influenced by information management. A well-equipped information processing technology will help clients in getting the desired information. The portfolio managers need to strengthen their operational system with the help of people considered to be efficient. Besides, they also need to provide a new shape and look to the service delivery system with the help of front-line staff. Managing both the back and front systems requires use of new generation of technology.

With the help of back staff, the portfolio managers are found in a position to offer the services to their clients. But if we find front office not managed properly, the perception of clients regarding the service quality is absolutely changed. The delivery system comprises of the constituents aimed at satisfying the customer in building a long continuing relationships by tuning the services to the specific needs of the customers. We cannot negate that the very success of delivery of services depends on the quality of people placed there. We also call it a moment of truth where the customers get an opportunity to witness the truth.

In the processing of services, the portfolio managers thus need to focus their attention on the both categories of staff — front-line and back-line. In both the areas, we find technology playing an important role. The people serving there need personal-touch-in-service. We find personalised services bearing the efficacy of winning the heart and soul of customers. The professionals managing the affairs need personal care.

The process remains incomplete if we find professionals not managing for service recovery. At each and every stage, we find scope for lapses. The working people may commit mistake or even the working machine and equipment may commit mistakes. We find nothing unnatural in the commitment process. But the most important thing here is redressal. If we find working people not redressing their grievances properly and decently, they may invite reactions. The most important thing thus affecting the process of creating and delivering the services is found related to the service recovery. The quality of processing is found improved if we find people acting as front line staff welcoming complaints and making the best possible efforts to redress them. The portfolio manager should not forget that the delivery of service can be standardised but the mistakes and lapses committed while redressing cannot be repaired. The service recovery in a true sense paves avenues for increasing the number of satisfied group of customers. If your clients feel that you are taking their grievances sincerely and redressing them properly, they turn to be your habitual customers. The portfolio managers need due attention on the above-mentioned facts for right processing of services.

PHYSICAL EVIDENCE AND ATTRACTIONS

The portfolio management services are of intangible nature. This makes it essential that the portfolio managers make efforts to tangibilise their services. This will help in getting the confidence of clients. The portfolio management firm needs to assign due weightage to the look of the décor of the premises. We are well aware of the fact that in the group of additional mixes of marketing, the physical evidence focuses our attention on service ambience. The providers need to generate the service fragrance and therefore the pleasant, professional-looking decor of the premises, exteriors and interiors, furnishing, display of machines and equipments for processing help in projecting a fair image of the firm. The clients visiting the office will evidence the service fragrance which will help the creation of positive feelings regarding the firm. Besides, the firm may also provide membership identity to the clients because as members they may feel privileged. Accessibility to the optional services of the firm will be an additional benefit because the clients witnessing the display may like to avail the optional services. Since we find the market competitive, it is pertinent that portfolio management firm in addition to other services also assign due weightage to the creation and exposition of service ambience. Since we find the corporate culture considerably depending on attractions and fragrance, the portfolio managers by making possible tangibility of their outstanding properties will be successful in influencing the customers or clients. The customers or clients believe and trust the facts they witness. The service ambience create service fragrance and this proves to be a point of attraction.

Another dimension related to this submix of marketing draws our attention on physical attractions. Service fragrance is not only the matter of service ambience but in addition, it is also related to the exposure of people serving the firm or delivering the services. This focuses our attention on the personal care dimension of people serving the firm in different capacities. Particularly the front-line staff having an one-to-one interaction with the clients need to be well dressed, neat and clean and interested in nurturing and aesthetic sense. This is also a process of tangibilisation of the intangible services. The portfolio managers may realise that they have nothing tangible in the name of services. And therefore our customer or clients visiting the office need an exposure.

In view of the above, it is right to mention that in the portfolio management services, the professionals need due attention on the creation of a positive impression. The transactional trust in the investors depends on the tangibilisation process and you have a number of things to tangibilise. What to exhibit with the motto of winning the heart and confidence of clients. As a professional, you cannot overlook it. The service ambience will help you in many ways. You need to distinct yourself. And distinction is also related to the fragrance.

PEOPLE

Either we talk about service ambience or our focus is on processing, the people working in the back and front offices determine the magnitude of success. The portfolio management firm can be successful in attracting and influencing the customers, if we find quality people working at different back- and front-line of service creation or service delivery. The servicescapes need due management; the portfolio managers have to accept this fact. Tangibilisation is an art which requires a professional touch and the quality people working there can make it possible. It is in this context that we go through the people mix in the portfolio management services. In the delivery of service, the marketing people play an outstanding role. The customers may not be aware of the process and in this respect, we find people making them aware. The sophisticated technology used in processing requires people who are well aware of managing, maintaining and operating the technology. The portfolio managers need to realise the significance of professional relationship. It is not only sufficient that portfolio managers are aware of the techniques of financial management for managing the portfolio. It is also important that they have knowledge of communication and behavioural skills. Particularly while managing service recovery, the people working there need to satisfy the customers. They are not only supposed to be factually sound but in addition they are also expected to be behaviourally decent.

The above-mentioned facts make it clear that in the portfolio management services, the people mix need an intensive care. An in-depth knowledge of portfolio management, no doubt, is an essential consideration for the people serving the portfolio management firm. But in addition, they also need to develop expertise in the field of marketing. Because we find almost all the problems directly or indirectly related to the customers or clients, it is significant that they have communication excellence. The problems of portfolio management are very much related to the emerging trends in the stock markets and also the money markets. This makes the working conditions much more complicated. Winning the trust of customers and retaining them in the business make it essential that the people serving the firm have a sense of personal commitment. They show personal-touch-in-service and are submissive to the customers. Further, it is also essential that the working people are sincere and honest. Misleading or miscommunicating clients will not solve your problems. Honest delivery and sincere recovery will help you in the image projection.

Another side of communication is with the brokers. The interaction with brokers help in getting a better deal in the market while channelising the money of clients. The custody function of portfolio management focuses our attention on making available the status report to the clients. Thus, on the one hand, the professionals need to develop relationships with the customers and on the other hand, they also need to interact with the brokers. Receiving and transmitting are the two sides necessitating high degree of communicative ability of portfolio managers.

PORTFOLIO SERVICES MARKETING IN INDIAN PERSPECTIVE

With the increasing pace of globalisation, the stock and money markets started becoming much more volatile. The economic liberalisation programme benefited the national economy of India to such an extent that masses developed a temptation for corporate investments. Since there was a significant increase in the level of income of almost all the segments, it was natural that we also witness a major change in the savings behaviour. It was against this background that the beginning of 21st century engineered a strong foundation for the development of national economy. Of course, the credibility for the same goes to globalisation and economic liberalisation.

With the emergence of corporate sector, we find development of corporate culture which paves avenues for the development of material culture in which masses start searching new avenues for savings mobilisation and investment channelisation. If we find markets witnessing much more volatility, the investors and potential investors need an in-depth study of changing market conditions so that their investments continue to be productive. It is not possible that all the investors develop excellence for channelising their investments. It was against this backdrop that investors realised the services of portfolio managers and the portfolio management services thus started developing formally.

Of late, we find development of portfolio management firm or even the in-house portfolio management services developed by some of the leading organisations found to be financially-sound. They are considered to be professionally-sound to develop portfolio for productive investments of their clients or customers for which they charge fee. They formulate a mix of different instruments in tune with the emerging trends in markets so that the customers get handsome returns for their investments and are found satisfied. The investment incentives inject life to their attitudes and the process of mobilising savings and channelising investments keep on moving.

The increasing activities in the stock markets testify that investors even in future will like to channelise their investments in the corporate sector. They lack expertise and expect a handsome return. This necessitates the services of portfolio managers and therefore the development of portfolio management services will be popular even in the years to come. We consider marketing an effective prescription to satisfy the customers. The persons using the services of portfolio management firms are considered to be their clients or customers. They have to keep themselves satisfied and for that, they have no option but to conceptualise innovative marketing. Thus, the portfolio managers and the portfolio management firms need to make it sure that the professionals not only have an in-depth knowledge of financial management but they are also potentially sound in the field of marketing.

The increasing level of income bears the efficacy of bringing an attitudinal change. The corporatisation was successful in changing the lifestyles. The masses developed temptation for material culture. And the investors preferred channelising their investment to the productive heads. It was essential for the portfolio managers that they develop their awareness of the changing attitudes of their clients and provide to them the benefits of expertise they have developed in the field of portfolio management.

The prime responsibility of a portfolio manager is to develop a portfolio in tune with the changing requirements of clients which provide to them handsome returns. The development of portfolio is considered a mix of different types of shares and securities of share and money markets which have high potential of generating returns and offering incentives. The expertise minimises the possibilities of risk. Hence, while conceptualising marketing, the most important task before a portfolio manager is to ensure handsome incentives for the investments of clients. With the help of marketing information, the portfolio managers will be in a position to formulate a sound product mix. Innovative portfolio commensurate with the needs and requirements of customers and in tune with the changing or emerging trends in markets need world-class professional excellence of marketers. The portfolio managers, thus, need to develop their marketing excellence.

It is significant that our customers are well aware of the portfolio services that we offer to them. All our efforts for making the services much more innovative and productive turn into a fiasco, if we find professionals not promoting their innovative services with the help of creative promotional measures. Informing, sensing, sensitising, persuading and transforming are the effects of our creative promotional efforts. The marketers have to understand the customers or clients in a right fashion.

In a number of cases, we find portfolio managers making use of the services of brokers. Of course, the brokers have an in-depth knowledge of stock markets and therefore they can make use of their services in the process of identifying the productive instruments. The customers expect time-honoured services and the portfolio managers need to ensure that their clients do not have any grievance or if they have, the service recovery processes are activated.

The portfolio management firms need to perceive that in the coming years, the market operations would considerably be increased. Charging moderate or reasonable fee for the services offered would help professionals in increasing the number of customers. They should not nurture exploiting attitude.

The marketers also need to practise the three additional submixes such as process, physical evidence and attractions and people while marketing the portfolio management services.

The time-honoured, accurate and decent processing of services help professionals in image projection. With the use of technology, we find even the activities in the stock and money markets considerably influenced by the new generation of information and communication technology.

Fig. 8.4: Stock Market Trend

The working people need to ensure decent processing of services. The back or front staff should make possible effective use of the machines and equipments so that any information reach to the clients as and when they demand. The communication excellence, body language and facial expression of front-line staff resolve delivery and recovery problems in a right way.

The servicescapes also need due attention. Service ambience play a positive role in generating service fragrance. The exteriors and interiors, furnishing, display of machines and equipments, lighting and ventilation, aesthetic management are some of the important aspects found very instrumental in attracting the clients. Since we find clients or visitors witnessing everything physically and enjoying the service fragrance personally, the creation of a positive impression cannot be denied.

The people working or serving the portfolio management firm in different capacities play a very meaningful role in managing, creating and delivering the services to the ultimate clients.

The professionals while conceptualising innovating marketing are supposed to be well aware of the multi-faceted changes in the stock and money markets. While developing a portfolio, they need to consider the amount of fund, objectives of investors, risk bearing capacity of clients and their preferences, although we do not find any set rule for formulating a mix of scrips or assets in portfolio, the portfolio managers may include 10-15 companies, specially for individuals.

The current phase of globalisation has been found paving avenues for earning more and investing more. In an age of material culture, you find yourself secured with sufficient money in your pockets. The investments, if professionally channelised, bring sufficient money in your pockets. Of course, you will have to face risk but here is an option that will help you in maximising the returns and minimising the risks. The professionally-sound portfolio managers are to help you in this endeavour.

Since the markets will develop and new opportunities will be created, it is pertinent that the portfolio managers develop their excellence in the field of marketing. Identifying the changing attitudes of customers or clients is a difficult task which makes it essential that the professionals are well aware of the emerging trends in the markets. A techno-driven information system may help professionals in enriching their knowledge bank. The day-to-day activities in the stock and money markets considerably influence the designing of a sound portfolio and this makes it essential that the portfolio managers make possible a microscopic audit of emerging trends. Volatility necessitates sound portfolio management (Fig. 8.4).

SUMMARY

In this chapter, you have gone through different dimensions of portfolio management. Before starting another chapter, be sure that the following facts are well versed:

Portfolio Management: The Conceptual Exposition: Portfolio management is a professional service meant for advising the investors. It is a method of distribution of total amount of investment by the investors in different securities with the motto of minimising the risks and maximising the returns.

Portfolio Management Services: An Overview: The portfolio services are of discretionary and non-discretionary nature. We also find firm providing optional services. In the discretionary services, the investors leave the responsibility of management of their investments in the hands of portfolio managers whereas in the non-discretionary services, the portfolio managers simply make available to their clients the advice regarding investments and execute the investment decisions of their clients. In the third category, we also find optional services in which both the discretionary and non-discretionary service are offered to the clients. We also find firm offering services like organising counseling sessions, borrowing against securities, circulation of odd lots within the client's portfolio, facility of temporary overdraft, etc.

Users of Portfolio Services and their Behavioural Profile: Both the individuals and institutions avail the portfolio services. We call them customers, users or clients. They pay fee to the portfolio management firm for using their services. The behavioural profile of different categories of users are found of diverse nature based on their expectations for getting the returns and facing the risks.

The Portfolio Managers: There are some guidelines and provisions for the portfolio managers because a layman cannot hold the position of a portfolio manager. He/she interested in acting as a portfolio manager, at least two in number, should must have the supporting infrastructural facilities in addition to the expertise. They work as per the provisions of SEBI.

Market Segmentation for Portfolio Services: We find different types of users coming from different segments. They come from public, private and trade sectors and are youths, or gray or senior citizens. They may be men and women with different levels of income. They reside in general or cosmopolitan towns, big or small towns and cities. A study of different segments is found essential.

Information for Portfolio Decisions: For managing and marketing the portfolio, the portfolio managers need quality information on time. The portfolio management firms need to include in their infrastructure, the new generation of sophisticated information and communication technology.

Marketing Mix for Portfolio services: The professionals marketing the services bear the responsibility of formulating a sound marketing mix combining all the seven mixes.

Product Mix: The portfolio management firms need to develop a sound portfolio combining a mix of share and money markets helping clients in getting maximum returns with the minimum risks. The discretionary, non-discretionary and optional services focus their attention in the very context.

Promotion Mix: While promoting, the professionals need to mix the different components of promotion in such a way that the measures prove to be highly effective. The advertisement measures or other components should not undermine the guidelines of SEBI. The investors are to be sensitised and persuaded in the face of their reception capacity.

Price Mix: While charging fee, the portfolio management firms need a legitimate approach. The terms and conditions must be in tune with the restrictions of SEBI.

Place Mix: The portfolio- management firms and their managers need to make use of the services of brokers and on the basis of their expertise and experiences have to develop a portfolio to fulfil the objectives of investors. The channelisation must be time-honoured and decent.

Process Mix: The front and back line staff serving the offices of portfolio management firms, with the help of new generation of sophisticated technology, should make possible right and decent processing of services so that customers or clients are found satisfied.

Physical Evidence and Attractions: The service ambience needs to generate service fragrance. In this context, the exteriors and interiors, the decor, furnishing, placing of equipments and machines, aesthetic management create a positive impression. This focuses on tangibilisation of your properties where professionals need due attention. In addition, the people serving the offices of firms need an attractive and impressive look.

People: All categories of people serving the portfolio management firms in different capacities need to develop their excellence. The portfolio managers need professional excellence both in finance and marketing streams. The other employees also need communication excellence and personal-touch-in-service. All of them need to be sincere and honest.

Portfolio Management Services in Indian Perspective: With globalisation, we find new trends in the Indian national economy. A change in the attitudes of all the segments is apparent. Increasing temptation to the corporate investments has been found making the share and money markets much more volatile. Boom and depression move in a cyclic order. It is in this context that we find portfolio management services becoming popular in the Indian context. The portfolio managers with the help of their professional excellence develop the art of designing a portfolio that maximises the returns from their investments and at the same time also minimises the intensity of risks. Since the share and money markets appear to develop, the portfolio services also need a professional touch so that innovative marketing processes are found effective in satisfying the customers.

KEY TERMS

- Volatility
- IT Networking
- Risk Phobia
- Capital Line
- Portfolio Management
- Scriptech
- SEBI
- Software Packages
- Disinvestment
- Modern Portfolio Theory
- Investment Advisory Services
- Times Guaranty
- Non-discretionary Services
- Brokerage
- Peripheral Services
- Techno-driven Processing
- Economic Offence
- Service Recovery
- Turpitude
- Physical Evidence
- Segmentation
- Servicescapes
- Behavioural Patterns
- Service Ambience
- Global Networking
- Transactional Trust
- Operational Mechanism
- Back and Front-line Staff
- Scrips
- Service Fragrance

Review Questions

1. What do you mean by Portfolio Management? Explain the different dimensions of portfolio management services.
2. Focus on the behavioural profile of users of portfolio management services.
3. What do you mean by Portfolio Management Marketing? Throw light on the role of portfolio managers in designing a portfolio.
4. Explain the role of information management in managing and developing the portfolio.
5. Focus on the different segments of clients using the portfolio management services in the Indian context.
6. What do you mean by Marketing Mix? Discuss the different submixes of marketing for the portfolio management services in Indian perspective.
7. Formulate a marketing mix for portfolio management services helping investors in minimising the risks and maximising the investment returns.
8. Focus on the extended marketing mixes in the context of marketing of portfolio services.
9. Write a descriptive note on the portfolio management marketing in the Indian perspective.
10. Explain the Portfolio Management Product in the face of recent developments in the global economy.
11. Throw light on the SEBI guidelines for portfolio management.

Application Exercises

1. Design an imaginary Portfolio for your client in the face of emerging trends in the stock markets.
2. As a Portfolio Manager, the customers need your expertise for making investments with the motto of getting high returns. Advice how he/she should make investments.
3. Do you feel that designing of a portfolio requires professional excellence? Present your arguments as a portfolio manager.
4. What properties you need to incorporate in your credentials for acting as a successful portfolio manager? Explain.
5. Develop a marketing mix for the portfolio services in the Indian perspective.
6. You are working as a portfolio manager in a reputed portfolio management firm. Suggest the role you need to play to satisfy the clients.
7. As a marketing manager, throw light on the service ambience and processing of services to your clients.
8. Explain the efforts you will like to initiate as a portfolio manager for providing tax reliefs and investment incentives to your customers.
9. Do you find it essential to use the services of brokers for protecting and promoting the interests of your clients? Focus on your role as a portfolio manager.

Endnotes

1. Basu B.K., *Lectures on Management Accountancy,* New Central Book Agency, Kolkata, 2008.
2. SEBI Guidelines for Portfolio Managers.
3. SEBI Guidelines, 1991 and 1996-97.
4. Gupta and P.K. Basu., Portfolio Optimisation in the Indian Stock Market, *Delhi Business Review,* Vol. 9/1, 2008, pp. 21-30.
5. SEBI Guidelines on Advertisement.
6. Gupta Rakesh and P.K. Basu, Weak Form Efficiency in Indian Stock Markets, *International Business and Economic Journal,* Vol. 6/3, 2007, pp. 57-61.

Factoring Services Marketing

Factoring Services particularly in the Indian perspective need a new look, a new vision and a professionalised approach because the worldwide economic depression has been found creating myriad of problems while collecting the receivables and improving the liquidity.

Chapter Objectives

Introduction – Factoring Services: The Conceptual Exposition – Typology of Factoring Services – Factoring and Forfaiting – Factoring Services Marketing: The Conceptual Exposition – Users of Factoring Services and their Behavioural Profile – Information Management for Factoring Services – Marketing Mix for Factoring Services – The Product Mix –The Promotion Mix – Pricing Decisions – The Channels – Process – Physical Evidence and Attractions – People – Factoring Services in Indian Perspective – Summary – Key Terms – Review Questions – Application Exercises – Endnotes.

Learning Objectives

This chapter aims at studying the marketing of factoring services. The motive of this chapter is to sensitise the readers to the various dimensions of factoring services marketing. The professionals come to know the conceptualisation of different mixes of marketing in the factoring services. The factoring organisations work as providers whereas the clients or the concerned companies are the users. The receivables are the amount to be collected by the factoring organisations. The marketing professionals come to know the process of application so that the customers or clients are found satisfied.

INTRODUCTION

It is essential for an organisation that its receivables are collected on time because this is to affect the mobility of finance without which the financial transactions are delayed and the image problem crops up. We find a number of cases where companies have experienced myriad of problems for delay in the collection of receivables and it is against this background that we talk about the factoring services.

Factoring service focuses our attention on the conversion of credit bills into cash. The accounts receivables, bills recoverable and credit dues in different forms keep the companies in the wrong box, if we find receivables not collected on time. We find factoring an arrangement in which receivables on account of sale of goods or services are sold to the factor at a certain discount. Because the factor gets the title of goods or services due to factoring contract, we find them responsible for all credit control, sales accounting and debt collection. The factoring services are found of great use, specially for the small and medium-sized companies. We find such type of services both at national and international levels. At the domestic level, we name them factoring whereas at the global or international level, we name them forfaiting. In the services, we also find offering of relevant consultancy services in the areas of finance and marketing. The debt insurance facility is also made available to the clients against the possible losses due to the insolvency of debtors. Besides, the administrative responsibilities of the client such as maintenance of books, accounting, management of asset, collection of debt and information reports to the client are also included in the services offered by factor. The factoring services are found risk-prone. The service providers need professional excellence for satisfying their clients.

In the Indian perspective, we find factoring services at a nascent stage. In 1988, a Study Group was constituted under the chairmanship of C.S. Kalyana Sundaram for examining the feasibility of factoring services in India. This study group recommended the setting up of specialised agencies or subsidiaries for factoring services in India. The Group felt that particularly for the SSI sector, the factoring will have tremendous opportunities in India. Later, the Vaghul Committee Report on the Money Market Reforms also made a strong advocacy in favour of factoring services but the factoring services could not take a concrete shape. Of course, the RBI allowed some of the banks such as the Canara Bank, SBI, PNB and a few others for setting up some factors in 1991 but the actual operations started in 1994. Thus, we find the year 1994, a beginning in the Indian context when we talk about the factoring services.

We find factoring services also known as Invoice Discounting to be very effective in the Indian perspective where we find a number of small and medium-sized industries facing numerous problems due to delayed collection or even pending collection of the receivables. In a true sense, such a condition keeps them at an indecisive stage. By assigning their book debts to a factor, we find the concerned companies in a position to take off them from the Balance Sheet. The operational mechanism allow companies in improving their liquidity position and to be in a position to take credit from the banks. The receivables, if not collected on time, accumulated in larger quantities contract the potentials of the companies to take loan from the banks. Thus, we find factoring helping in improving the credit potentials.

In the group of factoring services, there are a number of services such as purchase of book debts and receivables, administration of sales ledger of the customers, partial or full prepayment of debts, collection of book debts and receivables with or without documents, covering the credit risk of the suppliers and dealing in book debts of customers. At the outset, we find assessment of the credit standing of the client and thereafter setting of the limit of credit risk and opening of a line of credit. The factor is found responsible for fixing the limits to credit exposure and the time limits. The bills to be paid to clients are to be assigned to be paid to the factor. The copies of invoice and challans for delivery received are handed over to the factor for the necessary action.

The companies interested in factoring their receivables submit a list of customers containing credit rating, amount involved, date of maturity and other terms. When we find factor satisfied with the results of scrutiny, the decision is circulated to the client. The amounts to be discounted for factoring are disclosed. We also find cases where the factor takes all receivables on wholesale discount basis. In that condition, we find the factor taking all the documents concerned with the approved list and a major portion of the dues which may be even 80% to 90% to be paid to the clients. The factor also charges commission for the services rendered.

In India, the RBI has opened doors for the factoring services. But we do not find impressive results. This is also due to the fact that there are a number of conditions when we find the existing regulatory framework not in a position to protect the factor. Particularly in the global context, when we find forfaiting in place of factoring, the providers of the factoring services are found experiencing a number of problems. The magnitude of risk in factoring services is so high that the providers appear reluctant. But we find opportunities and the providers have to ensure that how and in what way they will capitalise on. The banks normally working as a factoring agency need to make use of their professional excellence.

FACTORING SERVICES: THE CONCEPTUAL EXPOSITION

Factoring is considered to be a financial service containing the financial and collection of receivables in domestic as well as the international trade. It is an arrangement between the providers and users in which receivables on account of sales of goods or services are sold to a factor at a certain discount. Factoring is also known as Invoice Discounting.

We find factoring as a non-banking service by a few of the banks who undertake this responsibility as an agent under the guidelines of the Reserve Bank of India. It is a financial arrangement to benefit specially the small and medium-sized industries. In the context of domestic services, we call it factoring whereas in the case of international services, we name them forfaiting. In the business world of today, the factoring has proved its positive contributions to the existence and development of small and medium-sized industries.

It is a result of financial deregulation which made ways for a number of non-banking functions such as leasing, hire purchase and factoring. It is a process of taking the risk of customers. It is a contract between the providers and users.

FACTORING: THE TYPOLOGY

The factoring services are of different types such as Limited Factoring, Selected Buyer-based Factoring, Selected Seller-based Factoring, Maturity Factoring, Full Factoring and Factoring with Resource as detailed below:

Limited Factoring: We also call factoring as Invoice Discounting. If we find factor discounting only certain invoices on a selective basis and converting credit bills into cash only in respect of the concerned bills, we call them limited factoring.

Selected Buyer-based Factoring: This type of factoring is related to the selected buyer in which we find the approved buyers of a company in the face of their reputation and creditworthiness contacting the factor for discounting their bills. The claims are paid by discounting the bills and the payments are made to the seller. Since we find involvement of selected buyers in the process, we call it selected buyer-based factoring.

Selected Seller-based Factoring: In this type of factoring, we find involvement of selected seller. In the process, the seller sells all their receivables to the factor. The invoicing of customers is done with the approval of the factor. In this case, the sellers make available to the factor important documents like the challan related to invoice delivery, contracts, etc. The factor now maintains the accounts, collects the funds and discharges other functions of situational nature.

Maturity Factoring: In this type of factoring, the clients do not get any advance credit or finance. The factor accepts the responsibility of collection of bills in the face of maturity date. The collection of funds may be with recourse or without recourse. If we find it without recourse, the payment is made to the client on a discounted basis. This also includes the coverage of risk and the factor may proceed against the debtor on the basis of the conditions mentioned in the contract. We call it maturity factoring because the collection of fund is found based on the maturity date.

Factoring with Recourse: In this context, we find factor acting as an agent for the collection of bills. The risk for the failure of non-payment of debt or interest on it is not covered by the factor. In case of non-payment, the factor has a right to recover the defaults from the seller.

Full Factoring: In this type of factoring, we find factor rendering all the related services such as collection of receivables, maintenance of sales ledger, collection of credit, credit control and credit insurance. In full factoring, we find the factor also making available the facilities for drawing up to a certain limit which is found based on the bills outstanding maturity-wise. Besides, the factor also takes the risk of default or credit risk and they will have claims on the debtor. Since we find the factor taking almost all the risks involved in the process, we call such type of factoring as the full factoring.

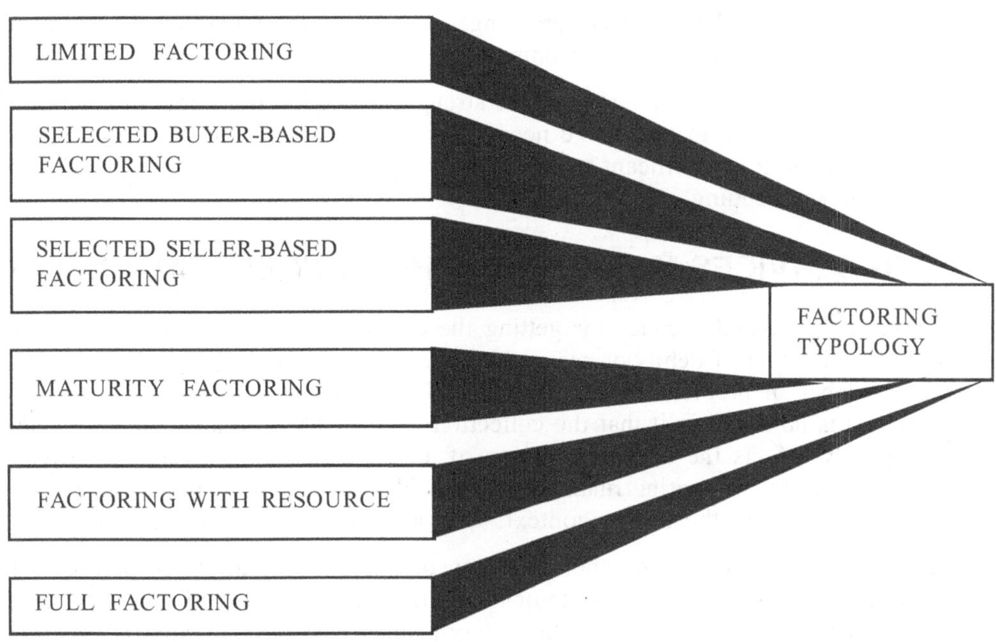

Fig. 9.1: Typology of Factoring

It is significant here to mention that in the Indian condition, we find factoring at a nascent stage and therefore it is a bit different to the developed countries where we find even insurance risk for the failure of debt collection. We cannot deny factoring to be risky an in the Indian perspective, welcoming a condition as found in the developed countries would not be considered a time-honoured step. Particularly when we find the public sector banks facing a number of problems, it is not proper to be very fast in the application process.

FACTORING AND FORFAITING

We are aware of the fact that factoring and forfaiting are almost the same but in the application processes, we find a few of the differences between the two. Of course, this is due to the application of forfaiting in the global context. The application of forfaiting is found specially in the international trade. In the forfaiting, the risks of debtor, debtor country, currency risk, goods at sea are the terms to be used when in the factoring we do not require to use these terms. The forfaiting services are offered mainly through the Exim Bank or it may also be in collaboration with Foreign Floating Agency. In the Indian context, the factoring services are offered mainly through the banks. In the process of forfaiting, we find acceptance of various types of risks such as risk of debtor, debtor country, risk of currency and risk of goods at sea. The forfaiting also includes discounting of the bills, promissory notes and other documents related to the international trade. The forfaiting services may be either with or without recourse but a majority of the exporters prefer forfaiting without recourse where risk is borne by the forfaiting agency. In the process of forfaiting, we find use of forfaiting bills with the support of foreign agencies or even importers. The Exim banks in addition to other services also offers forfaiting services to the users.

The forfaiting makes ways for a number of complications. The banker or forfaiter finds it difficult to take regulatory support except for the existing cover for the risks involved in any foreign trade transaction. Besides, they also find it difficult to manage the information which complicates the rating of foreign agencies. The political risks also complicate the forfaiting process. It is very natural that in the forfaiting services we find involvement of high costs. The time period, distance, nature of trade and the terms and conditions of contract vary from country to country and therefore, we find a variation in risks.

The above-mentioned facts make it clear that both the factoring and forfaiting are different due to application boundaries and geographical limitations. The method of credit assessment and the examination of documents are also found different in factoring and forfaiting. We find forfaiting creating numerous problems both to the users and providers. In the Indian context, the forfeiting services are yet to gain popularity. Of course, the EXIM Bank has been granted permission by the RBI to offer forfaiting services but the legal complications and implications have been found obstructing the process of development.

Because we find globalisation injecting new life and strength to the foreign trade, the forfaiting services may gain popularity in the days and years to come. We need to explore measures that how and in what way we can minimise the legal complications. It is significant here to mention that the forfaiting is a replaced form of consortium and government to government lending.

FACTORING SERVICES MARKETING: THE CONCEPTUAL EXPOSITION

An organisation needs to expand avenues for getting the credit facilities and we cannot deny a threat to its organisational goal if the collection of debits or receivables are delayed. Particularly the small-scale and medium scale industries face a number of problems on that account. The factoring is considered to be a prescription to resolve the problem. There is no doubt in it that the collection of receivables is a time-taking and risky operation which if failed considerably affects the creditworthiness of an organisation and resulting from which we find a vicious circle to be instrumental in inviting financial crunch. The developed countries have been found offering factoring services since long but in the Indian context, it is almost at a very nascent stage.

The marketing factoring services focuses our attention on the conceptualisation or application of modern marketing principles so that the customers or clients or the sellers in the context of factoring are found satisfied. The organisations or agencies buying the risks from the companies who have created it bear the responsibility of collection of receivables. Of course, they get a discount for that but the magnitude of risk is found of high order. It is in this context that we find marketing processes much more significant. The concerned agencies working or acting as a factor need to be professionally sound so that the collection processes are found complete without any delay.

The factor services marketing thus draws our attention on the two different terminologies. We are well aware of factoring and another term marketing is meant applying the principles so that you succeed in satisfying your clients or customers and earn discounts for that you have a legitimate right. The factoring services are found to be the results of the transactions between the two parties, viz., the factor who buys the risks for the collection of receivables and the users who sell the risks to the agencies for the collection of receivables for which they get discount and or commission as per the terms and conditions.

The factoring services marketing focuses on the professional excellence of agencies so that they succeed both ways, e.g., satisfying the companies or organisations from whom you have bought the right of factoring and the concerned debtors from whom you have to collect the receivables. In the process of factoring, the concerned organisations acting as an agent need to study and understand the needs and requirements of users. In a majority of the cases, we find small-scale and medium-sized industries as the users of factoring services. The factoring organisations while practising marketing also need to enrich their knowledge bank which focuses on management of information with the help of a techno-driven system. Actually, we consider it a managerial process for the formulation of a sound marketing mix. Thus, we call it:

- A managerial process for marketing factoring services.
- A professionalised effort to satisfy the clients and benefit the users.
- A financial service.
- A financial arrangement.

USERS OF FACTORING SERVICES AND THEIR BEHAVIOURAL PROFILE

In the group of users of factoring services, we include all those organisations who sell goods or services on credit and require the factoring services at post-sales stage. Generally, we find small and medium-sized units availing the factoring services. The factoring organisations need to study and understand the changing needs and requirements of their clients. An in-depth study of market will help factoring organisations in identifying the levels of expectations of the users of services. The existent and emerging opportunities if identified in a right way will help professionals in making the marketing decisions. The marketers need to know about the potential clients and their changing buying behaviour. The customers have certain level of expectations and the professionals need to identify the same. We also find clients expecting packages of services from the factoring organisations and in that condition what type of packages would be required by them need due attention of providers. We find multi-faceted studies related to the behavioural profile of users and the marketers making sincere efforts while studying their behaviour come to know about the levels of their expectations.

We are aware of the fact that in the Indian context, we find the factoring services at the nascent stage and therefore the intensity of competition in the market is found low. This in a very natural way makes it a seller's market. Presently, we find a few of the banks in the business of factoring and they provide limited services to the users. Keeping in view the high level of volatility in the global economy, the factoring organisations need a careful study of market. The small-scale units, no doubt, may be their customers but if we find their turnover not so high, the factoring organisations will not find them remunerative as the factoring cost will be non-optimal. Further, the factoring organisations may not prefer even those organisations in which we find high concentration of a few debtors because in that case the intensity of risk will be high. In addition, they may also not consider those organisations found new and untired as in that case, the operations would be risky.

The above-mentioned facts make it clear that the factoring organisations need to make a microscopic study of users of the services so that their decisions are not instrumental in inviting unremunerative factoring. They need to evolve stringent financial and non-financial criteria for identifying the clients. The important considerations necessitating prime attention of factoring organisations in the identification process are size or scale of the organisation, trends in turnover or capital employed type of product, nature of activities and profitability and image of the concerned organisation. The factoring organisations working in the Indian economy need to make it sure that only registered public and private limited companies are identified to be the potential clients for the factoring services. In case of an individual client, they need to mix a maximum exposure limit so that the diversification of risk is found easier.

The users in general expect immediate collection of their receivables so that they are in a position to improve their liquidity position. The providers contrary to it prefer low intensity of risk. Since we find both the parties having an opposite consideration, there must be an optimal point so that the factoring services protect and promote their interests and the financial activities keep on moving. The situational forces are found too much instrumental in the financial operations. The factoring organisations need to identify the clients making available to them the receivables bearing low risks. In that case, they may also offer packages of services to their clients to motivate them. The rate of discount may not be a consideration to take a decision because this may invite numerous problems in due course. While making contract, they should not forget the identity and image of the organisation who have to make payments of bills. To transact and contract with the organisations, we find turnover of the company an important consideration because with a high turnover, the intensity of risk is expected to be low.

Factoring services are availed by different categories of organisations and the providers need to take a decision in the face of facts narrated above. We cannot negate that when uncertainties in economy are found mounting, the factoring organisations cannot be liberal. In the Indian perspective, we find some of the banks such as SBI, PNB and Canara Bank engaged in factoring. The emerging trends in markets do not appear to be positive. Since we find global economy *vis-à-vis* the Indian economy witnessing economic depression, the collection of outstanding bills may be much more problematic. The factoring organisations need a careful decision and to initiate right steps for the mobilisation of resources. They need to identify their capital requirements and to pave avenues for mobilisation by getting funds from the IDBI and SIDBI under the rediscounting and refinancing schemes. The GIC may also help them credit insurance facilities for the debts to be factored.

The users of factoring services specially small-scale and medium-sized industries facing the problem of payments of outstanding bills or receivables find it difficult to get financing facilities from the banks. They expect due cooperation from the government and specially RBI so that banks and others acting as an agent for the factoring services resolve their problems.

INFORMATION MANAGEMENT FOR FACTORING SERVICES

For an effective marketing of factoring services, it is pertinent that the factor service providing organisations have a well developed information network. This is significant to enrich their knowledge bank, particularly related to the parties concerned with the book debts and receivables. At both the stages of offering the services, the factor organisations need up-to-date information. At the outset when before making a contract, they need to know about the concerned parties, the information networking is found essential and then after making the contract when the factoring organisations start the collection process, they again need the information. Hence, it is significant that the providers develop a network of information. In the Indian context, we find offering of factoring services, specially by the banks and fortunately a majority of the banks have a techno-driven information networking. This makes their task much more easier. Credit rating is found based on evaluation and the professionals find it convenient to activate the evaluation process with the help of a sound information management. It is against this background that we find information management playing an outstanding role in improving the quality of factor services.

Here, our focus is on the marketing decisions and this necessitates an in-depth knowledge of clients found to be the service-users and the marketplace where we find factoring organisations and the concerned parties interacting with each other. The clients expect quick disposal of their cases and the providers expect maximum possible discount and commission for the minimum possible risk. Keeping in view the changing market conditions, we find a change in the levels of expectations of both the parties. In the Indian perspective, we find the factoring business much more risk-prone. This makes it essential that the service providing organisations based on information networking make themselves aware of the creditworthiness of the users and the concerned parties. The information management will help the service providing organisations in many ways. A microscopic audit of the financial position of service-users will be found easier with the help of marketing research. The day-to-day collection processes may be evaluated with the help of marketing intelligence system. The creditworthiness of the concerned users and parties may be known with the help of internal reporting and internal marketing.

The most important thing in the very context is related to the potentials of factoring organisations to develop the information network and at the same time, the potentials of the clients or users to bear the service cost. Because we find the factoring services particularly in the Indian perspective offered by the banks; we cannot doubt their potentials. But so far as the users are concerned, we doubt their potentials to bear the high service cost. Despite all, it is in the interest of both the parties that the marketing decisions are information-based. In a volatile market, it cannot be overlooked because we find possibilities of unfair and unlawful practices in the business transactions.

MARKETING MIX FOR FACTORING SERVICES

The marketing professionals while conceptualising modern marketing principles need to formulate a sound marketing mix that helps in satisfying the clients. The factoring organisations may work independently or may act even as an agent. Because the volatility in the economy is increasing fast, it is pertinent that factoring services are professionally sound. All the seven submixes of marketing are practised here.

The Product Mix

By product mix, we mean the services offered by the factoring organisations. They actually act as a provider and make available to their customers a number of services. The factoring organisations need to study the emerging trends in the markets. In the process of formulating a package of services, they have to develop their awareness of the scale of market, the intensity of competition, the role of rivals, the national or international character, the concerned users and the concerned companies. While studying the users of services, the factoring organisations need to know about both the existing as well as the potential customers, their behavioural profile, levels of expectations, etc. A lot of groundwork is to be done before formulating the product mix. Creditworthiness of both the parties need due attention of marketing professionals.

The key services offered by the factoring organisation are purchase of book debts and receivables, administration of sales ledger, partial and full payment of debts, collection of book debts and receivables, covering the credit risk, credit control, credit insurance and situational functions or services necessitated by the changing condition. The factoring organisations may also offer other services such as making available a periodical statement on sanctioned limit, utilised credit and balance outstanding, the data on the list of book debt taken over and realised, agewise classification, collected and due for collection and those with recourse and without recourse, etc. It is significant to mention that the banker-customer relationships prove to be a guiding force when we talk about the additional services to be offered by the factoring organisations. Because we find the factoring organisations acting as an agent, they may render even other services if the clients or customers demand. The banks and subsidiaries generally working as a factor need to study the market conditions and to eliminate and incorporate the services found of innovative nature. To initiate and activate the process of innovations, they also need to have a microscopic study of the potential customers and to gauge their levels of expectations so that the innovative peripheral services are included in the product mix of the factoring organisations.

The marketers need to update themselves particularly to develop a package specially when we talk about the forfaiting services. The increasing intensity of economic depression makes it essential that the professionals do not prefer businesses having much more risk.

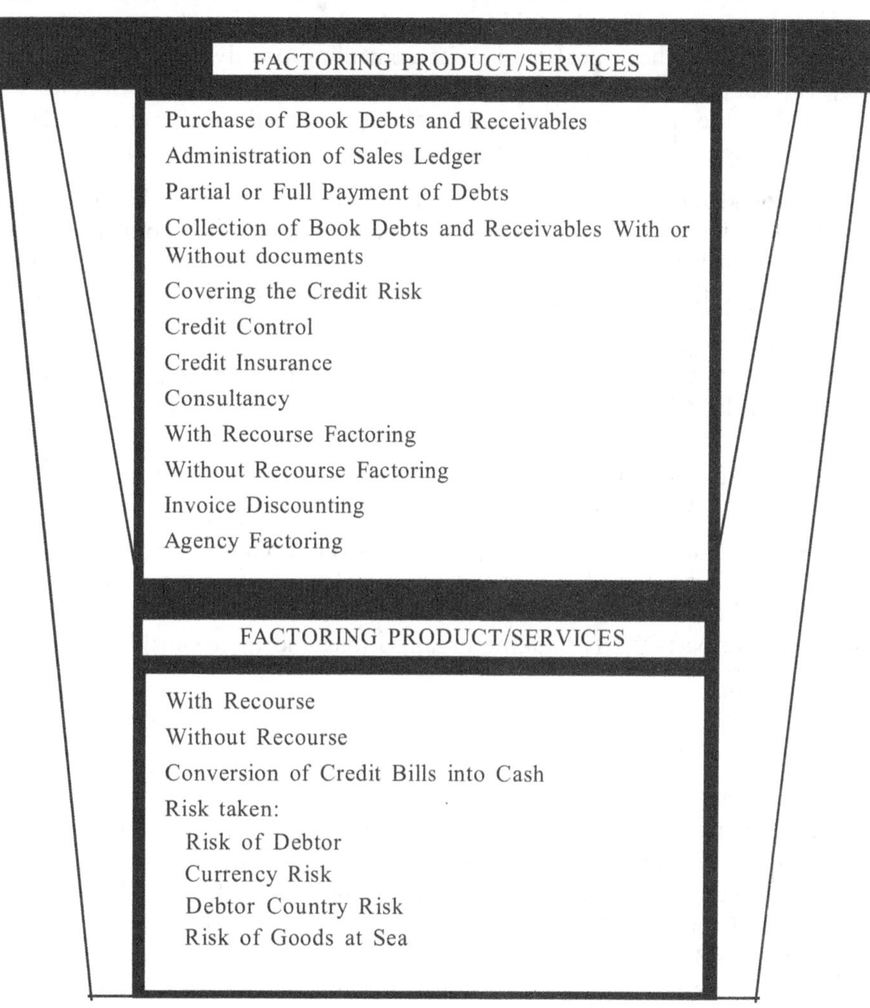

Fig. 9.2: Factoring/Forfeiting Product/Services

In Figure 9.2, we find different types of services offered by Factoring and Forfaiting Agencies. The concerned organisations accept the risks on debtors and receivables. In addition, they also offer other services in the face of contracts made by both the parties. The marketing professionals while formulating a product mix concentrate on the services mentioned in their contracts. They also formulate a package of services to make possible additional attractions in their services. The intensity of risk is found high in the forfaiting services. The development of product mix must be in tune with the intensity of competition in the markets. Since we find the intensity of competition low, the service providing organisations play an important role and dominate the process.

Promotion Mix

In addition to the formulation of a sound product mix, the marketers also bear the responsibility of promoting the factoring services so that the clients and potential clients develop their awareness of the quality of services to be offered to them. It is in this context that we go through the formulation of an effective promotion mix. The marketing professionals have to canvass the new business and to develop rapport with them. For this purpose, they will be required to visit their business houses. The different components of promotion are to be blended in such a fashion that results are effective but the processes are cost-ineffective. The professionals may take the support of advertising and for that the print media may preferably be used. This will help the marketing professionals even in minimising the cost of advertisement. Since we find the factoring services at the nascent stage, the cost economy needs priority attention. The circulation of printed literature will help clients and potential clients in knowing the details. Besides, the professionals may also think in favour of publicity for promotion. To publicise in an effective way, it is pertinent that the professionals develop rapport with the media people and make efforts to develop their awareness of the factoring services offered to the clients. In this context, the professionals may also develop contact with the academics so that they speak and write something positive about the factoring services of that factoring organisation. The cooperation of financial experts such as CA, CPA and Solicitors may be solicited for writing something positive in the newspapers and magazines preferred by the clients. They may also think in favour of direct mailing through blanket coverage and mailshot.

While formulating a sound mix of promotion, the professionals may also take support of telemarketers who will play an effective role in detailing out the information and removing the confusions. The queries of clients or others may effectively be answered with the support of telemarketers. Since we find sophisticated information and communication technology, the marketers with their high communicative ability may make this component much more effective.

For promoting the factoring services, the marketers may also take the support of personal selling because the factoring organisations for different purposes use the services of personal sellers. For convincing and motivating the clients, they may work as an effective link. So far as the word-of-mouth promotion as a component of promotion is concerned, if the factoring organisations satisfy the clients, they will transmit the messages to their counterparts and the process of transmission will keep on moving.

The marketing professionals are required to make use of different components of promotion so that the clients are informed, sensed, sensitised, persuaded and transformed in an effective way. The involvement of cost is an important factor which cannot be overlooked. The professionals need to make it sure that guidelines and regulations limiting factoring organisations, particularly banking organisations and their subsidiaries in the Indian perspective are not undermined.

Pricing Decisions

The marketing professionals while formulating a marketing mix also need to make sound pricing decisions so that the clients are motivated. It is significant here to mention that in the factoring services, the concerned organisation charges a number of expenses such as the discounting charges and the administrative charges. We find these two charges increasing the level of pricing for the factoring services. In the Indian context, we find banks and their subsidiaries factoring the services in the face of the recommendations in the Indian Banking Act, 1949. Accordingly, the SBI, PNB and Canara Bank have been found offering the limited factoring services with the help of their subsidiaries. The conventional bank financing is found cheaper because in the factoring services we find inclusion of other expenses. The factoring organisations, in case we do not find the services offered by banks, may initiate efforts to minimise the discounting charges by keeping them at par with the banks. But they have no option and to charge the administrative expenses which may vary from 1% to 2%. This in a very natural way may increase the pricing level. This makes it essential that the factoring organisations make efforts to minimise the overhead expenses which may help in rationalising the price structure.

In the Indian perspective, the factoring services mainly offered by a few selected banks need to think over the issue on a priority basis. This is essential because the clients in a majority of the cases come from the small-scale segments and the factoring services are offered to them to increase their potentials of mobilising the financial resources. Like other factoring organisations, the banks acting as a factor are not required to make additional expenses and therefore they may think in favour of minimising the factoring cost.

The above-mentioned facts make it clear that the pricing for the factoring services need due attention organisations or banks acting as providers. Receivables if not collected on time may contract their potentials of getting the credit facilities from banks or other financial institutions. If the users or clients have to pay high costs, this will affect their financial position.

The intensity of competition is considered to be an important factor for making the pricing decisions. We are well aware of the fact that in the marketing for factoring services, the intensity of competition is found very low. On the other hand, the magnitude of risk is high. Hence, the decisions related to factoring pricing ultimately rests on the changing market conditions. The professionals need to keep into consideration the multi-faceted changes and to make pricing decisions accordingly.

The Channels

The factoring services are used by the companies who are found interested in the collection of their receivables. The services are provided by the factoring organisations who for a certain percentage of discount make payments for the receivables to the users. The factoring organisations actually serve their users as an agent. The users reach to the providers.

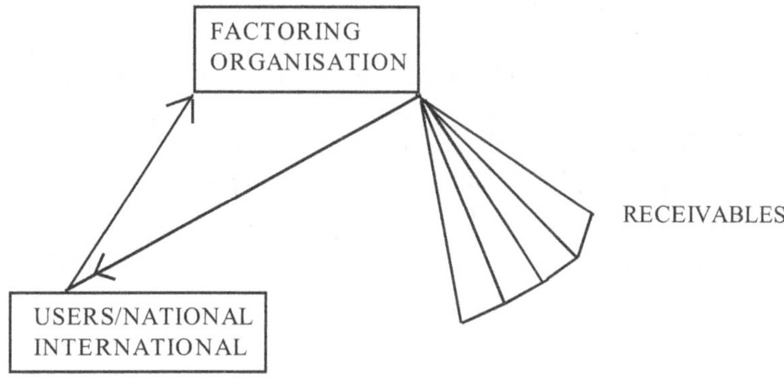

Fig. 9.3: The Channel for Factoring Services

It is clear from the Figure 9.3 that the users initially approach to the factoring organisations. The providers collect information regarding both, e.g., the companies to whom the factoring services are to be rendered and the companies or parties from whom the outstanding bills are to be collected. If they are satisfied with the information made available to them, a contract is made between the two. The factoring organisations collect the receivables and for which they get the discount. It is also significant to mention that on the basis of a contract, the factoring organisations deposit the amount to the accounts of the users after deducting the discount.

Thus, in the channelisation of factoring services, we find three different points of operation, viz., first, the users who may be companies, generally the small-scale and medium-sized; second, the factoring organisations who may be banks and/or their subsidiaries, financial institutions or other specialised organisation and third, the different parties from where the receivables are to be collected. The quality of services depends upon the professional efficiency of the factoring organisations and the team of people working for them. We find information networking an important centre for the channelisation of factoring services because the factoring organisations find it difficult to take decisions if they do not get right information on the right time. Since we find it a risk-averse business, the factoring organisations need to be very careful. Image problem is an important consideration guiding the decision making practices.

Process

The factoring services are processed by the professionals serving or working for the factoring organisations. We find factoring operations actually initiated by the concerned companies facing numerous problems on account of delayed or non-payment of book debts and the receivables. If that company appears interested in factoring services, a list of customers, credit rating, amount involved, maturity and other terms is submitted to the factoring organisations. And from there, we find involvement of factoring organisations.

After receiving the list of book debts and receivables and other details, the factoring organisations make a scrutiny of the list of buyers. If find the buyers in the approved category, they give the rate of discount for factoring along with the consent and make a contract. If the factoring organisations are unaware of the companies to be factored, they make a detailed enquiry of the financial position and business image of that organisation. Not only this, they also develop their awareness of the book debts and receivables and when they are found satisfied, a contract is made between the two parties for the factoring services.

For processing the factoring services, we find different methods of discounting. In some of the cases, the factor may take all the receivables on the basis of wholesale discounting. In that case, the factor takes all the documents related to the approved list and pays 80% to 90% of the amount due after deducting the discount and commission. After this, we find the companies availing the factoring services removing these instruments from its books of accounts and showing cash flow as against bills receivables written off.

The collection of book debts and receivables is an important process of factoring on which the quality of services and satisfaction of customers substantially rest. If the factoring organisations commit mistakes in identifying the parties related to book debts and receivables, the processing of services is found delayed and both the parties are found in trouble. This makes it essential that before making a contract, the portfolio organisations make an in-depth study satisfactory result; they accept the responsibility of factoring.

Thus, we find the key processes drawing our attention, e.g., assessing the credit standing of the client, setting a credit limit and opening a line of credit, fixing the limits to credit exposure and time period, selling the goods to the customer and invoicing the bills assigning them to be paid to the factor, handing over the factor the copies of invoice and receipt delivery challans for further action, paying upto 80% of the value of invoice after scrutiny of the documents, getting 20% from the customer and sending statements for the bills purchased, collection made and charges debited to the client.

The professionals serving the factoring organisations need a team of dedicated and committed people for processing the services to the best satisfaction of clients.

Physical Evidence and Attractions

The factoring services are offered by the factoring organisations, banks or their subsidiaries. The clients visit the offices of factoring organisations for different purposes. The impression of a client regarding the providers or in this case; the factoring organisations considerably rest on the servicescapes. The clients visiting the offices create a positive impression if they find the service ambience generating service fragrance. The exteriors and interiors, furnishing, lighting, aesthetic management play an important role in the service generation process. The professionals working for the factoring organisations need to make it sure that the different dimensions of service ambience are instrumental in activating the generation of fragrance by adding additional attractions through service ambience. The clients and their parties are found concerned with the factoring organisations. Creation of a positive impression are found important and with the help of service fragrance, the providers can make it possible. Since we find an amalgamation of a number of services in the factoring services, the techo-driven operations cannot be denied. In this case, the positioning and display of machines and equipments used in the process are also found important. We should not forget that display is an important dimension of projection and the professionals need not to forget the same. If clients or customers visiting your office evidence everything impressive due to your professionalised tangibilisation, the projection of a positive image cannot be negated. Hence, the professionals need to tangibilise the outstanding features or properties of their services.

Another dimension in the very context is related to physical attraction. This is also a process of tangibilisation of the people serving your organisation. The dresses used by them, their body language, facial impression, etiquette management, communication skill and overall personality play a significant role in the projection process. The clients visiting your organisation should create a positive impression regarding your credibility. They factor or are to factor with a strong sense of confidence and trust. Or even visitors coming here for other purposes provide you an opportunity for tangibilisation. Thus, the professionals need to make it sure that the employees working there as front or back staff tangibilise everything positive or fair.

We cannot negate the instrumentality of this submix of marketing in the factoring services. Both the above-mentioned dimensions need due attention of professionals. Creation, of course, is significant but if you minus projection from creation; the desired results cannot be achieved. It is in this context that marketers while formulating marketing mix also need due attention on this submix.

People

In the factoring organisations, we find involvement of a number of people coming from different segments and belonging to different echelons of management. While making contracts with the clients or while collecting money from the book debts and receivables, a number of formalities are required to be completed. The marketing professionals need cooperation of a full team with high communicative ability, verbal or written.

At the outset, the factoring organisations need to enrich their knowledge bank regarding the image of their clients and their receivables. The people need to be sincere and honest in the process of identification. The records of clients and their concerned organisations need a microscopic audit. Since we find people working in different capacities, the subjective knowledge of the emerging economic scenario is found essential for the working people. The increasing volatility in the markets makes it essential that people serving the factoring organisations have an in-depth knowledge of finance and marketing. On the one hand, they need to study the Balance Sheet while on the other hand, they also need to know the art of studying and understanding customers. In the factoring services, we find Balance Sheet of your clients helping you in knowing the financial position.

Collection of book debts and receivables sizeably depend on the involvement of people in the entire process. Telephonic call or written or verbal one-to-one communication with the parties play an important role in the collection process. The motive is to get the collection at the earliest. The behavioural profile of your people must be decent. People coming from or belonging to almost all the echelons need to be behaviourally sound. Irritation may delay the process of collection in addition to an increase in the cost of collection. Your back and front staff need personal-touch-in-service. They need to focus on the personal involvement of people in the process of servicing.

The different properties of people need due attention of marketers while formulating the people mix. Here, we also find sincerity, honesty and ethical dimensions of people serving the factoring organisations significant. The value engineering process of your organisation simplifies the task of image building and image projection.

The above-mentioned facts make it essential that the factoring organisations need to assign due weight age to the different properties of people and for that, they need to brush up their knowledge by imparting training facilities.

Thus, the above-mentioned additional submixes of marketing need priority attention of marketers working for or serving the factoring organisations. They need up-to-date and right information failing which the formulation process cannot be much more effective.

FACTORING SERVICES IN INDIAN PERSPECTIVE

The recommendations of a Study Group under the Chairmanship of Kalayan Sundaram, 1988 and further the recommendations of the Vaghul Committee Report (1991) engineered a foundation for the development of factoring services in India. But actually, the beginning could take place only in 1994 when banks were permitted to enter directly into factoring services. After 1994, we find banks free to enter or exit into any field on their commercial considerations and against this background; they started offering a number of non-banking services including the factoring services. However, we find the services at the nascent stage.

In the Indian context, we find the intensity of risk very high and this happens to be an important reason for the retarded growth and development aspect of factoring which focuses our attention on the conversion of credit bills into cash. In a true sense, it is a financial arrangement between the users and providers in which we find receivables on account of sale of goods or services sold to the factor at a certain rate of discount. The title of goods or services due to factoring contract is found transferred to the factoring organisations accepting the responsibility of credit control, sales accounting and debt collection. We find factoring services both at national and international levels. At the national level, we call them factoring whereas at international level we call them forfaiting.

The factoring services help companies in many ways. Due to delay in the collection of receivables, the companies find themselves not in a position to get the credit facilities which affect their normal functioning. If the factoring organisations accept the risk involved in the collection of receivables, we find an increase in the credit rating of companies. Since we find factoring organisations aware of the creditworthiness of clients, both of them enter into a contract. This leads to reduction in debts and expansion in credit potentials.

It is significant here to mention that in India, mainly due to the non-availability of credit information, the services of collection of book debts of clients are not made available to the clients. Of course, the banks finance the receivables but with recourse and even this one for limited periods as shown in their cash flow and funds flow statements. In a number of cases, we also find that funds are not received on time and the assets become non-performing assets of banks. Actually, we find companies in a straight jacket as they borrow from one and pay to another. The payment of old loan with a new loan creates a vicious circle in which we find companies trapped forever. By creating and aggravating the image problem, they make their task much more complicated and the factoring services prove to be ineffective.

The national economy of India has been witnessing a number of developments, no doubt some of them showing positive effects but at the same time, we also find a few of them of negative nature. The increasing uncertainties in the Indian economy have paved avenues for threats and challenges which has increased the intensity of risk. The small and medium-sized units have been found facing numerous problems on that account. This makes it essential that the factoring organisations offer to them opportunities to survive and thrive. They need to market the factoring services in such a way that the clients and potential clients are sensitised and persuaded. The credit insurance facility needs priority attention particularly in the Indian perspective where the delayed collection of receivables has been aggravating the problem of financial resource mobilisation. The banks acting as a factor need to be fair in dealings with the clients. The RBI needs to make provisions for the designing of a legal frame that regulates the unfair practices. The factoring organisations need to make ways for credit appraisal and rating which would let them know the realities and irregularities. The problem of non-performing assets has been increasing very fast which cannot be considered a healthy development with the viewpoints of both the providers or users.

To activate and reverberate the cycle of development, the organisations in general and the small-sized organisations in particular need high intensity in their cash flows which due to delayed or non-payment of receivables has been found contracting. The process of financial resources mobilisation starts taking rest when the liquidity position of an organisation is found adversely affected. We cannot negate that in the Indian condition a number of small organisations have been found facing the stage of financial bankruptcy due to delayed collection of dues from the large-sized organisations, government companies and government departments. This makes a strong advocacy in favour of factoring services especially with the support of public sector banks. We find unfair practices even promoted by the public sector banks and therefore they also need to strengthen their realisation that bidding a good-bye to the professional ethics may aggravate the image problem which may throw their business activities in the reverse gear.

With the increasing pace of globalisation, the economic activities in the national and global economies will be much more faster, and this will pave avenues for economic uncertainties and risk. Hence, the factoring services need due attention of banks or other factoring organisations so that the small units in particular get an opportunity to flourish. We cannot negate that credit insurance services may inject new life and continuity to the factoring services. The GIC in particular needs to come forward and to activate and promote the factoring services. The small-scale units in particular need suitable guidelines and suggestions to keep on moving the process of their smooth development and this necessitates strengthening of the consultancy services so that they get their financial and marketing activities considerably improved.

With the mounting momentum in globalisation, we find contours of development in global trade witnessing a rapid development. This has resulted into the emergence of a number of organisations evincing keen interests in foreign trade. Against this background, it is pertinent that sincere and honest efforts are made to expand the forfaiting services so that small organisations are efficacious of improving their liquidity position. The EXIM Bank accepting the responsibility of forfaiting services in the global trade need priority attention on this issue. The professionals working there need to develop their awareness of the incoming positive or negative developments in the international trade and credit rating of the potential clients to enable them to improve their business potentials. The RBI needs priority attention on the role of EXIM Bank so that the unfair or unlawful practices are regulated. Particularly when find worldwide economic depression signaling much more volatility, it is significant that the forfaiting services make ways for professional excellence.

The oscillating economic scenario, both at national and international levels, make it essential that the factoring and forfaiting services are no doubt promoted but at the same time, the business regulations are to regulate the possibilities of unfair practices. It is to be mentioned that the RBI and other investigating bodies have identified unlawful practices in bank dealings with the clients. It should not be forgotten that this may harm both the parties. We advocate factoring and forfaiting but in a regulated way.

Of course, the policy makers will realise it sooner or later that the foundation of SSI units is required to be strenghtened to provide to the national economy an umbrella of economic protection. They lack professional excellence and even the due support of regulations. They do not have a sound organisational set-up and they are not potentially sound to afford people having world-class excellence. Of course, the SSI units can show improved liquidity and financial solvency if the factoring organisations come forward to help them to take off the book debts from the Balance sheet. Since we find banks in a position to help them in many ways, a stage of financial bankruptcy can be regulated. In this context, the RBI will be required to reframe the regulatory control.

In view of the above, it is right to mention that factoring services particularly in the Indian context need a new look, a professional touch and sincere efforts to improve the liquidity position of business houses expecting red signals due to worldwide economic depression. By conceptualising innovative marketing principles, they will be successful in initiating and activating the process of qualitative transformation. Satisfying the clients, redressing their grievances, recovering the services as and when the circumstances necessitate are some of the tips to be perceived by the factoring organisations in the right perspective.

SUMMARY

Before starting another chapter, be sure that the following facts are well versed.

Factoring Services: The Conceptual Exposition: Factoring is a financial service in which the receivables on account of sale of goods and services are sold to a factor at a certain discount.

Factoring: The Typology: The factoring are of different types such as Limited Factoring, Selected Buyer-based Factoring, Selected Seller-based Factoring, Maturity Factoring, Factoring with Recourse and Full Factoring.

Factoring and Forfaiting: Factoring and forfaiting both of them are by and large the same. In the national perspective, we use factoring whereas in the international perspective, we use forfaiting.

Factoring Services Marketing: The Conceptual Exposition: This focuses our attention on the conceptualisation of the principles of marketing by the factoring organisations to satisfy the clients and to accomplish the organisational objectives.

Users of Factoring Services and their Behaviour Profile: The companies facing the problems of collection of receivables, specially coming from the small-scale units are the users of factoring services. They expect package of services from the factoring organisations.

Information Management for Factoring Services: The factoring organisations need detailed information regarding their clients and the concerned parties from where the dues are to be collected. On the basis of a sound information management, they find it easier to rate the creditworthiness.

Marketing Mix for the Factoring Service: The marketing professionals while practising marketing need to formulate a sound marketing mix in which all the seven submixes are included.

Product Mix: This makes it essential that the factoring organisations include a number of services or a package of services so that the customers or clients are motivated.

Promotion Mix: The professionals need to make use of the different components of promotion in such a way that the processes are cost-effective but the results are effective. The print media may much more effecting while informing, sensing and sensitising the clients and potential clients.

Pricing: The factoring organisations include in the price mix a number of costs. The discounting charges, administrative expenses and commission if charged are included in the costs.

Place Mix: The clients or potential clients interested in availing the factoring services reach to the factoring organisations who after a microscopic audit of receivables make a contract with them. The factoring organisations accept the responsibility of collecting the debts and receivables on the basis of contract between the two.

Process: The factoring services require right and time-honoured processing with the help of techno-driven information and sophisticated technology so that the promised services reach to the clients on time.

Physical Evidence and Attractions: When the services are found intangible, the professionals need to tangibilise their outstanding features in such a way that clients or customers visiting the offices are found impressed. The servicescapes, service ambience, service environment, service fragrance need due attention of professionals. Besides, the people working there as front or back staff need due emphasis on personal care services to add additional attractions to their services.

People: The people working for the factoring organisations need professional excellence, thematical competence, sincerity, honesty and personal-touch-in-service.

Factoring Services In Indian Perspective: In the Indian context, we find the factoring service at the nascent stage. In a true sense, the services were formally started by the banks in 1994 when the RBI permitted them to enter directly into factoring services. The EXIM Bank was permitted to offer the forfaiting services to the clients engaged in the foreign trade. The factoring services are especially for the small-scale and medium-sized companies who have been facing numerous problems on account of delayed collection of their receivables. The RBI and banks must pay due to attention on their problems.

KEY TERMS

Factoring
Receivables
Forfaiting
Money Market Reforms
Consultancy Services
Credit Rating
Typology
Hire Purchase
Invoice Discounting
Risk of Currency
Political Risks
Clients
Political Clients
Techno-driven Information
Marketing Mix
Package of Service
Credit Insurance
Consultancy
Telemarketers
Word-of-mouth Promotion
Discounting Charges
Administrative Expenses
Overhead Expenses
Service Channel
Information Networking
Book Debts
Physical Evidence
Servicescapes
Service Ambience
Service Fragrance
Tangibilisation
Personal Care Service
Etiquette Management
Thematically Competence
Volatility
Vicious Circle
Image Problem
Globalisation

Review Questions

1. What do you mean by Factoring Services? Do you find the factoring and factoring services identical? Justify your arguments.
2. Explain the different types of factoring services.
3. What do you mean by factoring services marketing? Focus on the behavioural profile of users of factoring services.
4. Do you find management of information essential for making the marketing decisions for the factoring services? Defend your arguments.
5. What do you mean by marketing mix? Explain the different sumbixes to be practised in the factoring services.
6. Throw light on the services offered by the factoring organisations to their clients.
7. How do you find additional three submixes of marketing relevant to the factoring organisations? Explain.
8. Write a note on the marketing of factoring services in the Indian perspective.

Application Exercises

1. The small-scale units have been facing the problem of delayed payments of receivables. Do you find for them the factoring service useful? Justify as a marketing professional.
2. How and in what way the factoring services help clients in improving their liquidity position. Defend as a marketer so that the task of persuading the potential client is found easier.
3. Formulate a marketing mix for the factoring and forfaiting services in the Indian perspective.
4. Design a package of service for your clients interested in availing the factoring services of your organisation.
5. As a professional of EXIM Bank, you have been assigned the responsibility of offering the forfaiting services to your clients. Explain how and in what way you can help them.
6. In the capacity of a marketer, explain the steps to be initiated by you for studying the behavioural profile of your potential clients.
7. Factoring Services in Indian are found at a nascent stage. Justify the role of RBI in the very context.

Endnotes

1. Report of Study Group, 1988 under the Chairmanship of Shri C.S. Kalyan Sundaram.
2. Recommendations of Vaghul Committee on Monday Market Reforms for Factoring Services to SSI units.
3. RBI Recommendations on Factoring Services, 1991, The SBI, PAN and Canara Bank and their subsidiaries permitted to work as factor.
4. Association of British Factors, 1986, *Factoring: A Financial Management Service for the Growing Business.*
5. Sengupta and Kuvalekar: *Factoring Services, Skylark,* 1992.

Transport Marketing

The discovery of fire, no doubt, was an important achievement but of all the inventions made so far, the wheel is probably the most important with far reaching effects. The Middle East, Egypt, Europe and other parts of the globe made use of wheel which made ways for speed and development. We accept challenges of nature and therefore we survive and thrive.

Chapter Objectives

Introduction – Transport Marketing – The Concept – Users of Transport Services – Behavioural Profile of Users – Market Segmentation for Transportation – Information Management for Transportation – Market Segmentation for Railways – Significance of Segmentation – The Indian Railways Product – Product Planning and Development – Planning for Freight Traffic – Planning for Passenger Traffic – Planning for Pipeline Transportation – Planning for Consultancy – Railways Mail Services – Marketing Mix for Railways – Marketing Rail Transportation Services in Indian Perspective – Marketing Management for Road Transport Organisations – Product – Product Planning and Development – Marketing Mix for Road Transport Organisations – Road Transport Services Marketing in Indian Perspective – Marketing Management for Civil Aviation – Product – Product Planning and Development – Marketing Mix for Air Transport Organisations – Air Transport Services Marketing in Indian Perspective – Transport Marketing in the Indian Perspective – Summary – Key Terms – Review Questions – Application Exercises – Endnotes.

Learning Objectives

The motive of this chapter is to sensitise the readers to the various dimensions of marketing the different modes of transportation. The transportation services play a catalytic role in the acceleration of economic transformation measures. Conceptualisation of modern marketing principles helps in satisfying the users which makes ways for organisational prosperity. The three modes of transportation are the three vital pillars of development. They need professional excellence and the implementation of marketing principles remains the most effective prescription in their hands. The readers will come to know the role of different submixes of marketing. Besides, they will also be successful in developing their awareness of the conceptualisation process. The motives are satisfying the users, accomplishing the organisational goals and contributing to the social transformation process.

INTRODUCTION

All biological laws support perishing of human beings with the first 'Ice Age'. The main reason for their survival was development of a healthy habit of accepting the challenge of nature at each and every step of development. When nature denied free gifts to other living beings, they soon vanished. But the human beings devised measures to remove the handicaps obstructing the flow of their development. The discovery of fire, no doubt, was an important achievement but it is also right to mention that of all the inventions made so far, the wheel is probably the most important with far reaching effects. Over five thousand years ago, the wheel was first invented in Mesopotamia. The new invention soon spread all over the world like a wildfire. At the outset, the Middle East and Egypt and later Europe and other parts of the globe made use of wheel for different purposes. In a true sense, this new invention promoted a new concept of development in which "speed" could receive an overriding priority.

A well managed system of transport acts as a catalyst of economic transformation. With the passage of time, the sophistication in the modes and process is a natural phenomenon. In India or elsewhere, the greatest revolution in road transport took place with the advent of mechanised road vehicle. Of late, we find transport the *de facto* barometer of social, economic and commercial progress. It has been successful in transforming the entire world into one unit. It has substantially contributed to the evolution of civilisation by transmitting ideas, inventions and feedback to the globe. It has proved to be an indispensable part of culture and hallmark of civilisation. It has removed barriers of physical separation besides maximising the frequency in the development of resource mix.

We can't check an acceleration in the process of socio-economic transformation when the different transport organisations make available to the society an effective transportation which is meant faster but safe movement of men, machines and materials from one place to another. Almost all the manufacturing, merchandising, banking, extracting and even other like businesses can't exist, if the wheels start taking rest. What to talk of the processes of socio-economic transformation even the process of cultural transformation is fantastically influenced if we stop the movement of wheels. Of course, there are a number of factors instrumental in the process of development but of all the factors, we find transportation contributing sizeably to the development processes since none of these exert even the tithe of influence upon economic growth that has come from transportation. Our most conspicious economic development achievements depend considerably on transport. A well-managed system of transport acts as a catalyst of economic development.

In the development of land transport, we focus on the configuration of soil or land surface. We prefer to construct roads where the land is even or surfaced. It is difficult to construct roads, specially in the hilly areas or flood-prone zones. The areas enjoying torrential rains are found not suitable for road construction. In the modes, we find different categories of carriages like bullock carts, buses, trucks, autorickshaws, cycle-rickshaws, tram-ways, bicycles, etc. In the Indian transport system, we find trucks occupying a place of outstanding significance because for short distance, we find them competing successfully with the railways. Besides, buses have also been found making a significant contribution for short distance journeys. The introduction of railways has revolutionised the process of development. The fast, safe, economic services of the Indian Railways have been successful in attracting almost all the segments.

The management and control of railways and roadways has undergone far reaching changes, particularly after the attainment of Independence in 1947. In respect of roadways, we find both public and private management but the railways are found managed by the public sector. With the establishment of State Road Transport Corporations, we find participation of public sector in the transportation of passengers. On the other hand, we find private road transport agencies engaged in transporting both the men and materials. We also find significant developments in the administration or management of railways. Of late, we find Indian Railways as the main artery of the nation's inland transport.

The Civil Aviation occupies a significant place in the transport management of today's world. Both for passenger and goods operation, the air transportation services have been playing an incremental role. The Indian Airlines for domestic flights and the Air India for the international flights are managed and controlled by the government. In the private sector, the scheduled airlines (passengers) are Jet Airways, Deccan Aviation, Spice Jet, Go Airways, Kingfisher Airlines, Paramount Airways and Indigo on the domestic sector. For cargo, we find Blue Dart Aviation. We can't deny the fact that civil aviation market is now more competitive which requires professional excellence and market the services.

In a country like India where the roadways and railways are important forms of land transport and the magnitude of dependence on them is also high, the marketing practices may help the service generating organisations in many ways. The mounting intensity of competition in the different modes of transport make it significant that we seek the co-operation of professionals for managing the services. It is in this context that we make a strong advocacy in favour of conceptualising marketing in almost all the three important modes, such as Road Transport, Rail Transport and Air Transport.

The mounting losses in the State Road Transport Corporations, the increasing dependence of the Indian Railways on the central exchequer, the deteriorating financial health of Indian Airlines and Air India make it essential that we think in favour of innovative marketing since this bears the efficacy of generating profits, satisfying customers and subserving the society in many ways. It is against this background that we find management experts supporting the application of modern marketing principles in the transportation services.

The State Governments, Union Government and private agencies engaged in the transportation business need to assign due weightage to the commercial considerations without which the generation of profit, satisfaction to customers/users and protection of the interests of weaker sections and backward regions would hardly be possible. The policy makers need to formulate such a policy that simplifies the task of executives. The construction of all-weatherproof roads, the insurance facilities, the protection to the transport assets and passengers are some of the important considerations failing which the transport organisations can't work profitably. The State Transport Corporations, the Indian Railways, the Indian Airlines and the Air India and in addition, the private sector organisations need an attitudinal change. The increasing cases of road accidents, the highways robbery, the ticketless travelling, the theft and pilferages in freight and cargo operations, the fare and freight structure, the processing of promised services to the end-users, promotional measures, the development of efficient personnel for transport generating organisations are some of the key issues requiring world-class professional excellence. The marketing principles bear the efficacy of developing the services in tune with the changing requirements of users, promoting the services to inform, sense and persuade the prospects, rationalising the fare and freight structures to make the services commercially viable and processing the services in such a way that the promised services reach to the end-users without making any distortion. It is in this context that we find it pertinent to formulate a sound marketing mix for the different categories of organisations offering different types of services to the different segments of users.

This chapter of the book goes through the marketing of transportation services. All the three modes of transportation, such as roadways, railways and airways need formulation of a sound marketing mix to strike a balance between the commercial and social considerations. So far as the users are concerned, by and large, we find them almost identical in the different modes of transportation. The first task before a professional is to develop their awareness of the changing needs and requirements of the users of different segments and thereafter to formulate a marketing mix. Either we talk about passenger or our focus is on the transportation of goods, the users expect punctual and safe services. Of course, they also expect affordable services from the transport organisations. The marketers need to make it sure that the promised quality of services are available to the users without any service quality gap.

In the process of formulating a marketing mix, the focus will be on all the seven mixes of marketing, e.g., product, promotion, price, place, process, physical evidence and attractions, and people. With the entry of private sector, particularly in the road and air transportation, we find intensity of competition high. This necessitates quality services at an affordable price. The marketing professionals while formulating the product mix need due weightage on safety and security measures. Not only the core but even the peripheral services also need due attention to excel competition. They need to promote the services with the help of different components of promotion but the promotional measures must be creative, effective and cost-effective. The fare and freight decisions need priority attention because the market is found to be competitive. But it is not meant that they bring down the price at the cost of quality. Informing, sensing, sensitising, persuading and transforming the potential users into actual and habitual users focus on creativity in promotional measures. The channelisation of passenger or goods transportation services need quality people and new generation of sophisticated technology. The processing of services must be time-honoured and decent without making any distortion in the quality. The servicescapes, service ambience, service environment and service fragrance help providers in adding additional attractions to the services. The employees serving there need to look smart, neat and clean and impressive. In addition, the transport organisations should have a team of dedicated, committed and professionally-sound people.

Thus, the formulation of a sound mix is, no doubt, a crying need of the hour and the Roadways, Railways and Airways need to make use of the new generation of information and communication technology for offering world-class services to the users of different categories. With the increasing pace of globalisation, we assign due weightage to sophistication and the service providing organisations cannot undermine it. The conceptualisation of marketing would help them in many ways.

TRANSPORT MARKETING — THE CONCEPT

Before anatomising other dimensions of marketing management, the conceptual exposition of transport marketing is presented. The term transport marketing is identification of the most profitable markets now and in future, assessing the present and future needs of the users, setting business development goals and making plans to meet them and further managing the services and promoting them to achieve the plans — all in the context of the changing business environmental conditions to cater to the changing socio-economic needs. It is a managerial device to formulate marketing mix which makes possible an optimal utilisation of the marketing resources to fulfil the changing needs and requirements of general as well as the industrial users. We consider marketing a customer satisfaction engineering and therefore the professionals bear the responsibility of making marketing decisions with the prime motto of satisfying the users. In addition, the marketing decisions make ways for the designing of a rational fare and freight structure that helps the transport organisations in maintaining the commercial viability. Besides, it is a managerial process to bridge over the gap between the services-promised and services-offered.

The aforesaid facts make it clear that the term transport marketing is application of marketing principles by the transport organisations in which the marketing professionals make sincere efforts to market the services in such a way that generation of profit, satisfaction to users and protection of social interests are made easier. Since we find the business environment more competitive, the marketing decisions help in excelling competition by making the services internationally competitive. It is a device that makes the ways for development and expansion. Since we find all decisions clustering around customers/users, the transport marketing proves to be a device to study the changing behavioural profile of both the categories of users. At the same time, we find transport marketing helping an organisation in making profits but in no case, we find a place for profiteering. We use profit as a tantamount of profiteering but both the terms have different meanings and implications. The transport generating organisations have a legitimate right of making profits since this simplifies the task of improving the quality of services and fulfilling the needs and requirements. A caged bird can't lay eggs of normal size. In the transport marketing or generally in the service generating organisations when we talk about making of profits, it focuses on profit making by promoting fair, ethical and legitimate practices. Profit that engineers a sound foundation for development and expansion helps in satisfying the users.

The marketing concept in the transport organisations focuses on some of the important problems as mentioned below:

- It is a managerial device to promote the transport business.
- It helps the transport generating organisations in making profits.
- It is a device to shape the perception of customer satisfaction.
- It is an effort to excel competition.
- It is a social process that makes a strong advocacy in favour of subserving the social interests.
- It is an attempt to make available world-class transportation services to the end-users.
- It is an organised effort to promote business.

USERS OF TRANSPORT SERVICES

In the transport generating organisations or even in other service generating organisations, it is pertinent that the users are given due weightage. The different categories of users use the services with different motives. The general users like safe, time-honoured and economic services and like this, the industrial or organisational users also prefer quality and fast services even if they are asked to pay more. We are well aware of the fact that in the Indian perspective both the public and private sectors have been found offering transportation services to the general and industrial users. In Figure 10.1, the different categories of users make it clear that in the service generating organisations like the State Road Transport Corporations, Indian Railways, Indian Airlines and Air India we find individual and general customers using the services.

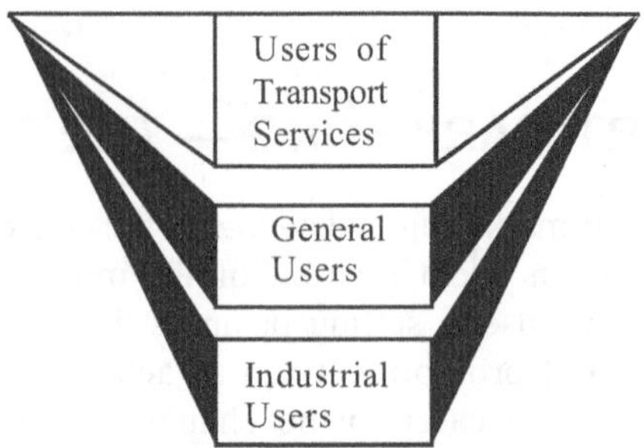

Fig. 10.1: Users of Transport Services

General Users: In this group, we include all users — rural or urban — availing the services of transport organisations for travelling or other purposes. Here, the potential users of the services like time-honoured and cost-effective services. The masses use different modes of transport and for the same, they are to be charged. An individual prefers to have fast, safe and economic services. The rural users/prospects avail the services with the prime motto of getting the services linked to the urban markets so that they succeed in getting a profitable return for their goods and services. In addition, they also use the passenger services. Sophistication is not an essential consideration for the rural users. On the other hand, the urban users prefer to avail quality services containing sophistication and offering to them more comforts and conveniences. They prefer to travel in AC, Deluxe, Super-deluxe buses. They like sleeper coaches or so. This makes it clear that the urban users are found influenced by sophisticated services where the rural users in a majority of the cases are found sensitised by the economic fare and freight structures. Safety is an essential consideration that requires due weightage. The rural users don't know about the safety element and therefore they are not serious to the violation of safety provisions. We also find cases where they promote risks by their own decisions. Thus, the rural general users are substantially influenced by price whereas the urban users are influenced by quality.

The distance of journey is also an important aspect influencing the requirements of potential users. Persons travelling for a long distance prefer to have quality services where different types of comforts and amenities are available. The users using the services for a short distance generally prefer time and safety. The Indian Railways, State Road Transport Corporations, Indian Airlines, Air India and other private transport organisations need to study the behavioural profile of users availing the passenger and freight traffic operations. It is natural that with the passage of time, we find a change in the hierarchy of needs and the transport generating organisations bear the responsibility of identifying the level of expectations and making multi-dimensional efforts to fulfil them.

Industrial Users: The industrial users avail the services of transport organisations with the motives of safe, economic and time-honoured transportation of their goods to the destination. With the development of primary, secondary and tertiary sectors, we find a significant increase in the requirements of industrial users. The agricultural sector uses the services of different modes of transport for the movement of inputs and outputs. In the face of changing requirements of this sector, it is pertinent that the transport organisations offer to them world-class transportation services. The safety provisions, insurance provisions need due weightage. The perishable and other agriculture produces are transported from one place to another. The transport generating organisations bear the responsibility of offering quality, safe and economic transportation of agricultural produces and inputs. On the other hand, we also find the industrial sector using the transportation services. The transportation of industrial inputs and outputs influences the functioning of industrial organisations. The perishable, bulky, consumer durables and non-durables, plants and equipments need due care of the transport organisations. Since we find different categories of industrial users availing the transportation services, it is pertinent that the transport organisations assign due weightage to the interests of cottage and small industries. The subsidised and cost-based services need due attention of transport organisations. The trade and commerce sector can't work smoothly if we find transportation organisations not working satisfactorily. The development of market, arrival and departure ratio of inputs and outputs, the demand and supply position would adversely be affected if the transport organisations fail in making available the quality, time-honoured, safe and economic services to the trade and commerce sector of the economy. We can't deny the fact that like the importance of circulatory system to the normal functioning of human bodies, the transportation services are found important to the socio-economic fabrics. The public as well as the private sector organisations need to identify the changing needs and requirements of industrial users and to make suitable arrangements to improve the services so that their expectations are fulfilled and the normal functioning of a market is not affected. It is the prime responsibility before the policy makers that they assign due weightage to the increasing demand and make the supply position optimal to their needs. The rural areas, urban areas depend substantially on the availability of transportation facilities. The availability of all-weatherproof roads is an essential consideration for improving the quality of road transportation services. The Indian Railways bear the responsibility of subserving the interests of all segments. The Indian Airlines and Air India bear the responsibility of offering quality services for transporting the valuable/expensive goods, equipments or so.

BEHAVIOURAL PROFILE OF USERS

We are well aware of the fact that the transport organisations also need to intensify an in-depth study of the behavioural profile of different categories of users so that they succeed in satisfying them. Business goes where it is invited but stays where it is well treated. For the development of an organisation or for expanding the transportation network both in the backward and developed areas, it is essential that the transport professionals study the changing behavioural profile, come to know the hierarchy of needs and make multi-cornered efforts to fulfil them. It is against this background that we talk about the behavioural profile of the users of transportation services. It is quite natural that multi-faceted developments in the socio-economic conditions influence the hierarchy of needs and requirements *vis-a-vis* the level of expectations. Yesterday, the users did not demand AC, Deluxe, Super-deluxe buses but today they demand. Yesterday, the users did not insist on door-to-door services but today they expect so. Yesterday, they did not raise their voice in favour of sophisticated and subsidised services but today they raise. Yesterday, they were not aware of the insurance facilities but today they are familiar with the same. These changes in the expectations of users make it essential that the transport organisations offer to them the services-desired. The providers are supposed to be more careful while offering the services so that the promised services reach to the end-users without making any distortion. For the success of a business, it is essential that users remain satisfied so that they successfully act as a hidden salesforce and activate the process of word-of-mouth promotion. To be more specific when we find both the public and private sectors engaged in the transportation business, it is important that the organisations keep their eyes open and minds active so that they are found in a position to make available to the users the world-class services. It is in this context that we need to study the behavioural profile of users of the transport services.

The most important thing in studying the behavioural profile is to identify the level of expectations which is substantially influenced by the multi-dimensional developments in the socio-economic fabrics. How to create the impulse using is an important exercise that requires professional excellence. To be more specific when the magnitude of competition is found at its peak, we need to increase the market share which requires services of world-class. We can't deny the fact that a change in the lifestyles of masses is considerably influenced by the development of corporate sector and emergence of corporate culture because this opens up new vistas for the development of different sectors and the transport sector is also one of them. The needs and requirements of industrial as well as the general users can't remain static. We also find a change in the perception of quality among the different segments. The general users prefer safe, time-honoured, comfortable services whereas the industrial users insist on services which help in activating the process of production. The demand and supply position, the transportation of inputs and outputs if delayed jeopardise everything. This makes it essential that the public sector as well as the private sector transport organisations keep themselves engaged in studying the behavioural profile of users/prospects. The main thing in the process is to keep on moving the process of qualitative-cum-quantitative transformation so that the task of excelling competition is simplified.

MARKET SEGMENTATION FOR TRANSPORTATION

An organisation offering to the masses the transportation services is supposed to be well aware of the specialities of a particular segment so that they are in a position to understand their preferences. It is quite natural that different categories of users avail different modes of transport for different purposes. If the transport professionals know about needs and requirements of a particular segment, the marketing resources can be developed accordingly. The users coming from the rural areas, illiterate persons, the agriculturists and industrialists the affluents availing the services and like this youths and women, kids and teens using the transportation services expect and behave in a different way. It is against this background that we need to segment the market in the face of changing socio-economic and business requirements.

The Indian Railways, State Road Transport Corporations, Air India and Indian Airlines have no option but to study the market and to divide it into small segments so that some of the identical properties are identified and necessary steps are taken. It is in this context that we talk about the market segmentation. The segmentation particularly in the transport sector needs to take into consideration a number of factors, such as regional, genetic are found important in the very context. The travelling teens, kids, men and women, the business community, and the small business houses feel that quality upgradation is essential and segmentation can make it possible.

The State Road Transport Corporations have been found generating losses since they are not aware of the changing needs and requirements of different segments. The needs and requirements of farmers, industrialists, traders, men and women, kids and teens, poor and affluents, rural and urban can't be identical. The segmentation let them know the level of expectations of different categories of users and the road transport generating organisations can improve the quality of services by formulating a sound marketing mix.

The Indian Railways offer services to the different categories of users, such as farmers, industrialists, general persons, rich and poor or so. It is essential that they are familiar with the hierarchy of needs and formulate marketing mix accordingly. The segmentation simplifies their task substantially. The service mix, the product profile, and the package can be designed to cater to the changing needs and requirements.

The Indian Airlines offering domestic air transportation services and Air India offering international services and other Airlines also need to segment the market. Since the market is competitive, it is significant that all the concerned organisations, private or public understand instrumentality of segmentation in making the right marketing decisions. To be more specific, the Air India is required to study and understand the different categories of national and international users so that the services are matched with the emerging trends in the international market. The Indian Airlines mainly offering the domestic services has to assign due weightage to the different categories of users availing their services. The market is found competitive and to be more specific, we find Sahara Airlines throwing a big challenge to the Indian Airlines.

The aforesaid facts make it clear that segmentation is a managerial process based on professional excellence. The segmentation helps the process sizeably. The policy planners, senior executives, and the managers need to assign due weightage to segmentation which would make the marketing efforts proactive.

INFORMATION MANAGEMENT FOR TRANSPORTATION SERVICES

In an age of information technology, the quality of transportation services considerably rests on the quality of information. All the modes of transportation partially or substantially make use of information technology for improving the quality of their services. We find civil aviation and railways sizeably depending on information and communication and even minor mistakes in the transmission jeopardise their normal operation then what to talk of the quality services. Information networking is found significant from the viewpoints of both safety and punctuality. A transformation in the quality of rail transportation services could be possible with the help of computer-driven operation. The air transportation services even cannot think of their existence, if we find something wrong in the transmission of information. It is against this background that the transport organisations need priority attention on the management of information.

In the management process, our focus is here on the marketing of transportation services and in this context, the professionals will find it difficult to study and understand the changing levels of expectation of users, if the information technology is not working properly. The revolution that we find in the communication services is also the result of new generation of information technology. The marketers with the help of new generation of technology find it easier to formulate a sound marketing mix helping them in offering the quality services. With the increasing intensity of competition, it is pertinent that the transport organisations make a microscopic study of the behavioural profile of users. This task is made easier with the help of new generation of information and communication technology. The marketing research helps them in forecasting the trend. Particularly, the civil aviation services where we find intensity of competition almost at its peak, it is essential that the air transport organisations not only focus on the quality of services but also concentrate on the cost. By striking a balance between the two, they would be successful in excelling competition. They have a tough task of increasing the occupancy ratio and it is not to be possible, if they undermine the management of information. A study of emerging trends is essential and for that, professionals have no option but to improve the quality of information.

We cannot deny that the road transportation services have not been making use of the information networking and this has considerably been affecting the quality of their services. If we find State Road Transport Corporations working on an organised basis, it is essential that they develop their information networking which would help them in many ways. Both for passenger and goods transportation, we find information networking essential. Of course, the rail and air transportation services have assigned due weightage to the management of information but the road transport services do not think over it on a priority basis. Information-based managerial decisions make ways for qualitative and quantitative transformation.

MARKETING MANAGEMENT OF INDIAN RAILWAYS

The Indian Railways are supposed to perform the dual role of a public utility service and a commercial undertaking simultaneously. This dual role imposes on them the obligation to fulfil the transport requirements of all sections of the society in conformity with the socio-economic objectives. Being a public utility undertaking, the Indian Railways don't have the freedom to adjust their fare and freight rates corresponding to increases in the prices of various inputs used by them. They also carry certain essential commodities passenger traffic at rates which don't cover even their cost of movement. This creates a big gap between the prices-paid for inputs and the prices-received from the outputs. We call it a cost-price-squeeze which questions the financial prosperity and ultimately the railways start generating losses which contract their efficacy of bearing the social costs.[1] Over the years, we have developed a peculiar perception regarding profit. A profit-making firm is branded as a blood-sucker, an exploiter, an enemy of the public and hence reprehensible. Whether we like it or not, it is a plain fact that albeit a public utility undertaking can't survive, unless it makes profits. In a true sense, the generation of profit is a matter of survival. A caged bird can't lay eggs of normal size. An undertaking generating loss or not making profits can't deliver goods to the society. We find an abnormal fall in its capacity of bearing the social costs. Particularly, for an utility undertaking, it is meant generating profit for raising the potentials of bearing the social costs.

The marketing practices answer to the problems of qualitative degeneration of services. It also makes the ways for increasing the earnings, satisfying the users and improving the technological base for securing safety and maintaining the time schedule. There is no doubt in it that the Indian Railways are the main artery of the nation's inland transport and Asia's largest and world's number one railway system under a single management. However, we find enough scope for initiating qualitative-cum-quantitative transformation to cater to the changing requirements of the users. We have to remain a leader and this requires application of modern marketing principles. We accept the fact that marketing principles if practised in a right fashion help management in striking a balance between the two opposite considerations of projecting a positive image and channelising the welfare facilities.

This draws our attention on the following:

- Formulation of a sound service mix for the Indian Railways which make available to the users world-class passenger and goods traffic services.
- Promoting the services with the help of innovative measures to inform, sense and persuade the users that they are offering the world-class services at a reasonable fare and freight structure.
- Offering promised services to the end-users and bridging over the gap between the services-promised and services-offered.
- Rationalising the fare and freight structures so that the commercial viability is maintained.
- Developing quality personnel for the Indian Railways who are supposed to be personally-committed and value-based.
- Adding additional attractions to the services so that the Indian Railways prove and continue to be number one.

MARKET SEGMENTATION FOR RAILWAYS

An organisation serving rich and poor, rural and urban, literate and illiterate, teens and youths, kids and grey, men and women finds it difficult to study the changing needs and requirements of the different segments. It is quite natural that all the users have their own likes and dislikes. The agriculturists and the industrialists, the traders, the institutions use the services of Indian Railways with diverse motives. If the market segmentation is right, the task of developing the marketing resources and satisfying the users is made easier. The modern marketing principles make a strong advocacy in favour of formulating the marketing mix in the face of changing needs and requirements, lifestyles, expectations of the different segments. It is against this background that we find it significant to study the problem of market segmentation in the Indian Railways. We can't deny that the expectations of the users of AC, first-class compartment can't be matched with the users of second-class. Similarly, it is natural that the users of Mail, Express or Ordinary trains would have different expectations. The farmers use the services and their expectations are found different to the traders or industrialists. The unemployed youths, students have different expectations. The weaker sections of the society have high expectations. These facts are a mute testimony to this proposition that for satisfying the different categories of users, it is pertinent that the Indian Railways have an in-depth idea of the behavioural profile. This necessitates market segmentation. The level of dissatisfaction moves upward when the organisations fail in assigning due weightage to the expectations. Of course, we don't find any direct competition since the Indian Railways have monopoly but the road transport corporations and companies have been found throwing a big challenge to the Indian Railways. In Figure 10.2, we find market segmentation for Indian Railways.

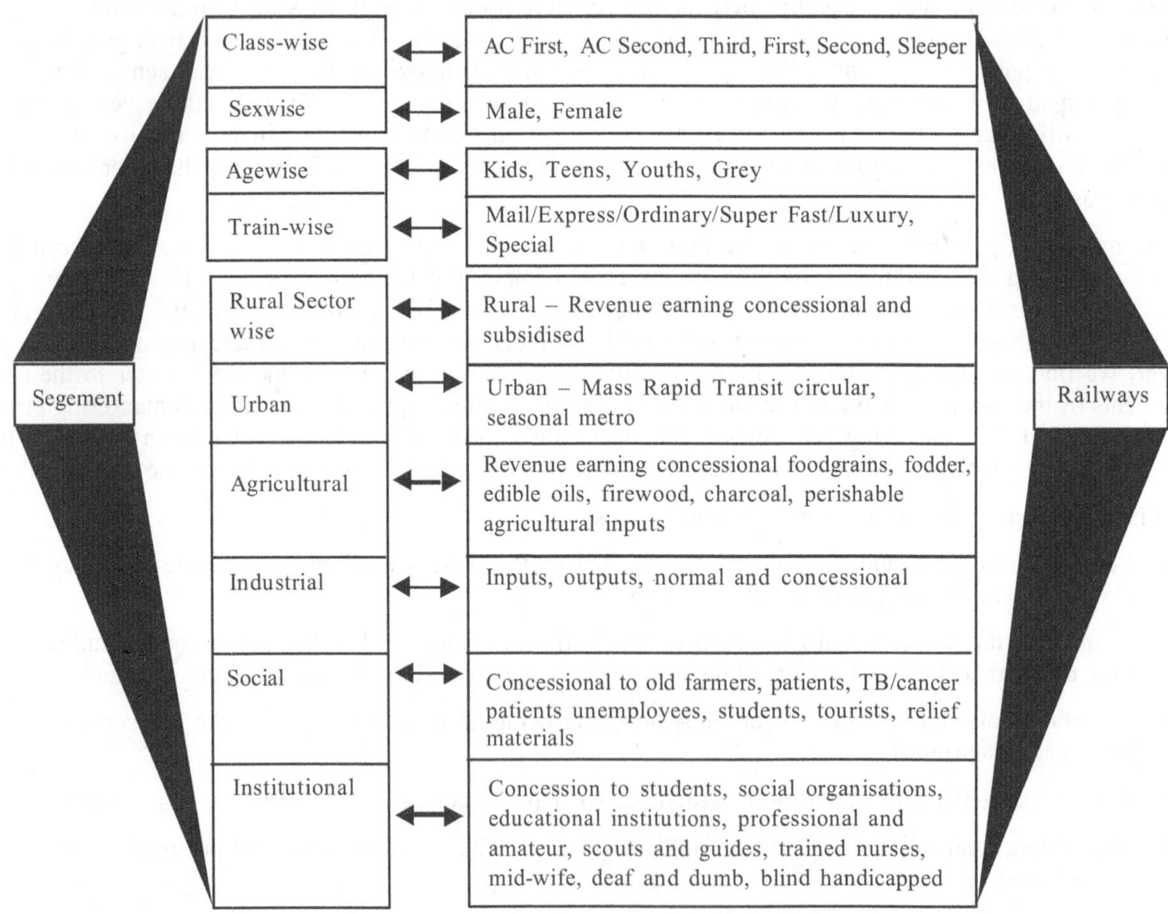

Fig. 10.2: Market Segmentation for Railways

SIGNIFICANCE OF SEGMENTATION

The Indian Railways are supposed to play the dual role of a public utility service and a commercial undertaking. This imposes on the railways an obligation to meet the transportation requirements of different segments in conformity with socio-economic objectives. Besides, they are also supposed to generate adequate revenue for expansion and development, discharging dividend and other liabilities. For maintaining commercial viability of an undertaking, it is pertinent that market segmentation is done, studied and perceived in a right fashion.

The marketing practices of even a public utility undertaking do not welcome a rigid or restraint pricing policy. It is right to mention that consistent efforts on the part of government to avoid the pressure on the budget have resulted into a big gap between the prices-paid and prices-received. The segmentation of market would help in assessing the incentives offered to a particular segment. The professionals would also be successful in identifying the level of their expectations which would help them in making possible an optimal development of the marketing resources. In the Indian perspective, the rural and agricultural sector, need an overriding priority. The spotting of rural opportunities and their optimal utilisation would make the ways for urbanisation which would establish a close link between the villages and towns.

The Indian Railways are supposed to provide a strong infrastructural support to the economy. This is possible when we know about the requirements. The high revenue generating fare and freight traffic operations can be fuelled which would improve the financial health of Indian Railways. The increase in the number of coaches, wagons, locomotives, and other technical or non-technical requirements is possible when we formulate a rational plan. We can't deny that segmentation paves avenues for identifying the emerging trends and formulating a plan in the face of available potentials and requirements. The corporate plan provides this perspective, spells out the objectives to be achieved and strategies to be formulated for each functional area for the time-honoured and cost-effective implementation of development-oriented policies and programmes. To be more specific in a public utility undertaking, we find it difficult to fulfil the requirements of all the segments since all of us shape a new perception of expectations.

In view of the above, it is right to say that market segmentation occupies a place of outstanding significance. The Indian Railways bear the responsibility of scanning the emerging trends in the face of needs and requirements of different segments. The task is not so difficult since of late we have sophisticated information technologies to manage the marketing information. We are in a position to rate our strength. We are also in a position to identify the intensity of competition generated by the road transportations, corporations and companies. We can also identify the profitable opportunities and thus the avenues for revenues can be broadened. The intensity of dependence on the central finance can be made dismal. It is in this context that we find it important to the development and prosperity of Indian Railways that marketing practices are in tune with the changing socio-economic needs. Of late when almost all the segments are found dissatisfied with the quality of services of the Indian Railways, it is essential that the Indian Railways assign due weightage to the segment-based development programme.

THE INDIAN RAILWAYS PRODUCT

Product is anything that can be offered to market for attention, acquisition, use or consumption which includes physical objects, services, personalities, places and ideas or anything else that has the capacity to provide the satisfaction, use of perhaps the profit desired by the customers/users. The main products of Indian Railways are services which have been defined as any activity or benefit that one party can offer to another that is essentially intangible and does not result in the ownership of anything. Although some of the products are also tangible like coaches, wagons, locomotives and tracks, the emphasis here is on the marketing of services since all the tangible products are used as inputs and the ultimate outputs are the passenger and freight traffic operations made available to the end-users.

PRODUCT PLANNING AND DEVELOPMENT

Before we go through the problem of formulation of a sound marketing mix for the Indian Railways, it is pertinent that we focus on the product planning and development. In an environment of rapid technological sophistication, faster economic growth and enhanced expectations of the people, a long-term perspective plan of the railway development is vital. The corporate plan of railways provides the perspective, spells out the objectives to be achieved and strategies to be followed. The corporate plan identifies specific strategies to be followed for each functional area for achievement of the corporate objective. The forecast of traffic projected by the National Transport Policy Committee, the Rail Tariff Enquiry Committee and Railway Reforms Committee[2] for the 2000 AD are yet to be fulfilled mainly due to the required expansion in the transporation capacity of India Raileays, what to talk of others when Indian Railways failed in fulfilling their own forecast.

The forecasts made by Railways is based on actual relationship established over the last four decades. In the case of passenger traffic, it is between the rate of population growth and the rate of increase in passenger kilometres. In the case of freight traffic, it is between the rate of growth in Gross Domestic Product and the rate of increase in Net Tonne Kms. To meet the colossal task of moving substantially higher volume of freight traffic, the Indian Railways have to make considerable efforts to make possible an increase in the capacity. This requires an increase in the quality and quantity of coaches, wagons, locomotives, tracks and other assests. All these eluate would be possible when we make decisions in tune with the anticipated growth in the traffic. We have to introduce new quality or special type of wagons helpful in maximising the loading capacity and have also to minimise piecemeal wagon movement as well as movement of small, specially for short distance. Besides, we also need to reduce the differential between speeds of Mail and Express trains by evolving better design of wagons on a stronger track. At the outset, we need to estimate our requirements and after this, the new product development strategies are to be formulated. We go through different plans, such as planning for passenger traffic, planning for goods traffic, planning for pipeline transportation, planning for consultancy, and the railway mail services. These dimensions aggregate the quality of outputs generated by the Indian Railways.

Planning for Passenger Traffic: Particularly after the attainment of independence, there have been radical changes in the transportation capacity of Indian Railways. Of late, we find Indian Railways operating a vast network of 65,000 route kms. The product planning and development is found essential to cater to the increasing number of passengers. This draws out attention on the introduction of coaches of new design having more accommodation and comforts. Till the early 1950s, we find steam locomotives dominating the motive power scene of railways so much that about 99 per cent of the passenger traffic and 99 per cent of the freight traffic were hauled by steam locomotion. The dieselisation and electrification resulted into the phasing out of steam locomotion. It is right to mention that diesel and electric locomotives are comparatively more efficient than steam locomotives. They provide greater hauling capacity, sharper acceleration and deceleration and are capable of higher speeds. They have less servicing needs and therefore we find availability of traffic in an increased position. The Indian Railways have undergone significant changes on the traction front. Track constitutes the basic infrastructure of the railways system which bears the brunt of the transportation of ever increasing traffic. The building up of a sound and reliable track structure constitutes a significant place in the smooth operation of railways. The servicing facilities to the travelling passengers need a new vision. The catering services, medical aid, supply of bed rolls, reservation facilities, lighting and sanitation, water are some of the important facilities found substantially instrumental in upgrading the quality of passenger services. Important trains on the Indian Railways have dining/pantry car facilities and the breakfast and meals are served to the passengers. This necessitates standard catering services. The cloak room facilities to the travelling passengers also divert a close attention. The most vital thing is to make possible quantitative transformation which draws our attention on the expansion of rail transportation facilities to the neglected and backward areas of the country. This in addition to the expansion also gravitates our attention on the quality of coaches having the maximum possible accommodation, safety provisions and amenities and facilities. The Indian Railways are supposed to make efforts to absorb the additional traffic demand by creating more transportation capacity through improvements in the design of the existing stock. It is right to mention that the new quality of coaches have more elbow and knee rooms besides inside finish with basins, mirrors and modern fittings.

The most important thing in the Indian perspective is to improve the quality of passenger services which require a close look on the multi-faceted amenities and facilities mentioned above. In addition to other aspects, the planners are required to keep into consideration the increasing demand for passenger transportation. The safety provisions need an intensive care. The increasing cases of accidents make it essential that sophistication in the technologies is made possible. New types of coaches and in a few of the cases even expansion of double decker coaches would be essential to make the supply position optimal. In addition, the services at the railway stations also need due care. It is right to mention that a majority of the railway stations lack even essential civic amenities. It is high time that the policy planners think over the development plans and formulate such a strategy for the development of passenger traffic that a fair synchronisation of qualitative-cum-quantitative improvement is made possible.

The information system would help management in estimating the demand position. We need to make an assault on the problem of overcrowding.

Planning for Freight Traffic: With the pace of economic growth picking up, the Indian Railways were called upon to provide a much higher and stronger infrastructural support to the national economy. The mounting contributions of Indian Railways to the emancipation of national economy has made it significant that the tempo is maintained. Of course, the growth is unparalleled, however the increasing developmental activities make a strong advocacy in favour of enriching the potentials. Always to touch the new heights should be our slogan. While one side of the coin narrates its positive contributions, another side confirms shortages of wagons, increased cases of theft and pilferages and unfair practices influencing the financial health of Indian Railways adversely. It is against this background that we need to plan for the freight traffic.

The agricultural and industrial development activities are inextricably interwoven with the development and fortunes of Indian Railways. In this context, the availability of wagon occupies a place of significance. To be able to cope with the pattern of traffic offering, it is pertinent that we activate the process of quantitative-cum-qualitative improvements. It is essential that we include special type of wagons fleet for having more accommodation and safety. The BOX wagon which is high-sided open bogie wagon with side discharge provision for transporting coal and other bulk traffic, the BOY type of wagon which is low-sided wagon to carry iron ore, the BCA wagon for the transportation of cattle, the BRH wagon for the transportation of rails, the TANK wagon for liquid consignments, the BCX water-tight wagon for foodgrains, cement, etc. need to be increased in number to meet the increasing demand. The container fleet for door-to-door services is also to be increased substantially. The significant task for the wagon supplying units is to increase the supply position and at the same time, intensify research activities to make available to the Indian Railways improved quality of wagons.

It is right to mention that the Indian Railways have taken certain measures to arrest diversification of traffic to road to some extent by introducing various user-friendly services, such as Domestic Container Service, Freight Forwarder Scheme, Quick Transit Scheme, Speed-link Express Trains, Street Collection or so. While planning for the freight traffic, it is essential that the wagon producing units promote research to improve the quality of wagons.

The dual role imposes on the Indian Railways the obligation to meet the transport requirements of all the segments in conformity with the socio-economic objectives and at the same also to generate sufficient revenues to meet the working expenses to discharge dividend and other obligations. The introduction of new technologies in the field of agriculture, the growing rate of industrialisation, the increasing performance of trade and commerce and other welfare activities aggravate the intensity of pressure on the Indian Railways. It is in this context that they are supposed to play a crucial role in the planned development of a country. In an age of high-tech, the Indian Railways need to intensify multi-dimensional steps for product planning and development so that the users coming from different segments are found satisfied and the possibilities of shifting of the profit generating traffic to the road transport are minimised.

The introduction of new wagons, inclusion of high-powered locomotives, technology-driven and user-friendly services, welfare orientation are some of key measures to improve the quality of services. The computerised services have virtually redefined the concept of quality in the Indian Railways. The rolling stock fleet of Indian Railways in service comprise almost 35 steam, 5,000 diesel and 3,500 electric locomotives.[3] The Indian Railways are in the process of inducting new designs of fuel-efficient locomotives of higher horse power, high speed coaches and modern bogies for freight traffic. Modern signalling control, automatic signalling and multi-aspect colour light signaling have made Indian Railways potentially sound. We cannot negate that the Indian Railways have made impressive progress regarding indigenous production of rolling stock and variety of other equipments over the years and is now self-sufficient in most of items.

Planning for Pipeline Transportation: We find pipeline transportation peculiar in the sense that it does not require any vehicle. It is a one-way method of transportation in which mechanical power is required for its operation. It is meant for the transportation of liquide commodities like urban water, gas, petroleum or natural gas. This mode of transportation is a recent development, particularly in the Indian context. In the Indian Railways, the pipelines carry white products mostly whereas black products are still carried by rail Guwahati to Silliguri, Barauni to Haldia, Barauni to Kanpur and Koyali to Sabarmati are the important pipelines. Keeping in view the increasing requirements, the Indian Railways would be required to expand the pipelines for carrying the crude oil to oil refineries.

Planning for Consultancy: Indian Railways have also been offering the consultancy services. The Research Design and Standard Organisation (RDSO), Indian Railways Construction Company Ltd. and Rail India Technical and Economic Services (RITES) have been offering national and transnational consultancy services of world-class.[4] RDSO is a unique institution carrying on research, development and standardisation work. To activate the process of innovation, the consultancy services would be required to be made of international standard. The multi-faceted aspects to be covered are research, design, indigenous development specification and standardisation, inspection, service engineering and consultancy.

The RDSO has been found making available to its clients the consultancy services to different Zonal Railways in addition to the assistance to industry for transportation of extra heavy and bulky consignments. The expansion of railways is the goal and therefore, the RDSO would also be required to vitalise and innovate its consultancy services. The Rail India Technical and Economic Services has steadily established itself as one of the leading total transportation consultants. Its recognition as consultant both in India and abroad testifies the quality of services offered by the RITES. Its services are in greater demand by a much larger spectrum of clients in the government, public and joint sectors. The RITES continue to attach special importance to extend support and assistance to the developing countries by providing wide range of activities, specially in Algeria, Bangladesh, Ethiopia, Ghana, Iraq, Jordan, Mozambique, Mexico, Mauritius, Sri Lanka, Zambia and Zimbabwe. Another undertaking is Indian Railways Construction Company Ltd. which is meant for taking up construction of railways projects including designing and construction of signalling and telecommunication, electrical system, railways tracks, etc. to meet the requirements of railways on turnkey basis and otherwise both in India and abroad. The overseas prospects are in Algeria, Saudi Arabia, Jordan, Bangladesh, Mauritius and France. The projects in India are with the Indian railways, PWD Punjab, PWD Maharashtra.

We can't deny that in the field of consultancy the aforesaid agencies have established world-class image. Almost all the countries have appreciated the outstanding contributions of these consultancy organisations in offering world-class consultancy services. It is hoped that even in future, the tempo and the quality remain maintained. This makes it essential that these units intensify research to initiate the process of qualitative transformation.

Railway Mail Services: Indian Railways are the mainstay of the present postal system. For carrying heavy mails and parcels and for linking the postal system with the remotest parts of the country, the Indian railways are and will continue to remain the most important means of establishing a postal network in the country. The development of economic postal system is due to the services rendered by the Indian Railways. In a true sense, the postal system would collapse if Railway Mail Services (RMS) are withdrawn. Prior to 1854, the post office was a medley of separate services in different provinces each having separate rules and different tariff. With the introduction and expansion of railways, it became the main channel of postal communication and mails are despatched for all post offices on the line as also for parcel beyond the terminal point. In past, there have been multi-dimensional developments in the mail services of the Indian Railways. It is essential that even in the years to come, the services are innovated and made competitive to counter the challenges and threats generated by the courier agencies. The increasing cases of late delivery, degenerating customer/user services has been found generating the image problem for the Department of Posts. With the co-operation of Indian Railways, the services can be made innovative as well as competitive.

For achieving the desired goals for providing the maximum possible satisfaction to the users of services, the marketing practices aim at planning for the development of product and formulating a suitable strategy which helps in transforming the potential users into the actual users. It is against this background that we make a strong advocacy in favour of innovation. Almost all of us are well aware of the quality of services offered by some of the world-class courier agencies. It is high time that the railway mail services are innovated to improve the workings of the Department of Posts. With the development of rail transportation, we expect that the RMS would be successful in maintaining speed, safety, time schedule or so. This necessitates professionalism in managing the mail services of the Indian Railways. It is significant that employees serving the wing are personally-committed.

MARKETING MIX FOR RAILWAYS

The Product Mix

The formulation of product mix is found significant to almost all the organisations either producing goods or generating services. Since the Indian Railways generate services, it is essential that the designing of mix is done professionally so that the users get the world-class services. Of course, we find the intensity of competition almost dismal but it is not meant that the Indian Railways don't assign any weightage to quality. We also agree with this view that the State Road Transport Corporations and the Inter-road Transport Agencies have been found throwing a big challenge to the Indian Railways in the form of snatching of business. It is a red signal that requires due attention of policy makers, senior executives and Railways personnel in general. There is no doubt in it that Indian Railways have tremendous potentials, the only thing they lack is dedication, value orientation. It is against this background that we focus on the formulation of an ideal product mix by the Indian Railways in which both the core and peripheral services are optimally synchronised. The product portfolio requires due attention of management. The profitable services for future are required to be included in the mix to counter the challenges and threats generated and aggravated by the road transport organisations. This requires the formulation of a sound product mix.

What Product to Offer?

Railways main products are fare and freight traffic services. Of course, some of the products of the Indian Railways are tangible but we find them inputs not the outputs for the Indian Railways. A few of the public sector undertakings under the Ministry of Railways are engaged in manufacturing locomotives, coaches and wagons. What product to offer is of course a dynamic concept that changes its shape in the face of multi-dimensional developments. Yesterday, the users were found satisfied with the ordinary wooden seats, today they expect cushioned seats. Yesterday, they were satisfied with the drinking water facilities, today they expect water refrigeration facilities. Yesterday, they did not make a demand for container services, today they expect. These significant changes in the level of expectations of different categories of users make it essential that we shape a new perception of quality by innovating the services. The innovation thus requires due attention of management. The product mix determines the magnitude of success. It is due to the fact that the product mix helps in satisfying the users, paving avenues for generating revenues, increasing the strength of the organisation to excel competition and paying handsome dividend to the investors.

While designing the product mix, it is pertinent that the professionals managing railways assign due weightage to the changing business environmental conditions. It is right to mention that till now we find a major change in the product mix of the Indian Railways but in light of developments made in the developed countries, we can't claim the services to be of world-class. The peripheral services have not been assigned due weightage by the Indian Railways. What to talk of the peripheral services when we find even the core services facing the problem of degeneration. The increasing cases of accidents, theft and pilferages, overcrowding, long waiting queues for reservation, late running of trains, etc. testify the poor quality of core services.

In Figure 10.3, we find the product mix of the Indian Railways.

It is right to mention that with the implementation of Five Year Plans and the resultant growth in the economy, the railways have increasingly become carrier of low-rated bulky materials like coal, iron ore, foodgrains, etc. It is a welfare-oriented scheme strengthening its base as an utility undertaking working in line with the holistic concept of management. In respect of high profit yielding commodities, the Indian Railways have been facing tough competition from road transport. This is in view of the inherent advantages which it enjoys over road transport such as freedom to pick and choose not only the commodities from carriage but also the destinations and the routes as well as customers and the liberty to give on the spot reduction of rates, etc. To make an assault on these problems, it is pertinent that user-friendly services are given an overriding priority. The peripheral services both at stations and coaches need due attention of management.

The selection of wagon is an important aspect to minimise the cases of theft and pilferages. Growing cases of theft and pilferages not only raise the financial burden on the railway exchequer but also aggravate the image problem. The units engaged in manufacturing wagons are required to intensify research to improve the quality of wagons. It is high time that the average carrying capacity of railways is increased.

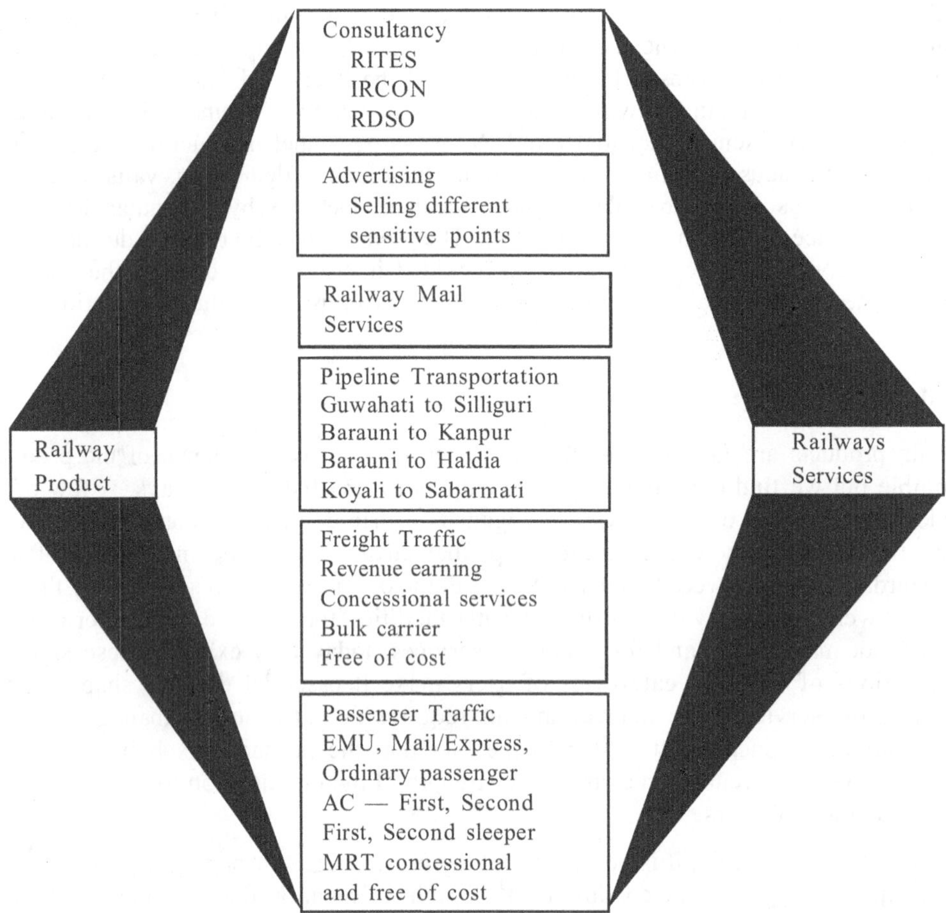

Fig. 10.3 : Product Mix of Indian Railways

The induction of BG wagons fitted with roller bearings which are much less liable to hot box failure than wagons with conventional bearings needs to be promoted. The workshop modernisation programme needs a new vision to activate the process of technological sophistication. We expect a lot from Central Organisation for modernisation of workshops. The Workshop Modernisation Project needs an intensive care.

The product mix of the passenger traffic operation needs a new strategy. This is essential to make possible qualitative-cum-quantitative improvements in the passenger services. Our focus is on both the core and peripheral services inside the coaches and at the railway stations. To improve operational efficiency, the automation is to be given due weightage. The electronics appliances need to be maintained properly. The electrification is to be speeded up. The peripheral services at the railway stations like safe drinking water, clean and well-managed sanitation, provision of dustbins, frequent washing and cleaning of tracks and stations, management of reservation counters, seating arrangements at the stations, proper lighting facilities, provision of electric fans, etc. are some of the services that would add additional attraction to the services offered by the Indian Railways. The safety provisions, protection to passengers and the railway staff need due attention. The management also bears the responsibility of adding additional attractions to the services inside the coaches while the trains are running, such as proper seating arrangements, lighting, sanitation and ventilation, safety to the travelling passengers, maintenance of the time schedule, etc.

The aforesaid measures would improve the quality of services. In addition, the Indian Railways also bear the responsibility of expanding the route kms., auto signalling and locking, conversion of MG into BG, special trains during the special season, proper announcements at the railway stations, etc. which would enrich the quality of services offered to the users. The following steps need due attention of management:

- Increase in the number of superior quality of coaches furnished with modern amenities and facilities.
- Increase in the number of superior quality of wagons having more accommodation and safety provisions.

- Activating the process of dieselisation and electrification.
- Special care to urban and semi-urban passengers by expanding or promoting the Mass Rapid Transit System.
- Plugging the leakages in the railway finance by intensifying the protective measures and checking the ticketless travelling.
- Optimising the social costs so that the deserving persons are offered concessional or free of cost services and at the same time, the misuse of concessional services used by the fake passengers are regulated.
- Promoting the consultancy services by intensifying the research activities and innovating the marketing practices.
- Synchronising the core and peripheral services optimally.
- Innovating the peripheral services by enriching amenities and facilities in the coaches and at the railway stations.
- Designing a sound product portfolio which helps railways to generate profits.
- Offering new packages for motivating passengers and tourists.

The Promotion Mix

If you offer quality services to the users, your task of building a positive image is simplified considerably. If you are performing well, you have a legitimate right of promoting the same. It is against this background that we talk about the promotion mix of the Indian Railways. The different components of promotion need due attention of management.

Advertising: We are well aware of the fact that it is a paid form of persuasive communication. There are a number of media used for advertising such as print media, broadcast media and telecast media. The railway professionals bear the responsibility of using all the three but not to make the process unproductive. While advertising, it is pertinent that we seek the cooperation of advertising professionals for sensitising the messages, slogans and appeals. The creativity is to be made possible and this makes a strong advocacy in favour of professionalising the whole process. You offer quality services and let others know about your positive contributions. The telecast media should be used to promote the business. You are bearing huge social costs and therefore the masses should know about your contributions. The advertisement messages should also be instrumental in inculcating mass awareness and civic sense. To check ticketless travelling, you need to advertise in right fashion. You need to advertise as and when special incentives are offered, attractive packages are designed, concessional services are given. In addition to the telecast media, we also need to use broadcast media for transmitting our positive contributions. Besides, it is essential that we also promote through print media for which dailies, weeklies, newspapers and magazines having larger circulation need to be used. The main thing in advertising is to make possible creativity so that the messages, appeals, slogans become effective in informing, sensing and persuading the users.

Publicity: While promoting, it is also important that the management assigns due weightage to public relations activities. Here, our emphasis is on developing rapport with media people, vocal leaders, opinion leaders and to motivate them. Just by developing a rapport with the media people, it is possible to publicise effectively. This dimension of promotion also gravitates our attention on sharpening the instrumentality of PROs, receptionists, announcers or so. We are aware of the fact that publicity requires development of sweet relationships with users or others so that we are not to face the image problem.

Sales Promotion: In the context of promoting the services, it is essential that we also think in favour of incentives to the users and travel agencies and to the front-line staff who are directly instrumental in increasing the business. The incentives to the users would be in the form of seasonal concessional services, circular trips, small gifts for high spending passengers or so. For the travel agents, front-line staff and the travelling ticket checkers, we need to offer special incentives linked to the generation of revenue.

Personal Selling: Personal promotion is found based on personal skill, ability, excellence and commitment. In the rail transportation services, we need to assign due weightage to the personal efforts of the provider of services. In a true sense, we find travel agents, tour operators, transport operators, hotels, front-line personnel helping you substantially while promoting the business. If we find travel agents and the railway personnel not favouring you, the task of increasing the business would be much more difficult. This makes it significant that the Indian Railways also think in favour of incentives to the personnel or agencies who promote the business.

Word-of-mouth Promotion: It is an important component of promotion in which the satisfied group of customers act as a hidden salesforce and keep themselves engaged in promoting the business without charging anything. The opinion leaders are also used for this purpose. This dimension of the promotion mix makes a strong advocacy in favour of improving the quality of services so that the satisfied users narrate to their friends and relatives the outstanding services offered to them. The word-of-mouth promoters if suitably motivated act as a sharpe-edged motivational tool. It is in this context that we need due priority to this dimension of promotion even by the Indian Railways.

Telemarketing: With the sophistication in the process of satellite communication, all of us have been witnessing significant developments in the field of telecommunication. The TV has been found adding an additional attraction to this dimension. It is a device to promote business with the help of telephones in which a person with high professional excellence is placed as a telemarketer who answers to the queries and questions raised by the users or the potential users. The important information and facts are transmitted to them on telephone. As an additional support, the televisions increase the instrumentality of telemarketing. In foreign banks and insurance companies, we find use of telemarketing. It is high time that even in the Indian perspective, we think over this dimension of promotion which would help the Indian railways and its users in many ways. We are aware of the fact that telemarketing would prove its instrumentality by informing, sensing and persuading the users. In this context, it is pertinent that person acting as a telemarketer is familiar with the code and culture essential for the effective telephonic talks. He/she is supposed to be a master of language with an attractive microphonic sound. It is also important that his/her temperament is not to generate tension rather to diffuse the tension of dissatisfied, aggressive, and short-tempered users. We hope that the Indian Railways think about this component of the promotion mix.

Cause-related and Sponsorship Marketing: Being a public utility undertaking, it is significant that Indian Railways make use of this component of promotion to project its image as a social transformer. A large number of services are offered by Indian Railways to the general masses. Almost all the segments of the society are found benefited with the product mix of Indian Railways.

This component of promotion focuses our attention on promoting with a particular cause and in a very natural way, we find social cause a focal point to be used by Indian Railways for promoting their contributions. The Indian Railways come forward as and when we find natural calamities or any other problem affecting the general masses. The display of posters and banners, slogans and messages become instrumental in sensitising the society. Since we find use of this tool of promotion to benefit the general masses and champion the social cause it is known as cause-related marketing. In this context, we find sponsorship marketing another term to be used for promoting the services. This draws our attention on sponsoring an event organised for social welfare and displaying banners and posters there so that the viewers assembling to witness the same get an opportunity to know the contributions of sponsoring organisation. The Indian Railways are potentially sound to make use of this component of promotion. We find strong justifications for such type of promotion by the Indian Railways.

The marketing professionals bear the responsibility of making use of different components of promotion in the face of emerging situations. An optimal mix of the promotional measures will help professionals in projecting the positive contributions of Indian Railways to the process of social transformation. Informing, sensing, and sensitising the masses become significant to build and project a positive image. We find Indian Railways bearing high social costs and promotional measures will help them in developing mass awareness. The problem of cost-price-squeeze needs to be promoted to sensitise the masses. The promotional measures need to be effective but at the same time we cannot make them cost-ineffective. Making use of a particular component of promotion depending on the prevailing conditions would make the promotional strategy result-oriented.

Particularly in the advertisement measures, the professionals bear the responsibility of projecting the outstanding features of organisational product services. The marketing professionals need to make possible creativity to activate the sensitisation process.

Price Mix

Pricing decisions occupy a place of outstanding significance, specially in an utility undertaking. In the context of Railways, our focus will be on fare and freight; the two different avenues for pricing the services. The pricing decisions make it essential that on the one hand, the Railways are successful in accomplishing the organisational objectives while on the other hand, they also find it convenient to meet the social considerations.

Making available the rail transportation facilities to the masses and strengthening the infrastructural base for an alround development of the country can't be possible unless railways contribute substantially to the development process. This necessitates due attention on the financial health of Indian Railways and for this, we can't underestimate the pricing decisions. Being a public utility undertaking, the Indian Railways don't have any freedom to adjust it fare and freight structure corresponding to an increase in the prices of various inputs used in the process of offering the services. The policy of price restraint followed by the Indian Railways on socio-economic considerations is the root-and-branch cause of continuing financial disequilibrium.[5] The Indian Railways have often been found facing the problem of financial constraint. This makes it essential that the pricing decisions are made rational. The pricing strategies need to establish a fair match between the social and commercial considerations.

We find some of the commodities used as industrial raw materials, some of the articles transported to face the natural calamities, some of the materials transported for welfare purpose and some of the users experiencing it difficult to pay even the cost-based or subsidised fare and freight rates. On the other hand, we also find big business houses and affluent persons using the services of Indian Railways. The motives are diverse and therefore, we can't recommend a uniform policy. If the railways start the process of offering concessional services to all, the process of expansion and development would hardly be activated. The operational efficiency would adversely be affected and the ultimate sufferers would be the weaker sections and the backward regions. There are six principles of railways rate making, e.g., cost of service principle, value of service principle, what the traffic will bear principle, principle of differential charging, equal mileage rate principle, telescopic rate principle and principle of zonal charging. The suitability of a particular principle depends upon the prevailing conditions *vis-a-vis* the emerging trends. According to the cost of service principle, the transport charges are based on the actual costs incurred on that services.[6] The value of service principle focuses on the fixation of rates on the value of service.[7] The principle of differential charging allows different charges on different commodities for the same distance.[8] The equal kilometrage principle is the flat rate principle in which the rate per km decreases as kilometer increases and the principle of zonal charging recommends division of area into several zones and discourages short hauls and encourages longer ones.

Price Restraint Policy vs. Pricing Strategy

Being a public utility undertaking, the Indian Railways need to assign due weightage to the fare and freight rates. The policy of price restraint generates a big gap between the prices-paid and prices-received. Traditionally, the Indian Railways have managed to finance some of the unremunerative services and other social costs through transfer of funds within the services by what is known as 'Cross Subsidy.' Of late, we find very limited scope for cross subsidy because the internal cross subsidy finds it difficult to make up the losses on account of increasing social costs. Hence, the policy makers need an attitudinal change.

The aforesaid facts make it clear that utility undertakings in general and the Indian Railways in particular need a rational pricing strategy. The policy panels have also favoured hike in passenger and freight structure in conformity with the rising pressure of inflation. The following points[9] are found important while revising the structure:

- There should be an adjustment of rising costs of inputs by adjusting the same with fare and freight structure.
- The subsidised services should exclusively be for weaker sections of the society.
- The average receipt for passenger km and average receipt per tonne km should be taken into consideration while fixing the costs of output or services offered.
- The high-spending users should be induced by offering to them lucrative incentives.
- The unremunerative lines are required to be regulated.
- The consultancy fees are required to be made internationally competitive.
- The operational expenses and the unproductive administrative expenses are required to be optimised.

In view of the above, it is right to mention that the pricing policy for the Indian Railways needs due attention of the policy makers. We are not opposed to the social costs. We even welcome the contributions of railways to the process of welfare orientation *vis-a-vis* social transformation but at the same time, it is not to be forgotten that only strong organisations or individuals bear the capacity to shoulder the social burdens. If the Indian Railways fail in bridging over the gap between the prices-paid and prices-received, the vicious circle would be formed which would make them financially bankrupt. You spend on other mixes whatever you get from the pricing. If we find the pricing decisions not instrumental in development orientation, the potentials of Indian Railways to bear the social costs would start diminishing. It is against this background that we find pricing decisions significant. If the pricing decisions are rational, the generation of revenue would start moving upward which would make the ways for initiating qualitative-cum-quantitative improvements. More revenue, more development and *vice versa.* The financial managers managing and controlling the railway finance need to realise the instrumentality of pricing in the development and smooth functioning of an organisation.

In the Indian perspective, it is more realistic that we take a decision in the face of emerging trends in economy. We are aware of the paying capacity of different segments using the services of Indian Railways. We need more care and precaution while setting fare and freight structures. The poorer sections should enjoy the benefits but at the same time the affluent sections should make up the losses generated by them. The pricing decisions also draw our attention on the mismanagement of funds since this is to influence the pricing policy. It is high time that the Union Government realises the implications of a price restraint policy and paves avenues for the generation of revenues so as to improve the financial health of Indian Railways. It is against this background that we need to assign due weightage to the pricing policy of the Indian Railways.

The Place Mix

This submix of the marketing mix focuses on the offering of services to the users. In the rail transportation services when we talk about the place mix, it gravitates our attention on the process of offering the services. The Indian Railways make provisions for offering the services and the railway personnel working at the different stages in different capacities offer the same to the users. In this context, it is pertinent that distortion in the process of offering is regulated and any gap between the service-promised and services-offered is bridged over. If the drivers are deliberate in running the trains late, if the users face difficulties at the reservation, booking and reception counters, if the front line staff misbehave with the users, if the booked goods are lost, if the users develop a fear psychosis, we find a gap which stands as a big barrier while promoting the business. It is against this background that we consider it essential to go through the submix related to the processing of services.

Politeness is a virtue. This aspect of the behavioural management needs an intensive care, specially while offering the services. In the rail transportation when we talk about the offering of services, the following questions are required to be answered suitably:

- Are railmen behaving decently with the users?
- Are receptionists polite? Do they know about empathy?
- Are conductors of different compartments/classes careful to the promised services?
- Are booking or reservation counters dealing things properly?
- Are parcel counters fair and cooperating the users?
- Are the traffic managing technologies and personnel working satisfactorily?

The users in general feel that railways have not assigned due weightage to the training of railway personnel which has been generating the behavioural problem. They need to be more particular at the sensitive points, such as booking/reservation counters, parcel counters, enquiry counters, coaches, refreshment or coffee houses, clock rooms, public grievances booths, retiring rooms. The services promised are channelised through the aforesaid windows. This makes it essential that the personnel working there are efficient and well aware of the behavioural management.

In respect of processing of services, we find time management playing a significant role. The late running of trains is an important aspect influencing the quality and generating a gap. The management is supposed to take suitable steps in order that the passengers reach to their destinations safely. The time management needs an intensive care in the whole process of offering the services. Of late, the Indian Railways have sophisticated devices to manage and control the men and technologies. In addition to passenger services, they also need to be sure that the goods booked for a particular destination reach on time without any damage. The marketing practices make an advocacy in favour of innovating the place strategy so that the promised services reach to the users without any distortion. We can't deny that rail users often complain about the poor quality of services mainly due to inefficient personnel. This makes it essential that we make an in-depth study of people working there in different positions and playing a big role in the process of degeneration.

Process

The services need to be processed to the target users in such a way that they remain satisfied and do not get an opportunity to complain. We find Indian Railways well equipped with the new generation of technology. The skilled and non-skilled people, professionally sound and technocrats with the help of machines and equipments process the passenger and goods services. We find involvement of back as well as the front-line staff in the service delivery process. The marketing professionals bear the responsibility of managing things with the motto of satisfying the users. The passengers visiting the counters for making enquiries or buying tickets or getting reservation expect time-honoured services and decent behaviour of the front line staff. At the counter whatever the services they buy are processed with the help of a number of people and assets of Indian Railways. The locomotives, coaches, wagons, management of track, operational control are some of the factors through which the services reach to the ultimate users. Actually, we find involvement of a big team and a number of phases for the processing of services. In addition to machines and equipments, we find information technology playing a commanding role in managing the multi-dimensional services of Indian Railways.

The professionals need to manage them in such a way that the promised quality of services reach to the ultimate users on time and without any distortion in the service delivery process. In an age of technology, the Indian Railways need to activate the process of automation. We cannot negate the service quality even in the rail transportation services considerably depends on the quality of technology used for operation. If we make a comparative analysis of technology in the global perspective, we find Indian Railways not at a respectable position. In some of cases, we make use of second generation of technology and in a number of cases we make use of traditional technology. This necessitates priority attention on automation.

The processing is found also related with the service recovery. We find users of the services coming to the counters if they have complaints or grievances for the poor quality of services. In the Indian Railways, we find complaints lodged by the users in a very limited condition. This is due to the fact that they feel there are none to redress. From one way, the services reach to the users and from another way, the complaints may reach to the front staff. But usually we do not find users very much honest to the posting of their grievances or complaints to the concerned authorities. The professionals need to manage with this perception that we have options for wrong or poor quality of services but we do not have any option for the poor quality of service recovery.

In view of the above, it is right to say that process as a submix of marketing is found to be significant in improving the quality of service delivery and service recovery. Processing and monitoring are the two important facets determining the quality of rail transportation services. Right processing, right delivery: least possibilities for service recovery.

PHYSICAL EVIDENCE AND ATTRACTIONS

The operational dimensions of Indian Railways are found diversified in nature. The users of the services are found mainly concerned with the railway stations where they witness multi-faceted services. The scope for tangibilisation is found at platforms of railways where either while originating or terminating their journeys the passengers witness the organisational performance. While visiting the counters for enquiries or reservation, they witness the performance of technology used for their conveniences. The signposts, lighting, ventilation and sanitation, safe drinking water are some of the amenities attracting the passengers. The services, of course, are intangible in nature but we find scope for tangibilisation. The service ambience, service environment, and service fragrance strengthen their perception regarding the service quality. The marketing professionals need due focus on the service tangibilisation and for that, they have to assign due weightage to service ambience. In addition, we also find coaches where they have been accommodated necessitating due attention of professionals. The lighting arrangements, ventilation, functioning of AC, availability of water in the lavatories are some of the basics drawing their priority attention. Thus, we find scope for tangibilisation at the platforms, in the waiting halls and inside the coaches, if we talk about the passenger services. Since we find some of the services to be offered to the passengers online, it is pertinent that technology used for this purpose has been working properly. With the internet services, we find much more scope for online services but the professionals in the very context would be required to make it sure that the available technology and the operating people are working properly. Thus, we find physical evidence an important mix of the marketing mix.

Besides we find attractions focusing our attention on the personal care dimensions of people working there in different capacities. The uniform code is partially practised in the Indian Railways. Even staff wearing civil dresses need to be neat and clean. The most important thing is maintenance of dresses by them. The different dimensions of personal care services are found important for the people working there. Particularly, the staff or front-line staff having a direct interaction with the users need an impressive look. If we talk about tangibilisation, it is also considered helpful in the process.

Thus, the marketing professionals serving or working for the Indian Railways need to assign due weightage to the physical evidence and attractions. In both the areas, we find scope for adding additional attractions helping in building and projecting a positive image. With the development of technology, we find enough scope for tangibilisation but it also depends on our vision and professional excellence. Particularly, important stations where we find foreign passengers boarding, the tangibilisation needs an aesthetic look and a professional touch.

The People

In an utility undertaking, the management of people is a difficult task that requires more professional excellence. The marketing experts feel that out of all the submixes of the marketing mix, we find people playing a decisive role in the whole process since they manage everything. If we talk about sophisticated technologies, the productivity rate would hardly be accelerated if we find people operating and maintaining the plants, machines and equipments not efficient and personally-committed. Even a sound policy decision proves to be ineffective, if we find employees not sincere to efficiency generation and value orientation. This makes it clear that the Indian Railways need to assign an overriding priority to the management of people or employees of different categories on a priority basis. This necessitates an ongoing training programme, refresher and capsule courses, seminars and workshops where employees in addition to efficiency are made aware of the value orientation processes failing which we can't expect performance orientation. It is in this context that we think about the quality of people serving the Indian Railways. It is right to mention that motivational plans bear the efficacy of generating efficiency and we can't deny the fact that the Indian Railways have been offering to their employees a number of incentives in addition to the salary and perks linked to price index and the inflationary pressure. However, we find a majority of the employees at almost all the levels making a good-bye to value orientation thus making smooth ways for unfair, unethical and even illegitimate practices just for personal gains. The virus of corruption has infected the people to such an extent that we consider Indian Railways more sensitive to corruption. It is against this background that we find even those employees preferring to join Indian Railways who have already been getting more salaries and perks in the ONGC where the infection process is yet to be switched on.

In view of the above, it is right to mention that management of people occupies a place of outstanding significance, especially in the Indian Railways. It is not sufficient that employees serving an organisation are efficient. Efficiency carries no meaning if employees are found promoting unethical and unfair practices. The policy makers and the senior executives need to think over the problem on a priority basis. We agree with this view that at the stage of maturity, it is much more difficult to inculcate a sense, to inject new properties but we have no option and to devise ways to counter the same. The training and refresher courses for employees of almost all the categories need due weightage to the professional ethics and codes in their curriculum. Besides, they can also think in favour of intensifying the control measures by frequent assessment of their properties and inspections and enquiries and punishments.

The generation of efficiency, of course, occupies an important place. This makes it essential that an ongoing training programme is practised. With a change in the nature of technology *vis-a-vis* the work culture we need to improve the quality of our training programmes. The task is to promote performance orientation. This requires a fair blending of professional excellence and value orientation. Here, it is also important that employees performing well, adopting fair practices are offered additional incentives so that even others are persuaded to adopt the same path. Thus, to improve the quality of services, the Indian Railways need to assign due weightage to the management of people failing which the technological sophistication would hardly carry any meaning. We need to prepare employees who prove themselves professionally-sound and personally-committed.

MARKETING RAIL TRANSPORTATION SERVICES IN INDIAN PERSPECTIVE

Striking a balance between organisational and social considerations requires professional excellence of world-class. It is well-known that Indian Railways have to perform a dual role. On the one hand, they are supposed to make profits while on the other hand, they also bear the responsibility of bearing the social costs. Like other profit making organisations, we cannot rate the performance of Indian Railways only with profit parameter. If we find an organisation like Indian Railways making high profits, this is meant that the users of services and the society have been denied justice. We cannot negate that any organisation working in a business environment where we find sellers' market can make profits to the extent it desires. Because the users have no option and willingly or unwillingly they have to use the services even if they feel that there is nothing in the name of service quality. Recently, it has globally been publicised that Indian Railways have been making huge profits.[10] It is not in good taste that we make it a debatable point. But the service quality of Indian Railways no doubt is a debatable point. The users find nothing in the name of punctuality, safety, security, decency, comforts then what to talk of services of global standard. What to talk of defining and redefining quality when we find them even not providing the basics. It is against this background that we go through the conceptualisation of marketing principles in the Indian Railways.

Today, we live in an age of speed. What about the average speed of Indian Railways? Today, we live in an age of time management. What about punctuality in the Indian Railways? Today, we find a number of automotive devices to ensure safety. What about safety elements in the Indian Railways? Today, we find aesthetic management an essential consideration for sound management of an organisation. What about the same in the Indian Railways? While practising marketing, the professionals will play a dual role. On the one hand, they will make profits while on the other hand, they will make ways for everything the users not only expect but globally avail. A fair mix of core and peripheral services at an affordable price will be possible.

The marketers, serving the Indian Railways, bear the responsibility of practising marketing principles. The different mixes of marketing are to be conceptualised in such a fashion that Indian Railways are efficacious of defining and redefining quality. While conceptualising, the marketers must be professional so that they succeed in satisfying the users.

The product mix or service mix is considered to be the most important submix of the marketing mix. We are well aware of the different types of services offered by the Indian Railways. Here, our focus is on the fact that how and in what way the services are to be innovated. A majority of the services of Indian Railways rest on the safe and fast movement of wheel. The tracks on the wheel run; the controlling devices that regulate the safety provisions; the coaches and wagons on which the services travel and the people who handle everything determine the service quality.

It is not pragmatic that we are not following the technology adopted in Japan, even we are not following the technology adopted in China, particularly in the context of rail transportation services. In an age of supersonic where speed determines the magnitude of success, the Indian Railways need to innovate their operational mechanism. Automation would make the ways for safety and innovative technology would pave avenues for speed. We do not find even a single train in India maintaining an average speed of 100 kms per hour. The old design of coaches and locomotives, the traditional track management, and manual operation at different stages make the Indian rail system almost defunct. The RDSO needs priority attention on these things. So far as the peripheral services are concerned, we can make it possible as and when we like so and even we are not innovating them. Thus, the prime task before the policy makers of Indian Railways is to initiate and activate the process of innovations. Let us realise innovations as part of our culture. The safe, fast and time-honoured services are the expectations of users of both the categories — individual or organisational.

An organisation or an institution contributing something concrete in the form of their performance engineers a sound foundation for promotion. We cannot negate the contributions of Indian Railways to the process of social transformation. A number of subsidised or free of charge services of Indian Railways are a staunch testimony to this proposition. If we offer quality services and bear high social costs, there are a number of components to simplify and justify our task of promotion. The professionals need to develop a sound mix of the different components of promotion but in the process of development, it is to be made sure that measures are cost-effective and effective *pari passu.* This requires high degree of professional excellence. Because we find print media, due to new generation of print technology, becoming much more attractive, effective and cost-effective; the marketers need priority attention on this component. For sensitising the insensitive segments, they need visual exposure and therefore the telecast media may be preferred in that case. Your marketers need to develop rapport with the media people for effective publicity.

The pricing decisions, of course, occupy a place of outstanding significance. The scale of operation is very large and you have a very good number of users. Even your investment on innovation is high; you have scope for cost economy. The customers/users expect quality services. Charging less and offering poor quality of services cannot be a right perception for a judicious fare or freight structure. If you call a train Garib Rath in which passengers pay even more than double the ordinary fare and you find high occupancy ratio albeit in that train; it is almost testified that users prefer the service of high quality. If Indian Railways succeed in improving the quality of services; the users will not hesitate in paying more. Since you have a number of services exclusively for deserving segments of society; the fare and freight structure can be rationalised in the face of prevailing financial health.

In the process of practising marketing, the professionals need to ensure that services reach to the users in a right way. At each and every stage, they need due care. The provision for passenger and goods transportation services move through different channels. The different zonal offices command the service delivery and service recovery through divisional offices. The people working in different capacities at different points make available the services to the ultimate users. The providers need to make it sure that the promised quality of services reach to the destination without any delay and distortion.

The Indian Railways professionals while conceptualising marketing process the services with the help of information and communication technology and the efficient people. In the offices or at the counters, we find a number of people involved in the process. We find cases where computers are available but in a non-functional condition; telephonic facilities are there but none to attend; counters or windows are open but none to receive your grievances; enquiries are open but none to answer. These conditions obstruct processing and the users suffer. In a true sense, we find right and decent processing a teamwork and result of a team culture. The front-line staff need care both for service delivery and service recovery.

The rail transportation services are of intangible nature and this makes it essential that the process of tangibilisation draws due attention of professionals. The poor furnishing, decor, lighting, sanitation and ventilation services have become common features in the Indian Railways. The visitors in absence of signposts are confused. The places for waiting the passengers are found ill-managed. The uniform and dresses of people are not well-maintained. Often, we find cases of indecent behaviour. Thus, services are poor and efforts for tangibilisation are inadequate. The professionals need due care. They need to make the service ambience user-friendly and to be instrumental in generating service fragrance.

The rail people need to work with a sense of dedication and commitment. They need to understand the relevance of punctuality. They need to perceive the significance of behavioural profile. They need to realise the importance of sincerity and honesty. On the one hand, they need thematical competence while on the other hand, they also need personal-touch-in-service. The professionals need to make it sure that people working with them know about the team spirit and they have temptation for team culture.

Thus, the different submixes of marketing need priority attention of marketing professionals. Services without professional touch; services without personal touch; services without fragrance; services without team culture and services without decency are sufficient enough to tarnish the image of an organisation even if it has been making a record profit. By conceptualising marketing, the professionals can define and redefine the services.

MARKETING MANAGEMENT OF ROAD TRANSPORT ORGANISATIONS

The excavations of Mohanjodaro have revealed that the ancient Indians not only realised the significance of roads but also developed the art of constructing the same even 5000 years ago. At Harappa, we have discovered a two-wheeled vehicle in miniature with the driver seated in front. It is obvious that a wheeled vehicle can ply only on roads. The term 'Road' is applied for all broad made ways leading from place to place. The term 'Street' is confined to roads through towns, villages and other inhabited places. In Kautilya's Arthashastra, a good deal of information is given on the subject of roads. Even during that time in India, a great trunk road connected the North-West frontier with the capital Patliputra now known as Patna.[11] During the British period, roads received greater attention of the policy makers but the wonderful development of railways obstructed the normal development of roads. A committee under the chairmanship of Mr. Jaykar was appointed in 1927 to investigate and report on the development of roads and since then, we find commencement of modern era of Indian roads.

Like water, the roads can be used for numerous purposes. Water is used for drinking, washing, cooking, irrigation, conversion into ice, electricity, steam or so. In the same way, when a road is constructed, we find its multi-pronged uses, e.g., it can be used by pedestrians, by animals, bullock, horse, camel carts, bullock carts and also by the mechanically-driven vehicles. A developed country possesses excellent roads since this opens for them new vistas of development. Contrary to it in a backward country, the roads present a very gloomy picture. The roads strengthen our infastructural base and so become instrumental in activating the process of development. As compared to other forms of transport, the road transport is found cheaper. Of course, in the Indian perspective, the Indian Railways have been offering economic services to the users which is found cheaper than the road transport. The operational cost of a road vehicle is very low as compared to the high operational costs of railway, steamship or aeroplane. Railways or steamship or aeroplane can be used only by those who pay for their services but a road can be used by anyone even without making a direct payment. This clarifies the significance of road transport in today's perspective.

In India or elsewhere, the greatest revolution in the road transport took place with the advent of mechanised road vehicle, e.g., motor bus, motor lorry and motor truck. These motor vehicles were coupled with the properties of speed and operational economy which helped them in expanding their network and serving almost all segments of the society. The development of roads can benefit the backward regions substantially since they are found successful in capitalising on the opportunities profitably. The increasing development pace necessitated organised development of road transportation facilities. The informal sector started operation which later on was made formal and not only the private sector but even the public sector started taking part in the business of road transportation. It was against this background that the State Road Transport Corporations was found accepting the responsibility of offering the passenger road transportation services to the users. It is right to mention that the intensity of competition was found high and the public sector transport organisations failed in establishing an edge over the private sector which ultimately resulted into the sickness of almost all the State Road Transport Corporations. This engineered a strong foundation for injecting professionalism in the management of road transport organisations.

The public and private sector road transport organisations, of late, are found mismanaged. It is amazing to mention that by and large almost all the State Road Transport Corporations are found in red. We can't deny that the private sector organisations have been successful in maintaining their commercial viability. If we make a comparative analysis of the services of public and private sectors, it is obvious that in terms of customer/user services, they establish an edge over the public sector. Of course, there are a number of factors responsible for the same but ultimately it is mismanagement or deficient management that is the root-and-branch cause of poor customer services or the financial insolvency. The private organisations are found maintaining the time schedule, offering more comforts and charging less for the services. Contrary to it, the State Road Transport Corporations are found not sincere to the time schedule, charging exorbitantly but offering substandard services to the users. This make it essential that the public sector road transport organisations practise marketing principles to bring the derailed systems on the rail. It is against this background that we make a strong advocacy in favour of innovative marketing for road transport organisation. The increasing cases of accidents, traffic density, mismanagement of traffic, poor conditions of roads, poor maintenance and operation of buses make it essential that we think over the problem with a new vision.

The important categories of roads in the Indian perspective are PWD Roads, Zilla Parishad Roads, Village Panchayat Roads, Municipal Roads, CD/Panchayat Samiti, State Highways, Forest Department Roads, Irrigation Department Roads, Sugarcane Authority Roads and Railway Roads. In all the roads, we find two categories, viz., surfaced and unsurfaced. This excludes Roads under JRY.

We have almost 66,000 kms of National Highways and 10,36,158 kms of unsurfaced roads. In the context of National Highways, we find UP at the top with almost 6,000 kms and next to that we find Rajasthan with almost 5,860 kms. In respect of surfaced roads, we find Maharashtra at the top and next to that is UP.

It is right to mention that after the attainment of independence, a number of steps were taken to improve the quality of roads, but even today we find Indian roads lagging far behind the global standard. In 1947 when we attained independence, the length of National Highways was 21,440 kms. Almost after more than sixty years of independence, we do not find ourselves in a position to meet the basic requirements of connecting all villages and towns with the all-weatherproof roads. This has been found obstructing the process of socio-economic transformation. Though we cannot deny that India has one of the largest road networks in the world aggregating to about more than 33 lakh kms at present. For smooth road transportation, it is essential that the roads are well developed and consistently maintained but poor quality of construction and lack of proper maintenance have made a majority of the roads prone to accidents. We expect a lot from Golden Quadrilateral (GQ) and EW-NS Corridor. 6-laning, 4-laning, 2-laning schemes for National Highway Development Project would no doubt improve the road conditions *vis-a-vis* smooth, safe and fast transportation.

A revolution in the field of automobile industry would benefit road transport services if we find development of all-weatherproof roads. Both for passenger and goods transportation, we find road transportation considerably contributing to the development process. About 65 per cent of freight and 80 per cent of passenger traffic is carried by road transport.[13] All the pillars of development primary, secondary and tertiary are found sizeably influenced by the road transport services. The strain on the network is increasing day by day. The number of vehicles have been growing at a rapid pace of almost 11 per cent per annum. The share of road in total traffic has been growing fast. These developments make a call for the rapid expansion and strengthening of the road network. To cater to the present and future traffic requirements, it is imperative that centre as well as the state governments make sincere and honest efforts to improve road transportation services.

Of late, the infrastructural base of the national economy is not in tune with the increasing pressure and in the coming years when we expect a significant increase in the traffic pressure on optimal development is not to be possible unless we find practising of public-private partnership gaining a rapid momentum.

The most urgent task before the policy makers is to strengthen the infrastructural base of the economy so that the process of socio-economic emancipation is vitalised. The establishment of backward and forward linkages would make an assault on the retarded growth of economy *vis-a-vis* the sick organisations. Further, the agricultural and industrial transformation processes would also gain the momentum with the availability of quality road transportation services. If we turn our eyes on the quality of road transportation services made available to the users in the developed countries, we find services very poor. This makes it essential that both the organisations make innovative marketing efforts to initiate the process of qualitative and quantitative transformation. We have completed Ten Five Year Plans and have already started Eleventh but our efforts for improving the quality of roads have received only a lukewarm response.[14] We can't think about quality services unless we have quality roads and quality buses. It is hoped that the application of marketing principles would simplify the task of public and private sector road transport organisations.

In view of the above, the following aspects need an in-depth study:

- Formulation of product mix by the road transport organisations in which making possible a fair blending of core and peripheral services. The formulation of an attractive package that induces the passengers. The availability of quality buses and efficient personnel who are well aware of the behavioural management.
- Taking the support of sophisticated devices for promoting the services and projecting a positive image.
- Paving avenues for making the fare structure sound that helps generation of profits.
- Processing the services in a right way to bridge over the gap between the services-promised and services-offered.
- Developing efficient, dedicated, personally-committed and value-based personnel who make possible performance orientation.

PRODUCT?

Product is a benefit that one party offers to another. It is essentially intangible when we talk about services. The Road Transport Corporations or Inter-State Transport Organisations or Travel Agencies or the individuals engaged in the road transportation business carry goods or passengers from one place to another. The State Road

Transport Corporations also offer the mail services. Thus, the three main products are passenger traffic, goods traffic and mail services. Like the Indian Railways, we find the State Road Transport Corporations offering the concessional services to the students and daily commuters.

PRODUCT PLANNING AND DEVELOPMENT

For offering quality services, it is pertinent that due emphasis is given to the planning and development of product. In an environment of technological sophistications, it is essential that the organisations or the individuals engaged in the transportation business formulate a long-term perspective plan. The depleted condition of roads, existing mismanagement in traffic control, increasing cases of high way robbery make it essential that the policy makers think over the issue on a priority basis. Of course, it is prime responsibility of the government to make available to the transport organisations or agencies suitable conditions for plying buses or trucks for which they are charged. It is amazing to mention that even the national highways, lateral roads are found mismanaged then what to talk of others. Despite an impressive growth in the spread of the transport network, a large number of villages in the country lack road connection. It is found that the capacity of the entire transportation system including the road network continues to fall short of demand. The capacity constraints are felt in several areas. The inadequacy of capacity and substandard infrastructure have led to the excessive transit delays, fuel wastage and higher operating costs. Spatial demographic and economic features greatly influence the pattern of transport demand in the country. Urban population and economic activities are concentrated in metropolitan areas or in a few other important cities. Major coal and iron ore deposits are in the eastern part of the country. It is the region where most of the steel and heavy engineering industries are also located. The road traffic density in these areas or on these routes is high. It is felt that it would not be possible to serve the traffic on these routes or corridors. A feasible solution lies in the development of alternative routes or in increasing the number of buses, trucks and also balanced spread of economic activity in the country. Till now we find the national economy agrarian in character and the settlement pattern rural-oriented. In this context, the planning for the road transport is found essential.

Since the inception of planning, the road network has expanded on an average by about 4.5 per cent. It is not an impressive growth rate to satisfy any one. Keeping in view the transportation demand to be generated in the coming years, it is indispensable that the existing deficiencies in the national highways, state highways, major district road systems are removed. The improvement in the road transportation system makes a call in favour of better productivity in the transport sector. The environmental quality of highways is required to be preserved. On high density corridors, there should be expansion of roads with a provision of divided carriage way facilities. Though the practise of user of local materials and low-cost specifications would have to be continued in future as well.

Selective upgradation of road making equipments and construction practices can achieve high standards of road quality demanded by the modern generation of road vehicles. It is found that large programmes of road construction have an adverse effect on the environment or ecosystem. Prevention of ribbon development, provision of wayside amenities, landscaping and drainage and the landslide areas need an intensive care. Maintenance through normal repairs, periodic renewals and rehabilitation divert a close attention. The thrust towards the modernisation of the road sector requires adequate backup in the form of computerisation, introduction of Management Information System and planning and monitoring agencies. The research and development efforts are also required to be strengthened. The National Highways gravitate a close attention because NH though only 2 per cent of the length of the total road system, they carry one-third of the total road traffic.[15]

We can't deny that over the years, there has been a substantial shift from rail to road. The motor vehicle population in the country has been continuously increasing with the development of corporate sector and emergence of corporate culture. While manufacturing buses, trucks, cars, autorickshaws, the production units need to accord due priority to the environment-friendly measures. In addition, they are supposed to make possible operational economy by rationalising the consumption of fuel, increasing accommodation and improving the technologies. The organisations engaged in designing and constructing bodies need to assign due weightage to safety provisions, attraction and comforts. We find truck industry predominantly in an unorganised private sector. The setting up of truck terminals and transhipment at identified locations should not be underestimated.

Particularly, the State Road Transport Corporations are found engaged in the Mail Services. In the years to come, the pressure on them is likely to go up. The introduction of special type of buses for this purpose is felt essential. The concessional facilities to the daily commuters and students are required to be continued. The inadequacy of buses has been found generating numerous problems in almost all the State Road Transport Corporations. Of course, we find a sharp increase in the demand position but the supply position is not to cater to the same. The following strategic decisions are found important to make possible multi-dimensional improvements:

- The road network is required to be expanded. We need expansion of all categories of roads. The pressure on National Highways is doubled and this makes a strong advocacy in favour of 4-lane system.
- Selective upgradation of road construction materials is urgent. The modern generation of road vehicles requires roads of superior quality without any jerk. The thrust towards the modernisation of road sector requires adequate backup. Prevention of ribbon development, provision of wayside amenities, plantation on both sides of the roads, landscaping and drainage are found essential.
- Keeping in view the scarcity of petroleum products, the modern generation of vehicles is required to be promoted by the organisations engaged in manufacturing vehicles in order that the fuel economy is maintained and the safety provisions are taken care.
- The organisations engaged in manufacturing bodies of bus and trucks need to accord due priority to safety and decency.
- The phasing out of old vehicles not maintaining the Euro I and Euro II standards needs to be practised on a priority basis.

MARKETING MIX FOR ROAD TRANSPORT ORGANISATIONS

Like other organisations, the road transport organisations also need to strengthen their realisation that marketing bears the efficacy of striking a balance between the organisational and social considerations. Unless we satisfy the users of our services, the task of accomplishing organisational objectives will remain unfulfilled. And we cannot be successful in satisfying the customers/users if the marketing processes remain neglected. It is against this backdrop that we make a strong advocacy in favour of the conceptualisation of modern marketing principles in the road transport organisations publicly or privately managed for passenger or goods transportation. In a true sense, the organisational prosperity rests on professional excellence and the road transport organisations have not been found assigning due weightage to the same. With the implementation of innovative marketing, the quality of services would be improved and in addition, the cost-effectiveness will also be possible which will make the services affordable.

The different submixes of marketing need due attention of marketing professionals while practising marketing in the road transport organisations. The focus here is on all the seven submixes helping the formulation of a sound marketing mix, viz., Product Mix — in which the organisations will attempt to offer quality services to the users; Promotion Mix — where the professionals will blend different components of promotion in such a fashion that measures are effective but the costs are economic; Price Mix — where the professionals will fix or set a structure of competitive nature; Place Mix — in which the services are to be rightly channelised; Process Mix — where the professionals ensure right and decent processing of services to the ultimate users; Physical Evidence and Attractions — where the focus will be on making the service ambience attractive and the tangibilisation process effective and People Mix — in which the professionals would develop quality marketing people helping them in satisfying the customers. Synchronising the different mixes of marketing no doubt requires professional excellence.

The passenger as well as the goods transportation need good time management and safety and security. The improved quality of roads and professional excellence of marketing managers will help both categories of users in fulfilling their expectations from the road transport organisations.

The Product Mix

The product mix for the road transport services focuses our attention on the offering of quality core and peripheral services to the customers so that they remain satisfied. There are a number of services related to the road transportation and in the process, we find the involvement of both public and private sector. This makes it essential that both of them pave avenues for innovations. It is pertinent that to improve the quality of services the organisations make available the product of new generation.

The professionals bear the responsibility of formulating a sound product mix for road transportation facilities so that world-class quality services are made available to the users. The services are required to be made commercially viable *vis-a-vis* environment-friendly. The users' interests are to be given due weightage. This gravitates our attention on the product mix. In Figure 10.4, we find the product mix of road transportation organisations.

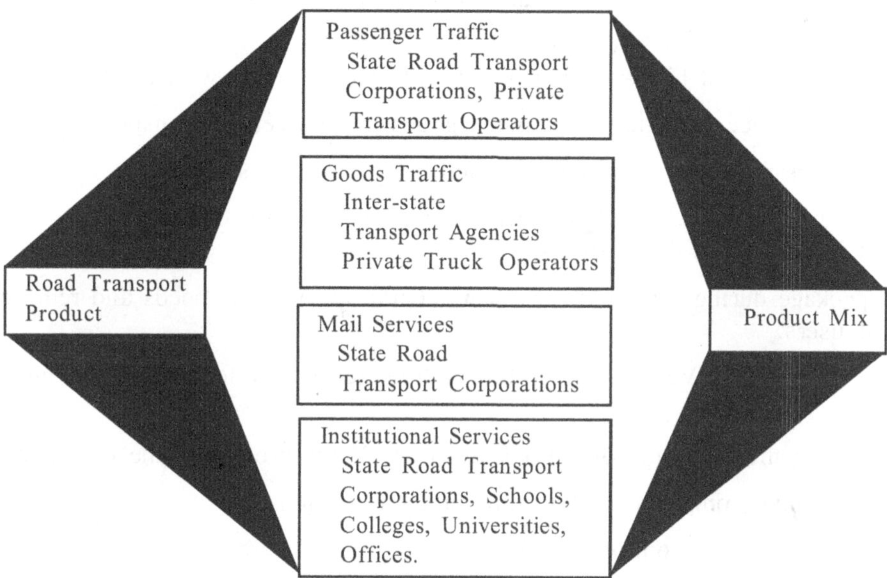

Fig. 10.4: Product Mix of Road Transport Organisations

The State Road Transport Corporations, Private Transport Companies, Travel Agencies, Transport Operators, Inter-State Transport Agencies and others engaged in the process need to assign due weightage to the formulation of a sound product mix for road transportation services. They while offering the services to the end-users are to make themselves sure that the process of formulation has made possible a fair blending of core and peripheral services. The State Road Transport Corporations are found engaged in offering the passenger transportation services. They also offer services to the society by bearing the social costs. Besides, the mail services are also offered by them. Of late, the users appear dissatisfied with the quality of services offered to them, specially by public sector transport organisations. The shortage of buses, poor maintenance, not maintaining the time schedule, frequent accidents, inadequacy of luxury buses, lack of insurance facilities are some of the important factors projecting the negative image of State Road Transport Corporations. Except a very few almost all the State Road Transport Corporations have been found facing the problem of financial crunch. The private sector transport organisations have been successful in establishing an edge over the public sector by improving the quality and maintaining the time schedule. These negative points divert our attention on the innovative efforts for reformulating the product mix.

The State Road Transport Corporations need to bear the responsibility of promoting tourism. Availability of superior quality of AC buses is urgently felt for capitalising on the opportunities optimally. So far as the mail services are concerned, the users have high expectations but the services made available are of poor quality. This makes it essential that they assign due weightage to the mail services. They are supposed to maintain the time schedule and to honour the safety and environmental considerations. Of course, the Inter-State Transport Agencies have been found doing well but even they need to innovate their service mix in the face of recent developments. The Travel Agencies have done well but keeping in view the emerging trends, they are supposed to initiate the process of qualitative improvements. The following points need a special mention while designing the service mix for the road transportation organisations.

- Increase in the number of superior quality of buses furnished with modern amenities and facilities.
- Introduction of new design of bodies for buses and trucks maintaining the safety provisions and adequate accommodation.
- Paying special attention to the daily commuters and students and unemployed youths.

- Expansion of transportation facilities to and fro to the tourist resorts.
- Attention on the construction of metal roads having the minimum possible jerks and proper maintenance of roads to minimise the costs on wear and tear.
- Minimising the side-effects of pollution due to the plying of buses and for that promoting afforestation on both sides of the roads.
- Concentration on national highways and linking the lateral roads with the highways.
- Expansion of insurance facilities to both the goods and passenger transportation services.
- Making provisions for civic amenities and facilities at the bus stations.
- Behavioural training to the front-line staff to make them aware of the instrumentality of behavioural management in promoting the business.
- Offering a package during a particular season keeping in view the needs and requirements of different segments of users.
- Amendments in the Motor Vehicles Act in line with the recent developments in the business environmental conditions.
- Strictly following the provision of Euro I and Euro II for protecting the environment.
- Developing shopping complexes at the important bus stations.
- Cushioned seats for more comforts to the travelling passengers.
- Intensifying the safety provisions and strengthening the protective measures to protect the passengers, vehicles against robbery and snatching.
- Expanding the services by promoting Inter-State Road Transport Services for the passengers.
- Strengthening maintenance and renewal measures and phasing out the old buses and trucks.
- Exploring avenues for promoting door-to-door services for the business houses using the freight transportation services regularly.
- In tune with the principles of social marketing bearing social costs in a rationalised manner.
- Promoting research for innovating the services.

The aforesaid measures would make the ways for quality services to the users. The formulation of a sound service mix requires professional excellence and the road transport organisations are required to professionalise the entire process.

Promotion Mix

Promotion an important submix of the marketing mix makes possible informing, sensing and persuading the customers/users. It creates impulse buying and transforms the potential users into the actual users. It helps in projecting a positive image. Like the rail transportation services, the road transportation services are also required to be promoted with the help of sensitive tools. It is against this background that we go through the instrumentality of different tools of promotion in promoting the business of rail transporation organisations. The different components of promotion on which we focus are advertising, publicity, sales promotion, word-of-mouth promotion, personal selling and telemarketing. The professionals serving the organisations bear the responsibility of identifying the real conditions and using the components helping them in increasing the market share, maximising the profit and subserving the social interests. The genesis of promotion lies in communicating the users/target audience in an effective way. Stimulation of demand becomes an easier task if the promotional strategies are sound. The public and private sector organisations offering the road transportation services need to make possible a rational use of different components.

Advertising: Advertising plays an incremental role in promoting the business of road transport organisations. The State Road Transport Corporations and the private transport operators need to advertise in a right fashion. Out of telecast media, broadcast media and the print media, they are supposed to select the most effective media or to make a mix of all keeping in view the budgetary provisions. We find State Road Transport Corporations bearing the social costs and this happens to be an important reason for their financial bankruptcy. A majority of the persons don't know about this dimension of profitability and therefore by advertising the professionals need to transmit the message to the users and masses. While advertising through the telecast media, they need to seek the co-operation of advertising professionals to make possible creativity in their messages, slogans and campaigns. The focus is required to be on the quality of services and their contribution to the subserving of social interests. In this context, it is right to mention that the effectiveness of advertising messages is substantially influenced by your efforts in building a positive image by offering the world-class services to the users. Unless the users or the potential users find a fair match between the advertisement slogans and the actual services availed by them, the sensitivity rate would hardly be accelerated. We can't deny that the quality of services offered by a majority of the State Road Transport Corporations is very poor which makes the task of advertisers much more difficult. The private transport operators are found offering superior quality of services to the users. And therefore, they have much more in their accounts to display. The Inter-State Road Transport Agencies are also found serious to the quality of services and therefore, they are also in a position to advertise. Thus it is pertinent that before advertising, the professionals make it sure that they have not allowed a big mismatch between the quality-offered and the quality-promised in the advertisement slogans. The broadcast media would also be suitable to the transport organisations since we find it economic and at the same time, a big network is existent. In addition, the print media can also be used for promoting the road transportation business. Of late, the latest developments in the print technology have sharpened the instrumentality of print media. It is this context that we find this media suitable to the road transport organisations.

Publicity: This dimension of the promotion mix bears the responsibility of developing rapport with media and the opinion leaders and getting their co-operation in promoting the business. It is found effective for those organisations who contribute substantially to the process of socio-economic transformation. We can't deny the positive contributions of road transport organisations to the process of socio-economic emancipation. By offering a number of concessional services to the different categories of users, the State Road Transport Corporations are found fuelling the process of social transformation. Since it is to affect the pricing policy of the State Road Transport Corporation, we need to develop rapport with media in order that they publicise it in a right way. It is quite natural that for seeking their cooperation, the transport professionals would be required to organise a press conference and to offer to them lunch/dinner/small gifts to motivate them to write in favour. The opinion leaders can also perform the responsibility of publicising the business of road transport organisations. It is the responsibility of professionals that they identify opinion leaders in a particular command area, develop a rapport with them and seek their co-operation to transmit their positive contribution to the masses. In the context of public relations, we can't devalue the instrumentality of Public Relations Officers who are supposed to be a professionally sound person to influence the users. The enquiry centres or the booking counters are also the sensitive points from there the process of image building takes off. The publicity thus can be helpful to all the organisations engaged in offering the services. Since we don't find financial involvement while publicising even the State Road Transport Corporations should attempt to make possible an optimal use of this component of the promotion mix.

Personal Selling: We are aware of the instrumentality of personal selling in promoting the business. In this context, we find professionally sound employees instrumental in promoting the business by informing, sensing and persuading the users. In the road transportation services, the private transport operators are required to use it. With the help of agents, brokers, branches, front-line staff; they can be successful in promoting the business. Since it is based on the personal excellence, it is pertinent that the road transport organisations identify and develop personnel who can discharge the responsibility in an effective way. The employees to be engaged are required to be professionally-sound having high communicative ability, handsome personality, patience and familiar with the behavioural management. To be more specific, the private road transport organisations can use this dimension of the promotion mix in an effective way since they are supposed to develop contact with different business houses for getting the business. We find its instrumentality both for the transportation of goods as well as for the movement of passengers. The personnel engaged should be aware of the points from which the profitable business is expected. The transport operators need to develop a rapport with the tour operators and the travel agents. We can't deny the instrumentality of personal promoters in getting the profitable business since by influencing the travel agencies, they can get a big business. In addition, the educational institutions also appear to be a sensitive point which can be capitalised on optimally. Thus, this dimension of the promotion mix is required to be used by both the public and private road transport organisations. Of course, they need to train and develop professionally-sound personnel for that purpose. While developing a programme, they are supposed to assign due weightage to the level of expectations of users *vis-a-vis* the changing business conditions.

Sales Promotion: The road transport organisations need to innovate the tools of sales promotion while promoting the business. We can't deny the fact that incentives make the ways for generation of efficiency. The high performers expect something more than the ordinary persons. The agents, brokers, front-line staff engaged in promoting the business are required to be given due incentives for their significant contributions to the promotion of business. The tools of sales promotion to be offered to the personnel engaged in promoting the business may be small gifts, free travelling facilities, subsidised services or so. Like other business organisations, the road transport organisations may think in favour of promotional incentives to the individuals, agencies, organisations helping them in touching the target, increasing the market share and maximising the profitability. The duration and measures would depend upon the prevailing conditions *vis-a-vis* the instrumentality of transport personnel or others taking part in the process.

In this context, it is significant that we also think about offering of incentives to the users of services. All categories of users — general or institutional, small-sized, or large-sized men or women — helping road transport organisations in increasing the business should be offered incentives like small gifts, a package, seasonal concessional facilities. The promotional incentives to the users of the services become significant with the viewpoint of retaining the business. To be more specific, the State Road Transport Corporations have been facing a critical situation *vis-a-vis* the financial crunch that need to offer incentives to the users. This would help them substantially in increasing the market share which is found going down with a good speed.

Word-of-mouth Promotion: This dimension of the promotion mix is based on the positive contributions of the road transport organisations. We are aware of the fact that the word-of-mouth promoters act as a hidden salesforce. They are satisfied group of users or the vocal persons or opinion leaders of the command area who have been offered additional incentives for promoting the business. When your friends, relations start communicating to you something positive regarding the instrumentality or the world-class services offered by a particular transport organisation, you trust on them blindly and prefer to use the services as and when the conditions require so. The advertisement slogans can be insensitive, the publicity measures can be ineffective, the sales promotion measures can also show a lukewarm response but the word-of-mouth communications are found proactive in all the conditions provided the hidden salesforce are not commercialising the process. It is against this background that we talk in favour of this component of the promotion mix. The transport professionals while using this component of the promotion mix are required to be careful that the persons identified as opinion leaders or vocal persons have a positive social image. On the other hand, it is also pertinent that they are serious to the quality of services and keep themselves engaged in innovating the services. Not only this, it is also significant that they increase the proportion of peripheral services in the product mix. This would add additional attractions to the service mix that would also act as a motivational tool. Thus, the word-of-mouth communication makes it essential that the transport organisations have been offering quality services and in addition have also been offering due incentives to the promoters. The road transport organisations offering world-class services to the users don't need to identify the opinion leaders since the users themselves act as a motivator.

Telemarketing: The business of transportation can substantially be promoted with the help of telemarketing. We are aware of the instrumentality of this component of the promotion mix in the present age of information explosion. With the development of satellite communication services, we find enough scope for the use of telemarketing for promoting the business. The television network has made telemarketing a more sharp-edged instrument of promotion. Like the rail transport organisation, the road transport organisations can also use it while promoting the business. This makes is essential that both for passenger and goods services, they have efficient, personally-committed and value-based telemarketers with a high communicative ability. It is a device to promote the business with the help of telephones in which we also find televisions playing an incremental role. The main thing in the process is to recruit such a person to act as a telemarketer who is well informed and is familiar with the dialogues to be transmitted on telephones. The transmission of information regarding the offering of new services in the service mix, launching of a new package, special discount or concession during a particular season help prospects to take a positive decision. The queries and questions asked by the prospects, users or even others are required to be transmitted suitably. It is against this background that the telemarketers require special skill of initiating and concluding the dialogues on phones. In the Indian perspective, we have enough scope and justifications for promoting this component of marketing. The Inter-State Transport Agencies are to be benefited substantially if they make use of telemarketing in a right fashion. This is due to the fact that they are required to transmit important informations to the users or prospects regarding the transportation facilities, safe arrival and delivery of goods. It is not possible that the users come to the business centres frequently. The telemarketing services would help them in knowing the actual position of their goods in transit. Even the private transport operators and the State Road Transport Corporations can make use of telemarketing their business.

In view of the above, it is right to mention that all the components of promotion have multi-dimensional uses for promoting the business. It is upon the transport professionals to explore avenues, opportunities and to select a suitable component or to formulate a mix and to use them rationally. Of course, they are supposed to assign due weightage to the budgetary provisions but at the same time, they can't ignore their requirements. We make a strong advocacy in favour of quality upgradation and feel that the road transport organisations should also keep the users/prospects well informed regarding their efforts. The task of image building is found complete when you offer to your prospects/users world-class services but the task of image projection remains incomplete unless you activate the promotional measures and keep on moving the process of sensitising the customers/users. We can't negate that more innovative the promotional measures, more positive are the results. This makes it essential that while synchronising the different components of promotion you keep in your minds a number of considerations, such as the financial health of your organisation, the intensity of competition in the market, the emerging trends in the market share, your image in the eyes of users at large or so. It is not supposed from you that a blind decision is taken. The innovation in the process of formulating a sound product mix becomes ineffective if you slow down the process of innovation in promotion. It is against this background that we make a strong advocacy in favour of a sound promotional strategy for activating the process of business expansion.

Price Mix

In the Indian setting where the users of road transportation services have high expectations with limited paying capacity, the task of formulating a sound pricing strategy is found much more difficult. Being a profit making organisation, the road transport organisations/agencies engaged in the business have a legitimate right of making profits. Whatever we spend or invest on different mixes of the marketing mix are managed by this mix of the marketing mix. Hence, the pricing decisions if not taken carefully stand as an obstacle while maintaining the commercial viability. Not only this, the task of shouldering the social burdens or bearing the social costs can't be made easier unless an organisation generates profit. It is in this context that we need more care and precautions while using the price mix of the marketing mix.

In the Indian perspective, we find both the public sector as well as the private sector engaged in the road transportation business. We can't deny the fact that both of them have miserably failed in making a rational pricing design. Our special focus is on the State Road Transport Corporations who have been facing the problem of cost-price-squeeze. With an increase in the pressure of inflation, the State Road Transport Corporations have no option but to make huge payments for the inputs used by them but they don't get a freedom while adjusting the price structure or fare and freight. This in a natural way obstructs the process of making profits and maintaining the commercial viability. It is against this background that we find almost all the State Road Transport Corporations facing the problem of financial crunch. They find it difficult to implement their development and expansion plans on account of poor financial health. On the other hand, we also find the private road transport organisations in the same boat. Even they are not in a position to fix their fare and freight rates independently since the general administration is found obstructing the process. A sound pricing policy is meant to be the policy which makes available to the undertakings a normal return on capital invested keeping in view the development and expansion plans.

The aforesaid facts make it clear that both the public and private road transport organisations need professional excellence while making the pricing decisions. We can't deny that in the Indian setting the fare and freight structure govern the pricing structure of general commodities. This makes it essential that the regulations for pricing assign due weightage to the emerging trends in the inflationary pressure. This makes the ways for using quality inputs which makes available to the users the quality outputs. Further, the pricing structure adopted by the travel agencies also draws our attention. It is generally felt that they violate the regulations frequently and deprive the exchequer of getting the tax. They charge more, earn more but show less. Here, it is important to mention that the term "Rate" is used to denote the charge that any transport organisation charges to move goods of any description while the term "Fare" is meant to be the charge that it makes to move passengers from one place to another.

In the setting of price structure, the scientific and right computation of cost is found significant. If the supplier of the services commits a mistake in computing the cost of production, a major adjustment is necessitated. We divide costs into two parts, viz., prime cost and supplementary cost and the two aggregated together constitutes the total costs. While computing cost of services charged by an organisation, there are a number of factors governing the same. Business is sometimes brisk as others slack. When we find it brisk, the profitable prices are generated but when it is slack, everybody suffers equally. It is felt that while determining costs, it is essential to focus our attention on the four elements, such as the vehicle or the vessel, motive power, the highway and the terminals. The theoretical basis of road transport rates and fares is cost of services. In a competitive environment, the rates and fares are fixed at such a level that the income earned generates ordinary profits and a normal return on capital. In this context, the rates and fares are different from the rates and fares in the railways whose basis is differential monopoly charging. The charges made by the road transport organisations conform broadly to the cost of service principle. In the road transport organisations, it is easier to determine the special or running cost of a service. The standing charges include interest on capital, depreciation, office expenses, rates of garages, licence fees and insurance charges. The running costs include fuel, lubricants like oil, greases, wear and tear of tyres, tubes, wheels and repair and maintenance of vehicles. In this respect, the convention or customs is found playing an important role in the setting of fare. In the process of excelling competition, the road transport organisations prefer charges helping them in making the price a motivational tool to attract the users. This paves avenues for charging less than the railways.

We can't say that the rates and fares on roads are determined solely on cost consideration. We find demand also playing a noticeable role and in the certain cases, it takes priority over cost. As for example, the offices, educational institutions start working at about 10 AM and therefore the demand for conveyance reaches at its peak between 9 AM to 10 AM. The charges released at this period only not covers the total costs of operating the service but also leave something extra to make up. This makes it clear that the demand factors also play an important role.

After the nationalisation of road transportation services, the private road transport organisations are required to consider the pricing structure followed by the State Road Transport Corporations. These facts make it clear that the process of setting of fare and freight is governed by a number of factors and the organisations are supposed to focus their attention on them so that the users of services don't feel themselves exploited. The cost of service principle is found applicable in the determination of fares and rates. The public or the private sector organisations are also supposed to bear the social costs. Of late, not only the public sector organisations but we also find even the private sector organisations bearing the social costs since the principle of social marketing has made possible an attitudinal change in the boardrooms.

To be more specific in the Indian perspective, we find this dimension of pricing playing an outstanding role. The losses incurred on the subsidised or the concessional services are required to be compensated by the provincial governments. The governmental regulations are required to be made liberal to adjust the increasing costs of inputs. The agricultural inputs need due attention of the road transport organisations since by doing such they can also counter the problem of regional imbalance *vis-a-vis* the sectoral imbalance.

In view of the above, it is right to mention that the pricing decisions need due attention of the road transport organisations. They can be successful in maintaining the commercial viability when the prices charged are reasonable and the moment they keep on moving the process of generating profits, the copious avenues are paved for shouldering the social costs.

The Place Mix

The road transport organisations while managing the marketing activities also need to formulate a sound place mix that makes possible time-honoured and cost-effective offering of services without making any distortion. In addition, they are also required to locate the bus stations at a point that is found easily accessible and safe. It is against this background that we go through the place mix. The absence of linkages between the forward and backward areas, the mounting dissatisfaction among the users of services, the emerging trends in the demand and supply, the neglected attitude towards the users' grievances are some of the important factors making a strong advocacy in favour of time-honoured and cost-effective services. Both the public and private road transport organisations are required to be careful to the social interests since the holistic concept of management makes it essential that an organisation paves avenues for bearing the social costs. For injecting life, strength and continuity to the development-oriented and welfare-sensitive plans or for countering the regional imbalance, it is pertinent that the backward areas of the country get a priority attention. The place mix would take into consideration a number of factors with the prime motto of making the service user-friendly.

The first problem is related to the process of offering the services so that the promised services reach to the users without any distortion. This focuses our attention on the gap between the services-promised and services-offered. We can't deny the fact that the quality of vehicles used in the process also plays an incremental role but ultimately it is the quality of people serving an organisation who govern everything. This gravitates our attention on the different categories of employees serving the road transport organisations. We can't deny the fact that particularly in the public sector road transport organisations, the employees at large lack professional excellence. Not only this, it is also found that they don't know anything about the behavioural management. The front-line personnel on the booking counters, the receptionists, the personnel working in the workshops, the drivers, conductors or even the managerial cadre lack professionalism. It is mainly due to the fact that a majority of them have been found facing the problem of a big gap between the services-promised and services-offered. The late running of buses, increasing number of complaints, accidents, increasing depreciation cost and operational costs are sufficient to testify their poor or substandard quality. On the other hand, the private sector transport organisations are found sincere to the time schedule, safety, maintenance or so. In addition, the personnel are found submissive, behaving decently and redressing the grievances of customers. Thus, they immensely succeed in minimising the gap and offer quality services to the users. We can't deny that the quality of buses used by the private road transport organisations also establishes an edge over the public sector and therefore the users also find the services comfortable and safe.

The aforesaid facts make it clear that the road transport organisations can't undermine the processing of services that plays a decisive role in satisfying the users. They need to make possible employee orientation that requires an ongoing training programme for almost all categories of employees. In addition to the professional excellence, the behavioural profile also assumes a place of outstanding significance. This necessitates an in-depth knowledge of behavioural management to all categories of employees. By doing such, they can make possible a fair blending of professional excellence and value orientation.

Another dimension of the place mix is related to the location points. The location of bus stations at a point that is found easily accessible, safe and equipped with infrastructure and communication facilities appear important in the very context. We can't think of locating the bus stations or the terminal points for the Inter-State Transport Agencies at a place lacking all-weatherproof roads. Thus, we find it the first consideration for locating the bus stations. Of course, the workshops can be located at the place found far off the populated area. This is also found with the terminal point for improving the loading and unloading facilities *vis-a-vis* the godowns or warehouses. The other infrastructural facilities, such as electricity, communications are also found important with the view-point of improving the quality of services. In the Indian context, we can't devalue the safety and protection measures. For strengthening the safety measures, it is essential that workshops make a routine check-up and supervision and the repair and maintenance provisions are given due weightage. In the protection measures, it is significant that the bus stations are close to the police stations or posts. While locating bus stations, it is also important that we select a place that is not close to the vulnerable areas where we find an unnecessary assembly of unwanted persons. There must be adequate space for making available to the users other facilities such as shopping complex, pay phones, medicare centres, small hotels and refreshment centres, sanitation, water or so. These facts make it clear that for improving the quality of services offered to the users, it is impact generating that the location points for bus stations, terminal, points, godowns, workshops, etc. need due care of transport professionals.

In view of the above, we find place mix, an important decision-making area for the road transport organisations. We talk about quality upgradation, we also talk about safety provisions. The motive is to improve the quality of services so that the users at large feel that they are availing the world-class services and at the same, also get it ensured that whatever the promises have been made by the transport organisations would in no case be distorted. This would help the road transport organisations in excelling competition and satisfying the users. We can't negate that in the years to come, the intensity of competition would go up since the Indian Railways have been found making sincere efforts to make the services competitive. The public transport organisations get a number of additional incentives. Hence, it is a matter of survival, especially for the private sector organisations who continue to remain in the race and can also think of getting a success if they start believing in making things happen. By offering quality services to the users by frequently shaping and reshaping the perception of quality, they can add additional attractions to their service mix. We find place strategy helping them in making available the promised quality of services to the end-users. This would make ways for increasing the market share since the public sector organisations in a majority of the cases appear disinterested to these problems. It is against this background that we talk about the place mix in the process of formulating a sound marketing mix for the road transport organisations.

The management of place thus needs due attention on the following:

- Locating bus stations at a point that is easily accessible, safe and equipped with the modern infrastructural facilities.
- Bridging over the gap between the services-promised and services-offered by improving the quality of employees.

Process Mix

The users of road transportation services expect punctual and safe services. The safety and punctuality elements become significant and in this context, the right and decent processing draw priority attention of professionals.

For passengers, it is pertinent that vehicles used for them are of quality so that the possibilities of their breakdown are minimised. In case of any breakdown, there should be sufficient arrangements for their immediate repairing and replacement. Right from the originating points to the points of their termination, there should be arrangements for proper checking and for that, the skilled personnel are to be deployed. In a true sense, they need networking with the help of a sound information management. Before boarding of the passengers, the vehicles need a thorough checking. For processing the services, the bus stations are also considered an important point. The front-line staff at the enquiry or booking counters play an important role in processing. The facilities for reservation or cancellation need due attention.

For goods transportation, it is essential that the suitable arrangements are made for loading and unloading. The loading and unloading must be safe. The transport agencies have a well developed network and they should assign due weightage to punctuality. The users of the services need to be communicated the date on which the goods are to be delivered. The cases of theft and pilferages are to be regulated. At both the originating and terminating points, there should be checking of the goods in the face of their consignment. In a number of cases, the users fail in getting information on time. The professionals need to take support of communication network.

The professionals found sincere to right and safe processing of services minimise the possibilities of complaints and service recovery. All possible efforts are to be made to minimise the cases of complaints but when the users complain, they should not delay their redressal.

Physical Evidence and Attractions

In the road transportation services, the servicescapes become significant particularly at the bus stations and transport offices of agencies. The professionals cannot undermine service ambience at the points where users assemble. The interiors, furnishing, lighting, sanitation, safe drinking water, ventilations, signposts, display of communication services are some of the important areas helping the creation of a customer-friendly service ambience coiling service fragrance and adding additional attractions to services. At different bus stops, we find scope for tangibilisation which simplifies the process of image projection. It is significant to mention that in the Indian perspective both the public and private sector road transport organisations have been found undermining service ambience. This has not only been creating inconveniences to the users but have also been making their task of image projection difficult. Here, the people particularly working as front-line staff need to look impressive. The dresses they wear or uniform they use must be neat and clean.

The People

Of late, we find people getting an outstanding place in the formulation of a sound marketing mix by almost all the organisations. Of course, the sophistication in the process of technology upgradation plays an incremental role in improving the quality of services but we can't negate that ultimately it is the quality of people serving an organisation that determines the magnitude of success. If we lack quality people even the world-class technologies fail in delivering goods. Contrary to it even if we have old generation of technologies but a team of dedicated, professionally-sound, value-based personnel, we succeed in offering the promised services. It is against this background that almost all the organisations either producing goods or generating services have been found assigning due weightage to the quality of people to be recruited.

Performance orientation plays a significant role to improve the quality of services and we can't think about the same unless we recruit people having faculties of development and adopt an ongoing training programme to develop and brush up their potentials or credentials. If we turn our eyes on the performance of State Road Transport Corporations, we find that by and large almost all of them have been offering to the users poor quality of services. Contrary to it, we find private transport organisations relatively in a commanding position by developing a new perception of quality. This is due mainly to the quality people engaged by them. Like other organisations, the road transport organisations, also need to employ quality people and to organise refresher courses, capsule courses to develop their credentials to make them high-performers. This, of course, gravitates our attention on the professional excellence or efficiency but in addition, we also need an intensive care on value orientation. A fair blending of professional excellence and value orientation can make ways for developing quality people who would be efficacious in serving the organisations; even the working conditions are not conducive. If we find the State Road Transport Corporations witnessing red, green and amber signals; if we find a grave problem of financial crunch; if we find frequent cases of misbehaviour by the employees; if we find the depreciation cost increasing sharply; if we find the operational costs going up, this is significantly due to the poor quality of people they have. This makes it essential that the public sector road transport organisations assign a transcendental priority to the people emerging as the most important mix of the marketing mix. The front-line staff, the managers need an in-depth knowledge of behavioural management. All of us are well aware of the instrumentality of value degeneration process in the State Road Transport Corporations. This needs a departure.

In view of the aforesaid facts, we find it essential that the road transport organisations in general and the public sector organisations in particular think about developing people on a priority basis. They need to make possible performance orientation which requires a fair mix of a number of attributes and properties as discussed above. It is also important to mention that the process of performance orientation can't be circled in a right fashion more so for the long time unless employee orientation is made possible. This focuses our attention on offering innovative incentives to the employees proving themselves as high performers. This keeps on moving the process of performance orientation because even the inefficient employees attempt to improve their efficiency.

ROAD TRANSPORTATION SERVICES MARKETING IN INDIAN PERSPECTIVE

India has one of the largest road network in the world aggregating to about more than 33 lakh kms. But if make a microscopic analysis of the quality of roads in global perspective, we find Indian roads lagging far behind the international standard. This in a very natural way has been affecting the performance of road transportation services. Because we find road transport contributing significantly to the passenger and freight traffic operations, the degeneration in quality is to affect the process of national economic transformation. The two-pronged measures such as development of quality roads and induction of quality buses and trucks in the fleet would make an invasion on the poor quality of services mounting day by day. It is against this background that we need conceptualisation of marketing principles in the road transportation services.

In the Indian context, we find private road transport services on an unorganised basis which stands as a barrier in the conceptualisation process. Hence, our focus is on the public sector because in almost all the states we find State Road Transport Corporations offering the passenger traffic services. Like the rail transport services, the users of road transport service also expect safe and time-honoured services which they are often denied. In a majority of the states, we find State Road Transport Corporations in red. This is mainly due to the fact that they fail in offering quality services to the users. The passengers in the prevailing conditions prefer the services of private transport services.

The conceptualisation of modern marketing principles may be helpful in improving the service quality and service recovery processes. It is significant to mention that the State Road Transport Corporations have been facing the image problem which can be removed with the help of quality service product. Though we find the working conditions of State Road Transport Corporations different to the Indian Railways who have freedom of managing their tracks. Thus, improving the quality of services with the poor quality of roads and inferior quality of buses is considered to be an acid test for the professionals or others serving the organisation. Formulating a sound marketing mix requires managerial proficiency and almost all the State Road Transport Corporations have been facing the problem of managerial deficiency. A stage of vicious circle if not reversed back traps the entire system and makes an organisation virtually handicapped. The public sector road transportation services have sufficient avenues for initiating qualitative improvements. There are a number of services at the bus stations and stops such as buying tickets, getting reservation, amenities like safe drinking water, sanitation, ventilation, reservation, cancellation and service recovery where they need professional and personal touch. Adding additional attractions to the service mix needs due attention but prior to that they are required to manage their core services which are virtually in a defunct condition.

The safety considerations at the bus stations and during the journey need priority attention. This will depend on the information networking.

Since we find image problem in a majority of the states, the task of promoting the road transportation services will be difficult. However, the transport corporation offer a number of subsidised services and this will be helpful while promoting the services. Advertisement may be a suitable component for them due to its cost-effectiveness feature. As and when they offer a package of services, this may be considered while promoting. The inclusion of new AC buses and sleeper buses may also be informed to the passengers.

The placement of services makes it essential that right from the head offices to the regional and divisional offices and to the respective micro-level offices, the provisions for services need time-honoured transmission so that the concerned offices deliver the services to the concerned passengers. The front-line staff offering the services need to maintain the flow. The policy decisions should move in the defined directions.

The decisions related to pricing/fare need due attention of professionals so that the transport corporations succeed in making profits while on the other hand, they also meet the social considerations. In the Indian context, we find State Road Transport Corporations facing a difficult situation while pricing because the private sector has been found making the market conditions much more competitive.

For processing of services in a right way, the back and front-line staff need to make use of the information and communication technology so that the promised quality of services are made available to the users. Service delivery and service recovery — both the dimensions need due care of front-line staff. The redressal of complaints cannot be overlooked.

In the offices, at the bus stations and even in the buses, we find scope for tangibilisation. The professionals need to make it sure the outstanding features are tangibilised for the projection of a positive image. The staff in general and the front-line staff in particular need to look impressive.

The different categories of staff working for the State Road Transport Corporations must be competent. They need a professional and personal-touch-in-services. The value engineering or ethical dimensions cannot be overlooked. It is right to mention that mainly due to unfair practices, the State Road Transport Corporations are becoming financially insolvent.

Thus, the State Road Transport Corporations have to conceptualise marketing principles so that the improved quality of services at an affordable price structure attract the passengers to avail the services. In the present market conditions when we find inflow and outflow of passengers increasing fast, the State Road Transport Corporations have tremendous opportunities to capitalise on. A sound marketing strategy will make the task of professionals easier.

In the Indian perspective where we find about 70% of the freight traffic and 85% of the passenger traffic carried by roads, it is pertinent that government policy makers strategically think over the poor quality of roads. It is also to mention that on an average we find 7% to 10% growth per annum in the road traffic. National Highways are found dominating the scence as almost 40% of the entire vehicular traffic are carried on by them.[16] With the increasing growth rate, we expect that the pressure on roads will increase further. This makes is essential that central as well as the state governments think over the issue on a priority basis.

The State Road Transport Corporations and the private sector organisations need to include superior quality of buses in the fleet. The State Road and National Transport Agencies require priority attention on improving the quality of trucks. The different categories of staff they have will determine the operational results. Since the State Transport Road Corporations in almost all the states have been found in financial crisis, it is imperative that the conceptualisation of marketing principles is made possible. The road transport organisations may be successful in arresting the problem of financial crunch if they practise marketing principles by using the expertise of professionals having world-class excellence.

In a majority of the states, the State Road Transport Corporations have proved to be a financial burden. The passengers prefer to avail the private services as they find them delivering safe and punctual services. Of course, in a few of the States, we find them in better condition but even in these states, the private sector services have an edge. This makes it essential that they develop a network and promote inter-state services. They should also involve themselves in the mail services which would make ways for financial resource mobilisation. A package of services to the passengers will be helpful in motivating them. Besides, they can also make use of their bus stations and buses as advertisement points. If the services are of quality, they will not have any problem of occupancy.

The unfair practices are found at its peak particularly in the State Road Transport Corporations. This makes it essential that professionals prefer to appoint people having a fair background and further link the earnings of a particular bus with the costs. In addition, they also need to monitor the day-to-day operations with the help of a squad to regulate the unfair practices.

The most important thing that they lack is managerial proficiency and by practising marketing, the professionalised efforts would help them in different ways. The quality of services would be improved and new doors would be opened for organisational prosperity. Breaking the vicious circle is an important task and the marketers can make is possible.

MARKETING MANAGEMENT OF CIVIL AVIATION

We can't deny the fact that man's conquest of air and now space represents one of the most glorious chapters in the annals of human achievements. The centuries of dreaming, aspirations, study, research, devotion, dedication by all kinds of men in all times and climes resulted into the emergence of sophisticated air transportation services. After the end of World War II, we find contours of development witnessing radical changes. In the Indian perspective, the progress in the field of civil aviation has been phenomenal. We can't negate that our domestic and international air transportation services have been making good strides. The economy of a country is substantially determined by the quality of air transportation services. Sophistication in the process the world over has been so fast that our services of late look of poor quality and even unsafe. Both the public sector organisations engaged in the process of offering the air transportation services, such as the Indian Airlines mainly for the domestic flights and the Air India exclusively for the International flights have been facing the problem of financial crunch. There are a number of factors responsible for such an unpleasant development no doubt but ultimately it is deficient management that draws our attention on a priority basis.

Aviation administration is an important area which has been found facing numerous problems. We need to realise that this is the root-and-branch cause for the present crisis which has been forcing Air Transportation Authorities to think over the problem with an open mind. The administrative lapses which used to invite different kinds of disasters can't be concealed. Of late, even for the domestic flights, we find the business environment competitive. So far as the international business environment is concerned we find the intensity of competition at its peak. This makes it pertinent that public and private sector air transport organisations innovate their strategic decisions. If they fail in doing so, the intensity of problem would be so much high that even the innovative strategic decisions would show a lukewarm response. It is against this background that we think over the marketing management of civil aviation.

The two important dimensions divert our attention in the very context, first is related to the technological sophistication which substantially determines the quality of services and the second is the managerial proficiency that plays an incremental role in making the services user-friendly *vis-a-vis* competitive. Since the Indian Air Lines and Air India have been facing the problem of financial crunch, the policy makers have no option but to activate the process of qualitative transformation. Aviation administration is inextricably and subtly linked up with the international airlines whose operations are managed in private as well as public sectors by nations friendly or otherwise. With the development of corporate sector and more so with the emergence of corporate culture, we find a profitable market for the civil aviation. Now not only the business elites or the political elites but we find even others using the services of air transportation. We accept the fact that a well geared aviation administration can bring about wonders and contribute to the national propsperity and international co-operation. We focus here on the different dimensions of air transportation services with the motto of making the services technology-driven *vis-a-vis* user-friendly. This would help the air transportation organisations in making the services internationally competitive.

Since we expect a positive increase in the business, the rate of profitability can also be maximised. The projection of a positive image would be possible which would help in making the services internationally competitive. Of late, we find aviation, not an isolated activity affecting only upper drawers of society but in a true sense, a key industry and key administration where world-class professional excellence is felt a must. In the competitive world of today, its neglect is not only self-defeating but immensely disastrous. In an age of Concord, it is essential that we make possible qualitative improvements so that world-class services are made available to the users. It is against this background that we find a study of market dimension important.

This study focuses on the formulation of marketing mix of air transport organisations or airways or airlines so that the system is made more sophisticated. At the outset, the task is to formulate a sound product mix that makes possible a fair synchronisation of core and peripheral services. In the core services, we go through the essential services inside the aircrafts as well as at the airports. In the peripheral services, we focus on the supportive services which make the journey comfortable, memorable and add additional attractions to your service mix. The professionals bear the responsibility of blending the core and peripheral services in such a way that product attractiveness keeps on moving. The formulation of a package tour would also be discussed in the very context. Since the aviation industry is to affect a number of allied industries, such as tourism, hotel, trade and commerce etc., our focus is on making the service mix internationally competitive. The second dimension to be discussed in the very context is designing of an ideal promotion mix which plays the role of informing, sensing and persuading the users. The different dimensions of promotion would be taken into consideration to make the promotional measures sensitive, creative, cost-effective and proactive. It is in this context that we go through the optimal blending of advertising, public relations, sales promotion, personal selling, word-of-mouth promotion and telemarketing. An optimally synchronised promotional measures simplify the task of promoting the business in a magnificent fashion. We also go through the pricing strategy that throws light on the various components of fare and freight or the tariff. There must be a close relation between the quality of services offered and the slab of prices charged for the services. We are aware of the fact that the International Airports Authority of India plays a contributory role while formulating the pricing strategy. The domestic tariff is regulated by the government whereas the international tariff is regulated by the International Authority. This component of the marketing mix plays an important role since all steps related to other mixes depend upon the revenue that we separate from pricing. The domestic and international tariffs depend upon a number of considerations. Since we find negative impact of the worldwide economic depression on the aviation industry, it is pertinent that the pricing decisions are made sensitive to profit *vis-a-vis* proactive to the expectations of users. In addition, the components related to place covering the offering of services and the location of airways or airlines offices would also be taken into consideration. Even in the aviation industry, we find management of human resources playing a commanding role and therefore the people would also be discussed as an independent submix of the marketing mix.

PRODUCT?

The air transportation multi-dimensional services found of intangible nature are known as the product. The passenger services, cargo services, mail services are the important products of air transportation. The individuals as well as the institutions or organisations are the users of the services. The product or the service product of air transportation are commercial as well as social. The sophistication in the air transport technologies determines the quality of product or standard specification. A number of inputs are used in offering the services and the quality of inputs used determines the quality of outputs. Since we find product a bundle of expectations, the increasing competition, sophistication, innovations shape and reshape the level of expectations of users. More high the level of expectations, more challenging we find the task of air transport professionals in developing and mixing the core and peripheral services. The core services product focuses on the essential services inside the aircrafts or at the airports whereas the peripheral services include the services to make the product mix attractive, comfortable, memorable or so.

PRODUCT PLANNING AND DEVELOPMENT

Planning and development become essential to cater to the changing needs and requirements of the users. We can't develop unless we plan and we can't plan unless we forecast. More competitive the business environment, more frequency we find in the development processes. Speed, safety, time, comforts are the main elements to be given due weightage while developing the air transportation services. The new generation of aircrafts, environment-friendly and fireproof seats, scientific control, development of new amenities and facilities, development of personnel in tune with technological sophistication are some of the constituents of development that require an ongoing, realistic, intelligent meticulous plan. The planning and development processes need team culture and a team spirit where skilled and unskilled, managerial and technical, financial and legal personnel are found involved. The technologies contribute substantially to the planning and development processes. The Marketing Information System, the technologies related to operation and control, the scientific development, intensive research immensely activate the development process. The most important of all is the policy and attitudes of the policy makers.

A balanced air system is the motive and we can't negate that policy makers have not been successful in activating the developmental efforts for making the services internationally competitive. The world has reached the stage in which a balanced system composes of air planes and sea planes, a composite type of machine which can taxi on the ground, run on water and fly in the air, helicopters which take of vertically and land on the pin point, stratospheric flying, rocket ships, Concord or so. The efforts in the Indian context are found very disappointing. It is a fact that we can't achieve that progress in air transport which has already been achieved by commericially and industrially advanced countries of the globe. Though we realise that with the attainment of independence, a number of steps have been taken to develop the system, still our efforts can't be said to be optimal to the changing business conditions. The development planners, policy makers, scientists, management experts virtually have failed in assigning due weightage to the developmental efforts already channelised by the developed countries.

The civil aviation services have undergone radical changes during the yester decades. Today, we find a number of companies providing passenger traffic and cargo handiling services in the country. The Air Transport Companies operate both in the public and private sector where we find the process of technological sophistication gaining a rapid momentum. The Air India, Indian Airlines and Air India Charters Limited (Air India Express) and Alliance Air are in the public sector whereas Jet Airways, Decan Aviation, Spice Jet, Go Airways, Kingfisher Airlines, Paramount Airways, Indigo, Sahara Airlines in the private sector. In addition, we also find Blue Dart Aviation operating as cargo private scheduled airline. The fleets operational are B747-400, B747-300, A310-300, B777-200LR, B777-300ER, B787-8 all power with GE engines and B737-8000W power with CFM engines. Besides, we also find a proposal of inducting aircrafts with CFM-56-B engines.[17]

We cannot negate during the yesteryears mainly due to globalisation and economic liberalisation, we find a significant increase in the level of income. Besides, the corporatisation has made ways for the development of corporate culture which has considerably influenced our lifestyles. The private sector companies have been found offering multi-dimensional incentives to their employees with the motto of minimising the mandays lost due to one or other factors and air travel incentive is also one of them. In addition, we find an attitudinal change in masses where sophistication is commonly found in their behavioural patterns. Thus, we find emergence of a big market for the air services in the days to come.

On the other hand, it is also right to mention that due to a major hike in the fuel price, the air transportation services are becoming unaffordable for the burgeoning middle class. In the days and years to come, the hike in fare and freight cannot be negated. Further, we also expect the side-effects of worldwide economic depression on the civil aviation sector which will bring a major fall in the occupancy ratio.

The emerging two adverse conditions are to make an invasion on the demand and supply position. However, the civil aviation sector cannot stop the development and expansion plan. The economic boom and depression move in a cyclic order. The global economy will once again come back on the rail. Hence, we do not find justifications for stopping the development and expansion plan. This is also due to the fact that once we cultivate the habit of leading a comfortable lifestyle, it becomes too much painful for us to switch over to the traditional patterns. This happens to be the most supporting factor in favour of development and expansion.

In view of the emerging facts, the civil aviation sector needs a facelift. World-class airports, aircrafts and staff having world-class excellence would make ways for qualitative developments in the air transportation services.

The research and development activities also need innovative efforts. The Civil Aviation Sector needs to make preparations for Commonwealth Games, 2010 to be held in Delhi. Thus, in view of the changing economic scene and market scenario, the development planners are required to initiate efforts to activate qualitative-cum-quantitative improvements.

The tasks before the development planners are:

- Rationalisation of fare structure, specially on short haul routes to make it cost-effective. It is advisable to adopt the Long Run Marginal Cost Principle of pricing for domestic air services.
- Acceleration in the rate of productivity of aircrafts by improving maintenance schedules so as to reduce aircraft down line to the minimum and improving the run round time at the airport.
- An element of competition in the provision of domestic air services is desirable. Private airlines need to operate on routes which cater to genuine passenger and tourist traffic. This would lead to improvement in the efficiency of air services.
- Strengthening the acquisition programme for the inclusion of sophisticated aircrafts.
- Assigning due weightage to the development of human resources who are supposed to be professionally-sound and personally-committed.
- Making possible sophistication in the process of maintaining and controlling the domestic as well as the international flights operations.
- Modernising the airports to ensure the world-class safety provisions.
- Developing peripheral services at the airports and inside the aircrafts to make the services internationally competitive.
- Time management, safety provisions and coordination to be given due weightage.
- Developing the technology-driven Marketing Information System with the help of sophisticated info-tech.

The aforesaid efforts are required to be intensified to improve the quality of both the passenger and cargo operations. In addition, they also need to streamline the mail services. The authorities managing and controlling the affairs are required to have world-class excellence that requires an ongoing programme for intensive training. We feel that there are tremendous opportunities and professional excellence would be instrumental in capitalising on the same optimally.

MARKETING MIX FOR AIR TRANSPORT ORGANISATIONS

The Product Mix

Since we find the air transport market competitive, it is pertinent that the core and peripheral services are innovated. The professionals bearing the responsibility of making possible frequency in the process of innovation are required to turn their eyes on the services of leading airways of the world. This would help them in making the innovative efforts of world-class. The product attractiveness is required to be made possible that requires designing of a sound product portfolio. With the globalisation and liberalisation, the foreign trade operations have been found increasing fast and this makes it essential that air services make possible an expansion in their capacity by including modern generation of aircrafts. In the service mix, we find passenger services, cargo services and the mail services. Airborne trade has been increasing in importance and now accounts for more than a quarter of total foreign trade in value terms. This makes it essential that the loading capacity is increased. The helicopter services are also an important part of the product mix and the primary users of helicopters are ONGC, NTPC, etc. Considering the high operation cost and foreign exchange outgo in maintenance and operations, it is necessary that the helicopter services are primarily restricted to oil exploration sector. With the development of foreign trade and increasing cultural exchange programmes, the Air Mail Services also need innovation. The services inside the aircrafts and at the airports are required to be made of international standard. Thus, in almost all the areas, we need to make the services mix competitive.

In Figure 10.5, the product mix of Air Transportation Services is presented. The three key services, such as passenger transportation, cargo services, and mail services make it clear that different categories of users, the individuals and the institutions use the air services. The formulation of a sound product mix is urgently needed. This is not possible unless we have new generation of aircrafts, sophisticated technologies managing and controlling the operations and the quality human resources offering quality services. The domestic and international services need professional excellence to maintain the time schedule and ensure the safety provisions. It is in this context that the service mix of air services has been discussed. Not only the core services but we also need to assign due weightage to the peripheral services. The users have developed high expectations. The food and drinks served in the international services, the entertainment and information management, the quality of seats and interior decoration, the passengers availing lay-off and using hotel and transportation services, the visa arrangements for entering a country during lay-off, the shopping complexes and the duty-free shops at the airports and even inside the aircrafts, the high behavioural profile of air hostess and their physical attractions are some of the neglected aspects requiring due care while innovating the process. In the domestic services, the private air transport organisations have been found enriching the quality of their peripheral services. We find an apparent change in the quality of services offered by the Indian Airlines Corporation and the Sahara India.

The aforesaid facts make it clear that the product mix of air transport service is required to be innovated to make the services nationally and internationally competitive. We can't deny the fact that to be more specific in the air transportation in addition to other aspects, we find aesthetic management playing an important role. This make it essential that to be more specific the airports assign due weightage to indoor and outdoor plantation, and beautify the lounge where users stay for a short interval.

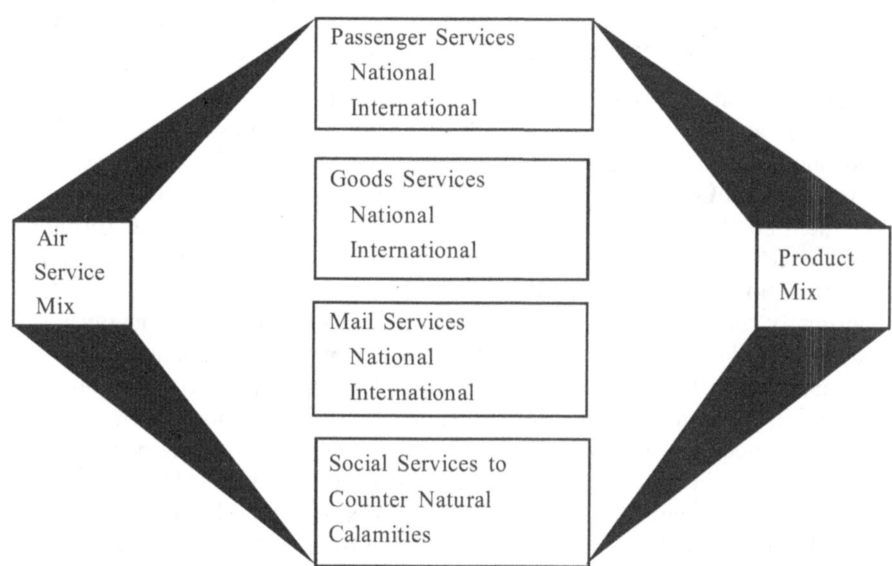

Fig. 10.5: Air Services Mix

On the basis of Figure 10.5, it is right to mention that the service mix covers passenger, goods and mail services to both the categories of users, organisations and individuals, national and international. The tourists are also found an important category of users of air services. It is important to mention that the civil aviation sector is structured into two distinct functional entities — operational and infrastructural. Indian Airlines offer domestic services and in addition, the Sahara India also offers the domestic services. The Air India offers international services. The infrastructural facilities are provided by the National Airport Authority (NAA) and International Airport Authority of India (IAAI). The important airports like Mumbai, Delhi, Kolkata, Chennai and Trivandrum are run by the IAAI. The NAA manages other airports. The services at different points, such as the services at the airports include transmitting important information to the passengers, making suitable arrangements for the security checking and weighing the goods, arrangements of temporary visa to enter the country to the international passengers, making available transportation facilities to the users from the airports to the hotels, custom checking, positioning of signposts to help the users, interior decoration, indoor plantation, seating arrangements, refreshments and cafeteria, sanitation and water, ventilation, lighting, etc. need due care of airport management. Further, the services inside the aircrafts include making provision for luggage, fireproof seat and interior decoration, entertainment provisions, food and drinks, tea and coffee, water and sanitation, transmission of necessary information, displaying the security and safety provisions, medicare services to the ailing passengers or so.

DESIGNING A PACKAGE FOR AIR TRANSPORT SERVICES

While managing the product for the air transportation services, it is pertinent that we also think in favour of designing a package for the users that acts as a motivational tool and simplifies the process of gaining and keeping the business. We can't deny the fact that incentives in any form fuel our efforts and sensitise the process of generation. By a package, our focus is on making a mix of different types of incentives for the prospects such as a trip for selected countries, concessional charges for children or reduced slab for parents, paying hotel charges or a lunch, a dinner, excursion, reduced charges for cargo services for a certain period or so. More profitable and attractive the package, more positive we find the results. This makes it essential that the air transport organisations, public or private, make sincere efforts to innovate the packages, and make it profitable to the extent we find the process commercially viable. Since the business environment is volatile and the intensity of competition is becoming high, it is essential that the air transport professionals managing the marketing portfolio keep their minds open, know and understand the strategic decisions of competitors and keep on moving the process of formulating a package while making the product decisions. This would help them in many ways. The new business would be motivated and the old business would also be retained. A consistent increase in the market share is need of the hour because a majority of the airways and airlines, of late, have been facing the problem of non-optimal occupancy ratio inviting numerous problems. What to talk of the Indian Airlines and Air India, if we find British Airways facing the problem of financial crunch. It is against this background that we make a strong advocacy in favour of designing a sound package for the different categories of users.

The marketing professionals are supposed to have an idea of the behavioural profile of different segments, such as kids and teens, youths and grey, men and women, students and professionals, married women and single married, technocrats and bureaucrats, intellects and artists or so. Today, we live in an age of nucleus marketing which is based on the principle of studying the behavioural profile of all the members in a family and making arrangements to satisfy them so that they continue to act as hidden salesforce. The formulation of a package requires professional excellence. As and when we talk about air transportation services, the industries like tourism and hotel attract our attention since a close link with the allied services/industries makes the ways for capitalising on the opportunities, optimally and profitably. Both the categories of tourists, domestic and foreign, economic and high spending and both the industries tourism and hotel can immensely be promoted if the package is attractive. This makes it clear that innovation in the process of package formulation is a must and the professionals are supposed to make it possible. We can't negate that transport, tourism and hotel form a chain and all of them while designing the product mix need to seek the cooperation of each other for making possible an optimal utilisation of the available opportunities. It is in this context that we need to assign due weightage to this dimension of the product strategy. The Indian Airlines and Air India have been facing the problem of financial crunch. They are supposed to show the world-class excellence while making the product decisions and activating the innovation process.

The Promotion Mix

The formulation of an ideal promotion mix is essential to inform, sense and persuade the users. In the Indian perspective, we need more creative efforts because the potential users in a majority of the cases don't prefer to use the air services. The business magnets, business executives, politicians, cine artists, high spending tourists, business houses using expensive inputs and trading the same, the Department of Posts, domestic and international tourists are some of the users of the air services. Of course, we find a qualitative difference between the users of other modes and the air transport. The users appear to be more conscious, aware of their rights and in a majority of the cases are found sophisticated. We can't deny the fact that albeit the labour class of the society use the international air services when they get a job in the overseas countries. However, a majority of the users are sophisticated and therefore our promotional efforts are required to be more creative. The professionals engaged in the air services bear the responsibility of blending the different components of promotion in such a way that the task of increasing the business is simplified. Since a number of airways and airlines have been facing the problem of financial crunch, it is pertinent that they make possible an optimal use of the different components of promotion. It is against this background that we focus on the different constituents of promotion.

Advertising: We are aware of the fact that air transportation services need creative advertisements to promote their business. This is the first component of the promotion mix which is based on professional excellence of the advertising agencies. In view of the rising cost of inputs and the increasing impact of worldwide economic depression on the air transportation, we need to make the advertisement budget optimistic *vis-a-vis* optimal. This is essential to regulate the multi-dimensional expenses found of unproductive nature and instrumental in making the services expensive. Though the airlines and airways don't have any freedom in setting the rate of fare or freight since NAA and IAAI regulate most of the activities, it is still impact generating that they think over the problem with an open mind and just to make the services economic don't violate the safety provisions. The telecast media and the print media are found important while promoting the air business.

While advertising through the telecast media, they need to consider the budgetary constraints and not to forget the budgetary provisions. We find television very much instrumental in sensitising the prospects and even in keeping or retaining the old business. We are supposed to keep in our minds the quality and nature of target market and the level of expectations. The advertising professionals need to make the advertisement slogans, campaigns, messages proactive to the generation of business. The airways and airlines have also to make it sure that whatever the strategic decisions they make to promote the business are in a position to establish an edge over the promotional measures of the competitors. This is essential to make the advertisement proactive to the expansion of business. They are also required to assign due weightage to the efforts made for the projection of a positive image. We can't deny the fact that the Indian Airlines as well as Air India have been facing the image problem. The advertisement may be efficacious in transmitting the facts and removing the image problem.

Since we talk about the air transportation services, it is essential that while advertising we also keep in our minds the image of our country, the natural scenes, the tourist attractions, rich cultural heritages or so which would energise the process of motivating the tourists and thus not only the airways but a number of industries are to be benefited, such as tourism, hotel, banks, insurance, trade and commerce, education or so. It is assumed that the advertising professionals while designing the advertisement layout, composing the scenes, positioning the events, designing the messages, developing the themes assign an overriding priority to make the advertisement processes creative. We are aware of the fact that both the domestic as well as the international flights have been facing the problem of poor occupancy ratio and therefore we can't expect something concrete or positive unless our products or services have been offering multi-pronged benefits or blending multi-dimensional attractions. It is against this background that we talk in favour of advertising with the support and cooperation of allied industries.

Of late, we find significant developments in the field of print technology since the laser printing, off-set printing, screen printing have made possible sophistication and economy in the process. The advertisement professionals are supposed to know the latest developments in the print technology and while advertising are required to make innovative efforts so that creativity is made possible. Promoting the use of world-class materials appears essential to make the process productive. They are also supposed to have an in-depth idea of the magazines, newspapers preferred by the different segments and to use the same for advertising. The print media being economic in nature and subjective in character would be proactive to the air transport business provided we make possible an optimal use of the same. Sophistication has made ways for attraction which is found paving avenues for business generation.

While advertising, it is impact generating that we select an opportune moment of flight, an attractive scene of take-off, high attractiveness of personnel in general and the air hostess in particular, the landscape of an attractive tourist centre, wildlife sanctuaries, lake, park or so. Since of late we have sophisticated photographic devices, the task is easier. The main thing is the instrumentality of the advertising professionals in adding attractions to the posters, leaflets, brochures, booklets or so. If the users/potential users are found sophisticated, we need sophistication at each and every stage of marketing. It is in this context that we talk so loudly about the creativity and sophistication. The print media being economic in nature would make the entire process cost-effective and the rate of profitability can also be maximised.

The air transportation services can also make use of broadcast media. To be more specific for the domestic flights, we need to advertise on radio where we find enough scope for audio attraction. The advertisement budget can't be made non-optimal to the general budget of the business and the domestic airlines are required to maintain economy, especially while managing the unproductive expenses. Thus, all the three vehicles, such as print media, telecast media and the broadcast media are required to be used for advertising the air business and the mode, scale, moment would depend upon the emerging trends in the domestic and global business conditions. In any case, we are not supposed to make the process unproductive.

Publicity: We find publicity an important component of the promotion mix. It is a process of persuasive communication for which we are not supposed to pay any thing. So far the sharpness of the tool is concerned, we find it very much instrumental in sensitising the persuasion process provided the media people, public relations officers, receptionists have been helping you sincerely and honestly. Strengthening public relations activities is found essential to promote the business of airlines or airways. The Public Relations Officers, Receptionists, Travel Agents, Travel Guides, Media people are some of the sensitive points of publicising the business. The air transport professionals or the marketing managers bearing the responsibility of promoting the business are supposed to have an in-depth idea of the different sources helping them effectively in publicising the business. Unless the prospects know about the quality of business from the authentic sources, the process of stimulation can't be geared up in the right direction. This makes it essential that the marketing professionals seek the cooperation of media people by organising a meeting, get-together, workshop, press conference, briefing, arrange for them lunch/dinner/excursion/small gifts and motivate them to motivate the prospects by publishing news items and advocating much in their favour. It is in this context that we focus on this component of the promotion mix.

The most important point in the publicity is the cooperation of media. The marketing professionals should have an idea of magazines, newspapers preferred by the prospects or users and they should develop rapport with the correspondents concerned. We agree with this view that developing rapport is an art and the professionals are supposed to be aware of the same. How to present the facts and figures related to your business? How to visualise the positive points and to conceal the negative ones? How to initiate the dialogues with the media people? How to oblige them? These aspects need due care of the marketing professionals since they are supposed to know everything about the stimulation process.

The Public Relations Officers play an incremental role in getting the publicity of your business. This makes it essential that personnel working as PROs, Receptionists, Front line staff know about the behavioural management and particularly about the EMPATHY. This would help them in influencing the impulse of prospects/users and increasing the market share. It is pertinent that they have high communicative ability; they are looking smart; their facial expression narrates optimism and they are also in a position to share the sorrows and sufferings of the users by using soft words with a smiling face. Business is not only the business of core services for which you charge. Business is something more than the core services for which you charge nothing. It is against this background that we find publicity an important dimension of promoting the air transport business.

The Airways, Airlines need to recruit efficient personnel for that very purpose who should have professional excellence no doubt but in addition they are also required to have the potentials of attracting the users/prospects. We can't negate that it is an art that requires an ongoing training programme for developing the faculties of personnel supposed to discharge the responsibility of publicising your business. The publicity thus proves to be an effective device of promoting the air transport business. You serve well, it is your business responsibility. You let your prospects know about the quality of your services; it is your responsibility as a world-class professional.

Sales Promotion: A component of promotion adopted for a particular period to touch the target and withdraw the measures when the time is over is known as sales promotion. The tool based on incentives is found instrumental in sensitising the users/prospects if the professionals innovate the process frequently. The sales promotion measures are meant for both the related sources of channelising and using the business, such as the travel agents, tour operators, transport operators, receptionists working in the offices of airways all of them who process the services and the passengers or business houses who ultimately use the services. In the first case, we call it trade promotion and in the second case, we call it consumer promotion or user promotion. The airways marketing professionals bear the responsibility of identifying the innovative tools which have not been used by the competitors so far.

The incentives to the personnel instrumental in processing the services need due attention of the professionals so that the positive contributions of providers is used as a base for determining the incentives to be offered. Such a base assigning due weightage to the business promotion would induce even those personnel who are not so efficient. The travel agents contribute a lot to the promotion of air transport business and therefore we need to think in their favour on a priority basis. In addition, the tour operators also contribute to the process and therefore we also need to think in their favour. Besides, the front-line staff in the offices of the airways and the receptionists working there also play the same role. This makes it significant that we offer to them some incentives which may be in the form of a holiday trip to a particular place, concessional services to their children or spouse or so. You can also think in favour of offering to them innovative gifts which have yet not been offered by your competitors. The nature and type of incentives would depend on the contributions of providers. If they make immense contributions, the incentives would be good in quality and volume. Contrary to it, the providers making insignificant contributions would get small benefits.

The users or prospects also deserve promotional incentives. Some of the users are habitual who frequently use the services whereas some of the users are occasional who use your services occasionally. It is judicious that you take a decision regarding the promotional incentives on the basis of the frequency that you find in using the services. The incentives may be in the form of concessional services, an attractive package as a holiday trip, small gifts or so. We also find organisation of contests for that purpose in which the winners are given prices.

The main thing in the sales promotion is offering due incentives to all who play a significant role in promoting the business. The air transport professionals are supposed to be aware of the sources from where the business comes. With the help of computers now they are in a position to identify the providers helping the process substantially or marginally. We find the business environment competitive and the mounting intensity of competition or the emerging trends in competition would let you know the scale of benefits to be offered. Since it is a part of your promotion budget, you are supposed to innovate the process in the face of changing business results. It is in this context that we think in favour of sales promotion helping the process of business promotion. Frequency in innovation would make your task easier and therefore instead of copying the tools offered by the competitors you need to try to offer something new.

Personal Selling: Personal selling is an important component of the promotion mix that is found based on personal credentials. Of course, the air transport organisations find this submix of the promotion mix instrumental in increasing the business. An art to influence, stimulate, sensitise the impulse buying is known as personal selling. It is against this background that we also call it personal promotion. In this context, the air transport marketing professionals are supposed to know about the behavioural profile of persons who act as personal promoters. The travel agents, tour operators, transport operators, travel guides, front-line staff on the booking counters, receptionists contribute substantially to the process of promotion. If they stop selling, the offices of airways would find it difficult to sell. This makes it clear that even the quality services fail in attracting the users, if the channels are not to cooperate. This makes it essential that we offer incentives to them so that they keep on moving the process of stimulation.

The management of people active in promoting the business requires that we select persons, agencies having a positive image. We can't expect something positive from the inefficient promoters. The travel agencies having a well established business can help you substantially and therefore it is your prime responsibility that while selecting travel agents you assign due weightage to the image of travel agencies. The tour operators and transport operators also help you considerably and therefore you need precautions in selecting the operators having a widespread network. Now you need to think about the incentives to be offered to the promoters. In this context, it is significant that you let them know in advance about your proposals, schemes so that they make innovative efforts to touch the target. We are aware of the fact that they get commission which is regulated by IATA and NAA. However, we find almost all the organisations offering additional incentives to the motivators or promoters.

In the personal selling, we find even the front line staff or personnel at the booking or reservation counter of airways offices playing an incremental role in promoting the business. Here, it is essential that you are aware of the credentials of persons supposed to discharge the business responsibility and try your best to brush up their faculties as and when the opportunities come. The personal selling is based on the behavioural profile. If we find cases of misbehaviour of indecent behaviour by the front-line staff, the task of getting the business is found much more complicated. This makes it essential that personnel working at the counters where we find a face-to-face communication with the users have high communicative ability and high behavioural profile.

The air transport organisations also need due weightage to the training programme for the front-line staff. It is significant that the personnel working as promoters know in detail about the product portfolio and the future plans. You have already included or propose to include in your fleet the Concord the most sophisticated aircraft of today but the promoters don't know about this development. This would create a communication gap and would generate misunderstanding among the users or prospects. Our focus is on the point that a detailed information regarding the latest development or development proposals is found impact generating to activate the stimulation process.

Word-of-mouth Promotion: This happens to be an important constituent of the promotion mix in which the promoters act as a hidden salesforce. The satisfied group of users, opinion leaders narrate outstanding merits or salient features of services used by them. We find narration to relatives, friends and therefore the rate of sensitivity is found high. The constituent focuses on the quality of services offered by the service generating organisations. The air transport organisations may also depend on this component of promotion if they feel that the quality of services offered by them is of world-class. If you travel by Air India and are satisfied with the quality of services, it is natural that you mention your experiences to your friends and relatives. They trust in you and therefore the stimulation process is on. The moment your friends and relatives get an opportunity to travel, they find Air India their first choice. Advertisements may be ineffective, publicity may also be ineffective but the word-of-mouth communications can't be ineffective if the communication processes are based on right exposition. It is in this context that we find this component of the promotion mix helping an organisation in promoting the business.

In the Indian perspective, the Indian Airlines, Air India, and others may use this component of the promotion mix if they realise that providers have not been distorting the quality of services promised. The distortion process at any stage by any person would make this tool of promotion ineffective. If the users at large feel that Emirates, British Airways, Air India have been offering quality services to the users without making any distortion, the prospects would prefer to use the services of these airways as and when they get an opportunity. In addition to the satisfied group of users, we also find opinion leaders acting as word-of-mouth promoters. This makes it essential that the air transport marketing professionals have an in-depth knowledge of the prospects/users living in a particular command area. In this context, it is pertinent that the professionals are satisfied with the behavioural profile of word-of-mouth promoters. The masses need to form a positive opinion regarding the opinion leaders. We also find cases where social reformists, popular cine leaders, regional artists succeed in acting as hidden salesforce. It is in this context that we need to seek the cooperation of high performers who with the help of quality personnel succeed in getting the profitable business.

The aforesaid facts make it clear that the positive efforts of air transport organisations for improving the quality of services would increase the instrumentality of this constituent *vis-a-vis* would minimise the advertisement budget. This makes it essential that the airways and airlines engaged in offering the services are careful to the quality element. For increasing or sharpening the instrumentality of this tool, it is pertinent that air transport organisations make possible total quality management which takes the shape of a quality circle. This requires involvement of all who directly or indirectly contribute to the generation process. Since we expect the airways and airlines having a team of efficient personnel and innovative marketing strategies, the word-of-mouth promotion can be effective. It is not to be forgotten that the dissatisfied group of users play a negative role. Thus, the instrumentality of this tool is vigorously influenced by the perception of quality perceived and practised by the air transport organisations.

Telemarketing: Of late, we find telemarketing playing an important role in promoting the business. Almost all the organisations have been found energising the selling activities with the support of telemarketing. Like other organisations, the air transport organisations also find enough scope for promoting telemarketing in different areas. The telemarketers can serve multi-dimensional purposes. They can play an outstanding role in informing, sensing and persuading the users even without making a big investment. A sophisticated telephonic instrument and a well trained telemarketer are found essential for intensifying the use of this component of the promotion mix. The queries and questions of users/prospects can satisfactorily be answered and misunderstanding, confusion and communication gap can also be removed if telemarketers are found professionally sound. It is against this background that we need promoting telemarketing even in the air transport business. The booking counters, the enquiry counters, the reception counters, the users' complaints and grievances cell, the announcers are found playing an incremental role in promoting the air business. All the sensitive points need the support of a professionally sound telemarketers. He/she is supposed to have a high communicative ability in addition to an attractive personality and microphonic sound. It is important that the telemarketers are well aware of the recent developments so that the users or prospects don't face any difficulties in getting the desired information. We find copious avenues for promoting telemarketing in the air transport business because a number of allied industries, such as hotel, tourism, travel agencies, tour operators, transport operators, banking, insurance play a contributory role in getting the business. The telemarketers are supposed to know all about the important windows from where they get the business or even expect to get the business. The information related to vacancy and occupancy, take-off and landing, hotel booking confirmation and cancellation, etc. can be transmitted to the concerned users with the support of telemarketers. In addition, the visa for the users in transit can also be arranged with the support of telemarketers. The cargo services, national or international, depend substantially on the instrumentality of telemarketers. The telemarketers can transmit to the trade and business representatives necessary information and can also answer to their queries and questions for smooth booking and delivery. These facts are a mute testimony to this proposition that the air transport organisations need to promote this component of business promotion on a priority basis.

With the sophistication in communication technologies, satellite communication service, increasing business flow and its expanding linkages with the allied industries, we find enough scope for developing telemarketing in the air transport business. The travel agencies, the hotels are found closely linked with the air services. The comforts and conveniences to the different categories of users can considerably be increased if the telemarketers are found supporting the air transport business. We can't deny the fact that with the development of telecast media and increasing instrumentality of television in almost all the areas, the telemarketing would continue to play an important role even in the years to come. This makes it essential that the national and international air transport organisations make use of telemarketing both for domestic and overseas, general and commercial purposes since economy in promotion is made possible. In the present age when we find managing the human resources a difficult task, it is pertinent that we think of channelising the use of telemarketing.

The Price Mix

Pricing decisions play a decisive role in managing the business of air transport organisations. The increasing operational costs, the mounting competition, the falling occupancy ratio, the imbalances in demand and supply, the increasing pressure of inflation are some of the important factors influencing the strategic decisions for setting fare and freight rates in the air transport business. We are aware of the fact that we have different authorities to manage and control the domestic as well as the international air transport businesses. The Ministry of Tourism and Civil Aviation, the Indian Airlines Corporation, the National Airports Authority, the International Airports Authority of India, and the Air India Corporation are the bodies directly or indirectly influencing the process of making the pricing decisions. The management of domestic pricing is not so much complicated but the management of international pricing is found much more complicated since a number of problems crop up while setting the fare and freight structures. We need to maintain the international standard of pricing but we find it difficult to optimise the expenses as found in the leading airways of the world. We can't deny the fact that in the Indian perspective, the pricing decisions need an intensive care of administration since we can't imagine of maintaining the commercial viability unless the pricing decisions are made rational.

For the domestic flights, we find Ministry of Civil Aviation playing a decisive role in making the pricing decisions. The operational expenses are found increasing fast to improve the quality of services or to follow the safety norms. The users expect a lot for the charges they pay. The air transport authorities find it difficult to rationalise the fare and freight structures since the falling occupancy ratio is found throwing a big impact on the revenue position. The inflationary pressure is found increasing which in a natural way influences the costs of inputs used for offering the services. The installed capacity is found facing the problem of a non-optimal utilisation. Thus, the task before the ministry is found tough since productive or unproductive expenses need to be rationalised. We have failed in making possible technological sophistication which has also been increasing the operational costs. The users at large are not in a position to pay more. These factors make the task of pricing a bit difficult. However, the Ministry of Civil Aviation bears the responsibility of rationalising the fare and freight structures in such a way that the revenue position is increased. The rationalisation of fare structure needs to be undertaken particularly on short haul routes to make it cost-oriented. We find it more judicious to adopt the Long Run Marginal Cost Principle of Pricing for domestic air services. Subsidisation of air services in regions other than the North East and in accessible areas is not desirable. The main problem is to make the pricing decisions competitive because we also find private air transport organisations involved in the process. Thus, while making the pricing decisions for domestic services, it is essential that we keep in our minds a number of considerations. We don't find it right to increase the operational expenses and to allow a frequent increase in the fare and freight structures. Of course, with the development of corporate sector, we find the demand position showing a positive sign of development still the gap between the demand and supply is found complicating the task of administration. It is high time that the air transport organisations, public or private, engaged in the domestic flight operations make the fare and freight structures proportionate to the increasing operational costs. This also makes a strong advocacy in favour of rationalising the operational expenses. With the use of sophisticated technologies and with the cooperation of personally-committed high performer employees, we find enough scope for optimising the operational costs. We find the market profitable provided the demand position is increased which makes it essential that we make pricing a motivational tool and bridge over the gap between the demand and supply. The domestic tourism is to be promoted, the air transport culture is to be developed, the quality of service is to be improved, the operational expenses are to be rationalised, the use of sophisticated technologies is to be encouraged and these steps would help marketing professionals in making a sound pricing decision which would be effective in maintaining the commercial viability of domestic air transport organisations.

The setting of international pricing is found much more complicated since it is not only upon the Air India to set the fare and freight structures. The International Airports Authority of India, International Air Transport Association (IATA) are some of the important organisations playing a decisive role in making the pricing decisions for the international air transport business. IATA divides the world into three areas, such as Area 1, Area 2 and Area 3. In the Area 1, the countries are North and South American continents, islands adjacent thereto like Greenland, Bermuda, West Indies, Caribbean area, Hawaiian Island, Midway. In Area 2, the countries like Europe, Africa, Islands adjacent thereto like Ascensian, the part of Asia situated in West including Iran. In Area 3, the countries are remaining part of Asia and the islands adjacent thereto like East Indies, Australia, New Zealand, Islands of Pacific Ocean. International Civil Aviation Organisations is also found playing an important role in process of making the pricing decisions.[18] Thus, we find involvement of a number of bodies and organisations in setting the international fare and freight structures but almost all the airways and airlines find it difficult to follow the international standard.

In view of the above, it is difficult to make the pricing decisions optimal to the increasing operational costs. The safety provisions need an overriding priority. The installation of sophisticated technologies and the services of high performer professionals are to aggravate the operational costs. In addition, the users at large have developed the levels of their expectations. Thus, we find it difficult for the Air India to make the business profitable. It is against this background that we need to innovate the marketing decisions. Optimising the operational expenses, increasing the occupancy ratio are the two important dimensions which would require more professional excellence. The civil aviation and tourism are found interrelated. The Ministry of Tourism and Civil Aviation bears the responsibility of promoting world tourism to increase the demand position for Air India. The inclusion of innovative peripheral services, the formulation of a lucrative package for the world tourists, the inclusion of new sophisticated aircrafts in the fleet are some of the steps making the task of increasing the business easier. We find the international business environment much more competitive and the Air India is not free to adjust the fare and freight structures independently. This makes it essential that we innovate the marketing practices and motivate the world tourists, organise international conventions and conferences, offer to the users a number of incentives to use the services of Air India and make ways for increasing the market share and paving the avenues for high productivity and profitability.

The Place Mix

This dimension of the marketing mix focuses on processing of services and selecting the location points for airways and airlines offices keeping in view the comforts and conveniences of the end-users. By the processing of services, our emphasis is on the involvement of channels, front-line staff, travel agency offices, offices of the tour operators or so from where the services flow and reach to the ultimate users. In addition to the services inside the aircrafts, we find a number of services as a part and parcel of the air transport services. Right from the buying of tickets and booking of seats till the users reach at the destination, there are a number of core and peripheral services in which a number of agencies and organisations are found involved. The main theme coiled in this mix is to make available to the ultimate users the promised services and to be sure that services are not distorted at any points by an individual or an organisation bearing the responsibility of making available the promised services to the end-users. It is against this background that we go through the place mix. Some of the passengers buy tickets from the travel agents whereas some of the passengers buy tickets directly from the offices of airways. Some of the flights are of general nature whereas some of the flights are chartered. The air transport organisations bear the responsibility of making it sure that the prospects don't face any difficulty while buying the tickets and make the necessary arrangements for the confirmation of booking. It is also to be confirmed that the users booking their luggages are not to face inconveniences. The behavioural profile of the personnel working in the offices of travel agents and in the offices of the airways and airlines requires due attention. It is also to be sure that the information network of the offices of travel agents is technology-driven and user-friendly. In addition, the airport authorities are found involved in the process of offering a number of services to the users when they start their journeys and report at the airports. The security checking, custom checking, and luggage checking are some of the formalities in addition to the checking of passport, visa, income tax clearance or so. The airport authorities with the support of a team of number of agencies and officials make available these services to the users. It is essential that all the windows or the counters offer the services as per the provision and promises. Your entry in the aircrafts equipped with all the amenities and facilities of core and peripheral nature draws a close attention of airways and airlines. Keeping in view the duration and nature of flights, the users are made available lunch/dinner, breakfast and drinks inside the aircrafts. It is almost all clear that air hostess looking attractive, smart, well dressed are at your disposal to make available to you the defined services. If in course of journey, you are supposed to change the aircrafts and the duration of stay is long, it is the responsibility of airport authorities and the concerned airways and airlines to make available to you the hotel accommodation and visa or so. Again from the start of your journey to the point of destination, the airways are supposed to offer you a number of facilities.

The aforesaid facts make it clear that a number of services are to be made available to the end-users and the airways and airlines have to be sure that the promised services reach to the end-users without making any distortion. This in a natural way requires professional excellence. The management bears the responsibility of making available the promised services to the end-users.

Another dimension of place mix is related to the location and management of the offices of airways, travel agents, tour operators, transport operators or so. We can't negate that the main thing in the selection of a place is easy accessibility. The place is required to be safe, well connected with all-weatherproof roads where all the required infrastructural facilities are to be available. We find cities precincts a suitable location point for the offices of airways and others. The offices of all the agencies and organisations concerned with the availability of related services need to be managed in a right fashion. The technology-driven booking system is to be ensured. It is also essential that the prospects, users get necessary information regarding cancellation and for that the computers, telephonic services are required to be made sophisticated. The water and sanitation facilities for the users and comfortable seating arrangements need due care of the travel agents or airways offices. The lighting, ventilation facilities need to be made available. The interior decoration, furnishing, plantation need aesthetic sense so that the users form a positive opinion regarding the airways services. The users of the airways services feel themselves alleviated and therefore the services and look of the concerned offices should magnify the same. The tour operators and the transport operators need more space and therefore, they have no option but to establish their offices essentially not in the cities precincts but at a place where all the facilities are required to be made available even in their offices. The positioning of posters of airways and airlines which look attractive and draw the attention of the users attending the offices for chartered flights, package tours need due care. There facts make it clear that in the management of place, the location point for a particular office occupies a place of significance and the concerned agencies, organisations need to realise the same. It is in this context that we find management of place an important component of the marketing mix.

In view of the above, it is right to mention that the air transport business is linked with a number of allied services offered by a number of agencies and organisations. If we don't find cohesion and coordination the promised services would hardly reach to the end-users.

Process

The processing of services in the air transport is found with three-tier arrangements. The first is aircrafts; the second, information technology and the third, people serving in different capacities. The Airports Authority of India (AAI) is a regulatory body which was formed in April 1995 and is responsible for ensuring safe and efficient air traffic services. The AAI is also responsible for providing air safety services and rescue facilities. Besides the responsibilities related to planning development, construction and maintenance of runways are also with the AAI. Thus, in the processing of air traffic services, we find AAI playing an outstanding role. The second aspect is management of aircrafts in the fleet. The concerned airlines make it sure that aircrafts in operation are in perfect order. The third dimension for processing is a team of people working as crew members, consisting of air hostesses pilots and the supporting staff. In addition, the people working as front-line staff for reception, enquiries, booking of air tickets and cancellation are also involved in the process. The service delivery and service recovery processes move through different stages. We are well aware that air traffic services considerably depend on the information and communication networks. The ultimate users are the passengers in the case of air transport services and individuals or organisations making use of the cargo services. The different levels of employees process the services in such a way that users are found satisfied. The promises made by the airlines need to reach to the users on time and in a decent way.

Physical Evidence and Attractions

In the air traffic services, we find this submix of marketing significant with the viewpoint of projection of a fair image. Keeping in view the users of high profile, it is imperative that the concerned professionals ensure tangibilisation. The service ambience draws priority attention where interiors play a very positive role. The furnishing, signposts, ventilation, lighting, sanitation and aesthetic sense help professionals in the projection of image. The service fragrance makes it essential that particularly in the airports and aircrafts; the professionals assign due weightage to tangibilisation. The lounge of airports needs due attention of professionals with the viewpoint of tangibilisation because we find there long stay of passengers. Besides, the aircrafts need to be well maintained. Innovative services in the aircrafts add additional attractions to the services.

In the air traffic services, we find physical attractions to be very instrumental in the projection of image. The staff working either in the airports or the crew members working in the aircrafts need to look neat and clean. The uniform need special attention in the air traffic services. The personal care dimensions are found very effective and in this context, the dresses, hairstyle, shoes, facial expression and body language of staff instrumentalise the tangibilisation process. The physique of air hostesses is found regulated and therefore they need special care.

If we combine both, the users feel fragrance. The service ambience thus needs priority attention.

People

Like other organisations, the air transport organisations also need an intensive care on the management of people serving airways in different capacities. Ultimately, it is the quality of people that helps air transport professionals in shaping the perception of quality or even in bridging over the gap between the services-promised and services-offered. Of course, we find sophisticated technologies simplifying their functional responsibilities substantially but nothing can be made sure unless we find professionally-sound, personally-committed and value-based employees serving airways or its supporting offices. It is against this background that of late almost all the organisations have been found assigning due weightage to the management of people. The marketing professionals feel that the air transport organisations need to make the ways for performance orientation which is not possible unless they have quality people. The technical, managerial, non-technical personnel bear the responsibility of perceiving the new perception of quality.

Since we don't find any limit for quality upgradation, the air transport organisations need to devise ways for innovating the core and peripheral services and in the process, the marketing resources would be required to be made proportionate to the changing level of expectations of users. We are well aware of the fact that professionally-sound, personally-committed, and value-based employees can be proved to be high performers who can make possible performance orientation. This draws our attention on innovating the recruitment methods, developing the intensive training programme, assigning due weightage to the behavioural studies while designing the syllabi and making the employees aware of the recent developments in the field of air transportation by promoting audiovisual exposure. The air transport management needs to intensify an ongoing training programme for almost all the categories of employees. We can't check sophistication in the process of technological advances; we can't check the increasing level of expectations of users of the services because the competitive organisations have been found promoting research for practising innovative measures in almost all the areas, the only thing that we can do is to improve the quality of our personnel. It is in this context that we find marketing professionals making a strong advocacy in favour of treating "People" as an independent submix of the marketing mix.

The main task before the air transport organisations is to make possible performance orientation without which they can't think in favour of accelerating the rate of productivity. The increasing operational costs need to be made optimal, the falling occupancy ratio is required to be given due weightage, the new generation of aircrafts is required to be included in the fleet, the promotional measures are required to be innovated, the increasing gap between the services-promised and services-offered is required to be bridged over and only high performers can make things positive. It is also right to mention that the air transport organisations need to improve the behavioural profile of employees so that they succeed in making an assault on the image problem.

We talk much about performance orientation but paradoxically don't consider it essential to think about employee orientation. In a true sense, we find a correlation between the two. By the employee orientation, our emphasis is on offering due incentives to the high performers in order that even the inefficient personnel are induced to generate efficiency. We can't deny the fact in the Indian perspective almost all the organisations expect performance orientation without employee orientation. They don't link incentives with efficiency which ultimately demotivates even the high performers and activates the vicious circle in which all of them start believing in promoting the unfair, unethical and even illegitimate practices just for their personal gains. The air transport organisations in general and the Indian Airlines and Air India in particular need to promote employee orientation by rationalising the salaries, job promotion schemes and other benefits. We need a transcendental priority to employee orientation since incentives make the ways for a positive change. An attitudinal change in employees is not possible unless the air transport organisations or the senior executives and the policy makers change their attitudes by innovating the incentives. It is against this background that we speak so loudly about employee orientation. Increasing cases of unrest in the public sector air transport organisations make it clear that the policy makers need an attitudinal change.

AIR TRANSPORT SERVICES MARKETING IN INDIAN PERSPECTIVE

Globalisation has changed our lifestyles. It has made ways for corporate culture in which we find sophistication an important dimension for image projection. The corporatisation has opened doors for the development of corporate culture in which we find high level of temptation for material culture. Earn more and spend more govern our behavioural patterns. Of course, the air transportation services is not a new thing even in the Indian context but the demand side has witnessed a galloping increase particularly after the emergence of a new wave culture substantially influenced by the cross-cultural society. It is against this backdrop that the airways need a new look, a new vision and a professional touch in the service delivery and service recovery.

The other side of the coin, no doubt, presents a gloomy picture. The global economy has been experiencing a threat and the corporate sector has been experiencing a number of threats and challenges on that account. This is likely to affect the demand side. During the yesteryears, the air traffic services witnessed qualitative-cum-quantitative improvements. This made possible a significant increase in the supply side. A number of airlines entered into the business and have been facing numerous problems due to worldwide economic depression.

Optimism paves the ways for development. The policy planners are hopeful that the reversal in trend is a must. Ups and downs are the inherent properties of development. The human minds never take rest and devises ways to counter the odds. We are hopeful that sooner or later, the economy will be back on the rail and once again the processes of development would be reverberated which would open new vistas for the development of air traffic services.

Professional excellence is considered to be an effective prescription for the sound development of national economy. Creating new opportunities and capitalising on the same with professionalised efforts are found essential in the present changing scenario. The customer services need priority attention either for organisational prosperity or for cost-effectiveness. If we find airways resolving the problem of low occupancy ratio, the services are to be economic. This focuses our attention on innovative marketing practices to be conceptualised by the airways. We need to keep into consideration the satisfaction of users *vis-à-vis* their temptation for air transportation. Even with a high growth rate, we find a majority of the users not preferring air services. The marketing activities will be successful in sensitising and persuading them. The airways may succeed in achieving 100 per cent occupancy ratio, if the users of even 2nd class AC of Railways find the air services affordable and this cycle will keep on moving the supply side.

In the conceptualisation process, the professionals need to formulate a package of services to be effective in attracting the potential users.

We are aware of the fact that market is much more competitive in which for excelling competition; services should have an edge over the rivals. Increasing the frequency, maximizing the occupancy ratio would simplify our task of minimising the fare which would act as a motivational tool. The professionals need to formulate a mix of different types of services combining mail services, cargo services in tune with the capacity and integrating or interlinking of services of different airlines for different places. The most important aspect in this context is networking with the help of information and communication technology so that users of diverse segments are combined and the concept of cost-effective services is practised. In addition to the commercial services, the airlines also need to mix social services, especially when we find cases of natural calamities. This in a very natural way necessitates inclusion of aircrafts in the fleet having maximum possible accommodation. The networking would benefit airlines in many ways, e.g., high occupancy ratio, earning through supplementary services, cost-effectiveness and high profit generation.

While making use of different components of promotion, the marketers once again need to maintain cost economy. The most important thing is developing awareness of the passengers regarding the outstanding features of your services. The different segments of users are to be approached and communicated with the help of print media. The display of posters must be at the points where we find potential users assembling in a very good number. The newspapers, magazines preferred by high profile segment are to be selected for advertisements.

Maintaining cost economy and making the fare structure, nationally and internationally competitive, are to be possible when we find professionalised efforts for increasing the occupancy ratio and bringing down the costs as and where we find the scope. We find almost all the airlines of the globe globe facing the problem of financial crunch and an important reason for the same is the falling occupancy ratio.

The services need to move through the prescribed channels. The airports, aircrafts, crew members and other technical and non-technical staff significantly contribute to the channelisation of services to the ultimate users of passenger and goods traffic services. The front line staff and the crew members are directly concerned with the users and they need to make it sure that the promised services reach to the users on time. The behavioural profile and body language of the concerned staff play an important role in the service delivery and service recovery processes. The performance of staff and delivery of services also depend on the information and communication technology used for this purpose.

The service ambience needs due care of professionals specially to add additional attractions to the product mix. The passengers find the services much more convenient with the help of signposts. The lighting, interiors and furnishing need due care of professionals. The servicescapes bear the efficacy of generating service fragrance.

The people serving the airlines must have communication excellence. The technological perfection and behavioural decency are considered essential in the very context. The elements like personal-touch-in-service and value orientation cannot be overlooked.

In view of the above, it is right to mention that conceptualisation of marketing in the airline services draws priority attention of marketers. The worldwide economic depression has considerably influenced the civil aviation sector not only in India but around the globe. But it is not meant that we stop our development plans and allow the civil aviation sector to invite a stage like financial bankruptcy. The retrenchment of employees cannot be the solution. We may not prefer even merger. The traffic markets need reorientation. Of course, a revised service agreement between India and USA signed in April 2005 replacing the earlier agreement signed in 1956 have granted unlimited access to the designated airlines. Besides, the liberalised agreements have also been concluded with some important traffic markets like UK, Australia, Germany, Netherlands, Canada, Singapore, New Zealand, UAE, Thailand, France and Russia. The opening of new traffic markets, no doubt, will benefit the civil aviation sector.

The "Open Sky Policy" for cargo services has allowed foreign airlines or association of exporters to bring any number of freighters to the country for the upliftment of cargo. The Government has also permitted the market forces to determine cargo tariff with IATA rates as the floor rates. The policy has made possible encouraging results. But the cargo operations need a boost and this requires policy decisions to be made liberal.

We find "Greenfield Airports" in Bengaluru and Hyderabad of world-class and further expect a lot from the restructured Delhi and Mumbai airports. Inclusion of new generation of crafts in the fleet needs priority attention of the policy makers. The Indian Airlines Limited expects qualitative transformation in its services with the induction of new aircrafts such as A319, A320 and A321, all powered with CFM-56-B engines. Of course, the delivery process is on and this is going to help the facelift of civil aviation services of Air India.[19]

It is imperative that the policy makers assign due weightage to the development of world-class pilots. Indira Gandhi Rashtriya Uran Akademi is an autonomous body under Ministry of Civil Aviation, Government of India to train pilots to achieve higher standards in flying and ground training. We expect that the recommendations of Dawar Committee specially related to modernisation, innovation and upgradation of infrastructure of IGRUA with a view to enhancing the number of trainees from 40 to 100 trainees per course for Commercial Pilot Licence will enrich the civil aviation sector. Besides, the private sector also needs to include new generation of aircrafts in the fleet.

The global economy will come back on the rail. The process of national economic transformation once again will witness acceleration. The corporate sector and corporate culture will continue to gain popularity in the development process. And resulting from which, the civil aviation sector will also have new life and strength.

TRANSPORT MARKETING IN THE INDIAN PERSPECTIVE

Marketing Rail Transportation Services: In the modern age, we can't think about a self-sufficient society. We depend on one another and the process of dependence is likely to continue since we find a frequent change in our needs and requirements, preferences, likes and dislikes, attitudes, lifestyles and expectations. Transportation has proved to be an indispensable part of culture and hallmark of civilisation. Manufacturing, merchandising, banking, extracting and the like businesses substantially depend on the quality of transport services made available to the process of development. It is against this background we need a well managed transport system which proves to be a catalyst of socio-economic transformation. Of late, we consider transport as a *de facto* barometer of social, economic, commercial and cultural advances. In the developing countries like ours, it is pertinent that the transportation system is created by means of a suitable network of backward and forward linkages. This helps a contraction in the regional imbalance and becomes instrumental in reversing the vicious circle of poverty and backwardness. We can't deny the fact that in the Indian perspective, we find rail transportation contributing substantially to the development processes. Of course, in the process of bearing high social costs, we find Indian Railways inviting the problem of financial crunch which has been making an assault on their potentials of serving the socio-economic infrastructure. This makes it essential that the Indian Railways conceptualise marketing and innovate the strategic decisions to activate the processes of qualitative-cum-quantitative improvements.

They need to make a sound mix of marketing in which all the submixes are blended optimally to cater to the changing expectations of users. The passenger and goods transportation services are required to be improved, the late running of trains is to be stopped, the cases of ticketless travelling are to be minimised, the cases of theft and pilferages need to be regulated, the increasing cases of robbery and accidents need to be checked, the speed is required to be increased, the users' services are required to be improved, the operational expenses are required to be made optimal, the rate of productivity is required to be accelerated and we can be successful in making possible all if the marketing practices are innovated. It is in this context that we think of marketing the services of Indian Railways.

Of late, we find technological sophistication essential for quality upgradation. This makes it essential that the policy makers think of initiating the process of technological advances. In addition, it is also essential that they assign due weightage to the development of employees. There must be a close relation between the technologies that we adopt and the employees that we have to operate, maintain and manage the same. This focuses our attention on the existing deficient management. It can't be refuted that the Indian Railways have been facing the consequences of unfair and unethical practices which have been promoted by their own employees. The policy makers find it difficult to bring the systems on the rail. In a true sense, we need to make possible a basic change in the system of operation where strong trade unionism has been found obstructing the process of development. The pre-conceived ideas of employees in favour of earning more by serving the railways, specially with the help of unfair practices need to be changed by intensifying the stringent measures failing which albeit the most sophisticated rail transport system would fail in delivering goods.

Marketing Road Transportation Services: All of us are well aware of the instrumentality of road transportation services in the Indian perspective where they have been contributing sizeably to the development processes. To be more specific, the Public Road Transport organisations have been facing the problem of financial crunch to such an extent that we find a majority of the State Road Transport Corporations collapsing. The private road transport organisations no doubt are found commercially viable but the quality of users services in both the categories are found very poor. This makes it essential that both the public as well as the private road transport organisations practise innovative marketing *vis-a-vis* improve the quality of services.

The Public Sector Road Transport Corporations have been facing the problem of deficient management. An overcrowded system, working with the support of old generation of buses and inefficient, unfair employees can't survive for a long time and this is the real thing that we find with the State Road Transport Corporations. Except a few, almost all the State Road Transport Corporations have been found in red. What promoted ailments need not to be revealed. What can bring the system on the rail need to be promoted. This makes it essential that the

State Road Transport Corporations improve the quality of services by improving the quality of buses, maintaining the time schedule, rationalising the fare and freight structures, optimising the operational expenses, minimising the wear and tear and the depreciation costs, increasing the revenue position and more so making an assault on their lost image by innovating the marketing practices. This makes it essential that the State Road Transport Corporations promote a technology-driven system and optimise the number of employees. A contractual job system appears important to make possible an attitudinal change. When employees at large start promoting unfair practices, the employers have no option but to revamp the system.

The Private Sector Road Transport Organisations, of course, are found in a better position. They maintain the time schedule, promote user-friendly devices and make available quality buses. They generate profits and succeed in improving their financial position. The employees serving private organisations have no option but to maintain profitability since they find themselves insecured the moment organisations start generating losses. Thus, it is the job insecurity which forces them to be fair at least to the extent the commercial viability is maintained. It is against this background that private sector road transport organisations have been surviving and even thriving. So far as the goods transportation services managed by them are concerned, we find the system relatively well managed. A number of inter-state transport agencies have been serving the users and at the same time generating profits. We can't negate that in the Indian perspective if they stop working, the entire socio-economic activities would be jeopardised.

In view of the above, it is right to mention that both the public as well as the private road transport organisations need to promote innovative marketing for increasing the operational efficiency and promoting the user-friendly services. The professional excellence needs an intensive care. They need performance orientation. The policy makers need to think in favour of employee orientation, of course, in the face of their contributions to the development processes. Improved quality of buses, trucks and value-based, personally-committed employees with the support of professionally-sound management can bring the derailed systems on the rail.

Marketing Air Transportation Services: In an age of speed, we talk about the air transportation services. We can't negate the positive contributions of air transport services to the development of national economy. Since a number of allied industries are benefited, it is high time that we think in favour of improving the operational efficiency of Indian Airlines and Air India facing problem of low productivity and financial crunch. Of course, there are a number of factors responsible for the poor financial health of air transport organisations but of all, it is deficient management that contributes substantially to the degeneration process. It is against this background that we need to revamp the air transportation system.

Of late, we find the business environment volatile and the intensity of competition at its peak. The pressure of inflation, the continuing worldwide economic depression, the poor technology, the inefficient employees, etc. are some of the factors making the task of initiating qualitative transformation in the system much more difficult. The degeneration in the quality of services can't be negated, the failure of time schedule can't be denied, the inadequacy of quality aircrafts and sophisticated control system can't be refuted and these factors contribute substantially to the deceleration in productivity forming a vicious circle of generating losses and inviting a condition in which financial health of an organisation would hardly be improved. Of course, it is difficult to manage the international air transport operation but not so difficult to manage the domestic air transport operation if we make possible professional excellence in the decision-making processes. We find enough scope for improving the operational efficiency in the Indian Airlines if we think in favour of a technology-driven, user-friendly operation. We need to promote the use of new generation of technologies to minimise the operational costs and we also need to make the services user-friendly to improve the demand position *vis-a-vis* the occupancy ratio. Rationalising the fare and freight structures by optimising the operational expenses would help management in making the services commercially viable. Since we find the business environment competitive, it is pertinent that both the public as well as the private air transport organisations assign due weightage to high productivity.

The Air India offering the international services has been facing numerous problems. The intensity of competition is high and we find a big difference in the systems to be managed by the global leading airways and the Air India. New generation of aircrafts, sophisticated control system, due weightage to allied industries like tourism, hotel and convention, innovative promotional efforts, a team of high performers may be efficacious in improving the productivity and increasing the profitability. Thus, the important task before the Air India is to make ways for qualitative improvements in almost all the areas. This necessitates professional excellence of world-class failing which even the most sophisticated technologies would fail in delivering goods. This focuses our attention on improving the quality of management and innovating the marketing resources.

In view of the above, we feel that the domestic as well as international air transport services need a basic change in their service mix. They are required to project a positive image that requires creativity in their promotional efforts. They need to process the services in a right fashion so that the gap between services-promised and services-offered is bridged over. They need to develop a team of high performers by intensifying an ongoing training programme.

SUMMARY

You have gone through the marketing of rail transportation, road transportation and air transportation. After going through the chapter, be sure that the following facts are well versed:

Transport Marketing — The Concept: Transport marketing focuses our attention on practising modern marketing principles in the transportation services so that the transport generating organisations succeed in satisfying the users and maintaining the commercial viability.

Users of Transportation Services: We find different categories of users using the multi-dimensional services of transport organisations. The passenger, goods and mail services are used by the individuals, organisations for general and commercial purposes.

Behavioural Profile of Users: For practising marketing principles in a right fashion, it is essential that the professionals have an in-depth knowledge of the changing needs and requirements and level of expectations of users so that the services offered to them fulfil their expectations.

Market Segmentation: The transport generating organisations need to segment market so that they succeed in studying and understanding the users and prospects and make proactive efforts to develop marketing resources which fulfil their expectations.

Marketing Rail Transportation Services: The rail transportation services are offered by the Indian Railways. Till now, we don't find a direct competition in the business environment which makes it a sellers' market. However, the Indian Railways have been facing a competition which is generated by the road transport organisations. This has been found throwing a negative impact on their business profile. This makes it essential that they practise innovative marketing principles and formulate such a marketing mix that makes the services competitive and the return on the invested capital profitable. The service mix, promotion mix, the price mix, the place mix, the people mix are the different submixes to be innovated in the changing business conditions.

Marketing Road Transportation Services: Both the public as well as the private sector organisations are found engaged in the road transportation business. The State Road Transport Corporations have been facing the problem of financial crunch resulting into sickness and a depleted condition. This makes it essential that particularly the public sector organisations practise marketing principles so that the system is made technology-driven and user-friendly. The quality of services is required to be improved by improving the quality of core services and enriching the peripheral services. They have been facing image problem and this necessitates innovative and creative promotional measures. They need to make their fare and freight structures proportionate to the increasing costs of inputs and further they also need to bridge over the gap between services-promised and services-offered.

Marketing Air Transport Services: The emerging negative trends in the business profile of Indian Airlines and Air India make it clear that they have been facing the stage of financial disaster. The poor quality of services make it essential that they assign due weightage to the application of marketing principle. They need to believe in making things happen and to innovate their service mix frequently. In addition, they are also required to take support of innovative promotional measures. The operational expenses are required to be minimised and the rate of productivity is required to be accelerated. The application of marketing principles appears to be a solution to initiate qualitative improvements.

KEY TERMS

Biological Laws
Mechanised Road Vehicle
Configuration
Bullock Carts
Tantamount
Profiteering
Consumer Durables
Information Networking
Blood-sucker
Mass Rapid Transit
Commercial Viability
Net Tonne Kms.
Brunt
Synchronisation
Knee Rooms
Elbow Rooms
Quick Transit Scheme
Panel Inter-locking
Route Relay
RDSO
RITES
RMS
Pilferages
Plugging
Social Costs
Microphonic Sound
Cause-related Marketing
Financial Disequilibrium
Telescopic Rate
Service Recovery
Physical Evidence
Tangibilisation
Service Fragrance
Miniature
Pedestrians
Golden Quadrilateral
Demographic
Wayside Amenities
Cost-price-squeeze
Holistic Concept
Signposts
Credentials
Front-line Staff
Civil Aviation
Commonwealth Games
Lay-off
Servicescapes
Service Ambience
Aesthetic Management
Occupancy Ratio
Empathy
Tour Operators
Package of Services
Satellite Communication
Interiors and Exteriors
Operational Costs
Galloping
Crew Members
Cargo Operations

Review Questions

1. What do you mean by Transport Marketing? State and explain the different categories of users availing the different types of services.
2. Focus on the behavioural profile of users of transport services.
3. What do you mean by Product? Throw light on the product of Indian Railways.
4. Write a note on the planning and development of the product services of Indian Railways.
5. Write short notes on the following:
   (a) Planning for Passenger Traffic
   (b) Planning for Goods Traffic
   (c) Planning for Pipeline Transportation
   (d) Planning for Consultancy Services

6. What do you mean by Market Segmentation? Explain the importance of segmentation to segmentation to the transport organisations in general and the Indian Railways in particular.
7. Focus on the Promotion Mix of Indian Railways.
8. Explain the different pricing policies for setting fare and freight rates in the Indian Railways.
9. Discuss the three additional/extended marketing mix in the context of Indian Railways.
10. Comment on the marketing mix of Indian Railways.
11. Write a note on the marketing management of road transportation services.
12. Write a note on the marketing management of air transportation services.
13. Throw light on the different components of promotion in the context of road transportation services.
14. Focus on the different components of promotion in the context of civil aviation services in India.
15. Write a note on the marketing of rail services in Indian perspective.
16. Write a note on the marketing of road transport services in Indian perspective.
17. Write a note on the marketing of civil aviation services in Indian perspective.
18. Explain the extended mixes of marketing in the context of road transport services.
19. Discuss the extended mixes of marketing in the context of civil aviation services.

Application Exercises

1. As a service marketer, formulate a marketing mix for the rail transportation services in the Indian perspective.
2. The State Road Transport Services in almost all the states of the country are found in red. Suggest measures to remove their problems as a marketing professional.
3. Formulate a package of services for the Indian Railways which would help them in justifying their role as a public utility undertaking.
4. Suggest measures to promote the rail transportation services.
5. As a marketing professional, formulate a marketing mix for the services of State Road Transport Corporations in Indian perspective.
6. Design a product mix for the road transportation services in the Indian context.
7. The Civil Aviation sector has been facing a number of problems in the global perspective. Suggest measures to improve their strength to counter the challenges.
8. The Servicescapes need due attention in the air transportation services. As a professional, how you would manage the service environment for the air transportation services for the domestic and international airports.
9. As a service marketer, focus on the considerations for studying and understanding the behavioural profile of high profile users for the air transport services.
10. Comment on the changing role of Indian Railways as a profit maker.
11. The Indian Railways need an improvement in the quality of services. Suggest measures as a marketing professional.
12. Focus on the role of People Mix in the marketing of transportation services in the Indian perspective.
13. The road transportation services cannot deliver goods without quality roads. Comment as a professional.
14. Justify the conceptualisation of marketing principles in the Indian Railways.
15. Justify the application of marketing principles in the air transportation services.

Endnotes

1. Jha S.M., Indian Railways Social Costs, *Lok Udyog,* Vol. XVI/11, 1983, pp. 45-52.
2. National Transport Policy Committee, Tariff Enquiry Committee Forecast on Traffic.
3. Indian Railway Year Book - 2008.
4. Jha, S.M., Indian Railways Transnational Consultancy Services, *Indian Railways*, January-March 1984, pp. 23-26, Railway Board, New Delhi.
5. Jha, S.M., *Making Rail Services Viable*, National Herald, New Delhi, April 12, 1983.
6. Johnson E.R., The Railroads and Public Welfare, p. 157.

7. William Accorth, *The Elements of Railway Economics,* p. 37.
8. Colson M.M., Quoted by K.C. Srinivasan, *Railway Freight Rates*, 1928, p. 20.
9. William Acworth, *op. cit.,* p. 84.
10. Indian Railway Year Book — 2008.
11. *The New Popular Encyclopaedia,* p. 126.
12. Indian Railway Year Book — 2008.
13. Manorma Year Book — 2008.
14. Eleventh Five Year Plan, Planning Commission, *Government of India*, New Delhi.
15. *Ibid.*
16. Monorama Year Book — 2008.
17. Indian Railway Year Book — 2008.
18. Jha, S.M., *Tourism Marketing*, Himalaya Publishing House, Mumbai, 1995.
19. Indian Railway Year Book — 2008.

☆☆☆

TOURISM MARKETING

"Sophistication makes the ways for complications. Of late, the market is sophisticated, the customers are sophisticated, the technologies are sophisticated and even the tourism industry is found developing in a sophisticated fashion."

Chapter Objectives

Introduction – Tourism: The Concept – Tourist: The Concept – Typology of Tourism – Tourism Marketing: The Concept – Users of Tourism Services – Behavioural Profile of Users – Product Planning and Development – Market Segmentation for Tourism – Marketing Information System for Tourism – Formulation of Marketing Mix for Tourist Organisation – The Product Mix – Salient Features of Tourism Product – Designing a Package Tour – Marketing the Brand Decisions – The Promotion Mix – Advertising – Publicity – Sales Promotion – Word-of-Mouth Promotion – The Price Mix – The Place Mix – The Process – Physical Evidence and Attractions – The People: Travel Agents, Travel Guides – Tourism Marketing in Indian Perspective – Summary – Key Terms – Review Questions – Application Exercises – Endnotes.

Learning Objectives

The present chapter aims at studying the different dimensions of tourism marketing. The tourism industry is considered to be an economic bonanza. The application of modern marketing principles will help tourist organisations in many ways. Since tourism is an amalgam of different industries, we find positive impact of development of tourism on allied industries. The marketing process helps in satisfying the tourists and projecting a positive image of tourism industry in the global map. The marketers know about the conceptualisation of marketing and formulation of a sound marketing mix for the development of tourism industry. The study aims at sensitising the readers to the various facets helping them in the application process.

INTRODUCTION

Change is a natural phenomenon. We cannot have a command on the cyclic order of taste, fashion, dislikes, needs, requirements and levels of expectations. This process, of course, is governed by the process of transformation which forces us to welcome a change and move strategically in the right directions. If we fail or delay the process, the seeds of dissatisfaction and monotony get a favourable milieu for their germination and proper development. To regulate the process, we welcome a change which influences our decision-making behaviour and force us to welcome a change of place. The motives are diverse such as entertainment, enriching the knowledge bank, religious and cultural considerations, adventure and pleasure and even health. The prime thing is our movement from one place to another, of course, for a temporary period. It is against this background that travelling has emerged as a business and recently as an industry. This process of transformation has caused so many ups and downs right from the very beginning of civilisation to the present time. Initially, we find tourism a matter of pilgrimage. The Roman Empire injected life and strength to travelling and credibility for the development of tourism as an industry goes to them.

With the passage of time, the contours of development underwent radical changes. The emerging corporate culture made ways for a change in the lifestyles. The sophisticated developments in transportation, information and communication helped a change in our behavioural patterns. The increasing domination of corporate culture made ways for the development of techniculture which has been paving avenues albeit for the development of robot culture. The emergence of new wave culture changed the concept of family and we find development of micro and satellite families. Not only this, we now also find emergence of live-in culture. The multi-dimensional developments in the socio-economic system and cultural patterns opened new vistas for the development of tourism industry. The volatility and competitiveness started touching new heights which necessitated development of professional excellence. It is in this context that the boardrooms and policy decision-makers have been found evincing keen interests in the development of tourism industry in a new fashion.

It is significant to mention that the fall of Roman Empire resulted into the downfall of tourism which continued at least till the end of Middle Age. The available facts reveal that Romans evinced interests in visiting temples, shrines, festivals and baths for health and amusement. Till 15th century, despite significant development in the field of trade and commerce, we find retarded development of tourism but when the industrial revolution gained momentum, the elite of the society preferred to go abroad for developing excellence and making possible cross fertilisation of thoughts and ideas. By the turn of 19th century, we find multi-faceted developments in transportation and communication which energised the process of technological sophistication and with the beginning of 20th century, the process of inventions and innovations engineered a sound foundation for the development of infrastructural facilities. These developments also injected life and strength to the tourism industry. No doubt that the World War I and War II obstructed the flow of development but the second half of 20th century proved to be the Golden Age since almost all the countries of globe started patronising tourism as an important economic activity. It is right to opine that the industrial revolution paved copious avenues for the development of tourism as an industry. In the face of its outstanding properties, the developed as well the developing countries assigned an overriding priority to tourism.

Thomas Cook was of the view that beauty is for the people. The opinion of Mr. Cook generated new dimensions in the tourism business which paved avenues for a number of developments. We cannot deny that since time immemorial, travel has been the first choice for masses. But due to inadequate transportation and communication services, they found it difficult to enjoy. This obstructed the process of development of tourism as an industry.

Monotony with high intensity is a natural phenomenon particularly in the present materialistic world where we are often beset with multi-dimensional problems. The emerging material culture proves to be an important reason for monotony where to avail amenities and facilities in tune with a modern lifestyle, we have no option but to work, work and work. This developed a sound base for traveling with pleasure and created tremendous opportunities for the development of tourism industry. The domestic as well as world tourism started witnessing a positive trend and the credibility for the same goes to qualitative improvements in the field of civil aviation industry. So far as the domestic tourism is concerned, the rail and road transportation services significantly contributed to the development process.

Both at national and international levels, it was considered essential to organise the industry in such a way that it shows multiplier effects and provides an opportunity for the development of transportation, communication, hotel and trade and commerce. International cooperation was found essential for the development of world tourism.

A number of organisations were found active in the development of tourism industry, such as World Tourist Organisation, Pacific Area Travel Association. International Union of Official Travel Organisation is important among them. In the Indian context, the Department of Tourism was found associated with the Ministry of Tourism which paved wider avenues for the development of tourism. The concept like Rural Tourism, Adventure Tourism, Health Tourism, Eco Tourism and Sports Tourism started gaining popularity day by day. The focus of Indian masses on pilgrimage tourism could get a new life due to sophisticated modes of transportation. With the development of a broader concept, significant developments could take place and the essence of tourism was further distilled and it was more a holistic approach. In the general theory of tourism, Walter Hunziker and Kurt Kraph (1942) considered it both a human as well as an economic activity. In 1974, this approach was again brushed up by Burk and Medlik because they viewed tourism as a composite phenomenon embracing a whole range of different relationships between travellers and the host population. The fun and excitement, no doubt, gained the momentum with the holistic approach. This new approach made possible development of tourism as an industry. The policy makers as well as the environmentalists pinpointed the side-effects of manufacturing industries specially on the front of ecological balance. This necessitated a focus on the development of non-traditional industries. The travelling business which was transformed into an industry was found efficacious of delivering goods to the socio-economic molecule due to their multiplier effects. Almost all countries of the globe started exploring new avenues for development so that they succeed in earning foreign exchange and tourism was found an effective option.

In the face of its succulent benefits, the policy planners assigned due weightage to the development of tourism industry. We cannot negate that with tremendous socio-economic potentials, the tourism industry is considered an economic bonanza which paves avenues for the development of a number of allied industries, such as hotel, transportation, communication, information banking, trade and commerce, etc. In addition, we also consider tourism a potential source for world peace through mutual appreciation and international understanding.

In the Indian perspective, we find tourism as the third largest foreign exchange earner for the country. The Travel and Tourism sector creates more job per million per rupee of investment than another sector of the economy and it has potentials of offering a number of job opportunities in its allied areas. The New Tourism Policy envisages a framework which is government-led, private sector driven and oriented towards community welfare. The government bears the responsibility of creating the legislative framework and basic infrastructure for tourism development. The private sector is considered responsible for providing the quality products and the community providing active support. For the implementation of New Tourism Policy, there are five key strategic objectives, viz., positioning tourism as a national priority, enhancing India's competitiveness as a tourist destination, improving and expanding product development, creating world-class infrastructure and effective marketing.

Of course, we have made a number of efforts to develop tourism but our share in international tourist arrivals is around 0.50 per cent which presents a gloomy picture of our development records. The World Travel and Tourism Council has identified India as one of the foremost growth centres in the world in the coming decades. How and in what way the professionals capitalise on the opportunities will determine the magnitude of success.

The first and foremost task before the tourist organisation is to increase the flow of foreign tourists. We have world heritage monuments with the high potentials to attract world tourists, such as Taj Mahal, Qutab Minar, Agra Fort, Group of Monuments, Ellora Caves, Elephanta Caves, Ajanta Caves, Fatehpur Sikri, Sun Temple Konark and a number of tourist centres in different parts of the country. The state of Maharashtra is number one with the highest number of foreign tourist arrival and thereafter we find Tamil Nadu, UP, Rajastan, Goa and Delhi.

In addition, we also need to increase the influx of domestic tourists. This draws our attention on the conceptualisation of marketing principles by the tourist organisations. We cannot deny that our efforts lack professional excellence. Incredible India — a slogan, of course, has activated the process but we have to practise innovative marketing so that the opportunities are capitalised on to the desired level. It is right to mention that tourism in India has been facing the image problem and therefore the marketers need creativity in their promotional efforts so that the image problem is removed. A package of services blending product of all segments in the face of the taste and temperament of domestic as well as the foreign tourists will help professionals in getting the desired results. Almost all the states in the country have potentials for the development of tourism industry but they fail in tapping the same.

With the high magnitude of worldwide economic depression, the influx of tourists is to be adversely affected both at domestic and global levels. Particularly when we find civil aviation sector facing a number of challenges and threats, it is likely to make our efforts insensitive. Hence, it is an acid test of professional excellence of marketers that they design such a marketing mix which is proved to be proactive. The transport operators and tour operators can play an incremental role in making the process cost-effective which would act as a motivational tool. The accommodation sector requires due focus on increasing the occupancy ratio but the emerging negative trends in national and global economies make it essential that the concept of Budget Hotel is made popular. The Indian Railways also need priority attention on promoting tourism and for that, they can offer a package during the season when the arrivals of foreign tourists are expected. The travel agents and travel guides need personal-touch-in-service. The information networking with the help of techno-driven information system needs due weightage for sensitising the potential tourists.

The government administration needs to make it sure that the law and order conditions are not to aggravate the image problem. The domestic as well as the foreign tourists need due protection. It is hoped that our concerted, sincere and honest efforts with personal and professional touch would benefit the tourism industry in different ways.

TOURISM – THE CONCEPT

Before studying other dimensions, we go through the concept of tourism. "Tourism denotes the temporary, short-term movement of people to destination outside the place where they normally live and work and their activities during their stay at these destinations."[1]

"Tourism is a pleasure activity in which money earned in one's normal domicile is spent in the places visited."[2]

"Tourism is the totality of the relationship and phenomenon arising from the travel and stay of strangers, provided the stay does not imply the establishment of a permanent residence and is not connected with the remunerated activities."[3]

"Tourism is an activity involving a complex mixture of material and psychological elements. The material one are accommodation, the attractions and entertainment available. The psychological factors include a wide spectrum of attitudes and expectations."[4]

"Tourism is a composite industry. It consists of various segments which can produce a wide range of products and services."[5]

In view of the aforesaid viewpoints of different experts, the following points emerge regarding tourism:

- Tourism is a temporary and short-term movement of people.
- Tourism is the totality of relationship.
- Tourism is an activity involving a complex mixture of material and psychological elements.
- Tourism is the activity concerned with the utilisation of leisure hours.
- Tourism is a composite industry consisting of various segments.

TOURIST – THE CONCEPT

The origin of the word "tourist" dates back to 1292 AD. It has come from the word 'tour.' A number of experts have defined the term:

"Tourists are the voluntary temporary travellers, travelling in the expectations of pleasure from the novelty and change experienced on a relatively and non-recurrent round-trip."[6]

Dictionnaire Universal says, "tourist is a person who makes a journey for the sake of curiosity for the fun of travelling."[7]

The League Committee finds tourists "a person visiting a country other than that in which he usually resides."[8]

Tourists are:

- Persons travelling for pleasure, health and domestic reason.
- Persons arriving in the course of sea cruise.
- Persons travelling for business purposes.
- Persons travelling for convention.

Not to be Tourists:

- Persons arriving without a work to take up an occupation.
- Persons coming from the rural areas to the urban areas.
- Students in boarding.
- Persons domiciled in one country and working in adjoining country.
- Persons passing through a country without stopping.

TYPOLOGY OF TOURISM

Tourism can be classified into different categories in the face of its motive, regional variations, number and arrangements. The professionals need to develop their awareness of the different types of tourism so that the task of formulating a sound package is considerably simplified.

Purpose as Base: The tourists may visit a place with diverse motives such as recreation, adventure or sports, health, convention, culture and incentive.

Recreational Tourism: The tourists spend their leisure hour at the hill stations, sea beaches, etc. In the recreational tourism, the tourists get an opportunity to get away from the day-to-day humdrum and refresh their mind and energy to enrich their potentials for delivery goods without developing monotony.

Cultural Tourism: The cultural tourism satisfies the cultural curiosity of tourists and for that, they visit ancient monuments, and places of historic and religious importance. It helps in protecting and promoting the cultural heritage and helps development of pilgrimages.

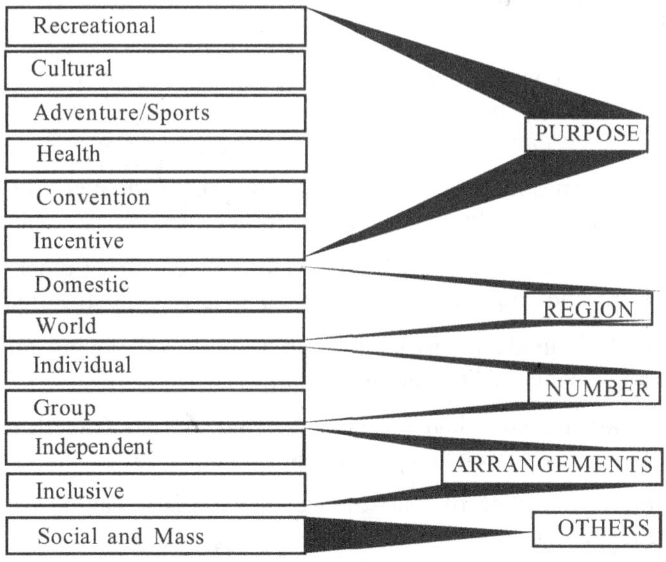

Fig. 11.1: Typology of Tourism

Health Tourism: Such type of tourism makes available to the tourists a suitable place for recovery or medical treatment such as places having curative potentials, e.g., hot springs, spas, yoga. The hill stations are also considered suitable for quick recovery of patients *vis-à-vis* for recreating and refreshing their mind.

Incentive Tourism: The incentive tourism offers holiday trips as incentives to dealers and salespeople specially by the big tourist organisations.

Sports Tourism/Adventure Tourism: With the emergence of corporate culture, we find emergence of new avenues of tourism in which Sport Tourism draws attention of professionals. The upcoming youths have developed their temptation to adventure sports because the corporate culture makes ways for the development of spirit of adventure. The new breeds of young professionals especially with the IT industry have lots of money to spend and this has opened doors for the development of sports tourism. Of late, we find a number of call centres making use of adventure sports as a team building exercise. We find adventure in air, water, snow and land and it is upon us to select the ideal one in tune with our taste and temperament.

In the Indian context, we find sport tourism an emerging area because we find its link with adventure for which the upcoming youths are found crazy. The Directorate of Mountaineering and Allied Sports, Manali has been imparting training in the various streams of adventure sports. The places such as Mussorie, Nainital, Haridwar, Rishikesh, Almora, Ranikhet are found suitable for adventure sports. In this context, we also find rock climbing an important area. Maharashtra Tourism Development Corporation has been organising mountaineering and rock climbing courses.

Flying is also found to be an emerging area instrumental in relieving stress. We find corporate sector tapping it for their employees and approaching flying clubs. Despite a number of constraints, we find young men and women showing their temptation to flying and therefore this is also an area to capitalise on.

Ballooning is considered a sport not only for the young but even for the grey segment. It is also not so much risky. We also call it a lazy cruise in the sky. It has adventure.

Paragliding is a mix of parachuting and handgliding and we find it one of the easiest aero sports to learn. The history of skiing is found very old in India because the Sky Club of India is in existence right from 1927.

A white water sport is also an important area which was started in Rishikesh. Rafting is found to be an Indian sport. The term white water refers to white foam which forms on the top of the water. Wind surfing has also gained popularity. Yacht race is also a new area. Zorbing, hot air ballooning, bungee jumping can be tried even in the rural areas.

The above-mentioned new areas in tourism need due care of professionals for which we have tremendous opportunities. The only thing they need is to promote these areas with professionalised efforts so that it is to add new features in the tourism industry. There are a number of areas which may help us in promoting Rural Tourism.

Convention Tourism: The convention tourism focuses our attention on the assembling of delegates in Conferences and Seminars which may be related to the different areas such as political, social, economic, trade and commerce, etc.

Domestic Tourism: The domestic tourism belongs to the normal domicile of tourists or to the areas in their own country and do not require any documentation for travel.

World Tourism: In the world tourism, we find travelling to countries other than their own with a different economic and political system and requires documentation to cross the frontiers.

Individual Tourism: In the individual tourism, the tourists are found moving individually. An individual finalises his/her programme depending on his/her means and requirements.

Group Tourism: Contrary to individual tourism, we find tourists travelling as a member of a group and therefore we do not find any separate schedule of an individual.

Independent Tourism: In this type of tourism, we find tourists making transportation, accommodation or other arrangements independently or are assisted by the travel agents.

Social Tourism: The tour arrangements for the weaker sections of society with the assistance of government or any other agency are found in this category. It is a type of tourism practised for low income groups who are not in a position to meet the costs on travelling unless they get support from an agency, association or government. We find the supporting services related to tourism offered in a subsidised form with the motto of enriching the knowledge bank of poor sections of the society. It is found common in the East European countries. Since in the Indian context, we find a number of subsidised services offered by the government to the weaker sections, the social tourism is also found gaining popularity here but it is not in the organised form.

Mass Tourism: The mass tourism refers to the participation of a large number of people in tourism. The developed countries like USA, Canada, France, Germany, Japan practise tourism as a part of their lifestyles. In the Indian context, we do not find tourism as a part of our lifestyles and therefore the concept of mass tourism is yet to gain popularity. The promotion of mass tourism is essential to meet the commercial considerations. Though the environmentalists are found critical to mass tourism because they feel that the increasing influx of tourists would create environmental problems. The centralisation of a large number of population within a certain point cannot be considered to be healthy particularly with the viewpoint of environment.

The above-mentioned types of tourism need due attention of tourist organisations. They need to develop a package and in the process of blending, the situational factors and existent potentials cannot be overlooked.

TOURISM MARKETING — THE CONCEPT

A clear perception of tourism marketing requires a brief analysis of marketing. We are well aware of the fact that there have been fundamental changes in the traditional concept of marketing which has been influenced by the multi-dimensional changes in the business environment. A transformation in the attitudes, lifestyles, expectations is the result of a number of developments. Professionalism paves the ways for excellence which opens doors for quality generation *vis-a-vis* competition. Almost all the organisations producing goods or generating services have no option but to assign an overriding priority to quality upgradation that requires innovations. This necessitates a change in the concept of marketing which determines its functional boundaries. We find satisfaction of users the focal point around which all the functional areas of marketing cluster. While clarifying the perception of tourism marketing, it is essential that we assign due weightage to the three important considerations, the first – generation of profits by the tourist organisations, second – world-class services to the tourists which help in satisfying them and the third – positive contributions of tourist organisations to the process of social transformation and ecological balance.

We consider marketing a human activity directed at satisfying the needs and wants through exchange processes. The American Marketing Association defines marketing as "the performance of business activities that direct the flow of goods and services from producer to consumer or users."[9] Kotler finds marketing a social and managerial process by which individuals and groups obtain what they need and want through creating and exchanging products and value with others.[10]

Krippendorf says, "Marketing in tourism is to be understood as the systematic and co-ordinated execution of business policy by tourist undertakings whether private or state, owned at local, regional, national and international levels to achieve the optional satisfaction of the needs of identifiable consumer groups and in doing so achieves an appropriate return."[11]

Burk Kurt and Medlick opine, "Tourism marketing activities are systematic and co-ordinated efforts extended by National Tourist Organisation and/or tourist enterprises at international, national and local levels to optimise the satisfaction of tourist groups and individuals in view of sustained tourism growth."[12]

In view of the above, the following points emerge regarding tourism marketing:

- Tourism marketing is a process of creating a product or providing a service.
- Tourism marketing comprises fact finding, data gathering, analysing (marketing research), communication to inform and promote (promotion), ensuring and facilitating sales, selection of marketing planning (distribution), coordination, control and evaluation (marketing planning and auditing), developing professionally-sound personnel (people).
- Tourism marketing is an integral effort to satisfy tourists and more so, it is a device to transform the potential tourists into the actual tourists.
- Tourism marketing is the safest way to generate demand, expand market and increase the market share.
- Tourism marketing is a managerial process to promote business.

USERS OF TOURISM SERVICES

We find different categories of users availing the services of tourist organisations. In Figure 11.2, we find classification of different categories which would help the tourism professionals in studying and identifying the level of their expectations *vis-a-vis* their behavioural profile.

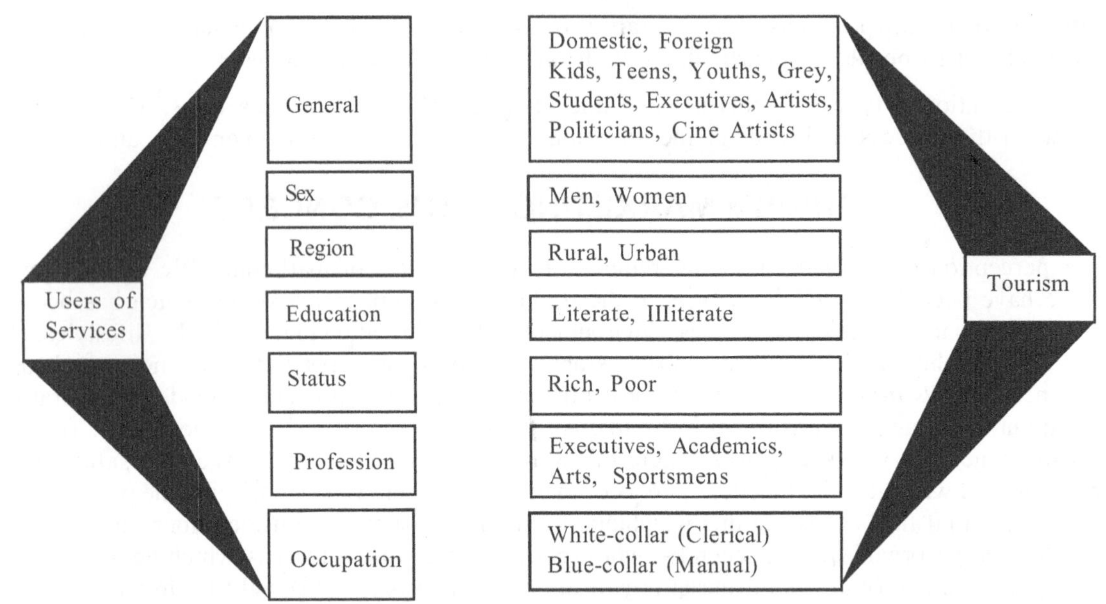

Fig. 11.2: Users of Tourism Services

Non-users: Persons not interested in using the services are known as non-users. They lack willingness, desire and ability and therefore, the level of income or even the availability of leisure hour is not to influence them.

Potential Users: We also call them prospects or the prospective users. They have willingness but the marketing resources have not been used optimally for influencing their impulse. They bear the efficacy and the marketing professionals are supposed to capitalise on their potentials by using creative promotional measures.

Actual Users: Persons already using the services generated by the tourist organisations are known as actual users.

Occasional Users: Users availing the services occasionally but not forming a habit to travel are known as occasional users.

Habitual Users: Users forming a habit and availing the services regularly are known as the habitual users.

It is right to mention that men and women; kids and teens; youth and grey; rural and urban; poor and rich; white-collar and blue-collar personnel; executives and technocrats; professionals and intellects; literate and illiterate are the different categories of users availing the multi-dimensional services of tourist organisations. It is quite natural that the behavioural profile of all the users can't be identical. This makes it essential that professionals study and understand their changing behavioural profile.

BEHAVIOURAL PROFILE OF USERS

For the successful and cost-effective execution of the marketing strategies or for translating the strategies into meaningful purposes, we realise the significance of an in-depth study of the behavioural profile of different categories of users. The tourist organisations need to understand their behavioural profile which simplifies their task of creating and stimulating the demand. We know that users have values, perceptions, preferences, expectations which are the result of environmental influences. There are a number of factors influencing the behavioural profile, such as the race, ethnicity, religion, nationality, leisure habits, health factors, lifestyles, age, life cycle stage, occupation, level of incomes, advances in communication technologies or so. We find management increasingly using new techniques to understand how users react to marketing and other influences on their behaviour. It is in this context that we find it important to assess the behaviour patterns and users' characteristics. In the recent years, the users have become more discriminating in their using habits and therefore we find their needs for different services, products and brands changing constantly. This makes it essential that the marketers analyse their behavioural profile and come to know the levels of their expectations.

In psychological terms, the whole range of the generation of wants and their transformation into buying or using decisions can be explained as behaviour. The multi-dimensional environmental considerations make the ways for generating a number of conflicting wants but it is difficult to transform all of them into effective demand. Thus, the core problem of the entire marketing process is to identify strategies bearing the efficacy of activating the transformation process so that a number of potential tourists are transformed into the actual tourists and further they prefer to be the habitual tourists. We can't deny the fact that the transformation process is activated by a number of factors. This raises the instrumentality of decision-making model of a tourist. The various elements of this decision-making model are flow of stimuli, opinion leaders, selector system, attitude, transformation of attitude into the behaviour and the feedback.

In a true sense, the transformation process is the transfiguration of attitudes into action. The marketers here are supposed to ensure the potential tourists that their attitudes are not to be destroyed. The relevant factors in the transformation process are the situational and organisational factors. The process remains incomplete unless the marketers make a microscopic study of feedback loop which helps in gauging the level of expectations or dissatisfaction. In the face of changing discretionary income, a change in the lifestyle and behaviour can't be ruled out. The lifestyle governs the level of expectations. If the lifestyle has been influenced by an increase in the discretionary income, it is natural that the level of expectations would remain high.

In view of the above, it is right to say that the marketing decisions can't be creative and proactive unless we have an in-depth knowledge about the behavioural profile of users. The most important problem is to satisfy the tourists. We consider marketing a customer satisfaction engineering. The inventions and innovations in the field of transportation and communication are to influence the process of innovation in the formulation of marketing mixes.

Arriving at creative marketing decisions is a challenging task that requires world-class professional excellence. Manifestation of perfection in the purest form is an essential criterion to achieving excellence. All marketing activities concerned with goods or services, tangible or intangible start and end with customers/users. In the tourism industry, the professionals are required to see that users are unaware or aware, interested or intend to try, trier or experimental, occasional or the habitual. An expert says, "the individual specific behaviour in the marketplace is affected by internal factors, such as needs, motivation, perception and attitudes as well as by external or environmental influences, such as the family, social groups, culture, economic and business influences.[13] Thus, we find sociological, economic and psychological factors instrumental in influencing the behavioural profile of different categories of users.

While studying the behavioural profile of users of the tourism services, we find a study of lifestyle essential. The term lifestyle was originally coined by Max Weber. It encompasses many of the sociological, cultural and psychological variables. William Lazer defines lifestyles as referring to a distinctive or characteristic mode of living in the aggregative and broadest sense of a whole society or segment thereof.[14] From a sociological standpoint, Fieldman and Thielber define lifestyle in terms of four characteristics, viz., lifestyle is a group phenomenon; it pervades many aspects of life; it implies a central life interest and it varies according to sociologically relevant variables. It is right to mention here that lifestyle concept is neither a model nor a theory of consumer behaviour. It is rather an organisational concept for understanding many of the determinants and processes of behaviour. We find an in-depth study of lifestyle essential since it draws a variety of analysis together and a variety of discipline together and more so, it pervades many aspects of life.

A study of behavioural profile thus makes it essential that the tourist professionals serving different categories of tourist organisations are aware of the behavioural influences and based on the changing level of expectations of users/prospects, they develop the marketing resources to make the process of influencing the behavioural profile cost-effective. In this context, the typology of users' behaviour would help them substantially as presented in Figure 11.3

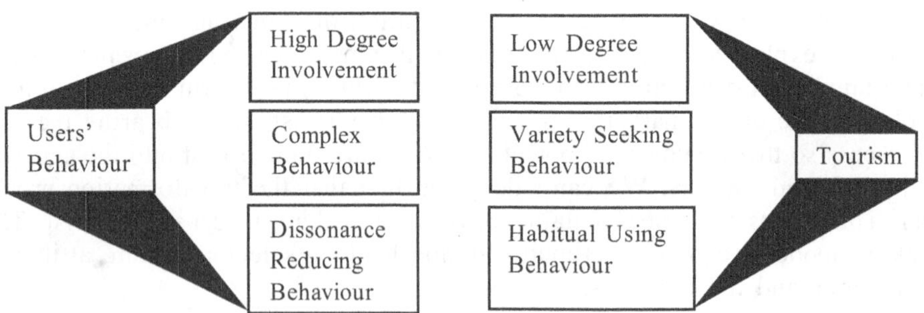

Fig. 11.3: Typology of Users' Behaviour

The aforesaid facts make it clear that arriving at sound marketing decision can't be possible unless we formulate sound marketing plans and develop optimal marketing resources. It is essential that before planning an organisation identifies its target users and the decision process they go through. This necessitates an in-depth study of users' behavioural profile.

PRODUCT PLANNING AND DEVELOPMENT

The tourism is a multi-segment industry. The essence of marketing is bringing together the mix of products, possessing the efficacy of satisfying the users. In the western industrialised countries of Europe and North America which generate the great majority of tourists, a conscious emphasis has been given to planning and development of tourism product. There is no doubt in it that the taste-oriented tourism products have a far reaching impact on the positioning of demand and supply. In addition, we find the process helping in maintaining the commercial viability. It is against this background that we need to assign due weightage to scientific product planning and development.

The tourism products are an amalgam of different tangible and intangible elements. The products have some salient features, e.g., the products are highly perishable, used for pleasure or speeding up the learning cycle and the users, a heterogeneous group of people who are required to come to the spot. The products can't be transported to the users and in no case, the providers can store or preserve the products. The demand is highly flexible and the products need world-class superstructure and infrastructure. The three basic elements of the products are attraction of the destination, facilities at the destination and accessibility to the destination. To the different members of the tourism industry, the tourism products are different, e.g., to the hotel industry, it is guest-nights; to the airline, it is the seats flown and the passenger miles that result; to the museum, art gallery or archaeological site, the product is the number of visits. In a true sense, it is a complete experience which complicates the task of careful planning and optimal development.

The development of tourism is the development of the process of social industrialisation. In a competitive market where the leading tourism generating countries of the globe have been successful in speeding up the process of socio-economic transformation through social industrialisation, it is essential that the developing and the less developed countries assign an overriding priority to the planned development process. Moreover when unplanned and haphazard developments pave avenues for the atmospheric pollution, this dimension of management needs a transcendental priority. The World Bank warns,[15] "In many areas of the world, tourism development has produced great disparities in the standards of amenities provided for the visitor and for the local population. This can't be entirely denied that in the long run, the improvement of standards for the local population is probably a condition of successful tourism development. The development of a new resort by the provision of infrastructure costing perhaps millions of dollars has a great impact on land values in the area affected."

Thus, it is important that the tourism planning whether at national or at regional level must be regarded as an integral part of country's overall economic and social planning. A plan for tourism can only serve its desired goal. The main target to such a plan would be to arrive at an optimum harmonisation of the interrelations between the two places of market while avoiding the creation of serious economic, social and territorial imbalances. The key steps in the planning are assessment of tourist demand and paving ways for an optimal supply.[16] Thus, in addition to other benefits, the tourism planning makes an assault on imbalances. The tourist organisations and the professionals find it convenient to have a fair blending of social and commercial considerations.

In the Indian perspective for developing the tourism products, we find tremendous potentials. The tourists from North America and West Europe or other developed countries prefer a fair mix of cultural and beach tourism. Of late, we find a craze for village tourism. If we develop important beaches and make available to the users an attractive landscape and regional cultural mixes in tourism products, they may opt for a package tour. The planning of tourism on the pattern of Sri Lanka may get a positive response.

Sri Lanka presents an impressive example where instead of development of this sector as a cultural tourism, we find efforts for developing as a beach tourism. The tourists of Europe are found in search of sun, surf and sand in remote typical islands. On the basis of the recommendations of experts, Sri Lanka developed this sector in a bit innovative way. A master plan was prepared for tourist which based on expensive marketing research, pioneered the concept of developing tourist resorts primarily at beaches. The liberal policy of the government attracted the high spending foreign tourists and injected fresh life and strength to the tourism industry. It is important to mention that development of tourism within the island was on a planned basis keeping in view the environmental conditions and regional planning. About 70 per cent of hotel development in Sri Lanka has taken place outside the urban areas or in the outskirts or in the rural areas where the problem of unemployment is found alarming. The development of Benotota, forty miles from Colombo, as national holiday sea resort is an example of scientific planning where more than one hundred acres of land have been converted into a bust economic centre, specially based on coconut. In addition, Sri Lanka has provided growth stimuli to a number of non-traditional industries like gems and jewellery. The tourism industry has been helpful in the development of handicrafts. Thus, the aforesaid facts make it clear that countries like ours need to develop tourism based on that style.

In the Indian perspective, we find tremendous opportunities for developing beach tourism, village tourism and heritage tourism. The forts, old palaces, havelis, etc. need an intensive care of tourism planners. Particularly the high spending tourists prefer village tourism and heritage tourism. The tourist organisations and the national and provincial governments need to formulate a plan for the development of tourism keeping in view the regional and local conditions where the sites are to be developed. A fair blending of heritage and beach tourism or village and heritage tourism would be efficacious in attracting a number of high spending tourists.

For formulating a scientific plan, it is pertinent that we assess the demand and supply position, set the objectives, identify potentials for territorial planning, develop superstructure and infrastructure, explore avenues for generating the financial resources, develop human resources in the face of changing level of expectations of the prospects, assign due weightage to the designing of organisational structure and market the services in a right fashion by injecting professional excellence in the personnel supposed to serve the tourist organisations, make an appraisal of our achievements and are careful to the corrective measure to remove the lapses. Environmental planning and regional planning are the two important facets necessitating due attention of planners.

MARKET SEGMENTATION FOR TOURISM

The behavioural scientists feel that appeal, strategy and tact vary from segment to segment which in a natural way necessitates a change in the strategic decisions. The modern marketing theory prefers the formulation of marketing policies and strategies for each market segment which an organisation plans to solicit. It is natural that different segments react in a different way. Segmentation makes possible tailoring of products and marketing programmes uniquely suitable for each sub-segment. A market is not only an aggregate demand for a product but the sum of demands of different market segments. For getting a positive response in the market, it is pertinent that the marketers or the tourist professionals are well aware of the different market segments. It is against this background that we need to study market segmentation for tourism services.

At the outset, it is essential that the tourist organisations select a suitable base for segmenting the market. The selection of base has a far reaching impact on studying the target market. Though there are a number of bases for segmentation, we find lifestyle an important base since the travelling decisions are fantastically influenced by the changing lifestyles. The emerging trends in the level of income, the availability of leisure hour of course influence the process but the main thing is the lifestyle. This is supported by the logic that if we earn more, we spend more. We prefer to utilise our leisure time for gaining pleasure or for enriching the knowledge bank. This necessitates an in-depth study of lifestyle for making segmentation proactive. The living styles of Americans and Indian can't be identical, the decision-making of both of them are to be different. The Americans prefer to travel and therefore they assign due weightage to the travelling decisions while scheduling or ordering their engagements. The Indians avoid to travel albeit we find them earning more or sufficient leisure time or holidays in their hands. This makes it clear that for segmenting market, we find this variable constituting a place of outstanding significance.

The aforesaid facts make it clear that for getting a positive response, the segmentation of tourism market needs an intensive care. The tailoring of products with the expectations of tourist or a fair synchronisation of tourists' expectations and potentials of the tourist organisations would hardly be possible unless we segment the market in a right fashion. The whole drama of marketing is prompted by the opinion leaders where the word-of-mouth promoters play an incremental role. The process of segmentation simplifies the task of marketers. The tour operators, the transport operators, the travel agents, the tourist guides, and the hotels find it easier to make the marketing decisions. They even with the minor intelligence and diligence are found successful in identifying the market or the potential tourists. It is right to mention that the needs and requirements as well as the levels of expectations can't be uniform. The segmentation benefits tourist organisations in different ways. An optimal marketing plan, a balanced development of marketing resources, true gauging of the level of expectations, formulation of creative strategies for getting a positive response make it clear that the tourist organisations assign due weightage to segmentation. They are supposed to select a suitable base for segmentation out of numerous bases like holiday base, purpose base, demand base, geographical base, psychological base, demography base, socio-economic base, sex base, age base or so.

These bases help professionals in studying and understanding the changing behavioural profile of users. In Figure 11.4, the market segmentation bases make it clear that geographic, demographic, psychographic and socio-economic aspects can't be underestimated to have a clear picture of the tourism users.

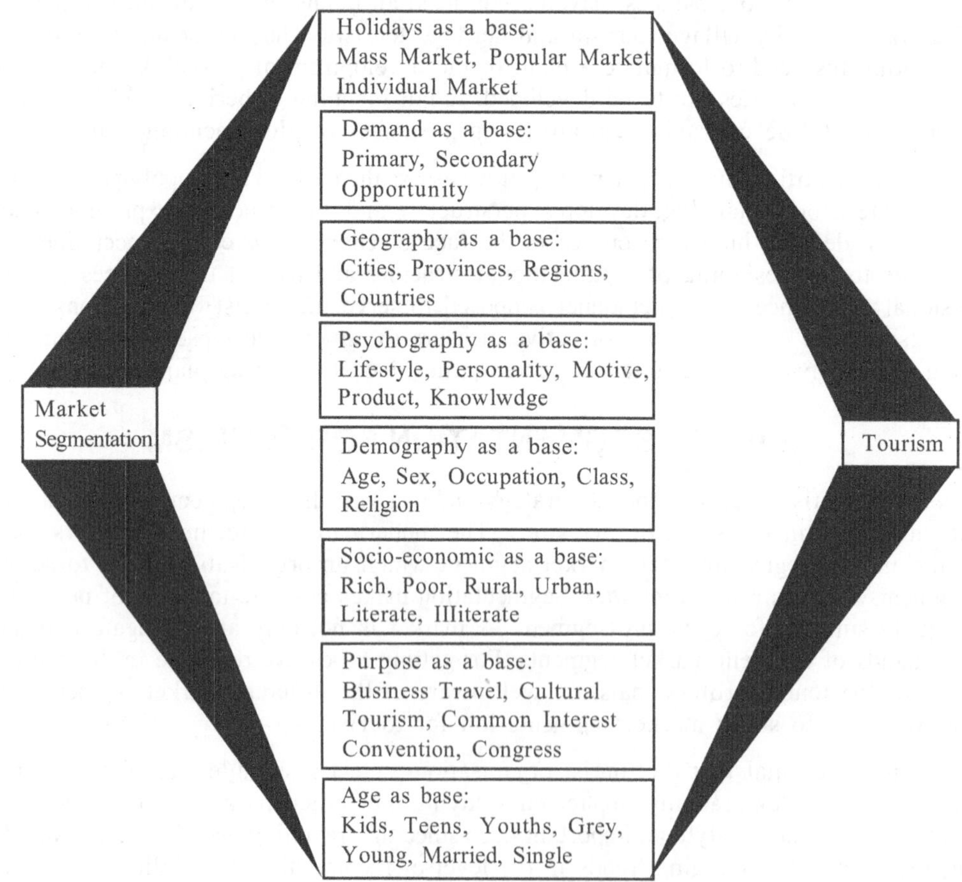

Fig. 11.4: Market Segmentation Bases

The holiday base focuses our attention on the fact that long-distance tours require availability of more leisure hours. The holiday market is classified in terms of demand. The different categories are the mass market, the popular market and the individual holiday market. The mass market involves largest number of vacationists who generally travel in long groups. They prefer all-inclusive tours. The users belong to the conservative group in which we find skilled and semi-skilled workers, blue-collar employees as the potential users. The popular market involves smaller groups going on inclusive or semi-inclusive tours. The users are generally class one and class two groups, pensioners and retired people. The individual holiday market involves "social group-A" like corporate chairman and senior executives. We find an apparent change in the behavioural profile of different categories in the holiday base. Another base is purpose in which we find business travel market, cultural tourism market, common interest tourism market and conference and convention. The demand base classifies markets into primary tourism market, secondary tourism and opportunity tourism. The geographic base includes lifestyle, personality, motives, product and knowledge. The demography base covers age, sex, occupation, class and religion. The socio-economic base makes classification like rich, poor, rural, urban, literate and illiterate. The age base classifies markets for kids, teens, youths, young married and old people market.

The aforesaid small segments simplify the task of tourist professionals. They know about the changing needs and requirements of different segments and innovate their strategic decisions accordingly. The development of marketing resources in tune with the changing levels of expectations make the ways for the stimulation of demand and simplify the task or marketeers. It is in this context that we need to segment the market for the different allied industries helping the tourism industry in many ways.

MARKETING INFORMATION SYSTEM FOR TOURISM

Knowledge is supposed to be the power. Of late, to manage a business is to manage the future and to manage the future, it is essential to manage the information. It is against this background that the tourist organisations assign due weightage to the MIS. The sophistication in the process of communication technologies has paved avenues for the development of a technology-driven MIS. In an age of information explosion, it is pertinent that an organisation develops and institutes MIS to have an easy access to information needed for planning, problem-solving and decision-making. The coordinated, systematic and continuous information gathering are the important purposes of managing the information related to the marketing activities. We can't deny that like other organisations even the tourist organisations have been found devaluing MIS for making creative marketing decisions. The mounting intensity of competition makes it essential that the tourist organisations are well aware of the emerging trends in the market conditions. This would help them in developing the marketing resources and making them responsive to the changing tastes and preferences of the users.

The key problem in the management of information is to establish a tourist information network. There is no doubt in it that we have developed sophisticated communication facilities and are also in a position to utilise the benefits of new generation of communication technologies. The MIS would help the tourist organisation in many ways, such as the formulation of scientific and intelligent plan would be possible which would make it easier to balance the demand and supply position. The emerging trends in the market can be identified and the marketing decisions can be made creative. The designing of package tour, innovation in the promotional measures, a change in the pricing strategy or using it as a motivational tool, the management of tourist organisations, tour operators, transport operators, travel agents would be made productive. Thus, it is essential that the tourist organisations take support of technology-driven MIS which would make the marketing decisions innovative.

We are well aware of the fact that quality of inputs plays a decisive role in determining the quality of outputs. In the MIS, if the tourist organisations fail in enriching the data bank, even the technology-driven system would hardly serve purpose of tourist organisations. This draws our attention on the fact that the research scientists or even the marketing personnel collect quality data to make available to the organisations quality information. The system analysts bear the responsibility of managing the infomation or transforming the data into information with the help of sophisticated computers. The tasks of storing, analysing, processing and disseminating are found on the shoulders of system analysts who are supposed to be world-class computer professional. Since the tourism industry is to influence a number of industries, it is pertinent that all the allied industries, such as hotel, communication, banking, trade and commerce, transport, insurance are familiar with the emerging trends in business *vis-a-vis* the changing expectations of users. The information related to the demand position help the related organisations in managing the supply position. The optimal development of resources is thus made possible which makes the process of development productive. These facts make a strong advocacy in favour of a well developed and technology-driven MIS.

Like other industries, the tourism industry also faces the problem of formulating and innovating the marketing mixes. This makes it essential that the system has been making available to the different allied industries the necessary information regarding the emerging changes in the business environment and the details regarding the users. The main thing in the process is to identify their lifestyles and level of expectations. If the researchers design their research plan in the face of emerging trends, the marketing research would help the allied industries in many ways. In the management of information, we find project planning playing an important role. There are different steps of project planning such as setting the research objectives, planning the required information to accomplish the organisational goals, identifying the sources to be tapped in seeking the information, employing the research design, sampling the procedures and selecting the method for analysing the data. Such a scientific project planning, in addition, to simplify the process of research also makes the result effective. In the tourism industry, we find different categories of users and an amalgam of different products which make it a multi-segment industry. This in a natural way complicates the task of a researcher. A researcher while collecting data and helping system analysts in managing the information is supposed to design the questionnaire consisting of tourist sites, users, products, promotion and competition. The following questions need an appropriate answer:

- Who are the users and where do they live?
- Who are the potential users and where do they live?
- What are their likes and dislikes?
- What are their travel preferences and interests?
- What do they prefer to buy while travelling?
- Where do they prefer to stay?
- Where do they prefer to take their foods and drinks?
- What are their transportation preferences?
- What are their entertainment preferences?
- What are the strategies of leading competitors?
- What type of marketing strategy would be suitable in the existing market?

We can't deny the fact that if there is one thing certain in the present world, it is change, We can't check the flow of change. This necessitates dynamism in our plans, policies and strategies to make possible necessary changes as and when the circumstances necessitate so. The multi-dimensional changes in the environmental conditions influence our lifestyles, living habits, tastes, preferences or so. Of late, almost all the leading tourist generating countries of the world have been found promoting research for innovating the process of making decisions which has been found making ways for value engineering. It is against this background that the MIS in general and the marketing research in particular has been found drawing due attention of the tourist organisations. In an age of information explosion, it is pertinent that the communication gap is bridged over. It is felt that the gap between the providers and the users has proved to be a major constraint in making the marketing decisions creative. A well designed, technology-driven, supported by world-class professionals MIS would be beneficial to all the allied industries contributing substantially to the development of tourism industry. An easy victory on the time gap is the result of a well developed MIS.

FORMULATION OF MARKETING MIX FOR THE TOURIST ORGANISATION

The Product Mix

Like the manufactured product, the potential tourists can't feel, taste, touch or sample a package tour. The tourism product is a non-material intangible thing. Every product is aimed at some market and its marketing success depends essentially on its 'fit' with the market. This makes it essential that the tourist professionals must continually strive for improving the effectiveness and increasing the profitability. More so when we find it a multi-segment industry, the task of formulating a sound product mix for the tourist organisations is found a bit difficult and challenging. The challenge for the marketers it to transform the dreams into the realities. We accept the fact that selling holiday is selling dreams. It is essential that the product offered to a target market must satisfy the users. Thus, the formulation of a sound product mix covers a wide range of activities like designing a package tour, branding, credit delivery services or so. Thus, the formulation of a sound product strategy focuses on the formulation of a sound product mix that makes possible designing of a profitable product portfolio by including and eliminating the core and peripheral services in the face of results received from the product portfolio. An optimal product strategy necessitates an in-depth study of the product life cycle. An amalgam of core and peripheral services requires a microscopic study of different services in order that the decisions related to inclusion, elimination are found productive. An expert rightly remarks, "Strategically, the core service is the primary benefit that consumers seek from the service provider. The core service often becomes a commodity as a service industry matures. Consumers expect the firm to be competent in providing the core service. The result is that peripheral services often become the way in which the customers' heart is won."[17]

The formulation of a product mix thus becomes an important task for marketing the tourism services profitably. The development of accommodation facilities by opening new classified and unclassified hotels, the channelisation of safe, comfortable and fast transportation facilities, availability of sophisticated communication facilities at tourist sites or hither and thither the sites and hotels, and the taste-oriented restaurants are some of the important components of an optimal product mix gravitating due attention of tourist organisations. We can't negate that the tourism product is a quite complex one, since it comprises a place (the holiday destination), services (a tour operator's package incorporating the temporary use of an airline seat, hotel room and sometimes other facilities and on occasion certain tangible product such as free flight bags or a complementary bottle of duty-free whisky to encourage booking. This makes it clear that the tourist organisations and to be more specific, the professionals working there need world-class excellence so that both the services are synchronised optimally and in the process, the peripheral services are innovated frequently to add additional attractions to the product. More attractions in the product, more positive results we expect from the tourism industry.

In view of the above, it is right to mention that the tourist professionals need excellence and we don't find any limit for the same. Sky is the limit for quality upgradation. A number of decisions are required to be made to make the product mix sound enough to stimulate the demand and increase the market share. It is against this background that we go through a number of issues, such as salient features of services, the product mix, the formulation of an ideal tour package or so.

James Gulliton described the marketing executives as a mixer of ingredients. This inspired Prof. Neil Borden to coin a new terminology in the marketing literature, i.e., marketing mix. He was of the view that without the help of quality submixes, the marketing executives would hardly be successful in accomplishing the organisational goals. This engineered a sound foundation for the frequent use of the term marketing mix in which initially the four submixes were included, such as the product mix, the promotion mix, the price mix, and the place mix. Gradually, we find inclusion of some other mixes, such as People, Process and Physical Attraction. While going through the marketing mix for the tourism services, we cover all the submixes.

The framing of product mix is, no doubt, a challenging task since the marketing professionals are supposed to blend the core and peripheral services optimally. In the tourism industry, a deeper product line is found a must. This is due to the fact that needs, expectations, preferences of different categories of users can't be identical. The tourism marketers are required to be captive to deepen the product line so that the products match to the expectations. The extent to which the marketers are found successful in deepening and innovating the product line have a telling impact on the net gain or satisfaction.

Innovation in the tourism product helps raising the sensitivity. There is nothing fixed and fundamental about the tourism product. The users of the services look forward to quality product. This increases the functional responsibilities of a marketing professional. Modifying the product without touching their physical properties and providing the management with more profitable opportunities to capitalise on are found significant in the very context. The marketing professionals while designing the product mix are to be careful that features like physical, psychological and peripheral are included in the mix. The content factors are within the jurisdiction of the government who bears the responsibility of developing, maintaining and conserving tourist attractions like parks, museums, beaches, historic and archaeological treasures or so. Unless these factors are developed in a right fashion, the marketing professionals would hardly be successful in making the marketing resources productive. The context factors are, of late, found managed by both the public as well as private tourist organisations. Earlier, this responsibility was on the shoulders of private sector tourist organisations.

The designing of an ideal product mix is significant but it is not possible unless we find governmental organisations extending the best possible cooperation to the tourist organisations. The direct or indirect patronage of government is found essential to get a positive response. The development of infrastructural facilities is found an important dimension of tourism product. Unless we find hotels, lodges, apartments, cottages, havelis, old palaces available in a good number, the task of promoting the world tourism would hardly be fulfilled. This makes it essential that for promoting tourism as an industry, the government extends to the different organisations the infrastructural facilities like road, transportation, electricity, water, medicare facilities, banking, insurance or so. The tourist organisations are also supposed to design a sound package so that the motivation to the tourists is found more creative. The synchronisation of different services needs an intensive care to the quality of services that we include in the marketing mix. It is in this context that we go through a sound product mix for the tourist organisations.

In Figure 11.5, we find the product mix for the tourism industry, The multi-dimensional services included in the mix are attraction, accommodation, transportation, recreation, restaurant, and shopping.

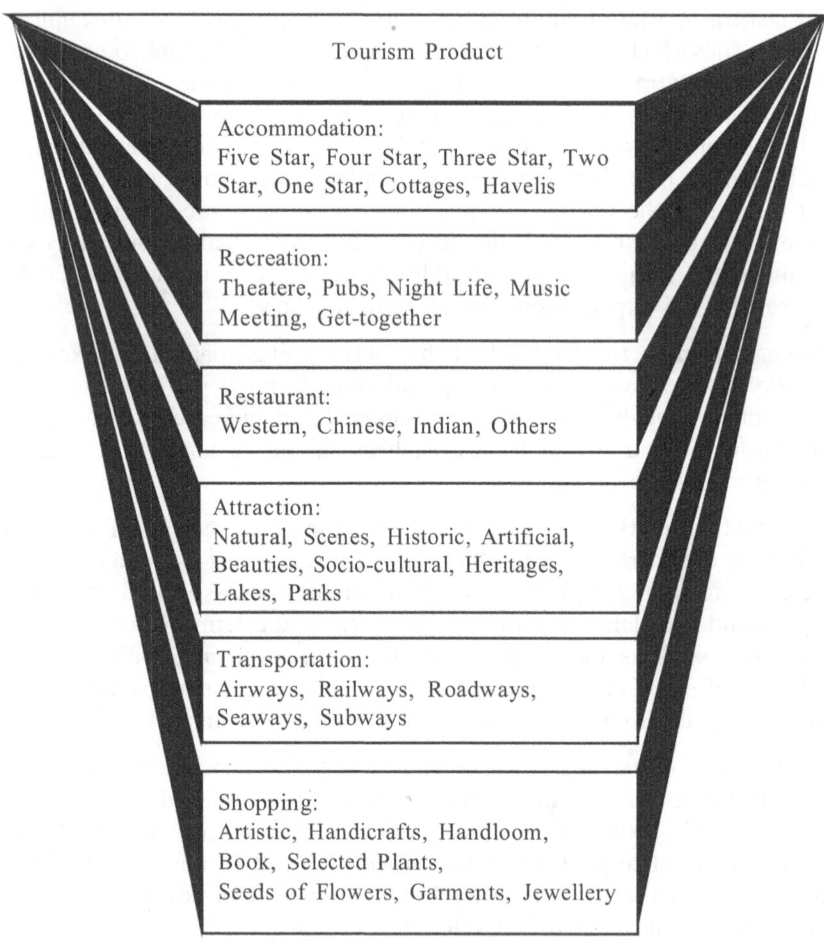

Fig. 11.5: Tourism Product

The tourists belong to varied cultural patterns, divergent desires, needs and requirements, different socio-economic strata or so. This makes it essential that the tourist organisations while managing the different services are careful to the emerging trends. Since all the tourists need the same core services, the width of the product is almost fixed. It is essential that the tourism marketers are captive to deepen the product line. The success of tourism business depends considerably upon the extent to which the marketers develop and make available the services. It is significant that the marketers are well aware of the quality promised and are particular that the gap between the quality-promised and quality-offered is bridged over. This in a natural way requires innovative efforts. The marketers here are not free to deepen the product line. They at best can catch up their cluster patterns and can forge their activities to serve one or more cluster, group of segments or so.

While formulating the product mix for the tourist organisations, it is pertinent that the tourist organisations are familiar with the strategies of leading tourist organisations and promote innovation to the extent it is possible.

Of late, we find a craze for village tourism, rural tourism, adventure tourism or so. We also find that the high spending tourists prefer to stay in cottages, havelis and old palaces converted into hotels having five-star amenities and facilities. They want peace and therefore prefer the outskirts or the villages. We find cottage culture establishing an edge over the multi-storeyed apartment culture. We find aesthetic sense playing an incremental role in adding additional attractions to the services. These aspects are found important while formulating the product mix.

SALIENT FEATURES OF TOURISM PRODUCT

For making the marketing decisions effective, it is pertinent that the tourist professionals are well aware of the salient features of the tourism product. This would help them in many ways.

1. Tourism product is highly perishable: Perishability is an important factor that influences the decision-making behaviour of the tourist professionals. The product is used just when it is offered and therefore, if it remains unused, the chance is lost, the business is lost. If the tourists don't visit a particular place, if the seats in hotels, aircrafts remain vacant, the business is lost. This makes the product highly perishable and makes it essential that the tourist professionals make the best possible efforts to promote the services in such a fashion that opportunities never remain untapped.

2. The tourism product is a service product: We find services the only product used and sold in the tourism industry. This makes it essential that the tourist professionals assign due weightage to creative marketing strategies which are found proactive. The levels of judgement and knowledge possessed by the individuals and related to tourism reflect on the satisfaction derived by the tourists after visiting a place. In this context, the marketers need to be high performers, personally-committed, imaginative and so. This helps them in capitalising on the opportunities optimally.

3. Intangibility complicates the task of marketers: We are well aware of the fact that tourism is a multi-segment industry in which the transportation and accommodation services constitute a place of outstanding significance. The tourist professionals find it difficult to persuade the users by displaying the seats in the aircraft and the bedrooms in the hotels. The users first use and then come to know about the quality.

4. The services are for pleasure: It is right to mention that the tourism services are used by the tourists to enjoy. By visiting tourist resorts, spots, sites, beaches, they get pleasure. We also find the services instrumental in enriching the knowledge bank of tourists or the crazy persons use the services to taste the flavour of adventure. This makes it significant that the tourist organisations make the centres attractive by adding additional attractions.

5. Users are supposed to visit the centre: For availing the services of the tourism industry, it is pertinent that the users visit the place physically. The users are supposed to come all the way to the spot. This necessitates setting of product features in a right way.

6. Adequate infrastructural facilities for the tourism product: No doubt that almost all the industries need infrastructural support, but the tourism industry can't exist if hotels, transportation services are found non-existent. Thus, we find infrastructural facilities essential to improve the quality of services. Efficient transportation facilities, hygienic hotel accommodation, and sophisticated communication services are some of the key infrastructural facilities, adding attractions to the tourism services.

7. The users are a heterogeneous group of people: It is important to mention that the tourism users come from different regions, income groups, sections, age groups, genders, professions or so. This makes it essential that the marketers are familiar with the different groups of people using the services.

Designing a Package Tour

In the process of formulating a sound product strategy, there are a number of factors to be given due attention. The designing of a package tour occupies a place of outstanding significance. For the profitable marketing of tourism services, it is pertinent that the different components of product are managed in a right fashion. This gravitates our attention on the offering of a package holiday product which necessitates management of the following factors:

Destination: The development of destination or tourist sites has a far reaching impact on attracting the tourists. It is essential that destination or the tourist sites are easily accessible. This necessitates safe, fast and reliable transportation facilities hither and thither the tourist sites. To be more specific for promoting world tourism or attracting the foreign tourists, it is essential that the flying time is made proportionate. The site should be clean, the beaches should be sandy; sunshine should be certain; the entertainment facilities at the site should be of quality; the site should be safe to walk about; the local people should be friendly; the tour operators, the travel guides and others should have competence of speaking English and other regional languages. These facilities at the destination would add attractions.

Management of Airport: While managing the tourism product, the airports are required to be managed carefully. The airport should be local and convenient. The arrangement for car parking should be safe and adequate. It should not be congested but it should be spacious. In addition, the shopping facilities should be duty-free. The airport should be clean and the vehicles should be available so that tourists don't face any trouble. Besides, the security arrangement should be tight to protect the passengers and their valuables. The aesthetic management occupies a place of significance in the very context.

Airlines: The flights should maintain the time schedule otherwise a dislocation may invite multi-faceted problems, not only to the tourists but even to the airport authorities. The services should be reliable, good and polite. The sophisticated modern aircrafts of new generation should be included in the fleet to attract the tourists. The safety record should also be up to mark to the remove the fear psychosis or psychofobia.

Road and Rail Transportation: For the tourists preferring to travel by buses of railways, it is significant that the stations are well managed. The booking and reservation counters should be managed scientifically. The enquiry window should be controlled by efficient and well-behaved staff. The safety and security arrangements should be adequate to counter the law and order problems. The signposts should be positioned at right places to help the travelling passengers.

Hotels: For managing the hotel services, it is essential that we are also careful to the hotel accommodation facilities. It is pertinent that hotels are easily accessible to the tourist sites or beaches or shops. The hotel personnel should be trustworthy and competent enough to speak English and other regional languages. They are supposed to be friendly. The management of facilities at hotels need due care. Though the standard of services, amenities and facilities depend upon the grade of hotels still it is essential that hotels offer the promised services to the users. The gap between the services-promised and services-offered should be bridged over. The hotels should be well maintained, the decor should be attractive; possibly a fair mix of eastern and western culture, the atmosphere should be calm and quiet; specially at the night time, public rooms should be adequate in number, the swimming pool should be neat and clean where inflow and outflow of water should be scientific to protect the danger of water contamination or pollution. There should be bar with good range of drinks. The bedrooms should be spacious in which balcony facilities should be made available. The child care services should also be made available. Particularly at the beach resorts, the sea view should be possible with all rooms, in-room telephonic services should be available, in-room TV should be provided. There should be adequate cupboard space. The hangers should be attractive and artistic, toilets should be neat and clean and well equipped with east and west provisions. The lighting and ventilation arrangements should be adequate. The intensity of light at different points should be given due weightage. While managing hotels, the restaurants and cafeterias also need due care. The restaurants and cafeterias should be well managed. The food and drinks should have taste orientation. The varieties of meals and drinks should be available. The seating arrangements should be comfortable, the meal hours should be flexible and the hotel personnel should be polite and friendly.

Resort Representatives: Regarding representatives of resort, they should be knowledgeable, friendly, accessible and competent.

Tour Operators: The tour operators should be reliable where the guaranteed services are made available to the guests without making any distortion. The price should reflect good value for money.

Tour Agents: The tour agents should be competent, friendly and conveniently available. They should also provide extra services to the tourists. The incentives need due weightage. Free transfer to airport and free insurance facilities induce tourists.

Miscellaneous: In addition, the fellow travellers should be like-minded. The main thing is to make the tour pleasant and memorable. If the tourists have companionable fellow travellers, the journey would of course remain memorable.

The aforesaid facts make it clear that being an amalgam of a number of industries and services, the tourism industry is known as a multi-segment industry in which the designing of a package which proves its instrumentality as a motivational force is found a bit difficult and challenging. It requires professional excellence so that we are in a position to assess the changing levels of expectations of the guests/tourists and all the required amenities and facilities are made available to help tourists to go to the destination, to enjoy and to come back safely. The tour operators and transport operators bear the responsibility of formulating a package tour and therefore they should have world-class professional excellence to know and understand their changing needs and requirements. The services are related to a number of industries managed by others and therefore, the tour operators and transport operators managing the affairs should make it sure that whatever the promises they have made on behalf of hotels, airways, railways, roadways are not to be distorted. This is likely to project the image of tour operators and therefore a gap between the services-promised and services-offered would make the task difficult. It is against this background that designing of a package tour occupies a place of outstanding significance and all the allied industries making the package are required to be careful that they are not inviting degeneration.

MAKING THE BRAND DECISIONS

The decision-making practices for introducing a brand, virtually influence the magnitude of effects. If an organisation decides to introduce a brand name, it can introduce a blanket or family brand. It can also introduce different brand names for each product. There are sufficient examples of these approaches in travel. "Accor Hotel" trade under a range of company names. Scheduled airlines may run charter off shoots under different brand names, such as Lufthansa, Condor, Iberia, etc. If any brand is too closely associated with a particular type of product, a new brand name may be preferred. In developing a brand, it is essential that a brand is not just a means of drawing attention. More so, it is remembered that a brand helps a tourist organisation in distinguishing the product and thus helping an organisation to establish brand loyalty. It must act as a cue to the product characteristics including the product's quality. Brand provides the opportunity for a company to enhance its corporate image. How the consumers feel about a brand reflects their feelings about the company. The travel companies such as Swissair, Cunard and Hilton Hotels are the suitable examples.

How to make a good brand name is a challenging task. There are a number of guidelines developed by the marketing professionals, specially for the development of a good brand name. The name and symbol should convey attributes with appropriate imagery, since one important function of the brand name is to obtain immediate recognition for both the products as well as their attributes. It should be easy to pronounce and remember the name. In addition, the name should communicate benefits of the product. The symbol should be distinctive and their design and colour should support the product concept. The words conveying the nature of product of having pleasant associations should help to reinforce the benefits in the purchaser's mind. The brand names, if catchy, retain the present organisation's name but reduce it to a more easily memorised logo. The simplicity of a word or illustration enhances recall and recognition. In the travel industry, this aspect is found important where the brand may have to be displayed on a fast moving object such as an aircraft or coach. A brand enhances the corporate identity of an organisation so that the products and company become inseparable in the minds of consumers. To make it more impact generating, it is essential to use it in all areas of the company's marketing such as on stationery, brochures, representatives' uniforms, shop front, literature racks and in promotional measures such as flight bags, carrier bags or other give-away materials.

While making the brand decisions, it is essential that all the four demands are given due attention. The existing demand which is the result of the adequate supply of products, the consumers want; the displacement demand which is the result of dissatisfaction experienced by the consumers; the created demand which is the result of unrecognised and latent wants and the future demand which is the result of demography or other changes in population are found significant, specially with the viewpoint of identifying the reason for the failure of products in the markets. It is essential that the products are well supported by the travel agents who bear the responsibility of racking your brochure and selling the product. It is also meant effective briefing of agents since a number of travel sales have been lost through inadequate briefing of retailers on new products and their benefits. In the formulation of product strategy, the making of brand decisions is thus found impact generating.

LAUNCHING A NEW PRODUCT

Launching of a new product is found significant while formulating a sound product strategy. In the tourism industry, be it aircraft, ferry route, hotel or tour package; we find risk elements and uncertainties of high magnitude. Of course, it is difficult to quantify the failure rate of new products, still a careful screening of the product remains an important tool in the hands of marketers. Before we go through screening, it is essential to clarify the concept of new product. An expert says, 'By new product, we mean improvement to an existing product, can render that product so new as to make it be seen by prospective purchasers as genuinely new product. Similarly if an existing product is launched to a new market unfamiliar with it, the product is also in all intents and purposes, a new product.'[18] In Figure 11.6, we find details regarding the same.

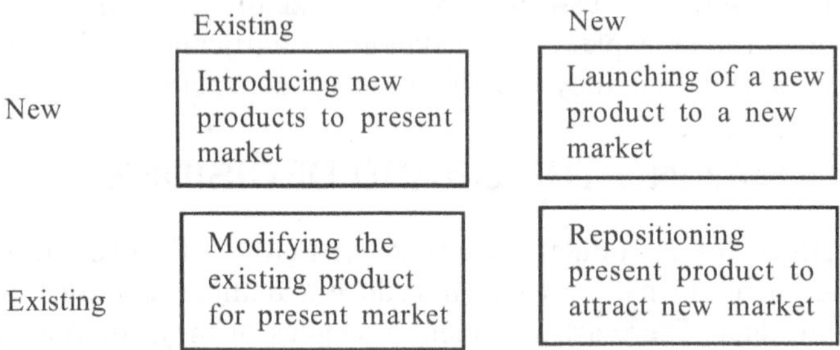

Fig. 11.6: Existing and New Product

It is right to say that a company prefers to modify the existing product to the present market and makes the product attractive to face the least possible risk. Some additional benefits are added in this case. Suppose if the product is losing its response in the existing market, then the repositioning may be preferred. This is meant to direct its appeal to a different market segment or to prefer overseas market. To make the product more appealing to a new type of customer, it is also suggested to change the concept of the product. Another alternative is to develop a genuinely new product (or new brand) to be sold to the existing users. In that case if a company succeeds in projecting a positive image, we find all possibilities of getting a trial even by the existing consumers. Finally, a company can choose to introduce a genuinely new product to a new market segment. Often, the new products are the extensions of the present product line. For example, the ready-to-eat cereal added to a line of regular cereals, or the additions of new flavours to an old product line as was done by Ovaltine.[19] In this context, it is difficult to determine exactly when a product can genuinely be new, since most of the products we buy are simply advances or modifications of existing products. In travel tourism, the Concord offered totally a new concept in air travel. Billy Butlin looking in the 1930s for a way of keeping seaside visitors entertained in all weathers, introduced the concept of holiday camp which was unlike any existing form of holiday at the time. The main thing in the launching of a new product is to find the market gap which is a product opportunity with a ready market which has not yet been tapped. The market-oriented approach line is found suitable for the development of a new product. In the Scandinavian hotels, the high cost of labour was instrumental in raising the hotel price structure for food. Here, the solution was to introduce self-service breakfasts.

The Promotion Mix

Creation of awareness has a far reaching impact. The tourist organisations bear the responsibility of informing, sensing and persuading the potential tourists in a right fashion. The marketers need to use the various components of promotion optimally so that they succeed in increasing the number of habitual users. We find several cases to quote when even the world-class goods or services fail in attracting the customers/users. Communicating the promotional messages to the target market is an important task before the marketing managers for which a number of ways and means are used. The tourism promotion is an effort to implement marketing plan formulated by the tourist organisations. It helps in maximising the duration of stay, frequency of visit by offering new tourist products in the same country to areas which hitherto have remained untapped or partially tapped. It is a marketing effort which consists of marketing communication to transmit information about the business to all participants as well as to the users. The communication process passes through different phases like creating awareness that the existing services are easily available and reliable. It makes possible comprehension of what the services can do for them and the conviction that the services would pay dividends in return for their investments. The promotional measures are based on what the tourist organisations can sell.

William L. Hewes Jr., publisher of Pacific Area Travel Association, a prestigious travel trade monthly published on behalf of Pacific Area Travel Association comments on the tourism promotional measures in the Asian countries. 'Most NTOs: (a) do not know their markets and (b) they do not have experienced competent marketing personnel. Only a very small portion of their budget is used for trade advertising which is an important area of promotion. The major costs of overseas tourist offices are on personnel and activities which are not cost-effective. A small country, for instance, may spend $100,000 for a cocktail party to entertain two hundred per cent PATA delegates. Imagine the results if this amount had been spent on trade advertising.' These comments regarding the non-optimal promotional efforts made in the field of tourism promotion make it clear that the tourist organisations have not been found making an optimal use of the different components of promotion which has been making the process cost-ineffective. It is against this background that we go through different dimensions of the promotion mix.

Advertising: We find advertising an important component of the promotion mix. The advertisement helps in furnishing important information to the actual and potential tourists and further simplifies the process of transformation. Its coverage is wide. It can be placed before a large number of potential tourists. Frequency generation is an additional contribution of creative advertising. For the promotion of tourism, we find creative advertisement slogans acting as a sharp-edged instrument. Advertising in tourism is similar to advertising for others. It essentially follows the AIDA principle of attracting the attention, creating interest, fostering desire and inspiring action. Advertising in a true sense is a communication link between the seller and the buyer. It is a positive device to increase or promote the business.

Categorically for tourism, the advertising is aimed at the public to create awareness of the travel offers available on a resort and its attractions to influence their business decisions. If we advertise well, we sell well. Though in the tourism industry, we find other components also instrumental but advertisement bears the efficacy of turning the negative into positive.

The whole thing in the advertisement is to make possible creativity. It is creativity that makes our slogans, messages, appeals proactive and we succeed in persuading the users. This requires world-class professional excellence because only the professional advertisers can make ways for creativity and sensitivity.

We consider advertising as paid public messages designed to describe or praise the products. In the tourism industry, the products are destination, accommodation, transportation or so. The advertisements are made in the newspapers, general and specialised magazines specially in the form of posters or billboards. In order to transmit a predetermined message to a predetermined audience, we also advertise in radio and televisions through the commercial services. Thus, the three measures – print media, broadcast media and the telecast media help in advertising.

With the sophisticated developments in the field of print technology, such as laser printing, offset printing, screen printing, we find print media active in throwing a positive impact. We find a number of trade and business newspapers and magazines in which the messages and slogans can be advertised. The advertising professionals bear the responsibility of making the advertisement slogans or messages creative which are found successful in influencing the tourism potential users. How to compose the slogans? How to select the events? How to select the magazines? These questions are found important when we take a decision regarding the print media. We can't negate the fact that due to economy, we find a majority or even almost all the tourist organisations advertising through the print media. This is also due to the fact that advertisers get more space for exposure and can inform and sense the target audience with the help of supporting facts and figures. The information regarding the particular resort, availability of hotel accommodation, transportation and shopping facilities can be transmitted in a right fashion when we advertise through the print media. We have quality papers, quality print devices, quality advertising professionals and these developments can help us substantially in making the advertisement messages proactive. On the other hand, we find economy and therefore it is not to throw a major financial burden on the promotion budget of tourist organisations. The circulation is wider and therefore it is found covering almost all the prospects albeit with a small investment. These facts make it clear that in today's world, we find print media gaining popularity and helping the tourist organisations considerably in making the process cost-effective *vis-a-vis* productive. It is against this background that we find a large-scale use of print media in the advertisement world of today. Of course, the advertising professionals need more care and precautions failing which the results can't be satisfactory.

In addition to print media, we find broadcast media also instrumental in advertising. The advanced and sophisticated transmission devices have increased the acceptability of print media fantastically. We are in a position to reach to almost 100 per cent of the target audience. The audio-exposure determines the magnitude of success of the broadcast media. We can't deny the fact that the effectiveness of broadcast media is not so high and therefore the advertising professionals need excellence to make the slogans and messages proactive. The intensity of acceptability is substantially influenced by the instrumentality of advertisement professionals. However, we find it right to mention that of late print media has established its edge over the broadcast media.

The most sensitive but expensive telecast media help tourist professionals in promoting the business substantially. The satellite communication facilities have virtually revolutionised the telecast media. With the sophistication and expansion of TV network, we find multi-dimensional improvements in the telecast media which has raised the sensitivity of advertisement slogans and appeals fantastically. It is against this background that we find almost all the organisations using this component of promotion. The tourist organisations also use it because audio-visual exposure help them in visualising the eye-catching tourist spots, resorts, natural scenes, swimming pool facilities, bedrooms arrangements or so. Since we find tourism a multi-segment industry, the tourist organisations find it easier to project events having more attractions. In this context, it is essential that the advertising professionals make possible creativity in the slogans and messages by understanding the behavioural profile of target users. Advertising for promoting world tourism, domestic tourism, adventure tourism, rural tourism, village tourism, social tourism need expertise so that the events become successful in sensitising the prospects. Being an amalgam of different industries, we find scope for making a consortium or syndicate to advertise through TV which make ways for frequency and economy.

The minus point that we find due to intangibility can be compensated with the help of visual exposure of scenes and events. We can project hotel bedrooms, well arranged restaurants and cafeterias, swimming pools, playing grounds, shopping complex or so. It is in this context that we make an advocacy in favour of telecast media. The tourist professionals need to take a decision regarding the selection of efficient advertising professionals who have an in-depth idea of the lifestyles of the segment for which the messages are transmitted. It is quite natural that sensitivity rate of all the segments can't be uniform.

The aforesaid fact make it clear that print media, broadcast media and telecast media are the different vehicles through which our messages travel. "I LOVE NEW YORK", a message transmitted by the tourist organisations of the New York changed the scenario, projected a positive image and increased tourism business considerably. The sensitivity rate of the message was so high that the image problem was countered successfully. In the Indian perspective, we also find image problem very much instrumental in forming a negative opinion regarding the tourism potentials and the safety and protection of tourists. Of late, the high spending tourists feel that it is not safe to travel in India. We find such a negative opinion even formed by other categories of tourists which has aggravated the image problem to such an extent that the tourism professionals in general and the advertising professionals in particular need to activate the process of brainwashing by intensifying the creative messages. This draws our attention on telecast media since this would help tourist organisations in transmitting the moments of travelling by the tourists safely. All the prospects can't have an opportunity to go through the magazines or the newspapers but a majority of them or almost all of them watch TV regularly. This increases the number of viewers. Thus, the tourist professionals need to formulate a fair mix of print media and telecast media and right from the very beginning need to think over the problem of budgetary constraint. The advertising, thus, happens to occupy a key position in the promotion mix if the tourist professionals advertise sensibly.

Publicity: Another dimension of the promotion mix is publicity which focuses our attention on strengthening the public relations measures by developing a rapport with the media people and getting their personalised support in publicising the business. It helps in projecting the positive image of tourist organisations since the prospects trust on the news items publicised by the media people. The public relations cover a wide range of activities. It is the art and science of planning and implementing honest two-way communication and understanding between a company or an organisation. It is also known as the reflection of organisational programmes and objectives. Its main purpose is to inform the masses about the activities and mission of an organisation. Its purpose is to create the best possible reputation. In the context of tourism, the promotional strategies can't be proactive unless we strengthen the public relations activities. It is against this background that we need to assign due weightage to this component of the promotion mix.

The tourism publicity plays a positive role in attracting the tourists and promoting the business. A well-planned publicity programme is found efficacious in the very context. The publicity programme include regular publicity stories and photographs to the newspapers, travel editors, contact with magazines on stories, ideas and the framing of outlines and pictures, etc. With the passage of time, the tourism publicity has occupied a place of outstanding significance. At the initial stage, the information publicity was considered important but of late, the commercial tourism publicity has established its edge over the information publicity. Of course, this has been due to an increase in the number of tourists and travel frequency. It has necessitated creative commercial publicity techniques so that a long-term publicity strategy is designed. In respect of tourism publicity, the motive forces are found sensitive because it is based on experience, instinct, routine and technique. Applied psychology and sociology are found not getting due weightage in the process even till now. Of late, the marketing professionals feel that an examination or a microscopic analysis of the behavioural profile of users is essential without which the publicity measures would show a lukewarm response. A tourism publicity programme can be perceived in the creation of the perception of satisfaction. This would form the tourist brand of the country *vis-a-vis* would make possible coordination among the publicity measures. The effectiveness of the publicity measures is sizeably influenced by the efficiency of the publicity technicians. If they are efficient, the rate of sensitivity of the programme would be at its peak. It is right to mention that words are not only the conveyors of thoughts and ideas but also of emotional contents and the travelling on right path makes possible the desired transmission not only to the intellects but also to the psychism of the recipient and finally are expressed to this end. There are different groups in the publicity, such as advertising publicity, projected publicity, structural publicity and personal publicity. The blending of all of them optimally makes the publicity mix sound enough to influence and sense the users.

The sales support activities draw our attention in the very context. Establishment of personal or indirect contact with the users or trade intermediaries are called the sales support technique. In the tourism industry, the promotional activities, furnishing or transmitting to the public at large some important informations related to accommodation, transportation, communication or outstanding attractions become significant.

This dimension of promotion is found very much effective, specially when we talk about the tourism industry. It also helps sellers to perform efficiently. We can't deny the fact that very success of tourism industry depends upon the instrumentality of retail travel agents. If they motivate well, the demand is stimulated *vis-a-vis* the market share is increased. The sales support activities inform the users or trade intermediaries, travel agents, tour operators, airlines, etc. regarding the potentials. The intermediaries need a number of information to inform and persuade the users, such as transportation and communication services, weather conditions, law and order situations, addition in the peripheral services, opening of new hotels with new amenities and facilities, the changing travel regulations, foreign exchange regulations, visa provisions or so. These informations are found relevant to the intermediaries as well as to the potential tourists who are planning to visit. The sales support techniques play an incremental role in the promotion of tourism business by using the print materials such as brochures, folders, direct mail material, display material, etc.

In view of the above, it is right to mention that publicity proves to be an important submix of promotion which simplifies the task of tourist professionals. The media, opinion leaders and national and international tourist organisations are benefited substantially by the publicity measures taken up in right fashion. A close examination of the behavioural profile of users or prospects is found essential to increase the instrumentality of the promotional measures. This suggests to cover the emotional world of a man and the conduct of his life. If we find tourism gaining popularity, the influencing factors are neither the beautiful landscape nor the past and contemporary culture of a country, nor the natural medical cures, nor the transport and the tourist plant, nor the appreciation of the authorities concerned rather than the need, interest and attitudes which can be influenced with the help of scientifically and intelligently campaigned publicity. The leading tourist generating countries of the world are found showing a constantly positive attitude towards publicity, of course, graded publicity initiated by the publicity of the individual trade firms, resorts, areas, provinces and countries. On the other hand, the upcoming or budding tourist generating countries of the world begin with the country's publicity to which regional and travel trade publicity is added.

The publicity need to satisfy the fundamental principles of clarity of objective and uniformity. The clarity of objective signifies that the entire range of national tourist policy should not show any contradiction whereas the uniformity helps in creating the impression abroad that the national publicity campaigns are part of uniform planning. There must be a single goal to put national tourism to the forefront and the regional and local features on the second.

The tourist publicity programme for a country may be:

- the creation of the concept of satisfaction which could form the tourist brand of the country;
- the coordination among the publicity measures of the economic, cultural and tourist institutions of a country in conjunction with brands coupling; and
- the contact analysis of satisfaction, market observations and research as well as the publicity effectiveness.

Sales Promotion: All the components of promotion except advertisement are found 'below-the-line.' We don't find a clear-cut distinction between below-the-line and above-the-line promotion. As for example, the window display is one of the merchandising techniques designed to promote products at the point of sales (PoS). Though it is argued that the windows of travel agencies are used to advertise the products like current bargain, offer for flights and holidays, the window display is still identified as a form of 'below-the-line' promotion. Paradoxically, we are all aware of the advertising and its uses but a majority of us appear disinterested in sales promotion which can be undertaken successfully if the tourist professionals are found imaginative. Sales promotional measures are the short-term activities seeking to boost sales at peak demand periods to ensure that the firms obtain its market share and are used to help launch a new product or support an ailing or modified one. There is no doubt in it that the money-back or money-off or bargain offers are also found effective but this can have the effect of demeaning the inherent value of the product. Roonie Carpett's joke that he remembers an event because it was the week Allied Carpets were not having a sale, carried an important message for the marketers that too much emphasis on 'deals' would degrade the products in the eyes of customers or users and at the same time would also undermine the level of profit. It is significant that we use sales promotion as complementary to advertising. This tool of sales promotion is designed to appeal particularly those customers who are price-sensitive. There are a number of techniques to promote sale and the tourist professionals need to use them in the face of their requirements *vis-a-vis* the emerging trends in the business. In Figure 11.7, we find the tools or techniques of sales promotion.

On the basis of Figure 11.7, it is right to mention that a number of techniques are used for promoting sale. In the tourism industry, a travel company offers give-aways to their clients, such as flight bags, wallets for tickets and foreign exchange and covers of passport. The hotels offer a number of facilities like shoe shine clothes, first aid sewing kits, shower caps and shampoo. Further, the VIP clients also get fruits and flowers in their rooms. There is no doubt in it that almost all the promotional measures generate goodwill and add values to the product but at the same time, the purpose may also be to make the product memorable. It is against this background that we find ash-trays the most effective give-aways to be made availabale to the travel agents. In addition, the paper weights and calenders are found effective.

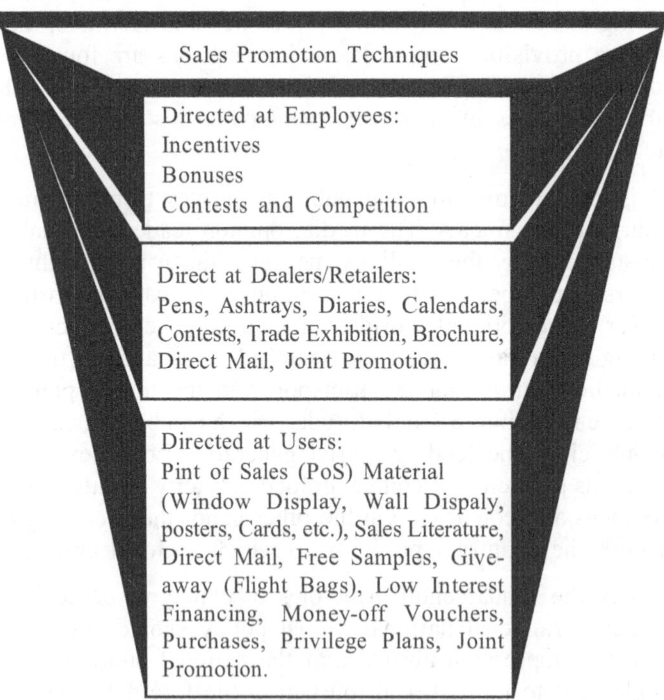

Fig. 11.7: Techniques of Sales Promotion

The promotional tools directed at the company's staff, directed at dealer or the retailers and directed at consumer through retailers or directed at the three facets of sales promotion drawing due attention of the tourist professionals. In case the products are sold through the retailers, the options are to aim the promotion at the consumer directly to build brand awareness and create demand. We prefer in that case the 'Pull Strategy' in which the promotional measures pull the users into the offices of the travel agents. This makes the ways for pre-sale. Alternatively, the sales promotion is also geared to the merchandising activities designed to persuade the retailers to promote the product. We call it 'Push Strategy' where promotional tools attract customers and the business we find in the offices of the travel agents. This is found useful, specially to the upcoming or budding tourist organisations not able to afford the national advertising. Here, they may opt for Push Strategy by identifying the important retailers and adopting 50-50 joint promotional expenses. Recently, we find co-operative promotion. The hoteliers, cross channel ferry companies and manufacturers of alcoholic drinks have promoted short back holidays on the basis of joint promotion. In addition, the price appeal has also proved its instrumentality in the very context. Thomas Cook offered three-tier sales promotion based on price and one more novel technique as detailed below:

- Cook agreed to match the price of any holiday they sold which was known as price promise.
- Money-back guarantee to the clients who purchase the product or any tour operator known as trading charter.
- Matching of customers' need with a particular holiday known as formal guarantee.
- A business travel challenge in which the details of expenditure on staff business travel booked through other agents over a three months' period were submitted by companies to Cook, specially to calculate the expected savings, provided the bookings are made through them.

The tourist professionals while promoting sale with the support of sales promotion measures are required to cover different stages like determining the objective, identifying the target audience, evaluating the alternative strategies, selecting the best, developing the programme, testing the programme, implementing the programme and evaluating the effects. This helps them in making the sales promotion measures productive. It is essential that we make an evaluation of the sales promotion tools so that the corrective measures are taken, innovation process is activated and cost-effectiveness is made possible.

Word-of-mouth Promotion: Much communication about tourism actually takes place by word-of-mouth information which in a true sense is word-of-mouth recommendation. In the tourism industry, it is found that the word-of-mouth promoters play the role of a hidden salesforce, who instrumentalises the process of selling but often we fail to recognise their contributions. If our friends, relatives and well-wishers communicate to us something positive or negative regarding the services they have experienced in the bed rooms of a hotel, in the restaurants or cafeterias, at the tourist sites by the travel guides, we find the process effective. If they make positive comments, we prefer to visit that particular place, hotels and the offices of the travel agents. Contrary to it, if they communicate the negative points or their bitter experiences, we avoid. It is in this context that we find word-of-mouth promoters acting like a hidden salesforce who helps the process of selling substantially but we fail to know their contributions. The advertisement, publicity, sales promotion may be insensitive but we can't doubt the sensitivity of word-of-mouth promotion. The high magnitude of effectiveness is due to high creditability of the channel, specially in the eyes of the potential tourists. The increasing sensitivity of this tool of promotion in the tourism industry makes it clear that the tourist generating organisations need to concentrate on the quality of services they promise and offer. If we assign an overriding priority to the satisfaction element, the word-of-mouth promotion would remain instrumental in the process of creating and expanding the market. This makes it essential that the marketers or the tourist professionals keep their eyes open, identify the vocal persons or the opinion leaders and take a special care of them so that they keep on moving the process of stimulating and creating the demand. We call it two-step flow of communication in which messages are directed to the opinion leaders rather than to the masses found insensitive to quality and promises.

An important question regarding word-of-mouth promotion is related to its magnitude of sensitivity and acceptability. Why do we find the hidden salesforce so much effective? A plain answer to this question is that the experiences, deliberations, expressions of the opinion leaders are based on direct or physical viewing. If our friends or relatives communicate to us the specialities of a particular tourist site, or positive feelings regarding their stay in a particular hotel, it is quite natural that we prefer to visit the site or to stay in that hotel as and when the opportunities are available. It is against this background that we find satisfaction to users a prerequisite for the success of hidden salesforce. The hidden salesforce help the tourist organisations in optimising the promotion budget by rationalising the expenses on advertisement. The tourist organisations get business being influenced by the word-of-mouth promoters.

In view of the aforesaid facts, it is right to mention that word-of-mouth is an important dimension of promotion, which makes a strong advocacy in favour of improving the quality of services. This also focuses on identifying the vocal persons and the opinion leaders who have high communicative ability and are aware of the art of influencing the potential tourists. We can't deny that the word-of-mouth promotion can't be effective if the perception of innovation in quality is not getting an important place in the marketing management of tourism industry. If you offer something new, innovative to your customers, the word-of-mouth promoters become instrumental and the process of persuasion keeps on moving.

Personal Selling: An important component of promotion mix, the personal selling is based on the personal skill of an individual. The oral representation in conversation bears the efficacy of transforming the motivation into persuasion. Hence, we find persuasion the main thing in the modern marketing management. A businessman persuades investors to invest, persuades the suppliers to supply the raw materials on reasonable terms and conditions and persuades markets to promote or patronise their products. Of course, no other tools of promotion are so much impact-generating as the personal selling. It is highly distinctive form of promoting sale with the help of two-way communication. The goods or services are half sold if their properties are well told. This art of telling-and-selling is the personal selling. Every business organisation – be it pharmaceutical, electronics, insurance, banking, travel and tourism, hotel – all of them need services of professionally-sound, personally-committed sales personnel having an in-built creativity, innovation and imagination. Persuasion through motivation is the main thing either for profit generation or for customers' or users' satisfaction.

The travel and hotel business depend considerably on the personal selling. The development of travel and tourism has been possible due to well educated and trained sales personnel. The development of tourism business has been influenced by the services rendered by the travel agents and travel guides since they work as information carrier.[20] The feedback help management in framing and finalising the development plans. Thus, we find personal selling a distinct form of promotion which involves social behaviour. The social characteristics of personal selling makes it an activity which is found difficult to manage. Foster says, personal selling is the personal presentation of a tangible product or intangible services or ideas to the personal customers.[21] The products, prices and markets in particular determine the form or nature of personal selling. As for example, for holidays, the personal selling takes place at the travel agents and at the sales office which a tour operator may have. For business travel accounts, the personal selling is required to influence the decision of travellers or the tourists. In the process, we find involvement of a number of personnel from the head of any travel department to the executives or secretaries. As for example, for important trips or conferences and exhibitions, the director of a firm may also be sold.

It is important to mention that in the tourism industry, the personnel who attend tourists form an essential ingredient of the product, such as the sales personnel are found responsible for dealing with the customers behind the counter, the resort representatives cater to the needs of tourists when they reach to the destination or other staff with whom the tourists come in contact, e.g., hotel waiters, barstaff, porters, hotel cleaners, coach drivers or airline cabin crew.[22] All of them play a vital role in ensuring that the tourism products satisfy the tourists. Services don't mean servility. The phrase – the customer is always right, applies specifically to the tourism industry. The sales personnel are required to be friendly in behaviour and careful in expression. To put it in another way, the travel product is indivisible from the personnel who deliver the services. No reduction in price would compensate for impolite and indecent travel guide, a solvent waiter and a surly or a haughty coach driver. These facts are a mute testimony to this proposition that the travel business is linked with the performance and behaviour of sales personnel or travel staff.

If they act well; if they perform well; if they behave well and if they don't generate a gap between quality-promised and the quality-offered, the tourism business would thrive.

Dealing with clients is found important to the sales personnel that requires a fair synchronisation of personal and social skill or interpersonal skill. Regarding the personal skill, it is right to mention that the tourism personnel are supposed to project a positive opinion regarding the tourist organisations *vis-a-vis* the destination. The travel clerks, hotel receptionists or resort representatives confronting with the tourists would of course form a negative impression which would affect future marketing adversely. The client relationship thus occupies a place of outstanding significance. We also find some of the tourist organisations imposing strict rules related to appearance and grooming. Though some of us don't find it judicious to impose restrictions on our rights of selecting hairstyle, dresses, cosmetics but here it is essential that the tourist personnel must learn to adjust the constraints under the services conditions. This is meant conforming to the dress-style and grooming that the employers need. As for example, the airlines make available uniform for their staff and issue guidelines in the acceptable level of grooming standards. Though the USA Continental Airlines were judged to have acted illegally when they dismissed a female employee with an exemplary professional record for refusing to wear make-up.[23] It is pertinent to mention that the travel staff coming into close contact with the customers must be fastidious about personal hygiene. This draws our attention on regular bath, wash, dental care, restrictions on food which may offend client such as garlic or onions and the use of anti-perspirants. The main thing that we find in the process is personal properties helping the personnel in throwing a positive imprint and making their task of persuasion easier. A fair blending of professional excellence and physical attractions is required to be essential. The sales personnel are supposed to look alert, evince interests in clients, avoid slouching when they walk. Clothes must be clean and well pressed. The hotels, airlines, car rental staff, couriers, resort representatives and travel agents need to assign due weightage to the dresses they use.

In addition, they also need social skill. It is essential that the sales personnel approach customers in a friendly and confident manner. It is meant welcome smile, eye-contact, attractiveness and a willingness to listen. Above all, our attitudes of mind towards services must change. The use of derisive terms such as punters is symptomatic forms a negative attitude to services which is indefensible. We are required to learn from Italy, Spain where the quality of service is high. We are supposed to be attentive to the needs and requirements of our users and to try our best to fulfil the same. We talk about the instrumentality of personnal selling in the process of promoting the tourism business and this makes it essential that our personnel working at different stages in different capacities know in depth about the behavioural management *vis-a-vis* the empathy. They on the basis of their service profile and with the help of behavioural profile can be successful in getting the business. The social skill focuses on understanding the customers, listening to them patiently, countering their pains and sorrows by using soft words and smiling facial expressions so that the users feel satisfied, form a positive opinion regarding destination and tourist organisations and prefer to visit the place frequently.

Telemarketing: In an age of communication superhighway, the existence of an organisation is substantially influenced by the use of sophisticated communication technologies in the process of making decisions. Of late, we find significant developments in the field of satellite communication which has made the process more sophisticated. The telephonic instruments of new generation are found helping the system sizeably. It is against this background that we talk about marketing with the help of telephonic services. It is pertinent to mention that latest developments in the field of telecast media and expansion in its network has paved avenues for the use of televisions in the process of selling. We are aware of the fact that telemarketing is a method of selling in which we find a professionally sound telemarketer instrumental in expanding the business. The quality of technology and the communicative ability of telemarketers determine the magnitude of success of this component of the promotion mix. We can't deny that the instrumentality of TV improves the quality of performance. In the tourism industry, we find a big scope for the use of telemarketing. The travel agents, offices of airways, receptionists, secretaries can't work efficiently if the telephonic services are not up to the mark. This makes a strong advocacy in favour of recruiting a person considered to be professionally-sound, personally-committed and having high communicative ability to receive, present and impress. A number of queries are required to be answered. The informations related to booking, confirmation, cancellation are required to be transmitted. The confusions and misunderstanding regarding the image problem are to be removed. The positive points regarding the destination or the peripheral services are required to be transmitted. And these functional responsibilities require due support of telemarketers. It is in this context that we find almost all the tourist organisations recruiting telemarketers for that very purpose.

Of late, we find management of personnel a difficult task. In an age of telemarketing, we find scope for minimising the number of personnel since with the help of an efficient telemarketer, it is possible to energise the process of selling. The travel agents, tour operators, transport operators, hotels find it convenient to expand their business by developing telephonic contacts which help them in transmitting the required information and removing the confusions and misunderstanding obstructing the flow of business expansion. To be more specific in the Indian context where we find tremendous opportunities for the development of tourism industry, it is pertinent that the allied industries fuelling the tourism industry seek the cooperation of telemarketers who would help them substantially. For making the process of telemarketing productive, it is essential that sophisticated instruments and well trained telemarketers are available. The telemarketers need patience because in the marketing process, they may expect a number of turning points where dialogues may generate tension. How to diffuse the tension? How to inform and sense the users? How to answer to their questions? How to explain their queries? How to remove their confusion and misunderstanding? If the telemarketers are in a position to answer to these questions satisfactorily, the business would come and this one with the minimum possible investment on personnel and process of selling.

The aforesaid facts make it clear that telemarketing has been found occupying an important place in the modern marketing management and we find justifications for the use of telemarketing even by the tourist organisations.

The Price Mix

In the tourism industry, the pricing decisions are found critical and challenging since it is a multi-segment industry. When a tourist proposes to visit a particular place, the total cost on his/her travelling includes the expenses incurred on transportation, accommodation, communication or so. Thus, the entrance fee charged at the destination becomes insignificant when we talk about the pricing decisions. We accept the fact that a change in the hotel tariffs, air fare structure or transportation cost influence the price structure *vis-a-vis* the travelling decisions. The stimulation of demand makes it essential that pricing strategy simplifies the process of motivation. This necessitates to use pricing as a motivational tool.

No marketing without pricing. The whole process of making a sound pricing decision, of course, is a play of manipulation. If we succeed in manipulating the variables influencing the pricing decisions, the success at the marketplace can't be denied. There is a no doubt in it that the controllable variables like product, distribution and promotion are well within the reach of the marketers but so far as the uncontrollable variables are concerned, they need more care and precaution. Here, we find an acid test of their excellence. The pricing decisions are made to fit the changing competitive conditions encountered by specific products and we call them pricing strategies. It is essential that the pricing decisions are consistent with the desired image. Pricing decisions must be wise since the unwise and irrational pricing decisions make the ways for image problem. Thus, it is right to mention that like other organisations, the tourist organisations are also required to make pricing decisions carefully.

While adopting the pricing strategy, the tourist professionals need to optimise the distribution and promotion costs. If we spend more on travel agents, tour operators, tourist guides, personal selling, advertising, sales promotion; the high pricing strategy remains the only solution. This would, of course, be a barrier to motivate the general tourists preferring economy in travelling. The high spending tourists are not sensitive to price but the general tourists are found price-sensitive. In addition, we also need to think in favour of social tourism which makes it essential that the pricing decisions are liberal to the economic class of the society. The pricing decisions also make it significant that we assign due weightage to package tour. The leading tourist generating countries of the world have been found charging more, but the mix of their package tour is so rich that the potential tourists are motivated. The tourist professionals bear the responsibility of identifying the target market and formulating a package accordingly. They are required to consider whether to trade-up market (high-priced packages for a limited elite of the potential tourists) or trade-down market (low-priced packages for the mass market). Thus, a fair blending of trade-up market and trade-down market is essential to make the tourism business profitable. This is possible when the tourist professionals have world-class excellence and they know how to establish a balance between the two so that select market and mass market both of them are tapped optimally. The marketers in addition to other aspects are also supposed to identify the value-sensitive and price-sensitive tourists. This would simplify their task of making the services commercially viable *vis-a-vis* mass market-oriented.

The tourist organisations need high sales volume for some reason or other. It is pertinent that they know about the potentials of an organisation supporting the tourism services. There are a number of questions to be answered suitably to avoid a crisis.

- Can it satisfy the demand that would be generated?
- Has it sufficient forward reservation of rooms and transport seats?
- Should prices be lowered when demand exceeds supply?
- Are tourists sensitive to price or to value?
- Are they politically associated?
- What is the price elasticity of demand?

The marketers in addition to other aspects have to be careful regarding the price and value sensitivity of the tourists. If they are price-sensitive, an increase in the price structure would gear back the demand position and would bring down the tourists' influx. This makes it essential that the tourist organisations follow a particular policy on the basis of sensitivity rate, lifestyle and behaviour pattern. Besides, we also find some of the tourists reacting to frequent changes in price. This makes a strong advocacy in favour of price stability. The tourist organisations while making the pricing decisions need to study the different categories of tourists, e.g., high spending tourists and the low spending tourists, foreign tourists and domestic tourists, adventure tourists and cultural tourists, village tourists and educational tourists. This would help them in adopting a rational pricing policy.

In the pricing decisions, the product or the service mix of the tourist organisations is found important. This makes it essential that the tourist organisations set prices in line with the quality of services to be made available to the customers. The market may view the cheaper product with suspicion and therefore an abnormal cut in the structure can't be advisable. We find a majority of the tourism products of homogeneous nature. A low-priced holiday diverts holiday makers from other countries. If the holiday benefits are promoted considerably, a change in the trend can't be denied. In the tourism product, we find that each product in the range faces entirely different market conditions, such as an airline may experience significant competition both in price and service on one route.

In view of the above, it is right to mention that the pricing decisions are influenced by the internal and external factors. The tourist professionals are supposed to watch the emerging trends in both the market conditions. To be more specific, the external factors complicate the task of professionals since they don't have any control on the external factors like governmental regulations, law and order situations, behavioural profile of the tourists, emerging trends in economic depression, code of practices and ethical considerations.

The tourist professionals while making the pricing decisions are required to think in favour of discounting price. The different forms of discount, such as discounting for cash payment, price reduction for quality, trade discounts, trade allowances, seasonal discount, distressed stock and similar discount tactics are the options. But while offering discount, it is not to be forgotten that it is also to create the image problem since some of the value-sensitive tourists may doubt your quality. The motive while setting the pricing structure is to increase the business.

The Place Mix

Offering of service has a far reaching impact on the organisational prosperity. This draws our attention on the processing of services by the different categories of personnel involved in the process. A sound distribution system is found essential to improve the quality of services or to bridge over the gap between the services-promised and services-offered. The distributors thus occupy a place of outstanding significance. The normal eyes fail in receiving the historical and cultural monuments and the travel guides engaged in the process or even the travel agents clarify the same. In the tourism industry, the distribution problem is concerned with the transmission of information about the services to the concerned users. As and when the bookings are made, the information regarding confirmation and cancellation become essential and a sound distribution system makes it possible. We can't deny the fact that with the use of sophisticated information technologies by almost all the tourist organisations, the task is simplified considerably. The introduction of computers, sales desk terminals and central reservation system have made the task easier. There are a number of factors instrumental in making the distribution process effective or productive. It is pertinent that the tourist professionals are well aware of the variables influencing the functional style of distributors or the intermediaries working as tour operators, transport operators and the travel agents. It is essential to make it clear that the transport operators and tour operators act as wholesaler whereas the travel agents acts as a retailer.

The tourism industry is a multi-segment industry where accommodation, attraction, transportation, and communication are found important. The product of these services include air, sea, road, rail carriers, hotels and other forms of tourist accommodation. In addition, the facilities like catering, amusement, skiing, shopping, etc. add attractions to the product. These services reach to the ultimate users through tour operators and the travel agents. The instrumentality of transport operators, tour operators and travel agents determines the processing of services.

The term chain of distribution denotes the method through which the services reach to the destination. The middlemen are the link and if the link is strong, the producers succeed in raising the influx of tourists. The middlemen are the tour operators and the transport operators who buy services like hotel rooms, seats in the aircrafts, railways, arrange chartered flights and sell the same either to the travel agents (retailers) or even directly to the tourists. The tour operators are also called the producers of a new product. The travel agents buy the services at the request of their clients and provide a convenient network of sales outlets catering to the needs of a local catchment area. In Figure 11.8, we find the distribution channel for the tourism industry which focuses on the different middlemen engaged in the process of distributing the services. The services are generated by both the public as well as the private sector. The services are supposed to be standardised where the middlemen make it sure that the promised services would be made available to the users without making any distortion. Of course, we find possibilities of distortion at different points by the different service generating organisations but all of them need to bridge over the gap.

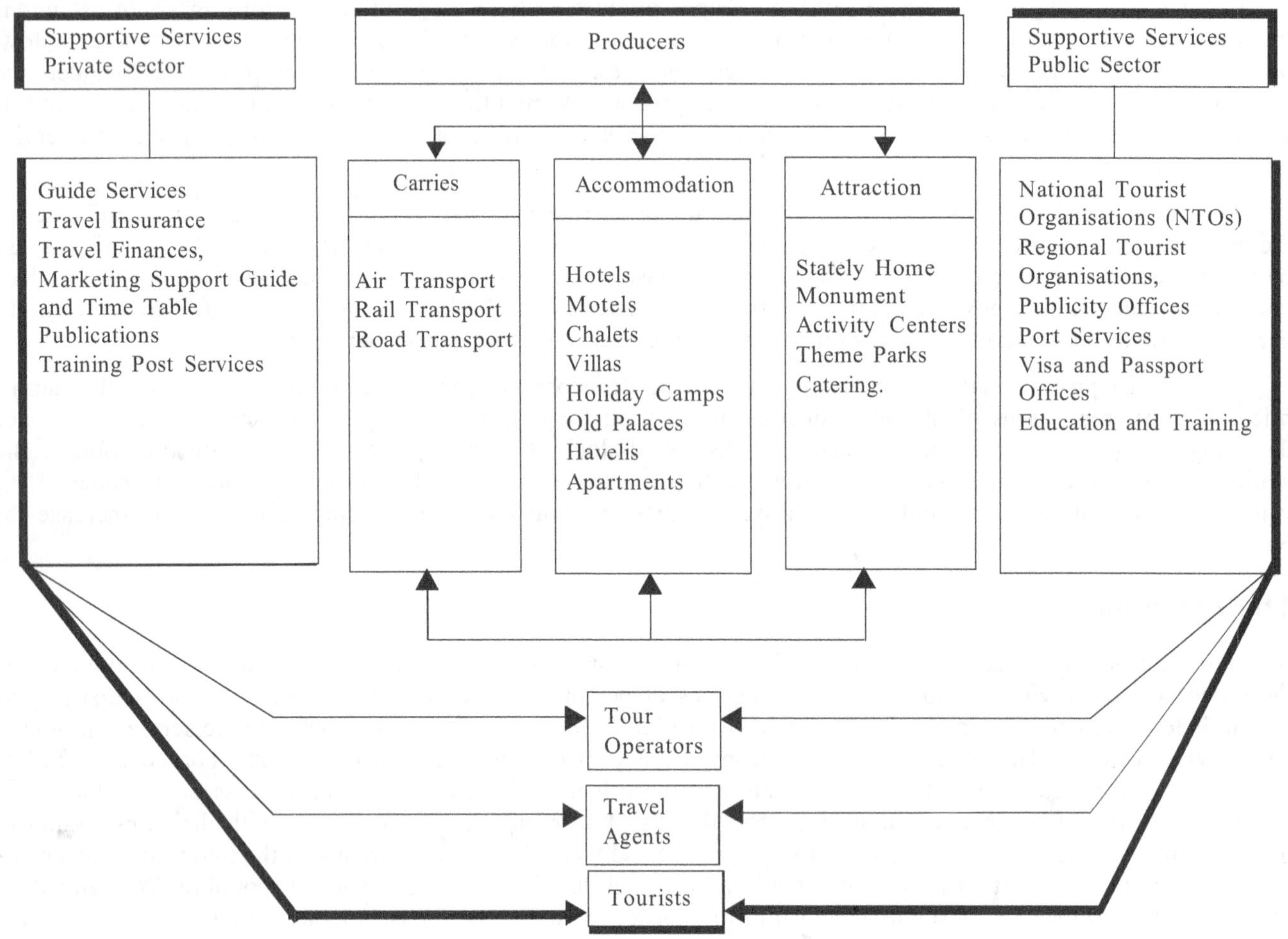

Fig. 11.8: Tourism Industry and the Channel of Distribution

One-stage System: The one-tier or one-stage system focuses on the direct selling of services by the providers to the ultimate users, such as the airlines selling directly to users through its own offices and reservation counters. We find a number of advantages of this system, since the providers can maintain the quality. The system is opposed by a number of experts due to high cost of operation. The stimulation of demand requires professional excellence and the travel agents are supposed to have world-class excellence to manage things to the expectations of users.

Two-stage System: In the two-tier system or two-stage system, we find involvement of middlemen between the providers and users, i.e., Travel Agent. The positive effects of the system are that a traveller while receiving professional services can also buy other products like airline ticket, hotel accommodation and transportation facilities. Besides, he/she gets a single bill for all the services. The price of advantage is an additional advantage since a travel agent gets higher prices in the case of group tours, conferences, conventions, etc. In addition, the services cost incurred on travel agent is found very nominal to the users as he/she receives a commission from the principal.

Three-stage System: The three-stage or three-tier system involves two middlemen, a retail travel agent and a wholesaler or a tour operator. An additional advantage of this system is that the wholesaler makes bulk purchases of the products for which he/she is paid adequate discount.

Four-stage System: The four-stage system is similar to the three-stage system but it has an additional middleman. Known as Speciality Chancellor, he is found instrumental in the development of tour packages.

The aforesaid channels of distribution of the tourism services make available the services to the ultimate users and therefore these are the different points where we also expect a distortion in quality. It is against this background that different providers of the services need to be careful while appointing the middlemen.

Tour Operators: A tour operator is one who buys the individual elements in the travel product on his own account and combines them in such a way that he is selling a package of travel, the tour to his clients.[24] In common parlance, he is also referred to as a travel agent. A tour operator bears the responsibility of delivering the services. He creates own packages by buying or reserving necessary supply elements and often retails through travel agents, their own offices and by direct mail via booking form in brochure or by direct enquiries from consumers.[25] He offers a number of packages known as tour programme. They are like a wholesaler. Some of us also call tour operators as producers of a new product but it is more appropriate to describe them as middlemen.

Travel Agent: The travel industry is found to be an uncoordinated people trying to achieve a coordinated result. A travel agent is one who acts on behalf of a principal, i.e., the original provider of the tourism services, such as hotel company, airline, tour operator or a shipping company. A travel agency is also called a manufacturer of tourist product, i.e., an inclusive package tour. Of late, a majority of the travel agents conduct regular package tour to set itineraries with a standard of services. Besides they design package tours to suit the needs of a group. Travel agents form the retail sector of the distribution chain.

In the channel decisions, the marketing institutions play a decisive role. The tourist organisations, tour operators, travel agencies are the main institutions helping the making of productive distribution decisions. We agree with this view that product innovation can't be the lone solution for demand penetration since innovation in the distribution process plays an important role. To be more specific in the tourism industry, the middlemen play a commanding role because the products are of perishable nature. This draws our attention on the characteristics of the product to determine the length of the channel. The market factors also occupy a place of importance in the distribution process. From the standpoint of producers, it is pertinent that we design a profitable channel and assign due weightage to cost and satisfaction. The channel involving the minimum possible costs but securing high level of satisfaction to the tourists may be effective. To put it in another way, the channel can't concentrate only on the profitability element. The aforesaid facts make it clear that the tourist organisations are required to make the channel decisions proactive so that the tourists get an opportunity to avail the promised services without any distortion. If the middlemen act well, perform well and behave well; we expect a considerable increase in business. The hotels, airlines can't work efficiently failing the cooperation of tour operators and travel agents.

The Process

The tourism services being an amalgam of different industries need due attention of all the concerned industries for right and time-honoured processing. The services reach to the ultimate users through the channels working as transport operators, tour operators and travel agents and guides. The transport operators, tour operators work as wholesaler whereas the travel agents work as retailer. Even the services of travel agents depend on transportation and accommodation and therefore, for processing, it is imperative that all the concerned agencies and people working thereon make it sure that the promised quality of services reach to the tourists on time. The front-line staff play an important role in the entire process. The travel agents and the front-line staff working there fail in offering the promised services if the rail transportation, road transportation and civil aviation services do not extend due co-operation. Since a number of information and communication technology are used by them, it is pertinent that they get due support of the networking so that information related to booking and cancellation reach to the tourists on time. We find time management playing an important role in the service delivery and service recovery processes. The complaints of tourists need a time-honoured redressal. In the entire process, we find travel agents playing a decisive role. The flow of services rests on the flow of information and communication technology and the people using the same. The operating systems adopted by the travel agents are the result of involvement of technology. The service delivery process considerably depends on the people working as front-line staff communicating directly with the tourists who may be face-to-face or online. The stages for service delivery are not so much complex in the tourism industry if we find information networking maintaining the flow.

The above-mentioned facts make it clear that the processing of services in the tourism industry becomes complex due to the fact that the services are not related to a particular organisation or agency. The failures at one stage obstruct the service delivery process even if we find other concerned organisations or agencies working satisfactorily. In a true sense, we find travel agents becoming a silent spectator when the transportation and accommodation sectors witness something wrong in their flow. Integrating all or combining all depend on a number of factors. The professionals serving the offices of travel agents need excellence in the integration process. In case of any dislocation, the information to the concerned tourists requires to be transmitted on time. They need a networking from the different agencies so that in case of service gap, the stand-by services are used.

Right and time-honoured processing thus determine the magnitude of satisfaction of tourists. Because we find word-of-mouth communication considerably influencing the tourism industry, it is imperative that all possibilities for the creation of image problem are ruled out.

Physical Evidence and Attractions

The professionals serving tourist organisations also need to practise this submix of marketing which focuses on a number of factors helping attractive tangibilisation of the inherent properties. The most sensitive point for the tourism industry is the office of travel agents from where the services reach to the tourists. The interior decoration, furnishing, display of information and communication technology, signposts, ventilation, lighting, leaflets, posters, business cards need right tangibilisation. Since we find tourists availing the services of hotel, it is pertinent that the outstanding properties are tangibilised even there. The hotel industry gets an opportunity for tangibilisation which is virtually gifted by the tourism industry. Like this, the railways and road transport organisations also need to tangibilise their properties throwing a positive impact on the behavioural profile of users. While tangibilising, the provisions related to service recovery also need due attention. As and when we find intangibility making the task of professionals much more difficult, they with the help of tangibilisation may be successful in projecting their image. In the tourism business image, plays an important role.

In this submix, the professionals also need to think about the dresses of employees. They need to look smart, neat and clean and wear uniform in the face of uniform code. The personal care services thus help professionals in adding additional attractions to the services they offer. The physique of employees working in the offices of travel agents or acting as travel guides or working in the hotels and airlines become significant in the very context. They need etiquette management and aesthetic sense.

The servicescapes if professionally-managed become instrumental in generating the service fragrance. The professionals cannot undermine the outstanding role of service ambience in all the three important sectors, such as hotel, transport and tourist. The high profile tourists are found very sensitive to aesthetic management. Managing offices and other sensitive points with the motto of projecting aesthetic sense to be helpful in generating services fragrance cannot be undermined. Service culture makes it essential that you have assigned top priority to the creation of service ambience.

In addition to service delivery, we also find it point for service recovery where tourists either online or face-to-face lodge complaints and expect quick and decent disposal. Cases of complaints need redressal on a priority basis. The potential tourists or others witness all the activities very minutely. If your tangibilisation is attractive, the process of image projection is found switched on. You need to seal avenues irritating the tourists or others.

THE PEOPLE

We can't deny the fact that sophisticated technologies have been successful in accelerating the pace of development. We also agree with this view that new generation of information technologies have simplified the task of decision-makers. At the same time, we have also to accept the fact that the sophisticated technologies can't deliver goods to the development process if the employees operating and maintaining these technologies are not of world-class. Whatever the inventions and innovations we find today are the result of our dedication, perfection and commitment. These facts make it clear that technologies need due support of human resources who invent, innovate and develop technologies. It is against this background that the marketing experts have been found making strong advocacy in favour of treating people as an independent submix of the marketing mix.

Like other industries, the tourism industry depends substantially on the management of human resources. We are well aware of the fact that tourism industry is an amalgam of different industries and therefore all the supporting industries need to assign due weightage to the management of people who bear the responsibility of accelerating the productivity of technologies used in the process. The tourism industry can't work efficiently if the travel agents, tour operators and travel guides lack world-class professional excellence. Of course, the offices of travel agents depend fantastically upon the new generation of computers and internet services but after all we find employees, staff contributing significantly to the process. The travel guides need professional excellence since the projection of a positive image regarding destination in particular requires their due co-operation, failing which even the world-class services offered by the travel agents are found meaningless. The tour operators also need to manage human resources efficiently.

In the management of people, the related organisations are required to think in favour of developing an ongoing training programme so that we find a close relation between the development of technologies and the quality of personnel who are supposed to operate and maintain the same. We find strong justifications for an overriding priority to this submix of the marketing mix. We focus here on the credentials they need to fulfil the expectations of customers. We also go through the developments making the environmental conditions conducive and focus on the incentives to them for energising the process of performance orientation. In addition, we make an anatomy of employee orientation that requires due weightage to efficiency generation, value orientation and perfection.

The travel agents are the focal points around which all the activities of the tourism industry cluster. The airways, the hotels, the roadways and others can't think of efficiency generation if they don't get enormous cooperation of travel agents. Of course, the tourism business can't thrive if the offices of the travel agents are not extending to all the allied industries their intensive cooperation. This gravitates our attention on the management of travel agents and the instrumentality of the staff managing the working of their offices.

Provisions take the shape of promises. Whatever the tourist organisations provide for are transformed into promises. It is essential that promised services are made available to the ultimate users without making any distortion.

Travel Agents: Travel agents form the retail sector of the distribution chain, buying travel services at the request of their clients and providing a convenient network of sales outlets which cater to the needs of the local catchment area. Normally, they don't charge any fee from the clients since they get commission from the principal for each sale they negotiate. In few cases, we also find them acting as wholesaler and in that case, he/she is supposed to be the specialist in putting together tour offerings marketed to the public through a network of retail agents or the airlines. As and when they act as a retailer, we find a direct deal with the clients/customers. He represents or acts as an agent for airlines, steamships, railways, hotels, car rental firms or so. He also designs a package tour for customers by assembling in pre-paid and pre-arranged packages. Thus, the functional responsibilities before the travel agents make it clear that they are required to be professionally-sound to manage their business in a right fashion. Since they make available to the tourists, the necessary information, it is pertinent that information management of the offices of travel agency is promoted by technologies and efficient, submissive, personally-committed employees perform the task. The receptionists working there, the computer professionals at the working desk, the doorman entertaining the guests or clients are required to work efficiently. The computers and super-computers, the internet and intranet, the fax and e-mail would hardly serve the guests if employees operating and maintaining them are not sound. This makes it clear that the travel agents bear the responsibility of managing technologies and managing the personnel who operate these technologies.

In view of the above, it is essential that the travel agents have a team of dedicated and personally-committed employees. We can't deny the fact that performance orientation is the main thing for improving the productivity of technologies used in the offices of the travel agents. The employees or the computer professionals need world-class excellence and the receptionists, secretaries need to be submissive. The behavioural profile of employees serving the offices of travel agents need a transcendental priority. They need to know about empathy. They need to be soft and submissive. They need to assign due weightage to physical attractions. This draws our attention on the personal care management of the employees serving the travel agents. They are supposed to be neat and clean, well-dressed and to wear the make-up projecting a cultural bias. They need to have high communicative ability and in a position to speak English, Hindi or other regional languages, specially of the catchment area and this one with a high frequency. They are supposed to be decent in behaviour. They are required to be friendly. These attributes play an incremental role in improving the quality of services of the travel agents.

On the one hand, the travel agents need to be careful while recruiting the personnel and on the other hand, they also need more care and precaution while developing an ongoing training programme. We find a number of professional institutes meant for that very purpose and in addition, a time-to-time refresher and capsule courses are also to be organised to enrich their credentials. Thus, this is the first task in the context of managing people for the tourism industry. Technology-driven offices require due cooperation of professionally-sound and personally-committed employees.

Travel Guides: There are a number of points where we need the services of tourist guides. The places having historic importance, cultural bias can't be perceived by ordinary persons in a right fashion unless quality tourist guides narrate. This makes it essential that in the tourism industry, the tourist organisations assign due weightage to the management of travel guides. In the distribution of tourism products, we can't underestimate the services of travel guides. The success rate of travel agency is sizeably influenced by the instrumentality of travel guides. If they act and behave well, the tourists are motivated and the travel business gains the momentum. If they misbehave with the tourists even the quality services of agency carry no meaning. It is against this background that while managing people for the tourism industry, we need to assign due weightage to the development of the potentials of guides. The modern marketing is found full of complications and uniqueness. The tourists are sophisticated, the tourist sites are sophisticated, they have high expectations and these things would be proved to be unproductive, if the tourist guides are inefficient. This makes a strong advocacy in favour of making available to the industry quality tourist guides.

- Patience is considered to be the most important aspect for a successful travel guide. They should have the capacity to adjust with the adverse conditions. If they are agitated, the tourists can't get satisfaction even if the destination is attractive.
- Sense of humour is another consideration for a successful travel guide. It is sense of humour that activates the process of motivation. If the travel guides are humorous, the tourists would not feel monotony. This would simplify the task of making the tour memorable.
- Tact is found essential for transforming the occasional tourists into the habitual tourists. If he/she is tactful, the tourists would be found satisfied. This draws our attention on the art of managing the odds.
- Knowledge draws our attention on the information bank of travel guides. He/she should have an in-depth information regarding destination and its connecting services. The historical monuments, modern paintings, cultural heritages are found insignificant to the general tourists unless the travel guides narrate to them facts and realities in the plain words.
- Language focuses our attention on the communicative ability of the travel guides. He/she should be competent enough to speak different languages frequently. This is essential to bridge over the communication gap. In this context, we need to divert our attention on body language. It is not to be forgotten that the travel guides in a number of cases can add attractions to their excellence, if they are familiar with the body language of the concerned tourists.
- Leadership is an essential criterion for an ideal travel guide. He/she should have the quality of leading a team of tourists so that whatever deliberations are made throw a positive impact on the behavioural profile of the tourists.
- Personal commitment is found essential to improve the quality of a travel guide. This gravitates our attention on performance orientation.

These attributes make an individual, an ideal travel guide and the professional institutes while developing travel guides need to assign due weightage to the aforesaid properties.

TOURISM MARKETING IN INDIAN PERSPECTIVE

Of late, tourism has emerged as an important sector of the economy. It is found to be an economic bonanza which contributes substantially to the development process. If the managerial decisions are creative, innovative and sensitive, we expect a lot from the tourism industry. The rate of success in the tourism industry is sizeably influenced by the instrumentality of supporting industries, such as hotel, transportation, communication, banking or so. The developed countries and to be more specific, the leading tourist generating countries of the world such as USA, UK, Germany, France, Australia, Spain, Singapore, Cyprus have assigned due weightage to the principles of modern marketing in managing the tourism industry. In the Indian perspective, we find tourism industry at the bottom of our development agenda which has been standing as a barrier while energising the process of qualitative or quantitative improvements. It is against this background that we need a basic change in the national development policy for tourism.

Of course, it was in the early 1950s that the Government of India decided to promote tourism industry but it had no clear objectives in terms of marketing. At the initial stage, the image problem was found at its peak and even till now we find it an important constraint. The government further activated efforts and new offices were opened in 1964. The beginning of the decade 1970s opened new vistas for the development of marketing concept in the tourism industry. The Pacific Visitor Survey conducted by PATA in 1967 revealed that it was only due to image problem that the tourism industry in India has not been successful in raising its contribution to the development of economy *vis-a-vis* generation of foreign exchange. The beginning of the decade 1980s paved avenues for the development of tourism industry. The management experts felt that if the contribution to the world tourism is to be increased, we have no option but to market the tourism services professionally. This necessitated launching of a National Image Building and Marketing Plan in key markets by pooling resources of the various public and private agencies instead of independent and disjointed efforts presently undertaken by these organisations to project a fair image.

The exploration of the new tourist generating markets particularly in the Middle-East, South-East and East Indian countries having a broad spectrum of cultural affinity with India and encouragement of ethnic tourism by launching programme of Discover Your Roots and vigorous marketing of conferences and conventions traffic could be possible during 1980s. Sustained efforts were needed to promote Buddhist pilgrimage tourism for which there is a great potential. Aggressive marketing was required to be taken up in the existing tourist generating markets abroad as well as to explore new markets. It was necessary to reorient the marketing projects and rationalise the locations of the tourist offices abroad keeping in view the market conditions and potentials. In order to cater to the needs of professionally-sound manpower for tourism marketing, the Indian Institute of Tourism and Travel Management was developed as a model institute.

In view of the above, it is right to mention that diversification of tourism from the traditional sightseeing to the more rapidly growing holiday tourism market within the framework of the country's milieu is need of the hour. The policy planners, the tourist organisations, the domestic and global agencies are required to realise gravity of the situation to capitalise on the opportunities optimally. This requires a basic change in the product development strategy *vis-a-vis* the innovative promotional efforts to project a positive image.

The beginning of the decade 1990s opened new areas for the development of tourism in the Indian perspective. This necessitated development of infrastructural facilities like transportation, communication, accommodation or so. In addition, this also required use of sophisticated information technologies by the tourist generating organisations so as to improve the quality of services at different points. In addition to the planning and development of tourism products, the promotional strategies thus require due attention of professionals. The creativity in messages, campaigns and appeals which probably could not get due treatment earlier is required to be made possible. No plans, policies, strategies and decisions are expected to be productive or proactive unless we assign due weightage to the behavioural profile of users. We can't deny the fact that till now the tourist organisations have devalued the instrumentality of behavioural studies and therefore we are supposed to do it on a priority basis. The emerging trends in the business environment make it essential that world-class professional excellence is to the industry without which all our efforts are to be ineffective. To be more specific when some of the fictions of today profess the emergence of evolutionary form of travel, such as monorails operated by magnetism and floating on a cushion air, or travel in vacuum tubes in which a vehicle will travel at a speed of 800 kms per hour, it is quite natural that the level of expectations of users keep on moving.

The thrust areas are the following:

- Making tourism industry a unifying force, instrumental in fostering better understanding through travel.
- Helping to preserve, retain and enrich our cultural heritages.
- Bringing socio-economic benefits to the community and the state, specially in terms of expanding the employment opportunities, generation of profits, tax generation, foreign exchange generation or so.
- Giving a direction and an opportunity to the youths of the country both through domestic and world tourism to perceive hopes and aspirations of others in a right fashion.
- Offering opportunities to the new generation in taking up the activities helpful in image building and strengthening the national image.
- Innovating the promotional measures and assigning due weightage to aggressive promotion to project a positive image.

- Development of people by advancing education and training facilities. Enriching their professional excellence by undertaking an ongoing training programme.
- Motivating the private sector to develop the superstructure.
- An overriding priority to adventure tourism, village or rural tourism, beach tourism, heritage tourism or so.
- Promoting the use of sophisticated information technologies to improve the quality of services.
- Enriching peripheral services to add additional attractions.

Despite a number of steps taken by the government policy makers, the contribution of India to the world tourism has not crossed the level of 0.50 per cent and this speaks of our lapses in the formulation and implementation of strategies. The New Tourism Policy[26] focuses on government-led drives, supported by the private sector and oriented towards community welfare. The government bears the responsibility of framing regulations to control unfair practices and generating the supporting infrastructural facilities. The strategic areas to activate the process of development are:

- **Positioning tourism as a national priority:** This makes it essential that government policy makers assign due weightage to the infrastructural constraints and make available to the tourists full protection. The District Administration comes forward and the media promote tourism so that masses come to realise that they are safe. World tourists need special treatment.
- **Enhancing India's competitiveness as a tourist destination:** This makes it essential that the tourist organisations *vis-a-vis* the organisations making available superstructure facilities focus on two-pronged measures, viz., first, improving quality and second, making the process cost-effective.
- **Improving and expanding product development:** This draws our attention on qualitative-cum-quantitative transformation in the multi-faceted services to be offered to the tourists. We are aware of the fact that tourism industry is an amalgam of different industries and therefore all of them need to strengthen the realisation that improving the demand position requires qualitative transformation whereas increasing the supply position requires quantitative transformation. Like other industries, the tourism industry cannot think of increasing the product, indeed they can think of adjusting and regulating the demand side which brings an increase in the supply side.
- **Creation of world-class infrastructure:** The development of tourism industry rests on the availability of quality infrastructural facilities. It is to be made sure that the quality of services in the hotels, buses, aircrafts, rails, sheep cruises are of world-class. The communication and information networks are available to them without any obstruction. The power and water services are uninterrupted. The entertainment devices are in tune with their taste and temperament.
- **Effective Marketing:** It is not only significant that we concentrate on improving the quality of our services. It is equally important that we market the services with help of world-class marketing professionals. They need to develop their awareness of the changing needs and requirements and the lifestyles of different segments and further making it sure that their expectations are fulfilled. This helps an increase in the number of satisfied group of tourists.

SUMMARY

You have gone through different components of tourism marketing. After reading this chapter, be sure that the following facts are well versed.

Tourism — The Concept: By tourism, our emphasis is on temporary and short-term movement of people. It is a composite industry consisting of various segments.

Tourism Marketing — The Concept: We consider tourism marketing a process of creating a product or providing a service. It is a managerial process to promote the business of tourism.

Users of Tourism Services: We find different categories of persons using the services of tourism industry. They are called users of the services. They are also known as tourists.

Behavioural Profile of Users: The needs and requirements, the attitudes, the lifestyles, the expectations are the different components of behavioural profile.

Typology of Tourism: The different types of tourism are Recreational, Cultural, Adventure/Sports, Health, Convention, Incentive, Domestic, World, Individual, Group, Independent, Inclusive, Social and Mass Tourism.

Product Planning and Development: The formulation of a plan for the tourism services and elimination and inclusion of services to cater to the changing behavioural profile of the users is the product planning and development.

Market Segmentation for Tourism: This focuses our attention on dividing and subdividing the different categories of markets for tourism to study and understand them in a right fashion.

Market Information System for Tourism: For making or innovating the marketing decisions, it is essential that we collect facts and figures or data from different sources and transform them into information. The Marketing Information System for tourism is to manage the data and to transform them into information, manually or with the support of technologies.

Marketing Mix for Tourism: It is the formulation of different submixes for marketing the tourism services. The different submixes are the product mix, the promotion mix, the price mix, the place mix and the people. We also call them ingredients to formulate the marketing mix.

The Product Mix: This draws our attention on the core and peripheral services in the tourism industry. We are aware of the fact that tourism is a multi-segment industry, such as hotel accommodation, transportation, communication are the services extended to the tourist organisations. We call them product mix.

The Promotion Mix: By the promotion mix in the tourism industry, our emphasis is on promoting the tourism business with the help of different constituents of promotion, such as advertisement, publicity, sales promotion, word-of-mouth promotion, personal selling and telemarketing. These components when aggregated take the shape of promotion mix.

The Price Mix: Since tourism is a multi-segment industry, it is natural that expenses incurred on different types of services are included in the price mix. Here, the entry fee charged at the destination is also included in the price.

The Place Mix: This focuses our attention on the process of distributing the services. We are aware of the fact that tour operators, transport operators and the travel agents distribute the services related to tourism. The tour operators and the transport operators are the wholesalers whereas the travel agents are the retailers. The tour operators buy services in bulk from the different supporting organisations and sell them to the travel agents. The travel agents sell the services directly to the tourists. In few cases, we find tour operators even selling directly to the users.

The Process: The tourism services are found related to a number of allied services and therefore right processing makes it essential that the travel agents ensure that the promised quality of services reach to the tourists without any gap in time or in quality. The front-line staff and technology used influence processing.

The Physical Evidence and Attractions: The tangibilisation of outstanding properties is found essential for the projection of image. The professionals need due attention on interiors, furnishing, lighting, ventilation, display of publicity materials and equipments so that the service ambience is found instrumental in generating service fragrance. The dresses and uniform need due attention to add additional attractions in services.

The People: This draws our attention on managing the marketing people working in different capacities. The travel agents, travel guides, front and back line staff need to enrich their knowledge bank. In addition, they need personal and professional touch.

Tourism Marketing in Indian Perspective: In the Indian context, we find tourism industry potentially sound but the existent opportunities have not optimally been capitalised. Our share to world tourism is around 0.50 per cent. This necessitates professional excellence so that we succeed in removing the image problem and motivate domestic as well as the world tourists to be persuaded by the slogan "Incredible India." Our promotional efforts need to be creative and aggressive. Our focus must be on the non-traditional areas such as Sports Tourism/ Adventure Tourism, Rural Tourism, Health Tourism, Convention Tourism and Cultural Tourism. The high spending world tourists prefer and enjoy innovative product.

KEY TERMS

Corporate Culture
Robot Culture
Pilgrimage
Socio-economic Molecule
Community Welfare
Incredible India
Budget Hotel
Image Problem
Recreational Tourism
Cultural Tourism
Sports Tourism
Adventure Tourism
Health Tourism
Rural Tourism
Social Tourism
Mass Tourism
Convention Tourism
Ballooning
Paragliding
White Water Sports
Surfing
Zorbing
White-collar
Blue-collar
Discretionary Income
Behavioural Profile
Environmental Planning
Opinion Leaders
Marketing Information System
Marketing Intelligence System
Heterogeneous Group
Tour Operators
Transport Operators
Travel Agents
Pull Strategy
Specialty Chancellor
Travel Guides
Live-in Culture
Boardrooms
Volatility

Review Questions

1. What do you mean by Tourism? Explain its different types.
2. State and explain the different types of users of tourism services.
3. What do you mean by Tourism Marketing? Focus on the behavioural profile of users of tourism services.
4. Write a note on the planning and development of tourism services in the Indian perspective.
5. Define Market Segmentation. Explain the different bases for segmenting the tourist markets.
6. What do you mean by Marketing Mix? Focus on the different submixes for tourism marketing.
7. Throw light on the extended marketing mixes for tourism.
8. Explain the significance of marketing research for making the marketing decisions for tourism services in India.
9. Discuss the tourism product and the promotional measures for persuading the potential tourists in the Indian context.
10. Explain the importance of personal selling to the development of tourism business in India.
11. Focus on the instrumentality of publicity for promoting the tourism services in India.
12. Focus on the considerations influencing the formulation of a tour package.
13. Discuss the distribution channel for tourism services.
14. Throw light on the instrumentality of travel agents in promoting the tourism business.
15. Explain the factors influencing the pricing decisions in the tourism business.
16. Discuss the non-traditional tourism to be suitable in the Indian context.
17. Write a note on the present problems and future prospects of tourism business in Indian perspective.
18. "The tour operators act as a wholesaler and the travel agents as a retailer." Comment on this statement.
19. "The pricing decisions in the tourism business are found critical as well as challenging." Discuss this statement.

20. Focus on the instrumentality of Marketing Information System for improving the quality of decisions.
21. Explain the role of safety measures in motivating tourists.

Application Exercises

1. As marketing professional, focus on the measures you would prefer to initiate to increase the influx of high spending tourists coming from abroad.
2. Formulate a product mix to motivate the domestic tourists.
3. You have been working as a service marketer and are asked to design a promotion mix for motivating the world tourists. Throw light on the measures you would take to discharge your functional responsibility.
4. As a travel agent, you need to develop your contact with the tour operators and transport operators. Explain the steps you will take for this purpose.
5. Being a professional, you are supposed to minimise the tourism costs by formulating an ideal package. Focus on the factors you would keep in your mind while designing a tour package.
6. As a travel agent, you have to make your office a point of attraction. Explain the efforts you will initiate to make the service ambience attractive.
7. Being a professional, you need to activate the publicity measures for persuading the tourists. Throw light on the steps you will take to get high publicity.
8. You need to recruit different categories of staff for your office. Explain the basics you would like to ensure for them.
9. The worldwide economic depression is throwing a challenge to the tourism industry. As a marketing professional, suggest the measures the government should initiate to increase the number of world tourists.
10. Do you feel that Indian tourism industry has been facing the image problem? Justify your opinion as a service marketer.
11. "Incredible India" — a slogan to motivate tourists has been found effective. Do you agree with this view? Defend your arguments.
12. "I LOVE NEWYORK" — a slogan helped changing the economy of New York. Comment as a professional.
13. As a marketing professional, suggest the different types of non-traditional tourism to be promoted by the government.
14. Do you feel that tourism industry in India has been facing an adverse condition due to bad law and order in some of the sensitive parts of the country? Justify your arguments and explain the role of safety measures for motivating the tourists.

Endnotes

1. Burk Kart A.J. and Medlik S., *Tourism – Past, Present and Future*, Heinemann, London, 1974, p. V.
2. US Study Travel, Quoted from Christopher J. Holloway, "*The Business of Tourism,*" Pitman, London, 1960.
3. Hunziker and Krapf, Quoted from Foster Douglas, *Travel and Tourism Management*, Macmillan, London, 1985.
4. Foster Douglas, *Travel and Tourism Management*, Macmillan, London 1985.
5. International Consultants and Technocrats Pvt. Ltd., National Committee on Tourism (Preface), Ministry of Tourism, Government of India, New Delhi.
6. Erik Cohen, Quoted from John Lea, *Tourism and Development in the Third World*, Rutledge, London 1988.
7. Dictionaries Universal.
8. The League Committee, The Committee of Statistical Expert of the League of Nations in 1937.
9. American Marketing Association, Chicago, 1990, Committee on Definition.
10. Kotler P., *Marketing Management*, PHI, New Delhi, 1990, p. 3.
11. Krippendorf J., *Marketing in Frendenverkehr Bern, 1971*, Quoted from Medlik S., Tourism – Past, Present and Future, 1988, pp.194-95.
12. Butkart A.J. and Medlik S., *op. cit.,* 1988, p. 195.
13. Walters C. Glenn, *Consumer Behaviour*, Homewood III, R.D Irwin, Inc., 1978.
14. Lazer Willlam, *Lifestyle Concepts and Marketing.*

15. World Bank Observation, Tourism Sector Working Pare World Bank, June,1972.
16. Jha S.M., *Services Marketing,* Himalaya Publishing House, Mumbai, First Edition, Chapter 5.
17. Jha S.M., Preface to the book "*Service Marketing*" by Morris L. Mayer.
18. Holloway J.C. and Plant R.V., *Marketing for Tourism*, Pitman, UK, 1992, p. 74.
19. Kelvin V. Brown, How to Make a New Product from an Old Product Management, December, 1976, pp. 26-31.
20. Jha and Singh, *Marketing Management in India Perspective*, Himalaya Publishing House, Mumbai, 1988, p. 544.
21. Foster Douglas, *Travel and Tourism Management*, Macmillan London, 1985, p. 256.
22. Holloway J. Christopher, *op. cit.,* p. 105.
23. *Ibid.*, p. 107.
24. Burk Kart A.J., and Medlik S., *op. cit.*, p. 163.
25. Foster Douglas, p. 258.
26. India – 2008.

☆☆☆

HOTEL MARKETING

Emerging corporate culture and the changing lifestyles have paved avenues for the development of hotel culture. The youths and upcoming youths have an opportunity to earn more and spend more. Corporatisation injects life and strength to the entire process.

Chapter Objectives

Introduction – Hotel: The Concept – Motel: The Concept – Hotel and its Typology – Hotel Marketing: The Concept – Marketing vs. Selling the Hotel Services – Users of Hotel Services – Behavioural Profile of Users – Market Segmentation for Hotel – Marketing Information System for Hotel – Product Planning and Development – Formulating Marketing Mix for Hotel – The Product Mix – The Promotion Mix – The Price Mix – The Place Mix – The Process – Physical Evidence and Attractions – The People – Hotel Marketing in Indian Perspective – Summary – Key Terms – Review Questions – Application Exercises – Endnotes.

Learning Objectives

This chapter aims at studying the different dimensions of Hotel Marketing. The readers come to know the process of formulating a sound marketing mix for the Hotel Services. They develop their awareness of the concept of hotel, its typology, concept of hotel marketing and its applications. The behavioural profile of users and segmentation of markets will help readers in studying the changing needs and requirements of users. With the help of information management, the marketers may be successful in formulating a sound marketing mix for the hotel services. In the process of formulation, the marketers will also come to know the three additional mixes. Besides they would study the emerging trends in the Indian perspective. Making possible an increase in the occupancy ratio and minimising the costs are the important considerations in the Indian perspective, specially when we find worldwide economic depression adversely affecting the hotel industry.

INTRODUCTION

God-fearing philanthropists or crusaders constructed temples, dharmshalas, sarai to the rescue of the devout who travelled on pilgrimages. This practice was followed even by churches, monasteries and cathedrals. Inns and taverns were found well developed till the downfall of Roman Empire by about 500 AD. For several hundred years, the travellers' inns lost to civilisation. Inn-keeping could not flourish because travel was infrequent and trade largely at a standstill. The crusades in Europe which started in 1095 AD lasted for over two hundred years. This provided for elbow rooms for engineering the foundation of a social revolution resulting into the development of trade and business that led to the emergence of a new class, i.e., Middle class. The impact of renaissance was visible firstly in Italy and gradually in several countries of Europe. Inn-keeping, thus, became a remunerative business. The first tavern was opened in USA in 1634. Hotels emerged from tavern. By 1820, hotel became the accepted term to describe a place where people stayed for the night and took their meals on a payment basis. Since then, there have been multi-pronged developments in the socio-economic parlance which has made ways for the emergence of hotel as an industry.

Significant developments in the field of transportation, sophistication in communications, growing importance of sophisticated information technologies in the business world, engineering of a strong foundation for industrialisation and urbanisation, increasing domination of corporate sector on the national and international economies, emerging corporate culture and changing lifestyles paved copious avenues for the development of hotel industry the world over. The officials on deputation, the business magnets on trade promotion mission, the foreign representative on peace mission, the domestic or foreign tourists interested in visiting a place for pleasure or for enriching the knowledge bank, the international events, etc. are some of the important reasons for the development of hotel industry. Restaurants, cafeterias and hotels offer food and lodging services to he/she, person/persons who develop the habit of eating and staying out of home. Modern hotels provide refined services to their guests. The customers or guests are always right. This principle necessitated application of management principles in the hotel industry and the hotel professionals realised the instrumentality of marketing principles in managing the hotel industry.

The growing significance of managerial proficiency in the hotel industry made possible innovation in the marketing decisions. Today, the services are planned, controlled, automated, audited for maintaining and controlling the quality. The concept of total quality management is found getting an important place in the marketing management of hotels. The inclusion of modern amenities and facilities in the hotel services is made possible by the leading hotel chains which has been opening new doors for innovation and competition. It is against this background that the hotel companies, of late, need world-class professional excellence.

The transformation of industrial economy has made possible multi-faceted developments in the business environment. Resulting from which we find migration of rural population to the big towns and metropolises. The newly emerging urban society has been found providing a fillip to the development of modern hotels. Travelling for religious purposes is an established custom and tradition, specially in the Indian society. The pilgrims are found visiting the sacred places. These developments make it clear that we find a conducive environment for the development of almost all categories of hotels.

The emerging positive trends in the tourism industry indicate that hotel industry is like a reservoir from where the foreign exchange flows. This naturally draws our attention on hotel management. In addition, the domestic tourism also indicates a positive sign of development. Thus, the emerging new developments in the socio-economic environment open new vistas for the development of hotel industry. Of late, the organisations engaged in the hotel business are required to conceptualise modern marketing principles. This makes it essential that they formulate a sound marketing mix which makes possible an optimal development of the marketing resources and makes the process of development cost-effective. Like other industries, the hotel industry also needs to explore avenues for innovation, so that a fair blending of core and peripheral services is made possible. It is not to be forgotten that the leading hotel companies of the world have been intensifying research to enrich their peripheral services with the motto of adding additional attractions to their service mix. It is against this background that we find their service mix more flexible in nature. The latest developments in the field of promotion have paved avenues for the introduction of innovative and aggressive promotional measures. The advertising, publicity, sales promotion, word-of-mouth promotion, personal selling and even telemarketing have been found used in the process of promoting the hotel business. The hotel tariff is found drawing due attention of the policy makers. All of them have been found attempting for making the pricing decisions motivational. The front-line staff, receptionists, waiters, housekeepers, sales executives are found responsible for offering the promised services to the guests. The gap between the service-promised and services-offered is required to be bridged over that draws our attention on the management of hotel personnel. The recruitment and training programmes are required to be developed in the face of technological sophistication. The leading hotel companies have been found promoting an ongoing training programme so that the personnel come to know about the use of sophisticated communication technologies. We feel that high performers would serve the purpose that makes a strong advocacy in favour of employee orientation. The decisions regarding incentives need due care. It is high time that we make possible a fair synchronisation of performance orientation and employee orientation. This requires world-class professional excellence.

Optimism paves the ways for development. If we are optimistic, it is natural that we succeed in generating opportunities and are also in a position to capitalise on them optimally. With the beginning of electronic revolution, the contours of development have undergone radical changes. We find corporate culture injecting new life and strength to the behavioural profile of customers which has been found very much instrumental in changing the level of expectations. New segments are found emerging everyday. Women are also found evincing their interests in the professional courses. Kids are found more bold. The population of fifty plus are now found interested in travelling. These developments open new vistas and the hotel companies need world-class professional excellence to identify and tap them to fulfil the expectations of different categories of customers.

The emerging trends in the global economy considerably influenced the strategic decisions for the hotel industry. If we find global economy thriving, the trade and commerce activities sizeably influenced by globalisation open doors for the development and prosperity of hotel industry. Contrary to it, the worldwide economic depression contracts avenues for prosperity. In a true sense, the corporatisation resulted into the development of corporate culture which made ways for the emergence of material culture assigning due weightage to the lifestyles based on western culture. More money in the hands of youths thus injected life and strength to the development of hotel culture. It was against this background that we find development of hotel industry in almost all the countries since the beginning of 1990s.

Presently, we find economic depression throwing a number of challenges and threats before the hotel industry. This is due to the fact that the corporate sector has been forced to regulate its budget to maintain its financial health which has adversely affected the business of hotels not only in India but around the globe. We find business houses in general preferring Budget Hotel or Economic Hotel. This makes it essential that the hotel sector brings a change in its strategy and assigns due weightage to the concept of Budget Hotel. The leading star groups of hotels have been successful in increasing its occupancy ratio. Even while developing budget hotels, they need priority attention on conference hall, wedding hall which would help them in earning more even if the economic depression continues further.

The hotel sector needs also to think about the concept of cottage and apartments preferably in the rural areas. It is significant to mention that high spending tourists coming from the developed countries of the globe prefer to live in cottages equipped with all the amenities and facilities in the star group of hotels. They want peace and prefer to stay for a long duration. Since we find the high earning youths of the corporate sector developing their temptation to the sports tourism or adventure tourism; the cottage or apartments would be comfortable and economic for them. Besides, we also find avenues for the development of Health Tourism and the cottage and apartments or budget hotels would be found comfortable and economic even for that segment. Of course, the policy planners and boardrooms would be required an in depth study of location for developing hotels in tune with the changing market conditions and users' preferences.

Boom and depression move in a cyclic order. Countering both the conditions successfully requires-world-class professional excellence. The marketing professionals managing hotel business need a microscopic study of the changing levels of expectations of users. In an age of techniculture, they can do it with the help of techno-driven information system. Optimism paves the ways for development. And the professionals need to be a sound strategist *vis-à-vis* tactful and optimistic.

HOTEL — THE CONCEPT

At the outset, we go through the concept of hotel. The common law says that hotel is a place where all who conduct, themselves properly and who being able and ready to pay for their entertainment, accommodation and other services including the boarding like a temporary home. It is home away from home where all the modern amenities and facilities are available on a payment basis.

The aforesaid viewpoints regarding the hotel clarify that hotel is a public place where all possible facilities are made available to a person or persons who stay. The facilities like entertainment, food, accommodation, etc.

thus become the core services of a hotel. It is also considered to be a large city house of distinction and a utility product for the tourists.

The American concept regarding the hotel considers it a place for business to gather.[1] Further, it is also considered to be a place where tourists stop, cease to be travellers and become customers.[2] The definition presented by hotel operators to authorities of the National Recovery Administration in Washington is found to be a more comprehensive definition, presented by Stuart Mc Namara. The definition says, primarily and fundamentally, a hotel is an establishment which supplies boarding and lodging not engaged in inter-state commerces or in any intra-state commerce, competitive with or affecting inter-state commerce (or so related that the regulation of one involves the control of other). It is a quasi-domestic institution retaining from its ancient and origin certain traditions and acquiring in its modern development, certain statutory rights and obligations to the public where all persons not qualified by conditions or conduct are prepared to pay for their accommodation, are to be received and furnished with a room or place to sleep or occupy if such accommodations are available with such services and attention as are incident to their use with or without contract as to duration of visit and which conducts within the confines of its physical locations the business of supplying personal services of individuals for profit. Incidental to such fundamental and principal business, the hotel may furnish quarters and facilities for assemblage of people for social business or entertainment purposes and may engage in retaining portion of its premises for shops and businesses whose continuity (i.e., proximity) is deemed appropriate to a hotel.[3]

We can't deny the fact that the definition formulated by Stuart Mc Namara expanded the functional areas for modern hotels. The assemblage of people for social business and entertainment purposes makes it essential that hotels are also furnished with a big conference hall where the maximum possible accommodation is available. We also call it the function room.

MOTEL — THE CONCEPT

Initially, the term motel was meant for local motorists and foreign tourists travelling by road. Basically, motels serve the needs and requirements of these travellers and meeting the demand for transit accommodation. We can also call motel a transit overnight stay. Some of the important services offered by motels are parking, garage facilities, accommodation, restaurant facilities. Motels are found equipped with filling stations, accessories, service of elevator to the automobile entrance restaurants, etc. Motels are found located outside the city, preferably by the side of highways and important road junctions. The accommodation available in a motel is more in the category of a 'chalet facility' which has a dining hall with fixed menu. In USA, the motel accommodation is ranked at par with hotel accommodation.

HOTEL AND ITS TYPOLOGY

Since time immemorable, there have been frequent changes in the concept and perception of hotel. There are a number of hotels offering different types of services. The variation in architectural facilities, the size, the

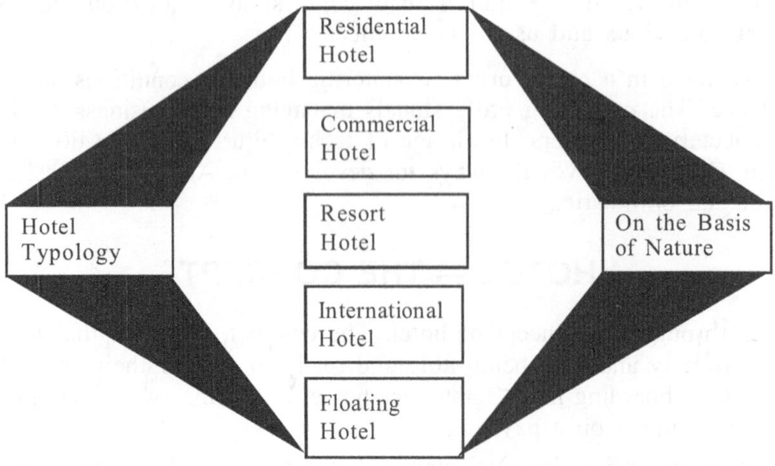

Fig. 12.1: Types of Hotel

facade, the facilities and amenities can't be overlooked. This necessitates a study of its typology. In Figure 12.1, we find different types of hotels offering different types of services to the different categories of users as per their promises.

1. Residential Hotel: The residential hotels work as an apartment house. Often, we call them apartment hotels. The hotels charge rent on monthly, half-yearly, or yearly basis. The hotels are generally found located in big cities and towns where no meals are served to the customers. Initially, the residential hotels were developed in the USA. The services offered in the residential hotels are comparable to an average well-managed home.

2. Commercial Hotel: The commercial hotels are meant for the people who visit a place of trade and commerce or business purposes and therefore these hotels are found located at the commercial or industrial centres. These hotels focus their attention on individual travellers and are generally run by the owners.

3. Resort Hotel: The resort hotels are meant for the holiday makers, tourists and for those who need a change in the atmosphere mainly on health ground. These hotels are found located near the sea, mountain and other areas having an attractive landscape and healthy climatic condition. The tourists visit hotels mainly to relax. The entertainment and recreation facilities like swimming pool, tennis courts, boating, golf course, self-riding and other indoor sports in addition to restaurant and cafeteria, conference room, lounge, shopping arcade, entertainment, etc. become significant in the resort hotels.

4. International Hotel: The international hotels are modern luxurious hotels, classified on the basis of international guidelines. These hotels are placed in various star categories, e.g., five star deluxe, five star, four star, three star, two star, one star. The international hotels are mostly owned by the public companies where a board of directors is constituted for its control. The overall management is found in the hands of senior executives.

5. Floating Hotel: The floating hotels are located on the water surface. The places are sea, river, lake. These hotels provide all the facilities and services made available in a good hotel. In the leading tourist generating countries of the world, we find the practice of using old luxury ships as floating hotels.

Classification on the Basis of Standard and Control

On the basis of standard and control, we classify hotels into two parts, such as approved and unapproved. The approved hotels are found of international standards where the accommodations are made available as per the criteria laid down by the Ministry of Tourism and Civil Aviation. Since they have the stamp of official recognition, the customers trust on them. The unapproved hotels may also offer quality services but they lack official recognition and therefore, the customers or prospects don't believe offering of services-promised without making any distortion. In Figure 12.2, we find classification on the basis of official stamp.

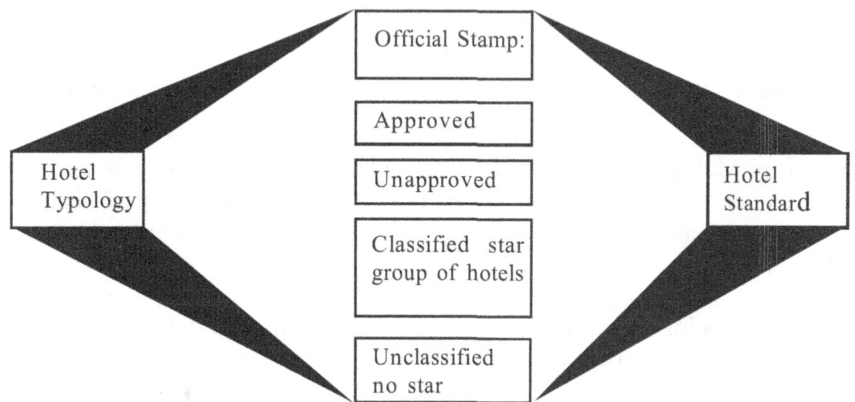

Fig. 12.2: Classification on the Basis of Official Stamp

We find a number of unapproved hotels where world-class services are made available to the tourists and even the foreign tourists prefer to stay in these hotels. Hence, the point of difference between the classified and unclassified hotels or approved or unapproved hotels is the official stamp and recognition. We find realities in the comment, 'the unapproved hotels are clean and those who spend money from their own pockets prefer to stay in the unapproved hotels because economy in operation is given due weightage. It is against this background that in the unapproved hotels, the customers get inexpensive accommodation.'[4] Thus, it is not right to say that the unapproved hotels don't offer quality services. The differences are in the group of users or guests attending the hotels. The foreign tourists in a majority of the cases prefer to stay in the approved hotels whereas the domestic tourists in a majority of the cases prefer to stay in the unapproved hotels.

Classification on the Basis of Star

One more basis for making a classification is the availability of star. The Department of Tourism is found responsible for fixing the criteria for everything from the size of the room to the qualifications of staff.[5] On this basis, there are two important types – classified and unclassified.[6] The star group of hotels are included in the classified group. Hotels having no star are deemed unclassified. The four major classification of American hotels are the commercial, the resort, the residential and the motel.[7]

The aforesaid classification makes it clear that different types of hotels are used by the different categories of users who make decisions on the basis of tariffs charged and services offered by the hotels.

HOTEL MARKETING — THE CONCEPT

The key points of difference in the hotel marketing as against other consumer products are that once customer has spent money in hotels, he/she has nothing substantial to show for his/her money except the bills, as compared with buying a television or a refrigerator. Effective marketing and dynamic selling become significant in the context of hotel marketing because once you have not sold a seat in a restaurant or a room in a hotel, the income is lost and lost forever. A hotel bedroom or a restaurant seat has no shelf-life. Generally, the hoteliers explain their marketing by showing their computer booking service or the advertising campaigns for the coming season. There is no doubt in it that these things are part and parcel of hotel marketing, but only one aspect of the continuous circle of marketing. For marketing hotel services, it is essential that marketing be understood fully by the executive at the top of a hotel group with total commitment on his part to the continuous need to market. A number of experts have gone through the concept of hotel marketing as summarised below:

Gerry Draper:[8]

"Ascertaining consumer needs, tailoring the product as closely as possible to meet those needs, persuading the customers to satisfy his needs and finally ensuring that the product is easily accessible when the customer wishes to purchase it."

The definition of hotel marketing consists of almost all aspects, right from ascertaining customer needs to getting the customers' satisfaction.

Melvyn Greene:[9]

"The ultimate in marketing is to establish brand loyalty so that eventually the consumer does not purchase the goods/services once, but continuously. This is achieved only by the product following the complete process of marketing."

The definition given by Melvyn Greene concentrates on the transformation process. Actually, the marketing practices in the hotel or other organisations focus on transforming the occasional customers into the habitual customers. This process is also known as transforming the light customers into the heavy customers.

Melvyn Greene added:[10]

"Marketing is basically seeking out a demand and then making the product or supplying the service to satisfy the demand. Selling is rather the other way round – creating a product or service and then trying to find a market for it."

In another definition, he clarifies the difference between marketing hotel services and selling hotel services.

Anerson & Lembke:[11]

"We believe that the real meaning of marketing is listening to the demands of the market and satisfying these demands at a profit, from that it follows that superior marketing is listening to the market more intently than your competitors and satisfying the demands more effectively."

This definition concentrates on creating the demand and satisfying the customers. Further, it emphasises on the formulation of competitive strategies for excelling the competition.

MARKETING vs. SELLING THE HOTEL SERVICES

According to the concept and perception of hotel marketing, it is right to mention that marketing and selling of hotel services can't be tantamount. The definition given by Melvyn Greene clarifies it. The continuous circle[12] of marketing as shown in Figure 12.3 clarifies it.

In Figure 12.3, the continuous circle of marketing clarifies the difference between marketing and selling the hotel services. In selling, the key areas are advertising including other aspects of marketing communication like telephones, letters, face-to-face communication. Often, the hoteliers explain their marketing strategies by showing computer booking services and the advertising campaigns planned for the coming tourists. As per the continuous circle, it is essential to keep into consideration the research required for data collection and on the basis of a sound marketing information system, transforming the data into information for making right marketing decisions. In addition, it is also essential that the strategies adopted by the competitors are given due weightage, specially while making and practising the strategic decisions. The threats and weaknesses in the markets are identified, if we have an in-depth information regarding the competitors. The pricing decisions are also significant keeping in view the seasonal fluctuations which play a significant role in the hotel industry.

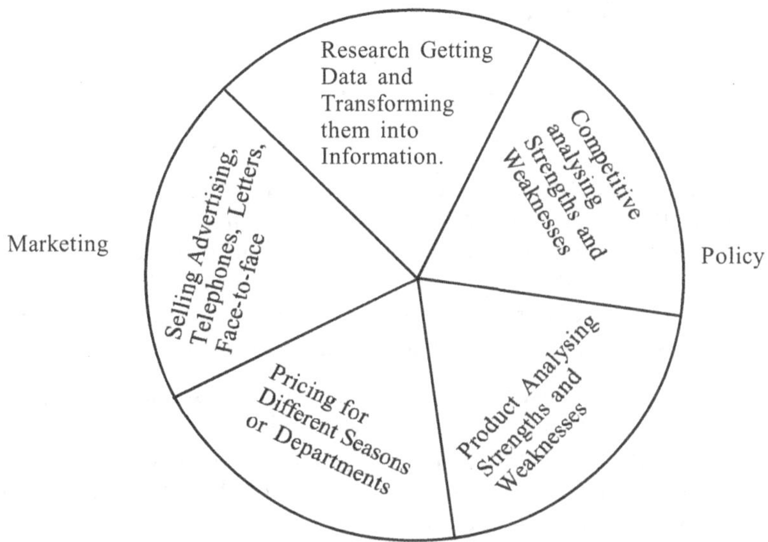

Fig. 12.3: Continuous Circle of Marketing

The major difference is marketing hotel services as against other consumer products, is that after a customer has spent money in hotels, he/she has nothing substantial to show except bills for his/her money as benefits as compared with buying tangibles, such as television and refrigerator. But if the rooms of a hotel remain vacant, it is unlikely that the same can be sold next day. While selling the hotel services, we cover the limited areas but while marketing the hotel services, we find unlimited areas. If we talk about marketing the hotel services, we include in its purview everything and almost all the dimensions directly or indirectly helping in promoting the business and this necessitates formulation of a sound marketing mix, such as an aggregation of different submixes like product, promotion, pricing, place and people. We manage services, we manage promotional activities, we manage pricing, we manage distribution process and we manage people serving as hotel personnel.

USERS OF HOTEL INDUSTRY

In marketing hotel services, it is important to know about the different types of users availing the services with diverse aims and objectives. This would ease the task of marketers specially while studying the behavioural profile. In Figure 12.4, we find classification of different categories of domestic and foreign users.

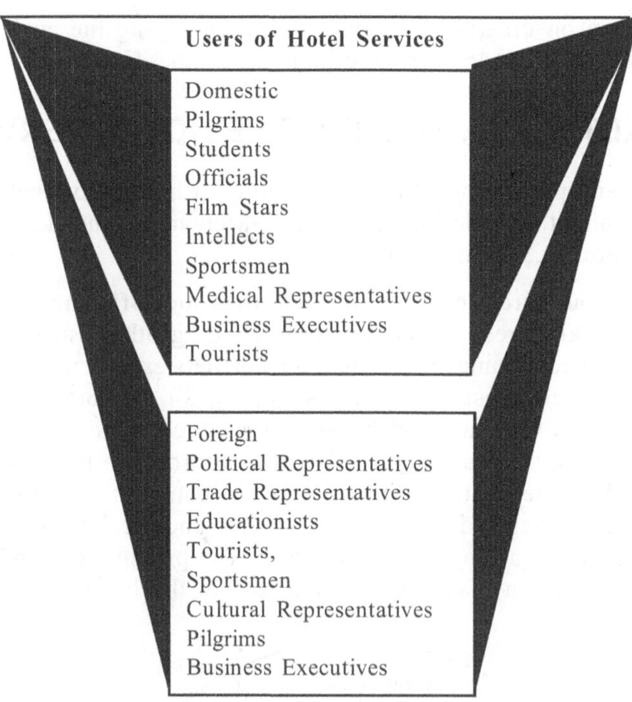

Fig. 12.4: Users of Hotel industry

It is natural that we find a difference in the intensity of both the categories of users.

Domestic Users: In the group of domestic users, the different categories are pilgrims visiting the sacred places, students on educational tours, officials on deputation, political representatives, film stars on location shooting, knowledge seekers on developing their credentials, sportsmen playing national games, etc. The domestic users stay in hotels with a different motive. We find a change in the level of domestic users. Generally, the domestic customers pay less attention on value and more on price. A majority of the domestic users are found price-sensitive and therefore the hoteliers are supposed to make pricing decisions motivational.

Foreign Users: In the group of foreign users, we find political representatives on peace mission, trade representatives on business promotion, educationists, sportsmen, cultural representatives, film stars, pilgrims, etc. These categories of foreign tourists visit hotels with diverse aims and objectives. They normally prefer to stay in the classified hotels where the services are found standardised. We also find cases where foreigners stay even in the unclassified hotels. To be more specific, the existing worldwide economic depression has made even the foreign users sensitive to price and this makes it significant that policy makers and the senior executives assign due weightage to this new development.

The main thing in the process is to study the levels of expectations of both the categories of users so that the marketers find it convenient to undertake an in-depth study of their changing behavioural profile, which would help them substantially in developing the marketing resources and formulating a sound product portfolio. The formulation and innovation of marketing decisions would be made easier when we are well aware of the emerging trends in the behavioural profile.

BEHAVIOURAL PROFILE OF USERS

Behaviour is like a mirror in which everyone sees his/her face/image. Purchase of a product or service and brand is rarely the result of a single motive. The users of hotel services come from different regions, strata, economic categories. Behaviour is not found static as it changes over time and specially in tune with demographic, geographic and socio-economic changes. Understanding the behaviour of hotel users is thus found essential but a difficult task which requires the hotel personnel to be professionally-sound. Particularly in the hotel services, we find lifestyles occupying a place of outstanding importance. From a sociological standpoint, we find lifestyles a group phenomenon. Lifestyles vary according to the sociologically relevant variables.

The emerging trends in the satisfaction index help a marketer in evaluating the sensitivity of marketing strategies. If the satisfaction index shows a positive trend, the existing strategies are supposed to be effective. Contrary to it, if the satisfaction index shows a negative trend, the marketers need to innovate their decisions. This calls for a microscopic study of the behavioural profile of users. It is not enough that the marketing managers react only to the given wants of customers. In a true sense, they are also supposed to play an active role in anticipating the needs, requirements and taste preferences in shaping and designing their desires and aspirations. The marketing philosophy should be the way of any business which would dictate every activity, operation and policy of an organisation with customer satisfaction at its roots. This task is found simplified fantastically when we have detailed information regarding the changing behavioural profile of users.

In psychological terms, the whole range of the generation of wants and their transformation into buying or using decisions can be explained as behaviour. The core problem of the entire marketing process is to identify strategies bearing the efficacy of activating the transformation process so that a number of potential guests are transformed into the actual guests and further the actual guests are transfigurated into the habitual guests. The marketers are here required to make it sure that their attitudes are not to be destroyed or ignored. The key factors in the transformation process are situational and organisational. We can't deny that customers have individual values, perception, preferences and a behaviour pattern based on environmental influences. The race, ethnic, religion, nationality, leisure habits, health factors and lifestyles have a substantial influence on the behaviour of users. The customers' age, life cycle stage, occupation, economic condition and personality influence the way in which they make the buying decisions. This makes it essential that the marketing professionals serving the hotels analyse their needs and identify the level of their expectations.

In the behavioural studies related to hotels and hotel companies, it seems appropriate that we make possible a segmentwise study of the behavioural profile. What motivates people to buy or spend money? What motivates guests to use hotels and restaurants? What prompts them to eat outside? What are their food habits? What are their drinks preferences? These questions are required to be answered suitably, specially with the motto of studying and understanding the behavioural profile of users. The marketing professionals, by intensifying the behavioural studies, find it convenient to know about the motivational factors, the hierarchy of needs and formulate the service mix accordingly.

We can't deny that arriving at a sound marketing decisions is a difficult task that requires world-class professional excellence. Manifestation of perfection in the purest form is an essential criterion for achieving excellence. All marketing activities concerned with goods/services start and end with satisfaction. If the customers/users are found satisfied, the process of increasing the business and expanding the market share keep on moving. Contrary to it, if they remain dissatisfied, the business is lost and lost forever. It is against this background that the marketing professionals are supposed to assign due weightage to the satisfaction element which requires due attention on the behavioural studies.

The needs and requirements of men and women can't be identical, the behavioural profile of kids and youths can't be the same, the behavioural profile of youths and grey can't be identical, the needs and requirements of business executives and the political representatives can't be similar. This makes it essential that the marketing professionals have made possible a microscopic study of the behaviour of different categories of customers belonging to different segments and in the face of their behavioural profile, attempt to develop the marketing resources and formulate a marketing mix.

In the hotel industry, the marketers are required to see that guests are aware or unaware, interested or intend to try. They are sensitive to price or pro to the quality. They are influenced by western culture or they like eastern culture. They like Indian foods or are tempted to western food habits. They are high spending or prefer to maintain economy. They have crossed the threshold barrier or are lacking something. They would eat in the restaurants of the hotels or would like to eat outside. These aspects would help marketers in identifying the level of expectations of users and they can tailor their marketing resources in tune with the preferences and options of guests. It is in this context that a study of behavioural profile is found essential.

We agree with this view that to understand marketing, we need to understand users and to understand users, we need to understand their behavioural profile. Marketing success or failures virtually depend on the reactions of target users expressed in the form of using patterns. There are a number of factors influencing the behavioural profile. The marketers found aware of the emerging trends can study and understand the behavioural profile. The society influenced by industrialisation, the economy influenced by the corporate sector, the development process influenced by sophisticated communication systems generate a particular set of behavioural profile. The needs and requirements in that set are found by and large the same. Contrary to it, the economy dominated by the agricultural developments, lacking sophisticated communication systems, the society not influenced by the corporate culture make ways for a particular set of preferences. Thus, the marketing professionals serving the hotel companies are supposed to be aware of these developments so that they are in a position to make their marketing resources optimal *vis-a-vis* proactive to the changing business conditions.

In view of the above, it is right to mention that the behavioural studies occupy a place of outstanding significance and the marketing professionals need to assign due weightage to these developments failing which the marketing resources can't be made optimal to the changing behavioural profile of users. It is against this background that we find a study of the behavioural profile of users important to the marketers.

MARKET SEGMENTATION FOR HOTEL

To make the marketing decisions effective, it is essential that the hotel professionals segment the market in such a way that the task of identifying the changing needs and requirements of different segments is made easier. Segmentation proves to be an important commandment of marketing since this helps in making and innovating the marketing decisions. All the users, of course, have their own likes and dislikes because the food habits are different; the drinking habits are different; the expectations are different. The kids, teens, youths, men, women, married and unmarried, youth and grey, technocrats and bureaucrats, business executives and political representatives stay in hotels with diverse motives. Segmentation makes the ways for knowing their uniqueness and formulating the submixes in such a way that an optimal development of marketing resources is made possible. It is against this background that we go through segmentation for the hotel organisations.

The ultimate motto of segmentation is to cater to the changing needs and requirements of the users. It is done with the motto of grouping and subgrouping the users so that their responses to the marketing inputs are similar. The success in marketing efforts lies in anatomising the needs and requirements of diverse segments. This allows the strategic marketing planner to be in a better position to spot opportunities, provide an orientation whereby service offerings can be turned to satisfy the guests and simplify the budgeting task through which marketing efforts are identified and monitored. There are different variables for market segmentation and the marketers are supposed to undertake micro and macro studies.

Normally, the hotel companies are found located at places of demand and therefore it is not realistic that the distribution is equal. The Federation of Hotel and Restaurant Association of India[13] has divided the country into four geographic regions, viz., Northern region covering Delhi, UP, Rajasthan and other northern states; Calcutta Region covering Orissa, West Bengal and other eastern states; and Eastern Union Territories including Andaman and Nicobar islands; Western Region covering Maharashtra, Gujarat, MP and Goa and Southern region covering Andhra Pradesh, Karnataka, Tamil Nadu, Kerala and the Union Territory of Pondichery. It is natural that the distribution is lopsided since all the regions are not conducive to the rich infrastructural facilities and the profitable marketing opportunities. The demand for accommodation is not uniform either due to non-accessibility or due to the non-availability of basic transport facilities. Some of the regions are better placed whereas some of the regions face a crisis-like situation.

In addition to the geographic consideration, we also find psychographic considerations important to segment the market. This is on the basis of psychographic variables which refer to life cycle, buying motives and knowledge of prospects regarding the services. The psychographic variables vary from segment to segment. The psychological considerations are found instrumental because the hotel professionals come to know about the behavioural profile of different users living in different segments.

With a view to maintaining standards and enforcing control, the Department of Tourism, Ministry of Tourism and Civil Aviation, Government of India has developed a system of categorising the available accommodation as per certain criteria. Accordingly, the hotels are either approved or unapproved.

The approved hotels are found of international standard and normally the foreign tourists prefer to stay in that category of hotels. This is due to the fact that the approved hotels have the stamp of official recognition. Approval in itself simplifies the task of promotion. The hotel professionals bear the responsibility of identifying the emerging segments.

Of late, we find a new trend even in the Indian condition because women have been found staying in hotels or eating in hotel restaurants. There are women executives and women going on holidays in all age groups, albeit without accompanying men. A number of married women have been found taking an extra holiday on their own. Middle-aged, divorced or single women have also been found staying in hotels. It is against this background that we find women segment emerging as an important segment for the hotel business.

The emergence of a short-break market also gravitates our attention in the very context. In a majority of the countries, we find 4-day or 5-day week. We also call it four-sevenths or five-sevenths. This has made possible development of a new market, i.e., weekend market. To improve future marketing, we find hotels and hotel companies successfully promoting weekend breaks. Though we find catchment area for this segment very much limited.

The single-parent market is also to emerge as a new segment for the hotel business. In this category, we find unmarried mothers with very little money. The separated and divorced men and women are also found in this category. This new segment is found profitable to the hotel industry since good number of single parents have been found spending more than they can afford. The propensity to spend of this segment is found at its peak.

With the passage of time, we find a change in the lifestyles. We can't deny that increasing domination of corporate sector in the national economy and developing new corporate culture in the Indian society has changed the lifestyles of prospects in general. A good number of persons now appreciate physical fitness. Both sexes are now found playing tennis or jogging. The increasing health consciousness has resulted in the emergence of a new segment, i.e., 'active leisure.' It is essential that the hotel professionals know about this segment and provide the essential facilities in the hotels like gym, sauna, the swimming pools including a circuit of exercise machines. The availability of personal care services close to the hotels or in the hotel complex itself would attract customers.

The emergence of Instant Market also draws the attention of hotel professionals. Today, we find everyone moving fast and no one likes to wait for long time. This has made ways for the development of the concept of fast food restaurants and quick access to service facilities in hotels. Increasing use of credit cards has actually changed the traditional concept of making payments. It is against this background that we find quick disposal of customers drawing the attention of hotel professionals. Buying at a short notice is now found increasing. This makes it essential that hotels have now in-built systems to take full advantages of this new development. Instant services are thus need of the hour and the hotels and hotel companies are required to perceive it in a right fashion and to innovate their services accordingly.

The aforesaid facts make it clear that multi-dimensional developments in the socio-economic parlance have paved avenues for the development of new segments and the hotel professionals have no option but to keep their eyes open and mind active.

To be more specific in the hotel industry, the lifestyle segment is found important. It has proved to be an internationally-accepted variable for targeting customers. In UK, A Classification of Regional Neighbourhood (ACORN) has been developed as a system for targeting customers. It has proved its instrumentality in determining the characteristics of different customer groups on the basis of their own records, specially the high spending tourists, habitual users, occasional users or so. ACORN[14] studies also simplify the task of profitable site location to attract tourists. In the hotel industry, the buying decisions are substantially influenced by the lifestyles of an individual or a family. The size of a family or the number of children in a family is found to be an important component, specially while taking decision. The nature of profession also becomes a dominating factor as it influences the activities offered for the leisure times which is directly related to the hotel industry. It is quite natural that lifestyle of a technocrat differ from the lifestyle of bureaucrat. The lifestyle of an individual engaged in business is found different to politicians. Thus, we can't deny the fact that for the hotel industry, the lifestyle has proved to be an important base for studying the needs and requirements of customers. In a true sense, we find lifestyle influencing the expectations and therefore the hoteliers need to have an in-depth study of lifestyle segmentation. A young single divorce lawyer views himself as something of a swinger. His attitudes and interests are translated into purchases such as yellow porsche, a custom-fitted wardrobe, a pent house apartment in a single complex. His monthly credit card statements list an expensive array of nightspots as well as several plane tickets. He is supposed to be an ideal potential guest for vacation packages augmenting his lifestyle and therefore he is important as a source of revenue generation. Another tax lawyer (family man) living in a small suburb and his house and station wagon reflect an orientation towards the home and children. Family vacations tend to be camping trips several times a year and an occasional trip abroad. Entertainment expenses include food and liquor and dinner at home with friends. Thus, he is found to be a suitable prospect for the life insurance companies first and then for the hotel industry.

In view of the above, it is right to say that hotel professionals need to have an in-depth study of market segmentation so that the needs and requirements *vis-a-vis* the level of expectations of different segments are studied and the marketing resources are developed accordingly. This would help senior executives and the policy makers in innovating new services or packages which are yet to be common in the hotel business. Hotels should have something better to serve. The guests should feel that they are getting additional, special comforts in the hotels. The availability of modern amenities and facilities, the construction of hotel apartments and cottages, the development of tennis courts and gym centres, are some of the new developments found very much instrumental in attracting the customers.[15] The hotels and hotel companies need to be aware of the emerging new trends in the society and are supposed to ensure that the guests get something more in hotels than those in their private homes. We can't deny the fact that even today we find a number of hotels without modern personal care amenities and facilities. If we find some of the hotels thriving, this is due mainly to the fact that hotels are old, unusual, nostalgic or historic. This makes it clear that if the hotels are with unique attractive features, the customers would be attracted. The old palaces and havelis are of late used as hotels and albeit the high spending tourists prefer to stay there.

MARKETING INFORMATION SYSTEM FOR HOTEL ORGANISATIONS

In an era of information explosion where sophisticated information technologies have been found making superhighway for communications, it is natural that almost all the organisations assign due weightage to the technology-driven Marketing Information System. This helps an organisation in making, screening, evaluating and innovating the marketing decisions. It is against this background that we find hotels and hotel companies assigning due weightage to the management of information. The MIS is supposed to be an important tool used by management personnel to assist in planning, problem identifying and solving, evaluating and innovating in the face of changing requirements. The emerging changes within and outside an organisation make it essential that marketing decisions are based on the sound management of information. The coordinated, systematic and continuous information gathering is an important strategy for managing and using the information related to marketing activities. The need of the hour is to be more effective in our marketing and sales efforts and an MIS makes it possible as much more marketing information is produced systematically and regularly. A management reporting system must be designed for the needs and requirements of every individual hotel. We find a hardcore of basic information which hotel management requires irrespective of the style and management strategies of the hotel.

The instrumentality of information system is involved in the essence of designing marketing strategies in tune with the changing taste preferences, lifestyles, likes and dislikes of the potential guests. Hence, the absence of an up-to-date information system with quick retrieval facilities will lead to poor services *vis-a-vis* dissatisfaction of the guests. We can't deny the fact that the process of innovation would be slowed down, if the process of technological sophistication in managing the marketing information is not getting an overriding priority. Our steps in the field of collecting, analysing and disseminating the information determine the intensity of positive or negative results. If the knowledge bank is rich, the latest developments in the field of tourism industry would be possible, the process of industrialisation would be accelerated and the hotel business would get a profitable market.

There is no doubt in it that change is the only constant thing in our lives. The world is changing with new market segments developing and new customers with new hopes and aspirations, with high level of expectations evincing interests in using the services of hotel industry. We accept the fact that social changes create opportunities and how we do capitalise on the new profitable opportunities is a challenging task before the hotel professionals. An MIS helps professional in identifying the profitable opportunities and in addition, also helps them fantastically in capitalising on the same optimally. This in a natural way gives a new boost to the hotel industry,

The different sources of business for the hotel are conference rooms for business purposes, recreational facilities for business tourists, restaurants, wedding halls, convention halls, exhibition halls, etc. Marketing information regarding the availability of accommodation occupies a place of outstanding significance in the very context. It is against this background that we find almost all the leading hotels and hotel companies making sincere efforts to develop a technology-driven information system which helps them in many ways.

In Figures 12.5, 12.6 and 12.7, we find marketing information for rooms, restaurants and function rooms. We are aware of the fact that availability of information is significant to get the best from the MIS.

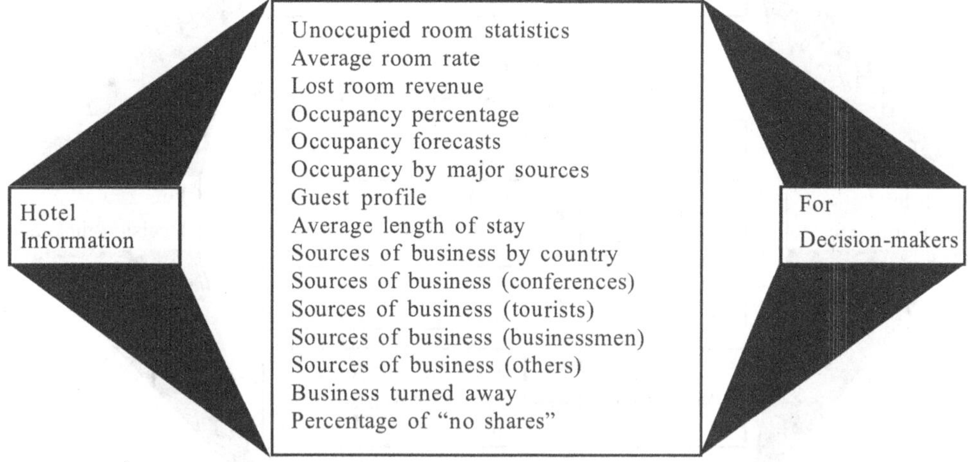

Fig. 12.5: Marketing Information for Bedrooms

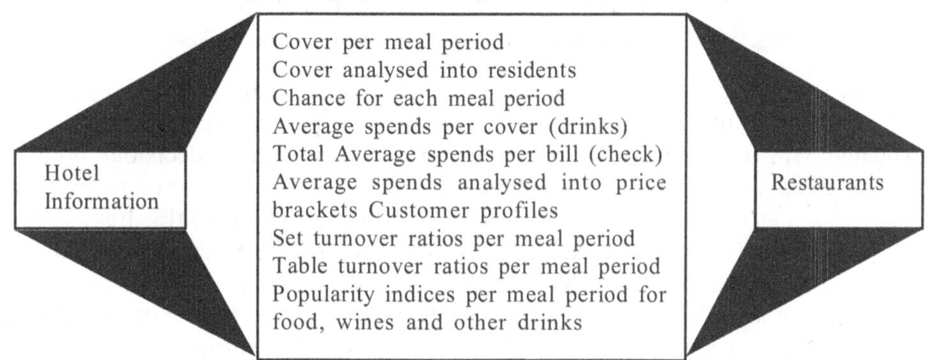

Fig. 12.6: Marketing Information for Restaurants

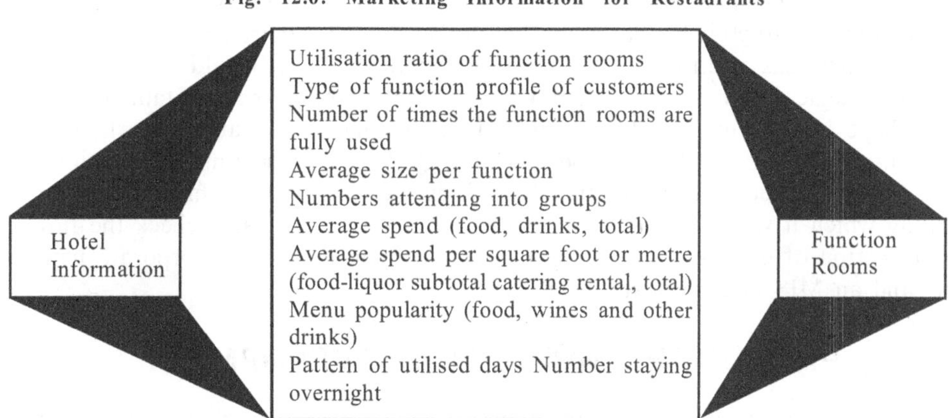

Fig. 12.7: Marketing Information for Function Rooms

The aforesaid facts and figures presented in 12.5, 12.6 and 12.7 make it clear that the hotel organisations need to have detailed information for managing the three important sources from where they get the business, such as the bedrooms where the customers stay, restaurants where the guests take their meals and breakfast and function rooms or convention halls where they deliberate upon important business problems.

The development of core and peripheral services in the face of MIS reporting would help hotels and hotel companies in attracting the customers. We can't deny the fact that in the management of marketing information, the system requires different types of information from different sources. A technology-driven MIS with a rich knowledge bank can serve multi-dimensional purposes of hotels. In Figure 12.8, we find information required by decision-makers.

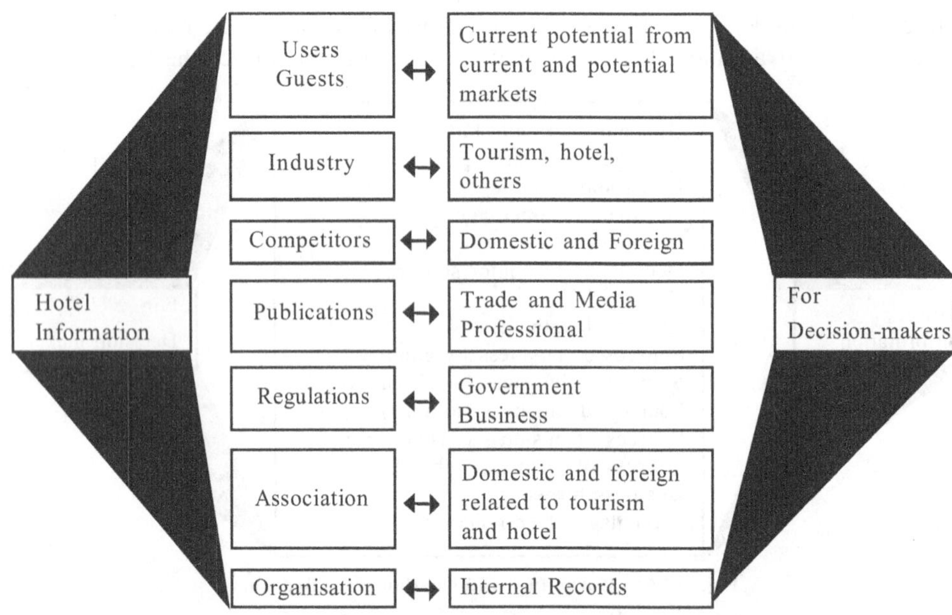

Fig. 12.8: Information Required by the Decision-makers

In view of the above, it is right to opine that in the coming years, the business environmental conditions for hotel business are likely to be more competitive and volatile. The professionals having world-class excellence and the most sophisticated MIS would be successful in making their marketing decisions proactive. On the other hand, the hotels not assigning due weightage to the new developments would have to make a good-bye. It is in this context that we make a strong advocacy in favour of a technology-driven MIS. Easy access to information, assisting the planning process for future marketing, co-ordinated systematic and continuous information, evaluation of performance, functional co-ordination, future orientation, projection of a positive or a fair image are some of the outstanding contributions of a well developed technology-driven MIS. It is high time that the hotel professionals realise gravity of the situation and assign an overriding priority to information management.

Like other organisations, the hotel companies also need to assign due weightage to future marketing. What would be the shape of future marketing? What would be the needs and requirements of different segments? What would be the level of expectations of different categories of customers? What would be the intensity of competition in the business? What strategic decisions would help hotels in capitalising in the profitable opportunities optimally? What would be the shape of strategic plan? What would be the shape of strategic marketing? These questions need to be suitably answered and a well-developed technology-driven Marketing Information System can make it possible. Thus, it is crying need of the hour that hotel industry interested in thriving assigns a transcendental priority to MIS failing which it would be difficult for them to survive. We can't check the flow of development. We can't turn the direction of change. The only thing that we can do is to incorporate new developments in our business plans and an MIS can do it successfully.

PRODUCT PLANNING AND DEVELOPMENT

Before dissecting other problems, it is pertinent that we have an in-depth idea of the product of the hotel industry. The emerging trends in the socio-economic environment occupy a place of outstanding significance. In the product management of an industry, the planning and development processes have a far reaching effect. We are well aware of the fact that hotels and hotel companies offer a number of core and peripheral services to the customers. It is also a well-known fact that by and large almost all the hotels offer the core services of identical nature and character and therefore, the hotel professionals are required to think more in favour of peripheral services that add additional attractions to their service mix.

In the management of product, the decisions related to elimination, modification, innovation, inclusion play a significant role. It is essential that based on the results of product life cycle and the MIS reporting, the hotel professionals, senior executives and policy makers think about planning and development which would simplify their task of managing the future. It is in this context that we focus on product planning and development for the hotels and hotel companies.

In an institution of commercial hospitality, the development of product has a telling impact on the marketing strategy. This is due to the fact that the magnitude of success is very much influenced by the quality of services offered to the customers. Sky is the limit for quality. The planning and development processes focus on quality upgradation so that the hotels are found in a position to make their services internationally-competitive. We are aware of the business rule about a new hotel. First year, it loses money; the second year, it breaks even and then in the third year; it shows a reasonable profit. If we plan the development of a hotel in a right fashion, a hotel can generate substantial profit. The development of hotel industry is the development of the process of social industrialisation. Coiling more dynamism in its nature, we find hotel planning a difficult as well as a challenging task. Hotel planning must be regarded as an integral part of the country's overall social and economic developed planning. The key steps in the planning processes are an assessment of hotel demand and profitable avenues for an optimal supply so that a situation like imbalance in demand and supply is arrested.

For the formulation of an intelligent as well as a realistic plan, it is essential that we forecast and for right forecasting, it is pertinent that we have complete information about the prospects, intensity of competition and the changing market conditions. If we think about hotel planning, it is quite natural that we also think about hotel building, furnishing, decor, ground development and aesthetic management. It is right to mention that particularly in the Indian perspective, the hotels and hotel companies have not been assigning due weightage to aesthetic management which focuses on managing and developing surroundings and premises in such a way that hotels look like a garden. If we think about hotel planning and development, it is not to be forgotten that in the 21st century, the prospects and markets are expected to be sophisticated. It is quite natural that the companies dealing directly with the customers would have to show particular flexibility to change as the consumer does. Yesterday, the customers preferred to stay in the cities' precincts, today they prefer to stay in outskirts or even in the rural areas.

Yesterday, the multi-storeyed complexes attracted attention and today, we find the cottage culture, equipped with modern amenities and facilities gaining popularity. The tourists in general and the high spending tourists in particular now prefer to stay in hotels away from the hustle and bustle of city life. These changes make it essential that the hotel planning and development get due attention of hotel planners.

Location: Location implies accessibility and conveniences to the users of hospitality services. The selection of a suitable place for hotel is found important. The main thing in the location of a modern hotel is accessibility and this gravitates our attention on the infrastructural facilities, such as availability of quality roads, electricity and communication facilities in addition to other services. Particularly in the western countries, the hotel planners assign due weightage to the management of surroundings or hotel premises. In the cities' precincts, it is not possible to develop modern hotels where we need a big playing ground, swimming pool, personal care centres, shopping complexes or so. Thus, to make an assault on the problem of space, we find outskirts or villages suitable location points for modern hotels. While developing premises, the hotel planners need to assign due weightage to aesthetic management. This focuses our attention on plantation. Making a decision for location is found significant as once a hotel is established, the development plans follow and the space constraint stands as a major obstacle. The hotel is an immovable fixture which has to use its skills in marketing to overcome any difficulties which may emerge after its initial location. In a true sense, the location tends to dominate all hotel operations substantially. It determines the customer mix which the business can achieve and therefore, the direction of marketing strategy and other business tactics. Thus, the hotel planners need to select a place which is calm and quiet, environment-friendly and easily accessible.

Hotel Building: Construction of hotel buildings is an important component of hotel planning. It is related to the planning of bedrooms, restaurant and a well-managed bar. In addition, it is also related to the development of peripheral services. The designing of hotel building no doubt is the concern of the architects but the management experts can identify the changing trends and the emerging preferences. The customers now prefer cottages, apartments with modern amenities and facilities. In the last few decades, we find significant changes in the likes and dislikes of potential users. In the 1960s, 1970s and 1980s, a majority of customers did not install central heating, double glazing, showers, extra bathrooms, extensions, play rooms and playgrounds, wet bars, wall-to-wall carpeting, tiled bathrooms and kitchens. Since the beginning of the decade 1980s, we find a change which could gain the momentum in 1990s. The hotel planners must be aware of the emerging trends so that they are in a position to provide to their hotels the facilities slightly better than in their private houses. It is found that in the hotel industry of today, we find 'nostalgia' playing an important role. Sentimental-longing for past is found influencing the hotel industry. It is against this background that even unusual, nostalgic or historic hotels are getting a positive response. It is in this context that we find development of old palaces and havelis as hotels. Since it is permanent investment and a capital-intensive project, a careful plan is a must, specially to make possible cost-effectiveness, *vis-a-vis* high productivity and profitability.

Hotel Bedrooms: In a hotel, we find bedrooms an important place where the guests stay for a long time. While planning for the bedrooms, it is essential that we keep in our minds the needs and requirements of users. It is quite natural that the needs and requirements of men can't be identical to the needs and requirements of women. Like this, needs and requirements of business executives would be different to the needs and requirements of cine artists. Hotel management is found saying all our rooms have a private bathroom, or we are the largest group in the world or we open a new hotel every week on an average, so they are found saying, "so what"? They also advocate that women want to avail hotel services like their male counterparts. Here, we need to make a microscopic study of preferences and requirements. Women often read different publications to men therefore the media preferred by women, the magazines, newspapers, novels of their choice should be made available in their bedrooms. We also find cases where business executives prefer to have a space for business purposes. In this context, the bedrooms should be designed in the face of their requirements. In addition, it is also important that bedrooms are well decorated where all the modern amenities and facilities are available. The cabling, wiring should be safe and the protective measures in case of accidents should be available.

Hotel Function Room: In the planning and development, we find hotel function room, conference hall, wedding hall important points. The hotel planners need to consider about the management of function rooms. With the development of corporate culture, we find enough scope for planning and organising the conference or convention halls. The infrastructural facilities keeping in view the business conferences and seminars need due attention of hotel planners. In addition, it is also essential that we keep in our minds the requirements of wedding halls because in the coming days there would be a profitable opportunity for the booking of wedding rooms. The hotel planners need to make provisions for the sophisticated communication facilities so that the required equipments are installed without generating problems. We find convention business as a backbone of modern hotel. It benefits the peripherals like travel and tourist agencies, the local community and above all hotels. More than 40 per cent of expenditure of the delegates coming for conferences is spent for hotel accommodation. In Singapore, we find hotels assigning due weightage to convention, Like this, we find France, USA, Germany and many countries managing hotels with the viewpoint of convention. Realising that the convention business is to benefit not only the hotel industry but a number of sectors and industries are benefited, the hotel planners the world over have been found thinking about this problem while planning hotels. It is against this background that the marketing of the convention business has occupied a place of outstanding significance in the recent years and even in the coming years, we expect the trend to continue. Currently, we find Americans spending billions of dollars annually for attending conventions and conferences. The convention industry has been found contributing substantially to the development of the economy of USA. It is high time that the hotel planners even in the Indian context assign an overriding priority to convention hall while planning and designing hotels.

The aforesaid facts need due attention of hotel planners. The hotels and hotel companies need to assign a transcendental priority to the planning and development.

FORMULATION OF MARKETING MIX FOR HOTEL ORGANISATIONS

The term marketing mix is the combination of what market offers and studies which help in identifying the actual point where marketing action can be taken to improve the acceptability of hotel product and stimulate demand. A modern hotel is a major establishment, a sophisticated job manned by trained personnel from hotel schools, an institution of commercial hospitality and a building or an institution where guests expect refined behaviour, excellent services and personal attention. This draws our attention on the combination of submixes in the hotel industry. With the viewpoint of marketing a hotel product, the combination of different submixes is found significant. The combination of core and peripheral services, the creative promotional decisions, the pricing strategies helping hotels in maintaining the commercial viability, the efficient hotel personnel instrumental in minimising the gap between the services-promised and services-offered, the education and training programme for the development of hotel personnel efficacious in enriching their excellence as high performers are important decision-making areas which gravitate our attention on the formulation of a sound mix for the hotel industry. It is against this background that we go through the different submixes of the marketing mix.

The Product Mix

In any organisation, we find product the focal point. The hotel services also require a fair combination of core and peripheral services. It is right to mention that in almost all the hotels of same category, by and large, the core services are found identical and therefore, the peripheral services divert a close attention where the hotel personnel need professional excellence. More innovative the peripheral services, more attractions we add to our product mix. This makes it essential that hotels and hotel companies assign due weightage to the formulation of an optimal product mix in which peripheral services prove to be a point of attraction.

The emerging trends in the socio-economic parlance necessitate an analogous change in the product mix. With the passage of time, it is quite natural that some of the services become outdated and therefore, we need to eliminate them. At the same time, it is essential that we keep our minds open and come to know the latest developments in the likes and dislikes of the customers, and while including new services in the product mix, assign due weightage to their preferences. While formulating the product mix, it is pertinent that we make the ways for frequent innovation. It is also right to mention that frequency in innovation is found essential and at the same time, easier in the context of peripheral services. The hotel professionals are required to formulate a package that helps in attracting the customers. Modifications in the existing services by adding a few outstanding properties is found to be a suitable strategy for the development of product. The generation of idea, the formulation of concept, the analysis of product cost and the testing of services before their final commercial launch become significant in the very context. This necessitates an in-depth study of product life cycle. A hotel manager bears the responsibility of adding attractions to the product mix and this is possible when they have world-class professional excellence.

While formulating the product mix for the hotel services, it is essential that catering management, restaurant and cafeteria management, management of bedrooms, management of convention halls are given due weightage. The boarding services are considered to be an important part of product mix. In addition, the lodging services also become significant. Here, it is essential that facilities like light, water, electricity, ventilation, entertainment, sanitation arrangement of bed, etc. are available to the guests. While formulating the product mix, the hotel organisations are required to make possible a fair mix of core and peripheral services. In Figure 12.9, we find the product mix for hotels.

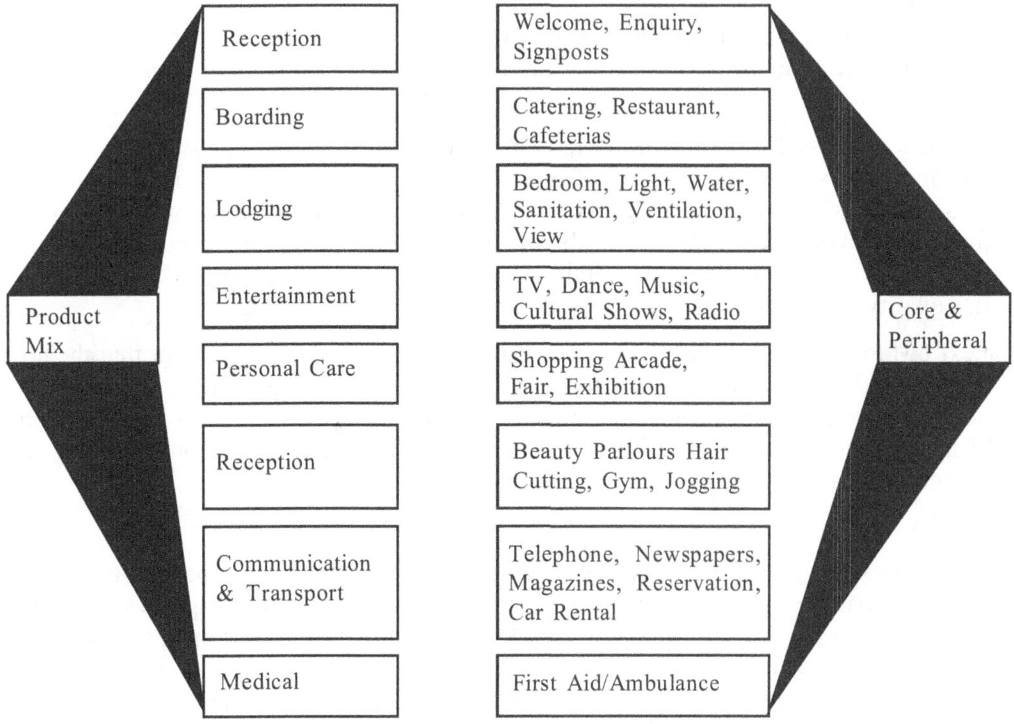

Fig. 12.9: Product Mix for Hotels

Before we think about introducing a new product, it is essential that we identify the reasons for its failure. The increasing intensity of competition in the hotel industry makes it essential that the hotel professionals attempt to innovate their service mix. The formulation of a sound product strategy becomes significant in the very context.

We can't deny the fact that as and when we talk about the services of hotel industry, our focus is on the tourism industry because from there we get profitable business. In addition, the industries and their executives also divert our attention since they help us substantially in getting the business. We can't devalue the instrumentality of educational institutions and business houses in getting business for our convention halls. These facts make it clear that while formulating product strategy, it is pertinent that the hotel professionals keep in their minds the users of services and their characteristics.

In the formulation of a sound product strategy, it is essential that we assign due weightage to the mix of services expected and desired by the potential customers. We need to make the information system strong enough to initiate suitable guidelines for the strategic decisions. What to offer? What to modify? What to alter? What to eliminate? These questions require suitable answers which are expected from the professionally-sound and high-performing team of hotel personnel. If we find that our competitors have been innovating their strategies, we have no option but to practise the same. If we want to project our image as a leader, we have no option but to make the ways for innovation. We need broad-based information related to the local community *vis-a-vis* the foreign and domestic tourists. In addition, the information regarding the facilities available in the hotel would be related to both such as areas producing revenue and areas not generating profitable financial returns. The information regarding the details of competition are also to be collected regarding the various facilities made available in a hotel including the prices, profile of potential customers, such as age bracket, sex, type of group, place of employment, place of residence, mode of transport, room popularity, new guest, first choice, length of stay, any complaints and who made the booking. Besides, we also need information related to hotel activities, such as occupancy statistics, seat turnover percentage, number of empty days, pattern of sales in restaurant and bar or so.

It is not to be forgotten that needs of the guests are the cornerstone of marketing analysis. An in-depth study of what the competitors are doing, implementation of unique selling proposition to fulfil the needs of customers, determination of objectives and the formulation of strategies, advertise a promise which is genuine and creditable and in which the customers can easily discern their own benefits can't be devalued in the very context. It is pertinent that we view everything from the customer's perspective. The accommodation facilities available and the housekeeping draw our attention to improve the quality of services. While formulating strategic decisions, it is significant that we include in our product mix, all the new services offered by our competitors. Not only the primary and auxiliary or core and peripheral but even the supportive services offered by allied industries divert our attention.

The development process can't remain static. This necessitates a continuous effort for incorporating the necessary changes in our service mix. The issue of concern here is how and what to incorporate? A sound product strategy is found a prerequisite for establishing a fair or positive image. Image is the way in which a hotel portrays itself. The factors like atmosphere, brand name, the status, type of people and corporate institutions patronising a hotel would be instrumental in building up a fair image. And the most important thing in the projection of a fair image is the quality of services and the behaviour of the front line staff.

In the context of formulating a sound product strategy for hotels, it is also pertinent that the hotel management promises the less and offers the more. This would be efficacious in bridging over the gap between services-promised and services-offered often found instrumental in generating dissatisfaction besides making an invasion on the image of hotels. The professionally-sound hotel personnel can take a decision regarding the promises and their offering patterns.

The Promotion Mix

For successful marketing, it is only not sufficient that we concentrate on the quality of services but it is also impact generating that we promote our business in such a way that our prospects come to know about the quality to be offered to them as hotel customers. This focuses our attention on innovative promotional measures. It is against this background that we talk about the promotional measures. There are a number of components for promoting the business and it is hoped that a professionally-sound employee would blend the different constituents in such a way that effects are proactive but the process of persuasion is cost-effective. The components like advertisement, publicity, sales promotion, personal selling, word-of-mouth promotion and telemarketing need due attention of hotel professionals.

The success rate of a hotel is virtually coiled in the essence of transforming the occasional visitors into the habitual visitors because this helps substantially the process of increasing the occupancy ratio. The sensitivity is vigorously influenced by creativity. This makes it essential that the decision-makers in the hotel industry make sincere efforts to formulate sound promotional strategy. We can't deny the fact that creation of awareness has a far reaching effect on the formulation of promotional strategy. If scientifically-formulated, optimally-blended promotional measures are used by the professionally-sound and personally-committed hotel personnel, the rate of success would be found satisfactory. We find a number of instances to quote that even quality services failed in creating and expanding market because the promotional measures failed in sensitising the prospects. This draws our attention on using the different components of promotion in such a way that we find them very much instrumental in throwing a positive impact.

Advertisement: We are well aware of the fact that advertisement is a paid form of communication which helps in informing, sensing and persuading the prospects or users. While advertising, it is significant that the hotel professionals make possible a productive use of print media, broadcast media and telecast media. In the face of potentials, requirements and the intensity of competition, we need to select media for promoting our messages and slogans.

Of late, we find significant developments in the print media since sophistication in the printing technologies has made ways for offset printing, screen printing and laser printing. These devices are found efficacious in attracting the prospects. We find a number of plus points in the print media. It is possible to be descriptive while advertising. We are in a position to attract the attention of prospects by displaying attractive scenes, events, landscape, comforts, costs, etc. To be more specific when we have advanced print devices, we find enough scope for using print media for advertising. In this context, it is pertinent that the hotel professionals advertise sensibly, intelligently and for that seek the co-operation of advertising professionals who can simplify and sensitise the process. Another plus point that we find in the print media is related to economy. We find it economic and therefore the promotion budget is not to be non-optimal. We have a big circulation of different newspapers, magazines and keeping in view the target market/audience to be covered, we can take a decision in the every context.

The services of advertising professionals would make possible creativity in the advertisement messages and appeals. While selecting the media for advertisement, it is significant that we keep in our minds the magazines, newspapers preferred by the target audience. The magazines, newspapers preferred by women and teens should be given due weightage since in a majority of the cases, the decisions regarding a particular tour hotel are taken by them. We can't negate the fact that with sophistication in print technologies, it is easier to gravitate the attention of target prospects provided the advertising professionals show their world-class excellence.

The broadcast media can also be used for advertising the hotel services but if we make a comparative analysis of this media with others, the effects are found of low intensity. Of course, with the advancements in communication technologies we have almost 100 per cent air network which may be used, specially for low class hotels where financial constraint stands as a barrier while advertising through expensive media. It is in this context that we talk about the instrumentality of broadcast media which though economic in nature help the hotels in advertising for pilgrims. The hotel professionals are supposed to select a suitable time for transmission when a majority of the target audience are supposed to be close to the radio set. We find a particular season during which the pilgrims prefer to visit the sacred places and the hotels located in that catchment area need to advertise on sensitive hours. The messages, themes need rural orientation in the very context. It is essential that the advertising professionals are well aware of the nature and requirements of target audience.

Of late, we find telecast media considered to be the most sensitive but expensive media of advertisement. In the world of marketing communication, we assign top position to the telecast media because scope for audio-visual exposure makes ways for sensitising the prospects in a right fashion. It is against this background that we find hotels advertising through TV. Here, it is important to mention that the telecast media while advertising assign due weightage to the sensitive hours when a majority of the viewers are found before their TV sets. The advertising professionals are required to consider the quality *vis-a-vis* reception capacity of audience and are supposed to compose the messages accordingly. The scenes of hotel location, the swimming pool, the shopping complex, the personal care centres, the arranged bedrooms, the restaurants and convention hall, the aesthetic management are required to be telecast in such a way that attractions are added in the events. The target prospects can take a decision regarding a particular hotel, if they are found satisfied. With the availability of a number of TV channels, we now find enough scope for maintaining economy provided the hotel professionals manage things properly.

In view of the above, it is right to observe that out of all the media, we find print media the most effective media for hotel advertisements. It is due mainly to the fact that in the print media, the advertisers get an opportunity to display facts and figures which may be very much instrumental in convincing and persuading the prospects. We can't deny the fact that while using print media, the materials used for advertising are found of world-class, such as quality papers, quality print, quality photographs, attractive scenes or so. The use of quality materials paves avenues for attractions.

Publicity

Another dimension of promotion known as an unpaid form of persuasive communication also plays an incremental role in promoting the hotel business. While publicising, the hotel professionals play a significant role by managing the media personnel for publishing news items related to the hotel. Public relations activities thus become instrumental in the process of publicising. The British Institute of Public Relations has defined it as "the deliberate, planned and sustained effort to establish and maintain mutual understanding between an organisation and the public. Public relations cover a wide range of activities. It is the art and science of planning and implementing a two-way communication and understanding between hotel companies and potential users of the services. It is also known as the reflection of the organisational programmes and activities."

In the hotel industry, we find public relations activities more instrumental in informing the clients the outstanding merits of different services offered. The specialities of hotel are presented in such a way that the prospects are motivated to avail of the facilities offered by a particular hotel. It also helps in creating an atmosphere where the users at large are convinced. Besides, it also helps in collecting the information on the preferences of the prospects. It is right to mention that we find a few or even a very few consumer industries to be benefited substantially by public relations as the hotel industry. The vast majority of hoteliers welcome publicity not only because it is free but because they know that most people buy a magazine or a newspaper to read the articles, news and editorials, rather than the advertisements unless they are looking for a product or are interested in booking a holiday or a restaurant or a convention hall or a wedding hall.

In the hotel business, we find a number of events which should be transmitted to the local press, such as the appointment of a new chef, list of cocktails, menus for certain functions held at hotel, particulars of certain important conferences or exhibitions to be held, menus for special days of the year, photographs of staff dressed up for special days and well-known people staying in the hotel. We find a number of hotels doing a lot of charitable work and helping in organising charitable fund-raising events. Of late, the sponsored events start and finish at hotels or are run even in the hotel grounds. Sponsored walks, sponsored car rallies, sponsored fashion designing events, sponsored entertainment programmes, sponsored beauty contest or so. We find all appearing in the newspapers and magazines. Hotels need press coverage for most of their activities – from the largest omelette to the longest sausage.

Journalists always prefer to visit a hotel as they get their full enjoyment free of cost. You can give journalists a write-up of your story and preferably a story with a photograph. Of course, the photographs cover a lot of space but if media use it, we find this the finest eye-catching free publicity. Sometimes, a stunt is also thought to obtain a write-up. Here, an example of Crest Hotel next door to Wembly Stadium, London where they arranged for a horse to check in at reception when 'Horse of the Year' show was on. In the magazine, it appeared as 'Horse and Hound!' This is an example of a right stunt, for the right location and in the right media. Another example is related to Carlton Tower Hotel in London. When this hotel open its Rib Room Restaurant, renowned for its roast beef, with a new menu and decor, they got a prize for Aberdeen Angus bull outside the hotel which received considerable free press publicity. We again find it a right publicity for the right theme.

The aforesaid facts are a mute testimony to this proposition that for the smooth and successful functioning of hotels, it is important to develop rapport with the media people, specially in the catchment area. Spending time and money for their entertainment would not be unproductive. Establishing a personal relationship with them is always found to be a paying proposition. A hotel manager was able to persuade a television crew to move the cameras six inches as they featured a story of a robbery at a bank next door to his hotel so that the shot included the hotel name and sign and the voice mentioned, "the bank was next to hotel." This appeared at peak viewing time just for a cold beer or a cake as they were working outside and the temperature was very high.

In view of the above, it is right to mention that press publicity plays a positive role in promoting the hotel business but creative thinking and planning are found essential for the same. An example is here related to the

London Tara with 844 rooms which could not get free publicity mainly due to the fact that there were a number of hotels. One day, they introduced a theatre show in the function room of the hotel. The show was 'Another Bride, Another Groom' which the General Manager had watched in a show in Australia. The slogan was 'Another Bride, Another Groom brought to London.' In addition to free press publicity, they also got bookings of their function room for a long period.

In the public relations, the activities range from a press release to newspapers and magazines, specially to create the interest of prospects in a holiday package in a good resort of a country. The holiday package tours and trips on familiarity with a tour spot, organised by tour operators for the travel agents help them in enriching their knowledge and making the travelling decisions. The "wine and cheese parties" organised by the British Airways to launch not required Seychelles as a new resort or other such functions with the motto of enriching the knowledge of the prospects. There are a number of media sources available for publicity. Illustration, copy and the spoken word are the primary publicity to media which are grouped into the following heads:

- Printed Publicity
- Advertising Publicity
- Projected Publicity
- Structural Publicity
- Personal Publicity

Thus, it is right to say that public relations activities occupy a significant place in the promotion mix of hotel companies. In the hotel companies, the tour operators, travel agents explore opportunities for educating the masses. In this context, it is important that hotel companies are getting the best co-operation from media and for which the Public Relations Officers or the marketers or the contact personnel bear the responsibility of developing rapport with them, organising for them lunch or dinner, offering to them small gifts and influencing them to write in favour. You spend nominal amount but get big coverage which help you substantially, if not at present of course in future.

Sales Promotion

In almost all the organisations, we feel the need of offering incentives for promoting the business. Like other organisations, the hotels and hotel companies also offer incentives to the users *vis-a-vis* to the personnel and organisations evincing interest in promoting the business. We consider sales promotion a temporary device to increase the business with certain objectives. It is a short-term activity seeking to boost sales during peak demand periods to make it sure that the firm obtains its market share and helps launch a new product or support an ailing or modified services. These facts make it clear that sales promotion is complementary to advertising. Sales promotion and advertising objectives do not conflict but reinforce one another. This tool of promotion is designed to appeal particularly to those customers who are found sensitive to price. It is quite natural that the tools of sales promotion attract buyers even having little brand loyalty. It is against this background that the promotional measures are found more effective where brand loyalty is a feature, such as certain cruise makers are holiday package operators but here it is essential that efforts are aimed at present clientele to attract more business from the existing market instead of trying to encourage brand-switching and targeting new clients. This is not to be a case of value addition to the business of tour operators and the travel agents. In the hotel business, we find perishability a risk and this factor is also given due weightage while offering off-season accommodation at low price tags.

We find repeated advertising and competitive market conditions two important reasons for the growing significance of sales promotion in the hotel industry. The techniques may be directed to the hotel staff, tour operator and the travel agents including the users of the services. In Figure 12.10, we find tools of sales promotion directed at the hotel staff, tour operator and travel agents and guests or clients. We find three-tier arrangements for sales promotion in the hotel business. There are a number of incentives offered to them. In addition, we also find some of the hotels offering concessional travelling and accommodation facilities, specially to their staff. Besides, we also find cases of organising sales contests.

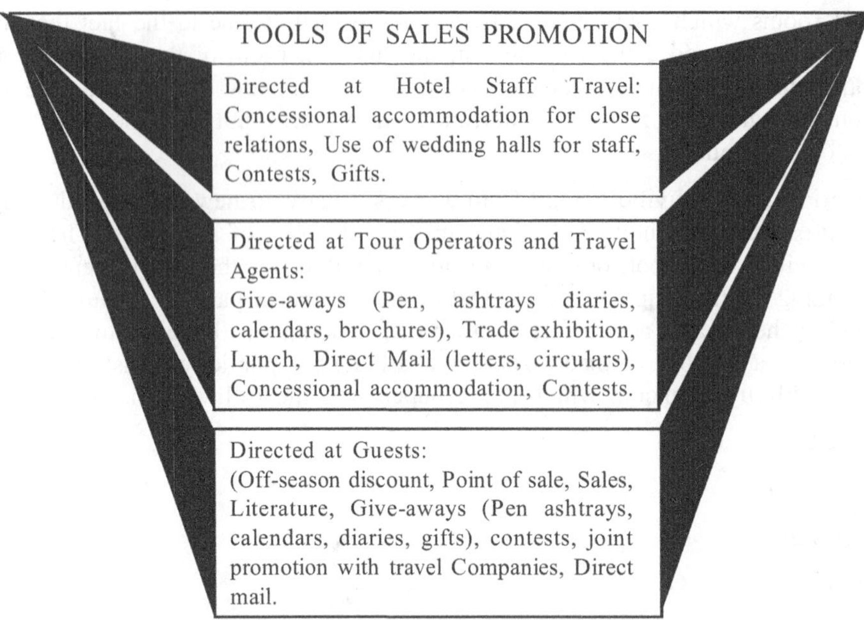

Fig. 12.10: Tools of Sales Promotion

The tour operators and travel agents are also given the incentives. We find give-away and concessional accommodation facilities for them. Besides, the guests or clients are also offered incentives. They are allowed off-season discount and a number of small gifts, specially the habitual guests for the purpose of keeping on the business. The following tools of sales promotion are used for all the three heads instrumental in promoting the hotel business.

1. Brochure: It is a device to stimulate customers and motivate them to visit a hotel and avail of the benefits offered by the management of the hotel. It is a detailed publication helping hotel companies in promoting their business. We also call it a pamphlet bound in the form of a booklet. It describes and illustrates the services made available by hotels. We find brochure different to folder in size and contents as well. It requires careful planning of the layout, colour and paper used for publishing the contents. The brochures are supposed to focus on the theme and messages of promotion areas. The guests, clients get detailed information from the brochure.

2. Folder: We find folder the most commonly used sales promotion tool. In this respect, it is essential that folders have an impressive appearance in totality. The particulars are required to be in brief but clear. We find it a single piece of illustrated paper which is found less voluminous than the brochure. The folders are usually printed on a single sheet of paper and then folded. The quality of paper and printing used for publication are found significant to make folders more attractive. The hotels can use folders for promoting the business.

3. Packaging: We call packaging an attractive wrapper of product. When we talk about packaging in the hotel industry, our emphasis is on the outer cover and internal layout of brochures and leaflets. We find it a final persuasive move on the part of hotels and hotel companies. The materials used for packaging are required to be attractive.

4. Attraction leaflets: This is exclusively meant for presenting a view of the different theme parks, museums, amusement parks, outstanding points of attraction in the hotels or so.

5. Merchandising: It is found helpful in promoting mass market. This tool is found significant to restaurants and bars. The merchandising involves displaying of foodstuffs and drinks in the right location. The restaurants and bars are required to place their important items at such point where the guest/clients get an opportunity to have a close view of special drinks or special menu.

6. Direct Mail Materials: The sales letters are found to be a direct mail material which can either be used alone or in combination with brochures and folders.

7. Display Materials: In the materials to be displayed at sensitive points are posters, dispensers, exhibits, etc. We can use these materials in the offices of the travel agents, tour operators or at the places where tourists come, such as tourists spots, resorts, airports, railway and bus stations.

8. Competition and Exhibition: We find organisation of competition and exhibition for promoting the business.

9. Special Offer: We also find a provision for special offer for all, such as users, travel agents, tour operators, and hotel personnel.

The aforesaid tools of sales promotion help hotels and hotel companies in increasing the business. The hotel personnel need professional excellence to make the tools of sales promotion productive.

Word-of-mouth Promotion

We consider word-of-mouth promotion very much instrumental in sensitising the prospects. In the hotel industry, it is much more significant that the satisfaction of users is given top priority. Of course, there are a number of components to promote sale but it is right to mention that other constituents may be ineffective but the word-of-mouth can't. The word-of-mouth promoters are those who are satisfied with the services of hotels or are motivated to motivate the prospects. We can't deny the fact that one bad meal would often do more damage by word-of-mouth than fifty good meals. Our guests take a good meal for granted but don't forget to narrate to their friends and relatives about a bad meal or the bitter experiences of menu fatigue. This speaks of the fact that word-of-mouth promotion can show more negative effects and therefore the hotels and hotel companies need to assign due weightage to this component of the promotion mix. Of course, the dissatisfied group of users are free to complain to the hotel management but often they don't act. We find them close-mouthed and stiff-lipped till they make a good-bye and after going back, they try their best to think twice before coming to that hotel again. Moreover, they start narrating to their friends and relatives their bitter experiences of menu fatigue even without taking a rest. It is against this background that high-level functions, refined behaviour and world-class services by the hotel personnel carry some meaning. These services pave the ways for oral communication and recommendation. The persons acting as word-of-mouth promoters are also called the hidden salesforce.

Almost all the hotels and hotel companies are found using oral communication or publicity for promoting the business. We can quote David Levin of the Capital Hotel, Basil Street, Knightsbridge as one of the most successful independent British hotel owners and operators. When he opened another restaurant, The Green House in Mayfair, he gave away a packet with a seed and instructions on how to sow and transplant them in a pot. The long-lasting plant was ornamental and a point of memory since people coming to that place asked about the plant and in a very natural way, the name of hotel supplying the same was promoted in a positive way. This speaks of the fact that word-of-mouth promotion is also possible when hotel companies in addition to the world-class services also offer some innovative gifts to their customers. The hidden salesforce or the oral publicists play an outstanding role in promoting the hotel business of which they are supposed to pay nothing.

We can't deny the fact that much of the word-of mouth communications are the result of your quality services, decent behaviour and innovative gifts. The hotel professionals bear the responsibility of identifying the opinion leaders or the vocal persons who can successfully act as a publicist. The persons with high communicative ability, having a domination in the society, acting as social activists, and popular leaders are found suitable prospects for publicising the services of hotels. If we talk about the effectiveness of this tool of sales promotion, we find it a two-step communication in which messages are transmitted to the opinion leaders. It is against this background that we make a strong advocacy in favour of word-of-mouth promotion. The hotels and hotel companies need to concentrate on the quality of services *vis-a-vis* the oral publicity which may be instrumental in promoting the business.

Personal Selling

Nothing happens unless anyone sells something and nothing is sold unless the buyers are motivated to purchase things of their choice. The oral representation in conversation bears the efficacy of transforming the motivation into persuasion. Thus, we find persuasion the main thing in energising the process of marketing. We can't deny the fact that personal selling has proved to be an important constituent of promotion. There is no doubt in it that the goods or services are found half sold when their properties are well told. The art of telling-and-selling is personal promotion which depends upon the personal excellence. Every business house — be it insurance, travel and tourism and hotel, we find professionally-sound salesforce or employees playing a decisive role in promoting the business. It is against this background that we talk about this constituent of the promotion mix.

The hotel business is substantially influenced by personal selling. The personal selling brings considerable momentum to the process of boosting the hotel business. The feedback received from the salesforce engaged in the process helps marketers in designing the development plans. Besides, the transmission of firsthand information is also an outstanding contribution of this tool of promotion. Service does not mean servility. The phrase 'the customer is always right', applies specifically to the hotel industry. The sales personnel are required to be friendly in dealings and cheerful in expression. They are required to be helpful and patient and above all, they should appear satisfied and work towards generating more satisfaction to customers.

For selling successfully and profitably, it is pertinent that we assign due weightage to Empathy. Here, our emphasis is on the process of projection. Ability to project yourself in a positive way, ability to convince others in a productive way are the important aspects when we talk about the instrumentality of personal selling. Projection is a combination of technique and psychology. The technique is related to the strategic words used by you while promoting the business. Psychology is related to one's ability to understand and deal with the people. We find more dynamism in technique because it is found to be always changing. If the circumstances are different; if the characters playing the role are different, it is quite natural that the dealings would also be different. As for example, if you are selling an identical product in your hotel, e.g., a four-day convention for 400 delegates, you are supposed to sell this directly by communicating in the actual function room, in the office of the buyers which might be private and quiet, or in an open office to a committee, in a foreign country. An important point to be clarified here is that the sales techniques are found changing with the changing business conditions.

We find personal selling very much instrumental in promoting the hotel business since we find in the process of selling instant communication. An opportunity to develop rapport with the prospects where we can project the best. Thus, face-to-face selling is an outstanding feature of personal selling that helps the salesforce sizeably. To be more specific in the hotel industry, it is difficult to motivate the guests since we need to use both verbal and non-verbal communication. For selling successfully, it is essential that salesforce managing the process are professionally-sound *vis-a-vis* the high performers. This makes it essential that persons with outstanding merits are given the responsibility of managing things.

A fair combination of personal and social skill is found essential for the salesforce to be engaged.

Personal skill: At the initial stage when the hotel receptionists, housekeepers, waiters, travel clerks encounter their clients or guests, the first impression projected by them would have a far reaching impact. The appearance and proper grooming of the personnel dealing with the guests play a significant role. We find a number of tourists organisations and hotel companies paying attention to regulate the same. Presenting a good show by the personnel goes a long way in influencing the image of your hotel. The hotel personnel need to realise that their way of dealing with customers would influence the business. They are supposed to adjust with the emerging constraints in the process. In almost all the leading hotels, we find that personal grooming of the staff is given due weightage and certain provisions are found for their appearance to attract the customers. Though we find that USA Continental Airlines were judged to have acted illegally when they dismissed a female employee with an exemplary professional record for refusing to wear make-up. In this context, it is significant to mention that hotel personnel coming into close contact, with customers must be fastidious about personal hygiene. This draws our attention on the basic hygiene criteria – with oral and dental care, restrictions on food which may offend clients or guests such as garlic, onion and in addition, a pleasing disposition which matters a lot in any client servicing industry and more so in a hotel industry. Hotel, airlines, car-rental staff, courier services, tourist resort representatives and travel agents are required to assign an overriding priority to a well written corporate image. If the hotel personnel succeed in projecting a fair image, it is substantially due to the personal skill.

Social skill: It is significant that the hotel personnel approach customers in a friendly and confident manner. It is meant welcome-smile, direct eye-contact, attractive disposition and willingness to listen. While shaking hands, we convey a sense of confidence and responsibility considered to be essential for opening the negotiations and transforming them into good business. Almost all the hotel personnel are required to have a well modulated and soothing voice, categorically while dealing with the guests or clients in totality. The waiters, housekeepers, porters, receptionists work in close association with the guests. They can ask a customer-attitude browsing through the brochures – is there any particular holiday you have in mind. This helps in generating a sales sequence. This speaks of the fact that the hotel personnel in general and the front-line personnel in particular need to show their professional excellence. Above all, the attitude of the personnel towards service must change. The use of derisive terms such as punter – is symptomatic of a poor attitude to service which is indefensible, if the hotel industry has truly to be professional in approach. Our concern for guests must improve.

The aforesaid facts are a mute testimony to this proposition that personal and social skills are found impact generating specially with the viewpoint of transforming the occasional customers into the habitual customers. Transforming the dialogues into a deal requires world-class professional excellence and the hotel personnels are required to be developed in such a way that they prove to be high performers. A rational plan for the recruitment and training is found a must.

Telemarketing

In an age of information explosion, we find frequent use of sophisticated information technologies for promoting the business. The telemarketing, of late, has been found gravitating the attention of a number of organisations where we find use of telephonic services for promoting the business. We can't negate the fact that even in the hotel industry, the telemarketing can play an incremental role. It is against this background that we talk about the instrumentality of telemarketing in promoting the hotel business.

We accept the fact that the instrumentality of telemarketing is substantially influenced by the skill of telemarketers *vis-a-vis* the instruments used in the process. A person with high communicative ability is to perform as a telemarketer who bears the responsibility of answering to the questions and queries of customers, prospects regarding the business transactions. In the hotel industry, the telemarketing can be helpful in promoting the business since the tour operators, transport operators, travel agents and the users develop a number of confusions and misunderstanding about booking, confirmation, cancellation, availability of package tour, a change in the hotel tariff or so. We are well aware of the fact that hotel is a multi-segment industry in which a number of industries are found involved in the process. The transport operators, the tour operators, the travel agents, and the users need multi-dimensional informations regarding the new provisions. If they have misunderstanding or they are confused, it is pertinent that the telemarketers remove their misunderstanding by answering to their questions suitably. It is in this context that we find telemarketers very much instrumental in activating the business transactions.

The hotel companies need the services of telemarketers. While recruiting/training the telemarketers, they need more care because communicative ability is considered to be the most vital aspect in the process of marketing with the help of telephones. This draws our attention on a rich communication network failing which the telemarketers would find it difficult to promote the business. We find technologies very much instrumental in influencing the process since poor quality of instruments and interruption in the process influences the quality of communication adversely. The hotels and hotel companies need to make it sure that the telephonic services are of quality. There are a number of sensitive points in a hotel where the telemarketers can play an important role. The reception and enquiries, the complaints and grievances redressal, the booking, confirmation, cancellation, the interruption in room services, the interruption in the services at the function rooms, the offering of a new package by a hotel, and the innovative tools of sales promotion to be used by hotels are some of the important points where an efficient telemarketer can serve both the hotels as well as the guests.

The aforesaid facts make it clear that in an age of satellite communication, the hotels and hotel companies are required to use telemarketing as an important constituent of promoting the business. This would only not be helpful in making the business environment conducive but in addition, the economy in operation is also to be made possible. The telemarketing, thus, simplifies the task of hotel professionals since the prospects think about a deal after getting the confusions removed. In this context, it is pertinent that they impart suitable training facilities to the telemarketers because a minor mistake committed by them may cause major injuries to the process of business promotion.

PRICE MIX

Pricing decisions are found critical, challenging and chaotic. Of course, no marketing mix is found so much critical as pricing. Pricing is not only the outcome of the marketing forces. It conveys something to customers even about the quality of a product. We also use pricing as a tool to manage demand. How to use this vital tool of the marketing is found important to the survival and prosperity of an organisation. There are a number of variables influencing the pricing decisions of an organisation. Like other organisations, the hotels and hotel companies also need to make pricing decisions. It is in this context that we go through the problem of pricing in the hotel industry.

The existence and prosperity of hotels and hotel companies are substantially influenced by the quality of pricing decisions. Of late, we find worldwide economic depression and the trend is not likely to be reversed in the near future. This makes it essential that the hotel companies also consider the emerging trends in the business environment *vis-a-vis* the mounting pressure of inflation. Talking about the pricing strategy is easier than writing about the same. The futurologist such as Henley Centre suggests that as discretionary income goes up, the systematic and emotional values attached to the brand name also go up. We accept the fact that symbolic value occupies a place of significance even in the hotel industry. The pricing decisions are beset with many problems. No doubt in it that fixing the hotel tariffs is just like pricing other goods and services. At the same time, it is also right to mention that the hotel professionals need more excellence while fixing the hotel tariffs since the services are found of perishable nature. In addition, the seasonal fluctuation in demand and increasing intensity of competition also complicate the task of professionals. They need world-class excellence while making strategical and tactical pricing decisions. It is in this context that we go through the problem of price mix.

Managing relatively volatile demand around a relatively fixed capacity of highly perishable product supply is identified as one of the principal characteristics of the hotel business. There are four elements in the strategic marketing response which accommodation suppliers make to their external business environment, such as planning the most profitable business mix of segments and products, deciding the position or image which each accommodation unit or chain of units should occupy, encouraging and rewarding frequent users of the services and developing marketing integration between units in common ownership (chains) or units in individual ownership (voluntary co-operatives). Strategic decisions are expected to generate a profitable mix of bookings and room occupancy through the production and distribution of appropriately priced distinctive products which match the needs and requirements of identified segments.

We accept the fact that pricing menus and drinks in hotel food and beverage areas to obtain maximum sales and profits is a very complex subject. While formulating the pricing strategy, the hotel professionals are required to take into account a number of factors, specially the diverse nature and character of dishes, involvement of costs and spending power of the customers. We also need to consider the economic criteria, target average spends, target covers per meal period, current menu and drink prices.

Pricing decisions are found important in both strategic and tactical sense. In the tactical sense, it plays an outstanding role. This is due to the inseparability and perishability of the hotel products. This is also due to the inability of the service engineering organisations to carry over unsold stocks as a buffer to cope with future demand as found in the goods manufacturing organisations. Also known as price deregulation, tactical pricing is found instrumental in promoting the hotel business. Experiences show that in the hotel industry, it is found to be a major selling tool. There are a number of ways for practising and benefiting from this tool:

- Seasonal Discounts — Found applicable in the hotel industry. Customary to charge lower prices, specially during the off-season.
- Trade Discounts — Found applicable in the hotel industry as tour operators and travel agents are offered discounts.
- Special Discounts — In the hotel industry, we find special function room rates for overnight convention.

Pricing for Room Tariffs

Here, we go through the guidelines for fixing reasonable room tariffs. While fixing room tariffs, it is essential that we assign due weightage to the price structure to be adopted. The average room rate should not be much higher than the competitive hotels otherwise the market will not welcome it. A hotel may also adopt a policy to give high payroll to provide a higher standard of services which the customers are ready to pay. There are some common factors considered by the hotel management and the public:

- current charges prior to a review,
- the established inflationary effect on cost,
- the general economic situation,
- the emerging trends in currency exchange, and
- the intensity of competition.

In the last few decades when the rate of inflation was not so high, a majority of our customers only looked at the current charges and the inflationary impact on cost. But now the situation is much more complex and therefore the customers consider all the aforesaid factors. In addition, it is also to be answered as to what tariff increase will the market bear. Right averages and average room rates are the two important aspects to be taken into consideration while fixing hotel tariffs. The following are the economic criteria on room tariffs:

- The total amount of net operating costs (after contribution from the food and beverage departments). Net operating costs, net operating cost plus rent (if payable), net operating cost plus interest and net operating cost plus a target return on capital.
- This helps in calculating the total room sales and to achieve various levels of profits with the assumption that room department cost ratios, staff numbers and staff standards are known.
- On the basis of the above, a schedule should be produced as per the average room rates required in order to break even and/or to achieve the profit targets at various occupancy levels.
- Budgets on room sales are to be planned based on sales mix taking into account the different sources of business.
- After this, based on the current quoted tariffs, it is possible to calculate the different sources of business, must not be exceeded if the average rate required is to be achieved.

Pricing for Food and Beverage

We can't deny the fact that pricing for food and beverage is much more complicated. In a majority of the hotels, there are three or four types of rooms but so far as the menus are concerned we can have dozen of dishes. There are some of the important points to be considered in the process:

- Do you find that your guests are eating in the hotel restaurant or coffee shop where the competitive restaurants are very close to the hotel. Generally, a proportion do eat in but a significant proportion go out.
- Where a hotel has two or more restaurants, they compete with each other and help splitting the market down the middle rather than offering a true price.
- The business in the function room.

Pricing for Function

Restaurants can get more business because the food, services or atmosphere is unique or just a little better than the competitors. But this aspect is found more complicated for function room services. Most of the functions are fairly routined which makes it difficult to produce a gastronomic experience. In addition, this aspect is found more competitive specially on the price front. Payroll is found to be a major cost on functions. Unless we move to the self-service (buffet style) functions, the payroll would remain an important dimension. A number of hotels are found fixing a staff standard for functions based on their style of hotel or one waiter to a table of ten people or one waiter to two tables. Yet, we find payroll more expensive.

In the pricing decisions for the hotel services, we find room tariffs of three types, e.g., the American Plan, Modified American Plan and European Plan. The American Plan includes the price of the room, breakfast, lunch or dinner. No meals are included in room rates under the European Plan. Room rates are quoted as per day. Double room rates quoted are for two persons per day. Some hotels have luxurious apartments, tariff of which is available on application. Some hotels add a service charge of 10 per cent. In hotels where the service charge is added, tipping is not encouraged by the management. The American Plan and the Modified American Plan give the impression that there is an element of compulsion. In making pricing decisions, it is also important that we are not under-quoting ourselves. A more pragmatic and realistic approach to tariff policy is the need of the hour. Quoting lower rates would, no doubt, increase the occupancy ratio. In tariff fixing, the psychology of users is also found significant. Some guests are found extremely sensitive to price and for them, the reduced rate would normally be stimulant. Yet the reduction in rate must be done carefully because we also find users considering high pricing a status symbol. We can't negate the fact that the pricing policy affordable to the guests and remunerative to the establishment is found to be a rational policy subserving the interests of all.

In view of the above, it is right to mention that the intensity of competition, emerging trends in economy and changing lifestyles are the important factors drawing due attention of the hotel management, specially while making the pricing decisions.

PLACE MIX

It is not only sufficient that we have a product mix of world-class; it is not only significant that we promise the best, it is much more impact generating that we bridge over the gap between the services-promised and services-offered. The hotels and hotel companies have been found innovating their service mix but they also bear the responsibility of making it sure that the promised services reach to the ultimate users in a right fashion. It is against this background that we focus on the place mix of hotel companies. The hotel personnel and the travel agents are found instrumental in offering the services related to hotels. The front-line staff, receptionists, enquiries, complaints and grievances redressal cell, the waiters, the porters, the doormen, the travel agents and the tour operators are found involved in the process. If they are professionally-sound and personally-committed, the promised services would reach to the users without any distortion that would generate satisfaction to the users and even the projection of a positive image would not be found much more difficult. Of course, the hotel institutes and travel and tourism institutes have been educating and training the personnel keeping in view the changing needs and increasing expectations of the users, still we find cases where they generate a gap while processing the services which results into dissatisfaction *vis-a-vis* projection of a negative image. This makes it essential that we assign due weightage to the processing of services.

A sound distribution system is found significant to the development of almost all the organisations either producing goods or generating services. In the hotel industry, the distribution of services is mainly related to the transmission of information by the related persons to the ultimate users. As an when the bookings are made of a bedroom or a function room or of a restaurant, the confirmation is found essential. The transmission of information related to cancellation is also found important. We can't deny the fact that with the introduction of sophisticated information technologies, the task is made easier but the professionals operating and maintaining the technologies have also been found generating the gap. This makes it essential that hotels, offices of travel agents and the tour operators are well connected with computers, internet services. A number of factors are found influencing the distribution process, such as location, point of sale, the cost of distribution, effectiveness of marketing resources, image of hotels and hotel companies, tactical strategy and the motivational schemes. For accomplishing the organisational goals or for bridging over the gap between the services-promised and services-offered, we need to innovate the distribution proceses, helping us substantially in purchasing the hotel bedrooms, function rooms restaurants, essentially through the chain of distribution. The hotels and hotel companies are here required to take a decision regarding a strong and efficient chain which maintains economy in the process and at the same time, also minimises the possibilities of distortion in the process.

A widespread myth persists till now that because the services can't be put on shelves and in warehouses as inventory, the distribution system or channels are found less impact generating in hospitality services. In marketing, the creation and manipulation of accessibility to the services is considered to be one of the principal ways to manage demand for highly perishable products.

We don't find anything wrong with the system, if hotels sell the services through tour operators and travel agents provided the in-house selling is not satisfactory.

The choice of location is, of course, the most important business decision, specially for proprietor-owned restaurants, guest houses and small tourist attractions. This is due to the fact that a well-located small business can often be sure of an adequate flow of customers to its catchment area. In this case, the consumers come to the producer directly and therefore, we find the distribution channels less significant. However, the fundamental attraction of well-located sites does not diminish. The more or less continuous search in the 1980s by international hotel companies seeking suitable hotel sites in major European cities provide some illustration of the power of location. The selection of tour operators and travel agents is an important decision-making area for hotels and hotel companies. If the hotels and hotel companies are well connected with the offices of the travel agents and the tour operators, the occupancy ratio can be increased. The tour operators buy a range of tourist products in bulk. This also includes accommodation facilities which is found relevant to the hotel industry. They also buy function rooms, specially for the organisation of conferences, seminars, exhibition, sales contests or so. After buying a number of services and making them a lucrative package, the tour operators sell them to the travel agents. Here, the tour operators play a decisive role in promoting the hotel business.

With the introduction of computers and increasing use of new generation of information technologies, we except a radical change in the distribution system. Of late, we find a number of hotels over a certain size computerised at least in the front office for guest billing, reservation, etc. Even while installing, operating and maintaining computers, they need more care. The software companies promoting computers advocate that by installing computers, the hotel management would register good business. But this is not the only thing since the computer professionals if not of world-class would fail in delivering goods. The front line staff whether they work on computers or manually are supposed to be high performers so that the sophisticated information technologies used by them deliver the best.

The distribution chain denotes the methods by which a product or services is processed from producers to the ultimate users. The middlemen are the link and if the link is strong, the service generating organisations find it convenient to increase the occupancy ratio. The middlemen are wholesalers buying hotel rooms in bulk and then selling the same to the retailers known as the travel agents. The tour operators are called the producers of services. The travel agents buy the services at the request of their clients and provide a convenient network of sales outlets which caters to the needs of the catchment area. In Figure 12.11, 12.12 and 12.13, we find three systems for distributing the services, e.g. two-level, one-level and zero-level. The three-tier distribution system is required to be managed properly so that the users expectations are fulfilled and the promised services reach to the ultimate users in a right way. It is in this context that the hotel management requires world-class professional excellence which would simplify the distribution process besides maintaining economy and making possible cost-effectiveness. The Figures presenting the three systems of distribution thus need due care of hotel companies. In Figure 12.11, we find zero-level distribution system.

This is a process of direct distribution without any middlemen. The hotels book, confirm and cancel with the help of their own system.

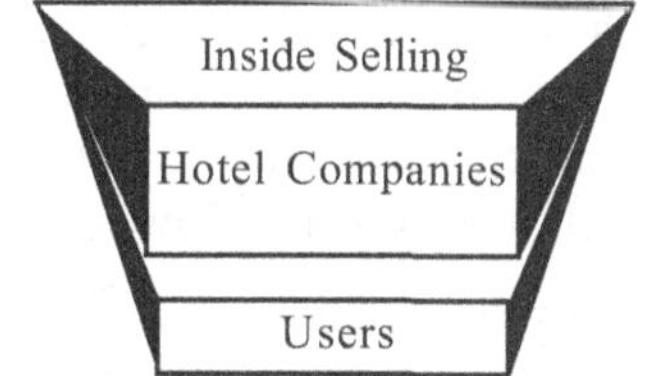

Fig. 12.11: Zero-Level Distribution

In Figure 12.12, we find one-level distribution system where between the hotel companies and their ultimate users, we find travel agents responsible for distributing or processing the services.

Fig. 12.12: One-level Distribution System

In Figure 12.13, we find two-level distribution system in which the tour operators act as wholesaler and the travel agents acts as a retailer.

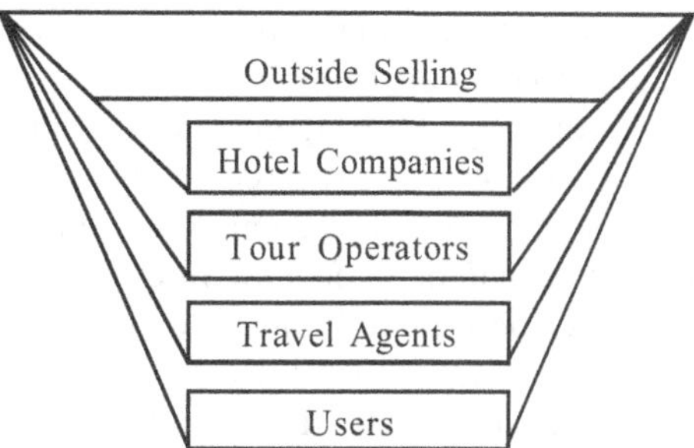

Fig. 12.13: Two-level Distribution System

The aforesaid facts and figures make it clear that all the three systems of distribution are found important to the hotel companies. They are supposed to seek the co-operation of channels failing which the task of increasing or optimising the occupancy ratio would be much more difficult.

Innovation of product can't be the lone solution for demand stimulation. Innovation in distribution occupies a place of outstanding significance. We can't negate the positive contributions of distribution processes in improving or degenerating the quality of services. Of course, the small hotels can promote their business even without taking the support of a distribution chain but so far as the big hotels and hotel companies are concerned, they can't work if the travel agents and tour operators don't make available to them the quality services. Building and maintaining the co-operation of middlemen is a critical decision-making area which requires more professional excellence. If the distribution chain is working satisfactorily, the hotels and hotel companies succeed and contrary to it, if they don't perform efficiently they suffer. This strengthens the hypothesis that tour operators and travel agents are customers for the product of hotels and hotel companies. This calls for a harmonious working relationships with the middlemen so that the hotel companies are not to face the multi-dimensional problems. For the hotel companies working on a large-scale, it is pertinent to select the best channel alternative. Of course, the most profitable channel is considered to be the best channel. But at the same time, it is also right to mention that in addition to profitability, we also find satisfaction to users playing a decisive role in the entire process and the world-class middlemen need to perceive it.

In view of the above, the hotel companies need to think about one-level or two-level distribution system. This is mainly due to the fact that they are supposed to transmit substantial information to the prospects, such as conventional customer access, providing brochure and leaflets and focussing on their services products, displaying and merchandising opportunities, itinerary planning, ancillary services, such as insurance, advice on other peripheral services, passport issues, visa issues, serving as marketing intelligence for hotel companies, supplementing hotel's promotional activities and lodging and redressing complaints from customers. The main problem before big hotels is to counter the challenges and threats engineered by the leading competitive hotel chains. Of course, the front-line staff also play an important role in the process of offering but their operational area is found limited. In the hotel industry, the distribution strategy is related to the following key issues:

- Will hotels prefer to sell directly to the users?
- Will they sell through clubs?
- Will they engage tour operators?
- Will they engage both tour operators as well as the travel agents?
- Will they engage only the travel agents?

Because of the choice and flexibility of distribution channels in service products in general and the hotel products in particular, the strategic choice between internal and external selling, domestic and international selling, direct and indirect selling occupy a place of significance. The world-class hotel professionals are supposed to make the decisions sound so that the process of distribution is made cost-effective. In addition, it is also important that they think about locational points since of late the high spending tourists prefer cottages located in the outskirts or even in villages. In an age of information explosion, the distance carries no meaning if well developed transportation facilities are available.

The Process

The hotel services reach to the ultimate users after processing in which we find involvement of a team of people and in addition, the information and communication technologies also play an effective role. The customers or guests as users of hotel services either directly or through travel agents book the rooms. When the customers start using the services, we find a number of people involved in the process, such as the receptionists making available to them the detailed information regarding the rooms and supporting them to ensure their convenient placement. The guests may be habitual or casual or even new and therefore the receptionists may instruct their concerned staff to take care. The selling may be outdoor, indoor or both or online. When the guests or customers reach to their rooms, they expect everything in order. This makes it essential that the professionals make it sure that before entry of a guest in the room even the small things are in perfect order. The bedsheets, pilo covers, cushions, curtains, lighting, ventilation, music, sanitation have been properly checked and the guests have nothing to complain. As per schedule, the guests are given the waking call. The telephonic and telecom services also need due attention.

If the guests avail the services of restaurants, the time schedule for breakfast, lunch and dinner requires to be informed and in the restaurants, a number of services are processed with the help of a team of people working in different capacities. The quality of food supplied, breakfast served, water on the table, performance of waiters determine the right and decent processing of services. The chef and his team play a decisive role in processing the food items to be served on table. The lighting arrangements on the table and the colour of light are also important in the very context. The music arrangements in the restaurants, the volume of music cannot be overlooked. Hence, even in the restaurants, a number of services are processed.

The services processed for guests may also include booking and cancellation of air tickets, if the circumstances necessitate or the customer's request. Even in the lounge, a number of services are processed, such as arrangements of furniture and lighting, music and scent, entertainment facilities, etc.

The above-mentioned facts make it clear that hotel services for right and decent processing need involvement of a team of quality people coming from different streams. In addition, the information and communication technologies and other equipments are also used for right processing. The promised quality of services cannot be made available to the guests or customers if we find even a small gap at one stage or point. The processing for service delivery, thus, needs a professionalised approach and personal touch.

Even for service recovery, we find processing and once again involvement of a full team. The professionals need to assign top priority to the service recovery processes so that transformation of dissatisfied guests into habitual guests is made possible. If guests feel that their complaints are redressed properly, they develop a high level of confidence.

PHYSICAL EVIDENCE AND ATTRACTIONS

The hotel business considerably rests on projection through tangibilisation of outstanding properties. The guests visiting hotels have high levels of expectations. There are a number of sensitive points considered significant with the viewpoint of tangibilisation such as reception, bedrooms, restaurants and lounge. The conference halls and wedding halls may also be a place for the projection of your image. The customers of high profile visiting and staying in hotels have high level of expectations and therefore while tangibilising, you need to consider their taste and temperament. Aesthetic management plays a significant role in the tangibilisation process. The marketing professionals managing these sensitive points need personal touch and a high degree of excellence.

The interiors, furnishing, signposts, ventilation, music and scent help you in making the service ambience customer-friendly. You need to consider the positioning and placing of music *vis-à-vis* the quality of music and its volume. Keeping in view the inflow of guests visiting your hotel, the music is to be selected. We find variations in taste and temperament and you cannot overlook it. The environmental dimensions have a big list and as a professional, you have to use them. The ambient conditions help you in generating service fragrance. Signs displayed on the exterior and interior of a structure are found acting as explicit communicators. We cannot negate that services cape can serve as a package and a visual metaphor for the service itself. It may also act as a facilitator in adding the accomplishment of customer and employees' goals. Besides, we also find it acting as a socialiser in prescribing behaviours in the environment and a differentiator to distinguish the organisation from its rivals.

In the hotel business, the marketing professionals need to strengthen their realisation that if we find habitual customer visiting hotels, we also find new customers visiting your hotel for the first time. The signposts help them in identifying or locating the service points desired by them. The positioning of signposts and lighting facilities there also become significant. The colour of light cannot be overlooked in the very context. In addition, the intensity of light also needs due attention.

There are a number of points for furnishing such as the lounge, reception, restaurants and rooms where guests stay. Generally, we find customers preferring furniture of artistic nature. At different points, you may place different types of furniture. Reception is considered to be the most sensitive point where you tangibilise. The information and communication technologies used there must be in order.

The bedrooms where your guests stay for the long time need your priority attention. The colour and intensity of light, quality and volume of music, the bedsheets and their colour, the cushion on the furniture, the ventilation, functioning of AC, the quality of sanitation services are considered important for room management. The scent used there and the ornamental plants inside and outside the room add aesthetic sense and generate service fragrance.

In the hotel services, the professionals need to add additional attractions and in the process, we find service ambience helping them in the tangibilisation of the outstanding features. Aesthetic management also needs due care which is found concerned with almost all the dimensions of service ambience. Right from the entrance of the compound of your hotel to the main gate and even inside, ornamental shadow plants, flowers with scent and intoxic fragrance simplify your task of image projection. You need not to forget that the service culture depends on service ambience.

In this context, it is also pertinent that the different categories of staff serving your hotel are sincere to the dress code. They need to make it sure that their dresses are neat and clean. A majority of the staff in the hotel have prescribed uniform. Since we find uniform symbolising your identity, you need priority attention on their maintenance. Besides, it is also essential that shoes used by them are well polished. The hairstyle also adds attraction to the personality of your staff. Thus, the different dimensions of personal care add additional attractions and you find yourself in a position to project your fair image.

Attraction is an important consideration in the hotel business. We find different sources for adding attractions to our services. Of course, we bear the responsibility of offering quality core services to our customers but it is not meant that we do not mind our peripheral services. The customers taking pleasure in lounge, enjoying breakfast and food in restaurants and getting peace in the bedrooms develop a perception regarding the service quality. As a professional, it is your prime responsibility to take care and not to provide an opportunity to them to complain. It is against this background that we focus on adding additional attractions to our services.

With the emergence of corporate culture, we find two more important places for tangibilisation, such as conference halls and wedding halls. Due to trade and commerce activities, we find frequent conferences related to different streams. At this place, we find a number of high profile customers assembling and therefore, the professionals need priority attention on the ambient conditions. They need to make it sure that all the amenities and facilities for presentation are available and can be switched on within a few seconds. We are aware of the fact that corporate culture has changed our lifestyles and due to time constraint, we find people preferring to organise their wedding and reception functions in the hotels. Again this provides you an opportunity for tangibilisation. As and where you expect assembling of high profile of your customers, you need special care there because a minor mistake in the creation of service ambience may cause a big financial loss *vis-à-vis* the image problem.

Thus, the marketing professionals while marketing hotel services need due attention on physical evidence and attraction simplifying their task of tangibilisation, adding additional attractions and ensuring fair projection.

THE PEOPLE

In an age of sophisticated information technologies when we have been making superhighway for communications, we find a basic change in the expectations of users. The personnel serving the hotel companies, no doubt, depend substantially on the instrumentality of information technologies but here it is also important that hotels and hotel companies assign due weightage to the development of personnel. Sky is the limit for perfection. This phrase is meaningful not only for the technologies but even for the people who manage them. It is against this background that the marketing experts the world over have been found making a strong advocacy in favour of an ongoing training programme for the personnel servicing the hotel companies.

In this context, our prime focus is on the front-line personnel working in hotels in different capacities. The receptionists, the porters, the housekeepers, the waiters and waiteresses and even the doormen play an incremental role in promoting the business. The sales executives, the marketing managers, the senior executives bear the responsibility of managing the front-line personnel in such a way that the promised services reach to the ultimate users without making any distortion. Of course, they are supposed to have proper education and knowledge regarding the services they need to offer but here, it is also important that we organise for them an ongoing training programme, refresher courses, capsule courses, lecture programmes, specially related to the behavioural profile. We find several cases to quote that even the five star hotels where the users stay with high expectations, a minor mistake committed by the receptionists or the housekeepers has resulted in a big loss. The front-line staff in particular need to identify the changing levels of expectations of users and in a majority of the cases, they virtually fail in doing such. A gap is generated between the quality-promised and the quality-offered. If the hotel personnels prove to be high performers, personally-committed, professionally-sound, value-oriented, aware of the behavioural management, familiar with the aesthetic management, they can satisfy the users even if the sophisticated technologies develop a fault. This makes it essential that the hotel personnels are made available an ongoing training facility efficacious in enriching their professional excellence. The cases of menu fatigue, power interruption, mismanaged bedrooms, function rooms and restaurants, indecent behaviour of doormen, poor information to the receptionists and enquiries can be minimised considerably if we assign due weightage to performance orientation.

We can't negate the fact that employee orientation makes the ways for performance orientation. This gravitates our attention on the multi-dimensional incentives to be offered to the hotel personnel. Incentives pave the avenues for the generation of efficiency *vis-a-vis* their personal involvement. But efficiency-based incentives need an overriding priority which on the one hand would induce efficients while on the other hand would also energise inefficients to perform their best. If we keep on moving the process of efficiency generation by offering incentives, a strong foundation would be engineered for generating the efficiency albeit by the low performers. It is against this background that we find it significant to make possible a fair synchronisation of performance orientation and employee orientation. We should not forget that the technologies in no case can replace the high performers.

SERVQUAL IN HOTEL INDUSTRY

Tangibility, reliability and responsiveness are a few of the important factors which the marketing professionals need to keep in their minds about the service quality of hotels. The hotel marketers bear the responsibility of marketing available to the guest's quality services and in the process of service delivery, they need due attention the dimensions mentioned below:

Tangibility: In this context, the hotel marketers focus on tangibilisation. Though we find hotel services of intangible nature but in the service delivery processes, there are a number of areas where tangibilisation is possible. Here, our focus is on the physical facilities, equipments and attractions generated by the hotel personnels. Particularly in the hotel industry, the professionals have to assign top priority to cleanliness. This is the minimum that the guests expect from the hotel industry. Besides, the availability of parking space and presentation of pamphlets and many cards are also found significant. We cannot negate that the tangibilisation varies from hotel to hotel. This is due to the fact that guests staying in Five Star Deluxe Hotels expect something distinct and therefore the tangibilisation process in that case would consist of a number of items such as quality of furnishing, interior and exterior decorations, quality of light, use of scent, aesthetic management, etc. The main thing here is to tangibilise the maximum that you can to impress upon the customers or guests.

Responsiveness: This focuses our attention on willingness of the hotel staff to provide time-honoured services to the guests. The SERVQUAL makes it clear that customers or guests expect from the hotel personnel, the quality of services in tune with their needs and requirements. Besides, the people are expected to be behaviourally-sound. Thus, punctuality and decent behaviour are the important considerations when we talk about service quality in the hotel services.

Reliability: The SERVQUAL regarding the reliability dimension makes it clear that in this context, the customers or guests have faith on the providers that they are going to keep their promises. In the hotel services, the services offered in restaurants are found concerned with reliability. The freshness and temperature of the food, the quality of food promised help in developing the faith of customers on hotel industry. In addition, it is also pertinent that the hotel personnel are very much sincere to the problems of customers and they make best of their efforts so that even new customers do not experience any problem. The gap between the services-promised and services-offered are to be bridged to gain the confidence of customers. The categories of employees determine the requirements for knowledge. A majority of the people serving hotel industry are expected to have basic knowledge of the industry.

Empathy: Personalised caring is known as empathy where the hotel personnels are supposed to work and serve with personal touch. There are two categories of employees serving hotels such as back-line and front-line. Particularly while placing people in the front line, it is imperative that they are aware of empathy and practise the same in the service delivery and service recovery processes. Developing friendly relationships and sharing personal feelings are some of the properties of empathy which help in building relationships.

Accessibility and Flexibility: This dimension of SERVQUAL focuses our attention on the ability of the providers of services concerned with location, operating hours, employees and operational systems to design and deliver the services efficacious of adjusting the demands of customers. The location point for hotels must have easy and smooth accessibility and in addition, flexibility is required for adjusting the operating hours. The occupancy ratio in a hotel is found during the season when we find high level of influx of tourists but this is not possible to increase the supply position. Hence, it is essential that hotel professionals are in a position to bring the demand and supply position at an optimal point.

Price: This dimension of SERVQUAL focuses our attention on the hotel tariff. The paying capacity of customers or guests is found important in the process of setting hotel tariff. When we find boom period, the customers particularly belonging to the corporate segment and specially from the software industry are found highly paid. In this context, the paying capacity of the corporate segment is found high. Contrary to it, when we find economic depression, the customers in general are found sensitive to price. This is due to the fact that we find a pay-cut drive in the corporate sector and resulting from which a fall in the paying capacity of customers. It is the general perception that if customers pay high price for the services, they expect high quality of services. Just reverse, when they pay low price, we find their expectations low. When the hotel industry becomes a status symbol, we find a paradox in the behavioural profile of customers. If they get high quality of services at low price, it becomes a general perception that service quality is not to be up-to-mark.

The aforesaid dimensions of SERVQUAL need due attention of hotel professionals for improving the quality of services in hotels. Actually, we find these dimensions as parameters to rate the Service Quality. The hotel marketers need to make an evaluation of the services in the face of aforesaid dimensions which would help them in identifying the weaknesses.

HOTEL MARKETING IN INDIAN PERSPECTIVE

The plantation of a western concept in the eastern environment was made initially by the British. The Taj Mahal Hotel built by Jameshedji Nauroji Tata in Bombay in 1903 is the only exception since till dawn of the independence, by and large, almost all the hotels in India were owned and managed by British or Swiss. After the attainment of independence and to be more specific with the beginning of the planned concept of economic development, the contours of development underwent radical changes. The policy makers realised the significance of hotel and tourism services in the emancipation of economy and gradually, we find a change in the development processes. UNESCO Conference organised in Delhi made the ways for the establishment of the Ashok Hotel in 1956, specially to accommodate the delegates attending the conference. Since then, we find a change in the development philosophy which encouraged albeit the private sector to participate in the development process.

The hotel industry particularly in the Indian perspective has often considered marketing as a tantamount of selling. We need to perceive that the marketing transplants the seeds and sales harvest the crops. We can't think of harvesting unless we think seriously about transplanting. The retarded development of hotel industry in the Indian environment is also due to the delayed application of modern marketing principles. Of late, the policy makers, the hoteliers, the tour and transport operators, the travel agents realise that to activate the process of development and to make the services internationally competitive *vis-a-vis* commercially viable; they have no option but to perceive and practise modern marketing principles in a right fashion. Such an attitudinal change has opened new vistas for the development of hotel industry.

Hotel marketing studies in its purview almost all the components directly or indirectly influencing the maintaining of commercial viability along with the generation of customer satisfaction.[17] We are aware of the fact that marketing is a process of engineering users' satisfaction and practising marketing in right perspective would make possible multi-dimensional qualitative improvements. The task before the hotels and hotel companies is to conceptualise marketing in the face of changing business conditions. Of late, we find the intensity of competition at its peak, the business environment highly volatile and the domination of sophisticated information technologies increasing very fast. The leading hotel chains have been found evincing their interests in the development of hotel industry in the face of new emerging trends which have been helping them in increasing the market share and establishing the leadership.

We have high potentials for the development of tourism industry which may be considered to be a positive sign for the development of hotel industry. In addition, we have also been successful in increasing the domination of corporate sector in the national economic transformation processes which has been opening new fronts for the development of hotel culture. Significant developments in the field of transportation, sophisticated communication technologies due to satellite communication have been found influencing our lifestyles fantastically. The kids, teens, women are now found crossing the threshold barriers. The professional education has been gaining popularity specially among the women and now we find them working as business executives. Women have also proved to be successful technocrats and bureaucrats. In almost all the areas, we find women contributing and sharing substantially.

These developments have made the business environment for the hotel industry more conducive. The opportunities are now available and we need professional excellence to capitalise on the same profitably.

The contribution of India Tourism Development Corporation (ITDC) to the development of hotel industry is found positive. The Ashok Chain is the largest hotel chain in India which is run by the ITDC, the public sector undertaking. Originally, the name of the chain was Ashoka but now it is Ashok. The Oberoi Chain is also found gaining popularity. The Taj Group of hotels are managed and controlled by the Indian Hotels Company Ltd. Besides, the Welcome Group is one of the fastest growing hotel chain in the Indian perspective. The Hotel Corporation of India – a subsidiary of Air India started with one hotel – Centaur at Mumbai Airport, presently has a number of hotels in different parts of the country. The Clark Group, Eastern Hotel International and Travotel are also emerging as important groups.

It is high time that particularly in the Indian perspective, the public as well as the private sector realises the relevance of economic hotels for burgeoning Middle Class. In addition, it is also important that the big hotel chains think about hotel accommodation facilities albeit for the low-income group of the Indian society. This is essential because the urban population is increasing fast. We find a profitable opportunity there which focuses on development of new economic hotels.

The intensity of competition is found mounting which makes it essential that the hotels and hotel companies think about innovative marketing. They need to blend core and peripheral services in such a way that the product uniqueness is made possible. Since we find least scope for innovating the core services, the hotel professionals need to think in favour of innovative peripheral services. Enriching the peripheral services is the first and foremost task before the hotel professionals. We can't deny the fact that a majority of the Indian hotels have been facing image problem which has been complicating their task of increasing the market share. Of late, we have sophisticated technologies and a big team of professionals having world-class excellence which simplify the task of innovating the promotional measure so that projection of a positive image is made possible. We need to make possible creativity in the promotional measures with the motto of sensitising the prospects and stimulating the demand. Of course, we find luxury hotels symbolising status but at the same time, economic hotels or say inexpensive hotels need due attention of hotel planners. The hotel personnel need an ongoing training programme. With the sophistication in the process of information technologies frequently used by the hotel companies, we need to redesign our personnel development programmes. We are living in an age of high performers where the human resources are supposed to be personally-committed and professionally-sound. This draws our attention on the motivational schemes for the hotel personnel.

In view of the above, it is right to mention that innovation in developing and using the marketing resources is felt urgent and the hotels and hotel companies have no option but to make it possible so that the process of quality upgradation keeps on moving. Perceiving right perception of marketing in a right fashion is crying need of the hour which is to be publicised and practised by the world-class hotel professionals on a priority basis.

With the new emerging trends in the global economy, it is pertinent that the policy makers bring a change in the concept of hotel. Since the poor occupancy ratio of luxurious hotels has been found adversely affecting their financial health, the concept of budget hotel or economic hotel is required to be promoted. Besides, we also need to promote the Heritage Hotel, a special category of hotels in palaces, havelis, castles, forts and residence carrying ancient values. The traditional structure reflects the ambience and lifestyles of the bygone and is found immensely popular in the foreign tourists. This will be in the category of functioning hotels. It is significant to mention that the Department of Tourism[18] classifies functioning hotels under the star system into various categories from one star to five star deluxe and Heritage Classic, Grand and Heritage Renaissance and Apartment Hotels from three star to five star deluxe, Time share Resorts from three star to five star and Guest Houses. Despite economic depression, we find a few of the selective high spending tourists who will continue to travel. The main thing is time-honoured identification of a change in the taste of users which cannot be overlooked.

The trade and commerce activities considerably influence the tourism and hotel sectors. We have no option but to accept that bringing back the global economy on the rail is a time-taking process and unless we find a reversal trend, the hotel industry will not get a conducive environment to thrive. Protecting the existence is the first consideration and this focuses our attention on Budget Hotel. Because the hotel business rests on the development of corporate sector and therefore till we find everything becoming normal, they will have to formulate their strategic plans very carefully.

Presently, we find almost all the star group of hotels facing the problem of occupancy ratio which has been making their task much more difficult. The corporate sector has also been found minimising their budgets. The trade and commerce activities are found shrinking. Thus, we find all the avenues showing red signal. At this juncture, it is not proper that hotels think in favour of any new plan for development and expansion at least for the time being. Maximising scope for budget hotel and making possible creativity in the promotional measures appear to be the solutions particularly in a volatile business environment.

Innovations in tourism may also be effective at this stage because adventure tourism, sports tourism, heritage tourism and village tourism are the options before the high spending foreign tourists who may prefer travelling for diffusion of tension. Economic depression brings tension and around the world, we find affluent sections of the society developing thirst for peace. The inflow of tourists, domestic as well as foreign if increased will meet the requirements of hotel industry.

SUMMARY

In this chapter, you have studied different dimensions of hotel marketing. After going through the chapter, be sure that the following facts are well versed.

Hotel – The Concept: Hotel is a place where all who conduct themselves properly and are ready to pay for their entertainment, accommodation and other services. It is home away from home where we get amenities and facilities, of course, on a payment basis.

Hotel and Its Typology: There are five types of hotel such as residential, commercial, resort, international and floating.

Hotel Marketing — The Concept: It is the application of marketing principles in the hotel industry so that the hotel services are made internationally-competitive *vis-a-vis* commercially-viable.

Users of Hotel Industry: The different categories of users availing the services of hotel industry are pilgrims, students, officials, intellects, sportsmen, trade representatives or so. The users may be domestic as well as foreign.

Behavioural Profile of Users: By the behavioural profile of users, our focus is on the needs and requirements, attitudes, lifestyles and expectations of users availing the services of hotel industry.

Market Segmentation for Hotel: The classification of users of hotel services on the basis of different variables so as to identify their level of expectations is known as market segmentation. It is a process of dividing and subdividing the market into different small groups.

Marketing Information System for Hotels: The management of information with the viewpoint of making the marketing decisions for the hotel industry is a managerial process of transforming the data into information.

Product Planning and Development: It is planning and development of hotel services with the motto of optimising the demand and supply. It is managing for future marketing. In this context, we go through the planning of hotel building, bedrooms, function rooms and convention halls.

Marketing Mix for Hotels: It is a managerial process of formulating the different submixes, such as the product mix, the promotion mix, the price mix, the place mix and the people.

The Product Mix: It is a process of formulating the core and peripheral services in the face of changing needs and requirements of the users. The elimination of outdated services and inclusion of modern services are found on the basis of marketing plan. The mix also goes through the problem of formulating a package holiday.

The Promotion Mix: This goes through the different constituents of promotion such as advertising, publicity, sales promotion, personal selling, word-of-mouth promotion and telemarketing.

The Price Mix: It draws our attention on the pricing decisions where we take a decision regarding the hotel tariffs and charge the services related to bedrooms, function rooms and restaurants.

The Place Mix: This goes through the problem of distributing the hotel services. The zero-level, one-level and two-level distribution system has been studied.

The Process: This submix of marketing focuses our attention on the different processes followed for making available the services to the ultimate users or guests. The processing of hotel services is found concerned with the services in bedrooms, restaurants and lounges where a team of people with the help of back-line staff and technologies process the services.

Physical Evidence and Attractions: In the physical evidence, we find our focus on tangibilisation of the outstanding properties of hotel services so that the users and visitors get an opportunity to evidence the quality. The interiors and exteriors, furnishing, lighting, ventilation, scent, aesthetic management and equipment and technology generate service fragrance and project a fair image. Besides, the uniform and dresses of employees and other personal care dimensions add additional attractions to the hotel services.

The People: This draws our attention on hotel people having professional excellence and personal-touch-in-service. Since we find a teamwork, there are a good number of people involved in the processing and service delivery and service recovery. They work manually and get the co-operation of technology for improving the service quality.

Hotel Marketing in Indian Perspective: With corporatisation, we have witnessed positive developments in the hotel industry. The emerging corporate culture changed our lifestyles and hotel culture started gaining popularity. A number of star group of hotels were found thriving in different parts of the country. But the worldwide economic depression has been found adversely affecting the national economy of India *vis-a-vis* the hotel industry. This necessitates innovative marketing strategy.

KEY TERMS

Philanthropists
Crusaders
Taverns
Pilgrims
Occupancy Ratio
Budget Hotel
Techniculture
Adventure Tourism
Sports Tourism
Residential Hotel
Commercial Hotel
Resort Hotel
Floating Hotel
Unmarried Mothers
Instant Market
Beauty Parlours
Gym and Jogging
Brochure
Folder
Porters
Waiters
Symptomatic
Transport Operators
Tour Operators
Speciality Chancellor
American Plan
Modified Plan
European Plan
Travel Agents
Travel Guides
Visual Metaphor
Apartment Hotel
Aggressive Promotion
Cottage Hotel
Nostalgia
Give-aways
Green House
Punter

Review Questions

1. Define Hotel. Explain its different types.
2. What do you mean by Hotel Marketing? Focus on the different categories of users availing the hotel services.
3. Throw light on the behavioural profile of hotel users.

4. What do you mean by Marketing Information System? Focus on the instrumentality of MIS in managing information for the hotel industry.
5. Discuss the marketing segmentation with a reference to hotel services in Indian perspective.
6. What do you mean by Marketing Mix? Explain in brief the different submixes of marketing mix for the hotel services.
7. 'The movement of marketing craft is slowed down if the management of information is poor.' In the light of this statement, explain the significance of information for making the marketing decisions.
8. Focus on the product mix of hotel.
9. Discuss the different components of promotion in the face of hotel services in the Indian perspective.
10. Write a note on the pricing decisions of hotel industry.
11. Explain the place mix for hotel services.
12. Focus on the extended marketing mix for the hotel services.
13. Focus on the marketing of hotel services in the Indian perspective.
14. Do you feel that worldwide economic depression is throwing a big challenge before the hotel industry in India? Define your arguments.

Application Exercises

1. You are working as a Hotel Manager. Suggest the measures you would like to take for increasing the occupancy ratio of your hotel.
2. Around the globe, we find hotel industry facing the problem of financial crunch. As a marketer, suggest measures to be effective in the very context.
3. You need to blend the different components of promotion in such a way that the costs are minimised but the effects are maximised. Elaborate how and in what way you will act.
4. As a marketing professional, focus on the package of services helping you in motivating the guests.
5. In the formulation of pricing strategy, you are supposed to play an important role. Comment.
6. As a marketing professional, throw light on the role of extended marketing mix for the hotel services in the Indian perspective.
7. As a marketer, explain the marketing decisions you would like to innovate in the face of changing trends in global economy.

Endnotes

1. Daniel J. Boorstern, *The American National Express,* Random House, 1965.
2. Charles K. Jr. and Larry E. Halber, *Tourism Planning and Development,* BBI Co., 1979, p. 174.
3. Definition Presented by Hotel Operator to the Authorities of the National Recovery Administration, 1933.
4. "*The Hindu*", May 15, 1983.
5. *Hotel and Restaurant Guide*, India, 1991, New Delhi, p. 17.
6. *Ibid.,* General Information.
7. Gerald W. Lattin, *The Modern Hotel and Hotel Management,* W.H. Freeman & Co., 1968.
8. Gerry Draper, Quoted from Melvyn Greene, *Hotel Marketing,* Heinemann Professional Publishing, p. 28.
9. Melvyn Greene, *Marketing Hotels and Restaurants into the 90s*, Heinemann Professional Publishing, Oxford, 1989, p. 29.
10. *Ibid.*
11. Anderson and Lembke, Advertising Agent of a Swedish Firm.
12. Melvyn Greene, *op. cit.,* p. 28.
13. The Federation of Hotel and Restaurant of India, New Delhi.
14. Jha S.M., *Hotel Marketing,* Himalaya Publishing House, Mumbai, 1998.
15. Jha S.M., *Hotel – The Sweet Hotel,* Rashtriya Sahara, New Delhi, October, 1997, pp. 93-94.
16. Vikas Singla and Amar Inder Singh, *Conceptualising Preceived Service Quality in Hotel Industry*, Indian Management Studies; Vol-12/1, pp. 61-81, 2008.
17. Jha. S.M., *Hotel Marketing*, HPH Mumbai, 1998.
18. India – 2008.

★★★

CONSULTANCY MARKETING

We find logic behind this argument that if an individual or an institution utilises our excellence for generating profits or for the projection of a fair image, our rights for sharing the benefits cannot be unjust.

Chapter Objectives

Introduction – Consultancy Marketing: The Concept – Rationale Behind Consultancy Marketing – Users of Consultancy Services – Behavioural Profile of Users – Market Segmentation for Consultancy Organisations – Marketing Information System for Consultancy Organisations – Formulation of Marketing Mix for the Consultancy Organisations – The Product Mix – Product Planning and Development – The Promotion Mix – The Price Mix – The Place Mix – The Process – The Physical Evidence and Attractions – The People – Consultancy Marketing in Indian Perspective – Summary – Key Terms – Review Questions – Application Exercises – Endnotes.

Learning Objectives

The present chapter goes through the different dimensions of marketing the consultancy services. This chapter aims at sensitising the readers to the process of formulating a sound marketing mix for the consultancy organisations. Particularly the consultancy organisations of big size would find the conceptualisation of marketing principles significant to them. The consultants in general and the management consultants in particular would be successful in studying and understanding the behavioural profile of clients considered as users of the services. The application of marketing principles with professional excellence would help consultancy organisations in many ways.

INTRODUCTION

Stretching out specialised services is not a recent phenomenon. It is as old as our culture and civilisation. This is supported by the fact that during ancient days, the Saints, Gurus, Prophets, Hermits and Philanthropists extended their meditated views for the welfare of masses but without charging any fee or even without accepting any obligation. After the organisation of a social system, a king used to keep ministers in various fields for consultation for which they were suitably paid. The materialism paved the ways for commercialisation. With the establishment of a society based on materialistic values, we find a basic change in the value engineering process. We find logic behind the arguments that if an individual or an institution utilises our knowledge or excellence for generating profits or for the projection of a fair image, our rights for sharing the benefits can't be unjust. This makes it clear that growing significance of specialisation made the ways for the commercialisation of consultancy services.

With the passage of time, the consultancy services were found organised. The business houses or even an individual started using the expertise to inject life, strength and continuity to their development plans. This helped engineering of a sound foundation for the development and prosperity of those organisations who evinced interests in using the world-class consultants. A firm required services of legal, technical, financial and management consultants for increasing the rate of profitability; an individual required medical aid to maintain his/her health; a person or an institution needed legal services to protect or safeguard their assets; an organisation required technical services to accelerate the rate of productivity or so. This basic change in the application and instrumentality of specialised services opened new vistas for the development of consultancy services on an organised basis.

We can't deny the fact that the pattern of development is substantially influenced by the emerging trends in competition. The acceleration of productivity, generation of profits, multiplication of assets, establishment of leadership are not only a thorny task but even a costly game of course not within the reach of everyone. All of us marginally or substantially, occasionally or frequently prefer to use the services of world-class consultants as and when the circumstances necessitate so. It is right to mention that we use the services of consultants even to promote unfair practices, profiteering, tax evasion, unfair computation of costs, exploiting others, grabing the properties of others or so. Generation of profit is, no doubt, our legitimate right but we are not supposed to promote profiteering. If we do so, it will form a vicious circle. We can't keep on moving the process of illegitimate or unfair practices for long time. By using the services of world-class consultants, we find fair avenues for the development and prosperity of an individual or an organisation. It is against this background that we find a formal development of consultancy organisations both on national and international levels.

Of course, we find some of the leading organisations having a separate wing for consultants in different areas but a majority of the organisations don't find it a commercially viable proposition and prefer to buy the services of consultants as and when they need to do such. Basically, an idea of selling expertise originated from here because some of the organisations or firms or an individual-explored avenues, capitalised on opportunities, opened service centres and tied themselves with the potential customers or clients. In addition, the firms or organisations experienced it profitable to seek the cooperation of consultants in lieu of establishing their own cell. In this way, the consultancy services were professionally-managed and organised which not only made ways for maintaining operational economy for making possible cost-effectiveness but also created job opportunities in different areas. Further, it opened doors for the generation of foreign exchange and projection of a fair image. If we get an opportunity to sell our knowledge and experiences, it is quite natural that we make best of our efforts to activate the process of quantitative-cum-qualitative improvements. And if we make a consortium or syndicate of a number of experts, the services are found of use to an individual as well as to an organisation which paves avenues for making the services commercially viable to both the selling organisations and the buying organisations *pari passu.*

To be more specific in the less developed countries like ours where small-scale entrepreneurs are found engaged in the business, the consultancy services need an intensive care. This is mainly due to the fact that they have limited potentials and the world-class consultancy services would help them in making possible an optimal utilisation of the available potentials. Not only the small business houses but even a big organisation also finds it profitable to use the services of consultants. And it is in this context that we find development of consultancy services in almost all the areas by almost all the organisations.

A consultant is required to assign due weightage to his/her clients. He/she needs to make an appraisal of the situation in which his clients has been working. It is right to mention that the profitability index of a client determines the success rate of consultants. It is against this background that a consultant is required to be circumspect while behaving with the clients. He/she is not supposed to work on the basis of his/her emotional feelings. The consultants or the consultative salesmen perform a product supply planning function. The former sells system of services with primary emphasis on services whereas the latter sells product with primary emphasis on quality.

In view of the above, it is right to say that the very success of consultancy marketing is influenced by the action and behaviour of consultants, the personalised services made available by them to their clients, the quality of services made available, the behavioural profile of consultants and the consultancy fee charged. A consultant is required to be careful particularly while managing information, preparing a data bank, identifying the profitable opportunities, making strategic decisions and tapping the potentials optimally. A microscopic study of the business environment is found essential. In the consultancy services, the product is 'Expertise.' Sky is the limit for quality. If the consultancy organisations offer world-class services, the task of marketing professionals is simplified fantastically. This in a natural way draws our attention on the marketing management of consultancy services since it simplifies the task of improving the quality of services for selling them profitably.

The formulation of a sound marketing mix for the consultancy organisations is found essential to identify the profitable opportunities and to capitalise on the same optimally. Creative marketing decisions govern the nature of service mix. The consultancy organisations find it convenient to innovate the services in the face of changing business conditions. The organisations may also be successful in formulating a lucrative package for the habitual customers using the services frequently. With the development of technologies and increasing sophistication in the information technologies, we find ample scope for energising the innovation process. The technical consultants, the management consultants, the legal consultants, the marketing consultants, the medical consultants and many others find it convenient to innovate the services with the help of information technologies. Thus, the consultancy organisations can be successful in innovating the strategic decisions related to their service mix and can make the services nationally and internationally competitive. The decisions related to promotion also bear an outstanding significance to increase the market share and to establish leadership. The conceptualisation of modern marketing would help consultancy organisations in innovating the promotional measures. The advertising professionals, the marketing professionals can make the promotional measures creative to sensitise the prospects and to transform them into customers. This makes it essential that the consultancy organisations practise modern marketing principles. In addition, the decisions related to fee or pricing is required to be made remunerative *vis-a-vis* affordable to the customers. The consultancy organisations can process the services in a right fashion with the help and cooperation of professionally-sound and personally-committed employees and thus a contracting gap between the services-promised and services-offered would open doors for fulfilling the high expectations of customers at large. The development of people would help the organisations substantially.

The aforesaid facts make it clear that like other organisations even the consultancy organisations need to think in favour of innovative marketing. We are well aware of the fact the consultancy services have a big potential market in the Indian perspective. In almost all the areas, we find opportunities. The main thing in the process is to identify and to capitalise on the same with the help of world-class professionals. We can't negate the fact that being an agrarian economy, we find consultancy services relevant even to the agricultural sector of the economy. The processing of agricultural produces has taken a new turn, the marketing opportunities are around the globe. The main thing in the process is to identify the world-class consultants who have a rich information bank and a well-developed information management system. We can't deny that to be more specific for the agricultural sector, we need the services of world-class consultants who at present are not in a good number. In addition, we find tremendous opportunities even in the services sector. The emerging services need due attention of world-class consultants.

It is high time that the consultancy organisations think in favour of practising innovative marketing which would help them in many ways. If you have developed your expertise, you have a legitimate right of selling the same profitably since for enriching your expertise you invest a lot of time and money. An individual or an institution if markets its services suitably, the avenues are paved for making profits.

CONSULTANCY MARKETING — THE CONCEPT

At the outset, it is essential to clarify the concept of consultancy marketing. The opinion expressed by the Institute of Management Consultancy, UK consider it the services provided by an independent and qualified person or persons in identifying and investigating the problems concerned with policy, organisation, procedures and methods; recommending appropriate action and helping to implement these recommendations.[1]

The aforesaid views make it clear that in the consultancy services, an expert of the related field or discipline or group of experts identify and investigate the problems and on the basis of their expertise, they make available suitable suggestions and further also help in the implementation of recommendations. As for example, person or persons having an outstanding excellence in the concerned areas like legal, medical, management, technical or so make available specialised services to a person or persons in the shape of knowledge and information. They make an in-depth study of the problems and offer to them appropriate suggestions to combat the problem. For the services rendered, they may or may not charge fee or commission.

The application of marketing concept in the consultancy services, of course, is a recent phenomenon. Though since time immemorial, the consultants have been found making available the specialised services, the variation in the nature and form can't be denied. The hermits, saints, gurus, philanthropists, prophets, etc. were invited to solve the problem but not on payment basis. This makes it clear that the consultancy services were available but the consultants were not found charging fee or commission for their services. Of late, we find its emergence as a full-fledged business. A number of consultants have been found engaged in the process and they have been found selling their views or expertise. This made ways for conceptualising marketing in the consultancy services. The growing significance of innovative ideas, expertise mainly to excel competition paved avenues for practising marketing. An individual or an institution started the process of marketing the consultancy services on national and international levels for making profits which made the business conditions competitive. Since then, the marketing concept has gained an outstanding significance. With the application of marketing concept, the professional excellence could get due weightage in the entire process of marketing the consultancy services.

The aforesaid facts make it clear that materialism paves the ways for selling the services which engineers a strong foundation for the application of marketing concept. Thus, by consultancy marketing, our emphasis is on marketing of expertise by an individual or an institution where they formulate the marketing mix and keep on moving the process of innovating the decisions to establish their edge on the competitors. The formulation of product mix makes it essential that they offer quality services to their clients or customers. In this context, they are supposed to act as a professional. They have to innovate their services as and when the business conditions necessitate so. In addition, they are also required to promote their services and for that, they need to use the innovative promotional measures. They help their clients in informing, sensing and persuading the prospects. Besides, they are also required to make decisions related to fee or commission. To be more specific when they work as an institution, the processing of services becomes significant to bridge over the gap between services-promised and services-offered.

RATIONALE BEHIND CONSULTANCY MARKETING

We find a number of points favouring the application of marketing principles in the consultancy services. The following points are given due weightage in the very context:

1. Growing significance of specialised knowledge: The mounting intensity of competition in the business environment makes it essential that we assign an overriding priority to specialisation or expertise. In the present-day world, we find specialisation gaining a place of outstanding significance in almost all the areas. We can't negate that increasing importance of competition is responsible for the same. The invention and innovation, growing importance of sophisticated technologies, continued efforts to keep on moving the process of qualitative transformation are some of the important factors making consultancy an immediate solution. It is not possible for an organisation to establish an independent cell for all the consultants but at the same time, we find expertise influencing substantially their business decisions. This necessitates developing services on an organised basis and practising marketing appears to be an effective solution.

2. Obtaining impartial view: It is right to mention that justification for obtaining impartial views necessitated application of marketing principles in the consultancy services. It is but natural that employees serving an organisation are influenced by a number of considerations which complicate the process of obtaining views without any prejudices. If we find faults, the employees may not reveal the truth. We agree with this view that only a person or an institution not directly concerned with the organisation may reveal the truths. The consultancy marketing gained popularity since it helped in getting the impartial views.

3. Justifying the predetermined measures: The significance of consultancy services is also due to the fact that we succeed in justifying the predetermined measures. The managers need the services of experts or specialists so that their reports or views or actions or decisions are stamped or authenticated by the authorities.

4. Limited number of consultants: The marketing practices in the consultancy services became essential to avail the services of efficient consultants. In certain cases, we find an organisation exercising the maximum possible pressure as the problems appear to be complicated and therefore can't be solved by consultants not having world-class excellence. The consultancy marketing helps them in getting the detailed information regarding availability of consultants in the different catchment areas. They can use their services in the face of available potentials and changing needs and requirements.

5. Making the consultancy services productive: We are aware of the fact that marketing principles bear the efficacy of making the services or products cost-effective found essential for accelerating productivity or maximising profitability. An individual or an institution invests substantially for enriching the credentials or developing professional excellence. An individual or an institution uses the services of consultants for making profits or personal gains. This engineers a strong advocacy for marketing consultancy.

The aforesaid facts are found justifying the application or marketing principles in the consultancy services. Individuals or institutions working as consultants need to conceptualise marketing.

USERS OF CONSULTANCY SERVICES

The consultants, in addition to other aspects, also need to assign due weightage to the nature and types of users of the services. This makes it essential that they are well aware of the changing attitudes and behavioural profile. This simplifies the task of understanding the expectations, developing the marketing resources in tune with their needs and requirements and making the marketing decisions proactive. Users may be an individual or an institution. The motives may be personal and commercial. The providers are supposed to make sure that customers and clients remain satisfied. At the same time, they have also to be careful that the services prove to be remunerative and very much instrumental in maintaining the commercial viability. They are supposed to think for the clients, move with the clients, work for the clients and go with the clients. The consultants are not supposed to lag behind their clients since they bear the responsibility of supporting them *vis-a-vis* to remove the psychofobia as and when the circumstances necessitate so. They need to subserve the interests of their clients. An individual or an institution seeking legal advice, technical or managerial suggestions or medical prescriptions needs support of consultants at different stages. If the consultants move with the clients, we find development of a sense of confidence among them which keep on moving the process of retaining the business. The clients in a majority of the cases feel that their goals would remain unfulfilled, if consultants are not with them physically, professionally and morally. This in a natural way increases the instrumentality of consultants.

The small-scale organisations substantially depend on the suggestions of consultants. It is right to mention that unless the consultants have an in-depth knowledge about the emerging trends in the business environment *vis-a-vis* the behavioural profile of users, the organisational goals would remain unfulfilled. In Figure 13.1, we find different categories of users using the services of different types of consultants.

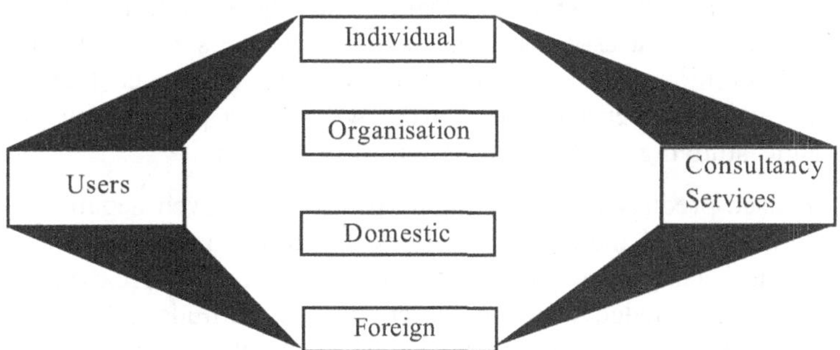

Fig. 13.1: Users of Consultancy Services

It is clear in Figure 13.1 that the users may be an individual or even an organisation/institution. It is also clear that motives may be personal, social and commercial. The services may be of different types, such as legal, medical, technical, financial, managerial or so. Generally, an individual requires the services of consultants to make an assault on the personal problems but an organisation seeks the cooperation of consultants for solving the business problems.

BEHAVIOURAL PROFILE OF USERS

A consultancy firm or organisation requires to study the users' behavioural profile because such a study helps them in identifying the needs and requirements. It is quite natural that psychology of different users can't be the same. An individual goes to the medical consultants for quick recovery and therefore his/her behavioural profile is, of course, based on quick recovery. If he/she is affluent, the financial consideration is not to govern his/her decision. Contrary to it, a poor person using the services of a medical consultant also keeps in mind the economy. A property holder or dealer seeks legal advice to secure ownership and therefore he/she is influenced by the protection of his/her assets. An organisation avails the services of technical consultants to accelerate the rate of productivity and therefore the important factors are cost-effectiveness, safety provisions, high-installed capacity or so. At the very outset, the consultants are required to study the needs and requirements of users and thereafter the level of expectations. We are well aware of the fact that the level of expectation is found dynamic in nature which is governed by the perception of quality developed by the competitors. If the competitive consultancy organisations offer world-class legal, medical, technical or other services to their clients, it is quite natural that their counterparts, avail the services with the same motive and develop a high level of expectation which if not fulfilled paves avenues for dissatisfaction. While studying the clients, they need to assign due weightage to the attitudes which in addition to other aspects also focus on the instrumentality of price/fee/commission in making the buying decisions. Some of the clients are found sensitive to price whereas we also find clients considerably influenced by quality. We can't deny the fact that a majority of the clients are found influenced by fee or commission charged.

The behaviour can't remain static. It moves with the changing personal and socio-economic conditions. The legal conditions also influence the process. The psychologists or the behavioural scientists are supposed to explore opportunities. The main thing particularly in the Indian perspective is to improve the quality. The stimulation of demand occupies a place of outstanding significance. The providers are required to be careful that their quality services are instrumental in attracting the clients. Only after studying the behavioural profile, the consultants find it convenient to develop the marketing resources. We are aware of the fact that the foreign users also avail the services of consultants and they are supposed to be high-spending clients but at the same time, a study of behavioural profile of foreign users is found a bit difficult. The providers are required to go through the quality of services of the competitive consultancy organisations and based on the perception of quality developed by the providers and perceived by the consultants, they are required to make a decision. Thus, in the behavioural profile of users, a number of problems are required to be studied.

In the domestic market, the intensity of competition is found not so high but in the foreign or overseas markets, we find the intensity of competition at its peak. In a majority of the cases, the foreign users have high level of expectations. Of late, we think everything in the global perspective and therefore, the consultancy organisations need to perceive a right perception of expectations. It is also right to mention that expectations can't remain static and therefore the consultancy organisations need a well developed information system to know the exact level. To be more specific in the consultancy services, we find projection of a fair image essential, specially for the consultancy organisations. This makes it essential that they promote the services in such a way that the prospects/ clients don't form a negative opinion. The users are required to be convinced that they are getting world-class services. By improving the quality of services, they make ways for a positive image. Attitude is considered to be an important aspect while studying the behavioural profile of users.

Attitude is an emotionalised predisposition to respond positively or even negatively to an object. Our response to a stimuli is governed by attitude. If the customers/users develop a name loyalty or brand loyalty, it is found difficult to change the attitude.[2] This makes it essential that the marketing executives serving the consultancy organisations have an in-depth knowledge which helps creation of attitudes. A brand or name loyalty can't be possible unless the providers communicate to the users the details about the services to be offered. This necessitates transmission of information with the help of suitable vehicles.

In addition to the institutional users, a consultant is also required to deal with an individual user seeking legal, medical, financial and technical advice to subserve his/her personal interest, such as the medical aids required for fast recovery, the legal aids required for protecting the valuables, the financial advice for channelising the investments into profitable heads or saving the tax liabilities. If an individual is found satisfied with the excellence of his/her consultant, we find scope for a repeat business. This makes it essential that not only the institutions but even an individual working as a consultant activates the process of projection of a fair image. The medical consultants succeed in getting the business because the clients develop a positive attitude, and like this, the legal consultants or other consultants get a business since they have been successful in developing a positive attitude. Here, it is also right to mention that projection of a fair image is fantastically influenced by the past records of consultants. If we find that a particular doctor succeeds in treating the patients successfully, the word-of-mouth communication becomes instrumental in the projection of his/her positive image. This makes it essential that the consultancy organisations or even an individual working as a consultant assigns due weightage to the quality of services which helps them considerably in projecting a positive image resulting into the generation of good name or brand loyalty. It is against this background that we find an in-depth study of the attitudes and behavioural profile of clients/users essential.

The aforesaid facts make it clear that in the consultancy services, the building and projection of a positive image is found essential to both the categories of consultants, such as an individual or an organisation. The marketing experts find marketing a customer satisfaction engineering that helps the consultancy organisations in many ways. It is in this context that we go through the problem of practising marketing principles in the consultancy organisations. An in-depth study of the behavioural profile of the users of different categories is found essential in the very context. The behavioural studies, thus, occupy a place of outstanding significance even in the consultancy services.

MARKET SEGMENTATION FOR CONSULTANCY ORGANISATIONS

Users or clients have their own likes and dislikes. They possess some uniqueness which complicate the task of a marketer, specially while assessing their needs and identifying the level of their expectations. In the consultancy services, there are a number of factors influencing the needs and requirements of the prospects. The behavioural scientists claim that segmentation would simplify the task of understanding the users. The modern marketing principles prefer formulation of marketing policies and techniques for each market segment which an organisation plans to solicit.[3] A market is composed of different customers who have different responses to market offerings. Each segment represents somewhat a different opportunity for the organisation. This makes it essential that an organisation makes possible grouping and subgrouping of customers which simplifies the identification process. The marketing strategies formulated on the basis of segment are found to be customer-oriented. In the consultancy services an organisation needs to segment the market on the basis of region, sector and geographical conditions. In Figure 13.2, we find regionwise segmentation.

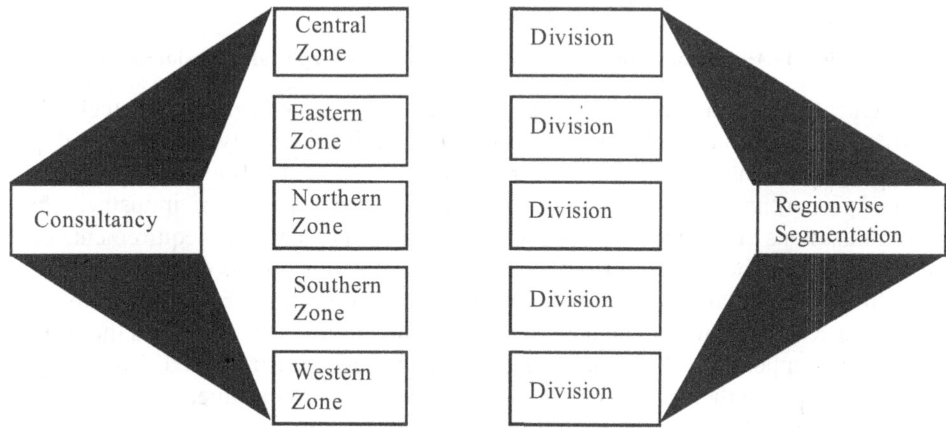

Fig. 13.2: Regionwise Segmentation

The Central Zone, Eastern Zone, Northern Zone, Southern Zone and Western Zone are the different market segments classified into different zones as per the requirements. Such a segmentation helps consultancy organisations in studying the needs and requirements of different zones and the development of marketing resources are thus made optimal to the users representing a particular zone.

In Figure 13.3, we find segmentation on the basis of sector. Such a sectorwise segmentation is divided into five parts, such as Legal Sector, Technical Sector, Financial Sector, Management Sector and Medical Sector.

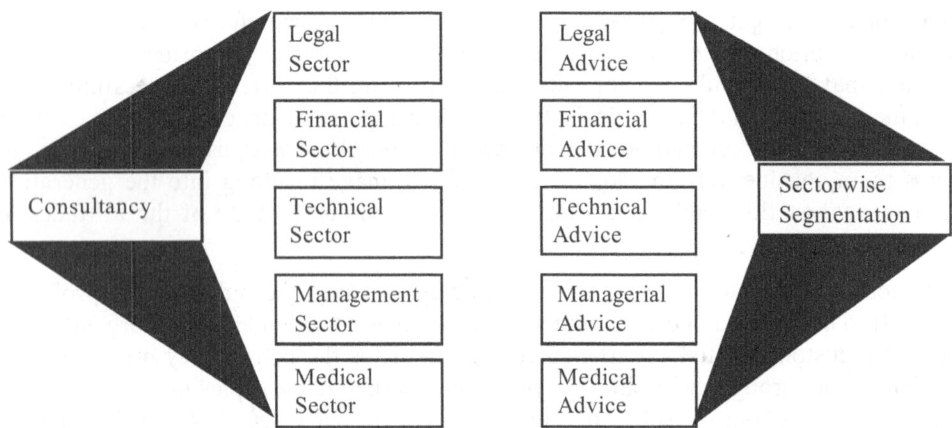

Fig. 13.3: Sectorwise Segmentation

It is quite natural that segmentation on the basis of sector helps the consultants and the consultancy organisations in understanding the expectations of different categories of users in a different way. The sectorwise segmentation presented in Figure 13.3 clarifies that in the consultancy services, a consultancy organisation needs to identify the needs and requirements of a client related to that segment. In some of the organisations, the legal advice is to be given and like this in some other organisations, the financial and technical suggestions are needed.

In Figure 13.4, we find segmentation on the basis of geographical considerations. In this respect, we find important categories as Rural, Urban, Individual and Organisational.

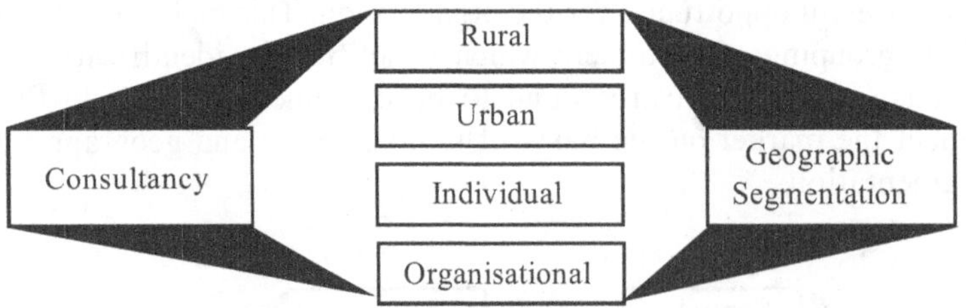

Fig. 13.4: Segmentation on the Basis of Geographical Consideration

The aforesaid segment shown in Figure 13.4 clarifies that in the rural segment, the technological requirements would not be so advanced as found in the urban sector. Like this, the individuals have different expectations from the consultancy organisations. In addition, the rural sector is found influenced by the developments related to agriculture whereas the urban sector is found related to the development of industry. Thus, the consultants or the consultancy organisations are supposed to study and perceive the changing requirements of different segments in a right fashion which would help them in developing the marketing inputs optimally. It is quite natural that rural prospects have limited expectations since their needs and requirements are different. We don't find the same thing with the urban prospects. They watch the latest developments in different areas and therefore their expectations are found high. They are supposed to be conscious, organised and well-informed. This makes it essential that the consultancy organisations keep their minds open, enrich the sources and management of information and formulate the service mix and other mixes in such a way that the changing needs and requirements are studied and the marketing decisions are tailored to the same in a right fashion. Thus, it is right to mention that like other organisations, the consultancy organisations also need to segment the markets. In the process of segmentation, we also find a big difference in the needs and requirements of domestic as well as the foreign users. The consultancy organisations while studying the level of expectation of foreign users are supposed to be more careful because we find their level of expectations relatively high, specially when we compare them with the domestic users. The bases for segmentation are required to be chosen in a right way and the markets are to be grouped and subgrouped in such a fashion that marketing decisions are made proactive.

MARKETING INFORMATION SYSTEM FOR THE CONSULTANCY ORGANISATIONS

The management of information plays a commanding role in making creative marketing decisions for the consultancy organisations. Unless the consultants have a rich information bank, the management of future would remain a difficult task. The marketing decisions of today are based on the trends in past and the marketing decisions of tomorrow would be influenced by the developments taking place at present. The multi-dimensional changes in the business environment make it essential that we manage the information system and innovate the process of making the marketing decisions in order that the decisions are creative *vis-a-vis* sensitive. The sophistication in the process of development of communication technologies, the changing governmental regulations, the mounting intensity of competition are some of the important developments making a strong advocacy in favour of a technology-driven marketing information system. We can't deny the fact that the consultancy business is substantially influenced by the quality of information made available to the consultancy organisations or the consultants. The task of decision-making is simplified considerably if they have a well-developed information system. The medical consultants, the management consultants, the legal consultants, the technical consultants or almost all the persons interested in selling their credentials profitably need latest information failing which they would hardly be successful in making available to their clients proactive measures which would make profit generation much more difficult. The doctors not aware of the developments in the field of medical sciences, the legal experts not aware of the changing acts, laws, rules and regulations, the technocrats not familiar with the latest technologies, the management scientists not getting day-to-day information can't be successful in making available to their clients the productive opinions. This makes it essential that the consultants and consultancy organisations keep themselves aware of the latest developments which would, of course, be found easier if the marketing information system is well managed. It is against this background that we need to gravitate our due attention on the instrumentality of marketing information system in making possible creativity.

An individual or an institution serving clients requires to develop a system which is well supported by the new generation of information technologies. The system analysts if professionally-sound and the researchers and the research scientists if personally-committed and value-based can successfully transform the data into information. With the help of decision supporting system and with the availability of microcomputers, the task of decision-making is now found easier. The important questions to be answered suitably in the very context are:

- Decision related to the sources for collecting the information or from where to collect the information?
- What sources would serve the purpose?
- What type of information would serve the purpose?
- What nature and types of technologies are to be used for transforming the data into information?
- What qualifications and credentials are essential for the computer professionals working as system analysts?

We accept the fact that the marketing information system would help the consultancy organisations in getting a suitable answer to the aforesaid questions. In the consultancy services, the consultants are required to manage the information in the face of following:

- The information related to the potential market to identify the same and to innovate the strategic decisions to capitalise on them profitably.
- The identification of areas of services found more profitable, less profitable and not profitable to formulate a sound product portfolio which helps consultants even if the business conditions are not conducive.
- The strategic decisions of competitors. The quality of information system available to them and the future plans of development.
- The decisions related to future marketing so that the marketing inputs are developed in tune with the emerging trends and the consultancy organisation get the required marketing outputs.
- The attitudinal change in the past and existing clients to identify the level of expectations.
- The emerging trends in the socio-economic environment which help consultants in identifying the emerging trends in the socio-economic conditions.

- The increasing instrumentality of technologies in making the decisions. The inventions and innovations in the field of development of new technologies and the sophistication in the process.
- The changes in the governmental regulations, specially related to business, foreign exchange, export marketing or so.
- The infrastructural facilities available and the future scenario.
- The incentives made available by the government to the business houses.
- The increasing level of expectations of customers in the face of the preception developed by the leading competitors.
- The instrumentality of specialisation in the business world.
- The attitudinal change in the boardrooms.

There are a number of sources for collecting the information. The consultants may collect information from branch offices, site offices, representatives, directly from the clients, subcontractors, journals and periodicals, government reports, national and international business publications and reports, the research reports of different organisations or so. We accept the fact that in the management of marketing information, the most important thing is the quality of facts and figures made available to the system. The consultancy organisations also need to take the support of researchers and the research scientists who conduct survey and make available to the system the latest information.

The pattern and criteria for the utilisation of the different sources of information would depend upon the changing needs and requirements of the consultancy organisations. For making possible creativity, sensitivity and acceptability, it is pertinent that right sources of information are used by the right personnel in a right fashion with the support of a technology-driven information system. The main task before the marketing professionals is to make possible frequency in the innovation process which is substantially influenced by the quality of information made available to them. Quality inputs make the ways for quality outputs. If we have quality facts and figures and the information system is well managed in which sophisticated technologies and quality professionals are given due place, we expect the available outputs to be of world-class helping the decision-makers in many ways.

FORMULATION OF MARKETING MIX FOR THE CONSULTANCY ORGANISATIONS

The formulation of marketing mix is an important decision-making area which requires professional excellence. An individual or a group of individuals engaged in the consultancy services is required to formulate a sound marketing mix that makes possible an optimal development of marketing resources. The marketing professionals based on the information received from a technology-driven information system can be efficacious in innovating the marketing inputs in the face of changing needs and requirements of prospects *vis-a-vis* business environment. It is in this context that we find the formulation process significant. We are well aware of the fact that the combination or mixing of recipes and their proportion play a decisive role in determining the quality of food items. Like this, it is the quality and quantity of different submixes that play a significant role in determining the quality of marketing decisions. This makes it essential that the marketers while formulating product mix, place mix, promotion mix, price mix and people keep in their mind the intensity of competition in addition to the level of expectations of clients.

The Product Mix

In the consultancy services, the important products are technical services, legal services, medical services and the managerial services. The providers and the clients may be an individual or even an institution. Customer orientation is considered to be an integral part of product development strategies. The consultancy organisations need to innovate their ideas in the face of the following:[4]

1. Selection of area: It is an important aspect in the formulation of product mix for the consultancy organisations. In the present day world, the magnitude of competition is found at its peak and the business environmental conditions are found more volatile. This makes it essential that consultants as well as the consultancy organisations have a well-developed information system which has been making available to them the information regarding the emerging profitable areas of the future. This would simplify their task of increasing their potentials or strength in the face of emerging trends. Of late, we find new generation of technologies playing an important role in almost all the areas. The organisations assigning due weightage to sophisticated technologies are found successful in capitalising on the opportunities profitably. This makes it essential that at the outset they identify the areas and only then design a marketing strategic plan.

2. Selection of clients: Another important step in the process is the selection of clients. The upcoming consultants or the budding consultants find it difficult to identify high-spending clients. Since we focus on the marketing of consultancy services, it is pertinent that our clients either an individual or an institution bear the potentials to spend as per their requirements. We don't find any sense in seeking the cooperation of medical consultants when the patients find it difficult to follow the prescriptions mainly due to the financial constraint. Like this, the legal consultants or the technical consultants point out the ways and the clients should be financially-sound to follow the same. This is directly or indirectly related to the performance or image of consultancy organisations because the doctors not getting a success in curing the patients, the lawyers not successful in winning the cases and the management experts not helping organisations in maintaining cost-effectiveness and securing commercial viability find it difficult to get the clients. It is against this background that the consultancy organisations while formulating the service mix also need due attention on the strength of their clients.

3. Studying the conditions and setting the objectives: We find a close relation between the changing business conditions and their impact on the formulation of the product mix. The changing business conditions influence the order of priorities *vis-a-vis* the objectives. After the selection of a profitable area and identifying the high-spending clients, the setting of objectives is found significant. The acceleration of productivity, optimising the costs, excelling the competition, increasing the market share, establishing the leadership and maximising the profitability and assets are the objectives to be given due weightage while setting the priority order. Thus, for setting the objectives, it is pertinent that the consultants or the consultancy organisations are well aware of the recent developments. The threats and challenges in the market influence the order of priority.

4. Discussing the proposal: The proposals are to be deliberated upon and the senior executives play a commanding role in the very context. The efforts taken for promoting the research activities can't be devalued. Further, the consultants need an in-depth knowledge of the behavioural profile of clients. Before accepting the proposal, the consultants are required to make it sure that their efforts in no case endanger the interests of clients. Of course, you need to be optimistic but it is not meant that you underestimate the instrumentality of feasibility studies which today or tomorrow would help you in projecting your image. It is in this context that we need an in-depth study or a microscopic analysis of projects before we accept the same.

5. Acceptance and implementation: After receiving acceptance of the proposal, the consultancy organisations are required to make suitable arrangements for the implementation of the same within the time-frame the specifications are there and you are supposed to assign due weightage to the promises that you make with the clients. The delayed implementation may invite numerous problems. This makes it essential that the marketing professionals assign an overriding priority to time management. Time-honoured and cost-effective implementation are the two important factors to be given a transcendental priority by the consultancy organisations.

The formulation of product mix requires a number of care and precautions. The consultants are required to be careful. The inclusion, elimination need due emphasis on the emerging trends in competition.[5] The innovative ideas, sophisticated technologies, intensive research need due care while formulating the product mix. To be more specific in the less developed countries like ours, it is pertinent that the consultants also think in favour of global efforts. The following questions need a suitable answer:

- How to make possible a long-term relationship with the clients?

  This simplifies the task of retaining the old customers and transforming the occasional clients into the habitual clients.
- How to follow the guidelines made available to the executives?

  This helps in designing a suitable strategy.
- How to make profits?

  This helps an organisation in enriching the potentials.

The formulation of a sound product mix makes it essential that the consultancy organisations make efforts to design a sound product portfolio in which different types of services are included. The medical consultants need to be aware of the latest devices of treatment and to offer to the patients the world-class medical aids. The technical consultants also need to innovate their product mix in the face of technological sophistication and to eliminate the traditional services from the product mix. The legal consultants need to be aware of the latest developments, such as amendments in laws, rules and regulations and to formulate the service mix accordingly. Thus, the elimination and inclusion processes need to be adopted even in the consultancy services. The management experts not aware of the latest developments in the business world would hardly be successful in serving the interest of their clients. These facts make it clear that like other organisations, the consultancy organisations also need to make possible innovation in the face of multi-dimensional developments in the business environment.

The main thing in the formulation process is making the service mix a point of attraction which stimulates the customers and further helps in innovating the marketing strategic decisions so that the profitable customers are retained. This activates both the processes – "winning and keeping" the customers. We can't deny the fact that ultimately it is the quality of service mix that considerably determines the sensitivity of our marketing decisions. Since the clients/customers take a decision in the face of benefits they get from the consultants, it is quite natural that the degeneration in quality makes the marketing decisions insensitive. If we find doctors successful in curing the patients, the advertisement or publicity measures are found effective. Thus, we find quality of service determining the success or failure of marketing decisions. Even the sophisticated promotional measures become insensitive if the consultant doctors fail in curing the patients. This speaks of the fact that all categories of consultants need to include quality services in their product mix.

The formulation of a sound package is also found important in the product mix of the consultancy organisations. Here, our emphasis is on the blending of different types of services keeping in view the needs and requirements of different segments availing the services. The packages become a point of attraction if the marketers show their professional excellence in the blending process. It is in this context that we talk about the designing of an attractive package for the consultancy services.

In view of the above, it is right to mention that the formulation of a sound product mix is required essential and the marketing professionals serving the consultancy organisations need to make it possible. This is easier when they are well aware of the changing needs and requirements and the increasing level of expectations of the clients/customers. In Figure 13.5, we find product mix of the consultancy organisations. Here it is important to mention that consultants of a particular wing or related to a particular area formulate their own service mix based on expertise, such as the medical consultants are required to formulate their service mix in the face of their own requirements. The legal and technical consultants are supposed to design their own mix. This is due to the fact that nature of service is found different in the different command areas. The medical consultants and the legal consultants can't act in the same way. The management consultants and the technical consultants are influenced by different considerations.

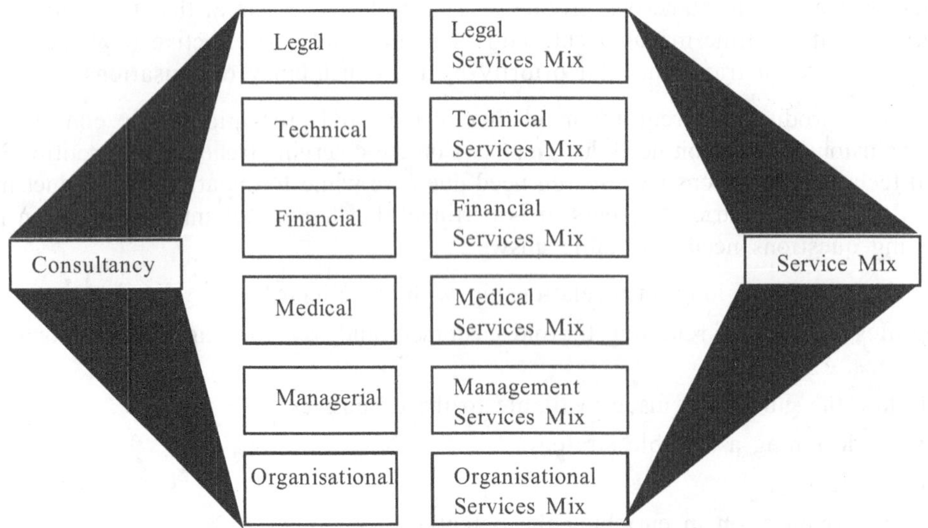

Fig. 13.5: Main Products in the Consultancy Services

PRODUCT PLANNING AND DEVELOPMENT

Consultants are termed to be the business planners. They in a true sense engineer the foundation for the development of an organisation. Almost all the consultancy organisations need to think about their future development plans. The medical consultants not well equipped with modern and sophisticated diagnostic devices, the technical consultants not well equipped with modern technologies, the legal consultants not well equipped with acts, laws and manuals and the management consultants not well equipped with the latest management literature find it difficult to offer the world-class services to their clients. This makes it essential that the consultancy organisations are well equipped with the supporting materials, technologies and the literature which simplify their task of offering quality services. If the consultancy organisations fail in serving the interests of business organisations, it is quite natural that it would be difficult for them to get the business in future. This makes it significant that the planning and development processes keep on moving.

The product planning and development strategies determine the magnitude of success. An important aspect in the very context is to define the client's market. After this, it is important that the consultants are aware of the potential users of the services. Here, it is impact generating that the consultants know about the services generated by their clients and the constraints experienced by them in the process. Defining the client's business is significant with the viewpoint of designing the strategic decisions. In addition, the steps taken by the concerned users in the field of research and development are found helpful to the consultants. The cash flow prepared by the clients is also required to be studied for getting a positive result.

Innovative strategies are the lifeline and therefore the consultants are required to channelise their efforts for collecting latest information. This gravitates our attention on the management of information. The consultants are required to show their interests in establishing long-term relationship since relationship marketing appears to be an important dimension of consultancy marketing.

The emerging trends in the socio-economic environment, the process of technological advancements, the global trade partnership, the mounting financial constraint, the changing governmental regulations, the increasing intensity of competition are some of the important aspects to be given due weightage while planning for the consultancy services. We can't deny that the business environment for future marketing is conducive and therefore an individual or an institution needs to plan for the development of services in such a way that the services are commercially viable *vis-a-vis* affordable to the different segments. Particularly in the Indian perspective where the state policy makers appear interested in the development of small-scale and cottage industries besides promoting the agro-based industries, it is pertinent that the product mix assigns due weightage to the interests of the concerned segment. In the consultancy services, the providers are required to make it sure that the clients get profitable results for their investments. This is essential because the avenues for profit generation to the clients would make ways for the generation of profits by the consultants. If the users or clients are benefited from the services of consultants, the future market would be secured, the retained business would gain momentum and avenues for profit generation to the consultancy organisations would be broadened. This makes it clear that the consultants begin their profit generation plan from the point where the users finish. This naturally necessitates a careful study or scanning of Balance Sheet, Profit and Loss Statement and Working Capital Management. In addition, the consultants would also be required to study the production costs and paying capacity of their customers. The experts suggest[6] that "80-20 Rule" is required to be practised. This rule focuses our attention on the identification of 20 per cent of the key accounts contributing 80 per cent of their turnover. In this context, a sensitive strategy is to follow the strategies which help the customers in strengthening their potentials and maximising the rate of profitability. When the clients start realising that their profit generation trend would be reversed failing the cooperation of consultants, we find business environment for the future marketing favourable. This makes it essential that the consultancy organisations assign due weightage to the commercial viability which would secure their future business.

We agree with the view that the development of product is not a static term. The multi-dimensional developments in the business environment make it essential that the consultancy organisations keep their eyes open and the mind active which would help them substantially, specially while tailoring the product mix to the changing needs and requirements of the clients. Of late, we find sophistication in transportation and communication technologies and frequent changes in the business regulations which make it significant that the consultancy organisations make possible qualitative improvements in their service mix. Almost all categories of consultants need to plan for innovation without which their efforts for excelling competition would hardly be successful in sensitising the prospects. It is in this context that the consultancy organisations have been found promoting intensive research for understanding the behavioural profile of customers. The upcoming consultancy organisations need to make their service mix productive.

The Promotion Mix

Like other services, the consultancy services are also required to be promoted which gravitates our attention on innovative promotional measures influenced by the new generation of marketing communication technologies. Of course, the consultancy organisations need to make the product mix innovative and attractive but here it is also impact generating that they keep on moving the process of informing, sensing and persuading the customers in a right fashion. It is against this background that we make a strong advocacy in favour of a sound promotion mix. There are a number of questions to be answered suitably as mentioned below:

- How to inform the clients?
- How to sense the clients?
- How to activate the stimulation process?
- How to persuade?
- How to increase the number of old clients?

These questions are rightly answered with the help of a sound mix of promotion which is a fair bending of the different constituents, such as advertising, publicity, sales promotion, word-of-mouth promotion, personal selling and telemarketing. We can't negate that professionally-sound marketing personnel are found successful in having a fair mix of the different constituents.

Advertising: We find advertising a paid form of persuasive communication. The latest developments in the field of marketing communication technologies have made advertising a sharp-edged weapon in the hands of consultants and the consultancy organisations. The sensitivity in advertising is found increased when the advertising slogans and messages prove to be creative. The advertising professionals having a world-class excellence can make it possible. The marketing experts feel that creativity paves avenues for sensitivity and sensitivity reserves elbow room for acceptability of the messages, slogans, appeals and themes. This makes it essential that messages have high degree of creativity. While advertising, the consultancy organisations need to draw their attention on some of the important problems as mentioned below:

- Composing slogans having creativity.
- Selecting suitable vehicles for travelling the messages.
- Injecting sensitivity to the messages, themes and appeals.
- Making the advertisement measures cost-effective.
- Increasing the life-span of advertisement slogans.
- Testing the advertising slogans before their final launching.
- Testing the advertising effectiveness.

The aforesaid issues are found significant with the viewpoint of making possible creativity in the advertisement decisions. A consultancy organisation is required to study the effectiveness of print media, broadcast media and the telecast media. The professionally-sound marketing personnel and advertising agencies, bear the responsibility of making the advertisement measures proactive.

The emotional persuasion mainly through impersonal communication bears the efficacy of attracting the attention of users. Where oral presentation in conversation fails in creating motivation, the advertising does it through emotional persuasion. In the armoury of today's business, the advertisement proves to be an effective measure.

As a propelling power, the advertisement thus is found to be a strategic device. The effectiveness of advertisement depends upon the decision of marketing professionals managing the business affairs. The development of a sound advertising theme is found to be an important decision-making area which necessitates a rational plan for advertisement.

In addition to other problems, the marketing professionals also bear the responsibility of selecting a suitable vehicle for advertisement. With the increasing sophistication in print technology, we find print media instrumental in informing, sensing and persuading the clients. The newspapers, magazines, posters, brochures, leaflets become the focal point in the very context. The world-class excellence of advertising professionals and the marketing executives can make this media effective when they are careful while selecting materials and media to be preferred by the target audience. Of late, we find sophisticated print devices, such as offset print, laser print and screen print. The quality papers are available and the leading newspapers and magazines have wider circulation. The professionals are required to select quality papers, quality print and media with wider circulation among the target audience. The advertising professionals would study the changing level of expectations of clients *vis-a-vis* the potentials of the consultancy organisations and based on study results would come to a conclusion. We can't deny the fact that the print media would also be economic besides a big circulation. These facts make it clear that the consultancy organisations need to prefer to advertise through the print media.

In advertising, we also find broadcast media instrumental in informing, sensing and persuading the clients. With the development of communication technologies, we have almost 100 per cent coverage of air transmission. The transmission is possible within short duration even to the remotest part of the country. The audience belong to almost all the segments. In the face of emerging trends, the consultancy organisations may advertise on Radio but the advertising professionals are supposed to make the messages and campaigns creative by using their excellence. The timing and duration of transmission is found significant and therefore the advertising professionals are required to study the expected time during which the audience are found playing with their radio sets. The frequency of transmission would also be decided by the advertising professionals.

Of late, we find telecast media establishing its edge over the print and broadcast media. This is due to the fact that televisions have the outstanding merit of audio-visual exposure. In the broadcast media, we have only audio-exposure facility which minimises its instrumentality in sensitising the prospects. At the same time, it is also right to mention that telecast media is found expensive which is not affordable to almost all the consultancy organisations. Of course, the leading consultancy organisations can afford advertising on TV. The marketing and advertising professionals bear the responsibility of making the advertisement slogans creative which succeed in influencing the prospects. The stimulation process is sizeably influenced by creativity and this makes it essential that the consultancy organisations are well aware of the expectations of target market.

Aggressive advertising is found essential when the normal processes become ineffective. The financial constraint draws our attention on the advertising budget which is required to be realistic.

Publicity: We find publicity instrumental in activating the process of persuasion for which the advertisers are not supposed to pay anything. The public relations activities are found important while publicising. Like other organisations even the consultancy organisations are required to use this component of promotion. The ultimate object of publicity is to transmit to the masses the news and information related to the effectiveness of the appeal. In the consultancy services, the publicity measures are required to be innovated. This requires support of academics and professionals in the field of creating creative literature and getting them published in the important newspapers, magazines and journals preferred by the target clients. The publicity measures simplify the task of consultative salespeople as the creative literature would be instrumental in raising the effectiveness. The services to be offered by a consultancy organisation would be published in a reputed media having wider circulation. The technical, medical, legal's management journal, and the important newspapers and magazines preferred by the prospects require due attention of marketing professionals.

The marketing professionals serving the consultancy organisations need to develop rapport with the media people so that they evince their personal interest and make possible a coverage of the developments made possible by the consultancy organisations or even by a particular consultant. We can't deny the fact that while publicising, the marketing professionals need to assign due weightage to the personnel having the skill of influencing the media people. The transformation of dialogues into a deal requires world-class professional excellence and the marketing professionals need to be careful that efficient personnel discharge this responsibility. Organising press conferences, displaying and visualising positive contributions, quality of services, benefits to the users are some of the important aspects requiring due attention of marketing professionals in general and the public relations officers or the contact persons in particular. They need to be professionally-sound and personally-committed besides having the art and tact of influencing the media people. It is in this context that we need to talk about LGD marketing where Lunch (L), Golf (G) and Dinner (D) play an incremental role in influencing the media, seeking their co-operation and getting the favour. We can also think in favour of offering to the media people small but memorable gifts. The main thing in the process is to get their favour which is hardly to be possible unless we convince and motivate them.

The aforesaid facts make it clear that publicity has proved its instrumentality in promoting the business provided the marketing professionals manage everything in a right way. We can't deny the fact that publicity measures succeed even when the advertisements prove to be ineffective. This is due to the fact that masses trust on media and whatever the positive or negative projection we find in the newspapers and magazines throw a telling impact on the impulse of prospects. The positive contributions of a medical consultant, legal consultant, management consultant, technical consultant if getting due coverage in the newspapers and magazines influence the impulse of prospects and the process of stimulation of demand is switched on. Thus, the marketing professionals need to explore avenues to make the publicity measures effective. This would also help them in optimising the promotion budget since the pressure on advertisement would considerably be minimised.

Sales Promotion: This component of promotion bears the efficacy of touching the target with the help of incentives offered to the middlemen and the clients or consumers. It is a temporary incentive with a certain motive found instrumental in promoting the consultancy business. We need to mention that in the consultancy business, the middlemen are also used to offer the services to the clients. The leading consultancy organisations have branch and site offices where a number of personnel are found engaged in offering the services to the clients. The services are offered directly to the users when we find an individual acting as a consultant. The marketing professionals are supposed to take decisions related to incentives to be offered to the middlemen as well as to the users. The branch personnel, site personnel play an incremental role in selling the consultancy services. We go through incentive measures to be offered to both.

The branch offices and site offices where a number of personnel work, play a significant role in offering the services. To improve the quality of services or make possible time-honoured implementation, it is pertinent that they are offered suitable incentives. We can't deny distortion in quality while offering the services that may even be deliberate. The consultancy organisations are required to influence the personnel supposed to offer the services to the clients. We find small gifts, travelling plan, subsidised or even free of cost service to the personnel practising sales promotion measures for the middlemen. The success rate of consultancy organisations is considerably influenced by the instrumentality of working personnel. If they cooperate and evince personal interests, the promised services reach to the users without any distortion that helps the consultants and the consultancy organisations in keeping and winning the users. Here, the marketing professionals need to select innovative promotional measures and the sensitive duration for offering the services.

In addition, the sales promotion measures are also for the users or clients. This may be in different forms, such as concessional services for a particular period, offering of small gifts to the customers, organisation of sales contests for the clients and users, package benefits to the customers for a particular period or so. Here, it is significant to mention that the consultancy organisations can be successful in promoting the business by innovating the promotional measures. To be more specific, the large-sized customers or industrial customers need due attention of the consultants. The incentives to customers may have a direct impact on the promotion of business. The marketing professionals bear the responsibility of identifying the measures and knowing the opportune moment for offering. This helps them in many ways. The business is increased and possibilities of getting the retained business are found wider. While offering incentives, the consultancy organisations also need to turn their eyes on the strategies adopted by the competitors so that they are in a position to offer the innovative measures, specially in the field of comparative advertising.

The aforesaid facts make it clear that in the promotion mix, we find consultancy services playing an incremental role. The important functional responsibility before the consultancy organisations is to make possible innovation in sales promotion. This requires professional excellence and the marketing professionals can make it possible. Memory value happens to be an important base while selecting the sensitive promotional measures for the clients.

Personal Selling: Personal selling needs personal excellence to influence the prospects. It has proved to be an important component of the promotion mix. The consultancy organisations find this constituent of the promotion mix effective in promoting the business. How to build confidence is an important aspect of personal selling in which the consultative salespeople are required to perceive the changing expectations of clients or users in a right fashion. They are supposed to perceive power, value and decision-making system in the client's organisations.

It is also essential that they develop personal relationship with the personnel engaged in the organisations of clients. In a true sense, they are required to move with the client. The success of personal selling substantially depends on the personality and excellence of an individual. Physical attractions are assigned due weightage in the very context. If they behave well, act well, move well, communicate well and receive well; the task of consultancy organisations is simplified considerably. It is against this background that we find personal selling an important component of the promotion mix.

Dynamics of personal selling has been found effective in activating the selling activities. For the actual sales, it is essential to assign due weightage to the sales preparations for initiating sales dialogues and transforming them into a deal. Pre-sale activities and post-sale services are found instrumental in making the process proactive. It is natural that all clients have varying degree of awareness. Some of them are fully aware of the latest developments; some of them are partially aware and some of them are totally unaware of recent developments. How to create awareness is an important functional responsibility before the personal communicators. Here, the consultative sales-people play an important role. They attempt to tailor the level of awareness of clients and adopt the measures to sensitise them. Not surprisingly, the highly conscious clients are found in a position to make an independent decision and know all about. While selling to the less aware customers, the consultant sales people are required to stress upon the main features of the services to be offered, the uniqueness of services, the relative merits or so.

Personal promotion helps consultants or the consultancy organisations in creating impulse buying. Sales do not occur automatically. Opportunities are always found in the market. The professionally-sound salespeople don't search and wait for the opportunities rather than they create the opportunities. A consultant salesman is required to devise new ways to move market into action so that impulse buying is generated in a right direction. The excellence of a consultative salesman occupies a place of outstanding significance. If the clients remain satisfied with the communicative ability of the consulting salespeople, the task of consultants and the consultancy organisations is simplified considerably. It is pertinent to mention that it is not only the consultants who generate the business but virtually it is the result of a joint endeavour of the consultative salespeople and the consultants that simplify the process of promoting the business. The consultative salespeople are required to create awareness and interest, reinforce to overcome cognitive dissonance, facilitate and cause the purchase to take place and ensure that the clients are satisfied with the services of consultants. It is against this background that personal selling occupies a place of outstanding significance in the promotion of consultancy services. We accept the fact that personal selling swamps advertising but it is essential that the salespeople are efficient, tactful, submissive, well-informed, intelligent, value-based, personally-committed and deliberating everything with more confidence and a high communicative ability. If we don't find image problem with the consultancy organisations, the results are to be positive.

In the consultancy services to break the ice, we find personal selling effective but its success rate is influenced by the support of impersonal promotion measures like advertisement and publicity. The magnitude of success is found high, if a consultant salesman perceives in a right fashion the emerging trends in the business environment. We can't deny the fact that personal selling is based on the concept of relationship marketing in which developing personal relations or rapport with the clients' own or trusted personnel appear impact generating. If they succeed in developing relationships with the big personalities, the dialogues are to be transformed into a deal. It is already pointed out earlier that the generation of profit by the clients paves avenues for the generation of profits by the consultancy organisations. It is in this context that they need personnel who happen to be professionally-sound.

How to influence the target audience? Of course, it is an important problem before the salespeople. This necessitates personal attention on the behavioural profile of clients. The following guidelines are expected to be important in the very context:

- They are expected to assign due weightage to the profit generation plan of the clients.
- They are supposed to help clients in defining their business, markets, products and the service system.
- They are required to maintain wide, multi-functional access inside the consultancy organisations.
- They are supposed to assign an overriding priority to quality.
- They need to bear the responsibility of bridging over the gap between the services-promised and services-offered by ruling out distortion in the process of offering.

- They are expected to draw a full complement of the product mix.
- They are supposed to accept the responsibility of informing, sensing and persuading the users. This makes it essential that they possess high communicative ability and in addition, they have an attractive personality and are also aware of behavioural management.
- They have patience and potentials for turning things in their favour.
- They know the art and tact of developing personal relationships.

The aforesaid facts are found essential to enrich the potentials of salespeople serving the consultancy organisations. The consultancy organisations need to review the performance and contributions of salespeople and to impart to them special training facilities as and when the circumstances necessitate. Thus, it is pertinent to mention that personal selling may be successful in promoting the consultancy business if the consultancy organisations assign due weightage to the development of salespeople. An ongoing training programme is found essential to generate the efficiency of salespeople.

Word-of-mouth Promotion: Quality of services is the main thing in promotion. If the services are of world-class, the customers/users start promoting your product. Contrary to it, if your services are of poor quality even the most sophisticated promotional measures fail in sensitising the users. It is against this background that we talk about this constituent of promotion mix. By word-of-mouth communication, our emphasis is on promoting the services by the hidden salesforce. It is pertinent to mention that the satisfied group of customers communicate to their close friends and relatives the outstanding properties of the services availed by them. Since we trust on our friends and relatives, the process of stimulation is found activated. If you are satisfied with the services of a medical consultant since he/she has successfully cured you on the basis of his/her expertise and in addition, his/her behaviour has also been decent; you talk to your friends and relatives regarding the same. In this context, you act as a hidden salesforce. In future, your friends and relatives prefer to use the services of the same doctor. Like this, if a legal consultant helps you in protecting the property, you talk to your friends and relatives the same. They prefer to use the services of the same legal consultant as and when they get an opportunity. These facts are a mute testimony to this proposition that quality goods or services are promoted even by the satisfied group of customers or users. It is in this context that we talk about the instrumentality of word-of-mouth promotion in promoting the consultancy services.

It is important to mention that in this context the marketing professionals also need to use the services of opinion leaders or vocal persons who have a high communicative ability. They identify such persons, offer to them concessional services in addition to small gifts and expect from them a strong advocacy in favour of their services. The consultancy organisations also need to use this component of the promotion mix since this helps them in many ways. The communication is likely to be effective since the processes are initiated and monitored by persons having a high social image. They know how to influence the masses and therefore they often succeed in promoting the business. The marketing professionals need to have an idea of opinion leaders in the concerned catchment area. This would determine the intensity of success of word-of-mouth promotion. It is against this background that we find medical and legal consultants using the services of brokers. Of course, we don't find the practice fair since in this context the narration is not based on personal experience of the promoter. Word-of-mouth communications need to be based on presentation of authentic facts and figures to the prospects. If we talk about the opinion leaders, it is supposed that they have used the services of consultants themselves and are satisfied with the same.

In view of the above, it is right to mention that like other organisations, the consultancy organisations also need to use word-of-mouth promotion but while doing such they are not supposed to use unfair and unethical practices. If the consultants offer quality services and the clients are satisfied with the same, we find promotion without making any efforts. This makes it clear that the main thing for effective promotion is world-class quality. Thus, the consultancy organisations need to initiate the process of qualitative transformation that activates the process of effective promotion, specially through word-of-mouth communication.

Telemarketing: Of late, we find telemarketing very much instrumental in promoting almost all types of goods and services. We are aware of the fact that telemarketing is based on the contribution of telephonic services and therefore, we can also call it marketing with the support of telephones. It is important to mention that with the satellite communication facilities, the telemarketing has proved to be an effective as well as an economic component of promotion. In some of the areas, we find a combination of telephones and televisions for promoting the services.

The main thing in telemarketing is the instrumentality of telemarketers. He/she should have a high communicative ability in addition to the art of telephonic talk. The consultancy organisations can use telemarketing for promoting the business. An individual consultant or the consultancy organisations need to recruit efficient personnel to act as telemarketers. The personnel acting as telemarketers need an ongoing training. An in-depth knowledge of the related services is found essential to the telemarketers. He/she bears the responsibility of answering to the questions and queries of clients, transmitting to them the required information, removing their confusion and misunderstanding on the basis of his/her communicative ability. It is natural that for discharging his/her functional responsibilities in a right way, the consultancy organisations need to make it sure that the personnel working as telemarketers are professionally-sound. We can't negate that even a minor mistake committed by the telemarketers can make an invasion on the image of the consultants and the consultancy organisations. The telemarketers are required to be patient. While initiating, activating and concluding the dialogues, he/she is supposed to diffuse the tension of prospects. If we find them short-tempered, the generation of tension can't be denied which would jeopardise our all positive efforts. This makes it essential that while recruiting personnel for telemarketers, the consultancy organisations are careful.

The medical, legal, management and technical consultants serving the consultancy organisations need the services of telemarketers. Of late, the leading consultancy organisations of the world have been found using the services of telemarketers. We find economy in promotion since the requirement for personnel is considerably minimised. While advertising or publicising, the users don't get an opportunity to raise questions and queries. But while practising telemarketing, we find it possible. Thus, the consultancy organisations need to promote their business with the support of telemarketers who would help them in different ways. But an ongoing training programme for the telemarketers can't be underestimated. To get the best result, it is also essential that the consultancy organisations make available to the telemarketers sophisticated instruments so that audio-disturbance is not to generate communication problem. Since we have advanced telecommunication network, we find justifications for promoting telemarketing.

In view of the above, it is right to mention that the consultancy organisations or the consultants need to blend the different mixes of promotion optimally so that the creativity is made possible, economy is maintained and the promotion budget is made optimal. The main thing in the promotion is to influence the impulse and to stimulate the demand. Our submixes of promotion are to be proactive, if we synchronise them professionally. But you need not to forget that creativity in promotion is not to serve your purpose, if the services are not of world-class. If we build a fair image, we have a right of projection. Image projection becomes insensitive, if the services are of poor quality.

The Price Mix

In the consultancy services when we talk about the price mix, our emphasis is on fee or commission charged by the consultants or the consultancy organisations for making available to the clients the services as per the promises or agreement. We agree with this view that a decision related to fee or commission plays a significant role. In this context, it is essential that the consultants are aware of the pricing objectives which may be either price competitor or non-price competitor. In the price competitor objective, the consultancy organisations offer lower price since the pricing decisions are required to be motivational. In the non-price competitor objective, we find stable price for individual services and for multi-service situation, a balance or an optimal point is searched in the high, medium and low price lines. In addition, the other objectives are discussed below:

1. Profit generation objective: The working out of fee structure with the viewpoint of generating profits may be a long-term objective. Generally, it is not appropriate that the consultants prefer to have price generating objective in the short-run since only in the long-run, the consultancy organisations may work with the objective of generating profit. It is against this background that we find a number of consultancy organisations preferring profit generation as a long-term objective. We agree with this view that in the short-run, the consultancy organisations need to concentrate on survival or break-even objective. This helps them in developing client's loyalty and once the process of generating the client's loyalty is on, the process continues further.

2. Market stability objective: The market stability objective helps in getting an average return even if the working conditions are not conducive. The decisive factors are market opportunities, special skills and positioning objective. It is found helpful in setting the risk aversive. This objective helps in minimising the possibilities of price fluctuation.

3. Market share objective: The objectives make ways for strategies. Before we formulate pricing strategy, it is essential that we concentrate on objectives. In the market share objective, the consultants work out fee structure in the face of annual revenue targets for business. The cost factor is not found so much important. In this objective, we find emphasis on linking of fees with the targets. It is in this context that the consultants attempt to work out such a strategy which helps them in accomplishing the organisational objectives. How to increase the volume or share is the main theme which needs due weightage while making the pricing decisions.

THE STRATEGIC DECISIONS

1. Strategy Allowing Fee Segmentation: The segmentation of fee focuses our attention on charging fee on the basis of segment which results into a variation in the structure. This is possible when consultants are found in a position to segregate their clients into homogeneous subgroups. In this context, the consultants are supposed to justify discrimination in the fee structure when the services are uniform. In this respect, the consultants are required to be careful specially regarding the movement of clients from one subgroup to another. We find such a strategy suitable when the end-result is the same but the efforts and constraints in achieving the end-result vary. As for example, the extent of basic information, data, drawings, collection and availability. The discrimination in the fee structure is also justified on the basis of spending capacity of the users of services.

We agree with the view that for those segments of the market who need the services but are not in a position to afford the high fee structure, the consultants are required to be liberal and the fee structure for such a segment would be different without a degeneration in the quality of services. It is against this background that we find medical consultants charging less from the weaker section of the society. The holistic concept of management makes it essential that the service generating organisations assign due weightage to the interests of deprived of section.

2. Price Lining Strategy: In this strategy, the consultants and the consultancy organisations charge different fee structure since the services vary. This is possible in the retail business. As for example, we find different price structure for shirts of different categories. Here, it is essential that the consultants are in a position to support price differentiation on the basis of service differentiation. The consultants serve in a different way such as they prepare feasibility report, daily project report, technical specification and so on. This strategy helps both the consultants as well as the clients in making cost analysis and revenue forecasting. The adjustment of fee is found difficult and therefore the consultancy organisations may face numerous problems in the long-run.

3. Leader Pricing Strategy: This pricing strategy helps in building volume and introducing as many clients as possible. It involves substantial reduction in price charged for goods or services having frequent demand. Here, the objective is to market additional services as full price, specially to the clients responding favourably to the leader priced services. In this strategy, the clients prefer to purchase exclusively the leader service. A number of clients like to negotiate which raises the possibility of shifting to other competitors. A dangerous stage like price war is expected which is not suitable to the development of an organisation. A stage like price war is to jeopardise everything.

4. Prestige Pricing Strategy: In this strategy, the consultants charge fee higher than the market. This is supported by the logic that they offer quality services and therefore charge high for the superior quality and less for the inferior quality. We find fee representing the status and this limits the number of clients having fee and status consciousness. If you offer world-class services, the high fee structure is found judicious.

5. Competition-based Strategy: Such a strategy is based on competition. Here, the consultants have three options, the first "to beat", second "to meet" and the third "to lead." In other words, in the "to beat" strategy, we find emphasis on lower price structure so that the price is used as a motivational tool and the clients are motivated. In the "to meet" strategy, we find focus on similar price structure whereas in the "to lead" strategy, we find emphasis on charging higher than the competitors. But this strategy is not suitable when the intensity of competition is high.

6. Skimming Strategy: In this strategy, the consultants recover their services and development costs. Here, the consultants get the maximum fee but the intensity of competition influences the pricing decisions. This strategy helps in the formation of a negative attitude where clients feel that fee has been reduced as the services are of substandard quality.

7. Penetration Strategy: The penetration strategy focuses on break-even point. Here, the fee structure is found a bit higher than the average. Here, the motto is to create trial, rapid acceptance and high volume of services for the consultants. In this strategy, the consultants and the consultancy organisations are required to increase the fee sooner or later which may act as a demotivational tool and the clients may be discouraged. Here, it is pertinent that the consultants show their excellence by justifying a change and this focuses our attention on modifying or improving the services so that the clients don't develop a negative attitude.

8. Discount Allowance Strategy: Of course, we don't find discount allowance strategy suitable for the consultancy organisations, however the consultants may offer discount or allowance when they act as subcontractors to another consultant. In this context, we find reduction in fee due to a reduction in the overhead costs.

The aforesaid pricing strategies are practised but the making of pricing decisions is a challenging task which requires world-class professional excellence. The consultants are first required to estimate the fixed and variable costs or expenses on the services offered to the clients and then need to search the break-even point. Information regarding the variable costs are obtained from different sources, such as past records, cost of machines, man-hour and the journals and reports. On the other hand, the fixed costs draw our attention on utility charges, insurance, rent, salaries, office equipments and furnishing. The break-even point determines the number of projects, the consultants would have at given levels so as to match the total cost and revenue. Cost plus approach is also an important way to set the fee where the consultants make estimate of the services on a case-to-case basis. Besides, the return on investment is also referred in a few cases. It is right to mention that all the strategies related to pricing can't be suitable in all the conditions and therefore, the consultants should have the potentials to identify the conditions in which a particular strategy is to be suitable.

A careful pricing is, thus, found important. Since we talk about even those services which are used by low income group or even by the weaker sections, it is important that the consultants and the consultancy organisations explore possibilities for a rational pricing policy which helps in maintaining the commercial viability besides subserving the social interests. It is against this background that they need world-class professional excellence. If medical consultants keep their fee structure so much high that the services remain confined to a particular segment or section, we can't call it a rational pricing policy. We are not making an advocacy in favour of generating losses, our prime focus is on the fact that when the services are of essential nature needed by almost all the segments, the medical consultants should explore avenues that how and in what way, a fair blending of commercial and social considerations is made possible. If the legal consultants keep their fee structure abnormally high, the poor and weaker sections of the society would fail in availing the same. This makes it clear that the consultants and consultancy organisations don't take pricing decisions in haste in order that the commercial considerations make the social considerations absolutely ineffective. At the same time, it is also essential that the social considerations are not to jeopardise the commercial considerations. Thus, the consultancy organisations need to make pricing decisions rational that establishes a balance between the two opposite considerations. Of course, it requires world-class excellence.

The Place Mix

In the consultancy services, the distribution mix also occupies a place of outstanding significance. By the place mix, our emphasis is on making available promised services to the clients on time. We are aware of the fact that an individual consultant offers the services directly to the ultimate users. But the consultancy organisations offer the services to the clients with the help of branch and site offices. To be more specific when we find the head office located far off, it is essential that the consultancy organisations make suitable arrangements for the offering of services so that time-honoured offering is made possible. The behavioural profile of personnel serving branch and site offices becomes significant in the very context. The opening of branch offices simplify the task of head office which also helps in improving the quality of services.[6] As an alternative arrangement, the consultancy organisations may also start a site office when we find a job contract or telemarketing, may also minimise the establishment expenses since a direct contact on telephone is possible. The nature of service and relationship with the clients are found here important.

Branch Offices: If the consultancy organisations find that the relationship with the clients is of permanent nature or it is not possible to have a direct contact with the clients due to their unmanageable number, cost-ineffectiveness or constraints in transmitting the information; the providers need to think in favour of a full-fledged branch. The opening of a branch would simplify the task of head office. In addition, the operational economy would also be possible. It is important to mention that when we find branch offices through which the services reach to the ultimate users, the head office bears the responsibility of managing the branch offices in such a way that the promised services reach to the users without making any distortion by the employees serving the branch offices. The employees serving the branch offices are required to be efficient and decent. If they use information technologies for offering the services, the head office bears the responsibility of making it sure that efficient personnel are operating and maintaining the technologies. We can't negate the fact that in the consultancy services, the instrumentality of branch offices is found significant. The location point for a branch office is also found important and the executives heading the branch are required to make it sure that branch offices are easily accessible where all the required infrastructural facilities are available. It is in this context that we talk about location point for the branch offices of consultancy organisations.

Site Offices: To be more specific when there is a job contract, the opening of site office is found essential. This brings momentum in the process of offering the services. There is no doubt in it that the relationship here is of temporary nature because the site offices are closed after the completion of a project. However, we can't devalue the importance of establishing site offices very close to the construction site where essential amenities and facilities are required to be made available. We can't deny the fact that opening of site offices increases the efficiency of consultancy organisation since proper monitoring and control make possible time-honoured implementation.

Through a Representative: It is important to mention that while distributing the consultancy services, we make an advocacy in favour of a representative where the establishment or opening of site office is not found to be a commercially-viable proposition. The offering of services with the help of a representative requires due attention on some of the essentials, such as nature of services, gap between the providers and clients and the relationship with the clients.

Through a Communication Media: We find distribution of consultancy services even through a communication medium. There are a number of services where the providers or the consultancy organisations are not required to open branch or site offices. Here, we find communication system or media playing an effective role since the telemarketers transmit necessary or desired messages to the clients.

In Figure 13.6, we find distribution channel for the consultancy organisations. While offering the services, the consultancy organisations are required to be circumspect so that a confidence of high level is generated and the process of transforming the potential clients into the actual and habitual clients is possible.

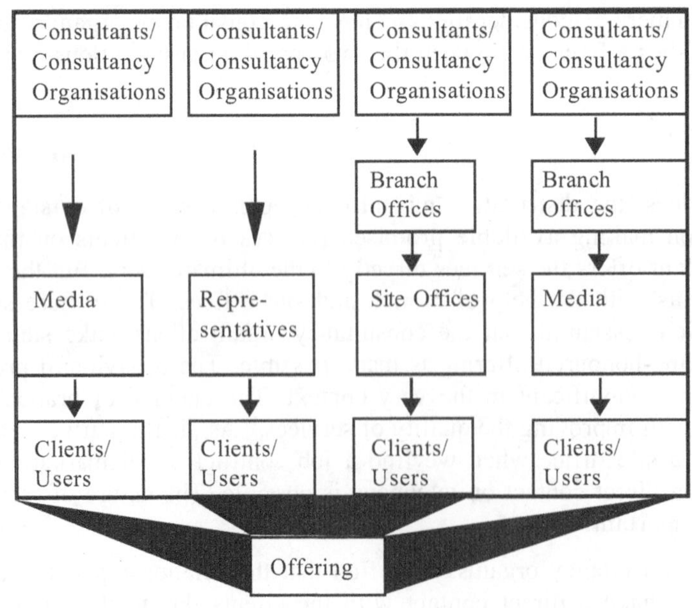

Fig. 13.6: Distribution Channel for Consultancy

We are well aware of the fact that responsibility of offering the services is found on the shoulders of consultative salespeople who play the game in a bit different way. The consultants or the consultancy organisations can't be successful in generating profits unless they get adequate support of consultative salespeople. This makes it clear that the consultancy organisations need precaution while employing the consultative salespeople. A client does not win alone indeed he/she/they win, along with the consultative salespeople. This clarifies the instrumentality of consultative salespeople in improving the quality of services. The consultative salespeople on behalf of the organisation attempt to maintain operational economy, accelerate the rate of productivity and thus make ways for generating profits for both – the consultancy organisations as well as the clients. It is in this context that we talk about the place mix for the consultancy organisations.

The Process

The providers in the consultancy services may be an individual or an organisation processing the services with the help of different experts where they use the services of technology if the circumstances necessitate so. The consultative salespeople play an important role in the service delivery process. We find different conditions for processing such as direct delivery of services by an individual consultant to the clients. We find there media playing an important role by informing and sensing the clients and the potential clients. The representatives of the consultancy organisations also work for them. The need to understand the needs and requirements of clients and to process them so that the promised qualities of services are made available to the clients. In the larger consultancy organisations, we find different branch offices and even site offices. Thus, the processing of services by the branch offices to the site offices and finally to the ultimate clients. We may also find one more category in which the responsibility of site office is discharged by the media people. The promised quality of services must reach to clients without gap and distortion. We also find possibilities that for delivering the services to the clients, the branch offices and site offices also make use of equipment and information technology. The professionals managing the affairs need to make it so that all the equipments and technologies used in the process work satisfactorily. The motive is to deliver the quality services in the face of promises made by the consultancy organisations.

The consultancy organisations also need to manage the service recovery processes. The clients if not getting the expected quality of services may complain the representatives, site offices or even directly to the head offices. The professionals need to identify the lapses in the service delivery process which may be either due to people or the technology used for this purpose. Sincere and honest redressals of complaints simplify the task of marketing professionals. The main thing in the process is to notice the complaints and satisfying the clients that all the measures are taken for their redressal.

The professionals need to strengthen this realisation that right processing is another form of evidence used by the clients to judge the quality of services delivered to them. The approaches for service delivery must be standardised. So far as the consultancy services are concerned, we find here consultants playing a decisive role. To complete the process, they may take the services of supporting staff and equipment and information technology but the ultimate responsibility lies on the shoulders of experts or specialists working as consultants. The flow in the processes are to be maintained and the quality gap due to technological faults is to be bridged.

Physical Evidence and Attractions

In the process of formulating a marketing mix, the consultancy organisations also need to divert their attention on physical evidence where we find focus on the properties tangibilising the image of the organisation. The consultancy organisations work with the support of consultants who for their operational efficiency take help of technologies. There are a number of services offered by the consultancy organisations related to the different streams. We find operations research, opinion surveys, market research, counselling, organisational development, organisational restructuring, production planning, financial planning, cost reduction, energy conservation, industrial relations, productivity acceleration, etc. Particularly the consultancy organisations of larger size offer a number of services and in that case, we find tangibilisation occupying a place of outstanding significance. They have a big team of experts or specialists related to the different areas of management. The clients and visitors are expected to visit the offices of consultants where tangibilisation is found essential for the projection of a fair image. Creation of reputation having service and quality fragrance appears essential for the consultancy organisations. This mix of marketing makes it essential that the offices of consultants have an impressive look. Our focus is here on the ambient conditions instrumental in throwing the service fragrance. The professionals can do it in different ways.

We find big consultancy organisations well organised and equipped with a number of devices for improving the operational efficiency. Particularly the information and communication technologies are found helping them substantially. Besides, the leaflets and cards, brochure, interior décor, ventilation display of equipment they have are some of the features which if properly and scientifically tangibilised would be helpful in the projection of image. Of course, we find consultancy service people-based but the perception of service quality is found high if they make use of the supportive technology.

We find consultancy services also offered by an individual and in that case, this dimension of marketing mix becomes insignificant because to make possible cost economy, he/she has no option but to minimise the expenses. However, they would also be required to generate a feeling about service quality with the help of different sources of projection, of course at a small scale. They cannot undermine the role of attractions with the help of personal care dimensions.

In the big consultancy organisations, it is feasible to develop different dimensions of personal care services which would simplify the process of adding additional attractions to the services offered. The dresses and physique of employees working there are found important in the very context. Motivating the clients and potential clients make it essential that professionalised efforts have been made.

The People Mix

In almost all the consultancy organisations, we find instrumentality of people to implement the policies and programmes in an effective way. We can't deny that technologies play an outstanding role in improving the quality and generating the efficiency but people who operate, maintain and control different types of technologies play a decisive role. Sophisticated technologies may fail but the quality people never fail. Sky is the limit for quality since multi-dimensional developments in the business world open new vistas for quality upgradation and the organisations believing in making things happen keep on moving the process of innovation which activates the process of quality generation. It is against this background that we find this mix of the marketing mix occupying a place of outstanding significance. Like other organisations, the consultancy organisations also need the services of quality people serving as consultants, consultant sales people, working in the branch and at site offices. We can't deny the fact that telemarketers play an incremental role in improving the quality of consultancy services. The instrumentality of people serving the branch and site offices is found significant because they may create a gap between the services-promised and services-offered by distorting the quality. Such a distortion makes an invasion on the image of consultancy organisations. It is against this background that the consultants and the consultancy organisations availing the services of branch offices, site offices and telemarketers need to assign due weightage to the quality of people engaged for offering the services. Since we find a big change in the expectations of clients, it is much more impact generating that the consultancy organisations develop an ongoing training programme for the employees offering the services to the clients.

While recruiting, training, compensating and controlling; they need professional excellence. After recruitment, a well-managed training programme changing with technologies and business conditions is found essential. It is quite natural that sophistication in technologies influences the whole system. Some of the consultancy organisations use the services of new generation of information technologies and therefore, they are in an advantageous position. This helps the shaping of the perception of quality which makes the task of marketing difficult to those organisations who don't use modern information technologies. We are aware of the fact that the consultancy services are based on excellence. A fair synchronisation of sophisticated technologies and quality employees makes the ways for quality upgradation. If the employees serving the branch and site ofices are satisfied with the incentives offered to them, the promised services reach to the clients or the ultimate users. This makes it essential that the consultancy organisations make possible employee orientation by offering to the employees incentives in different forms. Thus, while managing people, the marketing professionals need due weightage to the incentive plans for employees which would pave avenues for performance orientation. Since we talk about new information technologies, it is pertinent that the consultancy organisations seek the co-operation of telemarketers.

In view of the above, it is essential that the consultancy organisations think in favour of people. We can't deny that a majority of the consultancy organisations have been devaluing the instrumentality of quality people which has been found expanding the gap between services-promised and services-offered. It is high time that they take the support of quality people failing which we can't think about exciting future marketing.

CONSULTANCY SERVICES MARKETING IN INDIAN PERSPECTIVE

In the Indian perspective, we find management consultancy of course not at nascent stage but it is also right to mention that a majority of them have been found working on an unorganised basis. Consultancy services for managerial excellence draws priority attention of almost all the organisations. The IMCI, a professional association of individual management consultants and management consultancy firms comments that the quality of product of management consultants is not of world-class. A majority of them have not been found sincere to the professional ethics and service quality. An individual or an organisation working as a management consultant needs professional excellence and this is not to be possible unless we find them working independently, preferring it as a sole occupation and enriching their knowledge bank on a regular basis. A good number of management consultants are either from the segment of retrenched or retied management people or academics. The increasing unethical and unlawful practices in the consultancy services makes it essential that IMCI and governmental regulations come forward to regulate their unlawful behaviour. In almost all the streams of management, the consultants need to make available to their clients the services of world-class so that the benefits made available to the clients make ways for getting handsome fees for the services rendered.

We cannot deny that in the field of technical consultancy, the public sector has been found to be the clients whereas the private sector has also been found availing the consultancy services but at a very limited scale. With the beginning of economic liberalisation and globalisation, the corporatisation gained prominence which made way for privatisation. A number of private organisations emerging in different areas required the consultancy services of world-class which paved avenues for the development of consultancy services with professional touch of course on an organised basis. The increasing demand side made it essential that an analogous increase is found in the supply side and this resulted into the development of a good number of individual and institutional consultants.

Emergence of management consultancy as a service industry is found significant to improve the quality of consultancy services. Expertise of world-class to benefit the clients appears to be difficult unless we find consultancy organisations innovating quality and promoting ethics. We cannot deny that opportunities for the consultancy services would increase even in the days and years to come but failing the conceptualisation of innovating marketing they cannot be successful in making their services productive either to the providers or to the users.

The services of consultants play a crucial role particularly when we find the high level of volatility in the business environment. Surviving and thriving even in a rough weather requires professional excellence.

The emerging trends in society, economy, culture, technology, business regulations, competition, sectoral concentration influence the future marketing of consultancy services. The consultancy organisations are required to make an in-depth study of the changing environmental conditions so that the marketing decisions are found proactive and productive. The strategies found productive in the western countries are not to be effective in the Indian condition. This makes it clear that environmental changes substantially influence the marketing decisions. We can't deny the fact that consultancy services are found essential for almost all sectors of the economy. Competition makes the ways for sophistication. Sophistication invites complications resulting from which the managerial, financial, technological, legal and other decisions become complicated. An organisation needs more care while making the marketing decisions since even a minor mistake in the innovation process is to cause a big loss. It is not possible and even not essential that all the organisations have an independent cell for consultants. This gravitates our attention on the development of consultancy organisations.

Of late, a number of consultancy organisations are found engaged in offering the specialised knowledge and services helping the decision-makers in improving the quality of their business decisions. There are a number of problems complicating their decision-making behaviour.

- How to install and maintain the new generation of technologies?
- How to rationalise the depreciation cost?
- How to optimise the administrative expenses?
- How to make possible managerial excellence?
- How to improve the financial health of an organisation?
- How to make possible a sectoral balance in the industrial economy?

- How to solve the tax problems?
- How to make the process of communication effective?
- How to innovate the marketing decisions?
- How to counter the strategic decisions of competitors?

The aforesaid questions are to be suitably answered by the professionally-sound consultants. It is high time that organisations in general and the business organisations in particular use the services of consultants. The professionally-sound consultants are found successful in identifying the reasons for the lapses and making available the suggestive measures to counter the same. It is against this background that we find services of consultancy organisations used by almost all the organisations.

The rate of success of the consultancy organisations is considerably influenced by a number of factors. The most important thing in the process is to formulate a sound strategy. Strategy is supposed to be the additional decision rules which enables management to rate the performance. For the formulation of marketing strategies, a consultancy organisation requires to concentrate on the information management which helps them in perceiving the problems in a right fashion. With the increasing sophistication in the information technologies, we find a number of consultancy organisations selling information both at national and international levels. The professionals managing the consultancy organisations or the consultants working independently depend upon the information selling organisations. The formulation of a sound marketing mix is found important to the consultancy organisations and the availability of latest information simplifies their task considerably. To be more specific, the organisations offering the consultancy services need to innovate their marketing decisions which would not be possible unless they get detailed information. In the Indian perspective where the intensity of competition is found high, the consultancy organisations serving the business and domestic sectors need to improve the quality of their services. It is in this context that we talk about the formulation of marketing mix by the consultancy organisations in the face of changing needs and requirements.

Almost all the consultants and the consultancy organisations bear the responsibility of developing marketing inputs optimally so that their marketing efforts are found proactive. The first task before them is to formulate a sound product mix which makes possible a fair combination of different types of core and peripheral services. The medical consultants, the legal consultants or other consultants need to assign due weightage to the service mix they design. They have been found incorporating in the product mix a number of new services and at the same time, we also find them eliminating the traditional services. They need expertise regarding the elimination and inclusion of services in the product mix. We accept the fact that with the development of sophisticated technologies in almost all the areas, we find more frequency in the innovation process. The mounting intensity of competition makes it essential that we innovate and eliminate the services much earlier than the leading competitors. This helps consultancy organisations in adding attractions to their service mix. Further, it also helps them in activating the process of quality upgradation and injecting product attractiveness. The most important thing in the process is to have a sound product portfolio which is to secure future marketing. Old and new, high profit generating and low profit generating, profitable at present and profitable in future are the different considerations determining the formulation of a sound product portfolio. Thus, the consultants and the consultancy organisations need to realise the increasing instrumentality of innovative service mix. On the one hand, they need to concentrate on the quality of core services while on the other hand, they also need to explore avenues for the innovative peripheral services. This is due to the fact that peripheral services add additional attractions to our product mix which simplify the task of creating impulse and stimulating demand. Whatever the services we include in our service mix should be in the face of changing needs and requirements *vis-a-vis* the increasing level of expectations. This would help organisations in developing promotional measures found creative in nature and sensitive in action.

Of late, the promotional measures occupy a place of outstanding significance because almost all the organisations are found active in innovating the service mix. There are a number of constituents of promotion mix and they need to blend them optimally so that promotional expenses are made optimal to the potentials of an organisation. Advertisement, publicity, sales promotion, personal selling, word-of-mouth promotion and telemarketing are the components found instrumental in informing, sensing and persuading the prospects or users of the services. The professionals serving the consultancy organisations need to fix the proportion of a particular constituent.

They need here professional excellence to make possible creativity. When the consultancy organisations feel that their services are of world-class, nationally and internationally competitive, the promotional measures are required to be sensitised on a priority basis. We are aware of the fact that technological sophistication has also influenced the promotional measures and the leading consultancy organisations attempt to make the promotional decisions innovative. The efforts for building a positive image by improving the quality of services make it essential that the consultancy organisations innovate the process of image projection and this is possible with the support of innovative promotional measures bearing creativity. The advertising measures are required to be made creative, the publicity measures are required to be strengthened, the sales promotion measures need to be innovated, the personal selling needs due attention, the hidden salesforce are to be made instrumental and the telemarketing is to be made popular. These measures would help consultancy organisations in projecting a positive image. To be more specific in the Indian perspective, we need to create awareness and creative promotional measures make it possible. It is against this background that the consultancy organisations need to assign due weightage to the promotional measures to be practised.

The consultancy organisations also need to view the problem of setting fee and commission for the clients. This focuses our attention on the pricing decisions of the consultancy organisations. In the consultancy services, we also include the services of medical and legal consultants. In this context, it is pertinent that the consultancy organisations practise the holistic concept of management which makes a strong advocacy in favour of a rational pricing policy that also offers an opportunity to the weaker sections to avail medical and legal services. It is right to mention that some of the users belong to the affluent section whereas some others belong to the weaker section. The high fee strategy can't be suitable to the weaker sections of the society. The consultancy organisations may prefer a discriminatory fee strategy in which the weaker sections are charged subsidised or concessional services. In the Indian perspective, the rural sector needs the services of consultancy organisations for the development of rural economy. The management and financial consultants are supposed to offer specialised services to the rural sector and the fee structure is also to be made proportionate to the paying capacity of the organisations availing the services. In both the sectors, domestic as well as the institutional, this dimension of pricing decision occupies a place of outstanding significance. Thus, the consultancy organisations need to make a rational pricing policy which on the one hand maintains commercial viability to the organisation while on the other hand also makes the services affordable to the weaker sections of the society.

The place decisions focus our attention on offering the promised services to the clients. The leading consultancy organisations need the services of site and branch offices. We also find offering of services with the help of telemarketers. The main thing in the distribution process is to bridge over the gap between the services-promised and services-offered. The professionally-sound employees are to be engaged in branch and site offices. In addition, they need to recruit efficient personnel who act as telemarketers. The consultants and the consultancy organisations bear the responsibility of assigning due weightage to the behavioural management in the very context. Offering of quality services in a decent way makes available to the clients the services-expected. The employees serving branch and site offices need to be professionally-sound, personally-committed and value-based.

This makes it essential that the consultancy organisations assign due weightage to the development of people, working as consultants or acting as a consultative salesman. An ongoing training programme is found essential to enrich the credentials. The world-class services don't carry any meaning if the personal/employees working in the branch and site offices or acting as a telemarketer start making distortion in the process of offering. This makes a strong advocacy in favour of developing quality people for the consultancy organisations.

The aforesaid facts make it clear that the consultancy organisations need to make possible frequent innovation in the development of marketing inputs.[8] We can't expect the marketing decisions to be proactive and productive unless the marketing resources are made optimal to the changing needs and requirements. Thus, the consultancy organisations need to blend the different submixes of marketing in a right fashion.

An individual also needs the services of consultants in the areas like medical, legal and financial. Here, a consultant or a group of consultants need to adopt a bit different strategy. Particularly the medical consultants are supposed to be liberal while adopting the pricing strategy or charging fee. The medical consultants need to adopt a strategy in which the patients having high capacity pay more and like this, the persons having low capacity pay less. The legal consultants also need to keep in their minds the requirements of deprived of or poor sections of the society who find it difficult to protect their existence due to exploitation. Besides, the financial consultants also offer multi-dimensional services to the individuals for channelising productive investments. In this respect, it is right to mention that income structure draws due attention of the consultants serving the domestic sector in different areas. To be more specific in the medical and legal services, we find two extremes or outermost cases. One medical or legal consultant is found hard pressed and due to time constraint, he/she/they find it difficult to serve the users and at the same, we also find some of the legal and medical consultants using the services of brokers. These two outermost cases make it clear that the quality continues to be an important base for motivating the clients. If doctors offer to the patients the quality services which help them quick recovery, the satisfied group of patients start promoting the services. Like this, if we find legal consultants helping an individual in protecting his/her property on the basis of a strong advocacy, they get business even without making the promotional efforts. This is not meant that they don't need to promote. We find emphasis on the fact that the promotional decisions are based on the quality of services promised and offered to the users.

In almost all the areas, we find world-class individual and organisational consultants helping different sectors and segments of the society. It is high time that they practise innovative marketing to serve the clients and to help the consultancy organisations in thriving. It is in this context that we focus on some of the leading consultancy organisations serving the Indian economy and the Indian society.

SUMMARY

In this chapter, you have gone through different dimensions of consultancy marketing. After completing this chapter, be sure that the following facts are well versed:

Consultancy Marketing: The Concept: Consultancy marketing is the application of marketing principles in the consultancy services. The professionals bear the responsibility of formulating a sound marketing mix for the consultancy services. The providers may be an individual or an institution offering services in an organised way.

Rationale behind Consultancy Marketing: We market the consultancy services for availing the expertise, obtaining impartial views, justifying the predetermined measures and making the consultancy services productive.

Users of Consultancy Services: Both categories of users – an individual and an organisation – uses the services of consultancy organisations with diverse motives. They may be domestic as well as foreign.

Behavioural Profile of Users: The needs and requirements, attitudes, lifestyles and expectations are the different dimensions of behavioural profile.

Market Segmentation for Consultancy Services: The consultants and the consultancy organisations need to group and subgroup the market to identify and understand the behavioural profile of users.

Marketing Information System for the Consultancy Organisations: The marketing decisions need latest information and for managing the information, we find marketing information system which is a systematic and organised procedure for managing the information.

Formulation of Marketing Mix for the Consultancy Services: For marketing the services in a right fashion, we formulate marketing mix in which we find a study related to the different submixes, such as the product mix, promotion mix, price mix, place mix and the people.

The Product Mix: The product mix focuses on the services offered by the consultants and the consultancy organisations. It is a process of blending the core and peripheral services in such a way that the services are made attractive and competitive.

The Promotion Mix: It is a managerial device of blending the different constituents of promotion, such as advertisement, publicity, sales promotion, personal selling, word-of-mouth communication and telemarketing. The consultants and the consultancy organisations by promoting inform, sense and persuade the prospects/users.

The Price Mix: The consultants and the consultancy organisations charge fee/commission for the services offered. This focuses on making the pricing decisions rational.

The Place Mix: The consultancy organisation offer the services with the help of branch and site offices and therefore the employees working there play an important role in offering the services. This gravitates our attention on bridging over the gap between services-promised and services-offered.

The Process: In the marketing mix, the process focuses our attention on the service delivery processes adopted by the consultancy organisations with the help of consultants, their supporting staff and technology so that promised quality of services reach to the clients.

Physical Evidence and Attractions: In this submix, our focus on the tangibilisation of the outstanding properties of consultancy organisations with the motto of impressing upon the clients and visitors. The personal care dimensions related to the front line staff in particular cannot be overlooked to add additional attractions to the consultancy services.

The People: This submix is related to the consultating people involved in the process. In addition to the consultants, we find a team engaged in processing the services and therefore, they need thematical competence, personal commitment and sincerity and honesty for delivering quality services and projecting a fair image.

Consultancy Marketing in Indian Perspective: In the Indian perspective, the consultancy services is not of recent origin but so far as the management consultancy services are concerned, we find a momentum only after corporatisation when the corporate culture started gaining popularity to fulfill the temptation of upcoming youths to the material culture. However, the consultancy organisations working in India need to develop professional excellence.

KEY TERMS

Philanthropists
Hermits
Management Consultancy
Stimuli
Behavioural Scientists
Technocrats
Microcomputers
Clients
Habitual Clients
Legal Consultants
Winning and Keeping
Medical Consultant
Innovative Strategies
80-20 Rule
Creativity
Emotional Persuasion
Impersonal Communication
LGD Marketing
Memory Value
Consultative Salespeople
Target Audience
Telemarketing
Price Lining
Leader Pricing
Prestige Pricing
Skimming
Penetration
Discount Allowance
Break-even Point
Distribution Channel
Service Delivery
Service Recovery
Tangibilisation
Brochure
Leaflets
Thematical Competence
Personal Commitment
IMCI

Review Questions

1. What do you mean by Consultancy Marketing? Justify application of marketing principles by the organisations in the Indian perspective.
2. State and explain the users of consultancy services. Focus on the behavioural profile of users of consultancy services.
3. Explain the main services included in the consultancy services. Throw light on the instrumentality of peripheral services.
4. Discuss the segmentation of market within the viewpoint of marketing the consultancy services.
5. Explain the role of information management in the consultancy services. Write a short note on the formulation of marketing mix for the consultancy services.
6. Discuss the product mix for the consultancy services.
7. Explain the different components of promotion for promoting the consultancy services.
8. Focus on the pricing decisions for consultancy services.
9. Write a note on the extended marketing mix for the consultancy services.

10. Discuss the channel for distributing the consultancy services.
11. Write a note on the marketing of consultancy services in Indian perspective.

Application Exercises

1. To attract the clients, you need to offer a package of services. As a marketing professional, how you would formulate a product mix?
2. As a service marketer, you have to blend the core and peripheral services so that your clients get an additional attraction. Focus on the innovative peripheral services you would like to incorporate.
3. To promote the consultancy organisations in a right fashion, you need professional excellence so that the different constituents of promotion are synchronised and the process of persuading the potential clients is found effective. Comment as a marketing professional of a management consultancy organisation.
4. As a marketer, you need to make the fee structure remunerative to the consultancy organisations and affordable to the users. Suggest how you would act.
5. As a marketer, you need to make efforts for winning and keeping the customers. Focus on the management of site and branch offices to help you in the process.

Endnotes

1. Institute of Management Consultants, USA.
2. Engle Blackwell, *Consumer Behaviour,* pp. 21-22.
3. Donald Cowell W., *The Marketing Service*, CNA Foundations and Institute of Marketing, 1984, pp. 24-26.
4. Singh A. and Tyagi A.K., Strategy for Consultancy Service Marketing, *Business Environment (*Ed) by Ahmad and Ahmad, pp. 68-86.
5. *Ibid.*, p. 78.
6. Mack Hanan, James and Cribbin Herman Hesier, American Marketing Association.
7. *Economic Times* (ETM), July-August 1990, No.1, pp. 33-35.
8. Jha S.M., Indian Railways Transnational Consultancy Services, *Indian Railway,* Jan-March 1984, Ministry of Railways, Government of India, New Delhi, pp. 23-26.

RETAIL MARKETING

Corporate culture made ways for material culture. Material culture has opened new avenues for the shopping culture. Earlier, shopping was more of a choice but today it is an experience, a pleasure.

Chapter Objectives

Introduction – Retail Sector: A Service Industry – Emergence of Online or E-Retailing – Retail Formats – Retail Marketing: A Conceptual Framework – Behavioural Profile of Retail Customers – Managing Information for Retail Trading – Market Segmentation for the Retail Trading – Marketing Mix for Retail Services – Product Mix – Promotion Mix – Price Mix – Place Mix – Process – Physical Evidence and Attractions – People – Retail Marketing in Indian Perspective – Summary – Key Terms – Review Questions – Application Exercises – Endnotes.

Learning Objectives

This chapter aims at developing the awareness of professionals regarding the conceptualisation of marketing in the retail services. The readers will develop their knowledge bank related to the multi-dimensional developments in the retail sector. The motive of the study is to sensitise the readers to the process of formulating a sound mix for the retail services. Since we find it an emerging service industry, the readers will be successful in capitalising on the opportunities in the Indian retail sector. They will be aware of the marketing practices for increasing number of loyal shoppers to be helpful in increasing the profitability by satisfying the shoppers.

INTRODUCTION

Corporate culture considerably influenced by globalisation has engineered a sound foundation for the development of new culture believing in spending more for which they have no option but to earn more. The increasing domination of MNCs in the process of national economic transformation has been injecting new life, strength and continuity to consumerism in which comforts, amenities and facilities emerge as a status symbol. The burgeoning middle class, thus, makes a strong advocacy in favour of a market-place where shopping provides to them a pleasure. It is against this background that we have been witnessing multidimensional reforms in the retail trading. Emerging shopping mall and shopping plaza have been found attracting the upcoming youths who at present according to the NCAER survey happens to be 63 per cent of the Indian household. We cannot negate that modern urban India is substantially influenced by corporate culture in which we find a sophisticated lifestyle. The emerging new tracks of retail trading, no doubt, has been creating tremendous opportunities preferably to the budding youths but at the same time, we also find them much more sensitive to multi-faceted woes, e.g., problem of safety and security, shoplifting, data insecurity, lack of parking space and FDI. As found in Thailand, Malaysia, Brazil, Poland and China, the retail sector in India has not been motivating the foreign investors. In addition, the unorganised retailing has been throwing new threats and challenges. Today, attending mall is becoming a fashion. Earlier, shopping was more of a chore but of late, it is considered to be an experience. What to talk of the big towns and cities when we find mall culture spreading like a wildfire even in the small towns and cities.

The challenging new facets of retail trading are a staunch testimony to this proposition that the Indian retail sector has been moving in the new directions. We need not to question the justifications for such a structural transformation as the lifestyles not only in India but around the global has been sizeably influenced by the western culture in which shopping has emerged as a mode of getting pleasure and mall culture helps the upcoming youths of modern India in making a productive use of time and available money in their hands. The retail trading has been witnessing an upsurge and the foreign investors appear to capitalise on the opportunities.

We find new formats of retail trading considerably influenced by globalisation of fashion, culture and civilisation and therefore it is not possible to turn the directions. The only thing that we can do is to professionalise our efforts. The organised and unorganised — both the formats need a sound nexus for their development. The conceptualisation of modern marketing principles will help the professionals in many ways.

We consider retail marketing a process to identify the target market and to understand their changing needs and requirements. The services offered to the target market must be in the face of their changing lifestyles. The professionalised efforts in the process need due attention on the quality of services, promotional efforts to sense and sensitise the customers, pricing decisions keeping in view the purchasing capacity of customers, location points for the retail outlets, design of store and the tangibilisation, involvement of quality people efficacious of serving the customers and making it sure that their services have an edge over the rivals. When we make use of the term retail marketing, our focus is on studying and understanding the customers in a right fashion. Strategically decisions become significant in the entire process.

Of late, the organised retailing has been successful in serving the customers because they formulate a strategy providing much more comforts and conveniences to the customers. The customers get an opportunity to witness a number of products and services of quality and while shopping them get pleasure. The organised market comprises of Departmental Stores, Malls, Supermarkets, Hypermarkets and Discount Houses. The professionals serving the retail outlets also take into consideration the quality, value for money and convenience. They provide an opportunity to the customers to feel shopping a pleasure, motivating them to be loyal and developing a habit of visiting the retail outlets again and again. It is in this context that we find retail marketing based on professional excellence.

We cannot deny that the contribution of organised retailing is not more than 4 per cent of the total retailing industry. This speaks of the fact that in Indian perspective, we cannot overlook unorganised retailing. A large number of people are employed in the unorganised retailing and a majority of the customers avail their services. The development of organised sector of course cannot be regulated but at the same time, it is also pertinent that policy decision-makers do not undermine the interests of unorganised sector and the people employed in that sector. This makes an advocacy in favour of a policy that protects and promotes the interests of both the sectors.

Since we live in an age of globalisation, it is not proper that we restrict FDI in the retail sector. Willingly or unwillingly, the foreign direct investments will be found in the retail sector but it is to be made sure that they also keep into consideration the interests of unorganised sector contributing almost 96 per cent of the retail industry. The interests of both the sectors need due attention of government policy makers.

The Indian economy is found sizeably dominated by the agricultural sector and the retail sector cannot undermine the interests of agri-business. The farmers are found emotionally attached with their lands. Hence, the corporate farming cannot be promoted at the cost of those small and marginal farmers who make sincere efforts to make and keep them fertile. Exploitation of land by corporate farmers would invite multi-faceted problems and once the lands become barren; they would find it difficult to make them fertile.

With the passage of time, we find emergence of a number of formats for retail trading such as Chain of Stores, Convenience Store, Departmental Store, Speciality Store, Supermarket, Shopping Mall, Shopping Plaza, Discount Stores, Factory Secondary Stores and Kiosk. The emerging trends indicate that all the formats of retail trading have cropped up in tune with the changing lifestyles and the cultural patterns.

Presently, we find symptom of economic depression and it is difficult to forecast how long the trend will reverse or the intensity will increase and aggravate. Despite ups and downs, the retail industry will grow because the temptation for getting shopping pleasure has been developing as a habit. As per the estimate of AT Kearney Global Retail Index 2006 and according to the industry estimates, the organised and unorganised retail markets will grow to $427 billion by 2010 and $637 billion by 2015. Such a galloping increase in the retail trading is with the increasing pace of industrialisation to be instrumentalised with the help of corporatisation. Development as a big industry and injecting new lifestyles even amongst common people necessitate qualitative improvements in the marketing processes so that the satisfied group of customers keep on moving the process of development.

It is also significant to mention that we find development of retail trading even in the IT sector, a new emerging and prospering sector in the Indian economy. Since long we find medical services based on retail trading and the agriculture sector has also been found taking the support of retail trading. We cannot negate that whatsoever the innovations we find in the retail sector are considerably contributed by the IT sector and therefore the process of innovations will be found even in future.

The retail sector has also been found making ways for a number of woes such as shoplifting, problem of safety and security, data insecurity, increasing domination of FDI and emerging as a place for the development of immoral relationships. The upcoming youths particularly serving the IT sector have lot of money and they want to spend them this way or that way. In a majority of the cases, they are found unmarried and are influenced by western culture.

Thus, the retail sector has been emerging as a big industry and keeping in view the changes that we find in the behavioural profile of customers, it is imperative that avenues are paved for professional excellence. Whatsoever the volatility that we find in the markets, no doubt, would influence the customers' behaviour but both the organised and unorganised sectors would continue. In the changing conditions, the professionals need to conceptualise innovative marketing which would help the organised retailing in many ways. The retail sector *vis-à-vis* the customers would immensely be benefited and the satisfied group of customers would develop brand loyalty.

RETAIL SECTOR: AN EMERGING SERVICE INDUSTRY

Retail sector, one of the largest sectors in the Indian economy has witnessed different phases of its transition. We find such a transition in the entire globe. We consider retailer as a final chain in the distribution process through which we find delivery of goods to the ultimate customers. Right from "Mom-and-Pop stores" or in the Indian perspective "Kirana stores" to the development of shopping mall and shopping plaza; we find a long history. Both the organised and unorganised sectors contribute to the development of retail sector. In the Indian context, we find unorganised sector contributing almost 96 per cent of the total retailing though during the recent years we have also seen the organised sector increasing its contribution and thriving in its different formats. There are two segments in the organised retail trading such as In-Store Retailers and Non-Store Retailers. The in-store retailers operate at the fixed point of sales locations bearing the potentials of attracting a good number of walk-in customers whereas the non-stores retailers reach out to the customers at their doorsteps or offices.

In the Indian perspective, the retail sector is found emerging as a service industry just next to the agricultural sector. It has an impressive record of creating job opportunities and the turnover. During the yesteryears, the retail sector has emerged as an industry. Despite of significant development in the field of retail sector, the growth record in the Indian context cannot be claimed to be impressive because it is found much lower than USA, Brazil and China where the percentage is 80, 40 and 20 respectively. Our contribution even till date is around 4 per cent.[1] This makes a strong advocacy in favour of a policy that raises the contribution of organised sector.

Retailing is found emerging as a big service industry even in the Indian context and the credibility for the same goes to the development of corporate sector and emergence of corporate culture. The interests of small retailers, neighbourhood stores and mom-and-pop stores cannot be overlooked while formulating a retail policy. The strategical decisions make it essential that on the one hand we make ways for the development of new formats of retailing while on the other hand also protects the interests of a number of people retailing in the unorganised sector.

E-retailing an emerging sector in the retailing has been found serving multi-faceted interests specially in the medical services. The re-engineering of healthcare services has been possible due to e-retailing which is also known as e-tail. An e-tailer is a B2C business that executes a transaction with the final consumer. We find e-tailing, a subset of e-business. In plain words, we find focus on using Web for selling the products and services. It is an emerging area where we find tremendous opportunities to capitalise on.

In a number of areas, the concept of e-tailing has been practised and we find high level of satisfaction which the customers get from it.

Emerging as one of the important sunrise sectors, the retail sector needs priority attention of professionals. We cannot negate that India has been developing as an important retail destination which employs almost 7 per cent of the total workforce just next to agriculture.[2] The retail sector is now considered as an important industry and therefore the policy decisions need priority attention to keep on moving the process of development. The organised retailing, referring to the trading activities undertaken by licensed retailers and paying income tax, sales tax, etc. needs to increase its contribution to the retail trading. The unorganised retailing, referring to the traditional formats of low-cost retailing such as Kirana stores, owner-managed general stores, pan/bidi shops, convenience stores, handcart and pavement vendors, etc. need to be protected. Our policy decisions need not to close doors for the development of unorganised sector.

The above-mentioned facts make it clear that the retail sector has been emerging as a big service industry and therefore particularly the organised retailing has to pave avenues for professional excellence that qualitative improvements in the process of development of the retail sector are made possible. Let the boom industry develop with a professional touch and let the organised retailing practise innovative marketing principles. If we find people earning more, the contraction of opportunities for shopping cannot be a right step. Let people earn more and let them spend more. The development of retail industry cannot be and should not be checked when the economy is found prospering. Such a positive step would open doors for development which would benefit almost all sectors of the economy. The employment opportunities would be broadened and the development processes would be recycled. Let us prove ourselves cynosure of foreign eyes, specially in the retail sector in which we have potentials of world-class.

The marketers need to show their excellence in the retail sector. We need to identify the prospering avenues where our excellence would serve the national economy *vis-à-vis* weaker segments of society. The process of economic transformation *pari passu* social transformation can rapidly be accelerated with the development of retail sector. In the agrarian economy of India, the retail sector needs to be developed in a different fashion so that the agricultural produces get a profitable return; of course, the concept of corporate farming is to be checked. Corporate retailing would inject new life and strength to the retail sector and the prospering industry would benefit the society and the national economy in many ways.

EMERGENCE OF ONLINE OR E-RETAILING

With the increasing sophistication in technology, we find multi-faceted application of online devices and the credibility for the same goes to the new developments in the field of Information and Communication Technology (ICT). Due to time constraint, we find our temptation to online shopping increasing fast and the trend will continue and gain momentum even in the days and years to come. The experiences of e-shopping have been found positive and the retailers have been adopting innovative devices in the e-shopping to add additional attractions and fascinate new segments. Of course, it is due to its inherent outstanding features that we find the graph in its favour consistently moving upward.

The customers find Online Retailing much more convenient and it is on account of its additional feature that online shopping scores higher over the offline shopping. The e-retailing[3] provides to the retailers an opportunity offer to the consumer's customised products and services which is found different in the Brick and Mortar Store of typical nature. The e-retailers have also been found offering to their customers a number of incentives on website which may be in different forms such as discount in rate, auction option or other incentives. In the e-retailing, we also find e-retailers getting an opportunity of increasing the operational efficiency of their supply chain through online procurement or B2B (Business to Business) exchanges. We find such a provision facilitating integrated, near real-time reordering and replenishment from a decently-pruned, well-integrated vendor base. In a true sense, such a step makes possible an increase in the operational efficiency and saves the valuable time of its customers. An additional benefit of e-retailing is concerned with the availability of data related to the behavioural profile of buyers *vis-à-vis* the buying patterns. Thus, e-retailers and customers both of them find online shopping a convenient form of shopping making it a pleasure.

In view of the above, it is right to say that online shopping or e-retailing is gaining popularity and it is in this context that we find a number of companies preferring e-retailing. A survey conducted by International Data Corporation, a premier global market intelligence and advisory firm in the information technology and telecommunication industries, on the Indian e-commerce transactions market showed that B2C (Business to Consumer) business is to increase to ₹ 3,000 crores by 2010.[4] The important players in the very context are Rediff.Com, Baazee.com, Indiatimes.com, etc. who entered business through the online route and the LG Electronics, Indian Railways, Jet Airways, Indian Airlines who are the traditional brick and mortar companies.

Thus, we find a smooth playground for the online players and the process will continue with the increasing domination of techniculture. A new feather in the Retailing Sector has satisfied the customers and created a big market and even in the coming days, we expect it to be much more positive.

RETAIL FORMATS

Both the Organised and Unorganised retail sectors have different formats as shown in below.

Chain of Stores: Established by a single retailer exclusive store design and having a synergistic merchandising plan, promotion and service strategy.

Convenience Stores: Located close to residential are merchandising.

Franchise: Retail stores owned and operated by individual licensed by a big supporting organisation.

Departmental Stores: A store having several departments such as clothing, personal care, cosmetics, electronics, etc. all under a single roof.

Speciality Stores: Retail shops displaying merchandising having narrow product lines.

Supermarket: A store which is departmentalised with self-service offering.

Hypermarket: Very large in size varying grocery, hardware and general merchandising with self-service facilities usually located in warehouse type structure.

Shopping Mall: An arrangement of retail stores providing a right mix of shopping, food courts and entertainment and parking facilities. Retail space shared by an anchor stores and other retailers (tenants) who will pay the development of the mall rent or lease for putting up the shop within the mall premises.

Shopping Plaza: A configuration of many tenants using space of 1000 sq.ft. or so for putting up stores within a single building.

Discount Stores: A broad variety of merchandising offering limited services at low prices.

Factor/Secondary Stores: Owned and operated by the manufacturers.

Kiosk: A store as a concession format store placed within a mall/shopping centre, bus station, airport, free standing pavilion open on one or more sides.

In addition, we find Kirana Stores, Owner-managed General Stores, Pan/bidi Shops, Convenience Stores, Handcart and Pavement Vendors also as the formats of retail sector.

Both the formats need due attention of government policy makers because in a country like India where the retail sector has sizeably been contributed by the unorganised sector, we cannot undermine their interests.

If on the one hand, we professionalise the organised retail sector; on the other hand, we also need to protect and promote the interests of unorganised retail sector. The Indian conditions have a sound nexus for the development of mom-and-pop stores and even for the progress and prosperity of shopping mall.

RETAIL MARKETING: A CONCEPTUAL FRAMEWORK

At the outset, it is essential to go through the conceptual aspect of Retail Marketing.

Retail marketing is found to be a managerial process for identifying the target market. It is application of marketing concept in the retail sector where professionals study and understand the behaviour of customers and make available the quality product to the customers in the face of their changing needs and requirements. It is found related to the organised retailing where the professionals formulate a sound marketing mix and ensure that customers are found satisfied. The professionals in the marketing process make sure a location point having smooth accessibility, design stores in tune with the changing taste and temperament of customers, make possible creativity in the promotional efforts, keep the price structure profitable to the retailers and affordable to the customers, ensure right channelisation of services with the help of people and technology used in the process, regulate indecency and delay in the processing of service, tangibilise the outstanding properties of their outlets and serve and command everything with the help of a team of dedicated and committed people showing personal-touch-in-service. The decision-making practices clusters around the customers.

We find retailing a channel between the producers and ultimate customers or users to ensure to them the conveniences and comforts in the buying process. And when we make use of the term retail marketing, our focus is on the marketing processes for retailing. The retailers working in the organised sector take the help of professionals who bear the responsibility of practising marketing. In the process of formulating a marketing mix, the professionals keep into consideration a number of factors. For retail marketing, the most important thing understands the behavioural profile which simplifies the task of formulating a marketing mix.

In view of the above, the following facts emerge regarding the conceptual aspect of retail marketing:

- It is a managerial process because professionally-sound managers practise marketing.
- It is a process of identifying the target market.
- Retail marketing is considered to be a process of studying and understanding the behavioural profile of customers which focus on needs and requirements, likes and dislikes, priorities, and lifestyles.
- It is a process of formulating a marketing mix.
- It is found related to the organised retailing.
- It is practised in a number of areas because not only the goods manufacturing sector but service generating sector also makes use of retail marketing.

STUDYING AND UNDERSTANDING BEHAVIOURAL PROFILE OF RETAIL CUSTOMERS

Behaviour is considered to be an important dimension of marketing management simplifying the task of marketers in different ways. In the environmental conditions, a number of developments take place and all throw a telling impact on our behaviour. The needs and requirements, likes and dislikes, levels of expectations are influenced by the flow of discretionary income and techno-driven information. It is in this context that corporatisation has considerably influenced our behaviour. It is essential that the marketing professionals have an in-depth knowledge of changing behavioural profile so that they develop their awareness of the levels of expectations and make sincere and honest efforts to satisfy them. The retail sector is found concerned with almost all the segments. A number of products either goods or services are found concerned with the retail outlets. The professionals managing the affairs need an in-depth study of the changing levels of income, expectations and their impact on their lifestyles. After 1990, we find an attitudinal change in the Indian households and dominating factors influencing their attitudes are a significant increase in their disposable income and techno-based transmission of information.

The customers in general expect much more comforts and conveniences in availing the services. They prefer services at doorsteps due to time constraint. They like centralised services where it is possible to get everything they need. The two important considerations influencing their behaviour are the retailer and the merchandising. Of course, we find different stages in the buying process such as recognition of needs, search of information, evaluation of alternatives, selecting a retailer and selecting the merchandising, visiting a store or surf internet or going through catalogues and showing loyalty, if they are satisfied. But it is not essential that in all the cases, the buying decisions move in the fixed way. We find deviation in the process depending on the situational forces.

The retail market has been found experiencing competition of high magnitude and this has complicated the task of marketers while attracting the customers and retaining them for the long time. This in a very natural way makes it essential that the professionals study and understand their changing preferences and make sincere and professionlised efforts to fulfil them.

The first task before the professionals in the retail marketing is to make available to the customers high level of satisfaction. The customers are found to be loyal to a particular retailer when they are satisfied with their services. The marketers thus need to activate the process of value addition or enhancement. Values, we consider, an enduring belief that a specific mode of conduct or end state of existence is personally or socially preferable to an opposite mode of conduct or end state of existence. The value may be instrumental and terminal. The instrumental values refer to general beliefs related to desirable modes of conduct whereas the terminal value represent enduring belief related to end state of existence. Hence, the marketing professionals for satisfying customers need to offer both the instrumental as well as terminal. We assign priority attention to value because this makes the ways for achieving high level of satisfaction opening doors for retention of customers and high level of profit. In a true sense, we find shaping of the level of expectations before the buying decisions are made and when the customers get more than their prior expectations, we find them fully satisfied.

Thus, we find satisfaction, value and behaviour interrelated. We also find a relationship between the personal values and desired consumer benefits.[5] The values for the same attribute of product may vary from customer to customer. This makes it essential that the marketers consider different preferences of consumers and make use of them as a guideline for the formulation of a strategy. The SERVQUAL model[6] focuses on the same process of identification of different dimensions customers look for the selection of a retail store. The professionals need to concentrate their attention on some of the points such as distance from home, promotional measures, discount offered, availability of varieties, time taken for making the purchase, reliability in the terms of freshness, promptness of service ambience, credit facility, home delivery and availability of parking space considered to be major expectations of customers in the process of selecting retail store of their choice.

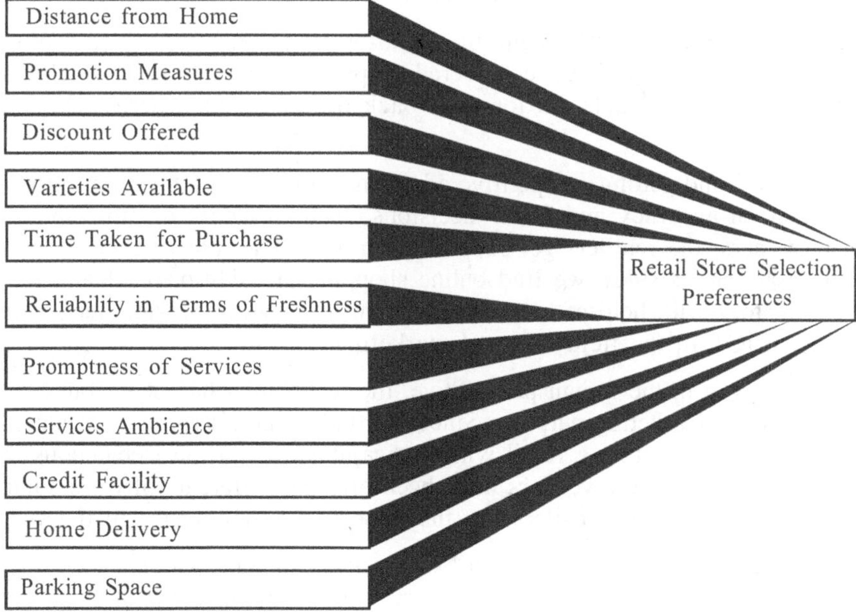

Fig. 14.1: Customer Preferences for Retail Store Selection

The above-mentioned facts make it clear that the marketers serving the retail sector have to assign due attention on the preferences of customers. In the eleven variables discussed earlier, we find three compositive factors such as value for money, store layout appeal and customer convenience. At the same time, we cannot deny that the recognising factors for consumer preferences are often based on needs and motives. This again focuses our attention on values making available to the marketer a very powerful tool in their hands for achieving the high level of satisfaction. This may also help them in the development of market segmentation strategy. And once the professionals get a success in segmenting the retail market on the basis of preference of consumers for the selection of retail store, it is found easier for them to design the new retail outlets and formulate a sound retail marketing strategy.

The eleven points as mentioned earlier, if given due weightage, will simplify the task of studying and understanding the behaviour of retail customers. Since the intensity of competition is to increase further, it is imperative that the marketing professional make their decisions on the basis of study results. Profitability is an important consideration for retailers and satisfaction is an important consideration for customers which sizeably rests on value addition.

An in-depth study of behavioural profile of retail customers help professionals in satisfying them. After completing the search for retail stores, the task rests on the shoulders of retail marketing people that how and in what way they make use of their communication excellence so that the customers feel satisfied.

Communicating with the customers belonging to different segments, e.g., different genders, different age groups, different educational background, different professions, different regions and different groups of income is considered an acid test of their excellence. Right from the doormen to the marketing professionals managing the affairs; each one of them need to show personal-touch-in-service. The personalised services make ways for satisfaction. If the customers feel satisfied, the task of developing loyalty is found easier. Hence, the professionals serving the retail outlets and getting a success in satisfying the customers open doors for profitability.

MANAGING INFORMATION FOR RETAIL MARKETING

In an age of information and communication technology, the retailers need to manage information with the help of ICT so that they get a success in satisfying the customers. Excelling competition is an important functional responsibility before the marketers which would be considerably simplified with information-based decisions. Bar-coding System, Electronic Data Interchange (EDI)[7] help retailers in achieving the productivity benefits for profit-oriented marketing. They are immensely benefited with the reduction in queuing time, lead time and operation costs. The scope for modifications in pricing and increase in the speed of transactions also simplify the productivity acceleration process. The data handling in an improved way, faster distribution, trading partnership, building database on consumer loyalty and quicker response to the changing market conditions simplify the marketing processes.

It is in the face of the increasing instrumentality of information that organised retailers have been found frequently using both the systems, POS which is considered simple in nature and ERP which is found to be complex. The large retailers make use of ERP packages for their back office system whereas the small retailers use the POS system.[8]

The retailers have been found getting competitive advantages due to ICT because automatic processing helps reduction in costs, increase in accuracy and faster decisions. In the context of developing loyalty programmes particularly for loyal customers, the retailers get support from data. The information technology also helps them adding value to their transaction. Besides, we find online shopping an additional advantage. The retailers find it convenient to manage inventory with help of a sound communication with the suppliers. Hence, the retailers get multi-faceted benefits from ICT in the field of retail marketing.

We cannot negate that even in the Indian perspective, the technology has been found throwing a big impact on the retail sector specially for marketing purpose. Since we find India emerging as a super IT power, a number of IT companies have been seen initiating a retail wing for capitalising on the tremendous opportunities in retail sector of India. We also find cases where vendors have been offering different software solutions to the retailers, specially single store and medium-sized retailers are the important beneficiaries in the very context.

The above-mentioned facts make it clear that retail sector needs to make use of IT for improving the marketing activities. Identifying the markets and activating the efforts for satisfying the customers are found the positive effects of IT. The retailers cannot undermine the role of IT in the present changing scenario because an important task before them is to excel competition which would be proactive with the help of information-based marketing decisions.

MARKETING SEGMENTATION FOR THE RETAIL SECTOR

Studying and understanding the needs and requirements of different segments of customers in a right way is the prime responsibility of marketers and the retail sector cannot overlook the same. An in-depth study of behavioural profile of customers is essential for the development of product mix and this draws priority attention of marketers on the different categories of customers, they have to face. Transforming the prospects into actual and habitual customers cannot be possible unless we develop our awareness of the customers. The different categories of customers cannot be identical in their lifestyles.

Heavy Buyers: The buyers under 45 years of age who have larger incomes are known as heavy buyers. We find their preferences different in nature as they prefer to shop from the large retail stores located out of town and generally later part of the day is selected for shopping.

Congestion Dislikers: This category of customer is found similar to the reluctant shoppers who have little interest in shopping. Since they do not like congestion, we find little interest of this segment on the shopping.

Local Shoppers: This segment prefers to shop at small stores locally available. Normally, they come from small households, belong to old age segment and maintain economy in shopping.

Compulsive Shoppers: This segment of customers frequently use the credit cards, belong to youth segment, usually are found women and have lower self-esteem. We find property of addiction in their shopping behaviour and they go for shopping with the prime motto of diffusion of tension, release of emotion even for repairing their mood.

Loyal Shoppers: We find this category of customer loyal to a particular store. The marketers on the basis of their professional excellence get a success in transforming the potential customers into loyal customers.

Technological Babies: The shoppers belonging to the age group 8-19 or budding youths are found technologically savvy, gadget loving, spending money freely on books, mobile phones, music, footwear and apparel, branded garments, eating out, personal care services.

Impatient Aspirers: We find this category of customers in the age group 20-25 normally known as upcoming youths found aggressive in behaviour, preferring independence in shopping and much more career-oriented. They prefer creativity and customisation while shopping.

Balance Seekers: The customers in the age group 26-50, normally found sober, preferring sophistication are found fascinated to high-end gadgets. We find them spending carefully and assigning due weightage to the convenience factor while shopping.

The needs and requirements, likes and dislikes, lifestyles of all the segments cannot be identical. The retailers need a microscopic study of their behavioural profile. We cannot negate that the shopping behaviour is considerably influenced by lifestyles which rest on our incomes.

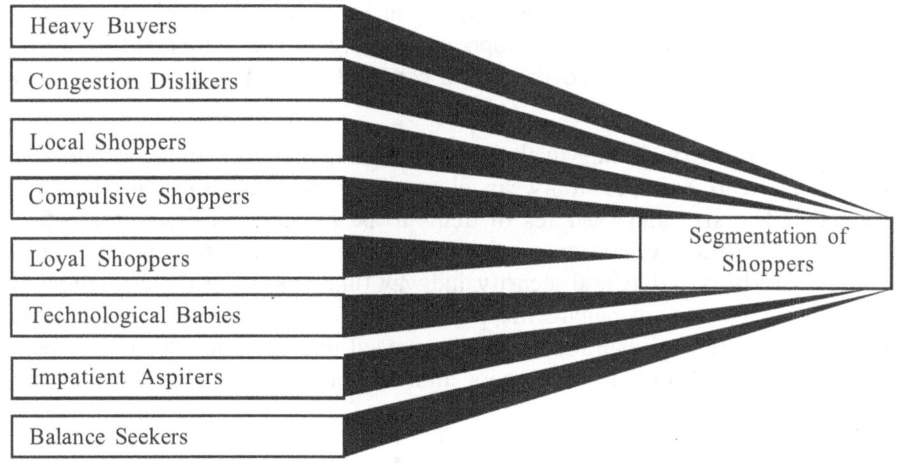

Fig. 14.2: Segmentation of Shoppers

The age group, gender factor, category of towns and cities, levels of income, professions are some of the factors determining the number of shoppers visiting the retail stores. The professionals serving the retail stores need to identify that how many shoppers, related to a particular segment with what frequency has been coming for shopping. The levels of expectations of all the shoppers cannot be identical in nature and character.

The task of formulation a sound marketing mix for the retail stores makes it essential that we have an in-depth knowledge of different segments. Transforming the potential shoppers into loyal shoppers necessitates a study of their expectations. The technological babies are found to be a profitable segment and therefore while developing a product mix their preferences need due priority, such as mobile phones, books and magazines, electronic gadgets, footwear, multiplexes, westernised garments and personal care services. The kids are also emerging as an important segment and therefore we need an outlet for toys. Another segment known as impatient aspirers cannot be overlooked because we find them of aggressive behaviour but shopping in tune with their preferences. They expect high level of customisation which the professionals need to remember. Even while designing the stores, we need to keep into consideration the preferences of different segments of shoppers.

With the emergence of material culture, we find development of mall culture and shopping has been found fascinating for those upcoming youths who earn more and want to spend more. Let's hope that retailers develop their awareness of the shoppers coming from different segments.

FORMULATION OF MARKETING MIX FOR RETAIL SERVICES

With the increasing domination of corporate sector, we find emergence of new formats for retail services. In a true sense, the material culture has been making ways for mall culture which is found spreading even in small towns and cities. The shoppers expect high level of services from the stores they shop. With the changing lifestyles, a number of new items get a place in our shopping list. The intensity of competition is also found at its peak. Thus, the levels of expectations of shoppers and the intensity of competition aggravated by the rivals are the two different conditions necessitating professional excellence. The conceptualisation of marketing principles in the retail sector will considerably help retail business not only in satisfying the customers but also in accomplishing the organisational goals. Our focus here is on the formulation of a sound marketing mix.

The shoppers visit a particular retail store to fulfil their multi-faceted requirements. Due to time constraint, it is not possible for them to visit different stores with a big list of shopping. More so, they prefer shopping with diverse motives to be fulfilled under one roof. It is against this background that we find shopping mall and shopping plaza gaining popularity day by day. The different segments of shoppers have different levels of expectations but all the segments expect quality products and quality services they shop and get from a store. This draws our attention on the different submixes of marketing.

Product Mix

In the process of formulating a marketing mix, we find product mix occupying a place of outstanding significance. How many outlets are to be included in a store depends upon the size of a store. And the decisions related to size are influenced by the different segments of shoppers residing in the catchment area. This necessitates an in-depth knowledge of the population to be covered. We cannot have a common policy for the formulation of a product mix.

Generally, we find retail stores including in their product mix, the food items, clothing, consumer durables, multiplex, hospitality, personal care services, footwear, electronic gadgets or other entertainment devices covering a large number of shoppers. The size and varieties of items to be included in the stores depend on the segments to be covered. The parking facilities, escalator services need due attention of retailers. In the management of parking services, our focus must be on safety and security and way finding to identify destination. Smooth accessibility needs to be ensured. Because we cannot negate the possibilities of some unforeseen incidents causing loss of valuable assets of stores and therefore insurance provisions need due attention. Due to tenant-driven feature, a number of aspects are the responsibility of developers and they need to develop their awareness of the needs and requirements of tenants.

The products and core and peripheral services need an optimal formulation. The service product particularly in the context of retailing is found an amalgam of products and services synchronising tangible and intangible features. The tangible features are physical surroundings, signs, displays, merchandise, uniforms, etc. as a part of physical evidence whereas the intangible services are type and timing of service delivery, communication excellence of the marketing people to interact with the shoppers or customers. Because in the retailing, we find an amalgamation of goods and services, the marketing processes are found a bit different to others.

Transaction with merchandising and transaction without merchandising are the two different conditions. In the transaction with merchandising, the ownership of goods is received from the retailers but when we find transaction without merchandising, the goods are received on rent for a particular period or we also find cases where extra services such as delivery, wrapping, giving credit are provided. In addition, we also find cases where the services are provided. In addition, we also find cases where the services are provided without goods or merchandising such as organising Holiday Travels, financial services or providing personal services such as dry-cleaning, hair dressing, and beauty treatment. We need to develop our awareness with and without merchandising transactions.

Retailing as a service is found to be intangible. We term retailing a service because the interpersonal skill of the providers is found here significant. The attributes like intangibility, perishability and inseparability need due care of retailers. Offering intangible services is found difficult and therefore the retailers need to make use of the creative selling techniques where we find scope for tangibilisation. When the retailers find the services of perishable nature, they bring a change in the service schedule to adjust the demand and supply position. In case of inseparability, the simultaneous production and consumption of services are preferred.

Thus, the retail marketers need to make it sure that goods available in the stores are of quality. We do not find any excuse for the poor quality of goods made available to the customers. Another important dimension is related to the quality of services offered by the marketing people serving the retail stores. Of course, with and without merchandising conditions make a difference but in both the cases, the shoppers or customers expect decent behaviour of sales and marketing people. This element constitutes an important position and for that, the marketers need to enrich the communication excellence of sales people even by organising a capsule course for this purpose. We find retail trading in a large number of items and the retailers also need to manage the supply position in order to avoid a gap between demand and supply. To maintain the quality of goods, it is also significant that management of inventory needs due attention and storage, warehousing and godowning services are up to the mark.

In view of the aforesaid facts, it is right to mention that retail marketers are supposed to play a commanding role in the entire process. The tangibles and intangibles are the features and making use of tangibles properties by strengthening the tangibilisation process so that value addition process adds additional strength to the intangibles requires managerial proficiency.

The retailers need to blend tangible and intangible properties in such a fashion that the shoppers feel pleasure in spending much more time for shopping. The lobbying is considered to be a important place where the shoppers have a time gap for entertainment. Movie theatres usually sell a number of stock foods and drinks. There may be a counter or self-service where one pays at the counter or coin-operated machines are also used. The lobby may be before or after the ticket check and may also include an arcade game area.

The food retail stores generally stock grocery items, vegetables, uncooked meat products, frozen products and daily needs like personal care, spices, snacks and sweets. We also find food retail stores working as a part of hypermarkets or supermarkets. The various types of food retailers are Conventional Supermarkets, Super Centers and Hypermarkets, Warehouse Stores and Conventional Stores. The Kiosk Stores are standalone trolley kind of stores with basic cooking, heating, boiling and dispensing facility. They are found located in malls.

Whatsoever the products or services are offered by the retail markets, it is the responsibility of marketers to make it sure that the promised quality reaches to the shoppers or customers without any gap. They need to ensure customised services which will help them in earning the competitive advantage. When we find customers satisfied with the services, they in a very natural way communicate the same to their friends and relatives and we find word-of-mouth communication bringing new customers to the stores. Just reverse to it, when they cerate a quality gap, the word-of-mouth communication works in a negative way. We cannot negate that it is a difficult task before the retailers. So far as the quality of product is concerned, they can make it possible because the merchandising is possible but when we talk about the quality of services, the task becomes too much difficult because it varies from person to person. Even in the same store, all the marketing people working there may not be identical in nature and behaviour. Here, the retailers need the services of marketing professionals who may help them in improving the quality of people.

Thus, in the formulation of product mix, the professionals need two-tier approaches, first — related to the quality of products available at different outlets and second — the services of sales and marketing people. It is significant to mention that a majority of the retailers succeed in managing the first-tier whereas only those succeed in improving the second-tier, i.e., the service quality where personalised and professionalised services are made available to the customers. The customisation prove to be an attraction, of course, based on professional excellence of marketers. The retailers cannot overlook this dimension of retailing on which projection of a fair image of the retail sector depends.

The Promotion Mix

With the mounting competition, it is pertinent that the retailers make the promotional measures creative so that the customers are sensitised and persuaded. The innovate package of service mix and creative methods of promotion would be instrumental in transforming the customers into habitual customers which would ensure profits to the retailers. The customers loyal to a particular retail store help an increase in the number of habitual customers. The promotional measures will have both the short-term and long-term objectives. In the context of short-term objective, the focus will be on increasing the sale during a particular period whereas in the long-term objective, the professionals will make efforts for creating a brand image for maximising the profits. Transmitting the information related to the available products, influencing the attitudes of customers and selling the benefits of their merchandising are some of important considerations while designing a promotional campaign. Influencing, and prompting the target market with the help of quality information related to the retail sponsor need due attention of professionals while promoting for the retail business.

Advertising: With the help of advertising, the professionals find it convenient to inform the target market even with a single message. This methods of promotion helps two-way communication through which the professionals come to know about the opinion of customers regarding stores and their offices with the help of opinion leaders. The marketers make use of different types of advertising.

Product Advertising: This helps in promoting merchandising where the outstanding features of the product are found in advertising.

Event Advertising: This focuses our attention on excitement about a particular product and period during which the retailer offers the product at a lower price.

Institutional Advertising: This type of advertising throws our attention on the benefits of a shopping centre or a shopping mall so that the customers enjoy their visits.

Co-operative Advertising: In the process of advertising, we find sharing of costs on advertisement by both the manufacturers and the retailers.

The intensity of competition in the retail market is found high and this makes it essential that the retailers devise new methods and in this context, we also find stealth marketing, a covert way of developing awareness of customers in which they are found unaware of the advertisement but the process of sensitisation is found effective as they are found completely unnoticed not only to the competitors but also to the customers.

Publicity: For promoting, the retailers may also use this component of promotion which is done with the help of media people, social leaders and reformists or academics who speak and write about the retail outlets and focus on the features of services offered by them. The professionals in this context need to develop rapport with the concerned sources.

The role of professionals while influencing the media people and developing personal relationships with them are found effective in publishing the retail business. Since we find it an unpaid form of persuasive communication, the professionals need to assign due weightage to publicity.

Sales Promotion: Offering incentives to customers is not a new phenomenon. In the retail marketing, the professionals also make use of this component of promotion which helps creating excitement, increasing footfalls and motivating people to enter and shop. They make use of two different strategies for this purpose such as pull promotion strategy and push promotion strategy. In the pull promotion strategy, the customers are offered various incentives which may be free samples, discount coupons or gifts whereas in the push promotion strategy we find offerings to the dealers which are found target-based. We also call them consumer promotion (pull promotion) and trade promotion (push promotion). In the sales promotion, the professionals make use of different tools such as displays, contests, prizes, gifts, coupon, sweepstakes, premium, etc. The sales promotional measures provide an opportunity to the customers to get some incentives whereas an opportunity to the retailers to touch the target. In view of increasing competition, the professionals need to offer innovative sales promotion tools to attract the customers.

Personal Selling: This component of promotion focuses our attention on face-to-face communication. The personal communication processes are used to influence the customers. The salespeople are found involved in the process. Of late, we find use of electronic devices for personal communication. The retailers can obtain more information with the help of database facilities found to be internet-based. Of course, we make use of e-mail for this purpose, however the face-to-face communication has some outstanding features keeping this component distinct to others. The communication excellence of promoters plays here an important role.

Word-of-mouth Promotion: This component is the outcome of the quality services offerred by the retailers. If the customers are found satisfied with the services of a particular retail store, they communicate the same to their friends and relatives. In the process, we do not find involvement of professionals, even not any expense but the results are found proactive because the communictors are not related to the retail segment indeed they happen to be our relative or friends. The customers virtually act as an opinion leader and prove to be a hidden salesforce.

Telemarketing: In the retail marketing, this component of promotion may be much more effective as sophisticated electronics media make the selling and promotional efforts result-oriented. The communication excellence of telemarketers and the quality of information and communication technology (ICT) need due attention of professionals.

Formulating a mix of different components and practising innovations will help retail professionals in throwing a positive impact on the target market. When to make use of a particular component and what amount to be spent for the same depend on the situational forces.

The Price Mix

With the increasing number of new formats of retail sector, it is natural that the intensity of competition is found high and this makes it essential that the professionals think over the pricing decisions with the motto of attracting customers. Of late, we find customers becoming much more sensitive to the vale addition and enhancement process. They expect good value for their buying decisions which focus on merchandising at a low price in addition to the services they get in the process. We also find one segment of customer not sensitive to price but very much sensitive to quality and service. While making pricing decisions, the long-term and short-term objectives are found instrumental. The long-term objectives divert our attention on the projection of a fair image so that the customers develop their temptation to a particular retail outlets and prove to be a habitual customer. The short-term objectives for pricing decisions are found throwing light on the increasing number of customers so that the target is achieved within the stipulated time.

The pricing decisions for the retail business are influenced by a number of factors which the professionals need to take into consideration.

1. **Product Uniqueness:** If the products are found unique to the customers due their outstanding properties, the customers are found not so much sensitive to price because they feel that high quality product costs high and therefore high level of pricing.
2. **Availability of Substitutes:** When the customers find a product of high price and at the same time, they also find substitutes having less price, their preference in a very natural way will be for the substitutes, provided we do not find a big difference in quality.
3. **High Quality Product:** We find a close relation between costs, quality and price. It is a general perception that when we want quality product we have to pay high price for that because the costs of the product will be high.

4. **Fairness Effect:** When the customers find the product reasonable and fair, the sensitivity to price is found high. In that case, we find association of the product with the quality and status.

5. **Perishable or Durable Product:** When the products are found of perishable nature, the price structure can not be kept at the high level but we do not find such a condition with the durable product.

6. **Fad Product:** When the products have fashion orientation, the customers show high degree of their temptation and therefore the price structure is found high.

The above-mentioned facts, no doubt, influence pricing decisions but it is also right to mention that reputation of a particular brand, provisions for after-sale services and guarantees, number of competing brands, urgency of the situation and the level of income also govern the pricing decisions. The volatility in the market also becomes a guiding force in the pricing decisions.

The retailers need to think in favour of strategical decisions for pricing which in a majority of the cases are influenced by the situational forces.

The pricing decisions may be Demand-oriented where the retailers keep into consideration the demand side. If we find an increase in demand, the retailers slash down the price. The Cost-oriented Pricing is found in relation to the costs incurred by the retailers. We also find Rate of Return Pricing which is found based on agreed rate of return on its investment. The Backward Pricing focuses our attention on the purchasing capacity of the customers. The Discriminatory Pricing throws our attention on flexible pricing where different structure is found for different segments of customers in different periods. The Skimming Pricing provides a condition where the maximum possible is charged from the customers and they have no option because the supply position is found low. The Leader Pricing focuses our attention on the price structure very close to the costs. With the motto of increasing the frequency of visits of customers, we find retail stores making use of leader pricing policy. Besides, we also find use of this policy on a festive occasion which helps retail stores in inviting and attracting the customers. The Competitive Pricing is practised with the motto of excelling competition. The Market Penetration Pricing draws our attention on a policy practised with the motto of penetrating the market. The setting of price structure is found below the level of competitors. The Psychological Pricing is practised with the motto of influencing the customers that they are buying at the level which is low enough for the customers to buy the same.

Of late, we find retailer also practising Everyday Low Pricing (EDLP) where we find the price structure for a particular day and the retailers try to set the level at a point which is lower than the rivals. This helps a retailer in establishing a market position ensuring the customers that they are making use of qualify merchandising at a reasonable price structure. The policy is followed throughout the year and therefore it may help a retailer in working out an image-building programme *vis-à-vis* the promotional activities. Besides, the customers also get higher level of service and the retailers find it convenient to manage the stock position to avoid the stock-out situations. This policy also helps in increasing profitability.

Today, we also find Internet Pricing due to online trading. In some of the cases, we find airways or airlines making use of this policy in which on the basis of online contacts the prices are fixed for different routes and day. There are a number of takers who buy the seats from the airlines on the lowest bid. This also helps in streamlining the supply chain efficiencies through online procurement. The customers find this policy convenient.

The pricing decisions in the retail business are influenced by a number of considerations and the retailers by making use of the professional excellence of marketers may be successful in adopting pricing as a motivational tool.

The Placement

We agree with this view that Indian organised retailing is experiencing a considerable momentum. It is against this background that we find leading domestic business houses and albeit global retail giants involved in this growing segment.

Whatsoever the significant developments that we find in the retail sector makes a strong advocacy in favour of evolving a format that suits the markets. Of course, the retail formats have evolved over a period of time and we need better positioning. We cannot negate that the new formats of retail sector may be a perfect sync with the potential markets if they are strategically placed and positioned in the minds of customers. The longevity and profitability are the two considerations for aligning the formats that we choose. It is essential that the retail formats are based on the adoption of markets. An in-depth analysis and understanding of the markets and consumer behaviour is found essential for the retail formats which may be proved to be money spinners. Keeping in view the considerations, the Reliance Retail has already displayed its strategies in rolling out the retail formats which focus on single or limited line products such as Reliance Fresh. We find it one-step solution model selling different lines of products ranging from vegetables to Plasma TV under one roof.

The different models for positioning are Mega Hyper Market Model (One Stop Model), Mega Cash-n-Carry Hyper Market Model (Metro Restricted to Business Owners), Mega Cash-n-Carry Hyper Market Model (SAM's Club Membership Model), Mega Single/Limited Line Category Model (Reliance Fresh, Food Bazar), Medium Limited Line Category Model (TriNetra, Fabmall), Medium Limited Line Discount Store Model (Subhiksha) Small/Single Limited Line Category Model (Yet to come could be TESCO Express Model).[9]

Increasing industrial and business activities are the essential considerations for the development of potential markets. The service potentials, employment opportunities, hubs for the sub-urban and rural areas may also be considered for this purpose. The markets are Industrial Hubs, The Business Hubs and The Mofussal Markets.[10] The Industrial Hubs have high-to-very high industrial presence, enormous service potentials and employment opportunities and high public and private sector presence. We find them acting as connecting hubs for semi-urban and rural areas. The Business Hubs are the markets which have high-to-very high business presence, enormous business prospects and they house a large number of entrepreneurs who generate revenue through goods and services sold to other places, states and countries. They have high level of potential for generating employment opportunities and act as a connecting link to sub-urban and rural markets. The Mofussal Markets are medium to small towns acting as connecting hubs to nearby rural markets. The available potential in these markets guide alignment of retail formats. Hence, the retailers need an in-depth study of the changing market conditions for locating the retail formats.

In the management of marketing processes, the retailers bear the vital responsibility of making the location decisions. In this context, we find Simulation exercise based on different models.

Huff Model is found based on the law of gravitation found suitable to a single warehouse or retail site. The quantity purchased becomes here the criteria for location. It is significant to mention that the probability of a given customer to shop in a particular store or shopping centre will increase with the growth in the size of a store. This model is based on the assumption that a particular customer residing in a particular area will prefer to shop at a shopping centre located in that area. It is also significant to mention that the larger the shopping centre more probability we find for visiting the customers because they find there varieties of items.

The Analog Approach is considered to be the most widely used technique to determine the physical location of the retail outlet. There are three steps in this approach known as Step a, Step b and Step c. Step a and Step b determine the current trade area where we find use of Customer Spotting Technique. The number of people and their areas of residence are taken into consideration. For the identification purpose, we find use of credit cards and cheques. In the Step c, we find matching of the current store with potential new store location for determining the best retail site. But it is difficult to find an analogous situation. If we find the analogous conditions weak, the task of location decision is found difficult.

Multiple Regression Method is found to be a common method for the determination of retail trade area. This method can be used to generate a relationship between store sales and a range of stores, population and competitor characteristics. Assessment of a systematic relationship between dependent variables such as sales and independent variables is found possible in this method.

Thus, we find use of different methods and models for location of retail outlets and the retailers while locating the same cannot undermine them. The different important considerations we find in the location process are Population, Accessibility, Competition and Costs. While making a study of population for location, we need focus on size, age, income, lifestyles, caste mix, housing which would provide to the retailers an in-depth knowledge of population where the retail stores are to be located. We find accessibility another consideration which draws our attention on flow of pedestrians, public transport facilities, accessibility of car parking space, accessibility of staff and accessibility for smooth delivery. The intensity of competition is also a consideration which gravitates our attention on the details about the rivals such as existing activity, turnover, age, design, facilities and future potential. The

Cost element draws our attention on the costs involved in acquisition, development of site, security, staffing, designing and delivery.

The retailers need an in-depth study of all the factors and to make location decisions which help them in getting high level of profits, excelling competition and providing much more conveniences and comforts to customers.

A retailer should not forget that choosing a store location is like choosing a location for your house. Any retailer or aspiring retailer needs three elements for making a store successful and these are location, location and location. You need to know about the target audience. A high-end speciality store will not find a price-sensitive area suitable for its location. If you create for classes, you need not to consider the masses. A residential area is considered suitable for a supermarket whereas a commercial area will be better for a Departmental Store. Like this, for a grocery store, we have to look at a residential area which is found to be heavily populated. The concept of in-house supermarket is gaining popularity in a single large apartment complex. Since the intensity of competition is found increasing fast, it is imperative that retailers think in favour of innovative locations for their offerings such as mobile locations, store-in-store, high traffic hotspots, occasion retailing and in-flight retailing. The retail formats like hotspots include services like Beauty parlours which may be located within large college campuses or ladies hostel, Sport goods and apparel inside or opposite the Gyms, Gift Shops opposite large wedding halls and Consumer Durables near High rise apartment complexes.

Thus, getting the right location is an important consideration for retail formats. The retailers cannot undermine them. The mistakes committed in location is to harm the retailers and their tenants in many ways. The locality may be commercial or residential which will vary with the retail formats.

The two important decision-making areas we find in this submix. One is related to the travelling of services from the providers to the shoppers. This focuses our attention on the deployment of salespeople at the required places so that they deliver the services on time. Another decision-making areas in this context is concerned with the use of technology for different purposes with the motto of delivery of quality services to the shoppers. The retailers need their attention on both the conditions.

The retailers with the help of developers need to make decisions regarding the placement of different outlets in the stores in tune with the comforts and conveniences of shoppers. This is essential because we find a mix of different outlets and all of them may not be required by all the shoppers.

The Process

In retail marketing, the processing of services occupies a place of outstanding significance. We consider service delivery an important dimension which after processing reach to the customers or shoppers either manually or with the support of technology specially for making payments of bill. The quality of product becomes insignificant when the quality of services offered by the marketing people is found poor. Thus, processing of goods and services to be delivered to the customers or shoppers needs due attention of retailers.

In large retail firms, the processing is found to be complicated because we find different separate divisions based on expertise knowledge. The buyers are found specialised in buying process whereas the sellers have specialisation of sales and marketing management. Actually, we find both the processes interrelated. The retailers for right processing need four-pronged measures. **First measure** focuses our attention on increasing buyers' contact with customers and improving informal communication between buyers and store personnel and selling the merchandising bought by them. In the process, we find three stages such as buyers develop contact with customers, develop contact with the people serving the stores and the store personnel sell the product to the shoppers or customers. Because we find buying in tune with the preferences of customers, the task of store personnel is considerably simplified. **Second measure** throws light on the fact that development of contact with customers should be based on the buyers visit to the store and their interaction with the department personnel who have to sell the product to the customers or shoppers. **Third measure** draws our attention on involving marketing people for coordination between the buying and selling processes. **Fourth measure** makes a strong advocacy in favour of improving coordination between buying and selling activities by involving the store people in the buying process.

The processing of services in the stores depend on the quality of store people and technology involved in the process. The marketers need to manage things in a right way so that the promised quality of services are made available to the customers or shoppers. It is not only significant that quality goods are available in the retail outlets. It is equally important that we find delivery of service without any gap. If we make use of technology for the required purposes, they need to work properly.

Customised merchandising paves avenues for increasing the number of satisfied group of customers, developing brand loyalty or store loyalty and simplifying the task of profit generation. The retailers need due care at different stages so that possibilities for any gap at any stage are considerably minimised.

Physical Evidence and Attractions

The retail stores and their management play an important role in managing the marketing activities. The servicescapes need due attention of marketing professionals managing the retail stores. The creation of service ambience helps in generating service fragrance. In the retail marketing when we talk about store design and layout,[11] our focus is on developing them in tune with the needs and requirements of customers which act positively on consumer behaviour. The emotional state of the customers visiting stores cannot be negated in the very context. In this sphere, we find Proactive Planning and Atmospheric to be much more effective. The use of space, colour walls, pillars, floor coverings, lighting, music, etc. considered important elements of service ambience need priority attention of retailers. The marketers need not to forget that the atmosphere or service environment is created by the combination of a whole series of cues and stimulants which focuses our attention on type of merchandising offered and the way it is displayed and are in a position to produce the desired store ambience and emotional response from the target customers. The marketers also need to develop this realisation that music plays an important role in creating the service ambience. They can make use of background music as a new tool to reach to the customers visiting the stores because we find music a big stimulant to influence the behaviour. It is also right to mention that the music can influence the speed with which people shop, their willingness to spend and even perceptions of the nature and behaviour, taste and temperament and likes and dislikes of customers visiting the stores and to place the music at a place that is found audiable and suitable. Audio Steam Solution is found significant in the process of throwing a positive impact of music on the shopping behaviour. We find a number of retail outlets such as McDonalds, Lifestyle, Adidas and many others realising the significance of ambience and making suitable arrangements for the same.

An efficient layout is found essential for the right use of space. This necessitates proper planning of the territorial areas, break up store areas into logical sales sections and functional areas. This focuses our attention on planning for encouraging customers to circulate around the space and visiting the merchandising areas to the possible extent. Suitable music or music in tune with their taste help customers in spending much more time in the store and making purchases. Besides, lighting also plays an important role in the service ambience and it can also act as a mood setter. Proper lighting is found helpful in influencing and creating a positive image of the store and its merchandising. The professionals need to strengthen their realisation that service ambience creates service fragrance and influences the behaviour of customers visiting the stores. In this context, they also need to make suitable arrangements for ventilation so that the customers find and feel comfortable while shopping. The interiors and exteriors also play a positive role in influencing the behaviour.

Tangibilisation helps in adding additional attractions to our services and therefore the marketers need to influence the customers by making use of a number of measures throwing a positive influence on their behaviour. We are aware of the fact that today the shopping has emerged as an important avenue for experiencing pleasure and if the customers visiting your stores get an opportunity to be there for three or four hours; our efforts made in this direction can satisfy them. The focus is on the value addition process and for that, we have a number of devices.

The environmental conditions and aesthetic management inside the store can be translated into the physical features with the help of layout, signs, displays, colours, lighting, music, visual merchandising, etc. which bear the potentials of influencing the customers. Creation of right appeal is found essential and this is to be possible with the help of service ambience. The more you tangibilise, the more you attract and the more you attract, the more they spend. It is in this context that the marketers consider service ambience very much instrumental in generating service fragrance. You need to design, develop and implement one of the most sophisticated satellite data delivery systems for in-store music for enhancing the customer's experience. The audio steam system is found providing to the customers a taste of international shopping experience. A number of retailers have practised the system in their stores and have also received a positive response of the same.

In the modern retail stores, we assign due weightage to the people working there in different capacities. In a few of the cases, we find them providing uniform with logo of their brand. We also find cases where they wear civil dresses. The focus here is on the development of their physical attractions and therefore it is pertinent that people serving the stores look impressive and keep themselves neat and clean. Aesthetic sense is considered to be an essential dimension for adding additional attractions and this needs due attention of marketers. Since we find a majority of the high profile customers visiting the stores, it is imperative that they project a positive impression. Fragrance not only in the ambiences but fragrance even in their personality need due attention of professionals. The main thing is throwing a positive impact on the customers' behaviour and in addition to other aspects, our focus must be on adding attractions to the different dimensions of aesthetic management.

In view of the above-mentioned facts, it is right to mention that this submix of the marketing mix needs priority attention of marketers. With the entry to the customers, it should be clear that they are witnessing here everything that they did not witness in other stores. Excelling competition becomes easier when we make efforts to establish an edge over the rivals. Looking distinct, behaving distinct, performing distinct and offering distinct would increase your efficacy of winning the hearts and minds of customers and they would feel pleasure while visiting your stores again and again.

The People

We cannot negate that even in the retail stores, the people serving there play an outstanding role. The customers buying goods or services from the retail stores take back home merchandising as well as the services delivered to them which is the result of interaction between the marketing people and the customers. If the people have played a big role in satisfying the customers, they do not hesitate indeed feel pleasure in patronising the stores again and again. Contrary to it when we find cases of indecent behaviour or poor communication, the customers change their options. Thus, the most important dimension for the retail staff is the behavioural profile which helps them in increasing the number of satisfied group of customers.

The marketing people serving the retail stores need communication excellence to impress upon the customers. They need sense of commitment and personal-touch-in-service. Besides, they also need sincerity and honesty. In the new formats of retailing, we find increasing cases of shoplifting and therefore they cannot overlook value-based efforts. In the big stores, we find different categories of people serving there and while recruiting people, it is to be made sure that they have all the properties and traits found essential for successful marketing people. On the other hand, the professionals managing the affairs bear the responsibility of developing their potentials so that they do not provide an opportunity to the customers for making complaints. One of the most important element determining the magnitude of success of the retail stores is the strong market people they have.

Of course, we assign due weightage to the elements instrumental in tangibilising our properties but often we forget that behavioural profile of marketing people is though intangible in nature but provides to the retailers a number of benefits which others fail to provide. The rivals can copy the tangibles which you display but it will be difficult for them to copy the quality of marketing people you have particularly in term of decency in behaviour. The personalised services are found significant in retail stores because there are a number of cases where they need your help. Selecting merchandising, making available the required information, assisting the customers, display of shelves and stock are found easier with the help and cooperation of marketing people.

The above-mentioned facts make it clear that in the formulation of a sound marketing mix for the retail stores, the marketers need to assign priority attention on the quality of people working there. High level of customer satisfaction is possible only with the help and cooperation of high level of marketing people.

Particularly when we talk about the mall management, it is right to say that one of the key functions is event management and therefore it is also significant that people have an in-depth knowledge of managing the events. In a true sense, the marketing people bear the responsibility of increasing the convertibility ratio which necessitates transforming the potential customers or customers into habitual customers making repeat purchases.

RETAIL MARKETING IN INDIAN PERSPECTIVE

With corporatisation of the Indian economy, there have been significant changes in the retail sector which has made ways for the emergence of new formats. The development of corporate sector has opened doors for the development of corporate culture, material culture and shopping culture. Of course, we find negative trends in the retail sector around the globe but in the Indian retail sector, we find significant developments. It was against this background that with the beginning of 21st century, the contours of development in the retail sector underwent radical changes and it could emerge as a service industry approximating the business of almost ₹ 1000 billion with a growth rate of 25% to 30% per annum. This in a very natural fashion has made the retail sector much more competitive where the retailers need high level of professionalism.

During yesteryears, the Indian economy has witnessed positive developments in the field of IT industry. We cannot negate that it has revolutionised the development character of almost all the sectors. The growing importance of information-based decisions has paved avenues for the use of IT by almost all the sectors and almost all the organisations. The retail sector has also been found making use of IT on an increased scale and the trend will continue even in future. Increasing pressure on the decision-makers for making right and fast decisions makes it essential that technology-driven decisions are preferred.

The multi-faceted developments in the field of retail trading have been found motivating not only the domestic business houses but even the global retail giants to this growing segment. The buoyancy in the purchasing power of consumer due to an increase in the level of discretionary income has made this segment much more lucrative. Despite the emerging negative trends in the global economy, the retail sector has been found prospering and this has been mainly due to the emerging corporate culture. The youths serving the corporate sector earn more and like to spend more which has been encouraging this sector for innovative services so that the increasing competition is successfully excelled. The spreading mall culture, developing shopping plaza have been injecting new life and strength to the retail sector which makes a strong advocacy in favour of professional excellence.

The changing new faces of retail trading are a staunch testimony to this proposition that the Indian retail industry has been moving in the new direction. The main reason for such a shift is the changing lifestyles considerably influenced by the western culture. The emerging new tracks of retail trading have been creating tremendous job opportunities preferably to the budding youths but at the same time, we also find them much more sensitive to multi-faceted woes such as problem of safety, shoplifting, data insecurity, lack of parking space and entry of foreign investors, specially in the sensitive areas which may be instrumental in aggravating the problems before the unorganised retailing. Since we find almost 96% of the retail business covered by the unorganised retailing, it is not proper that we allow foreign investors even in those segment of the retail trading where poor sections of the society has been getting tremendous job opportunities.

The emerging negative trends in the global economy are to throw myriad of challenges before the organised retail trading in India, such as identifying the right segment, increasing and converting footfalls (mind share) into money share (wallet share), acquiring appropriate location for retail outlets, ensuring the accessibility, maintaining sustainability, prioritising the product categories. In addition, motivating and increasing consumer footfalls are considered to be the biggest challenges before the retail industry. We also find cases where shoppers visit the retail stores for collecting knowledge and they ultimately visit their local stores for shopping. Wal-Mart, an internationally acclaimed brand used to set up huge superstores at the outskirts with this hope that the shoppers use their cars for visiting the stores and make large shopping. But in the Indian perspective, we find a different scenario because a majority of the customers may not prefer to travel beyond city and we find most of them even not having four-wheelers. This makes it essential that retailers assign priority attention to the location of stores.

In the Indian context, we find a majority of the customers found highly sensitive to price and therefore they frequently change their options for retail stores. In the retail trading, the most important aspect is concerned with an increase in the number of habitual customers, and the retailers find it difficult to transform the customers into habitual customers if they fail in providing better value for their money. Since the rivals offer to them better value, they do not take time in changing their options. Because the intensity of competition is found mounting, the retailers have no option but to make ways for better value proposition failing which they will find it difficult to increase the repeat purchases.

It is important to mention that in the Indian context we find food and grocery categories contributing 67% of the market share of the organised retailers and therefore the non-food categories need priority attention of retailers. The market is becoming much more competitive and the retailers will find it easier to excel when they shift to the non-traditional areas.

If we make a global survey, we find variations in the median age. It is about 25 years in India, 33 years in China and in Europe and America, it is much higher. A big difference exists in the taste preferences of older and younger population. The taste preferences of men and women are different. Ethnic and cultural considerations also influence their behavioural profile. Studying and understanding the behavioural profile of customers is found essential to gauge the level of their expectations. The marketers are required to play here an important role.

When we find western culture dominating the shopping behaviour, it is pertinent that our efforts are much more professionalised so that we provide to the customers quality goods *pari passu* the quality services. The marketers need to make it sure that shoppers visiting their stores carry with them a positive impression. They find the stores a place for gaining pleasure and the sales and marketing people take care of their likes and dislikes. The goods made available to them and the services delivered to them fulfil their expectations and they are found satisfied. While promoting, the marketers make it sure that the customers are sensitised and persuaded with the help of creative promotional measures. Increasing the cases of repeat purchase needs due attention of professionals. The sales promotional measures must be innovative to help you in touching the target. You also have options for using pricing as a motivational tool. The interiors and exteriors of your stores, the service ambience, lighting, music, entertainment, scent, signs generate service fragrance. The sales and marketing people look impressive and behave decently. The employees working there in different capacities show personal-touch-in-service. They are value-based and serve with a sense of commitment. Hence, the feelings of shoppers visiting your stores must be distinct to others so that they act as a hidden promoter.

The conceptualisation of marketing principles in the retail services thus requires priority attention of retailers. The professional excellence of marketers will simplify their task of satisfying the customers. The policy decision-makers also need to protect and promote the interests of unorganised retailers. We cannot undermine the interests of small players significantly contributing to the retail sector. The regulated entry of foreign direct investors is considered essential to protect the interests of agri-business. The e-tailing needs due attention of retailers. Thus, we need multi-pronged efforts to promote the interests of retail sector emerging and developing as a service industry.

Unique challenges need unique retailing. The retail density in India is on the increase whereas in other parts of the globe, we find it on the decline. This is due to our unorganised retailing. Providing a sound nexus for the development of both organised and unorganised retailing is found a crying need of the hour. Let our policy makers strengthen this realisation to emerge retail sector with the joint cooperation of both; small as well as the big players.

SUMMARY

In this chapter, you have gone through different dimensions of retail marketing. Before starting another chapter, be sure that the following facts are well versed:

Retail Sector: A Service Industry: The retail sector is found to be one of the largest sector in the Indian economy and has emerged as a service industry just next to the agricultural sector with an impressive record of creating job opportunities and the turnover.

Emergence of Online or E-Retailing: The retailers adopt innovative devices in the e-shopping to add additional attractions to their services. We also it e-tailing. It is found much more convenient to the customers. Besides, they get customised products and services from the retailers.

Retail Formats: The different formats in the retail sector are Chain of Stores, Convenience Stores, Franchise, Departmental Stores, Speciality Stores, Supermarkets, Hypermarkets, Shopping Mall, Shopping Plaza, Discount Stores, Factory Secondary Stores, Kiosk. In addition, Kirana Stores, Managed General Stores, Pavement Vendors, Handcart are also the retail formats.

Retail Marketing: A Conceptual Framework: It is conceptualisation of marketing principles in the retail sector so that the retailers find it easier to make available to the customers or shoppers superior quality of goods and services in tune with the levels of their satisfaction. It is a managerial process to formulate a marketing mix.

Behavioural Profile of Retail Customers: The marketers need to have an in-depth idea of shoppers visiting the stores. This necessitates study of their behavioural profile such as likes and dislikes, needs and requirements, lifestyles, attitudes and levels of expectations.

Managing Information for Retail Trading: The marketers for making the result-oriented decisions need information related to customers, competitors and the national and global economies so that they make available the goods and services to the customers in tune with their preferences.

Market Segmentation for the Retail Sector: For studying and understanding the markets in a right fashion, it is pertinent that the marketers are well aware of the different segments of retail customers such as Heavy buyers, Congestion dislikers, Local shoppers, Compulsive shoppers, Loyal shoppers, Technological Babies, Impatient aspirers and Balance seekers.

Marketing Mix for Retail Services: We find marketing mix a combination of different submixes such as product mix, promotion mix, price mix, place mix, process, physical evidence and attractions and people. All the seven mixes need an optimal blending to get the desired results.

Product Mix: The product mix in the retail sector draws our attention on both the goods and services. The retailers merchandise the goods available in their stores and deliver the services in the process of marketing.

Promotion Mix: It is a combination of different components of promotion. The retailers need to make use of different components for retailing in such a way that shoppers or customers are not only persuaded but further they are also motivated to make repeat purchases. The professionals need to make the process of promotion cost-effective.

The Price Mix: The marketers need to adopt this submix with the motto of using it as a tool for motivating the shoppers. The factors to govern the pricing decisions need due care. Today, we also find use of internet pricing due to online trading.

The Placement: The two important decision-making areas draw our attention in the very context such as the placement of goods and services to the customers and further the identification of a proper location point for the stores with the motto of smooth accessibility of all the concerned.

The Process: This draws our attention on processing of services to the customers. In the process, we find involvement of a good number of people. The availability of goods in the stores, delivery of goods and services to the customers with the help of sales and marketing people and other staff. We also find use of technology for certain purposes. The motive is to make available the promised services to the shoppers keeping in view their comforts and conveniences.

Physical Evidence and Attractions: This submix of marketing throws light on service ambience. The retailers need to make it sure that lighting and music arrangements, signs, interiors and exteriors, ventilation, scent, etc. are managed in such a way that the shoppers and people working there feel pleasure. The servicescapes help in generating service fragrance. In addition, it is also essential that sales and marketing people or other staff working there look impressive and are well-dressed.

The People: We find different categories of people working in the stores. This dimension of the marketing mix makes it essential that people working in the store show personal-touch-in-service. They need to work with a sense of commitment and are in a position to show empathy. They know about the behavioural profile and have a high level of communication excellence.

Retail Marketing in Indian Perspective: We find retail sector witnessing positive trends and emerging as a large service industry. The creation of tremendous job opportunities is an outstanding feature of this sector. With the development of corporatisation of Indian economy, we find a change in our lifestyles. The perception of shopping is now changed because the shoppers now go to the stores not only for buying but even for enjoying. Such an attitudinal change has made ways for the emergence of material culture *vis-à-vis* the shopping culture. A number of new formats have been included in the retail sector. Actually, we are developing our temptation or fascination to the market culture. But the policy makers here need to make it sure that development of organised sector of retailing is not to close doors for the unorganised retailing.

KEY TERMS

Burgeoning
Shopping Culture
Corporate Culture
Retail Outlets
Organised Sector
Unorganised Sector
Volatility
E-Retailing
e-Shopping
B2C (Business to Consumer)
B2B (Business to Business)
In-store Retailer
Mom-and-Pop Stores
Cynosure
ICT (Information and Communication Technology)
Value Addition
Heavy Buyer
Congestion Disliker
Technological Babies
Impatient Aspirers
Customised Services
Stealth Marketing
Pull Promotion
Push Promotion
Industrial Hubs
Business Hubs
Mofussal Hubs
Audio Steam System
Visual Merchandising
Aesthetic Sense
Logo
Rural Retailing
Agri-business
Wallet Share
Data Insecurity
Pari Passu
Ethnic
Pedestrians
Kiosk

Review Questions

1. Do you find retail sector an emerging service industry? Justify your opinion.
2. What do you mean by E-Retailing? Explain the different formats of retailing.
3. What do you mean by Retail Marketing? Discuss the significance of behavioural studies for the retail business.
4. Focus on the different segments of users with the viewpoint of retail business.
5. Explain the role of information for making decisions related to retail marketing.
6. What do you mean by Marketing Mix? Explain the different submixes for marketing the retail services.
7. Throw light on the importance of location and the important considerations for locating the retail stores.
8. Focus on the product mix in the face of retail business.
9. Explain the extended marketing mixes of retail services.
10. Write a note on the marketing of retail services in the Indian perspective.
11. Focus on the E-tailing in the context of retailing.

Application Exercises

1. As a marketing professional, focus on the important considerations to be taken care for locating a mall.
2. You are working as a marketer in a shopping mall. Explain the measures helping you in the tangibilisation process for attracting the customers.
3. Formulate a marketing mix for the retail business in the Indian perspective.
4. As a marketer, throw light on the relevance of studying the likes and dislikes of customers which may help you in formulating a product mix for your retail stores.
5. Do you find shopping mall to be successful in small towns and cities? Justify your arguments as a marketer.

6. Focus on the components you would prefer to use for promoting your retail stores.
7. Do you find e-retailing to be successful in the Indian perspective? Defend your arguments.
8. Focus on the impact of economic depression on the retailing business in the Indian setting.
9. Do you find it proper to promote the organised retailing at the cost of unorganised retailing in the Indian perspective? As a marketer, focus on the strategical decisions helping you in balancing the two.

Endnotes

1. Jha, S.M., Emerging Issues in Retail Management, National Seminar Paper on Retailing in India, Mahatma Gandhi Kashi Vidyapith, October 27-28 2007, pp. 36-39.
2. *Ibid.*
3. Mishra, S.K., Intervention in Retail, A Global Approach, *Indian Retail View,* BIMTECH, Greater Noida, July-Dec., 2007, pp. 19-29.
4. *Ibid.*
5. Verma, S., An Exploratory Study of Consumer Preferences for Retail Store Selection, BIMTECH, pp. 15-18, 2007.
6. *Ibid.*
7. Mishra, S.K., *op. cit.*
8. *Ibid.*
9. Sakkthival, A.N., Strategic Placement of Organised Retailing, *Indian Retail View,* BIMTECH, pp. 57-62.
10. *Ibid.*
11. Kaur, Banga, Kumar and Singla, Visual Merchandising and Store Design Strategies, *Indian Retail View,* BIMTECH, pp. 39-50, 2007.

PERSONAL CARE MARKETING

"There is nothing more appealing than a man with a sense of wit and fun. There is nothing more paying than an aesthete. Adding additional attractions to your personality necessitates personal care which may be managed personally or require institutional support."

Chapter Objectives

Introduction – Personal Care Marketing: The Concept – Users of Personal Care Services – Behavioural Profile of Users – Market Segmentation for Personal Care Services – Marketing Information System for Personal Care Service – Formulation of Marketing Mix for the Personal Care Services – The Product Mix – The Promotion Mix – The Price Mix – The Place Mix – The Process – The Physical Evidence and Attractions – The People – Personal Care Marketing in the Indian Perspective – Summary – Key Terms – Review Questions – Application Exercises – Endnotes.

Learning Objectives

The motive of this chapter is to sensitise the readers to the various dimensions of personal care marketing. The readers develop their awareness of the behavioural profile of users of services and the different segments of users emerging as the target market. Personality development is an important aspect for the development of corporate people and the different facets of personal care services help them in developing aesthetic sense. The seven mixes of marketing have been conceptualised in the personal care organisations so that they develop the potentials of protecting and promoting the organisational as well as the users' interests. A number of sectors need the services of personal care centers and so they need personal- as well as professional-touch-in-service in the service delivery process.

INTRODUCTION

The increasing pace of corporatisation has paved avenues for attractions. There is nothing more appealing than a man with a sense of wit and fun. There is nothing more paying than an aesthete. With the growing influence of corporate culture in the process of socio-economic emancipation, we find a basic change in the perception of personality development. Of late, the leading global organisations have been found assigning due weightage to Physical Attractions. The subjective knowledge or thematical competence, no doubt, plays an important role in developing our personality but we also need to take care of our look. The cine artists, technocrats, bureaucrats, corporate managers, intellectuals do not need an identical look. The corporate decision-makers need a look that is different to others. A look that generates a positive image, a look that magnifies optimism, a look that bears the efficacy of coiling your communication excellence and a look that visualises elegance. This makes it essential that corporate managers assign top priority to their dresses, physical fitness adding additional attractions. They are not supposed to look like a philosopher exposing pessimism. Actually their facial expression, movement of their eyes, their body language, *modus operandi* and *modus vivendi* add additional attractions to their personality considerably helping the process of image projection. It is against this backdrop that we find personal care services drawing priority attention in the formulation of a sound marketing mix.

Like women, we find even men of today developing a deep-seated fascination for using cosmetics or facial or preferring a beauty treatment. We find them very careful to the management of their physique. With a change in the lifestyles sizeably influenced by the corporate culture, it is very natural that we find each one of us sincere to look attractive. Of course, in almost all the job segments, we find make-up occupying a place of significance no doubt with a minor modification. In some of the segments, e.g., hotel, tourism, bank, insurance, music, entertainment, art and culture, retailing, civil aviation, etc., we find make-up becoming a situational compulsion. The professionals know about the requirements. We need to consider gender, age, profession, culture and occasion or so, while promoting make-up. Hairstyle cannot be overlooked because we find it instrumental in projecting a classic look throwing fragrance and adding additional attractions in the service ambience.

Our focus here is on sound physique with a make-up that suits the position which we hold. The organisation engaged in offering personal care services have a bright future, specially in the Indian perspective. Personality development, thus, is a combination of different dimensions and professionals need to inculcate and cultivate the habits of looking impressive which may help them in different ways. Willingly or unwillingly, we have to make ways for a corporate look.

Faculties of development rest on the development of our personality. Creativity transgresses the limits of physical boundaries. To look good, attractive and impressive, it is essential that we take care of our health, such as we keep ourselves neat and clean, well-dressed, smart and handsome and have fairly matched nature's creation with our creative actions. An affluent desires something more than a poor. The beauty need more than a beauty care. In a country like India or in almost all the developed and less developed countries, we find increasing domination of corporate sector which has been making ways for the development of corporate culture. We can't deny the fact that corporate culture substantially influences our lifestyles. It is against this background that we find western lifestyles gaining popularity in almost all the countries.

The increasing disposable and discretionary incomes, growing sophistication in the process of transportation and communication, increasing temptation for western culture, mounting craze for professional education, increasing number of working ladies in almost all the sectors are some of the recent developments throwing a major impact on our lifestyles. In a country like India where we find western culture outwitting eastern or Indian culture, we expect new developments yet to take place in the socio-economic parlance. We don't find anything wrong in the development of corporate culture provided the negative developments in the process are regulated. It is in this context that we talk about the development of personal care services.

The personal care services include beauty parlours, barber shop, dental care, dry-cleaner, laundry, garment making and repairing, shoemaking and repairing or all other services helping us in the process of adding physical attractions. To be more specific in the Indian condition, we find a profitable market for these services. In the Indian perspective, a majority of the personal care services are found of ancestral nature and character where a number of persons have been found employed. It is high time that we make possible a systematic *vis-a-vis* an organised effort for the development of these services so that the available potentials are capitalised on optimally. With the development of corporate sector, we expect personal care services to gain popularity. Not only women but even men have developed a craze for the personal care services. Like their women counterparts, they also like to maintain their physique and to add attractions in their physique so that they are found successful in throwing a positive imprint on their personality. The physical attractions have no boundaries. Like this, the expectations have no boundaries. Today, the boardrooms and customers want to see you smart and attractive. This makes a strong advocacy in favour of personal care services. Of late, we find emergence of a number of dimensions of personal care services and the trend is likely to continue since we find tidal wave of pop culture gaining popularity even in the Indian context.

The development processes influence lifestyles. The sophistication in the communication processes play an incremental role in making a society highly aware of the new developments. Of course, we find avenues for the negative developments but in the transformation process, the positive developments also take place. The sophistication in the telecast media play a commanding role in changing the lifestyles. There is no doubt in it that the print media play a successive role in the very context. The increasing level of education makes the society more sensitive. It is against this background that we find a change in the lifestyles of the Indian society. We can't deny that today we are more conscious to our health management. Nutritional awareness, physical attractions are now found getting an overriding priority in our healthcare agenda. If we find a craze for Gym and Jogging; if we find a temptation for Yoga; if we find attractions for looking smart and handsome; if we find persons evincing their interests in physical soundness, this is mainly due to the media. It is right to mention that sophistication in the process of transportation has fuelled the process of development. Internationalisation of fashion, culture and civilisation has considerably been influenced by sophistication in transportation and communication. In the present-day world, it is difficult that we spare time for managing things for maintaining a sound health. This has been making ways for the development of personal care organisations.

The aforesaid facts make it clear that it is need of the hour that we think in favour of a systematic and organised development of personal care services. Today, we talk about perfection which is the result of professional excellence. Like other services, the personal care services also need world-class professional excellence. There is no doubt in it that our words impress upon the target audience and throw a big impact on their psychology but the make-up narrates our feelings and ideas and satisfies an individual even without a conversation or a face-to-face communication. The physical attractions move with the lifestyles and the lifestyles move with the multi-dimensional developments in the socio-economic fabrics. Whatever we feel to express by our words is very smoothly expressed by our physical appearance. In the Indian perspective, we find a change in the lifestyles which, of course, has been the result of sophisticated media. The positive trends in industrialisation, urbanisation, communication and transportation make it essential that we think in favour of a planned and organised development of personal care services.

Gone are the days when we believed that physical attractions are exclusively for the women. Today, the senior executives like that their junior executives look smart and handsome and the junior executives don't hesitate in opposing the poor living conditions of their subordinates. They don't divide a line for men and women. Such a new perception in the development of personality focuses on physical attractions. Of course, we need to be professionally-sound and personally-committed but in addition, we are also supposed to look smart and attractive. Management of business is based on attractions. If we find product attractiveness essential to get a positive response in the market, we also find physical attractions essential to complete the process of personality development. Perfection, no doubt, is a fair synchronisation of professional excellence and physical attractions.

In view of the above, we find a profitable market for the personal care organisations. The development of personal care services focuses our attention on almost all the devices which help us in injecting attractions to our physique.

We agree with this view that physical attractions have no boundaries. However, there are some of the essentials and we go through the problem with this approach that an individual while serving an organisation looks smart and attractive. He/she is physically sound or maintaining a good health, looks smart and attractive and attempts to keep on moving the measures which help them in adding physical attractions. It is in this context that we find a number of services developed and offered by the personal care organisations.

Of late, we find aesthetic management getting a significant place in the business world. The personal care services bear the efficacy of developing aesthetic sense. A nicely dressed man/woman succeeds in attracting the attention of masses. A fairly managed physique keeps us smart. An individual with a high aesthetic sense makes the working conditions fair. He/she develops optimism which makes the ways for creativity. The aesthetic management has been found occupying a place of outstanding significance in the business world where we pay for satisfaction.

We find a big gap between the two categories of employees having aesthetic sense and lacking the same. We need to make it clear that different dimensions of personal care services help us in developing the aesthetic sense which makes the ways for practising aesthetic management in the business world.

With the growing importance of personal care in social as well as the business sector, we find development of a number of personal care organisations. In the Indian perspective, we find profitable potentials for the development of personal care services. Capitalising on the tremendous opportunities in a right fashion requires professional excellence. It is against this background that we need an organised development of personal care services. To be more specific in the Indian environment where the problem of unemployment is found at its peak, the planned development of personal care services would be instrumental in creating tremendous job opportunities. Thus, we find three-tier benefits; first — the aesthetic sense would be developed, second — the corporate sector would get employees looking smart and attractive and third — the job opportunities would be created.

The personal care organisations need a new vision, specially in the Indian condition where the corporate sector is found developing. We can't negate that till now, a majority of us lack aesthetic sense. Of course, it is influenced by the properties of intellects who don't assign any weightage to the external make-up or physical attractions. We find philosophers in a very limited number who develop theories. We find professionals in a very large number who practise the same. We talk about management, we talk about marketing and therefore, we also need to talk about attractions. We need to make our products attractive and like this, we also need to add attractions to the physique of our professionals who bear the responsibility of promoting and selling.

In view of the above, it is right to mention that the personal care services are to be marketed in a right fashion so that the services are remunerative to the personal care organisations and at the same time affordable to the target prospects. It is in this context that we go through the different dimensions of personal care marketing. By practising modern marketing principles, the personal care organisations would be successful in activating the process of qualitative transformation.

PERSONAL CARE MARKETING — THE CONCEPT

Personal Care Marketing is considered to be a managerial device to market the services in such a way that quality services are made available to the different categories of users at a reasonable price. It is an organised effort to formulate different submixes of the marketing mix which make possible a time-honoured *vis-a-vis* taste-oriented services in tune with the changing lifestyles. An optimal development of marketing inputs along with their productive utilisation helps the personal care organisations in making the services remunerative. It includes in its purview almost all the services which help an individual in adding physical attractions to his/her personality.

The Personal Care Services include the services of beauty parlours, barber shops, dry-cleaners, dentists, garment making and repairing, shoemaking and repairing, Gymnastic and Jogging for physical fitness, dieticians' services for standardising weight of the body, hair dressing and dyeing and Yoga for making the physique smart and attractive.[1] We can't deny the fact that these services contribute substantially to the addition of physical attractions helping an individual in looking young, smart, fit and active. Of late, we find these services neglected or developing in an unorganised way resulting into the poor quality of services found even not commercially viable. Personal care marketing focuses on the implementation of modern marketing principles in these services so that the services are made nationally and internationally competitive. Thus, the marketing principles make possible marketing of services by the personal care organisations in such a way that increasing expectations of users are fulfilled and in addition, the organisations also succeed in winning and keeping the customers for the long time. The development of personal care services may be by forming a consortium or syndicate in which a number of services are clubbed or offered even in an independent way where a particular service is made available. The marketing of personal care services makes it essential that the services are based on expertise where professionally-sound personnel are engaged. It focuses on the formulation of marketing mix. The formulation of product mix makes available to the users the world-class services. While formulating the product mix, the personal care organisations need to blend the core and peripheral services optimally so that they get an opportunity to use it as a motivational tool, specially by enriching the core and peripheral services. They need to promote in a right fashion so that the users as well as the prospects are informed, sensed and persuaded. This makes it significant that they blend the different constituents of promotion mix optimally. By marketing, the personal care organisations are also supposed to make the services remunerative, so that the organisations remain commercially viable and the charges affordable to the target segment. The marketing practices also make it essential that the personal care organisations are located at a place accessible to the prospects/users. The offering process makes it essential that quality personnel are engaged. Thus, we find personal care marketing an effort to formulate the marketing mix and based on the aforesaid facts we observe the following:

- Personal care marketing focuses on the application of marketing principles in the personal care services.
- We find it a managerial process where professionals are engaged.
- It is an organised effort.

USERS OF THE PERSONAL CARE SERVICES

There are number of users of different categories related to the different segments availing the services of personal care organisations. They are domestic as well as foreign tourists, corporate executives as well as cine and TV artists, youths facing interviews, persons attending functions and parties, athletes participating in national and international events, brides and bridegrooms preparing for wedding and reception parties, other persons interested in keeping themselves physically fit and attractive. The participants of beauty contests are also found using the services of personal care organisations. In Figure 15.1, we find different types of users of the personal care services.

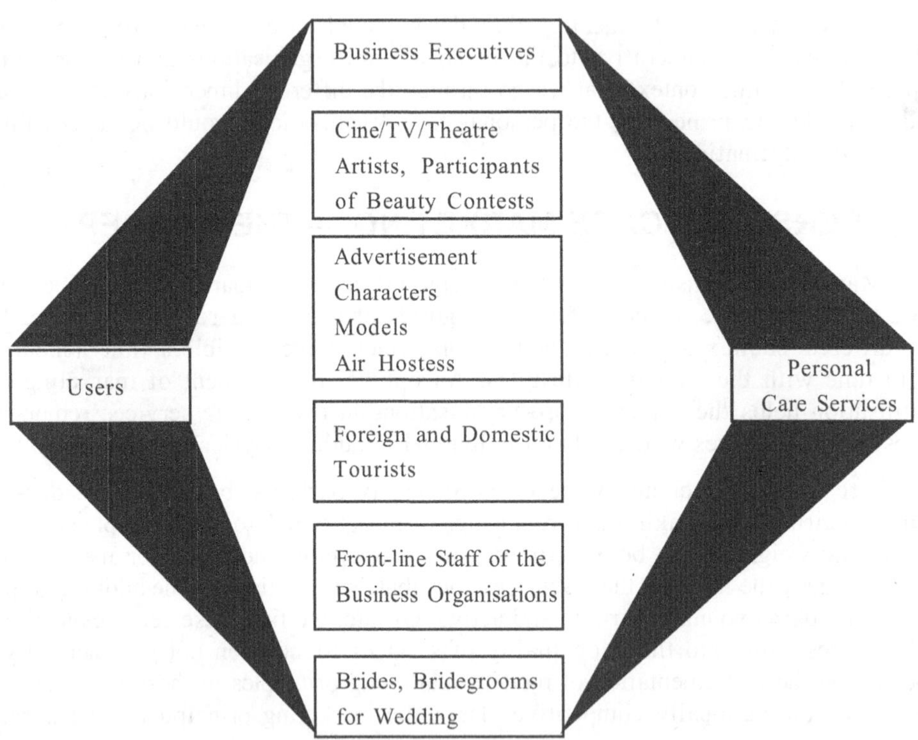

Fig. 15.1: Users of the Personal Care Services

On the basis of Figure 15.1, it is right to mention that almost all type of users use the services of personal care organisations. There is no doubt in it that some of the users are occasional whereas some others are habitual. The professionals engaged in different sectors, cine and TV artists are the habitual users whereas the rural brides and bridegrooms happen to be very occasional users who use the services while making preparations for wedding and reception functions. The youths getting professional education are also found emerging as a profitable segment for the personal care services. The foreign users generally avail the services when they visit a country as a tourist. The foreign corporate or trade representatives or different types of artists while conducting an event or visiting a country prefer to avail the services of personal care organisations. Since we include the services related to physical fitness, the masses prefer to use provided they can afford. Thus, it is right to mention that in the group of users we find different types and categories using the services, of course, all of them with the prime motto of looking attractive to influence others. This in a natural way complicates the task of marketing the services.

BEHAVIOURAL PROFILE OF USERS

We are aware of the fact that different types and categories of users use the services of personal care organisations. The needs and requirements *vis-a-vis* the level of expectations of different categories of users, substantially influencing the behavioural profile, can't be identical. Of course, there is no doubt in it that by and large almost all the users use the services with the prime motive of looking attractive but their expectations from the personal care organisations may vary. Like other organisations, the personal care organisations are also supposed to identify the level of expectations so that they succeed in tailoring the marketing resources to the changing needs and requirements of users. It is against this background that we find it relevant to study the behavioural profile of users availing the services of personal care organisations.

We agree with this view that a number of factors influence the behavioural profile and the professionals serving the personal care organisations need to go through the problem while making such studies. The beauty needs more than a beauty care. In the Indian perspective, we find a long history of using different types of herbals for adding attractions. In addition, the Yoga which has outlived its utility in the modern age was found popular in the ancient India. We don't need to mention, that of late, the personal care experts promoting Gym and Jogging also feel that an overriding priority to Yoga is essential to maintain the physique of an individual. The doctors confirm the instrumentality of Yoga in today's world and it is in this context that we find it gaining popularity once again. Thus, it is right to mention that in the Indian context, we don't find the personal care services a new development but a change in the process of managing the services can't be ruled out. Earlier, we find them in almost all the houses practised by a majority of the population and today, we find them disappearing from the houses and getting the shape of an organised business. Such a situational change in the development of personal care organisations is found generating numerous problems to the personal care organisations *vis-a-vis* to the users. This makes it essential that we go through the problem of marketing with a new vision.

The organisations engaged in offering the personal care service thus need to study the behavioural profile of different categories of users. The corporate employees in general and the executives in particular need to look smart and attractive. To be more specific, the front-line personnel working in different types of organisations where they are supposed to be face-to-face with the target prospects need to assign due weightage to the physical attractions. On the one hand, this is essential to promote aesthetic management in the corporate world while on the other hand, we also find it significant to project a positive image of the organisations that their employees are well paid and look a bit different to others. The boardrooms have been found assigning due weightage to the aestheic management since we find even the senior executives evincing their interests in the personal care services. With the development of tourism sector, we find foreign tourists coming to the country and even the trade representatives visiting the country for a deal are found interested in the services. They stay in five star hotels and we find personal care centres/ complexes also developing as a peripheral service of the hotel industry. They have the desire and the opportunities are there. In addition, we also find models contributing substantially to the marketing communication by adding attractions to the characters. We can't negate the fact that whatever the significant developments we find in the personal care services have considerably been generated by the advertising of late emerging as an industry even in the Indian condition. The sophistication in print and telecast media have been found energising the process of development. It is right to mention that the mounting intensity of expectations has fantastically been influenced by the sophistication in the process of marketing communication. The advertising professionals, models, beauticians have been found monitoring the make-ups for the characters to be advertised. The masses watch televisions or go through the newspapers and magazines from where they get the ideas which shape their expectations.

The aforesaid facts make it clear that the users of the personal care services are substantially influenced by the systems of development that we prefer. If we find a craze for western dresses and hairstyles; if we find a temptation for looking slim and if we find the use of cosmetics on a large scale; this is due to the messages transmitted and feelings generated by the creative advertisements. With the development of corporate sector, we don't find a sign of reversal in trend and even in the coming years, the trend is likely to continue. An important change that we find in the very context is the increasing uses of herbals in place of cosmetics. This is due to the side-effects generated by cosmetics. Thus, the expectations of a majority of the users using the services of personal care organisations are to be liberal to the western culture, civilisation and fashion. We can't deny the fact that globalisation of economy has made ways for the globalisation of fashion which has been found governing the behavioural profile of users.

The income index is considered to be an important dimension influencing the behavioural profile of users. We agree with this view that in the yesteryears, there has been a sharp increase in the disposable and discretionary incomes. In addition, we find a change in the lifestyles being influenced by the corporate culture. This makes it clear that even in the coming years, the users/prospects would keep in their minds the emerging trends and would take a decision in the face of latest developments.

An important change requiring due attention in the very context is regarding the craze for personal care services even among the men, specially youths working in the corporate sector. Most commonly used word "Shringar" was confined to women in past but of late, we find its relevance even to the men. It is in this context that we find development of beauty parlours for men. This makes it clear that the personal care organisations need to study the changes in the behavioural profile of the users due to a change in gender. It is quite natural that the taste and temperament of men and women are not to be one hundred per cent identical. The points of attractions in men for women and *vice versa* are naturally to be different. Further, we also find rural women in particular interested in a few selected services specially for decorating the brides for wedding. On this occasion, we find the urban women preferably living in the industrial towns and cities influenced by the ultra-modern fashion. The personal care organisations bear the responsibility of identifying the levels of the their expectations and formulating the marketing mix accordingly.

MARKET SEGMENTATION FOR THE PERSONAL CARE ORGANISATIONS

A number of users belonging to different categories and both sexes are found using the personal care services. Some of them work as business executives whereas some others work as trade representatives; some of them are cine artists whereas some others are models; some of them are domestic whereas some others are foreign tourists, some of them are women whereas some others are men; some of them come from the rural areas whereas some others come from the urban areas. The marketing professionals feel that the personal care organisations need to group and subgroup the markets so that they find it convenient to study and identify the level of expectations of different categories of users in a right fashion. It is in this context that we find market segmentation important to the making of creative marketing decisions. The marketing professionals bear the responsibility of dividing the markets on the basis of income, profession, region, education or so. These basis would help them in making the market small. As shown in Figure 15.2, we find segmentation of market for the personal care services.

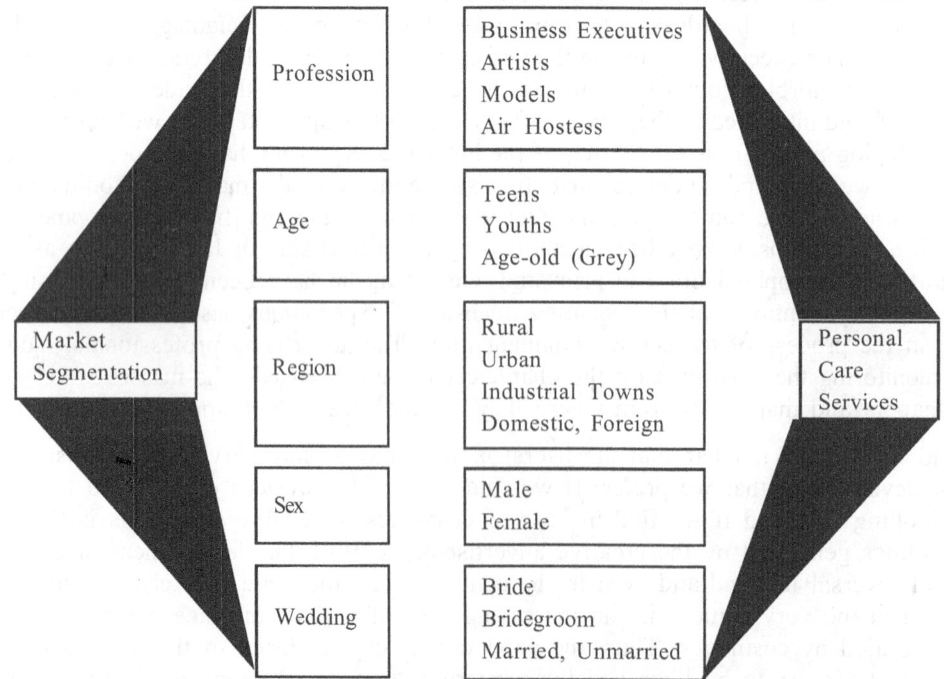

Fig. 15.2: Market Segmentation for Personal Care Organisations

We find both the men and women using the services of personal care organisations. The women like different hairstyles, make-up, physical therapy in comparison to the men. The teens, youths and grey have different preferences. The domestic users are found different to the foreign users. The business executives' preferences are different to the preferences of cine artists. The rural users have different likes and dislikes. The highly educated segment prefers different services. These facts make it clear that different users have different preferences and expectations. The marketing professionals are supposed to tailor the expectations of different categories of users to the development of marketing inputs. The age-old persons or grey segment shows special interest in Yoga, specially in the Indian perspective. The youths prefer Gym and Jogging. The persons living in the urban areas prefer jogging whereas the rural users or the segment believing in old values prefer Yoga.

The segmentation thus makes the ways for studying the changing preferences of different categories of users. The personal care organisations have a profitable future market and this makes it essential that they are careful to the changing expectations of users. They can't check the flow of development, they even can't change the order of preferences. The only thing they can make possible is developing their potentials in the face of emerging market conditions. This focuses our attention on the development of marketing resources which they can. If we talk about the formulation of product mix for the personal care organisations, it is essential that they know about the services not getting the desired response. This would help them in modifying, eliminating and including the services in tune with the changing needs and requirements. Since we expect development of personal care organisations even in the small towns and cities, it is significant that the marketing professionals are in a position to understand the differences in the expectations of users living in the metropolises, big towns and cities, industrial towns and cities and the small towns and cities. The segmentation is found important to the marketers in many ways. If they think of promoting the services, it is pertinent that they are aware of the receiving capacity of target market. This simplifies the task of advertising professionals, specially while making possible creativity in the advertisement messages. It is also significant that the personal care organisations think about the paying capacity of different segments and set the price structure accordingly. The services are likely to be expensive as of late we find use of expensive inputs by the personal care organisations. It is against this background that an in-depth study of different segments is found important to the personal care organisations.

In view of the above, it is right to mention that the personal care organisations need to make the market smaller. We can't deny that the small is beautiful since we can make possible an in-depth study of the small market whereas the identification of a big market is found much more difficult. If the users are found interested in quality services, it is the prime responsibility of the personal care organisations that they keep on moving the process of innovation which would make ways for the development of new services of world-class. If we talk about the rural users, it is quite natural that they can't afford expensive services and therefore the personal care organisations need to explore that how and in what way, the services can be made economic. If the users are found avoiding the use of cosmetics, the personal care organisations are supposed to explore the possibilities of using herbals.

The aforesaid facts make it clear that market segmentation is to be done in a right fashion. We don't find any wisdom in investing more but getting less. We talk about marketing and this focuses on investing less but getting more in return. The rural sector is found emerging as a big market, specially in the Indian perspective. The flow of industrialisation is also to gain the momentum in the rural market. With the increasing intensity of industrialisation in the rural areas, we expect the emergence of a big profitable market, specially in India. This makes it essential that the personal care organisations segment the market on the basis of different parameters as mentioned in Figure 15.2. The main thing in the process of development is segmenting the market in such a way that the users remain satisfied.

MARKETING INFORMATION SYSTEM FOR THE PERSONAL CARE ORGANISATIONS

Of late, we assign due weightage to the information-based decisions since the creative decisions need detailed, up-to-date and accurate information. Like other organisations, the personal care organisations also need to manage the information in such a way that the outdated services are innovated much earlier than the leading competitors. The needs and requirements are found changing, the income index is found changing and therefore, the expectations are also found changing fast. The multi-dimensional changes in the business environmental conditions influence the process of making the marketing decisions. Unless the decision-makers are well aware of the latest developments in the business world, the product uniqueness is not possible. This makes it essential that we manage the information in a right fashion so that we come to know about the emerging trend. It is in this context that we make a strong advocacy in favour of a technology-driven marketing information system for the personal care organisations.

With sophistication in the process information technologies, we find enough scope for managing information related to the different types of services and the users. Whatever the studies we undertake need information. If we talk about a study of the behavioural profile of users, we need the cooperation of marketing information system. If we segment the market, we need the cooperation of information system. Of late, even for quality decisions, we depend on the decision supporting system. These facts make it clear that for marketing different types of services by the personal care organisations, it is pertinent that we think in favour of a developed information system.

Personal care organisations are fantastically influenced by the changing lifestyles. The increasing level of income and the sophistication in the development of media are the two important factors considerably influencing a change in our lifestyles. If we earn more; we prefer to spend more; we enjoy by availing the modern amenities and facilities. We find a change in our food habits, hairstyles, dresses, perception regarding savings and expenses, development of personality or so. These things are related to lifestyles. The developments in communication remove the threshold barrier and we find kids, teens very bold. Even the age-old persons appear interested in keeping themselves physically sound. These developments pave avenues for the development of beauty parlours, hairdressing, jogging, garment making or so. Thus, we find a change in fashion which is substantially influenced by lifestyles. The personal care organisations need to enrich the information bank so that the developments around the world are collected and managed with the help of a system. They know about the preferences, likes and dislikes, expectations, lifestyles which simplify the task of formulating the marketing mix.

The instrumentality of marketing information system is coiled in the essence of formulating and innovating the different mixes in such a way that the personal care organisations succeed in offering world-class services to the users found remunerative to maintain the commercial viability and affordable to expand the market. Of course, it is not possible for a small organisation to develop an independent information system and therefore we may also talk in favour of a syndicate or a consortium.

But for the leading personal care organisations, it is not so difficult. They can make it possible with the help of a technology-driven system and to deliver the best, they can even seek the co-operation of leading information selling organisations. We don't talk here about an independent beauty parlour or Gym but the clubbing of a number of personal care services taking the shape of a personal care complex.

The marketing information system would help the personal care organisations in many ways. The information related to the emerging trends in the intensity of competition, high level of expectations, changing lifestyles, increasing health-consciousness or so would be made available by the system and the personal care organisations can develop their marketing mix in tune with the patterns of development. In the Indian perspective, we find tremendous opportunities for the development of Yoga as an important constituent of the personal care services. If we study the target market in a right way and advertise and publicise Yoga in a right fashion, the profitable opportunities would be identified around the world. It is against this background that we need to promote Yoga as an important constituent of the service mix of the personal care organisations.

While managing information, the marketing professionals need to be careful that the researchers or the research scientists collect information, conduct surveys and the world-class system analysts transform the data into information in such a way that accurate, time-honoured and quality information reach to them without any distortion. We find cosmetics generating a number of side-effects. The information system would inform the side-effects of cosmetics *vis-a-vis* the outstanding benefits of herbs which would make the masses aware of the regulated use of cosmetics. We find a code for Gym and Jogging and the users would be given a prescription related to the limitations. With the development of sophisticated computers, the system can also be successful in innovating the services by introducing new designs of fashion, hair dressing or so. In addition, the personal care organisations would also be successful in making an appraisal of the contributions of different types of services included in the mix. The management of finance, proper recording or documentation, formulation of marketing plan and many other activities would be managed properly.

The aforesaid facts make it clear that the marketing information system would improve the quality of services made available by the personal care organisations. It is against this background that we make a strong advocacy in favour of developing the information system. In the Indian perspective, we hardly find the organisations evincing interests in managing the information. When we talk about a systematic and organised development of personal care services, it is much more impact generating that we also talk about the management of information. We can't negate that in the coming years there would be multi-dimensional changes in the taste preferences *vis-a-vis* the lifestyles. The leading personal care organisations need to develop the services accordingly which would be made easier with the help of a well-developed technology-driven marketing information system. They need to manage information if not on large scale at least on a small scale. This would benefit the organisation in many ways.

FORMULATION OF MARKETING MIX FOR THE PERSONAL CARE ORGANISATIONS

We are aware of the fact that the formulation of a marketing mix is like the process of combining the different types of spices for cooking a delicious dish. The marketing professionals need to blend the different submixes in such a way that an optimal use of marketing inputs is made possible. The domination of corporate sector in the Indian economy and the emergence of corporate culture in the Indian society make the ways for an organised development of personal care services. It is in this context that the formulation of a marketing mix is discussed. Professionalism paves the ways for excellence which engineers a sound foundation for increasing the strength of an organisation. We can't deny that the formulation of a sound marketing mix for the personal care organisations requires professional excellence. The different submixes like the product mix, the promotion mix, the price mix, the place mix, the people mix need to be synchronised fairly so that whatever the marketing resources we develop are found instrumental in sensitising the prospects and winning and keeping them as a habitual customer for the years and years to come.

The Product Mix

The personal care services combine almost all the services which we use to add attractions to our personality where we find focus on the physical attractions. The services offered by beauty parlours, hairdressing and dyeing centres, garment making, shoemaking, dental care, Gym and Jogging centres, Yoga contribute substantially to our physical soundness. An organisation can combine different services or can concentrate even on a single service. Some of the services are found essential for which the users are charged and we call them core services. In the same context, we also find services blended to add attractions to the product mix and we call them peripheral services. The formulation of product mix requires a fair blending of the core and peripheral services. We can't deny that by and large almost all the organisations offer identical core services and therefore an organisation interested in establishing its edge innovates and enriches the peripheral services. While formulating the product mix, it is pertinent that the personal care organisations assign due weightage to the designing of a sound product portfolio in which different types of services found more profit-generating and less profit-generating are blended in such a way that a fair combination of present and future prosperity is made possible. In addition, it is also significant that different types of services are packaged with the motto of motivating the prospects. The marketing professionals are supposed to take a decision regarding the elimination of traditional and the inclusion of modern services so that product uniqueness continues for the long time. Thus, the formulation of a sound product mix is found essential and only the professionals having the world-class excellence can make it possible. Of late, we find a craze for a sophisticated living condition which influences the lifestyles. It is in this context that we find development of hotel culture, an increase in the number of working ladies and more consciousness for having a sound physique. The multi-dimensional developments in transportation and communication are found throwing a big impact on the lifestyles of masses. This also energises the process of developing high expectations and compelling the marketing professionals to innovate the services.

The personal care services due to high degree of fluctuation in nature and character complicate the inclusion and elimination processes. Gone are the days when we preferred simple living. Today, we find sophisticated lifestyle a status symbol and masses are found developing a craze for the same. The diversified group of customers with a number of taste preferences make it essential that the personal care organisations keep on moving the process of product innovation.

The beauty parlours should only not copy the western method of hairdressing but should also devise their own methods preferably in the face of ancient Indian values and taste. We can't say that prospects prefer western hairstyle in all the cases and regions. If at one place, the customers prefer bobbed hair, we also find attractions for long hair. They should promote the use of herbals in place of cosmetics found showing side-effects on skin. The barber shops, laundries, dry-cleaners need to diversify the nature and types of services in the face of Indian culture and civilisation. While formulating the product mix, the personal care organisations need to include in their service mix the Gym and Jogging, the Yoga, the nutritional awareness or so. An in-depth study of the changing preferences of customers is found essential to formulate a sound product portfolio. We can't negate that with the changing patterns of development, the profitable opportunities are available in the market. The economic liberalisation policy of the government, the increasing transportation and communication services, the mounting domination of corporate sector, the changing lifestyles are some of the factors engineering a sound foundation for the development of personal care services. This makes it essential that the personal care organisations activate innovative efforts to formulate a sound service mix that includes a number of services making the product mix competitive.

The aforesaid facts make it clear that personal care organisations are required to innovate the service mix assigning due weightage to Indian lifestyle. Of course, we find a difference in the lifestyles of people living in the different parts of the country. The preferences of people living in the southern part of the country is found different to their counterparts living in the northern parts. The lifestyles of people living in the industrial towns and cities is found different to the people living in the general towns and cities. We can't negate regional influences in the formation of taste preferences. The festive occasions are found different and the personal care organisations are expected to get profitable business on the occasions. We are well aware of the fact that fashion industry faces more fluctuations and therefore one style, one design gaining mass popularity today become outdated just tomorrow. With the high degree of acceptability and rejection, the fashion industry promotes frequent innovation. This makes it essential that the personal care organisations incorporate the necessary changes as and when the customers' preferences necessitate so. Not only this, they are supposed to be innovative and imaginative and to declare the services outdated much earlier the customers reject. They should also keep in their minds that the movement of fashion is found cyclic in order and therefore outdated services of today are likely to be popular just tomorrow. They need to promote change but in this context, it is also pertinent that they keep themselves ready to introduce even the most traditional and outdated fashion. Such an attempt would help personal care organisations in creating the profitable opportunities.

In Figure 15.3, we find product mix for the personal care organisations which make it clear that a number of services are included in the service mix. A change in the lifestyles is found significant to influence a change in the product mix.

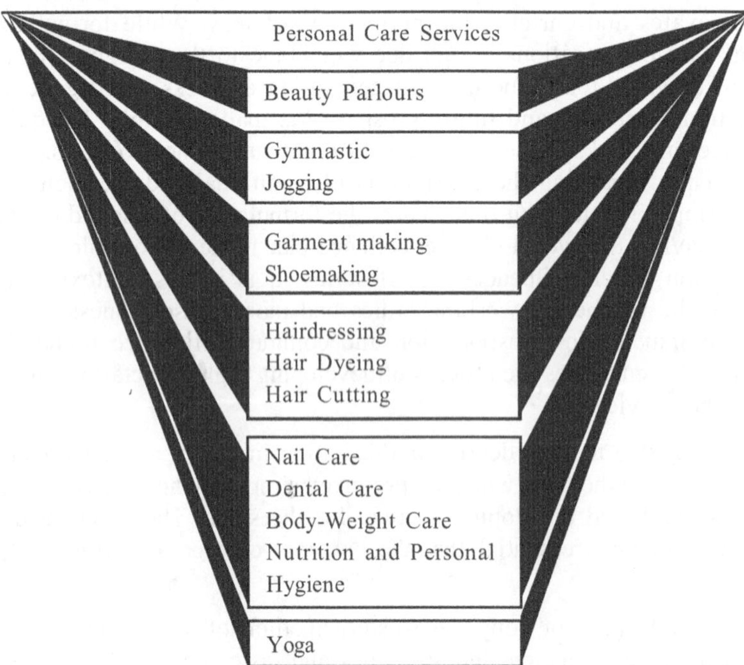

Fig. 15.3: Product Mix of the Personal Care Organisations

In the face of Figure 15.3, it is right to mention that the personal care services need to assign due weightage to the old values since the customers of late have been found developing a craze for the old fashion. It is also clear that the formulation of service mix should not only consider the preferences of women but they need to assign due weightage even to the preferences of men. This is due to the fact that of late we find its relevance for both genders and the different age groups. It is already clarified earlier that such a change has been influenced by the development of corporate sector and the increasing influence of media in influencing the lifestyles of masses. It is against this background that we need a service mix that is preferred by different segments of customers. The personal care organisations need professionalism, specially while formulating and innovating the service mix since we find more dynamism in the services of the personal care organisations.

In view of the above, it is right to mention that the personal care organisations need to make the services innovative. Such an innovation would be in the face of traditional as well as the modern style. If they need to include Gym and Jogging they also need to include Yoga. If they need to include modern hairstyles, they also need to promote traditional hairstyles. If they need to introduce western new design of dresses, they also need to promote Indian traditional designs. Such a blending process would make the service mix attractive *vis-a-vis* profitable and affordable. Of course, they need world-class professional excellence to formulate an innovative service mix. A well managed, technology-driven marketing information system would help them substantially in the innovation process.

The Promotion Mix

It is not only sufficient that we maintain our existence. It is much more impact generating that we thrive. This makes it essential that we evince our interests in offering the world-class services to the customers. While innovating the services, the personal care organisations are required to be careful to quality and while promoting the services, they need to assign due weightage to creativity. It is only not sufficient that we offer the best. It is also important that we let our target prospects know that we are really offering the best. It is against this background that we talk about the promotion mix of the personal care organisations. The different constituents of promotion need due attention of the professionals serving the personal care organisations.

Advertisement: Like other organisations, the personal care organisations also need to advertise their services in such a way that the prospects are informed, sensed and persuaded. They are required to make use of advertising in which creativity occupies a place of outstanding significance. The advertising professionals need to make the slogans, messages and appeals proactive to the target prospects. It is essential that they assign due weightage to the changing preferences of different segments and develop the services in the face of the emerging scenario. While advertising, we find print media the most sensitive and effective device to influence and stimulate demand. While selecting newspapers and magazines for advertising, the services, they need to assign due weightage to the circulation and popularity of a particular newspaper and magazine in a particular command area. Of late, we find sophisticated print technologies which make ways for sensitivity and acceptability. While advertising, the personal care organisations may also prefer to form a syndicate which would make the process cost-effective.

In this context, we also find broadcast media having a big network. The personal care organisations may use even broadcast media but here the advertising professionals need to assign due weightage to the time of transmission *vis-a-vis* the advertising materials. The duration of transmission should be in the face of leisure hour. It is essential that the radio players or listeners are free and they are in a position to gravitate their attention on the advertisement messages and slogans. We find economy in the broadcast media and therefore even the small personal care organisations may advertise through the broadcast media.

Of late, we find telecast media occupying a place of outstanding significance. With the development of satellite communication, we find a big transmission network and now even the private channels are found operating. We can't deny that the media being expensive would be suitable to only those organisations who have a big budget for advertisement. We can't negate the high intensity of sensitivity that we find in the telecast media. But at the same time, it is also right to mention that due to time constraint, it is not possible for the personal care organisations to make available to the target audience all the necessary informations and developments in the services.

The marketing professionals bear the responsibility of blending the different constituents of promotion optimally, of course in the face of the budgetary provisions and the financial constraints. The frequency of advertisement would also be influenced by the budgetary provisions. The main thing in the process is to inform, sense and persuade the target audience in a right fashion.

Publicity: This constituent of promotion mix is found suitable to the personal care organisations because they are not required to invest anything for publicising. The only thing they need is to develop rapport with the media people who by providing the eye-catching space for the news items would successfully publicise the services of personal care organisations. While developing rapport, the marketing professionals need to offer lunch, dinner and small gifts to the media people or to the opinion leaders found popular in the command or catchment area.

Sales Promotion: The instrumentality of sales promotion is found even for the personal care organisations where the employees serving the organisations and the customers using the services are offered innovative incentives. Such an offer becomes more effective specially when we find off-season or a downward trend in the use of services. The mounting intensity of competition and the existing market share of the organisation determine the frequency and duration of sales promotion measures. Even a small organisation can offer a small gift, specially to the habitual users. While offering incentives, it is pertinent that the personal care organisations keep in their minds the uniqueness as an important feature. The gifts should have a memory value. They also need to think in favour of concessional services to increase the demand and to touch the target.

Personal Selling: The leading personal care organisations having a big budget for promotion and offering varieties of services can promote even through personal selling. They need to use the services of salespeople having high communicative ability and in addition, who are also well aware of the art and tact of impressing upon the target prospects. The salespeople need to contact the target prospects in the command area. We can't negate that the personal care organisations are required to develop a training programme to the salespeople who are supposed to contact the target prospects.

Word-of-mouth Promotion: We can't devalue the instrumentality of word-of-mouth promotion in promoting the personal care business. Here, they are required to improve the quality of services. It is quite natural that if we find a person looking very attractive, the interested persons/prospects ask about the name of the beauty parlours or hairdressing centres, or a garment making centre whose services have been availed. The customers act here as a hidden salesforce and they promote your services without charging anything from you.

Telemarketing: In the present business world, the personal care organisations are found using the services of telephones and the excellence of telemarketers for promoting the business. Since we have a developed communication network, the personal care organisations may appoint telemarketers who by communicating, removing the confusions and misunderstanding of the prospects and customers, answering to their questions and queries, sensing and persuading them properly can make ways for stimulating the demand. In this context, it is pertinent that the personal care organisations have efficient telemarketers and sophisticated telephonic services along with the ultra-modern instruments.

The marketing professionals thus need to make a fine fusion of the different constituents of promotion which succeeds in influencing the impulse of prospects and stimulating the demand by making the promotional measures cost-effective.

The Price Mix

This dimension of the marketing mix focuses on the charges for the services offered by the personal care organisations. The pricing decisions for the personal care services become significant because the commercial viability of the organisations offering the services depends on the remunerative price structure. In addition, the decisions become important since in the Indian perspective, it is also essential that the price structure is affordable to the target segment. The emerging trends in competition and demand position influence the decisions substantially. In the metropolises, the users have a high spending capacity and therefore even a high price structure may be acceptable. The big industrial towns and cities also come under the same category. But so far as the small towns and cities are concerned, the same strategy can't be acceptable. To be more specific for the rural segment, we need special services and a special price structure. Thus, the personal care organisations are required to consider the economy of the location points or the catchment area. It is quite natural that quality of services also plays a decisive role in the very context. The beauty parlours located in the metropolises or big industrial towns and cities need to make the services internationally competitive because the foreign users may also buy the services.

The perception of quality for those personal care organisations would be different to the perception that we shape and perceive for the organisations located in the small towns and cities. In this context, we don't make an advocacy for using materials having side-effects. If we promote the use of herbals in place of expensive cosmetics, the services can be made cost-effective.

In view of the aforesaid facts, it is right to mention that the important guiding forces in the making of pricing decisions are quality or standard of services offered *vis-a-vis* the location points of the personal care organisations. The profit-oriented pricing strategy is the main thing. We can't negate that these services are used for gaining pleasure, adding attractions, and maintaining a sound health and therefore, the users are supposed to pay the charges for the same. The only thing regarding the economy is found judicious for the poor rural segment, specially using the services on the occasion of wedding. In this case, the personal care organisations located in the small towns and cities are supposed to offer cost-based services.

It is quite natural that the mounting intensity of competition would compel the personal care organisations to make the price structure competitive. They have to devise ways for making the services cost-effective by using inexpensive inputs. With the increasing competition, they would also be required to make the establishment expenses optimal. The scale of profit is required to be rationalised in the face of emerging trends in competition. We can't negate that particularly in the Indian perspective, we find the personal care organisations at the very nascent stage. This makes a strong advocacy in favour of using pricing as a motivational tool. Once the society is found forming the habits of using the services, the personal care organisations may change the bases for fixing the price. How to make it a motivational tool requires more professional excellence. The personal care organisations have a bright future and therefore, they need to show more patience while generating profits. The professionalism makes it essential that at the outset, an organisation makes the users habitual. It is in this context that we find pricing decisions critical as well as chaotic.

The Place Mix

The process adopted for offering the services plays a decisive role in satisfying the users. Promises carry no sense if the promised services don't reach to the ultimate users. A distortion in the process of offering degenerates the quality and engineers a strong foundation for dissatisfaction. It is against this background that we find a study of place mix occupying a place of outstanding significance in the marketing management of personal care organisations.

The leading personal care organisations make available the promised services to the ultimate users with the help of different centres located at different places where a number of experts and other personnel are found instrumental in offering the services. The small personal care centres offer the services directly to the users. This makes it clear that we find a possibility of distortion in quality, specially in the big centres where we expect a gap between the provider and the users. The place management becomes significant with the viewpoint of bridging over the gap between the services-promised and services-offered. In this context, it is pertinent that professionals assign due weightage to the management of employees serving the organisations. Like other organisations, the personal care organisations also need to make possible performance orientation and for this, they need quality personnel. The employees serving the organisation should have an in-depth knowledge of promises. The professionals managing the organisation need to make it sure that the users' expectations are fulfilled.

Another important dimension in the place mix is related to the Points of Location (PoL). We can't deny the fact that for the personal care organisations, the professionals need to assign due weightage to the place where the branch offices or the servicing centres are to be located. They are supposed to make it sure that places are easily accessible and the required infrastructural facilities are to be available. Since a majority of the personal care services are now based on electronics where technologies play a contributory role, the cases of breakdown or inadequate supply of electricity would make ways for a degeneration in quality. This makes it essential that necessary infrastructural facilities are available at the points of location. In addition, the professionals are also required to make it sure that at the points of location, the prospects/users would assemble in a good number. When it is a beauty parlour, the places close to the five star hotels, departmental stores, supermarkets or big shopping complexes, cinema halls, where we find assembling of persons a natural phenomenon would of course be suitable. Contrary to it when we talk about a personal care complex in which we find a mix of different types of services, the places are not required to be very close to the cities' precincts. In that case, the personal care centres, complexes need adequate s.pace which is also environment-friendly. Thus, the professionals managing the personal care organisations are supposed to make it sure that places selected are easily accessible, safe, environment-friendly and the required infrastructural facilities are available at the centres without an interruption.

In view of the above, it is right to mention that the personal care organisations need to manage place which would be instrumental in offering the promised services to the target users. The considerations as mentioned above draw a close attention of the professionals managing the organisations.

Process

In the processing of personal care services, we find involvement of people and technology through which the services reach to the ultimate users. The experts of their areas are found instrumental in the creation of services of beauty parlours, hairdressers, dentists, dry-cleaning, etc. The Gym centres also make use of experts for delivering the quality services. Earlier, all the services were manual-based but now we find use of machines and equipments for this purpose. The motive is to satisfy the users. Because we find masses developing a temptation for healthcare, the personal care centres have a bright future. The services need to be standardised and at the same time, we also need to consider the flow. The customisation of services needs due attention of personal care centres with the motto of motivating them for repeat visits. With the increasing demand for these services, we find personal care centres developing on an organised basis. In the metropolitan towns and cities, the general masses appear conscious to their physical fitness. Actually, we find it emerging as a professional requirement. The corporate sector in particular assigns due weightage to the physical soundness of their executives or others.

While formulating a sound marketing mix for the personal care centres, the actual procedures, mechanism and flow of activities by which the services are delivered need due attention. If we talk about the services offered by beauty parlours, a complicated and extensive series of actions are needed to complete the process. The customisation of beauty parlour services adds special attractions because if we find the services in the face of traditions and customs, it is to satisfy the customers. Today, we find a number of sectors assigning due weightage to the customs, traditions and culture; the beauty parlours and hair dressers by customising the services may be successful in creating a special segment making repeated use of services which will benefit the centres in many ways.

The operating system in the personal care centres is found mechanised. This makes it essential that the centres make use of new generation of technology for this purpose. A number of Gym centres, hairdressers and beauty parlours have been found using new operating system for service delivery. The services now need to be professionalised. It is very natural that the level of expectation of users will increase further because the corporate sector and entertainment sector would define and redefine the quality of services in tune with the professional requirements. We find emergence of a big market for the personal care services and therefore the personal care centres need to tap them. In addition, we also find increasing demand for beauty parlours and hairdressing services on special occasions such as marriage, wedding day, birthday, etc. Not only in the urban areas but we find development of market even in the rural areas. The right processing would improve the quality of services which is considered essential for satisfying them. In the process, the involvement of customers cannot be undermined as we find some of the customers playing an active role in the innovation processes.

Physical Evidence and Attractions

The personal care organisations while formulating a marketing mix also need to assign due attention on this submix which focuses on the servicescapes very much effective in creating service ambience considered essential for the development of personal care services. They need a professional-touch-in-service to satisfy the different categories of users of their services. The visitors or users coming to the point of service delivery are supposed to be an aesthete having a temptation for looking attractive and impressive. This necessitates designing of personal care centres in the face of the taste and temperament of users of services. The beauty parlours, hairdressing centres, Gym, dental care, dry-cleaner, garment making and repairing centres cannot have an identical look. Of late, we find use of information and communication technologies even in the personal care sector and therefore display of these items cannot be undermined. The tangible components facilitating performance or communication of the service must be displayed in an attractive way. The most important thing is tangibilising the outstanding features of your organisation *vis-a-vis* delivering your services in such a fashion that customers feel pleasure in waiting and availing. The lighting arrangements in the personal care centres need priority attention of professionals managing the affairs or providers offering the services. The colour of light, intensity of light and positioning of light help you in increasing the number of habitual customers. Arrangements for music cannot be undermined while managing the personal care centre. The volume of music and the quality and type of music would be in tune with the preferences of customers. Besides locating seating areas for the customers in queue also need our attention. It is to be made sure that the positioning of furniture for the waiting customers is not to create congestion. The decorative items need to be positioned at a place drawing the attention of all the customers. You need to throw a soothing and cooling effect. You also need to position the ornamental shadow plants to generate aesthetic sense. The curtains, cushion must be attractive but soothing. If the centre is found large-sized, the entertainment services may also be provided to the customers in queue.

The above-mentioned facts make it clear that managing personal care centre needs personal touch in creating, and managing the centre to be successful in attracting the customers. Occasional customers may be transformed into habitual customers, if you make the service ambience in tune with the taste and temperament of customers. So far as the use of equipment is concerned, we find even personal care services making use of the same for the satisfactory delivery of service. It is significant that whatsoever the equipment and machines you use in the centre are well maintained and considerably helping you in the value addition process. The interiors and exteriors both need attention of experts designing the service centre. The tangibilisation is considered to be an important dimension for image projection and the personal care organisations need to tangibilise their outstanding properties in a sophisticated way. The customers by encountering the displays are found attracted. The devices for displays need to prove a source for pleasure. The marketers need due focus on physical evidence because services are intangible and customers often rely on the tangible cues to evaluate the service before they use. The servicescapes draw our attention on physical facilities available to the customers in the personal care centres. The quality of air and temperature also need due care in the very context.

While tangibilising, the business cards and billing statements used by the personal care centres also become significant. In addition, brochures, web pages may help you in activating the process. Creating ambient conditions may vary from centre to centre depending on the profile of customers visiting the personal care centres. The dresses of staff serving the centre need to be of quality. They may also use uniforms and logo for the projection of image. In this context, the uniforms or dresses must be neat and clean. The marketers need to remember that the servicescapes are the outward appearance of the organisation and more so, it is a visual metaphor for the intangible services. By creating physical surroundings, the marketers provide to the customers an opportunity to convey an image. A well-designed functional facility can make the service a pleasure to experience. Just reverse to it, we find poor and inefficient design frustrating both the customers as well as the employees serving the centre.

With the emergence of corporate culture, we find wider avenues for the development of personal care centres which has been found increasing the intensity of competition. This makes it essential that the personal care centres establish an edge over their rivals. On the one hand, they need to improve the quality of services delivered by them whereas on the other hand, they also need to make their service ambience distint to their rivals. Innovative facilities add additional attractions to your services. Since we find people fascinated to the western culture, the personal care centres need to make it sure that their services have an imprint of the culture preferred by the users.

The dental care centres, dry-cleaners, garment making centres also need to make provisions for servicescapes in the face of their potentials. Today, we find a special attraction or even a craze for the Gym and yoga centres. Here, it is significant that the marketers focus on physical facilities available at the centres so that customers get an additional attraction. Because we find people becoming much more conscious to healthcare and a number of equipments and machines are used for the same, we find scope for their display even in Gym.

The above-mentioned facts make it clear that service ambience cannot be overlooked because it is found instrumental in generating service fragrance. The customers are ready to spend on personal care services and we need to capitalise on the opportunities in a right way so that personal- and professional-touch-in-services simplify our task of satisfying and retaining the customers.

The People Mix

The management of human resources plays a significant role even in the personal care organisations. We are well aware of the fact that a number of skilled and unskilled, trained and manual people offer the services which may even be technology-driven. This makes it significant that professionals managing the centres assign due weightage to the two important considerations, first the employees supposed to offer the services have world-class excellence and second, they get suitable incentives for the quality of services they offer. They need to make possible a fair blending of performance orientation and employee orientation. The performance orientation makes it essential that employees have the excellence to offer the promised services. Since we find the use of a number of technologies in the personal care services, they have to make it sure that employees know to operate and maintain the technologies to get the desired results. If new technologies are incorporated, frequently, the employees should be made available an ongoing training programme. This focuses our attention on the management of training which helps personal care organisations in making possible performance orientation.

In this context, it is also significant that professionals make possible employee orientation. This draws our attention on suitable incentives to the employees for offering the promised services. We can't negate that failing the payment of suitable incentives, we find degeneration in efficiency even among the personally-committed employees. In a true sense, we find a close relation between performance orientation and employee orientation. The professionals are required to make it sure that efficients get more to the inefficients. This would motivate inefficients to improve their efficiency.

In addition to professional excellence, the employees in general need to have an in-depth knowledge of behavioural management which would help employees in motivating the users and retaining them as habitual users even for the long time. We can't deny the fact that users getting quality services but facing indecent behaviour would avoid to use the services in future.

In view of the above, it is right to mention that people mix needs due weightage in the management of submixes of the personal care organisations. To be more specific in the Indian context, we find management not serious to the people management which has been found generating numerous problems. Of course, the use of technologies in the personal care services has shaped a new perception of quality which has raised the level of expectations of almost all categories of users using the services. This makes it essential that the professionals perceive the perception of expectations in a right fashion.

Thus, the different submixes of the marketing mix, such as the product mix, the promotion mix, the price mix, the place mix and the people mix need to be synchronised optimally so that the personal care organisations succeed in developing quality marketing inputs to offer the quality services to the users. The future marketing of personal care services requires a new vision, a new approach and a new strategy. Almost all the personal care organisations need to make their services innovative in which the peripheral services are required to be given due weightage. Since the core services by and large become identical, the professionals by enriching the peripheral services would be efficacious in adding attractions to their services. Product uniqueness would continue to be the focal point for the personal care organisations found interested in increasing the market share and establishing the leadership.

PERSONAL CARE MARKETING IN THE INDIAN PERSPECTIVE

Marketing of personal care services is found important in the Indian perspective since we find multi-dimensional changes in the socio-economic conditions. The business conditions appear to be conducive and this makes it essential that the personal care organisations view the problems in an innovative fashion. The increasing level of education, the significant developments in the economy, the sophistication in the process of transportation and communications, the increasing domination of corporate sector, the emergence of corporate culture, the liberalisation of economy are some of the positive developments in the Indian environment making the business environment favourable for the personal care organisations because these developments have been found changing the lifestyles. We find its imprint on a majority of the prospects. A craze for western lifestyles is the result of multi-dimensional developments found in the process of socio-economic emancipation. Thus, the personal care organisations need to market the services in a right way so that they, on the one hand, succeed in generating profits while on the other hand, also make the services affordable even to the low-income group of the society. It is against this background that we need to view the problem with a new vision.[2]

The formulation of a sound marketing mix is an important managerial responsibility before the professionals managing the services. In this context, the formulation of an innovative product mix is found significant. By innovation in the product mix, our emphasis is here on injecting new properties to the service mix which assign due weightage to Indian fashion, Indian lifestyle, Indian culture and for that, we need to promote Indian prescriptions. The beauty parlours, hair dressing and hair cutting centres need to think in favour of "Shringar" in which we find management of beauty with a different prescription. The contributions of milk, turmeric (a plant of ginger family), mustard in the shape of "Ongtan", neem plants, seeds, and many other medicinal plants need due attention of beauty parlours right now promoting cosmetics resulting into a number of side-effects. They have also to think in favour of "Kes Shringar" hair dressing found in ancient India where queens, female monarch were decorated. We can't negate that even today we find some of the Indian families using these devices for adding attractions. If we find some of the users fascinated to the bobbed hair, short hair; we also find users more crazy to the long hair. Of course, they need to feel that in the long hair, we find enough scope for changing the shape, size and direction and making them more attractive. Today, they have computers at their business desks and therefore, they can explore new devices by promoting graphics.

We are not opposed to the western hairstyles. Our emphasis in on the fact that specially in the Indian perspective, the beauty parlours, hair cutting and dressing centres need to make the services innovative and they can do it successfully by blending the devices used in the ancient India. The plus points that we find in the process are additional attractions with dismal side-effects, cost-effectiveness and a profitable international market.

Of late, we find a craze for Gymnastic and Jogging. We find development of a number of technologies for keeping the physique sound. Small and big exercise machines are used for making the body slim and reducing the weight of body. We find a craze for a balanced physique in the western world. Of course, we find it gaining popularity even in the Indian society.

Our focus is on promoting Yoga by the personal care organisations working in the Indian environment. The renewed interest in Yoga is a welcome step. It is, of course, an encouraging development that a number of western countries have been found promoting Yoga. We find Yoga a beneficial system and an elegant way of regulating and exercising the mind, brain, the respiration and almost all the vital functions of the body. Proper Yoga can give us a feeling of well-being in the systems which no drug can give. It is high time that the personal care organisations assign due weightage to Yoga and include the same in their service mix.

The garment making centres need to promote Indian fashion. We can't deny that, of late, the western world has been found developing a craze for the Indian dresses. Like this, the shoemaking centres also need to promote designs helping us in looking smart. The dental care is an important dimension of personal care services. The personal care organisations, in addition to the promotion of medicated toothpaste, need to consider the instrumentality of "neem sticks" for washing teeth.

The aforesaid facts make it clear that we find enough scope for promoting Indian values and Indian prescriptions in the personal care services where it is possible to make the services economic. In addition, we also find dismal side-effects. This gravitates our attention on blending the Indian and western devices in such a way that in the long run even the western world develops a craze for the Indian prescriptions.

We consider promotion an important constituent of marketing and the personal care organisations are supposed to promote the services in such a way that the latest sophisticated communication technologies play an incremental role in promoting Indian values by sensitising the target prospects in a creative way. We can't deny that, of late, we have world-class advertising professionals *vis-a-vis* the world-class marketing communication technologies. It is hoped that the professionals are familiar with the reception faculty of different segments using the services. The main task before them is to understand their expectations and to inform, sense and persuade them in a right direction. On the one hand, the personal care organisations need to promote their services while on the other hand, they also need to assign a transcendental priority to the Indian culture. The advertising messages, themes, dresses and styles of characters selected for promoting the messages and events need to explore avenues for promoting Indian culture. The fashion magazines in particular need due attention since in a majority of the cases we find scenes, events sensitising prospects in general and the teens in particular moving in the wrong direction.

Since they are found more gullible in nature, there must be a code which is to regulate their behaviour. Of course, they need to promote their services but it is not meant that in the name of promotion, they start promoting taste perversion. The promotional decisions need cost economy because in addition to other aspects, we are also supposed to make possible cost-effectiveness, specially for rationalising the cost of services. Of late even in the Indian context, we find quality print materials and the world-class print technology. We need to use them in the Indian condition.

Another dimension of the marketing mix is pricing which occupies a place of outstanding significance, specially in the Indian perspective. The personal care organisations are required to maintain economy and to make the price structure optimal so that even the ordinary persons get an opportunity to use the services.

In almost all the services, we find scope for maintaining economy and we don't find the personal care organisations an exception to it. This is found essential to increase the number of users *vis-a-vis* the market share. By promoting the use of Indian prescriptions, we find enough scope for rationalising the price structure. The personal care organisations working in the Indian perspective need to make it possible.

Since we find development of some of the personal care organisations on a large scale, the process of offering the services is found significant. In this context, it is essential that personal care organisations assign due weightage to the management of employees in different branches or working at the different centres. The employees are required to be high performers. This draws our attention on the imparting of training facilities in tune with the development and evolving technologies. We can't expect employees to show their excellence as high performers unless we offer to them adequate incentives. This draws our attention on an incentive plan which is linked to efficiency. We also find cases where the personal care organisations don't need the services of employees and the users get the services directly from the organisations. It is quite natural that the personnel offering the services keep in their minds all the essentials that we find significant to the big organisations.

In the process of formulating a marketing mix, we find process emerging as a submix. This draws our attention on the processes used for offering the services to the ultimate users. Since we find it an age of technology, we cannot negate the role of technology in improving the quality of services. The actual procedures, mechanism and flow of activities need due care of marketers in the process. Currently, we find operating system in the personal care services mechanised which makes it essential that the personal care centres make use of new generation of technology. The involvement of skilled people in the process cannot be underrated. The beauty parlours, hairdressing centres, Gymnastics, dental care services can be innovated with technological support and expertise. The most important thing in the processing is time honoured and world-class services in tune with the promises made by the personal care centres.

Another marketing mix necessitating due attention is Physical Evidence and Attractions. It is right to mention that in the personal care services, we find physical facilities or servicescapes also influencing the behaviour of customers. The corporate culture is considerably influenced by attractions. The marketers making efforts to add additional attractions succeed whereas others not realising its important role fail. The ambient conditions play a significant role in changing the preferences of customers. The tangible components like light, music, interiors and exteriors, ventilation, equipment if tangibilised properly throw a positive impact on customers. You need to throw a soothing and cooling effect by displaying the features you have. The decorative items must need due attention of professionals managing the centres. Ultimately, we need a fragrance in the service ambience which is found in tune with the taste and temperament of customers. The entertainment facilities need due attention but we cannot undermine the taste preferences of customers.

Tangibilising the business cards and billing statements also generate a positive effect. The dresses or uniforms of people working for the personal care centres must be neat and clean. They should look smart and impressive. The positioning of equipment used in the process need a place drawing the attention of all. The marketers need to remember that servicescapes or the physical facilities is an important dimension of marketing mix which help the personal care centres in different ways. We find them outward impression of an organisation very much effective in projecting a positive image.

Globalisation of economy has paved avenues for the globalisation of fashion, culture and civilisation. The westernisation of Indian economy is the main contribution of corporatisation which has thrown a telling impact on our lifestyles. We find an attitudinal change in masses. This has been engineering a sound foundation for the development of the different streams of personal care services. This necessitates a professional touch in the personal care services so that the corporate sector gets people to be effective in generating service fragrance and adding additional attractions. We have potentials for the development of personal care service in an innovative fashion and our professional excellence can market them in a right way.

In the Indian perspective, it is imperative that we promote personal care centres even in the small towns and cities. The sensitive location points are shopping complexes, colleges, universities and the areas close to studios and theatres. With the development of corporate culture, we find emergence of material culture which has changed our lifestyles. This has opened new markets for the personal care services. The centres can be developed even in the rural areas where the housewives can develop beauty parlours for women as a cottage industry. The school-going and college-going girls have been found developing a craze for using the services like facial and hair cutting. We expect expansion of markets in almost all areas and therefore the available opportunities are to be capitalised on.

The personal care centres working in the Indian setting need a new vision which will make ways for creativity. The potential customers are available in a very good number in almost all the segments and by making use of professional excellence and personal touch, they can deliver quality services to the users. The working ladies find it a professional compulsion because this is closely related with the image of organisation. The housewives make use of personal care services because they want to look attractive. Thus, men or women, teens or youths, grey or retired, urban or rural segments are the potential users and we need to transform them into actual and habitual users. This is mainly due to the fact that recent developments in the field of information and communication technology has injected new life to our taste preferences and therefore the process of demand creation will continue even in future. Actually, if we have a sense; we explore opportunities and conversely, if we lack aesthetic sense; we make even the productive opportunities impotent. If we develop aesthetic sense; we develop optimism and if we develop optimism, it is natural that we evince interests in nature which may partially be with the business motive and partially with the motive of impressing upon our spouse.[3]

To gèt a success in the job markets or to justify the position we hold, it is pertinent that we assign due weightage to our look which preferably be classic in tune with the changing corporate requirements. This focuses our attention on a sound physique. From the very beginning, an individual is required to be conscious to the structure of their body. Today, we find a number of Gym centres which may help us in the process. Besides, we also need to promote Yoga and Pranayam for sound physique. The dresses used by us need to have a correlation with our profession.

The wave of corporatisation will continue even in the days and years to come. We cannot negate that attraction is the most important thing in corporate management. We need fragrance in service ambience and for its creation, our aesthetic sense carry some meaning.

SUMMARY

In this chapter, you have gone through different components of personal care marketing. Before concluding the chapter, be sure that the following facts are well versed.

Personal Care Marketing — The Concept: Personal care marketing focuses on the application of marketing principles in the personal care services. We find it a managerial process where professionals are engaged to offer the services, such as the services offered by beauty parlours, hairdressing, physical soundness, dental care or so.

Users of the Personal Care Services: The different categories of users are business executives, cine/TV/ theatre artists, models, advertisement professionals, domestic and foreign tourists, front-line staff of the business organisations, brides and bridegrooms decorated for wedding and reception functions.

Behavioural Profile of Users: The sophistication in communication has changed our lifestyles *vis-a-vis* the expectations. The use of technologies has shaped new perception of quality. The professionals need to study behavioural profile so that they succeed in identifying the level of expectations.

Market Segmentation for the Personal Care Organisations: The professionals need to segment the market so that the expectations of different segments and sub-segments, such as teens and youths, men and women, business executives and cine artists, advertising characters and models or so are studied in a right fashion.

Marketing Information System for Personal Care Organisations: With the changing business environment, we find a change in our lifestyles. The emerging trends in income, education, transportation, communication, profession influence lifestyles substantially. The marketing information system helps in identifying the emerging trends.

Formulation of Marketing Mix for the Personal Care Organisations: The marketing professionals bear the responsibility of formulating a sound marketing mix in which product mix, promotion mix, price mix, place mix and the people mix are blended optimally.

The Product Mix: The formulation of a sound product mix necessitates a fair synchronisation of core and peripheral services. The marketing professionals need to innovate the product mix. The designing of a sound product portfolio is found important. They also need to develop a sound package that acts as a motivational tool.

The Promotion Mix: The quality services need to be promoted suitably. The different constituents of promotion, such as advertising, publicity, sales promotion, word-of-mouth promotion, personal selling and telemarketing need due attention of marketing professionals so that the users are informed, sensed and persuaded in an effective way.

The Price Mix: The marketing professionals find it significant to make the pricing decisions rational so that the price structure is remunerative to the personal care organisations *vis-a-vis* affordable to the target users.

The Place Mix: The channelisation of services for the personal care centres may also be direcly to the users with the help of people and technology used for service delivery. The leading centres may also have different branches for service delivery.

The Process Mix: The processing of personal care services are found with the help of experts. The actual procedures, mechanism and flow of activities are taken into consideration for delivering the promised quality of services.

Physical Evidence and Attractions: In this submix of the marketing mix, we find marketers concentrating on physical facilities available in the personal care centres which may also be known as servicescapes. The lighting, music, scent, ventilation, aesthetic management, equipment need tangibilisation for adding additional attractions to the services. In addition, the uniforms or dresses of people serving the centres need to be neat and clean. They should look attractive and smart.

The People: The people serving the personal care centres are found of two categories, such as technical people performing the services and administrative people managing the affairs. They need personal and professional touch in the service delivery process so that the customers are found satisfied.

Personal Care Marketing in Indian Perspective: With corporatisation, we find significant changes in our lifestyles. We find aesthetic sense occupying a place of outstanding significance for adding additional attractions. A number of services such as beauty parlours, hairdressing, gymnastics, jogging, garment making, dental care, body-weight care, nutrition, hygiene, yoga have been found gaining popularity because we find masses becoming much more conscious to the physique and healthcare. Emerging as a dimension of personality development, the personal care services have a profitable market even in the Indian perspective. Both the rural and urban people have developed temptation for that and therefore we need development of services on an organised basis. This will help us not only in capitalising on the opportunities available in the Indian markets but would also help people in developing health-consciousness. There are a number of special occasions when we find big demand for personal care services, specially the services of beauty parlours and hairdressing. If we develop them on an organised basis with a professional touch, the customers will get quality services. This necessitates conceptualisation of marketing principles in the personal care services so that the customers get services in tune with their taste preferences. The marketers in the very context need to develop their awareness of the lifestyles of customers which have been found changing very fast. The imprint of western culture on the personal care services makes it essential that the centres engaged in offering the services formulate a product mix commensurate with the professional, situational and personal requirements of customers. The craze for looking attractive will continue to develop even in the years to come and therefore, the personal care centres will require world-class excellence to capitalise on the tremendous opportunities.

KEY TERMS

Elegance
Aesthetic Sense
Aesthete
Beauty Parlours
Gym
Jogging
Corporate Look
Barber Shops
Yoga
Brides
Bridegrooms
Herbals
Front-line Personnel
Models
Air Hostess
Physical Therapay
Service Fragrance
Cosmetics
Peripheral Services
Nutrition
Hygiene
Metropolises
Catchment Area
Points of Location
Service Ambience
Servicescapes
Interiors
Tangibilisation
Ambient Conditions
Product Uniqueness
Efficacious
Ongtan
Turmeric
Classic Look

Review Questions

1. What do you mean by Personal Care Services? Focus on the marketing of personal care services in the face of corporatisation.
2. Define Personal Care Marketing. Explain the different categories of users of personal care services.
3. Throw light on the behavioural profile of users of personal care services.
4. State and explain market segmentation to identify the levels of expectations of users of personal care services.
5. What do you mean by Marketing Information System? Explain the relevance of information for personal care marketers.
6. Discuss the different submixes of marketing in the face of personal care services.
7. Explain the extended marketing mix for personal care services.
8. Focus on the personal care marketing in the Indian perspective.

Application Exercises

1. As a marketer, formulate a marketing mix for the beauty parlours.
2. You are working as a marketer in the personal care centres offering beauty parlour and hair dressing services. Suggest the measures to help the promotion of business.
3. As a marketing professional, you bear the responsibility of bridging the gap between services-promised and services-offered. Explain the various considerations to help you in the process.
4. Focus on the segments found profitable for the personal care services in the Indian perspective.
5. A beauty parlour centre wants to innovate its servicescapes. As a marketer, throw light on the measures to help an improvement in the service ambience.
6. Focus on the location points you find suitable for the beauty parlours and Gymnastic Centre.
7. As a marketer, focus on the target market to be touched in the rural areas for promoting the personal care services.

Endnotes

1. Jha, S.M., Marketing of Personal Care Services, *Planned Selling,* Annual Volume, 1989, New Delhi.
2. Jha, S.M. and Singh, L.P., Marketing Management in Indian Perspective, *Personal Care Service,* Himalaya Publishing House, Mumbai, 1988.
3. Jha, S.M., Looks Make a Man, *Hindustan Times*, April, 17, 2000.

EDUCATION MARKETING

Globalisation has been found opening new vistas for the development of thematical competence through new system of education but inculcation of ethical dimensions which happened to be the base of ancient Indian education system is found vanishing very fast. This necessitates structural transformation.

Chapter Objectives

Introduction – Innovative Education: Why and How? – Literacy: The Concept – Functional Literacy – The Concept – The Emerging Trends – Marketing Literacy: The Concept – Segmentation in Education – Understanding the Behavioural Profile – Education Information System – Marketing Mix for Adult Education – Strategic Marketing for Adult Education – Marketing Mix for Elementary Education – Strategic Marketing Mix for Elementary Education – Marketing Mix for Secondary Education – Strategic Marketing for Secondary Education – Marketing Mix for Intermediate Education – Marketing Mix for Higher Education – Strategic Marketing Mix for Higher Education – Changing Role of Marketing Professionals in Education Marketing – Consumer Protection Regulations for Educational Institutions – Summary – Key Terms – Review Questions – Application Exercises – Endnotes.

Learning Objectives

This chapter aims at studying the different dimensions of education marketing. The readers develop their awareness of the conceptualisation of innovative marketing principles in the educational services offered at different stages by the different organisations both in the public and private sectors. The motive of this chapter is to sensitise the readers to the role of innovative marketing in the improvement of quality. The globalisation necessitates a system of education which is to meet the changing global requirements. The government as well as the private educational institutions would immensely be benefited by applying the modern marketing principles with a societal approach.

INTRODUCTION

In an age of material culture where human capital formation plays a commanding role in accelerating the pace of economic transformation, the crying need of Indian society is to make the educational institutions highly productive. Particularly in the Indian society, the statesmen and social activists have been found very much critical to the privatisation of education. Of course, we find their critical views in the face of poor purchasing capacity of the general masses but what about the mounting cost of inputs used for innovating the system of education. Will the states exchequer bear the brunt due to mounting costs? Can we allow the educational institutions to offer substandard services, specially in an age of globalisation? Can we allow the educational institutions to face the stage of financial disaster? Can we allow the society to remain academically backward? Of course, the answers to all the questions in plain are "No."

Globalisation of economy has been opening new vistas for the globalisation of education where our focus is on developing education in tune with the changing global requirements. Our problem on account of high rate of demography will be considerably simplified if we make possible qualitative improvements in the system of education which necessitate the educational institutions to be financially sound but we find a majority of the educational institutions either in India or abroad facing the problem of financial of crunch. It is very natural that qualitative improvements in the system of education will require huge investments on input such as books, journals, magazines, audiovisual exposure devices, powerpoint presentation, internet services, facilities for audiovisual conferencing and so on. Besides, they will also need quality faculty and rich lab and the supporting infrastructural facilities. The statesmen are critical to hike in fee; the governments are not financially solvent to increase grants and the concept of charities and donations have not been getting smooth conceptualisation. This has been throwing the educational institutions, particularly managed by the public sector, in the reverse gear. We bear the responsibility of bringing the educational system back on the rail and this makes a strong advocacy in favour of applying social marketing principles in the educational institutions. Excellence in education is our motive which cannot be targeted unless we have world-class professional excellence.

We cannot negate that quality education would open new avenues to the upcoming youths because they can capitalise on the opportunities globally available and this will make the expenses on education an investment of productive nature for that the parents will have to bring a basic change in their attitudes.

An attitudinal change in the users of educational services necessitates a fundamental change in the nature and character of service profile. The educational institutions owing the responsibility of offering to the society culturally-sound, value-based, cost-effective and world-class services, need to perceive the emerging trends in a right fashion, Attitudes influence expectations which govern the formulation of marketing mix. The professionals bear the responsibility of orchestrating the marketing recourses found optimal to the emerging challenges and evolving developments. If the process of change keeps on moving in the right direction and you keep your eyes open, the marketing decisions are found proactive. Since you have identified the emerging trends and emerging challenges, the process of tailoring of marketing resources will, of course, be result-oriented.

During the yesterdecades, techniculture has been successful in having its telling impact on almost all the sectors. We find the business sector, international sector and the non-profit sector considerably influenced by the multi-dimensional change in the social environment. The sophistication in the process of transportation and communication and concerted efforts for transforming the information movement into knowledge movement has transformed the globe into a village in which the transmission process has been very fast. Against this background, we find developments taking place in one part of the world reaching to another part just in few minutes.

The users and potential users of educational services at all the levels and in almost all the segments have developed an awareness which has basically altered their expectations. The parents, of late, spend huge amounts for imparting educational aid and training facilities to their children with the hope that after the completion of education they would get a profitable return and this made possible transformation of expenditure into investment. The users are now sensitive to quality and if they get world-class educational aid, the fee structure will not be a barrier. The professionals need to perceive it and offer services in time in tune with the changing levels of expectations of users so that the interests of both the providers and receivers are optimally blended.

Of course, the process of quality innovation assumes an outstanding significance in almost all the areas but we find education at the top because by improving the quality of education, we open new vistas to all the sectors and organisations and the moment an organisation gets a team of quality people, the process of qualitative transformation *vis-a-vis* value engineering is not only switched on but is found moving forward with high speed and pace. If we talk about marketing education services, our focuses is not only on increasing the rate of literacy but a step ahead on world-class education which makes users potentially-sound to capitalise on the opportunities at both domestic and global levels.

Literacy paves the way for education which engineers a sound foundation for the development of knowledge. If we succeed in developing knowledge, our success in developing professional excellence cannot be negated. If we succeed in developing professional excellence, the managerial proficiency would help profit or not-for-profit making organisations in subserving the organisational interests *vis-a-vis* the interests of consumers and society. It was against this background that the great classical thinker Mahatma Gandhi focused on removing illiteracy and expanded its purview to the development of knowledge. He considered illiteracy a sin and strongly advocated assigning number one priority to its eradication on the agenda of social transformation.

The rate of literacy in India, it is about 76 per cent for males and 54 per cent for females (Census-2001). Of course, we have been successful in minimising illiteracy but our efforts and investments (inputs) are yet to establish an edge over the actual results (outputs). In addition to other aspects, we have also failed in formulating generally managed by the state governments and contributing to the literacy rate sizeably, bear the responsibility of offering to children elementary education. In addition, a number of private school and other formal and informal agencies also are offering elementary education to children. We also find adult education centres trying to erase adult illiteracy. Despite such multi-pronged efforts to promote elementary education, we are well aware of the non-optimal contributions of these centres of learning to the defined goals.

The parents living in rural areas, specially coming from weaker sections, promote their children to make a good-bye to schools and to support them financially. Thus, the drop-out ratio in these schools is increasing fast. The teachers do not evince personal interests in motivating children since the policy makers have not to put accountability on their shoulders. This necessitates innovation in the policy decisions where both the teachers and parents are made jointly responsible for the upward trend in drop-out ratio. The teachers should also be motivated to literate adults, of course, in the off hours. Thus, the need of the hour is to market literacy programmes in such a way that with the minimum possible investment, we succeed in getting the maximum possible result.

The secondary schools, colleges, institutes, universities bear the responsibility of educating and developing knowledge. Both the private and public sectors are found engaged in the process. The policies and strategies again stand as a barrier. We do not find a correlation between our requirements and potentials. A gap in the demand and supply position thus generates unemployment, poverty, social tension and so on. Except a very few, almost all the educational institutions are found in a depleted condition. The financial constraint stands as a major barrier since the costs of inputs have gone up and the mobilisation of internal financial resources from the outputs is very nominal. This imbalance in input-output and a mismatch in demand and supply make the educational institutions financially bankrupt which restrains their efficacy of delivering the goods to the society. How can we expect outputs to be productive when the mismatch in demand and supply position is to continue? The crying need of the hour is to remove the mismatch and imbalance which necessitates an innovative marketing strategy. This gravitates our attention on marketing education. Here, our emphasis is not on selling education since we name them not-for-profit-making organisations. In a very natural way, the emerging problems focus our attention on making such a provision or adopting such a policy for the fee structure which offers an opportunity even to the poorer and weaker sections of the society to taste the sweetness and fragrance of reputed schools, offering world-class services.

This chapter makes an attempt to study the various dimensions of marketing education. We start from the marketing of literacy since a strong foundation can only allow us to construct a strong building bearing the efficacy of facing the threats and challenges albeit in a rough weather. For activating the process of socio-economic transformation, it is pertinent to increase the rate of human capital formation. The educational institutions bear the responsibility of accelerating the rate by improving the standard of education. But here they also bear the responsibility of protecting the culture. The time-tested norms are required to be maintained and every chance of an invasion on culture is to be checked. This is not only essential to protect our cultural heritage, to safeguard the civilisation but also to promote ethical values, work culture, organisational culture and national excellence. If educational institutions do not assign due weightage to these components, how we can expect a statesman showing dedication and a sense of commitment to nation, the team of policy makers having a social orientation, an executive formulating a sound mix for the time-honoured and cost-effective implementation of policy decisions, the persons engaged in white-collar jobs working honestly and efficiently, and a teacher playing a decisive role in developing quality of human resources and transforming the society. Only professionally-sound cultured outputs can help us in these directions. In a true sense, culture is the most sensitive device to promote excellence and ethical values.

We go through the various dimensions of education marketing which necessitate a basic change in our policy decisions. Educational institutions, public or private, are supposed to accelerate the rate of human capital formation. This is possible when they have a defined goal, a set target and a well thought strategy. Right from the first stage of learning to the last stage of developing knowledge, they are supposed to subserve the social interests, *vis-a-vis* organisational and the national interests, of course, both are interrelated. The crying need of the hour is to innovate education and to market it in such a way that institutions and students both are found benefited.

INNOVATIVE EDUCATION: WHY AND HOW?

Innovation is to devise the way which simplifies the task of touching the target. If we talk about innovative education, our emphasis is on changing the system of education, of course, helping us in making the human resources productive. Carl Rogers (1962) and Shoemaker (1971) identified some important properties for innovation, e.g., relative advantage, compatibility, complexity, trialability and observability. The only thing that we find significant in the process is to have a new idea which succeeds in establishing an edge over the social evils. Of course, the idea should be efficacious in serving all the related persons/institutions, such as educational institutions, students, teachers, society and ultimately the nation. Against this background, we go through innovative education in the Indian setting. A number of social thinkers and educationists have gone through the problem and felt about education more or less in the same way. Mahatma Gandhi, Rabindra Nath Tagore, Bertrand Russell, Maria Montessori and Forabel are some of the noble thinkers whose views and ideas have been taken for developing a model for elementary education. As and when we try to activate the innovation process, it is very natural that we keep in our minds the changing national and international requirements *vis-a-vis* the socio-cultural factors. This is esessential to counter the multi-faceted social evils.

Let's start from the educational philosophy of Mahatma Gandhi.[1] To be more specific, for child education, his idea is found noble. He focused on self-sufficiency which paves ways for self-employment. He advocated that after the completion of school education, the students should be in a position to generate employment opportunities. This is possible when they are aware of the fundamentals of almost all the subjects. Even to a literate adult, men or women, we find his idea suitable. To be more specific, for rural India, the philosophy of Mahatma Gandhi is found more impact generating. Gandhiji wanted free and compulsory education for those in the age group 7 to 14. He preferred education which covers all the subjects which concern our own country, our people, our life and our physical and social environment. He strongly advocated crafts to be the main subject of education. He also emphasised that education must transfer the axge old spiritual traditions of our land.

If we go through his philosophy, it is right to opine that at least elementary education should be restructured in the face of Gandhian philosophy. Of late, we talk about unemployment, environment, ethical and cultural values and these properties are possible when we innovate the elementary education. Even we talk about technology, he always favoured appropriate technology that we can develop with the help of our own efforts and own materials.

Rabindra Nath Tagore's[2] idea is nothing but a matter of truth. Tagore substantially focused on informal education. He felt that education should be able to develop faculties in children. He was of the opinion that arts and crafts, drawing, painting, music, dancing should be a part-and-parcel of education. He believed that education should kindle the feeling of oneness in children. Developing spiritual unity in the nation was his main theme of education. He wanted science to be taught at higher level and world history to be learned by all children.

Bertrand Russell,[3] the British philosopher-cum-mathematician has also gone through the problem of education. He advocated to include discipline like language, history, geography, science, psychology, philosophy and sociology. He focused on the role of society in cultivating desirable and acceptable change or changes in the social order. He applied his mind equally, on the one hand, to the problems of logic and metaphysics and on the other hand, the social, political and educational issues.

Maria Montessori,[4] a doctor of medicine from the University of Rome, felt that education is the active help given to the normal expansion of the life of a child. Montessori believed that self-education is the best device to educate the children. Against this background, she emphasised the need for children's house where teachers are supposed to act as an observer.

Forbel,[5] a German educationist is known as the father of kindergarten concept which is meant a garden for children in which they can develop. He suggested pre-school education for children below 5 years. He advocated play way, songs, essential for their learning.

In view of the aforesaid thinkers, philosophers and educationists, it is right to say that the education system in India is not moving in the right direction. This draws our attention on the innovation process. Almost all the experts realise that social values, environmental conditions, extracurricular activities and informal education play an outstanding role in shaping the destiny of today's children in tune with the changing social, cultural, economic, national and international requirements. In the Indian perspective, where we find unemployment problem at its peak, social disorder gaining a rapid momentum, ethical values getting no place and an invasion on culture aggravated by almost all the organisations and institutions, we need to think about innovating the system of education at almost all the levels.

To be more specific, children's education and particularly in the rural areas, we need more concentration. In addition, we need a special task force to educate and train the females/women, living in villages. Both the formal and informal, public and private schools have to follow the guidelines. They need quality inputs to produce the quality outputs, since quality outputs bear the efficacy of acting like an atom in the socio-economic molecule.[6] If we succeed in innovating education, a number of socio-economic problems would automatically be thrown in the reverse gear. If we succeed in blending professional and ethical dimensions optimally,[7] our social and industrial organisations would pave ways for a qualitative transformation in which we do not find a place for socio-cultural confrontation. We are supposed to market education not as a profit making organisation rather than as a not-for-profit making organisation.

Of late, we find the environmental conditions more volatile. This in a very natural way complicates the task of a decision-maker since now he/she needs the efficacy of working efficiently even in a rough weather. If we succeed in developing human resources having more professional excellence, the task of facing the multi-dimensional changes and threats in the present business world would considerably be simplified. This is possible when the policy makers evince their interests in formulating a policy which paves ways for developing a service mix in which we find a fair blending of three important elements, e.g., profit generation, customer satisfaction and social orientation. Here, our emphasis is on education which is a product of not-for-profit-making organisation. The generation of profits by the educational institutions is till now a debatable topic. However, we find nothing wrong in the profit generation process, if it is based on a rational pricing strategy. The changing scenario across the country makes it essential that our outputs (human resources developed) are nationally and internationally competitive and at the same time, socially and culturally acceptable. It is in this context that we talk about a fair synchronisation of professional excellence and ethical values. Very surprisingly, we often talk about organisational culture, we frequently comment on the absence of dedication and commitment in the stock of our outputs, we always talk about zero work culture but never try to focus our attention on the roots. If we produce substandard outputs, how we can expect a fair return. To be more specific in the Indian condition, we find this problem at peak since by and large almost all the educational institutions find it difficult to make their value addition process cost-effective which decelerates the rate of productivity and ultimately questions their existence then what to talk of making them internationally competitive?

In view of the emerging problems, the crying need of the hour is to innovate the system of education. Right from the elementary education to the higher education, the innovation process is to be practised. No doubt, a number of constraints would crop-up on way but we have no option. The strategic marketing would help us in bringing things on the rail. The motive is to produce quality people who are high performers. We cannot deny the fact that we need more job opportunities and the sophisticated technologies would complicate our task. At the same time, we cannot allow stagnation in the development process simply to generate job opportunities. The need of the hour is to find out a solution which creates more job opportunities in the services sector. As for example, if we locate educational institutions, hospitals, personal care complexes close to the rural areas or in the outskirts of big towns and cities; a strong foundation would be engineered for urbanisation of rural areas. The villages would develop and migration of rural population to the urban areas would be checked sizeably. The main thing that we need to care is value engineering areas.

LITERACY — THE CONCEPT

The term literacy connotes a person able to read, write and understand or an educated person without a university degree. The term literacy is a condition of being literate. Thus, the actual meaning of literacy is basically related to knowledge of alphabets which helps a person to read and write. Against this background, we go through the marketing of literacy. The perception of illiteracy includes persons of all age groups (above 5) who should have the knowledge of alphabets but they lack. It is not confined to any gender or race. We consider it beneficial to all the human beings. Thus, in simple words, the knowledge which helps for the fulfilment of the objectives of life is known as literacy.

FUNCTIONAL LITERACY — THE CONCEPT

When we talk about the term 'functional literacy,' our emphasis is here on a certain level of literacy. If this certain level is absent, it is created through functional literacy as a basic instrument of change. Industrialisation and modernisation of agriculture require professional skills and real ability. This is not possible unless a person is functionally literate.

THE EMERGING TRENDS

Before we go through other problems, it is essential that we are aware of the present position *vis-a-vis* the past tren. During the last sixty years, a number of steps have been taken to increase the rate of literacy but till now we have not been successful in getting a satisfactory result. In 1951, it was about 25 per cent and even till the last census in 2001, it is 52 per cent only for males and 39 per cent only for females.[8] It is also significant to mention that earlier, we had included persons above 5 but in 2001 census we have included persons above 7 age group. This makes it clear that actually it is even less than 50 per cent for males and 30 per cent for females. The emerging trends testify the lukewarm response of our policies and programmes for increasing the rate of literacy. Our concern here is to market literacy in such a way that without any regional, race or gender bias, the illiteracy in all age groups above 5 is minimised considerably. Let's market it efficiently so that we succeed in having total literacy, latest by the end of 12th Plan.

MARKETING LITERACY — THE CONCEPT

An important question may be raised here that why we do use the term marketing for literacy. Since we have been investing huge amount of money and deploying a good number of personnel and sophisticated technologies to literate the masses, it is judicious to know about the results. If we invest more for removing illiteracy (inputs) but the literacy (outputs) is not increasing proportionately, the policy would be deemed to be unproductive since it is cost-ineffective. The very essence of marketing is to make our policies and programmes cost-effective so that we cross the target or at least even touch the target without crossing the financial and time limits. The marketing practices bear the efficacy of improving the input-output ratio since we frame a service mix keeping in view the sensitivity of target prospects, attempt to promote the same by using modern sophisticated devices, frame a fee structure in the face of holistic concept of management and channelise the services with the support of efficient and personally-committed personnel acting and behaving professionally, of course, in the Indian style, and Indian tone.

In view of the aforesaid facts, we use the term marketing for literacy, education and development of knowledge. Here, it is also to be clarified that by using the term marketing we are not bound to generate profits. Since most of the not-for-profit making organisations are now found liberal to the generation of profits, it is also significant to mention that whatever they generate as surplus should essentially be reinvested or ploughed back for the development and expansion of world-class services. The simple logic in using the term marketing is to make available to the prospects the quality services either free of cost or for the fee structure they are supposed to pay. The marketing practices would simplify the processes of qualitative-cum-quantitative transformation in the process of efficiency generation.

SEGMENTATION IN EDUCATION

Being a marketing professional, it is your prime responsibility to develop your awareness of the users of different segments so that you are in a position to identify the levels of their expectations. The rural, and urban, men and women, children, youth and grey segments as well as east and west; educated and illiterate and rich and poor segments need your due attention. Because you market the education services helping different segments while enriching their potentials — it is pertinent that you make an in-depth study of their preferences. You promote adult education and literacy; you promote primary, secondary and vocational education; you promote professional, technical, medical and general education and the priorities and preferences in all these areas may or may not be identical. One thing is, however, almost clear that in almost all the areas, we find users becoming sensitive enough to quality. This makes it necessary that you enrich your knowledge bank about the developments taking place globally. Your product should essentially be innovative and productive so that the parents investing on their wards, are able to get a return on their investments within a time-frame.

The process of segmentation will help you in understanding the users and their preferences which in turn will guide you while tailoring the marketing resources so that not only the quality is improved but the process of generation also becomes cost-effective. Because we find people coming from the poor segment, it is important that your professional excellence helps in rationalising the fee structure keeping in view the fact that the process is not to harm organisational interests. If we find educational institutions financially solvent, the process of innovation will not be delayed and this will serve different segments of the users in many ways.

Of late, we find government-managed educational institutions in a sorry state mainly due to the fact that they are financially bankrupt. On account of financial constraint, the process of innovation is delayed and degeneration starts. Of course, we find users charged nominally or get even cost-free services but whatever they get in the name of quality are not to help them to capitalise on the opportunities nationally or globally. Ultimately, they prove to be a liability both for their families and the society.

If you keep on moving the process of understanding the expectations of users, you will promote innovations paving the way for qualitative transformation, and resulting from which not only the users are benefited but also the educational institutions, society and ultimately the nation get the benefits in different ways. The task of satisfying the users is easier because your promotional measures have become not only cost-effective but even sensitive and proactive because you are creative.

In recent years, we find vocational, professional and technical courses gravitating due attention of users and potential users since they find it convenient to secure a job. Therefore, the educational institutions in general need to perceive the changing needs and requirements of the users and make possible a structural change in the system of education which would require due focus on making curriculum commensurate with their needs and requirements *vis-à-vis* the levels of expectations. Thus, we find segmentation a process helping professionals in understanding the users and potential users. An in-depth study of the behavioural profile, identification of lapses and shortcomings, elimination and inclusion processes are also easier because we process everything in the context of an advanced information system.

UNDERSTANDING THE BEHAVIOURAL PROFILE

Of late, we find behavioural studies drawing due attention of marketing professionals. The individual as well as the organisational behaviour require an in-depth study. As and when we talk about marketing, our prime attention is on satisfaction. Since you are aware of the levels of expectations of users, it is easier for you to satisfy them. Today's users are sensitive to the quality of services they are offered. They are fascinated not only by the quality but even decency. The marketing professionals have to understand users' expectations and offer services in a decent way. This draws our attention on the behavioural profile of providers. The faculty, receptionists, front-line staff in general, and the public relations officers are expected to be decent. The behavioural profile of people serving educational institutions has to be improved to add additional attractions to the service mix. The training facilities, refresher and orientation courses, and interactions will help in improving decent behaviour. When one thinks of improving the quality of services; a number of efforts are needed. A big budget is to be prepared and multi-faceted efforts are to be cultivated. When the people realise the instrumentality of decent behaviour in sensitising and influencing the users and potential users, it brings a change in their profile; you start getting the results. Of course, you need to promote training facilities to improve the behavioural profile of your people, specially subordinates but it should not be forgotten that if you do not invite or welcome ego conflict, they get an opportunity to study your behaviour and ultimately you become their model, They start learning from you and the process of training is completed without any investment. Conversely, if they find your behaviour indecent and aggressive even if the training programmes and refresher courses are creative; the results will be negative or lukewarm.

Studying and understanding the behaviour and making sincere and innovative efforts to improve the profile rest on your shoulders and you have to get the positive results. You have to act both as a professional and a trainer. Because you have an advanced education information system, the task will not be complicated since at each and every stage, you seek the co-operation of the system. Particularly, the institutions offering primary education have to pay due attention because the users of the services, being gullible, are very sensitive. They start copying your behaviour and the accountability of degeneration or deviation will be on your shoulders. But it is not meant that the educational institutions offering secondary and higher education are not concerned with the problem. The concept and perception of education marketing is gaining popularity even at the secondary and higher stages. Hence, you need to practise it without making any sectoral discrimination.

Emerging trends in income, increasing pressure of demography, impact of transportation, communication and information, instrumentality of education in the social system, orientation to customs, traditions and culture, regional and cultural bias are some of the indicators helping you while studying and understanding the behavioural profile of different segments of users, if you are well-informed, your functional responsibility will become easier.

EDUCATION INFORMATION SYSTEM

The soundness of managerial decisions is considerably influenced by the management of information. Educational institutions at all the levels and stages need to improve the quality of their decisions. And, for this purpose, they should be well supported by a technology-driven information system. The professionals with an in-depth study of the different segments will be in a position to know about the feedback and the elimination; inclusion processes can be made more result-oriented. The ultimate motto is increasing the number of satisfied group of users which will not be possible unless the educational institutions offer time-honoured services. A computer-driven information system will make their task easier. Whether we think about improving the quality of adult education, primary or secondary and higher education, getting a feedback at right time is significant and the information system makes it possible. The tailoring of the marketing resources to change the nature and character of service profile is based on reporting and the system helps even in this context. At all the stages of imparting educational aid and training facilities, we realise the instrumentality of informal education and how to process, the Decision Supporting System (DSS) is to guide you. Your efforts are always to be productive *vis-à-vis* result-oriented if we find them based on information system. In the system of education, we find extracurricular activities getting due place and whatever improvements you need to make, the system will let you know. The formulation of a sound curriculum will be impact generating, and with the help of a technology-driven information system, you do it in an effective way. In a true sense, the marketing professionals find it easier to improve the quality of their decisions, if the organisations assign an overriding priority to the development of a sound Education Information System (EIS).

In the context of vocational, professional, technical and medical courses, we find frequent changes and the educational institutions not incorporating them in their curriculum suffer a lot. On the other hand, the institutions promoting the same succeed in capitalising on the opportunities. Professionals who considerably depend on the education information system find it easier to increase frequency and promote accuracy. They are well aware of the changing levels of expectations of the users and potential users. Therefore, the opportunities are not only capitalised but even created. This helps educational institutions in becoming innovative because, at all the stages and levels, they derive the benefits of the innovations by offering new services which attract the users at large.

The promotional measures can also be made sensitive because the professionals make creativity possible. The task of developing mass awareness regarding child education, women and adult education becomes easier because you are able to make the advertisement and publicity media more and more sensitive. This also helps you rating the frequency of innovations, testing the duration of display, making promotion but only sensitive but cost-effective. You are also in a position to make your motivational plans more productive, because on the basis of information system, you link compensation to contributions of an individual or a group. Thus, it is imperative that the educational institutions make sincere efforts to develop a sound Education Information System (EIS).

MARKETING MIX FOR ADULT LITERACY

Product Mix: No doubt, the word "literacy" focuses on the knowledge of alphabets but keeping in view the changing needs of society and economy, it is pertinent that we change the perception. Unless we have a right perception of the subject, the service mix cannot be formulated in a right fashion. To frame a time-honoured syllabi, it is essential that we are well aware of the target. In modern society, an individual cannot protect his/her existence unless he/she is well aware of the fundamentals. Mechanisation of agriculture and domination of hi-tech driven industrial economy make it essential that we assign due weightage to the functional literacy and integrate the same with the formal education. It was against this background that way back in 1972, the UNESCO Tokyo Conference had suggested integration of adult education with the formal education.[9] This helps a person to develop the faculty to thrive even in a rough weather. So far as the adult education is concerned, the functional literacy can solve our problem but here it is significant that we blend even the informal education in the product mix or service mix. We go through elementary education exclusively since educational facilities for kids and children need an innovative approach, a new vision. We club child education or elementary education under the head marketing literacy since our literacy percentage is substantially contributed by them.

Thus, to market the literacy programme for adults, at the outset we go through the service mix which helps adults in capitalising on the opportunities. Since they bear the responsibility of contracting the unemployment problem, it is essential that right from the knowledge of alphabets to the imparting of vocational education, we do not underestimate the recent developments in the modern society. They should have a fundamental knowledge of the subject in tune with their aptitude. Besides, the service mix needs to assign due weightage to the informal education. This would pave ways for work culture *vis-a-vis* the organisational culture.

In Figure 16.1, we find a plan to formulate the product mix/service mix by the agencies involved in the process of promoting adult education. We find two important areas for adult education, e.g., formal and informal. In the formal education, the participating agencies are supposed to develop knowledge in tune with their aptitude. This would help adult literates in contributing to the process of making a sustainable society. The illiterates in this process are not only given the knowledge of alphabets but in addition, the functional education becomes an important part of the same. At this stage, they get a basic knowledge of the subjects and after this, the knowledge is developed in tune with their aptitude, specially to develop expertise in the face of changing environmental conditions.

In addition, we also make here informal education a part-and-parcel of adult education programme. This appears essential to generate civic sense, create nutritional awareness, health consciousness, cultural and ethical values and national excellence.

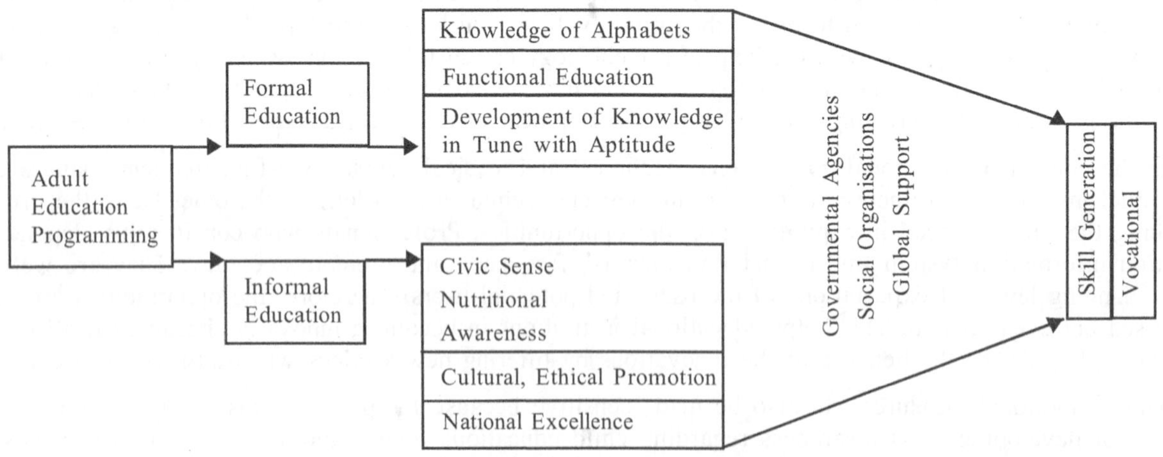

Fig. 16.1: Adult Education Programming

Thus, a fair blending of formal and informal education transforms the unproductive adult illiterates into a productive human capital. If we educate adult illiterates (women), we educate a family and keep on the circle of human capital formation moving forward. In addition to the central and state governments, a number of social organisations are also engaged in the process of removing adult illiteracy. Besides, UNESCO has also been supporting national agencies in the very context. Despite of huge investments and extensive efforts to eradicate illiteracy, we are lagging far behind USA, Canada, Japan, Switzerland, France, Netherland, Australia, UK where the rate of adult literacy is 99 per cent. What to talk of developed countries, even we are much behind Sri Lanka where it is more than 88 per cent.[10] The need of the hour is to improve the rate of literacy, to make the human resources productive, to accelerate the rate of human capital formation and to transform the liabilities into assets.

Promotion Mix: Promotion is considered to be the most sensitive mix of marketing which helps transformation of marketing policies and strategies into the meaningful actions. The participating agencies here bear the responsibility of informing and motivating the users (adult illiterates) in such a way that the turn-up ratio is increased considerably. The agencies to be more specific in the rural areas, find it difficult to promote the literacy programme since the prospects do not evince their interests. This draws our attention on creativity in the promotional decisions. For influencing the rural prospects, we find the instrumentality of audiovisual exposure of high magnitude and it is therefore the AIR and DD1 and other private TV channels are supposed to play here an effective role. The advertisement decisions need here an intensive care. The advertising agencies, media and the professionals engaged in the advertisement business have to make the adult literacy programmes more sensitive. The slogans, messages, appeals if positive, can make the advertisement programmes more effective. The professionals engaged in designing advertisement layouts, composing slogans, preparing TV serials or radio dramas should have an in-depth idea of the target prospects. The selection of characters and events also play here an important role. The cine artists or TV stars found more popular in the religious/devotional serials and movies have been found throwing positive impact on the rural prospects in particular. The media, TV channels are supposed to allot the duration time of televising a particular programme in the face of prospects. We cannot negate that after mid-1980s and to be more specific during 1990s, TV has gained popularity even in the rural areas. National Literacy Mission (NLM) has been found advertising through AIR/DD1. Besides, the private TV channels also need to promote Adult Education Programme.

It is not to be forgotten that for promoting adult literacy, the voluntary social organisations have also been instrumental. Since the audiovisual medium has been more effective, the concerned organisations should prefer TV/radio for advertising the messages, slogans or serials/telefilm. The professionals are not supposed to forget that rural prospects in particular are not so receptive. Against this background, they need to prepare a programme based on extensive research. The motive is to influence the prospects who are insensitive. To seek public participation in the activating process, it is also essential that we advertise in the popular daily newspapers. The songs and drama division of the central government, other drama/art centres/animation film, puppet show, folk songs, etc. are found more effective to sensitise the less receptive prospects. A vital task before the professionals is to motivate the rural women prospects. We expect something concrete from the creative advertisements. Aggressive advertisement strategy would be highly effective to influence the rural women illiterates.

The participating agencies, organisations, institutions are also supposed to develop rapport with the media to publicise their programmes. Such type of publicity would activate the process of brainwashing. In addition, this would also make the literacy programmes cost-effective.

National Literacy Mission, since its inception in 1988, has been successful in making a number of persons literate under Adult Education Scheme. The publicity materials of NLM are, no doubt, of good quality but the main hurdle to motivate the prospects is yet to be crossed. In addition to advertising and publicity, we should also think in favour of promotional incentives to prospects in general and rural women prospects in particular. The teachers and personnel engaged in the process are also required to be given due incentives. The target for total literacy is yet to be achieved. The existing promotional strategies would hardly be helpful in touching the target within the stipulated time. This in a very natural way draws our attention on aggressive promotion strategy. We need enormous cooperation of media to promote adult literacy programme. The voluntary social organisations, no doubt, can be successful in activating the process but even to simplify their task, the promotional decisions are required to be innovated. Fortunately, we have sophisticated communication technologies and an efficient team of professionals in different areas. The only thing that we need urgently is a strong sense of dedication and commitment without which our all efforts are likely to be turned into a fiasco.

The advertising agencies bear an important task of making creative advertisements. Creativity remains the enigma to most people. It is a complex process whose sensitivity depends upon the forces within the individual and outside. It is not just a gift. We can even inculcate the creative faculty. It is a range of abilities. It is both convergent and divergent thinking which responses to reality and thus succeeds in making the appeals positive. It bears the capacity to sensitise even insensitive persons. It is against this background that we find creative advertisements more instrumental in turning the negative into positive. Since the prospects (adult illiterates) are found generally less receptive, it is pertinent that while composing slogans, messages and appeals, the professionals attempt at making the advertisements more creative. To be more specific, the rural adult illiterates and specially the women fail to understand the slogans and messages, symbolic photographs or paintings. The professionals, if are found familiar with the lifestyles of target prospects, can be successful in motivating them. It is not to be forgotten that in developing advertisements the most significant aspect is visualisation. It is a process right from the designing of advertisements to the development of advertisement layout in print. It is related to art in advertising. This process is shared by the copywriter and the creative director of visualisation. Here, the professionals take a decision regarding the point or scene to be highlighted, e.g., product, people, event, background. We need more care while developing advertisements since both the subjects and prospects may be instrumental in generating monotony. How to design creative layout so that the locomotion process is right and the viewers are motivated to see, receive and act in the desired direction. Unless we find literacy programme activated as a social mission, our efforts would show a lukewarm response. National Literacy Mission established its edge over the National Adult Education Programme (1978) and let the Social Literacy Mission establish its edge over the National Literacy Mission (1988).

Price Mix: We find illiteracy a social evil which is to be eradicated at the earliest possible. Since a number of steps are to be initiated to activate the process, the mobilisation of funds needs due attention. So far as internal sources are concerned, we find a number of hurdles in the process. This draws our attention on collecting grants, charities and donations. We need to solicit the co-operation of Voluntary Social Organisations and global bodies for this purpose. The corporate sector may also sponsor the programme for removing illiteracy. So far as the sensitisation processes are concerned; the creative promotional measures may be effective in bringing the students to the adult education centres. We need to accept the Total Literacy Programme as a mission and therefore do not find any scope for charging fee, indeed realise the positive role of motivation to achieve the target within a time-frame. It is also pertinent that the users of the services realise importance of adult education and extend their best co-operation to the bodies or agencies involved in the process.

Place Mix: The channelisation of services need due attention of providers. A small gap or a minor mistake in the placement of services may transform even positive into negative. This draws our attention on the ways through which the services are offered. Our focus must be on adult women illiterates and to the extent it is possible, we need to minimise the length of channel or the gap between the programme funding agencies and the ultimate users. At the last level of distribution, we need more precaution because the teachers or the front-line staff making available educational aids or backup or supporting materials to the users are expected to be more sensitive. We may have permanent or part-time teachers for this purpose and keeping in view their contributions, the salary, honorarium or perks or other incentives may be offered. While channelising the services, it is advisable to make it small. This will also be helpful in minimising the cost and time for the distribution of services. Willingly or unwillingly, we need to accept that in the Indian perspective, the most sensitive segment of user women illiterates particularly living in the rural areas fail in getting the teaching aids and other incentives meant for them due to the sore-spots that we find in the channels.

Process Mix: The processing of adult education services need due attention on two important dimensions, e.g., first the quality of educational aid to be offered to the adults and the behavioural aspect of staff and teachers in the offering of services. The governmental, social and global agencies make a provision for the services. The services are found related to the generation of skill, vocational education, in addition to the knowledge of alphabets at the primary stage of learning. The agencies meant for offering the services either delay or distort the services and deprive the users of getting the real benefits. It is in this context that we talk about processing so that we don't find any gap between the services-promised and services-offered. The sources, measures, people for offering the services draw due attention. The concerned agencies need to monitor and review the offering of services.

Physical Attractions: We also talk about this submix of the marketing mix and here, our focus is on the make-up of the people instrumental in offering the services. The focal point is awareness of the target users of the services so that they with the physical make-up of the people serving them come to know about their identity. At the UNESCO, the people working with the agency are in their uniform, dresses and logo which makes it easier for the target users to know about their identity. A social organisation has to make clear its identity. If it is a government department, the clarification is needed. This would effectively counter the unfair practices. Since we find users coming from a particular segment, it is also significant that the agencies find it convenient to identify them so that the services reach to the destination within the time-frame.

People: A number of services are made available to the users and a number of people are involved for different purposes at different stages of offering the services. Formal education proves to be subject-oriented where we find focus on subjective knowledge in the face of the aptitude of users. The people engaged in offering the services should have a professional commitment and they should be patient. They should make honest and sincere efforts to motivate them. Since we talk about making a sustainable society, it is pertinent that the people making available the services are aware of the constraints and adjust timing keeping in view their conveniences and other engagements. In the context of functional education, we have to acquire knowledge of the basics and development of knowledge in tune with their aptitude. They are supposed to be an expert in a particular area. This helps them enriching their potentials to secure a job or to start their own venture. The people engaged for offering the services should be experts so that they can make the process of training interesting. Besides, they are also to be made available informal education in which we find emphasis on developing civic sense, nutritional awareness, health-consciousness and in this context, the people supposed to offer the services should be successful in convincing, sensing and influencing the adults. Because they have passed the stage of learning, the trainers/providers or teachers may face difficulties at each and every stage but they need to work with a mission using creativity in communications so that the self-sustainable programme or welfare agencies become result-oriented.

On the basis of Figure 16.2, it is right to say that a small channel would be suitable since the multi-level channel complicates the entire distribution process. It is more judicious that we minimise the involvement of bureaucrats in the process and establish a direct link with the Adult Education Centres. The leading global organisations, e.g., UNESCO (United Nations Educational Scientific and Cultural Organisations), UNICEF (United Nations Children's Emergency Fund), and UNIFEM (United Nations Development Fund for Women) are the global organisations directly or indirectly supporting the central government in the process. But the channel is so long (A) that the delay in distribution is very natural. Even in channel (B), we find a big gap. No doubt, the channel (C) is found partially effective. This proves that in the process of distribution, we prefer one or two-level channel.

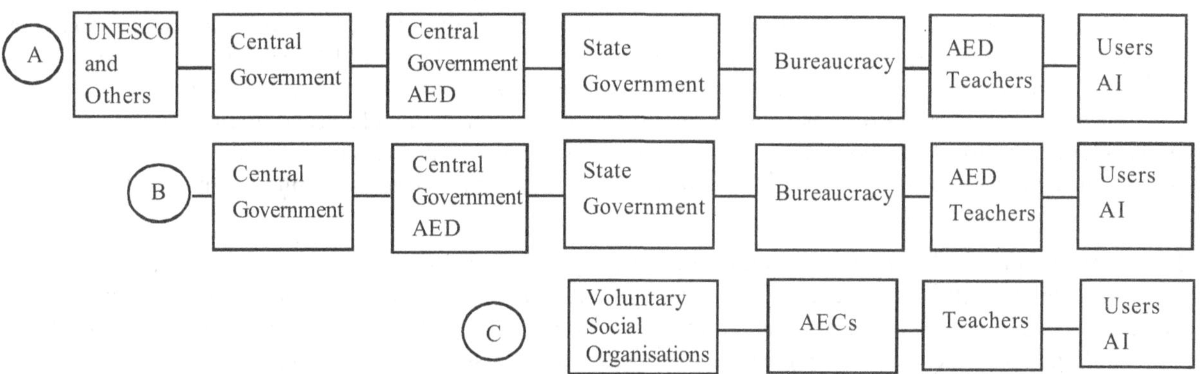

Fig. 16.2: Adult Educational Channel

The related organisations or agencies should have a direct link with the adult education centers so that they distribute the services to the target users without delaying the process. The related organisation should circulate a guideline for utilisation and the centres (AECs) should follow the same. There must be a general guideline regarding the service mix for the adult education and in addition, for rural areas and rural women, we should have a special task force. This is a special segment and for this, we need special strategic marketing. In a majority of the villages, we find that rural women due to shyness and their family tradition, do not like to come out which stands as a major barrier. We have talked about special visualisation scheme for this purpose while going through promotion. Our front line personnel need an in-depth study of behaviour so that they understand the psychology of target prospects and attempt to motivate them.

For educating the women illiterate, we need to take the support of women front-line staff, preferably of the same village. This would not only remove the problem of shyness but would also make possible personal-touch-in-service. We should fix individual target and group target and the front-line staff crossing the target should get due incentives. At the last stage of their education when they are supposed to cover vocational courses, we need the support of experts. If we assign to them the course according to their aptitude, the sensitivity rate would be high.

A structural change in the distribution process is urgently needed since almost all the organisations/agencies are of the view that a big gap between the funding agencies and ultimate users invite a number of problems. The participation of Panchayati Raj in the distribution process may be more effective to minimise the gap between funding agencies and the users.

STRATEGIC MARKETING FOR ADULT EDUCATION

United Nations Development Report (UNDR) 1994 reveals that India is categorised in the abysmally "Low Human Development" bracket. Proper definition defines an adult literacy rate as a percentage of persons aged 15 and over. Of course, we have taken a number of steps to remove illiteracy and the percentage from 1971 to 2001 has also shown a positive trend, i.e., from 36 in 1971 to 76 in 2001. However, we need more concerted efforts to eradicate this social evil. With changing socio-economic conditions, volatile environment and accelerated development processes and problems, increasing instrumentality of machines in the socio-economic transformation process, we need a new policy, a new strategy, a new vision and a new approach. In view of the recent developments in the socio-economic parlance, we need innovation in the marketing of literacy. Novel methods are required to be evolved, innovative strategies are preferably to be conceptualised, existing operational mechanisms are required to be revamped, suitably altered, enlarged and activated. The nurturing of a healthy, progressive and positive attitudes can make even the prickly path of eradicating illiteracy a complete success. This in a very natural way draws our attention on strategic marketing which can help us in formulating an action plan keeping in view the means, requirements of segment and target prospects. There are a number of key issues for strategic marketing since the motive is to achieve Total Literacy (TL) by 12th Five Year Plan.

1. Active Participation and Involvement: Since it is a programme related to the development of society, it is pertinent that at the very outset we talk about participation and involvement of society. Active participation and involvement of society is of vital importance not only to increase the sensitivity of our programmes but also to identify the loopholes or sore-spots. We need to generate the thirst for education and this is possible when all of us do not treat it as a programme but a social mission. It is very natural that a lay learner would not have a spontaneous thirst for education. It is in this context that we talk about incentives. The whole thing is to sensitise the target prospects. This process of sensitisation can be engendered through widespread implementation of information campaigns. Campaign for adult education responsive to the needs of particular area is vital. Of course, we find promotional measures to be innovated and we would talk about the same later but the most important thing is to seek the cooperation of society.

2. Visual Image to be Given Due Weightage in the Marketing Process: The visual image registers more readily and powerfully on the audience. The impact of the same is found more permanent and lasting. Its reach lends an aura of reality and renders it retentive to an unlettered mind. The reliance and employment of slides, television, video, street theatre are found sensitive techniques, instrumental in informing and creating attractive avenues for facilitation of the learner. Any visual mode which presents matters in a new way or innovative approaches like eye-catching, succinct slogans, triggers off a powerful influence resulting into a creditable and responsive feedback. In addition, a massive deployment of posters with popular characters magnifying the benefits of adult education would be successful in influencing the target prospects. The main thing is highlighting of and underscoring of a promise of amelioration of a learner's basic needs and responsibilities. We need to package the programmes in such a way that it ensures and assures the reactivating of a sustained and sustainable growth and qualitative transformation in their lifestyles.

3. Inclusion of More Incentives: While formulating the promotion strategy, we need to include new incentives both for the users and the front-line personnel. Realistic incentives are expected to be more effective. A concerted strategy to evolve mid-day meal schemes for users and their dependants, creche for children and other basic requirements which form the basic strands of the social safety net may be helpful in nurturing the potentialities of users. Not only to the adult illiterates but we need to offer more incentives even to the teachers, personnel engaged in the process.

4. Infrastructural Constraints to be Removed: In the strategic marketing, we also find infrastructural facilities playing an important role. This makes it essential that existing mechanism is upgraded. It is found that mere creation of school buildings, provision of attendant, paraphernalia like blackboards, chalks, books, etc. are mere cosmetic exercises throwing a very limited impact. This draws our attention on making available to the centres new facilities which they do not have in their own homes like, TV, electric fans, water coolers, etc. These incentives would only not generate and enrich infrastructural facilities but would also motivate the personnel and users.

5. Committed Pool of Volunteers: Even the rich infrastructural facilities fail in generating positive impact, if we do not have a zealous, committed pool of volunteers. In this context, we need active involvement of National Youth Bodies like the NSS and NSC. The physical presence of young educators would inspire confidence and trust. In addition, they are also found efficacious in activating persistent and sustained efforts. This would change the quality of distribution channel.

6. Undertaking Area Specific Programmes: In this context, we also realise the instrumentality of Area Specific Programme. This would help in determining the effectiveness of a learner's participation. We cannot deny the fact that methods applied in a hilly tribal area would not be effective in the plains. The vocabulary and contents must be local with a regional bias. We should assign due weightage to the needs and aspirations of the users, cultural-ethnic ethos, their motivations and aversions. Factors like values, attitudes, beliefs, customs of the users' community and its religious attributes, ethnic symbols and traditions, individual and social priorities, morality, rights and obligations should have a grass root touch.[11] Lack of these values can generate social reduction ranging from apathy to hostility which would make our programmes ineffective. This in a natural way diverts our attention on the service mix or curriculum that we approve for adult education in general and the adult women education in particular. An important task before the educationists is to frame such a curriculum, syllabi which create interest.

7. A Careful Equilibrium between the Carrot and Stick Policy: The motive is to achieve total literacy by 2017 and this makes it essential that we pave ways for optimising the Carrot and Stick Policy which can assist us in the achievement of the proposed goal. We can borrow successful models employed across the country[12] and make possible suitable amendments in the same in tune with our regional/local conditions. In Tanzania, the parental literacy campaign launched by various educational institutions increased the number of neoliterate parents. In addition, the private agencies can be instrumental in boosting adult education by creating special funds and infrastructure to facilitate the participation of learners in adult illiterates financed by workers' welfare trust. This in a true sense paves ways for the development of productive human resources which ultimately contribute a lot to the development of that organisation. The Musonda Women's Literacy Project in Kitwe, Zambia has successfully been supported by the Zambia Girl Guides since it came into shape in 1986. In addition to the literacy programme, they also promote cookery, nutrition, mothercraft and craft work. In the literacy campaign in Philippines, 10,000 people in Barangay with a literacy rate of 60 per cent have benefited immensely. The scouts have launched a project in training people in techniques for imparting literacy courses in villages. They are found involved in preparing course material. These illustrations are a mute testimony to this proposition that even in the Indian setting, we have to pave avenues for the involvement of masses. Even Pakistan has successfully implemented the 'each one, teach one' programme. We should not forget that literacy programme cannot be successful unless the educated people of the country, specially of rural bias evince their personal interests.

8. Special Weightage to Women Literacy: The task force should, of course, assign due weightage to women in general and rural women in particular. Educated wives and mothers are an asset to a nation. In villages, the women are yet to realise the importance of education of girls. Here, our emphasis is on the promotional strategy for women. The main thing is to create awareness and innovative promotional strategies can make it possible. The professionals have to accept it as a challenge. The industrial organisations are supposed to finance the scheme meant for women illiterate.

Thus, we bear the responsibility of achieving total literacy by 2017 which necessitates innovative marketing practices by all the organisations/agencies already involved or planning to involve in this social mission. It is not a programme but a mission which requires involvement of all.

MARKETING MIX FOR ELEMENTARY EDUCATION

Since elementary education system has been contributing substantially to the overall literacy rate, we find justification for discussing the marketing of elementary education under the head marketing literacy. In this education system, we find two categories, formal and informal. In the formal education, we find two levels, e.g., primary and upper primary. We are aware of the fact that both the government and private schools are involved in the process. The main problem in the elementary education is the drop-out ratio. A number of parents discourage their children and even the teachers fail in motivating them, resulting into a poor retention ratio jeopardising all our efforts to develop quality outputs. It is not wrong to mention that both at primary and upper primary levels, we need a structural change in the curriculum. The need of the hour is to make possible a fair synchronisation of formal and informal systems, specially to improve the quality of our coming generations. We cannot deny the fact that to be more specific in the rural areas, the government schools are almost all in a depleted condition. Students have neither a suitable space nor a dedicated teacher. No doubt, we find an increase in the enrolment position but if the retention rate is not improved, the enrolment rate would not serve our purpose. If we talk about the rural areas, willingly or unwillingly we have to accept that the results are very disappointing. Even today 95 per cent of rural population have a school within a distance of 3 kms and above. The system is meant for children above 5 age group and therefore, we can easily imagine the fate of enrolment. In addition to the revamping of government schools, we have to encourage private schools so that a competitive condition make ways for qualitative transformation. Against this background, we discuss here the problem of marketing elementary education.

Product Mix: At the very outset, it is pertinent that we go through the curriculum of elementary education. The changing environmental conditions determine the syllabi/curriculum for any educational system or organisation. Since it is a learning stage and therefore we cannot underestimate various dimensions of informal or non-formal education. While formulating mix and blending formal and informal education, it is significant that we pave ways for its further link with the secondary education system which would engineer a sound foundation for higher education. To make possible a contraction in the drop-out ratio or to increase the retention ratio, we need to make the curriculum more interesting. Since both the public and private sectors are involved in the process, it is essential that the services are made competitive. This would help users/students in many ways. In Figure 16.3, we find elementary education programming which is in the face of changing environmental conditions. We have a tough task to make our human resources internationally competitive. This is possible when we make our products more costly. By having a fair synchronisation of professional excellence and value engineering or say, in the beginning the blending of fundamentals and values, we pave ways for the development of their personalities. The productive human resources would pave ways for the development and prosperity of an organisation and *vice versa*. We cannot ignore the fact that the secret of Japanese developments are coiled in the essence of developing productive human resources. The image of an organisation is fantastically influenced by the quality of human resources. The elementary education is considered to be the most sensitive stage for engineering a sound foundation for the development of human resources.

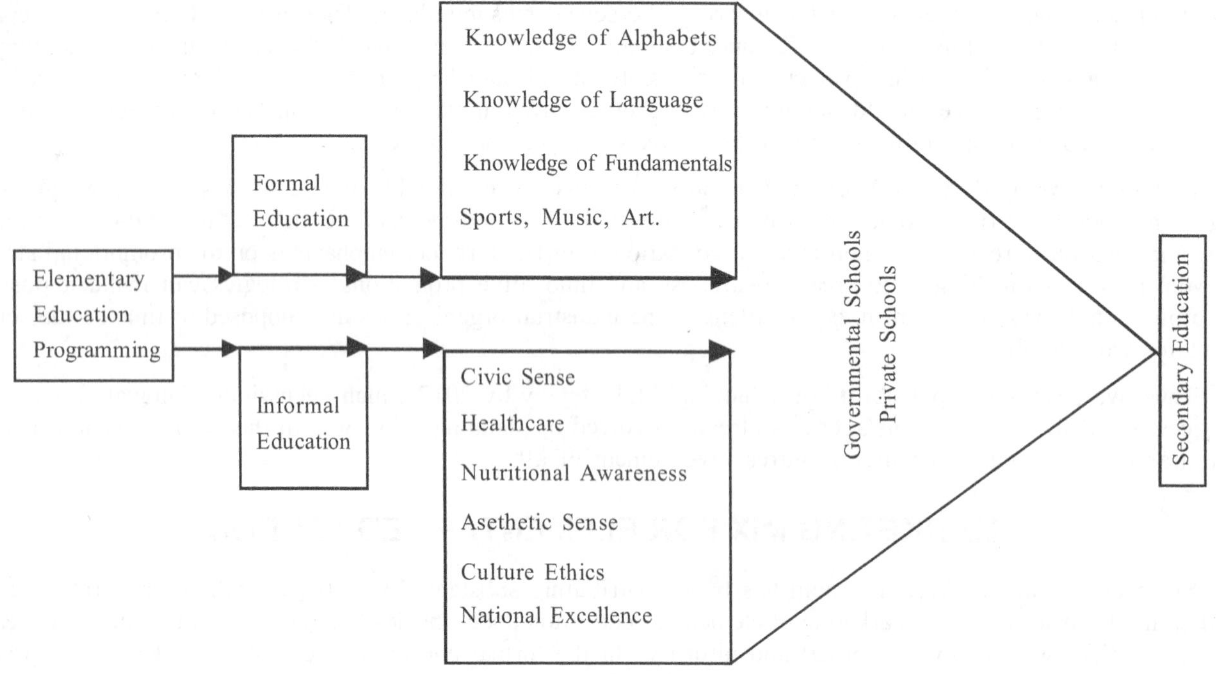

Fig. 16.3: Elementary Education Programming

At the outset, it is essential that we make available to them knowledge of alphabets so that they are in a position to read, write and understand. This draws our attention on the modern visualisation process so that they complete the first stage at the earliest possible. The primary stage of education would make them understandable, if sophisticated communication technologies are used. After this, at the upper-primary stage, we need to study their aptitude and based on the same, the fundamentals of the related area are to be made available to them. It is in this context that we find aptitude test significant to increase the effectiveness of our mission. Here, it is important to mention that while designing the syllabi or developing the curriculum, we should not forget the constraints that we find in the rural areas and the handicaps that we find with the rural children. Against this background, we should have a crash programme for brushing-up the rural children which would be helpful in removing the threshold barrier. Though they have the potentials still due to shyness or lack of exposure, they fail in delivering goods and make our programmes unproductive. The crash programme or special curriculum should be after the primary education.

Not only the formal but even we need to blend informal or non-formal education in our curriculum. Here, our emphasis is on social, cultural and ethical values by activating the brainwashing process. Since of late we have sophisticated communication technologies, the task is not so difficult. In Figure 16.3, we find civic sense, culture, ethics and national excellence as the key components of informal education. Our emphasis is here on value engineering. This is a value addition process in which we are supposed to be more careful. Though it is right to argue that mother is the best source to impart informal education to the children. Of course, we can't negate it but all of us are well aware of the emerging negative developments in our lifestyles. The urban mothers now prefer to work and so they do not get time to educate and train their children. And if we talk about rural children, their mothers in a majority of the cases are illiterate. It is in this case that we find a vacuum of values in the new generation. Most of us still believe that we do not need high weightage to social and cultural values. Against this background, it is right to mention that in this age of sophisticated technologies, we find socio-cultural and ethical values more impact generating since we cannot develop organisational culture unless our emphasis is on these components from the very first stage of learning. We cannot expect policy makers, decision-makers, white-collar personnel, blue-collar personnel, teachers, politicians, technocrats and others making value-based decisions till these traits are injected or inculcated in their personalities essentially at the learning stage. We find children more receptive. And it is also right that due to psychological factors, they receive negative traits very quickly. If they do not get knowledge of these components at the stage of elementary education, it is very difficult to inculcate these traits at the later stage. Of late, we find an adverse conditions. The parents in a good number do not realise these traits essential for the development of their personalities. They along with their kids/teens are found watching TV serials/movies full of violence and bedroom scenes. They themselves do not act and behave in the face of pop culture. The children do not get proper education regarding these traits in their schools. In the prevailing condition, it is not right to expect from our new generation to be value-based. It is against this background that we strongly feel inclusion of informal education promotion of value system in our curriculum.

Promotion Mix: Educating children is not a programme but a mission. Significant developments around the world make it essential that we innovate curriculum, make them interesting *vis-a-vis* thought provoking. The significant task here is to innovate the promotional strategies so that we succeed in creating awareness and increasing the enrolment and retention ratios. We are required to focus on two important areas, first to instrumentalise the personal promoters and second to innovate the non-personal promotional measures bearing more sensitivity. To be more specific in the rural areas, we have to be more careful since the parents are often found discouraging their children from going to schools. By educating children, we not only succeed in increasing the rate of literacy but also engineer a sound foundation for the development of productive human resources contributing to the process of human capital formation substantially and activating the development processes fantastically. It is against this background that we find promotional decisions playing an important role in strengthening elementary education.

The first task is found more impact generating since we find here the instrumentality of human resources. Our emphasis is here on the involvement of teaching and non-teaching personnel in motivating the children and their parents. For motivators playing a significant role in the motivating process, it is pertinent that they are getting adequate incentives. Hence, it is important that teachers get due incentives. It is also important to mention here that their incentives should be linked to enrolment and retention ratio. There must be a target and the teachers crossing the target should suitably be rewarded and should also be punished. On the other hand, the teachers failing in touching the target should be deprived of the additional incentives. Since the parents are also found here responsible for the increasing drop-out ratio, it is judicious that we think in favour of motivating the parents.

This is related to personal promotion since it is instrumentality of a personal promoter that determines the magnitude of success. We cannot negate that in the rural areas we need a special task force to motivate the parents. If we fail in the motivation process, we have no option but to punish those parents found responsible for discouraging their children. In this context, we need to assign due weightage to the behavioural dimension since it would help teachers in sensitising the motivation process.

The second task is related to non-personal promotion where we focus on advertisement and publicity measures. In the modern world, we have sophisticated technologies and sensitive media to make our slogans more effective. To be more specific, TV/audiovisual exposure need here a special mention. The government and private agencies evincing interests in this mission should come forward and contribute a lot to the advertising process. The professionals can play here an important role by making the slogans, messages and appeals proactive. Since it is a mission, they should work with the motto of subserving the social interests or should charge the minimum possible for the services they make available. The visualisation process needs due weightage, specially while designing the advertisement layout.

Like AIR and DD1, other private TV channels should also evince interests in advertising slogans related to child education. They should charge nominal, if not free of cost. Our special emphasis should be on motivating the girls living in rural areas. This necessitates special campaign exclusively to promote women education. The task, of course, is difficult but not so difficult if we have a strong sense of determination, dedication commitment and conviction. Women literates living in the rural areas should accept the responsibility of motivating the illiterate women.

In addition to advertisement, the publicity measures are also required to be strengthened. This requires developing a rapport with the media people. The governmental organisations or private organisations/agencies should pave ways for the same. They should organise seminars, conferences and workshops and should invite media people for an exposure. In most of the cases, publicity becomes more effective if the correspondents, press reporters, etc. are motivated. All possible efforts should be made to convince them that the child education programmes are being conducted efficiently or the constraints in the development process are identified carefully. They can advocate strongly for the right cause to bring things on the rail.

Price Mix: Since we find involvement of private schools in the process, it is judicious that we also talk about the fee structure. In the government schools, we find free of cost services but so far as the private schools are concerned, they charge exorbitant fees. Of course, they require to mobilise the financial resources but there must be a rational policy for the same. We should check commercialisation of education which is found exploiting the masses. We are not opposed to the charging of fees by the private schools meant for the children but they should not make it a source of making profits. According to the available seats, they should have a policy of charging fees on the basis of incomes of parents. In addition, they also bear a social responsibility of offering free of cost services to the poor and weaker sections of the society. Whatever the losses they generate due to cost-free services to the weaker sections would be charged from the high earning and middle-earning groups in proportion to their incomes. This is a rational pricing structure[13] which would maintain the quality of education in the private schools. While fixing fee, the computation of costs on education should be done honestly. The process of computation should not pave avenues for profiteering. Besides, the private schools should also make a provision for the creation of a development fund and a portion of surplus should be appropriated to this fund annually for quantitative or qualitative improvements found essential in the face of latest developments. The main thing is quality of services and either private or government schools should be very particular to "Quality." We cannot deny the fact that the ultimate motto is to strengthen the foundation which should be given an overriding priority. Of course, the government schools, except a very few, are found in a depleted condition mainly due to the financial crunch. The exchequer is not in a position to finance schools and the existing pricing policy does not allow them to generate adequate finance from the internal sources. It is against this background that they fail in managing expensive inputs for offering quality outputs. We do not find anything wrong in charging nominal fee from students who are well-off. If they pay at least ₹ 20/- as fee (per month) to the government schools, the avenues would be paved for quantitative or qualitative improvements even in the government primary schools. The motive is to improve the standard of education which would, of course, be futile failing the availability of adequate finance.

Place Mix: While making available the services to the users, the front line personnel play an impact generating role. Here, our emphasis in on the contributions of teaching personnel. It is right to mention that in a majority of the private schools, we find cases of exploitation. The teachers get poor salaries and they are supposed to put their signatures on the fake bills. Since we have the problem of unemployment willingly or unwillingly, they continue to work without raising any voice against the management. The labour and education laws fail to protect them since they are not in a position to lodge a complain. We cannot expect a sense of dedication and commitment unless we pay to them adequate incentives. So far as the teachers of the government primary and upper-primary schools are concerned, they get higher scale but make available to the institutions very disappointing services. To be more specific, in the rural areas where we find the most sensitive segment, i.e., rural poor, the students are found heavily affected. This draws our attention on managing government schools properly so that the services as per the mix reach to the users/students on time. We talk about ethical values at almost all the stages of education since failing this property, it is very difficult to expect a dedicated and committed teacher.

Process: In the context of elementary education, it is imperative to be decent and sophisticated in processing of services. Because the services are related to children found of gullible nature, the providers need additional care while offering so that the promised services reach the children without any distortion, The government-managed primary educational institutions are virtually in bad shape. The children fail in getting the services mainly due to the fact that the teachers distort the services in such a way that deprives the children of getting the educational aid promised by the government-managed schools. This mix of marketing the education services is significant with a view to satisfy the users. Though there are cases where, on account of inadequacy of supporting infrastructural facilities, the children don't get the services promised. In a number of cases the buildings of the primary educational institutions are in a dilapidated condition as can be seen during the rainy season; the teachers get an excuse for not conducting classes, The constraints in the process have to be removed to improve the quality and bridge the gap.

Physical Attractions: This mix of marketing focuses attention on the physical make up of teachers, students and other staff engaged by the educational institutions. It is a fact that users of the services are kids and minor children of gullible nature who naturally mind activities and behaviours. The dresses of teachers need due attention of the authorities managing the school affairs as otherwise we can't negate the insensitivity of our instructions. Of course, they have to wear neat and clean dresses so that the students get an opportunity to develop an aesthetic sense. There is no doubt that educational institutions managed by privately and missionaries have some dress code both for students and teachers. So far as the government-managed institutions are concerned, there is no such code prescribed.

People: When we talk about marketing of elementary and primary education services related to kids and minor children, it is necessary that an overriding priority is assigned to the teachers and other personnel serving there. It is really amazing that in the government-managed educational institutions, there is degeneration in the quality of services mainly on account of the fact that a majority of the people working there lack professional excellence. The teachers, unaware of the latest subjective knowledge, will fail in delivering the goods. Educational institutions particularly in the rural areas present a very gloomy picture because a good number of teachers abstain from their classes. This is instrumental in raising the number of absentees and drop-outs. Even in the urban areas, there is no positive sign of development because the poor quality of teachers and infrastructural facilities tend to degenerate the quality. There is an influx of students in the private schools mainly due to a degeneration in quality specially in the government schools.

We need to improve the quality of our teachers by making available to them the knowledge of latest developments in the discipline across the country. Our emphasis is here on behavioural management. Educating children is a tough task. Since we have an urgent task of achieving total illiteracy, it is significant that our strategies are innovative. Both the government and primary schools have to see that students get the best possible exposure and for that, the sophisticated communication technologies are used for imparting educational aid. This would increase our retention ratio since the curriculum would be made more interesting. Audiovisual exposure to the students would brush-up their potentials. But it is right to mention that in the rural areas, we find it difficult to install communication technologies due to power problem. For making the services effective, it is pertinent that we increase the instrumentality of teachers *vis-a-vis* an attempt to create interests of users of the services. Unless both of them interact and co-operate each other, the services would not reach to the target users in the desired way, and within the stipulated time.

STRATEGIC MARKETING FOR ELEMENTARY EDUCATION

All of us are aware of the sizeable contribution of elementary education to the present literacy rate. Our emphasis is on engineering a sound foundation for secondary education. The retention ratio is also to be increased. For marketing literacy efficiently, it is pertinent that we have an action plan which paves ways for qualitative-cum-quantitative improvements. We have a tough task of improving the quality of education, specially in the rural areas. We are also supposed to educate women on the priority basis. The multi-faceted constraints make our task more difficult and against this background, we talk about strategic marketing.

To start with, it is necessary to have a structural change in the curriculum. While going through the service mix, we have thrown light on the fair blending of formal and informal education. To be more specific, for rural students, we need a task force so that the existing threshold barrier is removed before they enter the secondary schools. The rural students lack exposure, they are shy and also lack a sense of confidence. Of course, they have potentials but due to these negative traits they often fail in fulfilling our expectations. This necessitates revamping of our syllabi in the face of latest developments across the country. In addition to the knowledge of alphabets, we bear the responsibility of making available to them the knowledge of fundamentals, sports and music. Our emphasis is here on making the process more interesting. This is essential to increase the retention ratio. We also focus on informal or non-formal education since we have miserably failed in making available to them the knowledge of culture, ethics, nutritional awareness, civic sense, afforestation and national excellence in our homes, i.e., learning initiation stage. In the modern competitive world, we frequently talk about organisational culture, work culture, ethical and moral values since these properties help us in increasing the rate of human capital formation *vis-a-vis* the organisational productivity. It is against this background that we need to innovate our product/service strategy. This would help us in many ways. The secondary schools would get quality intakes and the task of developing the human resources in a right fashion would be simplified considerably. Quality intakes can help us in getting the quality outputs. Both the government and private schools are required to innovate their services. The task of sensitising the users would not remain difficult, if the innovation process assigns due weightage to the regional affiliation of the target users.

In the strategic marketing, we also need to activate the innovation process in the context of promotion. Since we consider it an important dimension of marketing, it is significant that we innovate both personal and non-personal promotion. At the outset, we talk about personal promotion where teachers play a decisive role. Educating children is, no doubt, a tough task. This necessitates enormous cooperation of teaching personnel engaged in the process. Motivation is supposed to be the best device to activate the process. Here, it is essential that we link the motivation plan with the retention ratio. In addition, we should also think in favour of offering additional incentives to the teachers showing personal-touch-in-service and developing quality students. This would pave ways for the generation of efficiency. In addition, it is also essential that we punish those teachers who fail in discharging their duties efficiently. While planning, we also need to focus our attention on motivation to the students so that they are not only encouraged for enrolling themselves in the schools but continue education even when their parents oppose. In addition to the personal promotion, we also need a new strategy for the non-personal promotion. Since we have developed sophisticated technologies, the task is not so difficult. If the professionals are committed and the latest technologies are available, the advertisement slogans, messages and appeals are to be made creative. If we plan for promoting rural children in general and girls in particular, the creativity in promotion needs an intensive care. At this stage, the most important thing is to generate the thirst for education which requires creativity. The media have to extend their best possible cooperation in this mission. If they evince interest, the publicity measures can also be strengthened.

The fee structure is also a sensitive problem, to be more specific, in the Indian condition where a majority of the people are unable to pay even the nominal fee. Of course, we also find a change in our attitudes. The parents do not hesitate to pay ₹ 100/- or even more as a monthly fee to the private schools but they take it in a negative way, if the government schools charge even ₹ 20/- for the same standard of services. This necessitates attitudinal change. All of us feel that an important cause for the present degeneration in the educational institutions is the financial bankruptcy since the exchequer is not in a position to make available more finance. Hence, the policy planners have to think over the problem very seriously. Earlier, we have talked about a rational fee structure and this is the only way to bring things on the rail. On the other hand, the private schools have been found charging exorbitant fees and making profits against the set norms and ethics. The need of the hour is to regulate the same.

The organisations, agencies, institutions, teaching and non-teaching personnel have to devise ways for placing the services to the students. This necessitates a contraction in the distribution process right from the formulation of a service mix to its time-honoured distribution to the target users. In the Indian setting, we find a big gap of time between formulation of a policy and its field implementation. We need to minimise this gap which draws our attention on enriching the infrastructural facilities and instrumentalising the operational apparatus. And to fulfil the same, we again find financial constraint standing as a major barrier. Willingly or unwillingly, we have to pave ways for the generation of finance from the internal sources right from the elementary stage to the university stage. Since we find elementary education a mission, the governmental policies are required to be more liberal and the financial support is to be increased but ultimately the brunt of tax would fall on our shoulders.

MARKETING MIX FOR SECONDARY EDUCATION

After the completion of elementary education, we find the stage set for imparting secondary education which is considered to be an important ladder of education, specially with the viewpoint of making them understandable in the right perspective. We need to vibrate the positive trends in the enrolment and retention ratios. Since both the public and private schools are found engaged in the process, a sense of competition and co-ordination becomes inevitable. If we use seven years of imparting elementary education honestly and efficiently, the task further is not so difficult. The most important thing that we find at this stage is adopting a plan of education for teens with the least possible threshold barrier. The marketing of secondary education thus is found more critical and challenging. We need more professionalism in our decisions. The motive is to engineer a strong foundation for the higher education which helps us in developing knowledge in a right fashion.

Product Mix: Curriculum/syllabi bear the efficacy of making available to us a right or wrong direction. If we are very particular to the designing of an ideal syllabi, the direction is found right which paves ways for the development of social and cultural values in which ethical dimension gets an important place. We succeed in having a work culture, we succeed in maintaining organisational culture which help us in accelerating productivity and projecting a positive image. It is against this background that we assign due weightage to the development of services in tune with the changing requirements.

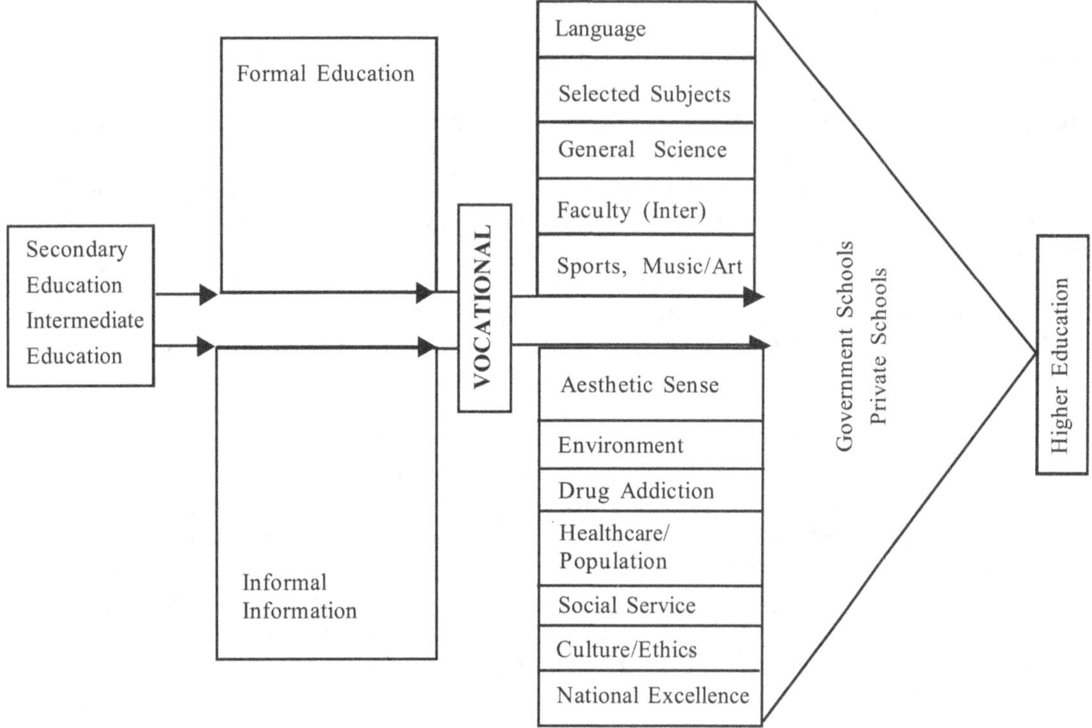

Fig. 16.4: Secondary Education Programming

In Figure 16.4, we find secondary education programming which focuses on the blending of formal and informal education for the development of an ideal citizen since this aspect of development of human resources determines the magnitude of success in our development efforts. While innovating the marketing practices, it is important that we have quality outputs and this is possible when we have quality inputs. Till now, we have undoubtedly been successful in developing knowledge but have miserably failed in producing an ideal citizen. This is found jeopardising our all efforts since the system now has started collapsing and the society is now found dying. If in Japan we find a work culture, it is mainly due to their success in developing an ideal citizen. No laws and regulations can make it possible. It is only the system of education that paves ways for the same. In the curriculum, we find both formal and informal education. While imparting formal education, our emphasis is on language, a few selected subjects, general science, sports, music and art. At the intermediate stage, we think about faculty programming. In the context of informal education, we find aesthetic sense, environment, vocational course, healthcare and population, culture and ethics and national excellence. It has already been pointed out earlier that we have a tough task of educating the teenagers who are found moving in the wrong direction. The government or private schools have to follow the syllabi approved by the national and provincial boards.

The certification boards have to see that their stamps have some values. The selection of different subjects should be in the face of global developments so that our products bear the efficacy of accepting the best and rejecting the worst. They would develop a strong elimination potential, if this stage of imparting education is managed properly. The knowledge of language is found essential to develop their reading, writing and perceiving skill. The knowledge of general science is found essential to make them aware of the latest developments around the world. The knowledge of a few selected subjects is essential to select a discipline for specialisation. We find sports, music and art in the formal education since we recognise the outstanding contributions of these traits in having a team spirit.

We focus on aesthetic sense since it plays a vital role in preserving values, generating efficiency and making an assault on monotony. Knowledge of environment to counter the problem of environment pollution; knowledge of healthcare and population to make our demographic structure optimal and sound; knowledge of social services to involve them in the social transformation process so that they oppose the destructive forces and conditions; knowledge of culture and ethics to sound their capacity of making a positive/creative decision and national excellence to think, plan and act in the best national interests. Thus, we need to think in favour of a fair synchronisation of formal and informal education.

Promotion Mix: If we make qualitative-cum-quantitative improvements in the system of education, it is essential that our target prospects get right information on right time. Promotional measures simplify the task *vis-a-vis* make our efforts productive. We cannot deny the fact that the task of motivating and persuading the prospects, to be more specific, when they are teenagers is very dificult. In an age of globalisation of economy, when we find its negative impact on the globalisation of culture, the protection of time-tested values is a challenging task. We need more professional excellence to transform the prospects into actual users of services. At the outset, we turn our eyes on the instrumentality of personal promotion in which the teaching and non-teaching personnel are supposed to play a decisive role. We have not only to increase the enrolment position but have also to increase the retention ratio. The prospects, specially living in the rural areas are found less receptive. Very surprisingly, the parents are found here playing a negative role. To be more specific, the rural women prefer to discontinue their education. It is a stage from where the retention ratio is found moving downward. A number of rural parents appear disinterested in educating their daughters in high schools. It is against this background, that the personal promoters have to make sincere efforts to motivate the prospects. If they succeed in generating thirst for education, the derailed system may come on the rail. We accept the fact that persuasion requires motivation and particularly in the present materialistic age, we need to assign due weightage to the financial incentives. Private schools do not face this problem since the teaching and non-teaching staff apprehend a threat to their job, if the number of students goes down. In the government high schools, the teachers and other staff feel that they are getting salaries even if the enrolment, retention and results are not satisfactory then why they should take trouble. It is in the wake of this that we need to link the incentives to the performance which includes three elements, e.g., enrolment, retention and examination results. To be more specific, we need special campaigns in the rural areas, preferably to motivate rural girls and their parents.

So far as the non-personal promotional measures are concerned, we need innovative efforts since we have sophisticated communication technologies. Of late, we find more than 90 per cent villages linked to national TV network and radio that make our task easier. The professionals while designing advertisement layouts or composing slogans, messages and appeals need more excellence and personal touch. The private high schools are now found advertising efficiently but so far as the government high schools are concerned, they do not find it essential. Against this background, we find it pertinent that advertisement campaigns are strengthened, innovated, conceptualised and visualised in a right fashion. Of late, we have sophisticated printing media and we can also use the same for this purpose. The media in general are required to be liberal to the advertisement campaigns related to education. Not only the DD1 and AIR but even the private TV channels need to extend their best possible cooperation. The administration and teaching and non-teaching personnel should attempt to develop rapport with media, specially to publicise their cause. This would also minimise the promotional budget of both the government and private high schools.

Price Mix: An important decision-making area related to marketing is the fee structure which appears to be a challenging task, specially in the Indian setting where a majority of prospects are not in a position to afford the expensive educational services. Since both the government and private high schools are engaged in the process, the need of the hour is to follow such a strategy which allows even poorer and weaker sections of the society to avail the services. Of course, the innovations in the process of education have been found increasing the input costs *vis-a-vis* the fee structure. Here, a rational pricing policy would make the ways for social orientation. It is against this background that we need more care while setting the fee structure. So far as the government high schools are concerned, they are neither charging fees nor making available to the prospects the standard services. The exchequer finds it difficult to finance the development plans and ultimately the worst sufferers are the students. This makes it clear that only a basic change in the pricing strategy would pave ways for the time-honoured development of government schools. If we find it essential to protect the dying government schools, the prospects have no option but to bear the burden. A rational pricing policy focuses on charging more from the affluents and the least possible from the poorer and weaker sections. Even we may think in favour of offering free of cost services to the students who deserve so. This income-based strategy would generate surplus to the schools and would make possible necessary developments to innovate the system. On the other hand, the private schools have been found charging exorbitant fees. It is necessary to mention that educational institutions are not supposed to make profits since we call them not-for-profit-making organisations. However, it is essential that they charge fees to maintain and develop the institutions. It is not possible that all the institutions offer the same quality of services. This makes it clear that educational facilities and quality of personnel would determine the fee structure. We can have different grades and the fee structure would be fixed accordingly. It is very natural that fee structure of both the government and private high schools cannot be uniform still the structure is to be made rational. Charging more from the high and medium income groups in proportion to their incomes and charging less from the low and marginal income groups again in proportion to their incomes would be a rational policy.

Place Mix: The problem of offering the services is complicated, specially in the government high schools where a big gap exists between the formulation and implementation of a particular plan. The bureaucracy and the teaching and non-teaching personnel form a long chain. It is necessary that government high schools are given more autonomy. The teaching and non-teaching staff are expected to make sincere efforts and to show a personal-touch-in-service. This means imparting special training to them so that they understand the behaviour and expectations of students and try to satisfy them. To be more specific, the students having a rural background have yet not crossed the threshold barrier. This questions their understanding capacity *vis-à-vis* retention ratio, If they remain dissatisfied for a long time or if teachers are not communicating with them effectively, they stop coming to the schools. This is a major problem, specially in the rural areas. The teachers are not accountable for the increasing drop-out ratio. The crux of the problem is that a majority of the weaker sections come under this purview which jeopardises all our efforts in making them educationally sound. If we are really interested in initiating qualitative-cum-quantitative transformation in the system of education, we have no option but to seek the best possible co-operation of teachers. So far as the private high schools are concerned, the magnitude of the problem is not so grave since the teachers who fail in motivating the students are forced to resign or, are sacked. In addition, there should be only a minimum gap between the formulation of policy and its implementation as desired. So far as the financial incentives to teachers are concerned, the government high schools have established an edge over most of the private high schools but so far as the services are concerned, a reverse is existent trend. The motive is to involve teachers in the time-honoured implementation of teaching plans. In the Indian condition, we find it difficult unless the teachers are honest and efficient. Here, we need to assign due weightage to the value engineering process right from the elementary stage, mainly to inject ethical values to receive the best and to deliver the services of world-class.

Process: We find secondary education also in the same boat. The government-managed schools are not working satisfactorily. The teachers avoid engaging classes and the students prefers to be enrolled in private schools. Of course, the government-managed schools also promise to offer the same quality of services but (on account of a gap), we find a distortion in quality. The processing makes it necessary that the teachers and other staff responsible to offer the promised quality of services to the students make it sure that there is no distortion at any stage. They are accountable to bridge the gap. This will be possible when they are punctual and follow the service code.

Physical Attractions: Teachers set an example to the students, therefore it is pertinent that we also assign due weightage to the dresses used by them and make possible uniformity in the management of educational 'institutions. In the government-managed educational institutions, there is no dress culture or code. The teachers wear whatever they like and the students follow suit. It is essential that teachers and other staff working there don't treat this casually and wear dresses having a cultural orientation. The students of even government-managed schools should be aware of it and the authorities have to promote code on dress culture as is found in the private schools. We can't negate the instrumentality of uniform in maintaining discipline and establishing separate identity.

People: This submix of the marketing mix is related to the people working in the secondary schools. In a majority of the cases, we find people of inferior quality. The teachers, if not of quality, will find it difficult to promote the same. They often lack even subjective knowledge then can we talk of conviction and promotion of ideas. They are not value-based and these constraints become instrumental in degeneration of quality. It is significant that the authorities managing government schools assign due weightage to the development of teachers so that they are well aware of the latest developments in the concerned area. Orientation and refresher courses are to be organised for this purpose. If students do not prefer to enroll in the government-managed high schools, it is also on account of the fact they get there poor quality of education and ultimately the teachers bear the responsibility of improving the quality. If we find them not up to the mark, the task will remain unfulfilled. Of course, a few of the educational institutions of special category have been successful in promoting quality but they are very negligible in number and therefore will not influence the process of development. It is high time that the government authorities realise the gravity of the situation and link contributions of teachers to compensation plans so that the efficients get motivated and inefficients get demotivated or forced to improve their potentials. The infrastructural constraints are to be removed. We find the management not assigning any significance to the lab and library. How then we can talk of modern supporting infrastructural facilities, extracurricular activities and entertainment facilities having just cosmetic values.

STRATEGIC MARKETING FOR SECONDARY EDUCATION

We have gone through different dimensions of marketing secondary education. It is an important stage from where we start talking about the development of knowledge. After the completion of this stage, the students are supposed to get intermediate education. At the secondary stage, we are supposed to teach and educate the most sensitive segment of the society. To be more specific when we find teenagers acting as prospects, the task becomes much more complicated. It is against this background that we need an action plan keeping in view the latest developments in the society. This would help us in making the educational plans more creative and productive.

Earlier, we have talked about the curriculum/syllabi. In addition to other aspects, we need to make the curriculum more interesting. It is in this context, we focus on music and art as an integral part of secondary education. Besides, sports also need here a special emphasis. Generally, in the rural areas, the students fail in getting due co-operation of teachers which ultimately force them to stop education. In the urban areas, the parents are conscious and willingly or unwillingly the teachers have no option but to extend their best co-operation to the students at different stages. Hence, the teachers working in the rural areas are required to be given additional incentives. This would motivate them and the results would be positive. But we need to link the incentive plans to efficiency.

In the face of recent negative developments in the society, it is pertinent that we assign due weightage to the informal education. We assign an overriding priority to the infrastructural facilities but fail in gravitating our attention on the human resources or say, the quality of teachers. We are not opposed to the use of sophisticated technologies for innovating the curriculum; we are not opposed to the beautiful buildings and furnitures; even we are not opposed to the amenities and facilities to the students inside and outside the classrooms but one thing cannot be negated that even if we lack these facilities but have a strong and dedicated team of efficient teachers; the students would get the standard educational aid. If we talk about Doon and Scindia schools, it is quality of the teachers, their dedication and commitment to their profession and a conducive atmosphere that counts much more and not so the material assets. Against this background, it is pertinent that we make available to the educational institutions the best lot of the society so that they contribute a lot to the process of human capital formation. Keeping in view the latest developments around the world, we need adequate financial resources to update and innovate our curriculum. If we make it possible, the fee structure would be abnormally high and a majority of people in the society would fail in using the services. This turns our eyes on charity, donation and we have also to think in this direction.

Strategic marketing advocates in favour of innovations in education. The government and private high schools are supposed to redesign their curriculum and to inform and persuade the prospects in a right fashion and therefore, they have to activate their efforts. The personal and non-personal promotion measures are to be made more creative in their efforts. Unless we have innovative services, we do not find any justification for investing a lot on promotion. If we have quality services, the word-of-mouth communication would simplify our task. The prospects and the parents would come to know the realities from their friends, relatives and so on. It is not meant that they should not think in favour of advertisement and publicity; but here our emphasis is on an optimal investment. We should have a budget for promotion but an overriding priority is to be given to the services that we make available to our students.

In the Indian setting, we need priority attention to the rural students and the rural high schools. It is on account of the fact that the condition in the rural areas is found very alarming. The conscious students and rich parents prefer urban high schools which promote migration of rural population to the urban areas. If we plan to develop a school in the villages close to the towns and cities, the "reverse exodus" cannot be denied which would only not encourage rural students and parents but would also engineer a foundation for the development of backward villages. In the beginning, it is very natural that the private sector would not follow it and therefore, the government high schools equipped with world-class amenities and facilities should preferably be opened in the villages not in towns and cities.

MARKETING MIX FOR INTERMEDIATE EDUCATION

After the completion of secondary education, we bear the responsibility of strengthening the foundation for higher education and this is made possible by enriching the intermediate education. Again we need to manage the teenagers, which complicates our task and requires more professional excellence. The selection of a particular discipline is made at this stage and therefore, it is an important decision-making area for career planning. The aptitude test is to solve the problem efficiently in selecting a particular area for developing knowledge. Like the secondary education, we find here the involvement of both the government and private plus-two schools. In addition, we find this stage also suitable with the viewpoint of vocational education since the prospects are now found at the threshold of maturity. In Figure 16.4, we have already talked about the curriculum development at this stage. Now, we go through the marketing problem so that the prospects get the quality services and the institutions get an opportunity to develop and flourish. Since the standard or quality of services is substantially influenced by the soundness of an organisation, it is important that educational institutions serve the society in the face of holistic marketing principles which allow them to develop and enrich their potentials, but not to make profits. It is against this background that we talk about the application of marketing principles in the educational institutions.

To start with, let us focus on the development of curriculum for intermediate education. At almost all the stages of education, the development of curriculum is found in the face of changing socio-economic and cultural requirements and this stage cannot be an exception to this well-established theory. While designing syllabi, we need to assign due weightage to the prospects and their background, specially to brush-up their potentials in tune with their counterparts living in the urban areas and coming from the highly educated families. As and when we find threshold barrier, the best solution is to start a crash programme/capsule course to remove it on a priority basis since it proves to be an important barrier to effective communication and further develops inferiority complex. Though the educational institutions assigning an overriding priority to this dimension from the very beginning do not face such problem but in the Indian setting, a number of institutions keep it at the bottom of their agenda which complicates their task and the students ultimately prove to be less receptive. Whatever the discipline they opt for should be in the face of their past records or in the face of an aptitude test since in some of the cases, we find students securing high marks in a particular subject but showing least interest in developing expertise and specialisation in that subject. We assign here due weightage to the vocational course since it is found helpful in many ways. To be more specific, the poor students who are not in a position to afford expensive education can get financial support by using their skills. Our focus should be here on linking the vocational courses with the latest developments so that we do not face any difficulties in developing expertise in the same area, if students like or the circumstances necessitate.

The promotional decisions also play here a significant role to motivate the prospects. The instrumentality of personal promotion determines the magnitude of success. The students are here more conscious and therefore the teachers are supposed to increase their communication ability. Of late, a number of technologies are available to focus attention on emerging sensitive problems and the teachers are expected to use the same to minimise the duration of credit hours for their core curriculum so they get enough time to go through the allied problems related to informal education.

At this stage, the drug addiction is found emerging as a big social evil and teachers, as a part of informal education, can highlight on its negative effects. In addition, advertisements are also used here to motivate students, particularly to seek admission. The private schools are found advertising through print media but again we do not find government schools showing interest in advertising. If the media support them, they can make it possible even without raising their budgets. We do not find anything wrong in advertising since through advertisements we provide an opportunity to our students to judge the best and to take a decision in tune with their requirements and potentials. The government as well as the private schools should attempt to develop rapport with the media so that they publicise efficiently even without influencing their budgets.

Again we find fee structure a critical decision-making area for private or public schools. Since the institutions are now required to invest more on inputs, it is judicious that they charge more for their outputs. Like secondary schools, the plus-two schools are also supposed to adopt a rational fee structure which provides an opportunity even to the poorer and weaker sections of the society to take admission and to get education. The motive is to subserve the social interests and we find holistic pricing policy suitable for educational institutions since it not only paves avenues for the development of schools but also provides an opportunity to the poor and intelligent students to get education. So far as the private schools are concerned, we again find a case of charging exorbitant fees by them. This turns our eyes on a code of conduct that regulates the private schools in particular to adopt a rational fee structure. So far as the generation of financial resources is concerned, we should open avenues for both the government as well as the private schools. They should be given a freedom to collect donations from big business houses, affluent sections of the society and so on.

In the context of distribution of services, it is significant that we concentrate our attention on the connecting chains. The teaching and non-teaching personnel are supposed to perform this role in a right fashion. The government plus-two schools again need an intensive care since like secondary schools, they have to cross a big channel for the offering of services or implementation of a development plan. It is also found that due to bureaucracy, the students also fail in getting scholarships in time. The need of the hour is to minimise the gap so that students, teachers and schools do not suffer on this account.

VOCATIONAL EDUCATION

Our strong emphasis is on the fact that higher education should not be generalised. The excellent and very excellent students should prefer higher education. In the Indian setting where we find unemployment problem at its peak, it is a crying need of the hour that we promote vocational education. It is against this background that we have included it in the service mix for both the students who have passed secondary school examinations or have completed intermediate education. This would help them in becoming self-sufficient. Not only this, the employment opportunities would also be generated for the blue-collar workers.

With a view to restructuring higher education, to delink degrees from jobs and to strengthen education to make it good enough to get a job, government and UGC have initiated a number of programmes for introducing vocational education both at the school and college levels. This is with the motto of diversifying the educational opportunities, enhancing individual employability, reducing the mismatch between demand and supply of skilled manpower and providing an alternative for those who are not interested in getting the higher education.

The vocational courses are offered at the plus-two stage in its major areas, e.g., agriculture, business and commerce, engineering and technology, health and paramedical services and home sciences. It is right to say that we have not been successful in marketing vocational courses successfully since till now only 4 per cent students have been allured. A number of colleges and polytechnics and institutions have been found offering this course.

We find vocational courses also for the degree students where the subjects are archaeology and musicology, advertising and sales promotion, mass communication and video production, travel and tourism management, actuarial science and several others which could provide added specialisation. We also find institutions offering a range of vocational and skill-based career development courses in areas such as gems and jewellery, footwear technology, plastics, food processing and construction management.

Here, it is essential to clarify the differences that we find between vocational and professional courses. At the beginning of skill-oriented education, we generally call it a vocational course that is based on practical knowledge but at the later stage when we develop excellence and expertise and concentrate on professionalism, we call it a professional course. It is in this context that postgraduate students are enrolled in the professional courses like MBA, MTA and others.

Of course, it is a difficult task to vouch for the credentials of all such institutions engaged in imparting vocational education but it is not wrong to comment that a number of institutions have not been successful in making available quality education to the students. Vocational or professional courses need specialised teaching personnel but by and large in almost all the institutions we find substandard teachers engaged in educating the students. This makes it essential that we are selective. The demand for competence in vocational skills is bound in time, to usher in a training revolution where people entering occupational areas would be recruited on the basis of their competence rather than their qualifications. Some of the students also opt for interior design, textile or accessory design, commercial art, graphic design or advertising. The professional courses require conceptual and intellectual skills but we do not find the same thing with the vocational courses. Here, the practical knowledge plays an important role. The students in getting the theoretical knowledge are supposed to know only the fundamentals. It is significant here to mention that computer industry has also been opening new vistas for vocational courses.

In India, the computer industry is found growing at a phenomenal rate of 45 per cent per annum. It is among the fastest growing sector of the Indian economy. By the turn of this century, this sector would employ approximately 2,25,000 fully qualified professionals, apart from 75,000 part-time operators. Just in the first decade of the 21st century, the requirement would be near 4,00,000 computer professionals. These facts are a mute testimony to this proposition that it is a growing sector and in near future would contribute sizeably to the job market. But the main thing is to maintain the international standard so that our professionals are efficacious enough to deliver world-class services.

Another expanding field is that of hospitality and travel. Or say, the hotel industry has also a bright future. We need a number of professionals for this industry. Food catering and beverage management, housekeeping, personnel and other hotel services are to create new job opportunities. The tourism industry would also get an important place which would require a good number of personnel in different areas like travel agents, tourist guides, tour operators, etc. Mass communication would also be a fast growing sector.

In a country like India where we have tremendous opportunities, our problems reach to an alarming stage since we often fail in capitalising on the opportunities in a right way. The policy makers are required to assign an overriding priority to the development of curriculum in the aforesaid areas by taking the support of experts. The motive is to impart quality education so that we contribute substantially to the processes of globalisation of economy.

Motivating the students in these areas is a crying need of the hour and therefore, we talk about creative advertisements so that the prospects are sensed and influenced in a right way. Once we succeed in speeding up the circle of vocational education, the copious avenues would be paved for lucrative jobs.

MARKETING MIX FOR HIGHER EDUCATION

Education for the development of excellence; education for the development of expertise and education for the development of knowledge are some of the motives which necessitate a sound strategy for the development of higher education in almost all countries of the world. Establishing leadership in the world is possible when we have a well-developed system for higher education in which efficiency remains the only criterion to evaluate the performance. The universities, colleges, institutes, studies and research centres are found engaged in the process of offering higher education. Scientific inventions and innovations, technological advances, professional excellence and managerial proficiency are some of the important dimensions playing a decisive role in shaping the destiny of a nation. The system of higher education is found efficacious in making available to the society a dedicated, committed, devoted and professionally-sound team of human resources who decide the future of a nation. Against this background, the crying need of the hour is to manage the system of higher education in such a way that sets a right direction for the development of human resources in the national and international perspectives. Quality outputs, in a very natural way, need quality inputs which generally are found expensive. We attempt to focus here on the problem of rising costs of inputs for producing the quality outputs. In the Indian setting, the problem is found a challenging one since the masses are not in a position to afford the high costs for getting the quality services. The universities, colleges, institutes and research centres are found in a depleted condition. The financial crunch is a major problem which has been disallowing these centres to incorporate the time-honoured changes in their curriculum even if they are found dying. Except a very few, almost all the centres are engaged in producing substandard outputs resulting into unemployment, poverty and backwardness. It is in this context that we talk in favour of marketing higher education which according to the holistic marketing principles attempt to enrich the efficacy of these centres *vis-a-vis* offer quality services even to the poor persons having an outstanding educational background.[14] This is based on the principles of societal marketing in which the educational institutions are not supposed to make profits. Thus, the marketing practices here pave ways for the development of human resources in the face of international specifications. Here, the qualitative transformation establishes an edge over the quantitative transfiguration.

Product Mix: In the process of marketing, at the very outset, we turn our eyes on the multi-dimensional services to be made available by these advanced centres of learning. We call it a service mix. This in a very natural way gravitates our attention on the curriculum which not only produce efficient persons but even the dedicated and committed persons. At the different stages of education, we have talked about ethical, moral, social and cultural values. If we have developed human resources in the face of curriculum discussed earlier, it is very natural that a sound foundation is already engineered for the subsequent developments. Important dimensions of the service mix are buildings, furniture, sanitation, water, electricity, library, equipments, laboratory and the teaching and non-teaching personnel. In the face of technological advances, the universities, colleges and institutes need to equip the information centre for data processing. These items increase the costs on inputs, though for innovations in education, we find them very much instrumental which have a far reaching effect on the communication ability of teachers. In addition, it is also found effective in increasing the receiving capacity of students. To be more specific, the institutions now need to have a well-established computer lab. For the development of premises, the plantation and gardening are also found important. The car parking, cycle parking, auto parking arrangements, of late, are found necessary in almost all the educational institutions. In the group of sophisticated communication technologies, we now find fax machines and internet services essential to transmit and receive important messages. The computers are required to be connected with internet. These recent developments are now making the educational services more expensive. If we have to make available to our students, the world-class teaching aid, we cannot underestimate the latest developments. On the other hand, the prospects are not in a position to bear the high fee structure. The educational institutions find it difficult to improve their core and peripheral services mainly due to financial crunch. The government colleges and institutes fail in mobilising finance from the internal sources. It is in this context that we talk about improving the quality of services even if the prospects have to bear some burden.

Promotion Mix: The universities, colleges and institutes across the country have been found making huge financial provision for promoting their services. In the Indian setting, the private colleges and institutes have also been following the same strategy but so far as the government-managed colleges and institutes are concerned, they are not in a position to follow the same due to financial constraints. Since we are discussing this problem with the notion that educational institutions have to make possible qualitative and quantitative improvements in the system, we do not find anything wrong in promoting the same. Here, the teaching and non-teaching personnel can play a significant role. The personal promotion is related to the instrumentality of teaching and non-teaching personnel who play a decisive role in motivating and influencing the prospects. The enrolment position is to be improved in the face of accommodation or the availability of seats. In addition to the personal promotion, we also need to advertise our services. The private institutions have been found advertising but the government institutions fail in doing so. While advertising, it is important that we focus on the quality of services and visualise the outstanding contributions of the institutions to the development of higher education. The audiovisual exposure has considerably been successful in sensitising the prospects. We can also take the support of printing media. The TV and radio should have a policy to promote the educational institutions, specially to motivate the rural prospects and categorically to influence the girls living in the rural areas. They are supposed to charge very nominal amount for this purpose and to advertise the messages and slogans during sensitive hours keeping in view the rural prospects. If we talk about a rational policy for fee, it is judicious that we also talk about bearing of social burdens by media. The publicity measures are also required to be strengthened and for this, we need to develop rapport with the media people. To be more specific for the government-managed colleges and institutes, we find it essential since they are found charging very nominal fees from the students. The motive in promoting the services is to inform, sense and motivate the prospects so that we succeed in getting the best intakes to impart the world-class education.

Price Mix: In a country like India where we find a majority of the persons poor and marginally poor, it is a challenging task to adopt a fee structure which is welcome by almost all the segments.[15] However, we find it essential to go through the problem and to adopt a strategy which is acceptable to the majority of our prospects. It is not essential that higher education facilities are made available to all. It is against this background that we have talked about vocational education. The students coming in the "average" category or even in "good" category should prefer specialisation in the vocational courses. On the other hand, the students under the "excellent" and "very excellent" categories should prefer higher education. We do not talk here about regional or rural bias. The facts are based on their credentials or say, outstanding merits. The colleges, universities and institutes should adopt a rational fee strategy which charges the least possible fees from the poor students. We can also think here regarding free of cost education to the students found extraordinarily meritorious but abnormally poor. On the other hand, the losses on account of this provision should be shared by medium and high income groups in proportion to their incomes. We can also think in favour of providing tax exemption facilities to the medium group parents paying high fees. The donations received from different sources should be meant for the development and expansion plans. Such a ratoinal fee strategy would make the educational institutions competent enough to initiate qualitative and quantitative transformation in the higher education. The students would be benefited and the educational institutions would contribute substantially to the formation of human capital. It is not wrong to mention that now parents are found more conscious to the education of their children and they make huge provision for the same in their family budgets. This is simply to focus that now prospects are very conscious to get quality education even if they have to pay more. In a country like India, it is essential that government colleges with all the latest facilities are located in villages so that the problem of urban congestion is minimised considerably.

In any case, the private or government colleges and institutes should not create such a situation which stands as a major barrier in promoting education to women. Contrary to it, they should formulate such a strategy which motivates and persuades them to come out to develop their credentials so that their contributions to the development of education and knowledge are increased substantially. We can use fee as a motivational tool for this purpose. In addition, we should also offer to them other incentives. It is against this background that such a strategy would pave ways for the development of the personalities of children. Since tomorrow when they become father and mother, they can educate and train their children.

Place Mix: Our emphasis is here on the gap that we find in between the formulation of an education plan and its implementation in the institutions concerned. In most of the cases, to be more specific in the government colleges and institutes, we find it acting as a major barrier. The policy makers frame policies and the bureaucrats in government and front-line staff in universities, colleges, institutes waste much more time in their implementation. The development and expansion plans, the scholarships to students, even salaries to teaching and non-teaching personnel are delayed on that account. At this stage when we advocate in favour of offering more financial and non-financial incentives to the students and teachers, such a situation is to jeopardise our all efforts. Once again, it is essential to focus on the problem that if the IITs and IIMs are making available to the society the best lot of human capital, it is not due to buildings, furnitures, and other material assets they have, but due to efficient, qualified and dedicated teachers they employ. The motive here is to make it clear that even with the least possible infrastructural facilities, we can be successful in producing the best, if we have a team of efficient and dedicated teachers. We cannot negate that motivation paves the way for the generation of efficiency. Of course, the infrastructural facilities make the process convenient and communicable but the most important part of education is the contribution of teachers. Against this background, we can imagine the frustration and disinterest among teachers when they are denied even their legitimate rights. In a true sense, we need a structural change in the distribution process and such a change should be practised with the motto that students and teachers are not denied at least their minimum rights.

In this context, it is also essential to turn our eyes on other side of the coin. We also find cases where teachers get due salaries and other incentives but fail to discharge even their defined duties then what to talk of their personal involvement in the process of energising the mission. The administration should not hesitate to punish those teachers.

The main thing is to seek the best possible cooperation of all who are acting as a chain in imparting education. We can make it possible by minimising the gap and fixing the accountability.

Process: Higher education, like other levels, is in a sorry state today. The universities and colleges managed by government have not been giving due weightage to this mix of marketing in which we find large-scale distortion in the process. In a true sense, the providers fail in offering the promised quality of services to the users and an important reason for the same is the distortion in the process made by both the teaching and non-teaching staff. The teachers are very much instrumental in degrading the quality of teaching and research. The non-teaching staff, by adopting and promoting unfair practices, have distorted the quality of services and dissatisfied the users at large. Of course, we find private-managed educational institutions even, in the context of higher education, gaining an edge over government-managed higher centres of learning. This submix of the marketing makes it necessary that the administrators, professionals with the responsibility of offering the services ensure that promised quality of services as published in the prospectus, information brochures and advertisement materials are made available to the ultimate users without any delay or distortion in the process. Both the sources of offering, the teachers and non-teaching staff, should be managed properly for bridging the existent gap between the services-promised and services-offered. Unless we fix responsibility for the same, the task would remain unfulfilled. The front-line staff managing the counters have an outstanding responsibility of satisfying the users by making available to them the administrative services, such as issue of certificates, degrees and marksheets or other requirements. In addition to the generation of efficiency, they also have to improve their behavioural profile, because, particularly in the government-managed colleges and universities, we find non-teaching staff in general have a low behavioural profile. They are totally unaware of behavioural management and on account of indecent behaviour of non-teaching staff, the situation in a few cases become explosive. This needs refresher courses or orientation courses for them particularly to develop their awareness regarding the need of behavioural management in improving the quality of services. In addition, the teaching staff/faculty also need to develop a high behavioural profile.

Physical Evidence and Attractions: In the formulation of marketing mix for higher education, this submix of marketing occupies a place of outstanding significance. The universities, colleges and institutes providing higher education need service ambience found distinct to others. The servicescapes need due attention of marketing so that the students or others visiting the centres for higher education form a positive impression and based on that make a choice for enrolment. Since in the higher centres of learning, we find students generally grown-up, they are found in a position to make a sense of judgement without seeking opinions of even their parents; the marketers need a professional touch so that the service fragrance adds additional attractions.

The designing of educational institutions must be in the face of recent developments so that the benefits of new generation of information and communication technology are made available to the students without any gap. If we find centres concerned with exact science and life science, there must be sufficient provisions for the development of lab. In the process of offering educational services, we also find use of equipment and this should be displayed with the motto of projecting a positive image of the institutions. The marketers need to assign due weightage to signage so that visitors or admission seekers coming to the educational institutions find it convenient to identify the different points where the services are made available. The positiong signposts should be at a place attracting the attention of all. The prospectus, brochures, newsletters should be attractive where detailed information should be furnished. The lighting arrangements, ventilation, sanitation must be up to the mark. The professionals need not to forget that by tangibilising physical facilities, they transmit strong messages to the students and visitors regarding the quality of services to be offered.

In the educational institutions providing higher education, the marketers need to focus on the ambient conditions helping students in developing their aesthetic sense. The tangible components bear the efficacy of facilitating performance or communication of services. The marketers need to make it sure that physical facilities are not only a facilitator but even a socialiser and more so a differentiator. Since we find intensity of competition gaining a momentum both at national and global levels, it is pertinent that the educational institutions providing higher education distinct their physical facilities with the motto of establishing an edge over their rivals.

The above-mentioned facts make it clear that physical evidence needs due attention of marketers with a different vision and mission. The surroundings, premises need fragrance to add additional attractions to the services. Impressing upon the admission seekers and visitors is found easier if we find professionals managing physical facilities keeping in view the ambient conditions successful in generating academic fragrance.

We find globalisation, internationalising not only the economic frontiers but also degenerating our social systems and culture. The impact of westernisation on our lifestyles is a staunch testimony to this proposition. If we watch the dresses of students in universities and colleges, you will notice an invasion on Indian culture. Thanks to the parents who promote this from the very beginning of the management of their children that vulgar dresses mean modernisation. They feel that if they wear dresses denoting Indian culture, they will not be successful in developing excellence as and when they enter the job market. In a true sense, culture and development both can be promoted simultaneously. We find successful women, of course, wearing Indian dresses and at the same time, also developing world-class excellence.

On the other hand, we also find women wearing ultra-modern dresses but not achieving any excellence. Of course, in modern business world, the corporate culture necessitates that people serving the organisations have a distinct look but it does not mean that they compel you to see vulgar dresses. Physical attractions and service conditions have a correlation with the external make-up of an individual. An impressive look does not mean a vulgar or an aggressive look. The teachers and non-teaching staff serving at the centres of higher learning have to assign due weightage to this submix of the marketing which advocates strongly in favour of personal care. Of course, an executive or a technocrat or a medico needs dresses in line with their working conditions and professional requirements but even in that case, there is scope for decency and cultural orientation. It depends solely on our perception of development and modernisation and a place assigned by you to the personality *vis-à-vis* cultural orientation in the behavioural profile.

People: Of course, the infrastructural facilities and new generation of technology play a significant role in improving the quality of services but ultimately it is the contributions of teachers serving educational institutions which establish an edge over all the constituents of efficiency generation. Where teachers are of poor quality, the university administration will find it difficult to satisfy the users. It is really amazing that a majority of the government colleges and universities have not realised the same which has been degenerating the quality of services and resulting from which all the sectors and areas get poor quality of people. We can't negate that degeneration in the quality of educational institutions is the most dangerous development of today. The teachers in a good number engage themselves in private tuition, political activities and all other engagements except the academic activities for which they are suitably paid. Improving the quality of people serving universities, colleges and institutes in different capacities, at different levels is the most important need of today. They can organise refresher and orientation courses for developing and enriching their excellence. For consistent increase in the potentials of teachers, it is necessary that motivational schemes are restructured so that the teachers having higher credentials, showing conviction and commitment to the profession and well aware of professional ethics are suitably rewarded. The process should discourage inefficients so that they improve their potentials. If we go ahead with the process of standard improving the quality of people serving centres of higher, the users will considerably be benefited as only world-class, decent, well-behaved and cultured teachers alone can deliver the goods to the society and can remove the image problem which is posing as a danger while marketing.

Privately-managed colleges and institutes are giving due weightage to the development of people which is helping them in improving the quality of services. Promotion of the efficients influence the inefficients to improve their quality. If we find teaching and non-teaching staff showing consistency in enriching their potentials; the task of top and middle-level management will be considerably simplified. In addition to professional excellence, teachers serving educational institutions have also to develop informal relation. By organising public relations activities, they can develop awareness among students about developing civic and aesthetic sense and value system.

STRATEGIC MARKETING FOR HIGHER EDUCATION

Globalisation opened new vistas for the development of higher education not only in India but around the globe. New doors were opened for qualitative-cum-quantitative improvements in the higher education which made ways for the conceptualisation of innovative marketing so that the organisational as well as the user's interests are protected. The mushroom growth of educational institutions also paved avenues for degeneration in quality. The mounting intensity of competition affected their enrolment position *vis-à-vis* the financial health. The world-wide economic depression has aggravated the financial position of educational institutions around the globe. What to talk of others when we find even Harvard, an internationally acclaimed institution, facing the financial problem. The policy makers, decision-makers, bureaucrats, statesmen, social scientists and activists, global and national bodies need to make a microscopic audit of the multi-faceted deficiencies found in the higher education.

Of late, we find lack of organisational culture and work culture in a majority of the educational institutions providing higher education. We cannot deny that a complete departure from the ethical and moral values has sizeably been responsible for the present degeneration in almost all the areas. If we find a stage of degeneration in the social institutions, specially in the educational institutions, it becomes too much difficult to bring the socio-cultural order back on the rail. If we educate our human resources without inculcating values and culture, it is natural that almost all the sectors suffer because all of us are the product of educational institutions. It is against this background that strategic marketing for higher education draws priority attention of professionals managing the affairs. We go through the problem in the Indian perspective where a number of persons, though otherwise very excellent, fail in getting higher education because they are poor and not in a position to afford the expensive higher education.

The educational institutions providing higher education need a drastic change in their syllabi. While restructuring curriculum, we need excellence in education found commensurate with the changing national and global requirements. Time-tested norms, modernisation of supporting infrastructural facilities, a team of dedicated and committed faculty, responsiveness to social interests, due weightage to social values, civilisation and culture, civic and aesthetic sense are some of the key areas necessitating priority attention. Unfortunately, we have awareness but only for personal gains. We have intelligence but only for manipulation. We need to confess it.

Value engineering process requires to be strengthened in the changing perspective. A fair synchronisation of professional and national excellence will serve the purpose of society and humanity. It we find educational institutions significantly contributing to the process of development, they have justifications for promoting their contributions. Informing, sensing, sensitising, persuading and transforming the target students need creativity in promotion. The educational institutions contributing something concrete find nothing wrong in advertising and publicising. Marketing of education services is not meant adopting it as a business. The educational institutions need a budget for promotion and the limits should not be exceeded. The advertisement messages and appeals may be insensitive but the publicity measures if adopted in a right way are found to be effective. We cannot negate that word-of-mouth promotion is considered to be the most effective component particularly for promoting the services of those educational institutions who have been contributing something concrete to the development of quality students. Actually, the word-of-mouth promoters act as a hidden salesforce and this depends on faculty responsible for improving or deteriorating the quality of education. If in the universities, colleges and institutes, we find excellent teachers, the prospects in general would prefer admission there. This draws our priority attention on the quality of teachers.

The most important dimension agitating the students in India are the expensive education services which become unaffordable to the masses. The government policy makers need due attention on the fee structure. The intelligent students who are poor need priority attention of educational institutions. The public as well as the private sectors need to accept it as a part of their social responsibility.

The marketing mixes like placement draws our attention on two important issues, such as channelisation of services to the students in such a way that promised quality of services reach to them on time. This also focuses our attention on identifying location point for higher education. Because the centres for higher education need a sprawling campus, it is better to locate them in the outskirts or even in the rural areas which would benefit the society in many ways.

The three extended marketing mixes like processing, physical evidence and attractions and people also need due attention of marketers in the very context. Because we raise a strong advocacy in favour of education marketing, it is imperative that the professionals focus on tangibilising the salient features of their services. Particularly, in the centres for higher education, we find use of a number of supporting facilities to add additional attractions, such as library, lab, auditorium, place for brainstorming session, classroom, centre for audiovisual presentation, lighting, ventilation, equipment, new generation of information and communication technology, playgrounds, water, gas, ventilation, sanitation, lounge, transportation, etc. We cannot negate that all these physical facilities make the ambient conditions friendly to the students. The professionals while managing service ambience need to make it sure that the students or others visiting the centres enjoy the academic fragrance.

The educational institutions need ambience found distinct to others. A place generating peace; a place diffusing tension; a place like Think Park may be a suitable place for meditation where we find excellence with distinction. Location, of course, is an important consideration for the world-class educational institutions efficacious of developing quality people.

CHANGING ROLE OF MARKETING PROFESSIONALS IN EDUCATION MARKETING

Gone are the days when we confined the functional responsibilities of marketing professionals only to making profits. It is significant to mention that the non-profit sector of the Indian society did not assign any weight-age to the professional excellence of managers and resulting from which they not only failed in improving the quality of education but also failed in increasing their efficacy of bearing the social costs. It is in this context that the educational institutions of modern India have started realising the importance of marketing. A majority of the technical and professional institutions now conceptualise innovative marketing having social orientation. This helps them in improving the financial health of the educational institutions and at the same time, also simplifies the task of offering world-class services to their students. The process in progress creates a condition in which institutions prove to be of world-class. The cycle of development goes ahead without any interruption.

Studying and understanding the changing behavioural profile of students as well as their parents are found essential for the formulation of a sound marketing mix for the educational institutions. The marketers are found successful in identifying their attitudes and offering the services in tune with their changing requirements. Earlier, the beneficiaries considered their spending as expenses but now we find them recognising the same as an investment. Such an attitudinal change has played an incremental role in the process of marketing the education services.

With the new generation of Information and Communication Technology (ICT), we find them efficacious of getting the right and up-to-date information considerably helping them in the innovation process. They get information related to demand and supply position and formulate a package commensurate with the requirements of changing global business environment. This helps them in keeping the demand and supply position at an optimal point.

The marketers find themselves in a position to segment the market in which we find a mix of potential users coming from different segments. Matching the requirements of a particular segment with the demands in the changing job markets simplifies the process of identifying the preferences of users. While advertising or making use of the other promotional measures; they are found successful in the sensitisation and persuasion processes.

Thus, in the modern business world, the professionals managing social institutions are supposed to play a catalytic role. All of us are well aware of the instrumentality of educational institutions in developing multi-dimensional faculties for the development of productive human resources. Almost all sectors of society and national economy go forward, if the educational institutions deliver goods to the society. Conversely, a degeneration in the services of educational institutions lead to degeneration at all the levels.

When we talk about elementary, secondary or higher education, our prime focus is on utilising the services of marketing professionals in all the areas so that innovations in the education system attract users both at the national and global levels. We should concentrate on developing a new perception of quality in tune with the emerging trends and challenges so that users at large benefit without any geographical boundary. Particularly while promoting the higher education, we have to work with this motto. The perception of quality devised by us would benefit everyone. In the goods manufacturing context, we talk about product innovations and promotion of research and development activities. It is high time that we make it possible even in the service generating organisations and more so in the non-profit organisations where the professionals have to go through an acid test.

You are responsible for orchestrating different submixes of marketing in such a fashion that the services are of quality and cost-effective. When we talk about the Indian society where masses find the expensive educational services unaffordable, it is to be made cost-effective. This can be done by regulating the unproductive expenses and by increasing the number of users specially of the affluent sections of the society. Of late, the affluent sections do not like their children to get education in the general institutions based on the assumptions that they will not get quality education. The moment general educational institutions show their worth, rich will also be motivated to enroll in those institutions.

The prime task is to improve the quality of service profile. You have to ensure value addition in the entire process of development. While developing the curriculum, you should ensure that your students are perfect; perfection is not related just to professional excellence. You have to inject additional properties by making them personally-committed and value-based. This, in addition to the curriculum, should be for informal education which need due emphasis on developing civic sense, nutritional awareness, aesthetic values and this needs promotion of informal education. Of late, the value system has been facing an adverse condition and this is due to the fact that educational institutions in general have failed in promoting the process of value engineering. In the education system, ethical dimensions play a significant role but a very few of the educational institutions have realised it. Therefore, marketing professionals, while managing educational institutions should assign an overriding priority to the development of value system. It is to be practised at all the three levels of imparting educational aids and training facilities.

Today, there is a fundamental change in the nature and character of education as professional courses have established an edge over the general courses. This is on account of the evolving developments in the job markets. The marketing professionals also need to promote general education but their prime focus should be on vocational, professional and technical courses as this will open new vistas for the generation and mobilisation of financial resources. If educational institutions are financially sound, the process of making them professionally excellent will be easy and without interruption. When they become financially sound, their contributions to social costs will also increase and thus they would be in a position to offer even cost-free services to a few of the poorest sections.

Transmission of information is an important dimension for effective promotion. When your service mix happens to be of world-class, it is necessary that the public also become aware of your positive contributions. This focuses your attention on creative promotional measures and you find yourself in a position to inform, sense, sensitise, and persuade the users and potential users about the quality of services proposed to be offered to them. Being a marketing professional, you are also able to be a creative promoter and your task would be easy even in an insensitive society. You have the sophisticated media for the transmission of information and you can make use of each one of them depending on your budget. Here too, you should not forget cost economy.

Of course, you belong to the non-profit sector but it does not mean that you do not realise the instrumentality of finance to increase your strength of bearing the burden of social costs. A rational fee structure subserving the interests of all the segments optimally is to be promoted and you can do it.

Quality teachers are the valuable assets. All the facilities and amenities prove to be dwarf before their positive contributions. Since they also live in a materialistic age, it is unfair to expect from them improved quality of services when they are not adequately compensated. This draws your attention on the motivational schemes that you can promote for attracting the outstanding and dedicated teachers. You have to reward them suitably as otherwise they would be discouraged and such type of demotivation over a period of time will lead to degeneration in quality. With well-developed marketing information system, it is easier to quantify the contributions of an individual or a team. Marketing intelligence system would be of considerable importance in rating and grading their contributions.

When we talk about the development of educational services, it is important that you assign a transcendental priority to the development of campus, beautification of surroundings to give it the look of a think park. In the generation of efficiency, surroundings play a constructive role, and hence we feel the need for cultivation of aesthetic sense. Gardening and plantation make the atmosphere healthy and natural. This exercise needs a peaceful and natural environment.

In this age of technology, you can't think about time-honoured development unless your institution is found tempted to techniculture. The rate of sensitivity is greatly increased through modern communication and information technology. Audiovisual exposure facilities help to sensitise even insensitive segments of society. This also helps while strengthening and imparting training facilities for an all-round development of the students. In a few selected areas, you need lab. facility and innovative devices have to be promoted to intensify research activities. Plants, equipments and instruments of the new generation should be incorporated for getting the desired results.

A number of cases have proved that educational institutions provide for qualitative improvements but the people working there may become a party to the degeneration process. It is necessary that you publish prospectus, information brochures, advertisement literature, newsletters, and it reports of your institution to get the expected cooperation of the people engaged in the process otherwise, the services degenerate and the ultimate users fail to get the promised quality. Therefore, it is essential that you are sincere to your behavioural profile as also of all the staff, so that they make honest efforts to develop an awareness.

The above facts make it clear that marketing professionals are expected to play a leading role in shaping the educational institutions. The professional excellence of the marketers will benefit the educational institutions in many ways. You make profits. You serve and subserve social interests. Both of them are significant but in marketing the services of educational institutions, you have to work with a service motive because the profit motive may lead to exploitation of the users especially when you manage a non-profit organisation.

The government as well as the private schools, colleges, universities, institutes and deemed universities need a change of attitude to bring back the derailed systems on the right track. In the Indian context, there are a number of educational institutions in all the categories and at all the levels who have been successful in producing world-class outputs. If we look at the first level, the Doon School, Scindia School, DPS, The Lawrence School (Shimla), Daly (Indore), The Mayo (Ajmer), Netrahat and a few of the schools managed by missionaries have earned good reputation because their students have proved their excellence in almost all the areas. They have been doing well and the most important fact that we find there is professionalism. They have stuck to the defined principles of marketing and all of us are well aware of their marketability. The parents have developed a craze to get their children admitted to leading schools of the country even if the fee structure is high. So also, we find a number of colleges, such as St. Stephen, Hindu, Sri Ram College of Commerce (Delhi), Presidency College (Chennai), Loyola College (Chennai), L.S.R. College (Delhi), R.A. Poddar (Mumbai), IIMC (Hyderabad), Presidency College (Kolkata) and many others well-known for their contributions have been attracting students desirous of getting quality education.

The technical and professional colleges and institutes have also proved their world-class excellence and we are well aware of the outstanding contributions of IITs and IIMs, though they have consistently been raising their fee structure, When we talk of others, we find coaching institutes preparing students for reputed educational institutions, specially for IITs attracting a good number of prospects seeking admission of their children and even there, the fee structure is no barrier. We know about the rush for FIIT JEE. In any discipline and stream, where there is motivation to parents and students, quality remains the lone factor attracting potential users. We agree with this viewpoint that while managing the educational institutions, all of them have acted very professionally and so they have been successful in improving their quality and increasing their marketability.

The government policy makers need to consider these cases in the changed scenario because the low fee structure of a majority of the educational institutions, managed by them have failed to attract prospects and despite the increasing pressure on the government exchequer, we find their contributions to quality moving downward. In the years to come, the potential users would pay for quality and it is high time that government schools and colleges change their attitudes. They have to open up new avenues for qualitative transformation which requires a structural change in the levels of management and a fundamental change in the policy decisions. Marketing educational services is an effective prescription that may help all the mismanaged educational institutions. Since a majority of them face a big image problem, it is necessary that they concentrate on improving the quality of their institutions by exploiting their potentials. The infrastructural constraints, financial handicaps and managerial deficiencies need intensive attention. All of them need to give top priority to the quality of their faculty because other supporting amenities and facilities may prove to be just of secondary importance. It is really amazing that a majority of them hardly think over the quality of their faculty as in a number of cases where quality people are working, they have been demotivated and inefficient, based on other considerations have been promoted and motivated. This strengthens the vicious circle of degeneration that shows disinterest in the transformation process.

Practising social marketing principles appear to be significant in the educational institutions at all the levels. Right from primary to the higher level, the transformation processes are required to be activated. The syllabi, instrumental in developing quality people, should be developed and adopted. The fee structure has to be made rational. The avenues for the mobilisation of internal financial resources deserve due attention. The individual and institutional donors are to be motivated. Since the educational institutions have the responsibility of contributing to the social costs, it is essential that different segments of society come forward and raise financial contributions to improve their financial health. Since expensive inputs are necessary to improve the quality of education, the hurdle of financial crunch is to be removed on a priority basis. There is no logic behind increasing the financial pressure on the state exchequer as the costs on the transformation of human resources into human capital has been non-optimal. The products of IITs and IIMs, because they have world-class excellence prefer to capitalise on the opportunities based on personal considerations. They do not assign any weightage to the social costs. They ignore the amount that poor tax payers have invested on their transformation. They are not influenced by social or national considerations. It leads to conclusion that a fundamental change is necessary in the education system which concentrates on quality upgradation and value addition. Of late, a number of banks and other financial institutions even private sector has come forward offering loan facilities to the students for enrolment in the IITs and IIMs. So financial constraint will no longer obstruct the process of transformation, if we have quality students. Hence, there is a strong case in favour of qualitative transformation.

The marketing professionals in the changed scenario, would be required to show their world-class excellence. The service profile of educational institutions in general need due attention. While designing syllabi or developing a curriculum, all the educational institutions need to orchestrate formal and informal education in an optimal fashion. It is necessary to mention that even educational institutions of world-class have not assigned due weightage to informal education. This is because the informal education is not getting any place in their curriculum development. It is high time that they assign number one priority to the value system and make provisions for value engineering in their syllabi. At all the levels, this is necessary as this would give impetus to the process of development as found in Japan. It is in this context that we should practise,[16] "Total Quality Management," which on the one hand, improve the quality of subjective knowledge while on the other, also engineer a sound foundation for value orientation. Truly, the educational institutions are responsible to develop quality people and "quality in totality" is required to be their motto. Perfection is not possible unless we give due weightage to value addition.

The holistic concept of management makes it necessary that organisations in general and the non-profit organisations in particular revamp their development agenda. They need to assign an overriding priority to social marketing which makes it essential that people contribute to the development of educational institutions and only then the educational institutions will become potentially sound and increase their contributions to the process of social transformation. One-way traffic will only aggravate the problems and in any case, it is not to be an effective prescription for social transformation.

CONSUMER PROTECTION REGULATIONS FOR EDUCATIONAL INSTITUTIONS

The marketing professionals managing educational institutions are also required to develop their awareness of the recent changes in the Consumer Protection Act because now education comes under the purview of consumer courts. The National Consumer Disputes Redressal Commission has finally given the green signal for hauling up educational institutions for offering the negligent services. In a recent order, the apex court has resolved the basic question of whether educational institutions come under the ambit of Consumer Protection Act held that they are also liable for rendering the poor quality of services. The instrumentality of this recent order of the National Commission can be understood from the fact that for more than 14 years, the issue of applicability of the Consumer Protection Act to educational institutions remained uncertain. A big question mark was found before the parents and ultimate users whether they could use the provisions of the Consumer Protection Act. The recent order of the National Commission in the case of *Bhupesh Khurana vs. Vishwa Buddha Parishad* has ultimately unlocked this basic doubt. It is right to mention that confusion in the issue arose from the order of the National Commission itself when in 1996 in the case of *Chairman, Board of Examination, Madras vs. Mohideen Abdul Kader,* the commission was not sure whether imparting of education would come under the definition of service in the Act. But in the case of Bhupesh Khurana, the National Commission states clearly and unambiguously, "Imparting of education by an educational institution for consideration falls within the ambit of service as defined in the Consumer Protection. Act. Fees are paid for services to be rendered by way of imparting education by the educational institutions. If there is no rendering of service, question of payment fee would not arise. The complainants (the students in the case) had hired the service of the respondents (the college) for consideration and so they are consumers as defined in the Consumer Protection Act. The order (OP no. 168 of 1994) came in response to a class action suit by twelve students complaining that the Buddhist Mission Dental College run by Vishwa Buddha Parishad

had in their advertisements given an impression that the college was affiliated to Magadh University, Budh Gaya and recognised by Dental Council of India. It was only when the college failed to conduct the examinations had they realised that both claims were untrue. Holding the service rendered by the college to be deficient, the National Commission directed it to refund the admission expenses of all the twelve students along with 12 per cent interest. In addition, it also directed the institution to pay ₹ 20,000 to each of them by way of compensation for the expenses defrayed on purchase of books, hostel expenses, etc. and for the loss of two academic years. It also awarded ₹ 10,000 as costs of the petition.

The aforesaid facts make it clear that policy makers and marketing professionals need to be aware of the provisions of the Consumer Protection Act. They bear the responsibility of offering quality services and if the services are deficient, the users may take the benefits of the changed provisions of the Consumer Protection Act. They need to make it sure that the promised quality of services reach to the ultimate users without any delay and distortion. While publishing advertisement and circulating publicity materials, they need more care and precaution. If they make available to the users and potential users wrong information, the users may make their task much more difficult.

In view of the evolving developments, the educational institutions are required to assign an overriding priority to the quality of education. This significantly increases the functional responsibilities of a marketing professional because professionalised efforts play a very effective role. Of late when we find the quality perception of education witnessing a fundamental change, the marketing professionals need to conceptualise marketing so that users at large get improved quality of services. The service mix of educational institutions occupy a place of outstanding significance because in view of evolving developments, they need to be innovative. While blending core and peripheral services, it is pertinent that they assign due weightage to informal education because in the Indian setting, the users fail to get informal educational aid at any stage of availing the educational facilities. By enriching informal education, the educational institutions would be in a position to add additional attractions to their services mix which would help increasing the number of students. Besides, the image problem is also to be removed.

The concept of Total Quality Management is found practised even in the education sector because the educational institutions of West have minimised the frequency of innovations and the incorporation and elimination processes, resulting from which the users and potential users develop a craze for the same. The world-class infrastructural facilities, faculty with high behavioural profile at almost all echelons taking part in the process of offering educational aid help them in the projection of a fair image whereas we find image problem complicating the task of professionals working in the Indian setting. With the increasing instrumentality of technology in the process of generating the educational services, the professionals need to change their vision and to work with an avowed mission so that all the segments of society get quality education.

SUMMARY

You have gone through the problem of marketing education. Before starting another chapter, be sure that the following facts are well versed:

Innovative Education: A new approach of imparting education which simplifies the task of touching the set target. We focus here on changing the system of education which is found to be more productive.

Marketing of Literacy: Literacy is related to the knowledge of alphabets to an individual. The functional literacy throws light on a certain level of literacy which is created through a basic instrument of education. Since the literacy rate is sizeably shared by child education, we discuss here both adult education and child education. The term marketing of literacy helps an organisation, government or private, to make the programme proactive. The emphasis is here on the four dimensions of marketing which go through the problem of innovating the curriculum in the face of prospects and environmental conditions, innovating the promotional strategies in the face of technological advances, innovating the pricing/fee strategy in the face of prospects' capacity and innovating the distribution process in the face of prospects so that the adult education programme is made productive. In the curriculum, we have advocated in favour of synchronising the formal and informal education.

Strategic Marketing: While going through the problem of strategic marketing, we focus on an action plan that helps us in reaching the target within the stipulated time and budget. This is an innovative process in the light of an action plan which is designed on the basis of forecasting results.

Marketing Elementary Education: We have included elementary education in the literacy programme since this system is contributing considerably to the literacy rate. We have discussed the seven mixes in the context of marketing of elementary education, both at primary and upper primary stages. While innovating the curriculum, we have advocated in favour of blending the formal and informal education. We find emphasis on informal education since this helps us in protecting the values considered to be a *sine qua non* for organisational culture *vis-à-vis* organisational productivity. We discussed the problem of promotion mainly to inform and motivate the prospects. Since the prospects are kids/children, it is natural that we assign due weightage to the innovative or sophisticated communication technologies to make the child education programme more effective. We also need special emphasis on rural students. Since the government elementary schools offer free of cost services, discussed in the context the role of private schools which generally charge exorbitant fees. There is a need for a rational fee structure. In the context of distribution of services, we have advocated in favour of minimising the gap, specially in the government schools.

Strategic Marketing: Since we have set a target of achieving total literacy by 2012, the strategic marketing focuses on strengthening the innovative process which helps in achieving the target and makes our programme productive. We need creativity in the system of education since the task of wooing the rural children and rural girls is found tough.

Marketing of Secondary Education: Our emphasis here is on secondary education. We need greater precaution here since the prospects are teenagers. In the curriculum, we need a blending of formal and informal education. The core papers are to be selected in the face of the latest developments. The latest communication technologies are to be used for making the system more effective. In the context of promotion, we have gone through the instrumemality of both personal and non-personal promotion. The advertising and publicity measures have been justified. Since both the government and private high schools are engaged in the process, the fee strategy again becomes a challenging task. A number of private high schools have been charging exorbitant fees which need a redressal. In the government high schools, there is a long chain of command for distributing the services which causes delay and against this background, we advocate in favour of bridging the gap to make our programme cost-effective and productive.

Strategic Marketing: In strategic marketing, we talk about the action plan which would make the system effective even for the rural students especially for the girls living in the rural areas.

Marketing Intermediate and Higher Education: At the stage of intermediate education, we have to strengthen the vocational courses. The higher education needs to be made selective, specially for excellent students. Since this stage contributes a lot to the development of knowledge, it is pertinent that we are very careful while designing the curriculum. In the communication process, we focus on scientific developments since this helps in consuming less credit hours. In the context of promoting the educational facilities, we have advocated in favour of strengthening the word-of-mouth communication which is found more effective, even without a budget. In addition, we also justify the advertising and publicity measures for both the government and private colleges, institutes and universities. In respect of fee structure, we focus on a rational fee structure which helps in initiating qualitative-cum-quantitative improvements in the system and makes available the facilities even to the poorer and weaker students. While distributing the services, we concentrate on minimising the gap, specially in the government colleges, institutes and universities.

Strategic Marketing: We have a target of initiating qualitative improvements in the system so that the products are more competitive and also contribute to the socio-economic transformation processes. The advocacy is in favour of enriching the curriculum. The government and private colleges and institutes and universities should advertise and publicise but there must be an optimal budget for that purpose. Essentially, we should ensure that educational institutions do not act as a profit making organisation. It is in this context, we have discussed a strategic plan for the fee-structure which allows even the poor and meritorious students to get education.

Changing Role of Marketing Professionals: Of late, the marketing professionals also need to market the services of non-profit organisations. The educational institutions are concerned to be managed under the non-business sector. While marketing the services of educational institutions, the professionals need to formulate a sound marketing mix protecting users' as well as the organisational interests so that a potentially-sound organisation keeps on moving the process of generating satisfaction.

KEY TERMS

Brunt
State Exchequer
Material Culture
Techniculture
Literacy
Trialability
Montessori
Zero Work Culture
Outskirts
Curriculum
Gullible
Ego Conflict
Lukewarm
Education Information System
Decision Support System
UNESCO
National Literacy Mission
Adult Education Programme
Total Literacy Programme
Sore-spots
Vocational Education
UNICEF
Panchayati Raj
Total Quality Management
Succinct Slogans
Amelioration
Zealous
Grass Root Touch
Apathy
Value Engineering
Threshold Barrier
Human Capital
Aesthetic
Exorbitant
Reverse Exodus
Intelligence Quotient
Copious
Brochures
Servicescapes
Ambient Condition
Service Ambience
Credentials
Mushroom
Academic Fragrance
Acid Test
Perception
Marketing Intelligence System
Consumer Protection Regulations

Review Questions

1. Define Literacy. Distinguish between Literacy and Functional Literacy.
2. Focus on the emerging trends in adult literacy. Explain the rationale behind marketing adult literacy.
3. Write a note on the marketing mix for adult education.
4. Explain the marketing mix for elementary education in the Indian perspective.
5. Focus on the strategic marketing for elementary education in India.
6. Discuss the marketing mix for secondary education in the Indian perspective.
7. Write a note on the marketing mix for intermediate education in the Indian setting.
8. Throw light on the marketing mix for higher education in the Indian perspective.
9. Focus on the changing role of marketing professionals in satisfying the users of educational services.
10. Write a note on education marketing in India.

Application Exercises

1. As a marketing professional, formulate a marketing mix for a leading technical institute.
2. In a Management Institute, you are working as a marketer. Design a marketing mix for that institute.
3. You have been assigned the responsibility of promoting a new course introduced in your institute. Design a mix of different components of promotion helping you in increasing the enrolment.

4. "United Nations Development Report (UNDR) 1994 reveals that India is categorised in the abysmally 'Low Human Development' bracket." In the light of this observation of the UNDR, focus on strategic marketing that you feel to be effective in the Indian setting.
5. "The elementary education substantially contributes to the overall literacy rate." Justify this argument as a marketing professional.
6. "Both the formal and non-formal education need an optimal blending in out curriculum. Justify this statement as a marketing professional specially in relation to primary education.
7. "In the Indian environment, a good number of educational institutions engaged in offering higher education are found in red." As a marketing professional, suggest a plan to be helpful in improving the financial position of financially insolvent educational institutions.
8. As a marketer, you bear the responsibility of improving the quality of education to the users and at the same time, ensuring subserving of social interests. Focus on your role as a marketer.
9. For a leading management institute, you have been asked to formulate a product mix commensurate with the changing global requirements. Suggest a model helping formulation of a sound product mix.
10. Globalisation requires a change in the system of education, specially in the Indian perspective. As a professional, suggest the marketing mix to be effective in the changing conditions.
11. Formulate a marketing mix for education services to be helpful in bearing the social costs.

Endnotes

1. Lakshmi, S., *Innovations in Education,* Sterling India, 1989, pp. 52-54.
2. *Ibid.,* pp. 38-41.
3. Bertrand Russell, *Education for a Better Social Order,* Quoted from Lakshmi S, pp. 55-57.
4. Montessori Martia, *Discovery of the Child,* Quoted from Lakshmi S., *op.cit.,* pp. 46-50.
5. Frederick W.A. Forbel, *The Education of Man: Pedagogies of Kindergarten, Education by Development,* Quoted from Lakshmi, S., *op.cit.,* pp. 41-46.
6. Jha, S.M., *Innovations in Education for Productivity Acceleration,* Proceeding of 8th All India Management Conference October, 1992 pp. 93-103
7. Jha, S.M., *Decision-making Criterion for the Productivity of Human Resources,* HRD Arhiant Productivity of Human Resources, HRD Arhiant Publisher, Jaipur, 1984 pp. 34-47.
8. Manorma Year Book, 2007.
9. Proceedings of UNESCO Tokyo Conference, 1972.
10. Manorma Year Book, 2008.
11. Frederick R. Kharonor, *Facilitation of Learners, Participation in Adult Education,* National Literacy Mission, Directorate of Adult Education, New Delhi, 1995, pp. 99-104.
12. *Ibid.*
13. Jha, S.M., *Privatisation of Education, Strategic Issues,* Employment News, October 1997, Cover Story.
14. Jha, S.M., Should We Market Education?, *The Hindustan Times,* January 25, 1997, Cover Story.
15. Jha, S.M., *Marketing Non-Profit Organisations,* Chapter-4, Himalaya Publishing House, Mumbai, 2003 pp. 367-382.
16. Jha, S.M., *Total Quality Management in Education,* National Seminar, Paper Published in Souvenir 2006, Kamla Nehru Institute, Sultanpur.

CHAPTER

HOSPITAL MARKETING

In the process of social engineering, a number of factors are found instrumental but of all the factors, the medicare and healthcare services assume a place of outstanding significance. We need professional excellence to make hospitals efficacious of bearning the social costs.

Chapter Objectives

Introduction – Hospital Marketing: The Perception – Rationale behind Practising Marketing in Hospitals – Segmentwise Users of Healthcare Services – Behavioural Profile of Users – Market Segmentation – Marketing Information System – Marketing Mix – Product Mix – Promotion Mix – Price Mix – Place Mix – Process – Physical Evidence and Attractions – People – Strategic Marketing – Consumer Protection Regulation – Hospital Marketing in Indian Perspective – Summary – Key Terms – Review Questions – Endnotes.

Learning Objectives

This chapter is to sensitise the readers to the various aspects of marketing hospital services. The readers aware themselves of the conceptual aspect of marketing medicare and healthcare services. They also come to know the justifications for marketing and the relevance of developing the Hospital Information System for different purposes. The hospital professionals go through the different submixes of marketing the healthcare services. The motive of this chapter is to sensitise the readers to the process of application of innovative marketing with the objectives of improving the quality of services, making the services cost-effective, increasing the potentials of bearing the social costs and satisfying the domestic as well as the foreign users so that we find hospitals becoming a centre for serving the society and earning the foreign exchange.

INTRODUCTION

The human capital formation on which our economic transformation programmes significantly rest considerably contribute to the process of material capital formation. In the Indian society, we find healthcare on the bottom of the welfare agenda. This in a very natural fashion obstructs the process of development and prosperity. A healthier 21st century is our target which focuses our attention on the availability of potable or safe drinking water, improved sanitation facilities, family welfare and quality healthcare and medicare services. We cannot negate the fact that scientific inventions and innovations have made possible multi-faceted transformation in the medical sciences which has made an invasion on a number of diseases. We have been successful in eradicating smallpox, we have also been successful in reducing the prevalence and incidence of leprosy but still polio, tuberculosis, cholera, typhoid and a number of communicable diseases, specially AIDS have been instrumental in increasing the death rate. In almost all the developed countries, the government hospitals bear the responsibility of subserving the social interests by making available quality medicare. They have successfully sensitised the masses to the devices essential for healthcare and resulting from which we find the food-prone and water-prone diseases almost at dismal point. Unfortunately, the hospitals in Indian perspective have failed in both the areas. Particularly the government-managed hospitals in a majority of the conditions are found in a depleted condition. When they miserably fail in providing even the basic medicare facilities, how can we expect from them activating the sensitisation process for developing mass awareness to the healthcare.

Sound mind develops in sound health and if we find our population not having a sound health, the task of developing them and transforming them into human capital would remain difficult. All our efforts for developing quality people commensurate with the global changing requirements will turn into a fiasco, if the social institutions like hospitals and healthcare centres are found managerially deficient. Of course, we find a few of the government hospitals of world-class but it is unfortunate to mention that they have been politicalised and facing the problem of quality doctors who are often demoralised and demotivated. Even the world-class supporting infrastructural facilities and equipments fail in delivering goods to the society, if we find social institutions like hospitals and educational institutions not having a conducive service ambience. It is also important to mention that medicare services cannot be productive if we find healthcare services not getting due attention of hospitals, educational institutions and the NGOs. Developing mass awareness needs priority attention and enormous cooperation of all of us failing which the sensitisation process cannot be effective.

Mounting pressure on the management of civic amenities on account of population explosion, increasing health hazards due to the insensitivity of the society and social welfare bodies, high magnitude of unawareness and environmental pollution due to poor rate of literacy and ineffective healthcare communication are some of the critical problems necessitating on overriding priority to medicare and healthcare management. The government policy makers, social reformists and activists and NGOs bear the responsibility for making available to the society quality services so that physically-sound human resources contribute significantly to the process of human capital formation. It is really amazing that even after over half a century, the policy planners have not been successful in ensuring even basic medical aid to the poorest of the poor. In the Indian villages we find the efficiency level of rural health centres almost dismal. The neglected women and children need due attention to activate process of social transformation.

Unawareness leads to multi-pronged degeneration. In the Indian context, we find even the educated segment of the society not well aware of the healthcare devices, then what to talk of illiterate and insensitive segments. The public even now fail to understand the instrumentality of food habits, nutritional awareness, potable water, sanitation services, Yoga and Pranayam in keeping a sound physique. This reduces their resistance power and they are prone to a number of diseases. We often talk about accelerating the rate of human capital formation but the task will remain unfulfilled unless the masses get healthy environment to make themselves stronger. The government exchequer finds it difficult to meet the increasing financial requirements of hospitals and health centres. They are not even allowed to mobilise finance from the internal sources by rationalising the fee structure. The task of mobilising donors and exploring possibilities of donations from different segments of the society have virtually stopped. These negative developments have aggravated the problem of financial crunch. It is because of this we find a majority of the hospitals and health centres almost dying.

Of late, we realised the contributions of professionals in improving the potentials of an organisation. The marketing professionals have the responsibility of satisfying the users of medicare and healthcare services and they are supposed to know the excellence of synchronising different mixes of marketing in such a fashion that interests of users and potentials of an organisation remain protested. We have twin responsibilities; first, to improve the quality of medicare services by enriching the service profile, and second, by making the healthcare communication processes more creative keeping in view the insensitivity, specially of the rural and women segments. The public as well as the private sectors need to fuel the process of development. The existing conditions make a case for the development of the private sector and we find good auguries because in some of the provinces they have been emerging fast; as in Maharashtra 3115, in Kerala 2040, in Himachal Pradesh 57, in Haryana 78 private hospitals have been making significant contributions to the medicare and healthcare services. In states like Andhra Pradesh, Maharashtra, Gujarat and Kerala, some 90 per cent of hospitals are owned privately. The remaining states need to follow the same.

In the process of social engineering, no doubt, a number of factors are found instrumental but, of all the factors, healthcare assumes a place of outstanding significance. 'Health is wealth.' This proverb was effective yesterday, is effective today and will remain effective tomorrow or even a day after tomorrow. This is mainly due to the fact that a sound health is a prerequisite for a healthy and productive mind. To accelerate the pace of economic transformation, we appreciate the contributions of human beings and to improve the quality and strength of human beings, we estimate highly the contributions of healthcare services.

In the Indian society, healthcare management is at the bottom of our personality development agenda and so it becomes instrumental in degenerating our productive efficacy. Of course, it is unfortunate, but the policy makers, healthcare experts, hospitals and healthcare organisations and even the non-governmental social organisations appear disinterested in bringing the derailed healthcare systems back of the rail. It is against this background that a majority of the hospitals and healthcare organisations have, of late, been facing multi-dimensional problems. If the providers become insolvent and poor and weak, it becomes very much difficult to fulfill the everchanging expectations of the users. Decades long neglect of the hospitals and healthcare centers have virtually made them bankrupt. The ultimate sufferers are the poor, since the private hospitals are found subserving the interests of affluents. It is against this background that we find it significant to go through the problem of hospital marketing.

It is true that task of improving their health is quite difficult and requires professionally-sound, and personally-committed team of hospital personnel. In addition, the boardrooms or the policy makers also need an attitudinal change. Gone are the days when the classical physicians, influenced by traditional practices, were successful in diagnosing just with the clinical investigations. Of late, the services of hospitals or healthcare organisations are considerably influenced by sophisticated equipment as also by apparatus, instruments and the world-class professional excellence of the hospital personnel. A number of expensive items are used in the process of diagnosing and treating the patients. Quality inputs generate quality outputs. Based on this principle, we find costs on different types of inputs have increased very rapidly. Again, the state exchequer finds it difficult to extend to the hospitals and healthcare centres adequate grants. The government hospitals are not free to charge even the cost-based fees. Thus, shrinking avenues for the generation of revenues has made the task of qualitative-cum-quantitative improvements much more difficult. The concept of hospital marketing is based on the perception that in lieu of offering poor quality of healthcare services, it is judicious and pragmatic to charge reasonably but to make available to the world-class services. Unless you are strong enough to resist the odds, you cannot survive. And in a materialistic age, unless you are financially sound, you are weak. Based on the same principle, an organisation or an institution also requires to assign due weightage to the financial soundness, since, if they become financially weak, the quality, strength, the confidence, their very existence would be in danger.

Management of marketing the hospital services draws our attention to the formulation of a sound marketing mix for the hospitals and healthcare organisations so that they are in a position to subserve social interests. Besides, the modern social marketing principles are essential, so that social costs do not cross the limits making an organisation or even an individual, financially sick. There are a number of submixes in the concerned area and a professional or hospital manager bears the responsibility of synchronising all the submixes in such a fashion that draws a safe compromising line between the two opposite considerations of subserving the social interests and developing an organisation of world-class. At the outset, we talk about the perception of quality since sky is the only limit to quality upgradation. In addition, we shall also go through the problem of behavioural profile since expectations cannot remain static. We believe in the principle of divide-and-rule in a positive sense and therefore, we prefer to segment the market. We live in an age of information technology and therefore, temptation to the development of a sophisticated marketing information system is quite natural.

The product mix for hospitals is necessary so that we keep ourselves engaged in making the services known to others by additional attractions and properties. The core services, supportive services, and peripheral services should be innovated in the face of evolving technologies and changing levels of expectations of the users. It is not only necessary that we improve quality. It is even necessary, more impact generating that we make available to the potential users the required information and keep them informed about the healthcare services offered by hospitals and healthcare organisations. This requires innovative promotional measures. We need to advertise with more creativity, to publicise by developing a rapport with the media, offer promotional incentives to the personnel as well as to the users. This draws our attention to the sales promotion measures. We need personal selling to inform users in a right perspective. And in an age of information and communication technologies, we can also use telemarketing for promoting and selling. If we offer quality services in a decent way, word-of-mouth promoters will do the rest. In addition to the product and promotion mix, we also have to adopt a reasonable fee structure based on a pocket-friendly fee strategy. This draws our attention to price mix. We should offer the promised quality of services in a decent way and this draws our attention to the price mix. In addition, the hospital personnel need to appear neat, clean an appear impressive which focuses on physical attractions. We need quality people quite effective in accomplishing the organisational goals. This leads to the question of New People Management (NPM). The gap between the services-promised and services-offered has to be bridged and this focuses our attention on time-honoured and decent processing.

An optimal mix of the aforesaid submixes is the prime responsibility of a healthcare manager and this chapter deals with a number of problems directly or indirectly influencing the orchestrating of a sound marketing mix for the hospitals or healthcare organisations, irrespective of the size and sectoral variations.

HOSPITAL MARKETING — THE PERCEPTION

Before we go through other dimensions, it is essential that our main focus is on the perception of hospital marketing. The changing time cycle necessitates a change in the perception and if we fail to conceptualise, or even delays the conceptualisation process, all efforts and strategies get only lukewarm response. Hence, we need to perceive the concept in the changing environmental conditions.

By hospital marketing or marketing healthcare services, we mean making available healthcare or medicare services to the different categories of users in such a way that they get quality services, at a reasonable fee structure, on right time and in a decent way.[1] The concept of Social Marketing principles focus on making available the services even to unaffordable segments of the users.[2] It is in this context that we find marketing medicare or healthcare services a managerial process that helps a professional in formulating a sound marketing mix in tune with fluctuating intensity of health problem. Social marketing also focuses on promoting the services in a creative way that informs, senses and motivates the users to manage healthy living conditions minimising the possibilities of illness or ailments. These principles throw light on inculcating mass awareness so that the patients or users change their living conditions, food habits, preferences, lifestyles and the harmful effects of environmental pollution. Thus, against other organisations, the healthcare organisations or hospitals are supposed to bring down the number of potential patients or users by injecting new life and strength in the preventive measures. If we improve the environmental condition, are aware of nutritional awareness, counter the food-borne, water-borne, noise-related diseases; regulate our living conditions, it is quite natural that several problems related to health will considerably be reduced.

A majority of us are confused with the conceptual aspect of marketing. During the yesterdecades, the contours of development have undergone radical changes which has changed the perception of marketing. Marketing is now focused on profit generation, stressing concentrated customer satisfaction, and on social orientation.[3] So profit generation is not the only thing that we expect from the functional areas of marketing. Of course, profit generation is an important condition but not an essential one. We are well aware of the fact that the changing social needs engineer a sound foundation for a change in the concept and perception.

It is true that the management principles have speeded up the process of industrial transformation which has substantially helped multi-dimensional social developments and at the same time, they have also created a fertile ground for the germination and growth of a number of health problems. The perception that marketing is to be conceptualised only in the goods manufacturing sector obstructed the development of service-generating organisations in general and the healthcare and educational institutions in particular. To put it in another way, the profit-making goods manufacturing organisations conceptualised the principles of modern marketing but the services generating profit-making organisations delayed the process. Later on, the profit-making service-generating organisations, viz., banks, insurance, transportation, communications, tourism, hotel and many other industries initiated the process but the non-profit organisations like healthcare or hospitals, educational institutions, social organisations, trade unions, police departments, religious organisations and political organisations continue to be in doldrums.

Of course, the non-profit organisations of the West have realised the instrumentality of marketing in increasing the efficacy of an organisation and have conceptualised marketing principles on a priority basis, but the less developed countries and developing countries are yet to develop a strong sense of relalisation. It is against this background that we find a major fall in the productive efficacy of non-profit organisations in general and the healthcare organisations in particular.

In a true sense, marketing is an important functional area of modern management helping all individuals or organisations and institutions for activating the process of qualitative-cum-quantitative transformation. As of today, marketing is considered to be a managerial process and more so, a social process, the conceptualisation necessitates alignment of marketing with the healthcare and educational services also.

Since hospital marketing is an aggregation or a compendium of two different areas, our focus should be on practicing the principles of modern marketing even in the non-profit organisations. It is in this context that we study the changing perception of marketing and its instrumentality in improving the productive efficacy of healthcare organisations or hospitals.

Since marketing is a managerial process, it sheds light on the formulation of different submixes of marketing. In the changing conditions, marketing experts, specially for the hospitals and healthcare organisations, find it proper to go through seven mixes, viz., Product Mix, Promotion Mix, Price Mix, Fee Mix, Place Mix, People Mix, Physical Attractions and Processing. Thus, when we talk about hospital marketing, it is necessary that we keep in our minds the creative developments in all the seven areas. By product mix, the focus is on the services generated by hospitals or healthcare organisations. A marketing professional is supposed to blend the different types of healthcare services optimally, e.g., the core services, supportive services, preventive services and the peripheral services. They have the managerial responsibility of considering quality upgradation as an ongoing process. This helps them in practising Product Uniqueness Proposition. Further, they are also responsible for promoting the services in an innovative fashion so that the patients or the potential patients understand it in a right perspective. This draws our attention on the different constituents of promotion such as advertising, publicity, sales promotion, personal selling, word-of-mouth promotion and telemarketing. By blending the different constituents, they are successful in creating mass awareness.

In addition, a marketing professional is also supposed to make the services affordable to the masses through cost-effectiveness. Besides, they need to locate the healthcare organisations or hospitals at strategic points found accessible and safe. Further, they should also resolve the problem of people management where sympathy, empathy are necessary in the hospital personnel. The physical attractions make it essential that they sense the hospital personnel regarding the dresses/uniform and personality development and the processing makes it essential that the hospital personnel with a decent behaviour bridges the gap between the services-promised and services-offered. Thus, a sound marketing mix is formulated. In the process of formulation, they also go through the marketing information system, behavioural studies, study of segmentation and so on.

In view of the above, it is right to conclude that hospital marketing is a managerial-cum-a social process helping society in tune with the proverb "Health is Wealth."

RATIONALE BEHIND MARKETING HEALTHCARE SERVICES

Of late, the concept of managing hospitals professionally has gained momentum the world over. The management of a non-profit organisation, no doubt, complicates the task of boardrooms and hospital managers in many ways. On the one hand, they need to offer world-class healthcare services to the patients while on the other hand, they are not expected to charge anything even a cost-based fee. The costs of inputs used in offering the services are increasing and they need to practise two-fold measures — first exploring the avenues for generating revenues and second, making the social costs proportionate or optimal to the potentials of the hospitals or healthcare organisations.

For successful marketing of services, it is necessary that hospitals are professionally sound. This helps hospitals in many ways, such as an increase in the organisational potentials to meet the social costs, use of internationally-accepted quality inputs in the process of generating the healthcare services and availability of smooth ways for modernisation, expansion and time-honoured development. Here, we find advocacy in favour of practising marketing principles in the hospitals or healthcare organisations.[4] The following facts testify the rationale behind such an application.

1. To keep users satisfied: We are well aware of the fact that the main purpose in the process of offering quality services is to satisfy the users and to go ahead with the process without gap. Like other profit-making organisations, the hospitals are also required to satisfy the customers and the principles of marketing help them substantially in the process. If the doctors and nurses are soft, sympathetic, decent and show empathy, the users would be satisfied. Of course, the quality of medical aid made available to them is actually significant but we cannot devalue the instrumentality of behavioural dimension in activating the process of satisfying the users. In the Indian perspective, the hospitals and healthcare organisations plan and act with this realisation that core services are the only thing they need to offer; but, this is not the only thing the users expect from them. By conceptualising marketing in a right fashion, they should build a strong foundation for both, viz., they offer quality medical aid and show personal-touch-in-service. Thus, with the fulfillment of their expectations, the users feel satisfied with the hospital personnel in general.

2. Time-honoured services: In the hospitals and healthcare organisations particularly, we find time management much more impact generating as this influences the success rate of treatment plans. With the passage of time, a number of developments have taken place in the medical sciences based on the contributions of new generation of biomedical equipments and apparatus. Sophisticated equipments and machines have virtually transformed the whole process on medicare management. The diagnostic and treatment devices have completely changed. We call them inputs which play a contributory role in the process of qualitative transformation. Generally, the hospitals find it difficult to install new generation of expensive bio-medical equipment mainly due to financial constraint. In the government hospitals, the results are very disappointing because they have not only failed in replacing technology but also in maintaining and managing the new generation of sophisticated technologies. No one can expect quality services mix from the poor, substandard, traditional equipment and apparatus. This makes it clear that hospitals have to give due weightage to the time-bound development plans to cater to the changing requirements and expectations of users.

3. Inculcating mass awareness: The hospitals and healthcare organisations should play a positive role in creating mass awareness since in the Indian society, the low rate of literacy complicates the task. A majority of the population are unaware of the food-borne, water-borne, pollution-borne, vector-borne and communicable diseases. To be more specific, the masses living in the rural areas are innocent, illiterate, taking least interest in the healthcare devices. The principles of social marketing are needed to make hospitals and healthcare organisations accept the responsibility of making the healthcare education or communications more creative with the support of audiovisuals and creative advertisement and publicity measures. The hospitals are not only responsible to offer the curative services but they also have to give an overriding priority to the preventive services. They should enlighten potential users or users about the impact of food, water and healthy living conditions on the disease profile. The hospitals, with the support of professionally-sound managers can succeed in inculcating mass awareness which would minimise the pressure on the hospitals. Then there will be a sharp fall in the number of patients coming to the hospitals. Unlike other profit-making organisations, the success rate of hospitals depend upon their contributions to bring down the number of its users.

4. Identifying the thrust areas: When marketing principles assign due weightage to the innovative measures in tune with the changing requirements, the identification of vulnerable areas is possible. In the context of medical services, viral diseases, communicable diseases, child care, women care, drug addiction are to influence the disease profile. In the Indian perspective, it is pertinent that we have a special task force to resolve the sensitive issues. We need to activate child immunisation, vaccination, pre- and post-maternity care, immunisation, a crash programme for eradication of malaria, cholera, leprosy, typhoid or so. The marketing principles accord an overriding priority to the thrust areas so that the possibilities of breaking out of disease are minimised. The principles of societal marketing advocate in favour of a transcendental priority to this segment of the catchment area which would simplify the process of making the services effective. An in-depth study of catchment areas, a survey and research into different disease profile will make it possible to learn about the thrust areas and vulnerable regions. This also supports the application of marketing principles in the hospitals. It is important to implement effectively disease control programme in the thrust areas.

5. Identifying the vulnerable segment: From the point of healthcare services, we find some of the segments of vulnerable nature necessitating special medical aid and care. The backward villages, urban slums, rural women and children, population close to the industrial towns and cities are considered to be the vulnerable zone. To make available the best possible medical aid to them, it is essential that we have detailed information regarding the nature and character of the problems. This draws our attention to the development of an information network so that hospitals get the news related to the required medical care. Earlier, we have talked about the management of information system and we find marketing information system an essential part of marketing activities in the healthcare organisations. The societal marketing principles favour a transcendental priority to this segment of the population and the modern hospitals assign due weightage to the development of information technology.

6. Behavioural dimension would be given due weightage: There are justifications for conceptualising marketing in the healthcare services because the behavioural dimension is an essential part of marketing management. To be more specific in a majority of the government hospitals, there is no place for behavioural dimension. In the syllabi for medical education, the behavioural dimension is neglected. The application of marketing principle opens avenues for behavioural studies even in the healthcare sectors. The hospital personnel are required to understand the changing behavioural profile of patients and attendants and they should be held responsible for decent, polite, sweet, sympathetic treatment.

7. Cost-effectiveness is made possible: Of late, we find almost all the organisations assigning due weightage to cost economy which is based on making the process of managing the services cost-effective so that the services are pocket-friendly or affordable. The marketing principle explores avenues for bringing down the costs on generating and distributing the services to the end-users. The management of hospital materials, stores, human resources and finance become significant for cost economy. Here, we find almost all the hospitals making sincere and honest efforts to maintain cost-effectiveness. It is essential that a hospital manager is able to get the right quality of hospital inputs, bought at a reasonable price and generating quality of outputs. Therefore, we practise hospital marketing.

8. A rational fee structure is possible: With the application of marketing principles, it is possible to make the fee structure rational. The principles of societal marketing show that the benefits of scientific developments and advancements should also be harnessed by weaker sections of the society. It is essential that the hospitals or healthcare organisations resort to a fee strategy that is acceptable to the masses. When we talk about pocket-friendly fee strategy, our focus is on subserving the interests of weaker sections on a priority basis. Income-wise, setting of a fee structure can be a judicious approach to improve the financial health of hospitals. It is an important managerial problem requiring due attention of the hospital policy makers. Shrinking financial avenues stressed that the hospital personnel make innovative efforts to generate and mobilise necessary finance.

9. Motivating personnel: The slogan of quality in totality cannot be translated into meaningful purposes unless the hospital personnel offer world-class services. Promotion in the services an important factor of motivation instrumental in influencing the different echelons of management. Showing empathy, personal-touch-in-service, decency in behaviour, etc. are substantially based on the motivational plans or schemes. The marketing principles argue for a plan which is linked to efficiency. When paramedical or medical personnel set up a camp in the rural areas in case of epidemics, the hospital manager is required to set up a camp with necessary precautions as per the required norms.

In view of this, it is right to mention that the process of application of marketing principles in the hospitals and healthcare organisations should be simplified, if the policy makers of government and private hospitals are really interested. We consider a hospital as social institution. The hospital capable of personnel should be made aware of the organisational goals to make sincere efforts to succeed. Besides the question of survival is more a problem of growth and prosperity. Hence, hospitals and healthcare organisations are a social institution, it is important to give due weightage to public interests. Marketing principles help in professionalising the services in tune with the defined goals and targets. Thus, the hospitals can generate their own financial resources. In the Indian perspective, the public are not in a position to afford the expensive services of private hospitals. Unless we allow the government hospitals to mobilise financial resources from the internal sources, the problem of financial crunch will not be solved. The marketing principles can help a manager in understanding the changing behavioural profile of the patients and attendants. A study of the behavioural profile is an essential part of marketing. Satisfying the customers/users/patients is the main objective of management of marketing. The hospitals and healthcare organisations thus need to give due weightage to the application of marketing principles. By conceptualising modern marketing and analysing the problem in the face of societal or social marketing, a hospital manager succeeds in solving a number of problems. It is against this background that we strongly advocate the application of marketing principles in the healthcare organisations. Even in private hospitals, marketing is essential as in the case of the government hospitals. By conceptualising marketing, we normally mean charging more or abnormal fees and earning profits but our focus in a true sense is on improving the quality of services, understanding the expectations of patients and attendants and thus processing the services in such a fashion that makes the task of satisfying the users easier. We find some of the leading private hospitals practising the same and hope that others would also promote such efforts. We do feel that even the government hospitals should implement and this needs an attitudinal change in the policy makers.

USERS OF HEALTHCARE SERVICES — SEGMENTWISE CLASSIFICATION

As we go through the problem of marketing healthcare services, it is right that we learn about the different types of users. It is quite natural that human beings belonging to different categories or segments act, expect and react differently. Since marketing professionals are responsible to satisfy the users, they should know about the changing levels of expectations of different categories of users/patients using the services of hospitals or healthcare organisations.[5] In Fig. 17.1, we find different types of users.

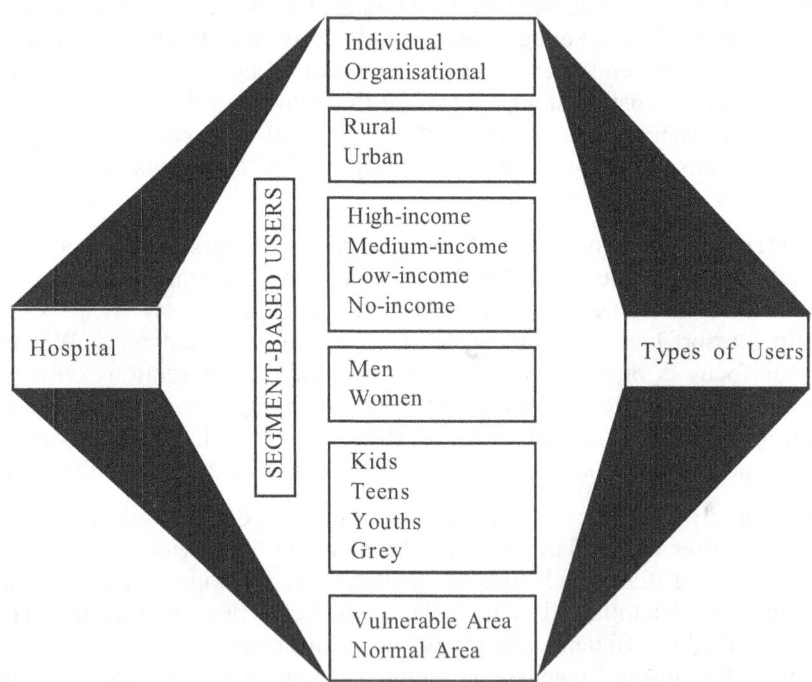

Fig. 17.1: Types of Users of Healthcare Services

We know that strategic decisions are substantially influenced by the quality of users availing of the services. It is essential that the hospital personnel have an in-depth study of different types of users. At the outset, we classify users into two parts, viz., individual and organisational or institutional. In the category of individual users, we find all of us availing the healthcare services directly without seeking institutional or organisational support. As for institutional or organisational users, we find industries or organisations or institutions making their own arrangements for the medicare or healthcare services of their employees. We find a link between a hospital or a healthcare institute where the employees get the services and the medical bills are reimbursed by the concerned organisations.

We also classify users on the basis of region such as those living in villages and coming to hospitals for medicare and the users in cities and towns and visiting hospitals for medicare. There is a difference in the expectations of both categories of the users. Similarly, we also classify users on the basis of their levels of income, viz., high-income group, medium-income group, low-income group and no-income group. The behavioural profile of rich and poor cannot be identical.

It is important that we know about the users belonging to different income groups. The gender and age are also important bases for making a classification of the users. The men and women act, react and expect differently. The kids, teens, youths and grey have different levels of expectations.

When we go through the problem of medicare or healthcare, it is also important that we are aware of the different categories of users living in vulnerable areas and in a healthy living condition. The users coming from rural areas and environmentally healthy areas have different problems. This makes it essential that the hospital personnel also know about the vulnerable and normal conditions.

The hospital personnel also happen to be users of these services. The professional users have different levels of expectations. If you serve in a hospital, it is quite natural that you have a different perception of expectations.

Since the hospitals and healthcare organisations subserve the interests of all, it is natural that they learn about the confessional groups, such as students and downtrodden sections.

The classification of the users is on the basis of the nature and types of diseases. Some of the users have normal or minor problems and while some others facing major health problems. It is natural that expectations and attitudes of all of them will not be similar. The hospital personnel are expected to know about them in detail so that they can fulfil or meet their expectations.

In view of the above, different categories of users use the services of hospitals or healthcare organisations and if we don't know about their behavioural profile, the task of satisfying them would be difficult. It is in this context that we need to understand the different categories and types of users/patients availing of the services of hospitals. While we talk about the marketing management of hospitals or the healthcare organisations, we should assign due weightage to the users' satisfaction. Of course, a hospital manager is primarily responsible to make available to the patients, quality medicare or healthcare facilities but this does not mean that they don't go through the problem of satisfaction or dissatisfaction. The hospitals are responsible to know about the significant changes in the disease profile of particular catchment or command areas. Problems of all the regions, all the personnel, all the patients are not identical. A study of the behavioural profile of different categories of users is needed while studying behavioural profile.

For the hospital personnel, the needs and requirements of patients assume great significance but with the same quality of services, you satisfy one segment, but dissatisfy another. Being a professional, it is your prime responsibility to inform, sense, influence, win and retain the users so that you are successful in projecting a positive image of your organisation. A study of the types of users of hospital services provides you important feedback of differentiates and generates unique service.

BEHAVIOURAL PROFILE OF USERS OF HEALTHCARE SERVICES

A study of behavioural profile is essential since it improves the quality of managerial decisions. The providers are required to understand the behavioural profile of users which is not static.[6]

The doctors attending on a patient, the paramedical staff helping them in the process, the nursing staffs simplify their task and the managerial staff arranging everything for them should understand the changing behavioural profile of patients and attendants. Of course, professional excellence of each of them plays a significant role in improving the quality of healthcare services but at the same time, their task of satisfying the patients and attendants will remain unfulfilled unless they do not have an in-depth study of behavioural management. Where two hospitals or healthcare organisations offer the same quality of medicare services to the patients but the personnel of one misbehave and another promote decency in behaviour, one generates tension, and another is instrumental in diffusing the same, one appears serious and keeps mum, and another shows sympathy and empathy — the users in general would prefer the latter most. The users with no option may use but you need to create a situation where they prefer to come even if they have a number of options. Thus, a study of behavioural profile assumes a place of outstanding significance.

In the Indian perspective, we find a changed scenario. It is really amazing that even world-class doctors offering quality healthcare services to the patients are misbehaving with them. Of course, we find a very few of them specially coming from the new schools having management orientation behaving decently with the patients and attendants. There is no sense in generating tension in the patients and attendants who are already tensed. In addition, generating tension complicates the responsibility of hospital personnel. We believe that our mental condition is closely related just to the treatment received at different places but it is not to be forgotten that decent behaviour of hospital personnel will also be impact generating. So, we need to give an overriding priority to the behavioural profile of hospital staff.

Attitudes, preferences, priorities, and expectations are important constituents of behavioural profile. A number of factors influence them generated at the places of processing. Of late, we find sophistication in the process of development of communication. The educated and conscious segments of the society know about the developments taking place in the different parts of the globe and therefore they have high levels of expectations. If we live on an island with a complete communication gap, our expectations would remain static. In a society where significant developments in the field of transportation and communication and concerted efforts for building a superhighway for information move forward, the expectations speedily proceed.

Against this background, we find the expectations of users and potential users of the healthcare services increasing rapidly. They come to know about the healthcare services made available to their counterparts in the leading hospitals, and expect the same standard and level where they turn customers. They, on the one hand, want world-class healthcare services while, on the other, also expect decent behaviour and multi-dimensional amenities and facilities for their comfortable stay at the hospitals or healthcare centres. The leading private hospitals have perceived it correctly and they are able to manage the hospitals in tune with the changing levels of expectations of patients and attendants, but the government hospitals have yet to realise those facts fully.

In the changing scenario, you are responsible to innovate the core services and at the same time, you have also to understand the instrumentality of peripheral services in the face of the expectations of patients and attendants. This would inject new life and strength to the hospitals which, of late, are in a deplorable condition. There is no doubt in it that the realisation of the situation by hospital manager will be meaningless if there is an attitudinal change in the policy makers. In a true sense, they are required to assign an overriding priority to the health sector. All our programmes for social engineering will end in a fiasco, if we don't succeed in offering at least the basic healthcare facilities.

Therefore, an in-depth study of the changing behavioural profile of users/patients is essential and all of us need to perceive it in a right perspective. The doctors attending on the patients, the nursing staff serving them, the paramedical staff assisting the process and the managerial staff simplifying the functional responsibilities, all of them need an attitudinal change. Specifically, we expect a lot from the doctors in this context as they are the leverspring of hospitals or healthcare organisations. May be that they have world-class professional excellence; may be that they are sincere and honest but their professional excellence, sincerity and honesty need to have a positive approach. So it is essential that they are also sympathetic to the patients and attendants and their behavioural profile change the realisation of the users and the attendants that doctors also happen to be decent, human and polite. It is amazing that in the Indian perspective, the doctors are yet to realise the instrumentality of decent behaviour, sympathy, and empathy in the process of speedy recovery of patients.

In view of the above, it is right to expect that the hospital personnel in general and the doctors in particular need an attitudinal change. The fact is that patients visiting hospitals are found in tension and we have to make sincere efforts to diffuse it. The motive behind understanding the behavioural profile of patients and attendants will change the functional character of hospital personnel. On the one hand, they need world-class professional excellence while, on the other, they also need a personal-touch-in-service. This is not possible unless they assign due weightage to the behavioural profile. In addition, the concept of hospital marketing makes it necessary to motivate the patients and attendants. You have to sensitise the patients and the process will help you in increasing the number of patients which lead to an increase in the revenue position of hospitals or healthcare organisation.

MARKET SEGMENTATION

Segmentation is a process to divide and subdivide the markets into small categories so that the process of identification of the changing expectations of users becomes easier. The expectations of even two persons are not found to be identical. However, there are some common factors which form an important base to divide them into the small categories. The rationale behind making segmentation is to understand correctly the users' expectation. Management experts and segmentation is to understand correctly the users' expectations. Management experts and marketing experts expect that if we segment the market, the task of undertaking an in-depth study of behavioural profile will become easier. Any change in the marketing mix without understanding the changing levels of expectations of potential users cannot be proactive. We need to segment the market for the healthcare services offered by hospitals or healthcare organisations.[7]

In Fig. 17.1, we have classified users into different segments. This is a segmentwise study which let you know the changing medical needs of the potential users. It is quite natural that when you come to know about their preferences and expectations, you innovate the process of formulating a sound marketing mix expecting a positive response. We view the latest developments in the field of information and communication technologies which are important reasons for an increase in the levels of expectations of users. Of late, a number of developments are taking place in the field of medical sciences which have made possible a basic change in the nature and form of diagnosis and treatment; at the same time, a technology-driven healthcare system has become very much instrumental in shaping the level of expectations. This makes it essential that the different types of mixes are innovated and the desired levels and standard of healthcare services are offered. The task will turn out to be more difficult if we do not assign due weightage to studies related to market segmentation.

We find logic behind the saying — *"Divide and Rule."* It is considered to be a strategy helping you in modifying, and developing the healthcare services. The level of awareness is substantially influenced by education. Educated persons act, react, expect and communice with a purpose. You come to know about their requirements and try to fulfil them by making adjustments in the marketing resources. This develops a sound marketing mix expecting a positive response from the different segments. It is quite natural that the needs and requirements of the high income group is different from the medium-income and low-income groups. The affluents have a high level of expectations and they favour in fulfilling the same. But the low-income group people find the process complicated. Besides, there are also variations on the basis of regional considerations. The prospects or the potential users living in the rural areas are not aware of the developments taking place outside the world and therefore they have limited expectations. The marketing experts feel that such variation is also influenced by the nature and character of a particular command area. It is quite natural that some of the areas are prone to diseases because the people living there are not aware of the healthcare requirements. The urban population knowing everything related to the developments in medical sciences has high levels of expectations.

Segmentation on the basis of age group reveals that the medical or healthcare requirements of different age groups cannot be identical. It is quite natural that kids and teens have problems which are different from those of youths and grey. A microscopic study reveals that kids living in the urban areas have different healthcare requirements compared to their counterparts living in the rural areas. Generally in the urban areas, we find mass awareness; therefore child care is getting an important place in their family healthcare budget. The same thing is absent in the rural areas because the people living in villages are not so much conscious of healthy living conditions. The requirements of grey group also will be different from other groups because of the different health problems.

Some of the areas are more vulnerable to diseases such as those heavily populated cities and towns and the industrialised cities and towns. They have different types of problems and therefore there is a difference in the disease profile. On the other hand, the people of the hilly areas or eco-friendly areas have different types of health problems. Thus, we find intensity of population and pollution also playing an important role.

The healthcare organisations or hospitals have some of the organisational or institutional customers. The institutions reimburse the medical bills of their employees who get medical aid in the hospitals. On the other hand, individual users who are not financed or supported by anyone and therefore there is change in the levels of their expectations in the case of the latter.

In Fig. 17.1, we find segmentwise classification of different types of users of healthcare services. We assign due weightage to segmentation because like other service generating organisations, the healthcare organisations also need to satisfy the users; for that, it is essential that they try to know about their expectations. If a hospital manager is found aware of the expectations of different segments of users living in the different catchment or command areas, he/she may simplify the task of medical and paramedical personnel and the nursing staff who will be responsible to offer the services. In addition, our awareness regarding the disease profile or healthcare problems of particular area will simplify the task of managing the services in the face of changing requirements.

These facts make it clear that market segmentation is an important dimension of marketing since it helps a decision-maker and the hospital personnel in understanding the users' expectations thus simplifying the task of innovating the services. The most important thing in the process is to satisfy the users which needs an in-depth study of different segments. Since we talk about sympathy, empathy and decency in the behavioural profile of hospital personnel, it is essential that they are well aware of the population living in a particular segment and facing a particular problem. If the hospitals or healthcare organisations fail in this, the service profile will not be in tune with the changing requirements of different segments. It is against this background that a study of market segmentation is necessary even in the context of healthcare organisations. Satisfying the users is your important functional responsibility and the segmentation would help you significantly.

MARKETING INFORMATION SYSTEM

In this information superhighway, an organisation has to consider the instrumentality of information system in making the marketing decisions creative which makes the ways for sensitivity and acceptability. Even the healthcare organisations have been facing the problem of competition requiring an improvement in the quality of decision. The formulation of a sound marketing mix is important to a hospital manager but the task is difficult because a number of changes have taken place. The diagnosis as well as the treatment drugs and medicines, equipment and apparatus are found changing all the time. Not only this, we also find a change in the expectations of hospital personnel who want more incentives in different forms. The increasing environmental problems lead to the water and food-borne and pollution related diseases and change the nature and character of the disease profile. Thus, in the face of multi-dimensional changes, it is pertinent that a hospital manager and other personnel are well-informed so that the quality of their services match the changing requirements of the users. It is in this context that we study the problem of marketing information system.

A technology-driven marketing information system is considered to be important to help a hospital manager and the hospital personnel in raising their awareness. We have talked about the management information system that studies the problems of all the functional areas of healthcare organisations. Here, we make an in-depth study of the marketing information system, specially from the viewpoint of making the marketing decisions. When we talk about a system, it is quite natural that we should know about its different subsystems. We find marketing information system an aggregation or combination of different subsystems in which analytical marketing, marketing research, marketing intelligence and internal reporting are important.[8] The processing of data into information is the main thing in its functional area which helps a hospital manager in knowing about the nature and character of a product or other mixes to cater to the changing healthcare needs of the society.

Of late, we also talk about the Decision Supporting System (DSS) which helps a decision-maker in selecting the best from the available alternatives. There is a basic change in the management of information today because different types of technologies are also used in the process. Information and communication technologies have virtually changed the management of information. With more speed, accuracy and memory, we find technologies helping the process fantastically in managing the information. It is essential that hospitals and healthcare organisations take the support of marketing information system for improving the quality of their marketing decisions which would help them not only in satisfying the users but also in developing the potentials of providers to bear the social costs. It is against this background that we consider the importance of marketing information system in the hospitals or healthcare organisations.

We are well aware of the fact that there are different subsystems helping the process of managing the information and therefore we need a brief idea of their instrumentality.

Internal reporting: Internal Reporting System is to help the information system in identifying the levels of inventory, accounts receivables and accounts payables, spotting important opportunities, data related to the performance of the hospitals or healthcare organisations. The base of internal marketing information is the accounting system. We also call the data collected as the result data managed with the purpose of spotting opportunities.

Marketing intelligence system: It is the second subsystem of the marketing information system which helps managers in getting information related to the current marketing environment besides identifying the emerging trends in the market. Census data, market news and reports, trade/health papers, health shows, medical books and journals, medical or health publications, publications of national and international health associations, publications of Medical Councils, Health Reports prepared at national and international levels are the important sources of getting the information. In a true sense, the intelligence system acts as a mirror of marketing environment. It is also considered to be an organised feedback process of marketing communication. This subsystem supplies happening data which has a far-reaching impact on the making of sensitive marketing decisions. We find a number of publications of different institutions and organisations or hospitals or healthcare organisations which help hospitals in knowing about the latest developments in the medical sciences. Of late, we find information superhighway helping a lot in enriching the information bank. The processes of developing marketing intelligence system are undesired viewing, conditioned viewing, informal and formal research.

Marketing research system: The marketing research system is also an important subsystem which offers special information on request when a manager is encountering numerous problems necessitating unique information for countering the problems. The marketing research studies are project-oriented. Generally, the information related to the behaviour profile and the changing levels of expectations of potential users/patients, advertising awareness, promotional efforts, emerging trends in competition, instrumentality or effectiveness of the publicity measures are collected through the marketing research.

Analytical marketing subsystem: This subsystem of the marketing information system is found useful for the collection of statistical procedures for extracting meaningful information from data. It is a computer-based marketing decision support system which helps a manager in different ways.

The above subsystems of the marketing information system are used for getting meaningful or relevant information for making the decisions. We are well aware that a hospital manager is responsible for collecting different types of information from different sources and with the support of a marketing information system, he/she is required to take decisions which help hospitals organisations in subserving the interests of patients. Of late, we find a number of changes in the medical sciences and we have the support of Health Information System nationally or internationally. We talk about a technology-driven information system in which the information and communication technologies are required to play a prominent role. It is the responsibility of a hospital manager to develop and enrich the marketing information system so that the qualitative improvements are made possible. The instrumentality of marketing information system is coiled in the essence of making available to a hospital manager the relevant information.

In Fig. 17.2, we find different subsystems of the Marketing Information System. These facts make it clear that marketing information system is meant to help a healthcare manager in many ways. With the increasing intensity of competition, it is essential that a hospital or healthcare manager keeps himself/herself well-informed so that whatever new developments take place in the medical sciences are incorporated in the marketing mix. The development of marketing resources depends upon the availability of information. If we have the latest information, the educational and research activities in addition to the service profile, can be innovated incorporating latest developments. With the developments of the concept of hospital marketing, we find marketing information system occupying a place of importance.

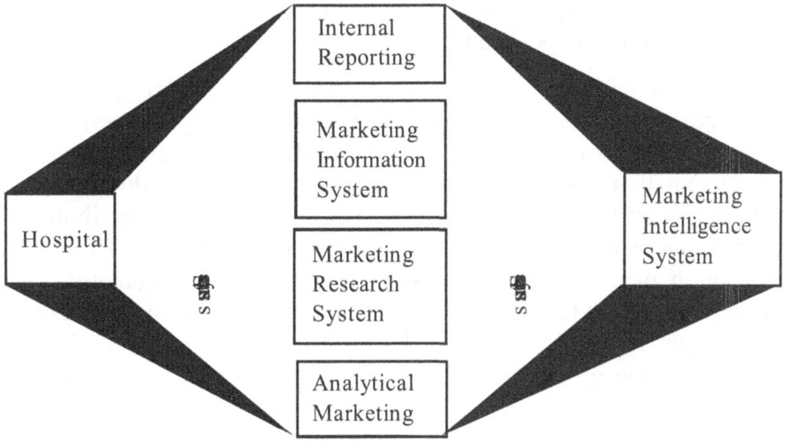

Fig. 17.2: Marketing Information System (Subsystems)

Of late whatever the developments are found in the health sector or medical sciences can be used with the support of information superhighways or internet operations. This makes it essential that a hospital manager assigns due weightage to the marketing information system. The main purpose of a healthcare organisation is to subserve the interests of the people by offering to them time-bound, economic/affordable, world-class healthcare communication services and this task would remain unfulfilled unless we take the support of a well-organised and systematically developed marketing information system. There is no doubt in it that all the subsystems of the marketing information system will be useful to the healthcare organisations but the analytical reporting and intelligence system will be of outstanding significance because the financial information would be received from the internal reporting and the external information would be received from the intelligence system.

In view of the above, it is right to say that like other organisations, the hospitals and healthcare organisations also need to develop an independent information system for marketing purposes. In view of the increasing costs of inputs, they have no option but to promote the concept of hospital marketing on the basis of the principles of social or societal marketing which, on the one hand would make available to the public affordable services while, on the other, would also ensure the time-bound expansion and development of hospitals. If an organisation is found financially sound, its efficacy to bear the social costs is found at its peak. It is high time that we make hospitals and healthcare organisations financially sound which requires conceptualisation of hospital marketing even in the government hospitals.

Marketing Mix: We are well aware of the fact that under product, we include both categories – goods well as the services. It is the prime responsibility of a marketer to make sincere efforts for merchandising customer benefit and services with the help of customer-oriented marketing decisions. It is the social responsibility of a marketer to be sure that the organisations for which he/she has been working contributes significantly to the process of social transformation. The holistic concept of management and the defined principles of social marketing make it essential that organisations irrespective of the fact that they have or do not have a legitimate right of making profits bear the burden of social costs. Of course, the healthcare organisations or hospitals don't have legitimate right of making profits, but it does not mean that they don't bear the social costs. It is against this background that we advocate in favour of marketing the healthcare services and purpose to formulate the marketing mix which accomplishes the organisational goals. The formulation of a sound marketing mix for an organisation requires professional excellence.

The term "Marketing Mix" was first coined by Prof. Neil H. Borden of the Harvard Business School.[9] Both the term and concept have since been adopted the world over. At the initial stage of industrialisation, an organisation targeted the production facilities first and then adjusted all the other functional activities around it. A number of authorities realised that marketing is something that takes place after the manufacturing process is over. With the passage of time, the pace of industrialisation was sufficiently accelerated which paved the avenues or opened new vistas for the inclusion of a number of products in the profile. Thus, the stress could no longer remain confined to manufacturing only and gradually we find development of service generating organisations. The conceptual framework of marketing mix has been designed by different experts in different ways but perception by and large is the same. Kotler, Keeley and Lazar, Davar and many others have gone through the conceptual aspect of the term but all of them agree that it is a fair blending of different submixes which in the course of development may change the ingredients and the composition process.

The ultimate goal of different submixes of marketing is to deliver standard goods or services to the customers/users. The product mix includes product line and quality, brand, packaging and services in the course of processing or others. This draws our attention to the formulation of a product or a service mix. We study promotion mix because it is not only sufficient that you contribute significantly to the production processes, it is much more important that your prospects/potential customers come to know about your contributions so that form a positive opinion about you and your product and make the buying decisions in your favour. There are a number of constituents to be included in the promotion mix, such as advertising, publicity, sales promotion, personal selling, word-of-mouth promotion and telemarketing. Both the categories of organisations — goods manufacturing or service generating should charge for their products. If they discontinue the process sooner or later, they have no other option but to forget it. This draws our attention on the price/fee mix which in a true sense is a reward for your excellence of mixing the different ingredients.

It is your responsibility to deliver the goods or processing the services so that they reach the ultimate end-users on right time and in a decent way. This focuses your attention on the place mix. Later, the mounting intensity of competition necessitated inclusion of more mixes change the fragrance of products and this included three more mixes in the marketing mix, viz., People, Physical Attractions and Processing. By the term People, we focus on New People Management which centralises our attention on the development of quality people or human resources who are not only professionally-sound but also personally-committed. A degeneration in the process of value-orientation has potentials to lay a sound foundation for the development of the concept of New People Management.

The increasing domination of the corporate sector in the process of socio-economic transformation paved the way for the development of a new culture influenced by the corporate sector and this made it necessary that your employees, human resources or working people project themselves in an attractive way so that the process of generating attraction is stimulated and it is against this background that physical attractions get a significant place in the marketing mix. It was also realised that goods/services are of quality but the people working there are not aware of decency or proficiency. This necessitates decent processing for making available the goods/ services to the ultimate customers/users and inclusion of processing as a mix is needed.

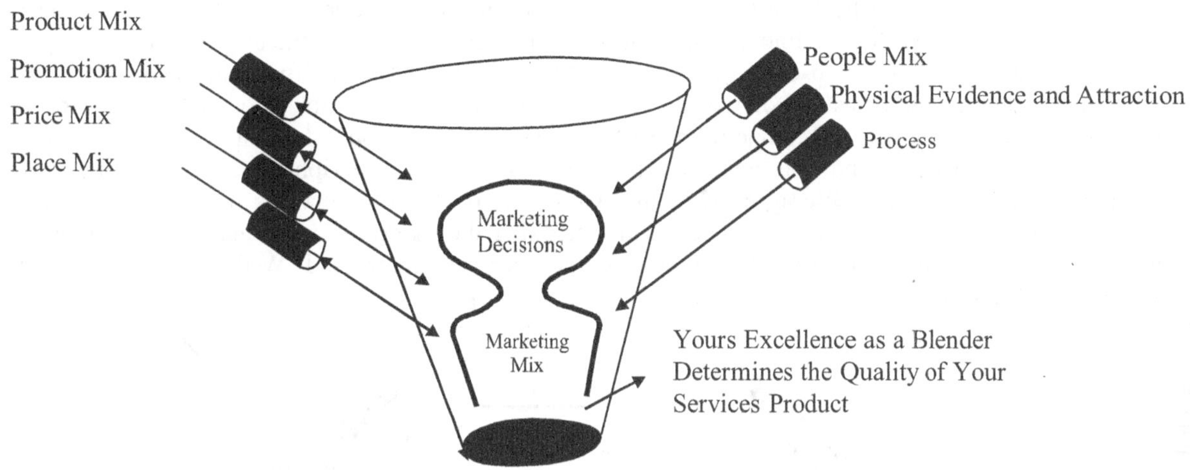

Fig. 17.3: Marketing Mix

In Fig. 17.3, we find the marketing mix which focuses on the fact that a marketer requires professional excellence for blending all the submixes like a cook who shows his/her excellence by mixing different ingredients or spices for preparing a delicious dish. It is quite natural that all the submixes in all the conditions and for all the purposes cannot be uniform; therefore based on your professional excellence, you are expected to identify the proportionate doses and the right time. If you have developed world-class professional excellence, it is quite natural that you are well aware of the taste, preferences, expectations of customers/users of different categories living in different areas and therefore you find yourself competent enough to market successfully not only in the national or domestic markets but even in the global markets. In this context, you need to remember that if you do not find a limit to quality of your goods/services, there is not any boundary for perfection or excellence or expertise you need to face the challenges and threats in the markets. Hence, you need to perceive that sky is the limit for quality (goods/services). Sky is also the limit for perfection/excellence. If you develop excellence with this notion, your task is greatly simplified because the competitors will find it difficult to accept your challenges and you succeed in the competition.

FORMULATION OF MARKETING MIX

The formulation of marketing mix requires professional excellence because it is a process of blending the different submixes, the development of marketing resources or the tailoring of marketing resources in tune with the changing requirements. It is in this context that the managers specially, serving non-profit organisations require world-class professional excellence. Whatever you offer today becomes outdated very soon and the process of elimination and inclusion continue. If you repeat the process, the concept of Product Uniqueness gets an important place and this simplifies your functional responsibility of winning and retaining the customers/users as long as you go ahead with the process. Conversely, if the process slows down or stops, the business is lost. Thus, the formulation of a sound marketing mix is an important managerial responsibility. Here, we study the problem of healthcare organisations and therefore a hospital manager requires world-class professional excellence, because based on his/her excellence, he/she would be successful in accomplishing the mission, goals and objectives.

Product Mix

In the service generating organisations, service mix occupies a place of outstanding significance; the high level of sensitivity and unfavourable conditions virtually prove to be an acid test of your expertise or professionalism. We are well aware of the fact that modern hospitals offer a number of services, such as core services, supportive, peripheral and the preventive services. In Fig. 17.4, we find the service mix/product mix of hospitals or healthcare organisations. It is an important functional responsibility of a healthcare manager to ensure that whatever the services profile/product profile they develop has the potentials of satisfying the users. How to make it possible is determined by the emerging trends in the medical sciences through the advancement in communications. Since formulation of a sound product mix is a managerial process of mixing different types of services in the profile, it is quite natural that the process is substantially influenced by the scientific inventions and innovations. Where research gets due weightage in healthcare sector, a basic change in the diagnostic and treatment process cannot be denied. It is in this context that we find a technology-driven diagnostic and treatment processes gaining popularity the world over. For generating world-class core services, you need the same quality of supportive services because unless the infrastructural facilities are of world-class, it is meaningless to think about the generation of quality services. The mounting intensity of competition makes it essential that you establish an edge over the strategic decisions of your competitors and it is against this background that the peripheral services draw the attention of a manager around the world. We agree with this view that if the core services help you in protecting your existence with the peripheral sources you succeed in increasing the market share. Since by enriching the quality of peripheral services, you create product uniqueness, the users are impressed. With this process, you succeed in establishing leadership.

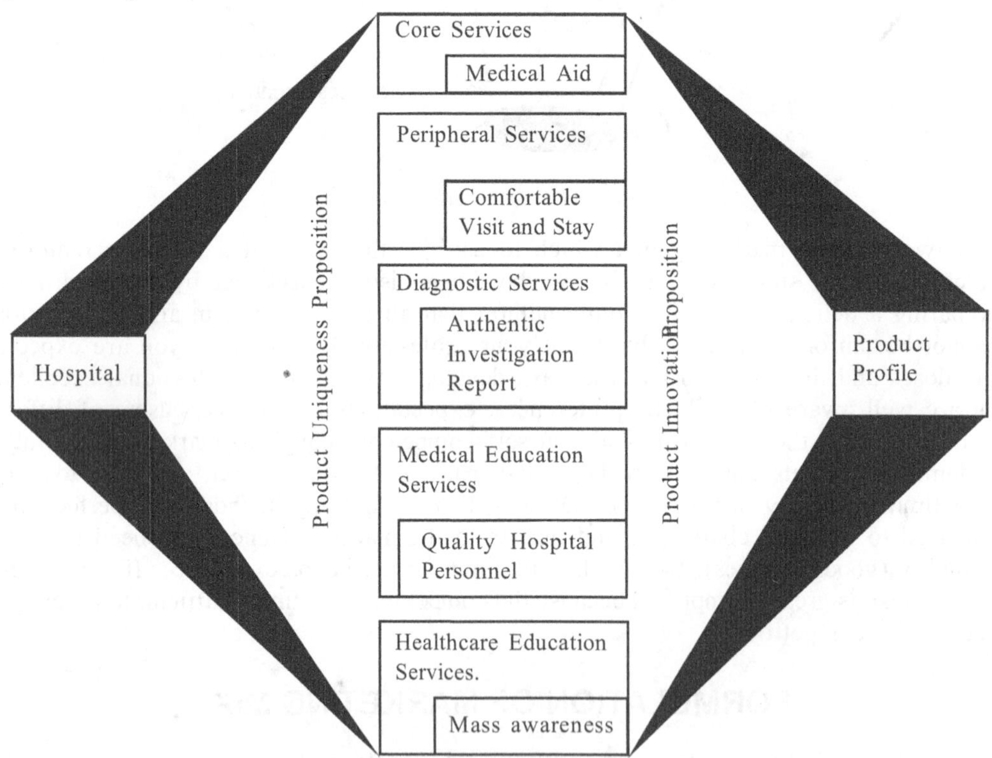

Fig. 17.4: Product Profile of Hospitals

In Fig. 17.4, we find the service/product profile of healthcare organisations which is a combination of different types of services.

The services have been classified into four parts, viz., line services, supportive services, auxiliary services and the preventive services.

It is your professional excellence to gauge the changing healthcare requirements of a particular catchment area and develop the mix accordingly so that the users experience uniqueness. Of course, it is important that you assign an overriding priority to the core and supportive services and assign due weightage to the auxiliary services but at the same, it is also necessary that you promote the communication services, specially focusing on the creation of mass awareness related to the healthy living conditions. It is really surprising that a majority of the healthcare organisations do not attach any significance to preventive services which aggravates the pressure on hospitals. In the Indian perspective, it is of prime importance that creativity is made possible in the preventive services so that the public come to know about healthy living conditions and develop an awareness regarding food and water-borne, pollution-related, vector-borne and communicable diseases.

It is right to remind you that professional excellence of a hospital or healthcare manager is the essence of minimising the pressure on the hospitals which would not be possible unless we make the preventive measures creative. Of late, we find modern healthcare organisations also innovating the peripheral services which focus our attention on a number of services making the stay and visit of patients and attendants comfortable and convenient. The seating arrangements, potable water, sanitation, power, transportation and communications, entertainment facilities, shopping complex, restaurants and cafeteria are to mention a few playing a big role in making the stay of patients and attendants comfortable. Of course, you bear the responsibility of innovating the core services but at the same time, you also need to innovate the peripheral services because in the healthcare organisations we find patients and attendants facing a number of problems very much instrumental in generating tension. It is your prime responsibility that you by the innovative peripheral services of your organisation instrumentalise the process of diffusing their tension.

The secondary, tertiary and other leading medical institutes not only generate different types of services but also product various categories of personnel. We talk a lot about the quality of doctors, paramedical staff and the nursing staff but keep their development plans at the bottom of health manpower development programme. This has caused degeneration in the quality of hospital personnel of almost all the categories. It is against this background that the hospitals and the healthcare organisations also need to take into consideration the quality of educational aid to be made available to the medical students. The training institutes for nurses occupy an important place because they play a leading role in improving the quality of services offered by you. The syllabi at all the levels and for all the hospitals offering educational aid and training facilities are to be updated according to emerging trends in the environmental conditions. In this context, it is also important to mention that we find educational institutions in general concentrating on developing the professional excellence of medical students. They do not understand that in addition to professional excellence, personal commitment also is to be given due weightage in the process of educating and training the medical students. It is mainly due to our neglected efforts and a negative attitude towards the development of ethics, human value, and humanity that we find doctors becoming inhuman and indecent. Even the unfair practices promoted by the hospital personnel are the result of the irrational educational policy. It is against this background that we make a strong advocacy for promoting medical ethics, which should be included in the curriculum to ensure that our products are not only professionally-sound and personally-committed but also value-based.

The formulation of a product mix or development of product profile for hospitals and healthcare organisations thus makes it essential that you optimally blend the different dimensions. Accreditation carries no meaning; professional excellence is of no use, if the patients and attendants feel that doctors or other paramedical staffs are playing the role of a blood sucker. Thus, the formulation of a sound product profile is your functional responsibility and you are supposed to perform excellently. Like other organisations, you also are responsible for satisfying the customers/users/patients; and this makes your product profile of world-class. Of course, you need more frequency in the innovation process; and in the process, the services should become affordable so that even the poor can afford.

Promotion Mix

It is only significant that you perform well. It is equally important that your customers/patients realise your constructive and positive contributions and this realisation will lead to promotion. You offer world-class healthcare services to your patients; you are not only sympathetic, but also show them empathy; you not only offer time-honoured services but your services are affordable too; unless these positive contributions of your organisation reach to the potential customers; your task of promoting services will become quite complicated. It is against this background that an organisation requires to adopt creative promotional measures to inform and sense; motivate and influence the public at large; the prospects of today are the customers of tomorrow. If you keep on winning and retaining the efforts; your market share will always move upward. Like other organisations, the hospitals and healthcare organisations also need to promote such endeavours and this makes it essential that they make sincere efforts, and show professional excellence in synchronising the different constituents of promotion.

With the passage of time, a number of promotional measures have been included in the list which has increased the promotional budget of all the organisations promoting in a right fashion. But in the context of healthcare organisations, you have to increase the effects and optimise the costs so that the services remain affordable to the public. This complicates the functional responsibility of a healthcare manager. How to blend the different constituents of promotion so that the prospects are sensitised but the costs remain proportionate is a challenging task and this means that you need to perform efficiently and effectively. Unlike other organisations, the success rate of the promotional efforts of hospitals or healthcare organisations is considerably influenced by the fact that they have been successful in bringing down the number of prospects. You have to ensure that your promotional measures have been so much effective that prospects feel that their living conditions are healthy, food contains nutritional values, drinking water is potable, environment is eco-friendly, sanitation is neat and clean and in addition, they have civic sense, aesthetic sense helping them in improving their health and increasing their resistance power to diseases. This makes it essential that your promotional measures are creative because creativity makes the way for sensitivity which leads to acceptability.

There are a number of components of promotion, such as advertising, publicity, sales promotion, personal selling, word-of-mouth promotion and telemarketing. In Fig. 17.5, we present the different constituents of promotion.

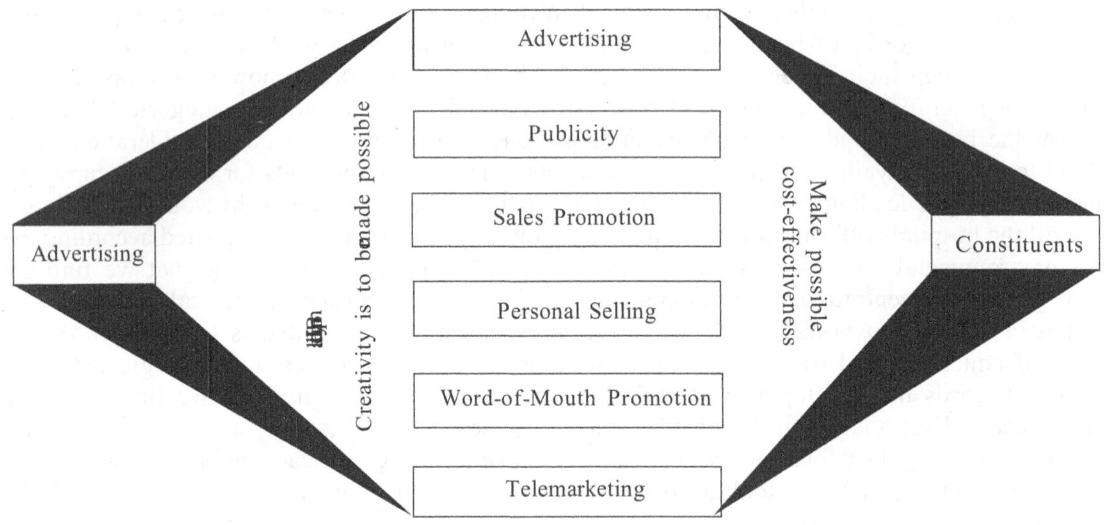

Fig. 17.5: Constituents of Promotion

Advertising: It is a paid form of persuasive communication. Like the goods manufacturing organisations even the service generating organisations also need to advertise and like other profit-making service generating organisations even the non-profit organisations like hospitals and educational institutions need to advertise. We find advertising a managerial process of informing and sensing the patients/prospects. In addition, we also find advertising a social process because the defined principles of social marketing make it essential that non-profit organisations assign an overriding priority to social advertising, though others too have the responsibility to contribute to the process of social transformation. Thus, the hospitals and the healthcare organisations need to assign due weightage to social advertising by making their slogans and campaigns more creative. By doing that, they bringdown the number of patients needing medical attention.

While promoting, the healthcare organisations need to instrumentalise the personal promotion measures but also to intensify the non-personal. For making available the right quality of services to the right users at the right time, it is essential that we focus on personal promotion. In this context, we find hospital personnel in general playing a meaningful role. To be more specific, the front-line personnel play a significant role in the very context. If the nurses start neglecting the patients, receptionists start miscommunicating with the patients and attendants, doctors do not show humanity; then the medical services even after the availability of world-class personnel and sophisticated technologies, fail in delivering goods to the society. Almost all of us are well aware of the most depressing contributions of personal promotion, specially in the healthcare sector. This makes it essential that we focus on advertising.

While advertising, it is important that we assign due weightage to creativity since this bears the efficacy of making the messages and campaigns effective. By creativity, our emphasis is on adjusting the advertisement programmes, campaigns, and slogans in tune with the receptivity of the prospects and in the face of changing conditions, the measures are to be made proactive. While advertising, a hospital manager or a healthcare manager is responsible for selecting the most effective media out of print media, broadcast media and the telecast media as per their requirements and budgetary limits. In the context of healthcare services, we need to take the support of print media and telecast media and also to make a fair mix of the two. We prefer telecast media as it has the potentials to sensitise even the insensitive rural and illiterate segments of the society. With the help of audio-visual exposure, and TV channels, the healthcare organisations — private or government, can be successful in creating mass awareness. To be more specific in the context of healthcare education for the rural segment, we find telecast media more effective in educating and informing, sensing and influencing the masses.

The health department, the hospitals, the healthcare organisations, and the social organisations are responsible for educating and sensing the public. Almost all the profit-making organisations have to promote healthcare education in a creative fashion so that the illiterate and poor segments of the society also come to know about the sensitive problems instrumental in solving their health problems. The main theme of social advertising focuses on health sector on a priority basis. The municipal corporations and non-governmental social organisations are also required to take keen interest in the process. Since we have a challenging task of sensing and influencing even the insensitive segments of the society, we find justifications for taking the support of professional advertising agencies that, with the help of creative messages, will boost the process of sensitising the public. Thus, the telecast media for the illiterate segment and print media for the literate segment would play a positive role in creating mass awareness.

We cannot deny the fact that in the Indian perspective we find even the literate and educated segment of the society, if not all of them, at least a majority of them do not give any importance to the healthy living conditions. They develop a food habit inviting numerous health problems. In addition, the rural women too have been facing health problems on account of the number of children. They are not fully aware of the family welfare/planning measures. In a true sense, we find them creating two types of problems, viz., first due to more children, the health conditions of rural women are poor and second on account of increasing population, the pressure on hospitals and healthcare organisations is increasing rapidly. This makes it essential that the concept of social advertising is given due importance in the boardrooms and the corporate sector of the country accepts the responsibility of creating mass awareness.

Publicity: We find publicity an unpaid form of persuasive communication because an organisation is not supposed to pay anything while publicising whereas the advertising is a paid form. It is in this context that we need to assign an overriding priority to this constituent of the promotion mix. The hospitals and healthcare organisations need to promote the same because they have been facing the problem of financial crunch. While going through this constituents of the promotion mix, it is essential to make it clear that the healthcare organisations/hospitals make use of the same in two ways, first by developing a rapport with the media people who would promote hospitals and second assigning due weightage to the public relations activities through a team of professionally-sound Public Relations Officers.

So far as the first step is concerned, the hospitals/healthcare organisations are required to develop a rapport with the media personnel and in this context, a public relations officer is more effective because he/she is expected to have an excellence of influencing and motivating the press correspondents for write-ups, news items related to the positive contributions to their hospitals. A tea party, get-together, lunch/dinner is organised for them, so that the process of sensitising the media is effective. Of course, a Public Relations Officer is required to have high communicative ability so that the media personnel understand the issue in the proper perspective.

The sensitivity of public relations activities in the hospitals makes it clear that a hospital manager should be well aware of the public requiring priority attention while publicising the services, viz., the patients and attendants, the government, the donors, the doctors, nurses, paramedical and managerial staff need to be influenced to activate the process. To enable hospitals to obtain a feedback on the present quality of services, it is essential that a hospital manager undertakes regular surveys with the support of professionally-sound researchers and research scientists. They need to accept the responsibility of designing questionnaires and selecting the respondents and further collate their opinions. The aim is to collect the opinions of selected respondents based on scientific sampling so that a hospital manager comes to know about the weaknesses and lapses and adopts corrective measures. It is quite natural that while selecting respondents, a hospital manager assigns due weightage to all the concerned segments as detailed earlier. Communication with the stakeholders occupies a place of outstanding significance, specially in the healthcare sector because all of them, partially or substantially, are influenced by the services of hospitals/ healthcare organisations. After achieving your goal, it is essential that you get a feedback of the stakeholders so that you are in a position to change your strategic decisions, if the feedback necessitates it. It is against this background that in the context of injecting new life to the publicity we need to communicate with the stakeholders. It is essential that we find communications comprehensive, open and even repetitive if conditions warrant so. We do not find any risk in being redundant when you repeat the importance of the task and underscore the basic objective you have been trying to achieve with your positive efforts.

In view of the above, it is essential that you have an independent Public Relations Department. If we find it significant that hospitals/healthcare organisations offer world-class healthcare services to the society and bear the social costs, then it is also important that they publicise their positive contributions so that the public at large come to know about the same. We are well aware that a hospital manager gets an opportunity to develop contact with almost all the segments of the society. May be that negative developments happen in the hospitals, indecent behaviour of the hospital personnel do not come to the notice of a hospital manager, therefore the hospitals have been facing the image problem. So, a hospital manager with the support of a professionally-sound Public Relations Officer comes to know about the feelings of stakeholders regarding the shortcomings of services and takes appropriate measures to resolve them. If you are interested in knowing about your positive or negative contributions, you need to develop proper rapport with the stakeholders. We do not find anything wrong if mistakes are committed, because it is quite natural that human beings working in an unfavourable condition fail to perform. We need to confess our mistakes to avoid repetition and their further transformation into blunders.

These facts make it clear that hospital/healthcare organisations need to strengthen the public relations activities through the Public Relations Department and the other health personnel working there. Projection of a positive image is, of course, impact generating and even hospitals or healthcare organisations cannot ignore it. And the task of image projection is successfully done with support of Public Relations Officer who is expected to be a star performer.

DIMENSIONS OF PUBLIC RELATIONS

An important and internationally acclaimed authority on marketing, Kotler has thrown light on the different components of public relations as presented in Fig. 17.6.

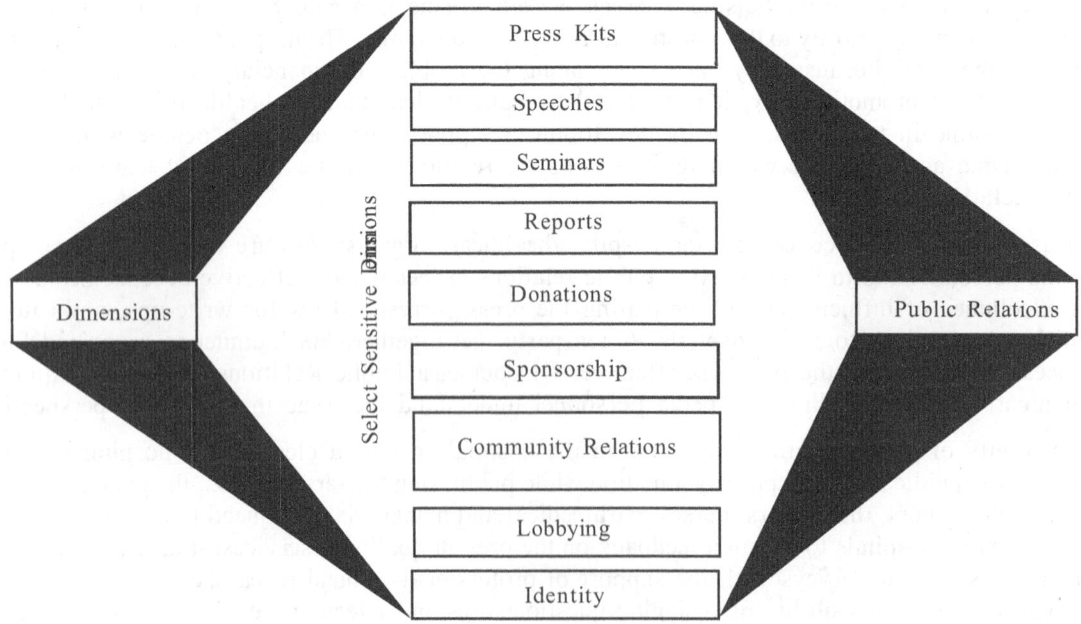

Fig. 17.6: Dimensions of Public Relations

Press kits: Whenever you organise a get-together, table talk, press conference, please distribute the kits containing writing materials to the press reporters which would influence them to write about your hospitals in a positive fashion.

Speeches: Since you have sophisticated information and communication technologies at the desk, please record them and make use of the same as and when the circumstances warrant it.

Annual reports: It is quite natural that you publish an annual report of your hospitals, specially in case of the private hospitals and prepare the reports mentioning the financial position of your hospital.

Seminars: You are also required to organise seminars, workshops frequently and invite prospects, patients, attendants, industrial customers or large-sized customers, vocal persons, social activists, intellects and others to participate and deliberate upon the performance of hospitals.

Charitable donations: In tune with the defined principles of social or societal marketing, you are also supposed to make significant contributions, to the development and welfare of the society. While organising conferences, conventions and seminars you may develop contact with industrial organisations making donations to your hospitals.

Sponsorships: To promote cause-related marketing, you are also required to develop rapport with the leading industrial organisations and business magnets showing interests in the promotion of social welfare and interested in sponsoring events for making available to you the financial support.

Community relations: You are also expected to develop community relations that would help you in projecting a positive image of your hospitals.

Lobbying: This focuses on lobbying with important personalities, VIPs, Social Reformists, Philanthropists, Political leaders with a clean image and so on.

Identify media: You are required to take support of media helping you in the projection of a positive image.

Being a hospital manager, it is your responsibility to ensure maximum use of all the components of public relations according to your requirements and situational needs. This would help you not only in the projection of a positive image but also in getting an opportunity to serve and get the financial support.

PUBLIC RELATIONS AND IMAGE PROJECTION

When there is a progress in your users, it is not difficult for you to regain the image, provided the innovative marketing practices are put to use. But if you fail to stop the process of tarnishing your image, your task becomes complicated. It is against this background that almost all the organisations have to apportion due weightage to the process of image projection. Like other service generating organisations, the hospitals/healthcare organisations also need to project a clean image. To be more specific when we find a majority of the government hospitals facing a lead image problem, it is necessary that the Public Relations Officer/hospital manager makes best possible efforts to project a fair image. We cannot negate the fact that tarnishing of image of hospital in general and the government hospitals in particular are mainly due to the degeneration found in the quality of their services. The public relations activities, if promoted in a right fashion, can be successful in erasing their tarnished image. Thus, we find image projection playing an important role specially in today's situations when hospitals in general are facing a poor image.

At the outset, it is essential that both the terminologies, viz., Image Projection and Image Building are clarified. A majority of us believe that image can't be built, but they are not correct in their observations. In a true sense, the term "image building" focuses on our positive efforts, deeds which change the perception of the receivers regarding the contributions of an individual or an institution. The purpose of image building is to project the proper image based on performance and contributions. The image building is a long-drawn result based on positive contributions, dedicated efforts, deeds and value-based services. To put it in another way, if we find hospitals/healthcare organisations offering world-class services, subserving the interests of weaker or poorer sections, bearing social costs, we create a condition for good image projection. This is one part of the process and therefore the hospitals/healthcare organisations are required to make positive contributions and make a case for image projection by activating the process of image building. If you are honest to the first process, it is quite natural that another part would also be completed successfully and your responsibility of image projection would be made considerably easier.

The above facts make it clear that a Public Relations Officer/hospital manager while organising, strengthening and innovating the public relations activities needs to concentrate on both. They have to ensure that their services are of world-class and therefore, they have been trying to build a positive image.

Now, the second task is to project your positive contributions specially with the help of sophisticated communication technologies so that you succeed in informing the public at large about your positive efforts to improve the quality and protect the interests of society. A hospital manager in the very context is required to go through the problems and if he/she feels the need for an efficient Public Relations Officer to hand over the responsibility of image projection they can do so. It is necessary to mention that in the entire process of image projection, you need to solicit the cooperation of media personnel and that depends upon your professional excellence in influencing and motivating them in the right fashion. Thus, the public relations activities can be helpful in projecting a positive image.

FACTORS CONTRIBUTING TO IMAGE BUILDING

Since your efforts for projection of a fair image are substantially influenced by your contributions to the process of image building, it is necessary that you are well aware of the following:

1. Behavioural profile of the hospital personnel: At the outset, you are responsible for studying and understanding the behavioural profile of different categories of personnel. This needs an in-depth study of their past records, reports from the user's grievances cell or so. The hospital personnel, in addition to the offering of quality services, are also required to behave decently. The cases of misbehaviour with the patients or attendants are to be gathered and based on the same, a report is to be prepared. In this context, you need to give due weightage to the behavioural profile of front line staff such as receptionists, cashier, paramedical staff and the centre for the collection of investigation reports, nursing staff or so on. This will make you aware of the behaviour profile of doctors attending on the patients. Unless the hospital personnel are decent in behaviour, it is difficult for you to project a positive image.

2. Quality of healthcare services offered: In the healthcare services, the qualities of core services occupy a place of outstanding significance. So, it is essential that you ensure that the different categories of hospital personnel are performing as per the defined norms. This focuses your attention on the quality of services to the patients.

There are cases where due to the negative attitude of front-line staff, the assured quality of services is distorted and a gap is created between the quality of services-promised and the quality of services-offered. Hence, you are required to ensure that your hospital offers quality services, assigning an overriding priority to the quality of core services, and, in addition, diverting due attention on the quality of peripheral services meant for the patients and attendants visiting the hospitals. Since we talk about quality in totality, it is essential that your professional excellence gives due weightage to the blending of core and peripheral services optimally so that the services are distinct. This helps you in creating product uniqueness simplifying your task of image building. We find a number of developments taking place everyday in the medical sciences, and you have you to ensure that your services are in tune with the evolving technologies and recent developments in the fields of medical sciences.

3. Performance of hospital personnel: It is also significant for you to ensure that the hospital personnel in general are performing excellently. On the one hand, they are offering world-class services based on their expertise, while on the other, they are also showing personal-touch-in-service. They are promoting ethical values, assigning due weightage to humanity and human values and thus have been successful in proving their excellence as a top performer. If your personnel are found making sincere and honest efforts to show personal commitments in addition to the professional excellence, your task of image building is easier. It is against this background that the hospitals and healthcare organisations need to assign due weightage to the level of performance of their employees working in different capacities at different points in different departments.

4. Fulfilling the expectations of public at large: We find healthcare services considerably influenced by their contributions to the process of social transformation. If they offer concessional or subsidised services and free services to the weaker sections of the society; and evince keen interest in promoting social advertising, It is quite natural that the public at large would remain satisfied. of late, we find the expectations of almost all categories of users of the services increasing fast, sizeably influenced by the sophistication in the process of development of communication technologies and the information superhighway. Being a healthcare manager, you need to identify the changing levels of expectations of prospects and to ensure that any gap between the expectations and potentials are bridged. Of course, you are required to subserve social interests by offering quality services to almost all the segments without making any discrimination.

5. You contribute substantially to social advertising: For propagating your positive contributions, in the aforesaid areas, you also need to make significant contributions to promote social advertising. In social marketing, we find social advertising getting an important place, which is to promote advertisements directly or indirectly contributing to the process of creating mass awareness, such as nutritional awareness, regulating food habits, realising the importance of potable water and sanitation, inculcating civic sense, promoting family planning measures, awareness related to immunisation programme and vaccination, communicable diseases, irresponsible sexual behaviour and so on. We are well aware of the fact that hospital/healthcare organisations also bear the responsibility of creating mass awareness and the social advertising would help them in the process. The signposts, slogans, the wall paintings, related to healthcare would be successful in creating mass awareness.

These facts are related to your positive contributions in promoting the healthcare services and therefore your deeds, contributions and mission lead to image building. On the basis of your services, you are in a position to project a positive image. Of course, the government hospitals have been facing image problem and it is difficult for them to project a positive image. But we also find a few of the government hospitals and a majority of the private hospitals offering world-class services and they would not find it difficult to project a fair image before the stakeholders or the public at large. With the sophisticated communication technologies, you will be in a position to project a positive image.

In a true sense, our deeds and misdeeds, positive and negative contributions, organisational and social considerations, decent and indecent behaviour, generation and diffusion of tension are the areas which make the task of image building difficult or easier. Where hospitals are offering quality services to the patients, subserving the interests of weaker sections, innovating the peripheral services frequently and assigning due weightage to social advertising, it is not difficult for them to project a positive image even if we fail in publicising, since our satisfied group of users act like a hidden salesforce and through word-of-mouth recommendations, they complete the incomplete task which remained incomplete even with the support of sophisticated promotional measures.

PROJECTION OF IMAGE

Since you have made positive contributions and achieved the mission by justifying your existence in the society, your right of promoting the same cannot be denied. Our emphasis is on adopting those measures which us in bringing an attitudinal change in the stakeholders. Of course, hospitals subserving the social interests bearing the social costs need to project a fair impact. The following measures may be helpful to you in activating the process of image projection.

1. Organising and participating in the exhibitions and seminars: It is essential that your Public Relations Officers or your representatives or you yourself participate in the conferences, seminars, workshops related to the health associations, medical council. In addition, you also organise seminars and workshops and inform the participants about the positive contributions of your hospitals. Since you have been making sincere efforts by subserving the social interests, the projection process would be proactive.

2. Organising patients relations programme: Being a manager, you are responsible for organising Patients Relations Programme where your get-together face-to-face communication with patients will help you in detailing and exposing the positive contributions of your hospitals, in addition, to the feedback that you get from them regarding the constraints and difficulties they feel. This would help you in undertaking opinion survey.

3. Get-together with the opinion leaders: For projecting the image of your hospitals, it is essential that you develop rapport with the opinion leaders, social activists, and academics, writing on health problems found almost in all the areas. Opinion leaders are those who have a say in the society and therefore whatever they feel about your hospitals will help you in the projection process. The main thing you have to remember is to influence them and on the basis of your professional excellence, you can do it effectively.

4. Contacting philanthropists: For the projection of a positive image, you need to influence the philanthropists who have love for mankind. To be more specific in the healthcare services, we find their feelings and comments more impact generating. Since the philanthropists are engaged all the time in the social welfare activities, it is quite natural that the people have trust on them.

5. Due weightage to social advertising: Since you contribute significantly to the process of social transformation by changing the nature and character of your advertisement, it is natural that you get the cooperation of stakeholders in general. You have to promote social advertising by creating mass awareness and narrating the positive contributions of your hospitals. Advertisements related to child care, rural women, family welfare, sanitation, healthcare in general, nutritional awareness, etc. would help you in many ways.

6. Rapport with educational institutions: For projection of a positive image, it is also essential that you develop rapport with local universities, institutes, colleges, schools and other institutions to inform the public about the positive contributions of your hospitals.

Sales Promotion: Since we talk about marketing the healthcare services, it is quite natural that we also discuss the sales promotion considered to be an important constituent of the promotion mix. In the hospitals/ healthcare organisations by way of sales promotion, we should gift or offer other incentives to both the parties, viz., the providers and the users. Hospital personnel play the role of providers and the stakeholders are the users. Of course, the hospitals or the healthcare organisations need to use this component of promotion with a fresh approach. If we advocate strongly in favour of professional and personal commitments, it is natural that we also talk about the incentives to be offered to them for their positive contributions to the development of organisations and subserving the interests of users. Here, we discuss the sales promotion tools even in the hospitals and healthcare organisations. The promotion incentives to the hospital personnel for their outstanding contributions will induce others also to contribute substantially. The low echelon of hospital personnel deserve due attention as their contribution to the process of development is found impact generating.

In addition to the hospital personnel, there is need for promotional incentives even for the users specially belonging to the low income group or poor segment of the society. When we talk about sales promotion, it is quite natural that limited incentives effective for limited period are offered when the pressure on hospitals or influx of patients in the hospitals is found low. Offering of small gifts and concessions during that period would help hospitals even in serving those segments who failed in availing of the services because of fee or other considerations.

Personal Selling: We find personal selling an important constituent of the promotion mix where the instrumentality of an individual plays a vital role in promoting services. We are well aware of the difference between the personal selling and salesmanship. By salesmanship, our focus is on the skill and excellence of sales personnel but in the context of personal selling, we find involvement or participation of not only the salespeople but even a hospital staff of high echelon is supposed to be involved in the process.

In the context of personal selling, it is important that the promoters communicate with prospective buyers or potential customers/patients/stakeholders in general regarding the outstanding services, salient features of hospitals or healthcare organisations which would, of course, be based on a comparative analysis of the contributions of other competitive hospitals. Essentially, you are not supposed to speak anything against your competitors but you have a right of making a comparative analysis of the features of your own services. Since we go through the problem of hospitals, it is quite natural that your communications, deliberations are based on specialities or the extraordinary facilities to the patients or attendants which are not made available by other institutions. The front-line professional of the hospitals, the receptionists, the nursing staff, the paramedical personnel and even the doctors and managers need to communicate effectively because there is nothing wrong in communicating the correct status.

In the context of personal selling, the managerial staff are expected to play a contributory role because they are supposed to be excellent and creative in communicating and influencing the prospects or the potential patients. A hospital manager needs to accept the responsibility of communicating with the industrial or organisational customers.

In the group of customers, they belong to the large-sized customers not directly but using the services indirectly. They provide an opportunity to their employees to avail of the services of hospitals and the medical bills are reimbursed to the hospitals or healthcare organisations. In this case, we find prospects for a big business and a hospital manager requires to motivate them so that they continue to make use of their services. We find personal selling very much instrumental in the process of getting large number of customers provided a hospital manager and his/her team evince interest in the process.

These facts make it clear that personal selling may be effective if the front-line staff, such as the receptionists, staff at the payment counters, nursing staff, paramedical staff and even the doctors and managerial staff give due weightage to influence and motivate the patients and attendants. The personal selling is based on personal relations in which the behavioural profile of employees play an effective role. It is against this background that we need to use this component of the promotion mix on a priority basis.

Word-of-mouth Promotion: This component of promotion mix is based on the positive or negative contributions of hospital/healthcare organisations. If we find hospital personnel offering quality services, showing sympathy and empathy, decency in behaviour, charging reasonably; the word-of-mouth communications act positively. Conversely, if we find hospitals offering substandard services, misbehaving with the patients and attendants, generating tension in them, it is quite natural that this tool of the promotion mix acts in negatively. This makes it clear that the instrumentality of word-of-mouth promotion is considerably influenced by the quality of product profile of hospitals, and, in addition, the behavioural profile adds additional attractions and you win the heart of patients and attendants who in exchange promote your services.

The advertising may be ineffective, the publicity may be insensitive, the sales promotion may be unproductive and even the personal selling may or may not be proactive but without exception, word-of-mouth promotion is extraordinarily effective — if you serve satisfactorily; it is a positive asset and if you serve half-heartedly; it is negative. This makes it essential that a hospital manager tries his best to improve the quality of product profile because this provides him an opportunity to show the excellence of hospitals.

Word-of-mouth promotion is an exercise of communicating favourably and therefore being a manager, you are supposed to make use of this component of the promotion mix. We also call this mix of the promotion word-of-mouth communication. The satisfied group of patients or attendants promote your business indirectly and know nothing about it. In the hospitals/healthcare organisations, we find this component of promotion very helpful in the promotion of business if the hospital personnel in general evince personal interests in offering quality services, showing decency in behaviour and making all possible efforts to fulfil the expectations of patients and attendants. But this component of the promotion mix also damages or harms your interest if you are not particular about the quality of product profile and no one would like to compromise with the quality. How to increase the number of word-of-mouth promoters is your important functional responsibility necessitating the cooperation of all the personnel engaged in generating and processing the services.

Telemarketing: Of late, telemarketing is contributing substantially to the process of promoting and selling. Scientific inventions and innovations open up new avenues for the development of information technology. Globally, telemarketing blossomed in the later part of 1960s. With the introduction of inbound and outbound Wide Area Telephone Services (WATS), the avenues could be broadened for the use of telephonic services for the marketing of goods and services. Gradually, we find development of television and this could inject new life and strength to telemarketing. Automated Dialing and Recorded Message Players (ADRMPs) can dial numbers, play a voice-activated advertising message and take orders from the interested customers or users on an answering machine device or by forwarding the call to an operator. Thus, we find telephone an important instrument playing a leading role in promoting the business. The sensitivity of telemarketing increased further with the advent of TV which is now a growing medium for direct marketing both through network and cable channels. TV is used in two ways for marketing goods or services, first – through direct response advertising and the second – through home shopping channels where an entire TV programme or even the whole channel is dedicated to selling goods or services.

Like other goods, manufacturing or service generating organisations even hospitals/healthcare organisations, can use telemarketing for promoting or even for business purposes. The big or large-sized hospitals can have an independent channel dedicated to the working of hospitals, fees for different types of services, accommodation available, arrangements for attendants, etc. The significant developments in the field of satellite communications have sharpened the instrumentality of telemarketing even in the Indian perspective. It is against this background that, of late, we find e-commerce or e-business gaining popularity. The Health Department of State Governments or the Union Government can promote leading hospitals of the country to inform and assess the prospects. We also find big hospitals efficacious enough in taking the support of telemarketing. If the big hospitals so desire, a separate network can be developed which would benefit even the smaller hospitals.

In the context of telemarketing, we find telemarketers playing an important role. The hospital/healthcare organisations telecasting their messages on the screen of TV are benefited in two ways; firstly, the patients or attendants come to know about the information, services, fee structure, amenities and facilities and secondly, the prospects can be persuaded effectively. If perceived in the right directions and persuaded with creative dialogues of telemarketers, they can transform the potential customers into actual customers. The instrumentality of telemarketing is substantially influenced by creativity. To be more specific in respect of healthcare services, we expect a lot from the telemarketers who are expected to stimulate the impulse of the patients or attendants interested in using the services of hospitals. We cannot deny the fact that the instrumentality of this new component of promotion substantially depends upon the quality of telephonic as well as the telecasting services. In the Indian context, the telemarketing may be useful to educate and influence the rural customers if we develop the network. It is the prime responsibility of a government to ensure quality healthcare services, the government hospitals promote telemarketing because this would not only be with regard to the government hospitals but the leading hospitals would also be included. To promote the health services, the telemarketing needs to be encouraged in government as well as the private hospitals.

STRATEGIC AREAS IN PROMOTION

Your task of informing, sensitising, influencing, winning and retaining the customers/patients need professional excellence of word-class. Since the users of the services in a majority of the cases have been educationally and financially weak, you need to promote creativity. You live in an age of technological sophistication where the pioneers and innovators are always promoted. By innovating the product profile, you have enriched the potentials of your hospitals to offer word-class healthcare services. Now, it is pertinent that you create mass awareness so that on the one hand, you succeed in attracting their attention while on the other hand, also minimise the possibilities of generating multi-dimensional diseases. It is essential that you promote with a sense. There are some thrust areas gravitating your priority attention and requiring due treatment. Being a professionally-sound manager, you are expected to formulate such a strategy that makes the promotional measures effective.

The following strategic decisions would sharpen the instrumentality of promotion:

Inculcating mass awareness: You are well aware that the society for which you promote the healthcare services has been facing the problem of high level of illiteracy which has made your task of creating mass awareness more difficult. Many health problems are due to ignorance or unawareness. We cannot deny that water-borne, food-borne, pollution-borne health problems can be substantially regulated if the masses develop awareness or consciousness. Contaminated water aggravates health problems and proves to be an important source for the water-borne disease. Like this, a number of diseases are caused by the consumption of unhealthy food items. What to talk of the illiterate segment of the society when we find even the educated and literate segments unaware of the nutritional value for maintaining a sound health. Of course, we find eating/food habits play an incremental role in the generation or regulation of diseases. With the passage of time and increasing impact of corporate culture on our food habits, we find a craze for fast food specially among the rich and the young. The latest, in the area is "FAST FOOD" which has resulted in nutritional deficiency and causing poor health conditions leading to the different types of diseases. Of course, we need variety in food since no single food item provides us with all the nutrients we need. Cereals like rice or wheat which form the staple food give us only a fraction of nutritional requirements. We need to supplement it with a number of vitamins and minerals to make our diet balanced or proportionate. We need to remember, "larger our diet sheet, the better out health will be." Carbohydrates, fats, water, minerals, vitamins are the different nutrients found in foodstuff and we need to make them proportionate to our requirements.

In Fig. 17.7, we find Energy Requirement Chart focusing on the importance of foodstuff in the maintenance of a sound health. It is your prime responsibility that while offering the preventive services you ensure that the promotional messages get due weightage. In the Indian perspective, we find most of us are consuming such food that provides us more carbohydrates and fats than proteins. This makes it necessary that we create mass awareness regarding the nutritional values. With the support of professionally-sound advertising personnel, we can create mass awareness to help us in many ways. In this context, it is significant that we seek the cooperation of dieticians or nutritionists. Also, we expect from doctors more positive efforts.

Category	Age	Height in cms.	Weight kgs.	Energy Allow Kcal	Protein gm
Infants	0-5	60	6	650	13
	5-1	71	9	850	14
Children	1-3	90	13	1300	16
	4-6	112	20	1800	24
	7-10	132	28	2000	28
Males	11-14	157	46	2500	45
	15-18	176	66	3000	59
	19-24	177	72	2900	58
	25-50	176	79	2900	63
	51+	173	77	2300	63
Females	11-14	157	45	2200	46
	15-18	163	55	2200	44
	19-24	164	58	2200	46
	25-50	163	63	2200	50
	51+	160	65	1900	50

Fig. 17.7: Energy Requirement Chart

The most important thing in the process of promotion is to generate mass awareness and our promotional messages need creativity in the process so that we find the public well aware of healthy living conditions. In addition to food, water, sanitation, environmental pollution, our messages also need to focus on the population problem. To be more specific, communicable diseases need a priority attention while creating mass awareness.

Instrumentalising personal promotion: In this process, it is necessary that we assign due weightage to personal promotion measures. The personal promoters like doctors, paramedical staff, nursing staff and even managerial staff have professional and situational responsibilities of activating the promotional measures. We need the constitution of a team of efficient, dedicated and committed hospital personnel related to almost all the echelons. If we find hospital personnel in general and the doctors in particular interested in promotion, the effectiveness of our promotional measures would be considerably increased. The secondary, tertiary hospitals and even the big private hospitals and institutes are required to promote healthcare services. The preventive services of hospitals/ healthcare institutions should make it essential that the hospital personnel with the help of creative promotional messages and appeals, make sincere and honest efforts to promote the services so that the pressure on hospitals is sizeably minimised. Your professional excellence would help in the stimulation process and the prospects would come to know about the measures to maintain a sound health.

Technology-driven promotion: In this information revolution age, it is quite natural that we utilise the information and communication technologies for activating promotional efforts. Of late, we find the print and telecast media in an advanced state. The hospitals/healthcare organisations need to advertise/and publicise with the support of communication technologies. We find audiovisual exposure more effective in sensitising the prospects. The rural segment, and specially the child and woman segment, need due care of a healthcare manager. We appreciate the positive contributions of modern print technology as a tool of promotion. The latest developments in the area are e-commerce and internet services found more effective in the process of informing and sensing the masses. In addition, the concept of telemarketing would help hospitals in promoting the services in a right fashion. The concept of cable marketing would be instrumental in the process. Thus, it is necessary that the hospitals/healthcare organisations take the support of advanced and sophisticated technologies not only for medicare but even for creative promotion for developing mass awareness and adding a new chapter in healthcare communications.

Innovations in promotion: Unless the hospitals and healthcare organisations further the process of promotional efforts to be innovative, the results are not likely to be satisfactory. Promotional efforts in a true sense should be a fair mix of curative and preventive measures. Of course, you have to innovate the product profile of the hospitals but at the same time, it will be effective if you make the processes of informing and sensing the patients/ prospects creative. Creativity bears the efficacy of sensitising the prospects. Out of the available measures for promotion, such as advertising, publicity, sales promotion, personal selling, word-of-mouth promotion and telemarketing, you need to select the most effective constituents in tune with your changing requirements. It is quite natural that the promotional strategy varies according to the changing segment and the disease profile. You have to make your promotional budget result-oriented because the services should be affordable. Maintaining cost-effectiveness in the process of promoting the healthcare services is your prime responsibility and being a manager, you bear the responsibility of ensuring that a non-optimal budget does not jeopardise your positive efforts. You need a fresh look, innovative measures and creative efforts. How to increase the sensitivity of your promotional efforts is an important functional responsibility before you which requires satisfactory performance.

An overriding priority to the organisational customers: While promoting, you have to be aware that the large-sized customers are sensitised effectively. We are well aware that some of the industries and institutions make provisions for treatment of their employees in a particular hospital. They reimburse the medical bills of their employees; and this is an important source for generating revenues for hospitals, specially under the private sector. Of course, you need to educate the rural masses at the same time, you have also the responsibility of exploring new avenues for revenues and to enrich your hospitals to bear the social costs on account of free medical treatment facilities to the weaker segments of the society.

These facts make it clear that as a manager you need to have to take strategic decisions to be result-oriented. Of late, this has become possible because we have professionally-sound advertising personnel in addition to sophisticated communication technologies.

The ultimate task before a hospital manager is to provide an effective promotional strategy that informs people successfully and play a dominating role in projecting a positive image of hospitals.

In hospitals/healthcare organisations, the word-of-mouth promotion or communication plays an outstanding role which is the result of a team work, team spirit and team culture. The satisfied group of patients/users acts like a hidden salesforce. If quality healthcare services are made available to them and they are satisfied with the behaviour of the hospital personnel there, naturally when they communicate their experiences to the friends, relatives, spouse who if motivated, prefer to use the services of that hospital as and when the circumstances warrant. Thus, hospital or healthcare services depend on the instrumentality of a team. In Fig. 17.8, we find promotion programming for the healthcare services.

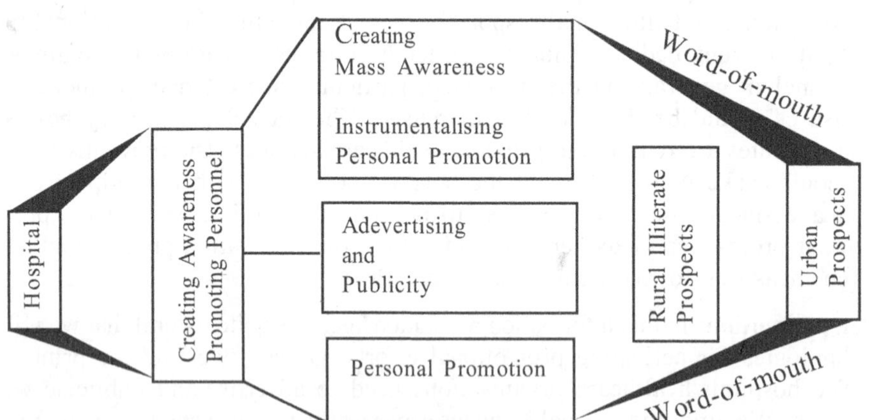

Fig. 17.8: Promotion Programming for Hospitals

These facts make it clear that almost all the constituents of promotion are instrumental but the word-of-mouth recommendations become more impact generating depending on the quality of services available to the users. The advertisement budget, public relations activities, tools of sales promotion, instrumentality of personal promoters and services of telemarketers will hardly motivate the uses it they feel that quality healthcare services are not made available to them. It is against this background that while formulating a strategy for promotion, a healthcare manager is not required to formulate a non-optimal budget for promotion. In a true sense, the quality of services of hospitals or healthcare organisations proves to be a base and if you find the base weak even if the promotional efforts are innovative and technologically-supported, the results or the sensitising processes will not be effective. However, a hospital manager is required to think about promotion and to formulate a strategy for the same so that the patients come to know about the changing service and behavioural profile. In the sphere of healthcare education for generating mass awareness, personal promotion occupies a place of outstanding significance and a hospital manager needs to show his/her professional excellence to sensitise the masses in the right directions.

Price Mix

In the Indian perspective, where a number of persons are below the poverty line, formulation of a price mix is a challenging task. A hospital manager, on the one hand, bears the responsibility of making the healthcare services affordable while, on the other, they are also expected to open new vistas for the development of hospitals and healthcare organisations. Striking a balance between the two opposite considerations requires world-class professional excellence. It is against this background that we study the problem of formulating a sound price mix for the healthcare services. Quality services need expensive inputs for which a hospital should be financially sound. Of late, costs of inputs used in the process are found increasing very fast. The Government hospitals in general are facing financial crunch because they are neither given a freehand while formulating a fee strategy nor adequate financial grants are made available from the state exchequer. They are expected to improve the quality but at the same time also to bring down the costs. Thus, a hospital manager requires professional excellence so that hospitals/healthcare organisations can thrive significantly to cater to the increasing healthcare requirements of the society. It is in this context that we study the problem of formulating a sound price mix.

The defined principles of social marketing make it essential that hospitals and healthcare organisations are given an opportunity to thrive so that they enrich their potentials of bearing the social costs on account of free services to the poorest of the poor. It is against this background that modern hospitals need an innovative pricing strategy. The fee strategy for hospitals, private or public, should be income-based. The quality of services would remain the same but the fee structure would be linked to the income structure. For this purpose, we need to classify the society into four subheads, viz., high-income group, medium-income group, low-income group and no-income group. In Fig. 17.9, we find a pricing/fee strategy for modern hospitals which would help them in generating finance from the internal sources. For a social institution like hospital, it is pertinent that we promote discriminatory pricing strategy, or what the traffic will bear or a pocket-friendly strategy. In the Indian context, we find it judicious because a majority of our population finds it difficult to avail of the expensive services of private hospitals. We don't find any logic in regulating the pricing strategy of government hospitals more so when we are not in a position to provide to them the financial support they need to cater to the increasing healthcare requirements of the society.

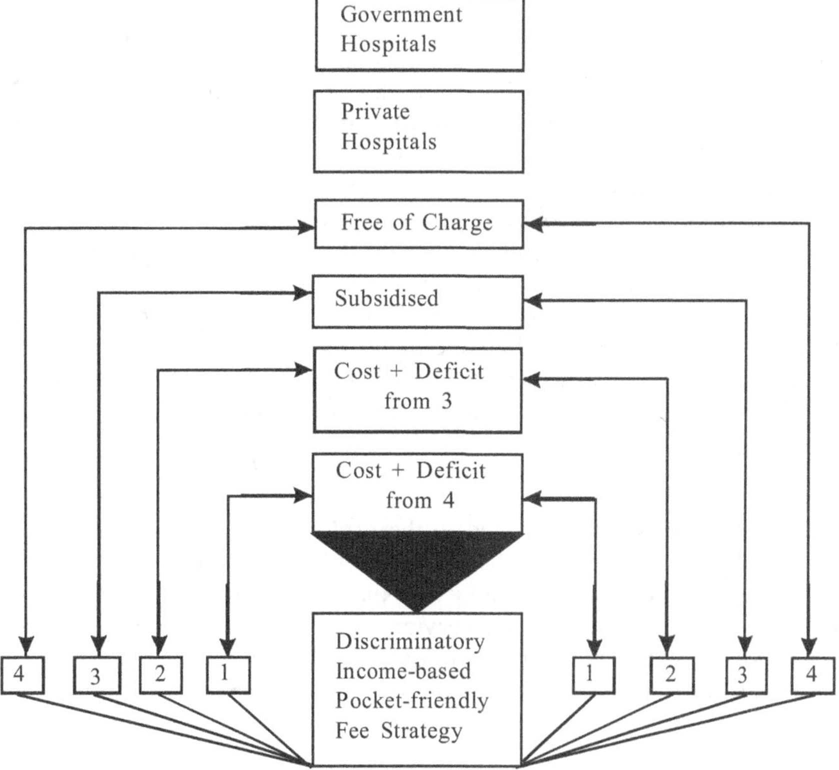

Fig. 17.9: Pricing/Fee Strategy for Hospitals

4 = No-income Group. He/she is not in a position to earn and therefore the free of charge services would be made available to them.

3 = Low-income Group. He/she earns something and therefore should pay a minor portion of their income to the hospitals as fee.

2 = Middle-income Group. He/she relatively earns more and therefore the fee structure for them would be enough to make up the losses on account of the low-income group.

1 = High-income Group. He/she earns well and therefore the fee structure for them should be sufficient to make up the losses on account of no-income group.

In Fig. 17.9, the fee strategy for hospitals makes it clear that four strategic decisions would be effective for the four different segments. At the very outset, we go through the problem of no-income group because specially in the Indian setting; we find this segment not harnessing the benefits of development in almost all the areas. They are not in a position to pay because whatever they earn is inadequate even to meet their family requirements of food and shelter. Hence, it is judicious that all of us who can afford partially or substantially contribute to the process by paying more proportionate to our incomes. The government hospitals as well as the private hospitals need a fresh look specially to subserve the interests of that segment. However, if we find a few of them even in that segment interested in contributing to the process of social transformation, we do not need to discourage them.

This would be positive in two ways, first there would be a very nominal increase in the revenue of hospitals and more important that a sense of participation will not demoralise them on this account that they are living or surviving at the cost of others. Of course, there would not be any limit to the same and the psychological and situational factors would guide them.

These facts make it clear that even from the internal sources, we find hospitals successful in making up the losses on account of concessional and subsidised services. So far as the development, expansion and modernisation programmes and in a few cases, meeting the deficits are concerned, the grants, charities, donations would be helpful.

We find rationale behind adopting such a strategy because even at the cost of all of us, the hospitals/healthcare organisations, private or government are required to be made available an opportunity to thrive and prosper so that qualitative and quantitative developments are possible to cater to the increasing healthcare requirements of society. We cannot move forward with the present strategy adopted by the government hospitals.

Place Mix

In the healthcare services, place mix draws our attention on two important issues, viz., first, the location point for hospitals and secondly, the process of offering the services. The location point for hospitals assumes a great significance because it is related to the time-honoured availability of services and the task is more complicated, if we find hospitals not located conveniently. Since the hospitals/emergency services are to be made available round-the-clock, it is important that the conveyance facilities are easily available so that emergency or even general patients and attendants or visitors do not face problem. In addition to the convenient location, it is also important that hospital is not located at places found hazardous to health. If we find hospitals located close to the big industries or population not having a civic sense; a number of problems can crop up. In addition to the pollution problem, anti-social elements may create different types of problems. Of course, the hospital planners, architects and consultants will help you in arriving at a right conclusion but one thing that you need to remember is trouble-free location. Since the patients and attendants are also expected to stay for a long time, if hospitals do not make available the facilities of shopping complex, and if the locations are very far the towns and cities, they may face complications.

Processing

Another dimension of marketing mix is related to the offering of healthcare services in a decent way. This drawn our attention to the behavioural profile of the personnel in general and the front-line personnel in particular. Being a manager, you bear the responsibility of satisfying the users and if the personnel start misbehaving, there will be a gap between the services-expected and services-offered. The personnel serving hospitals/healthcare organisations need not to forget that in addition to the quality of services, their behavioural patterns are also an important part of quality healthcare services. While offering or processing the services, they need to remember processing.

A degeneration in the behavioural profile of hospital personnel requires the formulation of a separate mix for the processing of time-honoured services and decent behaviour.

In the government hospitals, we find the problem of misbehaviour by almost all the categories of personnel and it is against this background that the management experts feel the need to give due weightage to the processing of services. This draws our attention on the knowledge of behavioural management to the different echelons of management or other personnel. It is, of course, necessary that you offer to the patients the promised quality of services but it does not mean that you are not aware of the terminologies, like "sympathy", "empathy", "humanity", etc. It is felt that an in-depth knowledge of behavioural management to the hospital personnel will lead to decent behaviour. To be more specific, the front-line staff like receptionists, nurses, paramedical staff need know about proper behaviour. This is mainly due to the fact that a number of services involve different categories of personnel and these are the points from where the process of service degeneration starts. Of course, almost all categories of doctors are also required to know about behavioural management but we need to ensure that front-line personnel working in the hospitals are decent. Particularly the personnel serving the government hospitals need to remember it because a large number of complaints are received against the behavioural profile of hospital personnel.

This necessitates due weightage to the behaviour profile of the personnel and medical superintendent serving the government hospitals is given to educate and train them in the changing perspective. There are different points where we need attention, such as the cash counter, admission, registration, investigation reports and reception. It is important that the patients or attendants at the sensitive counters are given due treatment so that any distortion in the process of offering the services is removed. A hospital manager/superintendent is required to bridge the gap between the services-promised or expected and services-offered and this is not possible unless a full team of hospital personnel coordinate with each other to provide good patient care.

Thus, while going through the place mix, it is important that a hospital manager devotes his/her attention on ensuring that the services reach the patients. He/she bears the responsibility of ensuring that different departments and personnel working there are careful, and in addition to the professional excellence, they also have the potentials to understand the changing behavioural profile of patients and attendants. Right processing, time-honoured processing, decent processing are some of the small things throwing significant impact on the level of efficiency of the personnel and satisfaction to the users and attendants. Here, we need a fresh look on the processing of services.

In the large-sized hospitals where local and outstation patients and attendants visit, it is essential that a hospital manager is particular about the influx of patients and the pressure on the outdoor and emergency services are minimised. In the specialised hospitals of excellence, patients from different parts of country or even from abroad arrive and so it is essential that overcrowding problem is taken care of intelligently. Increasing pressure on special category of hospitals makes it clear that there is a gap in the demand and supply positions of the hospital because the available facilities in the hospitals are not enough to cater to the increasing demand position. It is in this context that a hospital manager, while dealing with the problem of delivering the services to the ultimate users requires the support of a full team without which the services degenerate both at the micro and macro levels.

There are cases where the location point for a particular hospital assumes significance. In addition to the comforts of patients and attendants, a hospital manager is also required to study the constraints and difficulties before the hospital personnel specially while processing the services. There are a number of cases to prove that in the government hospitals, we find the problem of quality services and therefore a manager requires to ensure that quality is the most important aspect in the management of hospitals. But even if you improve the quality, and neglect the personnel, other constraints would influence the process. It is against this background that this mix of the marketing mix becomes significant.

In view of this, it is right to conclude that place mix requires due care of a hospital manager. He/she requires right processing of services so that the patients are satisfied. It is your professional excellence that would again determine the magnitude of your success.

Physical Evidence and Attractions

Ambient conditions bear the efficacy of projecting a fair image. Modern hospitals make use of a number of machines and equipments for offering quality medical aid to the patients. By physical evidence, our focus is on the physical facilities which the patients witness before using the services of hospitals. The patients, attendants and visitors come to hospitals with the motto of testifying their perception that the hospitals in which they are going to get the treatment are potentially sound. They have all the amenities and facilities for curing the patients. How and in what way, the hospital professionals satisfy them are found related to the servicescapes to be instrumental in creating service ambience. We should not forget that services of hospitals are based on the confidence of patients and attendants which they can gain and regain with the help of a number of displays attracting attention of potential users of services. It is in this context that hospital professionals need to manage the different dimensions of service ambience exclusively for hospitals.

The hospital services are based on cleanliness which is essential for impressing upon the patients and attendants and even for making the services ambience healthy disallowing scope for infection. This necessitates involvement of both machines and people. Of late, we find use of machines for disinfecting the hospitals where we find ample scope for infection at different stages. Besides, it is also essential that cleaning and disinfecting processes get necessary cooperation of people meant for this purpose. The operation should be round-the-clock. The sensitive points of hospitals need special care. In addition, the premises and surroundings need to look neat and clean. Management of aesthetics need due attention of hospital professionals and for that purpose, they need to ensure that hospital premises have a look of garden. We cannot negate the role of eco-friendly environment in minimising the duration of recovery.

The lighting arrangements at different points inside and outside the hospitals need due attention of hospital professionals. The colour and intensity of light *vis-a-vis* the positioning of light cannot be underestimated. This is essential for convenience and even for safety of patients and the assets of hospitals. This focuses our attention on non-stop supply of power. The signposts play an important role in guiding the new comers. The positioning of signposts and lighting arrangements for clean visibility cannot be overlooked. The lounge area of a hospital is found important with the viewpoint of diffusing the tension of patients and attendants. The furnishing of lounges, lighting and ventilation facilities, sanitation services, cleanliness of sanitation services, entertainment services, music, scent are some of the essential items making the place much more suitable for the waiting patients and attendants. The professionals need to make it sure that the lounges have the potentials of diffusing tension and generating fragrance. Since we find patients and attendants waiting there even for long time, the projection of image would also be easier.

The reception or enquiry centres play an effective role in the process of image projection. The availability, operation and display of information and communication technology for making available to the patients and attendants desired information on time and with decency simplify the task of marketing professionals serving the hospitals. The flow of action, quick disposal of cases, decent replies to the queries need not to be underestimated.

The circulation of information to the patients and attendants need due attention of professionals. The newsletters, leaflets, brochures, reports, successful treatment of patients, opinions of doctors, etc. play an incremental role in the tangibilisation process. The main thing is attracting the attention of patients to the service delivery processes to be followed by the hospitals so that they form a positive opinion regarding the service quality.

The hospital professionals need to perceive that the servicescapes play the role of packaging. The tangible products are packaged in an attractive way for diverting the attention of customers. Like this, servicescapes wrap the service and convey an external image of what is inside the hospitals. By making a mix of a number of stimuli, the professionals may be successful in conveying to the patients and attendants that they are going to be offered the medicare services more than their expectations. We consider servicescapes an outward appearance of the hospitals which may be instrumental in the formation of an initial impression.

The marketers need to strengthen their realisation that by tangibilising the outstanding features of their hospital, they will make efforts to establish their image as a differentiator. With the development of the concept of corporate hospitals, we find significant changes in the functional behaviour of hospitals. They make professionalised efforts to deliver services of quality which help them in establishing an edge over their rivals. While tangibilising, the professionals need to convince the potential users that what they are likely to get here not to be offered by other hospitals.

In the designing of servicescapes for hospitals, we find organisational goals constituting an outstanding position. The hospitals need to clarify their mission and objectives to impress upon the patients and attendants. The tangibilisation should be with the motto of transmitting a positive message to the patients and attendants that they are safe here and would be offered the best service. In the context of hospital, we find interpersonal services where both the users and providers are found involved. As a marketing goal, the hospitals need to promote their societal approaches for satisfying the users.

The above-mentioned facts make it clear that the hospitals also find this component of marketing mix important but at the same time, the professionals need special care so that the tangibilisation is not to create a negative image. Since the hospitals are found to be a sensitive place, we need to make it sure that tangibilisation succeeds in developing a right perception of the service quality to be delivered.

There is nothing more appealing than a man with a sense of wit and fun. There is nothing more paying than an aesthete. With the growing influence of corporate culture in the process of socio-economic emancipation, there is a basic change in the perception of personality development. Of late, the leading global organisations have been assigning due weightage to physical attractions.[10] The subjective knowledge, no doubt, plays an important role in almost all the organisations but at the same time, the organisations also expect that their employees have a classic look, an attractive look. A look that generates a positive image; a look that creates distinction; a look that magnifies optimism and a look that conveys elegance. In a true sense, we find the appearance of employees conveying the image of an organisation where they work. Poor, repulsive and pessimism generating appearance creates a negative attitude about both the employees and the organisation. It is against this background that physical attractions occupy significant place in the marketing mix of modern organisations either producing goods or generating services; either working with the aim of generating profits or working to subserve social interests. Like other organisations, the healthcare organisations also give due weightage to this submix of the marketing mix.

While going through the problem of hospitals or healthcare organisations, it is relevant that we view the problem differently. Of course, the dresses used by the hospital personnel indicate the culture of that institution. The professional requirements, situational limitations, circumstantial compulsion, cultural barriers are some of the important considerations influencing the nature and types of dresses used by them. It is quite natural that technocrats, corporate executives, cine artists, singers, doctors and others are not supposed to have an identical dress code and therefore the dresses used by them would have an apparent variation. The main thing in the process is to look smart and active and influencing the attitudes of users/customers/patients/attendants in a positive manner. In a majority of the hospitals, we find uniform culture not getting due significance. Of course, we find a very few of the healthcare organisations considering it significant. This makes it essential that the policy makers, boardrooms, top-level managers, senior doctors assign an overriding priority to the uniform culture.

Of late, we promote techniculture, develop human resources in the face of evolving technologies but overlook or ignore uniform culture. The Industrial Psychologists are of the opinion that there is a close relation between dresses used by us and participation expected from us. Where the Security, Police, Air Hostess, Hotel Personnel wearing the uniform/dresses made available to them here; a sense of participation is created and he/she finds himself/herself on duty and in action. Similarly, if we find doctors wearing uniform, nurses and other hospital personnel wearing dresses the look they have remind of their profession. Not only this, it is also significant that they are able to impress the patient's attendants and others too. The behavioural profile of patients and attendants witness a dramatic change the moment they find doctors and nurses in uniform. So, it is essential that hospitals or healthcare organisations irrespective of gender, age or sectoral variation promote uniform culture to activate work culture. The hospital personnel on duty should attach great importance of the uniform culture because a sense of responsibility is automatically conveyed to the users.

While promoting uniform code or culture, the main thing that should be taken care of is that the dresses (uniforms) used by the personnel are neat and clean, well-pressed and infection-free. A hospital or a healthcare manager is responsible to ensure that the linen used at different places should not cause any infection. It is in this context that laundry management gets an important place in hospital management. It is quite natural that the uniform supplied to the different categories of people should not create inconveniences rather should make the professional conditions proactive. Since you serve an organisation in which patients from diverse sections, groups, regions, cultural and family backgrounds come and stay for treatment, it is necessary that they form a positive opinion about the hospitals. It is not incorrect to mention that in a majority of the hospitals, uniform culture is neglected and presently except nurses a very few of other staff wear uniform. Even if they use, we find them not well maintained. The laundry section of the hospital is ill-maintained and deficiently managed and a medical superintendent find it difficult to improve the working conditions. The patients coming to the hospitals develop a negative attitude that the hospitals are financially insolvent and they have no fund to supply uniform and maintain them. In addition, the patients and attendants find it difficult to identify the hospital personnel. So it is necessary that particularly in the government hospitals, an attitudinal change is significant. The private hospitals have been giving due weightage to the uniform culture.

Since you serve an organisation promoting healthcare, educating and informing the public; it is essential that different categories of employees working there do not provoke to comment adversely about the different dimensions of physical attractions. Your dresses, physique, hairstyle, facial expression has significant impact on the behavioural profile of the patients, attendants and visitors. So it is essential that you are particular for the management of physical attraction and in promoting the same in the hospitals.

These facts make it clear that a hospital manager needs to treat Physical Attractions as a submix of the marketing mix where attractions carry some sensible meaning. Of course, your core services generate attractions; your peripheral services create additional attractions but we find physical attractions linked to both. We talk about the high performer, a super performer and this makes it necessary that all the dimensions are given a fresh look, a new vision, and an innovative treatment so that the uniqueness proposition leads to establishment of distinction in almost all the areas. It is against this background that we feel the need for including this submix of the marketing mix even in the hospitals and healthcare organisations. Unless you generate additional attractions, and unless you differentiate yourself, and your hospitals, the customers/patients would not be encouraged. Of course, we find quality of healthcare services motivating them significantly but when you offer quality healthcare services and in addition also make sincere efforts to generate additional attractions, the task of excelling competition; and of establishing leadership would be fulfilled satisfactorily. These facts make it clear that physical attractions need to be incorporated in the marketing mix of hospitals.

People Mix

Of late, we find people mix is of special significance in almost all the organisations. In the healthcare services, we find people playing a leading role. There is no doubt in it that despite innovative bio-medical equipment, apparatus, instruments, machines and robot, the techniculture becomes ineffective in establishing work culture if the people working there lack professionalism. It is against this background that we find developing the excellence of people an important task before the management of almost all the organisations. In the formulation of a marketing mix, the role of people mix has gained significance because the top-level managers and the boardrooms based on their experiences have come to this conclusion that people serving an organisation need top priority attention on your development agenda. We need to educate, train and develop people in such a way that they are not only professionally-sound but even personally-committed because professional excellence carries no meaning, if we lack personal care in services. This is substantiated by the fact that despite doctors having the world-class excellence, technocrats extraordinarily efficient, administrators exceptionally proficient, teachers well qualified and experienced, the results are almost all dismal, the level of efficiency coming down and the rate of productivity consistently declining due mainly to the fact that all of them lack personal commitment, ethics, values. This necessitates a fresh look, a new vision and an innovative strategy for the development of people. It is in this context that the concept of New People Management needs priority attention of the management experts.

It is time cycle that influences the nature and character of the developments and an individual or an institution not interested in conceptualising the same, suffers a lot. Change is a natural phenomenon. No one can stop the flow and change its directions. Hence, it is wise that we keep our minds active, eyes open and do our best to foresee the developments to take place and innovate strategic decisions accordingly. We have sophisticated world-class technologies, supporting infrastructural facilities, comforts-based buildings but the lowest level of efficiency. Like other organisations, we find hospitals and healthcare organisations also facing the identical problems. If we divert our attention on the level of performance of government hospitals, except a very few, by and large almost all of them present a disappointing result. The ultimate sufferers are the patients belonging to the poor segment because the private hospitals have been subserving the interests of those who can afford. Of course, we appreciate the contributions of medical scientists who have made possible significant developments in the disciplines but their mission would remain unfulfilled if we find the poorest of the poor not harvesting the benefits of development in the world of medical sciences. Hospitals or healthcare organisations do not have a legitimate right of making profits and therefore the boardrooms or the policy makers are mainly influenced by the social considerations. The government as well as the private hospitals needs to serve the patients with the same idea. Both of them need to find an equilibrium where time-honoured developments of hospitals and interests of stakeholders are given due weightage.

The formulation of a sound people mix particularly for hospitals or healthcare organisations make it essential that they have professionally-sound, personally-committed and value-based people who not only play a commanding role in accomplishing the organisational objectives but also contribute significantly to the fulfillment of organisational mission.

The most important task before a hospital manager is to develop a healthy and harmonious relationship with the employees to create a family and friendly feeling, a sense of belonging in the minds of employees, a feeling that employees and managers share the same ideals. Thus, in the face of degeneration levels of efficiency in the hospitals and healthcare organisations, it is necessary that an organisation has people with special attributes who fulfil the organisational as well as the social interests.

Since we face the problem of marketing the healthcare services, it is necessary that we make sincere and honest efforts to make available to the hospitals quality people and for this, it is significant that a fair synchronisation of the social and organisational goals is made possible. This would help or inspire the hospital personnel to show personal-touch-in-service in addition to the professional excellence. We talk about world-class excellence but it is not possible unless we find our incentive plans are competitive. A self-motivated manager bears the efficacy of making it a success.

The hospitals or healthcare organisations have been facing numerous problems. They need to make possible good patient care. They need to bear a considerable amount of social costs. They need to achieve world-class excellence. They need to assign an overriding priority to the satisfaction of patients and attendants. This makes it necessary that a self-motivated manager accepts the responsibility of building friendly, harmonious, value-based and inter and intra-departmental relationships. By doing that, he/she succeeds in making the environment at the workplace instrumental in generating the level of efficiency. It is in this context that we strongly advocate in favour of developing quality hospital personnel who play a leading role in increasing the number of satisfied group of patients/users.

A hospital manager faces a challenging task of making the process of generating and processing the cost-effective healthcare services so that the services are affordable even to the weaker sections of the society. Not only this, he/she also needs to make hospitals and healthcare organisations a centre of excellence which is very effective in promoting research and innovating the diagnostic and treatment measures to meet the multi-faceted necessary that an innovative fee/pricing strategy is practised so that the hospitals or healthcare organisations are in a position to enrich their potential of bearing the social costs. Of course, he/she bears the responsibility of enriching the quality of biomedical equipments, apparatus, instruments, machines, and infrastructural facilities but the important of all is the people that focus his/her attention on a priority basis. Unless we motivate people as per the international standards, it is difficult to achieve the world-class excellence and unless we are globally competitive, our dream of becoming a leader would remain just a dream.

In view of this, it is right to conclude that people mix of organisations in general and hospitals or healthcare organisations in particular need an overriding priority and in addition to a healthcare manager, the boardrooms or the policy makers also need an attitudinal change. Here, management experts promoting the new perception of "Quality People" require a fair blending of professional excellence and personal commitments.

STRATEGIC MARKETING

Increasing population, polluting environment, contaminated food and water, high rate of illiteracy, radiation caused by scientific inventions and innovations, use of plastic and glass material are some of the new developments, of course, slowly but surely have been laying a strong foundation for the development of a number of diseases. In addition, the cultural pollution, irresponsible sexual behaviour, drug addiction, increasing use of tobacco, craze for "Gutka" in the new generation are additional developments very much instrumental in aggravating the magnitude of the problem. On the other hand, the negligent attitude of the government to the health sector, inadequate support of public at large, delay in the process of conceptualising marketing in the healthcare services, increasing insensitivity among the masses to the healthcare services, degenerating work culture and falling rate of productivity of hospitals and healthcare organisations are fuelling the process of negative developments. Private hospitals are growing because they assign due weightage to the concept of modern marketing but so far as government hospitals are concerned, we find the picture very gloomy. The demand side is increasing fast while the supply position is facing qualitative-cum-quantitative degeneration. These facts make it essential that the policy makers, boardrooms, medical scientists, doctors, managerial staff make sincere efforts to find out appropriate solutions so that the dealing healthcare systems are set right.[11] It is against this background that we need an innovative marketing strategy.

During the yesterdecades, the contours of development have undergone radical changes in almost all the areas. The scientific advancements have led to a structural change in all the important areas of socio-economic transformation. If we look at the healthcare sector, the achievements appear very disappointing. India was one of the pioneers in health service planning with focus on primary healthcare. In 1946, the Health Survey and Development Committee headed by Shri Joseph Bhore recommended establishment of a well-structured and comprehensive health service with a sound primary healthcare infrastructure. This report not only provided a historical background to the development of a public health system but also laid down the blueprint of subsequent health planning and development in independent India.

At the time of Independence, the national healthcare infrastructure was mainly urban-based and clinically promoted. The hospitals and clinics provided curative care to patients who came to them. The reach out of the rural healthcare services was very limited. Gradually, we started development plans and during the last Five Year Plans, a number of steps were taken to improve qualitative-cum-quantitative developments. Improvement in coverage and quality of healthcare and implementation of diseases control programmes resulted in steep decline in the Crude Death Rate (CDR) from 25.1 in 1951 to almost 9.0 and we expect even further decline in the coming years. Life expectancy rose from 32 years in 1947 to almost 62 years now and the female life expectancy even higher than the male. Morbidity due to non-communicable diseases is showing a progressive increase because of increasing longevity and a change in the lifestyle. Morbidity due to common communicable diseases and nutrition-related diseases continue to be high. There is no doubt that India today has a vast network of governmental voluntary and private health infrastructure manned by a large number of medical and paramedical personnel.

Despite a number of positive developments in the healthcare sector, we find the masses not getting even the basic healthcare facilities then what to talk of the world-class services. We find a persistent gap in manpower and infrastructure especially in the primary healthcare services. Inadequacy of supporting infrastructural facilities, poor referral services, inadequacy of almost all categories of the hospital personnel, inadequacy of sophisticated biomedical equipments, apparatus, instruments, machines and technicians and engineers, massive inter-state and inter-district differences in the levels of performance, lack of intersectoral co-ordination, increasing dual disease burden, communicable and non-communicable diseases are some of the constraints standing as a major barrier while developing the healthcare services.

Of course, the state governments have been investing huge funds for the government hospitals but the level of efficiency is coming down. Even if they have bio-medical equipment of world-class, we find them of no use. On the one hand, the government hospitals complain about the inadequacy of personnel while, on other, we find them practising in the private clinics. Financial support by the government is steadily falling. The government hospitals do not have the freedom of generating revenue. Charities and donations are decreasing and ultimately we find them facing a financial crunch. The potentials of hospitals are decreasing whereas the requirements for healthcare services are increasing. The ultimate and the worst sufferers are the weaker sections of the society because the affluent sections get world-class healthcare services provided by the private hospitals. It is in this context that we find strategic marketing impact generation since innovative strategic decisions will lead to quantitative and qualitative developments.

Present century leads the next century. We have a long-run target of having a healthier 21st century and a short-run target of improving the quality of healthcare services. The hospitals today are responsible for protecting, and serving the human resources considered as precious endowment. The formation of human capital is sizeably influenced by the development of healthcare services. In the modern Indian society, marketing of healthcare services is difficult because a majority of us feel that it is the sole responsibility of government to promote the healthcare services. To improve the quality of diagnostic, curative and other services, the hospitals need to implement a number of capital-intensive projects in addition to the development of different types of infrastructural facilities. The heads of investment in a majority of the cases lead to quantitative improvements. At this juncture, we need to formulate a new strategy for the healthcare organisations.

These facts bear a staunch testimony to the promotion that despite innovative and strategic decisions, a marketer is expected to meet his/her professional requirements. The government exchequer finds it difficult to finance the students related to the education, training and research programmes. This draws our attention to some of the sensitive areas mentioned below. We have to reiterate that the hospitals or the healthcare organisations bear the managerial responsibility of bringing the detailed healthcare system back on the track. Since we talk about formulating strategic marketing, it is essential that we assign due weightage to the following suggestions so that the innovative strategic decisions prove successful.

• **Orchestrating the marketing resources:** Tailoring of marketing resources according to an action plan so that the marketing mixes prove to be proactive is known as strategic marketing. The fact makes it clear that the demand position is to increase and in addition, the disease profile would also be more hazardous. The hospital planners, architects, consultants, top-level doctors, top-level managers and the boardrooms or the government policy makers would have to change their attitudes and the line of action. They need to identify the thrust areas and to develop the marketing inputs accordingly so that the government and private hospitals are in a position to cater to the increasing health requirements. This requires qualitative as well as quantitative improvements in the healthcare sector of the country.

• **General and special hospitals need quantitative transformation:** In view of the increasing healthcare requirements of society, it is essential that we bring a substantial increase in the number of both the categories of hospitals, viz., General and Speciality. In almost all the state capitals, a large-sized general hospital is to be started and in the selected towns and cities or even in the easily accessible suburbs and rural areas, a number of speciality hospitals either based on the nature of disease or on the organism of body are to be set up. These would-be government-supported hospitals where cost-based, free-of-charge, concessional or even surplus-generating fee structure would be worked out. The hospitals would be well equipped with the sophisticated technologies and a team of committed and professionally-sound medical and paramedical personnel would be available. Modern management orientation would get top priority and different echelons of management would have the responsibility of developing them as a centre of excellence in their discipline. In the rural sector, the primary healthcare centres would be restructured and the concept of referral hospital would be rejuvenated. There would be a close link between the primary healthcare centres and the referral hospitals and speciality cases would be referred either to the general hospitals or to the speciality hospitals as the circumstances warrant. These hospitals would be in addition to the existing strength of hospitals and therefore we can expect a big increase in the potentials of healthcare organisations to meet the increasing healthcare requirements of the society. A special Health Care Fund would be created for which the State Governments, Union Government and public at large would make financial contributions in the face of their levels of income. It is important to mention that the corporate sector would also contribute as a Corporate Citizen in tune with the defined principles of Social Marketing.

• **The existing hospitals need qualitative transformation:** By and large, almost all the government hospitals are in a state of disarray. They have been facing the problem of financial crunch and so, financially bankrupt. And, naturally we find bankruptcy at almost all the levels. The traditional technologies and traditional management orientation has been found in the reverse gear. It is essential that a special task force is set up to overhaul them. The management orientation, upgradation of biomedical equipments, apparatus, instruments, availability of uninterrupted supporting infrastructural facilities, screening of the performance of almost all categories of medical and para-medical personnel, performance-based incentive plans need due attention of the policy makers. While dealing with the problems of government takes keen interest in the process of overhauling. So far as the financial requirements are concerned, the Union Government would be required to offer a matching grant. In addition, the global bodies taking part in the process would also be approached. An important task before the government would be to make possible one hundred per cent fair use of the financial resources.

• **Private hospitals to be promoted:** In this context, it is also essential that we promote the private hospitals. This means that formulation of policy decisions should be given due weightage in this context. Since we make a strong advocacy in favour of the bearing of social costs even by the private hospitals, it is necessary that they are offered special incentives for the development of such hospitals. It is necessary that we promote the corporate sector for the opening of new hospitals in the vulnerable areas of the country. Here, we need to stress a sense of co-ordination and co-operation between the government and private hospitals; specially to face the challenges caused by natural calamities or epidemics, immunisation and vaccination programmes. We agree with view that in terms of infrastructural facilities and quality of apparatus and equipments, we find private hospitals in general having an edge over the government hospitals and this is mainly on account of their management orientation which they practise on a priority basis. Of course, in terms of the quality of medical and paramedical personnel, we find government hospitals having an upper hand but this is not due to special incentives they get there but because of the well-established image of a few of the government hospitals and institutes. The government policy makers are required to study the problems of private hospitals and help them to solve the same. When they need to import biomedical equipment of world-class which are not available in the domestic markets, and when they need multi-faceted facilities, the government should come forward to help them. When they need financial support, the public sector commercial banks and other financial institutions should offer credit facilities on the reasonable terms and conditions. The supply of infrastructural facilities like power, water, communication should be ensured. The law and order problems and the safety and security measures need due support of government. The concept of small private clinics is to be given a shape so that they do not face problem. It is to be ensured that whatever fee they charge is fair according to the quality of the services they offer. At the initial stage, they need concessional services of infrastructural industries. Thus, we need to promote the private hospitals so that they develop and prosper and increase their potentials of bearing the social costs. In Andhra Pradesh, Maharashtra, Gujarat and Kerala, the private hospitals have been flourishing. It is a lesson for other states because the Government hospitals are not able to cater to the increasing healthcare requirements.

- **Government and private hospitals need to promote social advertising:** Since we talk about management of hospitals on the basis of the defined principles of social marketing, it is necessary that public as well as private hospitals both of them take keen interest in social advertising. By social advertising, our focus is on promoting social interests, viz., advertisements related to family welfare, child care immunisation, noise pollution, water contamination, irresponsible sexual behaviour, food habits, drug addiction, liquor consumption, use of tobacco or so. The messages related to the aforesaid problems would prevent health problems. Since different categories of patients and attendants are coming to the hospitals in large numbers from different parts of the country or even from abroad, the advertisement slogans and messages should be made creative and effective.

Whatever you expect from others, you should also need to fulfil the expectations of others. You expect that corporate citizen should promote the healthcare sector by extending to you the financial support and similarly, the society also expects that you promote and subserve their interests by inculcating mass awareness. The slogans related to social advertising would be efficacious in fulfilling or meeting the expectations of public at large. Besides, the society would be benefited considerably because a number of social problems would successfully be solved if the messages of social advertising become effective in sensitising and motivating the society.

- **Injecting needs for techniculture:** Except a very few, we find almost all the hospitals, private or government, creating healthcare services with the help of traditional technologies. The latest developments in the medical sciences have been successful in innovating biomedical equipment, apparatus, instruments, and, in addition, the information technology has been adding new dimension by innovating the diagnostic and treatment process. The patients are benefited because of authentic and quick diagnosis and the doctors are benefited by minimising the time gap between initiating investigations and coming to a final conclusion. It is against this background that we should try to promote techniculture which focuses our attention on aggravating the temptation for the new generation of medical technologies. Not only the government hospitals but even the private hospitals should promote the same to meet the increasing levels of expectations of users. Since we advocate strongly in favour of quality in totality; it is the prime responsibility of few of the leading hospitals of the country like Escorts Heart Institute (Delhi), AIIMS (Delhi), Institute of Reproductive Medicine (Kolkata), Tata Memorial (Mumbai), NIMHANS (Bengaluru) and Shankar Nethralaya (Chennai) to educate and persuade new as well as the old hospitals to promote technologies.

- **Creativity in healthcare communication:** A large number of diseases has been spreading like a wild-fire in the present society are self-generated. Since we find a majority of the population illiterate and unaware of wrong food habits, consumption of contaminated water, generation of noise and atmospheric pollution, drug addiction, family planning, early and late marriages, consumption of liquor, use of tobacco, irresponsible sexual behaviour invite a number of health problems. Hence, we talk about healthcare awareness. Even today, a majority of the hospitals have not given due weightage to the preventive services. It is the responsibility of all categories of hospitals to accept this vital social responsibility of creating mass awareness so that the health problems are considerably minimised. Since you as an expert know well about the instrumentality of creative messages and slogans in creating mass awareness, the slogans related to social advertising should be made creative. Of course, media have remained instrumental in the process but the messages and campaigns promoted by the doctors and hospital managers will have a greater impact.

- **Vaccination culture to be promoted:** In view of the emerging health problems, it is also significant that hospitals in general promote vaccination culture. Vaccines are the most cost-effective agents for controlling communicable diseases. Here, a revolution is needed on the vaccinology front. The immunisation programme will benefit the society in many ways.

A reduction in the infant mortality rate is the result of child immunisation. The Universal Immunisation Programme (UPI) is aimed at a healthier 21st century. This can certainly be achieved if the government and the core and paramedical personnel are actively involved in the immunisation programme. An aggressive marketing strategy is needed to make the immunisation programme a grand success. We are witnessing the positive results of Pulse Polio Programme and expect that in the near future, we also promote the Vaccination Programme for Hepatitis B. Tuberculosis is a major killer disease and in India, about half a million people are dying of this disease every year. Of course, we have vaccine like BCG in the immunisation programme but it is not so effective against Pulmonary Tuberculosis. It is essential that we develop more effective medicines against tuberculosis. Cholera is still around and often appears as an epidemic. The old cholera vaccine is no longer used. Typhoid is another problem which needs an antigen to counter this problem. Since we are studying the managerial problem, we should focus on the managerial lapses that we find in the process. Of course we are making efforts to promote immunisation programme but the vulnerable segments of the society specially the rural population have not been given due weightage. Thus, it is our prime responsibility to constitute a special task force for the benefit of the rural segment.

- **Yoga and pranayam need to be promoted:** Of late even the medically developed countries of the West have realised the significance of "*Yoga*" and "*Pranayam*" in countering a number of health problems. The revived interest in Yoga is a welcome the world over. We find Yoga, a beneficial and an elegant way of regulating and exercising the mind, the brain, the respiration and other vital functions. Proper Yoga can give us a feeling of well-being in the system which no drug can provide. So, we strongly advocate in favour of Yoga. The hospitals of all categories can successfully create awareness and interest in yoga among the masses. The involvement or participation of doctors in generating interest among the masses would benefit the society in different ways. To be more specific, the poor rural society right now faces a number of difficult health problems and they can substantially benefit if they realise and practise Yoga as a part of their health management programme.

- **Herbal products to be promoted:** In view of the increasing health problem, it is natural that we promote use of herbal products and create mass awareness regarding their efficacy in the treatment of a number of ailments and promote the cultivation of plants having medicinal value. In the Indian society where the masses find it difficult to buy the expensive medicines, it is essential that the hospitals and healthcare organisations shoulder responsibility of promoting herb-based medicines and cosmetics.

Hence, it is right to claim that to cater to the increasing healthcare or medicare requirements of the society, the healthcare organisations must activate qualitative-cum-quantitative measures. A gap between the demand and supply is to be bridged on a priority basis and this requires public participation.

- **An overriding priority to the quality system:** While discussing about quality in totality for marketing the healthcare services nationally and internationally, we should focus on developing quality system essential in meeting the quality objectives. It also helps in satisfying the internal managerial needs of hospitals and healthcare organisations. It is found broader than the requirements of a particular patient who for satisfaction only evaluates the relevant part of the system, such as the curative services made available to him/her. We find quality in totality a salient feature of an entity that depends on its ability to satisfy stated and implied needs. So it is essential that hospitals or healthcare organisations know about the quality policy as formally expressed by the policy makers or the boardrooms.

For maintaining quality, we find quality management essential in which all the activities of the overall management functions concentrate on quality policy. We find operational techniques and factors influencing or degenerating quality and therefore should get due weightage. These things help in shaping quality assurance which proves to be an important constituent to evaluate the performance because a gap between the quality-promised and quality-offered will dissatisfy the patients and attendants. Thus, it is significant that a healthcare manager for marketing the services in the future realises the right meaning of quality because any mistake committed in the process would lead to the marketing disaster. All the activities influencing quality are to be managed properly.

- **Behavioural management to be improved:** In addition to the world-class healthcare services, it is also essential that the hospital personnel improve their behaviour profile to minimise the gap between the services-promised and service-offered and also promote decency in processing. The hospital personnel in general need to show sympathy to the patients and attendants and in addition also to show empathy. This makes it essential that the behavioural profile of hospital personnel gets due weightage which needs restructuring of training and development programmes. With the increasing level of expectations of users, the hospital personnel need to improve their behavioural profile.

- **Uniform culture to be promoted:** To give a fresh look to the personality of hospital personnel, it is necessary that the hospital manager thinks of promoting the uniform culture. It should be made compulsory that all the personnel wear the uniform supplied to them by institutions. It should be ensured that the dresses are neat and clean and infection-free. The linen supplied by the hospitals should be washed, dried and pressed properly to counter the problem of infection. Sometimes, we find senior doctors not wearing and in this case, also the dresses they wear should be neat and clean and well pressed. Your look generates positive or negative image of hospitals and it is essential that you are very careful to the uniform of dress culture to promote physical attractions.

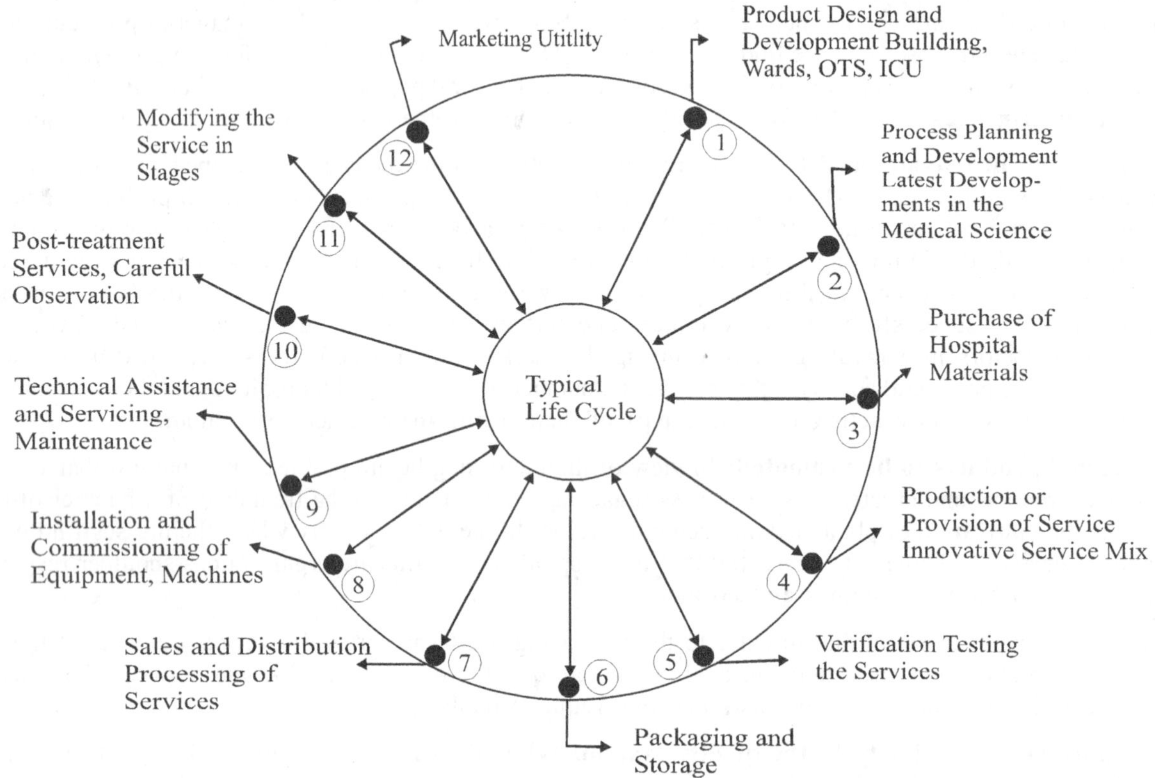

Fig. 17.10: Activities Influencing Quality

- **Social costs to be made optimal:** To improve the finances of hospitals, it is necessary that we make the social costs proportionate to the potentials of hospitals. The social costs are the losses on account of concessional or subsidised or free services available to the poor segments of the society. Government hospitals are generally facing problem of paucity of funds which make them financially insolvent. Of course, the poor sections need due care but it is not meant that in all the cases and for all the purposes, we promote free or subsidised services. A basic change in the pricing policy is imperative. The private hospitals also need to promote the concessional or subsidised services because they have to contribute to the process of subserving the social public interests optimally.

- **Concept of rural urbanisation to be promoted:** Strategic marketing makes it essential that for the development of new hospitals — both in the private and public sectors, the concept of rural urbanisation is to be promoted. This means opening and developing new hospitals in the rural areas or in the suburbs so that even the rural segment is benefited by the new developments in the field of medical sciences. If we develop big, specialised hospitals close to the villages or suburbs, the development of backward regions would be possible since a number of patients and attendants coming to the hospitals for treatment will include all the segments of the population. The multiplier effects would be found effective and a number of development centres would start functioning. But in this context, it is important that we locate hospitals at places easily accessible round the year.

These strategic decisions would bring multi-dimensional improvements in the workings of hospitals or healthcare organisations. The patients would get quality healthcare services, the hospital personnel would be motivated and the hospitals would thrive leading to the developments in the medical sciences.

CONSUMER PROTECTION REGULATION FOR MEDICAL SERVICES

In the context of professional services, medical services occupy a predominant place because we find them essential in nature and are required by each and every one in the society. Hence, a duty is cast on the medical practitioner to attend on the patient and exercise reasonable care while making treatment of such a patient. Any medical practitioner who is negligent in his professional career may be held liable for any mishap due to that negligence. Here, it is also significant to mention that mistaken diagnosis is not an act of negligence unless it is negligence *per se*. Similarly, paramedical services such as scanning centres, diagnostic centres and medical laboratories also come under the ambit of Consumer Protection Act.

A recent decision pronounced by the Andhra Pradesh State Consumer Disputes Redressal Commission throws light on the subject. In this case, an eleven-month old boy who was admitted in a hospital with fever and cough was advised blood transfusion. The patient's uncle donated blood which was tested by a blood bank and was found to be HIV I and II negative. Although blood was transfused to the child, there was no improvement in the condition of the child. When the child's blood was examined, the child was found infected with the HIV virus. The father and mother were tested and found HIV negative and hence the possibility of the child contacting the disease from parents was eliminated. It was held that the blood bank had issued the donor card without properly examining the blood of the donor and hence, there was deficiency in service. The child was given a compensation of ₹ one lakh.

Medical services rendered free of charge in a government hospital are not within the purview of the Act. The free services rendered by the municipalities in the form of facilities like sanitation, roads, street lights, parks and so on are also outside the purview of the Act. In a true sense, we find these services managed by the municipalities or other government agencies out of the taxes paid by the citizens. It has been held by the Supreme Court in *Commissioner, Hindu Religious Endowments, Madras vs. Sri Lakshmindra Thirtha Swaminar* case, that these taxes dot not constitute 'consideration' for the services ostensibly rendered gratis by the state to its citizens. Similarly, a claim of pension by an employee from his employer is not covered under the Act because he is not hiring the services of his employers for consideration.

The term 'service' has a variety of meanings. It may mean any benefit or any act resulting in promoting interest of happiness. It may be contractual, professional, public, domestic, legal, statutory and so on. The concept of service is thus very wide. In this context, the definition of service as given in Consumer Protection Act under Section 2(0) reads as under:

"Service means service of any description which is made available to potential users and includes, (but not limited to), the provision of facilities, in connection with banking, financing, insurance, transport, processing, supply of electrical or other energy, board or lodging or both (housing construction), entertainment, amusement or the purveying or news or other information, but does not include the rendering of any service free of charge or under a contract of personal service."

A service must be made available to potential users who are willing to pay for the service. The service must be rendered for remuneration. Services rendered free of charge do not come under the definition and therefore are outside the purview of the Consumer Protection Act. In the exclusionary clause of the definition for service the expression, under contract of personal service has been used but not defined in the Act. In the case of *Indian Medical Association vs. Vasantha P. Nair,* the Supreme Court held that the relationship between a medical practitioner and a patient carries within it certain degree of natural confidence and trust and therefore the services rendered by the medical practitioner can be regarded as service of personal nature but since there is no relationship of master and servant between the doctor and the patient, the contract between medical practitioner and his patient cannot be treated as a contract of personal service and a contract for services and therefore not covered by the exclusionary part of the definition of service.

The above facts make it clear that the medical services are included in the purview of the Consumer Protection Act when we find deficiency in service. The term 'Deficiency' has been defined by the Act. As per Section 2(i)(g) of the Consumer Protection Act, deficiency means any fault, imperfection, shortcoming or inadequacy in the quality, nature and manner of performance which is required to be maintained by or under any law for the time being in force or has been undertaken to be performed by a person in pursuance of a contract or otherwise in relation to any service. Deficiency is a breach of an obligation — statutory, contractual or otherwise to maintain a particular quality, nature and manner of performance of service. Deficiency in service may take many forms such as of substandard material in construction, other defects and deficiencies in construction, delay in delivering services, delay in settling the claim or belated repudiation of claim by an insurance company and so on. The expression of deficiency is synonymous with negligence. Service companies that do not care for these deficiencies not only lose customers but also need to pay compensation to them. The term deficiency in medical services focuses our attention on negligence in investigation. It was in this context that the Supreme Court ordered for a compensation of ₹ one lakh to the affected party in the earlier mentioned case.

The medical practitioners and diagnostic centres therefore need to make it sure that they have not shown negligence of duty while offering the services to the patients. If we find deficiency in the services offered due to negligence, the cases may be covered under the Consumer Protection Act.

HOSPITAL MARKETING IN INDIAN PERSPECTIVE

Healthier 21st century is our target. We cannot negate that despite intense pressure on the state exchequer and heavy brunt on bonafide tax payers, the general masses have failed in getting even the minimum healthcare and medicare services. It is, of course, a sore-spot on the Indian social system where the government bears the responsibility of making available each one of us at least the basic medicare services. We find a majority of the government hospitals and rural healthcare centres facing the problem of financial crunch in addition to the managerial deficiency. The infrastructural constraints, mismanagement of even expensive biomedical and medical equipments, inadequacy of dedicated, committed and professionally-sound doctors and paramedical personnel, increasing insensitivity among masses are some of the critical problems which require due attention of the government policy makers and hospital professionals.

Managing a non-profit organisation is, no doubt, a difficult task because the professionals managing the affairs not only bear the responsibility of protecting and promoting the interests of patients but are also supposed to make hospitals a centre of excellence in which we find patients getting the world-class services. The mission is to make the society fully aware of the healthcare and medicare services so that the sufferings of masses are considerably minimised. In an age of new generation of Information and Communication Technology, the world-class hospital professionals can benefit hospitals in many ways.

Paving the ways for the mobilisation of financial resources is an important functional responsibility before the professionals. It is imperative that in the face of increasing medicare costs, the hospitals specially managed and controlled by government need to mobilise finance from all the three sources, viz., fees from the patients, grants from the governments and charities and donations from the affluents. They may also explore avenues for getting funds from the global bodies. We find a majority of the hospitals both in the public and private sectors facing the inadequacy of quality medical and paramedical personnel. The rural healthcare centres or hospitals located in villages present a gloomy picture. In absence of quality equipments both for treatment and investigation or diagnosis, the hospitals fail in delivering goods to the society *vis-à-vis* to the nation.

Professional excellence bears the efficacy of bringing the derailed medicare services back on the rail. We cannot negate that despite intense pressure on state exchequer, the hospitals in the government sector have been facing myriad of problems. It is high time that we remove the problem of managerial deficiency and provide to them an opportunity to thrive. This will help us not only in serving the domestic users but also in generating foreign exchange by making available to the global users the world-class medicare services at a fee structure that would internationally be competitive. Of course, we find the process of attracting the foreign users of medicare services gaining a rapid momentum but still there are opportunities to capitalise on.

Regulating the unproductive expenses and soliciting the cooperation of medicare and healthcare professionals need priority attention to initiate and activate the process of qualitative-cum-quantitative transformation. The motive is to satisfy the users by improving the quality and minimising the cost. Though we feel that improving the quality and bringing down the costs are the two opposite considerations but the hospital professionals can make it possible. Besides, it is also significant that the problems on account of infrastructural constraints are resolved so that round-the-clock power and water services are available to the hospitals.

The service ambience for hospitals need a distinct look. The servicescapes or physical facilities significantly contribute to the process of development. The premises or surroundings of hospitals need priority attention of professionals. Keep your hospital clean because, it is to help you in many ways. The environment-friendly surroundings and clean atmosphere help in minimising the duration and rate of recovery. We find hospital a place friendly to infection and therefore you need to make best possible efforts to disinfect the floors, rooms, beds and clothes regularly.

The hospital professionals or medical and paramedical staff need not only personal touch but even human touch. It is really amazing that the doctors in a majority of the cases do not realise the role of behaviour in the treatment or recovery of a patient. An attitudinal change in behaviour appears significant and of course, we find it a matter of self-realisation. It is also painful to mention that a good number of doctors lack temptation to value system and ethics. Professional ethics inject life and continuity to professional excellence, the hospital personnel need not to forget it.

The most important task before the hospital professionals is to develop their awareness of the changing needs of patients as failing this the task of orchestrating the marketing resources will be difficult. It is in this context that the leading hospitals need to develop healthcare information system. They need to identify the gap between services-required and services-delivered and to make efforts to bridge the same. A majority of us have limited levels of expectations which can be fulfilled simply by offering the medical aid which we need.

Mobilising the donors is an important functional responsibility before the marketing professionals and in this process, they need the support of hospital information system. Both from the individual and corporate segments, they have to influence and motivate the donors and potential donors for charities and donations. Besides, they also need to develop contacts with national and global bodies or agencies for financial and infrastructural support.

Keeping in view the poor paying capacity of the Indian society, the medicare services are required to be made cost-effective. This is essential specially for the domestic users specially coming from weaker sections, who are not in a position to afford the expensive medicare services. It is in this context they can think in favour of income-based strategy.

Synchronisation of different submixes of marketing with the motto of serving the patients and developing the hospitals requires professional excellence. The core and peripheral services are to be blended in such a way that patients as well as the attendants feel themselves satisfied. The doctors as well as the marketing professionals need not to forget that improved quality of services at a competitive fee structure will help them in becoming a leader in the specialised area which would provide to them an opportunity to attract the foreign patients. This in a very natural way focuses our attention on intensifying the promotional measures so that the patients and attendants come to know about the outstanding features. Informing, sensitising and persuading the potential users need creativity. The hospitals need to promote even with the motto of developing mass awareness which would make the preventive measures much more effective. So far as the fee structure is concerned, it is imperative that in the Indian perspective they practise a different strategy which is in tune with the paying capacity of an individual. This will help hospitals in improving their financial position. Besides, they have to explore avenues for grants, charities and donations and for that, the marketers need to develop a distinct image so that the actual donors are found satisfied with the productive use of funds by hospitals. The channelisation and location are the two different areas for marketing decisions in which the professionals need expertise. Smooth accessibility and environment-friendly sites are to be their first choice. The professionals are required to ensure availability of promised quality of services to the users without any delay and distortion but with decency.

The professionals cannot overlook the role of extended mixes of marketing for hospitals because processing, physical evidence and attractions and quality of hospital people belonging to medical, paramedical and managerial cadre determine the magnitude of success. The hospital professionals have to ensure that while processing the medicare and healthcare services, the people as well as technologies and equipments have been co-ordinating each other and promised quality of services are made available to the patients on time. While processing, the front-line staff play an effective role. The marketers also bear the responsibility of tangibilising the outstanding properties of hospitals so that the patients and attendants or others visiting the hospitals get an opportunity to witness the same. We cannot deny that physical evidence or servicescapes play the role of a package by wrapping the services. This in a true sense is the exposure or display of the services that hospitals are going to offer to the users. The professionals need to make it sure that by tangibilising, they have been successful in adding additional attractions to the services. Like any organisation, the hospitals also need to assign top priority to the development of quality people. The medical, paramedical and managerial staff serving the hospitals need a number of properties as an essential part of their personality such as thematical competence, personal touch, sincerity, honesty, sympathy, empathy, professional ethics, humanity because they occupy a distinct place in the society where people consider them next to God. It is only on the basis of their service that they can justify their position.

It is also to be ensured that grants received from governments or other sources are used for productive purpose. The wastage of materials either in the process of offering or storing are to be regulated. The cases of theft and mandays lost are to be minimised.

The hospital professionals bear an outstanding responsibility of developing mass awareness so that we find masses sensitive to the healthcare problem. A number of diseases are either food-prone or water-prone and if they regulate their habits, the intensity of problem can be minimised. Sensitising masses to the hazardous problems like communicable diseases, nutritional deficiency, lack of vaccination culture, etc. need due attention of professionals. The innovative healthcare communication system may be effective in the sensitisation process. On the one hand, the marketing professionals need to sensitise the masses in support of preventive measures while on the other hand, the medical and paramedical personnel are required to activate the curative measures. Creativity proves to be much more effective in the sensitisation process and in this context, the marketing professionals need to practise innovative advertisement and publicity measures. The slogans, posters, messages related to medicare and healthcare services will make the process of developing mass awareness much more effective. In an age of technology, the marketers can make use of audiovisual exposure, powerpoint presentation for the sensitisation process. The communicative ability of professionals occupies an important place in bringing an attitudinal change.

Willingly or willingly, we need to accept the fact that medical, paramedical and managerial personnel considerably influence the magnitude of success. This focuses our attention on developing quality people for hospitals and healthcare centres. They need to be professionally-sound, value-based and personally-committed. The sympathy and empathy in behaviour and human-oriented approaches help achieving the desired results. It is not only significant that doctors are aware of the methods of treatment, it is equally important that they also know about humanity and human values. They need to serve with an avowed mission of serving the patients by being punctual, sincere, and honest to their profession.

The rural areas of the country present a very gloomy picture because doctors or other nursing staff do not prefer to work in villages. The government policy makers need to make it sure that working in the rural areas for a limited period is mandatory. A number of problems can be solved when they are on the spot. The health problem of rural women and children need priority attention. The supply of safe drinking water and sanitation services are to be channelised in the villages as a part of preventive measures. The vaccination culture is to be promoted and the cases of epidemics and natural calamities need special attention of professionals. Since hospitals and healthcare centres are supposed to work with the mission of serving the society, it is imperative that we conceptualise innovative marketing. This will immensely help hospital professionals in minimising the cost and improving the quality.

The conceptualisation of marketing in the hospital and healthcare services thus would be successful in satisfying the users. Besides, they would also be successful in sensitising the masses to control the water-prone, food-prone and communicable diseases. The team and work culture will lead to quality culture promoting quality philosophy required by all the hospitals and healthcare centres working in both the public and private sectors. The Indian healthcare and medicare sector thus will get right directions for development and prosperity.

Potentially-sound organisations would be financially sound to bear the social costs. If at the initial stage, we activate efforts to make them financially sound, the subsequent stages will increase their potentials of bearing the social burdens. The modern medicare services depend on expensive inputs and therefore we need to pave avenues for the mobilisation of financial resources. If we make them financially sound, the quality of services will be improved. The government policy makers need to bring a structural change for the development of hospitals and healthcare centres which presently are found in a sorry state of affairs.

In the context of hospital services, we find medical and paramedical staff playing a decisive role. If they are found of world-class, a number of problems will automatically be solved. The hospitals have been found facing the problem of infrastructural constraints, cleanliness and management of waste. To promote quality in totality, it is pertinent that we assign due weightage to aesthetic management, behavioural profile of doctors and paramedical personnel and quality of plants, machines, equipments and information and communication technology.

The performance of some of the leading hospitals of India are based on some of the parameters. Escorts Heart Institute — New Delhi (Cardiology), AIIMS — Delhi (Gastrenterology), Institute of Reproductive Machine

— Kolkata (Infertility), Tata Memorial — Mumbai (Cancer), NIMHANS — Bengaluru (Mental Health) and Sankara Nethralaya — Chennai (Eye Disorders); all of them are known for their world-class services and virtually they are quality leaders and star performers in their respective areas. The leaders, of course, bear the responsibility of increasing the number of quality hospitals. In addition, it is also essential that institutions promoting education and training facilities in the field of medical sciences develop their awareness of Total Quality Management and enrich the potentials of medical personnel to deliver goods to the society. A few selected names are AIIMS (New Delhi), Kasturba Medical College (Manipal), Maulana Azad Medical College (Delhi), Osmania Medical College (Hyderabad), Madras Medical College (Chennai), AAFMC (Pune) and the Christian Medical College (Vellur) and we expect from them to be instrumental in developing quality culture.

We cannot negate that a majority of the hospitals in India are in poor condition and we need to initiate the process of qualitative improvements. The healthcare centres in general and rural healthcare centres in particular need priority attention because in the rural areas we find people totally unaware of the health problem and on that account invite a number of water-prone, food-prone and communicable diseases. This makes a strong advocacy in favour of developing sophisticated healthcare communication system which may be successful in sensitising the masses.

Improving the quality of services and minimising the possibilities of diseases are the two important functional responsibilities before modern hospitals which need professional excellence, human orientation and personal touch. Innovating both the curative and preventive measures need due attention of hospital professionals.

A target of Health for All by the end of 11th Five Year Plan makes a strong advocacy in favour of strategic marketing which is not to be possible unless we initiate qualitative as well as quantitative improvements. Actually, we need a big push theory necessitating multi-cornered support in which public and private hospitals, healthcare centres, non-government organisations would be required to extend their cooperation. In addition, the public participation in financial resource mobilisation in the form of charities or donations will inject new life and strength to our efforts. It is significant to mention that India even after the completion of ten Five Year Plans has been lagging far behind in the healthcare services. The population-to-bed ratio in India is one bed per 1000 whereas the norm set by World Health Organisation (WHO) is at least one bed per 300. This testifies our failures on the front of improving the medicare services.

In view of the above, it is pertinent to mention that marketing medicare and healthcare services remains the only prescription to be much more effective in touching the target within the stipulated time-frame. We have to develop medicare services as an industry so that this sector proves to be a source for generating foreign exchange. There are a number of examples to prove that leading private hospitals achieving world-class excellence have been successful in wooing foreign users because for them the services are of quality but economic. This is to be possible at largescale when we keep on moving the process of qualitative improvements. We cannot negate that Indian doctors have a well-established global image which the modern hospitals can capitalise on with the motto of increasing their efficacy of bearing the social costs. Hospitals working under the public-private partnership will be successful in serving and subserving the social interests.

The motive is to serve the society;

The motive is to improve the quality;

The motive is to make the services cost-effective and

The motive is to minimise the medicare needs.

Let's hope that by initiating and activating world-class

professional excellence, we get a success in fulfilling our motives and achieving the mission.

SUMMARY

In this chapter, we have discussed the problem of marketing. The motive is to sensitise the readers to the instrumentality of marketing the healthcare services. After going through the chapter, the reader will become aware that the following facts are well versed.

Hospitals Marketing — The Perception: The hospital marketing focuses our attention on the conceptualisation of modern marketing principle in the healthcare services with a holistic approach.

Rationale Behind Practising Marketing in Hospitals: We find justification for the application of marketing principles in the healthcare services because this will ensure that users are satisfied, time-honoured services would be available to the patients, mass awareness would be created, thrust areas would be identified, vulnerable segment would be detected, behavioural dimension would be given due weightage, cost-effectiveness would be made possible, a rational fee structure can be introduced and hospital personnel can be motivated.

Segmentwise Users of Healthcare Services: We classify users of healthcare services on the basis of segment, viz., individual, organisational, rural-urban, high-income, medium-income, low-income and no-income, men and women, kids, teens, youths and grey, vulnerable and normal areas.

Behavioural Profile of Users: A hospital manager is required to know about the attitudes, lifestyles, preferences and level of expectations of the users.

Market Segmentation: It is managerial process of dividing and subdividing the markets into small groups and segments to identify the changing levels of expectations of the users.

Marketing Information System: It is a system to manage marketing information, specially with the help of the new generation of information technology. It is a process of transforming the marketing data into marketing information.

Marketing Mix: It is a managerial process of formulating the marketing mix to help a manager in developing marketing resources in tune with the changing needs and requirements.

Product Mix: This focuses on core, supportive, peripheral and preventive services of the healthcare organisations. It is a process of blending the different types of healthcare services against changing requirements.

Promotion Mix: This submix of the marketing mix focuses on the different constituents of promotion, e.g., advertising, publicity, sales promotion, personal selling, word-of-mouth promotion and telemarketing.

Price Mix: In this context, we study (or analyse) the problem of determining the fees by the hospitals and healthcare organisations.

Place Mix: This focuses our attention on the location for hospitals and the channels through which the services reach to the end-users.

Process: The process mix is related to the process of offering the services to the ultimate users. For processing the medicare services, we find involvement of a team of medical and paramedical staff who with the help of equipments, machines and information and communication technologies process the services.

Physical Evidence and Attractions: In the context of physical evidence, we find focus on the physical facilities adding additional attractions to the services. The hospital professionals create service ambience by tangibilising the outstanding features which generate service fragrance such as lighting, signposts, ventilation, sanitation, music, etc. Besides, we also find dresses and uniforms of paramedical and medical staff to be neat and clean for projecting a fair image.

People: The quality of medical and paramedical staff focuses our attention in this context. They need to be thematically-sound, personally-committed, value-based and professionally-sound.

Strategic Marketing: The concept of strategic marketing makes it essential that to cater to the increasing demand, we need an action plan and tailor the marketing resources accordingly.

Consumer Protection Regulation: In some of the cases, we find medical services under the purview of Consumer Protection Act.

Hospital/Marketing in Indian Perspective: In the Indian context, the medical and healthcare services need professionalism and for that, the hospital professionals need to conceptualise innovative marketing with a societal approach. This will help an improvement in the quality of services and in addition will also make the services cost-effective. The motive is to tap the foreign users with the motto of making the hospitals internationally competitive. If we find hospitals financially sound, this will increase their efficacy of bearing the social costs.

KEY TERMS

Human Capital
Service Ambience
Leprosy
Tuberculosis
Typhoid
Polio
NGOs
Yoga
Pranayam
Peripheral Services
Hospital Marketing
Social Marketing
Product Uniqueness
Apparatus
Biomedical Equipment
Disease Profile
Empathy
Leverspring
Divide and Rule
Decision Supporting System
Marketing Intelligence System
Hospital Information System
Holistic Concept
New People Management
Auxiliary Services
Vector-borne diseases
Communicable Diseases
Vaccination Culture
Potable Water
Aesthetic Sense
Biomedical Waste
Rapport
Press Kits
Community Relations
Lobbying
Image Building
Social Advertising
Superhighway
Sexual Behaviour
Telemarketing
Automated Dialing and Recorded
Message Players
Fast Food
Carbohydrates
Dieticians
State Exchequer
Pocket-friendly Strategy
Disinfecting
Signposts
Servicescapes
Service Ambience
Aesthete
Contours
Crude Death Rate
Orchestrating
Immunization

Review Questions

1. What do you mean by Hospital Marketing? Focus on the rationale behind practising the principles of modern marketing by the healthcare organisations.
2. Explain segmentwise users of the healthcare services.
3. Throw light on the behavioural profile of users and their influences on the level of expectations.
4. What do you mean by market segmentation? Discuss its instrumentality in satisfying the users of the healthcare services.
5. Explain the instrumentality of Marketing Information System in making and innovating the services of healthcare organisations. Focus on the role of information technology in increasing the potentials of the system.
6. What do you mean by Marketing Mix? Explain in brief the different submixes of the marketing mix in relation to the healthcare organisations.
7. Focus on the Product Mix of Hospitals. Do you find peripheral services instrumental in generating additional attractions to the hospital product? Define your viewpoints.

8. Explain in brief the different constituents of promotion mix in the context of the services of healthcare organisations.
9. Discuss the significance of word-of-mouth promotion to the process of motivating the prospects of hospitals.
10. What do you mean by Public Relations? Discuss the various dimensions of public relations.
11. Do you find public relations activities effective in image projection? Justify your answer with suitable examples.
12. "Image building makes the ways for image projection." In the light of this statement, explain the factors contributing to the process of image building and image projection.
13. Focus on the fee strategy to be adopted by the healthcare organisations, specially in the Indian perspective.
14. "You need to bridge the gap between service-promised and service-offered." In the light of this statement, focus on the instrumentality of processing in bridging over the gap.
15. People mix requires due attention of a hospital manager. In the light of this statement, explain the role of quality people in improving the quality of healthcare services.
16. "You need to promote uniform culture to promote work culture." Throw light on this statement and explain the importance of physical attractions as a submix of the marketing mix.
17. Focus on strategic marketing in relation to increasing demand of healthcare services and changing nature and character of the disease profile.
18. Explain the changing role of marketing professionals in satisfying the users of medicare and healthcare services.

Application Exercises

1. You are working as a hospital professional in a leading hospital. Formulate a marketing mix which helps you in satisfying the users.
2. As a marketing professional, throw light on the promotional measures you will adopt for initiating the preventive measures to control the water-prone, food-prone and communicable diseases.
3. You want to expand your services to the foreign users. Focus on the promotional measures you expect to be effective in the process of sensitisation.
4. What type of fee strategy you find suitable for medicare services in the Indian perspective, specially in tune with the societal approach?
5. What important considerations you need to keep in your mind while tangibilising the outstanding features of your hospitals.
6. Do you feel that medical and paramedical staff of hospitals need professionalised approach, personal touch, value commitment and human orientation? Comment as a hospital professional.
7. As a professional, you are supposed to develop rapport with the media people for publishing the services of your hospitals. Throw light on the measures you are going to initiate.
8. How you will develop a communication network for sensing and satisfying the users of healthcare services.

Endnotes

1. Jha, S.M., *Marketing Non-profit Organisations*, Chapter 5, Himalaya Publishing House, Mumbai 2003.
2. Jha, S.M., *Social Marketing*, Chap.1, Himalaya Publishing House, Mumbai, pp. 1-24.
3. Jha, S.M., *Services Marketing*, Edition, 2003.
4. Jha, S.M., *Social Marketing*, Chap.12, pp. 176-78.
5. Jha, S.M., *Services Marketing*, Chap.8, Hospital Marketing, pp. 306-07.
6. Jha, S.M., *Service Marketing*, Chap.8, Hospital Marketing, pp. 307-08.
7. Jha, S.M., *Hospital Management*, Himalaya Publishing House, Mumbai, 2000.
8. Jha, S.M., *Social Marketing*, Chap.12, Himalaya Publishing House, Mumbai, 1999.
9. Jha, S.M., Potable Water: A Mission for All, *The Hindustan Times*, January, 30, 1999.
10. Jha, S.M., Looks Make a Man, *The Hindustan Times*, April 17, 2000.
11. Jha, S.M., Strategic Issues in Medicare Services, *Employment News*, 16-22 May, 1998, Cover Story.
12. Kotler Philip *Marketing for Healthcare Organisations*, Eaglewood Cliffs, NT, Prentice Hall, 1987.
13. Jha, S.M., Activism in Parenthood, *The Hindustan Times*, August 22, 1998, Cover Story.
14. Jha, S.M., Hazardous Bio-Medical Waste, *The Hindustan Times*.

★★★

POLITICAL MARKETING

The political parties evincing keen interests in projecting a mass image; developing mass awareness by informing, sensing, sensitising, persuading the potential voters; managing the election campaigns; organising exit polls and opinion polls; publishing election manifesto; mobilising donors; developing volunteers and party workers and getting a feedback need conceptualisation of social marketing principles.

Chapter Objectives

Introduction – Political Ideologists of India – Political Organisation – A Social Institution – Political Environment in India – Political Marketing: the Perception and Misperception – Significance of Political Marketing – Dimensions of Political Marketing – Segmentation in Politics – Political Information System – Management of Behaviour in Politics – Marketing Mix for Political Services – The Product Mix – The Promotion Mix – Political Communication – Advertising – Political Advertising and TV – Media Strategy for Political Organisations – Publicity – Personal Selling – Word-of-mouth Promotion –Telemarketing – Mobilisation of Fee and Financial Process – Physical Evidence and Attractions – Managing the Party People – Strategic Marketing Politics – Political Marketing in Indian Perspective – Summary – Key Terms – Review Questions – Application Exercises – Endnotes.

Learning Objectives

The motive of this chapter is to sensitise the readers to the various aspects of marketing political services. The readers develop their awareness of the political environment in India and perceive the concept and percept of political marketing. The motive is also to help the professionals in the conceptualisation of marketing principles by the political organisations with the motto of increasing the membership, organising the election campaign, exit poll, opinion poll, designing the election manifesto, promoting the parties and serving the interests of society. The application is with a societal approach and in the face of holistic concept of management. The professionals while practising come to know the different submixes of marketing in the context of political services.

INTRODUCTION

All segments, regions, genders, races require equal opportunities to survive and thrive. The primary, secondary and tertiary sectors of the economy, of course, bear the potentials of accelerating the pace of development but they also need to be careful that their policy and strategic decisions, generation and promotional measures are not to create a condition paving avenues for socio-cultural and environmental degeneration. The policy makers play an important role in setting the directions. The political parties representing government or opposition benches bear the responsibility of studying the changing conditions and formulating a sound policy opening new vistas of development. Almost all the political parties, of late, have been facing the image problem. The marketing professionals may help them in different ways.

The political parties evincing keen interests in projecting a mass image; developing mass awareness by informing, sensing, sensitising and persuading the potential and actual voters; managing the election affairs; organising exit polls and opinion surveys; publishing election manifesto, brochures, newsletters; mobilising donors; developing volunteers and party workers and getting a feedback need to realise the instrumentality of marketing professionals and the marketing principles helping them in getting the desired results. It is in this context that the application of social marketing by the political organisations has attracted attention of political leaders.

The political parties are considered to be a non-profit making organisation and this deprives them of having a legitimate right of making profits. The political marketing is found related to social or societal marketing and this makes it essential that the marketing professionals while practising marketing assign due weightage to the social considerations. We find it a managerial process which may also be considered to be a social process (Jha, 2002). While going through the problem of non-profit organisations, we find Kotler (1994) talking about political parties and lobbyist groups.

The professional excellence of an individual or an institution paves avenues for a number of developments found positive in nature. The political organisations find it easier to impress upon and mobilise the donors, projecting their social image by making significant contributions to the process of social transformation and excelling rival parties by winning the hearts and minds of voters. It was against the multi-dimensional properties of social marketing that the political parties started thinking over the conceptualisation process for getting the desired results. The development of sophisticated technology for managing information and communication injected new life and continuity to the application process.

It was way back in 1960 that John F. Kennedy campaigned for the presidency and switched on a revolutionary approach to campaigning which later on laid a strong foundation for sophisticated marketing and communication strategies, not only in the USA but around the world. With the passage of time, the contours of development underwent radical changes and a number of developments took place in the information and communication network. Explosive innovations opened new vistas for quantitative improvements. With the development of technology, we find techniculture showing its imprints in almost all the walks of life. The advances and changes in political campaigning and marketing started attracting the attention of political parties in a number of advanced countries during 1970s and 1980s. It was during mid 1980s that late Rajiv Gandhi promoted management professionals for managing and campaigning for the elections and the positive results influenced even others to think about the conceptualisation of marketing in politics. The Indian National Congress started the process which was also promoted by Bharatiya Janata Party, and a number of regional parties also evinced keen interests in the process during 1990s. With the development of satellite communication, a new chapter was opened which revolutionised the communication network and almost all categories of organisations capitalised on the opportunities. At the beginning of 21st century, political marketing started gaining popularity since the info-tech redefined everything.

The political leaders, while representing the government, are also responsible for formulating development-oriented and welfare-sensitive polices making it easier to harness the benefits of development, especially by the weaker sections of the society. The opposition at the same time, is accountable to monitor and review the steps taken by the government so that they identify the lapses and shortcomings in the development process and make them an effective tool to tarnish ruling party's image. The sophisticated developments in the field of information and communications made their task easier. This motivated even the small and regional parties to conceptualise and practise marketing in politics. The election campaigning, advertisement and publicity, publication of election manifesto, annual reports of parties, information brochures and newsletters, cut-outs, posters and leaflets took an innovative form attracting the public and making management of election affairs much more interesting.

Since the political marketing practices are based on professional excellence, the political leaders find it convenient to organise party and manage elections. While managing elections, the professionals organise opinion polls, conduct surveys, design cut-outs and posters and sketches, draft election manifesto and information brochure, manage exit polls and with the help of promotional measures, advertise and publicise their contributions to the development and welfare of the society. Managerial proficiency thus helps them in different ways provided the party leaders, volunteers and workers are not influenced by materialistic gains and develop an awareness of the defined principles of social marketing guiding and regulating them in the development of value system by strengthening the process of value engineering.

Materialism necessitates identification of an opportune moment for capitalising on the opportunities in the face of faculties or potentials available in an individual or an organisation. With the multi-dimensional developments in the socio-political and cultural environment, a number of opportunities have been created, nurtured and found matured. If you have world-class potentials and professionalism, the task of an optimal tapping is found easier. If we turn our eyes on the development scenario taking place the world over, it is apparent that during yester-decades almost all categories of organisations have got a favourable milieu to survive and thrive. On the other hand, the process of technological advancements and sophistication has also been rapidly accelerated. Professionalism based on perfection has been perceived in the face of evolving changes. The organisations manufacturing goods or generating services, working with the motto of making profits or with the mission of serving the society albeit in a dismal profit condition, have paved avenues for qualitative-cum-quantitative transformation in almost all the areas. The professionals welcoming recent developments found of explosive nature and paving avenues for time-honoured conceptualisation and implementation have proved to be an innovator, a leader whereas others have remained just a follower and copier. In almost all the areas, the innovators have been successful in capitalising on the opportunities.

Like the profit-making goods-manufacturing and service-generating organisations, we also find non-profit making organisations activating sincere, honest and professionalised efforts to conceptualise and practise innovative efforts. It is against this background that we find educational institutions and healthcare organisations developing significantly and serving the interests both of mankind and different categories of organisations in many ways. In the developed countries of the world, we have witnessed innovations even in the management of political and non-governmental organisations (NGOs). An attitudinal change is found existent in almost all the segments. The political parties and political leaders have been found incorporating the latest developments while projecting their image, designing election campaigns, composing election slogans, developing posters and sketches, innovating promotional measures and sensitising the voters to be actual voters and getting, retaining and ensuring a place in the ruling bench. We can't negate that info-tech and communication technology have simplified their task fantastically resulting from which the sensitivity rate has been found consistently moving upward. A fair synchronisation of modern technology and world-class professionalism have been found helping them in resolving successfully even the critical problems. The less developed countries have also been found perceiving the same.

Of course, we don't find anything wrong with the innovative transformation opening doors for development by helping in making policies, formulating strategies and developing people in the face of evolving changes. But, in a majority of the cases, the principles of social marketing have not been assigned due weightage which has been aggravating the multi-faceted harmful effects on society, culture, economy and national and international relations.

The perception of social or societal marketing has gravitated due attention of all categories of organisations. The boardrooms have, of late, assigned number one priority to the concept of social marketing. Since we find political organisations also evincing interests in the modern marketing principles, it is pertinent that they conceptualise social marketing because an outstanding task of safeguarding public interests requires world-class excellence. Almost all the organisations involved in the process, political parties and social organisations in particular need to conceptualise marketing because in a number of cases we find political leaders representing and dominating different categories of organisations. The non-governmental social organisations, trade unions, civic bodies and public utility undertakings are sizeably represented by the political leaders. There is no doubt in it that the conceptualisation of marketing in politics would help political leaders in many ways because they would find it easier to sensitise the voters and potential voters. In this context, it is also significant that efforts taken in the process of informing, sensing and persuading the voters are not to promote unethical practices. The slogans, campaigns, speeches, promotional measures are required to be creative but not to misguide and miscommunicate the masses. The projection of the image of political parties is essential but they need more care while transmitting and narrating the wrongs, misdeeds, negative results, as only after honest confession, the corrective measures are to be considerably effective.

In the Indian perspective, we find political marketing at the very nascent stage. We find a number of political and social leaders personally committed, serving the society with a mission, projecting a fair image of the party and with their dedicated efforts making the task of rival parties much more difficult. Strategically, they have played an outstanding role in engineering a sound foundation for their parties without which the task of building a positive image would have been much more complicated. Lord Krishna as a strategist, Kautilya as a political guru, Mahatma Gandhi as a social reformist, Nehru as an architect of modern India, Ambedkar and Jaya Prakash Narayan as promoters of social justice have used politics as an instrument. Rajiv Gandhi engineered a foundation for the development of communication and information technology and like this, a number of political leaders have considerably contributed to the development process.

The process of technological sophistication gained momentum during 1970s and 1980s and in 1990s, we find it at the peak which transformed the nature and character of people and the concerned institutions and organisations. The significant developments in the field of communication and massive efforts for building a superhighway for communication, development of knowledge technology as a knowledge power, inventions and innovations in the field of communication and information technology made possible a number of qualitative-cum-quantitative improvements. The goods manufacturing and service generating organisations working with the motto of making profits used sophisticated technology and developed a new perception of quality. The non-profit making organisations like educational institutions, healthcare organisations, political parties and social organisations also explored new avenues for using communication and information technology. The merchandising of politics gained momentum that paved avenues for a large-scale use of technology even in politics. The developed as well as the less developed countries like ours also evinced interests in making use of new generation of information and communication technology which made possible a basic change in their nature and character. Political marketing thus could get a sound nexus but the process proved to be much more expensive.

With the increasing sophistication in communication technology, the political communication emerged as an important dimension of political marketing making use of advanced communication technology informing, sensing and motivating the voters and potential voters in a very effective way. Besides, the significant developments in the field of information technology helped them in managing the information system which simplified the task of identifying the weaknesses and diagnosing the shortcomings and strength of rival parties. The information system made possible an in-depth study of the attitudes and behaviour of voters coming from different segments and sections which made the strategic decisions much more impact generating. The world-class professionals engaged in the process of designing the election campaigns, drafting and composing election speeches, preparing the election posters, diagnosing the changing levels of expectations of voters and potential voters made possible effectiveness in the entire process.

The multi-dimensional developments in the socio-political and cultural environment have virtually changed the character of political leadership influenced by advanced education and training facilities. The chromosomes, family background, environmental conditions and situational factors have become insignificant to the development process. A number of educational institutions have been engaged in educating and training political leaders. The temptation and fascination for becoming a political leader have taken the shape of a craze and a large number of youths have also been found evincing their keen interests in developing political leadership. We can't negate that youths of today have sizeably been motivated towards political activities because they witness political leaders leading a comfortable and luxurious lifestyles. It is against this background that we find investment of huge money as election expenses. Though it is not an investment rather than an expenditure but an attitudinal change in the behaviour of political leaders makes it an investment. The management of political parties and elections prove to be much more expensive because all the rival parties develop a sense of competition and spend the maximum that they can. Of late, we find copious avenues for channelising election expenses and a majority of the candidates tap them in a non-optimal fashion. The process of mobilising financial resources gains momentum virtually crossing all the limits where ethics, values, humanity get no place.

It is in this context that social marketing bears the potentials to bring about the derailed political systems back on the rail. The political parties and leaders, no doubt, need to conceptualise social marketing which would regulate their attitudes and behaviour. While educating and training political leaders, we need to develop awareness regarding the ethics, values, humanity, personal commitment and dedication so that they conceptualise and practise marketing in the right directions. An optimal budget for political organisation is found essential to regulate the unproductive expenses. Though the recent developments have been instrumental in increasing the election expenses, the political parties need to strike a balance between the evolving changes and the situational requirements. The marketing colonisation of political campaigns becomes significant to show the right directions to make the process not only cost-effective but even proactive.

The political organisations need to promote research to have an in-depth idea of the related constituents or segments. The opinion polls are organised with the support of media and the potential candidates. The services of dedicated and committed workers, volunteers and professional researchers are also used for the said purpose. Pre-election polling, exit polls are practised for forecasting results and trends. The behaviour of voters are studied and researchers are engaged for that very purpose. Today, when we have an advanced system for information and communication, it is pertinent that like other organisations, the political organisations also promote the use of a developed and technology-driven information system. We can't negate the fact that to make the entire process result-oriented, the political parties need adequate fund and the resource mobilisation process appears to be complicated because the rival parties and public become critical to the process. Money does not grow on trees rather our efforts help generation and mobilisation of funds. Almost all the countries and by and large almost all the political parties existent there have been found raising funds from different sources and even in the Indian perspective we find raising of funds for election and other purposes. The main thing in the process is to make it sure that individuals or organisations offering financial help don't get undue benefits for charity and donations given by them.

We often talk about the behaviour of voters and potential voters. The political advertising is found instrumental in the transformation process where professionals play an outstanding role. The element of creativity determines the intensity of sensitivity. The services of world-class professionals may be used for that very purpose. Grabbing the non-voters is found to be a difficult task. The advertising campaigns managed and monitored by the world-class professionals may help the transformation process in which the potential voters would comfortably be transformed into actual voters. A predictive model of voter behaviour would help you in many ways. You also need a value-oriented model for making an appraisal of prospective candidates.

Development of political strategy and formulation of tactical issues would help political parties in getting the desired results. Image of non-verbal nature gravitates our due attention. The direct marketing is also practised for effective political campaigns. Of late, we have most sophisticated telecast media and we may also organise televised debates. It is not to be forgotten that telecast media would help you in the democratisation process. You may think in favour of formulating a fair mix by synchronising print media, broadcast media and telecast media in a manner that helps you in reflecting and shaping the public opinion. Strategic decisions are found significant because this helps you in resolving the tactical problems. For getting positive results, we find tactical issues significant and the political leaders and parties need to realise the same. The political parties need to make themselves strategically and tactfully sound which would help them in the projection of a positive image to capitalise on the opportunities. The policy decisions, no doubt, prove to be significant but the organisation at the national level would formulate the same and therefore the organisational structure at regional levels become pertinent to formulate a sound strategy keeping in view the regional conditions, behaviour of voters, strategic decisions of the rival parties and candidates, numerical strength of potential and non-voters. We find it essential that leaders, particularly at regional levels realise the instrumentality of tactical issues failing which the policies, and strategies are either to be ineffective or to show a lukewarm response.

The political marketing has been gaining popularity the world over and almost all the countries have been found conceptualising latest developments in the area. Of course, a number of changes influence the conceptualisation and implementation process but sophisticated developments in the communication and information technology has been found establishing an edge over others. This is mainly due to the fact that all the three sophisticated forms of media have been seen developing mass awareness and it is against this background that we find masses perceiving even the minor developments taking place in the globe everyday. The process of informing, sensing and sensitising the voters and potential voters has substantially been influenced by the increasing instrumentality of media. You need to work with the avowed mission of protecting and subserving social interests and in this context, you also bear the responsibility of publicising the same in an effective manner so that the public at large form a positive opinion about you and your party and the task of image projection is made much more easier. If you act and masses fail to know about your positive contributions, the task of capitalising on the opportunities is made much more difficult. While educating, training and developing political leaders *vis-a-vis* while organising the political party, it is pertinent that the educational institutions or other organisations engaged in the process of developing them realise the instrumentality of inculcation through transmission.

Since we find the globe witnessing multi-dimensional changes in almost all the areas, it is essential that we have an in-depth knowledge of developments taking place around the world. Because we find management of political organisation's large-scale operation, it is significant that we are aware of the principles of modern management. As we witness unethical, unfair, unlawful, irrational practices getting a dominating share in the modern politics, it is pertinent that political leaders know about the principles of social marketing on a priority basis. We go through both the political science and management routes so that the political parties and political leaders make an optimal use of their potentials.

In the Indian perspective, we find a few of the political leaders strategically and tactically-sound, professionally and personally-committed, ethically and morally value-oriented and therefore the political marketing would benefit the budding political leaders in developing their potentials in the face of evolving multi-dimensional changes. We have a rich political heritage and a large number of dedicated and personally-committed political leaders have also shown their worth even in a rough weather. The conceptualisation of political marketing would help them in making use of their positive contributions for the projection of a fair image.

We go through different dimensions of political marketing. The problems have been discussed in Indian perspective where the process of ethical degeneration has been found very fast.

POLITICAL IDEOLOGISTS OF INDIA

From the ancient to the modern age, we find a large number of ideologists making significant contributions to the Indian political systems by linking their effects to the development and welfare of society, protection and prosperity of living beings and generation and promotion of ethical dimensions for value orientation. They have acted as ideologists, social reformists, social activists, social scientists, strategists, diplomats and promoters of social justice. At the same time, we also find cases where they have acted as a manipulator, and a dexterous manager. On the one hand, we find some of them personally-committed, value-oriented and dedicated while on the other hand, we also find selected a few very much instrumental in activating the degeneration process. A brief analysis of their contributions would help us in diagnosing their attitudes and political ideologies.

Lord Krishna: A Strategist

Of late, Greek has earned the credibility of coining the word "Strategy" but if the word is considered to be coined from the world of battleground, Lord Krishna is found a pioneer who piloted and monitored the events of Mahabharat which just after eighteen days came to a logical conclusion. We can't deny that numerical strength, financial health, academic excellence, resourcefulness normally show a lukewarm response, if we find something wrong with our strategic decisions. When to use, how to use and how much to use our potentials become significant to get the desired success and therefore an individual or an institution, a group or a party can't be successful unless we find them potentially and strategically proficient. What to talk of the organisational efforts when efforts of an individual considerably influenced by the strategic decisions. It is in this context that in the battle-ground of Mahabharat strategically-sound Pandavas established an edge over the numerically and potentially-sound Kauravas. It was well formulated strategies of Lord Krishna that played a decisive role in defeating Kauravas. If we compare the numerical strength of both the sides, a big gap appears existent because a number of personalities representing the side of Kauravas were potentially sound but due to the lack of a strategist paralleling Lord Krishna, they failed in their efforts. This makes it essential that we assign due weightage to the strategic decisions because failing the same, our resourcefulness don't carry any significant meaning. Strategically proficient individuals or institutions succeed in establishing an edge even over the potentially sound but strategically deficient individuals or institutions and it is against this background that our policy decisions need not to undermine the sensitivity of strategic decisions.

The aforesaid facts make it clear that a political organisation can't survive and thrive unless a well formulated strategy influenced by situational requirements, guides and regulates them to develop and tap the potentials in the face of changing requirements. This makes it essential that you have a strong, dedicated, personally-committed, prudent, value-based leader because it was ultimately leadership that played a big role in Mahabharat. Formulation of strategy is, no doubt, important but implementation proves to be much more significant because it requires courage, patience, will power, team spirit, group culture failing which even time-honoured strategies prove to be ineffective.

This makes it essential that a strategist while activating the formulation process keeps in his/her mind the potentials of persons bearing the responsibility of implementation. The operational apparatus, if inefficient, makes the process of implementation much more complicated. Lord Krishna was confident that he leads a side which may numerically be weak but they are morally and potentially sound and therefore, a well formulated strategy would help them in achieving the target. An ideal strategist forecasts the results and estimates the efforts needed to get the desired results. He/she estimates the strengths of rival side and tries his/her best to make it sure that the strategic decisions establish an edge over them. This simplifies his/her task of formulating a sound strategy. We can't negate the fact that Lord Krishna was well aware of the potentials of Kauravas and he was also familiar with the weaknesses that the side of Kauravas is helpless before the craze of Duryodhan who would not allow them to move in the right directions. A classic strategist makes efforts to know the strengths and weaknesses of opponents. The strategies of superpower with the co-operation of top performers made the task of Kauravas much more difficult. This also speaks of the fact that strategists need to make it sure that performers included in the team have an outstanding calibre. They are not to be disheartened even if the results are not upto their expectations. May be that even a mass leader fails in getting the desired success but the teams need not be disheartened because this would make them morally weak. If we work with this attitude, the success can't be denied.

There are a large number of instances to quote that the instrumentality of Lord Krishna as a strategist played a dominating role in Mahabharat. At a number of places, we find even an outstanding hero like Arjun experiencing troubles in using the weapons, identifying an opportune moment to use the same and confronting with a stage of indecisiveness. Lord Krishna not only formulated a strategy but also helped Arjun and others in the implementation process. This makes it clear that an ideal strategist not only requires to use his/her excellence in the formulation process but also simplifies the task of teams, groups bearing the responsibility of implementation or acting as an operational apparatus. Excellence without prudence is found ineffective. And therefore, a strategist requires a fair synchronisation of both the attributes to win the battle.

In the game of politics, a strategist plays a commanding role because the well formulated strategies make and show the ways for sensitising the campaigns essential to win the election, rule the government and satisfy the opposition parties and the public/masses to retain the position for a long time. Thus, we find enough facts to confirm the role of Lord Krishna as a professional because the perfection was an outstanding feature of his strategy that was formulated on the basis of his excellence. The contributions of super strategists and top performers if synchronised optimally ensure positive results. A classic strategist bears the efficacy of making an optimal development and fair synchronisation. And Lord Krishna was a classic strategist.

Kautilya: A Political Guru

The transformation of Vishnugupta into Kautilya was mainly due to his political ideologies and political wisdom. He was friend, guide and philosopher of Chandragupta and by formulating a sound political strategy, he engineered a strong foundation for an all-round development of the Mauraya Kingdom. As a political guru of Mauraya Chandragupta, he managed the kingdom of Chandragupta. The political ideologies of Kautilya were so much sensitive and effective that even of late we name an individual Kautilya, if he/she shows his/her excellence in crafting and projecting a positive image. The establishment and prosperity of Mauraya Kingdom testifies his unparalleled prudence.

The period of Kautilya is 325 BC.[1] The birthplace of Kautilya is yet to be confirmed but he was educated at the Takshshila University. Simplicity was his outstanding quality which considerably influenced masses. He even though a Prime Minister in the kingdom of Chandragupta preferred to live in a cottage. Being influenced by his values, simplicity, dedication and commitment, Fayhan a wayfarer coming from China commented that the Prime Minister of a very big country lives in a cottage located in the outskirts, it is really very amazing. Kautilya, in response to his comment said that if ministers of a country live in a cottage or hut, the citizens of that country get an opportunity to live in a palace and conversely, if ministers start living in a palace, the citizens in a very natural way have no option but to live in a hut. This testifies the sense of commitment and sacrifice of Kautilya which became instrumental in crafting his political image as a guru.

The word "Diplomacy" focuses our attention on the art of negotiation specially in relations between States or tact of management of people in any sphere. We can't negate that diplomacy is not to coil in its essence unfair or unethical practices but to win the race by formulating a sound strategy with the support of excellence and expertise substantially influenced by diplomacy. The political ideologies of Kautilya focus on maintaining norms and honouring values in making the political decisions as a creativist. It is in this context that we find the ideologies of Kautilya even till now getting a respectable treatment. We can't negate that Mauraya Chandragupta succeeded in safeguarding the interests of public because the strategic decisions of Kautilya assigned an overriding priority to the welfare concept. At the same time, it is also right to mention that progress and prosperity of a nation was given due weightage which paved avenues for the channelisation of welfare-oriented development measures.

The emergence of Kautilya as a Mass leader was well supported by his political ideologies. In the face of his image, Chandragupta offered to him due place in the process of policy making and decision-making. The strategic decisions of Kautilya, on the one hand, became instrumental in the downfall of Nand Kingdom while on the other hand, also engineered a strong foundation for the development of Mauraya Kingdom. This speaks of the fact that political wisdom, diplomacy, practical wisdom, dedication, commitment and prudence are some of the traits helping a political leader in the projection of a positive image which he/she can use for the development of his/her party. It is ultimately image of a leader that crafts the image of a party/organisation. A particular party is known by the quality of its leaders, workers, volunteers, members working at different levels.

Mahatma Gandhi: A Saint Political Leader

We agree with this view that from the mid of 19th century to that of the 20th century, a galaxy of personalities having humanism, social orientation, academic fragrance, political wisdom emerged as a successful political leader. But we can't negate that the ideas and views of Mahatma Gandhi benefited the mankind and society in many ways. We find Mahatma Gandhi as an ideologist who served the society and nation with a mission. Gandhi's ideas on social reconstruction constitute an outstanding example of a courageous and insightful vision of a just and worthwhile social order.[2] He put forth succinctly and forcefully his views about the kind of society which India needed.

Technological progress can't be considered an end in itself because we consider it just the order of means. It is remarkable that Gandhiji was able to perceive many of the maladies caused by unplanned industrialisation even before the First World War when the colonial powers of the Europe were jubilant on the superiority of their civilisation. Though Gandhiji was not against the use of technology found instrumental in serving the interests of society. He says, "How can I be as I know that even this body is a delicate piece of machinery. The spinning wheel itself is a machinery, even little toothpick is a machine. When I object, it is actually craze for machinery, not machinery as such." All of us are well aware of the harmful effects of sophistication in the process of technological innovations because we find them not only aggravating the problem of unemployment but also showing a number of harmful effects on environment.

Human well-being and justice and liberty are the two important aspects of social transformation. We can't think about well-being of human beings unless we promote justice and liberty. It is right to mention that ideas of justice and liberty were borrowed from the West. His transformation as a political leader was considerably influenced by the exploiting attitudes of the British. He witnessed a number of events when the British promoted socio-economic inequity and degradation of the poor. This generated in his mind the ideas to protect the poor society of India.

Of course, Mahatma Gandhi was a man of religion but its perception was perceived by him in a different way. He was of the view that truth and love or non-violence are related to religion. If we evince our interests in showing love to mankind and promote truth and adopt non-violence as a tool to achieve our mission, we promote religion. Because we find truth identical to God, it is not possible that our efforts would subserve the interests of mankind just by worshiping God at the different points or centres. The ideologies of Gandhiji were logical which made him a mass leader who played a decisive role in attaining independence.

Honesty, simplicity, sincerity, humanity are some of the traits transforming Gandhiji as a superman who was found successful in bringing the movement of independence to a logical conclusion. There is no doubt in it that a large number of dedicated leaders made sincere and honest efforts to activate the independence movement but Gandhiji earned the creditibility because his attitudes, approaches, efforts, comments and logics were distinct to others. He was a saint who engineered a strong base for the development of Indian society. He promoted democracy with the notion that it would protect the interests of society. His political orientation was considerably influenced by socialisation.

Jawaharlal Nehru: An Architect of Modern India

With the attainment of independence, the contours of development underwent radical changes. It was high time that the political leaders acting as policy makers formulate a policy which activates the process of industrial economic transformation. We can't negate that before the attainment of independence, the British did not prefer plans that made the Indian economy stronger. This increased the functional responsibility before the policy makers working for an independent India. It was against this background that Pt. Jawaharlal Nehru formulated a plan considerably influenced by techniculture. It is right to mention that Pt. Nehru started the process of industrial and economic transformation which in a true sense paved wider avenues for the development of modern India.

We find, Pt. Nehru making significant contributions to the attainment of independence and at the same time, we also advocate his political wisdom based on practical wisdom. Having a strong hold in the organisation of party, Pt. Nehru worked as a leverspring of the Congress Party and in the face of his image found positive in the eyes of masses, he capitalised on the available opportunities in the best interest of the party and nation. The philosophy of Pt. Nehru was based on equality, social justice and security. Manufacturing image of his own as a procession of men,[3] Pt. Nehru established his image as a mass leader found interested in improving the quality of life of the Indian masses. As a philosopher, writer, historian, political thinker, Pt. Nehru established his mass image and even till last, he remained a mass leader.

Industrial transformation makes copious avenues for national economic transformation. Of course, the primary and secondary sectors of the economy contribute significantly to the development process but failing the development of a balanced industrial economy, we witness stagnation and contraction. It was in this context that Pt. Nehru activated the process of industrial transformation in which mechanised efforts made possible a basic change in the nature and character of the national economy. The problems like inadequacy of infrastructural facilities, poor technological base, high rate of illiteracy and regional imbalances gravitated due attention of Pt. Nehru and he did his best to minimise the same. The concept of planned economic development was initiated and promoted by Pt. Nehru.

As and when we find a political party having a leader with multi-dimensional traits and faculties, the party becomes the prime beneficiary. The task of organising, managing and controlling a party is fantastically simplified because the party organisation finds it easier to inform, sense and motivate the masses. We can't deny the fact that the image of Pt. Nehru helped Congress Party in mobilising the voters and potential voters and retaining the number one position for a long time. The advertisement and publicity measures were switched on and the positive image of party leaders was profitably encashed.

Dedication, sacrifice, imagination, optimism, sense of determination, strong will power, humanism, simplicity and diplomacy are some of the properties helping Pt. Nehru in establishing a positive image, transforming him as a mass leader, strengthening him in gaining popularity as a promoter and proving his excellence in building and projecting a fair image of the Indian National Congress.

Radhakrishnan: A Culminator of Indian Idealism

Academics with political orientation prove to be an asset to a political organisation if they are value-oriented and show their temptations to ethical dimensions. An organisation can use his/her services for promoting the interests of party. Conversely, if they make a good-bye to values and ethics, they prove to be manipulators and ultimately harm the interests of party *vis-a-vis* the society. It is in this context that we make comments regarding academics' contribution to the development of a party. Radhakrishnan basically an intellect was a promoter of ideologies. He has been internationally acclaimed scholar of philosophy and religion in the 20th century. It was his high academic calibre that helped him reaching to the highest position in public life in India. Sarvepalli Radhakrishnan culminated the idealist tradition of Indian philosophy and by becoming the President of India, he could be the first citizen of Indian national.

We agree with this view that Radhakrishnan was not a politician or even a political thinker. He was an educationist, a philosopher, and greatest interpreter of religion and culture.[4] He was a democrat and a great nationalist. He felt that Indian democracy must have basis in ethics and religion. This was based on the degeneration that he witnessed in the Indian politics. About science, Radhakrishnan said that science is a form of knowledge but it should not make us blind to the whole truth because it gives us only the formal structure of physical existence. It is not likely to help us in perceiving the truth in its totality.

Radhakrishnan evinced keen interests in promoting the interests of poorest of the poor. We find him concerned about the welfare of poor and downtrodden. He was of the view that the political leaders working as policy makers need to assign number one priority to national interests. Radhakrishnan, though not a political leader, had a clear vision of India's political future. On a number of occasions, he made advocacy to strengthen national defence and this was on account of the fact that after Chinese aggression, he became very critical to the foreign policy of Pt. Nehru related to the handling of Kashmir issue.

Radhakrishnan was fully aware of the developments taking place in the social environment of India. He apprehended that developments in the field of science would harm social interests because technological transformation would remain instrumental in the process of inviting multi-pronged degeneration. He opined that science is a form of knowledge but it should not make us blind to the whole truth. Since we find science not helping us in accepting the truth in its totality, we need a balance while promoting science and technology.

Sarvepalli Radhakrishnan could taste the fragrance of politics in 1946 when he was given an opportunity to represent and lead the Indian delegation to UNESCO. For the first time, he had a taste of diplomatic life. After that he was appointed Ambassador to Moscow. We agree with this view that whatever the political orientation we find in Radhakrishnan was the handiwork of Jawaharlal Nehru. Pt. Nehru was interested in having Vice-President and President with high academic profile and academic flavour and from there, we find beginning of his political career. Though basically not a politician, Radhakishnan performed the responsibilities assigned to him both as a Vice-President and President in a very effective manner. A promoter of Indian culture, Radhakrishnan helped projection of a positive image.

Jayaprakash Narayan: A Revolutionary Humanist

Total dedication and service to the cause of common man of India, transformed Jayaprakash Narayan as a revolutionary humanist.

We in general are influenced by self that guides us, motivates us and governs us but we find JP an exception to this. From the beginning of his life to the end, he served politics without any self. There are a number of examples when he testified that even in politics, an individual or a group based on positive contributions may serve social as well as national interests. The political orientation of JP could get a shape on the occasion of his marriage when a number of political leaders and thinkers were invited to attend the function. It was in 1917 that his father invited a number of political leaders to attend the function which was also attended by Mahatma Gandhi. In a true sense, we find it a turning point in the life and career of JP because on that very day he got an opportunity to meet and interact with important political leaders on social, national and other key problems. Non-violent Movement of Gandhiji also motivated JP because he was so much influenced by his perception that he started leading a simple life and worked for national interest.[5] In addition, the Non-cooperation Movement of Gandhiji also influenced JP and these developments helped a basic change in his life and philosophy.

As and when we talk about simplicity, sacrifice, personal touch and human values, we mention the name of JP. A leader promoting socialism, instrumental in solving the problems of poorest of the poor, evincing keen interests in promoting national cause could be successful in the projection of a fair image which was capitalised on by the political leaders at different times in different ways. From 1948 to 1951, JP and Lohia made joint efforts to promote and strengthen socialism. He could not get results as per his expectations in the election of 1952 and this disillusioned him about the party policies. After this, he joined the Sarvodaya Movement of Vinobha Bhave.

As an architect of Total Revolution in Bihar, JP could be successful in mobilising masses in favour of Janata Party and it was on account of his clean image that Janata Party could be successful in replacing the Congress Party. The total revolution was an attack on corruption, and an ethical degeneration in politics but JP was disheartened when he found political leaders very much instrumental in promoting corruption and making a good-bye to ethics. He dissociated from party and politics and the Janata Party failed in protecting its existence.

Jayaprakash Narayan was disappointed with the negative developments taking place in the political environment of India. He felt that the political parties and the political leaders and thinkers need to assign due weightage to the interests of the poorest of the poor. If they forget them, the society would not remain united and this would make their task of ruling the country much more difficult. He advocated for the welfare of weaker sections of the society who have not harnessed the benefits of development. He worked hard for the development of society and it was due to his dedicated efforts that a new chapter was started in the Indian politics in which the political leaders willingly or unwillingly started taking interests in subserving the interests of neglected sections of the society.

Ambedkar: A Promoter of Social Justice

Bhimrao Ramji Ambedkar acted as a promoter of social justice which was considerably influenced by treatment that he received at the different stages of his life and career. He himself belonged to an untouchable community and therefore was experiencing the opinions of masses about the neglected segment of the society. He deeply studied the history of human relationship in the Indian society. He was sizeably influenced by Lord Buddha and Kabir because both of them were opposed to the existent social systems in India. If we find pioneer in the field of social reform, we have no option but to talk about Budha because in a true sense, he has been the propounder of the concept of social justice. Mahatma Jyotiba Phooley, a great crusader of social justice of Maharashtra considerably influenced Ambedkar. Political reform is not to protect the interests of society unless we find social reform. Ambedkar was influenced by this philosophy that motivated him to work and live for untouchable segments of the society.

Ambedkar was of the view that class composition of a society is just a natural phenomenon almost in all societies of the world but economic and social considerations influence the process. He opined that in the Hindu system, it is based on birth with sanction of religion which has made the social system much more complicated.[6] Ambedkar was very much disappointed with the social systems and started advocating a classless society in which all the human beings need to be given equal rights and opportunities. From the very beginning of his career, he started promoting social justice and confronted with the political leaders opposed to his assumptions.

He earned distinctions as an intellectual and a scholar and it was against this background that he and his thoughts started gaining popularity all over the country. Though he got place in the highest governing body that was Executive Council of the Viceroy in 1942 where for the first time a person coming from the untouchable segment got a place, an attitudinal change was not found in Ambedkar. He perceived a number of negative points in the Indian social systems and felt that unless and until we promote a new society in which caste and religion don't get any place, the deliberations and policy decisions regarding social reforms would not serve social interests.

Ambedkar preferred to live as a leader of the weaker sections though masses supported his revolutionary ideas. If he failed in winning elections in 1952, it was considerably on account of his negative feelings about the few selected segments of the Indian society. We appreciate his contributions to the development of Indian society but he would have considerably been successful in promoting social justice if his feelings, remarks, comments, ideas, opinions, observations and perception would not have been governed by the bias which he narrated at different places on various occasions. All of us are aware of his invaluable contributions to the framing of Indian Constitution and actually we don't have words to explain the qualities, properties, traits making him a personality distinct to many others. We can't negate that of late masses have realised his feelings and reactions and in the days and years to come, a basic change in the nature and character of Indian social systems appears significant failing which the deprived of sections of the society would make the task of political system of the country much more difficult.

POLITICAL ORGANISATION: A SOCIAL INSTITUTION

Political parties and political organisations need to be considered a social institution bearing the responsibility of subserving social interests with the help of their policy decisions irrespective of the fact that they govern or act as an opposition. They are supposed to formulate a policy to be instrumental in accelerating the pace of socio-economic transformation. On the one hand, they are found accountable to an all-round development of the nation while on the other hand, they are also required to make it sure that their policy decisions are not to obstruct the process of social transformation. Whatever the policies they formulate are and would remain active in making the society educationally sound, economically developed, financially solvent, technologically advanced, culturally rich, environmentally friendly, demographically optimal, medically world-class and socially and nationally well-integrated. Of late, we find multi-dimensional degeneration and it has shown a far-reaching impact on the development and growth of political organisations. By and large, almost all the political parties have forgotten the defined role they are supposed to play in the society and it is in this context that the political organisations need to redefine their functional responsibilities. We talk about educational institutions, healthcare organisations and social organisations but we don't consider it significant to deliberate upon political organisations/parties. All the four organisations need to remember that they have to act as a non-profit making organisation because they don't have a legitimate right of making profits. They are supposed to act as a social institution.

Social institutions are directly related to the development of society. The perception of social development includes in its purview all the components directly or indirectly playing a positive role in protecting and promoting social interests. We can't imagine the society to be conscious unless the educational institutions strengthen both the wings of education – formal and informal. We can't expect the society to be physically sound unless the medicare and healthcare organisations work satisfactorily to counter the multi-dimensional health hazards. We can't expect the governmental organisations to be socially-committed and value-based unless the non-governmental organisations (NGOs) come forward and evince keen interests in regulating the unethical and unfair practices. And we can't think any of the organisations working to our expectations unless the political organisations are value-based. Since we find political organisations not playing the desired role, it is pertinent that they think about managing the affairs of party professionally.

We agree that political ideologies of different political parties can't be identical but in no case, the ideological variations should question the instrumentality of political organisations as a social institution because all of them bear the accountability of protecting and promoting social interests for which the ways may be different, strategies may be diverse, but the target remains the same. Increasing degeneration in the behavioural patterns and attitudes of political parties and their leaders make a strong advocacy in favour of professionalised management in which there would be least scope for degeneration. Any political party can't be freed from the responsibility of value generation and value addition. The formation of social capital, such as development of human and humane, expansion of infrastructural facilities, development of educational institutions, expansion of healthcare facilities, scientific inventions and innovations, channelisation of welfare measures and so on are some of the positive developments paving avenues for value addition. The generation of social capital which plays a very effective role in making the society productive requires an intensive care. It is on account of these bestowed responsibilities that we call political organisations a social institution.

The socially-committed political leaders need to develop their parties as a social institution. If the leaders start deviating from their goals, commercialisation and merchandising of politics can't be denied. If we talk about conceptualisation of marketing in politics, our focus is on professionalism not on commercialism and we are supposed to know the basic difference between professionalism and commercialism. We can't allow commercialisation of politics but professionalisation is to be promoted which would develop the excellence of political leaders while formulating a strategy that helps them in building and projecting a positive image besides expanding opportunities for the multiplication of social assets. The professionalism that makes possible an attitudinal change in the potential voters is the real thing that is to be made possible by the mass leaders of the party.

A social institution, like political organisation, can't be successful in subserving social interests unless the leaders belonging to almost all levels perceive that an organisation needs to work with an avowed mission of thinking and planning for the development and welfare of the society irrespective of the fact that they govern or act as an opposition. Of late, a large number of the political organisations have been found making a good-bye to the ethical dimensions and this has been opening new vistas for degeneration at almost all the stages and levels. An attitudinal change becomes must to bring things on the rail. If we start treating political organisations as a profit-making organisation, there would be multi-faceted change in the administrative mechanics and the scope for qualitative improvements would absolutely be freezed. It is in this context that we insist on treating political organisations as a social institution. Not only the ruling party but even parties related to opposition play an important role in making the policy decisions for the development and welfare of society. If we work with the attitude that they are part and parcel of the society; the party leaders would have no option but to pave avenues for an attitudinal change that would significantly influence their functional character. While mobilising funds for the development of party, they need not to forget that the process of mobilisation directly or indirectly is not to question social as well as the national interests. The constitution and by-laws of party are found significant to maintain and retain their character and behaviour. With a change in the social set up, they need to amend the provisions so that the public at large feel that the party would continue to safeguard their interests. The political parties working as a social institution would benefit the society *vis-a-vis* the organisation in many ways.

POLITICAL ENVIRONMENT IN INDIA

Your decisions, actions, strategic decisions make it essential that you are well aware of the emerging trends in the political environment which can't remain static. Since you have a well-developed political information system, your efforts for making an in-depth study of the emerging trends would not be difficult. You know about the strategies adopted by the rival parties; you know about the promotional measures practised by them; you have the feedback of voters and potential voters in your information bank; you know about the non-voters and thus with the help of a rich knowledge bank; you find yourself in a position to make your decisions more creative coiling much more sensitivity. It is in this context that we find it important to know about the changing political environment.

In the Indian context, we find a basic change in the political scenario particularly after the attainment of independence. Before the attainment of independence, by and large, all the parties worked with an avowed mission of activating the independence revolution. Irrespective of the ideological differences, the political parties in general were liberal to the efforts helping the process of attaining independence. Besides, they could not have alternatives to promote the development-oriented welfare measures and therefore with the help of a single point agenda of Independence, the joint efforts came to a logical conclusion. After the attainment of independence, the environmental conditions changed, behavioural patterns and attitudes changed, objectives changed, rivalism cropped up, system of communication changed and therefore the party at almost all the levels required a new vision and a new approach. We go through the problems in two parts covering a study of environmental conditions in politics before the attainment of independence and an in-depth study of emerging trends and evolving conditions after the attainment of independence.

Pre-independence Political Environment: As and when we start talking about the political environment before the attainment of independence, a large number of personalities come up before our eyes, such as Lokmanaya Bal Gangadhar Tilak, Raja Ram Mohan Roy, Sardar Patel, Mahatma Gandhi, Jawaharlal Nehru, Subhash Chandra Bose, Jayaprakash Narayan, Ambedkar, Swatantryaveer Savarkar and many others. The revolutionists like Khudi Ram Bose, Chandra Shekar Azad, Ram Prasad Bismillaha, Bhagat Singh injected life and strength to our independence movement. Acharya Kripalani, Shantirup Bhatnagar, Acharya Narendra Dev, Sarojini Naidu, Madan Mohan Malviya, Mohammed Ali Zinna, Dr. Ram Manohar Lohia, Abdul Kalam Azad, Dr. Zakir Hussain and others irrespective of attitudinal and ideological differences fuelled the movement for independence in a right fashion. The list is so big that identification of their names is not so much significant rather the most important thing is involvement and participation of all the political and social leaders who directly or indirectly created a condition that ultimately resulted into the attainment of independence.

Strategically, the ways were different but practically the destination was the same. The transformation of independence movement into the attainment of independence has a long history. The Quit India Movement speeded up the process which was activated under the leadership of Mahatma Gandhi. The participation of almost all the political and social leaders in the Quit India Movement forced the British to quit and we became independent. With the attainment of independence, we find multi-dimensional developments in the political environment of India. It is also right to mention that after the attainment of independence, the political parties except the National Congress Party were found unorganised which provided to the Congress Party an opportunity to thrive. The well-crafted image of Pt. Jawaharlal Nehru has helped the party in many ways.

Post-independence Political Environment: A study of the political environment of India during the post-independence period reveals a number of points making the environmental conditions unfriendly. The planned concept of development promoted by Pt. Nehru assigned due weightage to the development of industries which engineered a strong industrial base. The technology started playing a positive role in the development of national economy. Since the Congress Party fuelled the independence movement, they were in a position to capitalise on the opportunities and to occupy a position inside the government. The intensity of competition was very low because political parties in general were not so much strong to face the challenges and threats generated and aggravated by the Congress Party. When Indira Gandhi became Prime Minister, the development efforts were channelised which in addition to other aspects also increased rivalism and a number of political parties came into existence. For excelling competition, it was essential that promotional measures are strengthened. From here, we find beginning of the concept of political marketing. The transportation, communication, power sectors were found changing the strategic decisions of political parties. However, a change was not possible unless they formulated a joint or united front. The organisation and management of Congress Party was considerably influenced by the evolving changes.

Late Rajiv Gandhi played an important role in managing, monitoring and controlling the party affairs. It was during his time that use of technologies and marketing professionals in the field of election campaigns was found promoted. The significant developments in the field of media paved avenues for the use of management principles in the Congress Party in which the marketing practices were given due weightage. The designing of election postures, composition of election slogans, speeches, messages were done with the support of management professionals. This was a beginning and the credibility for the same goes to Late Rajiv Gandhi.

Bharatiya Janata Party promoted this concept because by that time we find a number of developments in the field of communication and information technology. The print media, telecast media and broadcast media were found in the most sophisticated form. The increasing significance of communication technology in the field of politics was also on account of the fact that by that time the intensity of competition was found at its peak. Almost all the political parties were found interested in channelising the uses of technology which required services of world-class marketing professionals.

In the decade of 1990s, we find the concept of marketing getting a place in the Indian politics which in the 21st century has been taking a new shape where innovative efforts of professionals play a decisive role. It is against this background that we find it a subject making use of political as well as the management tracks.

POLITICAL SOCIALISATION

Political socialisation is considered to be a process through which political culture is internalised and certain political orientations are developed in an individual. It is a process through which an individual develops his/her awareness related to the political system which ultimately determines his/her perception of politics. It is also known as a process of development through which an individual enriches his/her knowledge, attitudes, values and beliefs related to the political field.[7] Since we find political system closely associated with the multi-dimensional developments in the political systems, it is quite natural that emerging changes in society have a telling impact on the perception of political socialisation. It is against this background that a degeneration in values in society has paved avenues for an analogous degeneration in the attitudes of the political leaders. The behavioural patterns and the decision-making criteria of almost all the political organisations have now considerably been influenced by the changing perception of politics which, in a true sense, is found an invasion on their positive thinkings to the development process. The perception of political socialisation has not remained the same because from the ancient to the modern age, we find a fundamental change.

Kautilya, the political guru was influenced by a different perception which assigned due weightage to value orientation, personal commitment, sacrifice and dedication. We find imprint of the same on his policy and strategic decisions which motivated him to stay in an ordinary cottage even in the capacity of a Prime Minister. Gradually, we find a change in the perception because of a large number of changes taking place in the social systems. During the period of pre-independence, by and large, almost all the political parties and organisations worked with the motto of attaining independence and therefore the political rivalries and values could not be invaded. A basic change was visible after the attainment of independence in 1947 because almost all the parties and leaders started working with a different motive. The emerging multi-dimensional changes in attitudes, beliefs and values resulted into a change in the perception of politics which was sizeably influenced by materialism and self. Scientific advancements accelerated the pace of development which could be instrumental in changing the attitudes and lifestyles. The consumerism injected a new life and strength and changed the character and vision of the masses. All the political parties, organisations and leaders virtually are a direct products of the social systems and therefore we find imprint of a change in the social systems, particularly on the mental make-up of an individual. Since materialism prevailed and influenced the social systems and behavioural patterns, the political system was also influenced. It was in this context that a fundamental change in the attitudes of political leaders paved avenues for the muliti-dimensional negative developments. We can't negate that society remains to be the focal point around which all the organisations and their people cluster. If the society is value-based, the masses from the very beginning of the learning stage are given an opportunity to activate the process of value orientation. A line of difference between good and bad, right and wrong, deeds and misdeeds can't be drawn unless we find society assigning due weightage to the contributions of an individual or an institution and motivating or demotivating them in the face of their positive or negative contributions.

"Political socialisation refers to the learning process by which the political norms and behaviour acceptable to an ongoing political system are transmitted from generation to generation." Sigel (1965)[8] with this observation made it clear that value orientation is an ongoing process that should start from the very beginning of the learning stage. Rush and Althoff (1972)[9] made it clear that political socialisation is the process by which an individual becomes acquainted with the political system and which determines the perception of politics and his reactions to political phenomena. It is determined by the social, cultural and economic environment of the society in which the individual lives and learn by the interaction of experiences and personality of the individual. Once again, we find emphasis on the environmental conditions influencing us and playing a decisive role in the formation of attitudes. Greenstein (1968)[10] opines that narrowly conceived, it is the deliberate inculcation of political information, values and practices by instructional method and therefore he focuses on political learning — formal and informal, deliberate and unplanned at every stage of the life cycle including not only explicit political learning but also nominally non-political learning of political relevant personality characteristics. Dawson and Prewitt (1969)[11] find it a development process through which the citizens mature politically.

The aforesaid observations and views of different experts refer to the learning process through which from the very beginning of development of personality, the values are to be injected and in the process, we need involvement of all sections. We can't negate that in the Indian context, the educational institutions have not been successful in activating the process of value orientation. Further, the family where we live, the parents also appear indifferent to the ethical dimensions of personality development. Not only this, the parents often find it difficult to instruct and preach because they also happen to be a party to the process of value degeneration. Thus, at both the stages of learning, we find absence of ethical dimensions and values which in a very natural way make our task of value orientation much more difficult.

Of late, we find multi-dimensional degeneration in the political environment of India which makes it essential that we think over the problem on a priority basis. It is quite natural that in absence of socialisation of politics, we find comercialisation getting a place which has been forming a vicious circle of making investments and getting a profitable return. The political leaders are found developing a new cult which has been fuelling the process of commercialisation of politics. If they willingly or unwillingly spend huge money for managing elections or party affairs, they expect lucrative return and from here, we find the beginning of the degeneration process. The reversal of this cycle becomes difficult because they start merchandising politics. They are not aware of the fact that political organisations don't have a legitimate right of making profits. It is in this context that we need to conceptualise and practise political marketing which would require a prime focus on social marketing.

POLITICAL MARKETING — THE PERCEPTION AND MISPERCEPTION

Before injecting life and strength to the conceptualisation process, it is pertinent that we perceive the concept in a right fashion and develop the perception helping political organisations in crafting a positive image. The political organisations like other social organisations are supposed to subserve social interests and in addition, they also bear the responsibility of protecting and promoting public as well as the national interests. This makes it essential that they develop professionalism for an optimal blending of the different facets of social transformation. The modern management principles, substantially influenced by social marketing, make it essential that like other non-profit making organisations, the political organisations also take into consideration their accountability to the society as well as to the social institutions. The concept of political marketing thus draws our attention on practising modern marketing principles considerably influenced, guarded and regulated by the defined principles of social marketing.

Political marketing is a managerial process in which professional excellence of political leaders and their teams become instrumental in making public their contributions to the society so that masses come to know about their efforts and attitudes. Since the public at large need to make their decisions in favour of a particular party which is to decide the existence and prosperity of an individual and his/her party, it is significant that professionally-sound efforts are made to win the race. The available technologies, infrastructural support, strategies adopted by the rival parties, increasing significance of creativity in sensitising the voters are some of the facets to be given due weightage by the political parties and political marketing attempts to resolve their problems. This makes it a managerial process in which art, tact, ability, expertise, prudence and excellence are suitably rewarded.

Political marketing is considered to be a social process because the marketing strategies to be followed by the political leaders and their parties are considerably influenced by the principles of social marketing. The application of marketing principles in the games of politics is sizeably influenced by the social considerations. The slogans, campaigns, promotional measures, communication are not to miscommunicate or misguide the society. Whatever the practices they follow, are to be instrumental in informing and sensing the masses in a right fashion. The degeneration in any area is to be regulated. The advertisement and publicity measures are to be made innovative to sense the masses so that they come to know about the right ways to make the environmental conditions conducive. It is against this background that we find political marketing a social process. We can't limit the boundary of political marketing just to the winning of elections and occupying the ruling bench. Since the political organisations are considered to be an important social institution, it is significant that the social marketing principles make politicians fully aware of the responsibilities they owe to the different segments of society.

Political marketing is also considered to be a strong force to make the masses aware of their rights and duties. Unless we find social awareness, the voters and potential voters would not be in a position to judge the contributions of a party or an individual. This makes political marketing very much instrumental in creating mass awareness and sensing them in the right directions. With the development of technology, we find traditional marketing resources not so much effective in developing communicative ability. The slogans, campaigns, speeches and posters are made creative and informative with the help of marketing professionals.

The perception of marketing in no case necessitates generation of profits as an essential criterion and it is against this background that we find almost all the non-profit making organisations very much active in practising modern marketing principles. The healthcare organisations or hospitals, the educational institutions, the social organisations need to conceptualise modern marketing principles but with a new vision. The social considerations establish an edge over the commercial considerations and the marketing principles make them efficacious in protecting the national interests. Like this, the political organisations also practise marketing and the main reason for the same is to project a positive image. In no case, the political marketing believes in misguiding the gullible segments.

These facts regarding political marketing make it clear that the political organisations conceptualise marketing principles but while practising, the social considerations dominate and the strategic decisions are considerably influenced by the masses representing the different segments of society. Like other non-profit making organisations, the political organisations also need to practise marketing with the motto of making the organisations potentially sound to face the challenges and threats generated by the rival parties. Making the promotional tools more and more sharp edged to project right things in a creative fashion so that the normal flow is transformed into a wave, is the main thing that we find in marketing politics, specially in an age of communication superhighway. Newman goes through the problem in Handbook of Political Marketing (1999).[12]

In view of the above, the following facts are observed:

- Political marketing is an amalgamation of two words used in two different areas. This focuses our attention on the application of modern marketing principles in politics with due emphasis on social marketing, by fairly synchronising both the tracks — Management and Politics.
- Political marketing is a social process because all the constituents directly or indirectly, considerably or partially are related to the subserving of social interests. The marketing in politics thus is closely related to the activation of social transformation process.
- Political marketing is also found to be a managerial process because while practising marketing, the political parties or organisations need the services of world-class professionals who on the basis of world-class excellence make the processes sensitive *vis-a-vis* cost-effective.
- Political marketing is also considered a communication process where political leaders in addition to other attributes get an opportunity to develop their communicative ability. This also makes it a technological process because of late we find political parties taking the support of information and communication technology for sharpening and sensitising the promotional measures.
- We need to remove the misperception moving in the minds of a few of us that the concept of political marketing is to allow political leaders to promote merchandising and commercialise politics for getting a profitable return. The perception focuses our attention on practising the principles of social marketing where all our efforts need to be welfare-sensitive and development-oriented.

SIGNIFICANCE OF POLITICAL MARKETING

It is ultimately perception that portrays a clear picture of the outstanding significance of political marketing. We agree that a majority of us even till now have not perceived the concept of political marketing in a right way which creates confusion and misunderstanding regarding its importance. We can't negate that marketing by a social institution proves to be difficult because the organisations not having a legitimate right of making profits complicate the task of policy decision-makers. The educational institutions, healthcare organisations, political organisations and social organisations conceptualise marketing with a mission paving avenues for subserving social interests. It is against this background that political parties need to conceptualise marketing with a new vision. The political leaders need to make an assault on the image problem and for that marketing is found to be effective.

The following facts testify the instrumentality of political marketing in the Indian political environment where a number of political parties have not been found honest and sincere to the social considerations.

1. Strategic decisions are found proactive: As and when we talk about a game plan, our focus is found on strategy because strategies are considerably influenced by the defined principles of a battleground in order to make an attack and get a success. Our efforts in the process, if unproductive, become active in degenerating the level of efficiency and ultimately make us potentially deficient. This makes the ways for the formation of a vicious circle which necessitates a sound strategy for the reversal of a cyclic movement. The principles of marketing simplify the task of strategy formulation and a political party is found successful in designing campaigns and innovating promotional measures to be sensitive to inform and sense the voters. It is not only sufficient that we have a big budget for advertisement and publicity measures. It is much more impact generating that our strategic plans have a correlation with the changing temperament and attitudes of the behavioural profile of voters and whatsoever we desire to convey are transmitted to the target segment in a creative fashion. The strategic decisions of rival parties can't be overlooked because this helps injecting creativity.

2. Crafting of a positive image is possible: We can't negate that it is our image that throws a telling impact on sensing and attracting the masses. A political leader with a negative image finds it difficult to influence the voters even if we find party having a fair image. This makes it essential that the political organisations are careful while preparing the list of candidates. In an age of electronics, the rival parties find it difficult to promote the party affairs mainly on account of cost consideration. Of course, we find electronic media very much effective in advertising, propagating and publicising but a majority of the political parties find it difficult to afford. If you have a leader with a high profile and a mass image, the task of influencing and persuading is found easier. The efforts made by your party inside and outside the government, countering the sufferings of natural calamities, generating public awareness, guiding and sensing the society are some of the positive contributions helping you in building and projecting a positive image. Image becomes a focal point and political marketing simplifies the task of projection. If you are fair and make use of sophisticated promotional devices, your task of transmission and projection would be much more easier.

3. Cost-effectiveness is made possible: We are well aware of the fact that the political organisations need huge financial assistance for managing the election or other affairs of the party. They generate finance from different sources. The mobilisation of resources is to be done carefully so that the rival parties don't get an opportunity to make adverse comments and the masses are convinced. It is right to mention that in a majority of the cases, the political parties have been found adopting unfair, illegal, unethical measures for generating funds. Of course, they need funds for managing the party affairs but the persons, institutions, organisations extending financial support are not to be given undue weightage. The management of finance requires due attention so that unproductive expenses are considerably minimised. We agree that the marketing principles help them in quantifying the monetary requirements for a particular head because the strengths of rival parties can rightly be gauged. This makes your task of assessing the requirements much more easier. With the help of a computer-driven information system, the political organisations find it convenient to document the events to be useful in the days or years to come. You advertise and publicise but failing creativity and sensitivity, whatever you spend on promotion prove to be unproductive. The marketing principles help you in making your campaigns and slogans creative helping in establishing an edge over the strengths of the rival parties. You spend but with a sense which makes the entire process cost-effective.

4. Social considerations get an overriding priority: It is significant to mention that application of marketing principles is substantially influenced by the holistic concept of management in which social marketing principles are given due weightage. It is against this background that we find political marketing a social process. The political organisations not only need to manage the election campaigns but also to win the race and further to keep on moving the process of subserving the social interests. The creation of mass awareness, generation of civic sense and facilities, regulations related to social ills, protection of environment are some of the basic problems necessitating due attention of the political organisations. In a true sense, they bear the responsibility of protecting the social interests but of late, we find a majority of them making a good-bye to the accountability they bear to the society. We can't negate the fact that social marketing is the foundation on which we formulate the concept of political marketing. The political leaders and their parties need to accept the fact that the conceptualisation and application of marketing principles would open doors for the subserving of social interests which would help political organisations in building a positive image. In a majority of the less developed countries, we find political organisations unaware of their duties and responsibilities. This makes their task of building image *vis-a-vis* capitalising on the opportunities much more difficult. Even if they keep themselves engaged in protecting the social interests, the insufficient and insensitive election campaigns don't provide to them the results they expect. The unsystematic and unorganised efforts show a lukewarm response and despite their positive contributions to the social transformation process, they fail in mobilising the public opinion. The defined principles of social marketing make it essential that on the one hand, they contribute to the social transformation process while on the other hand also publicise positive contributions of their party in a creative fashion.

5. Loyalty to party is retained: The political marketing is considered to be a fair blending of social and managerial considerations in which an individual as a leader and party as an institution gets an opportunity to sensitise and win the heart of masses. We are well aware of the fact that with the help of creative advertisements and publicity campaigns, the task of persuasion is fantastically simplified. The political parties and the concerned leaders are supposed to keep on moving the process of social transformation irrespective of the fact that they are holding the opposition or ruling side. The masses witnessing their contributions would come to know about their attitudes and behaviour patterns which would develop softness and ultimately they would be loyal to a leader or a party. We can't negate that loyalty is found based on positive contributions and attitudes. If we find masses influenced by the fact that the leaders of a particular party have been pro to their interests, the loyalty is retained which helps the party in returning to power repeatedly.

These facts are a staunch testimony to this proposition that political marketing if conceptualised and practised in a right manner would make the task of leaders and their concerned parties much more easier. If we find positive contributions essential to project a fair image, the creative advertisement and publicity measures or promotional efforts become a must. It is not only essential that you keep on moving the process of serving the society. It is much more impact generating that you make the masses aware of your contributions, efforts, attitudes. It is but natural that in the developing or less developed countries, the masses lack sensitivity because of the low rate of literacy. The political marketing simplifies your task of sensitising because the professionals having world-class excellence with the help of sophisticated communication technology make your promotional efforts efficacious. Your campaigns, promotional devices, speeches and slogans, communicative ability come to a logical conclusion if we find political marketing considerably influenced by social marketing. Make your slogans, campaigns, posters, photographs, sketches, cut-outs so effective that masses are persuaded and stimulated in a desired way. Whatever you spend or invest prove to be productive because the results you get are found to your expectations.

The instrumentality of political marketing is thus found coiled in the essence of dedication of leaders, workers, members, volunteers; use of sophisticated communication and information technology; dedication and commitment of party members; strength of rival parties; image of leaders dominating the party; records of party leaders, positive contribution of party to the development of society and significant of all, the weightage given to the principles of social marketing. If we find political marketing gaining popularity in the West, it is mainly due to the strategic decisions they make in the face of social marketing. The less developed countries like ours can also be successful in making a productive use of marketing in politics, if they make sincere efforts to practise the same in the face of changes found in the East. To get the desired results, it is essential that we practise marketing in politics with a new vision so that masses don't form a negative opinion.

DIMENSIONS OF POLITICAL MARKETING

Change is a natural phenomenon. Change in the political environment; change in the business regulations; change in technology; change in attitudes and behaviour; change in the intensity of political rivalry; change in the rate of literacy and a number of changes in different areas necessitate an analogous change in the functional areas of political marketing. If the political parties and leaders delay the process of incorporation; the task of getting a success would be much more difficult. They would perform but would not get the reward. They would promote but the messages would remain insensitive. The opportunities would be there but they would fail in capitalising on the same. The various dimensions of political marketing would help political parties in many ways. They would have an in-depth idea of voters and potential voters living in the different segments of a constituency; they would come to know about the behavioural profile of candidates, members, workers, volunteers and voters and with the help of a technology-driven information system, they would also be in a position to develop a mix that would help them in informing, sensing and sensisting the voters. The task of transforming the potential voters into actual voters would considerably be simplified and they would keep on moving the process of winning the elections and retaining the position. The formulation of strategies would not be difficult because the information system would help them in gauging the strength and identifying the weaknesses of rival parties. With the help of a technology-driven political information system, they would find it easier to formulate a marketing mix that would help them in developing innovative services to the different constituencies. Thus, the key dimensions in the political marketing are:

- Segmentation to divide the constituencies into different small parts which would help them in studying the level of expectations of men and women, kids and teens, youths and grey, rural and urban, illiterate and literate segments of a particular constituency.
- Behavioural studies to know the changing attitudes, behavioural patterns of voters and potential voters or masses living in the society. In this context, also know about the attitudes of candidates, members, workers and volunteers.
- Political information system to collect facts, figures, data to transform them into information with the viewpoint of identifying the emerging trends, feedback, lapses and shortcomings. In this context, strengthening political communication to enrich the communicative ability of candidates, workers, members, volunteers. Taking the support of information technology to diagnose the developments taking place in the different areas.
- Formulating a sound marketing mix to offer time-honoured services to the different segments, promoting in a creative fashion to inform, sense and influence the voters and potential voters, bridging the gap and removing the possibilities of distortion in the services promised to the different segments, developing quality candidates, workers, members, volunteers by educating and training them in the face of changing levels of expectations of masses. Assigning due weightage to the formulation of a service mix in the face of quality of services offered by the rival parties. To be innovative in approaches and efforts.

SEGMENTATION IN POLITICS

Small is beautiful. Small is knowledgeable. Small is attractive. Small is manageable. It is against this background that we talk about segmentation because it is a process of dividing the areas and population into small segments so that the varying needs and requirements, attitudes, levels of expectation, preferences, satisfaction and dissatisfaction are studied minutely. A microscopic study of the changing level of expectations of voters living in different constituencies prove to be difficult if we make efforts to study all the segments with the help of a single variable. The men and women, kids and teens, youths and grey, voters and non-voters, literates and illiterates, rural and urban segments can't have identical needs and requirements. Since you have to identify their expectations, magnitude of satisfaction or dissatisfaction, it is pertinent that you divide your constituencies into different segments and with the help of political information system come to know about their needs and requirements and the levels of expectations. This would help you in formulating development-oriented and welfare-sensitive programmes. In the context of political marketing, it is also significant that you make efforts to satisfy the masses so that your voters and potential voters, non-voters, kids and teens, men and women, youths and grey don't feel discriminated. Potential voters of today and even non-voters of today are likely to be the voters of tomorrow; kids and teens of today are to be the voters of tomorrow and therefore you while channelising your welfare, development programmes need to make it sure that all the segments get due weightage on your development agenda. If you depend on today and don't think about tomorrow, it is difficult for you to be sure that tomorrow or a day after tomorrow there would not be any degeneration and a particular segment voting in your favour would continue to vote for you again and again.

Segmentation occupies an important place in the world of marketing. Almost all the organisations have been found making use of segmentation for making their efforts and steps more sensitive. It is a device that helps you while planning and securing future, formulating development plans, finalising strategic decisions, innovating services, increasing creativity and so on. You need to identify the representation of different segments in a particular constituency or area and also to know about their needs and requirements and expectations to formulate a mix that helps you in getting their support. It is essential that not only voters and potential voters get due treatment but even segments considered to be non-voters are given an intensive care. This is essential because non-voters of today may be the voters of tomorrow. The marketing resources would be instrumental in transforming them if you make sincere and profesionalised efforts to inform, sense and persuade them in a creative fashion.

Kids and teens upto 17 years: This segment of your constituency needs due attention because in a majority of the cases, they dominate the decision-making behaviour of their parents. The marketing professionals need to know about their needs and requirements, specially related to educational facilities, medicare services, recreational facilities, sports activities, formal and informal education, infrastructural facilities and financial services so that they develop a craze and form a positive opinion about your party. Sooner or later, today or tomorrow, they may be your voters and even promoters. You can solicite their best cooperation as a word-of-mouth promoter. By developing this segment, you develop a dedicated force to help you in many ways even in an unfriendly environment.

Men and Women Segment: It is but natural that in the face of gender, we find variation in the needs and requirements and expectations and this draws your attention on studying their behavioural patterns. Women segment has till now been found neglected in the political environment of India and therefore due weightage to this segment would increase the numerical strength of your voters and potential voters. It is easier for you to motivate the women segment by channelising a number of welfare facilities for their all-round development and protection. To solicit their co-operation, you need to expand educational facilities, drive against dowry, child and medicare, development of day-care institutions. Like this, we find men segment of your constituency having different needs and requirements and you need to study them.

Youth Segment: With the viewpoint of managing party affairs and elections, we find this segment of your constituency to be more effective provided you manage them properly. In the Indian perspective, the problem of unemployment is found at its peak and your development programmes instrumental in expanding the employment opportunities would help you in getting their co-operation. Since in the Indian context, we find youths completing 18 years of age having the right to vote, the youths upto 40 years of age may be considered as youth segment.

Grey Segment: This segment of your constituency is found different in tastes and temperaments. Persons crossing the age of 50 would be in this segment. They in a majority of the cases are found hard pressed specially on account of multi-faceted socio-economic problems and therefore you need to study their needs and requirements to transform them into the actual voters.

Old Segments: Persons crossing the age of 65 would be considered old aged segment. In a majority of the cases, we find them depending upon their children but so far as the casting of vote is concerned, we don't find them influenced by their children. They have their own understanding and a sense of judgement. For getting the co-operation of this segment, you need to promote the social security programmes such as development of medicare and entertainment facilities, subsidised transportation and communication services, financial services and social security so that they become your voters and keep on moving their favour and support your party for years and years to come.

Rural and Urban Segment: There are a large number of constituencies in the rural segment and therefore a majority of your rural voters considerably influencing the results need an intensive care. They live in villages and face a number of problems. For getting their support, you have to assign due weightage to the civic amenities and facilities in the rural areas on a priority basis. In the Indian context, the policy makers related to any party have not given due weightage to the rural segment though they have received their best possible support and co-operation as and when the circumstances necessitated. Besides, an optimal development of towns and cities requires due attention of your party.

New and Debatable Segments: It is really amazing and to some extent also painful that the policy makers have themselves created and promoted a segment which was virtually vanishing from the sight. Of course, we find this a sore-spot on the Indian Social Systems which has actually been the gift of political leaders who constitutionally bear the responsibility of making an assault on the same. Initially, the Census of India had been publishing caste-wise break-up of the population but keeping in view the fact that it is to pollute the social systems and also to generate a number of social evils, the same was abolished. Once again, we have started the process of caste-wise segmentation of population and the concerned leaders have also evinced their interests in publishing a community-wise break-up. This is to get share in the face of representation of a particular segment in the total population. We can't negate that it is not only to generate factionalism, aggravate casteism, promote communalism but also to motivate the segment to increase the population and get the maximum share. In a country like India where we find demographic pressure mounting at its peak, the policies motivating a particular segment to increase their representation by increasing population would fuel the process of population explosion which would have a long-term harmful effects. In a true sense, we need to control population *vis-a-vis* the demographic pressure.

But just to increase the vote bank, we find a few of the selected political leaders and parties making a strong advocacy in favour of such a segmentation that would make social environment unfriendly and would also generate social tension. Can we allow a particular segment to increase the pressure of population just for getting the political benefits and reserving their seats?

The political parties and leaders act as a policy maker. They bear the accountability of making available to the society right directions so that they move forward to protect the interests of mankind without making any discrimination on the ground of caste and religion. This is in a true sense the perception of secularism and we are constitutionally bound to follow the same. A particular segment or caste not getting due share mainly due to the fact that they have regulated the size of their families would considerably be motivated to increase the same, if we nurture, promote and protect the new segment.

It is right to mention that segment pro to a particular caste and religion is the result of additional and undue benefits offered by a particular party. All equations, calculations, principles, contributions become ineffective because they work with an avowed mission of favouring a particular party. The increasing tension in the social systems of India is considerably influenced by the voting patterns which the political parties and leaders conceptualise and practise to get the undue benefits. We can't consider it a healthy development and need to explore new solutions.

The national policy makers bear the responsibility of protecting the social and national interests on a priority basis. The prime motto is to establish a social system in which all of us without any discrimination get an equal opportunity to survive and thrive. Some of us need more financial and infrastructural support and the policy makers would do it considering the same as a number one priority. Haves and have-nots are only the two segments and if we work with this notion, the social systems would be regulated in which a classless, casteless society would emerge and in addition the mounting social tension would also be arrested.

POLITICAL INFORMATION SYSTEM

Policy and strategic decisions are considerably influenced by your knowledge and understanding regarding the multi-dimensional latest developments. You need creativity which requires to be innovative. Innovations can't be possible unless you have an in-depth knowledge of the evolving changes and emerging trends. You are supposed to know about your own strengths and weaknesses in addition to the diagnosis of threats and challenges generated by the rival parties. Since we find change an ongoing process and the sophisticated developments in the field of transportation, communication and information have made possible more frequency in change, you can't keep yourself indifferent and isolated. It is against this background that we talk about information system that of late is found substantially influenced by computers. Like other organisations, the political organisations also need to develop a technology-driven information system which would simplify their task of understanding the needs and requirements, level of expectations, intensity of competition in the different constituencies and regions. The information system is an organised set of procedures in which people and technologies play a meaningful role. It is a mathematical or scientific device of transforming the data into information. The party workers, researchers, volunteers, members collect facts and figures from different constituencies. The information system after making an analysis disseminates them which help political leaders in making and innovating the decisions. The party organisation finds the information significant to initiate a change.

We talk about segmentation but failing the cooperation of information system, the task would remain much more difficult. We need an in-depth study of the behavioural profile of leaders, workers and voters which require information related to the different facets of behaviour patterns. We have to formulate a sound marketing mix and even for that we need information because the development of marketing resources would be optimal where due attention is given to the requirements of constituencies and the types of population living there. Since the rival parties increase the intensity of competition, we need to know about their strengths and weaknesses and even for that we require information. With the mounting rivalry, the political organisations often need to innovate their strategic decisions and this would not be creative unless we find them information-based.

The leading political parties thus have to develop an information system which would essentially be technology-driven. The world-class computer professionals are to be engaged for managing the information system so that the strategic plans, operational apparatus, workers and volunteers are in tune with the changing requirements of the political parties. The ruling as well as the opposition parties — both of them are found benefited with the information system. The opposition parties with the help of information system are found in a position to identify the lapses and shortcomings of ruling party(s) at different stages of making and practising the policy decisions. They would find it convenient to counter the claims they make in their favour.

The above facts testify the instrumentality of a sound information system for the political organisations. Of course, the small parties would find it difficult to develop an independent information system but they can buy information from the information-selling organisations.

The quality of a product is influenced by the quality of inputs used in the process of production. If we use substandard or poor quality of inputs, the outputs in a very natural way would also be of poor quality. Whatever the facts, figures, data we use in the information system are the inputs and the system with the help of professionals and computers transforms them into outputs. This focuses our attention on the facts, figures and data made available by the researchers or workers related to a particular constituency. You need to be careful while managing the inputs so that up-to-date reporting of the developments, trends and intensity of threats generated by the rival parties, contributions of party leaders to the development of that constituency are made available to the system so that whatever the strategic decisions we make prove to be effective.

The opinion poll, survey and feedback would energise the process of making right decisions. Since we talk about a technology-driven information system, the computers and the computer professionals would simplify our task of managing the information. The political parties may expect positive results from the system and therefore the people engaged for the collection of data become significant. We need to use the services of dedicated and committed party workers and volunteers who make available to the system right facts and figures. It is also found that in some of the cases, the researchers failed in making right reporting that confused party organisation and the decisions could not be right which sizeably harmed the interests of party as a whole. Since we find information system responsible to make mid-term reporting, it is impact generating that at the required intervals, the concerned leaders and workers make available to the system the facts and realities.

There are a number of areas where you have to think and plan on a priority basis. The sensitive issues in a particular constituency or area focus on the contributions of party to the development of that constituency, existing strength of rival parties, professionalised efforts and their expected results. Since we talk about the political information system, it is much more significant that an in-depth knowledge of the changing political environment is regularly transmitted to the information bank of the system so that the decisions like selection of candidates, development of party workers and volunteers, contributions of party to the development of constituencies, impact of promotional measures on increasing the sensitivity of voters and the potential voters, challenges and threats generated by the rival parties are taken in a right fashion.

With innovative information technology, the system is found efficacious of making a detailed analysis of the rights and wrongs. The contributions of an individual or a team are analysed and the shortcomings are identified. An opportunity for making corrections minimises the risk element in forecasting the intensity of effectiveness. If you are in a position to forecast, the strategic plan can be formulated and necessary preparations can be made to accomplish the objectives. This makes it essential that party organisation strengthens the information system and makes it innovative to enrich the knowledge bank. The transformation of information power into the knowledge power would benefit the political parties in many ways.

MANAGEMENT OF BEHAVIOUR IN POLITICS

Behavioural studies occupy a place of outstanding significance even in the management of politics. Since we talk about political marketing, it is but natural that our prime focus is on the behavioural patterns found existent among the different segments of society. The perception of politics in the minds of society becomes an important consideration influencing the attitudes and behaviour. If we find masses developing a negative attitude regarding politics and the political leaders, the task of sensing and sensitising them proves to be much more complicated. On the other hand, the behavioural studies also necessitate an in-depth study of the behavioural patterns of party members, workers and volunteers. The behavioural profile of a candidate becomes significant to determine the effectiveness of our strategic decisions. If you know about others, the chances of resolving and correcting are there. If a majority of the population form a negative opinion/attitude regarding you and your party, the task of persuading them becomes much more difficult. The attitudes help expectations to take a shape. Significant developments in transportation and communication also help the process of shaping. Besides, the examples of the past play an important role in the formation process. If we find some of the party leaders setting examples, establishing new record of positive developments; it is quite natural that masses expect the same even from others. The behavioural studies thus require due attention of political parties because a majority of the political leaders and workers and volunteers are even not aware of the instrumentality of behavioural studies in transforming the negative attitudes into a positive behaviour. It is against this background that in the marketing literature, the behavioural management requires due attention.

The marketing strategies make it essential that while sensitising the target audience/market/voters, you know about the levels of expectations they have from you and your party. This would help you while formulating strategies and injecting creativity. Your service mix would be in the face of their requirements and while promoting, you would be successful in persuading them because you are well aware of their behavioural profile. What are the preferences, likes and dislikes, needs and requirements of the people of that constituency? What were the contributions of leaders representing them earlier? What significant developments did they expect in the face of evolving changes? You need to study them and based on the results your strategic decisions are to be made. In some of the constituencies, we find your party leaders performing well but you also find a number of constituencies where your representatives, workers, volunteers have not performed satisfactorily. The feedback that you get from different segments of the constituency would simplify your task of formulating strategies.

The leaders of a political party require to have some of the traits on a priority basis. They should have patience to receive the grievances of masses who may react even in an aggressive way. They need high communicative ability to express their views and comments in a very simple way which is to diffuse the tension of masses. They are not supposed to be short-tempered showing reactions, speaking harsh words, fuelling anger and anguish rather should be submissive and soft-spoken. The party workers, volunteers need to be active, sincere and value-based. The people engaged in different affairs of a political party require to have fascination to the ethical dimensions.

We can't negate that of late a majority of the party people have been found making a good-bye to the ethical dimensions resulting from which unlawful, unfair, fraudulent practices have become order of the day. They in a few of the cases, join politics because copious avenues are there to earn illegal money. This makes it essential that the party organisation conducts education and training programmes to promote values. We find political leaders also playing the role of policy makers particularly when they represent the ruling side. If they are found involved in the process themselves who would regulate. It is not only sufficient that the party leaders are educated, efficient and sincere. It is much more significant that they are value-based. They should be optimistic so that the task of countering the challenges and threats generated by the rival parties or others is found easier. Since they would face the public at different times, at different places on different occasions; it is significant that the party leaders and workers transform themselves into super performers so that the masses/public get an opportunity to quote. Not only this, the party would also be benefited as the image of leader has a direct bearing on the image of the related party. If in the party organisation, we find quality people, the projection of a positive image of the party is found easier which simplifies the task of winning elections and subserving social interests.

The behavioural profile is an aggregation of a number of aspects in which quality of people, their attitudes, likes and dislikes, ethics and values, sincerity and honesty, simplicity and communicative ability are found important and the party organisation has to make efforts to inject essential traits by innovating the education and training programmes. If you have leaders with a high behavioural profile, your task of getting a success is considerably simplified. Conversely, if you have leaders promoting unethical and unfair practices, the rival parties would make your task much more complicated. If you have leaders having sympathy and empathy; the masses would be allured. Conversely, if you have leaders found rough and aggressive, the masses would make your task much more difficult.

The aforesaid facts make it clear that management of behaviour assumes an outstanding place in the marketing politics and the party organisation needs to make it possible on a priority basis. Short-term gains often invite long-term pains. May be that some of the people found calculative and manipulative benefit you temporally but in the long run, they prove to be a liability and start harming your interests. In the goods manufacturing sector, an organisation can't thrive for a long time, if the goods produced by them are of inferior quality. Like this, in a political party, the domination of poor quality of people in the party affairs complicates the task of party organisation. It is in this context that we make a strong advocacy in favour of an in-depth study of behavioural management. The educational institutions developing students in the area of politics need to develop their behavioural profile by making available to them an in-depth knowledge of behavioural management. Besides, the party organisation also bears the responsibility of enriching the behavioural profile of party members and workers. People with high behavioural profile often prove to be assets. Since we find Mafia commanding political parties in a few of the provinces of India, it is high time that the Election Commission of India and the Supreme Court regulate the derailed systems in such a fashion that quality people start managing the party affairs and the anti-social elements are found behind the bar.

FORMULATION OF MARKETING MIX FOR POLITICAL ORGANISATION

The political organisations and the people engaged thereon in different capacities at the different echelons bear the responsibility of subserving social interest. We are also aware of the fact that the political parties don't have a legitimate right of making profits. In a true sense, the service motto is required to be the mission of all the political parties and party members, workers and volunteers. Either ruling the government or acting as an opposition, they need not to forget that their actions and decisions throw a telling impact on social, cultural, economic and technological dimensions which play a decisive role in the transformation process. You need to make it sure that the oaths you have taken in the names of God and Constitution are practised in a right fashion. You have to be innovative and explore new solutions so that masses are found satisfied. Your investments are not to get any return because virtually you spend don't invest. You need to be dedicated, personally-committed and value-based. You have to work with a new vision so that evolving changes are incorporated. You have to make it sure that masses of your constituency lead a comfortable life and are sincere to improve their quality. Since your policies and strategies determine the directions, you are not to allow the masses to deviate. On the one hand, you have to speed up the social transformation process by activating the process of technological and economic transformation while on the other hand, you have also to ensure that the process of socio-economic transformation would not make ways for cultural degeneration. You have to regulate the degeneration process. You bear the responsibility of removing social tensions and dissension and to maintain social and national harmony. You have to maintain the ecological balance and ensure that development efforts are not to make an invasion on environment.

Your policies and strategies need an intensive care on the problems of population explosion. You have to maintain communal harmony with the mission that racial, genetic, regional, geographical, family considerations don't promote discrimination. Your policy decisions need to make available to all an equal opportunity to survive and thrive. You would also be successful in protecting national boundary and would make sincere efforts to promote national excellence. The International relations would be based on your diplomatic efforts.

These functional responsibilities, of course, require people with high calibre to participate in politics because here nothing is possible unless you are personally-committed. Dedication and value orientation are the essential traits you need to inculcate in your people. You have to improve the quality of life for the present generation and have also to make it sure that the new generations appreciate your contributions. You need to be positive. You need to be optimistic. You need to be pragmatic. Your actions, decisions should be efficacious of engineering a sound foundation for the coming generations.

Since you contribute significantly to the development process, you need to promote. While promoting, you are required to be innovative. The creativity is to be an essential dimension of your promotional tools. By advertising and publicising in an innovative fashion, you of course, would be in a position to inform, sense, sensitise and persuade the masses. Because you have sizeably contributed to the social transformation process, the masses would work for you and your party as a word-of-mouth promoter.

Service Mix

We are well aware of the fact that political organisations bear the responsibility of subserving social and protecting national interests. As a policy maker when they are in the government or as a regulator when they are in the opposition; they are socially, morally and constitutionally bound to think and act for society. The party members, workers and volunteers bear the responsibility of making the working conditions friendly. This makes it essential that political parties in general keep themselves fully aware of the core and peripheral services they have to render. Since we expect them to be innovative, the inclusion and elimination would continue to be an ongoing process. With the help of political information system, they would come to know about the changing requirements and increasing levels of expectations of different segments living in a constituency. With a change in the regional, national, global, situational requirements, the nature and character of core and peripheral services would naturally be changed. Excelling competition is significant which requires to be informative and innovative. A fair blending of core and peripheral services would simplify your task of making an attack on rival parties and getting a success as per your expectations. The task of projecting a positive image would not be successful unless you assign due weightage to the quality of services offered by your party. You need professional excellence; you need expertise of world-class.

The core services focus our attention on your contributions to the process of social transformation. This makes it essential that you are aware of the basic needs of the weaker sections of the society, such as food, cloth and housing. They need primary medicare facilities and you have to be vigilant that non-profit organisations bearing the responsibility of offering medicare and healthcare services perform satisfactorily. The primary education facilities also need an intensive care and you bear the responsibility of making it sure that educational institutions have been offering the same. The essential infrastructural facilities need your priority attention so that all-weather-proof roads, transportation facilities, power, water gravitate your priority attention. The women and children segments need an intensive care because even till now we find them neglected.

While managing the core services, you have to be careful that the promises made by your party while facing elections, included in the election manifesto are fulfilled sincerely and honestly. If you belong to the opposition camp, it is your prime responsibility to make it sure that while implementing projects and programmes, the elected representatives, party people, government administration promote efficiency, establish work culture, motivate performers, regulate unfair practices and demotivate and punish dishonests and inefficients. You have to collect feedback of different sections and segments in addition to the information that you get from your network. You have to be innovative and make your service profile distinct to your competitors/opponents/rival parties.

In managing core services, the rural India or villages draw your priority attention because the expanding gap between rural and urban areas is required to be bridged which till now has failed in getting due attention. The long continuing social evils like dowry, exploitation of women, children, child labour, under-age marriage and demographic pressure need due care.

While formulating service mix, the party organisation also needs to develop the peripheral services. If we talk about peripheral services, our focus is found on supporting services which improve the quality of your services and provide you an opportunity to make your service mix relatively superior to the rival parties.

Adding attractions and improving quality should be your motto that would require enormous co-operation of the information system. The peripheral services include a number of services such as development of regions, constituencies and development efforts made by the ruling party. This includes development avenues such as management of water, availability of potable water, sanitation services, civic amenities and facilities, healthcare centres, transportation services, communication services, financial services, development of social security measures, strengthening of informal education to improve the quality of people, monitoring and supervision of welfare-sensitive programmes, entertainment and recreational facilities, development of park and think park, nutritional awareness, promoting vaccination culture and so on. Irrespective of regional and geographical limitations, the ruling and opposition parties need to make joint efforts to the process of cost-effective and time-honoured implementation of development-oriented welfare-sensitive governmental and organisational programmes. We can't have a boundary for the peripheral services because the willingness potentials of political parties become the determining factor. In Fig. 18.1, we find the blending of core and peripheral services.

The above facts are a staunch testimony to this proposition that a fair blending of core and peripheral services would help you in many ways. If you include innovative services, your task of image building would considerably be simplified. The dedicated party workers, volunteers, potential candidates need to be given an opportunity to show their excellence.

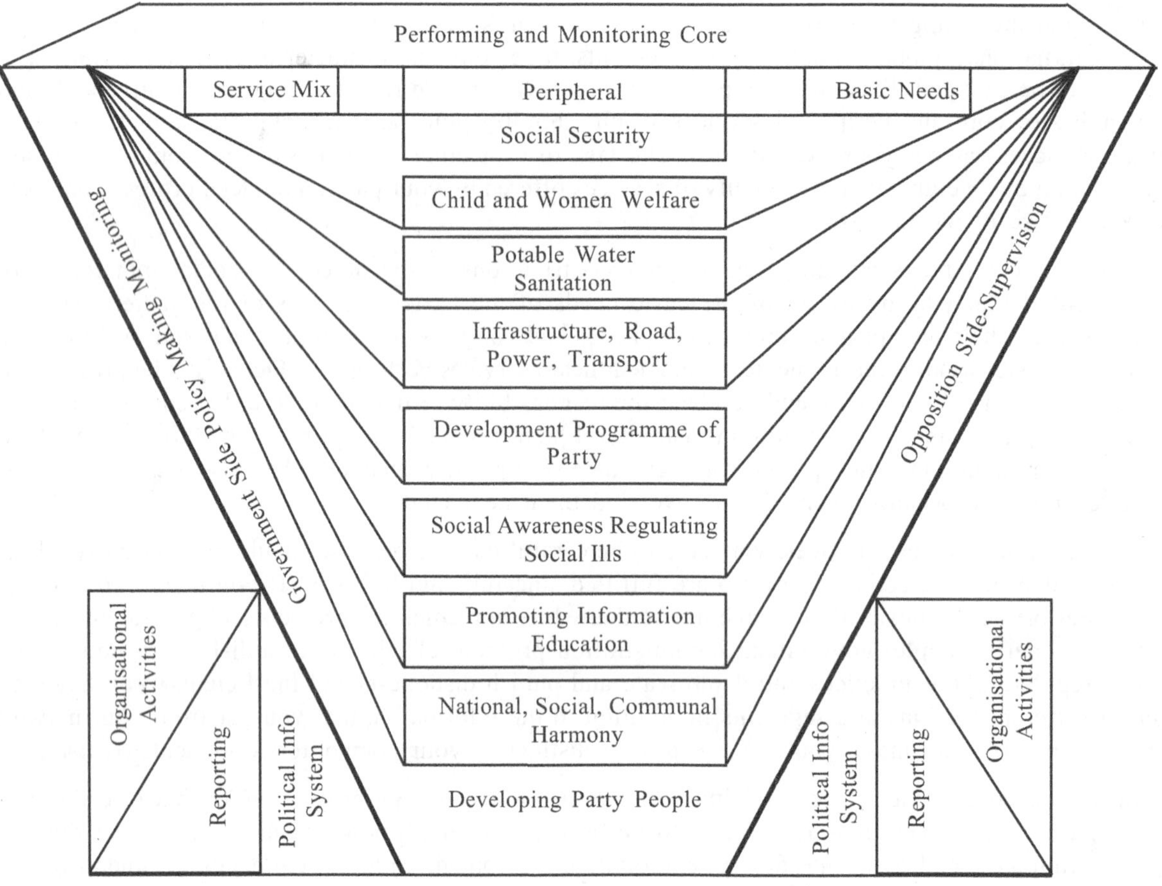

Fig. 18.1: Service Mix for Political Organisation

PROJECTION OF IMAGE

Image focuses our attention on the positive or negative contributions of an individual or an institution. By contributing in a positive fashion, we project a positive image whereas our negative contributions make our image negative. If we are positive and our efforts are concerned and consistent, we build and project a positive image. An individual or an institution requires to make positive contributions for the projection of a positive image.[13] Since we find political parties or organisations directly related to the masses, the image of people involved in the process portrays the image of a party. It is against this background that projection of image becomes significant to both — an individual or an organisation. Earlier, the communication processes were not so much fast and sensitive and therefore even the wrong decisions of an individual or a party consumed much more time for mass transmission, publicity and propagation. Of late, we find communication technology of the new generation very much instrumental and effective and therefore our deeds and misdeeds reach to the public with a supersonic speed. The ruling party commits mistakes, the opposition parties remain vigilant and start capitalising on the opportunities with the help and co-operation of sophisticated communication technology and world-class professionals. An individual or a party even performing excellently fails in sensitising, if we find a single unlawful decision testifying their involvement.

Since we consider image and appearance very closely resembling anything, our deeds and misdeeds form an opinion which may benefit or harm us. Building a positive image thus becomes much more impact generating because this simplifies our task of projection. The process of building a positive image is not to be the result of a day or two. Our consistent efforts coiling frequent innovations improve the quality of our contributions which form an opinion and decades long efforts without any distortion and interruption make the opinion positive. If we find the Indian National Congress successful in the projection of a positive image even till now, it is the result of their decades' long efforts for attaining independence and further in engineering a sound foundation for the Indian Nation.

By projecting a positive image, an individual or an institution succeeds in making the masses loyal to a particular party provided they feel that the party would keep on moving the process of development if favourable conditions remain existent in the socio-political environment. Thus, image helps us not only in capitalising on the opportunities but also creating and multiplying the same because an individual or an institution gets a sound nexus to develop optimally and turn things in their favour. The value orientation process helps strengthening the process of qualitative transformation albeit in a rough weather as the masses extend to them the best possible co-operation.

The political organisations are found closely related to the development of society. It is not possible that they for all the time continue to serve the society only as a ruling party. Even the opposition parties can do it very effectively. Of course, the ruling party has an opportunity to activate the manufacturing of image. With the help of development-oriented and welfare-sensitive programmes, the ruling political party gets an opportunity to transform the social system and the concerned leaders find an opportunity to build up their image which the leaders of opposition don't get. If the opposition leaders are sound, they formulate an innovative strategy to identify the lapses and shortcomings of the ruling party which would make their task of fighting elections easier.

The sensitivity of a particular issue varies with the passage of time and therefore either the ruling or the opposition parties bear the responsibility of identifying the needs of the hour. The ruling party may continue to rule for a long time if their efforts for identifying the needs establish an edge over the efforts of opposition parties. Conversely, the opposition succeeds in removing them from power, if they keep on moving the process of sensitising the masses to the lapses of ruling party. There is no doubt in it that some of the political leaders establish a strong mass image and this makes it essential that opposition makes efforts to identify their weaknesses because unless they make an attack on their image, the efforts would not be effective. United opposition thus remains the only solution because the unification process would make an assault on the ruling party. We agree that unification is a difficult task that not only requires a leader with strong social acceptability but in addition the feelings of sacrifice among all. The ruling or opposition parties having a leader with mass image make the task difficult to each other. In a true sense, the political leaders act as a strategists and sensitivity of strategies commands the success or failure of campaigns.

The service profile of a political organisation plays a meaningful role in the process of crafting and the parties assigning number one priority to social and national interests develops a positive image. If you perform honestly and efficiently and practise everything ethically, your image proves to be an asset. If the goods-manufacturing organisations and even a few of the service-generating organisations find it easier to business even in a rough weather, this is considerably on account of the benefits of brand image.

In the Indian context, we find some of the examples to quote because the image of Pt. Nehru, Indira Gandhi and Rajiv Gandhi could be helpful to the Indian National Congress and the opportunities were capitalised on by the party not once but several times. The BJP has capitalised on the image of A.B. Vajapayee and the United Front capitalised on the image of JP. Thus, there are two important areas, first the process of building a fair image and second projection of the same with the help of sophisticated and innovative promotional measures. The service profile having development and welfare orientation would be helpful to you if party workers and volunteers have been sincere to the implementation process.

The best solution to keep on moving the process of manufacturing quality leaders with mass image would be to activate the process of socio-economic transformation. The educational institutions and political organisations bear the responsibility of developing quality political leaders found professionally-sound, personally-committed and value-oriented. The time-honoured service profile under the leadership of a mass leader with a clean image needs an intensive care.

Promotion Mix for Political Organisation

If you work on the basis of your service profile; if you remain innovative to improve the quality of your services; if you add attractions to your service mix by enriching the quality of peripheral services and if your party organisation is confident that the promised services reach to the target segment without any distortion, you have a right of making them public so that masses come to know about your positive contributions. The promotional tools help you in the process and you need a fair mix of the different tools so that the sensitisation process is found as per your expectations and the cost-effectiveness is also made possible. In an age of superhighway for communication, it is but natural that promotional tools prove to be more sensitive but at the same time, it is to be very expensive. This makes it essential that your professional excellence is used in developing a fair mix in which all the tools get due share.

Political communication occupies a place of outstanding significance because the political leaders, workers, volunteers need high communicative ability to inform, sense and influence the potential voters for transforming them into actual and habitual voters. This focuses on personal selling because here the communicative ability of persons/people involved in the process determine the magnitude of success. The development-oriented and welfare-sensitive programmes of your party or government need to reach to the target segments on time without any distortion but a communication gap between the party organisation and party people makes your task much more difficult. You need to advertise and for that very purpose, you have print media, broadcast media and telecast media. In the face of your budget and requirements, you need to fix the share or proportion of a particular medium. You also need to publicise and this makes it essential that you and your people assign due weightage to the development of relationships so that media people are influenced and the publicity is done. Your party organisation needs to motivate word-of-mouth promoters. If you serve honestly and promote satisfactorily, the transformation of potential voters into the actual voters can't be denied. Since we live in an age of communication and information technology, it is quite natural that tools like cable marketing/telemarketing also get due representation.

Formulation of a sound promotion mix requires world-class professional excellence. Of late, we find a number of political organisations using the services of different organisations and professionals for advertising and publicising. While promoting, it is pertinent that you move in tune with your budget because making the promotional measures unproductive can't be a welcome step. You also need to divert your attention on the promotional strategies of the rival parties and for excelling competition, the budget can also be increased but the practice can't be generalised. Since we find public contacts playing an important role in the entire process of promotion, the measures like personal selling and word-of-mouth promotion need priority attention. This would not only expand possibilities of an increase in the number of your voters but the process would also be cost-effective and proactive. Creativity is an important dimension of promotion and you with the help of a technology-driven political information system and world-class professionals can make it possible.

POLITICAL COMMUNICATION

Creativity in communication is found impact generating for translating the strategies into meaningful actions. Almost all the organisations make use of creative promotional measures so that their messages, feelings, campaigns, ideas, thoughts reach to the target audience in a right fashion. It is in this context that we talk about the instrumentality of communication in politics. Political organisations and the leaders having mass acceptability need to think about communication so that they get the keys of access to power. Effectiveness with high intensity in election campaigns or other affairs can't be denied if elected or potential politicians assign due weightage to political communication. Your positive attitude, productive efforts and outstanding contributions to the process of social transformation don't benefit you and your party unless the masses come to know about the same. If you bear the responsibility of activating the process of socio-economic transformation and welfare channelisation; you are also supposed to sensitise the process of transmission. Communication makes the ways for effective transmission. Because you contribute significantly to the development process and transmit effectively by making the process of transmission innovative; the desired results can't be denied or delayed.

In an age of technology where we find techniculture proving its domination in almost all the areas, it is not only pragmatic but even judicious that politicians and potential politicians perceive the emerging dimensions of evolving changes in the management of communication which would simplify their task of increasing the sensitivity of messages and slogans and mobilising the masses in their favour. Sophistication in the process of upgradation of communication and information technology have made the task of political leaders much more easier provided they make use of the same with the help and co-operation of world-class professionals. Since you bear the responsibility of managing even the unmanageable, volatile and vulnerable sections of the society, it bears an outstanding significance that whatever you communicate would minimise scope for confusion and misunderstanding.

Language plays an outstanding role in making the process of communication more effective. It is pertinent for the political leaders that they keep themselves aware of the political language which of course would be a bit different to the language used by other sections of society. We can't deny that even for political leaders, the body language becomes significant because this helps them dramatising the events and sensitising and mobilising the masses because the process makes messages much more receptive. Simplicity is considered to be an important dimension of language and particularly for the political leaders who bear the responsibility of sensitising even the insensitive and illiterate segments more so in the Indian perspective, this property of language having mass acceptability is found carrying a special significance. A country coiling much more diversity in language and culture makes it essential that political leaders prove themselves to be the heroes of language because the knowledge of regional language would help them in making their speeches more sensitive and personalised which in a very natural way would have a fantastic positive impact on voters and potential voters.

The multi-dimensional channelisation of media and fast increasing sophistication in print media, broadcast media and telecast media have opened up new vistas for making the process of political communication much more effective. We can't ignore that advancements in telecast media have increased the sensitivity of communication because political organisations are now in a position to make use of the same in an effective way. In the Indian perspective where we find masses illiterate and carrying high intensity of insensitivity mainly on that account, it is pertinent that political leaders make themselves aware of the instrumentality of communication technology. The process of sensitising, sensing and influencing the masses would no doubt be expensive but at the same time would also be considerably effective. In addition, the advanced print technology has also been found making their task much also be efficacious while presenting and narrating their contributions to the transformation process. The posters, photographs, cut-outs, leaflets, etc., can be presented in an attractive form, if we make use of advanced print technology. Besides, the broadcast media also help political organisations in transmitting the messages and slogans. It is upon the political parties and their organisations to explore new avenues and enrich potentials for the productive use of communication technology which ensures positive results while capitalising on the opportunities.

When we go through the problem of marketing and view things as a marketer, the problem of political communication is to be studied in the face of creative attributes. Innovative measures are required to be practised in making use of media. An optimal use of media and the related technology would increase the potentials of political organisations. Because we talk about sophisticated communication technology, the organisations need the services of world-class professionals. Availability of technology carries no meaning if we don't find world-class professionals to manage them. Where to use, what type of technology to use and how to use are some of the aspects playing an effective role in sensitising the masses. Since dramatising of events and adding new attractions play an important role, the body language would also be included in its purview. It is significant to mention that body language for political leaders will be different from the body language required for other sectors. The political leaders need to inject the properties which help them attracting and persuading the masses. They need creativity in the very context so that language proves to be a source to help them in projecting a mass image.

The above facts make it clear that political communication makes it significant that the political leaders have high communicative ability and professional excellence. Irrespective of the fact that they belong to ruling bench or opposition side, they need a high degree of expertise which requires innovative education and training programmes. With the help of ancient and modern literatures and new generation of communication technology, the process of injecting potentials can be made more proactive. Since we find learning an ongoing process, the political leaders would considerably be benefited and the organisations would find it easier to project their contributions. Maarek (1994) goes through the problem in detail.[14]

Advertising: We find advertising a paid form of persuasive communication used by almost all the organisations. The political organisations have also been found making use of advertising as a tool to inform, sense and persuade the voters and potential voters. While advertising politics, it is pertinent that the advertising professionals keep them fully aware of the different segments of population living in different constituencies. You need to advertise for the political parties as well as for the political leaders commanding the responsibility of practising and monitoring the policy and strategic decisions. Because of the availability of a number of alternatives, it is essential that you also keep in your mind the infrastructural, financial and situational constraints failing which the results would not be as per your expectations.

The important media such as print media, broadcast media and telecast media accept the responsibility of political advertising. The political organisations need to formulate a fair mix so that a particular medium is used in a particular condition. Keeping in view the financial and situational limitations, you need to fix the proportion of a particular medium in your total promotion budget.

- **Political Advertising and TV:** With the significant developments in the field of satellite communication, we find advertising gaining wider popularity as an effective source of transmission. The evolving changes in communication, information and print technology have made TV incredibly effective in sensitising the masses.[15] In the Indian context, the rural and illiterate segments can effectively be informed and sensed with the help of television advertisements. You need to make public your positive contributions to the development and welfare of society and national economy and televisions makes your task easier. The image of noted political leaders of your party can be projected in an attractive way.[16] The significant developments in the telecast media have made possible multi-dimensional changes in the policy and strategic decisions but the main thing in the process is to identify the opportune moment and the potential segment. Since you have to transmit the contributions of your party and government, the composition of speeches, presentation of facts and figures, framing of slogans need due care. While advertising through TV, you need the co-operation of world-class professionals. Since we find the medium expensive, you also need to optimise the use of television and to prefer popular channels viewed by the target segments. While advertising, you also need to go through the TV advertisements of rival political parties with the motto of initiating a change in innovating the process.

In the Indian context, we find late Rajiv Gandhi promoting TV and further we also find BJP using TV as an important medium for TV advertising. If you have mass leaders, the TV advertising helps you in sensitising the target audience. It is in this context that the Congress Party projected the image of Pt. Nehru, Indira Gandhi, Rajiv Gandhi and Sonia Gandhi and we find BJP projecting the image of Atal Bihari Vajapayee and L.K. Advani, Trinamul Congress projecting the image of Mamta Banerji, RJD projecting the image of Laloo Prasad Yadav and JDU in Bihar projecting the image of Nitish Kumar. Both the national as well as regional political parties get an opportunity to advertise through television. Of course, the cost factor limits frequent use of TV for political advertising, however all the political parties have been found using the same. We can't negate that for rural and illiterate segments, the TV establishes an edge over other media.

• **Broadcast Media and Political Advertising:** In view of the significant developments in the transmission technology, we find the percentage of users coming almost to one hundred. This makes the broadcast media considerably productive to the political parties and leaders because they find themselves in a position to reach to the target segment not covered by the telecast media. Irrespective of age, income, gender, race and other barriers, we find broadcast media instrumental in promoting almost all the segments. In addition, we find cost-effectiveness an important reason for its popularity. With the help of broadcast media, we find transmission of election speeches, slogans and messages. The organisation is also found transmitting the achievements of party and contributions of leaders with the help of broadcast media. This makes it essential that the political organisations make an optimal use of this medium. The significant developments in the field of transmission technology have made possible sensitivity and low-cost transistor sets are now also affordable to a majority of the population. The transmission is found effective even when the audience don't assemble at a particular place. To get the desired results from the broadcast media, it is essential that we take the support of professionals who prepare election speeches, compose advertisement slogans, present positive contributions and strategic development plans of the party. Since we find even the rival political parties promoting through broadcast media, it is your prime responsibility to make an in-depth study of their advertisement strategies so that necessary changes are incorporated to initiate and activate the process of qualitative transformation.

Political advertising is different from business advertising, the distortion in communication can't be negated. This necessitates careful representation of facts. The script is to be made short and the services of professionals are to be used for this purpose. The instrumentality of announcer while presenting facts plays an outstanding role because even creative speeches and slogans become ineffective if announcers lack communicative ability. This draws our attention on the professional excellence of an announcer. The voice becoming insistent irritates audience and therefore quality of audio becomes significant to increase the sensitivity of messages and slogans. Despite a number of limitations, the broadcast media may be effective in informing, sensing and persuading the masses, through the services of world-class professionals.

Political advertising needs due attention while composing the speeches, slogans and messages. The simplicity of language, use of regional languages, the sound of announcer, the way of presentation and the quality of technology used in the process require due weightage while making use of the broadcast media.

• **Print Media and Political Advertising:** We agree that of late print technology of world-class has changed the quality of results and therefore, the political organisations need to make use of the same on a priority basis. We find this medium cost-effective but very much instrumental in informing, sensing and persuading the masses. The presentation of posters, slogans, contributions, messages, facts and figures are found more impressive and lasting in the print technology. The new generation of print technology has, of course, increased its significance in almost all the areas.

The political organisations need to narrate their development and welfare-oriented programmes in different constituencies for different segments and for this purpose, we find print media incredibly effective. They can't be so informative and narrative while using the broadcast and telecast media because the available time is found very much limited. Since latest developments in the print technology have paved new avenues for adding attractions, the political parties and leaders even with a low-cost advertisement budget can be successful in informing, sensing and sensitising the masses. Because of the availability of space, they can also be analytical while presenting facts and figures. The photographs, graphs, trends and facts can be presented in a very receptive form. Here, it is also right to mention that high rate of illiteracy stands as a barrier because in the rural areas of country specially among illiterate segment only posters and photographs are found effective. Despite some of the barriers and limitations, we find print media significant even while making political advertisements.

The aforesaid facts make it clear that you have three alternatives and based on a number of considerations, the decisions are to be taken so that on the one hand, the political organisations succeed in informing, sensing and persuading the masses while on the other hand, they also find the process of promotion cost-effective. This draw our attention on strategic decisions related to media because while organising and managing a party, your decisions need to be professionalised failing which creativity and cost economy would not be possible. In Figure 18.2, we find the promotion mix for political organisation.

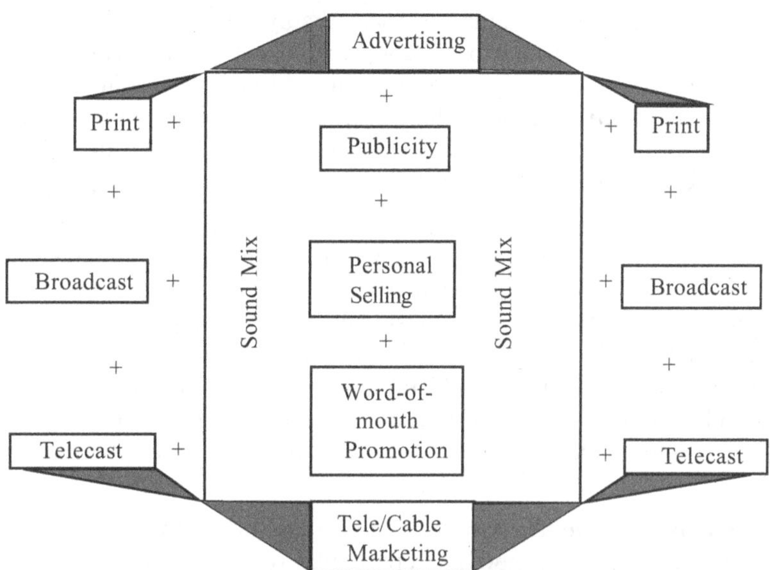

Fig. 18.2: Promotion Mix for Political Organisation

Figure 18.2 makes it clear that the political organisations need to assign due weightage to cost consideration. Since the telecast media would be expensive, they need to use it to transmit only important events and decisions. The rural and illiterate segments would find it effective and receptive. The broadcast media and print media are the two alternatives necessitating due share. Out of all, we find print media to be most effective and economic and therefore the political organisations except, in a very few selected cases, need to promote them to get the desired results. An optimal media mix is to be formulated which requires frequent reviewing and monitoring of the changing conditions.

MEDIA STRATEGY FOR POLITICAL ORGANISATION

Strategic decisions occupy a place of outstanding significance to get the desired results. Our plans and policies can't be practised in an effective fashion unless we formulate a sound media strategy. The political organisations also need to realise the increasing instrumentality of a strategy in achieving the mission. Your budget for advertisement and at the same time, the advertisement budget of the rival parties; the media mix formulated by you and that of your opponents; the usage, geographical allocation and scheduling of media are some of the important constituents of media strategy gravitating close attention of political parties failing which the processes of political communication can't be proactive and productive. It is against this background that we need an in-depth study of media strategy.

- **Formulating a time-honoured advertisement budget:** Of course, you need to promote and for this, advertisement coiling more creativity is essential but at the very outset, you need to think about advertisement budget. The budget of a party for all the constituencies and the same for a particular constituency need due attention so that constituency-wise requirements are studied and necessary provisions are made accordingly. It is not essential that advertisement budget for all the constituencies would be uniform and identical in financial or strategic terms. The regional conditions, situational requirements, intensity of competition generated by the rival parties, evolving changes are some of the considerations to be given due weightage. The new generation of communication technology also influences the size of the budget. The image of a party *vis-a-vis* the image of a leader becomes significant in the formulation of advertisement budget.

- **Designing an optimal media mix:** In the context of making strategic decisions, the designing of a media mix focuses our attention on the inclusion and representation of a particular medium keeping in view the regional and situational requirements. We are aware of the different types of media such as print media, broadcast media and telecast media. The main thing in the formulation of a mix is to fix the proportion or share of a particular medium in the face of reports received from the political information system. The involvement of cost and rate of sensitivity are the two important factors to be considered in the process of strategy formulation so that whatever the mix we develop serve the interests of a particular constituency as well as protects the interests of a party as a whole. It is quite natural that the sensitivity rate of telecast media establishes an edge over others but on account of high cost, it is not to be used frequently. Among the three alternatives, you have to make a choice and fix the share of each one so that advertisements are not only creative and sensitive but also cost-effective and attractive. The effectiveness of a particular medium is considerably influenced by the quality of persons living in a particular constituency or region. If we find a particular area, sizeably represented by the illiterate persons, the telecast media with audiovisual exposure facilities are to be sizeably effective. The print media would be more effective among the literate segment and broadcast media are to be effective in both the cases. The professionals on the basis of an in-depth study of different segments would formulate a media mix playing a positive role in informing, sensitising and transforming the masses in our favour.

- **Scheduling requires an intensive care:** In the process of formulating a sound strategy for media, we find scheduling significant which draws our attention on timing, duration, size, space with the prime motto of making the process cost-effective. If you transmit to broadcast or telecast media without scheduling, the advertisements would not only show a lukewarm response but would also prove to be cost ineffective. Your dedicated and personally-committed party workers and volunteers or professionals engaged by you for this purpose would let you know the feedback based on their in-depth studies. The professionals make the process of scheduling proactive and cost-effective and therefore you need to use their services on a priority basis. They can make a microscopic segmentation which would make scheduling action result-oriented and your party would considerably be benefited.

- **Geographic allocation is to be made:** Strategic decisions make it essential that you make the ways for geographic allocations which throws light on studying a particular segment in a particular region or constituency and understanding them in full length. Media strategists, in addition to other aspects, also need to think about the geography of the regions where the advertisement campaigns are to be launched, messages are to be conveyed, views are to be expressed, speeches are to be transmitted, posters are to be displayed, slogans are to be made public and so on. What would be the suitable region or constituency for print media and where the broadcasting media would be effective. The strategists would help the political organisations in many ways. The professionals may play the role of strategists.

In view of the above, it is right to say that political organisations need to promote advertisement very carefully. It is not only significant that you have a big budget and you spend huge amount for advertising. It is much more impact generating that your advertisement strategies are in the face of changing requirements. Earlier, we have talked about the formulation of a sound mix of advertisement. It is not to be forgotten that the nature and character of media mix would be governed by the intensity of competition generated by the rival political parties. Of late, we find electronics media increasing the instrumentality of advertisements but at the same time, the process is becoming more expensive. You have to strike a balance between the requirements and cost so that the advertisements succeed in persuading the masses but the process is not to make your budget disproportionate to your potentials. Since we are sizeably governed by the rural and illiterate segments, it is significant that our professionals while fixing proportion keep in their minds the magnitude of effects on the target audience or segment. The messages, slogans found effective among the urban and literate segments may or may not be effective among illiterate and rural segments. The slogans may be more effective among men but not so effective among women. Like this, the slogans may have a telling impact on grey but not on youths, kids and teens. While formulating strategies, you need to consider the intensity of sensitivity of the target segment and to incorporate necessary changes so that your messages are received in a right fashion.

Publicity: A form of persuasive communication for which you are not supposed to pay anything, in the marketing literature, is known as publicity. We consider it an effective tool of promotion provided the organisations make sincere, intelligent and tactful efforts to solicit the co-operation of media. Since we find the process considerably influenced by the relationships you maintain and develop with the media people, the political organisations and political leaders have been found making use of the same for sensitising and persuading the masses. It is a sharp-edged tool of promotion helping an organisation in many ways. If you perform satisfactorily, contribute substantially to the process of socio-economic transformation, act efficiently for maintaining social harmony and improving the quality of environment, promote national excellence and improve international relations; the media people project your achievements and the masses at large come to know about the same. When you advertise, your prime motto is to persuade the masses and even when you publicise, the motto remains the same with the only difference that for advertising you have to pay whereas for publicising you pay nothing. It is in this context that we find publicity requiring due attention of the political parties so that they succeed in persuading public even without increasing the financial burden.

In an age of relationship marketing, it is natural that publicity occupies a place of outstanding significance. Like other organisations, the political organisation also requires to have marketers professionally-sound for developing contacts with the media people. Occasionally, you invite them on lunch and dinner and offer to them small gifts, behave decently, assign to them due weightage and your task of influencing the voters and potential voters is considerably simplified. It is not a matter of favour or disfavour. It is not a matter of support or criticism. It is simply a matter of publicity based on facts and realities. The media people making a news item in favour of your party serve your interests fantastically. The professionals serving your organisation are supposed to have tact and ability of influencing the media people.

In the world of media, we find presentation and interpretation playing a very effective role. The reporting is an art, the actual presentation is a tact and the composition is a technique. The readers need to perceive in the same fashion as transmitted by the reporters or writers through newspapers and magazines. This would not be possible unless we find them writing with a positive attitude. The write-ups are considerably influenced by our attitudes. If we have a negative thinking, the write-ups would not be pro even if we find everything in your favour. This makes a strong advocacy in favour of an attitudinal change which requires an analogous change in your attitudes. Since you work for a party, it is but natural that you have everything positive in your mind. It is not essential that the media people would perceive in the same fashion as you perceive. We find psychologists making it clear that attitudes are substantially governed by behaviour. You perform excellently, contribute satisfactorily but don't assign any weightage to the media. The reporting may be in your favour but the presentation would not benefit you because we don't find anything special in the attitudes of media people. Thus, a political organisation needs to publicise and for this, they also need to create a position of a professionally-sound marketer who knows about the relationship marketing and makes sincere efforts to develop friendly relationships with the media people and manages everything in your favour as it is proved by Mr. Nitish Kumar, C.M. Bihar whose media management has been very productive where he succeeded in getting the unexpected results in 2010 Assembly Election.

Personal Selling: As a tool of promotion, we find personal selling helping political parties in motivating the voters and potential voters. The members of a party working in different capacities at different levels of an organisation promote the activities so that the masses come to know about their efforts to develop a particular region or a constituency. Right from the top of an organisation to the bottom, the selected party members, workers having a high communicative ability and skill to influence the masses are to be engaged in the process. They prepare informative and thoughtful speeches related to their contributions and at public places organise a meeting where persons from different walks of life assemble. As and when we find special occasions, such as convassing for elections, door-to-door campaigns for motivation, clarification of misunderstanding and confusions; the party workers and members not only act as communicators but also as motivators. A party having popular mass leaders finds it an effective device to promote the party affairs. Since we find quality of communications playing an impact-generating role, it is significant that party organisation selects person having a high communicative ability and also organises education and training programmes to enrich the process of communication. In the management of a political party, we find style of communication significant because here the events are dramatised and with the help of body language, the speeches are made interesting and effective. The communicative ability of Pt. Nehru and Atal Bihari Vajapayee and dramatising of events by Laloo Prasad Yadav have been found motivating masses. The presentation of facts, use of body language, use of proverbs and stories in tune with the taste and temperament of audience help a speaker in mobilising the masses.

We find personal selling making an outstanding contribution to the process of mobilising and motivating the masses. Even the negatives are transformed into positives, if we find speakers bearing the efficacy of dramatising the events. It is in this context that the political organisation needs to promote with the help of a few selected members of the party because all of us would not be in a position to communicate effectively. The oratorical art of an individual is, of course, a natural gift but can also be cultivated with the help of education and training and to the extent it is possible, the party organisation needs to make sincere efforts to inculcate the same.

In addition to the participation of party members and workers, an organisation may also use the services of social reformists for this purpose. The expression of a party member in a very natural way would be pro to its party and therefore the intensity of impact may or may not be high. If we find a popular social leader or reformist advocating for you and your party, there we find more scope for mobilisation. It is against this background that we find political parties using the expertise and skill of cine artists and national cricketers. They have a mass image and a natural capacity to attract the masses. We find a craze for them making it easier to collect people. If JP started speaking in favour of United Front, it was his image as a mass social leader that helped the United Front in getting a success. Of late, we find almost all the political parties tapping the potentials of cine stars. The main thing in the process is to invite a leader coming from different walks of life to speak in your favour and helping the party in the mobilisation process. The party organisation needs to design a network which could be used on special occasions.

Word-of-mouth Promotion: If you concentrate on your service profile and keep on moving the process of innovating the quality of services of your party in the government or outside; the users or others become promoter because they transmit words of appreciation to their friends and relations which ultimately help your parties in getting and retaining wider support. The process is known as word-of-mouth promotion which in the world of marketing is found to be the most effective tool benefiting you substantially but taxing you nothing. In almost all the organisations, the word-of-mouth promotion has proved its instrumentality and specially in the service-generating organisations, we find this tool of promotion occupying a place of outstanding significance because the services of intangible nature don't provide to the users an opportunity to testify or ascertain their quality unless and until they themselves use, realise and confirm. It is against this background that we make a strong advocacy in favour of word-of-mouth promotion which is found based on the quality of the service profile of your party. It is not to be forgotten that this tool of promotion is not to be effective if we find a gap between the quality-promised and the quality-offered and therefore distortion at any stage is to harm your party significantly. Generally, we find channels working at different stages or levels bearing the responsibility of improving or distorting the quality and this makes it essential that you while organising the party assign due weightage to the management of channel and people who may be party members, workers, volunteers and even anti-social elements.

We find word-of-mouth promoters acting as a hidden salesforce and therefore your prime responsibility is to make possible qualitative-cum-quantitative transformation in your service profile. The projects having welfare orientation are to be made innovative and the political information system is to be assigned the responsibility of making it sure that the services offered by your party establish an edge over the services of rival parties. It is to be made sure that the programmes liberal to the development of regions or constituencies reach to the target/ destination without any distortion and that would not be possible unless you have a team of dedicated and committed people who are considerably influenced by the process of value orientation.

Your prime responsibility is to make it possible to increase the number and quality of the party members and volunteers because in a majority of the services, party people are found very much instrumental in distorting the quality of services. With a technology-driven information system, your task of initiating and activating the process of qualitative transformation will considerably be simplified. Increasing the number of word-of-mouth promoters needs an analogous increase in the quality of your service profile. In this context, you have to synchronise core and peripheral services optimally. Also you have to be innovative and the political information system can help you in the process. You can utilise the service of social leaders, social activists and reformists for that very purpose and if they are satisfied with the contributions of your party, they will promote your party and the process will be effective as the masses trust their words unquestionably.

Telemarketing: In an age of technology, we find everything influenced by techniculture because in terms of speed, quality and innovation thus the new generation of technology makes your task easier. With innovative developments in the communication and information technology, we find their large-scale uses in marketing. We agree with this view that the political parties would substantially be benefited while promoting their cause because they would be in a position to telecast their contributions to the society in a very effective way. The communication technology and television are found directly involved in the process in which telemarketers while presenting achievements, messages, slogans, grievances and their redressal make efforts to increase the awareness of the masses. Since we find satellite communication playing a major role in improving the quality and coverage, the telemarketing has emerged and would continue to develop and grow as an effective way of promoting the business either for making profits or for subserving the social interests. It is against this background that we find almost all the organisations using telemarketing and even the political organisations can make a significant use of the same to promote the party.

The two important wings, telemarketing and cable marketing help political leaders and their parties in enriching the awareness among the public by improving the quality of transmission. Even in the remotest parts of the country where transmission facilities are found obstructed, the satellite communication has paved new vistas for cable marketing. It is right to mention that in the process not only the communication technology but even the services of professionals are used and with the co-ordination, co-operation and interaction of the two, we find transmission of messages to the masses. Of late, we have witnessed a number of qualitative improvements in the communication technology and recently the information technology has also been given due weightage. The telemarketing even in the coming years and decades would continue to play the role of a promoter which is found to benefit the political organisation in many ways.

The quality of technology and people play a decisive role in the transmission process and this makes it essential that we make concerted efforts to improve their quality. The management of technology makes it essential that we maintain and operate them in tune with the literature and educate and train people to deliver the best they can. This draws our attention on the communicative ability of telemarketers who with their effective and interest-generating communications enrich the quality of outputs. Since we talk about the technology-driven political information system, it is pertinent that both the aspects coordinate each other because the latest information regarding the performance of a party would be made available by the system. To be more specific while managing election and important party affairs, we find telemarketing very much instrumental in increasing mass awareness and it is in this context that in the developed countries of the world, we find more emphasis on this specially while managing the election activities. In the Indian context, the political organisation has been found evincing interest but presently it is at nascent stage that requires due attention of the party leaders making policy decisions. If you perform honestly, sincerely and efficiently; you have a legitimate right of making it public by promoting your contributions and we find telemarketing a sharp-edged tool proving its instrumentality in the process. But you need to formulate a sound mix of all the components and to fix the proportion of each one in the face of potentials and requirements.

MANAGING FEE AND MOBILISATION OF RESOURCES

In the Indian perspective, the political parties suffer a lot on account of poor fund position and mismanagement of fund. We do not find provision for government grants to the political parties even for managing elections. In the developed countries of the globe, an organised effort is made for the membership drive which helps them in creating a fund. Besides, we also find provision for grants which help them in managing their day-to-day activities. The conceptualisation of marketing principles in the political organisations is also with the motto of improving their financial position but in a fair way. Improving the financial health of political parties to enable them to serve the society in different ways requires multi-faceted efforts.

Membership drive is considered to be the most important dimension for resource mobilisation. The process of increasing membership drive can considerably be increased with the support of marketing professionals. It is also significant to mention that the concept of marketing initially when practised in the USA was with the prime motto of increasing the membership drive and at the later stage, it was implemented for managing the election affairs. In the USA, even the Churches have conceptualised marketing for increasing the membership. This makes a strong advocacy in favour of professionalised efforts for the membership drive by the political parties so that they succeed in increasing the membership. It is not meant that they initiate fake drive for increasing membership. If they are fair in enrolling the members, the task of getting their support would also be made easier. Besides, this will help political parties in improving their financial position. Influencing potential members needs due focus on political communication in which the professionals will throw light on the contributions and ideologies of the party for which they are working.

The political parties have also been found getting charities and donations from different individuals and organisations. In the Indian context, we find it emerging as an important source for resource mobilisation but we also find cases where political parties misuse their power and force or persuade the business houses or industrial organisations for hidden donations and charities. In a true sense, we find it turning as a sore-spot in the resource mobilisation process and creating a vicious circle. The business houses or industrial organisations extending financial help to the political parties expect undue favour from them and this proves to be a base for corruption. We cannot negate that this helps creation of a vicious circle affecting the national economy in an adverse way. Of course, we cannot check an individual or an institution for extending financial help to the political parties but at the same time, we cannot allow the hidden charities and donations both at individual and organisational levels.

The provision for grants by the government is a matter of policy decision on which we can deliberate upon at different levels and in different legislative houses but the most important thing is regulating the election expenses.

CHANNELISATION OF SERVICES IN POLITICAL ORGANISATION

You make efforts to generate; you make sincere efforts to innovate and therefore you promise the best quality of services to the masses either as a regulator or as a promoter. In this context, you also bear the responsibility of making it sure that whatever the quality you promise to the masses reach to them on time without making any distortion. The gap is bridged, the behaviour is decent and the quality is maintained. Since you act as a policy maker, you, in the capacity of opposition also act as a regulator and here, it is your prime responsibility to make it sure that right from the top to the bottom all the members, workers and volunteers working at different levels make the process time-honoured *vis-a-vis* cost-effective. The party organisation at national, regional, local levels are careful about the processes adopted by the operational apparatus while implementing the programmes and policies of government or a party or of any organisation and agency. This makes it essential that we assign due weightage to the channelisation of services.

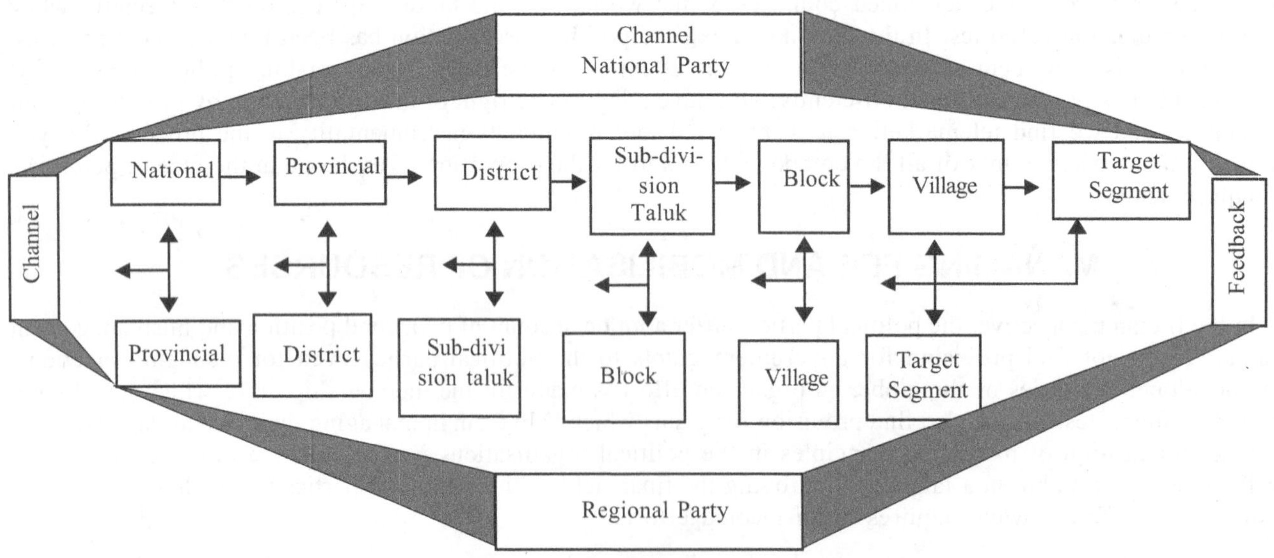

Fig. 18.3: Channelisation of Services in Political Organisation

A national party crosses bigger channels whereas a regional party crosses relatively smaller channels. In Figure 18.3, we find channel management in both the cases. Since the party organisation has to know about the implementation process, emerging problems in a particular constituency, feedback of masses regarding the programmes and policies, grievances related to implementation and unfair or unlawful practices, the strategic decisions of the rival parties and the management of channel need great attention.

In Figure 18.3, the channelisation of services focuses on two different categories of political party, viz., national and regional. In the face of a difference that we find in the functional areas and responsibilities, the national parties bear the responsibility of developing a network for the offering of services so that they succeed in promoting and regulating the norms and provisions.

A political party having national status and acting for promoting and protecting the interests of government requires a well-regulated channel with quality people. Right from the top to the bottom, they need to be vigilant so that they not only make possible effective utilisation of the policies and programmes of government but also set examples to the opposition. Because we find opposition party all the time active in identifying the lapses and shortcomings active in tarnishing the image of your leaders and party, it is significant that your people working as members, workers, volunteers, agents and contractors responsible for the implementation of policies and programmes don't provide to them an opportunity. Of late, the Panchayat Raj System has been given due weightage and therefore, the development or welfare programmes need to have a direct link particularly when we find the same for the rural areas of the country.

The government administration, the party people and the agencies for implementation have to develop a network. The programmes are allocated for a particular region or a constituency, rural or urban areas, weaker sections, women, children and in a majority of the cases, we find lapses generated by the dishonest and unfair people working for the party. If we find political party interested in keeping or maintaining a fair image, the only solution is to formulate an organisational structure with the help of dedicated, committed and value-based party people at different levels of the organisation.

A political party having regional status has to cross through smaller channels. Even in that case, we find instrumentality of party people. They, working at district, subdivision, block and village levels, have to remove the constraints in the implementation of policies and programmes of government. If they represent the opposition side, they have to identify lapses and shortcomings in the implementation process so that they are in a position to capitalise on the opportunities. Particularly at village level, they need to be more careful because the progammes of government or party fail to reach to the concerned segments mainly on account of the negligence of government administration and the party workers.

Thus, the important channels are found at national level, provincial level, district level, subdivision/taluka level, block level and village level. When we talk about the regional parties, the channels start from the provincal level. Since we find channels in both the categories responsible for the development of society, the party organisation is supposed to play an important role. They have to develop a network for collecting information so that on the basis of feedback and they receive from the different segments, the lapses, shortcomings, loopholes, grievances, complaints are redressed and the task of implementation is made proactive.

As and when we find a gap in the channelisation of services, the programmes or policies of party and government fail in reaching to the target segments. This creates a gap and the image of your party is considerably tarnished. It is really very amazing and painful that specially in the Indian context, the party organisation has not been successful in simplifying the task of implementation rather than in a majority of the cases, we find party people involved in promoting corruption. This in a very natural way gravitates our attention on the management of party people. The numerical strength of a party is not the only thing when we find something wrong with its quality. The party workers are there; volunteers are there, members are there but when a majority of them become instrumental in strengthening the unfair practices; the social systems start collapsing.

LOCATION POINT FOR POLITICAL PARTY OFFICE

Accessibility coiling smoothness attracts masses. Since you have to attract the public particularly to the different offices of your party, specially on occasions like election, convention, opinion survey, party meetings, and organisational activities, it is necessary that the location points of your party office is convenient to them. The availability of all-weatherproof roads, round-the-clock transportation and communication services, safety and security, supporting infrastructural facilities are some of the important features requiring your immediate attention. If the party office generates a number of problems to the workers, members, volunteers and visitors coming to the party office, you will fail in initiating co-ordination and soliciting co-operation. While marketing politics in addition to other submixes, we also need to plan for location of party offices at almost all the levels of organisation and administration.

It is essential to mention that in the Indian context, the party organisation has not been sincere to this problem which has made their task of interaction and inter- and intra-coordination very complicated. A communication gap develops and generates misunderstanding and confusion in the entire process. Irrespective of the fact that they belong to the ruling or opposition side, it becomes significant to give due weightage to the location and establishment of party offices. In this context, it is important that you think about the infrastructural facilities and the quality of people placed there. Earlier, we have talked about some of the attributes and traits required to be inculcated among the party people in which high behavioural profile of party members and workers was given top priority. While managing party offices, you need to place people having high behavioural profile. They should have the sympathy and empathy so that the problems, queries, information and grievances are noted and transmitted to the information system and redressal measures are initiated.We also find cases where the party workers managing offices have been indecent and have also irritated the visitors coming to them.

The sound management of party office would benefit the party organisation in many ways. The feedback would be received from different segments and constituencies. The reports related to opinion poll and survey would also be managed and regulated properly. The organisational activities would be made action and result-oriented. The communication gap would be bridged and policy and strategic decisions of party would be proactive.

We have also talked about telemarketing in the marketing of politics. Here, it is important to mention that party office is an important place for them from where the party activities can be energised. If we find management of party office sound, the coordination would be possible and particularly while managing, framing and regulating the election work and other development and welfare activities, the party organisation would be found successful in monitoring and controlling. The organisation of party meetings, transmission of information, collection of facts and figures are some of the key issues depending on the sound management of the party office. The party organisation at the top, middle and bottom levels of management needs to think over the problem on a priority basis.

Physical Evidence and Attractions: The formulation of this submix for the political organisations draws our attention on tangibilisation of outstanding features of the party for impressing upon the members and potential members visiting the offices of political parties. The political organisations need a distinct image focusing on their contributions to the process of social transformation. The ideologies of parties and their role as ruling or opposition need to be displayed at a place attracting attention of visitors and members or others. Besides, they also need to display the action plan of their parties so that members or others coming there develop their awareness of the prospects of the parties in the coming days. The image of noted leaders of the party also needs to be tangibilised. The newspapers, newsletters, brochures, leaflets, posters of the party cannot be overlooked for the projection of image. For the political organisation, the ambient conditions need focus on social orientation. Today in an age of sophisticated information and communication technology, the professionals managing the affairs need to tangibilise the flow of activities and transmission of information so that members and potential members are convinced that they have a well-connected communication network. The service fragrance here needs social image of political parties and their leaders. We find offices of political parties an important place for the delivery of services resulting from an interaction between the front-line staff and the members or visitors. The people working there need to be an excellent communicator showing professionalised approach and personal touch. They need to transmit a strong message to the visiting persons magnifying the objectives and ideologies of the party. Actually, this happens to be a suitable place for them for strengthening the perception of visitors. Particularly in the head offices where we find a good number of people visiting the offices, the signposts may be used for the convenience of visitors. The offices of political parties need to play an important role especially during the season. The publication and display of election manifesto need due co-operation of professionals.

The physical attractions for political leaders and professionals or others working in the offices of political parties need to focus on simplicity. They should, of course, look neat and clean but should not give a negative impression to the public visiting the offices. Simplicity in the dresses of employees working there and decency in their behavioural profile are some of the basics helping political parties in the projection of a positive image. The displays in the offices need due attention on the donations received and amount spent for protecting and promoting social interests.

The above-mentioned facts make it clear that marketing professionals working for a political party need a different approach in the tangibilisation process helping them in establishing an edge over the rival parties. The people coming there should be efficacious of developing the perception and strengthening their realisation that the party they are likely to join is number one.

The Process Mix

The political parties offer the services through their members and volunteers to the public and in the process, we find front-line staff and information and communication technology playing an important role. The development and welfare programmes of political parties are processed with the help and co-operation of different levels of management and ultimately reach to the regions or constituencies for which the services have been processed. The ruling as well as the opposition parties need to make it sure that their workers, volunteers, office bearers and members show conviction and generate a sense of confidence and trust. At an apex level, the promises are made by the political parties or their concerned leaders and if the promises are not processed in a right way, this will make the task of parties and their leaders much more difficult *vis-à-vis* will create an image problem. Today, we find new generation of information and communication technology to simplify the processing of services and therefore the office bearers are supposed to play a very positive role in order that the services are delivered to the target audience or public without any delay and distortion.

The processing of services focuses our attention on the flow of communication and services. The target public to whom the services are to be delivered need to be informed the progress and the expected gap between the services-promised and services to be delivered. The office bearers or the professionals managing the affairs need to consider the actual procedures, mechanism and flow which can be speeded up with the use of new generation of information and communication technology. We cannot negate that the services rendered by the political leaders or their parties cross a number of stages and therefore we find them of complex nature leaving scope for taking much more time for delivery. We also find cases where the services are found related to the government administration and therefore, the processing takes much more time.

Professionalised efforts and new generation of information and communication technology with the help and co-operation of dedicated and committed volunteers may be successful in minimising the time gap in the service delivery process. The political leaders before making promises need to be sure that they will be active in minimising the duration for increasing the flow with the co-operation of government administration. Time-honoured and promised quality of services if delivered to the target regions or public without any distortion and with personal touch simplify the tangibilisation process thenth the political parties find themselves in a position to display their sincere and honest efforts for service delivery.

Thus, this submix marketing needs due attention of political parties evincing interests in conceptualising the marketing principles. The techno-driven processing, time-honoured processing and behaviourally-sound processing help political parties in fulfilling their promises.

MANAGING THE PARTY PEOPLE

The existence and development of a political party is sizeably influenced by the contributions of party people working in different capacities at different levels of an organisation. We find some of them acting as party members, some of them as party workers and some of them as volunteers. In the organisation of a political party, we find different office bearers at different levels responsible for the implementation of the development programmes. It is not only sufficient that you formulate an ideal plan, constitute a team of professionals, involve party members and volunteers and make yourself sure that everything is going on smoothly and efficiently. This draws our attention on the quality of people involved in the entire process. The focus is on quality because we have witnessed a number of cases in which the party people have been involved in promoting unfair and unlawful practices. Efficiency and professionalism can't be tantamount of ethics. The party people may be sincere, efficient and punctual but if they don't perceive ethics and fail in developing the same in their personality, the results would either be negative or lukewarm. They need people who serve more but expect nothing. A party without dedicated, personally-committed and value-based people can't protect its existence, then what to talk about the progress and prosperity. Professionalism develops the potentials of increasing efficiency but in absence of virtues, ethics and values we find unproductive results. It is against this background that we make a strong advocacy in favour of developing quality people.

The quality people thus need three properties or traits, e.g., they need to be efficient which is possible when they are well educated and trained; they need to be personally-committed but it is possible when training programmes have been successful in transforming them as professionals showing personal-touch-in-service and the most important one, they need to be value-based which would not be possible unless we have recruited and selected people in the face of their family background. Unless we find pursuits or development faculties, the education and training programmes would prove to be failure. While enrolling members, nominating or electing party office bearers, selecting volunteers, you have to make it sure that the inculcation of potentials is done on a priority basis.

The party organisation bears the responsibility of developing a team in which we find team culture. There are a number of cases where the party organisation has nominated or selected people having a disputed or unfair image. The task of party members, workers and volunteers would be much more complicated when we find them advocating and canvassing for a person earning a bad name. Electioneering, channelisation of development and welfare facilities, countering the harmful effects of natural calamities, mobilisation of funds for the party, protecting the interests of neglected women and children are some of the sensitive issues found very much instrumental both way. If you work sincerely and honestly, the opportunities are in your favour for earning a good name and projecting a positive image. Conversely, if you work and promote unfair and unethical practices, the opportunities are again in your favour but not for you rather than in favour of the rival political parties. This necessitates concerted efforts, dedicated efforts, personally-committed and value-based approaches to develop quality people helping political parties and their leaders in many ways.

In the Indian context, we find a number of voluntary organisations and a few of them have also played a bigger role in the development of party. Almost all the political parties have been found making efforts to increase their numerical strength but we find a very few of them considering about quality. This is mainly due to the fact that often they play a negative role and even the positive contributions of a political party fail in the projection of a fair image which can be capitalised on. This gravitates our attention on the selection of volunteers, imparting of education and training facilities to them and inculcation of virtues and values which till now has not been given due place. We can't negate the contributions of Shiv Sena, RSS and Seva Dal to the development of Bharatiya Janata Party (BJP). Development of Student's Wing, Women's Wing also constitute a place of outstanding significance and we find almost all the political parties in the Indian context taking advantages of their contributions in different ways. It is right to mention that organisation of volunteers, party workers and members require due attention because failing it, we can't expect positive results. The management of party workers is thus found to be an important problem of political marketing and communication. It is high time that the political parties realise the instrumentality of people in the organisation and management of a party failing which their task of manufacturing of image and its effective projection would remain unfulfilled. It is in this context that we go through different dimensions of development of people for the political parties.

Selection, Nomination and Enrolment: Unless you have quality inputs, the education and training facilities offered to the party workers and members would not be productive. The political parties often commit mistakes and even blunders while selecting, nominating and enrolling members and volunteers which make their task of development of committed groups of people much more difficult. The team culture is not nurtured properly that creates problems while managing them. The transformation process can't be effective unless we start the process from the initial stage of selection. The party workers and volunteers need some of the traits or attributes on a priority basis, such as dedication and commitment, virtues and ethics, humanity and punctuality, sensibility and communicative ability, sincerity and honesty. At the first stage, we need to make it sure that the people to be selected have aptitudes related to the political track so that with the help of education and training facilities, they find it easier to brush up and develop. An in-depth study of population of different regions and constituencies would simplify the selection process. The prime focus is to be on pursuits, faculties, aptitudes and while switching on the selection process, you need to select people having these attributes without which the transformation process can't be effective.

Education and Training: Since we find education and training facilities very much instrumental in the development of people in different areas, the political parties also need to strengthen their training programme. The important functional responsibilities like electioneering, informing, sensing, sensitising, persuading and transforming would be discharged by them and therefore it is pertinent that workers and volunteers are educationally, professionally, ethically and potentially sound. We find training an ongoing process because the evolving changes in different areas require reforms and explosive innovations in the process or style of training facilities. While educating people, it is also essential that we sound them, particularly in the areas of informal education because a majority of the population even though educationally sound lack civic sense, aesthetic sense and traffic sense. The value orientation is also found to be significant and the trainers need to do it on a priority basis. The properties like honesty and integrity gravitate close attention of the political organisations.

Motivation: Though we don't find it right to offer to the party workers and volunteers financial incentives because this may promote unfair and unlawful practices, however to motivate them to deliver goods, the offering of a position in the organisation based on their credentials and contributions can't claimed to be irrational. The dedicated and personally-committed party workers and volunteers showing their worth-while managing election or other party workings, generating and mobilising funds for the party in a fair way, channelising welfare facilities, generating mass awareness need to be promoted so that others get a lesson and make sincere and honest efforts to develop.

Monitoring, Evaluation and Control: While managing volunteers and workers, you assign to them some responsibilities to be discharged within the time-frame and if they do it successfully, you can't and should not deny to them the promotional incentives. While monitoring individuals, groups and teams, you get an opportunity to rate their training and development programme meant for them. The target of an individual, a team or a group is to be fixed and after the completion of stipulated time; the results are to be reviewed. The groups, teams and individuals performing excellently need to be given an opportunity to discharge key or even critical responsibilities.

The above motives to develop people would help the political organisation in improving the quality of people. Because you have to counter the threats and challenges generated by the rival parties, it is pertinent that you keep on moving the process of protecting public interests, excelling the rival parties, projecting a fair image of the party and winning elections. Your people need a number of attributes that would be determined by the changing conditions in the political environment. You have to be imaginative and innovative so that whatever the policy and strategic decisions you formulate for the development of your party are practised in a right fashion. Your prime goal is to subserve social interests and this makes it essential that you keep on moving the process of adding attractions to the multi-dimensional personality of people engaged or to be engaged. Your party workers and members need to enrich their behavioural profile. They need not only sympathy but even empathy to win the heart of masses. They need to be ethically-sound so that whatever they speak throw some positive impact on the target segment. We can't negate that ultimately it is quality of people serving the party who determine the intensity of your success. In the society where process of multi-faceted degeneration has been found growing, it is significant that policies and strategies become instrumental in reversing the trend.

STRATEGIC MARKETING IN POLITICS

Environmental conditions considerably influence our policy and strategic decisions. Since we find change a natural phenomenon, the political environment also witnesses multi-dimensional changes. With a change in the social set up, economic conditions, generation of technology, cultural and behavioural patterns, we find the political environment sizeably affected. If the policy makers and strategists don't receive the evolving changes on time, whatever the decisions they make would not show the desired impact. An attitudinal change in the different segments of the society becomes the focal point when we talk about strategic decisions related to the marketing in politics. The drama of marketing in politics is considerably related to the transformation process in which the potential voters are transformed into the actual voters. With the passage of time, we find a change in the process of obtaining results because the voters of today become the non-voters of tomorrow and potential voters of yesterday become the voters of today. The political organisation needs to intensify its marketing efforts so that the voters are transformed into the habitual voters and the political voters and even non-voters are transformed into voters so that the election results are found in your favour.

You have already gone through the development of a technology-driven political information system and while formulating strategies your network should be efficacious of helping you in getting the right information regarding the emerging trends, changing attitudes and mounting competition. You need a well-developed information system and professionally-sound people to manage the same so that whatever the innovations you are likely to make remain secret till the last moment. You have to make it sure that the researchers, workers, volunteers of your party placed in different constituencies for collecting facts and figures or data are sincere and honest and value-oriented. Whatever the problems you face, information you get and solutions you need should be in the knowledge of system analysts so that they make available to you the desired information on time.

A constituency is found classified into different segments and the expectations of all of them can't be uniform or identical. On the one hand, you need to plan for the development of society while on the other hand, also need to develop the constituency you represent. Understanding the people of different segments in a constituency is found problematic but the information system would simplify your task. It is essential that you assign due weightage to the kids, teens and youths dominating the decision-making practices of their families. The management of election affairs is an important functional responsibility of a political party and even in this context, segments like women, youths and teens may offer to you enormous co-operation provided they feel that your party and you as a candidate would assign number one priority to their problems. If you act sincerely and understand the changing behavioural profile of different segments, the results are likely to be in your favour.

Since we talk about marketing in politics, it is pertinent that you show your excellence while formulating a sound marketing mix. This draws your attention on the different submixes. The service mix or service profile needs frequent innovation and a fair synchronisation of core and peripheral services. You act in the capacity of a policy maker and this makes you accountable to monitor and supervise the development and welfare programmes of government. You also act as an opposition and this makes you responsible to identify the lapses and shortcomings in the implementation process. The core services draw your attention on fulfilling the essential requirements of your constituency such as the civic amenities, infrastructural facilities and basic needs of society.

The peripheral services divert your attention on the supporting needs of the society, such as ecological balance, pollution of environment, recreational facilities, sports activities, nutritional awareness, healthcare, informal education to develop civic sense, promotion of vaccination culture, social and communal harmony, national excellence and many others to be instrumental in the development of society. The various components of core and peripheral services would be influenced and governed by situational requirements and changing conditions. The peripheral services of yesterday may be core services of today and therefore the innovation process is to be given due weightage and for this, you need enormous co-operation of the information system. You need to remember that ultimately the quality of service mix would help you in the process of image projection. The strategic decisions related to the service mix make it essential that you are aware of the evolving changes and offer the best to the society.

Since you offer quality and value-based services to the society, your right of channelising promotion can't be denied and for this purpose, you again need to formulate a sound promotion mix in which different constituents are to get the required share. You need to formulate a budget for promotion and because you have financial problems, the constituents found expensive in nature require a regulated use. In the face of behaviour of target audience and nature of changing conditions, you have to fix the share of a particular constituent. You need to advertise but in a creative fashion so that your messages, slogans, campaigns prove to be productive. Your professional excellence is coiled in the essence of assigning due weightage to publicity because for this, you don't pay anything. You need to develop relationships with the media people and to motivate them to write in your favour. They can turn things in your favour and make possible an attitudinal change in the masses, if they extend to your party the best co-operation that you need. Besides, you have also to think about other constituents of promotion. Personal selling would help you while motivating the voters and potential voters but you need to enrich your communicative ability. In an age of communication technology, you have also to think about its instrumentality in the transmission process. If you serve well, the masses come to know about your positive contributions to the development process and your friends, voters, social leaders, reformists and activists help you as a hidden salesforce. The word-of-mouth promotion thus helps you in the process of promotion. The telemarketing or cable marketing would also be effective and you have to assign due weightage to the same.

The mobilisation of membership fee, charities and donations become essential to make the political parties financially-sound to deliver goods to the society. The membership drive is, no doubt, an important aspect and the professionals may help you in the process. In addition, they also need to motive the donors and potential donors related to both individual and institutional segments. If the donors and potential donors witness that your party has been moving in the right directions and the persuasion process would be found proactive. In the name of cause-related marketing, the political parties may activate the process of social transformation by involving their parties in protecting and promoting the interests of victims of natural calamities or even war victims. You need to tap the potentials available in your segment or constituency and this helps identification of potential donors. With the help of a sound political communication system, you may be successful in transforming the potential donors into actual donors and further even in impressing upon the actual donors that their donations are used for productive purposes.

The processing of services should maintain and speed up the operational mechanism. The new generation of information and communication technology would help them in the transmission process. The front line-staff while processing need to make it sure that promised quality of services are delivered to the concerned segment or constituency on time. The political leaders need to assign due weightage to simplicity specially when we talk about dresses to be used by them. You should not forget that expensive dresses may tarnish your personal image *vis-à-vis* image of your party. We need to remember Kautilya who preferred simplicity and stayed in a cottage. He opined that if Ministers start living in palaces, the citizens have no option but to live in cottages. Conversely, if they live in cottages, the public get an opportunity to live in palaces. It is unfortunate that presently we find an adverse scenario. The political leaders lead comfortable and luxurious lifestyles from where and how, it is needless to explain.

The professionals serving the political organisations bear the responsibility of developing a brigade of dedicated volunteers and workers to be effective in delivering goods to the society. This necessitates training facilities by the professionals. Keeping in view the regional considerations, the potentials of party workers and volunteers are to be developed. In a majority of the cases, we find political parties facing image problem mainly on account of their workers and volunteers who lack sincerity and honesty. In the Indian context, we find almost all the political parties facing the image problem. Hence, the most important task before professionals is to develop the communication system and to constitute a team of like-minded persons working with a sense of conviction and commitment. The political leaders are found much more liberal while making promises but not so sincere while fulfilling the same. This draws our priority attention on promising less but offering more.

The experiences of past testify that in a majority of the cases, the political parties have failed in bridging the gap between services-promised and services-offered mainly due to the slackness and non-cooperation of the party people. This in a very natural way necessitates multi-dimensional improvements in the quality of people made responsible for offering the services to the target segments. You are supposed to set examples and if masses witness that you are directly or indirectly involved in the process of promoting unfair and unlawful practices, the marketing would not help you getting the desired results. The government policy makers, the party organisation, the election commission and judiciary need to think over the problem on a priority basis. You need to involve quality people, value-based people, professionally-sound people, personally-committed people at the location points for your party office. Smooth and convenient accessibility, safe and secured location, infrastructurally-sound location, healthy and environment-friendly location would be instrumental in promoting your organisation in an effective way.

There are a number of occasions when a large number of people assemble, such as organisation of party meeting, election campaigns, opinion poll, monitoring and supervision of organisational activities and if we find something wrong with the location points, your task would be made much more complicated. In view of the above, it is right to mention that in the Indian environment, political marketing would gain popularity in the days and years to come. Because we find rival parties, national and regional, instrumental in increasing the intensity of competition, masses becoming more conscious, innovative communication and information technology playing a significant role in the transmission process, unlawful and unfair practices becoming common, value-based people becoming indifferent to the political activities and forming a negative opinion about politics and the political leaders, it is high time that political parties think over the problem on a priority basis. Commercialisation or merchandising has been continuing since long in the political environment of India which would create a vicious circle that would pollute and degenerate everything. The political parties need an attitudinal change. The educational institutions bearing the responsibility of developing political leaders, political parties instrumental in promoting the masses voting for a candidate, office bearers working in different capacities in the party organisation need to promote values and virtues in the Indian political environment so that the process of degeneration is reversed.

Ultimately, we find society responsible for everything. Governmental regulations may be ineffective, regulations and codes of political parties may be ineffective and unproductive, acts and laws may also be insensitive but the social regulations can't be ineffective. This makes it essential that in the political environment of India to bring the political systems on the rail, the diverse sections of society come forward and take a lead to regulate the increasing unlawful and unfair practices in politics failing which the social systems would collapse. Let's hope that professionally-sound people, personally-committed people and value-based people evince keen interests in politics. Let's hope that they are considerably influenced by the holistic concept of management and conceptualise and practise social marketing.[17]

POLITICAL MARKETING IN INDIAN PERSPECTIVE

Politics without ethics; politics without professional excellence and politics without social orientation become very much instrumental in garboiling the social system.[18] The political leaders of India need to remember Kautilya who is considered as a political guru and his ideologies helped multi-faceted transformation in the kingdom of Mauraya Chandragupta and at the same time, his strategic decisions resulted into the downfall of the Nanda Kingdom. The moment you join politics you need a transformation in your nature, behaviour, character and personality so that you prove to be a mass leader and people witness transformation of Vishnugupta into Kautilya.

With the passage of time, the contours of development have undergone radical changes. The organisations generating services of critical nature should be financially-sound to achieve their objectives of serving and subserving social interest. They also need managerial proficiency to improve the quality of services and satisfy the users. In the group of non-profit organisations, we also talk about political organisation since without their commitments to the society, the process of social transformation would move in the reverse gear. It is on account of development-oriented and welfare-sensitive policy of a government that the process of socio-economic transformation starts going forward. The political parties have to mobilise funds for which they depend on the donors. Influencing the donor for getting donations is also an important functional responsibility of the professionals making a case for the donors and potential donors. Magnifying the positive contributions of the party to the development of the constituency requires professional excellence. Informing and sensitising the voters and potential voters can be sucessfully done, if the political parties make use of the services of marketing professionals. Besides, the management of election affairs, designing and preparing the posters and cut-outs, slogans and messages, organising and conducting opinion polls and surveys to assess the performance of party workers and volunteers are a few of the functional responsibilities needing due attention of professionals.

It is against this background, that developed countries are conceptualising and practising modern marketing principles and they have also been successful in accomplishing the organisational goals. In the Indian context, the process is on but the development is at the very nascent stage. Even now, a majority of the political leaders have not realised the instrumentality of marketing in getting the desired result. Of course, late Rajiv Gandhi initiated the process of conceptualising marketing in the Indian National Congress and now we find BJP evincing interests in promoting the same.

The political leaders work in different capacities. They represent government and are responsible for formulating a sound policy. They also act as opposition and in that event they identify the shortcomings and errors of government and the ruling party. In both the areas, the professionals can make the task of political leaders easier. With the help of a sound Political Information System, the professionals come to know about the emerging trends, participation of party workers and volunteers, instrumentality of operational apparatus in the implementation of development and welfare schemes, contributions of opposition party(s), the feedback of voters and the potential voters, the organisation and promotion of opinion poll and exit poll and all other monitoring and reviewing activities benefits the party. The professionals act as a friend, guide and philosopher of the party leaders and promoters of party interests.

All of us, partially or substantially, use the services of political parties. It is not necessary that the development and welfare activities channelised by the parties remain confined to a particular section or segment. The general masses also derive the benefits and thus all of us are the users. The marketing professionals have to ensure that we remain satisfied with the contributions of the party's performance.

The management of elections is the most significant functional responsibility of professionals. They help parties by making the entire process cost-effective and proactive. The formulation of a sound budget for election, mobilisation of finance, development and organisation of party members and volunteers conducting opinion polls, designing posters and cut-outs exclusively for election, drafting the speeches of important leaders etc., help in managing election affairs effectively. With the help of expertise and excellence, they can make everything informative, sensitive and productive.

In an age of electronics, the advertisement and publicity measures are required to be made more impact generating and the profesionals can make it possible. The audiovisual exposure facilities help sensitising the rural masses. The professionals can make the promotional measures more creative. In the Indian context, a majority of the population live in the village and therefore the professionals have no option but to concentrate in the rural areas to get the support of masses. The political parties also need to assign due weightage to the development and welfare programmes, specially for the rural areas and exclusively for the rural poor. The development of infrastructural facilities in the rural areas may help in winning the heart of the voters and potential voters. The transformation of potential voters and even non-voters into actual habitual voters will be easier if professionals assign due weightage to the development of rural areas. In the marketing literature, the Pareto-effect or Boston Matrix makes a strong case in favour of 80-20 rule. This speaks of the fact that marketing professionals need to intensify their promotion programmes in the areas where they, with the least possible efforts, get an opportunity to increase the market share. Since a majority of the population live in the rural areas, it is imperative that the professionals formulate their strategic decisions in tune with the needs and requirements of rural population. The rural population need lion's share of the benefits since the intensity of rural backwardness is at its peak. The political parties concentrating their energy in the rural areas will not only serve the interests of the society but would also be able to project a positive image of party leaders.

Monitoring and reviewing help professionals in identifying the mistakes and shortcomings and therefore they have to make a mid-term appraisal of all the development efforts initiated and activated by the party members and volunteers. The professionals act as strategists and therefore the formulation of strategy must be sound but the most important thing is the time-honoured and cost-effective implementation which will not be possible unless we have a team of dedicated, committed, sincere and value-based people. They need to make a mid-term evaluation so that the implementation is complete within the time-frame. This would help party organisation in promoting the development plans of the government. If they do not weed out from the party the dishonest and unfair workers vounteers at the very initial stage, all of the efforts taken by them will end in a fiasco.

The professional is supposed to be an effective communicator with an impressive and impact-generating oratory. The media people have to be motivated for publicising the positive contributions of the party so that the public come to know about the same. The news items regarding the development and welfare activities of the party will benefit everyone in many ways. With this trait, the professionals will also be efficacious of promoting event management. The organisation of important meetings of leading party leaders, dispaly of publicity and advertisement materials, soliciting the co-operation of social leaders, reformists and activists, impressing philanthropists and big business houses will be of outstanding significance. A sucessful professional can manage the events effectively and successfully.

The aforesaid facts make it clear that the marketing professionals not only promote the business of profit-making organisations but they also help the non-business sector or non-profit organisations in many ways. The main thing in the process is the excellence of professionals and interests of political parties in using the services of world-class professionals. We can't negate that political parties are accountable to the society and if they don't work for the development of society, the task of seeking their co-operation would be very difficult.

Satisfying the masses is an important responsibility and if the political parties use the services of professionals, they find the task easier. When the professionals promote fair practices, constructive efforts, development-oriented projects, welfare-sensitive programmes, the task of social transformation will be achieved fully. The masses will start harvesting the benefits of development that will lead to mass co-operation. Non-voters of today are the voters of tomorrow and the voters of today may be non-voters of tomorrow. So, it is essential that the party leaders keep moving the process of social development and welfare. Winning the hearts of the voters, making them positive and retaining them for the years to come is not an easy task. The political parties can make it possible; the professionals promoting it effectively succeed in securing a respectable position whereas others negating the same will have to bid a good-bye.

The political leaders as well as the political parties practising marketing in politics need not to forget that at each and every stage they have to keep in their minds the restrictions and limitations of socialisation and commercialisation of politics but at the same time have also to pave the ways for the protection of social and organisational interests with the help of world-class professionals who bear the efficacy of sensitising the voters and the potential voters. Developing mass awareness is an important dimension and professionals must be instrumental in informing, sensing and sensitising the target segments. The positive contributions of a party in the development process, fair and clean image of the party leaders make the task of the professionals more easier. They find themselves in a position to project a positive image. In marketing politics, the image problem is a major barrier which is the result of inefficient and dishonest party workers and biased development policies of the party. The top management with the responsibility of formulating policies and the marketing professionals, having the potentials of sensitising the masses cannot move in the opposite directions and therefore both of them have to follow the same path.

As a friend, guide and philospher, the professionals have to ensure that party leaders don't forget this as otherwise the task of managing elections would be complicated.

The sophisticated developments in the field of information technology have made it easier for the professionals managing opposition parties to identify the errors, lapses and shortcomings in the policies of government. With the help of a sound political information system, they can do it. The researchers and research scientists collect facts and figures and the feedback from the different segments of society which when made known may complicate the task of the ruling bench. Innovations in media considerably help the process of transmission. So, it is necessary that the political party(s) representing the government/ruling bench develop a strategy for implementation of the policies and programmes of government. The professionals working there should be vigilant so that unfair, unlawful fair and unethical practices are halted at the very initial stage.

When we talk about marketing politics, it is significant that professionals also consider the problem of finance because the process of managing a party is now becoming very expensive. The management of donation and donors is an important functional responsibility of professionals managing politics. The positive contributions of party leaders and organisation simplify the process of mobilising the donors. The task is complicated when the part and party leaders have not been sincere to the social and organisational problems. The individuals and corporations are the donors and the potential donors and they can be persuaded effectively when marketing professionals formulate an innovative service profile, adding additional attractions, and convince them that the donations collected earlier have been utilised for the development and welfare of backward regions and neglected segments. Contrary to it, if they misuse the funds, the persuasion will be difficult. This will aggravate the problem of financial crunch. Not only this, the opposition parties will also get an opportunity to tarnish their image. In the marketing liteature, we find cause-related marketing linked to donations for the development and welfare of the society.

The corporate sector prefers to donate for the welfare of the society but when they feel that the funds are being misused, the professionals find it difficult to influence them.

The political communication is an important dimension of political marketing in which the marketing professionals make use of the sophisticated devices for sensitising the masses. In a democratic set up, the media have the freedom to propagate and even a minor mistake of the ruling party may result in a major loss. The professionals have to mobilise donors because in absence of adequate donations, the organisation and management of political parties becomes difficult. The execution of political campaigns requires adequate finance. If the party is having an image problem, the mobilisation of fund from the party members will be complicated. The membership fee is an important source and new members can hardly be enrolled when masses start developing negative attitude.

We can't negate that political marketplace of today is more volatile. The impact of materialism is on the workers, volunteers and leaders. The value system is moving in the reverse gear. The ethical dimensions are neglected. This makes it necessary that the marketing professionals sensitise them in the changed scenario and let public know the realities. A frequent change in the attitudes of voters and potential voters is a testimony to this proposition that none of the political parties in the Indian setting have been promoting values and the voters change their options frequently.

In the present volatile political environment, the conceptualisation of marketing principles necessitates the formulation of a sound strategy. The development of political strategies makes it essential that the party organisation develops an awareness and helps in an attitudinal change. They need to perceive that materialism is not to find any place in politics as otherwise the value system will bid good-bye to the social system. If they evince interest in politics, the prime thing is social service not the personal gain. They are not supposed to invest to get a profitable return. Unless and until, we find an attitudinal change, the conceptualisation of social marketing principles will not only be difficult but would also be of no avail. If we make strong advocacy in favour of marketing politics, the prime thing is professionalism and the political parties are not supposed to think about professional excellence in the absence of value orientation. In the Indian context, we find the political system considerably influenced by value degeneration which had been making inroads leading to the collapse of all the subsystems. Corruption starts from the top. We find pollitical leaders involved in it, the bureaucrats, administrators and all of us find an excuse for the same. The wave of corruption and unlawful practices jeopardise all the efforts. The political marketing makes it essential that the political leaders pave the way for an attitudinal change. The professionals can make their task easier, work with a mission, vision and goal assuring protection of the social interests and development of value system. They need to follow values promoted by Kautilya as otherwise even world-class marketing professionals would find it difficult to promote the interest of society and project a positive image of the party for which they work.

SUMMARY

You have gone through different dimensions of political marketing. After going through the chapter, be sure that the following facts are well versed:

Political Ideologists of India: You have gone through the ideologies of some of the political leaders playing a contributory role in the process of socio-economic emancipation. Lord Krishna, Kautilya, Mahatma Gandhi, Pt. Jawahar Lal Nehru, Radhakrishnan, Jayaprakash Narayan and Ambedkar are a few of the leaders dominating the political scenario at different times, in different capacities and in different ways.

Political Organisation: A Social Institution: Since we find political parties playing a contributory role in the transformation of social systems, we have gone through the social character of political organisation.

Political Environment in India: Right from the ancient to the modern period, we find a number of turning points in the political environment of India which has substantially influenced the policy decisions of political parties.

Political Socialisation: Since political parties are supposed to play a decisive role in the development of society, a basic change in the attitudes of political leaders is found significant.

Political Marketing — The Perception and Misperception: Political marketing is a process of conceptualising and implementing marketing principles with the prime motto of satisfying the society and developing the social system in tune with the evolving changes. In no case, we find commercialisation to be practised in the process.

Significance of Political Marketing: Strategic decisions, building of a positive image, cost-effectiveness, overriding priority to social considerations, retaining the loyalty to a party are some of the aspects focusing on the significance of political marketing.

Dimensions of Political Marketing: Here, we go through different dimensions of political marketing in brief, such as segmentation, behavioural studies, political information system and the formulation of a sound marketing mix for the political organisation.

Segmentation: It is a process of dividing and subdividing the society into different segments, such as men and women, voters and potential voters, voters and non-voters, kids and teens, youths and grey, rural and urban.

Political Information System: It is a technology-driven organised set of procedures where people and technologies manage information with the viewpoint of helping the political leaders in making policies and formulating strategies.

Management of Behaviour: In this context, we go through the attitudes, behaviour and expectations of the different segments of society.

Marketing Mix: The formulation of different submixes, such as service mix, promotion mix, channel management, management of people, place and location have been discussed here. The political organisation makes available to the different segments of society in different capacities a number of services and we go through both the core and peripheral services. The constituents of promotion have been discussed in the promotion mix.

The mobilisation of membership fee by activating the membership drive and use of political communication system for motivating the donors and potential donors need professional excellence. The channelisation of services by the political organisations with the help of professionals to the target segment and processing of services with the help of information and communication technology and members and volunteers need due attention in the marketing mix. Further, the physical evidence focuses our attention on tangibilisation of the outstanding features and ideologies of political parties to impress upon the visitors and members. The political parties need a brigade of quality members and volunteers to be effective in making available the promised services to the target constituency or region. The professionals need to educate and train them in a right way.

Strategic Marketing: In this context, we discuss the problems in the face of evolving changes in the conditions of political environment. The professionals bear the responsibility of studying and understanding the emerging trends and to formulate an action plan helping the parties and leaders in projecting their image and excelling the rival parties.

Political Marketing in Indian Perspective: The conceptualisation of modern marketing principles in the Indian perspective needs due focus on social approach with a professional touch. Since we find multi-party system in the Indian political environment, the small parties will find it difficult to practise the same. The big political parties may implement it with the help of professionals who would considerably help them in the building and projection of a fair image.

KEY TERMS

Lobbyist Groups	Sensitivity
Social Marketing	Creativity
Contours	Attitudes
Election Manifesto	Expectations
Milieu	Fraudulent
NGOs	Anguish
Synchronisation	Behavioural Management
Boardrooms	Election Commission
Political Organisations	Core Services
Social Organisations	Peripheral Services
Chromosomes	Demographic Pressure
Political Guru	Communal Harmony
Strategist	Potable Water
Diplomacy	Election Campaigns
Architect	Body Language
Revolutionary Humanist	Persuasive Communication
Social Justice	Political Advertising
Social Capital	Broadcast Media
Political Environment	Print Media
Quit India Movement	Telecast Media
Political Socialisation	Media Mix
Consumerism	Social Harmony
Lucrative	Word-of-mouth Promotion
Image Drafting	Telemarketers
Image Projection	National Party
Political Information System	Regional Party
Political Communication Network	Taluk
Behavioural Studies	Target Audience
Volunteers	Tantamount
Kids and Teens	Political Ethics
Constituency	Voters
Grey	Potential Voters
Operational Apparatus	National Excellence
Commercialisation	Merchandising
Holistic Concept	Societal Marketing

Review Questions

1. What do you mean by Political Marketing? Throw light on the application of marketing in politics in Indian perspective.
2. Comment on some of the political ideologists significantly to the process of social transformation.
3. State and explain the complexities found in the political environment in India.
4. What is political socialisation? Comment on the socialisation of politics in India.
5. Explain the significance of political marketing in Indian perspective.
6. What do you mean by segmentation in politics? Focus on its instrumentality in the Indian context.
7. Throw light on the behavioural studies found significant to study the attitudes of voters.
8. Explain in brief the different submixes of marketing politics.
9. Discuss the different extended submixes of marketing in the context of political marketing.
10. Explain the instrumentality of advertisement in politics.
11. Discuss the media strategy helping the marketing professionals in making the promotion budget of political parties optimal.
12. Explain in brief the different constituents of promotion with special reference to publicity and word-of-mouth promotion.
13. Explain the role of personal selling and telemarketing in promoting the political parties.
14. Focus on the role of volunteers and party workers in managing the election campaign.
15. Explain the role of information in managing the party affairs.
16. Write a short note on political marketing in Indian perspective.
17. Focus on the changing role of marketing professionals in satisfying the party members and increasing the membership drive.

Application Exercises

1. You have been working as a professional of a leading political party in India. Design a plan for campaigning of election.
2. Formulate a Marketing Mix for your party.
3. As a marketing professional, you need to study the behavioural profile of voters. Explain the processes you will follow for dividing the voters of different segments.
4. Focus on the promotional measures you will adopt for informing, sensing, sensitising, persuading and transforming the potential voters into actual voters or retaining your voters.
5. You have been managing the office of a political party; focus on the servicescapes you will manage for attracting the persons visiting your office.
6. For making preparations for election, your party needs to publish and release Election Manifesto. Explain your role as a marketer.
7. You have been asked by the top management of your party to speed up the membership drive helping you in increasing the members and mobilising finance. Throw light on the measures adopted by you in the capacity of a professional.
8. The volunteers and members of your party need adequate training. Design a plan for imparting training facilities to them.
9. You have to publicise the outstanding contributions of your party. Focus on the steps you will like to initiate for developing rapport with the media people.
10. As a professional, you need to develop Political Information System. Throw light on the steps you will take for this purpose.

Endnotes

1. Rana Bhavan Singh, *Chanakya Sutra,* New Delhi, 1995, pp. 5-7.
2. Bali D.R., Modern Indian Thought, pp. 115-31.
3. *Ibid,* pp. 195-206.
4. *Ibid,* pp. 224-35.
5. *Ibid,* pp. 236-55.
6. *Ibid,* Alpana, *A Study in the Process of Political Socialisation,* HPH, Mumbai, 1989, pp. 1-2.

8. Siegal R.S., Assumptions About the Learning of Political Values, Annals of the American Academy of Social Sciences, 1966, pp. 1-2.
9. Rush and Althoff, *Political Sociology,* London, 1972, p. 16.
10. Greenstein F.I., *Political Socialisation in International Encyclopedia of Social Sciences,* 1968, p. 551.
11. Dawson and Prewitt, *Political Socialisation,* Boston, Little Brown, 1969, p. 17.
12. Bruce I. Newman, *Handbook of Political Marketing,* Sage Inc., 1999, p. 816.
13. *Ibid,* Chapter IV/19.
14. Phillippe J. Marraek, *Political Communication,* University of Luton Press, England, 1994.
15. Bruce I. Newman, *op. cit.,* Chapter 21/23.
16. *Ibid.,* Chapter. II/8.
17. Jha, S.M., *Social Marketing,* HPH, Mumbai, 1999.
18. Jha, S.M., Political Marketing in Indian Perspective, *Pratibimba* Vol. 3/1, 2003, pp. 45-49.
19. Jha, S.M., *Marketing Non-Profit Organisations,* HPH, Mumbai, 2004, Chapter 6.

CHAPTER

DAY-CARE MARKETING

The Corporate culture made ways for material culture and material culture injected life and continuity to the emergence of Day-care culture. Practising marketing principles appears to be essential to improve the quality of services of Day-care centres or Crèches.

Chapter Objectives

Introduction – Day-care Services: The Perception – Day-care Centre: The Perception – Day-care Marketing: The Perception – Rationale behind Day-care Marketing – Users of Day-care Services – Behavioural Profile of Users of Day-care Services – Segmentation in Day-care Marketing – Marketing Information System for Day-care Centres – Formulation of Marketing Mix for Day-care Organisations – Service Mix for Day-care Organisations – Promoting the Day-Care Organisations – Fee Strategy for Day-care Organisations – Channelisation of Day-care Services – Location Point for the Day-care Centres – Process – Physical Evidence and Attractions – People – Summary – Key Notes – Review Questions – Application Exercises – Endnotes.

Learning Objectives

This chapter aims at studying the day-care services. The readers will develop their awareness of the conceptualisation with the motto of improving the quality of services. Since we find users of services of gullible nature, the professionals need to take care in the process of formulating a sound marketing mix so that the parents or working mothers are found satisfied. They need a human touch and try to make the services much more personalised. In addition to the core services, the small kids belonging to a formative age group need parental affection which is to be possible when we find humanised leadership. This chapter aims at sensitising the readers that crèches or day-care centres need uniqueness in their service mix.

INTRODUCTION

Globalisation of economy has engineered a sound foundation for the globalisation of fashion, culture and civilisation. The new wave culture considerably influenced by western lifestyle is the gift of material culture in which money establishes an edge over relationships. We develop our temptation for modern amenities and facilities to lead a comfortable life and for that, our requirements for money move forward even without a gap. The emergence of such a culture in which earn more and spend more monitors our attitudes, it is found essential that both the units in a family, e.g., wife and husband prefer to work even at the cost of their small kids who need parental affection and personal care on a priority basis. They need utmost care and unfortunately are found much more neglected. The Indian Social System was found influenced by a different philosophy in which the commitment of a mother to her son or daughter was given topmost priority, and it was such magnitude of sacrifice of a mother to her children that the position of mother was found at top.

Time cycle necessitates a change because it is a natural phenomenon. We have no option but to follow. In the Indian Social System and cultural patterns, we find a major change particularly with the beginning of the decade 1990s when liberalisation made ways for globalisation and this resulted into an emergence of material culture. The corporatisation started dominating our economy and albeit our behavioural profile. This necessitated an increase in our income. The concept of housewives was replaced by working women. Since the size of a family was abnormally reduced in which even grandfathers and grandmothers were not accommodated; the working couples started witnessing a number of problems while nurturing and managing their small kids. It was against this backdrop that Crèches came into existence firstly in the developed countries of the globe and later even in the developing countries like ours.

Thus, the corporate culture made ways for material culture and material culture injected life and continuity to the day-care culture. We welcome or oppose; the day-care centres or day-care organisations are increasing in a very good number and such a mushroom growth has been paving avenues for a number of sore-spots in the operation and management of day-care centres. The small kids need utmost care but they fail in getting the parental care and affection particularly at the most sensitive formative stage of their life cycle. We cannot negate that such a treatment with them bring a change in their attitudes. Nurturing kids by parents help development of children in a right way leaving scope for the growth of a number of traits and faculties essential for the development of personality in totality. Increasing aggressiveness in our behaviour is also due to ill treatment with the kids which can be expected in day-care centres or crèches but the same cannot be imagined by the parents. Our focus is here on managing and marketing day-care centres or crèches with a professional touch sizeably influenced by human touch.

Mounting popularity of corporate culture has been found developing a craze for the westernised lifestyles which keeps working mothers engaged for earning more even at the cost of their degenerating and disintegrating family structure. Since we find both of them, wife and husband in job, they have a busy schedule for the whole day which engineers a strong foundation for the development of day-care culture in which they don't have time even to look after their small kids. Because the kids remain neglected, we find their transformation as teens in a very unregulated form. The youths thus are found moving without destination and directions. If we fail in managing our kids and teens, the cropping up of a number of social evils and bad habits is but natural which would stand, as a major barrier to the development process. The national policy makers, social scientists; reformists and activists; political leaders bear the responsibility of developing such a society contributing substantially to the process of socio-economic emancipation without any degeneration in our cultural patterns. We can't check the flow and directions of development. We can't force an individual or a couple to move in the defined directions. We can't regulate the flow of consumerism making available to us a comfortable and luxurious living condition. What we can do is to offer an alternative, an option to the working couples to take the support of day-care centres or organisations.

Pre-education age is found to be the most sensitive and receptive stage in our life cycle because this portrays a picture which can't be removed for the long-time. Day-care organisations bear the responsibility of making available multi-dimensional development avenues to the children of working couples who don't get time to look after them properly. If we keep on moving our fascination to reduce consumerism; we can't check day-care culture. Because we have to strike a balance between increasing temptation and changing situation; our prime focus would be on promoting the day-care organisations paving avenues for the safety, nursing and development of children. If we find a prosperous future for corporate culture; the day-care culture would also thrive and therefore, the day-care organisations would be required to be promoted.

Day-care marketing focuses our attention on marketing the day-care services. In a true sense, we find materialism paying new vistas for the development of modern culture and a majority of us have developed a craze for the same. Marketing of services offered by the day-care organisations has been found remunerative and of late, we find institutionalised efforts gaining momentum. The working couples are required to pay a small share of their incomes and for that, the day-care centres look after their tots and kids. It is a managerial process because we need world-class professionals to manage the centres for the time-honoured development of the pre-school children enrolled therein. It is also a social process because the institutionalised efforts need social orientation in which children get a conducive environment to grow and contribute substantially to the social transformation process.

Institutionalisation of day-care centres would make the ways for qualitative improvements. It is not only sufficient that we take care of the children enrolled for day-care. It is incredibly significant that we nurture them in a proper way. Of course, the services of parents to their children can't be replaced but the best possible efforts can be made to nurse them in an identical environment with the help and co-operation of people showing personal touch and parental affection in service. It is in this context that we focus on the instrumentality of day-care organisations in countering the problems generated by the day-care culture growing as an offshoot of corporate culture and consumerism.

Often maintained by Welfare Departments, Settlement Houses, Corporate Sector and Other Social Service Agencies; the day-care centre or a day-nursery takes care of the children of working mothers of limited income families. They prepare inputs for pre-primary or primary schools. The nuclear families under middle-income group are the prime users of the services of day-care centres/creches. The burgeoning middle class living in the urban areas for their tiny tots prefer to use the services of sweet and loving day-care centres. Since we find a significant increase in the number of middle class, it is but natural that in the days and years to come, the users of course in a very large number would be in search of a day-care centre efficacious of nursing their children in an environment where love, affection, sense of security and parental guidance are made available. The age group of children in the day-care centres vary from 2½ to 5 years, if they also include kindergarten.

Since we find a sound nexus for the development of day-care centres, it is essential that they practise marketing principles so that on the one hand, the users get quality services while on the other hand, the centres also prove to be remunerative. The centres need to conceptualise the principles of social marketing because whatever the services are offered by them prove to be a productive contribution to the process of human development *vis-a-vis* the human capital formation. World-class play-way method of pre-school education and training helps children in developing pursuits and enriching faculties. Development of an integrated personality is found essential and the centres if professionally-sound, infrastructurally-rich and objectively value-oriented serve the desired purposes in an effective way. The centres need to work for quality in the face of evolving challenges and changes. They need a service mix engineering a sound foundation for schooling. A fair blending of core and peripheral services is needed to add additional attractions to the service mix *vis-a-vis* to increase the number of users. You have to be innovative while including the peripheral services because this can also be used as a motivational tool.

The increasing urbanisation, burgeoning middle class, increasing domination of corporate sector in the transformation of national economy, mounting craze for westernised lifestyles are some of the key factors making the business environment conducive for the day-care centres. It is in this context that you have to promote day-care centres in such a fashion that users and potential users come to know about your centres and make decisions in your favour. Since you have remained innovative while formulating the service mix, the messages transmitted by your organisation for promotion would be effective in informing, sensing and sensitising the users and potential users. Your professional excellence needs to think about a result-oriented promotion mix.

While advertising you need to be creative and to formulate a sound mix of media so that your views, information, development programmes, specialities in the service mix rich to the users in an effective way. With the support of media people, you have to publicise so that the masses and specially the potential users come to know about your world-class services. For promoting your business, you have also to think about sales promotion and to offer gifts and other incentives to the users and potential users so that they act as a hidden salesforce. The word-of-mouth promotion is essential to keep on moving the process of qualitative-cum-quantitative transformation and the satisfied group of customers perform this responsibility in a fantastic way. You have also to solicit the co-operation of social reformists and activists who would substantially promote your organisation. In an age of sophisticated communication technology, you also need to develop telemarketing for promotion. Your professional excellence while formulating a mix would simplify the task of sensitising the users and potential users.

While developing a mix for the channelisation of services, you need to make it sure that the services promised by you to your users reach to them without making any distortion and for that, you need to be careful specially while recruiting, training and developing people responsible to offer the services. The gap between services-promised and services-offered is required to be bridged. The fee structure adopted by you need to be rational so that the users and potential users are motivated. Of course, you bear the responsibility of improving the quality of services and for that huge money would also be needed and your efforts to make the cost structure optimal would help you in many ways. The people engaged by you for different purposes need due weightage because they bear the responsibility of nursing kids and making available to them love, affection, parental guidance, sympathy and empathy, so that a sound foundation is engineered for their time-honoured development. Professional excellence, personal commitment and personal-touch-in-service are to be the essential traits of people serving the day-care centres. The location points for your centres should smoothly be accessible so that users and visitors don't face any problem and full protection is made available to the kids in a friendly environment. You need to develop aesthetic sense so that the enrolled children find the environmental conditions healthy, conducive, friendly and result-oriented.

In view of the above, it is right to observe that day-care centres need to develop a sound marketing mix. The focal point is the quality because the working parents send their children to the centres with high hopes that proper care and nursing would help them in an all-round development of character, career and personality. Because you have to nurse the small kids, it is pertinent that the children don't get anything wrong because whatever they witness at this formative stage throw a major imprint on their character and personality. You need to contribute substantially to the process of developing human, humane, human values and this makes it essential that the defined principles of social marketing are conceptualised by you while making the policy and strategic decisions. The day-care centres have a prosperous future but commercialisation and merchandising need not to dominate the decisions. There must be a correlation between the fee you charge, and the services you render; time schedule you maintain and the results that they get.

DAY-CARE SERVICES — THE PERCEPTION

The day-care services or day-nursery services or creches are related to the multi-dimensional services made available to the children of working parents of age group 2½ to 3½. The children get a number of services, such as love and affection, parental guidance, educational services, child care, recreational and sports activities. They offer to the children a friendly environment and ensure proper care for an overall development of children enrolled therein.[1] The services include almost all the services paving avenues for the development of character and personalities of children.

DAY-CARE CENTRE — THE PERCEPTION

The day-care centre or a day-nursery is an institution meant for the children of working mothers who due to lack of time find it difficult to look after them. The centres are either run independently or as a part of the kindergarten school. It is found located in the urban areas and offers to the children not only the essential services related to their education but also some of the peripheral services for preparing them for the primary or pre-primary schools. They make available composite day-care service and exclusive day-care service. By exclusive day-care service, we mean provision for only day-care service whereas the composite day-care service also includes kindergarten.[2]

DAY-CARE MARKETING — THE PERCEPTION

Day-care Marketing focuses our attention on marketing day-care culture developing as a craze. It is a process of conceptualisation of marketing principles within the framework of social marketing. It is a managerial process because the professionals bear the responsibility of developing children during their pre-schooling education and training. It is also considered to be a social process because the centres are supposed to engineer a sound foundation for child care not essentially as a commercial enterprise but preferably as a social venture. Of course, they have a legitimate right of making profits but their fee structure should not be non-optimal to the quality of services they offer to the children. It is an organised effort to inculcate some of the special traits required by an individual for the development of his/her personality. It is a process of formulating marketing mix in the face of evolving changes. It is a device to develop centres to make the services remunerative *vis-a-vis* cost-effective. We also find day-care marketing a suitable medium to project image. It is a source of inputs to the institutions offering kindergarten and pre-primary education. It is an approach to define the perception of quality in tune with the evolving changes in the social systems and culture patterns.

The aforesaid facts regarding the day-care marketing makes it clear that conceptualisation and implementation of marketing principles by the day-care centres draw attention of welfare departments, corporate sector, social organisations taking part in the process of establishing the centres with the motto of improving the quality of human beings, nurturing kids in a proper way and for that professionalism, personal-touch-in-service, ethics, virtues and human touch need an intensive care and in the process, the principles of social marketing need conceptualisation so that commercialisation is not to establish an edge on welfare orientation *vis-a-vis* social transformation.

RATIONALE BEHIND DAY-CARE MARKETING

A majority of us often raise the questions related to the reasons for the development of day-care centres and conceptualisation and application of marketing principles by them. Of course, we find justifications for conceptualisation and the following facts testify the same:

1. Promoting child care: Neglected, uncared, unregulated children prove to be a social liability. The parents have no option but to earn the maximum possible and this deprives the working mothers of taking proper care of their children. The age group for which we find day-care centres, 2½ to 3½ and in a few cases where we include kindergarten upto 5 have been found the most sensitive period in the life cycle of human beings. The imprints during this formative age group are found fast because children by nature are found conscious of perceiving and learning. It is not possible for the working mothers that they remain confined to their houses because unless they earn, the expanding family budget on account of lifestyles, consumerism and inflationary pressure would remain in deficit. It is in this context that we find justifications for the establishment and development of day-care centres. The conceptualisation of marketing helps them while improving the quality, making the process cost-effective, projecting the image, enriching the infrastructural facilities and so on.

2. World class education and training: Since we find day-care centres very much instrumental in improving the quality of their services by introducing innovative play-way system of education and training where the children in addition to educational facilities also get the recreational facilities sports facilities, and all the facilities for their proper development; incredible opportunities exist for their time-honoured development even in absence of their parents. We talk about marketing which helps the centres in developing the perception of services in the face of evolving multi-dimensional changes. We also talk about conceptualisation of social marketing which marginally regulates the freedom of commercialising the day-care services.

3. Eagerness to utilise specialised teaching: The day-care centres are established with the motto of making available to the children most sophisticated services which their counterparts get anywhere in the globe. A craze for adopting modern culture is found existent which would not be possible unless we find development of modern day-care centres. We talk about day-care marketing which opens new vistas for the development of centres in the face of international standard. The parents prefer that their children get specialised knowledge and whatever the education and training facilities they get at the centres are supposed to prepare a sound foundation for primary or pre-primary education to their children.

4. Increasing day-care culture: We are well aware of the fact that corporate culture has been making ways for the development of day-care culture which is fantastically fuelled by consumerism. Almost all of us are found interested in using the modern amenities and facilities which would not be possible unless wife and husband both of them increase the sources of their incomes. With the development of day-care centres, they are mentally free that the centre would look after their children in tune with the changing requirements. Even if they are not present, the centres would offer to their children the parental guidance, love and affection, educational and recreational facilities so that they feel at home, even if they are not in home.

5. Strong base for pre- and primary schooling: We are well aware of the fact that in the day-care services, the children of age group 2½ to 3½ are enrolled. This limit goes upto 5 when we find kindergarten. The process of primary education starts thereafter and by that time we find children of day-care centres potentially sound for schooling. The primary education for them proves to be very much productive because they are enrolled in the institutions where world-class educational aid has been made available to them. They are also aware of the extracurricular activities and therefore they get entry with a strong base.

6. Cultural orientation: Of course,we find the day-care centres making available to the children world-class educational and other supporting services but in this context the centres also bear the responsibility of making available to them the knowledge related to the cultural and behavioural patterns so that a perfection is found in their personality. It is, of course, significant that the day-care centres don't make a good-bye to the cultural and behavioural dimensions. We are not opposed to the modern and sophisticated developments, we also not disagree with advanced educational aid but cultural and behavioural dimensions make the ways for the development of social systems in addition to the protection of cultural heritage which in a majority of the cases have been found disintegrating. In the service mix of day-care centres, the value orientation and cultural and behavioural dimensions need a priority attention. The centres need to make it sure that modern educational aid would not deprive them of the Indian social and cultural values.

7. Modern lifestyles: The main focus is on the modern lifestyles and the increasing temptation or even craze for the same among the general masses. Of late, we find the middle class increasing in a very large number and with this, a good number of day-care centres are to be started by the different categories of organisations. The corporate sector, the social organisations, the political organisation need to promote day-care centres because the potential users of the services, specially the middle income group working wives have been found interested in the development of world-class day-care centres. Of course, we find the supply position particularly quality-wise not in a position to meet the increasing demand position. This necessitates a code for the development of day-care centres. There is no doubt in it that centres if managed properly would provide to the working couples an opportunity to even more because they find themselves free from the responsibility of managing their children in the formative age group. The consumerism thus would get a favourable environment and the lifestyles of the persons/couples who can afford would also be influenced.

The aforesaid facts testify the rationale behind conceptualising and implementing marketing principles by the day-care centres. In this context, it is also significant that the centres formulate a sound service mix and increase the awareness of users and potential users of the services in an effective way. If they practise the principles of social marketing, a number of evils that we find in a majority of the day-care centres would also be removed. Increasing competition would make available to the users improved quality of services. Besides, the centres in general would make sincere efforts to make the process cost-effective which would also result into a rational fee structure.

USERS OF DAY-CARE SERVICE

The Day-care centres need to understand the behavioural profile of users and this makes it essential that they also know about the different categories of users and potential users of their services so that they develop marketing resources in tune with the changing needs and requirements and the levels of expectations of the working wives. The different categories of users have different expectations and therefore, the day-care centres would also find it significant while formulating the service mix or while developing other submixes. In Figure 19.1, we find the different categories of users which in a majority of the cases have been classified in the face of their monthly incomes. of users and potential users of the day-care sevices.

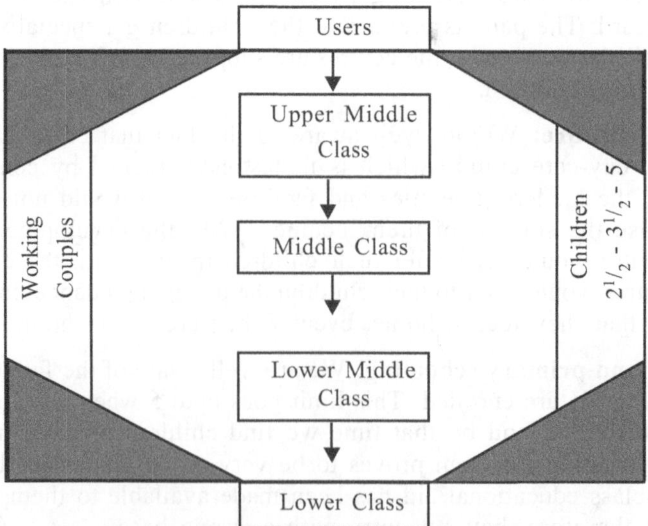

Fig. 19.1: Users of Day-care Services

Uppeer Middle Class, Middle Class, Lower Middle Class,Upper Lower Class are the different catagories of users and potential users of the day-care services.

Upper Middle Class: Monthly Income Above ₹ 1,00,000

Middle Class: Monthly Income Above ₹ 60,000 to ₹ 1,00,000

Lower Middle Class: Monthly Income Above ₹ 30,000 to ₹ 60,000

Lower Class: Monthly Income Above ₹ 30,000

Of course, the working couples are the users of the services because we find them in a very large number but in a few of the cases, we also find single earners. It is also to mention that a majority of the users of the services belong to the educated segment which is Graduation and above. In the face of the family structure, we find Nuclear families dominating but few of the users also belong to the Joint families. It is to make it clear that Nuclear family consists of husband, wife and their children. Extended family consists of Nuclear family plus parents and/or unmarried brothers and/or sisters of the head of the family member and/or of the spouse of both. Joint family includes all the blood relations living together in one household.[3]

It is but natural that the lifestyles, expectations, attitudes and temperament of all the categories can't be identical. Since you have to satisfy them, your prime responsibility is to identify their expectations and innovate the service accordingly. The behavioural profile of a segment plays a significant role in satisfying the users and the day-care centres need to have an in-depth knowledge of the sam

BEHAVIOURAL PROFILE OF USERS OF DAY-CARE SERVICE

The marketing practices can't be claimed to be effective unless the consumers/users are found satisfied. The marketers can't be successful in satisfying the users unless they have an in-depth knowledge of their expectations. The expectations can't remain static. There are a number of factors influencing the levels of expectations of users. The behavioural studies make the ways for identifying the changing levels of expectations of users and because expectations and satisfaction move together, you succeed in increasing the number of satisfied group of users, a prime consideration for increasing marketing share and becoming a market leader. It is against this background that we go through the behavioural profile of the users of day-care services.

Since a majority of the users of day-care services are educated and well aware of the evolving changes in the business around the world, it is but natural that they have a high level of expectations. This makes the task of day-care centres and marketers much more difficult. Because the day-care centres bear the responsibility of satisfying them, it is pertinent that they keep on moving the process of identifying the changing levels and make innovative efforts to develop the marketing resources optimally so that they not only satisfy them but even transform them to act as a hidden salesforce. Since we find small kids using your services, they can't evaluate and rate your performance. It is in this context that we find parents as users who send their children to your centres with new hopes and aspirations.

Earlier, we have gone through the problem of different categories of users of the day-care services. It is right to mention that even different categories could not have identical needs and requirements. We find a difference in their preferences, likes and dislikes and attitudes. The transformation of one level of users into another can't be negated. The expectations of upper middle class would naturally be high but if we find transformation of lower middle class into upper middle class, the difference in the level of two upper middle classes can't be denied. This is mainly due to the fact that expectations are considerably influenced by the profession that an individual acquires at the initial stage of his/her career. Like this, the expectations of lower class and another category of upper class would vary. This makes it essential that the marketing professionals have a detailed idea of different categories of users of the day-care services.

The working couples found highly educated and another group of couples relatively less educated would not have the same behavioural profile. Because we find income playing a significant role in the transformation process, it is essential that the marketing professionals make a microscopic analysis of the changing levels of income. This would activate the process of increasing the number of users of the day-care services. The developments in the field of communication and information play an important role in shaping the level of expectations.

At the very outset, you need to enrich your knowledge bank related to the latest developments taking place in the day-care services. The innovative services made available by your competitors are to be included in the service mix. The core services may be identical but to the extent it is possible you should distinct the peripheral services.

It is innovative peripheral services that would help you in adding additional attractions to your service mix that would act as a motivational tool. The users would considerably be motivated by the peripheral services. By improving the quality of both categories of your services in the face of the increasing expectations of users and potential users; you pave avenues for their satisfaction *vis-a-vis* the word-of-mouth promotion.

You need to be particular to the attitudes and preferences of the single earners. The behavioural profile of single earners is found distinct to the behavioural profile of double earners. In a majority of the cases, we find single earners more rigid and conservative. Like this, the behavioural profile of parents working in the leading multinational companies would be different to the working couples of government departments or other organisations. The professional background thus helps you in understanding the changing expectations of your users. The more reputed an organisation, the much more higher the levels of expectations.

An in-depth study of feedback that you get from the Information system would substantially help you in increasing the number of satisfied group of users. A number of cases testify that the users of day-care services are found dissatisfied because they feel that the centres have not been offering to their children the promised services. Lack of emergency child care, inadequacy of people showing personal-touch-in-service, lack of punctuality or poor record of time management, space constraint, poor quality of food served by them, non-optimal fee structure are a few of the reasons increasing the number of dissatisfied group of users. This makes it essential that you assign due weightage to the quality of services. Since we find day-care centres related to the problems of small kids, it is not only judicious but even ethical that you don't make any compromise with the quality of services.

The behavioural studies make it essential that you are aware of the changing levels of expectations of working couples and keep on moving the process of qualitative transformation. You need to feel that frequent innovations in the service mix would help you in increasing the number of users which would make the process cost-effective and further would expand scope for the development of day-care centres. The increasing commercialisation can't be accepted because it is to affect the society in an adverse fashion, viz., the small kids not in a position to comment would be exploited and a number of substandard day-care centres would also be motivated.

Of course, the day-care centres need self-regulations, specially to protect the interests of small kids sent to the centres with the hope that home-like treatment and parental guidance would be made available to them. If they fail in regulating their behaviour; the government would be required to regulate their activities. Since we don't find social organisations pro to the subserving of social interests, it is essential that the working couples or users of the services form an association or syndicate to regulate the working of day-care centres.

An in-depth study of the attitudes and expectations of users and potential users is significant and the study results would help the centres in many ways, provided they work with a positive attitude. Exploitation of parents and small kids is required to be checked on a priority basis.

SEGMENTATION IN DAY-CARE MARKETING

You need to improve the quality of your services; you need to promote your organisation so that the users and potential users come to know about the innovative efforts made by your organisation. You need to make yourself potentially-sound to excel competition and with the increasing market share, you have to establish leadership. This makes it essential that you understand the emerging trends, evolving changes, mounting competition, level of expectations so that the process of qualitative transformation speeded up by you move forward without any gap. It is in this context that we talk about segmentation.

Segmentation is a process of dividing and subdividing a market into different small groups so that the process of identification is found right. Of course, we don't find even two persons having identical nature and character, likes and dislikes, preferences and attitudes, needs and requirements, however the similarities among the different users found in a segment can't be negated. If you understand the segment, you understand the market and if you understand the market, you have opportunities to make yourself potentially sound to counter the threats and challenges generated by the organisations found nationally and internationally competitive.

The Day-care users belong to a particular section/group but the emerging trends in the social systems indicate that in the days and years to come, there would be a significant increase in the number of users and new segments would also prefer to use the services of day-care centres. The increasing level of income and the changing lifestyles are the key developments to pave avenues for the inclusion of new segments in the list of users of day-care services. The study of segmentation is found significant and the day-care centres need to develop their service/ product mix in the face of emerging trends. Since we find a change even in their expectations, an in-depth knowledge of the same would help formulation of a sound service mix. The innovation process would be made result-oriented because you have optimally blended expectations and offerings.

Segmentation helps you in many ways. It helps you understanding the users, their changing needs and requirements, levels of expectations, the demand position in a particular segment, the feedback of a particular segment, the intensity of competition generated by the rival centres, your market share and so on. The study results related to the areas mentioned would make your task of formulating a sound marketing mix much more easier. Destination determines the strategies to be followed to reach to the place without any risk and also within the stipulated time. Because awareness regarding the target helps you in identifying the dangers or obstacles, you make the necessary preparations accordingly. You find yourself potentially sound and make yourself mentally ready. Conversely, if you are unaware of the destination, the task of formulating strategies becomes much more complicated.

In the day-care service, the two important bases for segmentation are found important, e.g., the level of income and the concept of working wives. The low-income group virtually finds it difficult to afford and we find by and large the same problem with the single earner. Since a majority of the users belong to the educated segment, we may also make classification on the basis of education. Professional background also influences the process and therefore, we may also use it as a base. A microscopic classification of segment simplifies your task of formulating a sound service mix. Not only this, the strategic decisions related to the promotional measures for different segments would also be made, if the day-care centres make an in-depth study of different segments. The level of expectations and the needs and requirements and preferences of highly educated segment would be found different to the relatively low educated segment. The users working in the leading multinational companies behave in a different way and their expectations are found different. On the other hand, the users working in other organisations or government departments behave and expect in a bit different way. In Figure 19.2, we find different segments of users of day-care services.

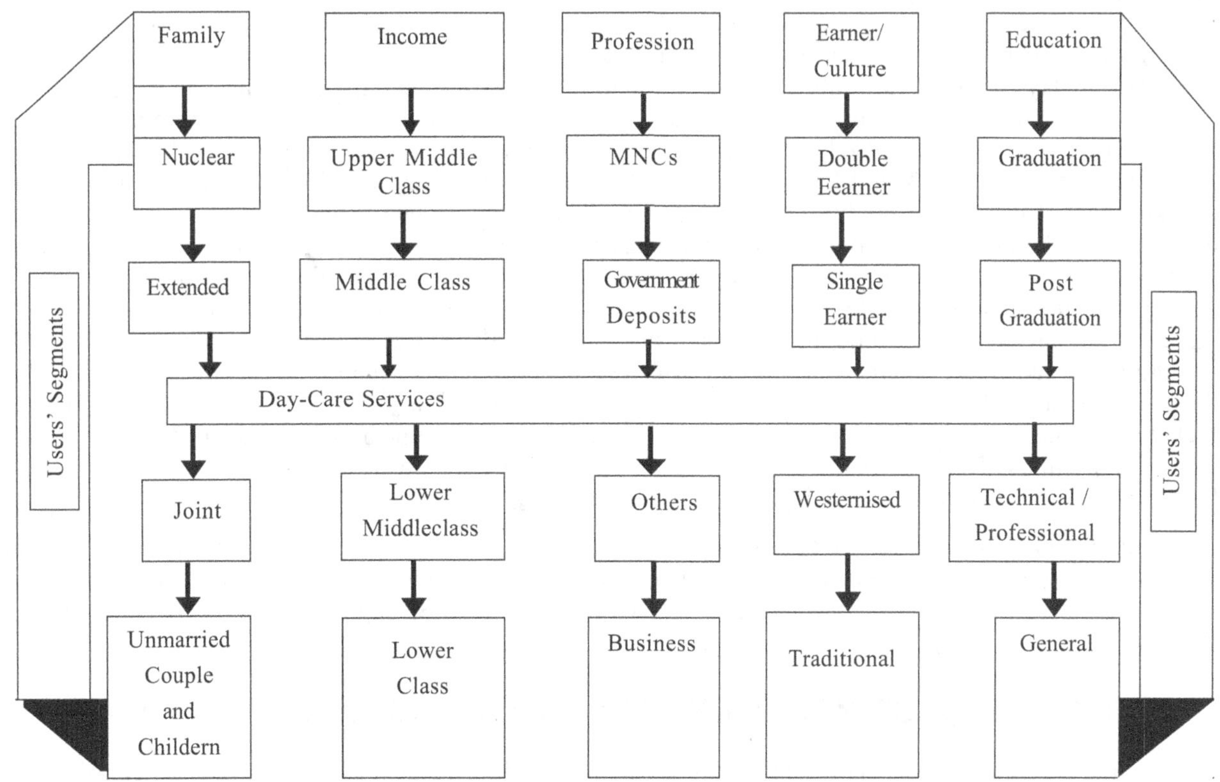

Fig. 19.2: Segement of Users in the Day-care Services

Since an in-depth study of segmentation is related to the level of expectations and marketers bear the responsibility of satisfying them, it is pertinent that we assign due weightage to the process of segmentation. You need to develop the marketing resources in the face of changing levels of expectations and a study of segments would simplify your task. Your ultimate motto is to satisfy the users and to transform the potential users into the actual users. This necessitates a careful and research-based study and for that you need to solicit the co-operation of information selling organisations if you are not in a position to develop an independent system to manage the information.

In a true sense, we find a close relation between the behavioural studies and the studies related to segmentation. You know about the different categories of your users on the basis of segmentation and based on segmentation, you understand the changing behavioural profile of different segments. And for both purposes, you have to take the support of information. The civic bodies, telephone directory, census reports are some of the sources helping you while segmenting. Since duration, profession, income, family and culture are the different bases; you need to collect information related to the concerned segments.

MARKETING INFORMATION SYSTEM FOR DAY-CARE CENTRES

Your success is considerably influenced by the quality of your decisions. You are also aware of the fact that the quality of your decisions is substantially influenced by the quality of information. Improving the quality of your information thus is found significant which requires a sound information system. Of late, we find information technology playing an outstanding role in the management of information in which computer professionals play a commanding role. If you work on a large-scale, it is possible for you to develop a sound information system but if you work on a small-scale, you have to depend on the information selling organisations. Since with the help of the information system, you know about the emerging trends, you enrich your knowledge bank regarding the different income groups, emerging trends in day-care culture, influence of corporate culture on the society, the level of education; you find yourself in a position to understand the users and the potential users, you have to manage. The policy and strategic decisions related to marketing can't be effective, if we find something wrong with the quality of information. This makes it essential that the day-care centres also manage the information system.

They while managing the information system would depend both on primary and secondary sources of information. On the one hand, they have to conduct research, opinion poll, survey of market; while on the other hand, they have also to depend on some of the published information, e.g., telephone directory, electoral rolls, census report, published literature in dailies, magazines and journals. With the support of both the sources of information, the day-care centres would be in a position to formulate a sound marketing mix. In the service product mix, the core and peripheral services would optimally be blended and the process of transforming the peripheral services into core services would also be made effective. The innovations would be found in developing the peripheral services and the efforts thus would keep on moving the process of adding additional attractions and alluring the users and potential users. The quality would be a prime consideration which at any cost would not be allowed a degeneration. The creativity in the promotional measures would be made possible to inform, sense, sensitise, persuade and transform the users into the habitual users and potential users and even non-users into the users. On the basis of information that we receive from the system, the different constituents of promotion would fairly be blended. The fee structure would also be taken due care and all possible efforts would be made to make the same optimal or judicious. There would be a close relation between the quality of services that we offer and the fee that we charge. The people engaged in the process of offering the services would not only be professionally-sound but would also be personally-committed and thus the sympathy and empathy would be found in their behavioural profile. The promises would be made carefully but whatever we promise would be made available to the users without making any distortion and delay.

The aforesaid facts make it clear that management of marketing information has a telling impact on the formulation of a sound marketing mix because the orchestrating of marketing resources with the fluctuating expectations of users can't be possible unless we understand the levels of expectations they have and the feedback they make available.

FORMULATION OF MARKETING MIX FOR DAY-CARE ORGANISATIONS

If we find corporate sector contributing substantially to the development process; if we find corporate culture taking a shape, the westernised lifestyles would continue to gain popularity and this would inject new life and strength to the day-care culture because the flow of consumerism would naturally be found increasing. If we find a consistent increase in the number of working mothers and the double-earners; an analogous increase in the demand of day-care services can't be reversed. If you are sincere and innovative to make the day-care organisations nationally and internationally competitive, you have a prosperous future. Your protto needs to be qualitative-cum-quantitative transformation in the different mixes of marketing so that a galloping increase in the number of satisfied group of users is made possible. It is against this background that we go through the problem of formulation of a sound marketing mix for the day-care organisations.

Even till now, we find a majority of us concentrating on four mixes of marketing, such as product, promotion, price and place but significant developments and emerging trends have made ways for the inclusion of three new mixes, e.g., people, process and physical attractions. We go through the problem of day-care services in the face of all the seven mixes so that transformation is made possible not only in the core services offered by you but also in the peripheral services to add additional attractions to your services mix to use the same as a motivational tool. Since you have a developed information system, you are supposed to know about the changing levels of expectations of users and the potential users. This is to help you to be innovative. You also know about their behavioural profile and this is to help you in identifying the levels of expectations. You have segmented the market and this is going to simplify your task of understanding their needs and requirements, likes and dislikes, taste and temperament, preferences, attitudes and expectations. Your task of formulating a sound marketing mix is found easier that would help you in satisfying the users, increasing the market share and becoming a leader by retaining and gaining the position. Your professional excellence as a marketer and the soundness of your information system are the important aspects determining the magnitude of your success.

The formulation of a marketing mix for the day-care organisations makes it essential that you have an in-depth idea of the needs and requirements and level of expectations of the working mothers, specially coming from the middle income group. They are in search of a day-care centre making available to their children, of the age group 2½ to 3½ to 5 years, proper and friendly environment for an all-round development.[4] Besides, they also make available to them love and affection and parental guidance and adequate arrangements for their safety and security. They provide to their children quality medical aid, healthy food, recreational and sports facilities so that play-way system of education plays an important role in shaping of their personalities and development of career helping them in perceiving world-class primary education. Since you need to make the supply position commensurateto their changing requirements, it is pertinent that your efforts for the formulation of a sound marketing mix prove to be result-oriented. We go through the different submixes to be formulated for the day-care services of world-class

Service Mix for Day-care Organisation

The day-care organisations offer multi-dimensional services to the small kids of working mothers. The single or double earners of the middle income group are the users of their services .The children before getting primary education get friendly environment for their development. It is right to mention that presently a majority of the day-care centres have not been making available to the users quality services[5] and therefore the problem of formulating a sound service mix requires an intensive care of marketers promoting the buisness. It is, of course, a commercial venture but the principles of social markiting are found instrumental in the formulation process and a centre not working with this motto can't get the desired success. Because a number of day-care centres have been offering poor quality of service, it is of prime significance that they practise innovation and synchronise core and peripheral services optimally. They need to keep on moving the process of transforming the peripheral services so that additional attractions to the service mix simplify their functional responsibilities of retaining and gaining the position and becoming a market leader.

The core services focus our attention on all the essential services made available by the day-care centres for which they charge, such as educational aid, recreational facilities, quality food, healthy environment, safety and security, trannsportation and communication facilities, infrastructural support. If we make a survey of the day-care centres working in India, we find a majority of them not making available even the core services. They serve poor quality of food, unfriendly environment, substandard healthcare services and resulting from which a large number of the users have been found dissatisfied. In Figure 19.3, we find a mix of core and peripheral services.

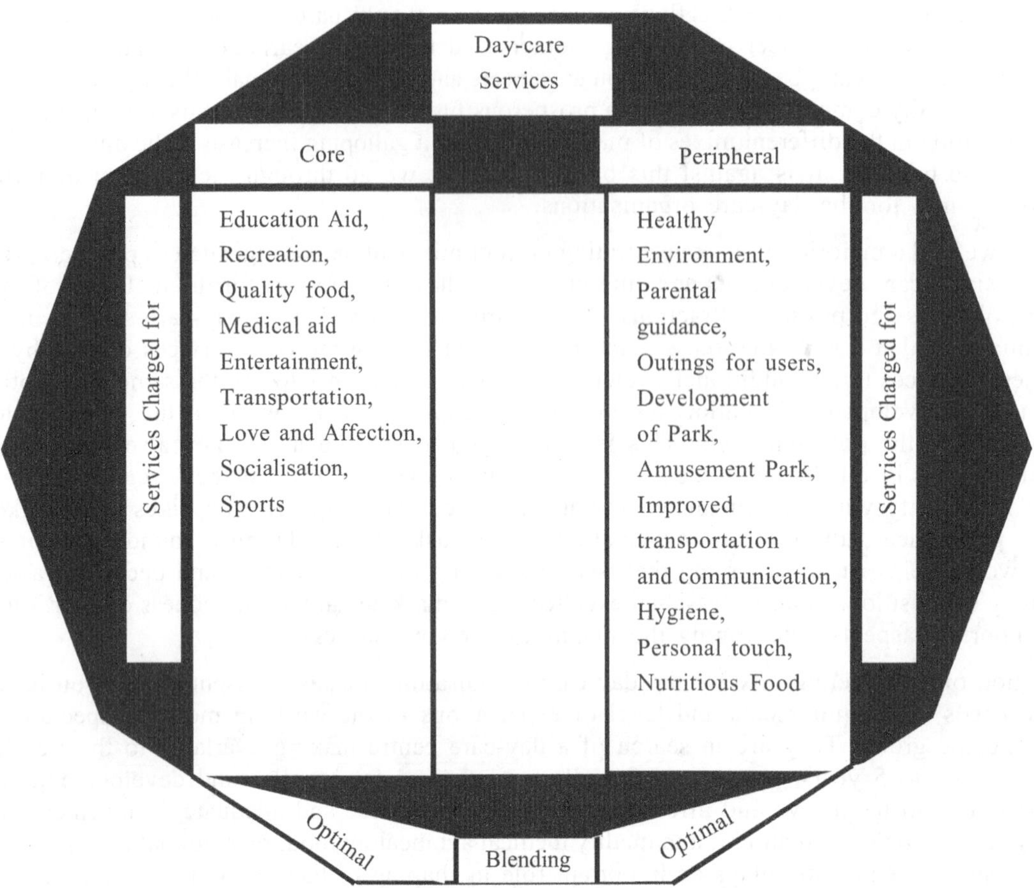

Fig. 19.3: Service Mix for Day-care Organisations

We can't have a boundary for the peripheral services. The prospering day-care organisations make sincere and honest efforts, innovative efforts to transform the peripheral services into the core services. If we talk about a sound nexus for the development of children; if we talk about parental guidance to the children; if we talk about personal-touch-in-service; if we talk about sympathy and empathy; if we talk about culturally-sound entertainment facilities, of course, a very few of them would be found injecting these properties in their service profile. The working mothers, single or double earners send their children to the day-care centres with this hope that they would get everything for their all-round development.

The increasing degeneration in the service profile of day-care organisations is a staunch testimony to this proposition that they need an attitudinal change. Being a commercial venture, you have no doubt a right to adopt a fee structure found optimally sound to the quality of services offered by you but it is not meant that you have a freehand in promoting profiteering. You have to be innovative and to pave avenues for cost-effectiveness so that you succeed in tapping the market potentials. With the help of marketing information system, you can enrich your awareness and can formulate a service mix helping you in many ways.

It is right to mention that a sound service mix of today may be transformed into traditional just tomorrow which may decrease your market share. This makes it essential that you make innovation an ongoing process and maximise the frequency of including new peripheral services in the mix.

The service mix includes pre-school discipline and training, encouraging pre-school socialisation, educational aid, recreational facilities, sports facilities, proper food, quality healthcare services, parental affection and guidance, safety and security. All the services mentioned are just the core services for which the users are charged.

The peripheral services have no boundary. The day-care organisations in all the services need to show personal touch, provisions for outings of children, conducive and friendly atmosphere and natural surroundings, development of park, nutritious food, spacious accommodation, convenient transportation and communication, hygiene and cleanliness and for that sophisticated sanitation facilities, regular check-up of children, good time management and for that, time-honoured services, day-care centre van, proper and adequate spread of day-care centres in the region, personal care by the owner and staff, regular supply of nutritious hot meals and milk, integrated day-care centre with kindergarten classes, and everything that the centres feel sufficient for children enrolled therein.

Sky is the limit for quality. With this notion and vision, we need to develop and establish the day-care centres. The quality of service mix is the real thing that matters. Since we find the services related to the small children, it is pertinent that we don't make any compromise with the quality of services. Whatever we include in the service mix turn them into our promises and the people serving the centres need to make it sure that there would not be any gap between the services-promised and services-rendered. The formulation of service mix is an ongoing process that requires frequent innovation. If you remain innovative, the users reward you and your organisation.

Promoting the Day-care Organisations

You need to serve best. You need to define the perception of quality. You need to be an innovator. But your innovative efforts resulting into the services of world-class also require to be promoted in a creative way so that the users and potential users come to know about you and make decision in your favour. We find promotion a device to inform, sense, sensitise, persuade and ultimately transform the potential users into habitual users. Because your services are of world-class and the working mothers are satisfied with your product and behaviour, they in a very natural way keep on moving the process of rewarding you and promoting your organisation as a hidden salesforce. There are a number of constituents of promotion and your professional excellence is coiled in the essence of formulating a sound mix of the different constituents so that even with a small budget a difficult task is performed by you effectively and successfully. The main thing is creativity that not only helps you in sensitising the potential users but also in making the process of promotion cost-effective. Like other organisations, the day-care organisations also need to promote but their promotional efforts need to be much more sophisticated because a majority of the users belong to the educated and affluent segments. While informing and sensitising them, you don't face any problem because the messages are transmitted to the users found highly receptive.

Since we find new segments emerging, the day-care organisations have a prosperous future. The advancements in the communication and information technology have opened new vistas for the promotional measures to be much more creative and innovative but expensive. A fundamental change in the lifestyles of different segments can't be negated. An attitudinal change that we find existent among masses is likely to increase the market potential. You need to develop your faculties to tap them and to become a market leader. It is against this background that we have talked about the formulation of a sound service mix and it is in this context that we make a strong advocacy in favour of innovative and creative promotional efforts. Of late, we have technologies to inform and sensitise and also the world-class professionals to make the entire process effective and cost-effective.

There are a number of components gravitating our attention and our professional excellence would blend them in such a fashion that the process of gaining and retaining keep on moving without any obstruction. We find advertisement and there are print media, broadcast media and telecast media to make our efforts result-oriented. We need to publicise and with the help of media people, we can do it successfully and effectively. The people engaged in the process of generating the services and making them available to the users are to be motivated and in addition, the working mothers found to be our potential users are also to be allured. We need to use the different tools of sales promotion in the face of emerging trends in the market. Earlier, we have talked about quality services and therefore the users if satisfied would oblige us by acting as a hidden salesforce. Besides, we have also advance communication and information technology to market the services that we generate. The different constituents of promotion, if optimally blended, help us in balancing the demand and supply position.

In Figure 19.4, we find different constituents of promotion and you need to fix the share of each component in the face of emerging trends.

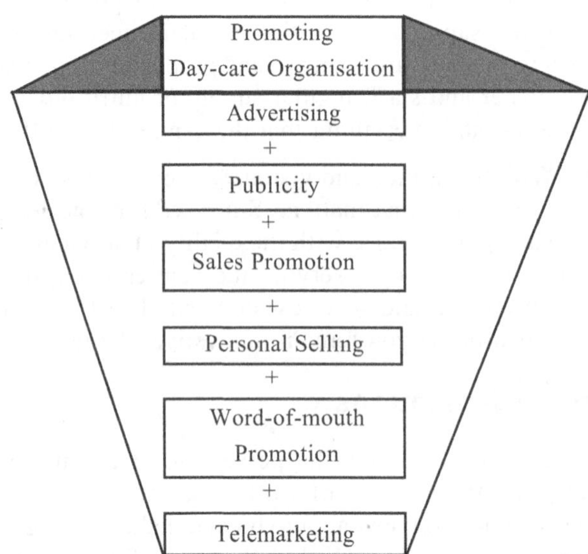

Fig. 19.4: Promotion Mix for Day-Care Organisations

Advertisement: As a paid form of persuasive communication, you need to advertise but with a sense so that on the one hand, you succeed in informing and guiding the users and potential users while on the other hand, also make the process cost-effective. Of late, we find sophisticated form of print technology and by making your messages, slogans, campaigns, facts, figures, achievements, development plans for the future creative; you find it easier to increase the awareness of potential users. With a change in the lifestyles, we find a few of the potential users also enrolling their children though they are not financially sound. This is on account of an attitudinal change. We also find even single earners now developing their fascination to the day-care culture. If we find world-class day-care centres even the high-income group would like to enroll their children. By making advertisement layout creative, you also succeed in motivating the emerging new segments. The print technology helps you in the process because you find sufficient space to inform and sensitise. It is your responsibility to be aware of the dailies, magazines, journals and periodicals subscribed by the target potential users and to publish effective advertisements having wider circulation amongst your users and potential users. The advertisement professionals would help you in the process. Even the day-care organisations not having a big budget for advertisement would be in a position to afford.

With the significant developments in the field of satellite communication and increasing innovations in the field of information and communication technology, we find broadcast and telecast media to be much more effective in today's world. The main thing in the process is to make the potential users fully aware of the developments taking place the world over and you have to perform this responsibility as a professional. Since a majority of your users belong to the well-educated segment, the print media would not only be effective but even cost-effective and therefore your priority attention should be on the same.

The broadcast media and telecast media found relatively expensive are to be used when special conditions necessitate. Because in the telecast media, you also find the visual exposure devices, the messages and photographs related to the peripheral services adding additional attractions can be displayed to inform and sensitise the users. The new emerging segments would find the telecast media much more effective.

You can't have a uniform policy for the media mix. With the changing situations and emerging segments, a particular medium would be found less or more effective. You need to identify the changes taking place in the environmental conditions everyday and to make decisions accordingly. In some of the cases, you would find print media effective whereas in some other cases the telecast media would establish an edge. Your decisions are influenced by two important conditions, e.g., your budget for promotion in general and advertisement in particular and the situational requirements. Since you have assigned due weightage to the formulation of an optimal service mix and your people with a personal-touch-in-service have bridged the gap between the services-promised and services-offered; the messages, slogans, campaigns are to be much more impact-generating.

The strategic decisions related to media play an effective role in increasing the sensitivity of a particular medium. Of late, we find a majority of the users dissatisfied with the performance of day-care organisations because they feel that their children at the centres are not made available even the core services for which they are charged then what to talk about the peripheral services. They also find cases where their children are not supplied quality food, required medical aid, emergency services, essential transportation and communication services, healthy environment. In that case, the strategic decisions related to media make it essential that at the outset you have to be active to identify the lapses in the services you have promised to your users and only thereafter, the advertisements are to be effective. It is also found that people engaged by you at the centres lack personal-touch-in-service and this makes it essential that you improve the behavioural profile of people serving the centres. There must be a correlation between the advertisement messages transmitted and the quality of services offered.

Since we find finance an important consideration before you, it is significant that you assign due weightage to the formulation of an optimal budget for advertisement. Spending much on advertisement and generating a gap between the services-promised and services-offered are the two opposite things making advertisements insensitive even we have made possible creativity with the help and co-operation of advertisement professionals. Projection without generation carries no meaning. Of course you need to advertise but you should have sufficient ground for the same which need your due attention on improving the quality of your services. Blending of print, broadcast and telecast media is essential but advertisement messages need not to be false and misleading.

Publicity: Instrumental in persuading users and potential users without taxing your organisation, the publicity occupies an outstanding place and the day-care organisations need to take the support of media people for that very purpose. It is an important constituent of promotion depending upon the instrumentality and excellence of your professionals. We find relationship marketing as an important base for intensifying publicity that requires your marketing professionals to be tactful and highly communicative. What you do publicise throw a telling impact on the users and potential users if the media people form a positive opinion about your organisation. This makes it essential that while formulating strategies for promotion, you assign due weightage to the personal excellence and communicative ability of the marketing professionals.

Publicity proves to be an effective device of promotion but the intensity of success is considerably influenced by the instrumentality of marketing professionals in motivating the media people. You need to invite media people on lunch and dinner and also to offer some small gifts on a particular occasion. This would induce them to write something in your favour. We can't negate that where advertisements fail, the publicity measures become effective. This is mainly due to the fact that the advertisement messages and slogans are designed and developed by you or your people whereas the publicity is done by the media people.

Since you have a competitive service mix and your services have been appreciated by the users; you can invite media people to witness the ground realities and if they are found satisfied; the news items developed by them would be found much more effective. Conversely, if we find everything wrong with your organisation, the users at large are found dissatisfied with the quality of services you make available to them either they would not write in your favour or even though they write the intensity of effects would be very low. For publicising effectively, you need to promote event management where organising workshops, exhibitions, sports would provide to you an opportunity to motivate media people. Your offerings need not to generate a feeling of flattering or servile attention. This practice in lieu of helping you may harm or jeopardise your interests.

Publicity is not required to give an impression of favour and for that the media people are required to be vigilant. The marketing professionals bear the responsibility of strengthening relationships with the media people which would be found positive to them but initially, they need to make it sure that whatsoever they have promised are offered to the users without making any distortion. If we find cases of complaints lodged by the users, your task of advertising and publicising become much more complicated. This makes it essential that before publicising, you ascertain that users at large are satisfied with your contributions to the process of nursing their small children.

In view of the above, it is right to say that in the day-care services, the publicity as a component of promotion requires more care and precaution because the direct users of the services, e.g., the small children of the age group 2½ to 3½ years draw due attention of all where false promises and lip sympathy don't carry any meaning.

Sales Promotion: If we find day-care a commercial venture, it is pertinent that promotional measures are intensified and in this context, the sales promotion measures need due attention of the marketing professionals. We find a number of people working and serving the centres in different capacities and if we motivate them properly; they would play a decisive role in improving the quality of services. Whatever the gap we find between the services-promised and services-offered would be bridged and the interests of users would significantly be subserved. Motivating people found active in serving the centres thus is an important consideration gravitating due attention of the day-care organisation. If we find an increase in the enrolment of children, there would be a direct increase in the business potentials of the day-care centres which would make them financially sound In any case, this is not to promote profiteering because we find services sizeably related to the social interests.

In addition, the day-care organisations may also think in favour of incentives to the users of the services, such as single earner couple, double earner couple, working mothers or others evincing interests in the day-care services. The offerings may be in the form of small gifts or a subsidised fee structure for a particular period. Outings of parents with their wards may also be successful in motivating them. It is in this context that we talk about excursion facilities for the parents of the children.

Word-of-mouth Promotion: The day-care services if of world-class bear the efficacy of increasing the number of hidden salesforce who act and promote your centre for which they don't charge anything from you. We are aware of the instrumentality of word-of-mouth promoters who in a true sense are the satisfied group of your users. In addition to the users, the social reformists, social scientists, social leaders, political leaders with a clean image may also act and promote your business. But the main thing in the process is the quality of services that you offer. Thus, the focal point in the entire process is the quality of services offered by the centres. If you are innovative and have optimally blended the core and peripheral services which your competitors don't offer, your task of promoting the centre is considerably simplified. The parents, working mothers if satisfied take part in the process. They communicate to their friends and relatives a few words of appreciation about your centres which help you in getting new children. Conversely, if they are dissatisfied, we also find possibilities of a negative trend.

We find word-of-mouth promotion a sharp-edged tool to promote day-care organisation. The advertisements may be ineffective, the publicity may also be found insensitive, the sales promotion measures may or may not help you but the word-of-mouth promotion can't be ineffective and insensitive. We, of course, are influenced by advertisements and publicity but if our friends or relatives communicate something, we trust them and prefer to act. It is against this background that we make a strong advocacy to improve the quality of service mix. Your promotional responsibilities are considerably simplified, if you keep on moving the process of innovations. Thus, you need to assign due weightage to your service profile and make an intensive research of individuals/groups establishing their image as a vocal social leader.

Personal Selling: For promoting day-care organisation, the people serving day-care centres in different capacities bear the responsibility of motivating the potential users. The communicative ability of people becomes an important factor. By narrating to them the different types of services to be made available to the children, they make efforts to influence their impulse. The potential day-care users work in different organisations and with the help of information system, you can document their residential addresses or address of organisations in which they work. Since we find it a process of one-to-one or face-to-face communication, the skill and expertise of people involved in the process determines the intensity of your success. In the process of one-to-one communication, the users may get clarification regarding the doubts and confusion. The queries of users may also be answered so that they don't carry any misunderstanding.

Telemarketing: We are well aware of the instrumentality of telemarketing in sharpening the effectiveness of promotional measures. In an age of communication superhighway, the day-care organisation may use the services of telephone and televisions. Both the measures with the co-operation of each other get an opportunity to promote. Here, it is pertinent that the communication technology and telemarketers both are of quality because instruments not in order and people not aware of the latest developments find it difficult to communicate. Since we find satellite communication getting an overriding priority in the management of communication and on account of that television gaining wider coverage and popularity, the telemarketers can be successful in channelising the information by effective transmission. The users and potential users get different types of information with the help of telephone or television. The day-care organisations find it convenient to promote because they don't need to make provision for enquiry as the telemarketers performance is satisfactory. If we find something wrong with the technology, the instrumentality of telemarketing would considerably be minimised. With the advent of cable marketing, we find wider expansion of transmission particularly in the segment where the market potential has remained untapped or partially tapped.

The aforesaid compenents of promotion need an optimal blending. The organisational and situational factors become significant in the blending process. In all the conditions and for all purposes, we don't find a particular constituent effective and this makes it essential that the marketing professionals undertake an in-depth study of the emerging trends and make use of particular component in the face of prevailing conditions. Since you have budget for promotion, it is essential that your efforts result into the allocation of funds for a particular components in a particular condition. The blending of promotional measures in an optimal fashion is an important managerial responsibility and you have to make it sure that the limitations related to time and finance are given due significance. Your motive is to inform, sense, sensitise, persuade and transform the potential users into actual users with the help of an effective medium.

Creativity in promotion is an important consideration and the day-care centres need not to forget the same. World-class professionals would not be successful in the accomplishment of organisational objectives unless they get enormous co-operation of information system.

Fee Strategy for Day-care Organisation

Inputs determine the quality of outputs. If you have quality inputs, the outputs offered by you would also be of quality and conversely, if you use substandard inputs, the outputs in a very natural way would be of poor quality which would harm your short-term as well as the long-term interests. Of late, we find day-care organisations using a number of expensive inputs for improving the quality of their services. They are supposed to offer healthy food, quality and convenient accommodation, sophisticated transportation and communication, frequent excursion and a number of supporting infrastructural facilities to enrich the quality of services. Unless they charge for that from the users, the task of improving the quality and making innovations frequently would remain unfulfilled. This would result into the emergence of a dissatisfied group of users making an invasion on the image and performance of day-care organisations. Of late, we less talk about creches and in addition, we also find other private welfare organisations not evincing keen interests in the development of day-care centres. This has paved avenues for the development of day-care centres by the private social organisations and the corporations but they have been facing the problem of financial crunch. The emerging negative trends make it essential that the day-care centres make innovative efforts to define and redefine the perception of quality that the children enrolled therein get world-class services and for which they are rationally charged.

Of course, we find day-care centres working as a commercial venture but they have been facing problems while adopting a fee structre striking a balance between the organisational problems and users' expectations. The users in general expect world-class services but they don't welcome an increase in the fee structure. On the other hand, we also find day-care centres, at least a majority of them, promoting profiteering by degenerating the quality of services and charging irrational fee structure from the users. Ultimately, we find small kids/tots the worst suffers who fail in getting the result for which they have been enrolled. Since the problem is related to the development of human and human resources; it is of prime significance that social organisations come forward and formulate social regulations to monitor and regulate the activities of day-care centres so that both of them are beneficiaries, e.g., the users by getting the world-class services and the centrs by having an opportunity to develop and prosper. The strategic decisions related to the fee structure make it essential that the day-care centres don't promote fee structure as a tool for exploitation rather than for motivation, qualitative transformation and value generation. A fair synchronisation of commercial and social consideration is felt essential.

We are aware of the fact that a majority of the users of the day-care services come from middle-income group. A very few of them are related to low income group and other segments. This makes it clear that users are potentially-sound to afford the quality services of day-care centres. The working mothers send their tots to the centres with high hopes and aspirations that their children would get all the services which their counterparts get in other parts of the globe and for which they are mentally and financially sound to welcome a decision favouring a rational fee structure.

Thus, Return on Investment (ROI) is considered to be a suitable fee strategy for the day-care organisation which focuses on assuming a fixed return on the investment made by an organisation. By following ROI strategy for setting fee, the day-care organisations get an opportunity to channelise investments on different heads with the motto of improving the quality of services. Some of us also opine that the day-care organisations while setting fee should prefer cost-based fee strategy but this would close doors for the development of day-care organisations. In the services of day-care centres, the main thing is the quality which can't be maintained and improved unless they generate finance in the face of costs they incur. Since they have a legitimate right of making profits, we find avenues for the minimum possible percentage of profit so that the organisations evince keen interests in channelising investment in the development of day-care centres. Of course, we don't find scope for profiteering. The creches mainly promoted by the welfare department of the government also makes provision for the day-care services, specially for the working mothers of low income and labour groups. In this case, the strategy would not have any relation to cost and a subsidised fee structure would be preferred that would, of course, be on the basis of what the traffic will bear. In a true sense, the fee structure needs to have a close relation with the costs on different types of services offered.

The users' paying capacity also influence the process of setting the fee structure but the welfare organisations would have to follow the discriminatory pricing strategy in which the income would be a base for charging fee. But this may invite a number of complications and confusions. Because there would be possibilities of degeneration in the quality of services, it is judicious that the day-care centres adopt a uniform pricing policy. A majority of the users belong to the group covering double earners and practically they are in a position to afford. The main thing they mind is the quality and therefore while setting fee structure, the day-care centres need to establish a correlation between the quality and fee. This would pave avenues for improving the quality of services.

Of late, we find users's expectations moving upward. They expect world-class services and therefore it is but natural that the fee structure would be high. But the day-care centres need not to work with the motto of exploiting the users and therefore the percentage of profit should be very nominal. There should also be provision for appropriation of profits to the different funds of the centres so that the expansion and development programmes and plans are not to face the problem of financial crunch. If we find day-care centres interested in promoting values, they may also adopt no-profit, no-loss strategy. Since we find it an organisation directly related to social interests, we find rationale behind promoting self-financing or no-profit, no-loss policy.

In view of the aforesaid facts, it is right to say that the day-care centres need a fee structure found sufficient to serve the users in tune with their changing levels of expectations and this would make an advocacy in favour of ROI strategy. The pricing or fee strategy becomes significant because all the mixes are governed by it.

Channelisation of Day-care Services

If you promise more and offer less; you invite dissatisfaction. If you promise less and offer more; you invite satisfaction. This makes it essential that any gap between the services-promised and services-offered makes your task complicated. You need to bridge the gap between the two so that the users get services in the face of promises. Generally, the people meant for channelising the services to the ultimate users generate a gap by distorting the quality or delaying the process. This is not only to affect the quality of your services but also to tarnish the image of your organisation. It is against this background that we find channel management playing a significant role in the entire marketing process. In the service generating organisations, we find the delivery process a bit different and therefore the people serving the organisation in different capacities responsible for making available the promised services to the ultimate users, if not managed and motivated properly, deliberately delay the process. This makes it essential that marketing professionals make it sure that right from the beginning to the last stage till the users get the services; they manage things with the motto of maintaining quality and ensuring punctuality.

In the day-care services, by displaying the notices and publishing the prospectus, brochures and the leaflets; the day-care scentres make some promises regarding the quality of services to be made available to the users. If the users feel that they have not been made available the same quality of services as offered or/and the time schedule has not been maintained; we find a gap that makes an invasion on the image and the users are found dissatisfied. The day-care organisations make available details of food to be made available to the children as per the schedule. If they don't get the same, we find a gap. Like this, they promise recreational and sports facilities but they don't offer. The provisions cross through different channels. If we talk about the quality of food — the suppliers of food materials, the cook, the required ingredients used; the time schedule; the way of offering food are the different channels managed with the support of back-line staff, through which the food items reach to the children. If we find something wrong with the food materials, or ingredients, or cook; the quality cannot be maintained.

The day-care centres also promise love and affection and parental guidance and instructions to the students. The people managing classes, rooms, bearing the responsibility of entertainment and recreation not showing personal-touch-in-service generate a gap and make distortion. This makes it essential that the day-care centres assign due weightage to management of people, monitor the process minutely, make supervision carefully and frequently so that at the different stages of offering of services, we don't find any distortion. The supporting infrastructural facilities and technical and skilled or unskilled people working there become a party to the process of distortion or degeneration.

The marketing practices make it essential that the children enrolled therein get all the services and facilities and in this context, the marketing professionals play a commanding role. You bear the responsibility of formulating the channel, deputing the people, monitoring and supervising their performance and making it sure that the promises are honoured at all the stages by all the concerned people.

Location Point for the Day-care Centres

We find day-care services of very sensitive nature because the services are related to the interests of tots/ small children not bearing the efficacy of resisting or countering the odds. They use whatever you offer. They live how and in what way you manage. This makes it essential that the policy and strategic decisions related to the location of day-care centres assign due weightage to the aspects standing as an obstacle to the safety, security and protection of children.[6] The location point needs to be smoothly and conveniently accessible and this draws our attention on the availability of all-weatherproof roads and the adequate, comfortable and safe transportation facilities. The working mothers, parents, visitors come frequently to the centres and therefore we find safe, convenient and frequent transportation facilities essential. They also need to meet their wards children frequently and this gravitates our attention on the availability of communication facilities. Since we talk about spacious accommodation, the centres would find it difficult to make it possible in the cities precincts and therefore the convenient location point would preferably be the outskirts. The day-care centres need spacious ground for developing park and promoting plantation to make the atmosphere environment-friendly and again the location point needs to be the outskirts of towns and cities. Proper sanitation, peace, sound location, free from the problem of noise pollution are some of the essential considerations necessitating due attention on the location points.

Of late, we find cases of kidnapping of children developing as a sunrise industry and this diverts our attention on the availability of police protection. The centres if close to the police station would make available to the children safety and security against the anti-social elements. The day-care centres are to be located keeping in view the conveniences and comforts of their parents so that the parents and children find it convenient to meet. The centres need a number of infrastructural facilities and this makes it essential that water, power, communication, healthcare centres or hospitals, and other services are available without interruption.

The aforesaid facts focus our attention on the place decision to be given priority attention while locating the day-care centres. Because the centres bear the responsibility of making available to the tots enrolled therein all the services and facilities making their stay comfortable, it is much more significant that they take a decision after obtaining the detailed information about the place where the centres are to be located. A few of us feel that location points for the day-care centres should be in the cities precincts but when we talk about availability of all the facilities within the campus and in addition, the problem of environmental pollution is also to constrain location at the central places, the location of centres in the outskirts would not be problematic particularly when we find round-the-clock transportation facilities. Because we find establishment of day-care organisation a capital-intensive proposition, it is essential that before selecting a place, we consider even small things which in the days and years to come may invite problems. Easy and convenient accessibility, peace and safety, environmental conditions, spacious accommodation are some the essential considerations gravitating close attention of day-care planners so that location proves to be a source of motivation.

Process

The processing of day-care services draws our attention on the different process through which the services reach to the ultimate users. The children enrolled in the creches or day-care centres and the parents both of them are the beneficiaries. Since we find direct users of services small kids or childern; they find it difficult to evaluate the quality of the delivery process. Due to a mix of number of services offered to the users, the professionals bear the responsibility of co-ordinating different types of services which are processed with joint co-operation of people and equipment. The teachers offering the educational facilities, the doctors offering the medicare services, the recreation and transportation services offered by the concerned agencies, the food services offered by the concerned staff and many other services need due attention for time-honoured and quality-based delivery. Keeping in view the age group of users, it is pertinent that day-care centres do not allow any leakage and make the services foolproof. Because we find a number of services mechanised, the flow can be maintained with the help of new generation of technology. In this context, it is significant that parents are satisfied with the quality of services made available to their children.

We cannot negate that the day-care services are found of complex nature. The approaches are required to be standardised and the operational flow is to be maintained. At each and every stage, the professionals need to make it sure that all the services are delivered to the users.

Physical Evidence and Attractions

Due to a complex nature of services offered by the day-care centres, the professionals also need to assign due weightage to servicescapes or service ambience or the management of physical facilities adding additional attractions to services and becoming helpful in generating services fragrance found very much instrumental in impressing upon the parents visiting the day-care centres. It is in this context that we focus on physical evidence and attractions as an important submix of the marketing mix. Ambient conditions in a very natural way depend upon the nature of services and the types of users using the services. If we find direct users not having the potentials to study the ambience, the parents as beneficiaries bear the responsibility of studying and understanding the same. The parents visiting the day-care centres for getting enrolment of their children need to be influenced so that they strengthen perception of the quality of services to be delivered to their children. In the context of day-care services, the tangibilisation draws our attention on the items, commensurate with the taste, temperament and preferences of children. Becauses the day-care centres make a mix of different types of services, the professionals need to display the technology used in the process, the items for entertainment, aesthetic management, sports, brochures, newsletters, the interiors and exteriors, the nutritional awareness, civic sense, etc. The tangible repesentation of the services to be delivered would be helpful in the formation of opinion of the parents or others visiting the day-care centres.

With the globalisation of economy, we also find globalisation of fashion, culture and civilisation. With the increasing importance of corporate sector, we find a craze for adopting the westernised lifestyles. It is felt that in the process of building a positive image, in addition to other dimensions, we also think about the living habits and conditions of people serving an organisation in different capacities. The physical appearance of our employees becomes instrumental in the formation of a positive or negative opinion. There is nothing more appealing than a man with a sense of wit and fun. There is nothing more paying than an aesthete. It is in this context that we find almost all categories of organisations assigning due importance to physical attractions. The day-care centres also need to think about this mix of the marketing because here people serving the centres also bear the responsibility of developing aesthetic sense. The children witnessing classic look and impact-generating appearance develop a sense in a natural fashion. When they find people serving them beautifully dressed, neat, clean, tempted to personal hygiene and adding additional attractions in their physical appearance, the children perceive and practise.

The children enrolled in the centres belong to different sections and groups. They also come from different regions and with a different family background. The lifestyles of working mothers and the lifestyles of housewives serving the centres, if of identical nature and behaviour, make the task of day-care centres much more easier. If we gravitate our attention on the types of people serving the day-care centres, we find housewives and retired teachers dominating the working in addition to cleaners that we find for the sanitation services. Aayah has also been found engaged in the process and in addition, we also find helper for receiving the children from their parents.

The physical attractions focus our attention on the dresses and make-up of people serving the centres. We also talk in the very context about the physical appearance of staff. If they don't live neat and clean and are not well dressed, the children and visitors would not form a positive opinion about the centre. Because we find children in the process of education and learning, they would not perceive aesthetic sense. This makes it essential that the day-care centres assign due weightage to the measures helping them in making the physical appearance of their employees attractive. So far as the sweepers and helpers are concerned, they need to be supplied uniform so that the projection of a fair image is possible. The teachers also need to be neat and clean and well-dressed. Since we find a majority of the staff coming from the segments, housewives and the day-care centres need mother-like behaviour with the children, it is essential that they with their dresses and behaviour give to the children an impression of mother. Besides, the visitors or potential users of your services coming to the centres would also have a positive opinion regarding the quality of the organisation. Since we need cultural orientation in the Indian perspective, the dresses and living conditions of staff should not give a negative impression.

In view of the above, it is right to say that in the process of formulating a sound mix for marketing the day-care services, the physical attractions need a priority attention.

People Serving the Day-care Centres

Ultimately people matter. We talk about the professional excellence of people serving the centres. We also talk about personal commitment and personal-touch-in-service. We even talk about sympathy and empathy which the staff need on a priority basis. We have also gone through the problem of physical attractions. But of all the properties that we need to inculcate, the human touch, humanity, human values contribute substantially to the development process. Since the services of day-care centres are found very much sensitive, it is pertinent that while managing different categories of people serving the organisation, we make possible a fair blending of all. In the face of cases of complaints lodged by the users and the efforts made by the organisation for their redressal, it is right to comment that they are not sincere to the management of people. Of course, the infrastructural facilities matter and you have made available the same but if teachers, helpers, aayas and others lack a high behavioural profile, the entire exercise would be turned into a fiasco. Because the centres bear the responsibility of developing children, satisfying the parents as users, improving the quality of the service mix; it is much more impact generating that the day-care centres assign an overriding priority to the management of people.

You need to be vigilant while recruiting because you need staff having a high behavioural profile. They are not to be aggressive in nature and rough in behaviour. They require personal-touch-in-service and in addition, the human touch. Of course, they should have professional excellence and teachers serving the centres should have an aptitude found pro to the attitudes of children. They need not to react and to be rough. They need not only sympathy but even empathy. While recruiting, you make it sure that all the properties are available or you incorporate the same by educating and training. Since the levels of expectations of users are found high, it is essential that whatever complaints are lodged are redressed quickly and properly.

The educational and family background of people serving the centre is found significant because if we find something wrong with their nature, character and behaviour; the children enrolled therein would be the worst sufferers. While educating and training, it is to be made sure that people serving the centre have conviction and personal commitment so that they perform excellently and efficiently. We find motivation, an important factor influencing the level of efficiency of people serving the centre. It is found that by and large almost all the centres have not been paying even reasonable salaries to their staff then what to talk of other incentives. The process of exploiting the staff needs a departure. Since you charge fee and generate finance; the paucity of fund is not to be an excuse for the payment of low salaries to the staff. In this context, it is essential that the day-care centres integrate motivation with contributions and staff serving satisfactorily are paid lucrative salaries so that they serve the centre sincerely and honestly. Conversely, the people against whom the users lodge complaints are either to be removed or punished. Control is an important dimension of the management of people and this makes it essential that very often you monitor and supervise their performance. This would help the process of transforming the inefficient people into the performer and top performer.

DAY-CARE MARKETING IN INDIAN PERSPECTIVE

We cannot regulate the flow and direction of wind. What we can do is to enrich our potentials to counter the same. The emerging negative trends in the society make it clear that there would be a galloping increase in the number of working mothers in the days and years to come. Our increasing temptation and fascination for material culture sizeably influenced by western culture cannot be fulfilled unless and until we promote the corporate culture. The corporate culture bears the efficacy of changing the social structure and influencing the behavioural patterns. It we find an increase in the number of working mothers the day-care centres of world-class would remain to be the only solution.

With the beginning of the decade 1990s, we find a fundamental change in our development patterns. The corporate culture started dominating the Indian economic system which paved avenues for the development of material culture. The consumerism trapped us in such a fashion that willingly or unwillingly a change in our lifestyles was found taking a strong shape. This injected new life and strength to the slogan, *Earn More and Spend More.* The concept of housewives was replaced by working women or mothers which, no doubt, helped them in leading a luxurious lifestyle but at the same also created a major problem that their small kids remained neglected and were deprived of the parental affection particularly at the age and stage when they need much more nursing. However, the new wave culture started gaining popularity and this opened doors for the development of day-care centres or crèches on an organised basis. Today, we find day-care culture emerging as a fashion, as well as a professional requirement *vis-a-vis* a situational compulsion.

The beginning of 21st century made ways for a number of development in the socio-cultural and economic systems. The increasing domination of Multinational Corporations (MNCs) mainly due to liberalisation helped emergence of a new wave culture which helped creation of a multicultural or cross-cultural society. In addition to a number of positive effects on our national economy, we also witnessed emergence of live-in culture which we may consider a sore-spot on the Indian culture. On account of material culture, the children remained neglected and on account of live-in culture we are making ways for an invasion on our culture and civilisation.

Truly speaking, it becomes much more difficult to regulate our behaviour if we find ourselves experiencing the taste of modern lifestyles and tasting the pleasure of unregulated sexual behaviour. The drama continues till the transformation of human culture into animal culture. But we have no option because once we taste the fragrance of luxurious lifestyles it becomes too much difficult for us to back because we reach to a no-return point.

Parents nurture a dream of developing the potentials of their children. They, of course, play a crucial role in the development of glamorous career and attractive personality. Since we find them working mothers, they find it difficult to spare time for the growth and development of their children. The anguish of working parents for not being in a position to provide the emotional support to their tots in absence of elders at home has been existent in a majority of the families. They have been found hunting for a sweet and loving day-care centre. A child around 2½ to 3½ years needs a social environment to be socialised outside the family and the day-care centres fulfil this need because they provide to the children conducive environment where he/she can learn new things, play, dance, interact and share with a group of children away from home. At day-care centres, the children colour, paint, play with blocks, wood, sand, clay and water and they carry out simple dramatisation, listen to stories and learn simple songs.

In mines, factories and plantations and also in the construction companies, we find the concept as a statutory obligation[7]. We don't find the concept for working women in the services and professions and it is in this context that we find rationale behind the development of day-care centres in the voluntary and private sector. Recently, the private sector and even leading corporations have been found evincing keen interests in the development of world-class day-care centres. With the development of private sector and with an increase in the temptation of women to be the working mothers, we find future of day-care centres very prosperous. This makes it essential that they improve the quality of services to be made available to the children of working mothers for which they don't hesitate to pay even high structure of fee. We find day-care centres being run either independently or as a part of kindergarten schools by the women in the urban areas to meet the pre-school educational needs of the children of urban middle class families.[8]

Since we find the concept of nuclear family gaining popularity, the day-care culture would have a potentially-sound market provided they keep on moving the process of qualitative transformation. Willingly or unwillingly, we need to confess that materialism has been opening new vistas of development for consumerism which no doubt would make our lifestyles much more sophisticated but at the same time would also deprive tots of the affection of mother which in any case can't be judicious. The social scientists have been found concentrating their attention on the problem but because we find opportunities in the market, an optimal tapping can't be wrong. This necessitates priority attention of marketing professionals because the centres managed by the hosusewives have not been found conscious of improving the quality of services. The strategic decisions make it essential that we think over the problem as a professional, explore new solutions to the emerging problems, make possible perfection in our decisions and make the entire process cost-effective partially to make profits but considerably to subserve social as well as the national interests.

A few of us may comment on the inclusion of the working mothers of a joint family in the group of users but here we talk about virtues, values, beliefs, humanity, morality, ethics, empathy and in a majority of the joint families, we find even close blood relations not having all the aforesaid properties in their own nature, character and behaviour then how and in what way they would nurture the children and would inculcate basic traits and if they practise what would be the intensity of impact, is a problem to be deliberated upon. If we find grandfathers and grandmothers, uncles and aunts, cousins and neighbours almost all of them promoting unlawful and unethical practices; they in a true sense, can't have a moral right of guiding and instructing their children. If they do it, the process would remain ineffective. It is high time that we confess on the prevailing situations and make available to our budding generations a conducive atmosphere in which they get an opportunity to learn, a base to develop and a very sound foundation to prosper. Failing which, we would develop professionally-sound people of course in a very large number but in absence of personal commitment and value orientation; they would often make a compromise with self-interests even at the cost of organisational, social and national interests.

Against this background, we need to make efforts to formulate strategies helping the day-care centres in perceiving the time-honoured perception of quality. Since they bear the responsibility of serving the children of working mothers, well educated mothers, fully aware and conscious mothers; the marketing professionals need to formulate a sound marketing mix in which we find a fair synchronisation of all the submixes. Ultimately, we are rewarded for the quality that we offer to our users. Innovators prove to be the leaders and this makes it essential that we activate sincere and honest efforts to develop core and peripheral services and keep on moving the process of transforming the peripheral services into the core services so that the process of adding additional attractions and increasing market share move forward on an equal footing. We need to enrich our information system which would benefit us fantastically. The prime motto is to improve the quality of services so that we promise more and offer much more. By doing such, we would be successful in building a positive image. We need to be innovative by celebrating the birthday of children and inviting parents, conducting ideal parent contest, and offering small gifts.

Since the users and potential users of the services are becoming more sensitive to quality, you need creativity in all the promotional measures you adopt. While advertising, you should have an in-depth knowledge of different segments and their changing levels of expectations. The print media would help you in informing the details of the services you offer and propose to offer. The telecast media would help you while showing the services that you offer, the environmental conditions of the centre, the natural surroundings that you offer to your children and everything at their disposal. Keeping in view the financial limitations, you need to formulate a cost-effective mix of media. The other tools of promotion such as publicity, users' promotion, word-of-mouth promotion, personal selling and telemarketing are also to be made innovative. While incorporating new properties, you need to know about the measures adopted by the competitive day-care centres. There must be a correlation between the services you offer and messages, slogans, information that you transmit and telecast.

In a majority of the day-care centres, we don't find a fair match between the fee that they charge and the quality of services that they offer. This in a very natural way dissatisfies them. While formulating the fee strategy, you need to make it sure that fee structure and quality has a correlation. We find the users sensitive to quality and therefore you have to adopt a reasonable fee strategy ensuring you the profit besides paving avenues for improvements in the quality of services.

The people serving your centre often create a gap between the quality that you promise and the services that you offer. This focuses your attention on the different channels through which the services reach to the target users. The staff working in different capacities at the different stages have to make it sure that they offer much more the services the centre had promised. In this context, you also need to ascertain that your employees are professionallysound, personally-committed and value-based. This would help you in many ways.

A majority of the centres have been found located close to the big housing colonies.[9] There is no doubt in it that with the viewpoint of accessibility and safety, we find it a convenient point but the modern concept of day-care centres makes a strong advocacy in favour of park, garden, sports ground, spacious accommodation and pollution-free environment which, of course, would not be possible there. It is in this context that the day-care centres need to change the location points which should be close to the cities and towns but in the outskirts. Of late when we find sophisticated transportation facilities, the users, staff and visitors would not find it difficult to reach to the centres or door-to-door services may also be offered. It is also to be made sure while locating the day-care centres that children enrolled therein are safe because we find sunrise industry thriving and kidnapping of children would not only tarnish the image of your organisation but would also complicate your task of nursing the children in a safe environment.

The people serving an organisation portray its image and therefore your employees should also be aware of the physical attraction which focuses on the dresses, make-up and physical appearance of your staff. Elegance and affluence should be maintained to the extent it is possible.

The strategic decisions in all the areas mentioned above need to assign top priority to the behavioural profile so that the children not only get the educational aid but also parental guidance, love and affection and personal and human touch.

SUMMARY

In this chapter, you have gone through different dimensions of day-care services. After going through the chapter, be sure that the following are well versed:

Day-care Services – The Perception: The day-care services are related to the small children of working mothers between the age group 2½ to 3 ½ years and in case of kindergarten 2½ to 5 years.

Day-care Centre – The Perception: Day-care centre or a day-nursery is an institutional effort to manage the services for the urban working mothers, specially coming from the middle-income group.

Day-care Marketing – The Perception: In the marketing of day-care organisation, the formulation of marketing mix is discussed in which all the seven mixes, such as service, promotion, channel, pricing/fee, people, processing and place and physical attractions have been gone through. It is a managerial process of marketing the day-care services with the help of marketing professionals.

Rationale behind Day-care Marketing: We market the day-care services for promoting child care, making available to the users world-class education and training, offering specialised teaching, increasing day-care culture, preparing a strong base for pre- and primary schooling, culture orientation and meeting the requirements of modern lifestyles.

Behavioural Profile of Users: The users are the working mothers belonging to the middle-income group and the children 2½ to 3½ years. The study of behavioural profile focuses our attention on studying the levels of expectations.

Segmentation in Day-care Marketing: While segmenting, we divide the market into different small groups so that the process of understanding their needs and requirements, attitudes and preferences and levels of satisfaction are found easier.

Marketing Information System for Day-care: The day-care centres need to develop information system so that facts and figures and data collected from different sources help in identifying the emerging trends to tailor the marketing resources in the face of evolving changes.

Formulation of Marketing Mix for Day-care Organisation: It is a process of formulating different submixes of marketing, such as service/product, promotion, channel, price/fee, physical attractions, people and process.

Service Product Mix: The day-care centres need to blend the core and peripheral services in such a fashion that the users feel satisfied and the organisational interests are also fulfilled.

Promoting the Day-care Organisation: While formulating the promotion mix, the marketing professionals bear the responsibility of blending the different constituents of promotion, sales promotion, telemarketing in an optimal fashion so that the task of informing, sensing, sensitising, persuading and transforming the potential users into actual and habitual users is considerably simplified.

Fee Strategy for Day-care Organisation: The marketing professionals bear the responsibility of adopting a fee strategy which on the one hand, meet interests of users while on the other hand, the commercial considerations are also fulfilled.

Channel Management and Location: We study here the different channels through which the services are delivered to the ultimate users. Besides we also go through the suitable location points for the Creches or Day-care Centres.

Process: This submix of marketing draws our attention on the processing of services with the motto of increasing the flow of operation. We also find use of technology for offering the multi-faceted services to the users with the help and co-operation of people belonging to different areas in which they have expertise.

Physical Evidence and Attractions: In this submix of marketing, our focuses is on the srevicescapes or service ambience or physical facilities which the interiors, exteriors, music, aesthetic sense, display of services to be offered are considered important in the very context. In addition, the professionals also need to consider the dresses and uniforms of people serving there which should be neat and clean to add additional attractions to services.

People: The teachers, helpers, maid servants, sweepers, cooks, physical instructors, musicians are the important dimension for which the day-care centres crèches need quality people. The professionals bear the responsibility of managing them in a right way so that they show personal-touch-in-services efficiencies of making available to the kids the parental affection. They also need human touch in their behaviour. Because the kids considered as users are found gullible in nature and at the very early stage, they need special care and treatment.

Day-care Marketing in Indian Perspective: We find day-care culture gaining a momentum even in the Indian context. With the development of corporate culture, we find increasing domination of material culture which has been creating a sound nexus for the development of corporate culture, we find increasing domination of material culture which has been creating a sound nexus for the development of crèches or day-care centres. The professionals managing the day-care centres need to conceptualise the principles of marketing with the motto of studying and understanding the changing behavioural profile of parents who need the services. The quality of services is to be improved and it is to be made sure that the promised services care made available to the kids and parents as guardians without any distortion and with personal touch. The day-care organisations need professional excellence because the users of the services are found gullible who can be deceived by anyone. The people providing the services need human touch in their behaviour. There are a number of cases to testify the ill-treatment of working people with the kids which we find inhuman and not only to tarnish the image of day-care centres but also to keep the users in a vulnerable condition. In the Indian perspective, it is pertinent that the day-care centres also strength and tighten safety and security measurements. With the mushroom growth of day-care centres or crèches, we find a big deterioration in the quality of their services and therefore the professional marketing the services need to involve themselves personally so that no scope is left for unpleasant development.

KEY TERMS

Crèche	Hygiene
Day-care Centre	Pre-school Discipline
Day-care Culture	Kindergarten
New Wave Culture	Satellites
Settlement Houses	Leaflets
Burgeoning	Kidnapping
Nursing Kids	Wit and Fun
Parental Affection	Fiasco
Nuclear Family	Pre-primary Education
Alluring	Heritage
Profiteering	Live-in Culture
Amusement Parks	Cross-culture
Material Culture	Empathy
Formative Age Group	Peripheral

Review Questions

1. What do you mean by Day-care Services? Focus on the Day-care Centres and the multi-faceted services offered to the children of formative age group.
2. Define Day-care Marketing. Explain the rationale behind conceptualisation and application of marketing principles by the day-care organisations.
3. Focus on the changing behavioural profile of users of Day-care services belonging to different segments.
4. Throw light on the different submix of marketing for the Day-care services in the Indian perspective.
5. Discuss the different extended marketing mixes in the context of day-care services.
6. Focus on the Services mix for the day-care services.
7. Comment on the different components of promotion for motivating the potential parents or working ladies.
8. Throw light on the strategies to be adopted by the Day-care organisations for striking a balance between the interests of Day-care centres and their users.
9. Focus on the location point to be suitable for the Day-care Centres.

Application Exercises

1. Being a marketing professional, formulate a marketing mix for the Day-care Organisations in the Indian context.
2. You have been asked to select suitable location point for the Day-care centres. Focus on the different considerations to help you in the selection process.
3. Do you feel that Day-care centres need a societal approach? Justify your arguments.
4. Focus on the promotional measures to help you in persuading the potential parents interested in enrolling their small kids in your centre.
5. As a marketing professional serving a big Day-care Centre, focus on the extended submixes of marketing to help you in processing, tangiblising and developing a team of dedicated people who play an important role in satisfying the users.
6. Working as a professional in a Day-care Centres, throw light on the service mix you will formulate in the face of emerging trends in the Indian society.
7. Do you justify application of marketing by the Day-care Centres? Define your argumentss as a professional.

Endnotes

1. Potokowaski, *Work and Family System: A Naturalistic Study of Working Class and Lower Class Families,* New York, 1979.
2. Felice Schwartz, *Management of Women and Facets of Family Life,* Harvard Business Review, January-February 1987.
3. Beliga Vamana B., *Issues, Strategy and Marketing Implications of Day-care Services — A Case,* Study Paper presented to All-India Commerce Conference, 1999.
4. Meena Swaminathan., Breast-feeding and Working Mothers, *Economic and Political Weekly,* May 1993, pp, 887-91.
5. Fran Suzzner, Rodger and Charles Rodgers, Business and Facts of Family Life, *Harvard Business Review*, pp. 121-29. November-December, 1989.
6. Baliga Vamana B., *op. cit.*
7. Meena Swaminathan S., *op.cit.*
8. Baliga Vamana B., *op.cit.*
9. *Ibid.*

COURIER MARKETING

Corporatisation accelerated the pace of development which increased the pressure of work on the Department of Posts. This made ways for the development of courier services. A mushroom growth of small and big players created quality gap. We expect that the world-class marketing professionals will bridge the same, and the courier world will perceive Just-in-time concept.

Chapter Objectives

Introduction – Courier Marketing: A Conceptual Framework – Rationale Behind Courier Marketing – Market Segment for Courier Services – Information Management for Courier Organisations – The Formulation of Marketing Mix for Courier Organisations – Product Mix – Promotion Mix – Price Mix – Place Mix – Process Mix – Physical Evidence and Attractions – People – Courier Marketing in Indian Perspective – Emergence of Department of Posts as a Big Competitor – Summary – Key Terms – Review Questions – Application Exercises – Endnotes.

Learning Objectives

This chapter aims at studying the different facets of courier marketing. The conceptualisation of modern marketing principles may be helpful in improving the quality of services. The readers after going through the problem develop their awareness of the application of different mixes such as product mix, promotion mix, price mix, people mix, process mix, physical evidence and people. Safe and time-honoured delivery to the destination requires professional excellence which would be possible with the help of marketers. The big players need to strengthen their realisation that the users have a high level of expectations from them which if not fulfilled will harm them and will benefit the Department of Posts in many ways.

INTRODUCTION

Our expectations for quality move forward even without a gap. The new processes of development, new generation of technology virtually are the gifts of since long continuing inventions and innovations by our scientists who always nurture a passion for defining and redefining quality. Thus, the cycle of expecting more and offering more keep on moving. The organisations identifying the right level of expectations succeed whereas others start struggling for their survival. With the development of corporate culture, the contours of development have undergone radical changes. Increasing temptation of masses to quality and speed has been found paving new avenues for new services bearing the potential of excelling competition. Thus, the innovators prove to be the leaders whereas the followers find no option but to copy. We reward quality and punish for not exercising creativity.

In almost all the countries of globe, we find public sector as an initiator and private sector as an accelerator. Acceleration is not to be possible in absence of initiation. From the time immemorial, we find provisions for formal or informal, organised or unorganised services playing an important role in satisfying the customers or users, specially related to the postal services with a variation in their forms. Till the development of transportation services, we used animals for sending our views, messages, letters. Mail was carried by runners or couriers who journeyed on foot, horses and camels and by bullock carts, horse carriages and country boats. There was no regular system of carrying parcels. With the introduction of railways, it become easier to carry mails to distant places safely and at short regular intervals. The prime focus is on the fact that development of transportation facilities injected new life and continuity to the mail services and helped a lot to the Department of Posts in minimising the duration and improving the quality of services. We cannot deny the fact that the services inexpensive in nature considerably served the socio-economic sectors of the country. Thus, we find Indian Railways as the mainstay of the postal system. Since 1907, when the Railway Mail Service (RMS) was established till present, the Department of Posts has been found using the services of Indian Railways both for quantitative and qualitative improvements in the postal system.

Corporatisation has accelerated the pace of development which has been found increasing the pressure on the Department of Posts. With the mounting pressure of work and decreasing operational efficiency, the Department of Posts found it difficult to improve the supply side. A degeneration in the quality of services was found aggravating the magnitude of problem. This raised a strong advocacy in favour of an alternative system to cater to the increasing demand side. It was against this background that we find emergence of courier services on an organised basis. A number of formal and informal organisations gradually started taking part in the process.

It is significant to mention that the process of development in the Indian context was initiated only after the beginning of the decade 1980s when SkyPAK, an internationally acclaimed courier organisation entered the Indian market with the motto of ensuring safe delivery of documents to the users. Since the Department of Posts was facing an image problem, the SkyPAK got a profitable market to prosper and by the end of the decade, its profitability reached to its peak. It was against this background that to innovate its services, the Department of Posts introduced Speed Post in 1986. Later on, we find DHL coming and becoming a market leader, particularly in the Indian perspective. Besides, we find Blue Dart, Elbee strengthening their market share and in addition, many others entered the courier market for which they had a well-established opportunities to capitalise on. Undoubtedly enough, the big players and small players snatched market from the Dept. of Posts. The safe delivery, time-honoured delivery were the outstanding features of their services which substantially helped them in increasing the market share.

With the beginning of the decade 1990s we find a major increase in the air fare which forced the courier organisations to increase the price. In addition, we also find one new development with the emergence of co-loaders working as middlemen which engineered a sound foundation for the development of small players. The co-loaders collect consignments from various small courier shops and fly them to the respective places. On account of a co-ordination and linking of services, the co-loaders helped small players in making the price of services much more competitive and challenging specially for the big players. We cannot negate that such a beginning in the courier market helped development of small courier organisations.

With the beginning of the 21st century, the market for courier services was found sizeably developed. A number of big players and a very good number of small players in the market made ways for some of the negative developments. The quantitative transformation if not well supported by professional excellence closes doors for qualitative transformation. The small players were not in a position to make possible professional services which resulted in unfair and unlawful practices in the courier services. The delayed delivery became a common feature due to inefficient people serving the courier organisations. Though due to corporatisation, we find the demand side increasing very fast but expect a very few almost all the courier organisations disappointed their customers.

It is high time that courier organisations realise gravity of the situation and make sincere and honest efforts to professionalise their services. Of course, we find nothing wrong in making use of the services of middlemen or co-loaders but the most important thing is the expectations of customers which cannot be fulfilled if we find small players not evincing interests in improving the quality of their services.

Positive and negative developments crop up in a natural process. However, we find courier organisations prospering and the trend will continue further because we find big players innovating their product portfolio.

The courier services thus started establishing an edge over the Department of Posts. A good number of courier organisations both at national and international levels have been offering quality services to the institutional and individual users. At the same time, it is also significant to mention that there has been a mushroom growth of courier organisations which has made possible a degeneration in the quality and resulting from which we find much more scope for dissatisfaction.

Professional excellence bears the efficacy of bringing a radical change in the quality. Besides, it also helps in making the process of service generation cost-effective. Minimising the duration of service delivery, making the fee structure nationally and internationally competitive and generating a sense of confidence amongst the service users need priority attention of professionals managing the courier organisations. It is hoped that application of modern marketing principles by the courier organisations would make the ways for qualitative improvements. The professionals need to study and understand the changing levels of expectations of users which are found high. In an age of speed, we find their expectations, of course, judicious and therefore it is to be made sure that their service mix is in tune with the changing requirements. It is also to mention that a few of the courier organisations have been found exploiting the users. Actually, they find this instrumental in tarnishing the image of courier organisations and increasing the temptation of users to the Department of Posts. The tariff structure of Department of Posts is found very much competitive and if the courier organisations delay the process of initiating qualitative improvements, the users may change their option.

Confining to the urban and neglecting the rural users or users living in suburbs or small towns and cities cannot to be a healthy sign of development. We find a good number of users particularly belonging to the individual segment not satisfied with the performance of courier organisations. Professionalism makes it essential that they develop a network and channelise the services in such a way that even the rural users are found satisfied. They need to promote the services with the help of professionals so that users and potential users are persuaded in an effective way. Processing of services with the help of new generation of information and communication technology would be instrumental in increasing the flow and minimising the duration. By managing service ambience, they may be successful in changing the perception of users. We cannot negate that the services of people play an incremental role in improving the quality and projecting a positive image.

The professional excellence of marketers would help courier organisations in many ways.

COURIER MARKETING — A CONCEPTUAL FRAMEWORK

Marketing the courier services focuses our attention on the application of marketing principle in the business process. It is a managerial process that makes possible a planned development of services. It is an organised effort to make the services commercially viable to the courier organisations *vis-a-vis* affordable to the users who make use of the multi-dimensional services. It is even a social process that draws our attention on subserving the social interests by offering concessional, subsidised services to the selected segments who deserve it. The courier marketing thus proves to be a device to promote the business by using fair practices. The marketing concept makes it essential that the organisations formulate a sound service mix in which we find a fair synchronisation of different types of services. The courier marketing practices thus make possible formulation of different submixes of the marketing mix, such as the product mix, the promotion mix, the price mix, the place mix and the people mix. In addition, the development of sound marketing inputs becomes a focal point which makes the ways for the development of quality outputs. The courier marketing draws our attention on studying the behavioural profile of users or prospects and tailoring the marketing inputs in tune with the changing preferences. The market segmentation, thus, happens to be an important aspect of courier marketing. Thus, the following facts emerge regarding the courier marketing:

- It is a managerial process that helps in managing the courier organisations in the face of changing market conditions.
- It is a planned effort that makes possible an optimal development of courier organisations.
- It is a professionalised game that requires professional excellence to make the service nationally and internationally competitive.
- It is a customer satisfaction engineering that makes the ways for winning and keeping the customers for the long time to come.
- It is a social process that paves avenues for subserving the social interests.

RATIONALE BEHIND COURIER MARKETING

We make an advocacy in favour of application of marketing principles in the courier services. A number of factors justify the same. It is right to mention that conceptualising marketing makes the ways for satisfying the users which happens to be the most important thing for increasing the market share and the level of profits. The courier organisations, thus, can maintain commercial viability. By formulating and innovating the marketing mix, the courier organisations can be successful in developing and perceiving a new perception of quality which makes possible qualitative improvements in the process. Generation of profits and satisfaction to the users are the two important dimensions which pave avenues for multi-dimensional quantitative-cum-qualitative improvements in the process. The organisations by making the services competitive can be successful in excelling competition. Since the marketing focuses on professional excellence, the courier organisations can also be successful in projecting a fair image. These facts make it clear that the application of marketing principles is to benefit the courier organisations *vis-a-vis* the individual or institutional users in many ways. The following facts justify the application of marketing principles.

1. Maintaining the Commercial Viability: The conceptualisation of modern marketing principle by the courier organisations is found justified because it helps them in maintaining the commercial variability. They are found in a position to tap the different segments of society with the help of marketing professionals which simplify their task of increasing the market share.

2. Improving the Quality of Services: When we talk about application of marketing principles by the courier organisations, the most important thing is improving the quality of services. The professional excellence of marketers formulate a product portfolio which offers to the users a package of multi-faceted services. The safe delivery, time-honoured delivery and decent delivery make the task of satisfying the customer much more easier. Of late, with the help of new generation of technology, the courier organisations have been successful in innovating the quality. They keep on moving the process of defining and redefining the quality which provide to the users high level of satisfaction.

3. Promotion and Image Projection: With the conceptualisation of innovative marketing, the courier organisations also succeed in building and projecting a positive image. We find it a natural process because once they succeed in satisfying the users, the promotional measures adopted by them are found much more effective. Particularly, the advertisement and publicity measures develop the awareness of users and potential users regarding the value addition processes in the product portfolio of courier organisations.

4. Helpful in Excelling Competition: It is well-known that courier market has become much more competitive due to the entry of a number of big and small players. We find the big players potentially of world-class and even the small players with the help and co-operation of middlemen like co-loaders succeed in enriching their potentials for excelling competition. Thus, in the process of excelling competition, we find users getting additional benefits. On the one hand, they get quality services while on the other hand, the price charged for the services offered is also found to be competitive *vis-à-vis* remunerative.

5. Globally Competitive Pricing: Since we find a galloping increase in the scale of operation, the big players are found in a position to make the task of small players a bit difficult. Of course, the small players get the co-operation of middlemen, but we cannot negate the possibilities of degeneration in quality due to multi-level channels operating the business.

The above-mentioned facts justify the application of marketing principles by the courier organisations. Here, it is significant that they make sure world-class professional excellence because failing it, they cannot ensure improved quality of services to the users. The marketing professionals would help them in innovating the services which would make the marketing processes much more effective.

MARKET SEGMENTATION FOR COURIER SERVICES

For studying and understanding the users of services in a right way, it is essential that the professionals managing courier organisations develop their awareness of the users coming from different segments. We find users coming from two main categories such as individual and corporate. We also find cases where even public sector and public sectors offices have been found using the courier services. Thus, on the whole, there are three different segments, viz., individual, corporate sectors and public sector. We find even individual making use of courier services either for domestic or official purpose. It is very natural that the levels of expectations of different segments of users cannot be identical. The situational forces also guide the level of expectations because in some of the cases, the users need urgent delivery of letters, packets or parcels. The courier organisations while formulating a product mix need to develop a package which combines services and schemes in the face of the changing requirements of users. This makes it essential that the professional serving the leading courier organisations have an in-depth knowledge of users living in different areas. The different categories of users coming from different segments are shown in Figure 20.1.

Fig. 20.1: Market Segmentation for Users of Courier Services

While diagnosing the levels of expectations of users of different segments, the most important thing that we find are the multi-faceted considerations governing the users. The courier organisations, big or small, need to remember that almost categories of users expect time-honoured and safe delivery of their despatches. It is not possible for courier organisations to adopt pricing as a motivational tool because the Department of Posts works with a different strategy. Being a Government organisation, the Department of Posts also follow the societal considerations which, of course, would be difficult for the courier organisations. An in-depth study of different segments and formulating marketing mixes in tune with their requirements requires professional excellence.

INFORMATION MANAGEMENT FOR COURIER ORGANISATIONS

In an age of information technology, it is very natural that like other organisations, the courier organisations also make use of new generation of information and communication technology to bring a qualitative improvement in the product mix. We cannot negate that the nature and type of services offered by courier organisations are found different to others. It is right to mention that the courier organisation cannot function properly failing the co-operation of information and communication. Right from the point of origination to destination, their services virtually play an incremental role in changing the perception of users and potential users regarding the service quality. This makes it essential that the courier organisations develop Marketing Information System if possible and if not they take help of new generation of computers and phone/fax services to update the information. So far as the leading organisations are concerned, they can afford and we also find them making use of the devices to some extent. Lining up the services and monitoring them frequently becomes essential to minimise the possibilities of a gap in service quality. The concerned people need to enter the despatches and thereafter monitoring as per the promised quality to be delivered to the users. All the despatches are to be stored in the data bank and on the information received from point of destination, the despatches are to be updated. The head offices bear the responsibility of getting the feedback from the branch offices regarding the delivery of services. The marketing professionals need to monitor the activities of branch offices and to prepare a list to know the gap.

The information management brings operational efficiency and also increases the possibilities for high level accuracy at each and every stage by coordinating the activities of receiving and delivering centres. The professionals managing the marketing wing need to play an important role by satisfying the users and increasing the number of satisfied group of users helpful in multiplying the number of potential users. Updating and informing processes sizeably rest on the instrumentality of information and communication technology. In case of large organisations, we do not find any problem in developing the information system but the small courier organisations that have financial problem can make it possible with the help of middlemen. They can manage it even with a small budget. The Marketing Intelligence System will help them in collecting the happening data to enable professionals to know the day-to-day developments. They can also take help of internal reporting for updating the data. The lapse at each and every point can be collected with the help of internal reporting. The leading courier organisations in particular bear the responsibility of intensifying the marketing research for knowing the changing levels of expectations of users and the emerging trends in the world markets.

Organising the information system with the help of new generation of information technology will bring multi-dimensional improvements in the services of courier organisations.

THE FORMULATION OF MARKETING MIX FOR COURIER ORGANISATIONS

The courier organisations are required to formulate a sound marketing mix for improving the quality of services. The courier services are required to be made competitive and this makes it essential that the courier organisations conceptualise marketing in such a way that the processes of qualitative-cum-quantitative transformation are activated in the face of emerging business conditions. It is against this background that the marketing professionals are supposed to make creative marketing decisions. This focuses our attention on the formulation of different submixes.

The Product Mix

Mounting intensity of competition makes it essential that the courier organisations formulate a sound product mix. By formulating a sound product mix, they would be in a position to understand the changing needs and requirements of different segments of users on prospects and the service profile would be made user-friendly.

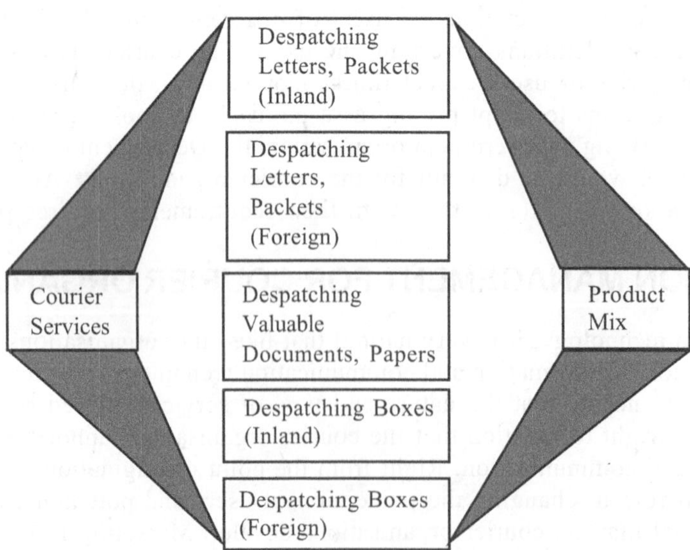

Fig. 20.2: Product Mix of Courier Organisations

The inclusion and exclusion processes, the innovation and alternation formalities would be tailored to the changing level of expectations of customers. The professionals would find it convenient to formulate a package to add attractions to the services which would simplify the task of excelling competition. We can't negate that multi-dimensional requirements of the domestic and the institutional sectors make it essential that the professionals are well aware of the emerging trends in the business conditions. This requires world-class professional excellence and a well-developed information system. With the increasing pace of industrialisation and urbanisation, it is quite natural that the users need due support of the courier organisations at different stages. Moreover, the degeneration in the efficiency of the Department of Posts has forced them to depend upon the services of courier organisations. This makes it essential that they make possible a time-to-time incorporation in their service mix. Inclusion of innovative services in the service mix would enrich the service profile and would also be instrumental in sensitising the prospects. The stimulation of demand makes it essential that the customers get the services which are not to be made available by the Department of Posts. This draws our attention on the formulation of a sound product mix for the courier organisations. The professionals are supposed to work with the service motive. They need to make it sure that the promised services reach to the users without making any distortion in the process. Of late, the users in general feel that their letters, packets, boxes are not delivered to the concerned parties on time. They realise a gap between the services-promised and services-offered and this is required to be bridged over. Ordinary letters or valuable documents should not be discriminated, specially in terms of time-honoured and safe delivery.

The formulation of a sound marketing mix makes it essential that the courier organisations are very much particular to the increasing level of expectations of users. We can't negate that the users have high expectations from the courier organisations and it is in this context that they prefer to use the services even if they find the tariff high.

The courier organisations need to minimise the time limit since we find it an important dimension of the service mix. They are also supposed to develop a package, specially for the habitual and large-sized customers. This draws our attention on the mixing of different types of services which add attractions to the service profile. We are well aware of the fact that the courier services are substantially influenced by the quality of services made available by their messengers acting as a courier. This makes it essential that in designing the services mix, they assign due weightage to the supporting services they need from the transportation and communication network. It is right to mention that the promises of courier organisations related to the time-honoured services are considerably influenced by the link they establish while designing the services. It is against this background that the courier organisations are required to make high promises and also to make it sure that whatever the promises they make are honoured without making any distortion.

Courier Organisations	Product Mix
DHL	Domestic and Global Service, Tie-up with Air Freight
SkyPAK	Domestic and Global Special Services like Kidglove for Fragile Item Night Bird for late night expressions for personal
Blue Dart	Domestic and Express Value-added Services – Just-in-Time
Elbee UPS	Domestic and Global DEPS, PACE and IN-PACE

Figure 20.3: Product Mix of Selected Courier Organisations

Of late, a number of small courier organisations are found operational. They lack supporting infrastructural facilities and fail in honouring the time schedule which has often been found making an invasion on the image of courier organisations. Such a negative trend in the courier business is to be reversed. The small courier organisations make high promises which can't be fulfilled. This makes it essential that the leading courier organisations make available to them the required infrastructural support and develop a network. Of course, they need to charge for the same. We can't check the opening of small courier organisations since in the Indian perspective, the leading courier organisations find it difficult to expand their network to the small towns and cities *vis-a-vis* the rural areas. We are not supposed to understand the instrumentality of courier organisations in serving the rural users. With the expansion of job markets in the urban areas, we find a major migration of rural population to the urban areas which has generated opportunities even in the rural areas.

The internationality acclaimed courier organisations such as DHL, SkyPAK, Blue Dart and Elbee are found offering a package of services to the users both at domestic and global levels.

In view of the above, it is right to mention that the courier organisations need to formulate a sound product mix. While formulating the product mix, they need to make it sure that the product portfolio of leading courier organisations in particular should include not only the high-profit generating services but even the low-profit generating services. Designing a package in tune with the regional and local conditions may be a sound strategy for the courier organisations. They need to assign due weightage to brand decisions particularly for formulating a marketing strategy for individual products. Value addition need priority attention of courier organisations. Keeping in view the increasing intensity of competition, the courier organisations bear the responsibility of initiating the innovation process which will make their product unique. In addition to the big players, the small players also need to bring a radical change in their product mix, of course, with the support of middlemen, otherwise they will find it diffiult to survive. Professional excellence remains the only solution to add additional attractions in their product mix.

PRODUCT MIX OF DEPARTMENT OF POSTS

The process of innovation has already been initiated by the Department of Posts which has resulted into the launching of a number of services in the product mix. All categories of Post Offices such as Head Post Offices Sub-Post Offices, Extra Departmental. Sub-Post Offices and Extra Department Branch Post Offices retail identical services but the delivery services are restricted to specific offices.

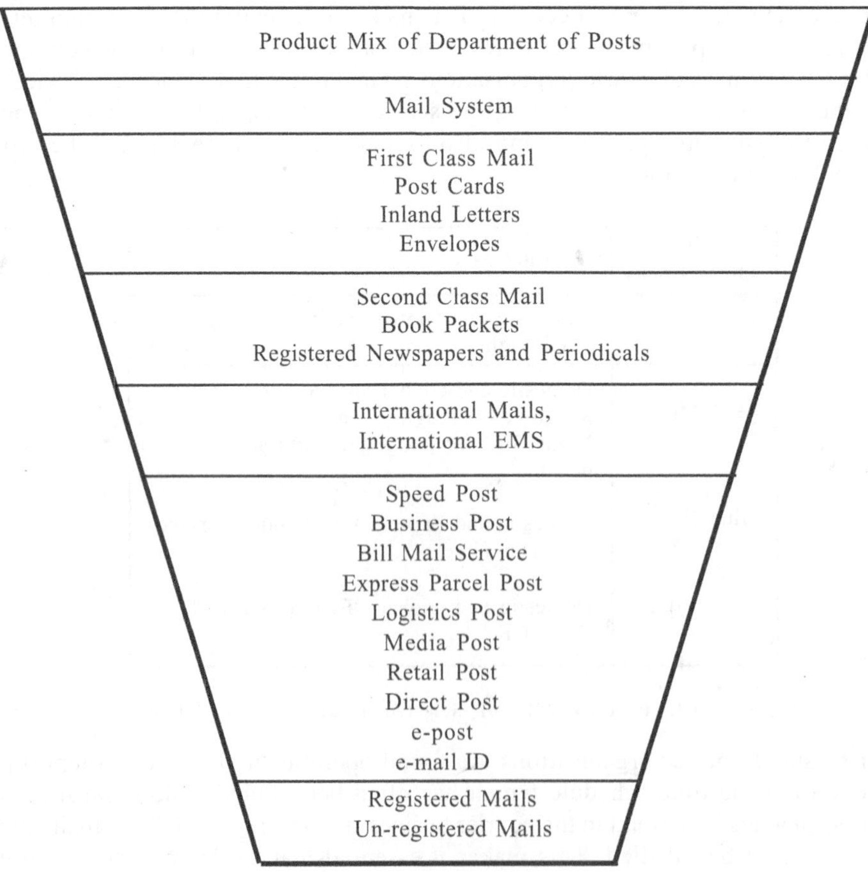

Fig. 20.4: Product Mix of Department of Posts (Mail Serivces)

An outstanding feature of the services of Department of Posts is rural orientation and societal approach which we do not find in the services of big or small courier organisations. We cannot negate that based on this feature, the Department of Posts may be successful in making their services distinct to their rivals. They have been building a distinct image in the society by serving the rural masses and charging the low postal tariff. The professionalised efforts and technological sophistication will help them in the projection of a positive image.

The big players were successful in snatching the business from the Department of Posts because during 1970s, the performance rate of Department of Posts was very poor. But since the mid of 1980s, we find a radical change and during the 1990s and even till date, we find the process of technological sophistication gaining a rapid momentum leading to qualitative transformation in the operational behaviour of Department of Posts. This has engineered a sound foundation for the marketing of the services of Department of Posts. The world-class professional excellence would be very much effective in capitalising on the tremendous opportunities available in the Indian markets.

The Promotion Mix

Your quality services lack any meaning unless the target prospects know about the same. You need to formulate a sound service profile and to use different constituents of promotion in such a fashion that the prospects are informed, sensed and persuaded in a creative way. It is in this context that we go through the different constituents of promotion for the courier organisations.

Advertising: The first constituent of promotion, i.e., advertising plays an effective role in promoting the business. To be more specific in the present age of sophisticated technologies, we find advertisement instrumental in promoting the business of courier organisations. In this context, they need to advertise through print media, broadcast media and the telecast media. The professionals are supposed to judge their potentials *vis-a-vis* the requirements and have to use the media found instrumental in promoting the business. Of late, the courier organisations find print media more effective because the sophistication in the development of print technology has opened doors for creativity. The offset print, screen print and laser print are some of the latest devices to be used by the courier organisations for that purpose. It is also right to mention that the availability of quality materials is found injecting additional attractions while advertising through the print media. The advertising professionals need to select the media preferred by the target prospects. The newspapers, magazines in big circulation may be effective since the services are used by almost all the segments of the market. In addition, the courier organisations also get an opportunity of making descriptive advertisements to inform in detail the target prospects. Further, we also find economy in the print media. It is due to the fact that of late print media have been found more effective. The marketing professionals and to be more specific the advertising professionals bear the responsibility of composing creative slogans so that messages, themes and appeals are found instrumental in sensitising the prospects. We can't deny that the frequency of advertisement would be determined by the intensity of competition. The broadcast media being economic in nature may also be used by the courier organisations. The small courier organisations are found using print media as well as the broadcast media. The telecast media can't be suitable for the small courier organisations mainly due to the budgetary constraint. There is, no doubt, about it that due to audiovisual exposure we find telecast media very much effective in stimulating the demand. The large-sized courier organisations are found using all the three media.

Publicity: We are aware of the fact that publicity occupies a place of significance because the courier organisations are not supposed to make any financial provision for publicising their services. Being an unpaid form of persuasive communication, the publicity makes it essential that the professionals attempt to develop a rapport with the media people and organise a get-together and offer to them lunch, dinner and the small gifts to influence them to write articles and news items in favour. If the media people are found satisfied with the quality of services offered by them, they may give suitable coverage as a news item which would considerably be instrumental in sensitising the prospects. The publicity measures are found more effective since the prospects at large feel that the media people are presenting right things regarding the services of courier organisations. Thus, the courier organisations may also use this component of the promotion mix.

Personal Selling: It is right to mention that for promoting the business of courier organisations, we find personal selling very much effective. The courier organisations may be successful in promoting the business in a right fashion, if the sales people have high communication ability. To be more specific, the large-sized courier organisations may engage agents, trade representatives for developing contact with the target prospects. If the sales personnel have high communicative ability, attractive personality and commitment to profession, the dialogues can be transformed into a deal. We can't deny the fact that the courier organisations need to recruit and train quality sales people for that very purpose. The instrumentality of messengers acting as couriers have been accepted by all. If the couriers, agents, representatives narrate to the prospects right things in a right fashion, we find enough scope for stimulation.

Word-of-mouth Promotion: Ultimately, we are rewarded for the quality of goods or services that we offer to the customers. If the courier organisations offer world-class services to the prospects or users; it is but natural that they remain satisfied and don't hesitate to communicate to their friends and relatives the plus and negative points. They in a true sense act as a hidden salesforce. If we come to know about the outstanding quality of courier services from our friends and relatives, we prefer to use the services of that very organisation as and when the circumstances necessitate so. In the world of marketing, we name it word-of-mouth promotion. The courier organisations may also take the support of opinion leaders for that very purpose.

Sales Promotion: This also happens to be an important component of the promotion mix. The courier organisations need to think about the innovative promotional tools for the sales personnel, marketing personnel and more so for the users of the services. In this context, they need to offer gifts, offer an attractive package, concessional services to the habitual users or so. The main thing in the process is to make the tools innovative because almost all the courier organisations are found offering small or big gifts.

Telemarketing: With the development of sophisticated communication technologies, we find scope for using the services of telemarketers. Of late, telemarketing has proved its instrumentality, specially in promoting the courier business. The information regarding the services, the queries, confusions would be transmitted and would suitably be removed on telephones. In this context, it is pertinent that the courier organisations recruit a person with high communicative ability so that he/she is in a position to convince the prospects. In addition, it is also significant that in the process of telemarketing, the courier organisations make available to the telemarketers sophisticated telephonic instruments effective in transmitting and receiving the messages without any interruption. Of late, the satellite communication has opened avenues for the use of telemarketing for promoting the business of almost all categories of services and therefore, the courier organisations are also found marketing with the support of telephones.

The aforesaid constituents of promotion are found available to the courier organisations and the marketing professionals are supposed to blend the different constituents in such a way that the prospects are stimulated and the dialogues are transformed into a deal. We can't negate that they need to keep in their minds the financial constraint since the promotional efforts are not supposed to make the business results unproductive. There must be a balance between the requirements and potentials failing which the promotion budget would prove to be a burden.

The Price Mix

In the Indian perspective, the pricing decisions become crtical because the organisations are supposed to make rational decisions which on the one hand maintain their commercial viability while on the other hand also subserve the interests of those segments of the society who find it difficult to pay the high tariff. Like other organisations, the courier organisations are also required to keep into consideration the fact that even weaker sections of the society find it convenient to use their services. It is against this background that we go through the price mix of the courier organisations.

The courier organisations buy the supporting services from the different categories of organisations which substantially influence their tariff structure. It is right to mention that whatever they charge as tariff from the users remains the only source of financing the business and therefore it is difficult from them to subserve the social interests by offering concessional or subsidised services. However, the courier organisations need to explore avenues for the same. Of late, the business environment is found volatile and the intensity of competition is also found to be high. At the same time, it is also right to mention that market potentials are available since a majority of the business is yet to be tapped. The pricing decisions are required to be made competitive so that they succeed in snatching the business from the Department of Posts. This requires professional excellence and it is against this background that we have been talking about the application of innovation marketing.

We can't deny the fact that the Department of Posts is yet to practise marketing and therefore a majority of the users right now using their services are found dissatisfied. It is in this context that the courier organisations need world-class professional excellence. How to snatch the business from the Department of Posts? The pricing decisions *vis-a-vis* the tariff structure of the courier organisations become significant in the very context. If professional excellence helps them in using tariff as a motivational tool, the snatching of business would be switched on. Earlier, we have talked about quality of services. Thus, offering quality services at a competitive tariff would help courier organisations in increasing the market share. Once they succeed in establishing the leadership in the market, the users would prefer to avail their services. Of course, the task is much more difficult because the courier organisations are also required to pay considerably for the inputs used by them in the process but they can make it possible by maintaining operational economy. They are required to regulate the unproductive expenses by rationalising the establishment expenses and promoting the use of technologies. If they succeed in increasing the market share even a small profit would be instrumental in increasing the total profit earned by the different branch offices. In addition, they need to assign due weightage to the large-sized customers.

The aforesaid facts make it clear that making of a rational tariff policy is a difficult task which requires professional excellence. The courier organisations are required to make the pricing decisions more scientific and progressive. This draws our attention on charging high structure from the users despatching valuable documents and papers, charging low structure from the habitual users, charging very low structure from the habitual large-sized users. The motive is to increase the market share and therefore in no case the tariff structure should cross the structure charged by the Department of Posts. If they improve the quality of services and make the structure competitive, the market share would automatically be increased.

The Place Mix

Quality services, promoted in a creative way and priced suitably would hardly reach to the target prospects in a decent way if the personnel and agencies instrumental in processing the services are not aware of their functional responsibilities. It is in this context that the place mix becomes significant and the courier organisations are required to manage the same in a right fashion. The place mix draws our attention on the two important issues — first, the services are processed in a right way in order that the gap between the services-promised and services-offered is bridged over and second, the courier organisations and their branch offices are located at a sensitive point so that the users as well as the personnel working there don't feel any trouble.

The first dimension of the place mix makes it essential that the professionals manage their head and branch offices properly. The personnel working there are efficient and the technologies used in the process of offering the services are sophisticated. The motive is to make available to the users the promised services without any distortion. This makes it essential that they recruit efficient personnel and also offer to them an ongoing training programme so that they come to know about the behavioural profile of the prospects. If the users feel that their letters, packets, boxes are not delivered to the concerned person on time, in a right condition, the dissatisfaction to the users can't be negated which would affect the business of the courier organisations adversely. They are also required to make it sure that the personnel working there behave decently with the users or prospects visiting the head and branch offices. While making promises, the professionals are supposed to go through the available potentials since it is not proper to make high promises and creating a gap by degenerating the quality.

The second dimension of the place mix draws our attention on the location points for the branch and head offices. We can't deny that the places selected for the offices of the courier organisations should smoothly be accessible. The required infrastructural facilities should be available at the centres and the offices should be managed in a right way. The interior decoration needs due attention of the professionals because this is the provision found instrumental in adding attractions to the services. In this context, it is also significant that proper furnishing is made possible and sophisticated communication services are available at the centres. To be more specific in the Indian perspective, we find safety and protection provisions requiring due attention of the professionals responsible for managing the branch offices as well as the head office. The availability of power and transportation facilities can't be underestimated.

The courier organisations while taking the support of branch offices need due attention on the channels instrumentalising the offering process. Since this is an important point from where degeneration starts gaining momentum if they neglect the same, a big gap between the services-promised and services-offered can't be denied. The management of place for the courier organisations need due attention of the policy planners failing which the new perception of quality can't be developed. Thus, it is right to mention that the courier organisations need to manage place mix with the help of efficient personnel and with the support of sophisticated technologies.

Process Mix

The processing of courier services needs due attention of professionals. Due to multi-level processing of services from originating point to the destination, the professionals managing the affairs at different stages need to speed up the operational flow. The processing of services needs supports of new generation of information and communication technology. Information, communication and transportation are the three different types of services required by the courier organisations for time-honoured and quality-based delivery. The processes are managed by the courier organisations but control rests on others. The different modes of transportation need effective coordination to reach to the destination. The failures may be while transporting, while informing and communicating and even while coordinating. The professionals responsible for marketing the services may find themselves completely helpless. The most important thing is delivery which is not beyond the control of professionals because there are a number of cases testifying the negative role of people bearing the responsibility of delivering the services to the concerned individuals or organisations. We cannot negate the Department of Posts has an edge over the courier organisations when we focus our attention on the personal touch, engaged for delivering. If we do not process in a right way, it is difficult for us to deliver as per the expectations of users. Developing a network is found essential for smooth and speedy processing. The small players need to solicit the co-operation of middlemen for this purpose and the big players have a strong network for this purpose.

Physical Evidence and Attractions

This submix of the marketing mix draws our attention on the number of factors concerned with service ambience and physical impression of people serving the courier organisations. The potential users or visitors coming to the office of courier organisations get an opportunity of witnessing the physical facilities used for generating the services such as interiors, lighting, display of equipments and information and communication technology used for processing the services, signposts for guiding the visitors, furnishing of office and reception, etc. Ambient conditions play an incremental role in the service generation and image projection. The marketing professionals bearing the responsibility of tangbilising the outstanding features of courier organisations need due attention on positioning. We are aware of the fact that in this submix of marketing, the potential users and visitors get an opportunity to strengthen, their perception of quality. Such a tangibilisation becomes instrumental in the shaping of the levels of expectations. Hence, the marketers on the basis of their professional excellence can be successful in influencing the potential users. The fragrance of services to be witnessed by them help in adding additional attraction to the services. The servicescapes of leading courier organisations are found very impressive but the small players find it difficult to afford the same.

The People Mix

In addition to other components of the marketing mix, we also need to gravitate our attention on the people mix because failing the availability of efficient personnel, a degeneration in the process of offering the services can't be ruled out. It is against this background that the professionals make a strong advocacy in favour of managing the people mix. This draws our attention on the different categories of employees serving the courier organisations at head or branch offices. To be more specific, the personnel working as couriers need due attention of the marketing professionals since they play an incremental role in sensitising the generation and degeneration proceses.

Of late, the people mix has emerged as the most vital component of the marketing mix. We talk about the instrumentality of sophisticated technologies, we also talk about the attitudes of the policy makers or the boardrooms and we talk more about the excellence of professionals managing the affairs but we less talk about the contributions of low echelon of employees playing a commanding role in improving the quality of our services. It is in this context that we need due attention on people mix in which the professionals are supposed to make possible a fair synchronisation of performance orientation and employee orientation.

By performance orientation, our emphasis is on improving the efficiency of employees involved in the process. This makes it essential that the marketing professionals assign due weightage to the management of employees serving the courier organisations. The employees working at the head and branch offices are required to be efficient, well aware of the operation and maintenance of technologies used in the process, sincere and punctual to the management of time and familiar with the behavioural profile of prospects or users. If they lack these properties, the quality of services would hardly be improved. By showing commitment to the profession, they can prove themselves to be high performers. The professionals are required to make it sure that by imparting to them proper training facilities the process of enriching the potentials is switched on in the right direction.

We talk about performance orientation but don't find it essential to assign due weightage to employee orientation. By the employee orientation, our focus is on motivating the employees suitably by offering to them efficiency-based incentive plans. In a true sense, we find a close relation between the two. Even the high performers may disappoint us if we continue the process of exploitation for the long time. And contrary to it even the inefficients would satisfy us if we train and motivate them suitably. The professionals need to realise that unless they offer to the employees suitable incentives, the process of efficiency generation would hardly be accelerated. This makes it essential that the courier organisations assign an overriding priority to the incentive plans for the employees which would make ways for performance orientation. Since the services offered by the courier organisations are found based on the instrumentality of employees, we don't find any scope for devaluing the same.

In view of the above, it is right to mention that the professionals bearing the responsibility of formulating a sound marketing mix also consider the instrumentality of people mix and they need to blend the different submixes in such a way that the marketing decisions are found proactive.

COURIER MARKETING IN INDIAN PERSPECTIVE

In the Indian perspective, the emergence of courier services is found of recent origin. We are aware of the fact that the Department of Posts, Government of India bears the responsibility of offering the services. With the increasing pressure of work on the Department of Posts, a degeneration in efficiency was felt by domestic as well as the business sectors which engineered a foundation for the development of courier services. There are a number of courier organisations right now serving regionally, nationally and internationally. Some of them are well organised but a majority of them are ill managed. This has been found making an invasion on the image of the courier organisations. We also find cases where the courier organisations are found generating losses. This makes it essential that they attempt to improve the quality of services. We can't deny that in the Indian perspective, the courier organisations have profitable market potentials. The only thing they need is to market the services professionally so that they on the one hand succeed in maintaining the commercial viability while on the other hand also make the services affordable to the masses who right now find it difficult to avail the expensive services of courier organisation. It is against this background that we find application of innovative marketing principles essential.

The task of professionals is considerably simplified, specially when the competitors start degenerating. We agree with this view that the Department of Posts is the only competitor making the task difficult to the courier organisations. A majority of the users avail the services of Department of Posts since the services are found inexpensive. Price sensitivity is found complicating the task of courier organisations in general and the small courier organisations in particular. This makes it essential that the courier organisations make possible operational economy, regulate the unproductive expenses and rationalise the tariff structure. Of course, they need to assign a transcendental priority to the quality of services. This necessitates application of marketing principles in the courier organisations.

The first task before the marketing professionals is to formulate a sound product mix that draws our attention on designing a service profile in which blending of different types of services is made possible. They need to work with the motto that product attractiveness is the main thing in activating the stimulation process in which new perception of quality based on the changing expectations of users is required to be given an overriding priority. The professionals, on the one hand, have to make it sure that the articles are delivered to the concerned person/organisation/institution on time and on the other hand, they are also supposed to make ways for developing the peripheral services which they would never get from the Department of Posts. Thus, a fair blending of core and peripheral services would be efficacious in attracting the prospects. In the core services, they need to concentrate on the quality of services and in the peripheral services, they need to add additional attractions to their services which the users don't get from the Department of Posts. They also need to design a package of benefits, specially for the small and large-sized habitual customers. They need to project a fair image on the basis of quality, the perception for which would be shaped in the face of emerging business conditions *vis-a-vis* the changing expectations of users. Time-honoured delivery is the main thing which is to be made possible despite of the multi-dimensional constraints they face in the process.

The next constituent of the marketing mix is the promotion mix that focuses on creativity in the messages, themes and appeal. In the Indian perspective, the courier organisations are required to optimise the promotional expenses which makes it essential that they use a particular component of promotion having more creativity, blend the different components optimally in the face of their changing requirements and make the entire process productive. This is essential to inculcate awareness. It is right to mention that a number of prospects are not aware of the services made available in their command area. The courier organisations need to promote the services in such a way that they succeed in informing, sensing and persuading the prospects. The promotional budget is to be made optimal. They need to seek the co-operation of advertising professionals having world-class excellence so that they spend less and get more.

While pricing, the courier organisations are required to have a rational price structure that helps them in maintaining the commercial viability. In this context, it is also pertinent that they make the tariff affordable even to those segments of the market who due to expensive services avoid to use the services. This makes it essential that they are very particular to the unproductive expenses and make efforts to regulate them in tune with the changing business conditions. By rationalising the price structure, the courier organisations would be successful in generating adequate financial resources. It is not significant that they concentrate on generating profits from the limited segments. It is much more productive that they generate less profits but expand the network, increase the market share and make ways for the profit generation in the long run.

The courier organisations in a majority of the cases have been found generating a gap between the services-promised and the services-offered. This is substantially on account of poor management. This makes it essential that the courier organisation seek the co-operation of marketing professionals. They are required to manage their head and branch offices by recruiting efficient personnel, making available the supporting infrastructural facilities and imparting to them training facilities in the face of evolving technologies and the changing level of expectations of the users. They need to promise carefully but to make it sure that whatever they promise are offered to the users without making any distortion. Thus, bridging over the gap between the promises and offerings is the most important functional responsibility of professionals bearing the responsibility of marketing the courier services. We can't deny the fact that in the Indian perspective the courier organisations in general make high promises which they can't fulfil. This makes ways for dissatisfaction *vis-a-vis* projection of a negative image.

The courier organisations find scope for processing the services with the help of new generation of information and communication technology. Besides, the fast mode of transportation simplifies their task of processing. The professionals need to make it sure that the promised quality of services are made available to the users on time and without any distortion. The service delivery considerably depends on processing.

While conceptualising marketing, it is pertinent that marketers make efforts to add additional attractions to the servicescapes by making the service ambient efficacious of generating the service fragrance. The leading courier organisations have a global network and therefore we find them in a position to manage the service environment but the small courier organisations find it difficult partially due to financial constraints and partially due to managerial deficiency.

The application of seven mixes of marketing with the help of marketers having professionals excellence would benefit the courier organisations in different ways. On the one hand, they will be successful in increasing their market share while on the other hand, the task of satisfying the users will also be found easier. They need to strengthen their realisation that in the Indian perspective, the courier organisations have tremendous opportunities. Capitalising on the available opportunities is to be possible if courier organisations activate professionalised efforts, show personal-touch-in-service and are value-based.

In view of the above, it is right to mention that the courier organisations working regionally, nationally and globally need to implement modern marketing principles. The small courier organisations are not in a position to practice marketing on account of financial consideration but to the extent it is possible, they need to professionalise they services. Big players or small players need not to forget that it is only uniqueness of the product and value addition that would simplify their task of excelling competition.

The process of technological sophistication has gained a rapid momentum in the Department of Posts which makes it essential that the courier organisations bring a radical change in their product mix by launching innovative services.

EMERGENCE OF DEPARTMENT OF POSTS AS A BIG COMPETITOR

During yesterdecades, we find significant developments in the field of courier services and the credibility for the same goes to the entry of big players such as DHL, SkyPAK, Blue Dart and Elbee. In addition, we find a mushroom growth of small players working with the help and co-operation of co-loaders acting as middlemen. The process of quantitative transformation, no doubt, gained a rapid momentum but at the same time qualitative degeneration was also witnessed which made ways for the Department of Posts that they by innovating their services throw a challenge to the courier organisations. The beginning was found with the introduction of Speed Post in 1986.

We cannot negate that since then, the Department of Posts by innovating their product mix has been emerging as a market leader specially in the domestic sector. With the beginning of the decade 1990s, the contours of development have undergone radical changes and now we find courier business emerging as an industry with an annual business of around ₹ 400 crores. It is right to mention that the Department of Posts mainly due to image problem has not been successful in regaining the confidence of high-paying sectors of the economy, however it has emerged as a big competitor. Of course, we find operational and attitudinal problems before the Department of Posts but the domestic business of Department of Posts in general and the Speed Post in particular has been found impressive.

The Speed Post, of course, lacks professionalised approach but we find a number of outstanding features in the product such as Book Now Pay Later Facility, Book Your Own Article Scheme, Contractual Service for any place in the country, Money Transfer facility, Money Back Guarantee, Round-the-Clock Booking Counters, etc. The International Speed Post Service (Documents) was also introduced in 1986 and the Merchandising International Speed Post was introduced in 1988. Based on bilateral agreements, we find International EMS Traffic. With the support of major partners like USA, UK, France, Hong Kong, Japan and UAE, the EMS has also emerged as an important product of Department of Posts.

The above-mentioned facts testify the emergence of Department of Posts as a big competitor and for excelling the high intensity of competition, it is imperative that the Department of Posts make possible professional excellence and conceptualise marketing for regaining their lost glory. This will also help them in projecting a positive image. In a true sense, the Department of Posts need aggressive marketing strategy which focuses on innovating the product mix and sensitising the masses to develop their awareness of the qualitative improvements initiated and activated by them. We find Proof of Delivery (PoD) an important tool to regain the confidence of masses, specially the high-paying segment. The advertisement campaigns need creative ideas and aggressive advertisement will help them in winning and maintaining the business. Of course, they need an innovative product and promotion strategy to bring back the derailed system on the rail.

The Department of Posts has an outstanding price strategy which may be used as an effective tool to motivate individual as well as the corporate users. It is not possible for the small and big players to introduce such a pricing strategy and this may be instrumental in safeguarding and promoting the interests of Department of Posts. We find a good number of potential users in both the individual and corporate categories but they are not aware of the facilities and tariff structure of Department of Posts. The channelisation of services need due attention so that at each and every point we find the minimum possible time-gap from one stage to another.

The big players have been making use of new generation of information and communication technology but we find the track records of Department of Posts not so impressive which obstructs the process of increasing the operational flow. The professionalised efforts would also make ways for tangibilisation of physical facilities for creating sound ambience. Let the high-paying users of services strengthen their realisation that Department of Posts would serve and subserve their interests and would show professional excellence and personal touch. This is not to be possible unless the Department of Posts assign due weightage to professional excellence. The point of service delivery and people working there need priority attention of marketing professionals because this is the point which has been very much instrumental in tarnishing the image of Department of Posts.

To attain a position of leadership, the Department of Posts have to leverage information technology which may be helpful in their emergence as a modern communication and financial agent. The key techno-driven initiatives such as computerisation of networking in all major Post Offices, mail offices, transit mail offices and head mail offices; transmission of money orders through the VSAT network; setting up of Automatic Mail Processing Centres and Synergy with e-governance initiatives of the Government of India need priority attention. We expect that these initiatives after proper acceleration would make Department of Posts potentially sound to counter the challenges aggravated by big players. An Internet-based track and trace service speed net launched in 2002 provides multiple services such as providing tracking facility for Speed Post articles, information to the management about the quality of service, business performance, marketing customer service, etc.

The innovative services like Business Post launched in 1997, Bill Mail Service launched in 2003, Express Parcel Post and Logistic Post launched in 2004, e-post launched in 2004, Direct Post launched in 2005 are the new feathers making the product mix of Department of Posts much more competitive. Besides, we also find Media Post, Retail Post and Expree Parcel Post services for attracting the users.

The concept of value addition has gained a rapid momentum and we find Department of Posts emerging as a big competitor. The most important thing necessitating priority attention of Department of Posts in today's context is world-class professional excellence which would make them potentially and strategically sound. This will help them in excelling competition.

Since early 1990, the Department of Posts has started computerising its Post Offices. This is with the motto of improving the quality of services, introduction of new value-added services to meet the expectations of the customers and strengthening its financial position. The computerisation of Registration as a part of the modernisation programme in the major mail offices and the computerisation of Transit Mail Offices have a vital role in the smooth handling and transmission of closed mail bags. The computerisation of Head Record Offices is for proper maintenance of valuable records, their prompt retrieval and efficient office management. The transmission of money orders through the VSAT Satellite Network is to cut down the transmission time for sending money orders across the country. The Automatic Mail Processing Centre helps sorting mails faster leading to quicker delivery. The modernisation of Operative Offices is for improving Ergonomics which is a study of people's efficiency in their working environment. The concept of service ambience has a now face lift. Besides, we find setting up of Business Development Directorate in 1996 with the objectives of marketing and promoting premium services for meeting the needs of specific segments. With effect from April 2005, it was reorganised into Business Development and Marketing Directorate for providing a sharper focus on marketing of the whole continuum of Post's products. A separate Parcel and Logistic Division has been created in the Business Development and Marketing Directorate for focusing attention on parcel products.

The above-mentioned facts are a staunch testimony to this proposition that Department of Posts has been initiating and activating innovative efforts to excel competition. The only thing they need is developing a brigade of dedicated and committed postal staff. On the one hand, we find technological advancements while on the other hand, we find operational inefficiency due to vanishing team spirit and work culture. This focuses our attention on multi-faceted efforts. The marketing professionals managing the postal services need to organise or constitute a team and to link incentive plans with their performance. The policy makers need a transcendental priority on the motivational schemes for the Department of Posts. If we go through the academic records of people serving the Department of Posts, a majority of them have a bright academic career. They are efficacious of receiving the aggressive strategies of professionals provided the marketing professionals manage them in a right way. Of course, they are low-paid staff in the public sector segment which obstructs the process of motivation and development.

The professionals need to educate and train them in the changed scenario and to motivate them by offering the financial incentives. Low-pay and high-working days cannot be considered an effective prescription to make use of the potentials of people serving the Department of Posts. If we are really interested in excelling competition, our professonalised efforts should reserve elbow rooms for performance-linked incentive plan.

SUMMARY

In this chapter, you have gone through the different dimensions of marketing the courier services. Before starting another chapter, be sure that the following facts are well versed:

Courier Marketing: A Conceptual Framework: It is a managerial process that helps in winning and maintaining the customers for the long time. It is a process of conceptualising marketing in the courier organisations in the face of changing market conditions. It is an organised effort to make the services commercially viable and further to satisfy the users by fulfilling their expectations.

Rationale Behind Practising Marketing: The conceptualisation of modern marketing principles by the professionals in the courier organisations is justified with the viewpoint of maintaining the commercial viability, improving the quality of services, instrumental sing the projection of a positive image excelling competition and adopting a globally competitive pricing policy.

Market Segmentation for Courier Services: The professionals segment markets for courier services into different parts such as individual, corporate sector, public sector companies and offices of Government Departments. All the users expect safe and time-honoured services.

Information Management for Courier Services: The courier organisations need to develop a sound information system particularly with the viewpoint of marketing will help professionals in developing a network for information and communication to ensure service quality. Besides, this will also help them in identifying the leakages and lapses for late delivery.

The Marketing Mix for Courier Organisations: The marketing professionals need to practise all the seven mixes.

Product Mix: The leading courier organisations have developed a profile file and packages for the services to be offered. The DHL and SkyPAK are considered leaders in the area. The services are despatching letters, packets both inland and foreign, despatching valuable documents and papers, despatching boxes both inland and foreign.

Promotion Mix: The courier organisations make use of different components of promotion such as Advertising, Publicity, Personal Selling, Sales Promotion, Telemarketing and Word-of-mouth Promotion. They develop a mix to persuade the potential customers. The process is made cost-effective with the help of professional excellence of marketers.

The Price Mix: The courier organisation buy the services from different organisations which considerably influence their tariff structure. However they need to make their pricing decisions nationally and internationally competitive. They also adopt differential pricing strategy where habitual or regular users of services get concessions.

The Place Mix: The place mix draws our attention on right channelisation of services and convenient location of offices so that places are smoothly accessible.

Process: This mix of marketing throws light on processing of services with the help of quality people and new generation of information and communication technology so that the promised quality of services are made available to the target users. The delay and distortion in the process of service delivery are to be removed.

Physical Evidence and Attractions: This submix of marketing focuses on the service ambience found in the offices of courier organisations where a number of users and visitors come. The servicescapes need due attention of professionals with the motto of generating service fragrance and adding additional attractions to servives. The leading courier organisations must need to assign due weightage to the dresses and uniforms which should be neat and clean.

People: The courier organisations need a mix of skilled and unskilled people. The persons managing information and communication should have an in-depth knowledge of new generation of professional technology used for this purpose. They need professional commitment and personal-touch-in-service. The behavioural profile of all categories of people working in the courier organisations should be decent.

Courier Marketing in Indian Perspective: In the Indian context, we find courier services of recent origin. However, they have developed and we find a good number of leading courier organisations working and serving the users. The focus is on implementation of marketing principles, specially by the leading courier organisations where the users have been found reporting the cases of delay in service delivery. The courier organisations working regionally, nationally and globally need to identify the changing levels of expectations of users of different categories. While formulating a sound marketing mix, they need to have an in-depth knowledge of changing market conditions. In a majority of the cases, we find image problem mainly due to the negligence of people supposed to deliver the services. By making use of new generation of information and communication technology, they would no doubt, be potentially sound but if the working force fail in maintaining. the time schedule for service delivery, our all efforts for improving and service quality would be turned into a fiasco. This necessitates professional excellence for managing the marketing activities of courier organisations. The big players and small players need to innovate their perception of service quality.

KEY TERMS

Courier	Fragile
Bullock Carts	Value-added
Horse Carriages	Ambient Conditions
Speed Post	Boardrooms
Co-loaders	Echelon
Department of Posts	Efficacious
Synchronisation	DHL
Middlemen	SkyPAK
Marketing and Intelligence System	Blue Dart
Internal Reporting	Elbee
Postal Tariff	Offset Print
Night Bird	Railway Mail Service
Kidglove	Command Area

Review Questions

1. What do you mean by Courier Services? Discuss marketing of Courier Services.
2. Throw light on the justifications for practising marketing principles by the courier organisations.
3. Explain the relevance of managing information for the courier services.
4. Throw light on the different segments of users of courier services.
5. Write a note on the origin and development of courier services in India.
6. Formtdate a marketing mix for the courier services.
7. Write a note on the marketing of courier services in the Indian perspective.
8. Focus on the extended marketing mix in the context of courier services in India.
9. Explain the product mix for the courier services in the light selected courier organisations of international repute.
10. Do you find Department of Posts emerging as a big competitor? Justify your opinion.

Application Exercises

1. As a marketing professional, design a product mix for the courier services found to be internationally competitive.
2. Suggest the pricing policy (tariff policy) adopted by courier organisations to be nationally competitive.
3. Formulate a marketing mix for the courier organisations in the Indian perspective.
4. Do you feel that servicescapes of courier organisations need priority attention of professionals? Justify your arguments.
5. Should the courier organisations tap the market potentials available in rural India? Justify your arguments.
6. How should you promote the courier services so that the task of winning and maintaining different categories of users is considerably simplified?
7. The big players need to make their tariff policy competitive. Comment on this statement as a marketer.
8. Do you feel that Department of Posts is throwing a challenge to the courier organisations? In the competitive business environment suggest the marketing mixes to be much more effective.
9. Suggest marketing strategy for courier organisations in improving the quality of services.

Endnotes

1. Jha, S.M., Courier Marketing, Chapter, 15 *Services Marketing,* HPH, 2003, pp. 635-47.
2. India, 2008.

☆☆☆

ENTERTAINMENT MARKETING

The emerging corporate culture has made ways for the tidal wave of pop culture. Getting our minds entertained to inject new life and strength for rejuvenation is essential for productive developments and positive behaviour. Let's be careful that entertainment is not making rooms for live-in culture.

Chapter Objectives

Learning Objectives

This chapter aims at studying the different dimensions of entertainment marketing. The motive is to conceptualise marketing in the entertainment services in such a fashion that the entertainment organisations succeed not only in meeting the commercial considerations but also in protecting and promoting the social interests. Since in the Indian perspective, we find a major change in the attitudes and behaviour of viewers, this chapter focuses on sensitising the masses to the perception of entertainment so that we find the entertainment programmes instrumental in refreshing and re-energising the viewers.

INTRODUCTION

In an age of material culture, we find ourselves beset of myriad of problems which upset us leading to monotony and fatigue. Temptation for recreation is a natural phenomenon. If we nurture a negative attitude regarding the law of nature; the process of concentration, meditation, efficiency generation would be reversed and resulting from which pessimism will take its root. It is also not possible that we bid a good-bye to the latest developments and deprive the society of witnessing the new devices of entertainment. This throws light on developing amenities and facilities bearing the potentials of entertaining the masses.

The human beings are found tempted to amenities and facilities helping them in leading a comfortable life which forces them to earn more. This results into monotony, pessimism and depression, if they find themselves not in a position to fulfil them. We cannot negate that corporate culture is found based on hard work. If we work hard and do not provide our minds an opportunity to refresh, the rejuvenation of energy would be difficult. A process of contraction in the development faculties would pave avenues for a number of negative developments which would adversely affect the working people and organisation *pari passu*. It is against this background that we find corporate policy makers realising the importance of entertainment facilities.

The multi-dimensional changes in our lifestyles have been due to a significant increase in our discretionary income. The globalisation of economy has made ways for globalisation of fashion, culture and civilisation. The sophistication in the development of communication and information technology has opened new vistas for the development of new multiplex culture. The opening of new air-conditioned picture palaces, open-air theatres, disco and pub, drama centres, music centres, new TV channels fascinate masses to entertain and enjoy. The increasing urbanisation, burgeoning middle class, domination of corporate sector, emergence of shopping culture make the business environment for the entertainment facilities much more conducive. A number of upcoming and budding entrepreneurs have been found evincing their interests in the development of these centres. Undoubtedly enough, we find it emerging as a profitable market *vis-a-vis* the productive investment.

Getting our minds entertained to inject new life and strength for rejuvenation is essential for productive developments and positive behaviour. The entertainment sector is found emerging as an industry and even in the days to come, the process of development cannot be reversed. Let's be careful that entertainment is not making rooms for live-in culture.

The entertainment services need professional excellence to capitalise on the opportunities expanding fast due to globalisation of culture. The emerging shopping culture has injected additional strength to the avenues for entertainment. In view of the emergence of a cross-cultural society, we find new opportunities and changing faces of entertainment. The marketing professionals bear the responsibility of diagnosing the behavioural profile of customers of different segments so that a sound marketing mix is formulated.

The product mix occupies a place of outstanding significance because we find customers with different professional and cultural background enjoying the entertainment services. It is pertinent to mention that the perception of quality is to be defined in tune with the taste and temperament of customers. A fair mix which on the one hand satisfies customers while on the other hand also opens doors for profit generation is to be designed by the professionals. The service mix will include in its purview the entertainment programmers efficacious of developing knowledge and instrumental in entertaining the viewers. The professionals also need to concentrate their attention on socio-cultural considerations. The presently emerging tidal wave of pop culture is found making an invasion on the Indian culture. We cannot negate that it is due to corporatisation which has made ways for the development of a new wave culture. The TV programmes and movies in a majority of the cases are found perverting the taste of teens and budding youths. An optimal product mix needs due attention on information, education, entertainment, cultural, ethical and human values.

The promotional measures need creativity to inform, sense, sensitise, persuade and transform the potential viewers into actual and habitual viewers. The professionals need to make use of different components of promotion in such a way that the sensitisation process is though productive but cost-effective.

A rational pricing policy keeping in view the quality of viewers is found significant. Since we find profit generation an important consideration, the marketing professionals need to make it sure that prices-charged and services-offered have a correlation.

The services need right channelisation so that at each and every stage, the viewers feel comforts and conveniences while using the services and the providers feel convenient while making the services ready for delivery.

Since we find imprint of technology on the entertainment services, it is imperative that new generation of equipments and machines are used for right processing and time-honoured delivery. The operational flow is to be increased but the quality is to be maintained.

The servicescapes become point of attractions for diverting the attention of customers regarding the quality of services to be delivered. The exteriors and interiors, lighting, furnishing, ventilation, sanitation, parking, cleanliness, aesthetic management help in making the service ambience successful in shaping the perception of viewers regarding the quality of services to be offered. The generation of service fragrance needs due care.

The people working in different capacities need excellence to perform in the desired way. The marketing professionals bear the responsibility of enriching their faculties and making use of the same with the motto of satisfying the viewers.

There are different sources for entertainment and a number of providers for organising and managing the programme in the face of changing taste preferences of viewers. The important sources are Movies, TV Channels, Theatres, Drama, Disco and Pubs, Circus, etc. We find a major impact of technology on production and marketing of entertainment programmes. A majority of the organisations come from the private sector but a few also belong to the public sector. Providing healthy entertainment is the joint responsibility of both the sectors. Entertainment for recreation or entertainment for sex orientation; this draws attention of marketing professionals. Of course, we find increased temptation of people to the western lifestyles; however, the government policy planners and the social reformists and activists have to make it sure that entertainment programmes are not making an invasion on our culture. To the extent it is possible, they should initiate efforts for promoting our cultural heritage and culture. The government-managed TV channels, National Songs and Drama Division, AIR, etc. bear the responsibility of sensitising the general masses. The private organisations producing entertainment programme pertaining to cultural degeneration makes ways for misleading the new generations, e.g., kids, teens, upcoming youths and this negative development plays a vital role in the derailment of socio-cultural systems. This happened in the developed countries of Europe; this happened in USA and this has started happening albeit in India. Of course, it is at nascent stage but the speed of degeneration is very fast.

It is very natural that private sector producing and marketing entertainment programmes work with profit motive but they should not forget that it is possible even by offering the healthy entertainment programmes. Attraction to sex and sex-generating events is a natural phenomena. The psychology of human beings is easily influenced by the programmes having sexual appeal and urge. This is an accepted fact that we cannot negate. But it is not meant that we forget the difference between human and animal. The entertainment providing organisations, public or private need to know the difference between human culture and animal culture.

Recently, we find sports also emerging as a source for entertainment. Of course, this is a healthy form of entertainment but the most important source for entertainment of general masses is TV channel which has gained popularity and is found throwing a negative impact on our culture. This makes a strong advocacy in favour of ethical dimensions in the functional character of entertainment providing organisations. Let's hope that government policy makers and social reformists realise gravity of the situation and monitor and regulate attitudes and behaviour of entertainment providing organisations.

ENTERTAINMENT MARKETING — A CONCEPTUAL FRAMEWORK

By entertainment marketing, our focus is on the application of marketing principles in the entertainment services. This gravitates our attention on the formulation of marketing mix for the services which help the entertainment organisations in improving the quality of services for satisfying and benefiting the users. It is a managerial process of making the services productive so that the organisations succeed in accomplishing the organisational goals. The marketing processes make the ways for profit generation since the optimal inputs make the services cost-effective by making possible operational economy. It is a planned effort to organise the business which requires world-class professional excellence. We find entertainment marketing a productive approach to fulfil the changing expectations of users. It is an intelligent effort to study and understand the changing behavioural profile of users based on the segmentation results. The making of creative marketing decisions is an important functional responsibility before the professionals which requires a well-developed and technology-driven information system. Thus, we observe the following facts regarding entertainment marketing:

- Entertainment marketing is a managerial process.
- It is also a social process since the entertainment organisations are supposed to subserve the social interests by inculcating mass awareness.
- It is an organised effort to manage the business.
- It is a device to help marketing professionals in developing quality marketing inputs which make possible quality marketing outputs.
- It is a process of customer-satisfaction engineering.

RATIONALE BEHIND ENTERAINMENT MARKETING

If we diagnose the rational behind the application of marketing principles in the entertainment services, there are a number of points to justify the same.

The following points are found in favour.

1. Satisfaction to Users: The application of marketing principles in the entertainment services helps in satisfying the users because the entertainment organisations offer the services to cater to the changing needs and requirements and increasing level of expectations of the users. By segmenting the market, the organisations get an opportunity to identify the preferences and to formulate the entertainment mix befitting to the changing taste of the users. This helps professionals in winning and keeping the users for the long time.

2. Generation of Profits: The application of marketing principles is found justified since the entertainment organisations succeed in marketing profits. The marketing practices help in increasing the business in addition to the cost-effectiveness which makes the ways for generating profits. An optimal development of marketing inputs makes the services productive.

3. Subserving the Social Interests: We can't deny that marketing professionals also make possible subserving of social interests. The entertainment organisations promote social advertising related to population control, drug addiction, afforestation, environment pollution, anti-smoking, AIDS, nutritional awareness are to mention a few helping society in may ways.

4. Making Possible Cost-effectiveness: It is also right to mention that application of marketing principles makes possible cost-effectiveness which regulates wastes of marketing resources playing a decisive role in rationalising the pricing policy.

MARKET SEGMENTATION FOR ENTERTAINMENT SERVICES

The marketing professionals need to study and understand the users belonging to different segments. This is essential to formulate a sound marketing mix for the entertainment services. We find people living both in rural and urban areas. We find viewers men as well as women. The kids, teens, youths and grey are also our customers. The affluent sections as well as the weaker sections of the society also watch the entertainment programmes. The viewers are not only the corporate people but even the people serving the government departments and unorganised sector. It is natural that taste preferences of potential or actual customers coming from the diverse segments cannot be identical. The marketing professionals will find it difficult to formulate a sound marketing strategy, if we find them unaware of their changing attitudes. This necessitates segmentation of entertainment markets. The different segments of entertainment markets has been shown in Fig. 21.1.

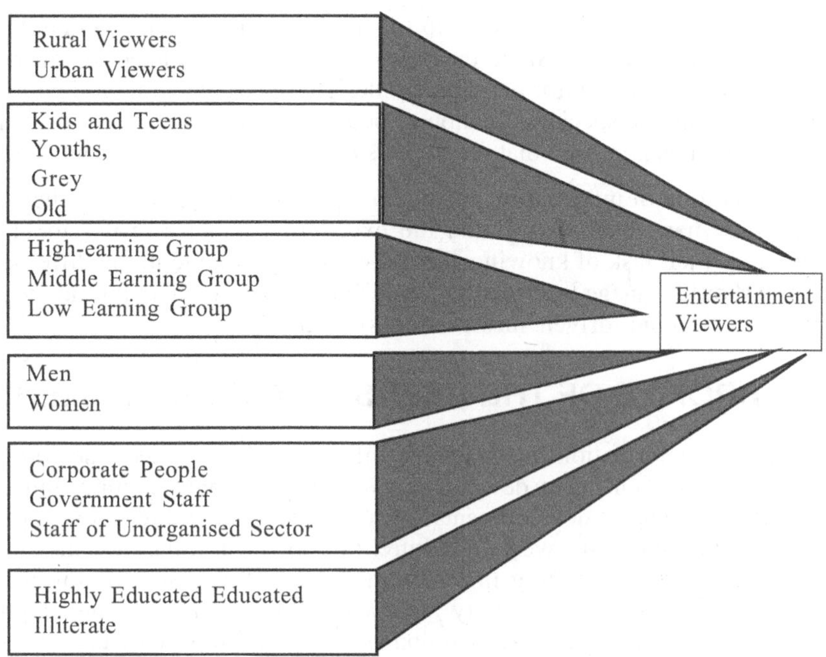

Fig. 21.1: Market Segments of Entertainment Viewers

We cannot negate the fact that attitudinal variation is governed by the mult-faceted changes in the socio-economic environmental conditions. In today's world, the economic transformation sizeably influences the behavioural patterns. The new generation of information and communication technology bridges the gap between the rural and urban viewers. It is due to the fact that we find almost all categories of customers showing their fascination to the western culture. The entertainment organisations offering to them the westernised programmes succeed whereas others underrating the same find it difficult to survive. The professionals have to see that how and in what way they can transform their attitudes by brushing up their minds. The creative ideas and creative messages can be successful in regulating the process of taste perversion.

MANAGING INFORMATION FOR ENTERTAINMENT SERVICES

The increasing flow of information throws a major impact on our lifestyles. We find imprint of changing lifestyles on our behaviour and attitudes. During the yesteryears, we have witnessed a large-scale use of information and communication technology (ITC) in almost all the areas and the entertainment sector has also been making use of the same to increase the operational flow and improve the quality of service delivery. The significance of managing information for marketing decisions is involved in the essence of collecting the information with diverse motives such as identifying the levels of expectations, attitudinal transformation, formation of behavioural patterns, segmenting the entertainment markets and formulating a sound marketing mix for delivering goods to the society and users *pari passu*. It is in this context that the marketing professionals need to assign due weightage to the management of marketing information.

We live in an age of globalisation which has been affecting our culture and civilisation. The intensity of impact on a particular segment can be studied with the help of information. The taste preferences of different segments of viewers can be studied in a right way with the help of information. Presently when we find emergence of a cross-cultural society, it is natural that professionals develop their awareness of the cultural background of viewers and potential viewers. The marketing professionals can also be successful in diagnosing the reasons for such an attitudinal transformation and developing the prescriptions or entertainment programmes efficacious to change the same. Perversion of taste is a natural phenomenon. It is natural that we copy the wrongs. In a true sense, the sensitivity rate is found at its peak when we talk in terms of copying the wrongs.

The professionals need to develop their awareness of the changing socio-cultural dimensions and their impact on the taste preferences and lifestyles of different segments of society. Since they bear the responsibility of formulating a sound marketing mix, it is pertinent that they undertake marketing research activities and also take help of marketing intelligence research activities and further also take help of marketing intelligence system to know the day-to-day developments in the marketing environment. Since they buy or borrow the concept or theme for programming, it is significant that on the basis of available information, they design a package combining a number of programmes. This will also help them in knowing the special attraction of people to a particular event or item. While undertaking the research activities, they should make it sure that researchers are sincere and honest and undertake the field survey.

Today, we find new generation of information and communication technology and therefore, the professionals need to make it sure that they have quality ICT and the excellent computer professionals to help them in the process. This will also simplify their task of knowing about the artists available in the different parts of the country. The marketing professionals should manage information for different purposes. The formulation of a sound marketing mix also requires support of a techno-driven information system.

BEHAVIOURAL PROFILE OF THE USERS OF ENTERTAINMENT SERVICES

The process of economic transformations considerably influences the process of socio-cultural transformation. The corporatisation made possible significant developments in the national economy but at the same time also paved avenues for a number of negative developments in the social system and cultural patterns. The corporate culture was found sizeably influenced by the western culture. In a true sense, the globalisation of economy opened doors for the globalisation of lifestyles resulting into the emergence of a multi-cultural or cross-cultural society. It was against this backdrop that the Indian society also winessed mult-faceted developments. The economic transformation as a positive impact and cultural degeneration as a negative impact are the two opposite considerations sizeably influencing the social system. In a very natural way, we find impact of these developments on the taste preferences of general masses in which temptation to the entertainment programmes having western influence have started creating a new opportunity and a new market. Almost all the entertainment providing organisations found these developments virtually a threat to their existence. Since this was a matter of their survival, it was quite natural that they make possible a radical change in their product mix having western orientation. We cannot negate that preferences of customers become the focal point while designing the product mix.

It is significant to mention that attitudinal change in the viewers of entertainment programme was found almost in all the segments. The increasing craze for westernised items even amongst the kids and teens has made it essential that the entertainment providing organisations overhaul their product mix and offer to them the programmes they need. The parents are helpless, the governmental regulations are not so much rigid and this has made the business environment much more conducive to profit generation. What to talk of the gullible segments of the society when we find even youths and grey segments of the Indian society evincing keen interests in entertainment programmes having vulgarity. The process of commercialisation thus gained a rapid momentum and all the organisations have started thinking in favour of offering more than they expect. Actually, we find negative developments very much instrumental in forming the vicious circle; be it social, economic or cultural.

The above-mentioned facts, thus, make it clear that the marketers serving the entertainment organisations need an attitudinal change. With this perception, they conceptualise marketing that anything can be included in the product mix, if the viewers like it or welcome. In the social system when we find social reformists becoming insensitive, the philanthropists becoming inactive and the regulations practically becoming ineffective; the task of throwing the cycle in the reverse gear is found difficult. The entertainment providing organisations cannot venture to go against the wind. And if they dare, we cannot deny their final departure from the entertainment world. Ethics, values actually we find these terms not getting any place in the Indian society.

The marketing professionals bear the responsibility of satisfying the viewers of entertainment programme. This makes it essential that they keep into consideration the changing levels of expectations of viewers in which we find a fundamental change. It is amazing that such change is found not only amongst the urban viewers but even amongst the rural viewers; not only amongst men but even amongst women; not only amongst affluents sections but also amongst the weaker sections. In a true sense, we find an invasion on our taste which has resulted perversion and vulgarity in our attitudes. While conceptualising marketing, the professionals have no option but to make an in-depth study of their behaviour and the study results indicate that their preferences, likes and dislikes are now completely changed. The professional excellence makes a strong advocacy in favour of ethical dimensions while the situational forces favour rejection.

The tidal wave of pop culture has virtually changed their behavioural profile. Aggressive behaviour is but natural when we find them all the time busy and not refreshing their minds by enjoying the fragrance of classical and light classical music. We find tension, dissension aggravating their depression and pop culture injecting new life and strength to them. The TV serials promoting bedroom vulgar scenes and violence are the first choice of today's society. The marketers have no option but to offer to them the items they like. We witness everything wrong; we do everything wrong; we watch everything wrong and we expect everything right.

The TV Channels, Multiplexes, Cinema Halls, Theatre Companies are the key providers of entertainment services and we find all of them making a compromise with the changing scenario. Of course, they have been successful in accomplishing organisational objectives by maximising profits but we find their contributions almost dismal in the context of societal responsibility. The most healthy source of entertainment, i.e., Circus has virtually been getting it difficult to survive because this fails in fulfilling the expectations of budding generations. Hence, we find it a problem to be given due weightage on the development agenda of government policy makers and social reformists that what should be the mission of entertainment organisations. Should they develop a product mix in tune with the changing attitudes of viewers? Or, they should explore avenues for brushing up the attitudes of viewers or potential viewers. If they move forward to the first option, the entertainment programmes promote illegitimate sexual behaviour *vis-a-vis* would make the society uncultured, specially in the Indian social system. And if they prefer the second option, there will be a threat to their commercial viability.

In view of the above, it is fair to say that the entertainment organisations cannot be spared of the social responsibility and therefore it is imperative that government policy makers make sincere and honest efforts to regulate the entertainment organisations so that they assign an overriding priority to healthy entertainment programmes. Attitudinal perversion cannot be allowed because this will spoil our new generations.

THE FORMULATION OF MARKETING MIX

Marketing professionals bear the responsibility of formulating a sound marketing mix for the entertainment organisations so that quality entertainment services are made available to the users. It is in this context that we talk about the formulation of different submixes, such as the product mix, the promotion mix, the price mix, the place mix and the people mix.

The Product Mix

In the entertainment services, the products are entertainment programmes made available to the viewers. The entertainment organisations offer different types of services to the different categories of users as shown in Figure 21.2.

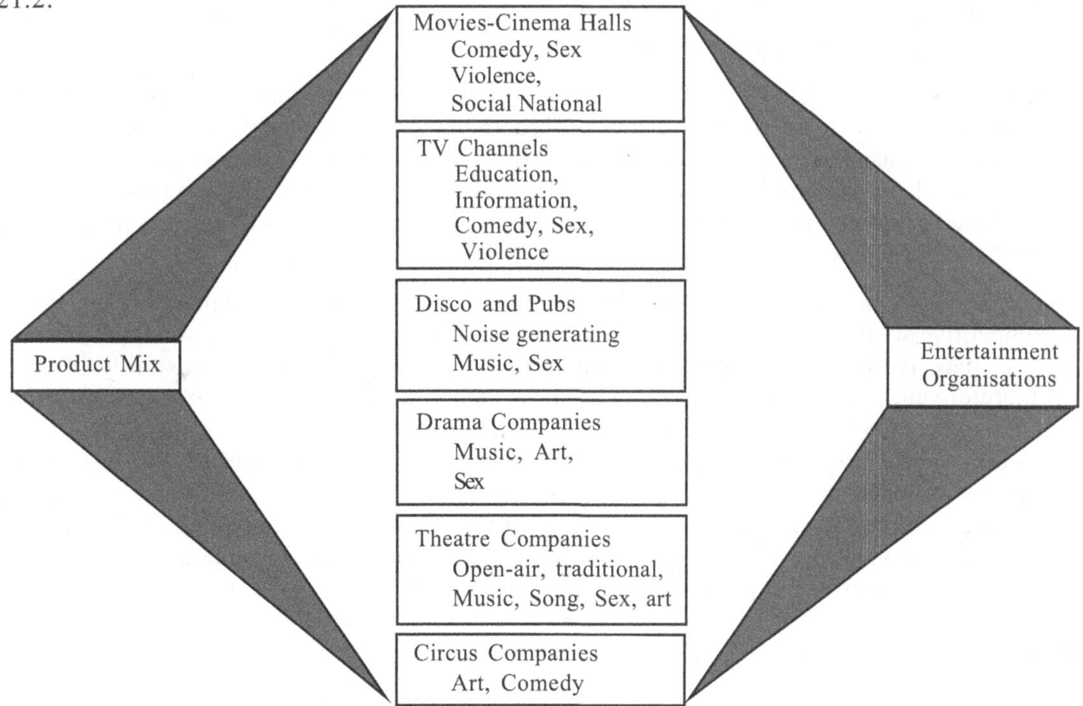

Fig. 21.2: Product Mix of the Entertainment Organisations

The different categories of organisations are Picture palaces, Open-air Theatres, TV Channels, Disco Halls, Pubs, Drama Centres, Dance Centres, Circus Companies, Theatre Companies and Amusement Centres. Some of the organisations are managed under the public sector whereas a large number of organisations are managed under the private sector. All the entertainment organisations are supposed to offer healthy entertainment items which on the one hand refresh the viewers while on the other hand also educate and sense them in a right perspective so that the possibilities of taste perversion, cultural invasion are regulated. This in a natural way draws our attention on the service mix or service profile of the entertainment organisations. We can't negate that of late a majority of the organisations are found engaged in activating the process of perverting taste and invading culture. The gaining popularity of pop-and-pub culture, the increasing attractions for violence and bedroom scenes, the expanding generation gap, the falling respect for elders, the increasing cases of AIDS are some of the negative developments for which the responsibilities fall on the shoulders of entertainment organisations. We don't find these developments a right sign. This makes it essential that the entertainment organisations in general formulate their entertainment mix in such a way that the process of social transformation is given a right direction.

They need to enrich their core services. The cine producers producing movies, the TV channels preparing TV serials, the Theatre Companies playing stories, the Drama Companies dramatising stories and others who entertain are supposed to assign due weightage to healthy entertainment programmes. In their service profile, they have to blend different properties in such a way that social awareness is made possible, informing and sensing tasks are carried on successfully, healthy comedy items are blended optimally, burning social, national problems are given an overriding priority and while doing such, the cultural values are not to be devalued. It was against this background that we had constituted statutory bodies to regulate their behaviour but it is amazing to mention that even they have perceived a new perception of quality entertainment in the name of art, freedom of expression or so. Of late, we find all of them acting, playing, producing, transmitting, telecasting with levity. This is found derailing the teens because they are gullible. This is found making an invasion on the Indian culture. This is found promoting sex, violence or so. The dresses and make-up they wear become a fashion, the themes they select become a lesson.

The aforesaid facts make it clear that whatever the negative developments we find in the present society have considerably been gifted by the different entertainment organisations. They often argue that we present because viewers like. Of course, they are not aware of the fact that human beings or even other living beings have some weaknesses in which temptation to sex is quite natural and therefore irrespective of the consequences and implications, we develop a craze for the same if our minds, eyes get an opportunity to view the same. In some of the cases, we also find them talking about art, freedom for expression and undoubtedly enough, majority of them don't know the real meaning of these words.

The product mix is required to be a fair combination of ancient and modern culture, no doubt, but we should not think like this that in the modern culture we have a freedom to promote open sex. The entertainment organisations in general and the TV Channels in particular need to assign due weightage to Indian culture. While formulating the product mix, it is also pertinent that they assign due weightage to the peripheral services, such as they develop other services close to the centres, they make world-class arrangements for the conveniences and comforts of the viewers and more so they make it a point of attraction.

In view of the above, it is right to mention that the product mix of the entertainment organisations is required to be made competitive so that the world-class services get a profitable market. We are not opposed to entertainment but they need to perceive the right perception of entertainment. They bear the responsibility of entertaining the masses and therefore they should entertain by presenting items which on the one hand refresh them while on the other hand also provide to them an opportunity to learn something positive. Of course, they need to produce the services selling more for generating profits and maintaining commercial viability but just for making more profits they are not supposed to derail the society, misguide the teens, promote sex and violence and invite and welcome the values making an invasion on the Indian culture, distorting social relationship or so. It is in this context that the entertainment organisations need a new prescription for the formulation of a sound product mix which refreshes viewers and develop their faculties.

The Promotion Mix

Like other organisations, the entertainment organisations are also required to engineer a sound base for the generation of profits which makes a strong advocacy in favour of effective promotional measures. Of course, they need quality entertainment programmes to satisfy the users and this requires the formulation of a sound service mix. In this context, it is pertinent that the users or prospects come to know about the quality of services which makes it essential that the entertainment organisations make possible creativity in the promotional measures. It is against this background that they need to use the different constituents of the promotion mix which would help them substantially in informing, sensing and persuading the users. The different components of promotion, such as advertising, sales promotion, publicity, personal selling, word-of-mouth promotion and telemarketing are required to be made effective to transform the prospects into the habitual users.

Advertisement: As a paid form of persuasive communication, the advertisement helps entertainment organisations in increasing the mass awareness. Almost all categories of entertainment organisations need to advertise with the support of advertising professionals having the world-class excellence. The effectiveness in advertising messages and themes is felt essential which draws our attention on creativity. We need to understand the level of expectations of the prospects which would help us in formulating and innovating the service profile. The marketing professionals need to formulate a sound product profile in which different types of entertainment programmes are included. In addition, they also require to design a package to motivate the users. It is not possible for all the entertainment organisations to have an independent wing for advertising. This makes it essential that they take the support of syndicate or the leading professionals who would help them in making the advertisement messages and themes creative. The print media would be suitable for almost all categories of the entertainment organisations because today we have sophisticated print technology and quality print materials which would add attractions to advertisement. In addition, the cost economy is also an additional benefit specially with the viewpoint of those entertainment organisations who find it difficult to advertise through the telecast media. So far as the big entertainment organisations are concerned, they have a big budget for advertisement and therefore, they can afford telecast media. There is no doubt in it that we find high intensity of effectiveness in the telecast media. The entertainment organisations may also advertise through the broadcast media. While selecting a vehicle, it is essential that they assign due weightage to the budgetary provisions and the financial constraint.

Publicity: We find publicity the most effective component of promotion since the entertainment organisations find it convenient to develop rapport with the media people. If they succeed in developing rapport with the media people. If they succeed in developing rapport and the media people are found influenced with the quality of entertainment programmes, an eye-catching coverage as a news item would promote their business even without making a substantial investment. The marketing professionals need to organise lunch, dinner parties or get-together functions in which the media people, opinion leaders and the popular artists are to be invited. If they succeed in impressing upon the media, the publicity would be possible which would help the entertainment organisations considerably in promoting the business.

Sales Promotion: The entertainment organisations also need to think about the sales promotion measures to promote the business. A temporary incentive to the sales promotion as well as to the users of services helps in boosting the sale. It is in this context that we make an advocacy for innovative tools of sales promotion, such as concessional services, offering of gifts, organisation of fair and exhibition by the entertainment organisations, specially for the sales people. In addition, they may also think in favour of such an incentive to the users of services. The offering of concessional services for the habitual users, organisation of sales contests, distribution of coupons, offering of small gifts would be helpful in increasing the business. We can't deny that such a provision would be more productive when we find the pressure on the ticket counters coming down. The promotional measures may be made operational by both — the entertainment organisations as well as the entertainment centres.

Personal Selling: We find this component of the promotion mix very much instrumental in promoting the entertainment organisations. The task of creating the impulse may be successfully carried on with the help and co-operation of sales personnel. The tact, ability and skill of sales personnel play here an incremental role. This makes it essential that the entertainment organisations are careful while recruiting, training and compensating the sales people. If they recruit personnel having faculties to impress and influence, train them properly in the face of changing behavioural profile of the users and remunerate them sufficiently depending upon their efforts for the promotion of business; the sales personnel may contribute significantly to the business of the entertainment organisations. The agents, dealers, brokers, sales personnel help substantially the promotion of business. They should have high communicative ability, attractive or handsome physique, dedication and commitment to the profession which would directly contribute to the business graph of the entertainment organisations.

Word-of-mouth Promotion: If you serve well; if the quality of your goods or services are of world-class; if your service profile succeeds in satisfying the users; your task of promoting the business is simplified fantastically.

It is against this background that we talk about the instrumentality of word-of-mouth promotion. The audience satisfied with the quality of entertainment programmes communicate their positive or negative feelings to their friends and relatives. If they are satisfied with your services, they advocate in your favour and such a positive remark helps in promoting the business because all of them prefer to watch the same as and when they get an opportunity. It is against this background that we find this constituent of the promotion mix playing a positive role, provided the quality of programme is superior.

Telemarketing: In addition to other components of the promotion mix, we find telemarketing emerging as an important constituent of promotion. With the development of sophisticated communication technologies, we find enough scope for promoting through telephones and televisions. This dimension of promotion requires the involvement of a successful telemarketer who should have high communicative ability to receive and transmit the messages related to the queries of the prospective customers or the users. Any confusion or misunderstanding in the minds of prospective customers is required to be removed by the telemarketers. But it is essential that the entertainment organisations make available sophisticated telephonic instruments to the telemarketers who bear the responsibility of influencing and impressing upon the users.

The Price Mix

In the formulation of marketing mix, the pricing decisions are found significant. If the users of the services come to view the open-air theatres, dance or music centres, cricket-show, car-racing or horse-racing, they are mentally prepared to pay high prices for the services. But for all the services, the entertainment organisations can't adopt the same strategy. The traditional theatres, the circus companies, movies and amusement parks need a pricing strategy that is found suitable even to the low-income group of the society. This makes it clear that high-pricing strategy is found suitable where the services indicate high status of viewers. Thus, the entertainment organisations need to assign due weightage to the category and paying capacity of the viewers. In a country like India where the entertainment services are viewed even by the weaker sections of the society, the entertainment organisations need to segment the customers and to adopt high-price structure for the high-income group and the low-pricing structure for the low-income group. While pricing, the entertainment organisations are required to take into consideration a number of factors, such as the cost of inputs, the slab of entertainment tax charged by the government, the social and economic status of the viewers or so. When the structure of entertainment tax charged by the government is found high, the entertainment organisations have no option but to charge more. Like this when the high-cost inputs are used in the process, the entertainment organisations charge high-pricing strategy. This makes it clear that the entertainment organisations can't take a decision in isolation since a number of facts influence the process.

The most important thing in the Indian perspective is the entertainment tax which is found throwing a big impact on the pricing decisions of the entertainment organisations. All of us feel that the masses find it difficult to view the movies, theatres, dramas regularly because the high slab of tax makes the price structure high. A rational tax structure is thus found essential to promote the entertainment organisations. To be more specific, the entertainment service used by the masses need due attention of the government. Besides, the entertainment organisations producing programmes visualising social, cultural and national problems need an overriding priority. The tax concessions, availability of subsidised infrastructural facilities or essential inputs, multi-faceted support in promoting the entertainment programme require due support of government. Of course, the exchequer requires due support of the viewers but at the same time, it is also right to mention that the viewers are required to be promoted since they have very limited means for entertainment. Moreover, the government also bears the responsibility of promoting the entertainment organisations and this needs due attention on the entertainment tax charged.

The pricing decisions can't underestimate the regional considerations since a uniform policy can't be adopted for the entertainment organisations established in the rural areas and others located in the big towns and cities. It is quite natural that for the entertainment organisations located in the rural areas, the pricing structure is required to be low which is possible when in addition to the low slab of tax, the supporting infrastructural facilities are made available at the subsidised or concessional prices. This is essential to promote entertainment service *vis-a-vis* the entertainment organisations. It is in this context that we need to develop an ongoing training programme for the personnel engaged in the process of offering the services.

Another dimension in the very context is related to the location points for the entertainment organisations. This dimension of the place mix becomes significant to make the service comfortable, safe and accessible. While selecting location points, it is pertinent that the entertainment organisations select a place which is smoothly accessible. The availability of supporting infrastructural facilities can't be underestimated in the very context. Since a majority of the entertainment programmes need adequate and uninterrupted power facilities, the marketing professionals need to make it sure that the problem of breakdown or inadequate supply is not to degenerate the quality of services. Further, it is also essential that the place selected for the entertainment centres is safe. We can't negate that a place where we find assembling of target prospects would be suitable and therefore cities' precincts draw our attention while locating the entertainment centres. To be more specific when the entertainment centres are meant for the children and women, the entertainment organisations need to make it sure that in addition to other aspects, the transportation and communication facilities are available specially during and after the show times.

The aforesaid facts make it clear that marketing professionals need to assign due weightage to the management of place which directly or indirectly influences the business prospects of entertainment organisations. To be more specific for the leading and large-sized entertainment organisations, it is also pertinent that they assign due weightage to the management of distribution channel. Since we find distribution process nationally and even internationally, it is essential that they are particular to the selection of distribution representatives, agents, dealers who have not been facing the image problem. It is important that they are offered reasonable incentives to promote sale. We can't deny the fact that representatives with a well-established image simplify the task of entertainment organisations. Contrary to it, the distribution representatives facing the image problem complicated the process of distribution. When we find the distribution network at the small-scale, the entertainment organisations are found directly involved in the entire process and therefore, they can manage the distribution process in tune with their own conveniences and potentials.

In view of the above, it is right to mention that the entertainment organisations bear the responsibility of making the distribution process convenient as well as economic. The marketing professionals need to make the distribution expenses optimal. While rationalising the expenses, they need to make it sure that they go to the places where the target audience are available in a good number. We don't need to locate distribution centres for all the services at all the place. When we produce entertainment programmes for the rural viewers, it is pertinent that we locate distribution centres where the rural prospects are available in a good number. Contrary to it when they locate distribution centres for the ultra-modern prospects, it is much more impact generating that they concentrate in metropolises or in the big industrial towns and cities. Thus, the place decisions require to take into consideration a number of factors which substantially influence the business prospects of the entertainment organisations. It is against this background that the marketing professionals are required to have a sound place mix.

In addition to other aspects, the pricing decisions of the entertainment organisations also need to consider the nature and types of services offered by them. The circus companies, traditional theatre companies promoting cultural heritage, folk songs deserve special support to be more specific by the government and the social organisations. It is not possible for the circus companies to bring down the price structure since they are required to spend huge amount for the inputs they use for offering the services. This requires a liberal policy of government in which the entertainment organisations of sensitive nature are supposed to make available multi-dimensional support.

In this context, it is also right to mention that of late the entertainment organisations in general have been found facing numerous problems mainly due to the popularity of TV channels. With the development of satellite communication, we find almost all the cinema halls or the picture places or others like drama and music companies facing the problem of financial crunch. They find it difficult to promote the business and unless we offer to them special incentives, the future marketing of a majority of the entertainment organisations would be in red. It is in this context that we find it significant to offer different types of incentives to the entertainment organisations.

In view of the above, it is right to mention that the entertainment organisations need to make the pricing decisions rational failing which the commercial viability of a majority of them would adversely be affected. We can't negate that such a negative trend in the business environment would close doors for the development of some of the entertainment organisations instrumental in entertaining the masses.

The Place Mix

In the making of marketing decisions, we find place mix an important decision-making area. This draws our attention on the two important problems, first the process of offering the services and second the selection of an appropriate place for the entertainment organisations. The process of offering the services is found significant with the viewpoint of making available the promised services to the audience. This makes it essential that personnel engaged in the process are well aware of the behavioural management. The personnel working at the ticket counters at the entry and exit points need due attention of the entertainment organisations since we find them acting as sensitive personnel or as the front-line staff. If they don't know about the behavioural management and start behaving indecently with the users or the prospects, the business would adversely be affected. In addition, the agents, dealers, also need due attention since they are found involved in the process. This makes it essential that the marketing professionals engaged are careful to their behavioural profile and offer to them an ongoing training programme so that they come to know how to behave. It is in this context that we talk about the instrumentality of offering the services. Like other organisations, the entertainment organisations also need to think over the problem that gap between the services-promised and services-offered is to be bridged over and this would hardly be possible unless we have a dedicated team of front-line personnel. By quality, our emphasis is on a number of factors just not the quality of entertainment programme. Your quality entertainment programmes fail in attracting the prospects/ users, if they come to know that their personnel lack a high behavioural profile.

The Process Mix

In an age of information and communication technology, the processing of entertainment services are found techno-driven. A number of equipments, instruments and machines are used in the process. Besides, we find a number of artists and supporting staff for presentation. Keeping in view the nature of programme, we find processing of services crossing different stages and phases. This submix of marketing makes it sure that people and technology work and perform in such a way that promised quality of services are delivered to the viewers as per their expectations. They should be sincere to the time and quality elements so that scope for delay and distortion is minimised. Programming of services and their proper presentation are the two important considerations influencing the service quality. In the entertainment services, delivery process is a bit complicated. The flow of activities is considerably influenced by the instrument and equipment used for this purpose. The marketing professionals are required to be sincere so that quality gap due to technology or working people are minimised. Thus, in the process mix, operating system through which service is delivered plays an incremental role.

Physical Evidence and Attractions

This submix of marketing draws our attention on the service ambience. The environment in which service is delivered determines the quality of programme to be delivered. In this context, the professionals need priority attention on servicescapes where we find focus on physical facilities becoming instrumental in adding additional attractions to the entertainment services. The interiors and exteriors, furnishing, lighting, ventilation, sanitation, parking, the designing of entertainment centres throwing architectural flavour, cleanliness, aesthetic sense are some of the aspects drawing due attention of marketing professionals. We cannot negate the fact that service ambience for entertainment organisations needs priority attention because the environment in which service is delivered and the tangible components through which the potential viewers go through become significant for the formation for positive or negative opinions. The ambient conditions facilitate performance if the tangibilisation process is found in order. The display of equipment used for service delivery also becomes effective in the formation of opinion. In a true sense, we find tangibles providing to the potential viewers cues on which they can depend. We cannot negate that physical evidence cues provide excellent opportunities for entertainment providing organisations to transmit consistent and strong messages regarding the quality of services to be delivered. The potential viewers strengthen their realisation through tangibilisation. The perception of service quality is found taking a shape to form the levels of expectations. This makes it essential that the marketing professionals study the potential viewers and make professionalised efforts to create service ambience helping the viewers in increasing their temptation to service.

The People Mix

Technologies, no doubt, play an important role in improving the quality of goods or services produced and generated by an organisation but ultimately it is the quality of human resources that plays a decisive role. It is right to mention that with the help of sophisticated communication technologies the entertainment organisations have been successful in improving the quality of their services but failing the world-class personnel working as characters or serving as distributors they would hardly be successful in accomplishing the organisational goals. It is against this background that we need to assign due weightage to the people mix of an organisation.

We are well aware of the fact that the entertainment organisations need a world-class service profile. This requires a fair blending of sophisticated technologies and quality personnel. The availability of super quality of camera would lack any meaning, if they lack super quality of photographer. The electronically managed light and song would hardly be successful in generating creativity and adding attractions, if they lack personnel to operate and monitor them. The supporting high quality of infrastructural facilities would fail in attracting the audience, if they lack world-class artists. The world-class entertainment items would hardly be successful in attracting the audience, if the distributors and to be more specific the front-line staff start misbehaving with the audience. These facts are a mute testimony to this proposition that the entertainment organisations also need to assign due weightage to the formulation of a sound people mix.

They need to manage different categories of personnel because some of them work as artists whereas some others work as distributors. While managing the marketing activities, the professionals are supposed to make it sure that quality artists are recruited, imparted an ongoing training facility, motivated sufficiently and controlled professionally. In addition to the core personnel, they also need to make it sure that the supporting personnel are of quality. They need to know how to behave, how to influence, how to convince and how to win. Since we find them working at almost all the stages, it is pertinent that they are efficient, sincere, dedicated, committed to the profession, value-based and prove themselves to be high performers. We can't negate that even they need an ongoing training to perform efficiently and decently. The marketing professionals bear the responsibility of improving their efficiency and enriching their faculties, specially related to the behavioural profile.

In both the categories of personnel, they need performance orientation which would hardly be possible, if they don't think about employee orientation. It is in this context that the professionals need to link their incentive plans to the efficiency index. The personnel proving their excellence as high performers and helping the entertainment organisations in promoting the quality and saleability need to be rewarded suitably. If the efficients, either acting as core personnel or serving as supporting personnel, get suitable incentives, even the inefficients would evince their interests in improving the credentials. Contrary to it, if the professionals start rewarding uniformly to both the efficients and inefficients even the efficients would start degenerating.

ENTERTAINMENT MARKETING IN INDIAN PERSPECTIVE

All of us have started perceiving the instrumentality of entertainment programmes in removing monotony, minimising fatigue, enriching credentials and generating efficiency. In a country like India where masses are unconscious, unaware, illiterate and insensitive, the entertainment organisations are supposed to play an outstanding role. The masses have limited discretionary incomes in their hands; the kids, teens and youths have become crazy. The multi-dimensional problems are found increasing the intensity of insensitivity. This makes it essential that the entertainment organisations significantly contribute to the process of qualitative transformation. It is against this background that we need to talk about entertainment marketing.

We can't deny the fact that India has rich cultural heritage, a strong rural background inhabiting a good number of innocent people. With the attainment of independence in 1947, we find a number of positive developments in the socio-economic fabrics. The sophistication in the process of technological advances has made ways for qualitative-cum-quantitative improvements in almost all the areas. The development of new generation of communication technologies has made possible sophistication in the process. We find significant developments in the entertainment facilities since a number of picture palaces, drama and theatre centres, disco clubs and pubs are found engaged in entertaining the different segments of the audience. Our honest confession makes it clear that these new developments in the entertainment world have engineered a strong foundation for an invasion on the rich cultural heritages of India. The masses now appear interested in the pop culture, disco culture, pub culture. Thanks to the new TV channels. Of course, we appreciate the positive contributions of DDI and Songs and Drama Division, Government of India who have played an outstanding role in educating the masses but now the negative contributions are found outwitting their positive contributions. The opening of new TV channels are found derailing the kids and teens. The lifestyles of ultra-modern society of today are found fuelling the process of negative developments. This makes it essential that the entertainment organisations in the Indian perspective conceptualise marketing which would help them in many ways.

The entertainment organisations in general and the TV channels in particular need to perceive right perception of quality entertainment programmes. This makes it essential that they assign due weightage to the formulation of a sound product mix or the service profile. They are supposed to educate the masses, inculcate mass awareness, impart to them proper training, entertain them properly so that their quality service profile is found successful in washing up their brains in which social values, ethical dimensions, national excellence need a transcendental priority. We agree with this view that masses have now high reception capacity but at the same time we also confess that they often prefer to receive the wrongs. A fair mix of different types of entertainment programmes is essential to improve the quality of service profile of the entertainment organisations. It is amazing to mention that the Circus Companies are of late facing the problem of financial crunch whereas the Disco and Pubs have been found successful in strengthening their financial health. This makes it essential that the entertainment organisations of almost all the categories assign an overriding priority to the formulation of a rich service profile in which Indian values are given due weightage. If the government appears disinterested in doing such the social regulations should make it possible.

In the Indian perspective, the promotional decisions need more creativity. Of late, the entertainment organisations have been found using different components of promotion. The professionals bear the responsibility of making possible an optimal use of different constituents so that the promotional expenses are regulated to make the pricing decisions rational. The advertising professionals need to study the changing preferences of prospects and further to sense them in a right direction. We can't negate that advertisement messages and themes are required to be made creative so that the task of sensitising the prospects or users is done in an effective way. The print media, broadcast media and the telecast media have to accept the responsibility of creating mass awareness. The existing perversion of taste is to be arrested and this requires concerted efforts of entertainment organisations *vis-a-vis* the media. While promoting, they need to be more careful.

In the Indian context, we find masses not in a position to afford the expensive entertainment services. Of course, a few selected segments can afford even the expensive services but the entertainment organisations also need to make the services economic so that even low-income group of the society is in a position to afford. We can't deny that in this respect, they need due co-operation of government while getting the supporting infrastructural facilities and specially while paying the entertainment tax. It is right to mention that high slab of tax makes the services expensive. In addition, the entertainment organisations are also required to regulate their unproductive expenses found instrumental in increasing the cost of services. The main thing in the process is to make the pricing structure rational. To be more specific, some of the selected ,entertainment organisations, such as the Circus Companies and the Drama and Theatre Companies promoting art and culture need due attention of government while imposing tax or while subsidising the supporting infrastructural facilities.

The entertainment organisations also need to process the services in a right fashion so that the users get the promised quality of services. The front-line personnel need an in-depth knowledge of behavioural management. The distributing agencies are required to channelise the services in' such a way that taste-oriented entertainment programmes reach to the target audience. We can't deny the fact that in the entertainment services, they play an incremental role. A number of quality entertainment programmes don't reach to the target audience because the distributing agencies, representatives show a lukewarm response. If they promote the services found instrumental in making high rate of profits, they should also promote the services having social, national and cultural orientation.

The flow of operation is required to be improved and for that, the professionals need support of sophisticated technology and quality people to take part in the process of offering the entertainment services. We are aware of the fact that entertainment services are found of coplicated nature because a number of stages and phases are required to be completed before presenting any show or event.

The marketing professionals need to create the user- and staff-friendly service ambience. Here, our focus is on the physical facilities and surroundings that we find for the delivery of services. The exteriors and interiors, furnishing, lighting, ventilation, sanitation, aesthetic management, equipments to be used, parking are some of the aspects drawing priority attention of marketing professionals while managing the servicescapes. The entertainment programmes are found a bit different to others where viewers come with the motto of diffusing their tension of getting themselves relaxed. This makes it essential that they get or view an ambience that generates service fragrance and strengthen their perception of service quality to be presented to them. The professionals also need to take care of the dresses they provide to the staff performing and the staff working at different counters as front-line staff or working at other places as the back-line staff.

The people concerned with the entertainment organisations are of different categories. The performing staff, front-line staff, back-line staff and other supporting staff need a sense of dedication for improving the quality of services.

In view of the above, it is right to say that in the Indian perspective, the entertainment organisations are supposed to play an outstanding role. They need to offer the entertainment programmes in tune with the taste preferences of customers or viewers while on the other hand are also supposed to assign due weightage to ethical dimensions. It is pertinent to mention that we find a basic change in the Indian viewers. In a majority of the cases, we find them preferring the westernised entertainment programmes. They are found tempted to the programme generating sexual urge and prefer to watch vulgar scenes. Such a major change in attitudes and preferences have made the task of professionals much more complicated. A sound entertainment profile focuses our attention on the fair blending of eastern and western values in which the programmes making the teens and youths crazy do not get any place. The entertainment providing organisations, of course, will find it difficult. But the government regulations and social reformists and philanthropists have to clarify the perception of entertainment. The healthy entertainment programmes refresh our minds and energise our strength whereas the entertainment programmes promoting noise, sex, violence make an invasion on our culture, derail the society and spoils the new generations. Let's exercise our minds and choose the best course of action in the larger interests of society.

SUMMARY

In this chapter, you have gone through different dimensions of marketing entertainment services. After going through the chapter, be sure that the following facts are well versed.

Entertainment Marketing: A Conceptual Framework: It is a managerial process and an organised effort to market the entertainment services. It is a device to help a marketing professional in developing marketing inputs which make possible quality marketing outputs.

Rational Behind Marketing Entertainment Services: The conceptualisation of marketing in the entertainment services helps satisfying the users, generation of profits, subserve the social interests and making possible cost-effectiveness to make the services competitive.

Market Segmentation for Entertainment Services: The different segments of society are the viewers of entertainment services such as rural and urban; kids, teens, youths, grey, old; high-earning group, middle-earning group and low earning group; men and women; corporate people, government staff and staff of unorganised sector; highly educated, educated and illiterate. The marketers need to segment and study.

Managing Information for Entertainment Services: The professionals need information to make the marketing decisions.The new generation of sophisticated information and communication technology and the services of excellent computer professionals are used for managing the marketing information.

Behavioural Profile of Users of Entertainment Services: Of late, we find a major change in the attitudes and behaviour of users leading to taste perversion. Increasing temptation for westernised entertainment programmes supported by sexual appeal and violence need priority attention of government policy makers, social reformists and philanthropists.

Marketing Mix: The seven submixes of marketing have been practised in the entertainment services.

Product Mix: This focuses our attention on the packages of entertainment services to be included in the product mix. The entertainment organisations need to pay attention on the organisational, social and cultural considerations while formulating the product mix.

Promotion Mix: This mix of marketing concentrates on combining the different components of promotion in such a way users and potential users of services come to know about the service quality. The professionals bear the responsibility of blending advertising, publicity, sales promotion, personal selling, telemarketing and word of-mouth promotion with the motto of sensitising and persuading the customers.

The Price Mix: Since we find entertainment services used by almost all the segments of society, the professionals need to adopt the pricing strategy found remunerative and competitive.

The Place Mix: This focuses our attention on the channelisation of services. The entertainment services cross different stages and the professionals need to minimise time and cost so that services reach to the destination on time.

Process Mix: The processing of entertainment services is found complicated. A number of processes are followed with the help of a team of people and number of information and communication technology. The professionals need to increase the operational flow and maintaining the quality so that promised quality of services is delivered to the ultimate viewers.

Physical Evidence and Attractions: In this mix of marketing, the professionals manage the servicescapes where we find focus on managing the physical facilities and surroundings such as interiors and exteriors, furnishing, lighting, music, ventilation, sanitation, parking, etc. In addition, they also need to be sincere while managing the dresses of performers and other staff.

People Mix: The entertainment services are offered with the help of a number of people. They need quality performers and the quality supporting staff.

Entertainment Marketing in Indian Perspective: In the Indian context, the marketing of entertainment services has complicated the task of marketers. This is due to the fact that we find a basic change in the attitudes and behaviour of almost all the segments. The professionals, of course, bear the responsibility of increasing profits but in addition, they also have to check an invasion of Indian culture. The increasing temptation of masses to the sex-oriented programmes cannot be considered to be a healthy sign. The entertainment organisations promoting programmes having sex and violence succeed whereas others promoting ethics and values face the problem of financial crunch. Synchronisation of both the opposite considerations require world-class professional excellence and in addition, the support of governmental regulations. We can allow, specially the kids and teens, found of gullible nature, to derail.

KEY TERMS

Monotony	Pub
Fatigue	Exchequer
Meditation	Amusement Parks
Rejuvenation	Financial Crunch
Multiplex	Prospects
Pop Culture	Front-line Staff
Burgeoning	Back-line Staff
Live-in Culture	Interiors
Human Culture	Exteriors
Animal Culture	Service Ambience
Marketing Outputs	Crazy
Kids	Confession
Teens	Cultural Heritage
Gullible	Target Audience
Western Culture	Ethical Dimensions
Philanthropists	Gravitate
Perversion	*Pari passu*
Vulgarity	Vicious Circle

Review Questions

1. What do you mean by Entertainment Marketing?Explain the rationale behind practising marketing in the entertainment services.
2. Explain the different segments of users of entertainment services and their behavioural profile.
3. Discus the relevance of managing information for studying the entertainment markets and users.

4. What do you mean by Marketing Mix? Focus on the different mixes of marketing to be practised in the entertainment services.
5. Explain the relevance of extended marketing mixes for the entertainment services.
6. Focus on the behavioural profile of users of entertainment services.
7. Write a short note on Entertainment Marketing in the Indian perspective.

Application Exercises

1. You are working as a marketer in a reputed TV Channel. Suggest a marketing mix for your channel.
2. As a marketing professional, focus on the changing attitudes and behaviour of users of entertainment, services in the Indian context.
3. In the capacity of a marketing professional serving a Theatre Company, suggest the marketing mix to be effective in the changing cultural patterns of Indian viewers.
4. Design a services mix for a TV Channel to be instrumental in meeting organisational as well as the social considerations.
5. Do you find the present developments in the entertainment sector healthy for Indian social and cultural systems. Comment as a marketing professional.
6. Suggest a plan for promoting the entertainment services in the Indian perspective.
7. As a marketing professional, focus on the service ambience to be instrumental in attracting the attention of viewers and potential viewers.
8. Do you find governmental regulations to be much more rigid to promote and protect the interests of Indian society? Justify your answer as a marketing professional.

Endnotes

1. Jha, S.M., Entertainment Marketing, *Services Marketing*, Chapter 15, HPH, Mumbai, 2003, pp. 647–60.

MASS COMMUNCIATION MARKETING

Scientific inventions and innovations, no doubt, have made possible a number of positive developments in the world of communication, but at the same time have also engineered a strong foundation for numerous negative developments. Conceptualising societal marketing may reverse the process.

Chapter Objectives

Learning Objectives

The present chapter aims at studying the different dimensions of mass communication marketing. The mass communication where we study both the information and entertainment media play an outstanding role in developing mass awareness. The motive is to sensitise the general masses to the social evils. The mass communication organisations need to realise the importance of conceptualising marketing with a societal approach. The professionals with the help of marketing processes may be successful in striking a balance between the organisational and social considerations. Creating mass awareness is an important functional responsibility which they can discharge by practising marketing.

INTRODUCTION

Sophistication paves the ways for complication. Scientific inventions and innovations, no doubt, have made possible a number of positive developments in the world of communication but at the same time have also engineered a strong foundation for numerous negative developments. The globalisation of economy gained a rapid momentum due to sophisticated communication technologies and the masses could get an opportunity to taste the fragrance of world-class goods and services. The hierarchy of needs and requirements, taste preferences are now found completely changed. Our food habits, dresses, family structure, choice for entertainment and lifestyles, of late are fantastically influenced by mass media. We cannot deny that globalisation of economy has substantially been successful in momentising the globalisation of fashion, culture and civilisation. Of course, we now get opportunity to taste the sweetness of a number of material assets which yesterday were not found in our family preferences but if not all of us, undoubtedly a majority of us feel the taste now turning sour. The mounting social tensions and dissension, upward moving graph of violence, paying respect to old people in the new generation, disintegrating Indian families, increasing selfishness, aggravating temptation for an open sexual behaviour, etc. are a mute testimony to this proposition that we are moving downward. If scientific inventions and innovations start paving ways for negative developments in the society which even make an invasion on our culture, the development processes need a microscopic audit. It is against this background that we go through the impact of mass communication on our society and culture.

This chapter includes in its purview mass media such as information media and entertainment media, e.g., telecasting, broadcasting and print media. There are a number of public and private sector organisations engaged in the process. They have been offering a number of services to the society. The study focuses on their positive as well as negative contributions and the professional excellence required by them for prioritising the business agenda. We welcome all the positive developments in the socio-economic panorama but if negative developments in culture and civilisation start dominating the entire process, the social scientists, policy planners and academics bear a moral responsibility of highlighting the issues so that wrongs are corrected in the face of defined principles of social marketing in which a professional is supposed to establish a balance between the social and commercial considerations. We are not opposed to the generation of profits but can't welcome an invasion on our culture just to generate profits. If we turn our eyes on the instrumentality of mass media, in degenerating the socio-cultural values, the graph is found as its peak.

During yesterdecades, there have been significant developments in the field of print technologies. The offset and laser printing devices have virtually changed the whole scene and this has made possible publication of a good number of attractive newspapers and magazines. The readers now get an opportunity to go through the multi-dimensional developments around the world. Business houses also succeed in adding attractions to their advertisement campaigns by using colourful photographs. The social organisations find it convenient to publicise their messages. Thus, the information media or print media or newspapers and magazines have been found benefiting the society in many ways. At the same time, we cannot negate that they have also been involved in degenerating social and cultural values. If we turn our eyes on their commercial advertisements, the aggressive dresses, poses, especially of women confuse us and we find it difficult to distinguish between Indian magazines and the magazines of western countries which appears to be an impact of globalisation of fashion and culture.

We have developed broadcasting services or say, radio services and now masses even living in the remotest parts of the country use the services of AIR. Of course, the transmission of news, talks, healthy entertainment programmes are found useful to the society. We come to know the latest developments around the world; we get an opportunity to publicise the slogans protecting the social interests; we get information regarding recent developments in different areas; the business houses get an opportunity to advertise but the transmission of sex provoking songs, noise polluting and tension generating pop songs have very much been instrumental in making an invasion on our culture *vis-à-vis* aggravating the noise pollution.

The beginning of the decade of 1980s started a new era, especially in the field of communications, i.e., telecast media. No doubt, we find television even much earlier than that but it was in 1982 that Asiad games organised in Delhi paved the ways for its expansion. The satellite communication services injected new life to the system and now more than 90 per cent of our population watch TV regularly. Initially, the DDI and gradually a number of private TV channels entered the scene. We accept the fact that audiovisual exposure is considered to be the best device to sensitise the viewers. We cannot negate that it has proved its instrumentality as the most effective entertainment medium. We know about the latest developments around the world; the students are benefited by watching the educational programmes; the business houses advertise and the task of informing, sensing and motivating the customers is simplified considerably; the social organisations publicise messages protecting the social interests; the weather forecasting helps farmers and others in many ways and so on. Anyone would naturally be shocked by viewing the other side of the coin. Before we depict the true picture, it is essential that we make it clear that cinema halls and private homes do not have the same environment. If we go to the cinema halls, there we have an option to be selective in viewing a movie or in selecting the viewers. We cannot make it possible in our homes where we live with the family members of different age groups and both sexes. The movies transmitted by them; the songs and music programmes televised by them compel us to come to the conclusion that the TV medium bears a major responsibility of degenerating and derailing the social system and values. We learn to promote violence; we come to know the art of making love with our boy and girl friends; we get an opportunity to view the bedroom scenes; we are informed about the latest developments in fashion; we are miscommunicated by their false and misleading promises in advertisements and what not.

UNESCO reports, 'Media violence has direct influence on children.' The reporting by UNESCO is based on two TV serials found very popular the world over, specially among children. The first serial, "Terminator" viewed by 88 per cent of kids and the second serial, "Rocky" viewed by 55 per cent of the kids have high aggressive environment. A joint project of UNESCO and the World Organisation of Scout Movement and Untreched Union come to the conclusion that both the serials have considerably changed the behaviour of kids viewing the serials because they are found more aggressive even with their parents, friends, brothers and sisters. This is just an example. We can get numerous examples where the business houses have misused this medium. Again to quote. Reynolds advertisement has been found encouraging teens for smoking. R.J. Reynolds, a leading cigarette manufacturing company of the world introduced Old Joe, a carton camel character in which the campaign rescued the flagging camel brand from obscurity. It was not simply to appeal to smokers over the age of 21 indeed to attract teenagers with a likeable cartoon character. The advertisement was so effective that there was an increase of 82 per cent in the Camel's market share, among teenagers since Old Joe was introduced.

Do we find it right?

Do we find it ethical?

Do we find it legitimate?

The psychologists confirm that children are more gullible in nature. They receive anything fast in their minds and copy the same very fast. The law of nature makes it clear that human beings in general are very receptive to wrongs they witness. We take more time to receive the right things but receive the wrongs quickly. All of us now feel a negative change in the behaviour of kids/teens/youths.

The aforesaid negative developments make it essential that we conceptualise social marketing principles in mass media in order that they play a very positive role in transforming the society, promoting socio-cultural values, injecting ethical values, generating national excellence and at the same time securing profits for strengthening organisational efficacy to keep on the process. Of course, we advocate transmission and telecasting of entertainment programme but of healthy nature; advertisement messages found socially and culturally friendly and not throwing an adverse impact on our teens in particular. We are not supposed to cross the limits. Thus, mass media in general and the TV media in particular need to think over the problem on a priority basis.

The government has reviewed the Print Media Policy and opened up the News Sector for FIIs, NRIs and PIOs. Earlier, only FDI upto 26 per cent in this sector was permitted. In the non-News Sector also, the limit has been enhanced to 100 per cent from the previous limit of 74 per cent. A new policy of expansion of FM Radio Broadcasting service through private agencies (Phase II) was approved in 2005. The Government of India issued policy guidelines for downlink of TV channels in 2005 which provide that no person/entity shall downlink a channel that has not been registered with the Ministry of Information and Broadcasting.

Today, we find digitalisation of air archive. News on Phone (NOP) and News on Internet are now available. A number of softwares have been developed for information exchange and improvement of efficiency in the working of the various units of AIR. Doordarshan's free-to-air Direct-to-Home service, DD Direct + was launched by the Prime Minister in 2004. DDI channel continues to make significant contributions to accelerate socio-economic transformation, promote national integration, scientific temperament stimulation, control of population, environment preservation, welfare to women and children besides promoting sports and artistic and cultural heritage of India. Apart from Public Service Broadcasts, it also telecasts entertainment programmes. DD-News channel, DD Sports, DD Bharati, DD India are the different wings of Doordarshan.

Mass communication plays an important role in sensitising the masses about national policies and programmes by providing information and education in addition to the healthy environment. In the nation-building endeavour, we find it playing an outstanding role. The Ministry of Information and Broadcasting is responsible for development and regulation of information, broadcasting and film sectors in the country. The information sector includes the print media which is regulated by the Press Council of India.

The above-mentioned facts make it clear that during the yesteryears, we find a number of developments in the field of mass communication. The benefits of new generation of technology are now also to the mass communication. This necessitates a microscopic audit of the performance of both the information and entertainment media. Emerging as Public Service Department, it has also been opening doors for profit generation by offering the commercial services. Aggressive marketing appears essential to improve their financial health but the professionals managing the affairs need not to forget that they are supposed to serve and subserve social interests and therefore while conceptualising marketing, the social considerations need an overriding priority. Adding new feathers to its cap, of course, is an ongoing process for a thriving organisation but not at the cost of social transformation. Both the information and entertainment wings of mass communication need to assign a transcendental priority to social considerations failing which the very purpose of mass communication is to be turned into a fiasco.

MASS COMMUNICATION OR MASS MEDIA?

At the outset, let us go through the conceptal aspects. Any medium of mass communication reahing a very large number of people such as newspapers, radio and television where we find transmission of message through a source and the diverse issues and problems are covered is known as mass media. From its earliest days, discussion on the media has regularly been thought of as the study of mass communication. The term communication was incorporated within ideas of ideology derived from the alternative traditions of interpretative, interactionist and Marxist sociologies.[1] We find interpretation of the term mass communication in different ways but one thing is almost all clear that it is a process of communicating to a very large number of people or say masses. The instrumentality of a communication organisation engaged in the process is substantially influenced by the quality of messages to be transmitted which rests on the quality of professionalism and equipment used for the purpose. We can also call it a vehicle to travel the messages not only for an individual but for masses. When we talk about newspapers, the news items related to different areas or views expressed to serve a purpose become a focal point. Using newspapers for advertisement is no doubt an outcome of significant developments in the process mainly to protect the commercial interests. The magazines are also a mass medium in which news items and experts' opinion are published. We also use this medium for advertisement. Gradually, we find development of broadcasting services which is also an important part of mass media. Here, the entertainment value is found significant but we also use this medium for news and business advertisements and publicity. The most recent addition in the entertainment media is TV which has entertainment value. Against this background, we also call it entertainment media.

The aforesaid facts make it clear that whatever media we use for this purpose, the communications are for masses. In the recent years, we have more sophisticated technologies for mass communication which have increased their instrumentality in informing, motivating, sensing, serving, guiding and even misguiding and miscommunicating the masses. Of course, the communication organisations play here a decisive role. We cannot negate the fact that mass media are specially to subserve social interests but when commercial considerations started dominating the social considerations, the mass media started playing a negative role. It is against this background that we focus on the emerging trends in mass media so that we find it possible to regulate the negative trends.

Thus, in the mass media, we find information media, specially newspapers and magazines and entertainment media or electronic media in which we find broadcast and telecast media or say, radio and television. It is a combination of both traditional and modern media which by coummunicating to the masses is supposed to play a significant role in the nation building endeavour.

EMERGING TRENDS IN MASS COMMUNICATION

In an age of information explosion, the spread in the dissemination of information have virtually become an index of a country's development. In a democratic set-up, we assign due weightage to public participation which in a true sense rests on the transmission of right information on right time. This calls for ensuring access to mass communication. Though the efforts in developing mass communication were initiated even before the attainment of independence, the significant developments took place only during the post-independence period. Since 1947, till present, we have witnessed different turning points. Inventions and innovations in communications have virtually revolutionised the entire process. Of late, we are so fast that we find conceptualisation of globalisation in almost all the areas.

An anatomy of the emerging trends in mass communication appears significant to identify the wrongs in order that remedial measures are taken and the contribution of mass communication to the process of socio-economic transformation is made spotless. It is against this background that we go through multi-dimensional developments in the different areas of mass communication, e.g., information media and entertainment media. In the group of information media, we include newspapers and magazines. We also call it print media. In the group of entertainment media, we include broadcast and telecast media. We also call it electronic media and go through radio and television. After the attainment of independence and to be more specific after the beginning of Five Year Plans, we find numerous developments in different areas of mass communication.

Information Media: The information media or print media or mainly newspapers and magazines that have information value bear the responsibility of making available to the society up-to-date and authentic information. We cannot deny that there have been significant quantitative-cum-qualitative improvements in the information media, specially during the last decade of 20th and first decade of 21st Century. Of late, we find more sophisticated technologies for printing which have benefited the society in many ways. The offset and laser printing devices have virtually changed the entire scenario.

The Registrar of Newspapers in India (RNI)-1956, allots newsprint and recommends import of printing machines for newspapers. As a part of new statutory functions, the Registrar's office issues Entitlement Certificates to the small and medium newspapers/periodicals whose annual entitlement of newsprint is less than 200 metric tonnes. Every newspaper/periodical has to be registered with the RNI. India has four news agencies, e.g., Press Trust of India (PTI), United News of India (UNI), Samachar Bharati and Hindustan Samachar. The Publications Division set up in 1941 under Home Department then called Foreign Branch of the Bureau of Public Information, a media unit of the Ministry of Information and Broadcasting (I&B) since 1944 has also been playing an important role in the context of information media.[2]

The Press Council of India was set up in 1966 which continued till 1975. The present Press Council was set up in 1978. It is to safeguard the freedom of the press and to improve and maintain the standard of newspapers and news agents.

The technological advances in the system have changed the functional capacity of information media. Of late, the transmission of messages through fax have made possible the task of updating news items fast. The new generation of machines have increased the publication capacity. Not only this, we also find an improvement in the quality *vis-à-vis* the accuracy. Computers have been successful in playing an incremental role in the process. The offset machines have made the publication of facts, figures and photographs very clear, accurate and attractive. The space constraint is also solved now because the new generation of sophisticated machines deliver more but cover less space. Thus, there have been qualitative-cum-quantitative improvements in the information media which has virtually changed the instrumentality of the entire system. In Figure 22.1, we find different dailies with the highest readership.

Newspaper Urban + Rural	Circulation in'000s
1. Dainik Jagran	2,12,44
2. Dainik Bhaskar	173,79
3. Enandu	113,50
4. Hindustan	105,57
5. Amar Ujala	104,69
6. Daily Thanti (Tamil)	94,45
7. Lokmat	88,20
8. Rajasthan Patrika	86,51
9. Times of India	80,92
10. Malayala Manorma	79,85

Fig. 22.1: Dailies with the Highest Readership

In Figure 22.1, we find dailies with the highest readership covering both rural and urban areas.[3] We find Dainik Jagran number one.

Languages	Languages with the highest number of monthly Registered Newspapers
1. Hindi	4,734
2. English	3,513
3. Bilingual	1,697
4. Tamil	1,267
5. Malayalam	933
6. Kannada	863
7. Telgu	791
8. Bengali	782
9. Gujarati	707
10.Marathi	697

Fig. 22.2: Languages with the Highest Number of Monthly Registered Newspapers

In Fig. 22.2, we find Hindi language having the highest number. It is due to multi-cornered concerted efforts made by personnel working in the print media that India's print media is described winningly as Asia's freest after Japan. India is a democratic country. Liberalisation in the field of newspaper publication should be treated separately from liberalisation in the field of manufacture of consumer goods. We should remember that freedom of expression and the right to information are not a commodity but a service. It is a crying need of the hour that right to information is interwoven with other rights. We find it more significant, specially in the social or national interests. Opening of this chapter occupies a place of outstanding significance since most of the prestigious foreign publications are found knocking at our doors for a clearance to start Indian editions or independent publications in India, e.g., the International Herald Tribune edited in Paris and published from many cities including New York, London and Tokyo, Living Media India and Time Warner Inc. as a joint venture for publishing an Indian edition and Financial Daily in collaboration with the Financial Times of London as a tie-up with the Anand Bazar Patrika Group of Calcutta.[4] We should not forget that even some of the developed European countries do not allow foreigners to own newspapers even though they have cultural similarities. In France, the Press Law does not allow foreigners even to own shares. This is the case in book publishing industry too. In Sweden, publishing rights are not extended to foreigners. Thus, an invasion by foreign media on the Indian horizon is required to be checked.

Of course, we appreciate the newspaper organisations for making possible multi-dimensional improvements in the system but at the same time also consider it right to mention that some of them have been found compromising with the situations. They hesitate to write the right things since lucrative advertisements given by the government or the business houses are likely to be stopped. No doubt, the mounting establishment expenses have been compelling them to generate more financial resources from commercial advertisements but such type of yellow journalism would jeopardise the real sense and there would be a direct attack on the credibility of newspapers and magazines. It is also found that just to mobilise financial resources, they publish advertisements which make an invasion on our culture and become instrumental in misguiding the new generation. Of course, they have a legitimate right of generating profits but at the same time they are not supposed to cross the limits.

The emerging trends in printing media thus make it clear that it is high time to regulate the negative developments so that they continue to play an important role in nation building. It is against this background that we go through the problem of marketing in mass media. If the social marketing principles are conceptualised in a right way, the organisations would, of course, be successful in having a fair blending of social and commercial considerations. This would help them in many ways, e.g., the readers would remain satisfied, the circulation would increase, the cost-effectiveness would be made possible and the avenues for profit generation would also be broadened.

ENTERTAINMENT MEDIA

Temptation for recreation is our nature. If we undermine or devalue the law of nature, the environment for concentration, meditation and efficiency generation would take a rest. Resulting from which the monotony would gain a rapid momentum and a sound base would be engineered for degeneration in efficiency, efficacy or potentials.[5] Particularly in the present materialistic age, the human beings are often beset with multi-dimensional problems. They on the one hand are expected to follow the busy schedule while on the other hand are also supposed to diffuse tension generated as a side-effect of their intensive efforts for multiplying the material assets. It is against this background that we assign due weightage to entertainment. Here, we go through two important media, e.g., broadcast and telecast media. In the broadcast, media, we focus on the services of AIR and in the telecast media, we concentrate on television. Of course, we find film media an important source of entertainment but so far as the impact of television on society is concerned, it is relatively of high magnitude. We also throw light on the movies telecast by TV and therefore, the contribution of film industry is also taken in the very context.

Broadcast Media: Akashvani broadcasting started in India in 1921. Initially, the transmission centres were privately managed and the process was started in Mumbai and Kolkata. The Indian Broadcasting Service came into existence in 1930 and it was transformed into AIR in 1936 and gradually into Akashvani in 19f7. The AIR is generally used in international perspective. The AIR is found servicing as an effective medium to inform and educate people in addition to entertaining the masses. The external service programmes are found in 27 languages. It serves in projecting Indian point of view in world besides disseminating information on Indian life, thought, culture, tradition and heritage.[6]

To be more specific Sixth Plan onwards, we find a rapid development in the services of AIR. The AIR network is now found through two transmitters, FM and AM. The FM transmission is found in Delhi, Mumbai, Chennai, Kolkata and Panaji. There are 185 broadcast centres, 293 transmitters, 30 Vividh Bharti commercial broadcasting, 148 MW transmitters, 51 SW and 94 FM. It is significant to mention that Vividh Bharati commercial broadcasting was introduced in 1967, specially to mobilise financial resources. Modernisation and greater application of the state-of-the-art of technology in all spheres of broadcasting could be possible specially during Seventh and Eighth Plans. Use of digital technology and Compact Disc Systems in all transmission booths of existing network are some of the important additions which made possible qualitative improvements in the broadcasting services.

It is important to mention that AIR is now on Internet. The Internet users numbering 80 million can now listen to AIR programmes at http://www, air code net in audio mode. The programmes are broadcast in mono, as stereo programme which cannot be transmitted over telephone. But the users having leased line on ISDN can receive stereo transmission. Thus, we find significant developments in the broadcasting services. Since more than 94 per cent of the population have been using the services, we also find a satisfactory broadcasting network which cannot be denied. The most important thing that we find here is the quality of services made available by the broadcasting media. Of course, we find a negative trend in the service mix since in most of the cases, they are found broadcasting sex-generating songs based on pop culture. They are trying to satisfy their users, an attempt which is found promoting the western culture. We are not opposed to the role they are supposed to play for entertaining the masses but at the same time they have also to honour the cultural values. If the tidal wave of pop culture is found spreading like a wildfire, the AIR should think over its service mix.

Telecast Media: In the entertainment media, we find this medium playing a very significant role in the present Indian environment. The television entered the Indian horizon in September 1959 with a limited transmission on three days a week. The regular service started in 1965. In 1976, TV was delinked from AIR and started working as an independent organisation. Internationally, we call it Doordarshan of India (DDI).[7]

DDI aims at promoting national integration, dissemination of message to promote family planning, afforestation, child immunisation, dissemination of knowledge to estimate agricultural production, projection of social protection for women and children promoting interest in games and sports to create values to appreciate artistic and cultural heritage. Of course, they have been successful on many fronts but at the same time have also been instrumental in making an invasion on our culture which is found degenerating socio-cultural values. We would go through the problem in detail later on.

The development scenario witnessed a radical change after 1982. It has now successfully reached to about 90 per cent of the population through a network of about 750 transmitters. There are 38 programme production centres in different parts of the country. There are 50 other transmitters giving terrestrial support to other channels and the Doordarshan uses large number of transponders on the INSAT. The International channel started its programme on a transponder on PAS-4. Doordarshan telecasts programmes more than 1,021 hours every week on its primary service. The Prasar Bharati Act is a new development in the area mainly with the motto of providing more autonomy to both AIR and DDI. The Act came into force on September 15, 1997. No doubt, there have been quantitative-cum-qualitative improvements in the services of DDI and we cannot negate their positive contribution in different socio-economic areas. At the same time, it is a crying need of the hour that we make an evaluation of its services in degenerating the social and cultural values. Despite a number of positive influences, the Doordarshan and other private TV channels have been found very much instrumental in making an invasion on culture. We would go through the problem in detail later on.

MASS MEDIA MARKETING

At the outset, let us go through the conceptual aspect of marketing mass media. We have already gone through the concept of mass media. The concept of mass media marketing focuses on the application of marketing principles by the concerned organisations so that they succeed in having a fair blending of social and commercial considerations.[8] In the process of conceptualising the principles of social marketing, we assign due weightage to their contributions to social, cultural and economic transformation. At the same time, we also make possible generation of profits in order that the mass communication organisations are found successful in enriching their efficacy to deliver the best and keeping pace with the changing development scenario. Thus, in plain words, we find marketing mass media a managerial device to promote the organisation *vis-à-vis* to serve the society. We should not perceive that the societal marketing principles close doors for profit generation. The principles are, of course, opposed to profiteering which throw light on yellow journalism and unfair practices followed in the process. Contrary to it, the social marketing principles advocate improving the quality of services and increasing the number of users. The commercial advertising should be promoted but it should not stand as a barrier, especially while generating the services.

In view of the aforesaid facts, it is right to mention that marketing mass communication is a managerial approach to achieve the defined aims and objectives. Of late, a number of print media are found facing a stage of financial bankruptcy. No doubt, there are a number of factors responsible for the same but the most important of all is the managerial deficiency. In tune with the defined principles of societal marketing, the users are supposed to get the best possible outputs which in no case are endangering social, economic, cultural and national interests. The print media or say, the information media, the entertainment media or broadcast media and telecast media, no doubt have been serving the society in many ways but at the same time have also been making an invasion on our culture. The societal marketing principles disallow it. They are supposed to play a positive role in the socio-economic transformation. They bear the responsibility of bringing the derailed social system on rail. They are supposed to promote national excellence. The marketing principles would help them in the related areas.

The concerned organisations or say, the mass media organisations know about their service mix, the promotional strategies in the face of changing socio-economic conditions, the pricing strategies which they should prefer, for their services and the distribution of services so that the users get right information on right time. The communication organisations by conceptualising the principles thus find it easier to have a fair synchronisation of social and commercial considerations.

JUSTIFICATION FOR MARKETING MASS MEDIA

The information media as well as the entertainment media are supposed to play an important role in the present society where values are found disappearing. There are numerous socio-economic problems where the positive attitude of media can help the policy planners in many ways. In the Indian society, we find a number of problems, e.g., population, pollution, illiteracy, child labour, drug addiction, communicable diseases, temptation for western lifestyles, contracting respect for old people, social tensions and dissension, etc. where the mass media can help the society substantially. The conceptualisation of societal marketing principles would enable mass communication organisations in increasing the potentials to deliver goods. There are a number of points to justify marketing mass media.

1. To Formulate a Sound Service Mix: Like other organisations, the communication organisations also need a service mix which helps them in establishing a balance between the social and commercial considerations.

When we talk about a sound service mix for mass media, our emphasis is on a balance between the core and supportive services. This is a subject of prioritisation or setting the order of priority in the face of emerging problems and defined responsibilities. The mass media, either we talk about information media or the entertainment media, have no option but to assign topmost priority to social services. The services liberal to economy and the commercial services would always get number two position in their service mix. We are aware of the fact that the marketing principles focus on the formulation of a sound service mix for the service-generating organisations and a product mix for the goods manufacturing organisations. We find it easier to prepare an action plan and to take the strategic decisions, if the service mix is formulated in a right fashion. Against this background, we justify the application of marketing principles in mass media.

2. Identifying in the Sensitive Problems and the Thurst Areas: It is very natural that mass media need an overriding priority to focus on some of the sensitive social problems and to throw light on the most neglected areas where a special task force is inevitable. Making a cover story is found important but unless we identify the areas and prioritise them suitably, the task would not be fulfilled satisfactorily. Information media bear the responsibility of informing the society and inculcating mass awareness. The entertainment media are supposed to entertain the masses. Unless they know about the social problems, the perception of entertainment and its relevance; they cannot be successful in discharging their defined responsibilities. The marketing principles help them in identifying the sensitive problems and in diagnosing the thurst areas on the basis of segmentation. If they segment their users scientifically, it is easier to identify the target. It is in this context that we argue for marketing mass media.

3. To Formulate an Optimal Promotional Strategy: For the smooth functioning of an organisation, it is pertinent that they have a rational plan to promote the business. Like other organisations, the mass media also need to promote in order that their prospects come to know about the services and take a positive decision. Whatever the services they include or eliminate in their mix should be informed to the users. The salient features of core and supportive services should be communicated to the prospects. The task of advertisement is not so difficult for them since almost all the mass media advertise even for other organisations. Such a promotional decision helps different related organisations in informing, motivating and sensing the users. We cannot negate that newspapers, broadcasting and telecasting services are required to be promoted in a right way. To the extent it is possible, they should try to make possible an integration in order that all of them extend to each other their expertise and advertise for each other with the help of a consortium or syndicate. It is very natural that innovation in promotion would help them in many ways and they can explore avenues for creativity. Innovation in promotion and creativity in advertisements can hardly be possible unless they take the support of marketing. Against this background, we make an advocacy in favour of practising marketing in the mass media or mass communication services.

4. Pricing Decision can be Rationalised: In almost all the organisations either producing goods or generating services, the pricing decision plays an important role. Of late, the administrative and establishment expenses are found going up. The market is becoming more competitive. The newspapers or broadcasting or telecasting services are now highly capital-intensive. The circulation of newspapers and magazines is hardly to keep pace with the mounting costs. The commercial services fail in generating adequate financial resources to meet the increasing expenses. The small agencies and organisations have been facing the problem of financial bankruptcy. These negative developments make it essential that the related organisations are very careful to the pricing decision. Cost-effectiveness is found essential to adopt a rational pricing strategy. On the other hand, the prospects are found not so positive since they avoid to buy a newspaper. The book publishing industry is also facing the same problem. The demand, the circulation, the viewers are found negative. The DDI is also facing numerous problems, specially after the entry of private TV channels. The facts make it clear that almost all the mass communication organisations need a rational pricing decision which helps them in motivating the prospects. It is in this context that we justify the application of marketing principles in mass communication.

5. An Optimal Distribution Strategy: In view of the emerging environmental conditions, it is pertinent that we offer the services to our users in a right way; in a decent way. The information media would hardly exist, if the distributors fail in activating the process. The hawkers are found working with a negative attitude and the press reporters and correspondents are not working properly. The broadcasting and telecasting media cannot survive, if the front-line personnel working there are not instrumental in motivating commercial advertisements. Thus, both the core and supportive services depend upon the instrumentality of intermediaries in the distribution process. The distribution process thus assumes a place of outstanding significance in surviving and thriving the mass media. The professional excellence is found significant to initiate qualitative improvements *vis-à-vis* to maintain economy in distribution. Such an important dimension of marketing can make possible multi-dimensional improvements in the whole system. Keeping in view the fact, we find it essential to conceptualise marketing in the mass media.

6. Cost-effectiveness is Made Possible: To be more specific when the intensity competition is found at its peak, it is essential that the concerned organisations make concerted efforts to maintain economy at almost all the levels. This is pertinent to generate profits and even to make possible sophistication in the system. If we succeed in having a sound service mix formulated in tune with the emerging socio-cultural and economic requirements; if we succeed in activating the right distribution process; if we succeed in maintaining economy in the process of distribution, it is very natural that we also succeed in maintaining economy at all levels. Against this background, we argue for practising marketing.

7. Satisfying the Users: The most important thing in managing an organisation is to keep the customers/ users satisfied so that the market is expanded, new segments are explored and tapped, excelling competition is found easier and a fair blending of social and commercial considerations is made possible. An increase in the circulation of newspapers or magazines or an increase in the customers of books makes it essential that users get the quality services at all the stages. They get standard materials, right information, authentic information and up-to-date information. In an age of information explosion, it is not so difficult, provided the mass communication organisations are well equipped. The computers, fax machines, internet and intranet services, advanced telephonic and electronic mailing facilities in a true sense have paved the way for quality services to users. Since we go through the problem in the face of marketing, it is very natural that decency in behaviour by almost all the personnel working in an organisation at almost all the stages is ensured. We cannot deny that our services, in a true sense, bear the efficacy of momentising word-of-mouth promotion. If the users/readers remain satisfied with the quality and behaviour, it is possible that he/she recommends his/her friends, relatives to be the users. Thus, the task of satisfying users is fantastically simplified if we conceptualise marketing in mass communication.

In view of the above, it is right to say that marketing principles would help mass media considerably. In the present competitive world, we expect professionalism in manufacturing goods or generating services since the customers'/users' expectations are found increasing. Marketing can simplify this task by transforming the prospects into habitual users.

PRODUCT MIX

Information Media: In the information media, we focus on newspapers and magazines. No doubt, there have been numerous developments in the system mainly due to technological advances and the publishing organisations are now found well equipped. At the same time, it is also right that a number of socio-cultural problems have cropped up which are very much instrumental in derailing the well established system. This makes it essential that while formulating the service mix, we also turn our eyes on the negative influences so that the remedial measures are taken to bring things on rail. The newspapers and magazines are basically known as information media. They bear the prime responsibility of making available to the society the authentic and up-to-date information. As shown in the Figure 22.3, we find a service mix for the publishing organisations where three-tier objectives make it clear. The society or to be more specific the users have a right to get time-honoured and authentic information. It is against this background, we assign topmost priority to this dimension while formulating a service mix. They have a big team of artists, engineers, photographers, printing craftsmen, maintenance engineers, mechanics and administrative staff. Unless we find a team spirit and a team culture, the services cannot be to the expectations of users. And so, the first task is to inculcate a team culture so that all the echelons co-operate and co-ordinate each other and deliver goods to the concerned organisation. The management of information is, of course, a difficult task that needs more professionalism so that right information is positioned at the right place. We cannot deny the fact that new generation of machines and equipment have simplified the process fantastically. The news collected from different sources related to different areas is required to be placed suitably.

In the context of sensing the users, the information media bear a responsibility of inculcating social awareness or mass awareness. We consider newspapers and magazines a social mirror and therefore, they are supposed to identify and highlight the sensitive issues and to select thrust areas for injecting special force. While prioritising, it is very natural that they assign due weightage to social problems. There are a number of sensitive issues such as population, illiteracy, child labour, prohibition, drug addiction, civic amenities, infrastructural facilities, civic sense, aesthetic sense, socio-cultural values and so on. Like this, we find thrust areas where they need to apply special force such as problem of villages, problem of pollution and civic amenities in big towns and cities, problem of hilly areas, problem of underprivileged segments of the society. The motive is to sense the society. They again need the co-operation and co-ordination among different levels of staff on their payrolls. We cannot deny the fact that newspapers and magazines in general have been found showing a lukewarm response to this problem. As and when they prepare a cover story, the positioning occupies a place of outstanding significance. The task of sensing the society would remain unfulfilled unless they are serious to the dissemination of information. Of late, it is not so difficult since the technological advances *vis-à-vis* the professional excellence have simplified their task substantially.

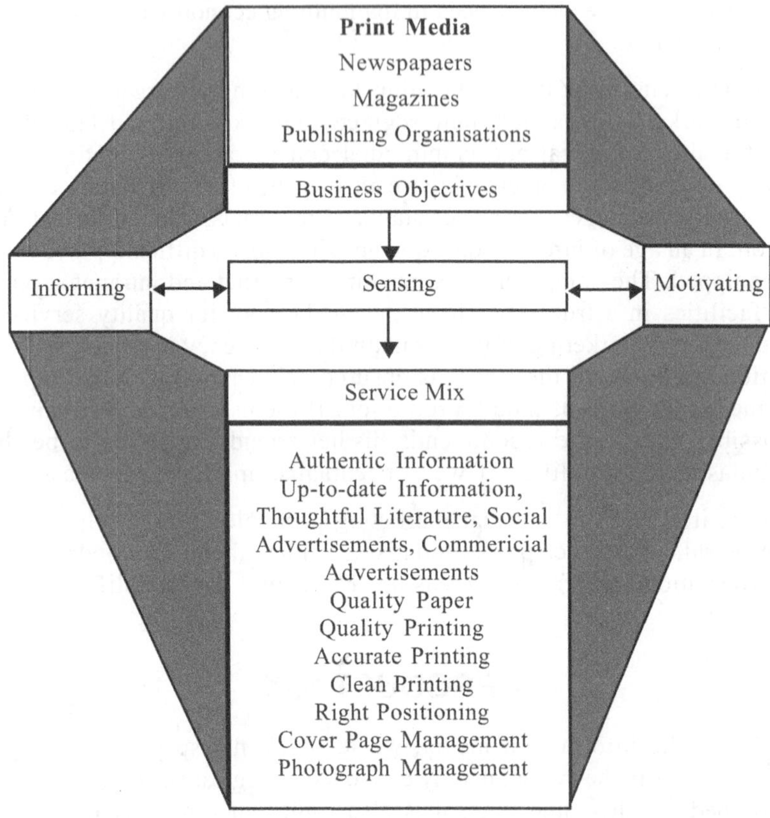

Fig. 22.3: Service Programming for Information Media

The next motive that we find in the Figure 22.3 is motivation. Here the our emphasis is on two facets, e.g., social advertising and commercial advertising. If they advertise to create awareness to counter the social problems, they are supposed to play a decisive role. They need creativity in slogans and messages so that the appeals are found positive. To be more specific in the Indian setting, they need more care since the masses are illiterate, unconscious and unorganised. The voluntary social organisations have even not been found making sincere efforts in the very context. The task of identification is very easy, specially in the Indian setting since they would find a problem as and where they focus their attention. Of course, they are supposed to prioritise them. Here, we throw light on the instrumentality of publishing organisations in the process. They are not supposed to publish commercial advertisements making an invasion on culture or touching the sentiments or image of a particular segment/section/sex/race.

It is very sad to comment that both the information and entertainment media just to generate profits are found compromising with the situations and publishing such advertisements which cannot be welcome in the Indian environment. To be more specific, the magazines are found promoting the same. They cannot defend their actions just by arguing that it is the concern of business houses. If they start censoring the same, the trend would be reversed in the positive direction.

Entertainment Media: For removing monotony or for generating efficiency, it is essential that we make available to the masses healthy entertainment. In the entertainment media, we go through broadcasting media and telecasting media. In the Indian setting, the broadcasting services are offered by the AIR.

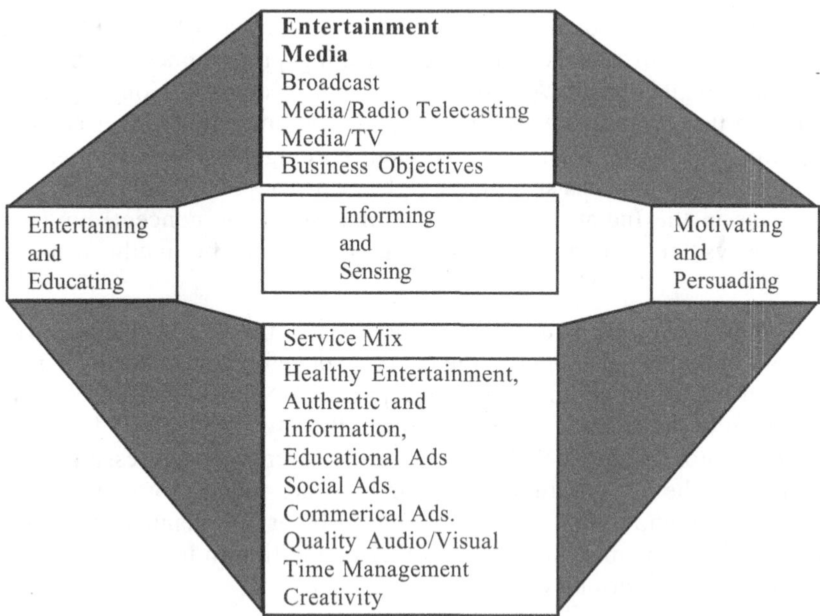

Fig. 22.4: Service Mix for Enteritainment Media

In Figure 22.4, we find a service mix for both. It is right to mention that AIR has three-tier objectives, such as entertaining and educating the society, informing and sensing the users and motivating and persuading the customers users. While broadcasting they are supposed to assign due weightage to the programme instrumental in making available to the users healthy entertainment. When they transmit music, drama, folk songs, the socio-cultural dimension needs an intensive. care. Of late, we find vulgar filmy songs and pop songs dominating their entertainment programme. It is a crying need of the hour that the AIR concentrates on transmitting healthy entertainment programme. In addition, they are also supposed to educate the masses. The motive is to offer to the users educational aid which they fail in getting in their classrooms. Another motive is related to information. They also bear the responsibility of making available to the users authentic and up-to-date information. They should, of course, cover the different areas while arranging the news items. In addition, the AIR should also be instrumental in sensing the users. Here, our emphasis is on creating mass awareness related to the sensitive social problems, e.g., family pl anning and pollution and afforestation, civic sense, child labour, health problems, child immunisation, clean living and so on. To be more specific when the society is illiterate, this dimension assumes a place of outstanding significance. Besides, we also find them responsible for promoting unethical commercial advertisements. While advertising for social issues, they should assign due weightage to the slogans and messages they transmit. They should try to make their slogans creative so that the appeals are positive. Further, the commercial advertising transmitted on Vividh Bharti should also not be overlooked. The motivation and persuasion in a right fashion gravitate our attention. It is important to mention that creativity simplifies our task considerably.

In the entertainment media, the telecasting media/TV has gained more popularity, specially during 1980s and 1990s.[9] We appreciate the contribution of DDI to the development processes. In addition to DDI, a number of private TV channels are now also operative. The users now get entertainment services. But this is an important area where we need a special attention. The DDI and other TV channels should realise the environmental differences that we find between a cinema hall and a private home. When we go to a cinema hall, of course, we have an option to be selective but we do not find the same thing in our homes where family members of different age groups and both sexes watch TV programmes together. No doubt except a very few almost all would agree that TV entertainment programmes and commercial advertisements have very much been instrumental in inviting numerous socio-cultural problems. The changing perception of modernisation is required to be reviewed. The tidal wave of pop culture is to be given a break since failing it make the globalisation of fashion, culture and civilisation would virtually aggravate the intensity of socio-cultural pollution to such an extent that a number of allied problems would automatically crop up to degrade the Indian civilisation.

We welcome entertainment but only healthy entertainment. It is not wrong to mention that just to generate financial resources the DDI and other private TV channels have been promoting vulgar commercial advertisements which have been found making an invasion on our culture.[10] We need to regulate the trend. The kids/teens/youths are the worst sufferers. While selecting or producing a programme by and large almost all the TV channels fail in diagnosing the negative impact of violence and sex-provoking programmes on the most gullible segment of the society who lack a sense of judgement. An apparent change in the behavioural profile of teens is a staunch testimony to this proposition that programmes in general and the commercial advertisements in particular should be given an overriding priority. Of late, the teens are found more aggressive in nature, they do not know about the perception of privacy but claim and insist on their right of privacy. No doubt, it is a global phenomenon but we need to view the effects in the Indian condition. The misuse of the concept, boyfriends and girlfriends, if not checked would make ways for an open sex which would only not be unethical but also be a threat to the Indian culture.

A crying need of the current society is to innovate the service mix of TV channels. If positive developments are welcome, it is very natural that we also oppose the negative developments. According to the UNESCO reports, media violence has direct influence on children. A joint report of UNESCO and the World Organisation of Scout Movement and Untreched Union have come to the conclusion that two TV serials found popular among children the world over, e.g., "Terminator" and "Rocky" have made children very aggressive in nature and behaviour.[11] We cannot negate that most of the TV programmes and movies are found promoting violence and sex, specially among teens and youths. The Indian movies telecast on DDI or other TV channels are generally found generating unethical feelings in the society. This makes it essential that in addition to telecast media, the Film Censor Board of India also thinks over the issue seriously.

We are not opposed to commercial advertising on TV channels since our advocacy is in favour of a fair synchronisation of social and commercial considerations. Indeed, the focal point of the study is Indianising the advertisement layouts. The advertisement professionals can do it very effectively. Unfortunately, the organisations in general have been found very liberal to the advertisements having a sex appeal. Even if the conditions do not demand, they select women characters and visualise their aggressive poses, uncultured behaviour and western dresses which attract users in general and the teens in particular. We cannot deny that human beings or living beings in general are found soft or sensitive to the opposite sex. This is a law of nature. It is also right that we search wrong things very fast. This makes it essential that we contract opportunities or avenues for the same.

It is also important to quote that some of the business houses even for their injurious and unhealthy products have been selecting characters attracting teens and youths in particular. Reynold advertisement has been found encouraging teens for smoking. R.J. Reynolds, a leading cigarette manufacturing company of world introduced Old Joe, a cartoon camel character in which the campaign rescued the flagging Camel brand from obscurity. It was not simply to smokers over the age of 21 indeed to attract teenagers with a likeable cartoon character. The advertisement was so effective that there was an increase of 82 per cent in the Camel's market share, specially among teenagers since the Old Joe was introduced.[12] If we make a survey, there are a number of examples to testify the same.

The aforesaid negative influences of TV programme and TV commercial advertisements make it essential that we have a code to regulate their services. Of course, the telecast media has played an important role in promoting social advertisements but the negative influences are found establishing an edge over their positive influences. The technological advances, no doubt, have made possible significant improvements in the quality of reception but the masses are now found badly affected. It is a crying need of the Indian society that telecast media start playing reduce a positive role.

PROMOTION MIX

Promoting Information Media

Promoting for others is easier since you have just to follow. Promoting for self is difficult since you have not just to follow but have also to fix direction for your movement. We are aware of the fact that newspapers and magazines act as an effective promoter. They play a big role in informing, sensing and motivating prospects. To be more specific when the intensity of competition is found at its peak, the small newspapers and magazines find it very much difficult to protect their existence. The leading newspapers and magazines have a big network, a well-knit team for distribution a well established image and a big promotional budget. Contrary to it, the small newspapers and magazines have been found struggling even for their existence. Against this background, we focus on some of the important issues for promoting information media so that both the small and big newspapers and magazines get a favourable business environment. It is important to mention here that some of the leading newspapers of the world have been making efforts to make the business environment more competitive and volatile since they are exploring avenues for getting an entry. If it is made possible, the task would be much more difficult. In the present context, we are required to be more vigilant to check it.

In Figure 22.5, we find different dimensions of promotion for the information media. At the outset, our emphasis is on personal promotion since the publishing business is sizeably influenced by the instrumentality of personal promoters. If the supportive personnel working for the newspapers and magazines stop extending their real support, the task of survival would be difficult. The agents, hawkers, front-line personnel play an outstanding role in promoting the business. This makes it essential that we get their best possible co-operation. An important question in the very context is related to the strategic decisions which make ways for motivating them in a right fashion. In the pharmaceutical industry, if the medical representatives do not extend their best co-operation, the task of promotion becomes complicated. We find almost all the same problems with publishing industry. It is very natural that an attractive incentive plan simplifies our task considerably and therefore we are supposed to make it possible. Your professional excellence in managing the personal promoters would play here a decisive role. Even if you pay more incentives but are behaving indecently, the results are not likely to be positive. Thus, a fair mix of decent behaviour and handsome incentives can activate the process satisfactorily. It is also significant to mention that the lowest level of personnel working for your newspapers and magazines are found playing the most positive role for you. If hawkers start acting against you, the task becomes much more difficult. It is against this background that we need to assign due weightage to the interests of personal promoters. Your motive is to increase the market share by increasing the circulation, and this is not possible unless supportive staff engaged in distributing and circulating your newspapers and magazines have a positive attitude. How to make it positive, this is your concern.

Sales promotion also constitutes a place of significance in promoting information media. Here, our emphasis is on motivating both the service personnel and users or readers. It is already mentioned earlier that agents, hawkers, distributors play an incremental role. This makes it essential that we think in favour of trade promotion and offer to the dedicated personnel due incentives. No doubt, they get a commission but in addition to the regular commission they are already paid, we should also think in favour of making the rate of commission progressive so that the distributors evince their personal interest in increasing the circulation of your newspapers and magazines. Besides, the offering of gifts would also be instrumental in getting their co-operation. No doubt, the costs on remediation would be high but we have no option since the market is more competitive. To be more specific when we advocate in favour of a progressive rate of commission, an increase in the market share would increase your efficacy to pay more. We should not overlook or underestimate the instrumentality of hawkers since they play a very effective role in increasing the circulation.

So far as the incentives to the users/readers are concerned, we should offer to them small gift, specially to the habitual users. Of late, we also find organisation of sales contests for readers. This is to help you in increasing the circulation. It is important to mention here that a provision for incentives to the potential readers in the new segments or regions would simplify the task of exploring avenues and capitalising on the opportunities considerably. An increase in the market share makes it essential that we are serious to the' expansion of market. Thus, the publishing organisations should think in favour of offering incentives to the users but at the same time should also be careful that unproductive expenses are minimised.

In view of the above, it is right to mention that promotional measures for the information media should be innovated frequently. Since the market is highly competitive and volatile, it requires professional excellence at almost all the stages of promoting the business. It is already shown in Figure 22.5 that out of all the promotional measures, we find personal promotion more sensitive. We cannot deny that if the publishing organisations concentrate on personal promotion and sales promotion, the advertisement budget can be minimised sizeably. We need to assign due weightage to our service mix and further we need to offer due incentives to distributors. It is not meant that the information media should stop advertising. Of course, they should go through the relative effectiveness of different dimensions of promotion and based on their impact on circulation should take a decision. Testing effectiveness thus would help them in getting a suitable solution. Once again, it is to be mentioned that if foreign publications get an entry, the task of promotion would be much more difficult.

The next dimension of promotion as shown in Figure 22.5 is advertisement. We are well aware of the instrumentality of advertisement in promoting the business. You are supposed to advertise on the most sensitive sensitise the prospects/users in a very effective way. Like, if newspapers and magazines advertise for a particular TV channel, this is also to be more effective. This engineers a strong foundation for the establishment of a consortium or syndicate. Since your prospects live both in rural and urban areas, it is very natural that creative advertisement slogans would help you in a big way. Of course, you should advertise effectively but should also take care of the advertisement budget which in no case should be non-optimal or disproportionate.

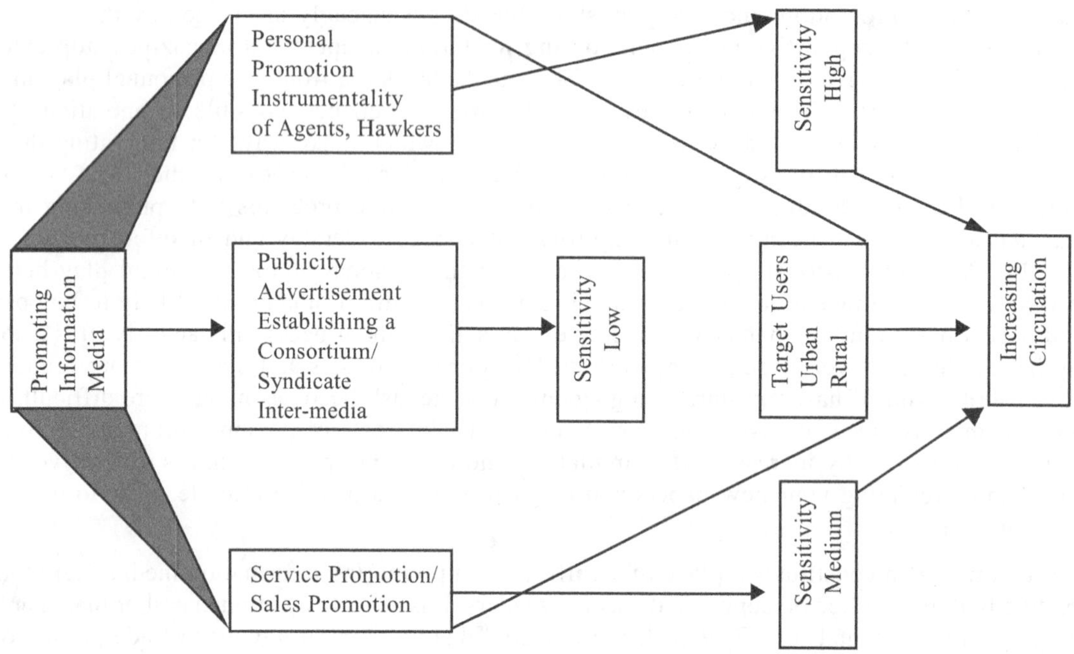

Fig. 22.5: Promoting Information Media

Despite a strong advocacy in favour of advertisement, it is also right to comment that the newspapers and magazines offering the authentic and up-to-date information and maintaining good relations with the users may survive and thrive even if they spend very little on advertisement. If they are making available to the readers, the news items, articles, and photographs related to the commercial advertisements in tune with their preferences or taste and temperament, the circulation is increased. It is against this background that magazines in general have been found publishing unacceptable, unethical and vulgar photographs for commercial advertisements. We should not welcome the trend and should regulate it in the best social interests. Of course, we should promote but our promotional efforts in no case should make an invasion our culture.

Promoting Entertainment Media

For making available healthy entertainment to the viewers, it is significant that we promote entertainment media in a right way. The AIR, DDI and other TV channels have been making available to the masses a number of services. They are found instrumental in creating mass awareness, informing to the masses authentic and up-to-date information and sensing the users in many areas. Though it is right that the services offered by them play a vital role in promotion, still we find justification for promotion since a number of services are includedm in the mix and the time of transmission and telecast is also changed. In Figure 22.6, we find different dimensions of promotion to be used by the organisations engaged in the process. It is very natural that sensitivity rate of all the dimensions cannot be uniform. The changing business environmental conditions would influence the rate of sensitivity of a particular dimension. However, we find service promotion and promotional incentives to viewers playing an incremental role and against this background, its sensitivity is found high.

The broadcast media or say the AIR has a big network. It is found available to the masses on account of its affordable cost. The motive of promotion is to increase the number of users living either in urban or in rural areas. Since we do not find any competition, the users willingly or unwillingly use the services of AIR. It is not meant that AIR should not promote its services. The incentives to front-line personnel as well as to the users would be helpful to improve the quality of services which would help AIR in getting commercial advertisements.

The mobilisation of financial resources is found essential since this is the lone source. Goods manufacturing organisations producing items of mass consumption prefer to advertise on AIR since the users are found even in the remotest part of the country. In addition, the service generating organisations also advertise on AIR. The AIR should offer due incentives to its personnel and users so that the revenue from the commercial advertisements is found helpful in implementing the development plans. For advertisement, they should also take the support of information media and telecast media. In a true sense, inter-media consortium or syndicate would simplify the task of advertisement *vis-à-vis* would also optimise its advertisement budget. While composing slogans, they should seek the co-operation of advertisement professionals so that the messages have a positive appeal. If AIR advertises for TV channels and TV channels advertise for AIR, the task of both the organisations would be simplified considerably. It is against this background that we talk in favour of a consortium or a syndicate. So far as the publicity is concerned, the AIR should seek the co-operation of information media. A rapport with information media would help AIR in projecting its image. Since a number of social advertisements are transmitted on AIR, the newspapers and magazines should extend their best possible co-operation. Though we talk about promotional measures, it is also right that the quality of services would simplify the task of promotion.

The growing popularity of telecast media is well-known to all of us. In addition to DDI, a number of private TV channels are now operative. The viewers reside both in urban and rural areas. We find a rapid increase in the number of viewers specially during 1990s. The satellite communication facilities have simplified the development and expansion process. However, we find different channels advertising since the business environment is found highly competitive. In Figure 22.6, we find different dimensions of promotion for both the broadcast and telecast media. It is right to say that out of all the dimensions of promotion, the promotion for staff and users/viewers is found more effective. Against this background all the channels need to offer due incentives to different categories of staff and viewers. The organisation of contests simplifies the task of promoting the users.

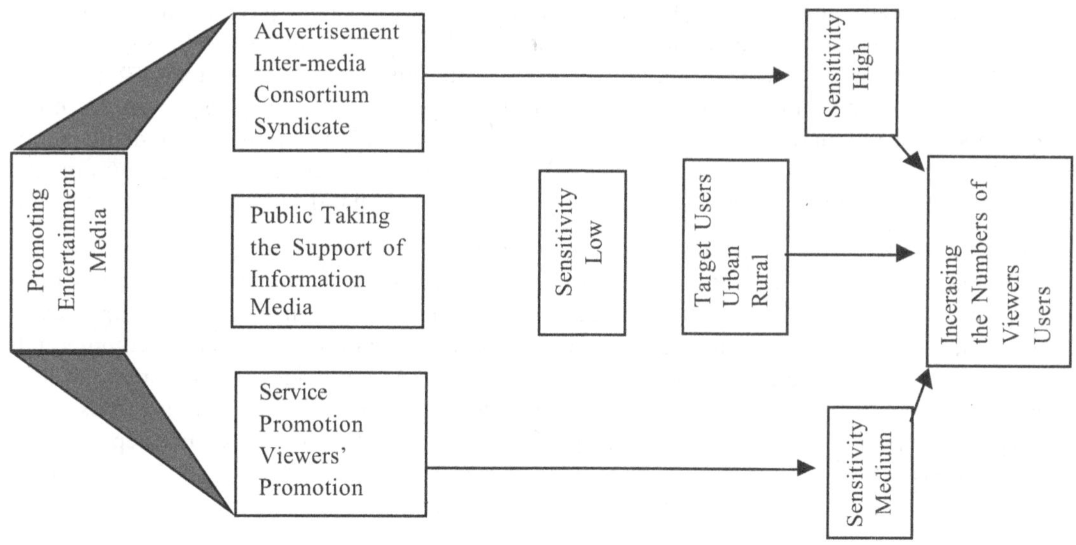

Fig. 22.6: Promoting the Entertainment Media

Of late, we find a race among different TV channels for raising the number of viewers. It is also an important reason for the emergence of a negative trend in the quality of service mix of different TV channels. It is very natural that goods manufacturing or service generating organisations prefer to advertise on a TV channel having the largest number of viewers. Currently, we find a reverse trend in the number of viewers of DDI which is, of course, due to some norms maintained by them while televising programme or commercial advertisements. Willingly or unwillingly, the DDI cannot make a good-bye to the time-tested norms. Though recently we find a change since the DDI has also been found compromising with the increasing competition. This makes it essential that the Ministry of Information and Broadcasting regulates the process otherwise the existing race for degenerating social, cultural and ethical values prevalent among different TV channels would donsiderably harm the value addition process.

Pricing Decision for Mass Media

Information Media: For almost all the profit or non-profit making organisations, this submix of the marketing mix is found critical, challenging but important. To be more specific when we talk about the organisations concerned with the publications of newspapers and magazines, this dimension assumes a place of outstanding significance since in the Indian perspective, a majority of the users/readers have developed a negative attitude. They can spend more on other heads but avoid to spend even the nominal amount for buying newspapers and magazines. If you have a newspaper in your hand, most of known and unknown persons would collect it from you; the neighbours would depend on you; they would go through the newspapers and magazines very minutely without enquiring the fact that you, the real owner, have or have not got an opportunity to go through even the headlines. Such a negative attitude is found affecting the demand position adversely. Against this baground, the publishing organisations often fail in utilising their installed capacity to improve the supply position which stands as a barrier in maintaining cost-effectiveness. Thus, an attitudinal change appears significant in the very context failing which any strategy for pricing cannot be effective. It is in this context that we go through pricing decision for information media.

The publishing organisations in general find it difficult to maintain economy since the establishment and intermediation expenses are found mounting disproportionately. The leading newspapers have a big market and therefore, they manage to survive and thrive but so far as the regional newspapers and magazines are concerned they find it difficult to protect their existence. All of us are witnessing the poor financial condition of small publishing houses. Though they get subsidised newsprints, still they fail in improving their financial position. We cannot say that prices of newspapers are abnormally high. A stagnation or even a proportionate contraction in the demand side makes it essential that we develop a culture of buying newspapers and magazines. In addition, it is also significant that the leading national newspapers avoid the discriminatory pricing policy. They charge less for their national edition charge more for their regional editions. So far as the reading materials are concerned, they make available more to the users/readers paying less and less to the users/readers paying more. Such a trend needs a departure. The main thing in optimising the pricing structure is the supply position and for that leading newspapers and magazines should attempt to inculcate buying habits by advertising creative slogans. We do not talk about reading habits or culture since almost all the persons prefer to go through the newspapers. Of course, we find avenues for minimising or rationalising the price structure but it is possible when the demand side shows a positive trend. If the publishing organisations utilise the installed capacity of their plants, machines, equipments, the supply position would be increased but it carries no meaning unless the demand side shows a green signal.

Entertainment Media: The AIR, DDI, and other private TV channels have been taken into the purview of the' study. When we talk about the pricing decision for entertainment media, it is right to mention that these organisations do not charge any fee for the services used by the users. Since they are supposed to entertain and inform the masses, the services made available to them act as a motivational force for the commercial advertisers. Sponsorship, thus, becomes an important area of the study. In the AIR services, the commercial advertisements become an important source for mobilising the financial resources. Earlier, there was a provision for licensing by both the AIR and DDI. Now, it is withdrawn and therefore both the organisations depend on commercial advertisements from where they get revenue. It is against this background that we go through the problem in a bit different way.

Since we advocate in favour of mobilisation of financial resources by both the public and private sector organisations, it is very natural that whatever the strategic decisions they take regarding commercial advertisements should have a fair blending of official and commercial considerations. It is very natural that the goods manufacturing as well as the service generating organisations prefer to advertise on a channel having the maximum number of viewers. So far as the AIR is concerned, we do not find any competition but now the telecast media have a very competitive market. This makes it essential that we regulate the services of telecast media. Of course, we favour autonomy but when an organisation starts misusing the same, the policy makers have no option but to think over the problem seriously. We cannot deny the fact that specially private TV channels have been found formulating such a service mix which attracts the kids, teens and youths. Even the goods manufacturing or service generating organisations also welcome such advertisement layouts found instrumental in attracting the sensitive segment. This is the root cause of a degeneration that we presently watch on TV channels in general and the private TV channels in particular. The aforesaid negative developments make it essential that commercial advertisements *vis-à-vis* the entertainment programme of TV channels maintain the time-tested norms. They bear the responsibility of sensing the society and in the name of sensing, we find them televising nonsense. This practice needs a departure.

We are supposed to protect our social values; we also bear the responsibility of contracting avenues for an invasion on our culture; we have an urgent task of inculcating mass awareness we have to promote the goods manufacturing and service generating organisations by offering to them an opportunity to advertise and motivate the prospects/ customers/users. This makes it essential that all the TV channels stop promoting the worst and activate promoting the best. We bear the responsibility of making available to our users the services which they can digest.

PLACE MIX

Distribution Strategy for Mass Media

Information Media: It is only not sufficient that we produce the best. It carries an outstanding importance that we distribute our services in a right way. Since the expectations are now found high, it is pertinent that we make ways for decency in behaviour. To be more specific, the service generating organisations are supposed to make it possible on the priority basis since they bear the responsibility of educating the masses. If they start misbehaving, the cycle would start moving in the reverse gear. It is against this background that we go through the problem of distributing the services by information media. The publication of newspapers and magazines is, of course, a difficult task but the distribution process is found much more difficult. The front-line personnel, the agents and distributors, the hawkers are the focal points from where the services reach to the target users. The newspapers and magazines, thus, need more care while selecting the agents and distributors. If they fail in doing such, the business is to be affected in an adverse way. On the other hand, the agents and distributors also need more care while selecting hawkers. We are aware of the fact that the distributors are paid commission on the newspapers and magazines sold by them. Thus, a decision regarding commission is found very much instrumental in influencing the distributors and getting their best co-operation.

The motives are multi-faceted publishing organisations need to optimise the distribution costs but the market is highly competitive. They need to offer more incentives to the concerned distributors but the cost-effectiveness is also to be made possible. They need best support of dealers and agents but their potentials to offer them more incentives are found contracting. The aforesaid developments need more professionalism while managing the distribution of newspapers and magazines. It is very natural that almost all the organisations take a decision with the only tool they have available, i.e., commission. No doubt, it simpifies the task of getting the co-operation of different levels of intermediaries engaged in the process but at the same time also increases the intermediation cost. This makes it essential that the publishing organisations in addition to protecting their own interests also think over the problem of small publishing newspapers and small magazines. It is right to mention that the demand side is substantially influenced by the quality of newspapers and magazines but the pricing policy also plays an effective role and the rising intermediation costs in a very natural way stand as a barrier. In a true sense, we need a team spirit right from the first stage of distribution to the last stage of making available the newspapers and magazines to the ultimate users/buyers. The motive is to make available the newspapers and magazines on time. The hawkers engaged in the process should behave in a decent way.

Entertainment Media: In the entertainment media, the focal point in the distribution process is the front-line personnel engaged in delivering the services to the users. In the broadcast media, the enquiry/reception, the personnel meant for producing the programme as well as the technical staff for recording the transmission, the announcer plays an important role. If we find a mistake at one stage, the entire process of distributing the services is affected in an adverse way. Even if the programme is produced decently, the transmission and announcement if found faulty would influence the quality. Thus, to deliver the best to the users, it is significant that the aforesaid personnel act efficiently and behave decently. The receptionists and enquiry counters cannot be overlooked since the artists, experts, visiting guests if not getting due treatment would be very much instrumental in forming a negative attitude about a transmission centre. Not only this, it is also essential that we talk about the instrumentality of Ministry of Information and Broadcasting since the movement of orders, instructions consuming more time would ultimately affect the quality of services to be offered to the users. Whatever the strategic plans, they have to implement and whatever the policy decisions they take for this purpose should be transmitted to the different Station Directors on time in order that they plan everything proportion to with their potentials and socio-economic requirements. The motive is to make the distribution systems scientific so that quality services are made available to the users uninterrupted.

In the telecast media, by and large, we find the same thing. The studios or the transmission or televising centres of course bear the responsibility of offering the services to the viewers but in the true sense, they are guided by a bureaucratic set-up which stands as a major barrier while practising professional excellence. No doubt, the private TV channels have their own policies but so far as the DDI is concerned. The Ministry of Information .and Broadcasting plays here a decisive role. The reception, enquiry, studio staff and the announcer play an incremental role. There must be a cohesion between the decisive and incremental wings failing which the users fail in getting the quality services. Of late, we are depending on sophisticated technologies and it is also found complicating the distribution process. We are not opposed to the technological advance but at the same time, it is also essential that our personal working at different levels or echelons know the skill of switching over. This would minimise the cases of interruption, poor reception, faulty delivery of services. We cannot deny the fact that in both the telecast and broadcast media, we find front-line personnel playing a very important role. Even if the programme is of quality an announcer can turn the televising process into a fiasco. This makes it a focal point for entertainment media in general. It is not only sufficient that we produce quality programme, it is also impact generating that users get the services in a right way.

PROCESS MIX

The processing of the services of information media are found with the help of new generation of information and communication technology. To process the services, we find a team of people combining technical experts, managerial professionals and supporting staff. The information and entertainment media have been successful in increasing the operational flow with the help of ICT.

The Information Media: The processing of information services are carried through Print Media, Broadcast Media and Telecast Media. All of them have been making use of technology for processing, editing and announcing. The collection of news is done by the reporters who collect news and photographs from different sources. The audiovisual devices are used by the reporters for the collection of news. The offset print technology has virtually revolutionised the process of printing for the newspapers, magazines and newsletters. Particularly for the news items, the print media are found much more popular. The readers to which the newspapers or magazines reach cross different stages and phases. For right processing of news items, it is pertinent that reporters in the field collected news on time and make them available to the news processing wing. With the internet services, the transmission of news items to the press has become easier. Here, it is important that technology used for transmission and reception are working properly. Further, editing of news includes a team under the leadership of editor who after editing makes available the same to the press. Since we find use of offset print technology, the processes are automated and skilled persons print the newspapers which are made available to the distribution wing. In the service delivery, we find hawkers playing a very important role because they bear the responsibility of making them available to the readers at their doorsteps.

For right, accurate and time-honoured processing, it is significant that professionalised efforts are made and the possibilities of gap between different processes are minimised.

We find broadcast media and telecast media also involved in the news services. They also collect the news items with the help of reporters. Particularly the news services of telecast media are considerably influenced by visual exposure. This makes it essential that they have been making use of sophisticated cameras and skilled personnel for that purpose. After collection, again we find processing and editing of the news items before broadcasting or telecasting. The news readers play a decisive role because they need quality communication excellence. In the context of telecast media, they also need attractive and impressive personality and impressive facial expression.

Thus, the processing of news services, of late, are sizeably supported by quality technology and the professionals need to process them in such a way that printing, broadcasting and telecasting devices make available to the readers and viewers the news items on time. The operational flow is required to be improved in all the cases.

The Entertainment Media: In the context of entertainment media, we find our focus both on movies and TV. They play a significant role in entertaining the masses. The processing of entertainment services in both the streams have almost the same phases. The viewers come to the cinema halls or multiplexes for watching movies or other entertainment programmes. The delivery of services makes it essential that different processes for developing a programme are followed and in addition, the skilled personnel with the help of quality technology transmit the same. In the process of developing a programme, we find different stages. Selection of story, writing of script, selection of artists, direction of play, visual recording are the different processes through which the programmes are developed. At each and every stage, we find experts involved in the process. The professionals bear the responsibility of processing the services in such a way that quality programmes are available to the viewers. Because we find use of new generation of technology at different stages of processing, it is imperative that operational flow is maintained. For delivering quality outputs, the professionals need to manage quality inputs.

PHYSICAL EVIDENCE AND ATTRACTIONS

This submix of marketing draws our attention on the service environment or ambience. In the information and entertainment media, we find their relevance in a different way.

The Information Media: In the information media, we find involvement of all the three streams. The service ambience in the information media is found significant with the viewpoint of working people and the performing staff. Because we find readers or viewers not having an accessibility to the studios or presses, the servicescapes remain confined to the people involved in the process. They, of course, need a suitable environment which focuses our attention on the lighting facilities, ventilation, sanitation, furnishing, parking which help them in performing in the required way. The dresses used by the performing artists and working people need due care. Particularly, the news readers while performing need an impressive dress.

The Entertainment Media: The servicescapes become significant when we find professionals managing cinema halls or theatres. So far as the televisions are concerned, we find people watching the same in their homes. In this context, the tangibilisation of stage for presentation is found impact generating. But while managing for theatres and cinema halls and multiplexes, the servicescapes play a positive role. This makes it essential that designers assign due weightage to interiors and exteriors so that viewers and visitors form a positive impression and feel pleasure in watching the programmes. A number of arrangements are to be made while managing service ambience for them. The lighting facilities, air-conditioning, music, the booking counters, furnishing, arrangements for parking of vehicles are found important in this context.

The entertainment services are considerably influenced by tangibilisation and the marketing professionals need to manage the service ambience in an attractive way. The quality, colour, and intensity of light at different points need due attention of professionals. Particularly in the multiplexes where we find a mix of different types of services, the professionals may use signposts. Of late, we find air-conditioning services found essential for entertainment services to be presented by cinema halls and multiplexes. Such arrangements are found significant even in the theatres. The provisions for music also occupies a significant position and this draws their attention on the quality of music, volume and positioning. The furnishing arrangements outside the theatres also become important for viewers. The provision for safe drinking water and parking facilities add additional attractions to the services. The focus here is on tangibilisation of outstanding properties of your theatres or multiplexes so that the potential viewers and visitors form a positive opinion regarding the services to be delivered. The professionals need not to forget that tangibilisation helps in publishing the services. If we find them tangibilising in an attractive way, the potential viewers develop a temptation for viewing.

The marketing professionals while managing the servicescapes also need attention on adding additional attractions by improving the quality of dresses or uniforms of performing and working people. They should look neat, clean and impressive. The reception counters, enquiries, booking counters are operated by the front-line staff and their physical appearance and facial expression throw a positive impact on the attitudes of potential viewers of services. The aesthetic sense needs due care of professionals.

In view of the above, it is right to mention that physical evidence and attractions needs due care of marketing professionals in the entertainment services. All your properties need an excellent tangibilisation. You bear the responsibility of generating service fragrance and this makes it essential that at each and every point, you show personal touch in the tangibilisation process. You need to realise the importance of posters, leaflets, publicity materials and their quality, offer of packaged services. The right positioning and quality of materials are the two important considerations where you need to focus. The display of lighting where you have displayed the posters should not be underrated. In the information media, we find this submix of marketing not significant to the viewers because they do not get an opportunity to visit the production centres. But service ambience is found important even for the performers and the working people and therefore, they should manage the same with the motto of making the working conditions much more conducive. Your motive is adding additional attractions and this is meant for both the service providers and the service users. It is not to be forgotten that with the changing levels of expectations of users for the service quality; they expect even the service ambience instrumental in generating service fragrance.

PEOPLE MIX

In the mass communication services, both for information and entertainment, a large number of people work together. In a true sense, the delivery of quality services rests on the availability of quality people working in different capacities.

The information media considerably depends on the role of reporters. In both the print and telecast media, the transmission of news cannot be possible if we find reporters not performing in tune with the service code. The time and quality elements need due care of reporters while making the news items. They should have a command on the concerned language and high degree of communicative ability to interact and conduct interviews as and when the circumstances necessitate so. They are not supposed to develop any bias or to show any prejudice. Commitment to profession is found an essential consideration for a successful reporter. Operation of camera adds additional attractions to the news items and therefore the reporters should also develop expertise in the related area. Since we find transmission of news items through the internet services, it is essential that they are aware of handling or operating the computers. When we talk about telecast media, the visual exposure becomes significant because the news items are supported by visual exposure.

In the entertainment media, we find a team of technical and non-technical persons right from the development of a programme to its transmission or broadcasting. The artists are considered to be the leverspring of an entertainment programme but in the process, a number of people are involved such as directors, script writers, musicians, camera operators, and a brigade of supporting staff. When we talk about the quality of people, it is essential that they are in a position to make their efforts much more professionalised. Besides, they also need a sense of dedication and personal-touch-in-service. They have a sound physique and costumes are managed with the support of expert of the related area. We are aware of the fact that quality of inputs determines the quality of outputs and in the context of entertainment media, it is not to be forgotten. Almost all the people working in different capacities need expertise in the related area and develop a passion to perform.

Undoubtedly enough, it is an age of technology where number of formalities are completed by the new generation of sophisticated technology but it is also right to say that ultimately people perform not the supporting technology. They are simply to assist and activate the process and therefore all categories of entertainment organisations need a team of performer.

The marketing professionals bear the responsibility of supplying quality people and making use of their services with the help and co-operation of experts or specialists. They need to constitute a team of different types of people found efficacious of developing and presenting the quality items getting a positive response in the markets.

MASS COMMUNICATION MARKETING IN INDIAN PERSPECTIVE

The mass communication have a task to activate the process of informing and sensing the society in such a way that the derailed socio-cultural system comes back on the rail. An outstanding responsibility of nation building by injecting national excellence; a task of transforming the society by inculcating social awareness; a task of safeguarding the cultural values and protecting and promoting the cultural heritage; a task of transforming the economy by strengthening public participation need professionals excellence. The technological sophistication cannot be meaningful unless we make possible sophistication in the process of value addition. Against this backdrop, it is a crying need of the hour that both the information and entertainment media innovate their marketing strategy in the face of multi-dimensional negative developments taking place in the Indian society every day.

Creativity makes ways for sensitivity. The professionals managing the affairs need to sensitise the masses. They need creative promotional measures so that a number of social evils cropping up in the socio-cultural systems are removed. The rural masses need an overriding priority where we find the magnitude of problems at its peak. National Rural Health Mission has not been successful in improving quality of life of rural masses. The goal of the mission is to improve the availability of and accessibility to quality healthcare specially for the women and children residing in the rural areas. But we do not find the results much more impressive. The National Rural

Health Mission (2005-12) seeks to provide effective healthcare to rural population throughout the country and the information and entertainment media need to prioritise the same.

The Directorate of Advertising and Visual Publicity is the nodal multimedia agency of the government to meet the publicity requirements of various Ministries and Departments in a cost-effective manner. Press Advertisements, Audiovisual Publicity, Printed Publicity, Exhibitions, Outdoor Publicity, Mass Mailing need due attention to sensitise the insensitive segments of society. Song and Drama Division can play a very effective role in the entire process.

A step taken for innovating the policy decisions paves the ways for innovating the marketing strategy. The long awaited Prasar Bharati[13] established with the motto of upholding the unity and integrity of the country, promoting national integration, safeguarding citizen's rights, creating awareness, promoting social justice needs an innovative strategy to accomplish the organisational objectives. Autonomous status is not only thing that we need. Practising autonomy draws our priority attention. The two constituents of Prasar Bharati have not been successful in making use of autonomy. Attitudinal forces play an incremental role in making use of the autonomy.

If we have a positive attitude the autonomy would help us in many ways. Contrary to it, if we develop a negative attitude, the autonomy is found helpful in jeopardising everything. More autonomy, more freedom, no intervention, no control and therefore you are free to do what you like. If media start derailing the society; if media start polluting the society; if media start making an invasion on our culture; if media start making the new generation more crazy, our all efforts for developing and strengthening a nation are to be turned into a fiasco.

It is already mentioned earlier that both the information and entertainment media bear the responsibility of sensing and guiding the society. And if they start misguiding by making available the viewers/users, the entertainment which they cannot digest, we can easily imagine the fate of Indian society, Indian culture. We cannot deny the fact that as and when we have been given more autonomy, we have misused it. The AIR and DDI failed in their goals of promoting social values, projecting the superiority of Indian culture and DDI started copying the functional properties of private TV channels influenced by western culture and civilisation. No doubt, they have been successful in promoting social advertisements but when kids start misbehaving; when teens start claiming privacy; when new generation is found more crazy, our slogans would hardly have a positive appeal.

We watch advertisements but fail in receiving the message since our values are found degraded. It is very natural that human beings have a temptation for opposite sex. They prefer to watch the programme providing them more satisfaction. And when expectations are influenced by the process of taste perversion our efforts to fulfil their expectations result into a disaster. If we watch the programmes televised by almost all the TV channels, willingly or unwillingly we come to this conclusion that things are not moving in the right direction.

The aforesaid negative developments make it essential that entertainment media/electronic media think over the problems in the Indian perspective. We welcome entertainment since it is an effective way of generating efficiency, diffusing tension and removing monotony. Entertainment for pleasure, not for deviation. Entertainment for satisfaction, not for tension. Entertainment for peace, not for unrest.[14] Earlier, we have focused on the TV programme changing the behaviour of kids, teens and youths. Of course, we appreciate the developments in the field of communication technologies since the concept of globalisation of economy is now conceptualised and practised more effectively but if globalisation of economy starts paving ways for the globalisation of fashion, culture and civilisation which becomes very much instrumental in derailing the society, deviating the new generation; it is high time to think over the issues seriously. We have autonomy and now it is upon us to use or misuse. We should take a lesson from Pakistan where all the private TV channels have been regulated. Of course, they appear very serious to their culture. Sooner or later, we have no option but to check the spreading tidal wave of pop culture.

The information media have less scope for such a deviation. The newspapers and magazines have hardly been successful in projecting social issues in the Indian perspective. To be more specific, the magazines with the help of commercial advertisements are found very much instrumental in the process. If we turn our eyes on the photographs in the magazines, it becomes difficult to identify the imprint of Indian civilisation and culture. Of course, they have a right to promote commercial advertisements but the dresses, poses of characters are found transmitting the message of vulgarity, nudeness or so. Of course, we need to promote oral contraceptive pills for controlling the birth rate but here we have to be careful that our messages are not encouraging teens for illegitimate, unethical sexual behaviour. Of course, we have a right to advertise our products but it is also essential that our products found unhealthy in nature and injurious in effect do not encourage teens to taste the same. Of course, we have a right to select characters but it is also essential that it is not to generate racial, regional discrimination. Thus, the magazines in particular have also been instrumental in making a good-bye to the time-tested norms.

The newspapers can play an effective role in promoting the socio-cultural values. But just to get more commercial advertisements, they have also been found compromising with the situations. The production of news requires professionalism. The three important requirements are the events occurring in the same rhythm as its own productive cycle, positioning of news in preconceived and pre-planned categories. The process of news selection also needs professional excellence. Galtung and Ruge offer six criteria to underline the process of news selection, e.g.., negativity, threshold, dramatic, continues, status and nation. They argued that news presentation should also be done professionally. They focus on unambiguity, personalisation and meaningfulness.[15] The reporters and correspondents while collecting news and the editorial staff while positioning the same should assign due weightage to the emerging socio-economic, cultural, political and other issues. The information media are supposed to play a meaningful role and the leading agencies like UNI and PTI in addition to protecting the interests of newspapers should also think about the instrumentality of newspapers in nation building. They are also supposed to make efforts for checking the entry of foreign newspapers. Of late, the publishing organisations are found well equipped. The only thing they need is. a strong sense of commitment to professional values. Since they have a direct contact with the masses, the task of identification of sensitive problems is not so difficult. Of course, they need to advertise specially to mobilise the financial resources but here it is meaningful that the advertisements do not make an invasion on our culture. If the concerned agencies make sincere efforts to promote socio-cultural values, the task is not so difficult.

The aforesaid facts make it clear that mass communication organisations need to innovate their strategies. They bear the responsibility of making available to the users/readers authentic and time-honoured information. They bear the responsibility of highlighting key social issues. They are also supposed to inculcate mass awareness. In addition, they have to pave ways for enriching the organisational efficacy so that the interests of personnel working there are subserved. Unless they make possible a fair blending of social and commercial considerations, it is not possible. It is against this background that we make an advocacy in favour of professional excellence. In addition to other aspects, the leading agencies should also think in favour of small and regional newspapers since most of them are found struggling for their existence. If they succeed in developing a culture; if they succeed in injecting values; if they succeed in sensing the society; if they succeed in guiding the policy makers, a strong foundation would be engineered which would also make ways for their development and prosperity.

SUMMARY

Mass Media: We also call it mass communication. Any medium of communication reaching a very large number of people such as newspapers and magazines, broadcast and telecast media where we find transmission of message through a source is mass media.

Emerging Trends in Mass Media: To be more specific after the attainment of independence, we find so many turning points in the mass media. There have witnessed quantitative and qualitative developments in information media, telecast media and broadcast media.

Mass Media Marketing: It is a managerial device to promote mass media so that the concerned organisations succeed in having a fair blending of social and commercial considerations.

Justification for Marketing Mass Media: There are a number of points to justify the conceptualisation of marketing principles in the mass media, e.g., formulating a sound service mix, identifying the sensitive problems and the thrust areas, formulating an optimal promotion strategy, rationalising the pricing decision, having an optimal distribution strategy, making possible cost-effectiveness and satisfying the users of the services.

Service Mix for Mass Media: In the formulation of service mix for mass media, we include both the core and supportive services offered by information media, telecast media and broadcast media. The information media have information value whereas the entertainment media have entertainment value.

Promoting Mass Media: Like other organisations, the mass communication organisations also need to promote their business so that they serve the society in a right fashion and at the same time also succeed in maintaining their commercial viability. Inter-media promotion may help them in optimising the promotion budget. While promoting, they are supposed to protect the social cultural values.

Pricing for Mass Media: To be more specific for the newspapers and magazines, the pricing dimension occupies a place of outstanding significance. The mounting establishment and intermediation costs have been found increasing the total cost but the demand side is not showing a positive trend. The information media thus need to inculcate habits of buying newspapers and magazines among the prospects which would increase circulation *vis-à-vis* would make possible cost-effectiveness in the services. For entertainment media, this dimension is found insignificant.

Place Mix: The information media in particular need to assign due weightage to this dimension of marketing because the agents and distributors play here an outstanding role. Both the media information and entertainment are supposed to assign due attention on reception, enquiry and service distribution centres.

Process Mix: To process the services related to mass communication, we find a team of people combining technical experts, managerial professionals and supporting staff. The operational flow is increased with the help of new generation of technology. The services are processed and offered to the users.

Physical Evidence and Attractions: This mix of marketing for the mass communication services draws our attention on the service ambience helping employees and performers in delivering and customers and visitors in strengthening their realisation about the services to be used. In the entertainment media, we find service ambience playing an incremental role in attracting the viewers and potential viewers. The employees working need to wear uniforms and dresses in tune with the situations and occasions inside and outside the studio.

People: In the mass communication services, we find involvement of a brigade of performing and supporting staff in different capacities. They need perfection and personal commitment to their profession and delivering with a sense of dedication. In a true sense, they need passion for their profession.

Mass Communication Marketing in Indian Perspective: The mass communication organisations bear an outstanding responsibility of informing and sensing the society in such a way that the derailed socio-cultural systems come back on the rail. Both the wings of mass communication such as information media and entertainment media, of course, are also involved in promoting their commercial considerations but basically they are taking part in the process of social transformation. In the Indian perspective, we find a qualitative reform in both the media during 1990s. The credibility for intensifying qualitative and quantitative reforms goes to the satellite communication and new generation of information and communication technology. But our prime attention is on their contributions to the process of sensitising the general masses so that mounting social evils are arrested. Of course, we appreciate their defined objectives but the results received so far are not so much impressive. We cannot negate that they lack professional excellence and therefore fail in delivering the desired goals. It is in this context that we make a strong advocacy in favour of conceptualising marketing with a focus on societal approach. They need creative promotional measures for effective persuasion. There is no doubt in it that are potentially sound in terms of supporting infrastructural facilities but managerially and strategically deficient. Both the media need a brigade of professionally- committed and value-based people. On the one hand, they need to intensify social advertisements while on the other hand also need to capitalise on commercial opportunities. This will make them financially solvent to enrich their potentials.

KEY TERMS

Mass Communication	Dissemination
Information Media	Drug Addiction
Entertainment Media	Communicable Diseases
Sexual Behaviour	Information Explosion
Social Marketing	Social Advertising
Offset Printing	Afforestation
Laser Printing	Tidal Wave
Satellite Communication	Pop Culture
Movie	Obscurity
Rocky	Teenagers
Terminator	Volatile
Digitalisation	Hawkers
Direct-to-home	Consortium
Free-to-air	Multiplexes
Marxist Sociologies	Jeopardising
Press Council of India	Vulgarity
Prasar Bharati	Nudeness
Vividh Bharati	Racial
Cultural Heritage	Panorama

Review Questions

1. What do you mean by mass communication? Focus on the different constituents of mass communication.
2. Explain the significant developments in the field of information media and entertainment media after the attainment of independence.
3. Define Mass Media Marketing? Throw light on the justifications for practising marketing in the massmedia.
4. Focus on the emerging trends in the mass communication in the Indian perspective.
5. Comment on the service mix for the information media.
6. Explain the product mix for entertainment media.
7. Focus on the promotion mix for mass communication.
8. Explain the price mix for mass communication.
9. Discuss the place mix for mass communication.
10. Focus on the extended marketing mix for mass communication.
11. Write a short note on mass communication marketing in the Indian perspective.
12. Focus on the marketing strategy for mass communication in the Indian perspective.
13. Write a critical note on the role of mass communication in protecting and promoting social interests.

Application Exercises

1. As a marketer, suggest a marketing mix for the information media which focuses on sensitising the rural masses.
2. You have been working as a marketing professional in AIR. Focus on the product mix to be formulated by the AIR for developing mass awareness.
3. Do you feel that DDI has been practising a right marketing strategy? Justify your arguments as a marketing professional.
4. A leading newspaper has been facing the problem of low circulation. Suggest a suitable marketing strategy.
5. A leading newspaper wants to innovate the service mix. Suggest a product mix.
6. A leading TV channel has been facing the problem of commercial advertisement. As a marketer, adopt the suitable measures helping in getting the advertisements.
7. Suggest a suitable social advertisement plan for DDI in the Indian perspective.
8. The increasing establishment expenses and mounting intermediation bill have been forcing a newspaper publishing company to increase the price of newspapers and magazines. Focus on the distribution strategy helping in making the distribution process cost-effective.
9. A TV channel wants to develop a mix for social advertisements. As a marketing professional suggest the promotional strategy to be effective in the Indian context.
10. As a marketing professional, you have been asked to design a marketing strategy helping a balance between organisational and social consideration. Suggest the strategy which you feel suitable for mass communication organisations.

Endnotes

1. Asher Cashdan & Martin Jordi, Studies in Communication, Part III, *Communication and the Media,* New York, 1987, pp.125-29.
2. Manorma Year Book, 1998, p. 570.
3. Indiastat, 2007.
4. Mathew K.M., Impact of Foreign Press on Domestic Media, Excerpts from Conference Paper.
5. Jha, S.M., *Social Marketing;* HPH, 2009.
6. India, 2008.
7. *Ibid.*
8. Jha, *S.M. Social Marketing*; HPH, 2009.
9. Eighth Five Year Plan.
10. Jha, S.M., New Wave Civilisation, *The Hindustan Times*, Patna, June 28, 1997.
11. *Times of India:* UNESCO — Media Violence has Direct Influence on Children, March, 1988.
12. Jha, S.M., Excerpts from the Paper presented to Marketing Education Group, 1996, Scotland.
13. Manorma Year Book, 2008.
14. Jha, S.M., Entertainment Marketing, *Services Marketing,* Chapter 15, 2004.
15. Critcher Chas, Media Spectacles, *Studies in Communication*, Blackwell, New York, 1987.

★★★

IT MARKETING

Complexity makes the ways for the development of sophisticated devices. The emergence of IT as a service industry is in the face of myriad of constraints experienced by large-sized organisations while managing their accounts.

Chapter Objectives

Introduction – IT: A Conceptual Framework – IT Marketing: A Conceptual Framework – Justifications for Practising Marketing in IT Services – Emergence of IT as a Service Industry – Behavioural Profile of Users of IT Services– Information System for IT Services – Market Segmentation for IT Services – Marketing Mix for IT Services – Product Mix – Promotion Mix – Price Mix – Place Mix – Process – Physical Evidence and Attractions – People – IT Marketing in Indian Perspective – Summary – Key Terms – Review Questions – Application Exercises – Endnotes.

Learning Objectives

The chapter aims at studying the different dimensions of marketing IT services. The marketing professionals need to develop their awareness of the changing levels of expectations of IT users found both at domestic and global levels. Since the markets for IT services are becoming much more competitive, they need to make use of world-class professional excellence so that their efforts for excelling competition are found proactive. The most important dimension particularly in the offshore marketing is bridging the communication gap. The marketers with professional excellence and high level of communication skill can make it possible. Conceptualisation of marketing will help in getting the repeat orders.

INTRODUCTION

In an age of sophisticated information technology, we find knowledge management occupying a place of outstanding significance. Why not we start our deliberations on knowledge management with the human brain considered to be the best model of knowledge management. Often we talk about five senses, viz., touch, taste, vision, hearing and smell. All of us are well aware of the fact that human brain acts as computer which computes the data, converts or transforms it into information and stores the same in the memory. The action of human brain is found very interesting. Interpretation and application are found in both parts of the human brain. The left part of brain is found active in interpretation whereas other right half applies logic and starts thought processing. So far as the feedback is concerned, it is collected from the environment and when we talk about intuition, it is found coming from somewhere. Now, we find formation of knowledge with the concoction of information, intelligence, intuition, investigation and inquisitiveness.

The technological revolution helped invention of computers to simplify out task of managing knowledge. Gradually, we have witnessed a number of qualitative improvements which has virtually increased its potentials and has also reduced its size. The development processes are so rapid that we find the least possible gap between new and old generation of computers. On account of its multi-faceted features, we find individuals and institutions making use of computers for professional, commercial and personal uses. This has made possible a significant increasing in the demand side. As and when we find demand side making a significant increase, the preparations are made for meeting the supply side. It was against this background that a large number of organisations even in the Indian perspective started taking part in the process.

Initially, we find IBM and ICL as the dominant players in the IT industry. Gradually, a number of small and big players have taken part in the process. The decade 1980s made ways for significant developments in the field of IT industry and the intensity of competition also gained a momentum. During the decade 1990s, we find technological advancements which resulted into the development of a chip and further the satellite communication technology made ways for cost-effectiveness. This helped a boom in the IT services. The intensity of competition started increasing fast which engineered a sound background for practising modern marketing principles in a multi-billion dollar IT industry. Software application, professional excellence, system integration, maintenance services, education and training, technology-oriented applications and software packages are the emerging areas in the context of IT services. The innovations in 21st century has made this industry potentially sound but the worldwide economic depression has been affecting this industry in a big way. The marketers need world-class professional excellence to deliver goods to the individual or institutional customers. The banking, finance, mining, steel, transportation and by and large almost all the sectors are found emerging as customers for the IT services.

Information Technology has tremendous marketing opportunities. It has a large product range such as educational games targeted towards children, business tools used by the office executives and offices, executive tools used for those interested in managing time and small amounts of information and data. Besides, we also find its uses by the Stock Exchange of India. Its uses for managing environment and monitoring the transmission of energy has also been appreciated. But these applications are just a few of the applications. In a true sense, we have a big list of users of services. This makes it essential that professionalised efforts are made to market the IT services.

The growth in the IT industry is found very fast. We find beginning of this industry as a hardware or computer-oriented industry but now it has proved to be a multi-dimensional force not only governing the success rate of economy but also influencing our lifestyles. We find IT emerging as a discipline and actually opening the floodgates of job opportunities to millions and millions of our youths both nationally and globally. The diversity of services demanded by IT is so large that one finds it difficult to identify its areas of operation.

Business Process Outsourcing (BPO) is a significant area absorbing people in a very good number with computer competence, good command of English knowledge and soft skills. BPO involves a contract with an organisation in US for providing a business or function. This process entails various kinds of efforts such as Accounting, Animation, Bank Office, Banking, Call Centre Operation, Chip Design, Clinical Research, Computer Programming, Content Development, Customer Services, Desktop Publishing, Engineering, Insurance Services, Invoicing, Knowledge Services, Management Consultancy, Medical Services, Product Design, Software, Taxation, Telecommunication, Transcription and Travel Agency Services. It is pertinent to mention that IT-enabled services which may be considered as a component of BPO has been offering bright prospects of employment. The persons acquiring higher qualitification can take up work known as KPO (Knowledge Process Outsourcing). We find wider avenues for developments in the context of KPO.

We find 21st century a landmark in the field of IT industry due to quantitative and qualitative developments in this sector. A number of organisations emerged and could prove their excellence nationally and globally. They did well in a number of areas such as earning foreign exchange, creating employment opportunities and sensitising the masses of the multi-faceted uses of IT. We are well aware of the multi-dimensional uses of IT in almost all the areas. Development of more than 7,500 Software Technology Parks in the country is a staunch testimony to this proposition that India developed a lot in the IT Sector. The states like Maharashtra, Andhra Pradesh, Karnataka were found the leaders in the process of initiating IT revolution in India. The emergence of IT sector as an industry made it essential that professionalised efforts are made to market the services so that industry *vis-à-vis* the national economy are substantially benefited. This made a strong advocacy in favour of conceptualising marketing in the IT sector.

The application of marketing principles in IT services makes it essential that the marketing professionals make an in-depth study of the emerging markets at national and global levels. They develop their awareness of the requirements of individual and institutional users and activate efforts to capitalise on the opportunities. The IT industry has a large number of product ranges and therefore formulation of product portfolio particularly for marketing purposes appears essential. The professionals need to ensure quality of product so that the organisations also have an international market. Since we find IT sector potentially sound, the efforts of professionals may be instrumental in getting the markets and increasing the profitability.

The marketers need to intensify the promotional acivities with the help of different components of promotion. The sensitisation and persuasion processes need creativity in the promotional measures. The different components of promotion are to be used in such a way that customers both in national and international markets develop their awareness of the available products. Besides, they are also supposed to sensitise the individual and institutional customers regarding the packages of services made available to them.

Since we find the market much more competitive, it is significant that professionals explore the possibilities of making the price structure competitive. The organisations need to produce quality product at an affordable price so that it is used as a motivational tool.

The distribution channels may be double-level where the wholesalers and retailers would make available to the customers the products on time. The professionals need to minimise the possibilities of high distribution costs.

The services are to be processed with the help of quality technology and efficient people so that the gap in service delivery is minimised. While processing, it is to be made sure that at each and every stage the professionals are sincere.

In the context of designing the servicescapes, the marketing professionals need to make it much more attractive. The tangibilisation of outstanding properties with the motto of adding additional attractions is found significant. They need to strengthen the realisation of customers regarding the service quality.

They need quality marketing people having communication excellence and to be in a position to influence the customers. Marketing in a competitive business environment makes it essential that marketing people show personal-touch-in-service.

Thus, the emerging IT industry by conceptualising marketing would be successful in marketing their product ensuring profits to the organisations *vis-a-vis* high level of satisfaction to the customers.

IT: A CONCEPTUAL FRAMEWORK

IT is the convergence of computer, information, intelligence, communication, internet and technical administration. IT integrates data, equipment, personnel and problem-solving methods in planning and controlling business activities. IT provides the means for collecting, storing, encoding, processing, analysing, transmitting, receiving and printing text, audio or video information. IT being a product and service of recent origin and having a large product range cover a variety of hardware, software, operating systems; facilitating easier interface with the users.[1]

IT MARKETING: A CONCEPTUAL FRAMEWORK

IT marketing focuses our attention on conceptualisation of marketing principles in the IT services with the motto of making profits and satisfying customers/users. This makes it essential that marketers have an in-depth study of national and global markets, they are well aware of users coming from different segments and are in a position to study their needs and requirements *vis-à-vis* the changing levels of their expectations. The approaches are professionalised and a sound marketing mix is formulated to make the marketing activities proactive to the changing needs of users. It includes in its purview the marketing research activities to study and understand the users. It is also considered to be a managerial device helping a marketing professional in making right decisions. Sensitising and persuading the users are important in the IT marketing which helps marketers in transforming the potential users into actual users and the actual users into the habitual users. It is based on professional excellence of world-class where marketers make efforts to improve quality, minimise the costs and increase profits. The marketing activities help increasing potentials for excelling competition.

In view of the above, the following facts emerge:

- IT Marketing is a managerial process where marketers need world-class professional excellence.
- IT is an organised effort for studying and understanding the users of IT services.
- IT marketing is a process of segmenting the markets helping professionals in dividing and subdividing the markets into small groups and subgroups.
- IT marketing includes in its purview formulation of a sound marketing mix.
- Sensitisation and persuasion are the two important dimensions of IT marketing based on creativity.
- It is a formal approach for satisfying the users and excelling competition.

JUSTIFICATION FOR PRACTISING MARKETING IN THE IT SERVICES

With the mounting multi-faceted uses of IT, we find emergence of this sector as a service industry. Almost all the sectors and a large number of individuals are the customers of IT services. At national and even at global levels, we find India as an important provider of IT services. Capitalising on the tremendous opportunities and satisfying the users to keep on moving the process make it essential that we conceptualise marketing in the IT sector. We find justifications for practising marketing in the IT services.

1. Identifying the Opportunities: By practising marketing, the professional may find it easier to identify the opportunities both at national and international levels. Both the segments of customers such as individual and institutional need due attention of marketers while activating the identification process. We cannot negate that the intensity of competition in the market is found high and this necessitates creation of opportunities. The professionally-sound marketers may be successful in both the areas. On the one hand, they will identify the opportunities where the marketing processes are to be intensified and on the other hand, they will also play a big role in sensitising the masses for making use of the services in different areas.

2. Innovating the Services: Since we find high intensity of competition, it is significant that the marketers formulate such a package of services which acts as a motivational tool. The innovation processes are to be frequent keeping in view the product mix of the rival organisations. The customers or prospects getting innovative services are attracted. At short intervals, the modifications in services are to be made. In the face of emerging trends in the product life cycle, the marketers have to take a decision.

3. Sensitising the Users: With the conceptualisation of marketing, the professionals succeed in developing awareness of the different categories of services by activating the sensitisation process. The creative promotional measure simplifies their task. The professionals by making use of their excellence may be in a position to use the different components of promotion. It is significant to mention that a good number of users are not well-aware of the multi-faceted uses of IT services. Sensitisation, persuasion and transformations measures may help organisations in creating and expanding markets. Aggressive promotional measures are found effective for those customers who are not well aware of the available services with the outstanding features, recently introduced in the market. The marketing professional with the help of a sound promotion mix may be successful in persuading and transforming the potential customers.

4. Helpful in Setting the Repeat Orders: It is not only significant that you create customers. It is much more important that you transform them into habitual customers by getting from them the repeat orders. Gaining and maintaining the customers make it essential that their past experiences have satisfied them.

There are a number of customers specially belonging to the institutional segment and once they are satisfied with the performance of services delivered to them, they keep on moving the process. The institutional customers also prove to be the individual customers because the organisations where they are making use of services and getting full satisfaction they prefer to use them even for personal uses. The IT professionals and marketing professionals both of them have to take part in the process.

5. Effective in the Export Marketing: The IT sector has tremendous opportunities in the global or offshore markets. It is upon the marketers to study the emerging global markets and to tap the opportunities. The professional services involve offering a variety of skills, specific to an individual which can be utilised on projects either at overseas sites or offshore. The services are found very expensive in the global markets and we can offer the users those services at a very reasonable price. The emergence of export services for IT has created profitable opportunities. The marketing professionals may identify the users and develop contact with them. We find offering of offshore services in a different way. The information related to the skills of an individual are stored which have an easy accessibility of the users. The demand and supply mechanism regulate the behaviour of price. The marketing professionals may play an incremental role in the entire process. We cannot deny that during yester-years, we have sizeably developed our potentials in terms of IT services. At the same time, we also find productive market opportunities. How to capitalists on the opportunities is an important problem and the marketing professionals have to simplify it.

6. Satisfying the Users: The most important task that marketing professionals successfully and satisfactorily perform are studying the needs and requirements of users, gauging the levels of their expectations and delivering to them the desired levels of services. This makes ways for satisfying the users. A global network is required to be developed for this purpose so that the marketers have an in-depth knowledge of the different segments of users.

7. Bridging the Communication Gap: In the IT services, the most sensitive problem if found related to the communication gap between software users and software marketers. The task of marketing professionals not aware of the IT jargon becomes too much difficult while persuading the potential users. This necessitates marketing experts having an in-depth knowledge of IT services and their productive uses. During 1990s and even in 21st century, the marketing experts developing expertise in IT concentrated on focusing the application of IT and their uses to the potential users which helped them in winning, gaining and maintaining the customers.

EMERGENCE OF IT AS A SERVICE INDUSTRY

Complexity makes ways for the development of sophisticated devices. The emergence of IT as a service industry is in the face of multi-faceted constraints experienced by large-sized organisations while managing their accounts. With the development of business, it was difficult for them to manage the accounting departments and therefore they started depending on their computers. Of course, the development in the process started taking a shape during 1980s because during the decade 1970s we find much more emphasis on the development of new generation of computers. It is right to mention that during the early part of 1970s, the IT industry was at its stage of infancy. When we find an organisation at its nascent stage and actually facing the stage of quality upgradation, the customers or users are found to be worst affected. There is no doubt that organisations concerned with finance, engineering and administration started making use of computers but so far as the customer services are concerned, they were found depending on the IT suppliers who were not taking much more interests in the redressal of problems. Hence, the IT found it difficult to emerge as a service industry.

The contours of developments underwent radical changes especially during the decade 1980s. There was a significant change in the nature and types of computers and simultaneously there was a basic change in the attitudes of providers. We cannot negate that increasing intensity of competition was an important reason for an attitudinal change. Not only the banking and airlines but a good number of organisations started realising the importance of IT for improving the rate of productivity and profitability. With the beginning of online applications, the replacement of manual legacy system was found possible. The increasing responses from the groups of users were due to the new generation of computers which benefited the users in many ways. The service providing organisations had no option but to perceive the concept of customer satisfaction in a right fashion which necessitated priority attention on customer services with the confines of a corporate structure. They were supposed to define and redefine the concept of quality in terms of customer services. And from here, we find emergence of IT services as an industry.

Of late, the organisations in general has been found assigning an overriding priority to customer services. The identity of an organisation is with the quality of IT Department. With the end of the decade 1990s or with the end of the 20th century, we find a number of organisations becoming users of IT services and computer literacy, PCs and the internet were found common fixtures either in office or at home. It is pertinent to mention that the thirst for IT increased to such an extent that till the end of 20th century, it was expected that people serving an organisation are aware of computer application.

The beginning of 21st century activated the process of quantitative and qualitative improvements and this resulted into a galloping increase in the demand side as almost all the organisations started making use of IT and for which, it was essential that we find a basic change in the concept and percept of customer services.

The IT organisation had no option but to redefine the concept of customer services to their desired levels. This in a very natural way made it essential that marketers develop professional excellence which make them efficacious of the applications of IT in the various sectors of the economy. They formulated innovative marketing strategy which is found unbeatable in the global markets. Against this background, the marketers required world-class professional excellence.

During the yesteryears, the IT sector has significantly contributed to the foreign exchange reserves and job markets. An industry exporting the software and ITES upto US $ 25 billion and expected to grow at a faster rate even more than 32 per cent in dollar terms has been creating profitable opportunities for the IT organisations both at domestic and global levels. We can easily imagine the contributions of IT sector to the job markets as the total number of IT and ITES-BPO professionals employed in India is nearing about 15,00,000. Thus, both in qualitative and quantitative terms, we find IT sector expanding and even in the days to come, it will grow and thrive.

The beginning of IT sector was for accounting and technical environment and now we find its transformation as a totally service-oriented industry. When we find supply side increasing fast, it becomes essential to sensitise the demand side. This draws our attention on the development of IT professionals having multi-dimensional faculties. On the one hand, they need to be a sound marketer while on the other hand they also need to develop their expertise in the field of its applications and uses. It is in this context that we find IT organisations hiring professionals having traits like empathy, helpfulness, patience, resourcefulness and team-orientation. Capitalising on the marketing opportunities in a productive way makes it essential that marketers are in a position to identify the changing needs and requirements of clients.

The above-mentioned facts make it clear that IT sector has emerged as a big service industry and the changing scenario makes a strong advocacy in favour of conceptualising innovative marketing. It is very natural that the intensity of competition in the IT markets is found mounting and to excel competition, the most effective prescription is to satisfy the customers /users/clients. Identify the key customers; identify the key services of the key customers; identify key processes supporting the key services and identify the key suppliers supporting the key processes are some of the important tasks before the marketing professionals. We cannot negate that marketers often commit a mistake in the identification process and therefore they find it difficult to make available to them the services to their desired levels. This results into dissatisfaction. Increasing the repeat orders is found essential but it is not to be possible unless we find customers oversatisfied. Exercising identification processes requires an in-depth knowledge, high communicative ability and uninterrupted availability of sound infrastructural facilities. Let's hope that marketers capitalise on the tremendous opportunities available in the IT sector.

BEHAVIOURAL PROFILE OF USERS OF IT SERVICES

We find users of IT services coming from different segments which in a very natural way complicates the task of marketers because the behavioural profile of all the users cannot be identical. This makes it essential that marketing professionals develop their awareness of the changing needs and requirements of users of IT services. The multi-faceted IT services are software application, professional services, system integration, maintenance services including hardware, software and facilities, education and training, techno-driven applications and software packages. The users may be individual or institutional. They come form almost all the sectors and are found in almost all the countries. The task of marketing professionals becomes too much difficult when they lack information related to the requirements of users and potential users. The marketing professionals by studying and understanding the niche markets would be in a position to fulfil and satisfy them. The users may expect specialised nature of services, they may come from a particular location, they may also require a package of services. The requirements of users regarding the operating systems they want to develop, the databases they want to tap are considered important in this context. The niches are to be identified before entering the market. It is right to mention that we find a different situation in the software marketing due to its multi-dimensional applications. Since the niche markets are found very specific in respect of software, the marketers find it difficult to promote them.

With the beginning of 21st century, we find a big increase in the number of users and uses of IT services. Today, we find microprocessors even in children's toys, word processors, pocket calculators, industrial robots, home applications, etc. just to mention a few of their innumerable uses and there is practically no new machine, instruments, control equipment or information system that does not have a microprocessor in it. Education at school and home, libraries, scientific research, office automation, report generation, banking, insurance, engineering colleges, management tool, industrial application, communication, traffic management, medicine, weather processing, space research, defence, stock and share market, games, payroll package, salary slip generation, tax calculation, fashion designing, product design, system analysis, hospitals architecture, mass mailers, online ticketing, booking vacation,[2] etc. Thus, we find a big list of users of IT services and therefore, the task of marketers while studying and understanding the behavioural profile of users is found difficult. We have entered areas of Article Intelligence or say, Fifth Generation Computers combining mainframe computers, minicomputers and microcomputers.

In the face of emerging trends in the IT sector, the marketing professionals bear the responsibility of developing their awareness of the multi-segment users expecting multi-faceted services from the service providers. Developing expertise in the field of marketing IT services focuses on an in-depth analysis of national and international markets. A microscopic study and anatomy of markets may help marketers in identifying the levels of expectations of users of IT services.

The task of IT service providing organisations is considerably simplified when we find business within geographical and cultural boundaries but we do not find the same scenario when we start marketing offshore. In the first case, it is easier for the marketing professionals to bridge the communication gap because geographical proximity makes possible face-to-face communication and interactions much more effective. Of course, we find online provisions but the task of coordination is not so easy due to cross-border cultural diversity. The offshore team finds it difficult to coordinate also on account of difference in time zones. The lead time may be even the whole day. This makes it essential that for studying and understanding the levels of expectations and requirements of clients, the marketing professionals at the very initial stage develop contact with the clients and do not commit mistakes in understanding their requirements. They need to make it sure that the requirements of clients are fulfilled to the best of their satisfaction otherwise the projects may be a success but the clients may remain dissatisfied. Increased level of communication is considered to be the most effective prescription to understand the behaviour of clients.

Management of the expectations of clients is considered to be an important dimension drawing priority attention of professionals. They need to deal with the problem of cultural diversity. Working with heterogeneous groups of individuals, no doubt, is a challenging task mainly due to cultural diversity. Crossing national, regional and cultural boundaries, of course, complicates the task of marketers. This makes it significant that the marketers develop their awareness of cultural diversity. The professionals also feel inconveniences due to infrastructural constraints because we also find cases of breakdown in the communication network. The professionals may take the support of collaborative technologies by developing regular contacts. The political turbulences and power shortage may also complicate the task of marketers while studying the levels of expectations of offshore clients. The intensity of risk is to be minimised by having a common configuration management and working on the latest version which may help them in working without any interruption. The marketers also need to assign due weightage to time management and this focuses on developing our awareness of the time zones. The teleconference meeting may help them because this simplifies the task of matching the offshore work hours.

While developing contacts with the domestic clients, the professionals do not face such problems but they should not undermine them. The most sensitive dimension of studying and understanding the behavioural profile of clients/users is to make use of effective communication. This focuses our attention on the knowledge bank of professionals regarding the clients. It is well-known that they are supposed to deal with the different types of clients coming from different segments and inheriting different levels of expectations. Unless you understand them, it will be much more difficult for you to include them in the group of clients known as habitual users making use of your IT services again and again.

The expectations of all the users cannot be identical. The professionals need to understand them. Generally, the institutional customers expect superset encompassing all the expectations of other segments of users. It is important to mention that the retail segment is found satisfied with the tool which can easily be used. They prefer products with appropriate alerts and reminders and also provide to them scenario analysis and a clear actionable advice. The middle segment or independent specialists want solutions that in addition to the functionalities mentioned earlier also facilitate more sophisticated strategies. The institutional segment expect highly evolved business intelligence data, customised solutions, structured product offerings, legally complaint advice and business enhancement tools like plan monitoring and control functionalities. In view of the changing requirements, it is essential that they are also provided software solutions. By making the solution configurable, the software providers can serve both sophisticated users such as institutional and independent specialists and retail users. We cannot negate the significant role of "Fast Track" solution helping in meeting the requirements of cross segment of users. In a true sense, the professionals need a Unique Selling Proposition. In general, we find their expectations clustering around high sophistication, cost-effectiveness and easy-to-use utility.

An in-depth study of different groups of segments of users may help professionals in understanding their changing requirements. The increasing sophistication and mounting competition have been inviting much more frequency in the levels of expectations. You may seek the co-operation of advisors, co-ordinators and marketing professionals for developing your awareness of the changing hierarchy of needs. It is also to be made sure that persons communicating and co-ordinating do not face the problem of language constraint and are in a position to receive the problems of clients related to costs, expectations and service quality. In addition, we also find unexpected obstacles due to communication gap. Time-to-time communication helps in understanding the real difficulties experienced by clients. Getting feedback thus becomes essential for fulfilling the desired level of expectations of users.

INFORMATION SYSTEM FOR IT SERVICES

Since the market is becoming much more competitive, it is essential that professionals enrich their knowledge bank with the help of a sound information system. What to talk of the offshore markets when they need information systems even for the domestic markets. This is due to mounting competition and changing needs and requirements of IT users. Knowing and understanding the niche markets is an essential consideration for formulating a sound marketing strategy. An in-depth knowledge of different segments will help the professionals in different ways.

The most important task in today's context is development of Offshore Information System[3] which has become increasingly important due to cultural diversity and time zones. It is found that a number of IT organisations suffer on that account which has complicated their marketing problems. For understanding the levels of expectations of IT users, it is essential that we have face-to-face communication but due to distance constraint and geographical barriers, the professionals find it difficult. It is against this background that we realise the instrumentality of developing an Offshore Information System. Development of a team specially for Offshore Marketing with the support of a local representative available on site and working as liaison member would make available to the Offshore Informations Systems related to the customers.

The Offshore Information Systems will simplify the task of marketers.[4] The marketing professionals will get the required information from the system specially related to the levels of expectations of IT users and potential users. There are a number of sub-issues simplifying the process of managing the expectations of IT users. Dealing with cultural diversity is the first consideration which focuses on studying the heterogeneous groups of individuals. With cultural variation, geographical boundaries and professional differences, we find a change in the levels of expectations. The differences are found hierarchical in nature. The system with the help of a coordinator would come to know the changing levels of expectations.

In the Indian perspective, we find divers groups or segments of IT users. Some of the organisations need the services on a large scale whereas some others need on a small scale. Both at domestic and offshore levels, we find management of communication playing an incremental role. The side-effects of communication are found very dangerous. Offshore sourcing involves coordination for managing information.

The development of sound information system both for domestic and offshore markets is essential for improving the quality of marketing decisions. The marketers bear the responsibility of satisfying the IT users and their tasks will remain unfulfilled if they lack information. In a competitive market, the professionals successful in gauging the levels of expectations of niche markets succeed in excelling competition.

MARKET SEGMENTATION FOR IT USERS

In a highly competitive market, the marketing professionals need to have an in-depth knowledge of the changing requirements of clients or customers. A number of customers coming from different segments are the users and in a very natural way the levels of expectations of all of them cannot be identical. Some of the customers are individuals where some of the users are institutional. Some of them are domestic whereas some of them are global. Some of them are teens whereas some of them are youth and grey. The attitudinal and situational variations *vis-à-vis* the situational forces determine the levels of expectations of customers. The marketing professionals need to prioritise the different groups of customers and thereafter to intensify their efforts to sensitise and persuade them. The task is difficult but the marketers have no option but to study and understand.

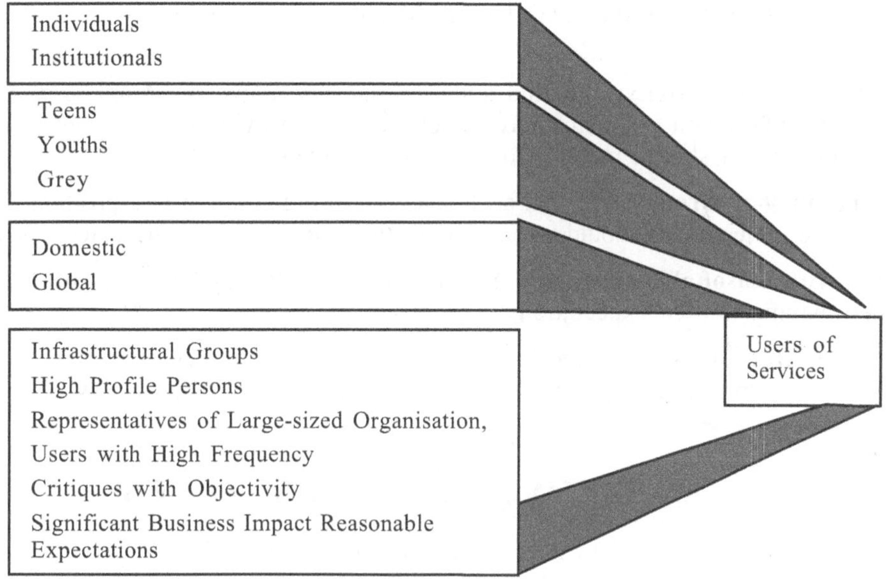

Fig. 23.1: Market Segments for IT Services

Though we find institutional customers making demands in larger quantity but it is not meant that the marketers undermine the individual customers. Even we find individual customers making ways for the institutional customers.

The teens in modern society have also been found using the services and their attitudes are found a bit different to others. The youths have been emerging as a customer bearing the potential to act as a word-of-mouth promoter. The grey also makes use of services and they have different temperament.

The marketing professionals need to understand both categories of customers, viz., domestic and global. The process of influencing the global customers is found a bit different because we find a number of constraints obstructing the process of persuasion. For the marketing professionals, it is easier to develop rapport with the domestic users of IT services because they find opportunities of developing face-to-face communication. We do not find this benefit with the offshore customers.

SEGMENT OF KEY CUSTOMERS

The marketing professionals bear the responsibility of assigning priority attention to the key or fat customers. They are considered potentially sound and identification of opportunities if done in a right way would make available to the marketers profitable opportunities to capitalise.

1. Customers belonging to Infrastructural Groups: We find infrastructural groups providing services to a number of departments in a company. Since they are considered as potential users for the IT services, it is important that the marketing professionals identify designated heads of the departments and develop a rapport with them to obtain the orders. They are considered as potentially-sound customers and with littlie efforts, the big orders may be expected.

2. Individuals holding high position: We find some of the people holding high position in an organisation and they are found efficacious of exercising their influence in an effective way. A number of persons hold significant position in that company who are considered potential customers and persons holding high position may influence them. Thus, the marketing professionals need to identify those persons holding high position in an organisation.

3. Representatives of large customers: The professionals also need to identify the representatives of large customers. In a large-sized organisation, we find working people in a very good number. They are also potential users of services and the professionals need to approach them to know their requirements. Since we find them frequently using services like e-mail, internet, and intranet, they may be approached through their representatives.

4. Frequent or Habitual Users: We also find some of the customers frequently using the IT services and the professionals need to identify them to develop contact. It is also possible that some of the organisations are frequently using the IT services and they may be considered as key customers. The major users of IT services are considered as key customers.

5. Critiques having objectivity: We find some of the customers, no doubt, criticising our services but with objectivity and therefore their criticisms may be helpful to the providers of services. The professionals should welcome their criticisms and should make efforts to resolve them.

6. Advance Technology Groups: We find such category of organisation in a position to place before you big orders and therefore the professionals should try to identify them. In aerospace and defense, we find a case like this.

7. Customers with reasonable expectations: The professionals may be in a position to identify and satisfy potential customers having limited expectations.

The marketing professionals thus need to identify the segment of key customers found to be potentially sound in business terms. Developing rapport and persuading them in an effective way depend on the professional excellence of marketers.

MARKETING MIX FOR IT SERVICES

The marketing professionals need to develop a sound marketing mix which will help them in identifying and satisfying the users. In the IT services, the professionals experience a number of problems while identifying the real and key customers. Due to a mix of customers coming both from domestic and global segments, they find it difficult to have face-to-face communication which complicates their task of sensing and persuading them. By formulating a sound marketing mix, they will be in a position to accomplish the organisational goals.

Product Mix

The development of a sound product mix by the IT organisations makes it essential that the multi-faceted services included in the package are commensurate with the changing needs of the IT users. In the Figure 23.2, we find the product mix of the IT services.

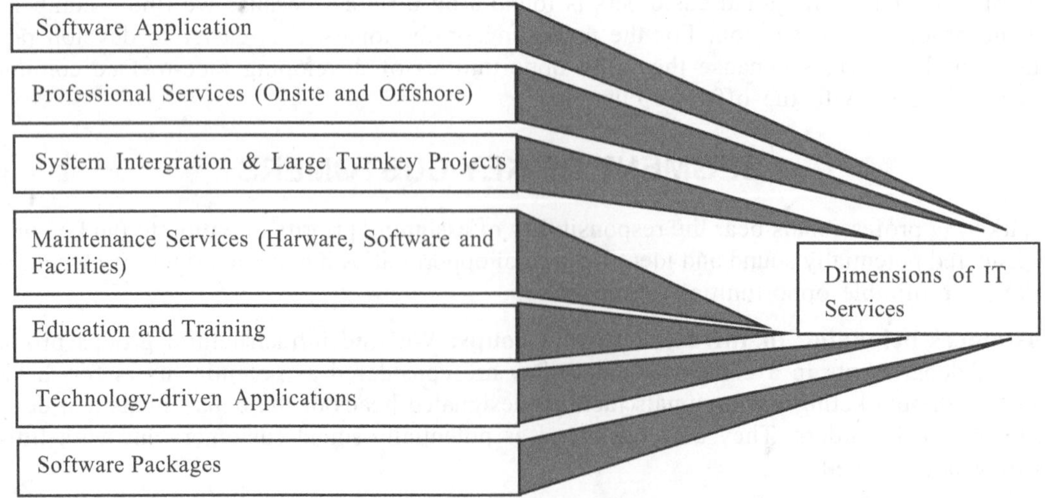

Fig. 23.2: Product Mix for IT Services.

1. Software Applications: Applications of software for a particular organisation is an important constituent of the product mix. This requires expertise related to both the areas. The IT professionals in consultation with the experts develop software for that organisation which helps them in increasing the efficiency and accelerating the productivity. It is pertinent to mention that IT professionals in consultation with the experts of banking, financial services, mining, transportation, steel, power and other sectors have developed software for them which is found in tune with their requirements. Almost all the sectors who have used IT services are found immensely benefited. Particularly the power sector is found an important beneficiary where generation and transmission of power was previously done manually and the sector was facing the problem of inefficiency. But the application of software commensurate with their requirements changed the scenario. The most important thing in this submix of marketing is to develop a contact with the experts of the concerned organisation and only then thinking about the development of software.

2. Professional Services: Another constituent of product mix focuses our attention on the professional services. This draws our attention on offering a number of services related to skill and expertise either at overseas sites or offshore. In the overseas locations, it is very much difficult to get the experts and even if we find them to be made available by the offshore suppliers, it is found to be very costly. The marketing professionals need to develop their awareness of the changing requirements of users and only then to make available to them the professionals or experts so that they get the world-class experts at the prices much below the levels of their expectations. We find subcontracting the process adopted in the very context. If your clients are satisfied with the quality of experts which you have made available to them, the process of repeat uses will keep on moving.

3. Systems Integration: This submix of the product mix throws light on the system integration. In a specialised segment of the industry, we find a number of items to be integrated as turnkey solutions. The IT users make use of multiple database choices, multiple applications, software vendors, multiple database choices, multiple applications and this necessitates services of experts for making the right choice. In this context, it is essential that the professionals have an in-depth knowledge of the capabilities of IT organisations. This necessitates "One Stop Shop" approach where the users are also made available other services. The professionals need to provide to the users the integrated services so that they are in a position to receive from them maintenance facilities and warranty facilities even after long period of establishment. This helps them in establishing the credibility of the IT organisations. Thus, the turnkey solutions provide to the users a good number of services.

4. Maintenance Services: We find IT services considerably resting on the maintenance service provided by the IT organisations. For the maintenance of existing hardware and software, the users require maintenance facilities. We also find subcontracting provisions for providing maintenance services to the IT users. It is right to mention that IT users find it difficult to have their own wing for maintenance and therefore the large-sized users have been seen making subcontracts for this purpose. They get a package of services related to hardware, software and communications. This helps users in saving time and money. The professionals, thus, while sensitising and persuading need to throw light on the maintenance facilities provided to the users as a package of services.

5. Education and Training: It is not only sufficient that we find IT organisations developing new generations of IT and not thinking about the professionals who are potentially sound to help the users in making use of them. It is in this context that we find education and training facilities becoming an important constituent of the IT product mix. The knowledge related to hardware, operating system or application are some of the basics required even for marketing purposes. The IT organisations also develop their special wing for educating and trading the professionals. We find a number of institutions for this purpose. The professional services and system integration are the important dimensions necessitating due attention while imparting education and training facilities.

6. Techno-driven Applications: Particularly when we talk about the software packages, the market is found to be much more competitive. In addition, we find much more frequent changes in the software packages. The process of technological sophistication is found gaining a rapid momentum in the IT sector. This makes it essential that IT organisations confine themselves to niche markets and concentrate on some of the basic technologies. It is not possible for all the IT organisations to develop their Research and Development wing because it is a capital-intensive project and requires much more time for the development of a new technology. Hence, a majority of the IT organisations prefer to concentrate on the niche markets with the support of basic technologies.

7. Software Package: We find a number of software packages such as Dbase, Lotus and Microsoft Windows. The intensity of competition is found very high in the software segment and therefore the marketing professionals need to develop a package having multi-dimensional applications. Keeping in view the frequency of change in the software, the marketing professionals need much more precautions and innovative strategic decisions.

Formulation of a product mix in the IT sector makes it essential that the IT organisations get a feedback from the marketing professionals specially to develop their awareness of the changing needs and requirements of IT users. In the domestic markets, the task is not so easier but in the offshore markets, it is a bit difficult. This makes it essential that the IT professionals think over developing offshore information systems. This will help bringing down the costs, improving the quality and a 24-hour development cycle by leverspringing difference in time zones. Further, it is also essential that professionals develop their awareness of cultural and geographical diversity. This makes a strong advocacy in favour of developing offshore teams represented by a member on-site bearing the responsibility of playing a liaison role. Studying and understanding the changing needs and requirements of IT users would be the functional responsibility of the representative member. They would be successful in gauging the levels of expectations of IT users and based on their feedback, the IT organisations would find it easier to develop a package in tune with the desired levels of expectations of users. The offshore developers need a distinct approach which may be different to the domestic requirements of IT users.

Thus, the formulation of a sound product mix is found essential because development of other marketing inputs would be in the face of product mix developed. It is very natural that while developing packages, the professionals would take into consideration the changing requirements of niche markets and professionalised efforts would be made to satisfy them.

Promotion Mix

The IT organisations also need to promote their services but in a different way. Keeping in view the frequency of change and cultural and regional variations, the marketers need to promote the services with professional touch and creative efforts. Sensitising the users and niche markets in an effective way cannot be possible unless the marketers show their world-class professional excellence. On account of technical services, the marketers face a number of problems while sensitising and persuading the users. The marketing professionals find a communication gap while influencing the IT users. Marketing software and particularly promoting software and using the same are the two different areas where the marketers find it difficult to influence due to communication gap. The persuasion process makes it essential that the marketers are in a position to explain to the users the cost-benefit components. It is in this context that the components of promotion are found less effective in the IT services. The most effective component that we find for promoting IT services is word-of-mouth promotion. The satisfied group of users is the best promoter of IT service. This makes it essential that IT organisations have been delivering quality services to the users. Further, it is also significant that marketers have consistently been taking care of the users for the long time. The quality services also include in its purview quality maintenance services. Of course, we find IT organisations making use of the different components of promotion but we do not find these measures becoming cost-effective. Hence, while promoting the IT services, the marketing professionals need to rationalise the uses of different components of promotion in such a way that users are informed but the uses of a particular service needs face-to-face communication. This process makes it essential that the marketers are well aware of the uses of IT services. The professionals may also think in favour of personal selling as a component for promoting the IT service. But in this context, it is essential that people engaged for activating personal communications have an in-depth knowledge of product to be marketed. This again focuses our attention on bridging the communication gap for effective promotion of IT services. We cannot negate that bridging the communication gap becomes difficult when we find two heterogeneous groups of individuals. Such a communication gap is found not only at national and regional levels but also at organisational and professional levels. In the process of bridging the gap, the co-ordinator onsite plays an important role in maintaining relationship between the two parties provided he is in a position to comprehend and communicate effectively without any interruption. If the clients fail in communicating their needs and expectations, the co-ordinator on site makes a clarification Managing expectations through co-ordination helps effective communication for promoting the IT business.[5]

Thus, the IT organisations for promoting the services need to strengthen the communication channel where marketing professionals and coordinators activate personal selling and become successful in convincing the clients. A majority of the IT organisations feel that their faulty communication process proves to be a barrier in promoting the business, particularly in the offshore dealings.

Price Mix

In the formulation of marketing mix, the pricing decisions are found complicated due to mounting intensity of competition. The IT organisations need to minimise their costs. We cannot negate that they have tapped the benefits of an increase in the demand side but now when the supply side is also found expanding fast, it is pertinent that they define the limits for profits by the IT sector which earlier or even till date is found abnormally high. The users in general are so much benefited with the services of IT that they do not hesitate while paying even the high price. The general pricing theory is found based on demand and supply mechanism and the IT providers have been found practising the same. Now, the intensity of competition is found mounting due to the entry of a large number of providers in the IT sector. This necessitates adopting a rational price structure to use it as a motivational tool both in the domestic and global markets.

The changing business environment and mounting economic recession have been throwing numerous challenges and threats before the IT sector. We agree with this viewpoint that the establishment expenses in the IT sector are found very high. The abnormally high pay and packages for the IT people unlike other sectors is also an important reason for high price structure. Of course, they need to spend a lot on the channel of distribution and it is their compulsion but we do not find justifications for making this sector or perceiving this sector as the superstructure. The IT organisations are getting it difficult to follow the strategy they have practised earlier and on the other hand, they are also setting it much more difficult to bring down their establishment expenses either by retrenchment or by pay cut. In a true sense, once when we follow the high structure, it becomes difficult to bring down. They brought a big jump in the financial and non-financial incentives of their employees and now they have been experiencing an invasion on their financial health.

The marketing professionals while adopting the pricing strategy are found preferring a differential pricing strategy in the face of scale of demand and frequency of using the services. Besides, they also keep into consideration the structure of their rivals and try to make it competitive. It is also right to mention that the IT sector will earn handsome profits even if the price structure is made abnormally low. But they have to strengthen their perception that they may be an important sector not a superstructure. The customers or users in almost all the segments will expand even in the days and years to come and therefore, they have a profitable niche markets. The only need to do is to study and understand the potential users and to bridge the communication gap. Transforming the actual users into habitual users and expanding the markets by minimising the price structure will help IT sector in thriving even in an age of economic recession moving towards depression. The marketing professionals need to use pricing as a motivational tool as and when the circumstances necessitate so. Being an important submix of the marketing mix, they need to make use of world-class professional excellence which will make them potentially and financially sound.

Place Mix

The multi-faceted IT services reach to the ultimate users through different channels. Due to complexity in the nature and types of multi-level service, we find involvement of representatives, salespeople, advisors and coordinators for making available the services to the ultimate users. It is well-known that users may be individual and institutional and domestic and offshore. The cultural variations, regional variations and language constraints stand as an obstacle specially while marketing the IT services across the national boundaries. A number of IT organisations are found involved in the process of generating the multi-dimensional services. The IT organisations are also found formulating a package and channelising the same to their users with the help of routes they find convenient. The domestic as well as the MNCs are found involved in the process. The process of delivering the IT services becomes complicated also due to a large product range such as educational games targeted towards children, business tools used by office executives and offices, executive tools used increasingly for those who need to manage time and small amounts of information and data, very large complex energy and environmental systems helping in monitoring of transmission of energy and using a census for managing the environmental and feeding data into computers, areas of artificial intelligence, areas of robots, financial and banking implications, stock markets, educational institutions and what not. It is due to a long range of product that we find IT organisations, distribution channels and even users experiencing a number of problems.

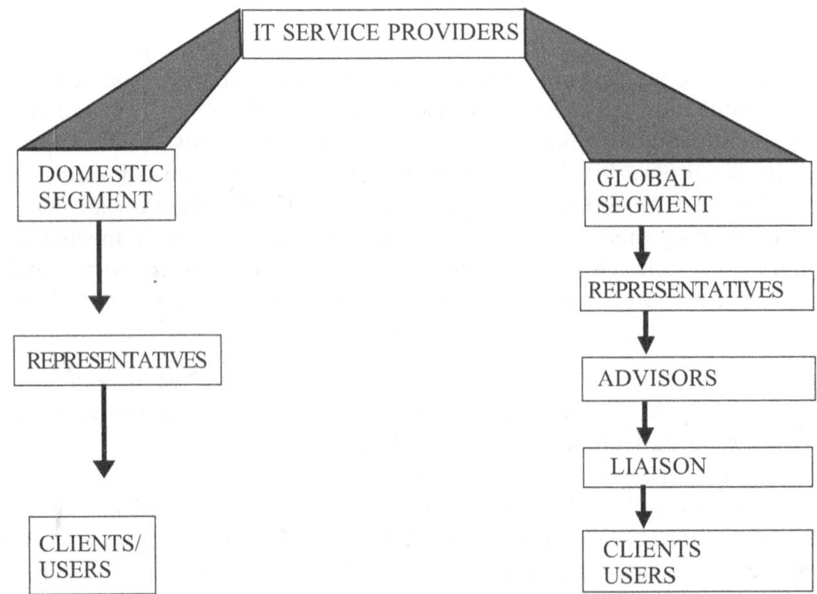

Fig. 23.3: Distribution Channel for IT Services

Of course, the IT organisations may be successful in minimising the costs by minimising or contracting the distribution channels but the nature and types of services *vis-à-vis* the users make their task of reducing the channel much more complicated. The intensity of competition is found high and therefore, the IT organisations and their representatives have no option but to minimise the time gap in the distribution process and reaching to the users the earliest possible. If this is their priority, it is very natural that the cost of distribution is found high and this is to affect the total costs of services. However, the marketing professionals should make efforts to minimise the distribution costs to the extent it is possible. The marketers, no doubt, find it difficult to minimise the distribution cost when they market across the national boundaries because in that case they need to take the help of coordinators and communicators at different stages, specially to minimise the language constraints. We cannot negate that even today we find a good number of users of IT services not familiar with the technology supplied and their outstanding features. The users and decision-makers both of them find the IT services of complicated nature and this focuses our attention on sensitising the masses and developing mass awareness to make the niche markets aware of the uses and complexities of IT services. This in a very natural way will require long distribution channel and will involve high distribution costs.

The IT organisations or IT service providers have been facing multi-faceted challenges in an age of globalisation. On the one hand, they face competition due to cost consideration while on the other hand, they also lag behind due to time element. For bridging the communication gap, they need the services of co-ordinators and communicators or even online liaison services and this is also to increase the cost of distribution. We cannot negate that the gap between costs incurred and prices charged is found much high but the mounting intensity of competition makes it essential that the IT organisations make sincere honest efforts to adopt a rational price structure. Initially, the IT organisations had been working and servicing the markets where the intensity of competition was low but now their tasks are likely to be much difficult. So far as the distribution costs are concerned, they have no option but there are a number of areas where they can bring down the establishment expenses.

We cannot negate that IT sector witnessing a galloping increase during the yester decades, has been facing multi-faceted problems due to worldwide economic depression and the only way to protect and survive is to make the price structure much more competitive. And this one also gravitates our attention on the costs of distribution. The marketing professionals may be successful in minimising the distribution costs specially in the domestic markets where it is much more easier to bridge the communication gap as the teams do not have to adhere to time differences and face-to-face interactions are found convenient due to cultural proximity.

The marketing professionals bearing the responsibility of formulating a sound marketing mix need to make sound managerial decisions for distribution or channelisation of services to the ultimate users and they need to explore avenues that how and in what way they can help a contraction in the process of distribution. When they market across the countries, a stage of helplessness is found due to regional, cultural and language barriers but in the domestic markets, they have avenues and sincere and honest efforts are to be made by them to minimise the duration and costs. This will help the IT sector in excelling competition.

Process

The processing of IT services from the IT organisations to the IT users or clients are found in a different way. For developing software for a particular organisation, it is essential that representatives, communicators, advisors or liaison officers develop their awareness of the needs and requirements of the concerned organisation for a particular purpose. The generation or creation of services are then processed by the concerned experts with the support of their team and other staff. In the process, we find involvement of IT and the computer professionals. When the services as desired by the clients or users are ready, the concerned representatives or channels meant for marketing deliver the same to them. Hence, we find processing very specific and therefore the marketing professionals get an opportunity to generate the services in tune with the changing needs and requirements of users. So far as the services related to maintenance are concerned, the liaison officers or communicators or advisors or the representatives attempt to get a feedback and based on their complaints and grievances redress them. The marketing professionals need to make it sure that promised quality of services are made available to the users or clients on time. In the context of education and training services, the concerned educational institutions need to ensure that whatsoever the educational aid and training facilities are imparted to the potential professionals would serve the larger interests of the concerned organisations. The maintenance and operation services considerably rest on the quality of services made available by the educational institutions. In the context of IT services, the processing found in different stages rest on the quality of people and computers. The professionals need to assure that possibilities of delay and distortion are regulated.

Physical Evidence and Attractions

In this submix of the marketing mix, we find our focus on the servicescapes. The physical facilities are found instrumental in creating a conducive service ambience. The two centres for the creation of servicescapes are the distribution centre where the representatives, dealers and salespeople are found involved in selling and display and the centres where we find actual creation of services. The IT organisations and their representatives play a very significant role in the creation of a positive impression through displays. The interiors and exteriors need special attention in both the cases. The ambience where we find quality of display and transmission or presentation of world-class may help IT organisations in projecting a positive image. The individual segment gets an opportunity to view the service ambience and the people managing the same may explain to them outstanding properties based on cost-benefit analysis. Since they get an opportunity of face-to-face communication, the task of influencing and convincing them is found easier. The focal point is creation of impression and for that, tangibilisation may be effective. Such a tangibilisation of physical facilities is also for the institutions imparting educational aid and training facilities related to the IT services. Here, the furnishing, lighting, ventilation, display of new generation of technology and parking may be effective in the persuasion process. The working professionals need to look smart and wear neat and clean dresses.

People Mix for IT Services

The IT sector emerging as a big service industry requires the services of a number of people with specialised knowledge of the related areas. The sector during the yesteryears has gained popularity and today, we find a craze for developing expertise in this area. Developing world-class knowledge in the field of hardware and software and maintenance is found an important consideration for the people serving this sector. A number of world class institutions even in the Indian context are found engaged in imparting educational and training facilities to the students. Increasing temptation and fascination for this sector is also due to this fact that IT sector, of late, has emerged as the most paying sector of the job markets. With the increasing process of technological sophistication, we find fewer gaps between two generations of IT and this has made it essential that the educational institutions engaged in the process of developing people keep on moving the process of enriching their knowledge bank, brushing up their potentials and inculcating the faculties which they lack. In a majority of the cases, we find IT professionals lacking high level of communication excellence and ethical and cultural properties turning them as a machine for minting the money. They are also not sound even in terms of civic and aesthetic sense and we also find cases when they lack etiquette. They have intelligence and their energy concentrate on earning more and spending more.

We are well aware of the fact that IT services considerably depend on channelisation of communication. At the different stages, the marketing professionals need to develop their rapport with the potential clients. They are supposed to explain to them the outstanding properties of services and their applications based on cost-benefit analysis. The coordinators and advisors or even representatives helping marketing professionals in persuading and satisfying the clients need communication excellence. Particularly when we find offshore services, the marketing professionals need to know about the basics of IT, benefits of its application and knowledge of regional language or to take the support of liaison office on the site. They need these properties in addition to the excellence in the field of marketing and therefore the IT organisations while recruiting marketing people need to make it sure that marketing professionals to be recruited have all the properties they need.

In view of the above-mentioned facts, it is right to say that the IT sector needs people having multi-dimensional properties. Since the market is becoming much more competitive, it is significant that they create and identify the opportunities and make use of their professional excellence while turning the potential clients into habitual clients. The repeat orders need due attention of professionals expected to gauge the changing levels of expectations of niche markets. Sensitisation and persuasion cannot be possible if the marketing professionals lack world-class excellence. The institutions imparting educational aids and training facilities need to assign due weightage to the multi-dimensional faculties required for quality marketing professionals.

IT MARKETING IN INDIAN PERSPECTIVE

The contours of development underwent radical changes specially during 1980s, 1990s and first decade of 21st century when we talk about development scenario in the Indian perspective. The pace and race of economic transformation gained a rapid momentum when the process of globalisation started benefiting the national economy of India in different ways. Inventions and innovations started minimising the gap between the two generations of technology. It was against this backdrop that we focus on the multi-dimensional development in the field of IT sector. We cannot negate that this sector of the economy virtually revolutionised the process of development. All the three sectors such as primary, secondary and tertiary made use of the IT services in different ways which engineered a sound foundation for the development of national economy of India.

During yesteryears, the IT sector has significantly contributed to the generation of foreign exchange reserves. A service industry exporting the software and ITES upto US$ 25 billion and expected to grow at a faster rate even more than 32 per cent in US dollar terms has been creating profitable opportunities for IT organisations both at domestic and global levels.[6] We can easily imagine the contributions of IT sector to the job markets as the total number of IT and ITES-BPO professionals employed in India is nearing about 15,00,000 which in the coming years is expected to grow faster.[7] The operational efficiency of almost all the sectors making use of IT services has been found making a galloping increase.

In view of the expanding scale of demand side, it is natural that a number of IT organisations will make efforts to increase the supply side. In a sector when we find processes of quantitative and qualitative transformation gaining a rapid momentum, it is pertinent that the IT organisations assign a transcendental priority to the marketing of services both at national and global levels. In the domestic markets, the marketing professionals find it easier to inform sense, sensitise, persuade and transform the niche markets to make repeat orders but their task becomes too much difficult in the global markets. They face numerous problems while developing contact and strengthening rapport due to variations in time zones, cultural patterns and language constraints. Bridging the communication gap is considered to be the most vital responsibility of marketing professionals specially in the global markets where a good number of opportunities remain partially or even fully untapped. We also find cases when the marketing professionals fail in explaining the uses and benefits of IT services.

The emerging trends make it essential that the marketing professionals make efforts to capitalise on the opportunities. Identifying the customers in a right fashion is considered essential for satisfying them. They are supposed to make an in-depth study of the changing levels of expectations and to make it sure that their professionalised efforts help in fulfilling the same so that they are found satisfied. They need to take the support of marketing information system for that purpose. The IT organisations need a feedback from the marketing professionals which they can get from the customers.They need to take support of coordinators, communicators, advisors and liaison officers on site for understanding the real problems of clients or users. Based on national and international levels, they have to divide the markets into different groups and subgroups. They need special attention on global markets. A package of services in tune with the changing needs and requirements of customers and in the face of the offering of rivals may be instrumental in getting the repeat orders. It is not to be forgotten that while promoting the services, the IT organisations need special efforts because advertisement is not likely to be much more effective. Making use of personal selling is found important and in this context, the marketers need to make use of representatives or advisors having communication excellence to satisfy the clients or users. They need face-to-face communication for satisfying the clients. A number of questions or queries may be raised and the communicators failing the knowledge of technology would find it difficult to convince. The marketing professionals need to depute people in the face of the cultural, regional and professional background. In the offshore dealings, they need special precautions. We also find telemarketers used as a tool of promotion in the IT services but this is just transmission of information not persuasion. The most effective tool is word-of-mouth promotion which depends on the quality of services and in addition, the experiences of clients regarding the services made available to them also help their decision-making process. Of course, a number of components are used for promoting the IT services but the marketers should not forget that developing personal rapport and convincing the clients have an edge over others. So far as the cost economy is concerned, the marketers should make the promotional measures proactive *vis-à-vis* cost-effective.

The pricing decisions are to be made in the face of clients and the intensity of competition in the markets. The marketing professionals are free to make use of pricing as a motivational tool. In the context of channelisation of services, there are a number of stages and it is significant that the marketers minimise the time gap *vis-à-vis* the cost on distribution. The most significant submix of the marketing mix for the IT services marketing is availability of people. There are a number of institutions and even IT organisations impart educational aids and training facilities. The most important consideration is developing world-class professionals both for the technical and marketing streams. In addition to other properties, the people serving the IT need communication excellence of world-class so that they are successful in sensitising and persuading the clients or users. Our focus here is on bridging the communication gap in the face of cultural, time and regional or geographical constraints.

Thus, the marketers need to formulate a sound marketing mix for IT services and for that, they have to develop a sound information system. In view of the recent emerging trends in the national and global economies, they have to redesign their strategic decisions particularly for marketing purposes. The clients or users in general are becoming much more sensitive to price and therefore the IT organisations need to initiate multi-faceted efforts to bring cost economy.

We find global economy much more positive for the Indian IT sector. This makes it essential that the marketing professionals innovate their strategic decisions. They need to take support of Offshore Information System which would help them in getting the benefits of lower costs, improved quality and round-the-clock development cycle. Offshore sourcing would help them in different ways. The professionals need to assign due weightage to effective time management. The co-ordinators may conduct teleconferencing when they have an idea of time zones. Efforts are to be made for gaining cost-quality competitive advantage. By leveraging lower labour rates and currency exchange rates with respect to the US dollar, the IT costs may be reduced. The communication channels also need sound management for bridging the communication gap found between the two heterogeneous groups of individuals. Management of client expectations is also found significant which will be possible with the help of co-ordinators.

We find tremendous opportunities both in onshore and offshore markets. Capitalising on the opportunities requires professional excellence. The marketers need to study and understand the changing needs and levels of expectations of clients or users. It is not only significant that we transform the potential customers into actual customers. It is much more impact generating that we get increased number of repeat orders. This focuses our attention on transforming the actual customers into habitual customers. This is not to be possible unless we make sincere and honest efforts to satisfy them.

With the new generation of IT, we find the levels of expectations of customers increasing very fast. The professionals need to know the changing levels and to innovate marketing strategy. Though the world-wide economic depression has been found showing red, green and amber signals to the IT industry, however, the negative trends would witness reversal specially in the Indian perspective. We have a long range of product and a large range of customers. Our services are cost-effective and our efforts in past have been found proactive. The IT organisations need to assign an overriding priority to cost economy. In addition to other expenses, they also need to curtail the establishment expenses. It is not proper that our levels of profits are abnormally disproportionate to the costs. We also need to be innovative and for that, our research and development activities need due focus. Defining and redefining quality need to be our motto. We would be successful where our rivals have failed.

SUMMARY

In the chapter, you have gone through different dimensions of marketing IT services. After going through this chapter, be sure that the following facts are well versed:

IT – A Conceptual Framework: It is the convergence of computer, information intelligence, communication, internet and technical administration.

IT Marketing – A Conceptual Framework: IT marketing is a managerial process where marketers need world-class professional excellence. It is a formal approach to conceptualise marketing principles in the IT services.

Justifications for Practising Marketing in IT Services: The application of marketing principles in the IT services is justified because it is helpful in identifying the opportunities, innovating the services, sensitising the users, helpful in getting the repeat orders, effective in offshore marketing, satisfying the users and bridging the communication gap for understanding the changing level of expectations of users.

Emergence of IT as a Services Industry: Of late, IT has emerged as a big services industry. The beginning of IT sector was for accounting and technical environment and now we find its transformation as a totally service-oriented industry.

Behavioural Profile of Users of IT Services: With the advancements in the field of IT, we find the levels of expectations of clients or users increasing very fast. They now expect sophisticated services from the providers and the marketing professionals are supposed to understand and satisfy them.

Information System for IT Services: For studying and understanding the diverse group of users, the marketing professional need to take support of information system. For the global markets, they need to develop the Offshore Information System which helps them in getting the requirements of users *vis-a-vis* their feedback.

Market Segmentation for IT Users: In the IT segments, we find a combination of different groups of users which may be individual and institutional. They may be domestic and even global. They are fat and thin or they are large-sized or small-sized.

Marketing Mix of IT Services: The marketing professionals bear the responsibility of formulating a sound marketing mix. Here, we find application of five submixes in the marketing mix.

Product Mix: The different types of services included in the product mix are software application, professional services, system integration, maintenance services, education and training, technology-driven application and software packages. The marketing professionals formulate a package in tune with the changing requirements of clients.

Promotion Mix: For the IT services, we find personal selling, telemarketing and word-of-mouth promotion very much effective in promoting the services. The personal selling based on face-to-face communication help in convincing and satisfying the users.

Price Mix: In the marketing of IT services, the pricing considerations become significant because the market is becoming much more competitive. The professionals need to adopt differential pricing strategy depending upon the nature and types of users. The IT organisations need to use pricing as a motivational tool.

Place Mix: In the placement or distribution of IT services, we find two different conditions in the domestic and offshore markets. In the domestic markets, we find short channel because the representatives succeed in making face-to-face communication with the users but in the offshore markets, we find representatives, communicators, advisors, liaison officer on site and through which the services reach to the IT users.

People Mix: A number of people coming from different streams take part in the IT services. It is significant that marketing people serving the IT sector also develop their expertise in the field of IT so that they are in a position to convince and satisfy the users.

IT Marketing in Indian Perspective: In the Indian context, we find IT emerging as a big service industry. We have been successful in earning the foreign exchange and in addition also in employing a large number of people in the IT sector. Thus, our contributions to job markets and foreign exchange reserves have helped development of this industry in the Indian perspective. Almost all sectors of the economy are found using the services and increasing their operational efficiency. It has played a very effective role in accelerating the productivity and profitability. Our services have got a positive response not only in domestic but even in the global markets. Of course, the worldwide economic depression has been adversely affecting this sector but the Indian IT organisations are potentially sound to face the challenges and threats both at domestic and global levels.

KEY TERMS

Knowledge Technology	IBM
Intuition	Desktop
Five Senses	Database
Concoction	Microprocessor
Inquisitiveness	Minicomputer
Computer	Macrocomputer
Outsourcing	Fast Track
Software	Aerospace
Hardware	Rapport
Desktop	Leverspringing
Chip	Telemarketing
Animation	Personal Selling
Internet	Offshore
Video	IT
Empathy	ITES
Architecture	BPO
Heterogenous	ICL
One Stop Shop	Turnkey
Overseas	KPO
Liaison	Lotus
Windows	Microsoft

Review Questions

1. What do you mean by IT? Do you find it emerging as a service industry? Defend your arguments.
2. What do you mean by IT Marketing? Justify application of marketing in the IT services.
3. Focus on the relevance of studying behavioural profile of IT users.
4. What do you mean by Market Segmentation? Segment IT markets.
5. Do you find Information system essential for IT marketing? Present arguments in favour of you opinion.
6. Focus on the marketing mix for IT services.
7. Write a note on the Product Mix for IT services.
8. Who are considered to be key customers of IT services? Explain.
9. Write a note on the IT Marketing in Indian perspective.

Application Exercises

1. Formulate a marketing mix for IT services in the Indian perspective.
2. Do you find IT a service industry? Give justification for your answer.
3. You have been acting as a marketing professional in a reputed IT organisation. Suggest the measures you will adopt for developing contact with the offshore users.
4. Design a promotion programme for IT industry.

5. Being a marketing professional, how you would form a team of communicators and advisors helping you in understanding the offshore customers.
6. Do you find pricing strategy in IT to be instrumental in getting offshore business? Explain your opinion as a marketing professional.
7. Identify suitable market segments for IT services in the Indian perspective.
8. We find IT industry facing numerous challenges on account of worldwide economic depression. Suggest marketing strategy to help them in surviving and thriving.

Endnotes

1. S. Banerjee, Manish Agrawal and H.R. Rao, Issues in IT-Offshore Outsourcing Coordination, *Journal* of *Marketing and Communication*, Jan-April, 2006, pp. 59-68.
2. Purna Pareek: Information Technology, *Financial Planning,* July-September, 2008, pp. 41-42.
3. Rajiv Kishore, H.R. Rao, Kichan Nam, S. Rajgopalan and Abhijit Choudhary, A *Relationship Perspective on IT Outsourcing; Communication of the ACM,* Vol. 46, 2003, pp. 86-92.
4. S. Banerjee, M. Agrawal and H.R. Rao; The Logistics of Going Offshore, *FS Outsourcing;* Vol. I, 2004, pp. 56-61.
5. L. Greenemeier, ABCs of Outsourcing Success, *Information Week*, 2001.
6. Manorama Year Book, 2008.
7. India, 2008.

ELECTRICITY MARKETING

Indian energy scenario is dominated by the feelings of discomfort and despair regarding the abysmally poor supply of power in most parts of the country. The pessimism is found growing amongst the different segments of users. The conceptualisation of marketing will make an assault on the pessimism and will help in increasing the number of satisfied group of users.

Chapter Objectives

Introduction – Electricity Marketing: A Conceptual Framework – Rational Behind Practicing Marketing – Behavioural Profile of Users of Electricity Services – Market Segmentation for Electricity Users – Managing Information for Marketing Services – Marketing Mix for Electricity Organisations – Product Mix – Promotion Mix – Price Mix – Place Mix – Process – Physical Evidence and Attractions – People — Electricity Marketing in Indian Perspective – Summary – Key Terms – Review Questions – Application Exercises – Endnotes.

Learning Objectives

This chapter of the book aims at studying the different dimensions of electricity marketing. The motive of conceptualising marketing is to improve the supply position and further to formulate a marketing mix helping in satisfying the users. The professionals while practising marketing need to manage expectations of electricity users and for that, they need to develop their awareness of the different segments of users. The application of marketing is also with the motto of improving the financial health of electricity organisations.

INTRODUCTION

The very existence of techniculture rests on energy. We cannot negate that energy is an essential input for energising the technology of new generation which has played a decisive role in accelerating the pace of economic transformation. The government policy makers bear the responsibility of making available to the national economy the supporting infrastructural facilities but it is painful to mention that a majority of the states in the country have been tasting the bitterness of energy imbalance. What to talk of the industrial or organisational requirements when we find even our domestic requirements hanging in balance. Energy, of late, is found to be the basic element of human activity. There are a number of sources to generate energy but our dependence on a particular source is considered to be an important reason for such an imbalance in the demand and supply position. The Union as well as the State Governments need a transcendental priority to resolve the energy problem. The public as well as the private sectors need professionalised efforts to make an assault on the aggravating problems of energy There are different sourcces for generation of energy but we have concentrated on coal and petroleum and have not made sincere efforts to tap the non-traditional sources available in different forms.

Energy is the basic element of human activity and an indispensable input to socio-economic transformation. It is against this background that the policy planners as well as the power experts have been found exploring avenues and advocating for exploiting different sources to generate electricity which caters to our changing socio-economic requirements. There are different organisations to generate and distribute electricity. They need to use conventional as well as the non-conventional sources to fulfil the increasing individual and institutional requirements. Presently, we find a big gap between demand and supply position. It is amazing that a number of organisations engaged in the process of generation, distribution and marketing are struggling for their survival. We cannot negate that a majority of the problems are due to managerial deficiency. Professionalism is yet to get due weightage in the managerial process. The organisations generate financial losses and the users continue to remain dissatisfied. This provides an opportunity to the informal sector which substantially contributes to the problem of environmental pollution. The emerging trends make it essential that the electricity generation process gets due care of policy makers. An optimal mix of conventional and non-conventional sources would improve the supply position.

The electricity organisations, specially managed by the public sector, have been found facing a number of problems. The conceptualisation of modern marketing principles would initiate the process of qualitative improvements. On the one hand, it will improve the supply position while on the other hand would also help the organisations in improving the financial health.

The changing lifestyles and expanding development activities have been found increasing the demand side but due to non-optimal generation, mismanaged transmission and managerially deficient distribution, we find supply side very poor. The problem of imbalance aggravates further when we find a majority of the users not aware of the problem of misuse of energy that becomes instrumental in contracting the supply side. The different sources of generation such as coal, petroleum, natural gas, biogas are found facing the problem of non-optimal utilisation. The current energy scenario and outlook in the coming future is clouded by concerns related to the multi-dimensional problems and only a few of them are mentioned here.

It is pertinent to mention that we have not assigned due weightage to the non-conventional sources of energy. The importance of renewable energy was recognised in the country in the early 1970s and we have today a large number of programmes for using renewable energy. We find several renewable energy systems and devices found to be commercially viable. The Ministry of Non-conventional Energy Source is the Nodal Ministry of the Government for all matters relating to new and renewable energy systems and devices. The renewable energy programmes cover the entire gamut of technologies, including biogas plants, biomass gasifiers, solar thermal and solar photovoltaic systems, windmills, small hydro plants, energy recovery from urban, municipal and industrial wastes, geothermal energy, hydrogen energy, electric vehicles and biofuels among others. During the yesterdecades, we find a significant increase in the development of expertise by different stakeholders such as State Nodal Agencies, State Electricity Boards, NGOs and Industries in planning and implementation of renewable energy projects. However, we need to do a lot to make available renewable energy to the masses at an affordable price. This focuses our attention on sensitising the masses to the potentials of renewable energy and availability of various systems and devices to make them less dependent on fossil oils. We need to move forward step-by-step. It is high time that we start renewable energy generation, otherwise it will be too late.

The policy planners also need to assign due weightage to Rural Energy, National Biogas Programme, Integrated Rural Energy Programme, Remote Village Electrification, Village Energy Security Programme, Solar Thermal Energy Programme, Solar Photovoltaic Programme, Wind Power, Biomass Power, Biomass Gasifier Programme, Small Hydro Power may play a contributory role in fulfilling the rural requirements of energy.

Maximising our dependence on non-conventional sources and minimising our dependence on the conventional sources would be a sound strategy to resolve the problem of energy crisis. We cannot negate that it is an important decision-making area for the marketing professionals that how do they market the conventional and non-conventional sources of energy. We find customers becoming much more quality-sensitive. They want uninterrupted services even if they have to pay more. Further, the professionalised efforts will also bring a radical change in the pricing policy. At the initial stage, the government support is found essential, specially to activate the process.

The Ministry of Power is primarily responsible for the development of electrical energy in the country. The Ministry is concerned with perspective planning, policy formulation, processing of projects for investment decisions, monitoring of the implementation of power projects, training and manpower development and the administration and enactment of legislation with regard to thermal and hydro generation, transmission and distribution.

The Government has launched the Accelerated Power Development Reform Programmes (APDRP) which aims at upgradation of sub-transmission and distribution system in the country and improvement in the commercial viability of the State Electricity Boards by reducing the aggregate technical and commercial losses (AT&C) to around 15 per cent as against the 50 per cent. This will ensure reliability and quality of power supply with adequate customer satisfaction. This involves a Six-level Intervention Strategy that encompasses initiatives at National Level, State Level, Feeder Level and the Customer Level. The strategy aims at technical, commercial, financial and IT intervention, organisation and restructuring measures and incentives mechanism for cash loss reduction. The investment component and incentive component are the two important components of APDRP. The investment component aims at strengthening and upgrading the sub-transmission and distribution systems whereas the incentive component aims at reducing the losses by providing the grant.

Here, we find main focus on the marketing of electricity distribution services by the different bodies and organisations under the public and private sectors. It is right to mention that in a majority of the states, the State Electricity Boards are found in red. We cannot deny that one of the most important reasons for the poor financial health is lack of professional excellence. This makes a strong advocacy in favour of managerial proficiency and application of marketing principles. Like other service-generating organisations, the State Electricity Boards and other private organisations have to conceptualise all the seven mixes of marketing with the diverse motives. On the one hand, they have to assign due weightage to commercial consideration while on the other hand have also to protect and promote social interests.

The formulation of service mix makes it essential that the electricity organisations make use of both the sources, viz., conventional and non-conventional. They need an integrated system combining generation, transmission and distribution. The customers expect quality services on time. The needs and requirements of individual and institutional customers *vis-à-vis* the changing levels of their expectations are to be studied and professionalised efforts are to be made to fulfil them. The marketing professionals are required to satisfy both categories of customers. In addition to the commercial considerations, they are also supposed to honour the social considerations.

ELECTRICITY MARKETING: A CONCEPUAL FRAMEWORK

Before we practise marketing in the electricity services, it is essential that we know its conceptual framework. The term electricity marketing focuses our attention on application of marketing principles by the electricity generating and distributing organisations. We consider electricity marketing a managerial approach to market the electricity services. Being a managerial approach, it is based on professional excellence. The electricity marketing is a systematic approach to distribute the electricity services to the different categories of users. It is an organised effort to make possible an optimal use of the different sources of energy.[1] On the one hand, the marketing practices make possible an optimal generation on the basis of changing needs and requirements of the different sectors while on the other hand also pave avenues for a rational distribution in which we assign due weightage to the interests of different segments. Thus, we find electricity marketing a device to strike a balance between the demand and supply. We also consider electricity marketing a social process because the organisations are supposed to assign an overriding priority to the subserving of social interests by increasing the supply to the neglected and the deprived sections. Thus, we observe the following facts regarding electricity marketing:

- Electricity marketing is a managerial approach to streamline the workings of the organisations engaged in the distribution process.
- It is a systematic effort to rationalise the demand and supply position.
- It is a customer satisfaction engineering in which the concerned organisations are supposed to assign due weightage to the quality of services which keep the users satisfied.
- It is a social process in which the organisations are supposed to regulate the sources of generation not found environment friendly and in addition, it also keeps in mind the interest of neglected segments and sectors.
- It is a guideline to formulate a sound marketing mix which makes the marketing decisions proactive.

RATIONALE BEHIND ELECTRICITY MARKETING

There are a number of reasons for the application of marketing principles in the electricity organisations. Making sure generation of profits to those organisations right now generating losses is an important consideration for conceptualising marketing. The private organisations engaged in the process have been found improving their financial health by practising innovative marketing. We can't negate that application of marketing principles is found logical also due to the fact that operational expenses can be made optimal. Marketing makes the ways for operational economy which helps in accelerating the rate of productivity. Thus, we find application of marketing principles judicious since the organisations find it easier to generate profits. Most of us call marketing a customer satisfaction engineering and we can't negate that marketing practices help in identifying the level of expectations of users and attempt to fulfil the same. The application of marketing principle paves avenues for the holistic concept of management in which we find social interests getting an important place. In addition, the electricity organisations are found successful in organising the future marketing. It is right to mention that the way of application would determine the intensity of positive or negative influences.

The following facts justify the application of marketing principles in the electricity organisations.

1. Quantitative improvement in the generation capacity: It is right to mention that the application of marketing principles would make possible a quantitative improvement in the capacity of generation of the electricity generating organisations. This is supported by the acts that after practising marketing, the professionals would be required to formulate a product mix in which the changing requirements of users would be given due weightage. A fair mix of conventional and non-conventional sources would be made possible. The mix of conventional sources would be made proportionate to the business environmental conditions, such as generation from thermal stations, hydroelectric stations, nuclear stations, diesel stations and gas power plants would be made optimal. It is pertinent to mention that in India more than 60 per cent of generation we find from coal-based thermal stations. There is no doubt in it that we have rich deposits of coal but we are supposed to preserve the same for the coming generations. This makes it essential that we minimise our dependence on coal and maximise the exploitation of other sources. An optimal utilisation of different sources would increase the generation capacity.

2. An optimal distribution is possible: We can't deny the fact that an optimal distribution would be made possible because the marketing principles would make an in-depth study of the changing requirements of different segments of users. The productive and unproductive sources would be studied. The management experts feel that the application of innovative marketing would make the ways for a rational distribution. The development sectors, the welfare heads would be given an overriding priority. A misuse by the domestic sector would be regulated. The neglected segment would be given due weightage. These efforts would make possible an optimal distribution.

3. Minimising the transmission and distribution losses: It is right to mention that we have been generating less and wasting more. The marketing principles would assign due weightage to productivity which makes it essential that the wastes at different stages are regulated. If we need operational economy and cost-effectiveness, we have no option but to control the transmission and distribution losses. Of late, we find wastes both at transmission and distribution stages which have been making the entire process unproductive. We are thus closing doors for high productivity. It is hoped that the application of marketing principles would make possible cost-effectiveness which would be very much instrumental in accelerating the rate of productivity. This would benefit both —the organisations since the rate of profitability would be high and the users — because the tariff would come down.

4. Minimising the gestation period: One important thing for minimising or rationalising the price structure or the tariff structure is to minimise the gestation period. This is due to the fact that if the gestation period is maximum, we find its impact on the estimated cost. The inflationary pressure throws a direct impact on cost and we find its impact on the users. This makes it essential that the projects are taken up with short gestation period keeping in view the feasibility. This in a natural way draws our attention on the availability of funds. It is right to comment that a number of generating organisations fail in making possible time-honoured implementation mainly due to the non-availability of funds. At the same time, it is also right to mention that in the Indian perspective we find a peculiar condition. The experts delay the implementation process deliberately with the motto of promoting unfair practices. In a majority of the cases in Bihar, we find such an unpleasant development increasing the financial pressure on the exchequer and making the task difficult to the users. The experts bearing the responsibility of time-honoured and cost-effective implementation create such a condition in which the process becomes cost ineffective. They design a project showing inflated estimate, delay the process of implementation, increase the estimate again and again and thus make the entire process cost-ineffective. It is against this background that the problem of efficiency level is found moving downward. The marketing practices would be instrumental in identifying the reasons for unproductive implementation which would make ways for fixing the accountability.

5. Location of thermal stations or other generating units: It is right to mention that the marketing practices would make possible right location of thermal stations *vis-a-vis* the distribution stations. A number of factors would be taken into consideration while selecting location sites, such as accessibility, availability of supporting infrastructural facilities, safety and protection to the personnel and the assets or so. We can't deny that the professionals by formulating a sound place mix would simplify the task of transmission and distribution organisations.

6. Conservation to gain the momentum: We accept the fact that in the Indian perspective, we underestimate this dimension of generation. If we stop the wastes, if we regulate the unproductive uses; we engineer a foundation for generation. The marketing practices would inculcate awareness and would sense the users who have been found promoting the same.

7. Satisfied group of users: If we talk about the application of marketing principles, the main emphasis we find on satisfaction to the different segments of users who right now are found dissatisfied. The lifestyles are found changing our needs and requirements. We need more electricity but get less. This is found generating dissatisfaction amongst the users. We can't deny the fact that the private sector organisations have been successful in satisfying the users and the credibility for the same goes to the aggressive marketing principles. They practise marketing, they assign due weightage to quality, they shape the perception of quality by innovating services, they make the entire process cost-effective, they pave avenues for high productivity and profitability and at the same time, they also keep in their minds the changing requirements and expectations of users and make sincere efforts to fulfil them. The professionalism thus makes possible high level of satisfaction to the users.

In view of the above, it is right to mention that the electricity transmission and distribution organisations, specially managed under the public sector need to practise marketing. The organisations right now generating losses would earn profits. The organisations till now instrumental in making the process cost ineffective would make possible operational economy. The organisations till present generating a quality gap would create a balance. The organisations at present dissatisfying the users would succeed in satisfying them. These facts are a mute testimony to this proposition that we need to practise marketing and to open new vistas of development.

BEHAVIOURAL PROFILE OF USERS OF ELECTRICITY SERVICES

The electricity distribution organisations have been facing plethora of problems. Almost all categories of users, of late, are found dissatisfied. This makes it essential that either public sector or private sector organisations develop their awareness of the changing behavioural profile of domestic, institutional, industrial and rural users so that by managing their expectations, they satisfy them and become successful in serving and subserving organisational as well as the social interests. With the changing pace of globalisation, we find even private sector taking part in the transmission and distribution processes and albeit in that context we find cases of dissatisfaction amongst the users. Actually, all of them have failed in managing expectations and therefore whatsoever the efforts they make are not bringing the desired results. While conceptualising marketing, the professionals would be required to have an in-depth knowledge of the needs and requirements and the levels of expectations which in the diverse segments of users are found different. But almost all the segments of users expect uninterrupted supply and in this term, we find their behavioural profile of identical nature.

With the increasing intensity of globalisation and corporatisation, there have been galloping increase in our needs and requirements for electricity. We find a change in our lifestyles and in addition to the domestic requirements, the institutional and industrial requirements have also been found increasing very fast. The increasing craze for electronics gadgets in the Indian society has been found an important reason for an increase in the domestic demand side. The increasing uses of IT in different sectors of the economy have also aggravated the intensity of demand side. Thus, the demand side is multiplying but the supply side is found disproportionate to our requirements. This creates an imbalance and proves to be an important reason for the mounting dissatisfaction.

The above-mentioned facts make it clear that application of marketing principles is found essential, specially in the public sector where we find magnitude of dissatisfaction at an alarming stage. The study of behavioural profile would also help them in rationalising the distribution process. The students have their different expectations, the domestic wives have their different expectations, the agriculturists, industrialists and other segments also expect in a different way. Since the electricity organisations have been facing the problem of non-optimal generation, it is pertinent that they also think over the problem of time and duration of distribution.

The needs and requirements of different segments of users will increase even in the coming years. The levels of expectations are found mounting without any gap. This makes it essential that the organisations managing electricity while practising marketing make an in-depth study of the behavioural profile of users and formulate marketing mix in such a way that they feel themselves satisfied. It is different to regulate the behaviour of users and therefore the electricity organisations need multi-faceted efforts to increase generation.

MARKET SEGMENTATION FOR ELECTRICITY USERS

For making an in-depth study of the users' behavioural profile, it is imperative that the marketers segment the markets into different groups and subgroups. In the context of electricity services, we find the following segments as shown in Figure 24.1.

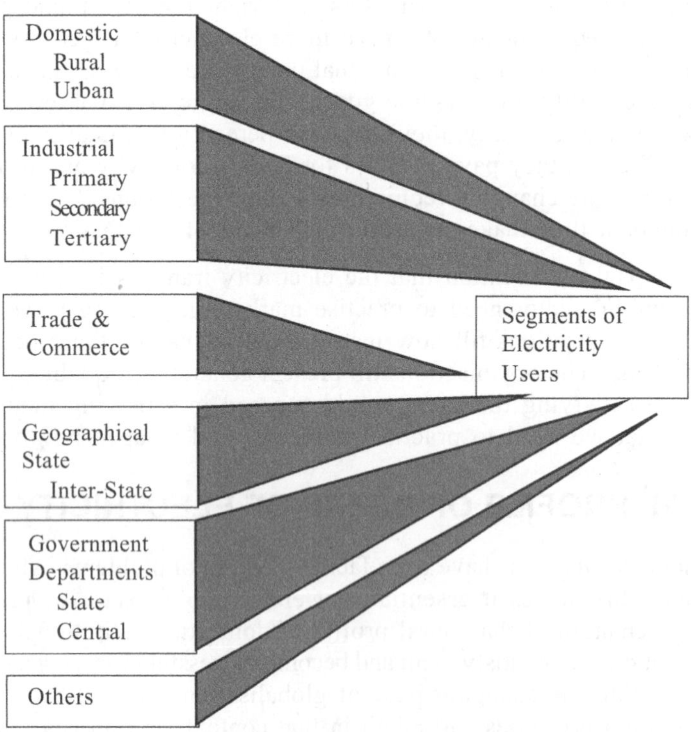

Fig. 24.1: Market Segmentation for Electricity Usersv

Domestic: The marketing professionals need to understand that their users come both from rural and urban segments. The needs and requirements and levels of expectations of urban people are found high. They are aware and sensitive. They have a different lifestyle. The rural users have limited levels of expectations.

Industrial: In this segment, we find three categories, viz., primary, secondary and tertiary. The primary sector mainly covers agricultural sector. Due to mechanised cultivation, we find the agricultural sector in need of electricity power, specially during the season. They need uninterrupted supply of power on a priority basis.

In the secondary sector, we find manufacturing industries. Due to a mix of different types of technologies used in the process of production, they need uninterrupted supply of electricity power. We consider it a segment which cannot survive without electricity power.

In the tertiary sector, we find both categories of services generating organisations, e.g., profit making and non-profit making. Due to a large-scale use of information technology, the power requirement for this sector has substantially been increased. Particularly, the non-profit organisations are considered as social institutions and they need power on a priority basis. During yesteryears, we have experienced radical transformation in the services sector which has opened new avenues for an increase in the demand-side. The marketing professionals need to make an in-depth study of the levels of their expectations.

Trade and Commerce: With the increasing pace of economic transformation, it is natural that the trade and commerce activities gain a rapid momentum both at national and international levels. In the Indian perspective, we find the trade and commerce sectors also increasing the demand side. The mounting intensity of export and import activities and a big jump in the trade and commerce has increased their power requirements.

Georaphical: In the generation of electricity power, we find some of the states having a surplus position. This has opened new doors for the demand and supply of electricity power from one state to another.

Government Departments: In both the state and central government departments, the conceptualisation of e-governance and even due to official or other requirements, we find demand of electricity power increasing very fast. The information technology is found uniting or integrating the entire country into one unit.

Others: In addition, we find increase in our requirements for electricity power even in other areas because we find all the sectors interested in increasing their operational efficiency and for that, they have no option but to make use of electricity power because other sources of power have non-optimally been used.

In view of the above, it is right to mention that the marketing professionals managing the electricity organisations need to activate multi-dimensional efforts. They need to be sincere in formulating the product mix opening doors for the tapping of non-traditional sources and to preserve the traditional sources for the coming generations. The different segments of markets make it clear that demand side has been increasing fast and even in the days to come, the trends will continue. We cannot regulate our behaviour; we cannot change our lifestyles; we cannot contract our requirements for power. And if we do not make possible a significant increase in the generation of electricity power, an imbalance will continue which will result into dissatisfaction.

Professional excellence bears the efficacy of turning the negatives into positives. The marketers bear the responsibility of rationalising the demand and supply side. On the one hand, the formulation of product mix needs an optimal mix of conventional and non-conventional sources while on the other hand, the strategic decisions requires sensitising the masses for regulating the misuse of energy. Because we find in majority of the conditions generating them losses, the marketing professionals may help them in improving their financial health.

MANAGING INFORMATION FOR MARKETING ELECTRICITY

In an age of information technology, it is very natural that like other organisations, the electricity organisations also make use of information for improving the quality of their managerial decisions. This is essential to develop a network for optimising the demand and supply side. The e-governance will also make ways for managing finance and plugging the leakages. A number of qualitative improvements can be initiated with the help of new generation of information technology. Collection and dissemination of information both for the demand and supply side is found essential for satisfying the users. The information related to the collection of outstanding bills may help them in improving the financial position. Thus, the marketing professionals need to manage information with the help of new generation of information technology which would help them in rationalising the distribution *vis-à-vis* the pricing policy.

The managment of information will simplify the task of marketing professionals while managing the expectations of users. The changing needs and requirements of different segments of users can be studied with the help of informtaion. The electricity organisations need to take support of marketing professionals who with the help of researchers may collect information related to the imbalance in demand and supply. The cases of interruption and breakdown may also be known with the help of information management. The cases of leakages and theft may be detected and the professionals may find themselves in a position to identify the individuals and institutions involved in the process.

With the help of information management, the professionals may find it easier to know about the mix of different sources of energy in the production mix. This may help them in making possible an optimal use of different sources. Of late, the electricity organisations have not been in a position to develop a network for the collection of bills in different banks. The information management may help them in developing a network making the task of depositing the bills much more easier to the users. This will also simplify the process of identifying the arrears and late deposits of bills by the users.

The services offered by both the back- and front-line staff would be of quality with the help of information management. The service delivery and service recovery would also be found easier with the help of new generation of information technology. The redressal of complaints would simplify the task of marketing professionals while satisfying the users.

The abovementioned facts make it clear that electricity organisation, particularly while distributing the services should make use of information technology which would simplify the task of marketing professionals. They will find information management effective in studying and understanding the changing needs and requirements of users. The formulation of a sound marketing mix considerably rests on the sound management of information.

THE FORMULATION OF MARKETING MIX FOR ELECTRICITY ORGANISATIONS

The formulation of marketing mix for the electricity organisations is a process that requires a fair blending of different submixes in such a way that an optimal development of marketing inputs is made possible. The marketing professionals bear the responsibility of formulating a sound mix that makes possible generation of profits to the electricity organisations and at the same time secures high level of satisfaction to the different categories of users using the services. It is in this context that we talk about the formulation of marketing mix. The different submixes are the product mix, the promotion mix, the price mix, the place mix and the people mix.

The Product Mix

The first important submix is the product mix that draws our attention on the quality of services. The organisations responsible for distributing the services need to shape the perception of quality. They are required to get the services from the organisations engaged in generating electricity. We are aware of the fact that there are different sources of generation, such as conventional and non-conventional comprising of coal, petroleum, natural gas, biogas, wind, sun, water or so.[2] The availability of resources is an important consideration which influences the process of generation. In the Indian perspective, we find adequate coal deposits and it is against this background that more than 60 per cent of power generation is by coal-based thermal stations. The next one is hydroelectric stations contributing about 35 per cent of power generation. And only 5 per cent we get from other sources. This makes it clear that till now we have made possible a non-optimal use of the available sources which if not at present of course in future would invite numerous problems. While formulating the product mix, it is important that we make possible an optimal use of different sources. The hydroelectric power has not been given due weightage till now and this makes it essential that we focus our attention on the same. The most outstanding advantage of this source is that we can generate electricity from water which is not to generate the problem of environment pollution. The generated electricity can be carried many kilometers by the connecting wires. For example, the power station built inside a mountain by the Kemano River in Western Canada sends its electric current 80 kms over the mountains to the huge aluminium works in the Kitimat Valley. Another power stations of the North of Scotland Hydro Electric Board, such as Pitlochry, Sloy and Cruachan send their electricity by wires over the greater part of Scotland. This makes it clear that expansion is possible even though the stations are located far-off. Another advantage is its cost-effectiveness. River water costs nothing since it comes from the rain draining into all the little streams that feed the river. Of course, the construction dams and power stations cost a great deal but once they are built, the electricity can be produced relatively at low cost. This makes it clear that we need to increase the contribution of hydroelectric and at the same time also require to minimise the contribution of coal-based thermal stations. We need to preserve coal for the coming generations and also to minimise the problem of pollution due to the same.

In addition, we also need to assign due weightage to the non-conventional sources and to increase the proportion of the same in the product mix. To be more specific, we need to make it popular in the rural areas where we waste cow dung, agricultural wastes or so.

In a bid to provide a simple and cheap method of energy generation, the Indian scientists have developed a number of designs of biogas plants which make use of the wide range of agricultural wastes such as animal dung, human excreta, vegetable waste, water hyacinth and produce fuel in the form of gas. Biogas is perhaps the most important component of renewable energy supplies. It is need of the hour that the electricity generating organisations change their preferences and develop a mix that establishes a balance. In Figure 24.2, we find the product mix for the electricity organisations.

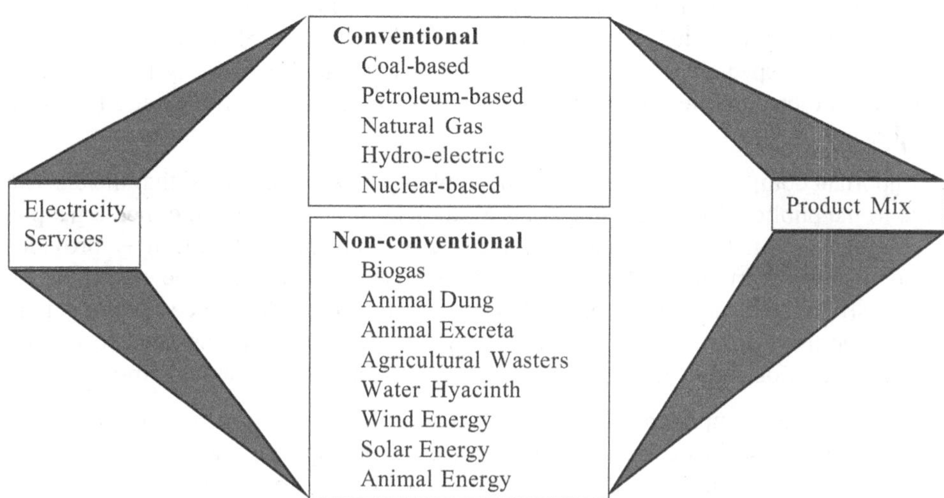

Fig. 24.2: Product Mix for Electricity Organisations

The fuel preferences need to be changed. This would minimise the pressure on the conventional sources. The solar and wind energy are found partially tapped. It is an emerging technology that enables conversion of solar energy directly into the electricity. But the system would work successfully in areas where sufficient sunny days are available ranging from 150 to 250 days in a year.[3] Particularly in the areas where more and more sunny days are available, we find waste of solar energy. Another important non-conventional source is wind energy. The efforts are needed to utilise the wind energy in the coastal areas.

The aforesaid facts make it clear that the electricity organisations need to formulate a sound product mix in which we find blending of different sources in such a way that excess pressure on a particular source is not to generate an imbalance in the resources mix. Of late, we exploit the coal deposits non-optimally which would generate resource-cum-environmental problems. We need to discourage it because we find rich potentials for the development of hydroelectric stations. Thus, a fair mix of conventional and non-conventional sources, renewable and non-renewable sources need due attention of the professionals and policy makers. The boardrooms need an attitudinal change and the policy planners are supposed to welcome and promote.

The Promotion Mix

A sound product mix would be instrumental in improving the supply position to cater to the increasing requirements of different segments of users. An uninterrupted supply in the face of increasing requirements makes it essential that the electricity organisations inform and sense the users in a right fashion so that the misuse is regulated by the users themselves. Since we don't find a competitive business condition in a majority of the areas, the promotional efforts need to focus on the rational use of electricity. It is in this context that we focus on the different components of promotion.

Advertising: We are well aware of the fact that advertising is a paid form of persuasive communication. The electricity generating and distributing organisations are supposed to play an outstanding role in the very context. Since the private organisations are found in a very limited number, the intensity of competition is by and large dismal.

Hence, the advertisng messages and themes need to focus on the conservation *vis-a-vis* a rational use of electricity. The users belonging to domestic as well as the institutional sectors have been found misusing electricity and aggravating the intensity of imbalance in the demand and supply position. In some of the areas, we find adequate supply whereas in some other areas we find frequent breakdown. Of course, the generation is non-optimal and therefore, it is pertinent that the transmission and distribution organisations while advertising make it essential that the users realise gravity of the situation and regulate their requirements. In addition, the advertising professionals are required to throw light on the way of rationalising the preferences *vis-a-vis* the implications of a non-optimal use or misuse. By making possible creativity in their messages, they can be successful in sensing them. They can use all the three media for that very purpose, such as print media, broadcast media and the telecast media. Besides, the advertising professionals also need to create awareness regarding the increased use of non-conventional sources of energy. To be more specific in the rural areas, we have tremendous opportunities for generating electricity from animal dung, agricultural wastes and solar energy. The private organisations need to promote the use of non-conventional sources. The government also requires to think in the direction of making available to them the supporting infrastructural facilities at subsidised prices. A deficit in the supply position necessitates a change in the attitudes of the advertising professionals. Since a majority of the organisations, specially under the public sector are found generating losses, it is difficult for them to spend for promotion and therefore the governmental communication organisations need to bear the responsibility of advertising the messages.

Publicity: An important component of promotion, the publicity makes it essential that the electricity organisations assign due weightage to the publicity measures and for that, they need to influence the media people. By publicising, they would be successful in regulating the misuse of electricity. The media people may provide a suitable place for news items or may also write articles promoting the rational use of electricity. The electricity organisations need to concentrate on intensifying the publicity measures since for that they don't need a budget. For nothing, they can sensitise and sense the users in a right direction. The government publications need to publicise the messages on a priority basis. We need not forget that the rational use or conservation would improve the supply position.

Sales Promotion: Another component of promotion, i.e., Sales Promotion focuses on offering of temporary incentives to the users and the sales people. In this context, it is important to mention that the private sector organisations engaged in operation need to offer innovative incentives to the users of the services so that they continue to buy their services which keeps on moving business promotion. Here, they also need to offer incentives to their own personnel for increasing transmission and optimising the operational expenses. The public sector organisations don't find this component relevant since in a majority of the cases, they are facing an imbalance in supply. Of course, they need to think in favour of incentives to the users for rationalising the demand position. The markets where we find both the public sector and the private sector organisations operational, a sense of competition may be existent and in this context, the organisations may think in favour of the innovative tools of sales promotion.

Word-of-mouth Promotion: This component of the promotion mix draws our attention on the instrumentality of hidden salesforce. If we find public and private sectors operational, it is natural that the hidden salesforce also become instrumental. This is advocacy made by the satisfied users in favour of the services of an organisation. If we find the services of private sector organisations establishing an edge over the public sector organisations, it is natural that the users would make a strong advocacy in favour of their own services as and when they interact with their friends and relatives. The messages, appeals are found here instrumental in stimulating the users or the prospects.

Personal Selling: We find the same case with the personal selling which is an important component of promotion. The communicative ability of sales people in promoting the business is found relevant to the private sector organisations. In this context, it is right to mention that personal selling would help the organisations in influencing the large-sized customers for buying the services.

Telemarketing: With sophisticated developments in the field of communication technologies, we find telemarketing occupying a place of outstanding significance in promoting the business. In the electricity services, the telemarketers can play a positive role in informing and sensing the users. The information related to the supply position, loadshedding, misuse or a rational use may be transmitted to the different categories of users. The telemarketers may be more instrumental in promoting the business of private sector organisations. Here, it is essential that they are made available sophisticated telephonic services and they have an outstanding communicative ability.

In view of the above, it is right to mention that the different components of promotion are to be used in a different way, specially in the electricity services where an imbalance in supply position and the domination of a sellers' market is making the business condition a bit different. The moment we find emergence of a buyers' market, all the components of promotion would be very much instrumental in promoting sale. Of late, the electricity organisations specially working under the public sector need to use the promotional measures for regulating or rationalising the demand position. Of course, it is also significant in the prevailing conditions and therefore the electricity organisations need to think over the problem with a new vision. They need creativity not for increasing the demand but for regulating the same. This would substantially help the organisations in improving the supply position since conservation in other form is termed to be generation.

The Price Mix

In the formulation of marketing mix, we find price mix influencing the survival and prosperity of an organisation. Like other organisations, the Electricity Organisations also charge price for the services they offer. The tariff structure of progressive nature is found based on the units of electricity consumed. Since both categories of the users, domestic and commercial use the services, we find a difference in the rate of tariff for both of them. The more you consume, the more you are supposed to pay. For the rural consumers, we find a special rate of tariff which is based on social considerations. The State Electricity Boards are found generating huge losses despite of the fact that they sell a valuable item of indispensable nature. This is mainly due to the fact that we find cases of theft of electricity consumption on a very large scale which is found promoted with the connivance of their own employees. The computation as well as the collection processes are found faulty. We can't deny the fact that the pricing decisions of the electricity organisations need due attention. It is amazing to mention that the private electricity organisations are found generating profits in the same market where the state electricity organisations generate huge losses. If we feel to bring the system on the rail, we have no option but to revamp the entire process of computing and collecting the tariff.

There are a number of sensitive issues while fixing the tariff structure. The generation and distribution costs are high, the administrative expenses are found mounting and the cases of theft are found increasing. We are aware of the fact that for having a rational tariff structure, the electricity organisations are required to regulate their costs. If the total cost is found moving upward, the tariff structure would go up. We find cases of poor maintenance of assets which aggravate the problem of pricing. In addition, the cases of theft of assets promoted by the staff make the pricing decisions critical. These emerging trends make it essential that the electricity organisations practise innovative marketing principles which would help them in many ways.

Whatever the strategies we follow, it is pertinent that some of the areas, some of the sectors, some of the segments get subsidised or concessional services. This is essential to promote rural industrialisation, regional equity and social balance. We can't think in favour of a uniform policy for pricing. The rural and urban segments, the weaker and affluent segments, the domestic and commercial segments, the small-sized and large-sized segments can't be treated equally, specially in terms of tariff structure. In this context, it is significant that the rural areas, backward regions, agricultural sector, entrepreneurs promoting villages and tiny industries are subsidised or concessional services. The subsidies offered would be adjusted by making the tariff structure progressive and adopting a high tariff structure from the commercial and affluent large-sized users. Like this, the entrepreneurs evincing interests in promoting industries in the vulnerable areas of the country would also be given concessional or subsidised services.

The aforesaid facts make it clear that the electricity organisations are supposed to make the tariff structure scientific which on the one hand would make the organisations commercially viable while on the other hand would also enrich their potentials of bearing the social costs. Such a principle of pricing is to be made effective even by the private organisations who in a majority of the cases have been found generating profits.

We can't deny the fact that the electricity organisations in general and the state electricity organisations in particular need to assign due weightage to professional excellence at different stages of their operation and management which would simplify the process of adopting a rational tariff structure.

The most important thing in the very context is to regulate the unproductive expenses. The electricity organisations are required to control the cases of theft of electricity and the assets. The computation process is to be rationalised which draws our attention on electronic metre. The organisations are required to change the system of traditional computation of units in which we find enough scope for theft. The use of technologies is to be channelised at the different stages of operation. It is amazing to mention that in the state electricity boards, except a very few, we find mismanagement at almost all the stages which makes the operational costs high. In addition, the high rate of service tax aggravates the magnitude of problem. This makes it essential that the electricity organisations regulate their operational costs by minimising the unproductive expenses. The cases of poor maintenance of assets increase the rate of depreciation *vis-a-vis* the lubrication and maintenance costs. The marketing professionals bear the responsibility of streamlining the system right now full of corrupt and unfair practices. The technical staff, the administrative staff, the white-collar and blue-collar staff; all of them are found involved in the process which has been found affecting the financial health *vis-a-vis* the quality of services. If they are surviving, this is mainly due to the fact that we find a seller's market. The moment we start promoting the private sector, they would have no option but to make a good-bye.

In view of the above, it is right to mention that the pricing decisions need more professionalism. The marketing professionals need to adopt a number of harsh measures to streamline the cases of theft and mismanagement. We can't negate the fact that whatever the unfair practices we find in the state electricity organisations are the result of inefficiency and corruption. This makes it essential that the professionals make an assault on the multi-dimensional problems very much instrumental in increasing the costs of services. The problem of overstaffing is found in almost all the state electricity organisations. At the outset, they need to retrench those employees who are found involved in the unfair practices. The system, in a majority of the cases, is found managed manually where we find enough scope for unfair practices. The boardrooms need to promote the use of sophisticated technologies at different stages. The technical staff bear the responsibility of optimising the operational costs on technologies but very sad to mention that they create such a condition deliberately in which the efficiency level of assets starts moving downward. This results into high depreciation, poor efficiency and low productivity. This makes it essential that we fix accountability right from the first stage of expansion of transmission facilities to the last stage of supply to the ultimate users. The billing process is to be computerised and the practices of fixing units need a departure. This draws out attention on computerised billing and electronic metres. We expect that these steps would make the ways for regulating the costs which would make the services economic. The practices of offering grants in aid need to be checked. It is right to mention that the marketing professionals may regulate everything if the boardrooms have a positive attitude. The technocrats have generated the problems. The management professionals need to show their world-class excellence to make an assault on the same.

The Place Mix

The marketing professionals bear the responsibility of making it sure that the promised quality of services reach to the ultimate users without any distortion. Bridging over the gap between the services-offered and services-promised requires due co-operation of almost all the channels through which the services are processed. This draws our attention on the formulation of a sound place mix. The electricity organisations after performing the responsibility of formulating a sound product mix need to make them available to the different categories of users. The place mix helps them substantially in the process of offering the services. It is in this context that we need to go through two important problems, first the services are processed in a right fashion and second the service generating and distributing organisations are located at right places where they get all the supporting infrastructural facilities.

The first problem is related to the processing of services. This is meant the involvement of different categories of technologies, units and personnel in distributing the services to the ultimate users. We are well aware of the fact that the transmission units are located far-off the cities' precincts and the grid and sub-grid stations are responsible to distribute the services. The involvement of technical and non-technical personnel in the very process plays a decisive role. The professionals are supposed to make it sure that a fair mix of quality personnel and the sophisticated technologies are used for that purpose. The generation and distribution processes need a close link. If the supply position is satisfactory, the users of all categories are made available round-the-clock electricity but failing the adequacy of supply, we expect from them to manage and monitor the loadshedding in such a way that the users get the services when they need. We can't deny that the agricultural and industrial sectors of the economy need adequate electricity and therefore, the professionals need to make it sure that production activities are not affected due to inadequate supply. The loadshedding programmes for the different categories of users are to be informed to them much earlier the implementation is switched on to enable them to reschedule the activities. The public relations officers need to inform the users the reasons for loadshedding. The technical personnel need to make it sure that connections to the different points are in order. The cases of leakages are to be detected and corrected at the earliest. They also need to be careful that metres of the concerned users where the units consumed by them are recorded are working properly. In addition to the distribution points, the professionals are also required to make it sure that the front-line personnel responsible for collecting the bills, listing the complaints, answering to the queries and confusions have a high communicative ability besides the high level of behavioural profile. The records are crystal clear, the bills are sent properly and collected regularly. We can't deny the fact that quality of services is a fair aggregation of a number of factors. It is only not sufficient that we offer quality services. In this context, it is also pertinent that the services are processed in a right fashion. Inefficient and indecent employees may generate numerous problems at different stages. The professionals bear the responsibility of making it sure that the users remain satisfied.

Another dimension in the very context is related to the location points for the generation and distribution units. In addition to this, they also bear the responsibility of locating offices at accessible points where the users don't face any problem. The supporting infrastructural facilities are to be available as per the requirements. So far as the generation and distribution units are concerned, we find places far-off the cities suitable, but the offices for managing things are to be located close to the cities where the users may conveniently reach for making complaints or for depositing the bills. In an age of sophisticated information technologies, we find enough scope for decentralising the bill collection centres. In most of the countries in the West, we find all the banks connected with a computer network and accepting the bills for the electricity organisations. Increasing crowd on the counters may generate inconveniences to the ultimate users. This is to be checked by managing the billing system.

The distribution of services thus makes it essential that we find a close link between the generation and distribution and the offices are located and managed properly. The technologies used in the process are working satisfactorily and the personnel placed there are high performers. The availability of electricity current carries no meaning if the distribution units fail in channelising the same in a right way. The management of grid stations is found significant in the very context which requires due co-operation of technical personnel. The place mix draws our attention on the availability of services to the ultimate users. The services aggregate a number of functional responsibilities made available by the transmission and distribution units in addition to the office management. Leakage at one point is to affect the quality of services at the subsequent points. Since failing adequate generation, we find inadequate distribution. If the offices are mismanaged, the users feel inconveniences while making complaints or depositing the bills. This makes it essential that the professionals manage the distribution channels in a right fashion. We can't deny the fact that in the Indian perspective, the distribution problem is of a complicated nature. The technocrats are found careless to the management and maintenance of technologies used in the process. The generation may be right but if distribution is not up to the mark, the users would hardly get the quality services. This makes it clear that the services are distorted at different points and the professionals have to be vigilant that a close link is established between the technical and non-technical personnel and more so between the evolving technologies and the recruited personnel.

The aforesaid facts make it clear that the marketing professionals need world-class professional excellence while channelising the services. The points of distortion are to be identified, the points of leakages are to be detected, the technical faults are to be diagnosed, the behavioural profile of non-technical and technical personnel is to be observed. The priority order *vis-a-vis t*he requirements of electricity to the different categories of users are to be scanned. We can't deny that by and large almost all the transmission and distribution units have been facing the problem of deficient management. Further, the offices are also found mismanaged where we don't find work culture. The white-collared and blue-collared personnel are found instrumental in promoting the unfair practices. These negative developments have been creating a big gap between the services-promised and services-offered. Hence, the marketing professionals need to bring the derailed system on the rail and this is not possible unless we find them professionally sound. It is against this background that we find place mix playing an important role in the marketing of electricity services.

The Process Mix

In the process of formulating a marketing mix, the process mix draws our attention on the different processes through which the services reach to the ultimate users. Though we find three important stages such as generation, transmission and distribution but when our focus is on the marketing of electricity services, the different process which may be included in this mix start from supply of power to the distribution centre for supplying the same to the different categories of users. The processing of services in the very context requires a large number of people and equipment. The supporting superstructure through which the power is transmitted plays an outstanding role in ensuring time-honoured and optimal distribution of services to the users. The leakages in transmission may complicate the task of marketing professionals. The cases of theft at different points are expected which may create a gap between the power received for distribution and power actually distributed to the ultimate users. With the development of electronics, we find possibilities for theft and leakages contracting very fast. However, the task is found to be complicated when we find involvement of employees in the process. We cannot negate that particularly the public sector organisations have delayed the process of technology upgradation specially in the distribution process. This has been found affecting the quality of services moving through different processes. The flow in distribution and service delivery cannot gain a momentum unless we find new generations of technology instrumentalising the distribution process. The counters or windows for service delivery also need support of technology for speeding up the flow. The operational as well as commercial both dimensions need a rapid increase in flow. Almost all the state managed electricity boards have been facing distribution problems and the working people and the operating technology have been found responsible for the same. The marketing professionals need to manage the dimensions related to the service delivery but at the same time, they cannot undermine the role to be played by the back-line personnel because this is directly related to the supply position.

The processing, thus, found an important submix of the marketing mix considerably influences the quality and timing of service delivery. The marketing professionals need to make it sure that possibilities of delay and distortion at the different processes of delivery are minimised. The professional excellence of marketers may help optimal distribution an important consideration for users' satisfaction. Non-optimal generation, faulty transmission and managerially deficient distribution make a strong advocacy in favour of techno-driven processing with the help and co-operation of professionally excellent marketers. It is against this background that we need to assign due weightage to the process mix. Right processing, time-honoured processing, techno-driven processing, decent processing and satisfaction generating processing are our motto.

Physical Evidence and Attractions

In the context of physical evidence and attractions as a submix of the marketing mix, the electricity organisations need to assign due weightage to a number of factors. The servicescapes are found impact generating both for the working employees and the visiting customers. In a majority of the cases, we find creation of a negative impression either regarding the quality services or related to the behaviour of staff. The marketing professionals need to create an ambience in which both the sides feel satisfied. To be more specific, the counters or windows related to the deposit of bills are found a sensitive point with the viewpoint of customers. In addition, the information related to installation, connection and disconnection, payment of arrears also create a condition for customers or users where they have no option but to be present. The working staffs are either forced to work manually or if they have computers; often not found in working order. Poor furnishing either for customers or for the working staff; inadequate lighting and poor quality of light; indecent behaviour of working staff and long waiting queues are the normal conditions where customers go for the payment of their electricity bills. The employees in general are found rough and aggressive then what to talk of showing sympathy and empathy. Poor sanitation, the ambience even without sanitation for users then what to talk of proper ventilation. Surroundings without signposts and even none to guide. No sign of civic sense then what to talk of the aesthetic sense.

Such an ambience is a common feature specially in the offices of government electricity departments. There is no doubt in it that the private sector organisations have managed their service ambience in an attractive way and we also find dress code and dress consciousness but the government-managed electricity boards are yet to realise the role of ambience in improving the quality and projecting the impression. Though it is right to mention that in the modern offices we find e-governance and IT culture managing our expectations and taking care of our needs and requirements. Willingly or unwillingly, they create an ambience where employees feel pleasure in performing and customers do not feel any problem in using or even they feel pleasure in waiting and sitting.

Thus, the marketing professionals need to draw attention on the creation of service ambience efficacious of generating service fragrance and stimulating employees for performing so that the customers or visitors coming to the offices feel pleasure in using and are found satisfied with the services delivered. They also visit offices while making complaints or for service recovery and once again we find the process of projection and stimulation in action. Of course, the electricity services reach to the doorsteps of customers but there are a number of occasions when they need to visit the offices of electricity department and the marketing professionals are required to develop an ambience found conducive for all. Thus, the formulation of this mix goes through the problem of ambience and dresses and uniforms of employees working there. Attraction is the essence of this submix of marketing.

The People Mix

While formulating different submixes, it is also essential that the marketing professionals assign due weightage to the people mix. We can't deny that sophisticated information technologies and high quality of plants and equipments are engaged in the process but at the same time, it is also right to mention that in almost all the electricity organisations, specially under the public sector, we find a crowd of inefficient, indecent and unethical value-degenerating personnel found promoting inefficiency in operation, indecency in behaviour *vis-a-vis* the unfair practices. We don't find work culture and in this respect, we find it difficult to distinct the technical and non-technical personnel. It is right to mention that the marketing professionals need due co-operation of the boardrooms while managing the personnel very much instrumental in degenerating the level of efficiency. It is amazing to mention that with the connivance of technical and non-technical personnel, a number of unfair practices are promoted at different stages of operation. The increased cases of theft, cutting of electric wires, fixing of low units, poor maintenance of technologies or so are the result of poor quality of personnel working in the electricity organisations. This makes it essential that the marketing professionals assign an overriding priority to the management of people. It is against this background that we find people mix occupying a place of outstanding significance in the marketing mix of the electricity organisations.

The professionals, thus, bear the responsibility of managing the people in such a way that quality personnel are made available to the organisations. We can't limit the boundary of quality only to the generation of efficiency. In a true sense, we find quality personnel a fair mix of different properties and attributes, such as efficiency, behaviour, dedication, commitment and value orientation. We need high performers, value-based and committed employees to make the ways for performance orientation. The vital task is to increase the productivity of technologies and employees. An acceleration in the rate of productivity of different inputs used in the process requires a special attention on the quality of human resources. We need to impart training facilities to the different categories of personnel. In addition to efficiency and behaviour, the value engineering is also to be given due weightage.

To make possible performance orientation, it is pertinent that the professionals gravitate their attention on employee orientation which focuses on incentive management. In a true sense, we need to link incentives with efficiency. We often talk in favour of productivity-linked bonus but now the prevailing conditions compel us to think in favour of efficiency-linked incentive plans. The technocrats managing the technologies are to be made accountable for the poor maintenance and operation. The concerned technical staff should be charged for high depreciation costs and the poor efficiency levels. The non-technical employees should be made responsible for fake billing and poor collection. On the other hand, the professionals need to reward suitably the personnel showing the high level of efficiency. Adequate incentives to the efficients and punishment to the inefficients remain the lone solution in the hands of professionals managing the affairs. They need to establish a fair mix of performance orientation and employee orientation which would make ways for efficiency generation *vis-a-vis* value orientation. Thus, the people mix needs due attention of the marketing professionals. The boardrooms, no doubt, need to be positive in the very context.

ELECTRICITY MARKETING IN INDIAN PERSPECTIVE

Indian energy scenario, of late, is dominated by the feelings of discomfort and despair regarding the abysmally poor supply of power in most parts of the country. The pessimism is found growing amongst the different categories of users. The generation and distribution problems are found alarming. The future projections of demand emphasise the wide-ranging challenge in arranging adequate supply of energy for almost all segments of market. Expansion of the energy sector requires a large infusion of capital across the board, such as for power generation at one end and strengthening of transmission and distribution systems at the other. Substantial investments are expanding the refining capacity and the existing marketing network for supply of petroleum products.[4] The production and use of energy involves major environmental impacts which in several cases have been ignored in past. The major project called GREEN India 2047 (Growth with Resources Enhancement of Environment and Nature) carried out by the TERI establishes some of the high economic costs of continuing neglect of environmental impacts in the energy management of today and the related decisions of the past. It is estimated for instance that approximately 2.5 million persons die prematurely each year as a result of indoor and outdoor air pollution. Indoor air pollution is caused essentially by burning of inferior fuels for cooking purposes, ill-ventilated dwellings and using very poor designs of cookstoves. Outdoor pollution particularly in the industrial towns and cities results largely from the use of motor vehicles. The security of supply of energy is a matter of concern. The country's dependence on oil imports has been growing significantly in recent years and the outlook seems even more grim for the future. The sources of supply of crude oil and petroleum products for India are confined largely to a small region of the world. The answer lies in restructuring energy supply in a manner so that dependence on the imported oil is considerably minimised. The current outlook for energy development in India is clearly not very heartening and even the outlook in the coming future is clouded by concerns related to the areas discussed above. On the other hand, the demand is increasing very fast. The changing lifestyles influences the requirements of domestic sector and the increasing sophistication in technologies is governing the power requirements of the industrial as well as the agricultural and service sectors. These facts make it essential that we view the problem with a new vision and in this context, we make a strong advocacy in favour of application of the principles of innovative marketing. It is against this background that the marketing of energy or electricity services is found occupying a place of outstanding significance.

The generation as well as the distribution systems are to be revamped. The gap between the demand and supply is to be bridged over. The misuse of electricity is to be regulated.[5] The cases of theft are to be checked. The decreasing level of efficiency is to be reversed. The behavioural profile of different categories of employees is to be made high. The measures instrumental in aggravating the problem of environment pollution need an intensive care. The rate of profitability is to be increased. The increasing needs and requirements of users are to be fulfilled. The social costs are to be made optimal. Thus, we find multi-faceted functional responsibilities before the electricity organisations which require world-class professional excellence. This makes it essential that the boardrooms favour aggressive marketing.

The marketing professionals at the very outset need to formulate a sound product mix that paves avenues for the use of non-conventional sources of energy. The agrarian economies make available tremendous opportunities for the use of non-conventional sources of energy. Another aspect in the very context is to minimise our dependence on the coal-based and petro-based thermal stations. We need to increase the percentage of hydro-based thermal stations. Atomic energy is to be given due weightage. Thus, an optimal mix of different sources of energy is essential to increase the supply position to cater to the increasing demand. This draws our attention on the formulation of a sound product mix.

Another problem in the very context is to use the creative promotional measures in such a way that users at large are made aware of the emerging problems. We need to sense them in a right fashion. The emergence of a seller's market, no doubt, aggravates the magnitude of problem. The electricity organisations working under the public sector don't care the misuse of electricity. The private organisations are in a very limited number and therefore not efficacious in throwing a positive impact. The marketing professionals bear the responsibility of managing the promotional measures effectively so that mass awareness is inculcated. The media managed and controlled by government bear the responsibility of promoting the messages and themes to be instrumental in sensing the different categories of users.

The tariff structure requires due attention of the marketing professionals.[6] We agree with this view that increasing level of inefficiency decelerates productivity since we don't find cost-effectiveness in the operational system. Thus, the operational expenses are found mounting. The service tax is also found complicating the task of rationalising the tariff. The electricity organisations are also supposed to bear the social costs since the principles of social marketing make it essential. A rational tariff structure is thus found a difficult task which necessitates cost-effectiveness. Our pricing or tariff decisions are to be efficacious in securing commercial viability but at the same time they also bear the responsibility of making the services economic. The professionals, thus, need world-class excellence to bring the operational economy without which the pricing decisions can't be made productive.

The marketing professionals are required to bridge over the expanding gap between the services-promised and services-offered. This makes it essential that the services are channelised with the help of supporting technologies and value-based efficient employees. The level of efficiency of technologies and employees is found coming down. Thus, the marketing professionals are supposed to make it sure that services are channelised in a right way and the distribution costs are made optimal. Again, we need to talk about the instrumentality of professionals who are required to be high performers.

In addition to the above, the professionals also need to assign an overriding priority to the formulation of a sound people mix. This draws our attention on the quality of technologies and the quality of employees. We find a close relation between the evolving technologies and the training facilities for the employees. Value engineering needs top priority, to be more specific, in the formulation of a sound people mix.

The aforesaid facts make it clear that the professionals need to increase the level of efficiency which would hardly be possible if they delay application of modern marketing principles.

To be more specific when we find the level of efficiency even below 20 per cent, the decision-makers need world-class professional excellence to speed up the process of development.[7] The State Electricity Boards present a very disappointing performance level. There are a number of factors found responsible for the same but the managerial deficiency appears to be the number one. A cohesion between technocrats and management is felt essential.

We need liberal pricing policy for some of the sensitive sectors and segments. The agricultural sector and the poor farmers, the industrial sector and the upcoming and budding entrepreneurs, the weaker sections of the society and the cottage industries are some of the segments of the users deserving subsidised or concessional electricity services. This is likely to increase the pressure on account of social costs. The management experts feel that an organisation financially sound may bear high social costs and therefore, the first and foremost task is to improve the financial health of the electricity organisations. This requires plugging of leakages found at different stages and an improvement in the level of efficiency.

The changing lifestyles and the evolving technologies would increase the demand side generated by almost all the sectors. This makes it essential that in addition to generation we also promote conservation. In US, through a process called COGENERATION, the energy conservation has been made possible.[8] The cogeneration is the production of two useful forms of energy from the same source. The steam generated in a factory's manufacturing process can be used to produce electricity which is piped to nearby homes where the heat is used to heat the space or water. The electricity can be used at industrial site where it is produced or it can be distributed to other sites. Thus, the need of the hour is to educate and sense the masses about energy conservation. It is in this context that we expect more from the marketing professionals in general and the advertising professionals in particular. They need more creative efforts to sensitise unaware and illiterate segments of the users.

In view of the above, it is right to say that in the Indian perspective the generation and distribution processes need to be reviewed. The technocrats as well as the management experts need to activate multi-dimensional efforts. In addition, the boardrooms also need an attitudinal change. This is essential to improve the supply position *vis-a-vis* the awareness related to conservation. While formulating the product mix, it is also to be remembered that the environment-friendly measures and sources are given due weightage. At the same time, the private organisations are also required to be encouraged. The moment we find the business environment competitive, the public sector organisations would have no option but to increase the level of efficiency failing which they would hardly survive. At almost all the stages whatever the problems we find are substantially on account of seller's market. They feel that the users have no option but to make a demand since the intensity of competition is almost dismal. In addition, the boardrooms need to change their preferences and the government requires to promote the non-conventional sources for which we have rich potentials. The marketing professionals bear the responsibility of establishing a balance between the demand and supply position partially by increasing the productivity of generating units, partially by promoting non-conventional sources and partially by momentising conservation.

SUMMARY

In this chapter, you have gone through different dimensions of marketing electricity services. After going through the chapter, be sure that the following facts are well versed:

Electricity Marketing: A Conceptual Framework: It is a managerial process to study the levels of expectations of users and to satisfy them by delivering quality services on time. It is a process of rationalising the demand and supply position. It is also a social process which helps in minimising the side-effects of generation.

Rationale Behind Practicing Marketing: The application of marketing principles in the electricity services is found justified. There are a number of factors justifying its application such as quantitative improvement in the generation capacity, optimal distribution, minimising the transmission and distribution losses, minimising the gestation period, making possible right location, conservation of energy and increasing satisfied group of users.

Behavioural Profile of Users of Electricity Services: This makes it essential that marketers develop their awareness of the changing needs and requirements of customers and manage their expectations in such a way that they are found satisfied.

Market Segmentation for Electricity Users: The different segments of users are rural and urban, industrial, trade and commerce, state and inter-state, central and state governments.

Managing Information for Marketing Services: For studying and understanding the behavioural profile of users, the marketing professionals need support of information.

Marketing Mix for Electricity Organisations: The public as well as private organisations need to formulate a marketing combining the different submixes.

Product Mix: There are a number of sources for generating electricity and the electricity organisations need to develop a sound mix in which the conventional and non-conventional sources are included.

Promotion Mix: The marketing professionals need to make use of different components of promotion in such a way that masses are sensitised and misuse of electricity by individual or institutional segments is checked. The cases of theft may also be minimised by developing mass awareness. The promotional measures are to be made cost-effective and proactive.

Price Mix: The tariff structure need due care both on organisational and social considerations. A differential pricing strategy is found suitable to meet the desired goals.

Place Mix: The services move through different stages and at each and every stage, the professionals need to minimise the time and cost. There must be a link so that wastage of energy is regulated.

Process Mix: The professionals need to process the services in such a way that possibilities of delay and distortion are removed. Use of new generation of technology will increase the flow and improve the operational efficiency for quality service delivery.

Physical Evidence and Attractions: In this mix of marketing, the professionals make efforts for creating a service ambience which is found conducive both for the working people and the visiting users. This also focuses on the dresses and uniforms of staff.

People: While going through this submix of marketing, the professionals make it sure that electricity organisations have a team of committed people. In addition to operational efficiency, they also need to be honest and value-based.

Electricity Marketing in Indian Perspective: With the increasing pace of corporatisation, we find multi-faceted efforts for socio-economic transformation which has changed our lifestyles. The multi-dimensional developments in almost all the sectors has made possible a significant increase in the demand side but so far as the supply side is concerned, we find development non-optimal to our changing requirements. At all the three stages such as generation, transmission and distribution, our efforts are not commensurate with the levels of expectations. In addition to other factors, we find managerial deficiency an important reason for the present energy crisis found at an alarming stage. This in a very natural way makes a strong advocacy in favour of conceptualising innovative marketing so that the marketing professionals succeed in satisfying the users and rationalising the supply position. The life cycle once geared starts moving forward and its reversal gets a lukewarm response. This necessitates innovative sensitisation process which the world-class marketing professionals can make possible.

KEY TERMS

Transcendental	Nuclear Energy
Conventional Energy	Animal Energy
Non-conventional Energy	Stakeholders
Biogas	Human Excreta
Solar Energy	Natural Gas
Wind Energy	Water Hyacinth
APDRP	Tariff
Hydro Generation	Electronic Metre
e-governance	Boardrooms

	Front-line Personnel	NGOs
	Back-line Personnel	Generation
	White-collared	Transmission
	Blue-collared	Distribution
	Theft	Dissemination
	Leakages	Agricultural Wastes
	Green India	Renewable Energy
	Cogeneration	Grid

Review Questions

1. What do you mean by Electricity Marketing? Justify application of marketing by the electricity organisations.
2. Focus on the behavioural profile of different segments of users of electricity services.
3. Explain the role of information helping marketing professionals in studying the behavioural profile of users of electricity services.
4. Formulate a marketing mix for the electricity services in the Indian perspective.
5. As a marketer, focus on the product mix to be suitable in the Indian context.
6. Throw light on the different components of promotion for promoting the electricity services.
7. Do you find extended mixes of marketing essential for marketing the electricity services? Justify your arguments.
8. Focus on the pricing strategy to be adopted by the electricity organisations in the Indian perspective.
9. Write a note on Electricity Marketing in the Indian perspective.

Application Exercises

1. You have been working as marketing professional, in the State Electricity Board. Suggest the measures they need to adopt to improve the quality of services.
2. As a marketing professional throw light on the changing levels of expectations of the users of electricity services in the Indian context.
3. You have to sensitise the general masses for controlling the cases of theft and misuse in the electricity organisation. Explain the steps you would like to initiate as a professional.
4. As a marketer, throws light on the product mix you will prefer to develop with the motto of preserving the conventional sources of energy.
5. As a marketer, focus on the pricing strategy you will like to introduce for striking a balance between organisational and social considerations.
6. Almost all the State Electricity Boards in India has been facing the problem of financial crunch. Suggest measures as a marketer.
7. Do you find expanded marketing mix essential for the electricity services? Defend your arguments.
8. How would you justify application of marketing principles in the electricity organisations?
9. Do you find efforts of government for generating electricity adequate? Justify your arguments as a professional.

Endnotes

1. Jha, S.M. & Singh, L.P., *Marketing Management in Indian Perspective,* Himalaya Publishing House, 1988.
2. Balkrishna & Thakur C.P., *Glimpses of Indian Technology: Non-Conventional Sources of Energy,* Publication Division, Government of India, New Delhi, pp. 204-23.
3. *The Hindu,* Survey of Indian Industry: Power: Unfolding Power Scenario by S. Rajgopal, pp. 97-102.
4. V. Uma Bhaskara Mani: Energy Conservation; *Yojana,* 32/16, 1988, pp. 15-16.
5. Srinivasan G., Non-Conventional Energy: The Tasks Ahead, *Yojana,* 32/16, pp. 6-7
6. Manorma Year Book, 2007.
7. India, 2008.
8. Indiastat, 2006.

☆☆☆

AUTOMOBILE SERVICES MARKETING

With the increasing sophistication in transportation, we find automobile services emerging as an important service-generating sector. The management experts feel that application of marketing principles would not only make possible offering of quality services to the users but would also be instrumental in making the services profitable.

Chapter Objectives

Introduction – Automobile Services Marketing: A Conceptual Framework – Rationale Behind Practising Marketing in the Automobile Services – Market Segmentation for Automobile Services – Behavioural Profile of Users of Services – Marketing Mix for the Automobile Services – Product Mix – Promotion Mix – Price Mix – Place Mix – Process – Physical Evidence and Attractions – People Automobile Services Marketing in Indian Perspective – Summary – Key Terms – Review Questions – Application Exercises – Endnotes.

Learning Objectives

This chapter of the study aims at practising marketing by the automobile servicing stations. The readers develop their awareness of the different mixes of marketing in the Indian perspective. The motive is to help professionals in practising marketing with the motto of improving the quality of service. With the increasing intensity of competition, we find application of marketing becoming significant so that the services are found competitive and affordable. The professionals need to develop their awareness of the changing behavioural profile of users with the motto of managing expectations.

INTRODUCTION

By definition, an automobile or car is a wheeled vehicle that carries its own motor and transports passengers. The automobile was not invented in a single day by a single inventor. It is in a true sense an evolution that took place worldwide. The automobile industry encompasses the business of producing auto-powered vehicles and includes manufacture and sale of two-wheeler motor cycles, cars, trucks and other commercial vehicles. Compared to big global players like Japan and USA, India is still emerging in the production of automobiles. In terms of total production of passenger cars, India still produces one-tenth the cars that Japan produces. Japan is in the list of the top ten car manufacturers of the world and produces more than ten per cent of the global requirements. The recent developments in the Indian automobile industry are found very encouraging and we find the industry poised for an exponential growth.

When we talk about the automobile industry, the decade 1990s is considered to be the golden period in which the process of technological sophistication gained a rapid momentum. For long, the Indian companies as well as the foreign companies could not get a favourable environment particularly in the Indian perspective. In the early 1990s, the Sujuki of Japan was given permission to set up its small car manufacturing unit in India together with the Government of India which is now Maruti Udyog Ltd. and since then we could engineer a foundation for the development of automobile industry.

We cannot negate that Indian has the potential to be a global automotive power. The Government of India has formulated an automobile policy with a mission to establish and strengthen automobile industry which is found globally competitive. With the development of automobile industry, we find development of a number of areas such as automobile components, automobile battery and automobile servicing centres. Thus, the automobile industry provides tremendous job opportunities because there are a number of areas where we find multiplier effects.

Our focus is here on the servicing facilities which grow up with the development of automobile industry. It is in this context that with the development of car manufacturing companies, the manufactures as well as the users realised the significance of servicing centres. Particularly in a country like India, it is imperative that we promote those industries which can create and provide job opportunities both to the skilled and unskilled people. Of course, the worldwide economic depression has been throwing a challenge to the automobile sector but we have a big market and therefore we find ourselves potentially sound to counter the emerging challenges and threats.

The Indian automobile industry will thrive even in the coming years and therefore both the car manufacturing companies and private agencies have to pave avenues for the development of automobile servicing centres making available to the users quality services. If we find automotive industry prospering, the demand for servicing will naturally increase.

With the increasing sophistication in transportation, we find automobile services emerging as an important service-generating sector of the economy. A number of skilled, semi-skilled and manual workers are found getting employment facilities. Of course, it is right to mention that in almost all the countries we find automobile servicing centres playing a big role in improving the level of efficiency and life of our motor vehicles. There are different categories of users availing the services of automobile servicing centres, such as the individuals, institutions, organisations. It is felt that a hazardous and unplanned development of servicing centres has very much been instrumental in aggravating the problem of environment in addition to the traffic barriers. This makes it essential that we focus our attention on the organised development of automobile services in order that the automobile centres develop in a right way and the users get the eco-friendly quality services. It is against this background that we focus on the marketing of automobile services.

It is right to mention that the automobile manufacturing companies offer after-sale services and therefore we find one category of automobile centre which is sponsored by the concerned company. The development processes are found systematic and therefore these centres develop as a formal sector. On the other hand, we also find second category of automobile servicing centres developing as an informal sector. It is developed independently and therefore the focal point of attraction is the category of servicing centres developed in an unorganised way as an informal sector. There is no doubt in it that a number of workers are found engaged and therefore these servicing centres contribute substantially to the job market but at the same time we also find high magnitude of child exploitation in the informal sector. In addition, the problems like environment pollution and traffic congestion complicate the task of city planners and the environmentalists. This makes it essential that we think over the problem with a new vision.

The management experts feel that application of marketing principles in the informal sector in particular would not only make possible offering of quality services to the users but in addition would also be instrumental in making the services profitable. The cases of exploitation of child labour by almost all the automobile servicing centres — formal and informal, make it significant that the management experts think over the problem on a priority basis. We are not opposed to the development of automobile servicing centres indeed we make an advocacy in promoting the same but there must be a code for operations and development. A majority of the automobile servicing centres are found engaged in unfair and illegal practices. In addition to exploiting the workers and users, they are also found promoting the cases of theft of motor vehicles. This makes it significant that we gravitate our attention on some of the sensitive problems generated by the automobile servicing centres. It is felt that the application of marketing principles would make possible multi-dimensional improvements, such as the cases of exploitation of child labour, pollution of environment, traffic congestion, poor quality of services to the users, cases of theft or so would be controlled. It is in this context that we go through the marketing problems of automobile servicing centres. We need to promote them but in a right fashion.

AUTOMOBILE SERVICES MARKETING — A CONCEPTUAL FRAMEWORK

At the outset, we go through the conceptual aspect of marketing the automobile services. We find automobile services marketing a managerial process that makes possible an organised development of the servicing centres. It is to help the servicing centres in planning, organising, staffing and controlling the marketing processes so that they succeed in generating profits and at the same time also ensure quality services to the users at large. The marketing of automobile services focuses our attention on the development of optimal inputs for making possible cost-effectiveness which help them in making the price structure competitive.[1] We can't deny the fact that the market is competitive since a number of servicing centres are found operational, especially in the big towns and cities. We find marketing a customer satisfaction engineering and therefore the marketing process helps the servicing centres in identifying the needs and requirements of the users and making the necessary arrangements accordingly which help them in increasing the market share and establishing the leadership in the command area. The marketing is also known as a social process since the servicing centres are required to make environment-friendly arrangements so that intensity of environment pollution due to the smoke generated by the centres is countered in an effective way. Further, it is also to minimise the problem of traffic congestion because the servicing centres are required to focus on the location points *vis-a-vis* the aesthetic management. In view of the above, we observe the following points regarding the concept of marketing automobile services.

- It is a managerial process that makes possible a planned development of the servicing centres.
- It is a customer satisfaction engineering that helps in identifying the level of expectations of users and to fulfil them to satisfy.
- It is a social process that helps in countering the problems of environment and traffic congestion. In addition, it is also to create job opportunities to skilled, semi-skilled and manual workers.

RATIONALE BEHIND PRACTISING MARKETING

The marketing experts feel that both the formal and informal sectors, organised and unorganised sectors, small and big organisations need to practise marketing since this helps all the concerned in many ways. If the servicing centres are started, the main thing influencing the organisers is the profitable market potentials. If they practise marketing, the opportunities are to be capitalised on optimally. The following facts testify the implementation of modern marketing principles in the automobile services.

1. To improve the quality of services: It is right to mention that the application of marketing principles makes the ways for qualitative improvements in the service mix of the automobile servicing centres. Generally, they are found offering repairing, denting, painting, cleaning services. In this context, it is pertinent that they take care of quality of workers of different categories they employ. In addition, they also need to assign due weightage to the tool management and the materials used for the different types of services. They need to formulate a service mix that helps users in getting the integrated or centralised services. The marketing makes an advocacy in favour of a package that includes integrated services. We can't deny the fact that the application of marketing principles would help them in improving the quality of services.

2. Satisfaction to the users: We are well aware of the fact that different categories of users avail the services and the marketing professionals need to identify the changing level of expectations of users. It is right to mention that the process of technological sophistication has also influenced the management of servicing. Of late we find the use of computers for painting and even for denting. The cleaning services are found automated. The repairing services also need a number of expensive tools and technologies. The servicing centres need to satisfy the users and this is possible when they make available quality services. In some of the servicing centres, we find more efficient skilled employees whereas in a majority of the centres, we find employees below the level of efficiency. The marketing practices make it essential that the different categories of workers engaged in the process of offering the services behave decently with the users. They are supposed to employ only those employees who have a high level of efficiency and behavioural profile. These arrangements simplify the task of satisfying the users.

3. Increasing the market share: The application of marketing principles also helps the servicing centres in increasing the market share. It is natural that in the big towns and cities, a number of servicing centres are found operational. The centres offering quality services, behaving decently with the users and charging a reasonable price for their services succeed in increasing their business which make it easier to increase the market share. With the increasing pace of industrialisation, we find a basic change in our lifestyles and therefore, we find the emergence of a profitable market. If you offer quality services, the market share would considerably be increased.

4. Maximising profitability: The most important thing in marketing the services of automobile centres is to pave avenues for generating profits. We accept the fact that if they keep on moving the process of offering the quality services, the avenues for generating profits would sizeably be broadened. For maximising the rate of profitability, it is essential that the servicing centres make possible cost economy by regulating the unproductive expenses. Thus, the automobile servicing centres find it convenient to make profits which help them in recycling the process of development and expansion. We don't favour generation of profits by using poor quality of materials or by misleading the users.

5. A planned development: Of late, in almost all the towns and cities, we find a mushroom growth of automobile centres. Such a haphazard and unplanned development is found creating numerous social and environmental problems. The unplanned location of automobile servicing centres in the cities' precincts invites a number of problems, such as pollution of environment, traffic congestion or so. In addition, we also find the servicing centres ill-informed about the changes in the technologies of new generation of automobiles resulting from which the staff can't be made available the required training facilities which may affect their business.

The aforesaid facts make it clear that application of marketing principles is justified because the servicing centres, society, users are benefited in many ways. It is not essential that only the big servicing centres think in this direction. In a true sense, we find its instrumentality even for the small servicing centres.

MARKET SEGMENTATION FOR AUTOMOBILE SERVICES

The marketing professionals need to study and understand the automobile sector and its multi-segment customers having multi-faceted objectives. It is in this context that they need to segment the automotive markets. The two different categories of users — personal and institutional — make use of automotive services and they need to visit the servicing centres as and when the circumstances necessitate. The users have no doubt different levels of expectations but all of them prefer time-honoured and quality-based services. We find some of the segments very much sensitive to price whereas some others are influenced by quality of services. The persons or organisations making use of vehicles for commercial purposes expect quick services. The men and women both of them make use of automotive servicing centers and we find their expectations not of identical nature. Even the youths and grey are not identical in terms of levels of expectations. Thus we find automotive servicing centres delivering services to the diverse groups of users and due to variations in the levels of their expectations; the professionals bear the responsibility of understanding them in a right fashion. In Figure 25.1, we find market segmentation for automobile servicing centres.

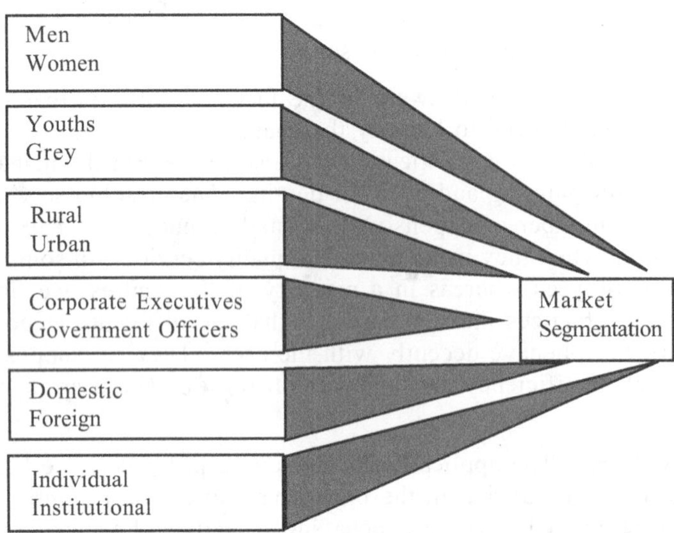

Fig. 25.1: Market Segmentation for Automobile Servicing

The users of automobile servicing centres come from public and private sectors and we find their levels of expectations different in nature. The users working as corporate executives in the private sector and the same rank of users working in the public sector have different levels of expectations. The domestic as well as the foreign users have different levels of expectations. Like this, the rural and urban users expect and behave in a different way.

The marketing professionals need to segment the users for studying and understanding the levels for their expectations so that they are in a position to formulate a sound marketing mix and to satisfy them by offering the services of world-class. The business of automobiles servicing centres rests on confidence and trust.

BEHAVIOURAL PROFILE OF USERS OF AUTOMOBILE SERVICING CENTRES

The levels of expectations of customers or users cannot remain static. We find multi-dimensional developments in the society and economy both at national and global levels and our behavioural profile is considerably affected by these developments. With corporatisation of Indian economy, we find a significant change in our lifestyles because the level of income of a few selected segments of society started increasing very fast. The corporate sector strengthened the foundation for the emergence of corporate culture in which maintaining a car became a compulsion. The car manufacturing companies produced cars for almost all the segments depending on their status and income. The financial institutions were found liberal in financing which made possible a significant increases in the number of car owners followed by an analogous increase in the demand for servicing centres. On the one hand, the car manufacturing companies started offering incentives in the form of after-sale services while on the other hand, there was a significant increase in the number of servicing centres in the informal sector.

The upcoming youths serving the corporate sector in general and the software sector in particular were found tempted to a different lifestyle considerably influenced by western culture. This made possible a basic change in their attitudes and resulting from which they started thinking and behaving in a different way. The luxury vehicles were used less for business and more for personal pleasure. We witness attitutional transformation in almost all the segments of users, no doubt, but not of that intensity and not with that diversity. Our focus is on the fact that much more frequency in the uses of cars increased demand for the servicing centres making available to them fast and quality services.

Since the impact of technology was found on the servicing centres, the users started developing high levels of expectations which they could not get in all the centres. The new generation of vehicles necessitated highly skilled mechanics which were found in the servicing centres of car manufacturing companies but in other centres both in terms of technology and mechanics, the users failed in getting standard quality of services resulting into dissatisfaction. The inadequacy of place, safety and security provisions aggravated the magnitude of problem.

The abovementiond facts make it clear that behavioural profile of almost all segments of users was found changed followed by a high level of expectations from the automobile servicing centres but a majority of the centres due to potentially deficient condition failed in delivering the services upto the desired level. It is significant that the marketing professionals develop their awareness of the changing levels of expectations and manage them in such a fashion that a mismatch between services-expected and services-delivered is bridged. This requires an in-depth study of behavioural profile and formulation of a marketing mix in tune with the study results.

FORMULATION OF MARKETING MIX FOR THE AUTOMOBILE SERVICES

While formulating marketing mix, the automobile servicing centres need to go through the different submixes. The formulation of marketing mix is found significant with the viewpoint of developing optimal marketing inputs. This draws our attention on the product mix which focuses on the different types of services to be included in the service profile, the promotion mix that helps the servicing centres in promoting the business, the price mix that helps them in adopting a rational structure for pricing which helps them in making profits, the place mix that simplifies their task of processing quality services to the users and the people mix that helps them in getting efficient personnel of different categories.

The Product Mix

In the formulation of product mix, the automobile servicing centres need to include the services found essential to increase the efficiency level of the automobiles in addition to the attractions and clearing operations. In Figure 25.2, we find the product mix of the automobile servicing centres.

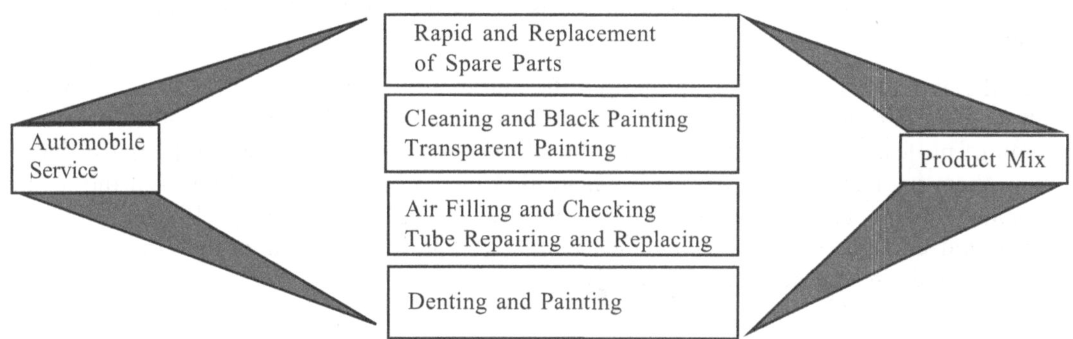

Fig. 25.2: Product Mix for Automobile Servicing Centres

On the basis of Figure 25.2, it is clear that the automobile servicing centres offer diversified services like cleaning of the automobiles, repairing and replacement services, denting and painting services, air filling and checking. These services are found significant to keep the motor vehicles in perfect order. Some of the servicing centres offer a particular service whereas we also find servicing centres where all the related services are available. On account of financial and space constraints, it is found difficult to include all the services in the product mix but we find it profitable to offer the integrated services so that the users don't need to go to the different servicing centres for the different types of services they need. While formulating the product mix, the servicing centres need to develop a package of benefits so that the users are induced to avail even the services they right now don't need. It is against this background that we make a strong advocacy in favour of integrating different services in the product mix. The users go to a particular centre and if all the services are available, they would prefer to avail the required services for which they would not be required to spare extra time. In addition, the package benefits would also make the services economic that would act as a motivational tool. It is quite natural that the service profile assigns due weightage to the nature and types of vehicles used in the command or catchment area.

It is essential to make available to the users the desired services. With the evolving technologies, we need a change in the management of tools and equipments to offer to the users the quality services. Not only this, the skilled group of employees also need training facilities in the face of emerging changes in the nature of technologies. The automobile servicing centres bear the responsibility of offering quality services and this is not possible unless we find a close link between the generation of motor vehicles and the knowledge and skill of employees working at the centres. In the servicing centres bearing the responsibility of cleaning and washing the motor vehicles, we find use of technologies and therefore the leading servicing centres also need to be aware of the service profile in the countries manufacturing the motor vehicles. In addition to the skilled and unskilled personnel, we also find a number of child labour working at almost all the servicing centres. In this context, the automobile servicing centres need to stop the practice of employing the child labour.

The formulation of an ideal package draws our attention on the blending of some of the related services so that the users find it convenient to use the same. In this respect, the automobile servicing centres need to link cleaning with the inside black painting, particularly at places where due to rains and poor roads the motor vehicles are found developing a number of faults. It is quite natural that the denting and painting services would be offered at the same centre to make the process of servicing compact and convenient to the users. Like this, the air filling and tube repairing services would be made available at the same place. While formulating an ideal package, our main emphasis is on making the package a motivational tool. And this makes it essential that the servicing centres integrate the different types of services, offer one free service who avails all the services or formulate the same in the face of intensity of competition in the market.

While formulating the service mix, the automobile servicing centres are required to make it an additional point of attraction by making provisions for the sale of some of the small attractive accessories. The users of the services may not be in need of these items but since they get an opportunity to view the same, the process of demand generation may be switched on. We can't deny that the intensity of competition is high because a number of servicing centres are found located even in the small towns and cities and therefore the automobile servicing centres need to add attractions to their service mix by enriching the peripheral services. Here, our focus is on small services related to the motor vehicles, or decorative items for the same, or items for the kids or so. Since the core services are found of identical nature, it is the quality of peripheral services that would make your product mix distinct *vis-a-vis* attractive.

In view of the above, it is right to mention that the automobile servicing centres need to formulate a sound product mix in which a fair blending of core and peripheral services are to be made possible. Of course, it requires due co-operation of professionals and therefore they need to seek the opinion of consultants for that very purpose who would help them in many ways. We can't negate that in the Indian perspective even the leading servicing centres don't manage their services properly which invite a number of complications. If you offer quality services to the users, we find enough scope for using the creative promotional measures to inform and persuade them to visit the centres and use the services frequently.

The Promotion Mix

Like other service generating organisations, the automobile servicing centres also need to promote the business which makes it essential that they focus on the different constituents of promotion, such as the advertising, publicity, sales promotion, personal selling, word-of-mouth communication and telemarketing. It is right to mention here that the promotional budget and the use or significance of a particular constituent depends upon the business potentials. If the automobile servicing centres are working on a large-scale, they can promote their business with the support of a number of constituents but if they are working on a small-scale, they need to concentrate on a particular component in the face of business potentials.

Advertising: The automobile servicing centres need to advertise and for this purpose, they need to take a decision in the face of their budget. We can't negate that even the small servicing centres may advertise through print media. The local newspapers and print materials are found sensitive for the automobile servicing centres. This would even be economic to advertise in the local newspapers or take support of leaflets and pamphlets to be inserted inside the newspapers. The main thing is to inform the users regarding the nature of services offered to them. The leading servicing centres would also find local advertisements suitable since the main task is to inform to the users and prospects regarding the services. Thus, we find print media economic as well as effective, specially for the automobile servicing centres. In addition, they can also advertise through the broadcast media if the transmission station is locally available. So far as the telecast media is concerned, it is more expensive and we even don't find it essential to take support of this media.

Publicity: The automobile servicing centres may use this component of promotion to publicise the business. In this context, they need to develop rapport with the local correspondents and opinion leaders who would help them in publicising the business. Since we find publicity a non-paid form of communication, the automobile servicing centres can publicise even by spending nominal amount for entertaining the media personnel. They are supposed to convince the media people that their services are of quality.

Sales Promotion: While promoting the business, the automobile servicing centres should offer innovative promotional gifts to the users or prospects. In addition to providing incentives to the users, they should also think in the direction of offering incentives to their own employees, specially when we find the business period sensitive. Of course, the promotional incentives to the users would have a far reaching impact on increasing the business. The small gifts to the users during some of the selected off-period or duration when the business is found stagnant, the automobile servicing centres can speed up the process of generating the business with the support of innovative promotional tools.

Personal Selling: We are aware of the fact that the personal selling is influenced by the instrumentality of sales personnel who have a face-to-face communication with the users or the prospects. While using the personal selling, the automobile servicing centres need to take the support of some of the dedicated sales personnel. They need to develop contact with the owners and agencies and to impress upon them regarding the quality of services available in the concerned centre. The main thing is to have a detailed knowledge of the command area so that they succeed in informing and persuading the users or the prospects. It is pertinent that they take the support of personnel having high communicative ability.

Word-of-mouth Promotion: In promoting the automobile servicing business, we find word-of-mouth promoters instrumental who in a true sense act as a hidden salesforce. The satisfied group of users and the opinion leaders of the command area may play an incremental role in the very context. If the automobile servicing centres are found offering quality services and the users are found satisfied with the performance and behaviour of the different categories of personnel working there, it is quite natural that as and when they meet with their friends and relatives or the colleagues they make a positive communication. This helps in stimulating the users and prospects to use the services of the centre about which their friends and relatives have made recommendations. It is against this background that we also call this component of the promotion mix word-of-mouth recommendation. The salesforce are found working without charging from you anything for transforming the prospects into the users. In this context, it is essential that the services are of quality and the behavioural profile of different categories of personnel working there is decent. You spend nothing for promotion, however, you succeed in promoting effectively. We can't deny that the level of effectiveness of word-of-mouth promotion is high because we may not trust upon the advertisement slogans but we often trust on the statements and comments of our friends and relatives. It is in this context that the automobile servicing centres are required to assign due weightage to the quality of services.

Telemarketing: In an age of sophisticated communication technologies, we find telemarketing emerging as an effective component of promotion. In the telemarketing, the concerned organisation uses the services of telemarketers who are supposed to be a successful communicator. In this context, it is significant that the automobile servicing centres have the telephonic facilities and persons with high communicative ability act as telemarketers. The telephone instruments are required to be of quality which don't interrupt the process of communication. The telemarketers should have an in-depth idea regarding the different types of services offered by the centre because they bear the responsibility of answering to the queries raised by the users or the prospects.

The aforesaid constituents of promotion would help the automobile servicing centres in promoting the business. It is quite natural that a majority of the automobile servicing centres would not be in a position to spend substantially for promotion and therefore they should take a decision in the face of available potentials because the market is competitive. We can't deny the fact that there are some of the servicing centres having rich potentials and therefore they can use a particular component depending upon their financial health *vis-a-vis* the intensity of competition. Thus, the automobile servicing centres not only need to offer the quality services but they also need to inform and persuade the users and prospects and for that, we find local advertisements to be economic as well as effective. The promotional measures would help them in getting more business, if they offer the quality services and develop a package of services which acts as a motivational tool to instrumentalise the process of stimulation.

The Price Mix

This component of the marketing mix is found to be the most sensitive component since it considerably influences the business of automobile servicing centres. The pricing decisions become significant also with the viewpoint of generating profits and motivating the users. In the Indian perspective, we find a majority of the users sensitive to price and therefore the automobile servicing centres bear the responsibility of identifying the nature of users or prospects living in the command area. If they feel that price is to be a dominating factor, they have no option but to adjust the cost accordingly.

With the increasing costs of inputs used in the process, such as management of tools, machines, personnel, we find the price structure high. This makes it essential that the automobile servicing centres assign due weightage to the operational costs and try to make the process cost-effective. The market is found to be competitive and therefore if other competitors have been charging less, you have no option but to adjust and set the structure accordingly. Even if others charge more, you should pave avenues for charging less so that you use pricing as a motivational tool. Here, it is pertinent that just for optimising the price structure, they should not bring down the quality of services since ultimately it is the quality of your goods or services that makes the marketing resources effective or even ineffective.

The Place Mix

In this component of the marketing mix, we focus on the processing of services. This makes it essential that the employees working there are not to generate a gap. They are required to be efficient, prompt and aware of the behavioural management. Since a number of factors influence the level of efficiency *vis-a-vis* the quality of services, it is essential that all the related factors are managed carefully. The technologies used in the process, the tools required for services and the personnel, specially the skilled labour need a priority attention. The main thing in the place mix is the right processing of services to the ultimate users.

Another important aspect in the very context is the location point for establishing the servicing centres. The automobile servicing centres are required to go through a number of factors, such as easy accessibility, good quality of roads, the problem of traffic congestion, scope for further development and expansion, the problem of environment and noise pollution or so. The locational factors determine the quality of services made available by the automobile servicing centres. The availability of adequate supporting infrastructural facilities increase the level of efficiency of the servicing centres. In any case, they are not supposed to select a place where the users find it difficult to reach in the absence of smooth accessibility. The places are also required to be safe since of late we find the problem of theft specially of small motor vehicles. In addition, they also need to think about the problem of pollution. If the centres are close to the cities' precincts or in the cities' precincts, the problem of pollution would crop up. Thus, the automobile servicing centres are required to select a place which is found environment-friendly and therefore a place close to the cities with a big space would be suitable for them. It is pertinent to mention that the places should not be close to the schools for children. While selecting a suitable place, the automobile servicing centres need to make it sure that a spacious road is connected to the centre.

The big centres should be close to the cities whereas the small centres can be located even in the cities' precincts. They have to make necessary arrangements so that the problems related to traffic congestion and pollution are countered successfully by developing plantation in the available space. In addition, they need to clean the premises regularly and the wastes are to be removed at the safe place very far from the towns and cities. The light and ventilation facilities at the centre should be adequate. The shopping complex should be close to the centre where at least the spare parts and light refreshment facilities are available.

The Process Mix

With a significant increase in the number of different types of vehicles, we find an analogous increase in the number of automobile servicing centres where the users go for the servicing of their vehicles. Since users expect quality and time honoured services, it is imperative that the servicing centres take support of new generation of technology for increasing the flow of services. We find involvement of a number of skilled and unskilled personnel in the process of service delivery. So far as the servicing centres of automobile manufacturing companies are concerned, they make use of new generation of technology and therefore their services have been found quality-based. The skilled mechanics with the help of new generation of technology replace the automotive spares and the cleaning centres wash the vehicles. A majority of the users fell that despite qualitative improvements in technology, the servicing centres take much more time for the disposal of vehicles which is mainly due to a gap between the requirements for servicing centres and the availability of the same in a particular town or city. In the processing of automobile services, quality and time are the two elements which need due care of professionals. Since we find development of a number of automobile servicing centres in the informal sector, the service providers fail in delivering quality services to the users. The services offered are found of complex nature because we find different stages through which the services cross. At each and every stage, the professionals need to ensure quality and time so that they succeed in increasing the number of habitual users. In the process of delivering the services, we do not find involvement of users because the processes are found very much technical. It is very much difficult for the general users to identify the lapses in the processing of services. Smooth and fault-free operation after servicing remain the only bases for customisation of services.

The after-sale services within the warranty period offered by the car manufacturing companies need due care of professionals. In this context, the users lodge complaints and the vehicles go through different processes. Because this is to tarnish the image of car manufacturing companies, the professionals managing the affairs need much more care and precaution. The redressal of complaints also go through different processes and at each and every stage, the working personnel need their personal involvement. The delayed processing may cause delayed delivery and therefore the operational flow is required to be increased.

The automobile servicing centres working independently or not linked with the car manufacturing companies also need to be careful while processing the services. It is right to mention that a number of servicing centres cannot afford new sophisticated devices for processing and therefore they have been facing image problem. Hence with a change in the nature and generation of automotives, the servicing centres also need to equip themselves with new technology so that they make possible time-honoured and quality-based processing found important considerations for customer satisfaction.

Physical Evidence and Attractions

In the context of automobile serving centres, this submix of marketing focuses our attention on the physical facilities available in the servicing centres. The servicescapes or service ambience are found here significant with the viewpoints of both the parties, viz., potential service users and the working people. Here, the professionals need due attention on the environment in which the services are delivered to the customers. The tangible components become here significant to shape the perception of potential customers regarding the service quality. The different components of servicescapes also help working people in increasing their operational efficiency. The potential customers visiting the servicing centres evidence the properties tangibilised and form an opinion regarding the services to be delivered to them.

In the automobile servicing centres, we find designing an important dimension and the experts are required to keep into consideration the comforts and conveniences of potential customers, working people and further the safety security of vehicles specially from theft and fire. Since the services are found techno-driven, it is pertinent that new generation of equipment and technology are used and displayed so that the working people find it convenient to work and the potential customers get an opportunity to view. They need furnishing and ventilation facilities to make the working conditions conducive. To the extent it is possible, the facilities for parking of vehicles are to be given due weightage. When we find servicing centres of large size, the professionals may also think in favour of signposts to guide and help the customers. The counters for making payments should also be equipped with new generation of technology. The business cards, visiting cards used by them must be attractive. The drinking water facilities and sanitation services cannot be undermined. The professionals need not to forget that ambient conditions generate service fragrance found essential for adding additional attractions to the services.

In addition to other aspects, the professionals also need to assign due priority to the dresses and uniforms of working people. We find automotive servicing centres using uniforms and they need to make it sure that their uniforms are of quality. Since we find them working with automotives, it is natural that the servicing processes make their uniforms dirty. The staff working front-line need to look smart and impressive.

The above-mentioned facts make it clear that the automobile servicing centres while formulating a sound marketing mix need to make the servicescapes in the face of changing generation of vehicles will find their task of impressing upon the potential customers much more convenient, if they are sincere and take help of experts while designing and managing the servicescapes.

The People Mix

This submix of the marketing mix is related to the management of human resources for the automobile servicing centres. We can't negate that even in the automobile servicing centres, we find human resources playing a decisive role in improving the quality of services. It is the instrumentality of skilled labour that plays an outstanding role in the very context. If the automobile servicing centres employ trained personnel, the problems would substantially be minimised. Of course, the availability of tools and machines also influence the level of efficiency but we can't devalue the contribution of trained personnel in the very context. It is pertinent that with the evolving technologies, the servicing centres need to make available to their staff the necessary ongoing training facilities for the short duration. The personnel working as unskilled labour should also be efficient because they influence the performance of skilled personnel. In addition, almost all categories of personnel need to have knowledge about the behavioural management so that the cases of indecent behaviour by the staff are not to stand as a barrier in getting the business. This makes it essential that we establish a link between performance orientation and employee orientation. We employ quality personnel and pay to them suitable incentives to prove themselves high performers.

In view of the above-mentioned facts, it is right to mention that the formulation of a sound marketing mix is essential for the smooth functioning of the automobile servicing centres. With the sophistication in the process of transport technologies in general and the road transport technologies in particular, we expect significant development in the service profile. In addition, the changing lifestyles also makes it clear that in the coming days, there would be a substantial increase in the number of users of the motor vehicles. For domestic or even for commercial purposes, a significant increase in the number of vehicles would make future marketing profitable. This makes it essential that the automobile servicing centres assign due weightage to professionalism that would help them in many ways. Not only the big servicing centres but even the small centres need to conceptualise marketing for improving the quality of services or for satisfying the users. It is only not sufficient that you get the business. It is much more impact generating that you keep on moving the process of getting the business and this task of winning and keeping the users for the long time would be simplified considerably if we practise marketing. It is against this background that we make a strong advocacy in favour of practising modern marketing principles by the automobile servicing centres.

AUTOMOBILE SERVICES MARKETING IN INDIAN PERSPECTIVE

Emerging trends in the lifestyles, increasing sophistication in the motor vehicle technologies and mounting domination of corporate sector in the economic transformation processes indicate good auguries for the automobile services in the Indian perspective. With the development of a new culture in which comforts and luxuries are getting top priority, we expect a sizeable increase in the number of different categories of motor vehicle users in the years to come. A close relation between the number of motor vehicle users and the development of automobile servicing centres is but natural. Of late, we find a good number of servicing centres but the unplanned mushroom growth has resulted into the emergence of a number of problems. Of course, there are some of the servicing centres generating more profits but a majority of them are found struggling even to protect their existence. They lack supporting infrastructural facilities to manage the business. Of late, we also find a few of them promoting unfair practices. The increasing cases of theft of motor vehicles are to testify the involvement of servicing centres in the unethical and illegitimate practices. This makes it essential that the automobile servicing centres develop their services on an organised basis. Haphazard and unplanned development would hardly solve the problems generated by the centres. The application of marketing principles would help them substantially in improving the quality of services, fulfilling the expectations of users and increasing the market share which would pave copious avenues for making profits. It is in this context that the management experts feel a planned development of this sector.

The marketing principles would benefit all the servicing centres either working on large scale or serving on a small scale; either located in the big towns or cities or serving the small towns and cities; either serving the domestic sector or working for the commercial sector. The main thing in the process of marketing automobile services is improving the quality of services by formulating a sound service mix, and making possible product attractiveness by formulating a sound package. Since a majority of the centres are found developing as an informal sector, we don't find the efforts systematic. The professionals feel that unplanned development and expansion has been inviting multi-dimensional problems. This is only not to degenerate the quality of service offered by the automobile servicing centres but even to close doors for satisfaction to the users and generation of profits to the servicing centres. In the Indian perspective, we find significant increase in the number of users of motor vehicles, specially during 1990s and first decade of 21st century. The emerging trends indicate that even in the second decade of the 21st century the trend would continue to remain positive which would bring a considerable increase in the number of users.[3] The new generation of motor vehicles are flooded in the market even right now and a number of financial agents are also there to finance them. This makes it clear that the market potentials would increase at its peak in the second decade of this century.

The aforesaid developments engineer a sound foundation for the development of automobile servicing centres. If they are interested in making profits; if they are interested in satisfying the users; if they are interested in contributing substantially to the job market; they need to make possible implementation of marketing principles. Of course, the formulation of a sound product mix is a difficult task but they have to make it possible.

The automobile servicing centres need to promote their business in an effective way. They need to advertise but not to make the process of promoting the business unproductive. The intensity of competition and the financial health of the servicing centres determine the scale of promotion. If the automobile serving centres fail in offering the quality services even creative messages would prove to be ineffective. This makes it clear that they need an optimal budget and a rational decision for promotion.

A motivational price structure is felt essential because a majority of the users are found sensitive to price. This necessitates to regulate the unproductive expenses. We can't deny the fact that increasing cost of inputs is making the task of centres a bit difficult. However, they have no option but to keep in their minds the strategies followed by the competitors, and to formulate a price structure that helps excelling competition.

It is also essential that the services are processed in a right way. This requires employee orientation. The servicing centres in the very context need to offer due incentives to the employees. Performance-based incentive plan would help generation of efficiency. The location point for a centre is an important decision-making area. They need to locate the servicing centres at the places found accessible, safe and environment-friendly. It is also significant that the supporting infrastructural facilities are available at the point of location.

While formulating the people mix, they need more care. This is due to the fact that quality people play an incremental role in improving the level of efficiency. There is no doubt in it that the availability of tools and machines play a big role but if the servicing centres don't have skilled personnel, the quality of services can't be improved.

In view of the above, it is right to mention that we find future marketing potentials profitable, provided the automobile servicing centres conceptualise modern marketing principles. If we lack quality marketing inputs, the task of capitalising on the oppportunities would be much more difficult. This makes it essential that they develop the servicing centres in a planned way. Like other businesses, they also need care while formulating the marketing mix. In the process of blending of different submixes of marketing, they need professional excellence. The marketing consultants would help them considerably in tapping the profitable opportunities in the market.[4] We find scope for developing automobile servicing centres even in the small towns and cities since because even there we find a considerable increase in the different types of users. Besides generating profits, they can contribute fantastically to the job market by creating job opportunities for skilled, semi-skilled and manual workers. Thus, the application of modern marketing principles in the automobile services would benefit different segments of society. We don't find any sense in promoting unplanned, haphazard and unorganised development to be more specific when we have a team of efficient professionals. Let's hope that the automobile servicing centres help users in getting quality services.[5] Let's hope that they contribute substantially to the job market. Let's hope that the automobile services are made commercially viable *vis-a-vis* eco-friendly.

SUMMARY

In this chapter, you have gone through different dimensions of marketing automobile servicing. After reading this chapter, be sure that the following facts were well versed:

Automobile Services Marketing: A Conceptual Framework: We find marketing of automobile servicing centres a managerial process making possible a planned development of the servicing centers helping in managing expectations and satisfying the users.

Rationale Behind Practising Marketing in the Automobile Services: The conceptualisation of marketing in automobile servicing is justified because it is to improve the quality of services, satisfy the users, increase the market share, maximising profitability and making possible a planned development of automobile serving centre.

Market Segmentation for Automobile Services: We find users of the services an amalgam of different segments such as men and women, youths, grey and old, rural and urban and people serving the different sectors and departments having different levels of expectations.

Behavioural Profile of Users of Services: The marketers for gauging the levels of expectations need to have an in-depth knowledge of the changing behavioural profile of users helping them in satisfying them.

Marketing Mix for the Automobile Services: The marketing professionals need to practise all the seven mixes of marketing.

Product Mix: The multi-pronged services included in the product mix are repair and replacement of spare parts, cleaning of vehicles, different types of paintings, air filling and checking, tube repairing and replacing, denting and painting.

Promotion Mix: The marketing professionals need to make use of different components of promotion such as advertising, publicity, sales promotion, personal selling, telemarketing and word-of-mouth promotion in such a way that the users and potential users are sensitised and persuaded in an effective way.

Price Mix: The charges for servicing must be affordable. Since a majority of the users are sensitive to price, the professionals cannot undermine this submix.

Place Mix: This focuses our attention on the channelisation of services. The technology, skilled and unskilled people are found the routes through which the services reach to the users. The location point for the servicing centres should be smoothly accessible.

Process: The professionals need to assign due weightage to the flow of operation so that the users get the time-honoured and quality services. The gap between services-promised and services-delivered must be bridged.

Physical Evidence and Attractions: In this mix of marketing, the designing of servicing centres and the physical facilities need due attention of professionals. The working people need uniforms of quality and the front-line staff to look smart and impressive.

People: In the people mix for automobile servicing, it is essential that the skilled staff working there are aware of the new generation of technology and they are value-based. The unskilled staff must have personal commitment to the profession.

Automobile Services Marketing in Indian Perspective: In the Indian context, we find significant developments in the field of automobile especially during the decade 1990s and after that the foreign as well as the domestic car manufacturing companies have energised the process of development. Here, we focus on the services offered by the automobile servicing stations. With the increasing number of motor vehicles both in the domestic and foreign segments, we find a rapid increase in the number of users which has increased the demand for automobile servicing. With the increasing competition in the sector, we find now the automobile servicing stations offering a package of services to the users. The car manufacturing companies have their own servicing stations and in terms of quality, we find them having an edge over the private servicing stations generally working in the informal sector. The conceptualissation of marketing principles will help them in satisfying the users. Since we find the intensity of competition increasing very fast, it is pertinent that professionals make the services competitive *vis-à-vis* affordable to the users. They need professional excellence for innovating the marketing practices.

KEY TERMS

Automotive	Pamphlets
Automobile	Leaflets
After-sale- Services	Opinion Leaders
Informal Sector	Precincts
Traffic Congestion	Signposts
Child Labour	Conducive
Haphazard	Mechanics
Software	Auguries
Upcoming Youths	Mushroom
Marketing Inputs	Manual Workers
Marketing Outputs	Servicing Stations
Denting	Telemarketing
Package	Word-of-mouth Promotion
Accessories	Servicescapes
Black Painting	Service Ambience
Transparent Painting	Automobile Components
Air Filling	Formal Sector
Maruti	Suzuki

Review Questions

1. What do you mean by Automobile Servicing Marketing? Justify application of marketing principles by the automobile servicing stations.
2. Do you find market segmentation essential for studying and understanding the behavioural profile of users? Defend your arguments.
3. Formulate a marketing mix for the automobile servicing station of a car manufacturing company.
4. Focus on the product mix found suitable for the automotive services.
5. Do you find the expanded marketing mix to be significant to the automobile servicing stations while practising marketing? Defend your arguments.
6. Explain the promotion mix the professionals need to design for the automobile servicing stations.
7. Explain the automobile services marketing in Indian perspective.

Application Exercises

1. You have been working as a marketer in a reputed car manufacturing company. Suggest for them a plan for the marketing of services.
2. As a marketing professional, focus on the measures you will like to follow for promoting the automobile services.
3. As a marketer, formulate a marketing mix for the automobile servicing stations of a reputed car manufacturing company.
4. Do you find servicescapes essential for the automobile servicing station? Defend your arguments.
5. Focus on your strategic decisions for the development of a servicing station in the Indian perspective.
6. You have been asked by a car manufacturing company to formulate a package for the users of automobile services. Focus on the services you will like to include in the product mix to motivate the users.

Endnotes

1. Jha S.M., Automobile Services Marketing, HPH, Mumbai, *Services Marketing*, 2003.
2. Srinivasan Suresh, *The Automobile Industry*; Advance Edge, pp. 42-48, August, 2006.
3. Sumitro Mukherjee & Dipankar Dey, The Indian Automobile Component Industry: Opportunities and Challenges, *The* ICFAIAN *Journal, of Management* pp. 116-29, Vol. V, No. 11, November, 2006.
4. Cugnus,Industry Monitor — Automobiles, *Economics & Business Research*, Vol. 10, 2004.
5. Department of Heavy Industries and Public Enterprises, Government of India: Auto Policy Vision to Establish a Globally Competitive Automotive Industry in India and to Double its Contribution by 2010.

BIBLIOGRAPHY

Allen Louis A. : Concept and Principles of Professional Management; L.A. Associates, 1970.

American Marketing Association : Hospitality for Sale, 1980.

Anand M.M. : Tourism and Hotel Industry in India; Prentice-Hall, 1976.

Andhea Rogres H. & Diana K. Phipps : Economics for the Hotel Catering Industry; B&J Ltd., London, 1977.

Anderson R. : Marketing Communication; Prentice-Hall, 1986.

Anderson W. : The Analysis Framework for Marketing Proceedings of the Conference of Marketing Teachers forms the Far Eastern States.

Argyle M. : The Psychology of Interpersonal Behaviour; Penguin, 1984.

Aronson S. : The Sociology of the Telephone and Telephoners; Prentice-Hall, 1976.

Asher Cashdan & Martin Jordin : Studies in Communication; Part III, Communication and the Media, New York, 1987.

Bali D.R. : Modern Indian Thought; Sterling Pub. Pvt. Ltd., 1996.

Balkrishna & Thakur C.P. : Glimpses of Indian Technology: Non-conventional Sources of Energy, Publication Division, Government of India, New Delhi.

Basu B.K. : Lectures on Management Accountancy; NCBA, Kolkata, 2008.

Bennett K. : Consumer Behaviour; Prentice-Hall, 1972.

Bennett P.D., Kassarjian and Harold H. : Consumer Behaviour, 1981.

Bennet R.C. : The Services Sector in India; Some Heretical Thoughts, Indian Management.

Bhatti S.S. : Hospital Administration Vol. I, Deep & Deep, Delhi.

Bruce I. Newman : Handbook of Political Marketing; Sage Inc., 1999.

Burkart and Medlik : Tourism: Past, Present and Future, London, 1974.

Carman James M. & Kenneth P. : Marketing Principles and Methods; Homewood III, Richard D. Irwin, 1973.

Coffman C.D. : Marketing for a Dull House: A Complete Guide to Hotel, Motel Operations Planning; Cornril University, N.Y.

Colin J. Coulson & Thomas Collier : Marketing Communication; Heinemann, London, 1983.

Service Management Operating Decisions; Prentice-Hall, 1990.

Corner J. : Three Introductions to Communication; Prentice-Hall, 1987.

Daniel M. : The Price of Transport Service, 1932.

Davidoff & Davidoff : Sales and Marketing for Travel & Tourism; National Publications, 1983.

David Stewar : The Theory and Practice of Transport; Heinemann, London, 1980.

Donald W. Cowell : The Marketing of Services; CAM Foundation, Heinemann, London, 1984.

Dorfman : Introduction to Insurance; Prentice Hall, 1987.

Drucker P.F. : Management Task and Responsibilities, 1973.

Edward W. Wheatly : Introduction to Mass Communication, N.Y., 1970.

Emery, Ault and Agree : Scanning the Business Environment; Macmillan, N.Y., 1967.

Evert Gummesson : Total Relationship Marketing; Oxford, England, Heinemann, 1999.

Foster Douglas : Travel and Tourism Management; Macmillan, London, 1985.

Francis J. Aguilar : Macmillan, N.Y., 1967.

Gale J. : Human Factors and the Telephone, Telesis, 1970.

Gerald W. Lattin : The Modern Hotel and Motel Management, W.H. Freeman, 1968.

Goel S.L. : Hospital Administration, Deep & Deep, New Delhi.

Gray-Liguori : Hotel and Hotel Management; Prentice-Hall, 1990.

Greenfield : Successful Management Consultancy; Prentice-Hall, 1990.

Greenstein F.I. : Political Socialisation in International Encyclopedia of Social Sciences, 1968.

Greiner Metzger : Consulting to Management; Prentice-Hall, 1990.

Gronroos C. : A Service Quality Model and Its Marketing Implications.

Gupta and Basu : Portfolio Optimisation in the Indian Stock Market, 2007.

Gupta Kalpana : A Study in the Process of Political Socialisation; HPH Mumbai, 1989.

Haselfield Y. & Richard A.E. : Human Service Organisation; The University of Michigan Press, 1974.

Harper B. Jr. & William F. Massy : Marketing Management, 1972.

Hawkins, Shafer & Rovelsrad : Tourism Marketing and Management; Washington, 1980.

Holloway J.C. & Plant R.V. : Marketing for Tourism; Pitman UK, 1992.

Howard : Consumer Behaviour in Marketing: Sterling India, 1989.

Hudman Hawkins : Tourism in Contemporary Society; Prentice-Hall, 1990.

Jain S.C. : Marketing Planning and Strategy, 1981

Jha S.M. & Sing L.P. : Marketing Management in Indian Perspective; HPH, Mumbai, 1988

Jha S.M. : Tourism Marketing; HPH, Mumbai, 1995.

Jha S.M. : Hotel Marketing, HPH, Mumbai, 1998.

Jha S.M. : Social Marketing, HPH, Mumbai, 1999.

Jha S.M. : Bank Marketing, HPH, Mumbai, 2000.

Jha S.M. : Hospital Management, HPH, Mumbai, 2001.

Jha S.M. : Marketing Non-Profit Organisations; HPH, Mumbai, 2003.

Juran J.M. : Upper Management and Quality; Juran Institute, N.Y., 1982.

John M. Rathwell : Marketing in the Services Sector; Cambridge, 1974.

Khan M.E. : Paying for India's Healthcare Organisations; Prentice-Hall, 1987.

Khurana K. & Yadava : Marketing of Services, IGNOU, 1997.

Kotler Andreasen : Strategic Marketing for No Profit Organisations; Prentice-Hall, 1987.

Kotler Bloom : Marketing Professional Services; Prentice-Hall, 1987.

Kotler Clarke : Marketing for Healthcare Organisations; Prentice-Hall, 1987.

Kotler F. Labm : Strategic Marketing; Prentice-Hall, 1985.

Kotler Fox : Strategic Marketing for Educational Institutions, Prentice-Hall, 1985.

Kotler Philip : Marketing ofr Non-profit Organisations, EEE, PHI, 1985.

Lai H. : Organisational Excellence through Total Quality Management; New Age International, 2008.

Lakshmi S. : Innovations in Education; Sterling India, 1989.

Lane V. Hartesvelt : Essentials of Hospitality Administration; Prentice-Hall, 1990.

Lenk K. : Information Technology & Society, 1982.

Leonard. L.Berry : Discovering the Soul of Service; The Free Press, New York, 1999.

Lickorish L.J. & Kershaw A.G. : The Travel Trade; Practical Press, London, 1950.

Lovelock : Service Marketing; Prentice-Hall, 1984.

Lovelock : Managing Services; Prentice-Hall, 1988.

Lundberg D. E. : The Hotel and Restaurant Busines, Medalist Pub. Inc., 1970, The Tourist Business, Boston, 1974.

Mack Hann J. & Cribbin Herban Heiser : Consultative Selling; AMA COMPublications, AMA.

Malcom H.B., McDonld & Mayor M. : How to Sell a Service; Heinemann, London, 1986.

The Telephone and the Users of Telephone; MIT Press, 1977.

Medved : Food Preparation and Theory; Prentice-Hall, 1990.

Morrison James W. : Travel Agents and Tourism; ARCO Publication, NY, 1980.

PATA : An Introduction to Marketing and Its Application to Tourism; A Marketing Division Handbook, 1973.

Pitrokowski : Work and Family System: A Naturalistic Study of Working Class and Lower Class Families; New York; 1979.

Pits R.E. : Prentice-Hall, 1986.

Philippe J. Maarek : Political Communication; University of Luton Press; England, 1994.

Poynter : Corporate Travel Management; Prentice-Hall, 1990.

Rachman D.J. & Romano E. : Modern Marketing; 1980.

Rana B. Singh : Chanakya Sutra; New Delhi, 1995

Rao A.V.S. : Services Sector Management in India; Allied Hyderabad, 1986.

Redman J. Barbara : Consumer Behaviour: Theory and Application; 1979.

Reidenback E.R. & Rush & Althoff : Bank Marketing, Political Sociology; London, 1972.

Sasser W.E. Olson R.P., Wyckoff D.D. : Management of Service Operations; Allyon and Bacon Inc., 1978.

Seglin : Marketing Financial Advisory Services; Prentice-Hall, 1988.

Sengupta & Kuvalekar : Factoring Services; Skylark. 1992.

Simyar Lloyd Jones : Strategic Management in the Healthcare Centre; Prentice-Hall; 1990.

Smalley : Hospital Management Engineering; Prentice-Hall, 1990.

Smithson : Business Communication Technology; Simon and Schuster International Group; Prentice-Hall, 1990.

Singh R.B. : Chanakya Sutra; New Delhi, 1995.

Sullivan M.P. : Bankers Magazine, 1981.

Van Harssel : Tourism: An Exploration; Prentice-Hall, 1990.

Walter A N Henry : Cutural Values do correlate with Consumer Behaviour, 1976.

Warren K.E. : Long-range Planning; The Executive Viewpoint; 1966.

Wheatley : Marketing Financial Services; Prentice-Hall, 1983.

Wigger : Catering to Every Whim; Prentice-Hall, 1990.

Witt Moutnho : Tourism Marketing and Management; Prentice-Hall, 1990.

Zeithmal & Bitner : Services Marketing; Tata McGraw-Hill Publishing Co. Ltd., New Delhi, 2003.

JOURNALS AND MAGAZINES

Harvard Business Review	: July-August, 1960 April, 1964 March-June, 1981
Prajanan	: September, 1982
The Economic Times	: 19th September, 1985 20th November, 1985 12th February, 1987 14th April, 1988 28th April, 1988 1st September, 1988 11th June, 1989
The Financial Express	: 2nd October, 1984 29th June, 1984
The Business Standard	: 24th July, 1987 March-April 1987 November-December, 1985
Planned Selling	: Annual 1988
The Bankers	: 16/12 1990
Lok Udyog	: XVI/ll, 1983
Magazine of Institute of Bankers	: March-April, 1984 April, 1986
Indian Banking Today & Tomorrow	: June, 1982 August, 1983
Indian Railways	: January-March, 1984
National Herald	: April 12, 1983
The Economic Studies	: 23/4, 1983
Journal of Marketing	: July, 1971 October, 1985
SBI Monthly Review	: August 1982 February, 1985
The Indian Journal of Commerce	: Conference No. 1983, 1984
Yojana	: 32/16, 1988 33/17, 1989
Proceeding of 8th All-India Management Congress	: October, 1992
The Hindu	: Survey of Indian, Industry, 1989
India 2000	: Birla Institute of Scientific Research, 1976
SCANN	: October-December, 1979
Pigmy Economic Review	: 33/12, 1989
Hotel and Restaurant Guide India 1991	: The Federation of Hotel and Restaurant Association of India, New Delhi
Siemens Review	: 57/1, 1990 58/2, 1991, Published by Siemens Akiengesellschaft Berlin and Munich

Modern Management	:	IIMS, Calcutta 11/3, 1986 IV/1 1987
Modern Marketing	:	Institute of Management and Marketing Studies Cuttack June-November, 1993 May, 1998.
The ICFAIAN Journal of Management Research (Different Issues)	:	The ICFAI Business School, Hyderabad
Advance' Edge		
Management Insight	:	IBS, Mumbai, 2006 and Other Issues
(Different Issues)	:	IP SAR, Cuttack
Pratibimba (Different Issues)	:	IMISt, Bhubaneswar
Financial Planning (Different Issues)	:	The Official Publication of FPB India

International Journal of Bank Marketing (Different Issues)
Indian Journal of Finance (Different Issues)
Indian Journal of Commerce (Different Issues)
International Business and Economic Journal (Different Issues)
Delhi Business Review (Different Issues)
Rashtriya Sahara Magazine (Different Issues)
Indian Retail View (BIMTECH, Greater NOIDA)

INDEX

– C –

– G –

– H –

– I –

– N –

– O –

– P –

– Q –

– R –

– U –

– V –

– W –

– Y –

– Z –